THE COOKBOOK **W9-BPJ-974**

THE NEW GOOD HOUSEKEEPING
COOKBOOK
IS BETTER THAN EVER
Revised and Updated for Healthier Eating
and Easy Preparation

From beginning cook to gourmet chef, America has counted on *Good Housekeeping* for generations. From cooking basics that include nutritional guidelines and measuring equivalents to clear, easy-to-follow recipes that contain preparation, cooking times, and calorie counts, *The New Good Housekeeping Cookbook* assures delicious, dependable family friendly cooking—with all recipes triple-tested in the kitchens of the Good Housekeeping Institute.

Sample a hearty bowl of *Butternut-Apple Soup*, prepared in just 35 minutes. Or, for a quick and original idea, try *Turkey Cutlets a l'Orange*— ready to eat in just 16 minutes. A complete section on *Beans, Rice & Other Grains* provides plenty of ideas for healthy eating. From wonderful appetizers to mouth-watering temptations for desserts *The New Good Housekeeping Cookbook* is the one cookbook you can always turn to when you want a recipe you can count on.

THE NEW GOOD HOUSEKEEPING
COOKBOOK
#1 for Generations of American Cooks

THE NEW
Good
Housekeeping
COOKBOOK

HEARST BOOKS

NEW YORK

Food Pyramid Guide appears courtesy of *Evista* ®
(raloxifene), Mark Stolar, M.D. and Greg A. Annussek,
Avon WholeCare, New York © CMD Publishing, 1999.

2 3 4 5 6 7 8 9 10

Printed in the U. S. A.

To subscribe to Good Housekeeping magazine visit
www.goodhousekeeping.com or **www.hearstmags.com**

Contents

Cooking Basics

❧

Eat Well to Stay Well • How to Measure
Equivalents • Substitutions
Guide to Herbs and Spices • Glossary

Here are the good cook's ABC's, the how-to's for successful cooking and meal planning:

Before you prepare a new dish, read the recipe all the way through, to make sure you have allowed enough preparation time, have the necessary ingredients and utensils of the right size on hand, and understand the techniques involved. Then, before you start to cook, assemble the utensils you'll need; measure all the ingredients and set them out in order of use so that you do not forget anything. In an emergency, some ingredients can be substituted for others (see Substitutions, pages 22–23); but it is best not to substitute unless the recipe suggests an alternate ingredient. That goes for package sizes and product forms—instant and regular, too.

Be careful about doubling a recipe. Some recipes can be increased successfully, but many more cannot. It is safest to follow the recipe as written and repeat it until the desired amount has been prepared. Seasonings and spices can be varied safely; it is a good idea, however, to try the recipe first as written to discover your family's tastes before changing it.

Prepare as much ahead as you can. Chop, cut, grate, melt, etc., before you start to mix. Grease and flour pans. When preheating is called for, turn the oven or broiler on when directed in the recipe—that will give it time to reach the required temperature before you put the food in, and it will save energy too.

Cook at the temperature specified in the recipe; but start

checking for doneness a few minutes before the end of the suggested time.

Finally, clean up as you work. The less cluttered the work area, the less chance of your making a mistake.

TO COOK AT HIGH ALTITUDES

Recipes in this book have been perfected for use at sea level; between sea level and altitudes of 2,500 to 3,000 feet, they probably need no modification. At high altitudes, however, some adjustments in cooking time and temperature and recipe ingredients may be necessary.

At sea level, water boils at 212°F. With each 500 feet of increased altitude above sea level, the boiling point drops 1°F. Even though the boiling point is lower, it takes longer to develop the heat needed to cook foods. Therefore, at high altitudes, foods boiled in water will take longer to boil and will require longer cooking times than those suggested in our recipes.

At high altitudes, cake recipes may need slight adjustments in the proportions of flour, leavening, liquid, eggs, etc. These adjustments vary from recipe to recipe, and no set guidelines can be given. Many cake mixes now carry special directions on the label for high-altitude preparation.

High altitudes also affect the rising of doughs and batters, deep frying, candy making, and other aspects of food preparation. For complete information and special recipes for your area, call or write to the home agent at your county cooperative extension office or to the home economics department of your local utility company or state university.

❧Eat Well to Stay Well

Don't put good eating habits—for yourself or your family—on hold. Forming poor dietary habits when you're young can lead to health problems later. It's essential to go beyond the "basic four" food groups to get the nutrients you need without too many calories, or too much fat, saturated fat, cholesterol, sugar, or sodium.

∾Dietary Guidelines for Americans

* Eat a variety of foods to get the calories, protein, vitamins, minerals, and fiber needed.
* Balance the food you eat with physical activity to maintain or improve your weight.
* Choose a diet low in fat, saturated fat, and cholesterol.
* Choose a diet with plenty of vegetables, fruits, and grain products (these fill you up healthfully).
* Use sugar, salt, and alcohol only in moderation.

∾The USDA Food Pyramid

The Food Pyramid is an outline of what to eat each day. The research-based plan, developed by the United States Department of Agriculture, is meant to serve as a general guide—not a rigid prescription—that encourages you to pick and choose from a vast range of foods to create a healthful diet that's right for you.

* The Pyramid calls for eating a variety of foods to get the nutrients you need along with the right amount of calories to maintain a healthy weight. The Pyramid focuses on controlling fat intake, because most American diets are too high in fat, especially saturated fat.
* The Pyramid emphasizes foods from five major food groups shown in the three lower sections of the Pyramid. Each group provides some—but not all—of the nutrients you need for a balanced diet. Foods in one category can't replace those in another (and no one group is more important than another); for good health, you need them all.
* When planning meals, choose fresh foods whenever possible. Processed foods tend to have fewer nutrients and

higher amounts of sugar, fats, and sodium than home-prepared ones. When you eat packaged foods, check labels to see that the fat content fits your fat budget (see What's Your Fat Limit?, page 10).

Bread, cereal, rice, and pasta. These foods—all from grains—form the base of the Pyramid. You need the most servings (6 to 11) of these foods each day.

Fruits and vegetables. The next level up also comes from plants. Eat fruits (2 to 4 servings daily) and vegetables (3 to 5 servings daily) for vitamins, minerals, and fiber.

Meats and dairy foods. Most of the foods on this level of the Pyramid come from animals. The "meat" group foods include meat, poultry, fish, dry beans, eggs, and nuts. Meats, poultry, and fish are rich in protein, B vitamins, iron, and zinc. Dry beans, eggs, and nuts provide protein along with other vitamins and minerals. Dairy foods—mainly milk, yogurt, and cheese—provide protein, bone-building calcium, and other nutrients. In general, animal foods are higher in fat than plant foods, but it's not necessary to cut out all meat and dairy products just to keep fat intake low. Low-fat versions of dairy foods and lean, well-trimmed meat and skinless poultry provide the same amounts of vitamins and minerals as their fattier counterparts. Most individuals should aim for 2 to 3 servings daily from each of these two groups. Vegetarians who do not eat animal foods can substitute extra servings of dry beans and nuts for their protein needs but will also need fortified foods, extra servings of other plant foods, or supplements to get adequate calcium, iron, and vitamin B_{12}.

Fats, oils, and sweets. At the small tip of the Pyramid are foods such as oils, cream, butter, margarine, sugars, soft drinks, candies, and desserts. To maintain a healthy weight, eat them sparingly.

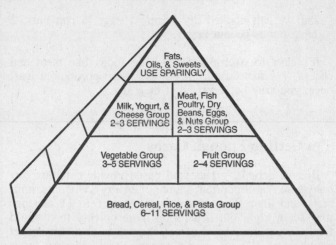

✎What is a Serving?

The Pyramid suggests a range of servings for each food group. The number that's right for you depends on your calorie needs, which in turn depends on your age, sex, size, and how active you are. What counts as a serving? There's no need to measure everything, but here are some guidelines:

Bread, cereal, rice, and pasta: 1 slice bread; 1 ounce ready-to-eat cereal; ½ cup cooked rice, pasta, or cereal.

Vegetables: 1 cup salad greens; ½ cup chopped cooked or raw vegetables; ¾ cup vegetable juice.

Fruits: 1 medium apple, banana, orange, pear, or peach; ½ cup cooked, canned, or frozen fruit; ¼ cup dried fruit; ¾ cup fruit juice (100 percent juice).

Dairy foods: 1 cup milk or yogurt; 1½ ounces natural cheese; 2 ounces process cheese.

Meat group: 2 to 3 ounces cooked lean boneless meat, fish, or poultry (3 ounces is the size of a deck of playing cards). Or, count as 1 ounce of meat any of the following: ½ cup cooked dry beans; 1 egg; ⅓ cup nuts; 2 tablespoons peanut butter.

It's easy to overdo calorie-dense foods like meat and cheese. Try measuring out the suggested portions at least once; you may be surprised at their size.

∾Getting Enough Carbs

Breads, cereals, grains, and pasta provide complex carbohydrates (an important source of energy), vitamins, minerals, and fiber. The recommendation of 6 to 11 servings may seem high, but it adds up more quickly than you'd think: A generous bowl of cereal or pasta or a hefty bagel could equal 2, 3, or even 4 servings each! Starchy foods are often blamed for adding extra pounds, but high-fat toppings (butter on bread, cream sauce on pasta) are the more likely culprits. Stick with lean carbohydrates like peasant bread or pita bread instead of rich croissants and buttery crackers. Whole-grain breads and cereals offer the most fiber.

∾Fruits and Vegetables

Five servings of fruits and vegetables daily (at least) is the rule to remember. Follow these ideas to help get your daily quota:

- For the best range of nutrients—and for delicious variety—don't eat the same fruits and vegetables day after day.
- Include choices high in vitamin C (citrus fruits, kiwifruit, strawberries), and those rich in vitamin A (carrots, winter squash, spinach, kale, cantaloupe).
- Research links cruciferous vegetables such as broccoli, cabbage, cauliflower, and Brussels sprouts with a reduced

risk for certain cancers, so have them several times a week.

• Frozen produce is convenient, and it may be more nutritious than fresh produce that has been stored or shipped.

∽Choosing Your Proteins

Top of the class. Chicken and turkey without skin, fish, and dry beans and peas are the slimmest selections.

Leanest red meats. *Beef* eye round, top round, tenderloin, top sirloin, flank steak, top loin, ground beef (90 to 93 percent lean); *veal* cutlets (from leg), loin chop; *pork* tenderloin, boneless top loin roast, loin chop, boneless sirloin chop; *lamb* boneless leg shank half, loin roast, loin chop, leg and shoulder cubes for kabobs.

Super seafood. Most fish and seafood is low in fat and rich in helpful Omega-3 oils.

Go easy on egg yolks. They're high in cholesterol. Many health experts recommend a limit of 4 egg yolks per week.

Don't go nuts. Nuts and seeds like sesame or sunflower are high in fat; eat in moderation.

∽Is There a "Good" Fat?

Yes. No healthy diet is without some fat; however, all fats in foods are a mixture of three types of fatty acids: saturated, monounsaturated, and polyunsaturated. Saturated fat, found in meat and dairy products, and coconut, palm, and palm kernel oil, should be limited to 10 percent of calories (about one third of your total fat intake) or less; too much raises cholesterol and the risk of heart disease. Monounsaturated fats, found in olive, peanut, and canola oil, and polyunsaturated fats, found mainly in safflower, sunflower, corn, soybean, cottonseed oils, and some fish, are healthier.

∾What's Your Fat Limit?

Here's an easy way to calculate the maximum amount of fat you should consume each day. For a diet containing 30 percent fat calories, divide your ideal body weight by 2. So if your ideal weight is 120 pounds, limit your total daily fat intake to 60 grams (120 lbs divided by 2=60). For a diet with 20 percent fat calories, divide your ideal body weight by 3. Fat is an essential nutrient, so don't cut it out completely. Remember that it's your average intake over a few days—not in a single food or meal—that's important. If you eat a high-fat food or meal, balance it with low-fat foods the rest of the day or the next day.

∾The Mediterranean Diet

For centuries the traditional diet of the sunny countries around the Mediterranean has succeeded in prolonging life and preventing disease. Health experts have taken notice— and suggested that the culinary habits of these countries could help Americans in their quest to cut fat and eat more nutritiously. The result: The "Mediterranean Pyramid," a plan not too different from the USDA Pyramid. Both have a foundation of grains, fruits, and vegetables. But the Mediterranean model highlights beans and other legumes, limits red meat to a few times per month, and promotes the use of olive oil. The model also encourages daily exercise— and even a glass of wine with dinner.

Go with grains (and pasta!). Bread, pasta, bulgur, and rice are staples on the Mediterranean table. This is a jump-start to good health, because grains are naturally high in complex carbohydrates and low in fat. Whole grains boast another healthy bonus—fiber.

Pack in the produce. The Mediterranean diet abounds in seasonal fresh fruits and vegetables—significantly more than in the typical American diet.

Amazing olive oil. For centuries, people in Mediterranean countries have enjoyed generous amounts of olive oil with no evidence of harm. They cook with it, drizzle it in soup and on salads, and even use it on bread in place of butter. What makes olive oil so great? The main difference between olive oil and other fats is that it's predominantly a heart-healthy monounsaturated fat. When substituted for fats that are more saturated, "mono" fats tend to lower artery-clogging LDL cholesterol while maintaining levels of the protective HDL cholesterol. But remember, all types of fat are high in calories and excess weight increases the risk of heart disease.

Focus on fish. Red meat is saved for special occasions (and then usually added in small amounts, combined in grain and vegetable dishes). Fish—low in saturated fat and rich in healthful Omega-3 fatty acids—is eaten several times a week, instead.

Get lean with beans. A key ingredient in Mediterranean salads, soups, and stews, these inexpensive foods are low in fat and high in protein, fiber, and complex carbohydrates.

Savor wines. Wine with meals is traditional in Mediterranean cultures, but overindulgence is rare. Studies have shown that moderate drinking (usually defined as one drink per day for women, two for men) raises "good" cholesterol levels and may make blood less likely to form clots in arteries. But moderation is the key—"one drink" is a 4 ounce glass of wine (½ cup), a 12-ounce serving of beer, or 1 ounce (2 tablespoons) of hard liquor.

Finish with fruit. Sweets have a place in the Mediterranean diet, but meals typically end with fresh or dried fruit rather than sugar-laden, high-fat desserts.

Let yourself relax. Quality of life can't be overlooked as a contributing factor to health and happiness. Meals are savored slowly with family and friends, and physical activity is part of daily life.

ᐧᐧLearning From Food Labels

Food labels help consumers make informed choices and understand how a particular food fits into their daily diet.

- The Percent Daily Values on labels tell you the percentage of the recommended daily amount of a nutrient in a serving (based on 2,000 calories daily). You can ''budget'' your intake of nutrients simply by adding up these percentages. For example, the following label shows a food containing 20 percent of the daily value for fat. If the next food you eat has a 10 percent daily value for fat, you've had 30 percent of your total fat allowance for the day. For fat, saturated fat, sodium, and cholesterol, it's good to keep daily values below 100 percent. Fiber, vitamins A and C, calcium, and iron are listed because American diets often fall short. For these, do aim for the 100 percent mark. Other vitamins and minerals may also appear on some labels.
- Food labels must also carry an ingredient list. Ingredients are listed on food labels in descending order according to their weight. This allows you to, for example, choose muffins with flour, not sugar, at the top of the list.

Nutrition Facts

Serving Size 1 cup (228g)
Servings per Container 2

Amount per serving

Calories 260 Calories from Fat 120

	% Daily Value*
Total Fat 13g	20%
Saturated Fat 5g	25%
Cholesterol 30mg	10%
Sodium 660mg	28%
Total Carbohydrate 31g	10%
Dietary Fiber 0g	0%
Sugars 5g	
Protein 5g	

Vitamin A 4% • Vitamin C 2%
Calcium 15% • Iron 4%

*Percent Daily Values are based on a 2000-calorie diet. Your daily values may be higher or lower depending on your calorie needs:

		Calories: 2000	2500
Total Fat	Less than	65g	80g
Sat Fat	Less than	20g	25g
Cholesterol	Less than	300mg	300mg
Sodium	Less than	2400mg	2400mg
Total Carbohydrate		300g	375g
Dietary Fiber		25g	30g

Calories per gram:
Fat 9 • Carbohydrate 4 • Protein 4

ᎥᏌUsing the Nutritional Values in This Book

With each recipe, you'll find nutritional information that can help you plan a balanced diet. To help you use this information, see "Learning From Food Labels" (see previous page) for recommended daily nutrient levels. Aim to balance higher-fat recipes with leaner choices: For example, serve lasagna with a green salad with a low-fat dressing and a glass of skim milk.

- Our nutritional calculations do not include optional ingredients or garnishes.
- When alternative ingredients are listed (e.g., margarine or butter), our calculations are based on the first ingredient mentioned.
- Unless otherwise noted, whole milk has been used.

ᎥᏌHow to Measure

All measurements should be level, unless (as rarely happens) the recipe directs otherwise.

Pay special attention to the wording used in recipes. For example, 1 pound shelled, deveined shrimp is a different measurement from 1 pound shrimp, shelled and deveined; there are more shrimp to the pound when they are weighed after the shells are removed than before, and this will affect the resulting number of servings.

USING THE CORRECT MEASURING EQUIPMENT

Accurate measurements are essential if you want the same good results each time you make a dish.

For dry ingredients, use a set of 4 graduated nesting measuring cups, consisting of ¼, ⅓, ½, and 1-cup measures.

For liquids, use a 1-cup liquid measuring cup that is also marked for smaller amounts; 2-cup, 4-cup, and 8-cup liquid measuring cups are helpful for measuring larger amounts.

A standard set of ¼-, ½-, 1-teaspoon, and 1-tablespoon measuring spoons is used for both dry and liquid ingredients.

MEASURING LIQUIDS

Always read the line on a measuring cup at eye level when checking the volume of liquid in a cup.

With the liquid measure on a level surface, slowly pour the liquid into the cup until it reaches the desired line.

If using measuring spoons, pour the liquid just to the top of the spoon without letting it spill over. Don't measure liquids over the mixing bowl; extra liquid could spill into the bowl.

MEASURING SHORTENING

Liquid shortenings such as vegetable oil and melted margarine or butter can be measured in the same way as liquids. Measure solid shortenings such as lard, vegetable shortening, and even peanut butter as described below.

Pack the shortening, firmly, right to the top of the measuring spoon or graduated dry ingredient measuring cup.

Level off shortening with the straight edge, not the flat side, of a knife or spatula.

MEASURING BUTTER OR MARGARINE

Each ¼-pound (4 ounce) stick of margarine or butter measures ½ cup; the wrapping is usually marked off in tablespoons for measuring smaller amounts.

With a sharp knife, just cut off the number of tablespoons needed, following the guidelines on the wrapper.

For margarine or butter not wrapped in this way, measure and level off as for solid shortening.

MEASURING FLOUR

In the recipes in this book both all-purpose and cake flours are measured and used straight from the flour package or canister without being sifted. Before measuring, lightly stir the flour in the package to aerate.

On a sheet of waxed paper, lightly spoon the flour into a graduated dry ingredient measuring cup or spoon. Never pack flour down or shake or tap the measuring cup.

Then, level off the surplus flour in the cup with the straight edge of a knife or spatula.

MEASURING SUGAR

Lightly spoon granulated white sugar into a graduated dry ingredient measuring cup or spoon and level off with the straight edge of a knife or spatula.

Brown sugar: Pack the sugar lightly into the dry ingredient measuring cup, then level off; it should hold its shape when inverted onto a flat surface from the cup.

HOW TO MEASURE PANS

Be sure your pans are the kind and size specified in the recipe. The size of some cookware is expressed in liquid measure at its level full capacity.

Measure the top inside of bakeware for length, width, or diameter; measure the perpendicular inside for depth.

Sizes for skillets and griddles are taken from the top outside dimensions, exclusive of handles.

HOW TO CHOP, CUBE, MINCE

Chop: to cut food into small irregular pieces.
Cube: to cut food into square pieces.
Mince: to cut food into very small irregular pieces.

～Equivalents

Almonds, 1 pound
    in shell   *1-1¼ cups nutmeats*
    shelled   *3 cups*

～Equivalents (Cont'd)

Apples, 1 pound   *3 medium; about 3 cups sliced*

Bacon, 16-ounce
package, chopped,
cooked   *1½ cups pieces*

Bananas, 1 pound   *3 medium; 1⅓ cups mashed*

Barley, 1 cup
medium   *about 4 cups cooked*
quick-cooking   *about 3 cups cooked*

Beans, dry
1 pound   *2 cups (uncooked)*
1 cup   *2-2½ cups cooked*

Berries. See individual
varieties.

Blackberries, 1 pint   *about 2 cups*

Blueberries, 1 pint   *2 cups*

Blue cheese, 4 ounces   *1 cup crumbled*

Brazil nuts, 1 pound
in shell   *1½ cups nutmeats*
shelled   *3¼ cups*

Bread, 16-ounce loaf
regular   *14-18 slices*
very thin   *28 slices*

Bread crumbs, dried
8-ounce package   *2¼ cups*

Bread crumbs, fresh
1 slice bread with
crust   *½ cup bread crumbs*

Bulgur, 1 cup   *3-3½ cups cooked*

Cabbage, 1 pound   *about 4 to 5 cups coarsely
                                              sliced*

Cashew nuts, 1 pound
shelled   *3¼ cups*

Celery, 1 medium
  bunch   *about 4 cups chopped*

Cheese, hard 4 ounces *1 cup shredded*

Cherries, 1 pound *about 2 cups pitted*

Chicken, cooked
  2½- to 3-pound
  chicken   *about 2½ cups coarsely*
                chopped cooked meat

Chocolate, semisweet
  1 ounce   *1 square*
  1 6-ounce package
  chips   *1 cup*

Chocolate, unsweetened
  1 ounce   *1 square*

Cocoa, unsweetened
  8-ounce can   *2 cups*

Coconut
  flaked, 3½-ounce
  can   *1⅓ cups*
  shredded, 4-ounce
  can   *1⅓ cups*

Cookies, crushed
  chocolate wafers,
  20 2¼-inch wafers *about 1 cup fine crumbs*
  chocolate wafers,
  2½-ounce package *scant ⅔ cup crumbs*
  gingersnaps, 15   *about 1 cup fine crumbs*
  vanilla wafers, 22 *about 1 cup fine crumbs*

Cornmeal, 1 cup *about 4 cups cooked*

Cottage cheese,
  8 ounces   *1 cup*

Couscous, 1 cup *about 2½ cups cooked*

Crackers, crushed
  graham, seven 5"
  by 2½" crackers *about 1 cup fine crumbs*
  saltine, 28   *about 1 cup fine crumbs*

∾Equivalents (Cont'd)

Cranberries, 12-ounce
  bag   *3 cups*

Cream, heavy or
  whipping, ½ pint
  carton (1 cup)   *2 cups whipped cream*

Cream cheese
  3-ounce package *6 tablespoons*
  8-ounce package *1 cup*

Currants
  dried, 10-ounce
  package   *about 2 cups*
  fresh, 1 quart   *about 3¾ cups*

Dates, pitted, 10-ounce
  container   *about 2 cups*

Egg noodles, 8-ounce
  package, 6 cups *about 4 cups cooked*

Egg whites, large
  1   *about 2 tablespoons*
  1 cup   *8-10 egg whites*

Egg yolks, large,
  1 cup   *12-14 egg yolks*

Farina, 1 cup
  regular   *about 6½ cups cooked*
  quick-cooking *about 6 cups cooked*

Flour, 1 pound
  all-purpose   *about 3½ cups*
  cake   *about 4 cups*
  rye   *about 3½-5 cups*
  whole wheat   *about 3¾ cups*

Gelatin, unflavored,
  amount needed to
  gel 2 cups liquid *1 envelope*

Green pepper, 1 large   *about 1 cup chopped*

Hazelnuts, 1 pound
  in shell   *1½ cups nutmeats*
  shelled   *3½ cups*

Hominy grits, 1 cup
  cooked   *about 4½ cups*

Honey, liquid,
  16 ounces   *1⅓ cups*

Kasha, 1 cup   *about 3 cups cooked*

Lemon, 1 medium   *3 tablespoons juice; about*
                   1 teaspoon grated peel

Lentils, 1 cup   *about 2½ cups cooked*

Lime, 1 medium   *2 tablespoons juice;*
                   about 1 teaspoon grated
                   peel

Macadamia nuts,
  7-ounce jar   *1½ cups*

Macaroni, elbow,
  1 cup   *about 2 cups cooked*

Margarine or **butter**
  ¼-pound (4-ounce)
  stick   *½ cup or 8 tablespoons*
  1 pound   *4 sticks or 2 cups*

Mushrooms, fresh   *about 2½ cups sliced or 3 cups*
  white, 8 ounces   *chopped; scant 1 cup sliced,*
                   cooked

Nectarines, 1 pound   *3-4 medium; about 2-2½ cups*
                   sliced

Nuts. See individual
  varieties.

Oats, 1 cup
  old-fashioned   *about 2 cups cooked oatmeal*
  quick-cooking   *about 2 cups cooked oatmeal*

Olive oil, 16 ounces   *2 cups*

∾Equivalents (Cont'd)

Onion, 1 large,
  6 ounces   *³/₄-1 cup chopped*

Orange, 1 medium   *¹/₃-¹/₂ cup juice; about*
                               1 tablespoon grated peel

Parmesan cheese,
  3 ounces   *1 cup freshly grated*

Peaches, 1 pound   *3-4 medium; 2-2¹/₂ cups peeled*
                               and sliced

Peanuts, 1 pound
  in shell   *2-2¹/₂ cups nutmeats*
  shelled   *3 cups*

Pears, 1 pound   *3 medium; about 2¹/₄ cups*
                               sliced

Peas, green,
  fresh in pod,
  1 pound shelled   *1 cup*

Pecans, 1 pound
  in shell   *1³/₄-2¹/₄ cups nutmeats*
  shelled   *4 cups halves;*
                               3¹/₂-4 cups chopped

Pineapple, 1 large   *about 4 cups pieces*

Pistachios, 1 pound
  in shell   *2 cups*
  shelled   *about 4 cups nutmeats*

Plums, 1 pound   *6 medium (about 2-inch*
                               diameter); about 2¹/₂ cups
                               sliced

Popcorn, ¹/₄ cup
  (unpopped)   *about 4 cups popped*

Potatoes, white, all-
  purpose, 1 pound   *3 medium; about 3 cups sliced;*
                               about 2¹/₄ cups coarsely
                               chopped; about 2 cups
                               mashed

Raisins, 15-ounce
   package   *about 2 cups*

Raspberries, ½ pint   *about 1 cup*

Rice, 1 cup
   (uncooked)
   parboiled   *about 4 cups cooked*
   precooked   *about 2 cups cooked*
   regular long-grain   *about 3 cups cooked*
   brown   *about 4 cups cooked*
   wild   *3-4 cups cooked*

Romano cheese,
   3 ounces   *1 cup freshly grated*

Shortening, 1 pound   *2½ cups*

Sour cream, 8-ounce
   container   *1 cup*

Spaghetti, 8 ounces   *4 cups cooked*

Split peas, 1 cup   *about 2½ cups cooked*

Strawberries, 1 pint   *about 3¼ cups whole; 2¼ cups
      sliced*

Sugar, 1 pound
   granulated white   *2¼-2½ cups*
   confectioners'   *about 3¾ cups*
   light brown, packed   *about 2¼ cups*
   dark brown, packed   *about 2¼ cups*
   granulated brown   *about 3 cups*

Sweet potatoes,
   1 pound   *2 medium; about 2¼ cups
      sliced; about 1½ cups
      mashed*

Swiss cheese, 4 ounces   *1 cup shredded*

Syrup
   corn, 16 ounces   *2 cups*
   maple, 12 ounces   *1½ cups*

Tomatoes, 1 pound   *3 medium*

∾Equivalents (Cont'd)

Vegetable oil,
16-ounce bottle   *2 cups*

Walnuts, 1 pound
in shell   *2 cups nutmeats*
shelled   *about 3½ cups chopped*

Yeast, active dry,
1 package   *about 2½ teaspoons*

∾Substitutions

Baking powder: For each 1 teaspoon called for, substitute ¼ teaspoon baking soda and ½ teaspoon cream of tartar (make fresh for each use).

Buttermilk, 1 cup: Place 1 tablespoon vinegar or lemon juice in cup and stir in enough milk to make 1 cup; let stand 5 minutes to thicken. Or use 1 cup plain yogurt.

Cake flour: For each 1 cup called for, use 1 cup minus 2 tablespoons all-purpose flour.

Chives: Substitute green onions, including the tops.

Chocolate, semisweet chips, melted, one 6-ounce package: Use 6 tablespoons unsweetened cocoa plus 7 tablespoons sugar and ¼ cup shortening; or use six 1-ounce squares semisweet chocolate.

Chocolate, unsweetened, melted, 1 ounce: Use 3 tablespoons unsweetened cocoa plus 1 tablespoon vegetable oil, shortening, butter, or margarine; or use 1 envelope unsweetened baking chocolate flavor.

Cornstarch (for thickening), 1 tablespoon: Use 2 tablespoons all-purpose flour or 2 tablespoons quick-cooking tapioca.

Ginger, fresh, minced, 1 tablespoon: Use ¼ teaspoon ground ginger.

Herbs: For each 1 tablespoon fresh, use ½ teaspoon dried.

Light brown sugar: For each 1 cup, substitute 1 cup granulated sugar and 1 tablespoon molasses; or use dark brown sugar.

Mustard: For each 1 tablespoon prepared mustard, use 1 teaspoon dry mustard mixed with 2 tablespoons wine vinegar, white wine, or water.

Pancetta: Substitute Canadian bacon or ham.

Pepper, ground red, ⅛ teaspoon: Use 4 drops hot-pepper sauce.

Pine nuts (pignoli): Use walnuts or almonds.

Prosciutto: Use ham, preferably Westphalian or country ham.

Shallots: Use onion.

Tapioca (for thickening), 2 tablespoons: Use 1 tablespoon cornstarch or 2 tablespoons flour.

Vanilla extract: Use brandy or an appropriate flavored liqueur.

Yeast, active dry, 1 package: Use 0.6-ounce cake; or use ⅓ or 2-ounce cake compressed yeast. Add to lukewarm liquid.

SMALL VOLUME EQUIVALENTS

Spoons	Cups	Fluid Ounces
1 tablespoon/ 3 teaspoons		½ fl oz
2 tablespoons	⅛ cup	1 fl oz
4 tablespoons	¼ cup	2 fl oz
5 tablespoons plus 1 teaspoon	⅓ cup	2⅔ fl oz
6 tablespoons	⅜ cup	3 fl oz
8 tablespoons	½ cup	4 fl oz
10 tablespoons plus 2 teaspoons	⅔ cup	5⅓ fl oz
12 tablespoons	¾ cup	6 fl oz
14 tablespoons	⅞ cup	7 fl oz
16 tablespoons	1 cup	8 fl oz

LARGER VOLUME EQUIVALENTS

Cups	Fluid Ounces	Pints/Quarts
1 cup	8 fl oz	½ pint
2 cups	16 fl oz	1 pint
3 cups	24 fl oz	1½ pints/¾ quart
4 cups	32 fl oz	2 pints/1 quart
6 cups	48 fl oz	3 pints/1½ quarts
8 cups	64 fl oz	2 quarts/½ gallon
16 cups	128 fl oz	4 quarts/1 gallon

◖Guide to Herbs and Spices

HOW TO STORE

Fresh herbs should be stored in the refrigerator for a few days. Basil and sage leaves can be plucked from their stems and stored, covered with olive or vegetable oil in a covered jar, for several months in the refrigerator. Red spices such as paprika, chili powder, and ground red pepper will hold their color and keep their flavor longer if refrigerated. Dried herbs, and ground or whole spices, should be stored in a cool, dry, dark cabinet, away from the heat of the range, the refrigerator exhaust, or under-cabinet lighting units. Once a year, give dried herbs and ground spices the "sniff test" by passing the opened container quickly under your nose and seeing if the contents can be identified; if not, discard the container and replace it. Whole spices will retain their flavor and aroma almost indefinitely.

ALLSPICE: Allspice is sold as smooth, brown, pea-sized whole berries or ground; the flavor resembles a blend of cinnamon, cloves, and nutmeg.

ANISE SEEDS: Small, oval, grayish-brown seeds are available whole or ground. They have a strong, sweet licoricelike flavor.

BASIL: An aromatic annual of the mint family. With many species, basil ranges in leaf color from bright green to dark purple. Sweet basil is the variety most found in this country. Its flavor is faintly aniselike and its aroma is sweet. It is sold fresh and also comes dried in leaf or ground form.

BAY LEAVES: These are glossy, smooth 1- to 3-inch-long leaves of the sweet bay or laurel tree, native to Mediterranean areas. The strong, distinctive flavor mellows in long-cooking dishes. Bay leaves are available whole or ground. (Do not use leaves of mountain laurel; they are toxic.) Be sure to remove whole bay leaves from cooked foods before serving.

CARAWAY SEEDS: These dried whole seeds have a warm, sweet, slightly sharp taste.

CARDAMOM SEEDS: Creamy-white dried cardamom seed pods, each containing 2 clusters of small brown seeds, are sold whole. The seeds are also sold ground but lose their essential oils rapidly. The flavor is sweet and the seeds are highly aromatic.

CELERY SEEDS: These are the very small brown seeds of a wild celery called ''smallage'' and not from the cultivated celery used as a vegetable. The flavor is similar to that of cultivated celery but stronger and more intense. The seeds are often ground and mixed with salt to make celery salt.

CHERVIL: An aromatic herb with lacy leaves and a delicate flavor reminiscent of tarragon, chervil is one of the classic *fines herbes* (along with parsley, chives, and tarragon) used in French cooking. It is readily grown in the home garden and is also available dried.

CHILI POWDER: An American invention, chili powder is a blend of ground chile peppers, ground cumin seeds, ground oregano, garlic powder, and, usually, salt. Other seasonings, such as ground cloves or chocolate, are added to some brands. Chili powders range from red to very dark red with varying degrees of hotness. Store chili powder in the refrigerator.

CHINESE FIVE SPICE POWDER: This aromatic, predominantly licorice-flavored, reddish-brown spice mixture is made of equal parts of finely ground Szechwan peppercorns (also known as "anise-pepper"), star anise, cassia or cinnamon, cloves, and fennel seeds; it is used in Chinese and Southeast Asian dishes.

CHIVES: Long, slender, hollow dark-green leaves that have a delicate onion flavor; chives are a favorite herb in the home garden. They are sold fresh, freeze-dried, or frozen. If fresh, the bulbs and purple flowers can be eaten as well as the leaves. Chinese or garlic chives have larger, flatter leaves and stronger flavor and may be served stir-fried as a vegetable dish.

CINNAMON: This sweet and pungent spice is the dried inner bark of evergreen trees native to Southeast Asia. In this country, cinnamon from the cassia tree is preferred. It is sold ground or as reddish-brown sticks of the rolled bark.

CLOVES: These dried, rich-brown, unopened flower buds of a tropical evergreen tree are sold whole or ground. They have a pungent, warm, sweet aroma, and a strong, sweet flavor.

CORIANDER: Fresh coriander is also known as "Chinese parsley" and "cilantro." It resembles parsley with its lacy leaves, but the flavor is much stronger and more pungent. Coriander seeds are sold whole or ground; they have an aromatic, slightly citrus flavor and aroma.

CUMIN SEEDS: Small (⅛- to ¼-inch-long), oval yellowish-brown cumin seeds taste somewhat like caraway, but their flavor is stronger. They provide the dominant tone in chili powder and are used in curry powder. Buy them whole or ground.

CURRY POWDER: This is a blend of many spices, including ginger, coriander, cumin, turmeric, black pepper, and dried red chilies. It gives foods a flavor characteristic of Indian cooking.

DILL: Fresh dill has feathery, fernlike leaves; when dried, it is called "dillweed." Dill seeds are tan in color, oval, and about ⅛ inch long; they are sold whole or ground.

FENNEL SEEDS: Small (about 5⁄16 inch long), yellowish-brown fennel seeds have an aniselike flavor but are not so sweet. They are sold whole or ground.

GINGER: This is the root of a tropical plant, available fresh, dried and ground, preserved in syrup, or crystallized (candied). Ginger has a pungent, sweet aroma and a hot taste. Refrigerate fresh ginger and use it within a week. For longer storage, peel ginger, slice or cut it into pieces, and place in a jar. Add enough dry sherry to cover, cover the jar, and refrigerate. Remove ginger as needed, and use the sherry (now ginger-flavored) in recipes.

MACE: Mace is the dried, lacy membrane surrounding the whole nutmeg. It has a flavor and aroma similar to nutmeg, but stronger and less delicate; it is light golden in color. Mace is sold ground and whole in supermarkets, as "blades" in specialty markets.

MARJORAM: An aromatic herb, sweet marjoram has small, gray-green leaves and a spicy, slightly bitter flavor, similar to oregano, to which it is related.

MINT: Of the many varieties of mint, spearmint and peppermint are the two most widely used. Both varieties have a strong, sweet aroma and cool aftertaste.

MUSTARD: Small seeds that come in two main varieties: white or yellow, and brown or Asian; the seeds are sold whole or ground (dry mustard). When dry, mustard has no aroma; it must be stirred with liquid (usually water), and allowed to stand for 10 to 15 minutes, to develop its pungent aroma and sharp, hot flavor, which has bite.

NUTMEG: Large (1 inch long) oval wrinkled seeds of the nutmeg tree; sold whole or ground. The flavor is warm, sweet, spicy.

OREGANO: Light grayish-green leaves of this herb have a strong, aromatic flavor with assertive undertones, similar to but stronger than the flavor of marjoram. It is available fresh, and dried, as whole or ground leaves.

PAPRIKA: A bright to brick-red powder, paprika is made by grinding the pods of mild sweet chiles or peppers; its flavor ranges from mild and sweet to hot, with a slight bite, depending on which chiles are used, and where they were grown. Hungarian paprika has the most warmth. Store paprika in the refrigerator.

PARSLEY: There are three main types of parsley: curly, with ruffled leaves and a mild flavor; Italian, with flat leaves and a more pungent flavor; and Chinese (see Coriander). Curly-leaf parsley is a favorite garnish. Italian flat-leaf parsley has become more popular and available, used as a seasoning. Parsley is always included in the *fines herbes* of French cooking, and its stems make up part of a *bouquet garni*. Dried parsley is sold as parsley flakes.

PEPPER: The world's most popular spice, pepper comes from the small, dried berries of a tropical vine. Black pepper is made from the underripe whole berries, which, when allowed to dry, shrivel and turn black. Pepper is sold as whole or cracked peppercorns, and as coarsely or finely ground pepper. White pepper is made from the core of mature berries; it is lighter in color, milder in flavor, less aromatic, and usually more finely ground. Green peppercorns (*poivres verts*) are pepper berries that have not been dried; they are usually packed in water or brine or are freeze-dried. They have a pungent, fresh flavor. Szechwan peppercorns are not related to the pepper vine. They are the dried reddish-brown berries of the prickly ash tree; also known as "anise pepper." They have a slightly aniselike aroma and flavor, and a mild peppery taste. They are one of the ingredients of Chinese five-spice powder.

POPPY SEEDS: The tiny, crunchy, blue-gray seeds of the poppy plant have a pleasant, nutlike flavor. They are sold whole, but may be purchased ground in specialty food shops. Store in the refrigerator or freezer. Toasting the seeds in a dry skillet before using them will crisp them and bring out the full nutty flavor.

RED PEPPER: Dried, ripe, hot chile peppers are used to make ground red pepper (cayenne pepper) and crushed red pepper flakes. Both are very hot and pungent. Ground red pepper is an orange-red powder; crushed red pepper comes as small dark-red flakes.

ROSEMARY: The grayish-green fresh or dried needlelike

leaves of this herb have a pungent, tealike aroma and a bittersweet flavor.

SAFFRON: Used as much for its rich, orange gold color as for its pleasant, slightly bitter flavor, saffron is the dried stigmas of a member of the crocus family. It is very expensive. The reason for its high price is that it requires more than 80,000 hand-harvested blossoms to make one pound of the spice. It comes as threads or powder, and must be stored in a cool, dark place.

SAGE: Aromatic, grayish-green, 1- to 3-inch-long, slender leaves which are soft and velvety when fresh, and turn silvery gray when dry. Rubbed sage is ground sage with a fluffy, cottonlike consistency; ground sage is a finer, nonfluffy powder. Dried whole leaves are also available.

SAVORY: Of the different varieties of this herb, the two principal kinds used in cooking are summer savory and winter savory. Summer savory has the more delicate flavor and is the type generally sold dried, as leaves and ground. It has a pinelike, almost peppery aroma, and slightly resinous taste, somewhat like thyme.

SESAME SEEDS: Known in some areas as "benne," sesame seeds are small, somewhat flat, oval seeds, about ⅛ inch long and pearly white in color, with a mild, sweet, nutlike flavor. They are sold whole and untoasted. Black sesame seeds are popular in Middle Eastern and Asian cooking. They have a more pungent taste. Sesame seeds should be stored in the refrigerator or freezer, because their natural oils turn rancid if left at room temperature. To toast sesame seeds: In a small skillet, toast sesame seeds over medium-low heat 1 to 2 minutes, stirring and shaking the pan often to prevent burning, until the seeds are lightly browned.

STAR ANISE: The licorice-flavored seeds grow in a star-shaped cluster of 8 pods or "cloves." Both the seed and its barklike covering are used. Star anise has a strong flavor similar to anise but more pungent. It is an ingredient of Chinese five-spice powder.

TARRAGON: The slender, pointed, dark-green leaves of tarragon have a piquant, aniselike flavor. Sold fresh and dried, tarragon is one of the *fines herbes* of French cuisine.

THYME: There are many varieties of this great culinary herb, but the most popular ones are garden thyme, a shrubby perennial with small, fragrant gray-green leaves, and lemon thyme, with a delicate lemon flavor. Thyme is an essential ingredient of a *bouquet garni*.

TURMERIC: When ground, turmeric, the root of a plant related to ginger, is brilliant yellow in color, with a pepperlike aroma, and slightly bitter, musty flavor. It is often used instead of saffron as a less expensive coloring agent for food, but not as a substitute for its flavor.

VANILLA BEAN: The unripe seed pod of an orchid, the vanilla bean is tasteless when picked but develops a strong, sweet flavor and dark brown, tough covering after curing. Store in a tightly covered jar. If the bean dries out, it can be grated and used in desserts.

GLOSSARY

al dente: Italian for "to the tooth," describes perfectly cooked pasta and vegetables. If pasta is *al dente*, it is just tender but offers a slight resistance when it is bitten.

baste: To spoon or brush a liquid over food—typically roasted or grilled meats and poultry—during cooking to keep it moist. The liquid can be a sauce or glaze, broth, melted butter, or pan juices.

beat: To briskly whip or stir a mixture with a spoon, wire whisk, or electric mixer until it is smooth and light in texture, and sometimes, color.

blanch: To cook foods briefly in boiling water. Blanching locks in texture and color for tender-crisp vegetables, loosens tomato and peach skins for peeling, and mellows salty foods. Begin timing as soon as the food hits the water—the water needn't return to a boil—then drain and cool in ice water to stop the cooking.

blend: To combine two or more ingredients until smooth or uniformly mixed. Blending can be done with a spoon, or an appliance such as an electric mixer or a blender.

blind bake: To bake a piecrust before it's filled to create a crisper crust. To prevent puffing and slipping during baking, the pastry is lined with foil which is filled with pie weights, dry beans, or uncooked rice; foil and weights are removed shortly before the end of baking time and the crust is baked a few minutes longer, until browned.

boil: To heat a liquid until bubbles break vigorously on the surface. You can boil vegetables, cook pasta in boiling water, or reduce sauces by boiling them. Never boil meats (they'll be tough) or custard sauces (they'll curdle).

braise: To cook food in a small amount of liquid in a tightly covered pan, either in the oven or on the stovetop. Braising is an ideal way to prepare less-tender cuts of meat, firm-fleshed fish, and vegetables.

broil: To cook food with intense, direct, dry heat under a broiler. For broiled meats, use a rack so the fat drips away. Always preheat the broiler, but don't preheat the pan and rack, or the food could stick.

broth: A thin, clear liquid produced by cooking poultry, meat, fish, or vegetables in water with aromatic vegetables, and used as a base for soups, stews, sauces, and many other dishes. Canned broth is always convenient as a substitute for homemade.

brown: To cook food quickly on top of the stove (in fat), under a broiler, or in the oven to develop a richly browned, flavorful surface, and help seal in natural juices.

butterfly: To split a food, such as shrimp or a boneless lamb leg or pork chop, horizontally in half, cutting almost, but not all the way through, then opening it up like a book to form a butterfly shape. Butterflying exposes more surface area so the food cooks evenly and more quickly.

caramelize: To heat sugar in a skillet until it becomes syrupy and deep amber brown. Sugar toppings on desserts such as crème brûlée can also be caramelized (by heating under the broiler until melted), as can onions (by cooking slowly until deep golden and very tender).

chop: To cut food roughly into small, irregular pieces about ¼" to ½" in size.

core: To remove the core or center of various fruits and vegetables. Coring eliminates small seeds or tough and woody centers (as in pineapple).

cream: To beat a fat, such as margarine or butter, alone or with sugar, until fluffy and light in color. This technique whips air into the fat, creating light-textured baked goods. An electric mixer makes short work of creaming.

crimp: To pinch or press dough edges—especially piecrust edges—to create a decorative finish and/or to seal two layers of dough so the filling doesn't seep out during baking. The edges of a parchment or foil packet may also be crimped to seal in food and its juices during cooking.

curdle: To coagulate, or separate, into solids and liquids. Egg and milk-based mixtures are susceptible to curdling if they're heated too quickly or combined with an acidic ingredient, such as lemon juice or tomatoes.

cut in: To work a solid fat, such as vegetable shortening, margarine, or butter, into dry ingredients by using a pastry blender, your fingers, or two knives used scissor-fashion. The fat and flour should form pea-size nuggets or coarse crumbs for flaky pastry.

deglaze: To add a liquid (e.g., water, wine, broth) to a skillet or roasting pan in which meat or poultry has been cooked to release the caramelized meat juices. After removing the meat, pour the liquid into the pan and heat, scraping up the flavorful browned bits from the bottom of the pan, to make a quick sauce.

devein: To remove the dark intestinal vein of a shrimp. Use the tip of a sharp knife, then rinse the shrimp with cold running water.

dot: To scatter bits of margarine or butter over a pie, casserole, or other dish before baking. This adds extra richness and flavor, and helps promote browning.

drizzle: To slowly pour a liquid, such as melted butter, olive oil, or a glaze, in a fine stream, back and forth, over food.

dust: To sprinkle very lightly with a powdery ingredient, such as confectioners' sugar (on cakes and pastries) or flour (in a greased cake pan).

eau-de-vie: French for "water of life," describes any colorless brandy distilled from fermented fruit juice. Kirsch (cherry) and framboise (raspberry) are two popular varieties.

emulsify: To bind liquids that usually can't blend smoothly, such as oil and water. The trick is to add one liquid, usually the oil, to the other in a slow stream while whisking vigorously. You can also use natural emulsifiers—egg yolks or mustard—to bind mixtures like vinaigrettes, mayonnaise, and sauces.

ferment: To bring about a chemical change in foods and beverages; the change is caused by enzymes produced from bacteria or yeast. Beer, wine, yogurt, buttermilk, vinegar, cheese, and yeast breads all get their distinctive flavors from fermentation.

fold: To incorporate a light, airy mixture (such as beaten egg whites) into a heavier mixture (a cake batter). To fold, use a rubber spatula to cut through the center of the mixture. Scrape across the bottom of the bowl and up the nearest side. Give the bowl a quarter turn, and repeat just until blended.

fork-tender: A degree of doneness for cooked vegetables and meats. You should feel just a slight resistance when the food is pierced with a dinner fork.

julienne: To cut food, especially vegetables, into thin, uniform matchstick pieces about 2 inches long and ¼-inch wide.

knead: To work dough until it is smooth and cohesive, either by pressing and folding with the heels of the hands or in a food processor or an electric mixer with a dough hook. Kneading develops the gluten in the flour, an elastic protein that gives yeast breads their structure. If kneading biscuit dough, use a light touch so the dough just comes together, and the gluten is *not* developed.

leavening: Any agent that causes a dough or batter to rise. Common leaveners include baking powder, baking soda, and yeast. Natural leaveners are air (when beaten into eggs) and steam (in popovers and cream puffs).

liqueur: A sweet, intensely-flavored high-alcohol beverage made from fruits, nuts, seeds, spices, or herbs infused with a spirit, such as brandy or rum. Traditionally served after dinner as a mild digestive, liqueurs can also be used in cooking and baking.

marinate: To flavor a food by letting it soak in a liquid that may contain an acid ingredient (e.g., lemon juice, wine, or vinegar), oil, herbs, and spices.

mince: To chop or cut food into tiny, irregular pieces.

panfry: To cook food in a small amount of hot butter, margarine, or oil in a skillet until browned and cooked through.

parboil: To partially cook a food in boiling water. Slow-cooking foods, such as carrots, are often parboiled before they're added to a mixture composed of quicker-cooking foods.

pare: To cut away the skin or rind of a fruit or vegetable. You can use a vegetable peeler or a paring knife—a small knife with a 3- to 4-inch blade.

pasteurize: To sterilize milk by heating, then rapidly cooling it. Most milk sold in the United States is pasteurized, which both destroys bacteria that can cause disease and improves shelf life. Ultrapasteurized (UHT) milk is subjected to very high temperatures—about 300°F—and aseptic-packed for extended storage. It will keep without refrigeration for up to 6 months, but must be refrigerated once it's opened. Ultrapasteurized cream, however, is not aseptic-packed, and should be refrigerated even when unopened.

pinch: The amount of a powdery ingredient or dried herb that you can hold between your thumb and forefinger—about 1/16 teaspoon.

pipe: To force a food (typically frosting or whipped cream) through a pastry tip to use as a decoration or garnish, or to shape dough, such as for eclairs. You can also use a zip-tight plastic bag with a corner snipped off.

poach: To cook food in gently simmering liquid; the surface should barely shimmer. If you plan to use the cooking liquid for a broth or sauce afterward, poach in a pan just large enough to hold the food. That way, you can add less liquid and avoid diluting flavors. Poaching liquid is often seasoned or contains aromatic vegetables for flavor.

pound: To flatten meats and poultry to a uniform thickness using a meat mallet or rolling pin. This ensures even, quick cooking and also tenderizes tough meats by breaking up hard-to-chew connective tissue. Veal and chicken cutlets are often pounded.

prick: To pierce a food in many or a few places, usually with a fork. You can prick a food to prevent buckling—an unfilled piecrust before it is baked, for example—or bursting—a potato before it is baked, or sausages before they are cooked.

proof: To test yeast for potency: If you're not sure the yeast is fresh and active, dissolve it in warm water (105° to 115°F) with a pinch of sugar. If the mixture foams after 5 to 10 minutes, the yeast is fine to use. Proofing also refers to the rising stage for yeast doughs.

punch down: To deflate yeast dough after it has risen, to distribute gluten (the elastic protein in flour that gives bread its strength) and prevent dough from overrising. Punch your fist into the center of dough, then pull the edges toward the center.

puree: To form a smooth mixture by whirling food, usually a fruit or vegetable, in a food processor or blender, or straining through a food mill.

reduce: To rapidly boil a liquid, especially a sauce, so a portion cooks off by evaporation. This creates a thicker sauce with a deeper, more concentrated flavor. If you use a wide pan, the liquid will evaporate faster.

render: To slowly melt animal fat (e.g., duck and chicken skin, pork rinds) down to a liquid. The clear fat is poured through a sieve before being used in cooking. The crisp, brown bits left in the skillet—delicious but high in fat—are called cracklings.

roast: To cook food in the oven, in an uncovered pan, by the free circulation of dry heat, usually until the exterior is well browned. Tender cuts of meat, as well as poultry and fish, are suitable for roasting; so are many vegetables, such as potatoes, parsnips, peppers, and even tomatoes.

sauté: To cook or brown food quickly in a small amount of hot fat in a skillet; the term derives from the French sauter ("to jump"), and refers to the practice of shaking food in the pan so it browns evenly.

scald: To heat milk until tiny bubbles just begin to appear around the edge of the pan—it should not boil. Before milk was pasteurized, scalding was a safeguard used to destroy bacteria and prolong freshness. Today's recipes specify scalding for other reasons, such as dissolving sugar or melting shortening.

score: To make shallow cuts (usually parallel or crisscross) in the surface of foods before cooking. This is done mainly to aid flavor absorption, as for marinated meats, chicken, and fish, but sometimes also for decorative purposes, as for hams and breads.

sear: To brown the surface of meat quickly in a hot pan or in the oven to caramelize the meat and enrich the flavor.

shred: To cut, tear, or grate food into small narrow strips. For some recipes, cooked meat is shredded by pulling it apart with 2 forks. Cheese is shredded on the large holes of a box grater.

shave: To cut wide, paper-thin slices of food, especially Parmesan cheese, vegetables, or chocolate. Shave off slices with a vegetable peeler and use as a garnish.

shuck: To remove the shells of oysters, mussels, or clams, or the husks of corn.

sift: To pass ingredients such as flour or confectioners' sugar through a fine-mesh sifter or sieve. This incorporates air, removes lumps, and helps the flour or sugar to mix more readily with liquids.

simmer: To cook liquid gently (or to cook food gently in liquid), over low heat, keeping it just below the boiling point. A few small bubbles should be visible on the surface.

skim: To remove fat or froth from the surface of a liquid, such as broth or boiling jelly. A large kitchen spoon or a skimmer, with a flat wire mesh or perforated bowl at the end of a long handle, is ideal for removing foam. Use a ladle or large spoon for removing fat..

steam: To cook food, covered, in the vapor given off by boiling water. The food is set on a rack or in a basket so it's over, not in, boiling water—since it's not immersed, it retains more nutrients, and maintains bright colors and fresh flavor.

stir-fry: To cook small, evenly cut pieces of food quickly in a small amount of oil over high heat, stirring and tossing almost constantly. Vegetables cooked in this way retain more nutrients because of the short cooking time. Stir-frying is much used in Asian cooking; a wok is the traditional pan, though a skillet or Dutch oven will do just as well.

temper: To heat food gently before adding it to a hot mixture so that it doesn't separate or curdle. Often eggs are tempered by mixing with a little hot liquid to raise their temperature before they're stirred into a hot sauce or soup.

tender-crisp: The ideal degree of doneness for many vegetables, especially green vegetables. Cook them until they're just tender but still retain some texture and bite.

toss: To lift and drop pieces of food quickly and gently using two utensils, usually to coat them with a sauce (as for pasta) or dressing (as for salad).

whip: To beat an ingredient (especially cream) or mixture rapidly, adding air and increasing the volume. Whip with a whisk, egg beater, or electric mixer.

whisk: To beat ingredients (e.g., cream, eggs, salad dressings, sauces) with a fork or more often, the looped wire utensil called a whisk so as to mix or blend, or incorporate air.

Appetizers &
First Courses

Canapés, hors d'oeuvres, dips, spreads, relishes, nibbles—they are all appetizers. For parties where appetizers are the only food served, offer both hot and cold kinds, assembling a variety of shapes, colors, textures, and flavors, from crisp nuts and cool dips to savory hot pastries and meats or seafood with zesty sauces. Appetizers that precede a meal should be chosen with the rest of the menu in mind, so similar flavors are not repeated in dishes served later.

Black Bean Dip

Prep: 5 minutes
Cook: 3 minutes

4 garlic cloves, peeled
1 can (15 to 19 ounces) black beans, rinsed and drained
2 tablespoons tomato paste
2 tablespoons olive oil
4 teaspoons fresh lime juice
1 tablespoon water

¼ teaspoon salt
⅛ teaspoon ground red pepper (cayenne)
½ teaspoon ground cumin
½ teaspoon ground coriander
Assorted crackers or cut-up vegetables

1. In 1-quart saucepan, heat *2 cups water* to boiling over high heat. Add garlic and cook 3 minutes to blanch; drain.

2. In food processor with knife blade attached, process garlic, beans, tomato paste, oil, lime juice, water, salt, ground red pepper, cumin, and coriander until smooth.

Spoon dip into bowl; cover and refrigerate up to 2 days. Serve with crackers or cut-up vegetables. Makes about 2 cups.

Each tablespoon: About 20 calories, 1 g protein, 3 g carbohydrate, 1 g total fat (0 g saturated), 0 mg cholesterol, 55 mg sodium.

Green Goddess Dip

Prep: 10 minutes
Cook: 5 minutes

2 garlic cloves, peeled
1 container (8 ounces) sour cream
1 cup fresh parsley leaves, chopped
2 green onions, finely chopped
2 tablespoons light mayonnnaise
2 teaspoons fresh lemon juice
1½ teaspoons anchovy paste
1 teaspoon dried tarragon
Assorted crackers or cut-up vegetables

1. In 1-quart saucepan heat *2 cups water* to boiling over high heat. Add garlic and cook 3 minutes to blanch; drain. Finely chop garlic; place in medium bowl.

2. Stir in sour cream, parsley, green onions, mayonnaise, lemon juice, anchovy paste, and tarragon. Spoon dip into bowl, cover and refrigerate up to 2 days. Makes about 1 cup.

Each tablespoon: About 35 calories, 1 g protein, 2 g carbohydrate, 3 g total fat (2 g saturated), 7 mg cholesterol, 40 mg sodium.

GH Guacamole

Prep: 20 minutes

2 medium or 1 large ripe avocado*
2 tablespoons minced onion
2 tablespoons chopped fresh cilantro
2 serrano or jalapeño chiles, seeded and minced
1 tablespoon fresh lime juice
½ teaspoon salt
¼ teaspoon coarsely ground black pepper
1 plum tomato (4 ounces), finely chopped
Tortilla wedges, chips, or cut-up vegetables

1. Cut each avocado lengthwise in half; remove pits. With spoon, scoop pulp from peel into medium bowl.

2. Add onion, cilantro, serrano chiles, lime juice, salt, and pepper. With potato masher, coarsely mash mixture. Stir in tomato. Transfer to small serving bowl. Serve with tortilla wedges, chips, or cut-up vegetables. Makes about 1½ cups.

Choose perfectly ripened avocados that yield to gentle pressure when lightly squeezed in the palm of the hand.

Each tablespoon: About 35 calories, 1 g protein, 2 g carbohydrate, 3 g total fat (1 g saturated), 0 mg cholesterol, 45 mg sodium.

Roasted Red Pepper and Walnut Dip

Prep: 30 minutes plus cooling
Broil: 10 minutes

4 medium red peppers
½ cup walnuts
½ teaspoon ground cumin
2 slices firm white bread, torn into small pieces
2 tablespoons balsamic or red wine vinegar
1 tablespoon olive oil
½ teaspoon salt
⅛ teaspoon ground red pepper (cayenne)
Toasted pita triangles

1. Preheat broiler. Line broiling pan with foil. Cut each pepper lengthwise in half; remove and discard stems and seeds. Arrange peppers, cut side down, in prepared broiling pan. Place pan in broiler 5 to 6 inches from heat source. Broil until skin is charred and blistered, 8 to 10 minutes. Wrap peppers in foil and allow to steam at room temperature until cool enough to handle, about 15 minutes. Remove peppers from foil. Peel off skin and discard.

2. Meanwhile, turn oven control to 350°F. Spread walnuts in baking pan and bake until toasted, 8 to 10 minutes. In small skillet, toast cumin over low heat, stirring, until very fragrant, 1 to 2 minutes.

3. Cut peppers into large pieces. In food processor with knife blade attached, process walnuts until ground. Add roasted peppers, cumin, bread, vinegar, oil, salt, and ground red pepper; process until smooth. Transfer to serving bowl. Cover and refrigerate if not serving right away. Remove from refrigerator 30 minutes before serving. Serve with toasted pita triangles. Makes about 2 cups dip.

Each tablespoon: About 25 calories, 0 g protein, 2 g carbohydrate, 2 g total fat (0 g saturated), 0 mg cholesterol, 40 mg sodium.

Blue-Cheese Ball

Prep: 20 minutes plus chilling

1 package (8 ounces) cream cheese, softened
4 ounces blue cheese, crumbled (about 1 cup)
2 teaspoons bourbon (optional)
¾ teaspoon dry mustard
2 tablespoons sesame seeds, toasted (see page 29)
Assorted crackers

1. In small bowl with mixer at medium speed, beat cream cheese and blue cheese until blended. Beat in bourbon, if desired, and mustard. With hands, shape cheese mixture into a ball. Wrap in plastic wrap and refrigerate overnight.

2. To serve, with hands reshape cheese ball and roll in sesame seeds. Serve with crackers. Makes about 12 appetizer servings.

Each serving: About 110 calories, 0 g protein, 0 g carbohydrate, 0 g total fat, 0 mg cholesterol, 0 mg sodium.

Pimiento-Studded Deviled Eggs

Prep: 40 minutes

12 large eggs
¼ cup sliced pimientos, drained and chopped
¼ cup light mayonnaise dressing
4 teaspoons Dijon mustard
¼ teaspoon salt
½ teaspoon ground red pepper (cayenne)

1. In 4-quart saucepan, place eggs and enough *cold water to cover by at least 1 inch*; heat to boiling over high heat. Immediately remove saucepan from heat and cover tightly; let stand 15 minutes. Pour off hot water and run cold water over eggs to cool. Peel eggs.

2. Slice each egg lengthwise in half. Gently remove yolks and place in small bowl; with fork, finely mash yolks. Stir in pimientos, mayonnaise, mustard, salt, and ground red pepper until well blended.

3. Place egg-white halves in jelly-roll pan lined with paper towels to prevent eggs from rolling. Spoon yolk mixture into egg-white halves. Cover and refrigerate until ready to serve. Makes 24 stuffed-egg halves.

Each stuffed-egg half: About 45 calories, 3 g protein, 1 g carbohydrate, 3 g total fat (1 g saturated), 107 mg cholesterol, 100 mg sodium.

Tortilla Spirals

Prep: 35 minutes plus chilling

Smoked Salmon Filling
1 ½ packages (8 ounces each) cream cheese, softened
4 ounces thinly sliced smoked salmon, chopped
¼ cup loosely packed fresh dill, chopped
3 tablespoons capers, drained and chopped

Sun-Dried Tomato Filling
1 package (8 ounces) cream cheese, softened
1 container (5.2 ounces) spreadable cheese with pepper
10 sun-dried tomato halves, packed in herb-seasoned olive oil, drained and chopped
⅓ cup packed fresh basil leaves, chopped
8 (10-inch) flour tortillas

1. Prepare Smoked Salmon Filling: In medium bowl, stir cream cheese, smoked salmon, dill, and capers until well blended.

2. Prepare Sun-Dried Tomato Filling: In medium bowl,

stir cream cheese, spreadable cheese with pepper, sun-dried tomatoes, and basil until well blended.

3. Spread each of the fillings evenly over 4 tortillas (4 with salmon, 4 with tomato). Roll each tortilla up tightly, jelly-roll fashion. Wrap each roll in plastic wrap and refrigerate until firm enough to slice, at least 4 hours or overnight.

4. To serve, unwrap tortilla rolls and trim ends. Cut rolls into slightly less than ½-inch-thick slices. Makes about 4½ dozen appetizers.

Each appetizer with salmon filling: About 85 calories, 3 g protein, 6 g carbohydrate, 5 g total fat (3 g saturated), 15 mg cholesterol, 155 mg sodium.

Each appetizer with tomato filling: About 85 calories, 3 g protein, 7 g carbohydrate, 5 g total fat (3 g saturated), 13 mg cholesterol, 155 mg sodium.

Salmon Pâté

Prep: 15 minutes plus chilling

1 can (15½ ounces) salmon, drained
1 package (8 ounces) cream cheese, softened
2 tablespoons chopped green onion
1 tablespoon fresh lemon juice
½ teaspoon salt
⅛ teaspoon ground black pepper
⅛ teaspoon dillweed
2 tablespoons capers, drained
Assorted crackers

1. In blender or in food processor with knife blade attached, process salmon, cream cheese, green onion, lemon juice, salt, pepper, and dillweed until smooth. Spoon mixture into small bowl; stir in capers.

2. Cover bowl and refrigerate pâté until well chilled,

about 2 hours. Serve with crackers. Makes about 2½ cups or 12 appetizer servings.

Each serving: About 115 calories, 0 g protein, 0 g carbohydrate, 0 g total fat, 0 mg cholesterol, 0 mg sodium.

Pork Rillettes

Prep: 30 minutes plus chilling
Cook: 3 hours

3 pounds boneless pork
    shoulder blade roast (fresh
    pork butt), trimmed and cut
    into ½-inch pieces
1 cup water
1 garlic clove, crushed with
    side of chef's knife

2 teaspoons salt
1½ teaspoons coarsely ground
    black pepper
1 teaspoon marjoram
½ teaspoon thyme
1 bay leaf
Unsalted crackers

1. In 5-quart Dutch oven, stir together pork, water, garlic, salt, pepper, marjoram, thyme, and bay leaf. Heat to boiling over high heat. Reduce heat to low; cover and simmer, stirring occasionally, until meat is very tender and falls apart when tested with a fork, about 2 hours 30 minutes.

2. When meat is tender, remove cover from Dutch oven and simmer meat over low heat, stirring often, until liquid has been evaporated. Discard bay leaf.

3. With two forks, pull meat into shreds. Spoon mixture into 2-cup crock; pack down well. Cover with crock lid or plastic wrap and refrigerate until well chilled. Serve spread with unsalted crackers. Makes about 2 cups spread or 10 appetizer servings.

Each serving: About 175 calories, 22 g protein, 0 g carbohydrate, 10 g total fat (3 g saturated), 77 mg cholesterol, 645 mg sodium.

Pastry Fingers with Cream Cheese and Caviar

Prep: 35 minutes plus chilling
Bake: 25 minutes

4 tablespoons margarine or butter
½ cup water
½ cup all-purpose flour
2 large eggs
1 package (8 ounces) cream cheese, softened
½ cup sour cream
1 ½ teaspoons grated onion
¾ teaspoon dillweed
1 jar (2 ounces) red salmon caviar, drained

1. Grease large cookie sheet. In 2-quart saucepan, heat margarine and water over medium heat, until butter melts and mixture boils. Reduce heat to low; vigorously stir in flour all at once. Continue stirring until mixture forms a ball, and leaves side of pan. Remove from heat; stir in eggs until blended and smooth. Refrigerate dough 20 minutes for easier piping.

2. Preheat oven to 375°F. Spoon dough into pastry bag fitted with ½-inch plain tip. Pipe onto prepared cookie sheet into 2½" by ½" strips, about 1 inch apart. Bake until golden, about 20 minutes. Transfer pastry fingers to wire racks and cool.

3. To serve, in small bowl with mixer at medium speed, beat cream cheese, sour cream, onion, and dillweed until smooth. With serrated knife, cut each pastry finger horizontally in half. Spoon some cream-cheese filling onto each half; top with some caviar. Makes about 60 appetizers.

Each appetizer: About 30 calories, 1 g protein, 1 g carbohydrate, 3 g total fat (1 g saturated), 16 g cholesterol, 35 mg sodium.

Pickled Shrimp Appetizer

Prep: 45 minutes plus overnight to marinate
Cook: 5 minutes

¼ cup dry sherry
4 teaspoons salt
1 bay leaf
¼ teaspoon whole black
  peppercorns
3 pounds large shrimp, shelled
  and deveined, leaving tail
  part of shell on, if you like
  (see page 366)

1 cup vegetable oil
⅔ cup fresh lemon juice
½ cup distilled white vinegar
3 tablespoons mixed pickling
  spice, tied in cheesecloth
  bag
2 teaspoons sugar
2 sprigs fresh dill
Crushed ice (optional)

1. In 4-quart saucepan, heat *6 cups water*, sherry, 2 teaspoons salt, bay leaf, and peppercorns to boiling over high heat. Stir in shrimp; heat to boiling, stirring frequently. Shrimp should be done when water returns to boiling or cook 1 minute longer, just until they are opaque throughout. Drain.

2. In large bowl, combine oil, lemon juice, vinegar, pickling spice, sugar, dill, and remaining 2 teaspoons salt; stir until blended. Add shrimp and toss well to coat with marinade. Cover and refrigerate shrimp overnight to marinate, tossing occasionally.

3. To serve, arrange shrimp in chilled serving bowl; discard marinade. To keep shrimp well chilled, place bowl of shrimp in larger bowl of crushed ice, if you like. Makes 24 appetizer servings.

Each serving: About 55 calories, 10 g protein, 0 g carbohydrate, 2 g total fat (0 g saturated), 90 mg cholesterol, 150 mg sodium.

Parmesan Toasts

Prep: 15 minutes plus cooling
Bake: 35 minutes

1 loaf dense sourdough bread (about 1 pound)
1¾ cups freshly grated Parmesan cheese
2 tablespoons olive oil
¼ teaspoon dried thyme
¼ teaspoon crushed red pepper
Pinch dried rosemary, crumbled
Pinch salt

1. Preheat oven to 300°F. With serrated knife, cut off ends from bread; reserve for another use. Cut loaf into slices, slightly thinner than ¼-inch thick. Place slices on 2 large cookie sheets. Bake about 30 minutes, until dry and toasted, turning slices halfway through baking. Remove toasts from oven. Turn oven control to 400°F.
2. Meanwhile, in medium bowl, with fork, mix Parmesan, oil, thyme, crushed red pepper, rosemary, and salt until blended.
3. Top each toast slice with 2 rounded teaspoons cheese mixture; spread mixture slightly. Bake toasts until cheese melts, 3 to 5 minutes. Cool on cookie sheets on wire racks until topping dries out, at least 2 hours or overnight. Store at room temperature in tightly covered container up to 2 weeks. Makes about 24 toasts.

Each toast: About 90 calories, 5 g protein, 9 g carbohydrate, 4 g total fat (2 g saturated), 6 mg cholesterol, 240 mg sodium.

Sesame Pita Toasts

Prep: 25 minutes plus chilling
Bake: 8 minutes

½ cup sesame seeds, toasted (see page 29)
2 tablespoons chopped fresh parsley leaves
2 teaspoons freshly grated lemon peel
½ teaspoon salt
¼ teaspoon coarsely ground black pepper
2 teaspoons dried thyme
1 package (7 ounces) mini pitas, 2-inch diameter
2 tablespoons extra virgin olive oil

1. In blender blend sesame seeds, parsley, lemon peel, salt, pepper, and thyme until seeds are ground, stopping blender occasionally, and scraping down sides with rubber spatula. Transfer mixture to medium bowl.

2. Brush tops of pitas with oil. Sprinkle top of each pita with about 1½ teaspoons sesame-seed mixture, pressing mixture on gently. Place pitas on large cookie sheet; cover and refrigerate up to 6 hours before serving.

3. To serve, preheat oven to 450°F. Bake until pitas are crisp and golden, about 8 minutes. Makes 24 toasts.

Each toast: About 50 calories, 1 g protein, 5 g carbohydrate, 3 g total fat (0 g saturated), 0 mg cholesterol, 75 mg sodium.

Cheddar Straws

Prep: 45 minutes plus chilling
Bake: 15 minutes per batch

2 cups all-purpose flour
½ teaspoon salt
Ground red pepper
1 cup (2 sticks) margarine or butter, cut into pieces
8 ounces Cheddar cheese, shredded (about 2 cups)
½ cup ice water

1. In large bowl, stir together flour, salt, and ¼ teaspoon ground red pepper. With pastry blender or two knives used scissor-fashion, cut in margarine until mixture resembles coarse crumbs.

2. Stir in cheese and water just until mixture forms a soft dough that holds together and leaves side of bowl. On lightly floured surface, with floured hands, pat dough into 6-inch square. Wrap dough in plastic wrap and chill in freezer 30 minutes for easier handling.

3. On lightly floured surface, roll chilled dough into 18" by 8" rectangle. Starting from one 8-inch end, fold one-third of dough over middle one-third; fold oppposite one-third over both to make a 6" by 8" rectangle.

4. Repeat rolling and folding as in step 3. Wrap dough in plastic wrap; freeze 30 minutes longer.

5. Preheat oven to 375°F. Remove dough from freezer; roll and fold again as in step 3. Then roll dough into 18" by 12" rectangle. Sprinkle dough lightly with ground red pepper; cut lengthwise in half. Cut each half crosswise into thirty-six 6" by ½" strips.

6. Place strips ½ inch apart on ungreased large cookie sheets, twisting each strip twice, and pressing ends against cookie sheet (this prevents strips from uncurling during baking).

7. Bake cheese straws until golden, about 15 minutes, remove from cookie sheets and cool on wire racks. Store in tightly covered container. Makes about 6 dozen straws.

Each straw: About 50 calories, 1 g protein, 3 g carbohydrate, 4 g total fat (1 g saturated), 3 mg cholesterol, 70 mg sodium.

Christmas Quesadillas

Prep: 40 minutes
Bake: 8 minutes

1 tablespoon vegetable oil	¼ teaspoon ground cumin
1 large onion, chopped	2 tablespoons chopped fresh
1 medium green pepper,	cilantro leaves
chopped	12 (6- to 7-inch) flour tortillas
1 medium red pepper,	6 ounces Monterey Jack cheese
chopped	with jalapeño chiles,
1 garlic clove, finely chopped	shredded (about 1½ cups)
¼ teaspoon salt	

1. In nonstick 10-inch skillet, heat oil over medium heat. Add onion and green and red peppers and cook, stirring often, until golden and tender, about 15 minutes. Add garlic, salt, and cumin, and cook, stirring often, 5 minutes longer. Remove skillet from heat; stir in cilantro.
2. Preheat oven to 450°F. Place 6 tortillas on 2 large cookie sheets. Spread pepper mixture on tortillas; sprinkle with cheese. Top with remaining tortillas to make 6 quesadillas.
3. Bake quesadillas 8 minutes, until lightly browned on both sides, turning once halfway through baking. Transfer quesadillas to cutting board; cut each into 8 wedges. Serve immediately. Makes 48 wedges.

Each wedge: About 50 calories, 2 g protein, 6 g carbohydrate, 2 g total fat (1 g saturated), 4 mg cholesterol, 75 mg sodium.

Spiced Nut and Pretzel Mix

Prep: 5 minutes plus cooling
Bake: 30 minutes

1 large egg white
2 tablespoons sugar
1½ teaspoons salt
¾ teaspoon ground red pepper (cayenne)
2 teaspoons ground cumin
1 pound natural almonds
8 ounces unsalted cashews
1 package (9 to 10¼ ounces) pretzel sticks

1. Preheat oven to 350°F. Spray 15½" by 10½" jelly-roll pan with nonstick cooking spray.

2. In large bowl, with wire whisk, beat egg white, sugar, salt, ground red pepper, and cumin until well blended. Add almonds and cashews; toss to coat with egg-white mixture.

3. Spread nut mixture in prepared pan. Bake 30 minutes, lifting and stirring nuts with wide spatula every 5 minutes.

4. Spread hot nut mixture on large cookie sheet; place cookie sheet on wire rack and cool nuts completely. (Nuts will be crisp when cool.) When cool, toss nuts with pretzels. Store in tightly covered container for up to 1 week. Makes about 9 cups.

Each ¼ cup: About 140 calories, 5 g protein, 12 g carbohydrate, 9 g total fat (1 g saturated), 0 mg cholesterol, 220 mg sodium.

Firecracker Mix

Prep: 10 minutes
Bake: 30 minutes per batch

¼ cup Worcestershire sauce
4 tablespoons margarine or butter
2 tablespoons brown sugar
1½ teaspoons salt
½ to 1 teaspoon ground red pepper (cayenne)
12 cups popped corn (about ⅓ to ½ cup unpopped)
1 package (12 ounces) oven-toasted corn cereal squares
1 package (8 to 10 ounces) thin pretzel sticks

1. Preheat oven to 300°F. In 1-quart saucepan, stir Worcestershire, margarine, brown sugar, salt, and ground red pepper over low heat until butter melts; stir to combine.

2. Place half each of popped corn, cereal, and pretzels in large 17" by 11½" roasting pan; toss with half of Worcestershire mixture.

3. Bake popcorn mixture 30 minutes, stirring once halfway through baking. Cool mixture in very large bowl or on counter covered with waxed paper. Repeat with remaining ingredients. Store in tightly covered container for up to 1 week. Makes about 25 cups.

Each ½ cup: About 65 calories, 1 g protein, 13 g carbohydrate, 1 g total fat (0 g saturated), 0 mg cholesterol, 245 mg sodium.

Spicy Ground Beef Empanaditas

Prep: 1 hour 15 minutes
Bake: 15 to 17 minutes per batch

Flaky Turnover Pastry (see page 58)

2 teaspoons vegetable oil
1 small onion, finely chopped
1 large garlic clove, finely chopped
¼ teaspoon salt
¼ teaspoon ground red pepper (cayenne)
¼ teaspoon ground cinnamon
¼ pound ground beef

1 cup canned tomatoes with juice
3 tablespoons chopped golden raisins
3 tablespoons chopped pimiento-stuffed olives (salad olives)
1 large egg, beaten with 2 tablespoons water, for glaze

1. Prepare Flaky Turnover Pastry. Wrap in plastic wrap and set aside.

2. In 10-inch skillet, heat oil over medium heat. Add onion and cook, stirring frequently, until tender, about 5 minutes. Stir in garlic, salt, ground red pepper, and cinnamon; cook, stirring, 30 seconds. Increase heat to medium-high; add ground beef and cook, stirring frequently, until beef begins to brown, about 5 minutes. Stir in tomatoes with their juice, raisins, and olives, breaking tomatoes up with back of spoon. Increase heat to high and cook, until almost all liquid has evaporated, 7 to 10 minutes. Remove skillet from heat.

3. Divide dough into 4 equal pieces. On lightly floured surface, with floured rolling pin, roll one-fourth of dough ¹⁄₁₆ inch thick (keep remaining dough covered with plastic wrap). With 3-inch round biscuit cutter, cut out as many rounds as possible, reserving trimmings. On half of each dough round, place 1 level teaspoon filling. Brush edges of rounds with some egg mixture. Fold dough over filling. With fork, press edges together to seal. Prick tops; brush egg mixture lightly over turnovers. With wide spatula, transfer turnovers, about 1 inch apart, to ungreased large cookie sheet. Repeat with remaining filling and dough, rerolling trimmings. If not serving right away, cover with plastic wrap and refrigerate.

4. About 25 minutes before serving, preheat oven to 425°F. Bake turnovers, in batches, just until golden, 15 to 17 minutes. Repeat with remaining turnovers. Serve hot. Makes about 4½ dozen turnovers.

FLAKY TURNOVER PASTRY: In large bowl, stir together *3 cups all-purpose flour, 1½ teaspoons baking powder,* and *¾ teaspoon salt* until well blended. With pastry blender or two knives used scissor-fashion, cut in *1 cup shortening* until mixture resembles coarse crumbs. Sprinkle with about *6 tablespoons cold water,* 1 tablespoon at a time, mixing with fork after each addition, just until dough holds together. Shape dough into a ball; wrap in plastic wrap. Refrigerate if not assembling turnovers right away.

Each turnover: About 70 calories, 1 g protein, 6 g carbohydrate, 5 g total fat (2 g saturated), 5 mg cholesterol, 80 mg sodium.

Mushroom Turnovers

Prep: 1 hour 20 minutes plus cooling and optional freezing
Bake: 12 to 20 minutes per batch

Turnover Pastry
1 package (8 ounces) cream cheese, softened
½ cup (1 stick) margarine or butter, softened
1½ cups all-purpose flour

Mushroom Filling

3 tablespoons margarine or
    butter
8 ounces mushrooms, trimmed
    and chopped
1 medium onion, finely
    chopped
1 garlic clove, crushed with
    garlic press
1 tablespoon all-purpose flour
½ teaspoon salt

¼ teaspoon coarsely ground
    black pepper
¼ teaspoon dried thyme
1 tablespoon dry sherry or dry
    vermouth
3 tablespoons sour cream
1 large egg, beaten with 2
    tablespoons water, for glaze

1. Prepare Turnover Pastry: In medium bowl, with hand, knead cream cheese, margarine, and flour until blended and dough just holds together. Shape dough into 2 disks; wrap each in plastic wrap and refrigerate until firm enough to handle, about 30 minutes.

2. Meanwhile, prepare Mushroom Filling: In 12-inch skillet, melt margarine over medium heat. Add mushrooms and onion and cook, stirring frequently, until onion is tender and liquid has evaporated, about 20 minutes. Stir in garlic, flour, salt, pepper, and thyme, then sherry; cook, stirring, 1 minute longer. Transfer mushroom mixture to bowl to cool. Stir in sour cream.

3. On lightly floured surface, with floured rolling pin, roll half of dough ⅛ inch thick (keep remaining dough refrigerated). With 3-inch round biscuit cutter, cut out as many rounds as possible, reserving trimmings.

4. On half of each dough round, place 1 rounded tea-spoon Mushroom Filling. Brush edges of rounds with some egg mixture. Fold dough over filling. With fork, press edges together to seal. Prick tops, brush turnovers lightly with egg mixture. With wide spatula, transfer turnovers, about 1 inch apart, to ungreased large cookie sheet.

5. Repeat with remaining filling and dough, rerolling trimmings to make about 48 turnovers.

6. Cover cookie sheets tightly with plastic wrap or foil and refrigerate turnovers up to 1 day. Or, to freeze, place unbaked turnovers in jelly-roll pan; cover and freeze until hard. With wide spatula, transfer turnovers to freezer-safe containers with waxed paper between each layer. Cover and freeze up to 1 month.

7. To serve, preheat oven to 450°F. Bake refrigerated turnovers until golden, 12 to 14 minutes. Or, place frozen turnovers about 1 inch apart on ungreased cookie sheets and bake until golden, 15 to 20 minutes. Serve hot. Makes about 4 dozen turnovers.

Each turnover: About 60 calories, 1 g protein, 4 g carbohydrate, 5 g total fat (2 g saturated), 10 mg cholesterol, 75 mg sodium.

Bite-Sized Bacon Quiches

Prep: 50 minutes plus chilling
Bake: 20 to 25 minutes

1 package (10 to 11 ounces) piecrust mix
1 tablespoon margarine or butter, melted
8 ounces bacon, chopped
3 large eggs
1 cup half-and-half
¼ teaspoon salt
8 ounces Swiss cheese, shredded (about 1 cup)

1. Grease and flour thirty-six 1¾-inch muffin-pan cups. Prepare piecrust mix as label directs.

2. On lightly floured surface, with floured rolling pin, roll dough about ⅛ inch thick. Using 3-inch round fluted biscuit cutter, cut dough into 36 rounds, rerolling trimmings.

3. Line muffin-pan cups with pastry rounds; brush pastry lightly with melted margarine. Cover and refrigerate until pastry is firm, about 1 hour.

4. In 2-quart saucepan, cook bacon over medium heat, stirring frequently, until crisp and brown. With slotted spoon, transfer bacon to paper towels to drain; cool. Wrap in plastic wrap and refrigerate if not baking quiches right away.

5. About 35 minutes before serving, preheat oven to 400°F. In medium bowl, with wire whisk, beat eggs, half-and-half, and salt. Into each pastry cup, sprinkle some chopped bacon and some cheese. Spoon about 1 tablespoon egg mixture into each cup. Place muffin pans on foil-lined cookie sheets to catch any overflow. Bake quiches until knife inserted in center of a quiche comes out clean, 20 to 25 minutes. Remove quiches from pans and serve immediately. Makes 3 dozen quiches.

Each quiche: About 95 calories, 4 g protein, 5 g carbohydrate, 7 g total fat (3 g saturated), 27 mg cholesterol, 140 mg sodium.

Shrimp Toast

Prep: 15 minutes
Cook: 4 minutes per batch

1 package (12 ounces) frozen shelled and deveined shrimp, thawed or 1 pound small shrimp shelled and deveined (see page 366)	1 teaspoon salt
	1 teaspoon finely chopped green onion
	⅛ teaspoon ground ginger
	6 very thin slices firm white bread, crusts removed
1 large egg white	Parsley leaves
2 tablespoons dry sherry	Vegetable oil for frying
1 teaspoon cornstarch	

1. If using frozen shrimp, drain very well. If using fresh shrimp, shell and devein. In blender or in food processor with knife blade attached, process shrimp until finely chopped. In medium bowl, with spoon, mix shrimp, egg white, sherry, cornstarch, salt, green onion, and ginger until well blended.

2. Cut each bread slice into 4 triangles. Spread 1 heaping teaspoon shrimp mixture evenly on each triangle with small spatula; scrape edge so filling will be neat. Gently press a parsley leaf on to each.

3. In 12-inch skillet, heat about 1 inch oil over medium heat, until temperature reaches 325°F on deep-fat thermometer (or, heat oil in electric skillet at 325°F).

4. Carefully place 5 or 6 triangles, shrimp side down, in hot oil; cook until lightly browned, about 3 minutes. Turn and cook until bread is golden, 1 minute longer. Transfer to paper towels to drain; keep warm. Repeat with remaining triangles. Serve hot. Makes 2 dozen Shrimp Toasts.

Each Shrimp Toast: About 45 calories, 3 g protein, 2 g carbohydrate, 2 g total fat (0 g saturated), 22 mg cholesterol, 145 mg sodium.

Chilled Lemony Mushrooms

Prep: 15 minutes plus chilling
Cook: 5 minutes

1 medium lemon
¼ cup olive oil
1 pound medium mushrooms, trimmed and sliced
2 tablespoons water
1½ teaspoons soy sauce
¼ teaspoon sugar
¼ teaspoon salt
¼ teaspoon dried sage
2 small heads bibb lettuce

1. From lemon, cut 6 very thin slices and squeeze 2 teaspoons juice.

2. In 3-quart saucepan, heat oil over medium-high heat. Add mushrooms and toss to coat with oil. Stir in water, soy sauce, sugar, salt, sage, and lemon slices and juice; heat to boiling. Reduce heat to medium and cook, stirring often, until mushrooms are tender, about 3 minutes. Spoon mushroom mixture into bowl; cover and refrigerate until well chilled.

3. To serve, cut each head of bibb lettuce into 4 wedges. Arrange two lettuce wedges and some mushrooms on 8 small plates. Makes 8 first-course servings.

Each serving: About 80 calories, 2 g protein, 4 g carbohydrate, 7 g total fat (1 g saturated), 0 mg cholesterol, 140 mg sodium.

Caponata

Prep: 30 minutes plus cooling
Cook: 40 minutes

2 small eggplants (1 pound each), trimmed and cut into ¾-inch pieces
½ cup extra virgin olive oil
¼ teaspoon salt
3 small red onions, thinly sliced
1½ pounds ripe tomatoes (4 medium), peeled, seeded, and chopped
1 cup Mediterranean olives, pitted and chopped
3 tablespoons golden raisins
3 tablespoons capers, drained
¼ teaspoon coarsely ground black pepper
4 medium stalks celery with leaves, thinly sliced
⅓ cup red wine vinegar
2 teaspoons sugar
¼ cup loosely packed fresh flat-leaf parsley, chopped
Assorted crackers or melba toast

1. Preheat oven to 500°F. Place eggplant on two 15½" by 10½" jelly-roll pans. Drizzle with ¼ cup oil (2 tablespoons per pan) and sprinkle with salt; toss to coat. Roast eggplant 10 minutes; stir, then roast about 5 minutes longer or until browned.

2. Meanwhile, in 12-inch skillet, heat remaining ¼ cup oil over medium heat. Add onions and cook, stirring, until tender but not browned, about 10 minutes. Add tomatoes, olives, raisins, capers, and pepper; reduce heat to low, cover and simmer 15 minutes.

3. Add eggplant and celery to skillet. Uncover and increase heat to medium. Cook, stirring occasionally, until celery is just tender. Stir in vinegar and sugar and cook 1 minute. Spoon into serving bowl; cool slightly to serve at room temperature or cover and refrigerate to serve cold later. Sprinkle with parsley. Serve with crackers or melba toast. Makes about 5 cups or 10 first-course servings.

Each serving: About 185 calories, 2 g protein, 16 g carbohydrate, 14 g total fat (2 g saturated), 0 mg cholesterol, 345 mg sodium.

Shrimp Cocktail with Tangy Dip

Prep: 15 minutes plus chilling
Cook: 2 to 3 minutes

1 teaspoon salt
1 pound medium shrimp, shelled and deveined (see page 366)
⅓ cup chili sauce
⅓ cup ketchup
2 teaspoons bottled white horseradish
1½ teaspoons fresh lemon juice
⅛ teaspoon ground black pepper
1 lemon, cut into wedges
6 Boston lettuce leaves

1. In 2-quart saucepan, heat *2 cups water* and salt to boiling over high heat. Stir in shrimp; heat to boiling. Reduce heat to medium; cook shrimp, stirring frequently, just until opaque throughout, about 1 minute. Drain.

2. In small bowl, stir together chili sauce, ketchup, horseradish, lemon juice, and pepper. Cover shrimp and sauce and refrigerate until shrimp are well chilled, at least 1 hour.

3. To serve, cut lemon into six wedges. On six small plates, arrange lettuce leaves, shrimp, and lemon wedge. Spoon sauce over shrimp. Makes 6 first-course servings.

Each serving: About 85 calories, 13 g protein, 7 g carbohydrate, 1 g total fat (0 g saturated), 111 mg cholesterol, 560 mg sodium.

Country Pâté

Prep: 40 minutes plus cooling and overnight to chill
Bake: 1 hour 15 minutes

3 slices bacon, finely chopped
8 ounces mushrooms, trimmed
 and finely chopped
1 medium onion, finely
 chopped
2 tablespoons margarine or
 butter
2 garlic cloves, finely chopped
2 tablespoons brandy
1½ teaspoons salt
1 teaspoon coarsely ground
 black pepper

1 teaspoon dried thyme
¼ teaspoon ground allspice
12 ounces ground chicken
 meat
8 ounces ground pork
4 ounces chicken livers,
 trimmed and finely chopped
⅔ cup packed fresh parsley
 leaves, chopped
¼ cup pistachios

1. In 10-inch skillet, cook bacon over medium-low heat, stirring occasionally, until browned.

2. With slotted spoon, transfer bacon to paper towels to drain. To drippings in skillet, add mushrooms, onion, margarine and garlic, cook, stirring frequently, until vegetables are tender, 8 to 10 minutes. Add brandy, salt, pepper, thyme, and allspice. Reduce heat to low; cook, stirring occasionally, 5 minutes longer. Remove skillet from heat; let mixture cool to room temperature.

3. Preheat oven to 350°F. In large bowl, combine ground chicken, ground pork, chicken livers, parsley, pistachios, mushroom mixture, and bacon. With wooden spoon, beat mixture until well blended.

4. Grease 8½" by 4½" loaf pan. Spoon meat mixture into prepared pan, packing it carefully with back of spoon to press out any air pockets. Bake pâté until thermometer inserted in center of pâté reaches 175° to 180°F and juices run clear, about 1 hour 15 minutes.

5. When pâté is done, transfer to wire rack; cover pan with foil. Place another 8½" by 4½" loaf pan on top of foil-covered pâté. Place two 16-ounce cans in top pan to weigh down pâté. Let weighted pâté cool 30 minutes at room temperature, then refrigerate overnight or up to 3 days.

6. To serve, remove weighted pan from pâté. Dip pan of pâté in hot water 15 seconds. With small metal spatula, loosen paté from sides of pan. If pâté doesn't release easily, dip pan in hot water again. Invert pâté onto cutting board and cut into thin slices. Makes 16 first-course servings.

Each serving: About 125 calories, 10 g protein, 2 g carbohydrate, 8 g total fat (3 g saturated), 68 mg cholesterol, 275 mg sodium.

Prosciutto with Melon

Prep: 15 minutes

1 small ripe honeydew melon or 1 medium cantaloupe, chilled
4 ounces thinly sliced prosciutto
Freshly ground black pepper

1. Cut melon in half and remove seeds. Slice each half into 4 wedges; cut off rind.

2. Arrange 2 melon wedges on each of 4 salad plates; arrange prosciutto alongside melon. Serve with freshly ground pepper. Makes 4 first-course servings.

Each serving: About 155 calories, 9 g protein, 23 g carbohydrate, 5 g total fat (2 g saturated), 19 mg cholesterol, 715 mg sodium.

PROSCIUTTO WITH OTHER FRUIT: Prepare as above but instead of melon, serve prosciutto with *8 large green* or *black figs,* halved; or *4 large kiwifruit,* peeled and sliced; or *2 medium papayas,* peeled, seeded, and sliced.

Chicken Liver Pâté

Prep: 15 minutes plus chilling
Cook: 10 minutes

1 pound chicken livers, each cut in half and trimmed
½ cup (1 stick) margarine or butter, cut into 1-tablespoon pieces
⅓ cup finely chopped shallots
½ teaspoon salt
⅛ teaspoon ground black pepper
¼ teaspoon dried thyme
⅛ teaspoon ground nutmeg
¼ cup sweet vermouth
Toast, crackers, or thinly sliced apple

1. Pat chicken livers dry with paper towels. In 10-inch skillet, melt 1 tablespoon margarine over medium heat. Add shallots and cook, stirring frequently, 1 minute. Stir in chicken livers, salt, pepper, thyme, and nutmeg. Cook, stirring frequently, until livers are no longer pink in center, 4 to 6 minutes. Stir in vermouth and cook 30 seconds.
2. Transfer mixture to food processor with knife blade attached, and puree until smooth. With machine running, add remaining 7 tablespoons butter through feed tube, 1 tablespoon at a time; puree until smooth. Transfer to serving bowl, cover and refrigerate until cold, about 6 hours or overnight. Serve with toast, crackers, or thin apple slices. Makes about 2 cups.

Each tablespoon: About 35 calories, 1 g protein, 1 g carbohydrate, 3 g total fat (1 g saturated), 21 mg cholesterol, 80 mg sodium.

Alaskan Salmon Spread

Prep: 30 minutes plus cooling and chilling
Cook: 8 to 10 minutes

1 teaspoon salt
8 ounces salmon fillet, skin and
   bones removed
1 medium lemon
8 ounces smoked salmon, finely
   chopped
½ cup (1 stick) margarine or
   butter, softened

2 tablespoons chopped fresh
   chives
1 teaspoon Dijon mustard
1 teaspoon capers, drained
   and chopped
⅛ teaspoon coarsely ground
   black pepper
French bread

1. In 10-inch skillet, heat *4 cups water* and 1 teaspoon salt to boiling over high heat. Add salmon fillet; heat to a simmer. Reduce heat to low; cover and simmer just until salmon is opaque throughout, 8 to 10 minutes. With slotted wide spatula, carefully remove salmon from water; drain salmon (still on spatula) on paper towels. Transfer salmon to medium bowl; cool slightly.

2. Meanwhile, from lemon grate 1 teaspoon peel and squeeze 2 tablespoons juice.

3. With wooden spoon, stir and mash poached salmon to an almost smooth paste. Add smoked salmon, margarine, chives, mustard, capers, pepper, and lemon peel and juice and stir until thoroughly blended.

4. Spoon spread into crock or serving bowl. Cover and refrigerate at least 2 hours. Before serving, let stand at room temperature until soft enough to spread, about 30 minutes. Serve with sliced French bread. Makes about 2½ cups.

Each ¼ cup: About 135 calories, 9 g protein, 0 g carbohydrate, 11 g total fat (2 g saturated), 17 mg cholesterol, 655 mg sodium.

Oysters Rockefeller

Prep: 30 minutes
Bake: 10 minutes

1 package (10 ounces) frozen
chopped spinach
3 tablespoons margarine or
butter
1 tablespoon finely chopped
onion
1 tablespoon chopped fresh
parsley
⅛ teaspoon ground red pepper
(cayenne)

¼ cup plain dried bread
crumbs
18 large or 24 small oysters
shucked and on the half
shell (see page 362)
2 slices bacon, chopped
Grated fresh Parmesan cheese
Lemon wedges

1. Unwrap frozen spinach. With serrated knife, cut spinach in half; place half in zip-tight freezer bag. Freeze for another use.

2. Preheat oven to 425°F. In 2-quart saucepan melt margarine over medium heat; add remaining frozen spinach, onion, parsley, and ground red pepper. Cover and cook, stirring occasionally, until spinach is heated. Stir in bread crumbs.

3. Arrange oysters in ungreased jelly-roll pan and spoon some spinach mixture on top of each. Sprinkle oysters with bacon and some Parmesan. Bake until bacon is crisp and edges of oysters are curled and they are opaque throughout, about 10 minutes. Serve with lemon wedges. Makes 6 first-course servings.

Each serving: About 180 calories, 5 g protein, 8 g carbohydrate, 14 g total fat (4 g saturated), 22 mg cholesterol, 330 mg sodium.

Shrimp and Avocado in Roasted Red-Pepper Sauce

Prep: 45 minutes plus cooling
Cook: 20 minutes

3 medium red peppers
1 ½ pounds large shrimp, shelled and deveined, leaving tail part of shell on, if you like (see page 366)
1 ½ teaspoons salt
½ cup chicken broth
3 tablespoons olive oil

1 tablespoon balsamic vinegar
1 small shallot, cut up
1 teaspoon sugar
2 medium ripe avocados, each pitted, peeled, and thinly sliced
2 large lemons, each cut into wedges

1. Preheat broiler. Line broiling pan with foil. Cut each pepper lengthwise in half; discard stems and seeds. Arrange peppers, cut side down, in prepared broiling pan. Place pan in broiler 5 to 6 inches from heat source. Broil until skin is charred and blistered, 8 to 10 minutes.

2. Wrap peppers in foil and allow to steam at room temperature until cool enough to handle, about 15 minutes. Remove peppers from foil. Peel off skin and discard.

3. Meanwhile, in 4-quart saucepan, heat *8 cups water* to boiling over high heat. Add shrimp and 1 teaspoon salt; heat to boiling. Cook just until shrimp are opaque throughout, 1 to 2 minutes. Drain shrimp well.

4. Place peppers in blender; add broth, oil, vinegar, shallot, sugar, and ½ teaspoon salt; puree until smooth.

5. Spoon pepper sauce onto 10 small plates. Arrange shrimp and avocado slices over sauce. Serve with lemon wedges. Makes 10 first-course servings.

Each serving: About 165 calories, 13 g protein, 6 g carbohydrate, 11 g total fat (2 g saturated), 105 mg cholesterol, 340 mg sodium.

Soups

~~~~

First-Course Soups
Main-Dish Soups

Soup has many uses. In servings of a cup or less, almost any kind of soup makes a good appetizer or between-meal snack. Clear soups and smooth cream soups, hot or chilled, are favorite first courses. Served in a cup or mug, these same soups can take the place of a beverage and be sipped along with the meal. For a main course, choose a hearty soup made with vegetables and meat, poultry, or seafood.

Glossary of Soups

Bisque: A thick, rich, creamy soup, usually made with shellfish, sometimes with pureed vegetables.

Bouillon: The French word for stock.

Broth: A thin, unclarified soup made by slowly simmering meat, fish, poultry, or vegetables in water with seasonings and aromatic vegetables.

Chowder: A hearty, thick soup made with solid chunks of fish or shellfish and/or vegetables. Most chowders are milk or cream based.

Consommé: Stock (see below) that has been clarified so that it is crystal clear.

Gumbo: A thick, southern-style soup containing seafood, meat, or poultry, tomatoes and other vegetables, and spices. It is thickened with okra or filé powder.

Stock: A flavorful liquid used as a base for soups, sauces, or gravies, made by slowly simmering meat, poultry, and bones, or fish trimmings, with vegetables in water, then straining.

∾First-Course Soups

Gazpacho

Prep: 10 minutes

2 pounds ripe tomatoes
(6 medium), each cored and
cut into quarters
2 medium English (seedless)
cucumbers, each peeled
and cut into 2-inch chunks
1 cup fresh corn kernels (cut
from about 2 medium ears)
½ cup loosely packed fresh
cilantro leaves

6 large ice cubes (about
1 cup)
2 tablespoons fresh lime juice
¾ teaspoon salt
¼ teaspoon ground black
pepper
Hot pepper sauce to taste
Lime wedges (optional)

In food processor with knife blade attached, in batches, coarsely chop tomatoes, cucumbers, corn, cilantro, and ice cubes. Transfer chopped vegetables to large bowl after each batch. Stir in lime juice, salt, pepper, and hot pepper sauce to taste. If not serving right away, cover and refrigerate up to one day. Serve with lime wedges, if you like. Makes about 7 cups or 8 first-course servings.

Each serving: About 50 calories, 2 g protein, 12 g carbohydrate, 1 g total fat (0 g saturated), 0 mg cholesterol, 215 mg sodium.

Oyster-Corn Chowder

Prep: 20 minutes
Cook: 10 minutes

1 pint shucked oysters (about 24) with their liquid
1¼ pounds all-purpose potatoes (4 medium) peeled and coarsely
    chopped
2 bottles (8 ounces each) clam juice
1 cup half-and-half
2 cups milk
1 can (15¼ to 16 ounces) whole-kernel corn, drained
1 teaspoon salt
¼ teaspoon coarsely ground black pepper

1. Drain oysters in sieve, reserving ⅔ cup liquid; or add
enough *water* to oyster liquid to make ⅔ cup.

2. In 4-quart saucepan, combine potatoes, clam juice,
and reserved oyster liquid. Heat to boiling over high heat.
Reduce heat to low; cover and simmer until potatoes are
fork-tender, about 10 minutes. Remove saucepan from heat.

3. With slotted spoon, remove enough potatoes to equal
1½ cups. In blender, covered, with center part of blender
cover removed to let steam escape, blend potatoes and half-
and-half until smooth. Pour potato mixture back into saucepan. Stir in milk, corn, salt, and pepper. Heat mixture just
to boiling over medium-high heat. Add oysters and cook,
stirring frequently, just until edges curl and oysters are
opaque throughout, about 5 minutes. Serve immediately.
Makes about 9 cups or 8 first-course servings.

*Each serving: About 190 calories, 8 g protein, 26 g carbohydrate,
6 g total fat (3 g saturated), 33 mg cholesterol, 650 mg sodium.*

Oyster Stew

Prep: 10 minutes
Cook: 15 to 20 minutes

1 pint shucked oysters (about 24) with their liquid
¼ cup all-purpose flour
1 tablespoon Worcestershire sauce
2 teaspoons salt
1 quart (4 cups) milk
2 pints (4 cups) half-and-half
3 tablespoons margarine or butter
2 tablespoons chopped fresh parsley

1. Drain oysters in sieve, reserving ⅔ cup liquid; or add enough *water* to oyster liquid to make ⅔ cup.

2. In 4-quart saucepan, with wire whisk, beat flour, Worcestershire, salt, and ¼ *cup water* until smooth. Heat mixture to boiling over medium-high heat, stirring constantly. Cook 1 minute. Gradually stir in milk until blended. Stir in half-and-half, margarine, oysters, and reserved oyster liquid; heat mixture just to boiling. Reduce heat to medium-low; cook, stirring frequently, just until oyster edges curl and oysters are opaque throughout, about 8 minutes. Stir in parsley and serve immediately. Makes about 10 cups or 10 first-course servings.

Each serving: About 255 calories, 9 g protein, 14 g carbohydrate, 18 g total fat (10 g saturated), 60 mg cholesterol, 695 mg sodium

Shrimp Bisque

Prep: 30 minutes
Cook: 1 hour 10 minutes

3 tablespoons margarine or
    butter
1 pound medium shrimp,
    shelled and deveined, shells
    reserved (see page 366)
2 cans (14½ ounces each)
    reduced-sodium chicken
    broth
1 cup dry white wine
½ cup water
2 medium carrots, peeled and
    chopped
2 medium stalks celery,
    chopped

1 large onion, chopped
2 tablespoons regular long-
    grain rice
1¼ teaspoons salt
⅛ to ¼ teaspoon ground red
    pepper (cayenne)
1 bay leaf
1 can (14½ ounces) diced
    tomatoes
1 cup half-and-half or light
    cream
2 tablespoons brandy or dry
    sherry

1. In 5-quart Dutch oven, melt 1 tablespoon margarine over medium heat. Add shrimp shells and cook, stirring often, 5 minutes.

2. Add broth, wine, and water; heat to boiling over high heat. Reduce heat to low; cover and simmer 15 minutes. Strain broth mixture through sieve into 4-cup measuring cup or small bowl, pressing on shells with spoon to extract any remaining liquid. Discard shells.

3. In same Dutch oven, melt remaining 2 tablespoons margarine over medium-high heat. Add shrimp and cook, stirring occasionally, until just opaque throughout, about 3 minutes. With slotted spoon, transfer shrimp to another small bowl. Add carrots, celery, and onion to Dutch oven; cook, stirring occasionally, until lightly browned, 10 to 12 minutes.

4. Return broth mixture to Dutch oven; stir in rice, salt, ground red pepper, and bay leaf. Heat to boiling over high heat. Reduce heat to low; cover and simmer until rice is very tender, about 20 minutes. Add tomatoes with their juice, cover and cook 10 minutes longer. Remove Dutch oven from heat; discard bay leaf and add shrimp.

5. In blender, covered, with center part of blender cover removed to let steam escape, puree shrimp mixture, in small batches, until smooth. Pour pureed soup into bowl after each batch. Return soup to Dutch oven and add half-and-half and brandy; heat through over medium heat (do not boil or soup may curdle). Makes about 10 cups or 10 first-course servings.

Each serving: About 145 calories, 10 g protein, 9 g carbohydrate, 7 g total fat (2 g saturated), 65 mg cholesterol, 750 mg sodium.

Miso Soup

Prep: 20 minutes
Cook: 35 minutes

1 tablespoon vegetable oil
2 large carrots, peeled and
  thinly sliced
1 small onion, chopped
2 garlic cloves, finely chopped
1 tablespoon grated, peeled
  fresh ginger
½ small head napa cabbage
  (Chinese cabbage), about
  ½ pound, cut crosswise into
  ½-inch-thick slices
  (4 cups)

1 tablespoon seasoned rice
  vinegar
¼ teaspoon coarsely ground
  black pepper
6 cups water
¼ cup red miso*
¼ cup hot
  tap water
1 package (16 ounces) firm
  tofu, drained and cut into
  ½-inch cubes
2 green onions, sliced

*Miso comes in a variety of flavors, colors, and textures that fall into three basic categories: Red, which has a strong flavor; golden, which is mild; and white, which is mellow and slightly sweet. Miso can be purchased in health-food stores and Asian markets.

Each serving: About 185 calories, 14 g protein, 13 g carbohydrate, 10 g total fat (1 g saturated), 0 mg cholesterol, 510 mg sodium.

1. In 5-quart Dutch oven, heat oil over medium heat. Add carrots, onion, garlic, and ginger and cook, stirring occasionally, until onion is golden brown, about 10 minutes.

2. Add cabbage, vinegar, pepper, and water; heat to boiling over high heat. Reduce heat to low; cover and simmer until vegetables are tender, about 20 minutes.

3. In measuring cup, dilute miso with hot water. Stir tofu and miso mixture into soup; heat through, about 2 minutes. To serve, sprinkle with green onions. Makes about 9½ cups or 8 first-course servings.

Cream of Mushroom Soup

Prep: 12 minutes
Cook: 18 minutes

½ cup (1 stick) margarine or butter
1 pound mushrooms, trimmed, stems removed and reserved, and caps thinly sliced
1 teaspoon fresh lemon juice
1 small onion, sliced

⅓ cup all-purpose flour
2 cups chicken broth
1½ cups water
1 cup heavy or whipping cream
1 teaspoon salt
¼ teaspoon ground black pepper

1. In 4-quart saucepan, melt margarine over medium-high heat. Stir in sliced mushrooms and lemon juice and cook, stirring occasionally, until mushrooms are just tender.

2. With slotted spoon, transfer mushrooms to bowl. Add onion and reserved mushroom stems to saucepan; reduce heat to medium-low, and cook until onion is tender.

3. Stir in flour until blended; cook, stirring, 1 minute. Gradually stir in broth and water; cook, stirring constantly, until mixture has thickened and boils.

4. Spoon half of mushroom mixture into blender; cover, with center part of blender cover removed to let steam escape, and puree until smooth. Pour mixture into bowl. Repeat with remaining mushroom mixture.

5. Return mixture to same saucepan; stir in cream, salt, pepper, and mushroom slices; heat just to boiling. Makes about 7 cups or 8 first-course servings

Each serving: About 250 calories, 4 g protein, 9 g carbohydrate, 23 g total fat (9 g saturated), 41 mg cholesterol, 650 mg sodium.

Crème Vichyssoise

Prep: 25 minutes plus chilling
Cook: 35 minutes

3 medium leeks (1¼ pounds)
3 tablespoons margarine or butter
1 pound all-purpose potatoes (3 medium), peeled and thinly sliced
2 cups chicken broth
1 cup water
1 cup heavy or whipping cream
1 cup milk
1 teaspoon salt
¼ teaspoon white pepper

1. Cut off roots and trim dark green tops from leeks; cut each leek lengthwise in half. Cut the white part of the leeks and enough of the green tops crosswise into ¼-inch slices to make 2 cups. Rinse leeks in large bowl of cold water, swishing to remove sand; transfer to colander to drain, leaving sand in bottom of bowl.

2. In 4-quart saucepan, melt margarine over medium heat. Stir in leeks; cook 5 minutes. Stir in potatoes, broth, and water; heat to boiling. Reduce heat to low; cover and simmer 30 minutes.

3. Spoon half of leek mixture into blender; cover, with center part of blender cover removed to let steam escape, and puree until smooth. Pour into 3-quart saucepan. Repeat with remaining leek mixture.

4. Stir cream, milk, salt, and pepper into leek mixture; cook over low heat until soup is just heated through.

5. Pour soup into large bowl; cover and refrigerate until chilled, since vichyssoise is usually served cold.

Vichyssoise is also delicious served hot; serve it right after cooking, or reheat to serve later. Makes about 7 cups or 12 first-course servings.

Each serving: About 145 calories, 3 g protein, 9 g carbohydrate, 11 g total fat (6 g saturated), 30 mg cholesterol, 385 mg sodium.

Quickie Vegetable Cream Soups

Master Recipe
Prep: 5 minutes
Cook: 20 minutes

1 tablespoon margarine or
    butter
1 medium onion, finely
    chopped
1 can (14½ ounces) chicken
    broth
1 package (10 ounces) frozen
    vegetables (see chart)

¼ teaspoon dried thyme
⅛ teaspoon salt
⅛ teaspoon coarsely ground
    black pepper
1½ cups milk
2 teaspoons fresh lemon juice
Optional garnish (see chart)

1. In 2-quart saucepan, melt margarine over medium heat. Stir in onion and cook, stirring occasionally, until tender, about 5 minutes. Add broth, frozen vegetables, thyme, salt, and pepper; heat to boiling over high heat. Reduce heat to low; simmer 10 minutes.

2. In blender, cover, with center part of blender cover removed to let steam escape, and puree vegetable mixture, in small batches, until smooth. Pour pureed soup into bowl after each batch.

3. Return soup to same saucepan; stir in milk. Heat through over medium heat, stirring often. Do not boil, or soup may curdle. Remove saucepan from heat; stir in lemon juice. Garnish, if you like. Makes about 3¾ cups or 4 first-course servings.

Each serving corn, lima bean, or pea soup: About 170 calories, 9 g protein, 20 g carbohydrate, 7 g total fat (3 g saturated), 13 mg cholesterol, 515 mg sodium.

Each serving asparagus, cauliflower, kale, or squash soup: About 130 calories, 8 g protein, 11 g carbohydrate, 7 g total fat (3 g saturated), 13 mg cholesterol, 480 mg sodium.

Type of Frozen Vegetable	Extra Ingredient	Additional Cooking Steps	Optional Garnish
Asparagus Cuts or Spears	¼ tsp. dried tarragon	none	snipped fresh chives
Cauliflower Flowerets	½ tsp. curry powder	Add curry powder after cooking onion; cook 30 seconds.	chopped fresh apple
Chopped Kale	1 garlic clove, finely chopped	Add garlic after cooking onion; cook 30 seconds. Add milk to kale mixture before pureeing.	crumbled crisp-cooked bacon
Lima Beans	none	none	chopped fresh thyme
Peas	¼ tsp. dried mint	none	swirl of sour cream
Whole-Kernel Corn	¾ tsp. chili powder	Add chili powder after cooking onion; cook 30 seconds.	chopped fresh cilantro
Winter Squash	¼ tsp. pumpkin-pie spice	Add spice after cooking onion; cook 30 seconds.	chopped tomato

Broccoli and Cheddar Soup

Prep: 35 minutes
Cook: 25 minutes

1 tablespoon olive oil
1 medium onion, chopped
¼ cup all-purpose flour
½ teaspoon salt
coarsely ground black pepper
¼ teaspoon dried thyme
⅛ teaspoon ground nutmeg
2 cups reduced-fat (2%) milk
1 can (14½ ounces) chicken
    broth

1½ cups water
1 large bunch broccoli
    (1½ pounds), cut into
    1-inch pieces (including
    stems)
6 ounces sharp Cheddar
    cheese (about 1½ cups),
    shredded

1. In 4-quart saucepan, heat oil over medium heat. Add onion and cook, stirring occasionally, until golden brown, about 10 minutes. Stir in flour, salt, ¼ teaspoon pepper, thyme, and nutmeg; cook, stirring frequently, 2 minutes.

2. With wire whisk, gradually mix in milk, broth, and water. Add broccoli and heat to boiling over high heat. Reduce heat to low; cover and simmer, stirring occasionally, until broccoli is tender, about 10 minutes.

3. In blender, cover, with center part of blender cover removed to let steam escape, and puree broccoli mixture, in small batches, until smooth. Pour pureed soup into bowl after each batch.

4. Return soup to same saucepan; heat to boiling over high heat, stirring occasionally. Remove saucepan from heat; add cheese and stir until cheese has melted and soup is smooth. Sprinkle each serving with coarsely ground black pepper. Makes about 8 cups, 8 first-course, or 4 main-dish servings.

Each first-course serving: About 185 calories, 12 g protein, 12 g carbohydrate, 11 g total fat (6 g saturated), 27 mg cholesterol, 485 mg sodium.

Butternut-Apple Soup

Prep: 35 minutes
Cook: 40 minutes

2 tablespoons vegetable oil
1 small onion, chopped
2 medium butternut squash
(1¾ pounds each), peeled,
seeded, and cut into ¾-inch
chunks
12 ounces Golden Delicious
apples (2 medium), peeled,
cored, and cut into ¾-inch
chunks
1 can (14½ ounces) vegetable
broth

1 tablespoon fresh thyme leaves
or ¼ teaspoon dried thyme
1½ cups water
1 teaspoon salt
⅛ teaspoon coarsely ground
black pepper
1 cup half-and-half or light
cream

1. In 4-quart saucepan, heat oil over medium heat. Add onion and cook, stirring occasionally, until tender, about 10 minutes. Stir in squash, apples, broth, water, thyme, salt, and pepper. Heat to boiling over high heat. Reduce heat to low; cover and simmer, stirring frequently, until squash is very tender, 20 to 25 minutes.

2. Spoon one-third of squash mixture into blender; cover, with center part of blender cover removed to let steam escape, and puree until smooth. Pour mixture into bowl. Repeat with remaining squash mixture.

3. In same saucepan, cook squash mixture and half-and-half, over medium heat, stirring occasionally, until heated through. Makes about 9 cups or 8 first-course servings.

Each serving: About 150 calories, 2 g protein, 23 g carbohydrate, 7 g total fat (2 g saturated), 10 mg cholesterol, 305 mg sodium.

New England Clam Chowder

Prep: 30 minutes plus cooling and standing
Cook: 36 minutes

1 dozen large cherrystone)
   clams (see page 346)
4 ounces salt pork or bacon,
   cut in ¼-inch pieces
1 medium onion, chopped
1 tablespoon all-purpose flour
½ teaspoon salt
⅛ teaspoon coarsely ground
   black pepper

1 pound all-purpose potatoes (3
   medium), peeled and cut
   into ¼-inch pieces
4 cups (1 quart) half-and-half
1 tablespoon margarine or
   butter
Paprika

1. With stiff brush, scrub clams under cold running water until free of sand. In 4-quart saucepan, heat *1 cup water* to boiling over high heat. Add clams; heat to boiling. Reduce heat to low; cover and simmer, stirring occasionally, just until clams open, 5 to 10 minutes, transferring clams to bowl as they open. Discard any clams that have not opened.

2. Reserve clam broth. Cool clams until easy to handle. Discard shells; coarsely chop clams and reserve.

3. Clam broth can be sandy at times. Let broth stand a few minutes until sand settles to bottom of saucepan. Carefully strain clear broth through sieve lined with paper towels into measuring cup; add water to equal 2 cups, if necessary. Rinse and dry saucepan.

4. In same saucepan, cook salt pork over medium heat until lightly browned. Add onion; cook, stirring occasionally, until tender, about 5 minutes. Stir in flour, salt, and pepper until blended; cook, stirring, 1 minute. Gradually stir in clam broth until smooth; add potatoes and heat to boiling. Reduce heat to low; cover and simmer until potatoes are fork-tender, about 15 minutes. Stir in half-and-half and clams; heat through.

5. Stir in margarine; sprinkle chowder with some paprika. Makes 9 cups or 9 first-course servings.

Each serving: About 300 calories, 8 g protein, 14 g carbohydrate, 24 g total fat (12 g saturated), 59 mg cholesterol, 385 mg sodium.

VARIATION: Prepare as above but use *2 cans (10 ounces each) whole baby clams,* instead of fresh clams. Drain clams; reserve clam liquid. Add water to equal 2 cups. Omit steps 1 through 3.

Manhattan Clam Chowder

Prep: 40 minutes plus cooling and standing
Cook: 55 minutes

3 dozen large cherrystone
   clams (see page 346)
5 slices bacon, cut into
   ¼-inch pieces
1 large onion, chopped
2 large carrots, chopped
2 medium stalks celery,
   chopped
2 tablespoons chopped fresh
   parsley

1 pound all-purpose potatoes
   (2 large), peeled and cut
   into ¼-inch pieces
1 can (28 ounces) tomatoes
1 bay leaf
1½ teaspoons salt
¼ teaspoon coarsely ground
   black pepper
1 teaspoon dried thyme

1. With stiff brush, scrub clams under cold running water until free of sand. In 8-quart Dutch oven, heat *1 cup water* to boiling over high heat. Add clams; heat to boiling. Reduce heat to low; cover and simmer, stirring occasionally, just until clams open, 5 to 10 minutes, transferring clams to bowl as they open. Discard any clams that have not opened.

2. Reserve clam broth. Cool clams until easy to handle. Discard shells; coarsely chop clams and reserve.

3. Pour clam broth into bowl. Clam broth can be sandy at times. Let broth stand a few minutes until sand settles at bottom of bowl. Strain clam broth through sieve lined with paper towels.

4. Rinse and dry Dutch oven. In same Dutch oven, cook bacon over medium heat, until lightly browned. Add onion and cook until tender. Add carrots, celery, and parsley; cook, stirring often, 5 minutes.

5. Carefully pour clear clam broth into bacon mixture in Dutch oven. Add potatoes, tomatoes with their juice, water, bay leaf, salt, pepper, and thyme; heat to boiling, breaking up tomatoes with side of spoon. Reduce heat to low; cover and simmer, stirring often, until potatoes are tender, about 20 minutes.

6. Stir in chopped clams and heat through, stirring often, about 5 minutes. Discard bay leaf. Makes about 14 cups or 14 first-course servings.

Each serving: About 135 calories, 6 g protein, 10 g carbohydrate, 8 g total fat (3 g saturated), 17 mg cholesterol, 445 mg sodium.

VARIATION: Prepare as above but use *3 cans (8 ounces each) minced clams,* instead of fresh clams. Drain clams; reserve clam liquid. Omit steps 1 through 3.

Creamy Corn Chowder

Prep: 25 minutes
Cook: 40 minutes

6 medium ears corn, husks and silk removed
4 slices bacon, cut into ½-inch pieces
1 medium red onion, finely chopped
1 jalapeño chile, seeded and minced
1 garlic clove, finely chopped
2 tablespoons all-purpose flour
½ teaspoon salt
⅛ teaspoon ground black pepper

2 cans (14½ ounces each) chicken broth
2 cups half-and-half or light cream
1 pound red potatoes (6 medium), not peeled, cut into ½-inch cubes
2 small ripe tomatoes, peeled, seeded, and chopped
thinly sliced basil leaves

1. Cut kernels from cobs, about 3 cups; reserve 3 corn-cobs.

2. In 5-quart Dutch oven, cook bacon over medium heat, stirring frequently, until browned. With slotted spoon, transfer bacon to paper towels to drain.

3. To drippings in Dutch oven, add onion and jalapeño chile. Reduce heat to low and cook, stirring, until tender but not browned, about 6 to 8 minutes. Add garlic; cook, stirring, 1 minute. Stir in flour, salt, and pepper and cook, stirring, 1 minute.

4. Stir in broth, half-and-half, potatoes, and reserved corncobs; heat to boiling over high heat. Reduce heat to low; cover and simmer until potatoes are fork-tender, 10 to 15 minutes.

5. Discard cobs; stir in corn kernels and heat through. Remove Dutch oven from heat; stir in tomatoes and bacon. Sprinkle with basil. Makes about 9½ cups or 8 first-course or 4 main-dish servings.

Each first-course serving: About 275 calories, 9 g protein, 31 g carbohydrate, 14 g total fat (7 g saturated), 27 mg cholesterol, 570 mg sodium.

Black-Bean Soup

Prep: 10 minutes
Cook: 20 minutes

1 tablespoon vegetable oil
1 medium onion, finely chopped
2 garlic cloves, crushed with garlic press
2 teaspoons chili powder
1 teaspoon ground cumin
¼ teaspoon crushed red pepper

2 cans (16 to 19 ounces each) black beans, rinsed and drained
1 can (14½ ounces) chicken broth
2 cups water
½ cup loosely packed fresh cilantro leaves, chopped
Lime wedges

1. In 3-quart saucepan, heat oil over medium heat. Add onion and cook until tender, about 5 minutes. Stir in garlic, chili powder, cumin, and crushed red pepper; cook, stirring, 30 seconds. Stir in beans, broth, and water; heat to boiling over high heat. Reduce heat to low and simmer 15 minutes.

2. In blender, covered, with center part of blender cover removed to let steam escape, blend mixture, in small batches, until almost smooth. Pour soup into bowl after each batch.

3. Return soup to same saucepan; heat through. Sprinkle with cilantro and serve with lime wedges. Makes about 6½ cups, 6-first course or 4 main-dish servings.

Each serving: About 265 calories, 22 g protein, 46 g carbohydrate, 6 g total fat (1 g saturated), 0 mg cholesterol, 965 mg sodium.

∾Main-Dish Soups

Shrimp and Sausage Gumbo

Prep: 10 minutes plus cooling
Cook: 40 minutes

1 cup regular long-grain rice
1 pound hot Italian-sausage
    links, casings pierced with
    fork
3 tablespoons vegetable oil
¼ cup all-purpose flour
2 medium stalks celery,
    chopped
1 medium green pepper,
    chopped
1 medium onion, chopped
1 can (14½ ounces) chicken
    broth

½ cup water
1 package (10 ounces) frozen
    whole okra
2 teaspoons hot pepper sauce
¼ teaspoon dried thyme
¼ teaspoon dried oregano
1 bay leaf
1 pound large shrimp, shelled
    and deveined, leaving tail
    part of shell on, if you like
    (see page 366)

1. Prepare rice as label directs; keep warm.

2. Meanwhile, heat 5-quart Dutch oven over medium-high heat. Add sausages and cook until very brown, turning often, about 10 minutes. Transfer sausages to plate to cool slightly. Slice each sausage into thirds.

3. Discard all but 1 tablespoon drippings from Dutch oven. Add oil and heat over medium heat until very hot. Stir in flour until blended and cook, stirring frequently, until flour is dark brown but not scorched. Add celery, green pepper, and onion and cook, stirring occasionally, until tender, about 8 to 10 minutes.

4. Return sausages to Dutch oven. Gradually stir in broth, water, okra, hot pepper sauce, thyme, oregano, and bay leaf; heat to boiling over high heat. Reduce heat to low; cover and simmer 15 minutes. Add shrimp, remove cover, and cook, just until shrimp are opaque throughout, about 2 minutes. Discard bay leaf. Serve gumbo in bowls with a scoop of hot rice in center of each bowl. Makes 6 main-dish servings.

Each serving: About 470 calories, 28 g protein, 37 g carbohydrate, 22 g total fat (17 g saturated), 138 mg cholesterol, 970 mg sodium.

Caldo Verde

Prep: 15 minutes
Cook: 45 minutes

2 tablespoons olive oil
1 large onion, chopped
3 garlic cloves, finely chopped
2½ pounds all-purpose potatoes (about 8 medium), peeled and cut into 2-inch chunks
2 cans (14½ ounces each) chicken broth

3 cups water
1 teaspoon salt
¼ teaspoon coarsely ground black pepper
1 pound kale, coarse stems and veins removed, cut crosswise into very thin slices

1. In 5-quart Dutch oven, heat oil over medium heat. Add onion and garlic; cook, stirring occasionally, until lightly browned, about 10 minutes.

2. Add potatoes, broth, water, salt, and pepper; heat to boiling over high heat. Reduce heat to low; cover and simmer until potatoes are fork-tender, about 20 minutes.

3. With potato masher, mash potatoes in broth until they are lumpy.

4. Stir in kale; simmer, uncovered, until tender, about 5 to 8 minutes. Makes about 10 cups or 5 main-dish servings.

Each serving: About 250 calories, 8 g protein, 42 g carbohydrate, 7 g total fat (1 g saturated), 8 mg cholesterol, 925 mg sodium.

New England Cod Chowder

Prep: 20 minutes
Cook: 30 minutes

4 slices bacon
1 medium fennel bulb (1 pound), trimmed and coarsely chopped, or 3 celery stalks, coarsely chopped
3 medium carrots, peeled, each cut lengthwise in half, then crosswise into slices
1 medium onion, chopped
1 pound all-purpose potatoes (3 medium), peeled and cut into ½-inch pieces

3 bottles (8 ounces each) clam juice
1 can (14½ ounces) chicken broth
1 bay leaf
1 piece cod or scrod fillet (1 pound), cut into 1½-inch pieces
1 cup half-and-half or light cream

1. In 5-quart Dutch oven, cook bacon over medium heat, stirring frequently, until browned. Transfer bacon to paper towels to drain; crumble.

2. Discard all but 2 tablespoons drippings in Dutch oven. Add fennel, carrots, and onion, and cook, stirring occasionally, until lightly browned, 6 to 8 minutes. Add potatoes, clam juice, broth, and bay leaf; heat to boiling over high heat. Reduce heat to low; cover and simmer until vegetables are tender, 10 to 15 minutes.

3. Add cod, cover and cook just until opaque throughout, 2 to 5 minutes. Carefully stir in half-and-half; heat through. Discard bay leaf. Serve soup with crumbled bacon. Makes about 10 cups or 5 main-dish servings.

Each serving: About 335 calories, 24 g protein, 30 g carbohydrate, 14 g total fat (6 g saturated), 72 mg cholesterol.

Turkey Soup Creole Style

Prep: 30 minutes
Cook: 1 hour 20 minutes

1 turkey carcass with about 2 cups meat left on or 1 turkey carcass and 2 cups bite-size pieces cooked turkey	11 cups water
	2 teaspoons salt
	1 teaspoon dried thyme
	¾ teaspoon hot pepper sauce
¼ cup vegetable oil	1 can (14½ to 16 ounces)
½ cup all-purpose flour	tomatoes
3 medium stalks celery, thinly sliced	1 cup regular long-grain rice
2 medium onions, chopped	1 package (10 ounces) frozen cut okra
1 large green pepper, chopped	

1. Cut turkey meat from carcass into bite-size pieces; cover and refrigerate. With kitchen shears, cut carcass into several pieces.

2. In 8-quart Dutch oven, heat oil over medium heat, until very hot. Stir in flour; cook, stirring constantly, until flour is dark brown but not scorched. Add celery, onions, and green pepper; cook, stirring frequently, until vegetables are tender. Stir in turkey carcass, water, salt, thyme, and hot pepper sauce; heat to boiling over high heat. Reduce heat to low; cover and simmer, stirring occasionally, 45 minutes.

3. Remove carcass from broth; discard. To broth, add tomatoes with their juice, rice, and okra, breaking up tomatoes with side of spoon. Heat to boiling over high heat. Reduce heat to low; cover and simmer, stirring occasionally, until rice and okra are tender, about 20 minutes. Add cut-up turkey meat; heat through.

4. To serve, skim fat from broth and ladle into deep bowls. Makes about 14 cups or 8 main-dish servings.

Each serving: About 285 calories, 19 g protein, 36 g carbohydrate, 7 g total fat (2 g saturated), 40 mg cholesterol, 870 mg sodium.

Chicken-and-Corn Soup with Rivels

Prep: 20 minutes
Cook: 1 hour 5 minutes

1 chicken (3½ pounds)
1 large onion, chopped
8 cups water
1 tablespoon salt
¼ teaspoon pepper
1 package (10 ounces) frozen
  whole-kernel corn
1 package (10 ounces) frozen
  chopped broccoli
1 cup all-purpose flour
1 large egg
1 tablespoon milk

1. Rinse chicken, its giblets and neck inside and out with cold running water. Place chicken, breast side down, in 5-quart Dutch oven. Add giblets and neck; stir in onion, water, salt, and pepper; heat to boiling over high heat. Reduce heat to low; cover and simmer until chicken is fork-tender and loses its pink color throughout, about 35 minutes. Remove chicken, giblets, and neck to large bowl; refrigerate until easy to handle, about 30 minutes. Discard skin, bones, and neck from chicken; cut meat and giblets into bite-size pieces.

2. Skim and discard fat from broth. Heat broth to boiling over high heat. Add chicken, corn, and broccoli; heat to boiling.

3. Meanwhile, prepare rivels: In small bowl, with fork, mix flour, egg, and milk to make a crumbly dough. With fingers, crumble small pieces of dough into simmering soup. Reduce heat to medium and cook, stirring often, until rivels and vegetables are tender, about 5 minutes. Makes about 12 cups or 6 main-dish servings.

Each serving: About 285 calories, 30 g protein, 24 g carbohydrate, 8 g total fat (3 g saturated), 19 mg cholesterol, 1,050 mg sodium.

Hearty Mushroom-Barley Soup

Prep: 20 minutes
Cook: 1 hour 15 minutes

¾ cup pearled barley
2 tablespoons olive oil
3 medium stalks celery, sliced
1 large onion, chopped
1½ pounds mushrooms, trimmed and thickly sliced
2 tablespoons tomato paste
2 cans (14½ ounces each) beef broth
¼ cup dry sherry
5 medium carrots, peeled, each cut lengthwise in half, then
    crosswise into ¼-inch-thick slices
1½ teaspoons salt

1. In 3-quart saucepan, heat barley and *4 cups water* to boiling over high heat. Reduce heat to low; cover and simmer 30 minutes. Drain barley; set aside.

2. Meanwhile, in 5-quart Dutch oven, heat oil over medium-high heat. Add celery and onion; cook, stirring occasionally, until golden, 8 to 10 minutes. Increase heat to high; add mushrooms and cook, stirring occasionally, until liquid has evaporated and mushrooms are lightly browned, 10 to 12 minutes.

3. Reduce heat to medium-high; add tomato paste and cook, stirring, 2 minutes. Add broth, sherry, carrots, salt, barley, and *4 cups water;* heat to boiling. Reduce heat to low; cover and simmer until carrots and barley are tender,

20 to 25 minutes. Makes about 12 cups or 6 main-dish servings.

Each serving: About 80 calories, 3 g protein, 12 g carbohydrate, 2 g total fat (0 g saturated), 0 mg cholesterol, 385 mg sodium.

Split-Pea Soup

Prep: 20 minutes plus cooling
Cook: 1 hour 15 minutes

¼ teaspoon whole allspice
¼ teaspoon whole black peppercorns
1 bay leaf
1 package (16 ounces) dry split peas, rinsed
7 cups water
1 ham bone with 2 cups meat left on (left over from cooked whole or half smoked ham)

2 large carrots, peeled and thinly sliced
2 large stalks celery, thinly sliced
½ teaspoon salt
¼ teaspoon ground black pepper

1. Tie allspice, peppercorns, and bay leaf in piece of cheesecloth.

2. In 5-quart Dutch oven, stir split peas, water, ham bone, carrots, celery, and spice bag. Heat to boiling over high heat. Reduce heat to low; cover and simmer, stirring occasionally, until split peas are very tender, about 1 hour. Discard spice bag.

3. Transfer ham bone to cutting board to cool slightly. Cut off meat and discard bone. Cut meat into bite-size chunks and return to soup. Stir in salt and ground pepper and heat through over medium heat. Makes about 7 cups or 4 main-dish servings.

Each serving: About 545 calories, 45 g protein, 74 g carbohydrate, 8 g total fat (3 g saturated), 44 mg cholesterol, 1,465 mg sodium.

Curried Lentil Soup

Prep: 30 minutes
Cook: 1 hour

2 tablespoons olive oil	2 teaspoons curry powder
4 medium carrots, peeled and cut into ¼-inch pieces	¾ teaspoon ground cumin
2 large stalks celery, cut into ¼-inch pieces	¾ teaspoon ground coriander
	5 cups water
1 large onion, chopped	2 cans (14½ ounces each) vegetable or chicken broth
1 medium Granny Smith apple, peeled, cored, and cut into ¼-inch pieces	1 package (16 ounces) dry lentils, rinsed
1 tablespoon grated, peeled fresh ginger	¼ cup chopped fresh cilantro
	½ teaspoon salt
1 large garlic clove, crushed with garlic press	Plain low-fat yogurt

1. In 5-quart Dutch oven, heat oil over medium-high heat. Add carrots, celery, onion, and apple; cook, stirring occasionally, until lightly browned, 10 to 15 minutes.

2. Add ginger, garlic, curry powder, cumin, and coriander; cook, stirring, 1 minute.

3. Add water, broth, and lentils; heat to boiling over high heat. Reduce heat to low; cover and simmer, stirring occasionally, until lentils are tender, 45 to 55 minutes. Stir in cilantro and salt. Serve with yogurt. Makes about 10 cups or 5 main-dish servings.

Each serving without yogurt: About 370 calories, 20 g protein, 60 g carbohydrate, 7 g total fat (1 g saturated), 0 mg cholesterol, 315 mg sodium.

French Onion Soup

Prep: 15 minutes
Cook: 1 hour 40 minutes plus baking

3 tablespoons margarine or butter
7 medium onions (2½ pounds), each cut lengthwise in half and
  thinly sliced
¼ teaspoon salt
4 cups water
1 can (14½ ounces) beef broth
¼ teaspoon dried thyme
4 slices (½ inch thick) French bread
4 ounces Gruyére or Swiss cheese, shredded (about 1 cup)

1. In 12-inch skillet, melt margarine over medium heat. Add onions and salt and cook, stirring occasionally, until onions are very tender and begin to caramelize, about 45 minutes. Reduce heat to low; cook, stirring often, until onions are deep, golden brown, about 15 minutes longer.

2. Transfer onions to 3-quart saucepan. Add ½ cup water to skillet; heat to boiling over high heat, stirring to scrape up browned bits. Pour water from skillet into saucepan with onions. Add broth, thyme, and remaining 3½ cups water; heat to boiling over high heat. Reduce heat to low; cover and simmer until onions are very tender, about 30 minutes.

3. Meanwhile, preheat oven to 450°F. Place French-bread slices on small cookie sheet; bake until lightly toasted, about 5 minutes. Place four 2½-cup oven-safe bowls on jelly-roll pan for easier handling. Spoon onion soup into bowls; top with toasted bread, pressing toast lightly into soup. Sprinkle toast with cheese. Bake until cheese has melted and begins to brown, 12 to 15 minutes. Makes 6½ cups or 4 main-dish servings.

Each serving: About 375 calories, 15 g protein, 38 g carbohydrate, 19 g total fat (7 g saturated), 31 mg cholesterol, 835 mg sodium.

Minestrone with Pesto

Prep: 20 minutes plus overnight to soak beans
Cook: 1 hour

8 ounces dry Great Northern
  beans (about 1⅓ cups)
2 tablespoons olive oil
3 medium carrots, peeled and
  sliced
2 stalks celery, sliced
1 large onion, coarsely
  chopped
2 ounces sliced pancetta or
  bacon, coarsely chopped
1 pound all-purpose potatoes
  (3 medium), peeled and cut
  into ½-inch cubes
2 medium zucchini (8 ounces
  each), each cut lengthwise
  into quarters, then crosswise
  into ¼-inch pieces

½ medium head savoy
  cabbage (1 pound), cored
  and sliced (4 cups)
1 large garlic clove, crushed
  with garlic press
2 cans (14½ ounces each)
  chicken broth
1 can (14½ ounces) diced
  tomatoes
½ teaspoon salt
Pesto (see page 99) or ½ cup
  bottled pesto

1. Rinse beans under cold running water and discard any stones or shriveled beans. In large bowl, place beans and *6 cups water.* Allow to stand at room temperature overnight. (Or, in 4-quart saucepan, heat beans and *6 cups water* to boiling over high heat; cook 2 minutes. Remove from heat; cover and let stand 1 hour.) Drain and rinse beans.

2. In 4-quart saucepan, heat beans and enough *water to cover by 2 inches* to boiling over high heat. Reduce heat to low; cover and simmer, stirring occasionally, until beans are tender, 40 minutes to 1 hour. Drain beans.

3. While beans are cooking, in 5-quart Dutch oven, heat oil over medium-high heat. Add carrots, celery, onion, and pancetta; cook, stirring occasionally, until onion begins to brown.

4. Add potatoes, zucchini, cabbage, and garlic; cook, stirring constantly, until cabbage wilts.

5. Add broth, tomatoes with their juice, and *1 cup water;* heat to boiling over high heat. Reduce heat to low; cover and simmer until vegetables are tender, about 30 minutes.

6. In blender, covered, with center part of blender cover removed to let steam escape or in food processor with knife blade attached, puree ½ cup beans with 1 cup soup until smooth. Stir salt, bean puree, and remaining beans into soup; heat to boiling. Reduce heat to low; cover and simmer 10 minutes.

7. Meanwhile, prepare pesto, if you like. Serve soup with Pesto. Makes about 13 cups or 6 main-dish servings.

PESTO: In blender, process *⅔ cup packed fresh basil leaves, ¼ cup olive oil, ¼ cup grated Parmesan cheese, 1 tablespoon water,* and *¼ teaspoon salt* until smooth.

Each serving of soup with pesto: About 425 calories, 16 g protein, 45 g carbohydrate, 22 g total fat (5 g saturated), 17 mg cholesterol, 955 mg sodium.

Meats

~~~~~

Beef • Veal • Pork
Smoked Pork • Lamb • Sausages

All meat sold in the United States is checked for wholesomeness by government inspectors. The USDA monitors quality by grading meat according to the age of the animal and the amount of marbling (streaks or flecks of fat) in the flesh. Select meat with a good color and even marbling; any fat should be creamy white. Be sure to note the sell-by date on the label; cuts in vacuum packaging have a longer shelf life.

❧How Much Meat to Buy

For boneless cuts and ground meat, figure about ¼ to ⅓ pound per serving. For cuts with some bone, such as chops, allow ⅓ to ½ pound; for bony cuts such as ribs, ¾ to 1 pound.

❧How to Store Meat

Store raw meat in the coldest part of the refrigerator (generally the bottom shelf), away from cooked and ready-to-eat foods. Refrigerate uncooked meats 2 to 3 days or freeze up to 6 months. Ground meat won't last as long; refrigerate only 1 to 2 days or freeze up to 3 months.

For short-term storage (up to 2 days in the refrigerator or 2 weeks in the freezer), leave the meat in its original wrapping if intact. For longer freezing, or if wrapping is torn, carefully rewrap meat in zip-tight freezer bags pressing out air. Package together enough chops, steaks, patties, and other small cuts for a single meal, placing plastic wrap or a double thickness of waxed paper between pieces to facilitate separation during thawing. Label packages with the name of the cut, the weight or number of servings, and the date.

Thaw frozen meat (on a plate to catch drips) overnight in the refrigerator—never on the counter. Use thawed meat as soon as possible; never refreeze, or the texture will suffer.

ᒍHow to Cook Meat

With appropriate cooking methods, any cut of meat can be tender. Cook lean cuts by dry-heat methods (roasting, broiling, grilling, panfrying); for less-tender cuts use a moist-heat method (stewing, braising) until meat is butter-soft.

Cooking times in our recipes are based on meat at refrigerator temperature.

ROASTING: When roasting boneless cuts, place the meat on a rack in the roasting pan. That way, the heat can circulate under the meat and prevent it from steaming in its juices. For some cuts, such as rib roasts, the bones act as a built-in-rack.

Use a meat thermometer to determine doneness. Insert it into the thickest part of the meat without touching bone.

Remove the roast from the oven when it reaches 5°F to 10°F less than the desired temperature; the temperature will continue to rise as the meat stands.

PANFRYING AND SAUTÉING: Pat meat dry with paper towels. Use a heavy-bottomed pan, which will conduct heat evenly. Use just enough oil to prevent meat from sticking and make sure the pan is hot before adding the meat. Do not cover.

Avoid crowding the skillet, or meat will steam, not brown.

For a quick pan sauce, after cooking meat, pour off any fat and then deglaze the pan by adding a little liquid to release the caramelized meat juices.

BRAISING AND STEWING: Cut meat into cubes of about the same size for uniform cooking, then pat dry with paper towels before browning. Simmer over low heat; do not boil or meat will toughen. Use a pan with a tight-fitting lid to keep in steam. To test braised or simmered meat for doneness, pierce with a fork; the fork should slip in easily.

Many stews taste even better if cooked a day ahead, then chilled overnight to allow flavors to build and mellow. Remove any surface fat before reheating.

BROILING AND GRILLING: Preheat the broiler or prepare the grill. Broil or grill thinner cuts close to the heat. Thicker cuts need more distance so the inside has time to cook through before the outside burns.

To prevent flare-ups while broiling, do not line the rack with foil. The fat must be able to drip through. If you like, for easy clean-up, line the pan below the rack with foil. To avoid piercing meat and releasing its flavorful juices, use tongs rather than a fork to turn.

Stove-top grill pans may be used for both thin and thick cuts of meat, require little oil and give meat appetizing grill marks.

STIR-FRYING: Pat meat dry with paper towel. Cut the meat into small pieces or strips of uniform size, shape, and thickness. In a skillet or Dutch oven, heat a small amount of oil over medium-high heat until very hot. Add the cut-up meat; cook, stirring and tossing quickly and frequently, until the meat is coated with oil. Continue stir-frying just until meat is tender. If desired, make a sauce with a small amount of water or broth mixed with seasonings and cornstarch; cook, stirring, until the sauce thickens.

ᐁHow to Use a Meat Thermometer or an Instant-Read Thermometer

Once a piece of meat is removed from the oven, insert a meat thermometer or an instant-read thermometer into the thickest part of the meat without touching bone. Cook the meat until the thermometer registers an internal temperature 5° to 10° below the indication for doneness. The temperature will continue to rise as the meat stands.

ᐁBeef

Beef is graded by the USDA according to how much marbling (streaks of fat) the cut contains. Prime beef has the most marbling and is usually sold to restaurants. Choice beef has moderate marbling and is the grade most available in supermarkets. Select beef, the least expensive grade, has the least marbling and is often sold as a house brand. Cuts of beef including the words "round" or "loin" are lean-top round and tenderloin, for example.

Ground beef is labeled with the percentage of lean meat to fat. This ranges from 75 percent lean to 90 percent extralean; 80 to 85 percent lean, juicy and flavorful, is the most popular. To eliminate the danger of E. coli and other bacteria, ground beef (lean or otherwise) should always be cooked to medium doneness—until barely pink in the center.

HOW TO BUY BEEF

For all beef, color is a good indicator of quality. Beef should be bright to deep red. Any fat should be dry and creamy white. Cut edges should look freshly cut and moist, but never wet. Ground beef should look bright and cherry-red. Don't worry if the center of the package looks darker than the exterior. The darker color comes from a lack of oxygen; when exposed to air, the dark meat should return to red. Vacuum-packed beef is darker and more purple in color.

All beef is aged to improve its texture and flavor; for supermarket beef the process is quite short. Traditional aging can take up to six week; such cuts are more expensive and are generally found only at fancy butchers and restaurants.

CHOOSING THE RIGHT CUT

BROILING, GRILLING, OR PANFRYING: Lean, tender cuts work best for these quick methods. When broiling or grilling steaks 1 inch thick or more, position them farther from the heat source so the outside isn't charred before the inside is done. Porterhouse, T-bones, top round, top loin, rib-eye, sirloin, tenderloin, flank steak, and ground beef are the best choices for these methods.

BRAISING AND STEWING: Less-tender and generally less expensive cuts of beef become tender when simmered in a flavorful liquid for a long time. Chuck roast, bottom round, brisket, short ribs, and shanks are best cooked this way. Cubes for stew are usually cut from boneless beef round or chuck.

ROASTING: Large, tender cuts with some internal fat will give best results. Roast boneless cuts on a rack in a shallow pan so the meat doesn't stew in its juices; bone-in roasts don't need a rack. Standing rib roast, tenderloin, rib-eye, or eye round are best cooked this way.

POPULAR BEEF CUTS

Beef rib roast small end (roast). Also called standing rib roast.

Beef rib-eye roast (roast). Large center muscle of rib with bones and seam fat removed.

Beef bottom round roast (braise, roast). Also called beef bottom round pot roast.

Beef chuck boneless shoulder pot roast (braise). Also called English or cross rib roast.

Beef chuck 7-bone steak (braise). Named for bone which resembles number 7; also called center chuck steak.

Beef chuck short ribs (braise, cook in liquid). Also called barbecue ribs.

Beef shank cross cuts (braise, cook in liquid). Crosswise cuts from foreshank or hindshank.

Beef top loin steak (broil, grill, panbroil, panfry). Also called shell, strip, club, and Delmonico steak.

Beef loin porterhouse steak (broil, grill, panbroil, panfry). Includes at least 1¼ inches diameter of tenderloin.

Beef rib-eye steak (broil, grill, panbroil, panfry). Also called fillet steak; cut from beef rib-eye roast.

Beef top round steak (broil, grill, panbroil).

Beef loin tenderloin roast (roast, grill, broil). Cut from tenderloin muscle; very tender, boneless, with little if any fat covering.

This tender cut of beef tapers from a broad butt end to a narrower, thinner tip. To roast it whole, tuck the narrow end under to make the meat uniformly thick.

Beef tenderloin is also cut into smaller pieces, all of which are prepared somewhat differently:

Chateaubriand, the first cut after removing the butt of the tenderloin is a cut about 2 to 3 inches long, like a small roast. It is cooked whole (grilled or broiled), and sliced.

Tournedos are filet steaks, cut from the center of the beef tenderloin into about 1-inch-thick slices. The steaks are grilled, broiled, or panfried.

Filet mignon, a small cut of beef close to the narrow end of the tenderloin, is cut into about 1-inch-thick slices. It is grilled, broiled, or panfried like tournedos.

Start with meat at refrigerator temperature. Remove roast from oven when it reaches 5° to 10°F below desired doneness; temperature will continue to rise as roast stands.

Roast Beef Roasting Times
(Approximate Cooking Time)

Cut	Weight	Oven temp.	Medium-rare (145°)	Medium (160°)
Rib roast (chine bone removed)	4–6 lbs	350°F	1¾ hrs– 2¼ hrs	2¼–2¾ hrs
	6–8 lbs		2¼–2½ hrs	2¾ hrs– 3 hrs
Rib-eye roast	4–6 lbs	350°F	1¾–2 hrs	2–2½ hrs
Whole tenderloin	4–5 lbs	425°F	50–60 mins	60–70 mins
Half tenderloin	2–3 lbs	425°F	35–40 mins	45–50 mins
Round tip roast	3–4 lbs	325°F	1¾–2 hrs	2¼–2½ hrs
	6–8 lbs		2½–3 hrs	3–3½ hrs
Eye round roast	2–3 lbs	325°F	1½–1¾ hrs	–

ROASTS

Herb-Crusted Rib Roast with Yorkshire Pudding

25 minutes
Roast: About 3 hours

1 (3-rib) beef rib roast, from small end (5½ pounds), trimmed and chine bone removed
1 teaspoon salt
¼ teaspoon coarsely ground black pepper
½ teaspoon dried rosemary, crumbled
1 medium lemon
1 tablespoon olive oil
1½ cups fresh bread crumbs (about 3 slices white bread)
½ cup chopped fresh parsley
2 garlic cloves, finely chopped
2 tablespoons Dijon mustard
Yorkshire Pudding (see page 110)

1. Preheat oven to 325°F. In medium roasting pan (14" by 10"), place beef rib roast, fat side up. Sprinkle salt, pepper, and rosemary over roast. Roast beef 1 hour 30 minutes.

2. After beef has roasted 1 hour 30 minutes, prepare coating: From lemon, grate ½ teaspoon peel and squeeze 1 tablespoon juice. In small bowl, combine lemon peel and juice, oil, bread crumbs, parsley, and garlic. Remove roast from oven; evenly spread mustard on top. Press breadcrumb mixture onto mustard-coated roast.

3. Roast beef about 1 hour longer or until coating is golden and meat thermometer inserted in thickest part of roast (without touching bone) reaches 140°F. Internal temperature of meat will rise to 145°F (medium-rare) upon standing. Or roast meat to desired doneness.

4. When roast is done, transfer to warm large platter and let stand 15 minutes to set juices for easier carving. Reserve drippings. Meanwhile, prepare Yorkshire Pudding. Carve roast (see below) and serve with Yorkshire Pudding. Makes 10 servings.

YORKSHIRE PUDDING: In small bowl, with wire whisk, beat *1 cup all-purpose flour, 1 cup milk, 2 eggs, and ½ teaspoon salt,* until smooth. Spoon *2 tablespoons beef drippings* into pudding batter. Pour off all but ¼ cup beef drippings from roasting pan. Return pan to oven; turn oven control to 450°F; heat drippings in oven until very hot, about 3 to 5 minutes. Quickly pour batter onto hot drippings in pan; bake 10 minutes. Turn oven control to 350°F; bake until pudding is lightly browned and puffed, about 20 minutes longer. Cut into squares to serve.

Each serving without Yorkshire Pudding: About 510 calories, 31 g protein, 4 g carbohydrate, 40 g total fat (15 g saturated), 114 mg cholesterol, 410 mg sodium.

Each serving with Yorkshire Pudding: About 130 calories, 5 g protein, 15 g carbohydrate, 5 g total fat (2 g saturated), 71 mg cholesterol, 200 mg sodium.

Rib Roast Tips

- Purchasing a rib roast with the chine bone removed simply means the backbone has been cut from the rib bones, making it easy to carve the roast between the ribs.
- You don't need a rack to roast this cut; the bones act as a natural rack, making cleanup much easier.
- To carve a beef rib roast: Place roast, rib side down, on cutting board. With a carving knife, cut down toward ribs to make a slice about ¼ inch thick. Release the meat slice by cutting along edge of rib bone. Transfer slice to warm platter. Repeat to cut more slices. After whole roast is carved, cut between the bones to separate them. Add bones to platter, if you like.

Royal Rib-Eye Roast

Prep: 10 minutes
Cook: 1 hour 20 minutes

¼ cup Dijon mustard
1 teaspoon salt
½ teaspoon ground black pepper
1 beef rib-eye roast (4 pounds), trimmed
3 pounds potatoes (9 medium), peeled and cut in 1-inch chunks

1. Preheat oven to 350°F. In small bowl, stir together mustard, salt and pepper. Place roast, fat-side up, on small rack in large roasting pan (17" by 11½"). Spread top of roast with mustard mixture. Roast 20 minutes.

2. Meanwhile, in 4-quart saucepan, place potatoes and enough *water to cover*; heat to boiling over high heat. Reduce heat to medium-low, cover and cook 10 minutes; drain. Arrange potatoes around roast in pan, turning to coat with pan drippings.

3. Roast meat and potatoes, turning potatoes occasionally, about 50 to 60 minutes longer, until potatoes are fork-tender, and a meat thermometer inserted in center of roast reaches 140°F. Internal temperature of meat will rise to 145°F upon standing. Or roast meat to desired doneness. Transfer meat to warm large platter and let stand 15 minutes to set juices for easier slicing. Keep potatoes warm.

4. To serve, slice meat thinly, arrange on platter, and serve with potatoes. Makes 12 main-dish servings.

Each serving: About 430 calories, 31 g protein, 16 g carbohydrate, 27 g total fat (11 g saturated), 95 mg cholesterol, 300 mg sodium.

Pepper-Crusted Beef Tenderloin with Red-Wine Gravy

Prep: 30 minutes
Cook/Roast: 50 minutes

Tenderloin Roast
3 tablespoons cracked black pepper
1 tablespoon olive oil
1 teaspoon salt
1 whole beef tenderloin, trimmed and tied (4½ pounds)

Red-Wine Gravy
2 tablespoons margarine or butter
4 medium shallots (6 ounces), minced (½ cup)
1 can (14½ ounces) chicken broth
1 cup dry red wine
½ cup loosely packed fresh parsley leaves, chopped

1. Prepare Tenderloin Roast: Preheat oven to 425°F. In cup, combine pepper, oil, and salt; use to rub on tenderloin. Place tenderloin on rack in large roasting pan (17" by 11½"). Roast tenderloin 50 minutes or until meat thermometer inserted in center of roast reaches 140°F. Internal temperature of meat will rise to 145°F (medium-rare) upon standing. Or roast to desired doneness.

2. About 20 minutes before tenderloin is done, prepare Red-Wine Gravy: In nonstick 2-quart saucepan, melt mar-

garine over medium heat. Add shallots and cook, stirring
often, until tender and golden, about 10 minutes. Add broth
and wine; heat to boiling over high heat. Boil until sauce
is reduced to about 2⅓ cups, about 10 minutes. Remove
saucepan from heat.

3. When tenderloin is done, transfer to warm large platter and let stand 10 minutes to set juices for easier slicing.
Meanwhile, remove rack from roasting pan. Skim and discard fat from pan juices.

4. To serve, add pan juices and any meat juices on platter to gravy; heat through. Stir in parsley. Remove string
from tenderloin, and cut meat into thin slices, and arrange
on platter. Serve tenderloin with gravy. Makes 10 main-
dish servings.

*Each serving of tenderloin: About 360 calories, 43 g protein, 1 g
carbohydrate, 19 g total fat (7 g saturated), 1 g fiber, 127 mg
cholesterol, 130 mg sodium.*

*Each ¼ cup gravy: About 40 calories, 1 g protein, 2 g carbo-
hydrate, 3 g total fat (1 g saturated), 0 g fiber, 0 mg cholesterol,
165 mg sodium.*

Beef Stroganoff

Prep: 20 minutes
Cook: 10 minutes

1 ½ pounds beef tenderloin, trimmed and cut into
    2" by ½" strips
4 tablespoons margarine or butter
1 large onion, finely chopped
8 ounces mushrooms, trimmed and sliced
½ teaspoon salt
1 tablespoon all-purpose flour
⅓ cup beef broth
½ cup sour cream
1 tablespoon mustard

1. Pat meat dry with paper towels. In 12-inch skillet, melt 1 tablespoon margarine over medium-high heat. Add half of beef and cook, stirring, until lightly browned, about 1 minute, using slotted spoon to transfer beef to bowl as it is browned. Repeat with 1 more tablespoon margarine and the remaining beef.

2. In same skillet, melt remaining 2 tablespoons margarine over medium heat. Add onion, mushrooms, and salt and cook, stirring frequently, until vegetables are tender, about 5 minutes.

3. Drain meat juices from bowl into a cup. Add flour to skillet and cook, stirring constantly, 1 minute. Gradually stir in broth and meat juices and cook, stirring frequently, until sauce has thickened slightly and boils. Remove from heat; stir in sour cream and mustard until blended. Add meat; heat through gently (do not boil). Spoon into warm dish and serve. Makes 6 main-dish servings.

Each serving: About 440 calories, 22 g protein, 6 g carbohydrate, 36 g total fat (13 g saturated), 87 mg cholesterol, 630 mg sodium.

Sauerbraten

Prep: 30 minutes plus cooling and 2 to 3 days to marinate
Cook: 4 hours

3 medium onions, sliced
3 medium carrots, sliced
2 large stalks celery, sliced
2½ cups dry red wine
2 cups water
¼ cup red wine vinegar
6 whole black peppercorns
¼ teaspoon mustard
    seeds

1 beef bottom round roast
    (5 pounds), trimmed
2 tablespoons all-purpose flour
1½ teaspoons salt
¼ cup vegetable oil
⅓ cup fine gingersnap crumbs
    (about 5 cookies)
½ cup sour cream

1. Peel and slice 2 onions and 1 carrot. In 3-quart non-stick saucepan, combine sliced onions, sliced carrot, celery, wine, water, vinegar, peppercorns, and mustard seeds. Heat to boiling over medium heat. Reduce heat to low; cover and simmer 10 minutes.

2. Pour into large nonaluminum bowl, cover, and cool. Add meat, turning to coat. Cover and refrigerate 2 to 3 days to marinate, turning meat once each day.

3. About 4 hours before serving, remove meat and pat dry with paper towels; coat meat with flour and 1 teaspoon salt. Strain marinade through sieve into bowl, reserving liquid.

4. In 8-quart nonstick Dutch oven, heat oil over medium-high heat, until very hot. Add meat and cook until browned on all sides, 15 to 20 minutes. Remove meat to plate; pour off and discard all but 1 tablespoon pan drippings.

5. In drippings, over medium heat, cook remaining sliced onion and carrot, stirring often, 3 minutes. Add browned meat. Pour in marinade; heat to boiling. Reduce heat to low; cover and simmer, turning occasionally, until roast is fork-tender, about 3½ hours.

6. Remove meat to warm large platter; keep warm. Skim and discard fat from pan juices. Add gingersnap crumbs and remaining ½ teaspoon salt to pan juices. Cook over medium-high heat, stirring until mixture has thickened.

With wire whisk, blend in sour cream. Cook, stirring until just heated through (do not boil).

7. To serve, cut meat into thin slices, arrange on platter, and spoon some sour-cream gravy over meat. Pass remaining gravy separately. Makes 12 main-dish servings.

Each serving: About 225 calories, 28 g protein, 4 g carbohydrate, 10 g total fat (4 g saturated), 86 mg cholesterol, 235 mg sodium

Filet Mignon with Mustard-Caper Sauce

Prep: 7 minutes
Cook: 14 minutes

6 beef tenderloin steaks (filet mignon), each 1½ inches thick
2 tablespoons olive oil
½ cup dry vermouth
2 tablespoons chopped green onion
½ cup chicken broth
½ cup heavy or whipping cream
2 tablespoons capers, drained
2½ teaspoons Dijon mustard
½ teaspoon salt

1. Pat meat dry with paper towels. In 12-inch skillet, heat oil over medium-high heat until very hot. Add steaks and cook 4 to 5 minutes per side for rare or to desired doneness. Transfer to large warm platter; cover loosely with foil to keep warm.

2. Reduce heat to medium. To drippings in skillet, add vermouth and green onions; cook, stirring until browned bits are loosened from bottom of skillet. Stir in broth, cream, capers, mustard, and salt; heat, stirring, to boiling.

3. Pass sauce in gravy boat to serve with steaks. Makes 6 main-dish servings.

Each serving: About 430 calories, 22 g protein, 1 g carbohydrate, 37 g total fat (15 g saturated), 107 mg cholesterol, 440 mg sodium.

Spinach and Mushroom-Stuffed Tenderloin

Prep: 1 hour
Roast: 45 minutes

Spinach-Mushroom Stuffing
  (recipe follows)

2 teaspoons chopped fresh
  thyme leaves
1 teaspoon salt
1 teaspoon coarsely ground
  black pepper
1 whole beef tenderloin,
  trimmed (4½ pounds)
2 tablespoons margarine or
  butter

¼ cup plain dried bread
  crumbs
2 tablespoons dry vermouth
1 can (14½ ounces) chicken
  broth
8 ounces medium mushrooms,
  trimmed and sliced
2 tablespoons all-purpose flour

1. Prepare Spinach-Mushroom Stuffing.

2. In cup, mix thyme, salt, and pepper; use to rub on tenderloin. Turn thinner end under tenderloin to make meat an even thickness. Holding knife parallel to surface, cut a 1½-inch-deep slit in tenderloin, starting 2 inches from thicker end and ending 2 inches from thinner end.

3. Preheat oven to 425°F. Spoon Spinach-Mushroom Stuffing into slit in tenderloin. With string, tie tenderloin at 2-inch intervals to help hold its shape. Place stuffed tenderloin on rack in large roasting pan (17" by 11½"); roast tenderloin 30 minutes.

4. Meanwhile, in small saucepan, melt 1 tablespoon margarine over low heat. Remove saucepan from heat; stir in bread crumbs. Set bread-crumb topping aside.

5. Remove tenderloin from oven; sprinkle bread-crumb topping on tenderloin. Roast tenderloin 10 to 15 minutes longer, until bread-crumb topping is golden and meat thermometer inserted in center of meat (not in stuffing) reaches 140°F. Internal temperature of meat will rise to 145°F upon standing. Or roast to desired doneness. When roast is done, transfer tenderloin to warm large platter; let stand 10 minutes to set juices for easier slicing.

6. While tenderloin is standing, prepare gravy: Add vermouth and ½ cup broth to drippings in roasting pan. Place pan over low heat and stir until browned bits are loosened from bottom of pan. Pour pan juices into 4-cup measuring cup; let stand a few seconds until fat separates from pan juice. Skim and discard fat from pan juices; add remaining 1¼ cups broth and enough *water* to equal 2½ cups.

7. In 12-inch skillet, melt remaining 1 tablespoon margarine over medium-high heat. Add mushrooms and cook, stirring often, until golden brown and liquid has evaporated, about 12 minutes. Stir in flour and cook, stirring, 1 minute. Gradually stir pan juices into mushrooms and cook, stirring constantly, until gravy boils and has thickened slightly; boil 1 minute.

8. To serve, remove string. Slice stuffed tenderloin and arrange on platter. Serve with mushroom gravy. Makes 10 main-dish servings.

SPINACH-MUSHROOM STUFFING: In 12-inch skillet, heat *4 tablespoons margarine or butter* over medium-high heat; add *1 pound mushrooms,* trimmed and coarsely chopped, and cook until golden brown and liquid has evaporated, 12 to 15 minutes. Stir in *2 tablespoons dry vermouth;* cook 1 minute longer. Remove skillet from heat; stir in *1 package (10 ounces) frozen chopped spinach,* thawed and squeezed dry, *2 tablespoons grated Parmesan cheese, 2 tablespoons plain dried bread crumbs, 1 teaspoon chopped fresh thyme leaves, ¼ teaspoon salt,* and *¼ teaspoon ground black pepper.*

Each serving: About 440 calories, 48 g protein, 9 g carbohydrate, 23 g total fat (7 g saturated), 108 mg cholesterol, 685 mg sodium.

Spicy Tangerine Beef

Prep: 25 minutes
Cook: 25 minutes

4 tangerines or 3 medium navel oranges

1 boneless beef top sirloin steak (12 ounces), trimmed and thinly sliced crosswise

3 tablespoons vegetable oil

2 tablespoons plus ½ teaspoon cornstarch

1 large bunch broccoli (1½ pounds), cut into flowerets, stems peeled and cut into ¼-inch-thick slices

2 tablespoons water

1 medium red pepper, thinly sliced

3 medium green onions, cut diagonally into 2-inch pieces

3 garlic cloves, finely chopped

1 tablespoon minced, peeled fresh ginger

3 tablespoons soy sauce

¼ teaspoon crushed red pepper

1. Remove peel and white pith from 1 tangerine. Holding tangerine over small bowl to catch juice, cut sections from between membranes and add to bowl. From remaining fruit, with vegetable peeler, remove eight 3-inch-long strips of peel (each about ¾ inch wide). With knife, remove any pith from peel. From fruit, squeeze ¾ cup juice.

2. Pat meat dry with paper towels. In 12-inch skillet, heat 2 tablespoons oil over high heat until very hot. Add tangerine peel and cook until lightly browned, about 3 minutes. With slotted spoon, transfer peel to large bowl.

3. Meanwhile, on waxed paper, evenly coat beef slices with 2 tablespoons cornstarch. Add half of beef to skillet and cook, tossing often, until crisp and lightly browned, about 5 minutes, using slotted spoon, to transfer beef to bowl with peel as it is browned. Repeat with remaining 1 tablespoon oil and beef.

4. Add broccoli and water to skillet. Reduce heat to medium; cover and cook 2 minutes. Increase heat to high. Remove cover and add red pepper and green onions; cook, stirring, 2 minutes. Add garlic and ginger; cook, stirring 1 minute longer.

5. Meanwhile, in cup, stir tangerine juice, soy sauce, crushed red pepper, and remaining ½ teaspoon cornstarch until blended.

6. Add juice mixture to skillet and cook, stirring, until sauce has thickened slightly and boils. Return beef mixture and any meat juice in bowl to skillet. Add tangerine segments with any juice in bowl; gently toss to combine. Makes 4 main-dish servings.

Each serving: About 335 calories, 22 g protein, 24 g carbohydrate, 19 g total fat (4 g saturated), 42 mg cholesterol, 860 mg sodium.

Steak Pizzaiolo

Prep: 15 minutes
Cook: About 25 minutes

2 boneless beef strip (shell) steaks, each ¾ inch thick (10 ounces each), well trimmed
½ teaspoon salt
¼ teaspoon coarsely ground black pepper
1 tablespoon olive oil
1 large onion (12 ounces), cut lengthwise in half and sliced
1 small red pepper, cut into 1-inch pieces
1 small green pepper, cut into 1-inch pieces
2 garlic cloves, crushed with garlic press
½ cup chicken broth
2 tablespoons red wine vinegar
1 teaspoon sugar
8 cherry tomatoes, each cut in half
½ cup lightly packed fresh basil leaves, chopped

1. Pat steaks dry with paper towels. Sprinkle ¼ teaspoon salt and black pepper on steaks.

2. Heat nonstick 12-inch skillet over medium-high heat until hot. Add steaks and cook 4 to 5 minutes per side for medium-rare or until desired doneness. Transfer steaks to warm plate; cover loosely with foil to keep warm.

3. In same skillet, heat oil over medium heat. Add onion, red and green peppers, garlic, and remaining ¼ teaspoon salt, and cook, stirring often, until vegetables are tender and golden, about 10 minutes.

4. Increase heat to medium-high. Stir in broth, vinegar, sugar, and cherry tomatoes; heat to boiling. Cook, stirring, 1 minute. Remove skillet from heat and stir in basil.

5. To serve, slice steaks and arrange on 4 dinner plates; top each with some pepper mixture. Makes 4 main-dish servings.

Each serving: About 315 calories, 32 g protein, 16 g carbohydrate, 13 g total fat (4 g saturated), 88 mg cholesterol, 450 mg sodium.

Mustard Steak au Poivre

Prep: 10 minutes
Cook: 10 minutes

½ teaspoon salt
2 teaspoons cracked black pepper
4 beef tenderloin steaks (filet mignon), each 1 inch thick
   (4 ounces each)
⅓ cup brandy
1 tablespoon Dijon mustard with seeds

1. On waxed paper, mix salt and pepper; use to rub on steaks. Heat nonstick 12-inch skillet over medium-high heat until hot. Add steaks and cook 4 to 5 minutes per side for medium-rare or until desired doneness. Remove steaks to plate; keep warm.

2. Remove skillet from heat; add brandy and mustard and stir to combine. Return skillet to medium-high heat and cook, stirring frequently, until sauce boils; boil 30 seconds. To serve, pour sauce onto 4 warm dinner plates; place steaks on top of sauce. Makes 4 main-dish servings.

Each serving: About 210 calories, 24 g protein, 1 g carbohydrate, 8 g total fat (3 g saturated), 70 mg cholesterol, 425 mg sodium.

Lemon-Pepper Steak

Prep: 10 minutes
Broil: 16 minutes

1 tablespoon freshly grated lemon peel
1 tablespoon margarine or butter, softened
1 garlic clove, finely chopped
1 teaspoon salt
1 to 2 teaspoons cracked pepper
1 beef top round steak, 1¼ inches thick (2 pounds)

1. Preheat broiler. In small bowl, stir together lemon peel, margarine, garlic, salt, and pepper.

2. Pat steak dry with paper towels. Place steak on rack in broiling pan. Spread half lemon-pepper butter over top of steak; broil at closest position to heat source, 8 minutes. Turn steak; spread with remaining lemon-pepper butter. Broil about 8 minutes longer for rare or until desired doneness. Transfer steak to cutting board and slice thinly. Makes 8 main-dish servings.

Each serving: About 200 calories, 26 g protein, 1 g carbohydrate, 10 g total fat (3 g saturated), 72 mg cholesterol, 360 mg sodium.

Beef Stir-Fry with Arugula

Prep: 10 minutes
Cook: 10 minutes

4 teaspoons vegetable oil
1 bunch green onions, cut into 1½-inch pieces
1 package (8 ounces) sliced mushrooms
1 pound sliced beef for stir-fry (or round steak, trimmed and cut into thin slices)
3 tablespoons soy sauce
3 tablespoons balsamic vinegar
2 tablespoons brown sugar
2 bunches arugula or 2 packages (8 ounces each) prewashed spinach

1. In nonstick 12-inch skillet, heat 2 teaspoons oil over medium-high heat. Add green onions and mushrooms and cook, stirring often, until tender and brown, about 5 minutes. Transfer to bowl.

2. In same skillet, heat 1 teaspoon oil until very hot. Add half beef and cook, stirring constantly, until beef just loses its pink color, using slotted spoon to transfer beef to bowl with mushrooms as it is browned. Repeat with remaining 1 teaspoon oil and remaining beef.

3. In cup, with fork, mix soy sauce, vinegar, and brown sugar. Return beef mixture and any juice in bowl to skillet; stir in soy-sauce mixture. Cook 1 minute, stirring, until heated through. Remove from heat; stir in half the arugula.

4. To serve, place remaining arugula on platter and spoon beef mixture over. Makes 4 main-dish servings.

Each serving: About 260 calories, 29 g protein, 18 g carbohydrate, 15 g total fat (5 g saturated), 48 mg cholesterol, 875 mg sodium.

Steak and Pepper Fajitas

Prep: 10 minutes
Cook: 20 minutes

1 beef top round steak,
    1 inch thick (12 ounces)
1 bottle (8 ounces) medium-hot
    chunky salsa
1 tablespoon light corn-oil
    spread
1 medium red onion, thinly
    sliced
1 medium green pepper, thinly
    sliced
1 medium red pepper, thinly
    sliced

2 tablespoons chopped fresh
    cilantro
8 (6- to 7-inch) low-fat flour
    tortillas, warmed as label
    directs
1 container (8 ounces) fat-free
    sour cream
8 ounces fat-free sharp
    Cheddar cheese, shredded
    (about 2 cups)
Lime wedges

1. Pat meat dry with paper towels. Preheat broiler. Place steak on rack in broiling pan; spread steak with ¼ cup salsa. Broil at closest position to heat source, 8 minutes. Turn steak and spread with ¼ cup salsa; broil 8 minutes longer for medium-rare, or until desired doneness.

2. Meanwhile, in nonstick 12-inch skillet, melt corn-oil spread over medium-high heat. Add red onion and green and red peppers; cook, stirring frequently, until vegetables are tender-crisp. Stir in cilantro. Spoon mixture into serving bowl.

3. To serve, place steak on cutting board; holding knife almost parallel to surface, thinly slice steak. Serve sliced steak with pepper mixture, flour tortillas, sour cream, shredded cheese, remaining salsa, and lime wedges. Makes 4 main-dish servings.

Each serving: About 450 calories, 45 g protein, 55 g carbohydrate, 7 g total fat (1 g saturated), 51 mg cholesterol, 1060 mg sodium.

Seared Rosemary Steak

Prep: 5 minutes
Cook: 12 to 15 minutes

1 beef flank steak (1 pound), trimmed
½ teaspoon salt
¼ teaspoon coarsely ground black pepper
¾ teaspoon dried rosemary, crumbled
4 cups loosely packed arugula

1. Pat meat dry with paper towels. Heat 10-inch cast-iron skillet over high heat until very hot.

2. Sprinkle salt, pepper, and rosemary on steak. Add steak to hot skillet; reduce heat to medium-high, and cook 6 to 7 minutes per side for medium-rare, or until desired doneness.

3. To serve, arrange arugula on warm large platter. Thinly slice flank steak on an angle and place on arugula. Pour any meat juices from cutting board on top. Makes 4 main-dish servings.

Each serving: About 200 calories, 28 g protein, 1 g carbohydrate, 9 g total fat (4 g saturated), 47 mg cholesterol, 330 mg sodium.

Flank Steak with Red-Onion Marmalade

Prep: 10 minutes
Cook: 35 minutes

3 tablespoons margarine or butter
2 medium red onions (1 pound), thinly sliced
3 tablespoons sugar
3 tablespoons distilled white vinegar
1 teaspoon salt
¼ teaspoon coarsely ground black pepper
1 beef flank steak (1¾ pounds), trimmed

1. In nonstick 12-inch skillet, melt 2 tablespoons margarine over medium heat. Add onions and cook until very tender, stirring occasionally, about 15 minutes. Stir in sugar, vinegar, and ½ teaspoon salt. Reduce heat to low; simmer 5 minutes. Spoon red-onion marmalade into small bowl; keep warm.

2. Rinse skillet and wipe dry. Pat steak dry with paper towels. Sprinkle remaining ½ teaspoon salt and the pepper on steak. In same skillet, melt remaining 1 tablespoon margarine over medium-high heat. Add steak and cook 6 to 8 minutes per side for medium-rare or until desired doneness. Transfer steak to cutting board. Return red-onion marmalade to skillet; heat through.

3. Thinly slice steak on an angle and serve with red-onion marmalade. Makes 6 main-dish servings.

Each serving: About 265 calories, 29 g protein, 13 g carbohydrate, 17 g total fat (6 g saturated), 56 mg cholesterol, 515 mg sodium.

Chili Con Carne, Texas Style

Prep: 35 minutes
Cook: 1 hour 30 minutes

1 beef chuck blade roast
  (3½ pounds), well trimmed
  and cut into ¼-inch cubes,
  discarding bones
¼ cup vegetable oil
3 medium onions, chopped
2 medium green peppers,
  chopped
2 garlic cloves, finely chopped
1 teaspoon crushed red pepper
2 cans (28 ounces each)
  tomatoes

1 can (12 ounces) tomato paste
2 cups water
1 tablespoon sugar
1 teaspoon salt
1 teaspoon ground cumin
½ teaspoon dried oregano
½ teaspoon coarsely ground
  black pepper
4 ounces Monterey Jack or mild
  Cheddar cheese, coarsely
  shredded (about 1 cup)

1. Pat meat dry with paper towels. In 5-quart Dutch oven, heat oil until very hot over medium-high heat. Add beef, in batches, and cook, stirring frequently, until beef is well browned, using slotted spoon to transfer beef to bowl as it browns.

2. Reserve ½ cup chopped onion for sprinkling over chili later. In drippings remaining in Dutch oven, cook, green peppers, garlic, crushed red pepper, and remaining onions over medium heat, stirring occasionally, until vegetables are tender and adding more oil, if necessary.

3. Return browned beef and any juice in bowl to Dutch oven. Stir in tomatoes with their juice, tomato paste, water, sugar, salt, cumin, oregano, and black pepper, breaking tomatoes up with side of spoon. Heat to boiling over high heat. Reduce heat to low; cover and simmer, stirring occasionally, until beef is fork-tender, about 1 hour.

4. To serve, spoon chili into bowls. Pass shredded cheese and reserved chopped onion to sprinkle over each serving. Makes 10 main-dish servings.

Each serving: About 365 calories, 31 g protein, 20 g carbohydrate, 19 g total fat (6 g saturated), 93 mg cholesterol, 660 mg sodium.

Margarita Steak

Prep: 10 minutes
Cook: About 25 minutes

2 boneless beef strip (shell) or
  Delmonico steaks, each
  ¾ inch thick (10 ounces
  each), well trimmed
¾ teaspoon salt
⅛ teaspoon ground red pepper
  (cayenne)
1¼ teaspoons ground cumin
1 teaspoon olive oil
2 medium red onions, sliced

1 lime
2 tablespoons orange-flavored
  liqueur or orange juice
½ cup chicken broth
¼ cup packed fresh cilantro,
  chopped
1 medium avocado, pitted,
  peeled, and sliced (optional)

1. Pat steaks dry with paper towels. In cup, combine ½ teaspoon salt, ground red pepper, and 1 teaspoon cumin. Use to rub on steaks.

2. Heat nonstick 12-inch skillet over medium-high heat until hot. Add steaks and cook 4 to 5 minutes per side for medium-rare or until desired doneness. Transfer steaks to plate; cover loosely with foil to keep warm.

3. In same skillet, heat oil over medium heat. Add onions; sprinkle with remaining ¼ teaspoon salt and remaining ¼ teaspoon ground cumin and cook, stirring occasionally, until onions are tender and golden, 8 to 10 minutes.

4. Meanwhile, from lime, with vegetable peeler, remove 3 strips of peel (2" by 1" each) and squeeze 2 tablespoons juice.

5. Add lime peel to skillet with onions and cook 30 seconds. Stir in orange liqueur and cook 30 seconds longer. Add broth and lime juice. Heat to boiling over medium-high heat; boil, stirring, 1 minute. Remove and discard lime peel.

6. To serve, slice steaks and arrange on 4 dinner plates; top with onions and pan juices. Sprinkle with chopped cilantro. If you like, serve with avocado slices. Makes 4 main-dish servings.

Each serving without avocado: About 265 calories, 31 g protein, 8 g carbohydrate, 11 g total fat (4 g saturated), 88 mg cholesterol, 580 mg sodium.

Cubed Steaks with Caper Sauce

Prep: 7 minutes
Cook: 17 minutes

1 pound beef cubed steaks
3 tablespoons margarine or butter
1 medium onion, thinly sliced
⅓ cup chicken broth
1 tablespoon capers, drained
1 tablespoon prepared mustard

1. If steaks are large, cut them into serving pieces. Pat steaks dry with paper towels. In nonstick 12-inch skillet, melt 2 tablespoons margarine over medium heat. Add half of steaks and cook about 2 to 3 minutes per side or until browned. Transfer browned steaks to a warm medium platter; cover loosely with foil to keep warm. Repeat with remaining steaks.

2. In same skillet, melt remaining 1 tablespoon margarine over medium heat. Add onion and cook, stirring occasionally, until tender. Stir in broth, capers, and mustard; cook, stirring constantly, until mixture has thickened and boils.

3. Spoon onion mixture over steaks and serve. Makes 4 main-dish servings.

Each serving: About 255 calories, 26 g protein, 3 g carbohydrate, 15 g total fat (4 g saturated), 55 mg cholesterol, 375 mg sodium.

London Broil

Prep: 5 minutes
Broil: 10 minutes

1 beef flank steak (1½ pounds), well trimmed
1 tablespoon olive oil
1 tablespoon finely chopped onion
1 teaspoon salt
1 tablespoon margarine or butter, softened

1. Preheat broiler. With sharp knife, score both sides of steak for even broiling. Pat steak dry with paper towels. Place steak on rack in broiling pan. In cup combine oil, onion, and salt. Use to rub on steak.
2. Broil steak at closest position to heat source, 5 minutes per side for rare or until desired doneness.
3. To serve, place steak on cutting board; spread with margarine. Holding knife almost parallel to surface, cut steak into thin slices. Makes 6 main-dish servings.

Each serving: About 215 calories, 23 g protein, 0 g carbohydrate, 13 g total fat (4 g saturated), 57 mg cholesterol, 485 mg sodium.

Beef Bourguignon

Prep: 35 minutes
Cook: 2 hours 30 minutes

3 to 4 tablespoons olive oil
2½ pounds beef for stew, trimmed and cut into 1½-inch chunks
1½ pounds mushrooms, each trimmed and cut in half
6 slices bacon, cut into ¼-inch pieces
1 pound small white onions, peeled and quartered

2 medium carrots, peeled and cut into ¼-inch pieces
1 medium stalk celery, peeled and cut into ¼-inch pieces
1 cup dry red wine
½ cup chicken broth
2 teaspoons sugar
1 teaspoon salt
2 tablespoons all-purpose flour
¼ cup water

1. Pat beef dry with paper towels. In nonstick 5-quart Dutch oven, heat 3 tablespoons oil over medium-high heat until very hot. Add beef, in batches, and cook, until beef is well browned, using slotted spoon to transfer beef to bowl as it is browned. In drippings in Dutch oven, (adding remaining 1 tablespoon oil if necessary) cook mushrooms, over medium heat, 5 minutes; with slotted spoon, transfer mushrooms to another bowl. Cover loosely.

2. In same Dutch oven, cook bacon, onions, carrots, and celery, over medium heat, stirring frequently, until browned. Stir in wine, broth, sugar, and salt. Return meat and any juice in bowl to Dutch oven; heat to boiling over high heat. Reduce heat to low; cover and simmer until meat is nearly tender, about 1 hour 30 minutes.

3. Stir in mushrooms. Cover and simmer until meat is fork-tender, about 15 minutes longer.

4. Skim and discard fat from pan juices. In small bowl, gradually whisk water into flour until smooth. Gradually stir flour mixture into stew. Cook over medium heat, stirring, until pan juices have thickened and boil. Serve in deep bowls. Makes 10 main-dish servings.

Each serving: About 295 calories, 32 g protein, 11 g carbohydrate, 13 g total fat (3 g saturated), 73 mg cholesterol, 400 mg sodium.

Beef and Wild Mushroom Stew

Prep: 30 minutes
Bake: 1 hour 45 minutes

2 tablespoons vegetable oil
1 pound medium mushrooms,
    each trimmed and cut in half
1 package (½ ounce) dried
    shiitake or porcini
    mushrooms
2 pounds beef for stew,
    trimmed and cut into
    1½-inch pieces
¾ teaspoon salt
1 large onion, chopped

2 garlic cloves, finely chopped
2 tablespoons tomato paste
2 medium carrots, each peeled
    and cut lengthwise in half,
    then crosswise into thirds
1 cup chicken broth
¾ cup dry red wine
¼ teaspoon dried thyme
1 bay leaf

1. In 5-quart Dutch oven, heat 1 tablespoon oil over medium-high heat. Add fresh mushrooms and, stirring occasionally, cook until tender and lightly browned, and most of liquid has evaporated, about 10 minutes; transfer to small bowl. Cover loosely.

2. Meanwhile, in small bowl, pour 1 cup *boiling water* over dried mushrooms; let stand until softened, about 30 minutes. With slotted spoon, remove mushrooms. Rinse to remove any grit, then coarsely chop. Strain mushroom liquid through sieve lined with paper towels.

3. Pat beef dry with paper towels; sprinkle salt on beef. In same Dutch oven, heat remaining 1 tablespoon vegetable oil until very hot. Add half of beef and cook until browned, 10 to 12 minutes, using slotted spoon to transfer beef to bowl as it is browned. Repeat with remaining beef.

4. Preheat oven to 350°F. In drippings in Dutch oven, cook onion with *2 tablespoons water*, stirring occasionally, until onion is tender and lightly browned, about 10 minutes. Add garlic and cook 2 minutes longer. Stir in tomato paste; cook, stirring constantly, 1 minute.

5. Return beef and any juice in bowl to Dutch oven; stir in dried mushrooms and mushroom liquid, carrots, broth, wine, thyme, and bay leaf. Heat to boiling over high heat. Cover, place in oven and bake 1 hour 30 minutes. Add sautéed fresh mushrooms; cover and bake until beef is fork-tender, about 15 minutes longer. Discard bay leaf and serve. Makes 6 main-dish servings.

Each serving: About 370 calories, 30 g protein, 13 g carbohydrate, 18 g total fat (6 g saturated), 87 mg cholesterol, 480 mg sodium.

Beef Stew Milanese

Prep: 15 minutes
Cook: 1 hour 45 minutes

2 pounds beef for stew, trimmed and cut into 1¼-inch pieces
2 to 3 tablespoons olive oil
1 large onion, coarsely chopped
1 large carrot, coarsely chopped
1 large stalk celery, coarsely chopped
1 garlic clove, finely chopped
1 can (14 to 16 ounces) tomatoes
⅓ cup dry white wine
1½ teaspoons salt
¼ teaspoon pepper
½ teaspoon dried basil
1 tablespoon chopped fresh parsley
1½ teaspoons freshly grated lemon peel

1. Pat beef dry with paper towels. In 5-quart Dutch oven, heat 2 tablespoons oil, over medium-high heat, until very hot. Add half of beef and cook until well browned, using slotted spoon to transfer beef to to bowl as it is browned and adding 1 tablespoon more oil, if necessary. Cook remaining half of beef the same way.

2. In drippings in Dutch oven, cook onion, carrot, celery, and garlic over medium heat until lightly browned, about 5 minutes. Stir in tomatoes with their juice, wine, salt, pepper, and basil, breaking up tomatoes with side of spoon. Return beef and any juice in bowl to Dutch oven; heat to boiling. Reduce heat to low; cover and simmer, stirring occasionally, until meat is fork-tender, about 1 hour 15 minutes.

3. To serve, spoon stew into warm large serving dish; sprinkle with parsley and lemon peel. Makes 8 main-dish servings.

Each serving: About 255 calories, 26 g protein, 6 g carbohydrate, 13 g total fat (4 g saturated), 56 mg cholesterol, 600 mg sodium.

Orange Beef and Barley Stew

Prep: 30 minutes
Bake: 1 hour 45 minutes

1½ pounds beef for stew, trimmed and cut into 1½-inch pieces
2 tablespoons vegetable oil
4 medium carrots, each peeled and cut into 2-inch pieces
2 medium onions, each cut into 6 wedges
2 garlic cloves, crushed with garlic press

1 can (28 ounces) plum tomatoes
1 can (14½ ounces) beef broth
1 cup dry red wine
3 strips (3" by 1" each) orange peel
1 bay leaf
½ teaspoon salt
¾ cup pearled barley

1. Preheat oven to 350°F. Pat beef dry with paper towels. In 5-quart Dutch oven, heat 1 tablespoon oil over medium-high heat, until very hot. Add half of beef and cook until browned, using slotted spoon to transfer beef to bowl as it is browned. Repeat with remaining beef.

2. In same Dutch oven, heat remaining 1 tablespoon oil. Add carrots and onions; cook until browned. Add garlic; cook, stirring, 1 minute. Return beef and any juice in bowl to Dutch oven; add tomatoes with their juice, broth, wine, orange peel strips, bay leaf, and salt. Heat to boiling, over high heat, breaking tomatoes up with side of spoon.

3. Cover, place in oven, and bake 45 minutes. Stir in barley; cover and bake until beef and barley are tender, 45 to 60 minutes longer. Discard bay leaf and serve. Makes 6 main-dish servings.

Each serving: About 385 calories, 31 g protein, 32 g carbohydrate, 14 g total fat (4 g saturated), 55 mg cholesterol, 720 mg sodium.

Oven-Barbecued Short Ribs

Prep: 12 minutes
Cook/Broil: 1 hour 40 minutes

4 pounds beef chuck short ribs
2 medium onions, 1 cut into quarters, 1 finely chopped
1¼ teaspoons salt
2 tablespoons vegetable oil
1 medium green pepper, chopped
¾ cup ketchup
2 tablespoons brown sugar
½ teaspoon Worcestershire sauce
½ teaspoon hot pepper sauce

1. In 5- to 6-quart saucepot, place short ribs and one onion; pour in enough *water to cover* and 1 teaspoon salt; stir, and heat to boiling over high heat. Reduce heat to low; cover and simmer until short ribs are fork-tender, about 1 hour 15 minutes. Transfer ribs to platter and cover loosely. If not using ribs right away, cover and refrigerate.

2. Meanwhile, prepare barbecue sauce: In 2-quart saucepan heat oil over medium heat. Add green pepper and remaining finely chopped onion, cook, stirring occasionally, until tender. Stir in ketchup, brown sugar, Worcestershire, hot pepper sauce, *⅓ cup water,* and remaining ¼ teaspoon salt. Heat to boiling over high heat. Reduce heat to low; cover and simmer 5 minutes to blend flavors.

3. Preheat broiler. Broil about 5 inches from heat source, brushing ribs with some barbecue sauce, and turning them occasionally, until heated through and glazed. Serve with any remaining barbecue sauce. Makes 8 main-dish servings.

Each serving: About 615 calories, 30 g protein, 12 g carbohydrate, 49 g total fat (20 g saturated), 100 mg cholesterol, 545 mg sodium.

Mustard-Glazed Corned Beef
with Cabbage

Prep: 15 minutes
Cook: 3 hours 20 minutes plus cooling

1 corned-beef brisket (6 pounds), well trimmed
1 medium onion, cut in half
1 celery stalk, cut up
1 large carrot, cut up
2 garlic cloves, each cut in half
½ teaspoon whole black peppercorns
⅔ cup packed brown sugar
2 tablespoons prepared mustard
2 tablespoons ketchup
Sautéed Cabbage (see page 137)

1. Remove corned beef from package and rinse. Place in 8-quart Dutch oven; add onion, celery, carrot, garlic, and peppercorns. Pour in enough *water to cover* meat; heat to boiling over high heat. Reduce heat to low; cover and simmer until meat is fork-tender, about 3 hours. Transfer corned beef to platter to cool until easy to handle. Discard cooking liquid.

2. Preheat oven to 350°F. Cut meat into slices. Arrange meat, slices overlapping, on oven-proof platter or large roasting pan (17" by 11½").

3. In bowl, with fork, mix brown sugar, mustard, and ketchup; spread on top and between meat slices. Bake 20 minutes or until glaze is browned, and meat is heated through. Meanwhile, prepare Sautéed Cabbage. To serve, place cabbage on platter with meat. Makes 16 servings.

Each serving: 335 calories, 19 g protein, 14 g carbohydrate, 23 g total fat (7 g saturated), 97 mg cholesterol, 1,335 mg sodium.

SAUTÉED CABBAGE: Core, quarter, and coarsely slice *2 small heads green cabbage (each 1½ pounds)*. In 8-quart Dutch oven, heat *¼ cup vegetable oil*, over high heat, until very hot. Stir in cabbage, *1 teaspoon salt,* and *¼ teaspoon sugar;* cook, stirring often, until cabbage is tender-crisp, about 5 to 10 minutes.

Oven-Barbecued Beef Brisket with Mop Sauce*

Prep: 10 minutes
Bake: 3 hours 10 minutes

½ cup water
¼ cup cider vinegar
¼ cup Worcestershire sauce
   (yes, this much)
¼ cup ketchup
¼ cup dark corn syrup
2 tablespoons vegetable oil
2 tablespoons prepared
   mustard

2 teaspoons instant-coffee
   granules
1 teaspoon salt
⅛ teaspoon hot pepper sauce
   or to taste
1 beef brisket (3 pounds), well
   trimmed

1. Preheat oven to 325°F. Prepare mop sauce: In nonstick 1-quart saucepan, stir together water, vinegar, Worcestershire, ketchup, corn syrup, oil, mustard, coffee granules, salt, and hot pepper sauce until blended. Heat to boiling over medium-high heat, stirring occasionally; cook 5 minutes. Remove from heat.

2. Place beef brisket in 13" by 9" baking dish. Pour mop sauce over brisket. Cover baking dish with foil and bake about 3 hours or until brisket is fork-tender, turning brisket once during baking.

3. Transfer brisket to cutting board and slice thinly; arrange on warm large platter. Skim and discard fat from sauce; pour sauce into bowl. Serve brisket with sauce. Makes 8 main-dish servings.

*Mop Sauce is traditionally prepared for Texas ranch-style barbecues in batches so large it is brushed on the meat with a mop.

Each serving: About 325 calories, 34 g protein, 12 g carbohydrate, 15 g total fat (4 g saturated), 105 mg cholesterol, 605 mg sodium.

GH's Best Burgers

Basic Burgers

Prep: 5 minutes
Cook: 12 minutes

1 ¼ pounds ground beef chuck

Shape ground beef into four ¾-inch-thick oval patties, handling meat as little as possible. Heat 12-inch skillet over high heat until very hot. Arrange beef patties in hot skillet; cook 4 to 5 minutes per side for medium, or until desired doneness. Makes 4 burgers.

Each burger: About 275 calories, 25 g protein, 0 g carbohydrate, 19 g total fat (7 g saturated), 87 mg cholesterol, 75 mg sodium.

GREEK BURGERS: Prepare Basic Burgers as above but before shaping into patties, with a fork, mix the following into ground beef: *¼ cup chopped fresh parsley, 1 teaspoon dried mint, 1 teaspoon salt, and ¼ teaspoon ground black pepper.* Cook as above. Makes 4 burgers.

Each burger: About 275 calories, 25 g protein, 0 g carbohydrate, 19 g total fat (7 g saturated), 87 mg cholesterol, 615 mg sodium.

ROQUEFORT BURGERS: Prepare Basic Burgers as above but before shaping into patties, with a fork, mix the following into ground beef: *1 tablespoon Worcestershire sauce* and *½ teaspoon coarsely ground black pepper.* Shape mixture into 4 balls. Make indentation in center of each ball; place one-fourth of *2 ounces crumbled Roquefort* or *blue cheese* into each indentation. Shape mixture around cheese; flatten each into ¾-inch-thick patty. Cook as above. Makes 4 burgers.

Each burger: About 330 calories, 28 g protein, 1 g carbohydrate, 23 g total fat (10 g saturated), 100 mg cholesterol, 370 mg sodium.

TERIYAKI BURGERS: Prepare Basic Burgers as above but before shaping into patties, with a fork, mix the following into ground beef: *¼ cup chopped green onions, 2 tablespoons soy sauce, 1 tablespoon brown sugar,* and *¼ teaspoon ground red pepper* (cayenne). Cook as above but during last 2 minutes of cooking, brush burgers with a mixture of *2 tablespoons apple jelly, 2 teaspoons minced, peeled fresh ginger,* and *1 teaspoon soy sauce,* glazing both sides. Makes 4 burgers.

Each burger: About 320 calories, 26 g protein, 12 g carbohydrate, 19 g total fat (7 g saturated), 87 mg cholesterol, 680 mg sodium.

TEX-MEX BURGERS: Prepare Basic Burgers as above but before shaping into patties, with a fork, mix the following into ground beef: *2 tablespoons finely chopped onion, 2 tablespoons bottled salsa* or *Tomato Salsa* (see page 770), *1 teaspoon salt,* and *1 teaspoon chili powder.* Cook as above. Makes 4 burgers.

Each burger: About 280 calories, 25 g protein, 1 g carbohydrate, 19 g total fat (7 g saturated), 87 mg cholesterol, 650 mg sodium.

The Perfect Burger

• The best ground beef for burgers has some fat in it, for juiciness and great flavor, so forego the leanest ground beef.

- Gentle handling is another key to juicy burgers. Be sure not to overmix the meat when adding ingredients (like chopped onion) and to use a light hand when shaping the patties, so the burgers won't come out compact and dry.
- If grilling, get the grill good and hot before putting on the burgers so the meat will be seared and won't stick.
- Never flatten or score burgers with a spatula as they cook on the grill. This, too, forces out juices.
- For safety's sake, cook thoroughly, until there's just a trace of pink in the center (medium doneness, 160°F). Burgers don't have to be well-done to be safe to eat, just not rare. It's risky to eat rare or raw burgers because any bacteria that might lurk on the surface of meat before it's ground can be transferred to its interior during the grinding process. Cooking times vary, depending on the thickness of the burgers and the heat of the grill, so the only way to be sure they're done is to make them all the same size, then fork into one of them to check for doneness.
- For the best cheeseburger: Wait until burgers are done, then top with cheese and continue grilling just until the cheese melts.
- How long to keep ground beef in the fridge: Two days, in its supermarket wrap. For longer storage, rewrap in freezer wrap or a zip-tight freezer bag and freeze; use within 3 months.

Deluxe Open-Faced Cheeseburgers

Prep: 15 minutes
Cook: 12 minutes

1 small avocado, pitted and peeled
3 tablespoons low-fat mayonnaise
2 teaspoons fresh lemon juice
1¼ teaspoons salt
1 tablespoon olive oil
1 medium onion, sliced
1 small green pepper, cut into thin rings

1 pound ground beef chuck
½ teaspoon chili powder
2 ounces Monterey Jack cheese, shredded (½ cup)
4 slices whole-wheat bread, toasted
4 lettuce leaves
1 small tomato, sliced
Bottled taco sauce

1. In small bowl, with back of spoon, mash avocado. Stir in mayonnaise, lemon juice, and ½ teaspoon salt; cover and reserve.

2. In 12-inch skillet, over medium heat, heat oil. Add onion and green pepper, cook, stirring occasionally, until tender. Remove onion mixture to another small bowl; cover and keep warm.

3. In medium bowl, combine ground beef, chili powder and ¾ teaspoon salt just until well blended but not over-mixed. Shape beef mixture into 4 patties, each about 4 inches in diameter, handling meat as little as possible. In same skillet, over high heat, cook patties 5 to 6 minutes per side for medium, or until desired doneness. Top each patty with some cheese; cover and cook until cheese melts, about 2 minutes. Remove skillet from heat.

4. For each serving, spread a slice of toast with one-fourth avocado mixture; top with a burger, lettuce leaf, some tomato slices, one-fourth onion mixture, and some taco sauce. Makes 4 main-dish servings.

Each burger: About 560 calories, 29 g protein, 24 g carbohydrate, 40 g total fat (13 g saturated), 92 mg cholesterol, 1,185 mg sodium.

Steakhouse Burgers with Horseradish Sour Cream

Prep: 10 minutes
Cook: 10 minutes

1 ¼ pounds ground beef chuck
⅓ cup sour cream
2 ½ teaspoons bottled white horseradish
4 English muffins, split and lightly toasted
4 Boston lettuce leaves
Salt
Coarsely ground black pepper

1. Shape ground beef into 4 patties, each ½ inch thick, handling meat as little as possible. Sprinkle patties with ½ teaspoon salt, then 1 teaspoon pepper, pressing pepper lightly into patties.

2. Heat nonstick 12-inch skillet over medium-high heat until hot. Add patties and cook, shaking skillet occasionally, about 4 to 5 minutes per side for medium, or until desired doneness.

3. Meanwhile, in small bowl, combine sour cream, horseradish, ⅛ teaspoon salt, and ⅛ teaspoon pepper.

4. Serve burgers on English muffins with lettuce and horseradish sauce. Makes 4 main-dish servings.

Each serving: About 505 calories, 32 g protein, 31 g carbohydrate, 27 g total fat (11 g saturated), 104 mg cholesterol, 880 mg sodium.

Danish Meatballs

Prep: 10 minutes
Cook: 25 minutes

1½ pounds ground beef chuck
½ cup plain dried bread crumbs
1 large egg
1 tablespoon grated onion
1 teaspoon salt
2 tablespoons margarine or butter
2 tablespoons all-purpose flour
1 cup milk
1 cup water

1. In large bowl, combine ground beef, bread crumbs, egg, onion, and ½ teaspoon salt, just until well blended but not overmixed. Shape mixture into 24 meatballs.

2. In 12-inch skillet, melt margarine over medium-high heat. Add half of meatballs and cook until well browned, using slotted spoon to transfer meatballs to bowl as they are browned. Repeat with remaining meatballs. Pour off all but 2 tablespoons drippings from skillet.

3. Into drippings in skillet, over medium heat, stir flour and remaining ½ teaspoon salt; cook, stirring, 1 minute. Gradually stir in milk and water; cook, stirring, until mixture has thickened. Add meatballs and heat to boiling. Reduce heat to low; cover, and simmer, stirring occasionally, until meatballs have lost their pink color throughout, about 10 minutes. Makes 6 main-dish servings.

Each serving: About 415 calories, 24 g protein, 11 g carbohydrate, 30 g total fat (12 g saturated), 121 mg cholesterol, 810 mg sodium.

Auntie Lynette's Meat Loaf Surprise

Prep: 30 minutes
Bake: 1¼ hours

1 ½ pounds all-purpose
potatoes (about 3 large),
peeled and cut into 2-inch
chunks
¼ cup milk
2 tablespoons margarine or
butter
1 ¼ teaspoons salt
¼ teaspoon ground black
pepper
1 can (14½ ounces) diced
tomatoes

2 pounds ground beef chuck
2 large eggs
¾ cup seasoned dried bread
crumbs
¼ cup grated Parmesan cheese
1 garlic clove, finely chopped
1 package (10 ounces) frozen
chopped spinach, thawed
and squeezed dry

1. In 3-quart saucepan, heat potatoes and enough *water to cover* to boiling over high heat. Reduce heat to low; cover and simmer until potatoes are fork-tender, 10 to 15 minutes. Drain potatoes and return to saucepan. Add milk, margarine, ½ teaspoon salt, and ⅛ teaspoon pepper. With potato masher, mash potatoes until smooth; cover loosely and reserve.

2. Preheat oven to 350°F. In blender or food processor with knife blade attached, puree tomatoes with their juice and *½ cup water* until smooth.

3. In large bowl, combine ground beef, eggs, bread crumbs, Parmesan, garlic, ½ teaspoon salt, ⅛ teaspoon pepper, and ½ cup tomato mixture just until well blended but not overmixed.

4. Onto long sheet of waxed paper (14" by 12"), pat meat mixture into 11" by 9" rectangle. Spread mashed potatoes over meat rectangle, leaving a 1-inch border all around. Place spinach over potatoes; sprinkle with remaining ¼ teaspoon salt.

5. Starting at a narrow end, roll meat with potatoes and spinach, jelly-roll fashion, lifting waxed paper and using long metal spatula to loosen meat from paper. Carefully place meat loaf, seam side down, in 13" × 9" glass or ceramic baking dish.

6. Pour remaining tomato mixture over and around meat loaf. Bake meat loaf 1¼ hours. Let loaf stand 10 minutes before slicing. Makes 8 main-dish servings.

Each serving: About 400 calories, 28 g protein, 26 g carbohydrate, 21 g total fat (8 g saturated), 127 mg cholesterol, 1,015 mg sodium.

Home-Style Meat Loaf

Prep: 20 minutes
Bake: 1 hour 30 minutes

2 medium onions
2 pounds ground beef chuck
2 large eggs
2 cups fresh bread crumbs
 (about 4 slices bread)
½ cup water
¼ cup ketchup
2 tablespoons chopped fresh
 parsley

1 teaspoon salt
¼ teaspoon ground black
 pepper
½ teaspoon dried basil
2 tablespoons margarine or
 butter

1. Preheat oven to 350°F. Finely chop ½ onion and slice remaining 1½ onions; wrap sliced onions in plastic wrap and refrigerate.

2. In large bowl, combined chopped onion, ground beef, eggs, bread crumbs, water, ketchup, parsley, salt, pepper, and basil, just until well blended but not overmixed. Place meat mixture in 13" by 9" baking pan; with hands, shape mixture into 9" by 5" loaf, pressing firmly. Bake meat loaf 1 hour 30 minutes. When meat loaf is done, let stand 10 minutes to set juices for easier slicing.

3. About 15 minutes before meat loaf is done, in 10-inch skillet melt margarine over medium heat. Add reserved sliced onions, and cook, stirring occasionally, until tender.

4. To serve, with two large spatulas, carefully transfer meat loaf to warm large platter. Top with sautéed onions and slice.

5. To serve meat loaf cold, or for sandwiches, omit sautéed onions; cover and refrigerate and eat within 3 days. Makes 8 main-dish servings.

Each serving: About 315 calories, 23 g protein, 9 g carbohydrate, 20 g total fat (7 g saturated), 107 mg cholesterol, 530 mg sodium.

Whole Stuffed Cabbage

Prep: 30 minutes
Cook: 2 hours

Tomato Sauce (see page 147)
1 large head green cabbage (4 to 4½ pounds), tough outer
   leaves discarded
1 pound ground beef
1 medium onion, chopped
1 garlic clove, finely chopped
1 teaspoon salt
½ teaspoon ground black pepper
1 cup cooked rice
2½ cups water

1. Prepare Tomato Sauce.

2. Meanwhile, carefully remove 2 large leaves from cabbage; set aside. With sharp knife, carefully cut out stem and center of cabbage, leaving a 1-inch-thick shell. Discard stem; coarsely chop cut-out cabbage.

3. In 5-quart Dutch oven, cook ground beef, onion, garlic, salt, pepper, and 1 cup chopped cabbage, over medium-high heat, stirring frequently, until meat is browned and cabbage is tender, about 15 minutes. Stir in rice and 1 cup Tomato Sauce; remove from heat.

4. Spoon beef mixture into cabbage shell. Cover cabbage opening with reserved 2 cabbage leaves. With string, tie cabbage securely to hold leaves in place.

5. In same Dutch oven, pour in water; stir until browned bits are loosened from bottom of pan. Add remaining chopped cabbage and remaining Tomato Sauce. Place stuffed cabbage, stem end down, in sauce. Heat to boiling over high heat. Reduce heat to low; cover and simmer, basting occasionally with pan juices, until cabbage shell is fork-tender, about 1 hour 30 minutes.

6. To serve, place cabbage, stem end down, on deep, warm platter; discard string. Spoon sauce over cabbage; cut cabbage into 6 wedges. Makes 6 main-dish servings.

Each serving: About 395 calories, 19 g protein, 36 g carbohydrate, 21 g total fat (8 g saturated), 64 mg cholesterol, 905 mg sodium.

TOMATO SAUCE: In 3-quart nonstick saucepan, combine *1 can (28 ounces) tomatoes* with their juice, *1 can (6 ounces) tomato paste, 1 tablespoon brown sugar, ½ teaspoon salt, ½ teaspoon Worcestershire sauce,* and *⅛ teaspoon ground allspice.* Heat to boiling over high heat, breaking tomatoes up with side of spoon. Reduce heat to low; cover and simmer, stirring occasionally, 20 minutes.

Chili with Beans

Prep: 15 minutes
Cook: 1 hour 15 minutes

2 pounds ground beef chuck
1 large green pepper, coarsely chopped
1 large onion, chopped
1 large garlic clove, finely chopped
⅓ cup mild chili powder
2 cans (15 to 19 ounces each) red kidney beans

1 can (28 ounces) tomatoes
1 can (6 ounces) tomato paste
¾ cup water
1½ teaspoons salt
1 teaspoon sugar
1 bay leaf
Ground red pepper (cayenne) or hot pepper sauce

1. In 5-quart Dutch oven, cook ground beef, green pepper, onion, and garlic, over high heat, stirring frequently, until pan juices have evaporated and beef is well browned, about 15 minutes.

2. Stir in chili powder; cook 1 minute. Drain liquid from kidney beans into meat mixture; reserve beans. Stir in tomatoes with their juice, tomato paste, water, salt, sugar, and bay leaf. Heat to boiling, over high heat, breaking tomatoes up with side of spoon. Reduce heat to low; cover and simmer, stirring occasionally, 45 minutes.

3. Stir in reserved kidney beans. If you like chili hotter, add ground red pepper or hot pepper sauce, to taste. Cover and simmer 15 minutes longer to blend flavors. Skim off and discard fat from chili. Discard bay leaf. To serve, spoon into bowls. Makes 10 main-dish servings.

Each serving: About 355 calories, 24 g protein, 29 g carbohydrate, 17 g total fat (6 g saturated), 61 mg cholesterol, 950 mg sodium.

Chili Potpie with Cheddar-Biscuit Crust

Prep: 30 minutes
Cook: 1 hour 45 minutes to 2 hours

1 pound boneless beef chuck, trimmed and cut into ½-inch pieces
1 tablespoon plus 3 teaspoons olive oil
1 medium onion, chopped
2 garlic cloves, finely chopped
½ teaspoon salt
1 tablespoon chili powder
1 teaspoon ground coriander
½ teaspoon ground cumin
1 can (16 ounces) tomatoes in puree

1 can (4 to 4½ ounces) chopped mild green chiles
¼ cup water
1 tablespoon dark brown sugar
1 tablespoon tomato paste
1 can (15 to 16 ounces) pink beans, rinsed and drained
¼ cup chopped fresh cilantro leaves
Cheddar-Biscuit Crust (recipe follows)
2 teaspoons milk

1. Pat meat dry with paper towels. In 5-quart Dutch oven, heat 1 tablespoon oil over medium-high heat until very hot. Add half of beef and cook until browned and juices have evaporated, using slotted spoon to transfer beef to bowl as it is browned. Repeat with 2 teaspoons more oil and remaining beef.

2. Add remaining 1 teaspoon oil to Dutch oven. Reduce heat to medium. Add onion and cook, until tender and golden, about 10 minutes. Add garlic; cook, stirring frequently, 2 minutes. Add salt, chili powder, coriander, and cumin; cook, stirring, 1 minute.

3. Add tomatoes with their puree, breaking tomatoes up with side of spoon. Stir in chiles with their juice, water, brown sugar, tomato paste, beef and any juice in bowl, and heat to boiling over high heat. Reduce heat to low; cover and simmer, stirring occasionally, 30 minutes.

4. Add beans; heat to boiling over high heat. Reduce heat to low; cover and simmer until beef is very tender, 30 to 45 minutes longer. Stir in cilantro.

5. Preheat oven to 425°F. Meanwhile, prepare Cheddar-Biscuit Crust.

6. Spoon hot chili mixture into round deep 2-quart casserole or 9-inch deep-dish pie plate. Top with biscuit crust, tucking in edge to fit. With tip of knife, cut out 5 oval openings in crust to allow steam to escape during baking. (Do not just make slits; they will close up as crust bakes.) Brush crust with milk.

7. Place casserole on foil-lined cookie sheet to catch any overflow during baking. Bake pie until crust is browned, about 20 minutes. Cool slightly on wire rack before serving. Makes 6 main-dish servings.

CHEDDAR-BISCUIT CRUST: In medium bowl, stir together *1 cup all-purpose flour, ⅓ cup shredded sharp Cheddar cheese, ¼ cup yellow cornmeal, 2 teaspoons baking powder,* and *½ teaspoon salt.* With pastry blender or two knives used scissor-fashion, cut in *3 tablespoons cold margarine or butter* until mixture resembles coarse crumbs. Stir in *½ cup milk;* combine just until dough holds together and leaves side of bowl. Turn dough onto lightly floured surface; gently knead about 5 times, just until thoroughly mixed. With floured rolling pin, roll dough into a round 1 inch larger in diameter than top of casserole.

Each serving: About 515 calories, 24 g protein, 45 g carbohydrate, 27 g total fat (8 g saturated), 58 mg cholesterol, 1,320 mg sodium.

ᖰVeal

No matter how you cook veal, do it with care. Lean and delicate, veal should actually be cooked more like poultry than beef. As with other meats, the proper cooking method depends on the cut. Whether you broil a thick, juicy chop or create a fragrant stew, remember not to overcook veal, or you'll toughen its delicate texture.

Veal calves are raised to an age of 12 to 16 weeks. The finest and most expensive of all veal is milk-fed. It comes from animals that are fed on their mothers' milk or a special milk formula. The meat is light pink—almost white—and mildly flavored, with a firm but velvety texture. Grain-fed veal comes from calves that are reared to a similar age but fed a diet of grain or grass. It has a rosier color and a slightly stronger flavor than milk-fed veal.

HOW TO BUY VEAL

Look for fine-textured veal that's pale to creamy pink with little marbling. Any fat should be firm and very white. The bones of milk-fed veal will have a reddish marrow. Some veal carries a USDA grade of Prime, which is usually milk-fed veal, or Choice, typically from grain-fed calves and of slightly lower quality. Because veal is a moist meat, it is fairly perishable. It will last for only two days in the refrigerator, tightly wrapped.

CHOOSING THE RIGHT CUT

Veal is especially good cooked by moist-heat methods such as braising so the meat stays juicy and flavorful. Roasting at moderate temperatures also works well, and panfrying (in butter or oil) is ideal for thin cutlets.

BROILING, GRILLING, OR PANFRYING: These dry-heat methods are suitable for a variety of thin cuts. For broiling and grilling, choose fairly thick chops and steaks; cuts that are too thin will dry out. Use veal cutlets for panfrying only. Since they'll cook very quickly, keep a close watch. Best bets: Arm or blade steaks, loin chops, rib chops, ground veal, and cutlets.

BRAISING AND STEWING: Bone-in pieces are especially suited to long cooking, as they yield the best flavor. Veal shanks have meaty-tasting marrow in the center, which helps enrich stews. When done, braised or stewed veal should be fork-tender. Best bets: Shanks, shank crosscuts, arm or blade steak, breast, shoulder. Veal cubes for stew are cut from the leg or shoulder.

ROASTING: Many large cuts of veal will roast nicely. Since veal roasts are generally very lean, ensure juicy results by cooking only to medium doneness (160°F), basting occasionally with the flavorful pan juices. Best bets: Shoulder, rib roast, loin roast, round, and breast.

Veal Roasting Times
(Oven Temperature 325°F)

Start with meat at refrigerator temperature. Remove roast from oven when it reaches 5° to 10° below desired doneness; temperature will rise as it stands.

Cut	Weight	Meat thermometer reading	Approximate cooking time (minutes per lb)
Boneless shoulder roast	3-5 lbs	160°F	35-40 mins
Leg rump or round roast (boneless)	3-5 lbs	160°F	35-40 mins
Boneless loin roast	3-5 lbs	160°F	25-30 mins
Rib roast	3-5 lbs	160°F	30-35 mins

POPULAR VEAL CUTS

Veal shoulder roast, boneless (braise, roast). Shoulder cut with bones removed; rolled and tied to keep shape.

Veal breast (braise, roast). Also called breast of veal, it contains lower ribs; quite lean with some layering of fat.

Veal breast riblets (braise, cook in liquid). Also called veal riblets; long, narrow cuts containing rib bones with thin fat covering.

Veal shoulder blade steak (braise, panfry). Also called veal shoulder steak or veal shoulder chop.

Veal rib chops (braise, panfry). Contain big rib-eye muscle.

Veal loin chops (braise, panfry). Muscles include top loin and tenderloin.

Veal top loin chops (braise, panfry). Same as veal loin chops except do not contain tenderloin.

Veal cutlets (braise, panfry). Very lean, thin, boneless slices from leg; pound thin for scallopini.

Veal shank cross cuts (braise, cook in liquid). Cut crosswise from foreshank or hindshank, 1 to 2½ inches thick.

Veal Rib Roast Marsala

Prep: 10 minutes
Roast: 2 hours 8 minutes

1 veal rib roast (5 pounds), trimmed and chine bone removed
1 teaspoon salt
¼ teaspoon coarsely ground black pepper
¼ teaspoon dried oregano
¼ teaspoon dried thyme
1 ¼ cups chicken broth
8 ounces mushrooms, trimmed and thinly sliced
2 tablespoons all-purpose flour
⅓ cup dry Marsala wine

1. Preheat oven to 325°F. In medium roasting pan (14" by 10"), place roast bone side down. In cup, combine salt, pepper, oregano, and thyme; use to rub on veal roast.

2. Roast about 1 hour 45 minutes to 2 hours, or until meat thermometer inserted in thickest part of roast (without touching bone) reaches 150°F. Internal temperature of meat will rise to 160°F upon standing. When roast is done, transfer to warm large platter and let stand 15 minutes to set juices.

3. Make gravy: Skim fat from pan juices in roasting pan; spoon about 4 tablespoons into 2-quart saucepan, discarding remainder, if any. Pour broth into roasting pan; stir over medium heat until browned bits are loosened from bottom of pan. Remove from heat. Heat drippings in saucepan over medium heat; add mushrooms and cook, stirring frequently, until tender. Stir in flour until blended; cook, stirring, 1 minute. Gradually stir in broth mixture and Marsala. Cook, stirring, until gravy has thickened and boils; boil 1 minute. Pour gravy into gravy boat.

4. To carve veal roast, with rib side facing you, insert meat fork into top of veal roast to anchor meat, then slice meat, holding knife close to rib bone as each slice is cut. One slice of meat will contain a rib bone; the next slice will be boneless. Serve roast with gravy. Makes 10 main-dish servings.

Each serving: About 265 calories, 31 g protein, 3 g carbohydrate, 14 g total fat (5 g saturated), 136 mg cholesterol, 440 mg sodium.

Vitello Tonnato

Prep: 20 minutes plus chilling
Cook: 2 hours 30 minutes

1 rolled boneless veal rump roast (3¼ pounds), trimmed	1 can (2 ounces) anchovy fillets
2 tablespoons olive oil	¼ teaspoon ground black pepper
2 medium stalks celery, coarsely chopped	¼ teaspoon dried basil
1 large onion, sliced	3 tablespoons capers
1 garlic clove, finely chopped	1 can (6 ounces) tuna packed in olive oil
½ cup dry white wine	½ cup mayonnaise
	Lemon wedges

1. Pat veal dry with paper towels. In 5-quart Dutch oven, heat oil over medium-high heat until very hot. Add veal roast and cook until well browned; transfer to plate. In drippings in Dutch oven, over medium heat, cook celery, onion, and garlic, stirring occasionally, until tender, about 5 minutes. Return veal roast to Dutch oven; add wine, 8 anchovy fillets, 1 tablespoon capers, pepper, and basil; heat to boiling. Reduce heat to low; cover and simmer, turning veal occasionally, until veal is fork-tender, about 2 hours.

2. When veal is done, transfer to clean plate; cover with foil and refrigerate until chilled. Boil mixture remaining in Dutch oven over medium-high heat, until reduced to about 2 cups. Strain mixture through sieve, discarding vegetables. (There will be about ¾ cup broth.)

3. In blender, covered, with center part of blender cover removed to let steam escape, or in food processor with knife blade attached, puree broth and tuna with its oil until smooth. Pour into small bowl; cover and refrigerate (mixture will become thick).

4. To serve, unwrap veal roast, remove string, and cut into ¼-inch-thick slices. Arrange veal on large platter. Stir mayonnaise into tuna mixture until blended; spoon over veal. Sprinkle veal with 2 tablespoons capers and remaining anchovy fillets. Serve with lemon wedges to squeeze over servings. Makes 12 main-dish servings.

Each serving: About 235 calories, 27 g protein, 0 g carbohydrate, 13 g total fat (2 g saturated), 98 mg cholesterol, 430 mg sodium.

Veal Forestier

Prep: 15 minutes
Cook: 15 minutes

1 pound veal cutlets, each ¼ inch thick
¼ cup all-purpose flour
4 to 6 tablespoons margarine or butter
8 ounces mushrooms, trimmed and sliced
½ cup dry vermouth
2 tablespoons water
¾ teaspoon salt

1. With meat mallet or between two sheets of plastic wrap or waxed paper with rolling pin, pound each cutlet to ⅛-inch thickness. Cut cutlets into pieces about 3" by 3". Place flour on waxed paper, use to coat cutlets, shaking off excess.

2. In 12-inch skillet, over medium-high heat, melt 4 tablespoons margarine. Add cutlets, in small batches, and cook until lightly browned, turning once. Use tongs to transfer cutlets to plate as they brown. If pan gets dry, add remaining 2 tablespoons margarine.

3. To same skillet, add mushrooms, vermouth, water, and salt, stir until browned bits are loosened, and heat to boiling. Reduce heat to low; cover and simmer 5 minutes. Return veal and any juice on plate to skillet; heat through. Serve veal with mushroom sauce. Makes 4 main-dish servings.

Each serving: About 335 calories, 26 g protein, 9 g carbohydrate, 21 g total fat (4 g saturated), 88 mg cholesterol, 740 mg sodium.

Veal Cutlets with Peppers

Prep: 17 minutes
Cook: 24 minutes

⅓ cup olive oil
1 garlic clove, sliced
2 medium onions, sliced
3 medium green peppers, sliced
3 medium red peppers, sliced
2 tablespoons red wine vinegar
1 teaspoon dried basil
½ teaspoon dried oregano

1 ½ teaspoons salt
½ teaspoon ground black pepper
2 pounds veal cutlets, each ¼ inch thick
⅓ cup all-purpose flour
3 to 4 tablespoons margarine or butter

1. In 12-inch skillet, heat oil over medium-high heat. Add garlic and cook until browned; with slotted spoon, discard garlic. Add onions, green peppers, and red peppers; cook, stirring frequently, 2 minutes. Stir in vinegar, basil, oregano, ½ teaspoon salt, and ¼ teaspoon pepper. Reduce heat to medium; cover and cook, stirring frequently, 10 minutes. With slotted spoon, transfer vegetables to warm large platter; cover to keep warm.

2. Meanwhile, with meat mallet or between 2 sheets of plastic wrap or waxed paper with rolling pin, pound cutlets to ⅛-inch thickness. Sprinkle 1 teaspoon salt and ¼ teaspoon pepper on cutlets. Place flour on waxed paper; use to coat cutlets, shaking off excess.

3. In same skillet, over medium-high heat, melt 3 table-

spoons margarine. Add cutlets, in small batches, and cook
until lightly browned, turning once. Use tongs to transfer
cutlets to platter of vegetables as they brown. If pan gets
dry, add remaining 1 tablespoon margarine. Serve cutlets
with peppers. Makes 8 main-dish servings.

*Each serving: About 325 calories, 26 g protein, 14 g carbohydrate,
18 g total fat (4 g saturated), 88 mg cholesterol, 730 mg sodium.*

Veal Scallopini Marsala

Prep: 5 minutes
Cook: 12 minutes

1 pound veal cutlets, each ¼ inch thick
¾ teaspoon salt
¼ teaspoon ground black pepper
¼ cup all-purpose flour
3 to 4 tablespoons margarine or butter
½ cup Marsala wine
2 tablespoons chopped fresh parsley

1. With meat mallet or between two sheets of plastic
wrap or waxed paper with rolling pin, pound each cutlet to
⅛-inch thickness. Cut cutlets into pieces about 3" by 3";
sprinkle ½ teaspoon salt and the pepper on cutlets. Place
flour on waxed paper; use to coat cutlets, shaking off excess.

2. In 12-inch skillet, melt 3 tablespoons margarine over
medium-high heat. Add cutlets, in small batches, and cook
until lightly browned, turning once. Use tongs to transfer
cutlets to large warm platter as they brown. If pan gets dry,
add remaining 1 tablespoon margarine.

3. Discard fat in pan. Stir in Marsala and remaining ¼
teaspoon salt; stir over medium heat until browned bits are
loosened from bottom of pan; boil 1 minute.

4. To serve, pour pan sauce over veal and sprinkle with
parsley. Makes 4 main-dish servings.

*Each serving: About 265 calories, 28 g protein, 7 g carbohydrate,
13 g total fat (4 g saturated), 89 mg cholesterol, 580 mg sodium.*

Wiener Schnitzel

Prep: 15 minutes
Cook: 15 minutes

6 veal cutlets (1½ pounds), each ¼ inch thick
2 large eggs
1 teaspoon salt
½ teaspoon coarsely ground black pepper
⅓ cup all-purpose flour
1½ cups plain dried bread crumbs
½ cup (1 stick) margarine or butter
⅓ cup capers, well drained
3 tablespoons chopped fresh parsley
2 lemons, each cut into 6 wedges

1. With meat mallet, or between two sheets of plastic wrap or waxed paper with rolling pin, pound cutlets to ⅛-inch thickness.

2. In pie plate, with fork, beat eggs, salt, and pepper. On waxed paper, place flour; on another sheet of waxed paper, place bread crumbs.

3. Coat veal in flour, shaking off excess, dip in eggs, then coat with bread crumbs, firmly pressing so crumbs adhere.

4. In 12-inch skillet, melt 4 tablespoons margarine over medium heat. Add cutlets, two at a time, and cook 3 to 4 minutes per side, until browned and crisp. Use tongs to transfer cutlets to warm large platter. Repeat with remaining cutlets and margarine.

5. Top cutlets with capers and parsley; serve with lemon wedges. Makes 6 main-dish servings.

Each serving: About 390 calories, 30 g protein, 25 g carbohydrate, 18 g total fat (4 g saturated), 159 mg cholesterol, 1,145 mg sodium.

Veal Parmigiana

Prep: 15 minutes plus preparing Marinara Sauce
Cook: 40 minutes

2 cups Marinara Sauce (see page 478)
1 cup plain dried bread crumbs
1 teaspoon salt
⅛ teaspoon ground black pepper
2 large eggs
6 veal cutlets (1½ pounds), each ¼ inch thick
5 tablespoons olive oil
1 package (8 ounces) mozzarella cheese, cut into 6 slices
¼ cup grated Parmesan cheese

1. Prepare Marinara Sauce.

2. On waxed paper, combine bread crumbs, salt, and pepper. In pie plate, with fork, beat eggs lightly. Dip cutlets in eggs, then bread crumbs; repeat, coating each cutlet twice, firmly pressing so crumbs adhere.

3. In 12-inch skillet, heat oil over medium-high heat. Add cutlets, two at a time, and cook about 5 minutes per side, until browned and crisp. Using tongs to transfer browned cutlets to plate. Repeat with remaining cutlets. Arrange browned cutlets in same skillet. Spoon some Marinara Sauce over each cutlet; top each with slice of mozzarella, and sprinkle with Parmesan. Cover and cook over low heat until cheese is melted, about 5 minutes. To serve, use a large, wide spatula to transfer cutlets to plates. Makes 6 main-dish servings.

Each serving: About 455 calories, 38 g protein, 21 g carbohydrate, 24 g total fat (9 g saturated), 191 mg cholesterol, 1,180 mg sodium.

Veal Piccata

Prep: 10 minutes
Cook: 20 minutes

2 lemons
2 pounds veal cutlets, each ¼ inch thick
⅓ cup all-purpose flour
¾ teaspoon salt
3 to 5 tablespoons olive oil
2 tablespoons margarine or butter
1 cup chicken broth
½ cup dry white wine

1. From 1 lemon, squeeze 3 tablespoons juice. Cut other lemon into thin slices. With meat mallet or between two sheets of plastic wrap or waxed paper with rolling pin, pound cutlets to ⅛-inch thickness. On waxed paper, combine flour and ½ teaspoon salt; use to coat cutlets, shaking off excess.

2. In 12-inch skillet, heat 3 tablespoons oil and margarine over medium-high heat, until margarine has melted. Add cutlets, in small batches, and cook until lightly browned, turning once. Use tongs to transfer cutlets to plate as they brown. If pan gets too dry, add 1 to 2 tablespoons more oil, if necessary.

3. Discard fat from pan. Stir in broth, wine, and ¼ teaspoon salt; stir over medium heat until browned bits are loosened from bottom of pan. Return cutlets to skillet; cover and simmer until cutlets are fork-tender, about 5 minutes. Transfer cutlets to warm large platter; keep warm. Stir lemon juice into skillet; heat to boiling over high heat. To serve, spoon pan juices over cutlets; garnish with lemon slices. Makes 8 main-dish servings.

Each serving: About 230 calories, 25 g protein, 5 g carbohydrate, 12 g total fat (3 g saturated), 88 mg cholesterol, 425 mg sodium.

Veal Chops in Creamy Anchovy Sauce

Prep: 10 minutes
Cook: 20 minutes

4 veal rib chops, each ¾ inch thick (8 ounces each), trimmed
2 tablespoons olive oil
½ cup chicken broth
2 tablespoons dry vermouth
1 ounce anchovy fillets, drained and chopped
2 teaspoons fresh lemon juice
3 tablespoons milk
1 tablespoon all-purpose flour

1. Pat veal chops dry with paper towels. In 12-inch skillet, heat oil over medium-high heat, until very hot. Add veal chops and cook until browned. Add broth, vermouth, anchovies, and lemon juice; heat to boiling. Reduce heat to low; cover and simmer, turning chops occasionally, until juices run clear when chops are pierced with tip of knife, about 15 minutes.

2. Place chops on warm platter. In cup, stir milk and flour; gradually stir into pan juices in skillet. Cook over medium heat, stirring, until sauce has thickened; boil 1 minute. To serve, spoon pan sauce over chops. Makes 4 main-dish servings.

Each serving: About 285 calories, 34 g protein, 3 g carbohydrate, 14 g total fat (3 g saturated), 137 mg cholesterol, 510 mg sodium.

Stuffed Veal Chops

Prep: 15 minutes
Grill: 10 to 12 minutes

Veal Chops
4 veal rib chops, each 1 inch thick (10 ounces each), trimmed
¼ cup drained and chopped bottled roasted red peppers
2 tablespoons chopped fresh basil leaves
2 ounces Fontina cheese, sliced
½ teaspoon salt
½ teaspoon coarsely ground black pepper

Arugula Salad
1 tablespoon olive oil
1 tablespoon balsamic vinegar
1 tablespoon chopped fresh basil leaves
½ teaspoon Dijon mustard
⅛ teaspoon salt
⅛ teaspoon coarsely ground black pepper
4 ounces arugula, watercress, or baby spinach,
   tough stems removed

1. Prepare grill. Prepare Veal Chops: Holding knife parallel to surface, cut a horizontal pocket in each chop with as small an opening as possible.

2. In small bowl, mix roasted red peppers and basil. Place Fontina cheese slices in veal pockets; spread red-pepper mixture over cheese. Sprinkle salt and pepper on veal chops.

3. Place chops on grill over medium-high heat and grill 5 to 6 minutes per side, or until chops are lightly browned and just lose their pink color throughout.

4. Prepare Arugula Salad: In medium bowl, with wire whisk, mix oil, vinegar, basil, mustard, salt, and pepper; add arugula, tossing to coat.

5. To serve, spoon arugula mixture onto platter; arrange chops on top. Makes 4 main-dish servings.

Each serving: About 435 calories, 40 g protein, 3 g carbohydrate, 29 g total fat (11 g saturated), 180 mg cholesterol, 635 mg sodium.

Breast of Veal with Vegetables

Prep: 25 minutes
Cook: 2 hours 30 minutes

1 veal breast (4½ pounds),
   trimmed
¼ cup all-purpose flour
¼ cup olive oil
1 small onion, chopped
1 garlic clove, chopped
1 can (14 to 16 ounces)
   tomatoes
1 cup water

1½ teaspoons salt
1½ teaspoons sugar
1½ pounds small all-purpose
   potatoes, each peeled and
   cut into halves
3 small zucchini (about
   1 pound), cut into 1-inch
   chunks

1. With sharp knife, cut veal breast into individual ribs. Place flour on waxed paper; use to coat veal ribs. Reserve leftover flour. In 8-quart Dutch oven, heat oil over medium heat until very hot. Add ribs, in batches, and cook until well browned, using tongs to transfer ribs to bowl as they are browned.

2. In drippings in Dutch oven, over medium heat, cook onion and garlic until tender. Stir in reserved flour until blended. Add tomatoes with their juice, breaking them up with side of spoon. Return veal ribs and any juice in bowl to Dutch oven; stir in water, salt, and sugar. Heat to boiling over high heat. Reduce heat to low; cover and simmer, stirring often, 1 hour 30 minutes.

3. Add potatoes; cover and cook 15 minutes. Add zucchini; cover and cook, stirring occasionally, until veal ribs and vegetables are fork-tender, about 10 minutes longer. Skim and discard fat from pan juices. Serve veal ribs with vegetables and the sauce. Makes 6 main-dish servings.

Each serving: About 490 calories, 56 g protein, 27 g carbohydrate, 17 g total fat (5 g saturated), 218 mg cholesterol, 850 mg sodium.

Veal and Mushroom Stew

Prep: 40 minutes
Bake: 1 hour 15 minutes

1½ pounds veal for stew, trimmed and cut into 1½-inch chunks
¾ teaspoon salt
¼ teaspoon ground black pepper
3 tablespoons vegetable oil
1 pound medium white mushrooms, each trimmed and cut in half
4 ounces shiitake mushrooms, stems removed
½ cup water
⅓ cup Marsala wine
1 package (10 ounces) frozen peas, thawed

1. Pat veal dry with paper towels. Sprinkle salt and pepper on veal. In 5-quart Dutch oven, heat 2 tablespoons oil over medium-high heat until very hot. Add half of veal and cook until browned, using slotted spoon to transfer veal to bowl as it is browned. Repeat with remaining veal.

2. Preheat oven to 350°F. In same Dutch oven, heat remaining tablespoon of oil over medium-high heat. Add white and shiitake mushrooms, and cook, stirring occasionally, until lightly browned.

3. Return veal and any juice in bowl to Dutch oven; stir in water and Marsala, stirring until browned bits are loosened from bottom of Dutch oven. Heat veal mixture to boiling.

4. Cover, place in oven and bake, stirring occasionally, until veal is fork-tender, about 1 hour 15 minutes. Stir in peas; cook until heated through. To serve, spoon into soup plates. Makes 6 main-dish servings.

Each serving: About 300 calories, 26 g protein, 13 g carbohydrate, 15 g total fat (4 g saturated), 93 mg cholesterol, 405 mg sodium.

Veal Stew with Orange Gremolata

Prep: 20 minutes
Bake: 1 hour 15 minutes

2 pounds veal for stew,
   trimmed and cut into
   1½ inch pieces
2 tablespoons vegetable oil
4 medium carrots, each peeled
   and cut into 2-inch pieces
1 medium onion, chopped
1 cup chicken broth
1 can (16 ounces) tomatoes in
   puree

¾ teaspoon salt
¼ teaspoon coarsely ground
   black pepper
¼ teaspoon dried thyme
2 garlic cloves, minced
2 tablespoons chopped fresh
   parsley
1 tablespoon freshly grated
   orange peel

1. Preheat oven to 350°F. Pat veal dry with paper towels. In 5-quart Dutch oven, heat 1 tablespoon oil over medium-high heat until very hot. Add half of veal and cook until browned, using slotted spoon to transfer veal to bowl as it is browned. Repeat with remaining veal.

2. In same Dutch oven, heat remaining 1 tablespoon oil over medium heat. Add carrots and onion and cook, stirring frequently, until browned, about 10 minutes.

3. Add broth, stirring until browned bits are loosened from bottom of Dutch oven. Return veal and any juice in bowl to Dutch oven; add tomatoes with their puree, salt, pepper, and thyme. Heat to boiling over high heat, breaking tomatoes up with side of spoon. Cover, place in oven, and bake until meat and vegetables are fork-tender, about 1 hour 15 minutes.

4. In small bowl, combine garlic, parsley, and orange peel; stir into stew before serving. Makes 6 main-dish servings.

Each serving: About 305 calories, 31 g protein, 11 g carbohydrate, 15 g total fat (5 g saturated), 126 mg cholesterol, 640 mg sodium.

Osso Buco

Prep: 25 minutes
Cook: 2 hours

¼ cup olive oil
4 veal shank cross cuts, each 2 inches thick (1 pound each), trimmed
1 large onion, coarsely chopped
2 medium stalks celery, chopped
2 medium carrots, peeled and chopped

1 garlic clove, finely chopped
1 can (14 to 16 ounces) tomatoes
¼ cup dry white wine
1½ teaspoons salt
½ teaspoon dried basil
2 tablespoons finely chopped fresh parsley
2 teaspoons freshly grated lemon peel

1. In 8-quart Dutch oven, heat oil over medium-high heat until very hot. Add half of veal shanks and cook until browned, using tongs to transfer veal to a plate as it is browned. Repeat with remaining veal. In drippings in Dutch oven, over medium heat, cook onion, celery, carrots, and garlic, stirring frequently, until lightly browned and tender.

2. Return veal to Dutch oven; add tomatoes with their juice, wine, salt, and basil, breaking tomatoes up with side of spoon. Heat to boiling over high heat. Reduce heat to low; cover and simmer, stirring occasionally, until veal is fork-tender, 1 hour 30 minutes to 2 hours.

3. When veal is done, skim and discard fat from pan juices. Sprinkle veal with parsley and lemon peel. Serve veal shanks in shallow bowls with pan juices. Makes 4 main-dish servings.

Each serving: About 440 calories, 62 g protein, 13 g carbohydrate, 14 g total fat (3 g saturated), 247 mg cholesterol, 1,230 mg sodium.

Veal Nuggets with Sour Cream and Dill Sauce

Prep: 20 minutes
Cook: 25 minutes

3 to 5 tablespoons margarine
   or butter
1 small onion, finely chopped
1½ pounds ground veal
1 cup half-and-half
1 large egg
1 cup fresh bread crumbs
   (about 2 slices white bread)

1 teaspoon salt
2 tablespoons all-purpose flour
¾ teaspoon dillweed
¾ cup water
½ cup sour cream

1. In 12-inch skillet melt 1 tablespoon margarine over medium heat. Add onion and cook, stirring occasionally, until tender.

2. In large bowl, combine onion, ground veal, ⅓ cup half-and-half, egg, bread crumbs, and ¾ teaspoon salt until well blended but not overmixed. Shape veal mixture into 1-inch meatballs. Flatten each to ½-inch thickness.

3. In same skillet, melt 2 tablespoons margarine over medium-high heat. Add half of flattened meatballs and cook until browned, using slotted spoon to transfer meatballs to bowl as they are browned. Repeat with remaining meatballs, adding more margarine to skillet, if necessary.

4. Into drippings in skillet, over medium heat, stir flour, dillweed, and remaining ¼ teaspoon salt until blended. Cook, stirring, 1 minute. Gradually stir in water and remaining ⅔ cup half-and-half, stirring to loosen browned bits from bottom of skillet. Cook, stirring constantly, until mixture thickens and boils.

5. Return meatballs and any juice in bowl to skillet; heat to a simmer. Reduce heat to low; cover and simmer, stirring occasionally, 10 minutes. Stir in sour cream and gently heat through. Do not boil or mixture will curdle. Serve meatballs with the sauce. Makes 6 main-dish servings.

Each serving: About 375 calories, 26 g protein, 9 g carbohydrate, 26 g total fat (10 g saturated), 150 mg cholesterol, 675 mg sodium.

Veal and Sage Meat Loaf

Prep: 30 minutes
Bake: 1 hour 15 minutes

1 tablespoon olive oil
2 slices pancetta or bacon, chopped
2 medium carrots, peeled and chopped
2 medium stalks celery, chopped
1 large onion, chopped
1 large garlic clove, crushed with garlic press
1 pound ground veal
1 pound ground beef chuck
1 cup bottled marinara or spaghetti sauce
2 large eggs
1½ cups fresh bread crumbs (about 3 slices white bread)
4 teaspoons chopped fresh sage leaves
1½ teaspoons salt

1. In nonstick 12-inch skillet, heat oil over medium heat. Add pancetta or bacon, carrots, celery, and onion and cook, stirring frequently, until vegetables are tender and golden, 10 to 15 minutes. Add garlic; cook, stirring, 1 minute. Set vegetable mixture aside to cool slightly.

2. Preheat oven to 375°F. In large bowl, combine ground veal, ground beef, marinara sauce, eggs, bread crumbs, sage, salt, and cooked vegetable mixture just until well blended but not overmixed.

3. In 13" by 9" baking pan, shape meat mixture into 9" by 5" loaf. Bake meat loaf 1 hour 15 minutes. When meat loaf is done, let stand 10 minutes for easier slicing. To serve, cut into slices. Makes 8 main-dish servings.

Each serving: About 310 calories, 24 g protein, 12 g carbohydrate, 18 g total fat (6 g saturated), 135 mg cholesterol, 775 mg sodium.

ᴄ◟Pork

HOW TO BUY PORK

Look for fresh pork that's pinkish-white to grayish-pink. The flesh should be firm to the touch and moist but not wet. Fat marbling should be minimal; any fat should be white, firm, and well-trimmed.

Cured and smoked pork products are darker in color due to the curing process. They should be rosy pink.

Check the label for the cut you need, remembering that meat from the loin, especially the tenderloin, or leg is the leanest.

HOW TO TEST FOR DONENESS

The rule used to be to cook pork until it was well done—and often overdone—to eliminate the risk of trichinosis, a disease caused by parasitic worms that are killed at 138°F. But modern production methods have virtually eradicated trichinosis. According to the USDA, today's fresh pork will be juicy and succulent—and perfectly safe to eat—if it's cooked to an internal temperature of 160°F (170°F for very large cuts, such as fresh ham).

Medium or well-done? Pork cooked to medium (160°F) has a pink-tinged center and is slightly deeper pink near any bone. Avoid overcooking pork or the meat will be dry and tough. Ground pork should be cooked until no pink remains.

The right test to check pork chops and other small cuts for doneness? Make a tiny slit near the center with a sharp knife; the meat is done if the juices run clear. To test roasts, use a meat thermometer inserted in the thickest part but without touching any bone (which would throw off the reading). Remove roast from the oven when the temperature reaches 5 degrees below the desired doneness, then let it stand 10 to 15 minutes. The meat will continue to cook as it stands.

POPULAR PORK PRODUCTS

Fresh: Fresh pork has not been salted, brined, smoked, or cured in any way. Fresh ham is uncured leg of pork.

Cured: Pork is cured by salting with a dry rub or brine; once cured, it can be smoked for added flavor. Curing and smoking were originally developed as methods of preserving pork, enabling it to be stored at room temperature; today they're mainly intended for flavor.

Smoked: Smoking takes place after curing and is generally done as a separate process to impart flavor to the pork. Wrap and seal smoked products before storing.

Ham: Cut from the hind leg of pork, ham is usually cured and then smoked. Some hams are aged several months for even more flavor. Country hams are heavily salted and require soaking before they are cooked. Italian prosciutto is cured, dried ham that is not smoked.

Bacon: Pork belly is used to make bacon, which is cured and sometimes smoked. Smoked bacon has a deeper pink meat and yellower fat than unsmoked bacon. Italian pancetta is a type of unsmoked bacon that is often sold rolled in a jelly-roll shape, then sliced.

Salt pork: Like bacon, salt pork is cut from pork belly. It is salt-cured but not smoked, and is fattier than regular bacon.

Canadian bacon: Closer in flavor and texture to ham rather than to bacon. Canadian bacon is cut from the loin rather than the belly, and is therefore much leaner than regular bacon.

CHOOSING THE RIGHT CUT

Pork doesn't vary as much in tenderness as beef, so many cuts are equally suitable for dry-heat and moist-heat cooking methods. If broiling, grilling, or roasting pork, take care not to overcook it, or it will be tough and dry.

BROILING, GRILLING, OR PANFRYING: A wide range of lean pork cuts lend themselves to these quick cooking methods. Best bets: Tenderloin, rib chops, loin chops, sirloin chops, sirloin cutlets, and blade chops are ideal. Spareribs, back ribs, and country-style ribs are good for broiling and grilling (after precooking).

BRAISING AND STEWING: Many cuts of pork stand up well to long, slow cooking in liquid. Well-marbled cuts are especially succulent when braised or stewed. Avoid using very lean cuts, such as tenderloin; they'll toughen from long cooking. Best bets: Rib chops, loin chops, sirloin, loin blade chops (below right), sirloin cutlets, pork or ham hocks, spareribs, back ribs, country-style ribs. Pork cubes for stew are cut from the shoulder or leg.

ROASTING: Use tender cuts for roasting. Cuts from the loin (the back of the pig from shoulder to hip) are especially suitable. Good cuts also come from the leg and shoulder. Best bets: Rib crown roast, shoulder arm roast, arm picnic roast, leg (bone-in, i.e., fresh ham, and boneless), whole tenderloin, bone-in loin, boneless loin, spareribs, country-style ribs.

Pork Roasting Times
(oven temperature 350°F)

Start with meat at refrigerator temperature. Remove roast from oven when it reaches 5° to 10° below desired doneness; temperature will continue to rise as roast stands.

Cut	Weight	Meat thermometer reading	Approximate cooking time (minutes per lb)
Fresh pork			
Crown roast	6-10 lbs	160°F	20
Center loin roast (with bone)	3-5 lbs	160°F	20
Boneless top loin roast	2-4 lbs	160°F	20
Whole leg (fresh ham)	12 lbs	160°-170°F	25-30
Leg half, shank or butt portion	3-4 lbs	160°-170°F	40
Boston butt	3-6 lbs	160°-170°F	45
Tenderloin (roast at 425°-450°F)	½-1½ lbs	160°F	25-35 total
Smoked, Whole ham cook before eating	14-16 lbs	160°F	15-18
Smoked, Whole ham fully cooked pork (heat at 325°F)	14-16 lbs	130°-140°F	1-1¾ hrs total
Half ham	6-8 lbs	130°-140°F	1 hour total

POPULAR FRESH PORK CUTS

Pork shoulder arm roast (roast). Also called pork arm roast.

Pork shoulder arm picnic (roast). Also called picnic or whole fresh picnic.

Pork leg roast, boneless (roast). Also called rolled fresh ham.

Pork loin center rib roast (roast). Contains loin eye muscle and rib bone; also called center cut pork roast.

Pork loin tenderloin (roast, broil, panfry). Very tender and lean; cut into slices for panfrying or stir-frying.

Pork spareribs (roast, bake, broil, cook in liquid). Contains long rib bones with thin covering of meat on outside and between ribs.

Pork loin country-style ribs (roast, bake, braise, cook in liquid). Also called country-style spareribs.

Pork loin rib chops (braise, broil, panfry). Also called center cut chops.

Pork loin chops (braise, broil, panfry). Also called pork chops or loin end chops.

Pork loin sirloin chops (braise, broil, panfry). Also called sirloin pork chops or sirloin pork steaks.

Pork loin sirloin cutlets (braise, broil, panfry). Boneless tender slices cut from sirloin end of loin.

Pork loin blade chops (braise, broil, panfry). Also called pork loin blade steaks.

Fresh Ham with Spiced Apple Glaze

Prep: 15 minutes
Bake: About 4 hours 30 minutes

1 whole pork leg (fresh ham, 15 pounds), trimmed
2 teaspoons salt
1 teaspoon coarsely ground black pepper
2 teaspoons dried thyme
2 teaspoons ground cinnamon
½ teaspoon ground nutmeg
½ teaspoon ground cloves
1 jar (10 ounces) apple jelly
¼ cup balsamic vinegar
Assorted mustards, relishes, and chutneys
Rye and pumpernickel breads

1. Preheat oven to 350°F. Remove skin and trim excess fat from pork leg, leaving only a thin fat covering. Place pork leg, fat side up, on rack in large roasting pan (17" by 11½").

2. In small bowl, combine salt, pepper, thyme, cinnamon, nutmeg, and cloves. Use to rub on pork. Roast pork 3 hours. Cover pork loosely with a tent of foil. Continue roasting until meat thermometer (without touching bone) reaches 150°F, about 1 hour longer.

3. Meanwhile, in 1-quart saucepan, heat apple jelly and vinegar to boiling over high heat; boil 2 minutes. Remove saucepan from heat; set glaze aside.

4. When pork has reached 150°F, remove foil and brush with some glaze. Continue roasting pork, brushing occasionally with remaining glaze, about 30 minutes longer, until meat thermometer inserted in thickest part reaches 155°F. Internal temperature of meat will rise to 160°F upon standing. (Pork near bone may still be slightly pink.)

5. When pork is done, transfer to warm large platter; let stand 20 minutes to set juices for easier slicing. Carve pork and serve with assorted mustards, relishes, and chutneys, and rye and pumpernickel breads. Makes 24 main-dish servings.

Each serving without condiments and breads: About 315 calories, 42 g protein, 9 g carbohydrate, 11 g total fat (4 g saturated), 98 mg cholesterol, 290 mg sodium.

Fresh Ham Half with Parsley-Crumb Crust

Prep: 15 minutes
Roast: About 3 hours 45 minutes

1 butt- or shank-half pork leg (fresh ham, 7 pounds), trimmed
1¼ teaspoons salt
2 tablespoons prepared mustard
½ teaspoon Worcestershire sauce
⅛ teaspoon ground ginger

3 tablespoons margarine or butter
2 slices white bread, torn into small pieces
2 tablespoons chopped fresh parsley
3 tablespoons all-purpose flour
½ cup milk

1. Preheat oven to 325°F. Remove skin and excess fat from pork leg, leaving only a thin fat covering. Place pork leg, fat side up, on rack in large roasting pan (17" by 11½"). Sprinkle 1 teaspoon salt on pork. Roast about 3 hours 30 minutes or until meat thermometer inserted in thickest part of roast (without touching bone) reaches 155°F. Internal temperature of meat will rise to 160°F upon standing. (Pork near bone may be slightly pink). Remove pork leg from oven.

2. In small bowl, combine mustard, Worcestershire, and ginger. In 1-quart saucepan, melt butter over medium heat; remove saucepan from heat. Add bread and parsley to margarine; stir to combine.

3. Skim 1 tablespoon fat from pan juices in roasting pan; add to mustard mixture. With pastry brush, brush mustard mixture on pork leg. With hands, carefully pat bread-crumb mixture on pork. Bake pork until bread is browned, about 15 minutes longer. Transfer pork to large warm platter. Let stand 20 minutes to set juices for easier carving.

4. Meanwhile, prepare gravy: Remove rack from roasting pan; pour pan juices into 2-cup measuring cup (set pan aside) and let stand a few seconds until fat separates from meat juices. Skim 3 tablespoons fat from pan juices; spoon into 2-quart saucepan. Skim and discard any remaining fat from pan juices. Pour *¼ cup water* into roasting pan; stir until browned bits are loosened from bottom of pan. Add to pan juices in cup. Pour in enough additional *water* to equal 1½ cups.

5. Into drippings in saucepan, over medium heat, stir flour and remaining ¼ teaspoon salt; cook, stirring, 1 minute. Gradually stir in pan-juice mixture and milk; cook, stirring, until gravy has thickened slightly and boils. Boil 1 minute. Pour into gravy boat. Carve ham into thin slices, arrange on platter and serve with gravy. Makes 14 main-dish servings.

Each serving: About 325 calories, 29 g protein, 4 g carbohydrate, 20 g total fat (7 g saturated), 98 mg cholesterol, 355 mg sodium.

Roast Pork Loin with Apricot-Cranberry Pan Sauce

Prep: 30 minutes
Roast: 1 hour 30 minutes to 2 hours

Pork Roast
2 large lemons
2 garlic cloves, crushed with garlic press
1 tablespoon olive oil
1 teaspoon salt
2 teaspoons coarsely ground black pepper
1 bone-in pork loin roast (5½ to 6 pounds), trimmed and chine bone cracked

Pan Sauce
2 tablespoons margarine or butter
1 small onion, finely chopped
1 can (14½ ounces) chicken broth
1 cup dry Madeira wine
½ cup dried cranberries
½ cup dried apricots, chopped
½ cup loosely packed fresh parsley leaves, chopped

1. Prepare Pork Roast: Preheat oven to 350°F. From lemons, grate 2½ teaspoons peel and squeeze 1 tablespoon juice. In cup, combine lemon peel and juice, garlic, oil, salt, and pepper.

2. Pat pork loin dry with paper towels. Place pork in medium roasting pan (14" by 10"); rub lemon mixture on pork. Roast pork 1 hour and 30 minutes to 2 hours or until meat thermometer inserted in thickest part of roast (without touching bone) reaches 155°F. Internal temperature of meat will rise to 160°F upon standing.

3. When pork is done, transfer to warm large platter. Let stand 15 minutes to set juices for easier carving.

4. While pork is roasting, prepare pan sauce: In nonstick 2-quart saucepan, melt margarine over medium heat. Add onion and cook, stirring occasionally, until tender and golden, about 10 minutes. Add broth, Madeira, cranberries, and apricots; heat to boiling over high heat. Boil, stirring occasionally, until sauce is reduced to 2⅔ cups, about 8 minutes. Remove saucepan from heat.

5. Skim and discard fat from pan juices. Add pan sauce to roasting pan and cook over medium heat, stirring to loosen browned bits from bottom of pan, about 1 minute. Stir in parsley.

6. To serve, pour any juice on platter into sauce. Carve roast and arrange on platter; serve with sauce. Makes 10 main-dish servings.

Each serving of roast: About 300 calories, 34 g protein, 1 g carbohydrate, 17 g total fat (6 g saturated), 0 g fiber, 77 mg cholesterol, 300 mg sodium.

Each ¼ cup pan sauce: About 70 calories, 2 g protein, 10 g carbohydrate, 3 g total fat (1 g saturated), 1 g fiber, 0 mg cholesterol, 190 mg sodium.

Spiced Pork Medallions

Prep: 8 minutes
Cook: 12 minutes

2 pork tenderloins (12 ounces each), trimmed
1 teaspoon salt
¼ teaspoon ground black pepper
½ teaspoon dried thyme
½ teaspoon ground cinnamon
⅛ teaspoon ground nutmeg
⅛ teaspoon ground cloves
1 tablespoon vegetable oil
¼ cup red currant jelly
⅔ cup chicken broth

1. Cut each pork tenderloin crosswise into 4 pieces. With meat mallet, or between two sheets of plastic wrap or waxed paper with rolling pin, pound each piece of pork to ½ inch thickness. Pat meat dry with paper towels.

2. In medium bowl, combine salt, pepper, thyme, cinnamon, nutmeg, and cloves. Add pork medallions to spice mixture; toss to coat.

3. In 12-inch skillet, heat oil over medium-high heat until very hot. Add pork medallions; cook 5 minutes per side or until they just lose their pink color throughout.

4. Transfer pork to warm large platter. Into drippings in skillet, add jelly and stir until melted; stir in chicken broth and heat to boiling. Spoon sauce over pork and serve. Makes 4 main-dish servings.

Each serving: About 280 calories, 34 g protein, 14 g carbohydrate, 9 g total fat (2 g saturated), 92 mg cholesterol, 730 mg sodium.

Glazed Pork with Pear Chutney

Prep: 10 minutes
Broil: About 20 minutes

Pork Tenderloins
2 pork tenderloins (about 12 ounces each), trimmed
¼ cup packed brown sugar
1 tablespoon cider vinegar
1 teaspoon Dijon mustard
¼ teaspoon salt
¼ teaspoon coarsely ground black pepper

Pear Chutney
1 can (28 ounces) pear halves in heavy syrup
⅓ cup pickled sweet red peppers, drained and chopped
¼ cup dark seedless raisins
2 teaspoons cider vinegar
1 teaspoon brown sugar
¼ teaspoon ground ginger
¼ teaspoon salt
⅛ teaspoon coarsely ground black pepper
1 green onion, chopped

1. Prepare Pork Tenderloins: Pat pork dry with paper towels. Preheat broiler. In small bowl, stir together brown sugar, vinegar, and mustard. Sprinkle salt and pepper on tenderloins; place on rack in broiling pan. Broil 5 to 7 inches from heat source 8 minutes. Brush with brown-sugar mixture and broil 2 minutes longer. Turn tenderloins and broil 8 minutes. Brush with remaining brown-sugar glaze and broil 2 minutes longer or until tenderloins are still slightly pink in center and meat thermometer inserted in center reaches 155°F. Internal temperature of meat will rise to 160°F upon standing. When pork is done, transfer to warm large platter and let stand 5 minutes to set juices for easier slicing.

2. Meanwhile, prepare Pear Chutney: Drain pears through sieve, reserving ½ cup syrup. Cut pears into ½-inch pieces. In nonstick 2-quart saucepan, combine red peppers, raisins, vinegar, brown sugar, ginger, salt, pepper, and reserved pear syrup; heat to boiling over high heat. Reduce heat to medium and cook 5 minutes. Reduce heat to low; stir in pears and green onion; cover and cook 5 minutes longer.

3. To serve, thinly slice tenderloins on an angle. Arrange on platter and spoon warm chutney over pork slices. Makes 6 main-dish servings.

Each serving: About 350 calories, 28 g protein, 39 g carbohydrate, 10 g total fat (3 g saturated), 70 mg cholesterol, 410 mg sodium.

Spice-Rubbed Pork Tenderloin

Prep: 5 minutes
Broil: 20 minutes

¾ teaspoon salt
2 teaspoons vegetable oil
1 tablespoon curry powder
1 teaspoon ground cumin
¼ teaspoon ground cinnamon
1 pork tenderloin (1 pound), trimmed

1. Preheat broiler. In small bowl, stir together oil, curry powder, cumin, salt and cinnamon; use to rub on pork tenderloin.

2. Place tenderloin on rack in broiling pan. Broiling 5 to 7 inches from heat source, broil tenderloin 15 minutes. Turn tenderloin and broil 5 minutes longer or until slightly pink in center. Let stand 5 minutes before slicing. Makes 4 main-dish servings.

Each serving: About 225 calories, 27 g protein, 1 g carbohydrate, 12 g total fat (4 g saturated), 70 mg cholesterol, 465 mg sodium.

Ginger Pork Stir-Fry

Prep: 15 minutes
Cook: 12 to 15 minutes

1 pork tenderloin (12 ounces), trimmed and cut into thin slices
2 tablespoons grated, peeled fresh ginger
1 cup chicken broth
2 tablespoons teriyaki sauce
2 teaspoons cornstarch
2 teaspoons vegetable oil
8 ounces snow peas, strings removed along both sides of each
1 medium zucchini (8 ounces), cut in half lengthwise and
    thinly sliced
3 green onions, each cut into 3-inch pieces

1. In medium bowl, toss pork and ginger. In cup, stir together broth, teriyaki sauce, and cornstarch.

2. In nonstick 12-inch skillet, heat 1 teaspoon oil over medium-high heat until very hot. Add snow peas, zucchini, and green onions and cook, stirring frequently, until lightly browned and tender-crisp, about 5 minutes. Transfer to bowl.

3. In same skillet, heat remaining 1 teaspoon oil; add pork mixture and cook, stirring quickly and constantly, until pork just loses its pink color throughout. Transfer pork to bowl with vegetables. Stir cornstarch mixture; add to skillet and heat to boiling, stirring constantly. Boil 1 minute until sauce thickens. Stir in pork and vegetables and any juice in bowl; heat through. Makes 4 main-dish servings.

Each serving: About 170 calories, 21 g protein, 10 g carbohydrate, 5 g total fat (1 g saturated), 51 mg cholesterol, 550 mg sodium.

Honey-Soy Glazed Pork Chops

Prep: 10 minutes
Cook: 15 minutes

4 boneless pork loin chops, each ¾ inch thick (4 ounces each),
    trimmed
¼ teaspoon coarsely ground black pepper
3 tablespoons honey
2 tablespoons soy sauce
1 tablespoon balsamic vinegar
½ teaspoon cornstarch
1 garlic clove, finely chopped
2 green onions, sliced

1. Pat pork chops dry with paper towels. Sprinkle 1 side
of each chop with pepper.

2. Heat nonstick 12-inch skillet over medium-high heat
until hot. Add pork chops, pepper side down, and cook until
browned, about 4 minutes. Reduce heat to medium. Turn
and cook until chops just lose their pink color throughout,
about 6 to 8 minutes longer. Transfer pork chops to warm
medium platter; cover loosely with foil to keep warm.

3. Meanwhile, in cup, stir together honey, soy sauce,
vinegar, and cornstarch until smooth.

4. To same skillet, add garlic; cook, stirring, 30 seconds.
Stir honey mixture into skillet (mixture will boil), and cook,
stirring, 1 minute. To serve, spoon sauce over pork chops
and sprinkle with green onions. Makes 4 main-dish servings.

*Each serving: About 230 calories, 25 g protein, 15 g carbohy-
drate, 7 g total fat (3 g saturated), 61 mg cholesterol, 585 mg
sodium.*

Herb-Coated Pork Chops with Apple and Onion Sauté

Prep: 25 minutes
Broil: About 10 minutes

Breaded Pork Chops
⅓ cup plain dried bread crumbs
¼ teaspoon salt
¼ teaspoon ground black pepper
¼ teaspoon dried thyme
1 large egg
4 bone-in pork loin chops, each ¾ inch thick (6 ounces each), well
    trimmed
Olive oil nonstick cooking spray

Apple and Onion Sauté
2 teaspoons olive oil
2 medium onions, sliced
2 Granny Smith apples, each cored and cut into ¼-inch-thick
    wedges
2 teaspoons light brown sugar
¼ teaspoon salt
¼ teaspoon ground black pepper
¼ teaspoon dried thyme
¼ cup water
2 teaspoons cider vinegar

1. Prepare Breaded Pork Chops: Preheat broiler. On waxed paper, combine bread crumbs, salt, pepper, and thyme. In pie plate, with fork, lightly beat egg. Dip each pork chop into beaten egg, then coat with crumb mixture, firmly pressing so mixture adheres. Spray both sides of chops generously with nonstick cooking spray.

2. Place pork chops on rack in broiling pan. Broil 7 to 9 inches from heat source 4 to 5 minutes per side, until chops are golden on the outside and juices run clear when chops are pierced with tip of knife. Transfer chops to warm medium platter.

3. Meanwhile, prepare Apple and Onion Sauté: In nonstick 10-inch skillet, heat oil over medium-high heat. Add onions and cook, stirring frequently, until lightly browned, 5 minutes. Add apples, brown sugar, salt, pepper, and thyme; cook, stirring occasionally, until onions and apples are tender, 8 to 10 minutes longer. Stir in water and vinegar; heat through. To serve, spoon sauce over pork chops. Makes 4 main-dish servings.

Each serving: About 325 calories, 21 g protein, 29 g carbohydrate, 14 g total fat (4 g saturated), 110 mg cholesterol, 415 mg sodium.

Southwestern Pork Chops with Warm Corn Chutney

Prep: 5 minutes
Cook: 15 minutes

4 bone-in pork loin chops, each ½ inch thick (6 ounces each), trimmed
¼ teaspoon salt
2 teaspoons vegetable oil
¾ cup medium-hot bottled salsa
1 can (15¼ to 16 ounces) corn, drained
¼ cup packed cilantro leaves, chopped
3 tablespoons water

1. Pat pork chops dry with paper towels. Sprinkle salt on chops.
2. In nonstick 12-inch skillet, heat oil over medium-high heat until very hot. Add pork chops and cook about 4 minutes per side or until cooked through; juices will run clear when chop is pierced with tip of knife.
3. Transfer pork chops to 4 plates. In same skillet, over medium heat, heat salsa, corn, cilantro, and water to boiling. To serve, spoon warm corn chutney over pork chops. Makes 4 main-dish servings.

Each serving: About 480 calories, 30 g protein, 17 g carbohydrate, 33 g total fat (11 g saturated), 88 mg cholesterol, 680 mg sodium.

Spicy Peanut Pork

Prep: 15 minutes
Cook: About 15 minutes

4 boneless pork loin chops,
    each ¾ inch thick (5 ounces
    each), well trimmed
½ teaspoon salt
¼ teaspoon coarsely ground
    black pepper
8 ounces snow peas, strings
    removed
4 green onions, cut into
    1-inch diagonal slices

1 tablespoon finely chopped,
    peeled fresh ginger
3 garlic cloves, crushed with
    garlic press
¼ cup creamy peanut butter
¾ cup water
1 tablespoon soy sauce
1 tablespoon sugar
⅛ teaspoon ground red pepper
    (cayenne)

1. Pat pork chops dry with paper towels. Sprinkle ¼ teaspoon salt and pepper on chops.

2. Heat nonstick 12-inch skillet over medium-high heat until hot. Add pork chops and cook 3 to 4 minutes per side or until lightly browned and still slightly pink in the center. Transfer pork chops to plate.

3. In same skillet, place snow peas, green onions, and remaining ¼ teaspoon salt. Reduce heat to medium and cook, stirring frequently, 4 minutes. Stir in ginger and garlic; cook, stirring, 1 minute. Return pork and any juices on plate to skillet.

4. Meanwhile, in small bowl, stir together peanut butter, soy sauce, sugar, and ground red pepper until blended.

5. Pour peanut-butter mixture into skillet; stir to mix well and heat to boiling over medium-high heat. Reduce heat to low; simmer 1 minute. Serve chops with vegetables and pan sauce. Makes 4 main-dish servings.

Each serving: About 350 calories, 37 g protein, 13 g carbohydrate, 17 g total fat (5 g saturated), 76 mg cholesterol, 685 mg sodium.

Spicy Shredded Pork in Lettuce Cups

Prep: 25 minutes
Cook: 10 minutes

8 pork cutlets, each ⅛ inch
   thick (1¼ pounds)
2 tablespoons soy sauce
1 tablespoon cornstarch
¼ teaspoon ground ginger
¼ teaspoon ground red pepper
   (cayenne)
3 tablespoons vegetable oil

4 ounces snow peas, strings
   removed
1 medium onion, thinly sliced
1 carrot, peeled and cut into
   2" by ¼" matchstick strips
4 large Boston or iceberg
   lettuce leaves

1. Cut pork cutlets into 2" by ¼" matchstick strips. In bowl, combine pork, soy sauce, cornstarch, ginger, and ground red pepper; toss until well blended.

2. In 12-inch skillet, over medium-high heat, heat oil until very hot. Add snow peas, onion, and carrot, and cook, stirring frequently, until tender-crisp. With slotted spoon, transfer vegetables to bowl. Add pork mixture to skillet; increase heat to high, and stir-fry until pork is browned and has lost its pink color throughout.

3. Add vegetables and any juices in bowl and gently reheat. To serve, place a lettuce leaf on 4 plates; spoon some pork mixture into each leaf. Makes 4 main-dish servings.

Each serving: About 280 calories, 26 g protein, 9 g carbohydrate, 15 g total fat (3 g saturated), 71 mg cholesterol, 530 mg sodium.

Orange-Ginger Pork Medallions

Prep: 10 minutes
Cook: 10 minutes

2 large oranges
1 pork tenderloin (1 pound), trimmed and cut into ¾-inch-thick
    slices
¼ teaspoon salt
3 teaspoons vegetable oil
3 green onions, sliced
1 tablespoon grated, peeled fresh ginger

1. From 1 orange, grate the peel and squeeze ½ cup juice. Cut remaining orange into ½-inch-thick slices; cut each slice in half.

2. With meat mallet, between two sheets of plastic wrap or waxed paper with rolling pin, pound each piece to a ½-inch-thickness. Pat pork dry with paper towels. Sprinkle salt on pork.

3. In nonstick 12-inch skillet, heat 2 teaspoons oil over medium-high heat until very hot. Add pork and cook about 2 minutes per side or until pork just loses its pink color throughout. With tongs, transfer pork to plate.

4. In same skillet, heat remaining 1 teaspoon oil. Add green onions, ginger, and orange peel and stir-fry until green onions are lightly browned and tender, 2 to 3 minutes. Add orange slices and juice to skillet; cook 1 minute. Return pork medallions and any juice on plate to skillet; heat through. Makes 4 main-dish servings.

Each serving: About 220 calories, 26 g protein, 9 g carbohydrate, 8 g total fat (2 g saturated), 60 mg cholesterol, 215 mg sodium.

Sweet and Savory Pork

Prep: 15 minutes
Cook: 8 to 10 minutes

2 tablespoons brown sugar
¾ teaspoon salt
¼ teaspoon ground black
    pepper
3 garlic cloves, crushed with
    garlic press
1 pork tenderloin (1 pound),
    trimmed and cut into 1-inch-
    thick slices
2 teaspoons olive oil
½ cup dry white wine

2 tablespoons red wine vinegar
1 teaspoon cornstarch
¼ teaspoon dried oregano
½ cup pitted prunes, coarsely
    chopped
¼ cup pitted green olives,
    coarsely chopped
2 tablespoons capers, drained

1. On waxed paper, combine brown sugar, salt, pepper, and garlic; use to coat pork slices.

2. In nonstick 12-inch skillet, heat oil over medium-high heat until very hot. Add pork slices and cook 2½ to 3½ minutes per side, until lightly browned, and pork just loses its pink color in the center. With tongs, transfer pork to plate.

3. In 1-cup measuring cup, stir together wine, vinegar, cornstarch, and oregano until well blended. Add cornstarch mixture to skillet; cook, stirring constantly, until slightly thickened, about 1 minute. Return pork slices to skillet; add prunes, olives, and capers; heat through. Makes 4 main-dish servings.

Each serving: About 245 calories, 25 g protein, 22 g carbohydrate, 6 g total fat (1 g saturated), 64 mg cholesterol, 840 mg sodium.

Oven-Barbecued Spareribs

Prep: 7 minutes
Roast: 1 hour 30 minutes

6 pounds pork spareribs, cut
  into 2-rib portions
1 can (6 ounces) tomato paste
½ cup water
¼ cup cider vinegar
¼ cup honey

¼ cup packed brown sugar
2 tablespoons vegetable oil
1 tablespoon grated onion
2 teaspoons salt
2 teaspoons chili powder

1. Preheat oven to 325°F. Arrange spareribs in single layer in large roasting pan (17" by 11½"). Roast until fork-tender, about 1 hour.

2. Meanwhile, prepare glaze: In medium bowl, stir tomato paste, water, vinegar, honey, brown sugar, oil, onion, salt, and chili powder until well blended.

3. Roast 30 minutes longer, brushing ribs frequently with some glaze. To serve, arrange ribs on warm large platter. Makes 6 main-dish servings.

Each serving: About 745 calories, 45 g protein, 27 g carbohydrate, 51 g total fat (17 g saturated), 182 mg cholesterol, 955 mg sodium.

PORK FOR STEW

Latin American Pork Stew

Prep: 30 minutes
Bake: About 1 hour 30 minutes

2 pounds boneless pork loin,
    cut into 1-inch pieces
2 teaspoons olive oil
1 large onion, chopped
4 garlic cloves, finely chopped
2 cups water
1 can (14½ ounces) diced
    tomatoes
1 cup loosely packed fresh
    cilantro leaves and stems,
    chopped

¾ teaspoon salt
1 teaspoon ground cumin
½ teaspoon ground coriander
¼ teaspoon ground red pepper
    (cayenne)
3 medium sweet potatoes (1½
    pounds), peeled and cut into
    ½-inch chunks
2 cans (15 to 19 ounces each)
    black beans, rinsed and
    drained

1. Preheat oven to 350°F. Pat pork dry with paper towels. In nonstick 5-quart Dutch oven, heat oil over medium-high heat until very hot. Add pork, in batches, and cook until lightly browned, about 5 minutes, using slotted spoon to transfer pork to bowl as it is browned.

2. Reduce heat to medium. In drippings in Dutch oven, cook onion, stirring frequently, until tender, about 10 minutes. Add garlic and cook, stirring, 1 minute longer.

3. Add water, tomatoes with their juice, cilantro, cumin, salt, coriander, and ground red pepper; heat to boiling over high heat, breaking tomatoes up with side of spoon. Stir in pork and any juices in bowl; cover, place in oven, and bake 30 minutes.

4. Stir in sweet potatoes; cover and bake until meat and potatoes are very tender, about 40 minutes longer. Stir in black beans; cover and bake until heated through, about 15 minutes longer. To serve, spoon into shallow soup plates. Makes about 10 cups or 8 main-dish servings.

Each serving: About 340 calories, 36 g protein, 36 g carbohydrate, 9 g total fat (3 g saturated), 58 mg cholesterol, 735 mg sodium.

Hungarian Pork Goulash

Prep: 40 minutes
Bake: 1 hour 30 minutes

2 tablespoons vegetable oil
2 large onions, chopped
1 garlic clove, finely chopped
¼ cup paprika (yes, this much)
2 pounds boneless pork shoulder blade roast (fresh pork butt), trimmed and cut into 1½-inch pieces
1 package (16 ounces) sauerkraut, rinsed and drained

1 can (14½ ounces) diced tomatoes
1 can (14½ ounces) beef broth
½ teaspoon salt
¼ teaspoon ground black pepper
1 container (8 ounces) light sour cream
Hot cooked egg noodles (optional)

1. In 5-quart Dutch oven, heat oil over medium heat. Add onions; cook, stirring frequently, 10 minutes. Stir in garlic; cook, stirring frequently, until onions are very tender, about 5 minutes longer.

2. Preheat oven to 325°F. Stir in paprika; cook, stirring, 1 minute. Add pork, sauerkraut, tomatoes with their juice, broth, salt, and pepper; heat to boiling over high heat. Cover, place in oven, and bake until pork is fork-tender, about 1 hour 30 minutes.

3. Remove goulash from oven; stir in sour cream. Heat through on top of range over medium heat but do not boil. Serve over noodles, if you like. Makes 6 main-dish servings.

Each serving without noodles: About 525 calories, 31 g protein, 15 g carbohydrate, 39 g total fat (14 g saturated), 104 mg cholesterol, 920 mg sodium.

Adobo-Style Chili

Prep: 20 minutes
Cook: 2 hours 30 minutes

2 pounds boneless pork
    shoulder, trimmed and cut
    into 1½-inch pieces
2 teaspoons vegetable oil
1 large onion, finely chopped
4 garlic cloves, crushed with
    garlic press
3 tablespoons chili powder
1 tablespoon ground cumin
¼ teaspoon ground cinnamon
¼ teaspoon ground red pepper
    (cayenne)
⅛ teaspoon ground cloves
1 can (28 ounces) Italian-style
    plum tomatoes
¼ cup cider vinegar
¾ teaspoon salt
½ teaspoon dried oregano
1 bay leaf
2 tablespoons chopped fresh
    cilantro leaves
Warm corn tortillas (optional)

1. Pat pork dry with paper towels. In 5-quart Dutch oven, heat 1 teaspoon oil over medium-high heat until very hot. Add half of pork and cook until browned, using slotted spoon to transfer pork to bowl as it is browned. Repeat with remaining oil and remaining pork.

2. Reduce heat to medium. To pan drippings, add onion and cook, stirring frequently, until tender, about 10 minutes. Stir in garlic, chili powder, cumin, cinnamon, ground red pepper, and cloves; cook, stirring, 1 minute. Return pork and any juices in bowl to Dutch oven. Add tomatoes with their juice, vinegar, salt, oregano, and bay leaf. Heat to boiling over high heat, breaking tomatoes up with side of spoon. Reduce heat to low; cover and simmer until pork is fork-tender, about 2 hours.

3. Discard bay leaf. Skim and discard fat from pan juices. To serve, sprinkle with cilantro and serve with warm tortillas, if you like. Makes 8 main-dish servings.

Each serving without tortillas: About 325 calories, 30 g protein, 9 g carbohydrate, 19 g total fat (6 g saturated), 72 mg cholesterol, 475 mg sodium.

Picadillo "Salad"

Prep: 12 minutes
Cook: 22 minutes

¼ cup slivered blanched
  almonds
1 pound ground pork
1 medium onion, coarsely
  chopped
1 medium green pepper,
  coarsely chopped
1 can (8 ounces) tomato sauce
¼ cup water
½ cup dark seedless raisins

¼ cup chopped pimiento-
  stuffed olives (salad olives)
¾ teaspoon salt
⅛ teaspoon ground black
  pepper
¼ teaspoon ground cumin
1 small bunch (10 ounces)
  spinach, tough stems
  trimmed, washed and dried
  very well, and sliced

1. In 12-inch skillet, toast almonds, tossing frequently, over medium heat, until lightly browned. Transfer almonds to plate.

2. In same skillet, over high heat, cook ground pork, onion, and green pepper, stirring frequently, until all juices have evaporated and meat is well browned. Stir in tomato sauce, water, raisins, olives, salt, pepper, and cumin; heat to boiling. Reduce heat to low; cover and simmer 10 minutes. To serve, spoon pork mixture, hot or cold, over the spinach and sprinkle with toasted almonds. Makes 4 main-dish servings.

Each serving: About 325 calories, 30 g protein, 26 g carbohydrate, 13 g total fat (3 g saturated), 69 mg cholesterol, 1,080 mg sodium.

Breakfast Patties

Prep: 30 minutes plus chilling
Cook: 20 minutes per batch

3 pounds ground pork
⅓ cup chopped fresh parsley
2 teaspoons salt
½ teaspoon cracked black pepper
2 teaspoons dried sage

1. In a large bowl combine pork, parsley, salt, pepper, and sage; mix well. Shape into twenty 4-inch patties and place on waxed paper-lined jelly-roll pan. Cover and refrigerate until well chilled, about 2 hours or overnight.

2. In one or two nonstick 12-inch skillets, over medium-low heat, cook patties in small batches, about 10 minutes per side or until browned and they lose their pink color throughout. With tongs, transfer cooked patties to warm large platter; cover loosely with foil to keep warm. Makes 10 main-dish servings.

Each serving: About 230 calories, 29 g protein, 0 g carbohydrate, 12 g total fat (4 g saturated), 79 mg cholesterol, 860 mg sodium.

Pork Loaf

Prep: 35 minutes
Bake: 1 hour 40 minutes

4 large eggs
2 tablespoons vegetable oil
3 medium stalks celery, chopped
1 medium onion, chopped
1½ pounds ground pork
⅓ cup water
1 cup fresh rye-bread crumbs (about 2 slices bread)
2 tablespoons chopped fresh parsley
½ teaspoon salt
4 tablespoons chili sauce

1. In 2-quart saucepan, place 3 eggs and enough *cold water to cover by at least 1 inch;* heat to boiling over high heat. Immediately remove saucepan from heat and cover tightly; let stand at least 15 minutes. Pour off hot water and run cold water over eggs to cool. Peel eggs.

2. Meanwhile, in 10-inch nonstick skillet, heat oil over medium heat. Add celery and onion and cook, stirring occasionally, until tender. Transfer to large bowl.

3. Preheat oven to 350°F. To celery mixture, add pork, water, bread crumbs, parsley, salt, 2 tablespoons chili sauce, and remaining egg; mix with hands just until well blended but not overmixed.

4. In 12" by 8" baking pan, place half of pork mixture. Shape into 8" by 4" rectangle. Arrange hard-cooked eggs in lengthwise row on top of pork mixture. Top with remaining pork mixture and shape into an 8" by 4" loaf, pressing firmly. Brush top and sides with 1 tablespoon chili sauce. Bake 1 hour 30 minutes. When meat loaf is done, transfer to warm medium platter and let stand 10 minutes to set juices for easier slicing.

5. To serve, brush loaf with remaining 1 tablespoon chili sauce (use sauce that has not touched raw pork) and cut into slices. Makes 6 main-dish servings.

Each serving: About 355 calories, 30 g protein, 11 g carbohydrate, 21 g total fat (6 g saturated), 223 mg cholesterol, 510 mg sodium.

Porcupine Meatballs

Prep: 30 minutes
Cook: 40 minutes

1 tablespoon vegetable oil
½ small red pepper, finely chopped (½ cup)
3 green onions, finely chopped
2 garlic cloves, crushed with garlic press
1 tablespoon minced, peeled fresh ginger plus four ¼-inch-thick slices
1 pound ground pork
½ cup regular long-grain rice
1 large egg
1 tablespoon soy sauce
⅛ teaspoon ground red pepper (cayenne)
1 can (14½ ounces) chicken broth
¼ teaspoon Asian sesame oil
Thin strips green onion and red pepper

1. In deep 10-inch skillet, heat oil over medium-high heat. Add chopped red pepper and cook, stirring occasionally, just until tender, about 5 minutes. Add chopped green onions, garlic, and minced ginger, and cook, stirring, 1 minute longer.

2. Transfer vegetable mixture to medium bowl; cool to room temperature. Stir in ground pork, rice, egg, soy sauce, and ground red pepper until blended.

3. Line jelly-roll pan with waxed paper. With damp hands, shape meat mixture by rounded tablespoons into about thirty-two 1½-inch meatballs (mixture will be soft); place in lined jelly-roll pan.

4. In same skillet, heat broth, sesame oil, ginger slices, and *1½ cups water* to boiling over high heat.

5. Carefully arrange meatballs in simmering broth mixture (skillet will be very full); heat to boiling. Reduce heat to low; cover and simmer 30 minutes.

6. Serve meatballs with broth in shallow bowls; top with strips of green onion and red pepper. Makes 4 main-dish servings.

Each serving: About 475 calories, 25 g protein, 22 g carbohydrate, 31 g total fat (10 g saturated), 126 mg cholesterol, 680 mg sodium.

ᔕSmokedᔕSmoked Pork

Smoked pork comes in a wide variety of cuts, from whole hams to smoked pork chops, to bacon.

HOW TO STORE SMOKED-PORK PRODUCTS

Ham and other smoked-pork cuts should be refrigerated in their original wrapping, and they will keep for at least a week. Ham slices should be used within 3 or 4 days, opened packages of sliced boiled ham will keep for 3 days, and bacon remains good for 5 to 7 days.

Check the label on canned ham before you store it. Some canned hams have been pasteurized during processing and, like milk, must be refrigerated before and after opening. Small canned hams are usually "sterilized"—brought to a high temperature during processing—and may be stored with other canned goods in a cabinet.

Freezing changes the flavor and texture of smoked-pork products. If freezing is necessary, wrap the meat tightly in freezer wrap or a zip-tight freezer bag and freeze it at 0°F. or lower. Use frozen smoked pork within 1 month.

SMOKED HAMS AND SHOULDER PICNICS

Smoked hams labeled "fully cooked" can be bone-in or boneless, partially boned, boiled, canned, or picnic varieties. While such hams cans be eaten as is, additional heating will improve their flavor and texture. For the best eating, and for thoroughly heated meat, bake ham until a meat thermometer inserted in the center registers 130° to 140°F. (Smoked hams that are not marked "fully cooked" must be cooked to an internal temperature of 160°F.)

COOKING IN LIQUID: In a large saucepot, in enough *water to cover*, simmer a picnic until meat is tender, about 3 hours 30 minutes to 4 hours. To glaze a simmered picnic, place the meat on a rack in a large roasting pan (17" by 11½") and bake it in a 400°F oven 15 to 30 minutes, brushing 2 or 3 times with the glaze.

BACON

Packaged bacon is available sliced thin, regular, or thick; check the label. Slab bacon is unsliced, with the rind left on, to be sliced at home as needed. Bacon is either lean or fat, depending on the cut from which it is taken, and its flavor depends on the curing and smoking process used. Bake, broil, or panfry bacon slices.

HOW TO COOK BACON

BAKING: Preheat oven to 400°F. Arrange bacon slices on a rack in roasting pan, overlapping the lean edge of each slice with the fat edge of the next. Bake until browned and crisp, about 20 minutes. Drain on paper towels.

BROILING: Preheat broiler. Separate slices carefully, and place them on rack in broiling pan. Broil 5 to 7 inches from heat source 10 minutes per side or until browned. Drain on paper towels.

PANFRYING: In a cold, heavy skillet, place slices without separating them. Cook the bacon 5 to 8 minutes, over medium-low heat, separating slices with tongs so that they lie flat, and turning them occasionally to evenly brown both sides. Drain on paper towels.

Canadian-Style Bacon

Canadian-style bacon is a cured and smoked boneless pork loin. Boneless and lean, it is sold in 2- to 4-pound pieces or as slices. Large pieces can be roasted (see time-table). Broil, panbroil, or panfry slices until lightly browned on both sides, turning the slices occasionally.

Brown Sugar and Ginger-Glazed Ham with Two Sauces

Prep: 45 minutes
Roast: About 3 hours 30 minutes

Ham and Glaze
1 fully cooked smoked bone-in whole ham (14 pounds)
½ cup honey
½ cup packed light or dark brown sugar
1 teaspoon ground ginger

Mustard Sauce
1 cup sour cream
¾ cup mayonnaise
1 jar (8 ounces) Dijon mustard with seeds
1 teaspoon Worcestershire sauce
½ teaspoon coarsely ground black pepper

Cranberry-Cherry Sauce
1 large orange
1 can (21 ounces) cherry-pie filling
1 bag (12 ounces) cranberries (3 cups)
¼ cup sugar
¼ teaspoon ground allspice

1. Prepare Ham: Preheat oven to 325°F. Remove skin and trim some fat from ham, leaving about ¼ inch fat.

2. Place ham on rack in large roasting pan (17" by 11½"). Roast ham 2 hours 30 minutes.

3. After ham has roasted 2 hours 30 minutes, prepare glaze: In 1-quart saucepan, stir together honey, brown sugar, and ginger; heat to boiling over medium-high heat. Boil 1 minute. When bubbling subsides, brush ham with some glaze. Roast ham 30 minutes to 1 hour longer, brushing occasionally with remaining glaze, until meat thermometer inserted in thickest part of roast (without touching bone) reaches 135°F.

4. Meanwhile, prepare Mustard Sauce: In medium bowl,

stir together sour cream, mayonnaise, mustard, Worcester-shire, and pepper. Cover and refrigerate until ready to serve. Makes about 2½ cups.

5. When ham is done, transfer to large cutting board; let stand 20 minutes to set juices for easier carving.

6. Meanwhile, prepare Cranberry-Cherry Sauce: From orange, grate ½ teaspoon peel and squeeze ½ cup juice. In nonstick 3-quart saucepan, combine orange peel and juice, cherry-pie filling, cranberries, sugar, and allspice. Heat to boiling over high heat, stirring occasionally. Reduce heat to low; simmer, stirring occasionally, until most of cran-berries pop, about 10 minutes. Makes about 3½ cups.

7. To serve, carve ham into thick slices and arrange on warm large platter. Serve ham with the two sauces. Makes 24 main-dish servings.

Each serving of ham without sauces: About 325 calories, 36 g protein, 10 g carbohydrate, 15 g total fat (5 g saturated), 95 mg cholesterol, 2,400 mg sodium.

Each tablespoon mustard sauce: About 50 calories, 1 g protein, 1 g carbohydrate, 5 g total fat (1 g saturated), 4 mg cholesterol, 170 mg sodium.

Each tablespoon cranberry-cherry sauce: About 20 calories, 0 g protein, 5 g carbohydrate, 0 g total fat, 0 mg cholesterol, 1 mg sodium.

CARVING A WHOLE, BONE-IN HAM

- When shopping for ham, look for "fully cooked" on the label. This means it's ready to serve. To improve the flavor and texture, heat ham to an internal temperature of 135°F. to 140°F. If the label says "cook before eating," the meat must be cooked to 160°F.

- To carve a whole, bone-in ham: Place ham on cutting board. Using carving fork to steady ham, cut a few slices from the thin side to form a level base. Turn ham onto cut surface. Starting at the shank end, slice down to the bone and cut out a small wedge of meat. Continue slicing, perpendicular to bone, cutting thin slices until you reach the bone at the other end. Then, cut meat along the leg bone to release slices. For more servings, turn ham to its original position and cut slices to bone.

Whole Smithfield Ham

Prep: 5 minutes plus overnight to soak
Cook/Bake: 5 hours 30 minutes plus cooling

1 cook-before-eating bone-in Smithfield or country-style ham
   (14 pounds)
½ cup dark corn syrup

1. Prepare ham as label directs, or prepare as follows:

2. Place ham, skin side down, in saucepot large enough to hold the whole ham; add enough water to cover ham completely. Let ham stand in water at room temperature at least 12 hours, or overnight.

3. About 6 hours before serving or early in day, remove ham from water. With vegetable brush, briskly scrub ham; rinse ham well. Return ham to same saucepot, cover ham with fresh *water*. Heat to boiling over high heat. Reduce heat to low; cover and simmer until the bone on small end of ham (shank bone) pokes out about one inch from skin and feels loose, about 4 hours 30 minutes. Cool until easy to handle.

4. Transfer ham to rack in large roasting pan (17" by 11½").

5. Preheat oven to 325°F. With sharp knife, remove skin and trim some fat from ham, leaving about ¼ inch fat. Brush ham with corn syrup. Bake until glazed, about 15 minutes. Serve Smithfield ham warm or refrigerate to serve cold later. To serve, place ham on cutting board and carve into very thin slices (see page 000). Arrange on large platter and serve. Makes about 35 main-dish servings.

Each serving: About 175 calories, 21 g protein, 4 g carbohydrate, 8 g total fat (3 g saturated), 54 mg cholesterol, 1,350 mg sodium.

Honeyed Ham Steak

Prep: 3 minutes
Cook: 12 minutes

2 tablespoons prepared mustard
2 tablespoons honey
1 tablespoon margarine or butter
1 fully cooked smoked-ham center slice, ½ inch thick,
   about 6 ounces

In 10-inch skillet, over medium heat, warm mustard, honey, and margarine, stirring, until blended. Add ham steak; cook 5 minutes per side or until heated through. Remove ham to warm medium platter; pour pan juices over ham. To serve, cut ham into portions. Makes 1 main-dish serving.

Each serving: About 105 calories, 7 g protein, 9 g carbohydrate, 5 g total fat (1 g saturated), 20 mg cholesterol, 640 mg sodium.

Ham and Cheese Grits Casserole

Prep: 25 minutes
Bake: 45 to 50 minutes

3½ cups nonfat (skim) milk
2¼ cups water
1 teaspoon salt
1¼ cups quick-cooking grits
4 ounces cooked ham, coarsely chopped (¾ cup)
3 ounces low-fat Monterey Jack cheese, shredded (about ¾ cup)
2 tablespoons grated Parmesan cheese
1 pickled jalapeño chile, finely chopped
2 large eggs
3 large egg whites

1. Preheat oven to 325°F. Grease shallow 2-quart casserole. In heavy 3-quart saucepan, heat 1½ cups milk, water, and salt to boiling over medium-high heat. Gradually add grits, beating constantly with wire whisk. Reduce heat to low, cover and simmer, stirring occasionally, 5 minutes. Remove from heat; stir in ham, cheeses, and jalapeño.

2. In large bowl, with wire whisk, beat whole eggs, egg whites, and remaining 2 cups milk until well blended. Gradually stir grits into egg mixture (mixture will be lumpy).

3. Pour mixture into prepared casserole. Bake until top is set and edges are lightly golden, 45 to 50 minutes. Remove from oven; and place on wire rack. Let stand 10 minutes before serving. Makes 6 main-dish servings.

Each serving: About 300 calories, 19 g protein, 34 g carbohydrate, 9 g toal fat (5 g saturated), 98 mg cholesterol, 870 mg sodium.

Ham-Spinach Ring

Prep: 20 minutes
Bake: 40 minutes

2 tablespoons margarine or butter
2 tablespoons all-purpose flour
1½ cups milk
2 packages (10 ounces each) frozen chopped spinach, thawed
   and squeezed dry
3 large eggs
8 ounces cooked ham, coarsely chopped (1½ cups)
½ teaspoon salt
Cheese Sauce (below)

1. Preheat oven to 350°F. Grease 5½-cup ring mold. In 3-quart saucepan, over low heat, melt margarine. Stir in flour until blended; cook, stirring, 1 minute. Gradually stir in milk; cook, stirring constantly, until mixture thickens and is smooth. Remove from heat. Stir in spinach, eggs, ham, and salt until well blended. Spoon mixture into prepared ring mold.

2. Set ring mold in 13" by 9" baking pan; place pan on oven rack. Pour *hot water* into pan to come halfway up side of mold. Bake until knife inserted in center of mixture comes out clean, about 40 minutes. Meanwhile, prepare Cheese Sauce.

3. To serve, with small spatula, loosen edges of mold. Invert mold onto warm platter. Pour Cheese Sauce over mold and cut into pieces. Makes 6 main-dish servings.

Each serving: About 275 calories, 20 g protein, 13 g carbohydrate, 17 g total fat (6 g saturated), 148 mg cholesterol, 1,035 mg sodium.

CHEESE SAUCE: In 1-quart saucepan, over low heat, melt *1 tablespoon margarine or butter*; stir in *1 tablespoon all-purpose flour*, and *dash ground red pepper* until blended. Cook, stirring, 1 minute. Gradually stir in *¾ cup milk*; cook, stirring constantly, until sauce thickens and is smooth. Stir in *⅓ cup shredded Cheddar cheese* until blended.

Choucroute Garnie

Prep: 25 minutes
Cook: 2 hours 30 minutes

1 boneless smoked pork shoulder roll (2 pounds), trimmed
1 boneless pork shoulder blade roast (fresh pork butt)
   (2 pounds), trimmed
2 cups dry white wine
1 can (14½ ounces) chicken broth
8 juniper berries or 2 tablespoons gin
6 medium onions (about 2 pounds), each cut in half
8 medium all-purpose potatoes (about 2½ pounds), unpeeled,
   each cut in half
6 bratwurst or frankfurters
2 bags or cans (16 ounces each) sauerkraut, well drained

1. Remove stockinette casing (if any) from smoked pork roll or follow label directions regarding stockinette casing. In nonstick 10- to 12-quart saucepot, place pork shoulder roll, pork shoulder blade roast, wine, chicken broth, and juniper berries. Heat to boiling over high heat. Reduce heat to low; cover and simmer 1 hour 30 minutes.

2. In layers, add onions, potatoes, bratwurst, and sauerkraut. Heat to boiling over high heat. Reduce heat to low; cover tightly and simmer until the meat and vegetables are fork-tender, 35 to 40 minutes.

3. With slotted spoon, place the sauerkraut, bratwurst, potatoes, and onions on warm large platter; keep warm. When pork roll is done, remove casing, if any, from pork roll. Transfer to cutting board. Slice pork roll and shoulder blade roast, and arrange on platter with vegetables. Skim and discard fat from pan juices; discard juniper berries. Pour pan juices into gravy boat and serve with meat and vegetables. Makes 16 main-dish servings.

Each serving: About 405 calories, 24 g protein, 20 g carbohydrate, 25 g total fat (9 g saturated), 137 mg cholesterol, 1,055 mg sodium.

Smoked Pork Chops with Sweet-and-Sour Cabbage

Prep: 15 minutes
Bake: 1 hour 45 minutes

1 tablespoon margarine or butter
1 medium onion, chopped
1 medium head green cabbage (2½ pounds), quartered, cored,
    and coarsely sliced
2 tablespoons all-purpose flour
2 tablespoons sugar
1 teaspoon caraway seeds
¼ cup cider vinegar
6 smoked pork loin chops, each 1 inch thick (8 ounces each)

1. Preheat oven to 325°F. In 1-quart saucepan, melt margarine over medium heat. Add onion and cook, stirring occasionally, until tender.

2. In 13" by 9" baking pan, lightly toss onion, cabbage, flour, sugar, and caraway seeds until combined; pour vinegar over mixture and place chops on the top. Cover pan tightly with foil. Bake until cabbage and pork chops are fork-tender, 1 hour 45 minutes. Serve chops with the cabbage and pan juices. Makes 6 main-dish servings.

Each serving: About 500 calories, 52 g protein, 17 g carbohydrate, 25 g total fat (9 g saturated), 139 mg cholesterol, 2,050 mg sodium.

ᗑLamb

Whether you're roasting a whole leg for a festive holiday centerpiece or using lamb shanks for a homey weeknight stew, flavorful lamb is both elegant and earthy. Once a symbol of spring, lamb is now bred so it can be enjoyed year round.

HOW TO BUY LAMB

Select lamb that's pinkish-red. Darker meat is from an older animal and will have a stronger flavor. Any fat should be white, firm, and waxy. Bones should be porous and un-splintered, with a reddish tinge at the cut end.

A leg of lamb may be covered with "fell," a moist and pliable paper-thin membrane that surrounds the fat and may be strongly flavored. You can trim it off or not, as you prefer. Each 1 pound of raw lamb serves the following: Boneless roasts, 3 to 4 servings; bone-in roasts and chops, 2 to 3 servings; bony cuts like riblets and shanks, 1 to 2 servings.

CHOOSING THE RIGHT CUT

When preparing any cut of lamb, remember that it can dry out quickly if overcooked. So unless you prefer well-done meat, cook lamb just to medium-rare for the best results.

BROILING, GRILLING, OR PANFRYING: Tender cuts work best; avoid overcooking. Best bets: Rib chops, loin chops, sirloin, arm, and blade chops, leg steaks, butterflied leg.

BRAISING AND STEWING: These moist-heat cooking methods are best reserved for slightly less-tender—and more economical—cuts. Remember to cook at a gentle simmer. Best bets: Neck slices, arm chops, blade chops, bone-in shoulder pieces, shanks, breast, breast riblets. Lamb cubes for stew are cut from the shoulder.

ROASTING: Many tender cuts of lamb are good for roasting, but the leg and rib sections are the most popular. Place lamb roasts fat-side up on a rack in a roasting pan, which will help keep the meat moist and flavorful.
Best bets: Whole leg of lamb, leg shank half, rack.

Lamb Roasting Times
(Oven temperature 325°F)

Start with meat at refrigerator temperature. Remove roast from oven when it reaches 5° to 10° below desired doneness; temperature will rise as it stands.

Cut	Weight	Approximate cooking time (minutes per lb) Medium-rare (145°F)	Medium (160°F)
Whole leg	5-7 lbs	15 mins	20 mins
	7-9 lbs	20 mins	25 mins
Leg shank half	3-4 lbs	30 mins	40 mins
Leg sirloin half	3-4 lbs	25 mins	35 mins
Leg roast (boneless)	4-7 lbs	20 mins	25 mins
Rib roast or rack (cook at 375°F)	1½-2½ lbs	30 mins	35 mins
Crown roast unstuffed (cook at 375°F)	2-3 lbs	25 mins	30 mins
Shoulder roast	4-6 lbs	20 mins	25 mins
Shoulder roast (boneless)	3½-6 lbs	35 mins	40 mins

POPULAR LAMB CUTS

Lamb rib roast (roast). Also called rib rack and rack roast.

Lamb shoulder neck slices (braise). Cross cuts of neck with bones in. Also called neck of lamb and lamb for stew.

Lamb rib chop (broil, panbroil, panfry, roast, bake). Also called rack lamb chop.

Lamb loin chop (broil, panbroil, panfry). Meaty area has both rib-eye muscle and tenderloin.

Lamb leg sirloin chop (broil, panbroil, panfry). Also called lamb sirloin steak.

Lamb shoulder arm chop (braise, broil, panbroil). Cut from arm portion of shoulder. Also called arm cut chop or round bone chop.

Lamb shoulder blade chop (braise, broil, panbroil, panfry). Also called shoulder lamb chop or blade cut chop.

Lamb shank (braise, cook in liquid). Cut from the arm of shoulder.

Lamb leg whole (roast). Also called leg of lamb—oven ready.

Lamb leg shank half (roast). Sirloin half removed. Lower half of leg and round leg bone included.

Lamb breast riblets (braise, cook in liquid). Cut from breast, containing long and narrow ribs with meat and fat in layers.

Lamb breast (braise, roast). Also called breast of lamb. Part of forequarter, containing row of ribs.

Herb-Marinated Leg of Lamb

Prep: 20 minutes plus marinating
Roast: About 2 hours 15 minutes

1 cup dry red wine
¼ cup olive oil
3 tablespoons Dijon mustard
1 medium onion, chopped
1 garlic clove, finely chopped
2¼ teaspoons salt
⅛ teaspoon ground black
  pepper

1 teaspoon dried rosemary,
  crumbled
¾ teaspoon dried thyme
1 whole lamb leg (8 pounds),
  trimmed
3 tablespoons all-purpose flour

1. In large stainless steel, enamel, or glass pan, stir together wine, oil, mustard, onion, garlic, 2 teaspoons salt, pepper, ½ teaspoon rosemary, and the thyme until blended. Add lamb leg and turn to coat with marinade. Cover and refrigerate lamb at least 12 hours to marinate, turning lamb occasionally.

2. Preheat oven to 325°F. Place lamb, fat side up, on rack in large roasting pan (17" by 11½"). Reserve marinade. Roast lamb, basting occasionally with reserved marinade, about 2 hours 15 minutes, until a meat thermometer inserted in thickest part of roast (without touching bone) reaches 140°F. Internal temperature of meat will rise to 145°F (medium-rare) upon standing. Or roast to desired doneness. Discard any remaining marinade.

3. When lamb is done, transfer to warm large platter or cutting board; let stand 15 minutes to set juices for easier carving. While lamb is standing, prepare gravy: Remove rack from roasting pan; pour pan drippings into 4-cup measuring cup (set pan aside); let stand a few seconds until fat separates from pan juice. Skim 3 tablespoons fat from pan juices and spoon into 2-quart saucepan; skim and discard any remaining fat. Add *¼ cup water* to roasting pan and stir until browned bits are loosened from bottom of pan. Pour into pan juices in cup; add enough additional *water* to equal 2½ cups.

4. Heat drippings in saucepan over medium heat. Stir in flour, remaining ½ teaspoon rosemary, and remaining ¼ teaspoon salt until blended. Cook, stirring, 1 minute. Gradually stir in pan-juice mixture and cook, stirring constantly, until gravy thickens slightly and boils; boil 1 minute. Pour gravy into gravy boat. To serve, carve lamb into thin slices (see below) and arrange on platter. Serve lamb with pan gravy. Makes 16 main-dish servings.

Each serving: About 360 calories, 30 g protein, 2 g carbohydrate, 25 g total fat (9 g saturated), 108 mg cholesterol, 420 mg sodium.

HOW TO CARVE A LEG OF LAMB

Place meat with shank bone to your right. Cut some slices from thin side of leg. Stand leg on this cut surface. Starting at shank end, slice down to leg bone; cut slices until you reach bone at other end of leg. Then cut along leg bone under slices to release them.

Leg of Lamb with Pistachio Topping

Prep: 30 minutes
Roast: 2 hours 30 minutes

1 whole lamb leg
  (7 pounds), trimmed
2 large garlic cloves, sliced
1½ teaspoons salt
2 tablespoons margarine or
  butter
1 small onion, chopped
1½ slices white bread, torn into
  small pieces
½ cup pistachios, finely
  chopped

2 tablespoons fresh mint leaves,
  coarsely chopped
¼ teaspoon coarsely ground
  black pepper
½ cup port wine
3 tablespoons all-purpose flour
1 can (14½ ounces) chicken
  broth

1. Preheat oven to 325°F. With knife, cut about a dozen
½-inch-wide slits in lamb, and place a slice of garlic in
each. Sprinkle 1 teaspoon salt on lamb. Place lamb, fat-side
up, on rack in large roasting pan (17" by 11½").

2. Meanwhile, in small saucepan, melt margarine over
medium heat. Add onion and cook, stirring occasionally,
until lightly browned and tender, about 10 minutes; remove
from heat. Stir in bread, pistachios, mint, pepper, and remaining ½ teaspoon salt. After lamb has roasted 1 hour,
with hands, carefully pat bread mixture on top of lamb.

3. Roast lamb 1 hour 15 minutes to 1 hour 30 minutes
longer, until meat thermometer inserted in thickest part of
roast (without touching bone) reaches 140°F. Internal temperature of meat will rise to 145°F. (medium-rare) upon
standing. Or roast to desired doneness. When lamb is done,
place on warm large platter; let stand 15 minutes to set
juices for easier carving.

4. While lamb is standing, prepare gravy: Remove rack
from roasting pan; pour pan juices into 2-cup measuring
cup. Add port to roasting pan, stirring until browned bits
are loosened from bottom of pan. Add to pan juice in cup;
let stand until fat separates from pan juice. Skim 2 tablespoons fat from pan juices and spoon into roasting pan;
skim and discard any remaining fat.

5. Stir flour into drippings in roasting pan and cook over
medium-high heat, stirring, until blended. With wire whisk,
gradually mix in pan juice and chicken broth and cook,
stirring constantly, until gravy has thickened slightly and
begins to boil; boil 1 minute. If you like, pour gravy
through sieve into gravy boat. To serve, carve lamb (page
210) and arrange on platter. Serve lamb with pan gravy.
Makes 14 main-dish servings.

*Each serving: About 385 calories, 36 g protein, 6 g carbohydrate,
23 g total fat (8 g saturated), 122 mg cholesterol, 360 mg sodium.*

Marinated Butterflied Lamb

Prep: 10 minutes plus marinating
Broil: 30 minutes

1 boneless lamb leg shank half (4 pounds), trimmed
1 tablespoon whole black peppercorns
⅓ cup dry red wine
3 tablespoons olive oil
1½ teaspoons salt
1½ teaspoons dried oregano, crumbled
1 garlic clove, slivered

1. Using sharp knife, cut lamb leg lengthwise almost in half, being careful not to cut all the way through. Open and spread flat like a book.

2. Place peppercorns in small zip-tight plastic bag. With meat mallet or rolling pin, pound peppercorns until coarsely cracked. Place peppercorns in 12" by 8" baking dish; add wine, oil, salt, oregano, and garlic and stir to combine. Add lamb and turn to coat evenly with marinade. Cover and refrigerate lamb at least 12 hours to marinate, turning occasionally.

3. Preheat broiler. Remove lamb from marinade, reserving marinade. Place lamb on rack in broiling pan. Broil lamb 5 to 7 inches from heat source, basting occasionally with reserved marinade, about 15 minutes per side for medium-rare or until desired doneness. Discard remaining marinade. When lamb is done, transfer to warm large platter and let stand 10 minutes to set juices for easier slicing.

4. To serve, cut lamb into thin slices and arrange on platter. Makes 10 main-dish servings.

Each serving: About 265 calories, 30 g protein, 0 g carbohydrate, 15 g total fat (6 g saturated), 102 mg cholesterol, 250 mg sodium.

Roast Rack of Lamb

Prep: 10 minutes
Roast: 1 hour 15 minutes

1 lamb rib roast, 8 ribs (2½ pounds), trimmed (ask butcher to
  loosen backbone from ribs)
1 teaspoon salt
3 tablespoons margarine or butter
⅔ cup plain dried bread crumbs
2 tablespoons chopped fresh parsley
½ teaspoon dried oregano
2 tablespoons prepared mustard

1. Preheat oven to 375°F. In medium roasting pan (14"
by 10"), place lamb roast on rib bones. Sprinkle salt on
lamb. Roast lamb 50 minutes.

2. Meanwhile, in small skillet, melt margarine over medium heat. Add bread crumbs and cook, stirring, until
golden brown. Stir in parsley and oregano.

3. Remove roast from oven; spread top of meat with
mustard. Sprinkle crumb mixture on roast and press onto
roast. Roast about 25 minutes longer or until meat thermometer inserted in thickest part of roast (without touching
bone) reaches 140°F. Internal temperature of meat will rise
to 145°F (medium-rare) upon standing. Or roast until desired doneness.

4. When roast is done, transfer to warm large platter and
let stand 10 minutes to set juices for easier carving. To
serve, cut off backbone from ribs and carve between ribs
being careful not to disturb crumb coating. Makes 4 main-
dish servings.

*Each serving: About 540 calories, 27 g protein, 14 g carbohy-
drate, 41 g total fat (15 g saturated), 109 mg cholesterol, 1,030
mg sodium.*

Glazed Rosemary Lamb Chops

Prep: 10 minutes
Cook: 10 minutes

8 loin lamb chops, each 1 inch thick (4 ounces each), trimmed
1 large garlic clove, cut in half
¼ teaspoon salt
¼ teaspoon coarsely ground black pepper
2 teaspoons chopped fresh rosemary or ½ teaspoon
    dried rosemary, crumbled
¼ cup apple jelly
1 tablespoon balsamic vinegar

1. Preheat broiler. Pat chops dry with paper towels. Rub both sides of each lamb chop with cut sides of garlic; sprinkle with salt, pepper, and rosemary. In cup, stir together apple jelly and vinegar.

2. Place chops on rack in broiling pan. Broil at closest position to heat source 4 minutes. Brush chops with half of apple-jelly mixture; broil 1 minute. Turn chops and broil 4 minutes longer. Brush on remaining jelly mixture and broil 1 minute longer for medium-rare or until desired doneness. Skim and discard fat from pan juices. Serve lamb chops with pan juices. Makes 4 main-dish servings.

Each serving: About 460 calories, 32 g protein, 15 g carbohydrate, 30 g total fat (3 g saturated), 128 mg cholesterol, 235 mg sodium.

Lamb Steak with Red-Pepper Relish

Prep: 30 minutes
Broil: 10 minutes

⅓ cup cider vinegar
¼ cup sugar
1¼ teaspoons salt
Pinch dried thyme
Pinch fennel seeds, crushed
2 small red peppers, coarsely chopped
1 medium Golden Delicious apple, peeled, cored, and coarsely
    chopped
2 jalapeño chiles, seeded and finely chopped
1 center-cut lamb steak, 1 inch thick (1 pound), trimmed or
    8 loin lamb chops, each 1 inch thick

1. In nonreactive 2-quart saucepan, combine vinegar, sugar, 1 teaspoon salt, thyme, and fennel; heat to boiling over high heat. Add red peppers, apple, and jalapeños; heat to boiling. Reduce heat to medium-low; simmer, stirring occasionally, until relish is thickened and liquid has evaporated, 15 to 20 minutes.

2. Meanwhile, preheat broiler. Pat lamb dry with paper towels. Sprinkle remaining ¼ teaspoon salt on lamb. Place lamb on rack in broiling pan. Broil at closest position to heat source, 5 minutes per side for medium-rare or until desired doneness. Serve lamb with warm red-pepper relish. Makes 4 main-dish servings.

Each serving: About 320 calories, 18 g protein, 21 g carbohydrate, 19 g total fat (8 g saturated), 75 mg cholesterol, 720 mg sodium.

Breaded Lamb Chops

Prep: 5 minutes
Cook: 15 minutes

2 large eggs
1 tablespoon water
¾ teaspoon salt
½ teaspoon dried rosemary, crumbled
1 cup plain dried bread crumbs
4 lamb shoulder blade chops, each about ¾ inch thick, trimmed
2 to 3 tablespoons olive oil

1. In pie plate, with fork, beat eggs, water, salt, and rosemary. Place crumbs on sheet of waxed paper. Dip chops into egg mixture, then into crumbs, pressing firmly so mixture adheres. Coating each chop twice.

2. In 12-inch skillet, heat 2 tablespoons oil over medium heat. Add chops and cook about 5 to 6 minutes per side for medium or until desired doneness, adding additional 1 tablespoon oil if pan gets dry. Serve chops hot. Makes 4 main-dish servings.

Each serving: About 540 calories, 35 g protein, 20 g carbohydrate, 34 g total fat (12 g saturated), 221 mg cholesterol, 775 mg sodium.

Broiled Lamb Chops with Red-Currant Sauce

Prep: 8 minutes
Broil: 12 minutes

1 large lemon
½ cup red currant jelly
1 ½ teaspoons prepared mustard
½ teaspoon salt
4 lamb shoulder blade or arm chops, each ½ inch thick, trimmed

1. Preheat broiler. From lemon, grate 2 teaspoons peel and squeeze 1 tablespoon juice.
2. In nonstick 1-quart saucepan, heat lemon peel and juice, jelly, mustard, and salt over low heat until jelly melts. Remove from heat.
3. Place chops on rack in broiling pan. Broil at closest position to heat source 5 minutes. Turn chops; brush with sauce and broil 5 to 7 minutes longer, for medium-rare or until desired doneness, brushing occasionally with sauce. Makes 4 main-dish servings.

Each serving: About 335 calories, 20 g protein, 27 g carbohydrate, 16 g total fat (6 g saturated), 81 mg cholesterol, 400 mg sodium.

Lamb with Green Beans

Prep: 25 minutes
Cook: About 1 hour 20 minutes

2 pounds boneless lamb for stew, well trimmed and cut into
    1½-inch pieces
2 tablespoons olive oil
1 large onion, chopped
1 teaspoon salt
½ teaspoon coarsely ground black pepper
½ teaspoon ground allspice
¼ teaspoon ground nutmeg
1 can (28 ounces) tomatoes
2 pounds green beans, stem ends trimmed, and cut into
    2-inch pieces

1. Pat lamb dry with paper towels. In 5-quart Dutch oven, heat 1 tablespoon oil over medium-high heat until very hot. Add half the lamb and cook, stirring occasionally, until browned, about 5 minutes. Using slotted spoon, transfer meat to bowl as it is browned. Repeat with remaining lamb.

2. In same Dutch oven, heat remaining 1 tablespoon oil. Add onion, salt, pepper, allspice, and nutmeg; cook, stirring frequently, 5 minutes. Add tomatoes with their juice; heat to boiling, breaking them up with side of spoon.

3. Return lamb and any juice in bowl to Dutch oven; add green beans and heat to boiling. Reduce heat to low; cover and simmer until meat is fork-tender, about 1 hour. To serve, spoon into shallow soup plates. Makes about 10 cups or 8 main-dish servings.

Each serving: About 245 calories, 26 g protein, 14 g carbohydrate, 10 g total fat (3 g saturated), 80 mg cholesterol, 485 mg sodium.

Greek-Style Lamb Shanks

Prep: 30 minutes
Bake: 2 hours 45 minutes

4 small lamb shanks (1 pound each), trimmed
1 teaspoon salt
1 tablespoon vegetable oil
2 medium onions, coarsely chopped
1 large carrot, chopped
2 garlic cloves, finely chopped
1 can (14½ ounces) diced tomatoes
1 cup chicken broth
1¾ pounds all-purpose potatoes (4 medium), not peeled, each cut into quarters
12 ounces green beans, ends trimmed and cut into 2-inch pieces
2 medium lemons
2 tablespoons chopped fresh dill
2 tablespoons chopped fresh parsley

1. Pat lamb shanks dry with paper towels. Sprinkle ¼ teaspoon salt on lamb shanks. In 8-quart Dutch oven, heat oil over medium-high heat until very hot. Add half of lamb shanks and cook until browned, using tongs to transfer shanks to bowl as they are browned. Repeat with remaining lamb shanks.

2. Preheat oven to 350°F. In drippings in Dutch oven, cook onions and carrot, stirring occasionally, until tender and lightly browned, about 10 minutes. Add garlic; cook, stirring, 2 minutes.

3. Return lamb shanks and any juice in bowl to Dutch oven. Add tomatoes with their juice, broth, and remaining ¾ teaspoon salt; heat to boiling over high heat. Cover, place in oven, and bake 1 hour 30 minutes. Turn lamb shanks over; add potatoes and green beans. Cover and bake until lamb and potatoes are tender, about 1 hour 15 minutes longer.

4. Meanwhile, from lemons, grate 1 tablespoon peel and squeeze 2 tablespoons juice.

5. When lamb shanks are done, skim and discard fat

from pan juices. Stir in lemon peel and juice, dill, and parsley. To serve, place lamb shanks and vegetables on plates and spoon pan juices on top. Makes 4 main-dish servings.

Each serving: About 625 calories, 50 g protein, 53 g carbohydrate, 24 g total fat (9 g saturated), 159 mg cholesterol, 995 mg sodium.

Eggplant and Lamb Casserole

Prep: 55 minutes
Bake: 35 to 40 minutes

2 small eggplants (1¼ pounds each), trimmed and cut lengthwise into ½-inch-thick slices
5 tablespoons olive oil
2 pounds ground lamb
1 large onion, chopped
2 garlic cloves, finely chopped
1½ teaspoons salt
½ teaspoon coarsely ground black pepper

1 teaspoon ground cumin
½ teaspoon ground cinnamon
1 can (28 ounces) plum tomatoes in puree
4 large eggs
⅓ cup all-purpose flour
3 cups milk
¼ teaspoon ground nutmeg

1. Preheat oven to 450°F. Spray 2 small cookie sheets with nonstick cooking spray. Place eggplant slices on cookie sheets; brush with 3 tablespoons oil. Bake 20 minutes, rotating cookie sheets between upper and lower racks halfway through baking time, until eggplant is soft and browned. Remove eggplant from oven; turn oven control to 375°F.
2. Meanwhile, in 12-inch skillet (at least 2 inches deep), heat 1 tablespoon oil over medium-high heat, until very hot. Add ground lamb, onion, and garlic and cook, stirring oc-

casionally, until browned, about 15 minutes. Stir in 1 teaspoon salt, ¼ teaspoon pepper, cumin, and cinnamon; cook 1 minute longer. Remove skillet from heat; add tomatoes with their puree, breaking them up with side of spoon.

3. Break eggs into small bowl; beat lightly with wire whisk. In 3-quart saucepan, heat remaining 1 tablespoon oil over medium heat. Stir in flour and cook, stirring, 1 minute; (mixture will appear dry and crumbly). With wire whisk, gradually beat in milk; cook, stirring frequently, until mixture boils and has thickened, about 15 minutes. Remove saucepan from heat. Gradually beat small amount of hot milk mixture into eggs. Add egg mixture to saucepan, beating to combine. Stir in nutmeg, remaining ½ teaspoon salt, and remaining ¼ teaspoon pepper.

4. In shallow 3½- to 4-quart casserole or 13" by 9" baking dish, arrange half of eggplant slices, overlapping slices to fit if necessary; top with half of meat mixture. Repeat with remaining eggplant slices and meat mixture; pour egg mixture over top. Bake casserole until top is puffed and golden, and casserole is heated through, 35 to 40 minutes. Let stand a few minutes before serving. Makes 10 main-dish servings.

Each serving: About 460 calories, 22 g protein, 19 g carbohydrate, 33 g total fat (13 g saturated), 162 mg cholesterol, 570 mg sodium.

Greek Meat Loaf

Prep: 20 minutes
Bake: 1¼ hours

1 pound ground lamb
1 pound ground beef chuck
2 large eggs
2 tablespoons olive oil
1 tablespoon red wine vinegar
1 cup fresh bread crumbs
  (about 2 slices white bread)
2 bunches green onions, finely
  chopped (about
  1 cup)

4 ounces feta cheese, finely
  crumbled (about ½ cup)
¼ cup chopped fresh parsley
2 garlic cloves, finely chopped
½ teaspoon salt
¼ teaspoon ground black
  pepper
1 tablespoon dried mint

1. Preheat oven to 375°F. In large bowl, with hands, mix ground lamb, ground beef, eggs, oil, vinegar, bread crumbs, green onions, feta, parsley, garlic, salt, pepper, and mint just until well combined but not overmixed.

2. In 13" by 9" baking pan, shape meat mixture into 9" by 5" loaf. Bake meat loaf 1 hour and 15 minutes. Let meat loaf stand 10 minutes to set juices for easier slicing. To serve, remove from pan, place meat loaf on warm medium platter and cut into slices. Makes 8 main-dish servings.

Each serving: About 335 calories, 25 g protein, 5 g carbohydrate, 24 g total fat (9 g saturated), 142 mg cholesterol, 405 mg sodium.

Moussaka

Prep: 55 minutes
Bake: 30 minutes

4 to 5 tablespoons olive oil
2 large eggplants (2 pounds each), trimmed and cut into ¼-inch slices
1½ pounds ground lamb
1 large onion, chopped
1 garlic clove, finely chopped
½ cup dry red wine
¼ cup tomato sauce
1 large egg

4 ounces feta cheese, crumbled (about ½ cup)
½ cup plain dried bread crumbs
¼ cup chopped fresh parsley
1½ teaspoons salt
¼ teaspoon ground black pepper
¼ teaspoon dried thyme
Creamy Sauce (below)
Ground nutmeg

1. In nonstick 12-inch skillet, heat 4 tablespoons oil over medium heat. Add eggplant slices, in batches, and cook until golden, using tongs to transfer eggplant to paper towels to drain as they are browned. Add remaining 1 tablespoon oil to skillet if it gets dry.

2. In same skillet, cook ground lamb, onion, and garlic over medium heat, stirring occasionally, until meat is browned, about 10 minutes. Remove skillet from heat. Skim and discard fat from meat mixture. Stir in wine, tomato sauce, egg, feta, bread crumbs, parsley, salt, pepper, and thyme until well blended.

3. Preheat oven to 350°F. In 13" by 9" baking dish, arrange half of eggplant slices; spoon meat mixture evenly over eggplant. Top with remaining eggplant slices. Spoon sauce evenly over eggplant and sprinkle lightly with nutmeg. Bake until heated through, about 30 minutes. Let stand a few minutes before serving. Makes 10 main-dish servings.

Each serving: About 400 calories, 20 g protein, 23 g carbohydrate, 26 g total fat (8 g saturated), 84 mg cholesterol, 945 mg sodium.

CREAMY SAUCE: In 2-quart saucepan, over medium heat, melt 5 tablespoons margarine or butter. With wire whisk, beat in *½ cup all-purpose flour* and *½ teaspoon salt* until blended. Cook, stirring, 1 minute. Gradually stir in *1 can (14½ ounces) chicken broth* and *1 cup milk* and cook, stirring constantly, until mixture has thickened and boils.

∽Sausages

Sausage is meat such as pork or beef that is ground and seasoned and usually stuffed into a casing. The more than 200 varieties sold in this country can be grouped according to the ways in which they are processed:

Fresh Sausage. Made from uncured fresh meats, principally pork and beef. Refrigerate fresh sausage and use it within 2 or 3 days. Cook thoroughly before eating. Pork sausage, fresh kielbasa (Polish), bratwurst (German-style veal sausage), bockwurst, Spanish and Mexican chorizo (link or bulk), fresh Thuringer.

Uncooked Smoked Sausage. Made from fresh or cured meat and smoked but not cooked. Refrigerate uncooked smoked sausage and use it within a week, cooking the sausage thoroughly before eating. Smoked pork sausage, smoked kielbasa, mettwurst.

Cooked Sausage. Usually made from fresh meats, which are cured during processing and fully cooked so that they are ready to eat. Refrigerate and use it within 4 to 6 days. Some of these are heated before they are eaten. Blood sausage, blood-and-tongue sausage, bockwurst (precooked), bratwurst (precooked), Braunschweiger, liverwurst.

Cooked Smoked Sausage. Made from fresh meats, which are cured and fully cooked. Refrigerate cooked smoked sausage and use it within 1 week if the package is opened, longer if unopened; check the date on the package. Beef salami, bologna, mettwurst, cotto salami, frankfurters, German-style mortadella, smoked kielbasa, knackwurst, Vienna sausage.

Dry and Semi-dry Sausage. Made from fresh meats by a

carefully controlled drying process; they may be smoked or unsmoked, and are ready to eat. Store dry sausage in a cool place; refrigerate semidry sausage. Use unsliced dry and semidry sausage within 3 to 6 weeks. Summer sausage, cervelat (farmer), salami, chorizo, Lebanon bologna, mortadella, pepperoni.

Specialty Deli Meats. Made from fresh meats that are cured during processing and fully cooked. Use sliced meats within 3 days. Unopened vacuum packages will keep longer; check the freshness date on the package. Ham-and-cheese loaf, olive loaf, head cheese, luncheon meat.

HOW TO COOK FRESH AND UNCOOKED SMOKED SAUSAGE

All fresh sausages should be thoroughly cooked at low to moderate temperatures. Sausages are ready to eat when the inside color turns from pink to gray.

PANFRYING: In a heavy skillet, heat a small amount of oil over medium heat. Cook the sausages, turning them occasionally with tongs or a wide spatula, until they are done throughout.

BRAISING AND BROWNING: Place links in cold skillet with *2 to 4 tablespoons of water.* Cover and cook over low heat 5 minutes. Uncover; cook, turning occasionally, until water has evaporated and sausages are browned and done throughout.

BAKING: Preheat over to 400°F. Place links or patties on a rack in a roasting pan and bake until browned and done throughout, about 20 to 30 minutes, depending on their size.

HOW TO HEAT FULLY COOKED SAUSAGE

SIMMERING: Add the sausages to a saucepan with enough *boiling water* to cover. When the water boils again, reduce the heat; cover and simmer the sausage (don't boil) until they are heated through, about 5 minutes, depending on their size.

PANFRYING: In a skillet, over medium-low heat, heat the sausages, turning them occasionally, until browned on all sides and heated through.

BROILING: Place sausages on rack in broiling pan; broil 3 to 5 inches from heat source, turning with tongs, until evenly browned and heated through.

Sausage and Pepper Grill

Prep: 15 minutes
Grill: 15 to 20 minutes

⅓ cup balsamic vinegar
1 teaspoon brown sugar
½ teaspoon salt
¼ teaspoon coarsely ground black pepper
2 medium red peppers, cut into 1½-inch-wide strips
2 medium green peppers, cut into 1½-inch-wide strips

2 large red onions (about 8 ounces each), each cut into 6 wedges
1 tablespoon olive oil
¾ pound sweet Italian-sausage links
¾ pound hot Italian-sausage links

1. Prepare grill. In cup, mix vinegar, brown sugar, salt, and pepper. In large bowl, toss red and green peppers and onions with olive oil to coat.

2. Place sausages and vegetables on grill over medium heat. Grill sausages, turning occasionally, until golden brown and cooked through, 15 to 20 minutes. Grill vegetables, turning occasionally, until tender, about 15 minutes, brushing with some balsamic mixture during last 3 minutes of cooking. Use tongs to transfer vegetables and sausages to warm large platter as they are cooked; cover loosely with foil to keep warm.

3. To serve, cut sausages into 2-inch diagonal slices. Drizzle any remaining balsamic mixture over vegetables. Makes 4 main-dish servings.

Each serving: About 450 calories, 22 g protein, 24 g carbohydrate, 30 g total fat (10 g saturated), 78 mg cholesterol, 1,200 mg sodium.

Kielbasa and Red Cabbage

Prep: 20 minutes
Cook: 45 minutes

2 medium McIntosh or Rome Beauty apples
2 tablespoons margarine or butter
1 small onion, coarsely chopped
1 small head red cabbage (1½ pounds), cored, quartered, and
  thinly sliced
½ cup apple juice
3 tablespoons red wine vinegar
1 tablespoon sugar
1 teaspoon salt
1 pound kielbasa or knackwurst, cut into 2-inch slices

1. Core and coarsely chop 1 apple. In 12-inch skillet at least 2 inches deep, melt margarine. Add onion and cook, stirring occasionally, until tender. Stir in cabbage, apple juice, vinegar, sugar, salt, and chopped apple; heat to boiling. Reduce heat to low; cover and simmer 15 minutes.
2. Add kielbasa to cabbage mixture; heat to boiling over high heat. Reduce heat to low; cover and simmer 15 minutes. Cut remaining apple into wedges; add to skillet and heat through. Serve kielbasa with the cabbage mixture and apples. Makes 4 main-dish servings.

Each serving: About 520 calories, 18 g protein, 31 g carbohydrate, 37 g total fat (12 g saturated), 76 mg cholesterol, 1,895 mg sodium.

Sausage and Pepper Loaf

Prep: 30 minutes
Bake: 1 hour 10 minutes

1 tablespoon olive oil
2 medium red peppers, chopped
1 large onion, chopped
1 large garlic clove, crushed with garlic press
1 pound sweet Italian-sausage links, casings removed
1 pound ground beef chuck
1 can (8 ounces) tomato sauce

2 large eggs
1½ cups fresh bread crumbs (about 3 slices white bread)
⅓ cup grated Parmesan cheese
½ teaspoon salt
2 ounces shredded Fontina or mozzarella cheese (about ½ cup)

1. In nonstick 12-inch skillet, heat oil over medium heat. Add red peppers and onion and cook, stirring occasionally, until tender and lightly browned, 10 to 15 minutes. Add garlic; cook, stirring, 1 minute. Set vegetables aside to cool slightly.

2. Preheat oven to 375°F. In large bowl, with hands, mix sausage meat, ground beef, tomato sauce, eggs, bread crumbs, Parmesan, salt, and cooked vegetables just until well combined but not overmixed.

3. In 13" by 9" metal baking pan, shape meat mixture into 9" by 5" loaf. Bake meat loaf 1 hour. Sprinkle cheese down center of loaf in a 2-inch-wide strip. Bake 10 minutes longer. Let meat loaf stand 10 minutes to set juices for easier slicing. To serve, transfer to warm medium platter and cut into slices. Makes 8 main-dish servings.

Each serving: About 370 calories, 25 g protein, 10 g carbohydrate, 25 g total fat (10 g saturated), 132 mg cholesterol, 915 mg sodium.

Poultry

~~~~~

Chicken • Capon • Cornish Hens
Turkey • Duckling • Goose • Stuffings

HOW TO BUY POULTRY

Choose fresh whole birds that seem plump, with meaty breasts (meatier birds are a better buy because you're paying for less bone per pound). Chicken parts should also look plump. Poultry skin should be smooth and moist, and free of bruises or pinfeathers; bone ends should be pinkish-white. (The color of the skin can range from creamy white to yellow; it depends on the bird's feed and breed and has no effect on taste.) Avoid packages that are broken or leaking. The USDA inspection sticker or tag is a guarantee that the bird was reared and processed under strict conditions. Grade A birds, the most common variety sold in supermarkets, are the highest quality. More than 90 percent of all broiler-fryers (2½- to 4-pound chickens) are marketed under a brand name, a further assurance of quality.

To check freshness, note the "sell-by" date on the package. You can safely buy poultry through that date, and then refrigerate it for up to 2 days afterward.

Free-range chickens are those fed on a grain-only diet free from antibiotics and allowed to roam freely in the farmyard (unlike most chickens, which are caged). As a result, they develop more muscle, which creates fuller-flavored meat. Free-range chickens are usually much more expensive than regular chickens.

When buying frozen poultry, be sure the meat is rock-hard and without signs of freezer burn. The quick commercial freezing process should guarantee that poultry hasn't absorbed excess water; check by making sure there are no ice crystals. The packaging should be tightly sealed and intact; frozen liquid in the bottom can mean the bird was thawed and refrozen.

Poultry Sense

Poultry/Ready-to-Cook	Weight	Servings	Stuffing
Broiler-fryer	2½-3½ lbs	4	1-3 cups
Roasting chicken	5-7 lbs	6-7	3-6 cups
Capon	6-8 lbs	6-8	3-6 cups
Cornish hen	1-2 lbs	1-2	¾-1½ cups
Turkey	8-12 lbs	6-8	6-9 cups
	12-16 lbs	12-16	9-12 cups
	16-20 lbs	16-20	12-15 cups
	20-24 lbs	20-24	15-18 cups
Turkey breast	4-6 lbs	5-8	
Turkey breast (boneless)	2½-3 lbs	6-9	
Duckling	4-5 lbs	4	3-4 cups
Goose	10-12 lbs	6-8	6-9 cups

∽Handling and Storing

Raw poultry can harbor salmonella, a prime source of food poisoning, so always wash your hands, cutting board, and all utensils in hot, soapy water after handling it. Cutting boards should be bleached occasionally with a solution of 1 tablespoon bleach to 1 gallon water.

Store raw poultry in its original wrapping in the coldest part of the refrigerator for no more than 2 or 3 days, keep it separate from cooked and ready-to-eat foods.

If poultry is wrapped in butcher paper, or if the wrapping is leaking, unwrap it, place in a dish, and cover loosely with foil or waxed paper before refrigerating.

Some wrappings can transfer their odor to poultry. After unwrapping, check that any smell disappears quickly. Do not use if any off odors linger.

Rinse poultry inside and out with cold running water and pat dry with paper towels before using.

Store any giblets separately in the refrigerator and use within a day. They are an excellent addition to gravy.

Freeze whole uncooked poultry up to 6 months and pieces 3 to 6 months. Ground poultry will keep in the refrigerator 1 day, or in the freezer up to 3 months.

Cool cooked poultry as quickly as possible, then cover and refrigerate 2 to 3 days, or wrap and freeze up to 3 months. Any leftover stuffing should be promptly removed from the bird (to avoid potential bacterial growth), covered and refrigerated separately, and used within 3 days. It can be frozen for up to 1 month.

∾Thawing

For safety, it's important to thaw poultry in one of two ways: either in the refrigerator or by immersing it in cold water (see below). Never thaw poultry on the kitchen counter, because bacteria can multiply rapidly at room temperature. Also, do not thaw a commercially stuffed frozen turkey before roasting—bacteria can flourish in the thawed stuffing. Follow the label instructions for cooking. Keep these important guidelines in mind.

Frozen poultry should be thawed completely before cooking, so allow sufficient time, especially for large birds. Remove giblets as soon as possible during thawing, then wrap and refrigerate and use for stock or gravy, if desired.

If all ice crystals have disappeared from the body cavity and the legs are flexible, then the bird has thawed. Once thawed, cook the bird within 12 hours. Wipe out the body and neck cavities with paper towels; pat the skin dry. For reasons of texture, not safety, do not refreeze poultry once it has been thawed.

Thawing in the refrigerator: For refrigerator thawing, leave the bird in its original wrapper and place it on a tray to catch drips. Thawing time will depend both on the size of the bird and the temperature of the refrigerator (ideally 35° to 40°F). As a general rule, allow about 6 hours per pound. Thawing in cold water: If there's no time to thaw the bird in the refrigerator, try the cold-water method, which takes less time but requires more attention. Place the bird (in its original wrapper or a watertight plastic bag) in a large pan or in the sink with cold water to cover. (Warm water thaws poultry too quickly and can cause bacteria to grow.) Change the water regularly—every 30 minutes—to maintain the temperature. Allow about 30 minutes of thawing time per pound, then add 1 hour to that total.

∽Tips on Stuffing Poultry

You can prepare stuffing ingredients ahead and refrigerate them, but do not mix the stuffing or stuff the bird until you are ready to roast it. Never partially roast a bird one day and finish it the next. And never stuff a bird the day before you roast it. If you do, harmful bacteria are very likely to multiply.

Allow ¾ to 1 cup of stuffing per pound of bird.

Spoon the stuffing lightly into the bird so that it has room to absorb juices and expand during roasting. Bake any leftover or extra stuffing in a greased covered casserole along with the bird during the last 45 minutes to 1 hour of roasting time.

As soon as the meal is over, remove the stuffing and refrigerate the bird, stuffing, and gravy separately.

∽Tips on Roasting Poultry

All kinds of poultry can be roasted either stuffed or unstuffed; an unstuffed bird will take a little less time than a stuffed bird. Plan to finish cooking large birds about 15 minutes before carving, small birds about 10 minutes. During the resting time the meat will stabilize, and the juices will set, making carving easier, and preventing the juices from running out, so that the meat stays juicy and tender.

If bird begins to brown too quickly during roasting, cover loosely with foil. Remove foil during last 30 minutes of roasting, and with pastry brush, brush bird with pan drippings, vegetable oil, melted margarine or butter (unless roasting a duckling or prebasted bird) to give it an attractive sheen.

Poultry Roasting Times
(Oven temperature 350°F)
Start with bird at refrigerator temperature

Poultry type	Weight	Cooking time (unstuffed)	Cooking time (stuffed)
Chicken	2½-3 lbs	1¼-1½ hrs	1¼-1½ hrs
	3-4 lbs	1½-1¾ hrs	1½-1¾ hrs
	4-6 lbs	1¾-2 hrs	1¾-2 hrs
Capon (at 325°F)	5-6 lbs	2-2½ hrs	2½-3 hrs
	6-8 lbs	2½-3½ hrs	3-4 hrs
Cornish hen	1-2 lbs	1-1¼ hrs	1-1¼ hrs
Turkey (at 325°F)	8-12 lbs	2¾-3 hrs	3-3½ hrs
	12-14 lbs	3-3¾ hrs	3½-4 hrs
	14-18 lbs	3¾-4¼ hrs	4-4¼ hrs
	18-20 lbs	4¼-4½ hrs	4¼-4¾ hrs
	20-24 lbs	4½-5 hrs	4¾-5½ hrs
Duckling	4-5 lbs	2½-2¾ hrs	2½-2¾ hrs
Goose	10-12 lbs	2¾-3¼ hrs	3-3½ hrs

∾To Skin or Not to Skin

Chicken skin gets 80 percent of its calories from fat, so it makes sense to serve your bird without it. But you don't have to remove the skin before cooking. According to the

U.S. Department of Agriculture (USDA), it makes little difference in the fat content whether the skin is removed before or after cooking. But tastewise, especially when roasting whole chickens, you'll get a moister, more tender result if you cook with the skin still intact. Some skin-removal incentives:

	Calories	Fat (g)	Saturated Fat (g)
Breast, with skin	197	8	2
without skin	165	4	1
Drumstick and thigh, with skin	232	13	4
without skin	191	8	2

∾Chicken

Chicken is among the least expensive meats, but it is one of the most versatile, and it can be served in hundreds of different ways. Here are the basic cooking methods:

ROASTING: Preheat oven to 350°F. Use whole chickens, either stuffed or unstuffed. Place on rack in shallow roasting pan and roast about 30 minutes per pound, until meat thermometer inserted in thickest part of thigh, next to body, reaches 175° to 180°F and juices run clear when thigh is pierced with tip of knife.

BAKING: Similar to roasting but requires higher oven temperatures (375° to 425°F). Baking is recommended for chicken parts but not for whole birds. If desired, marinate parts before or brush with a sauce during baking; or coat pieces with flour or crumbs, and bake in a shallow pan drizzled with melted butter or olive oil.

BROILING: Preheat the broiler. Place chicken on the rack in the broiling pan. Broil 7 to 9 inches from the heat source, brushing the chicken as desired with marinade, seasoned olive oil, or margarine or butter during broiling.

BRAISING: Brown chicken first in hot oil or butter, then add a small amount of liquid, and cook slowly, covered, over low heat.

SIMMERING OR STEWING: Simmer, don't boil, a whole or cut-up chicken over low heat in a large amount of liquid.

STEAMING: Cook chicken in either a steamer or in a deep heat-safe bowl set in shallow water in a covered saucepot. Either way, chicken is cooked *above* simmering liquid.

BARBECUING: For chicken cooked over an open fire, as on the barbecue grill or on a spit, use only medium heat. To test for medium heat, hold your hand, palm down, at cooking height over the heat; you should be able to hold it there for about 4 seconds. Baste chicken with a sweet sauce only during the last 5 to 10 minutes to avoid scorching.

DEEP-FRYING: Deep-fry chicken in only enough vegetable oil to cover it, and maintain heat at moderate temperature. Too-high heat dries out chicken and over-browns it before it is cooked. Too-low heat results in greasy chicken.

PANFRYING AND SAUTÉING: Panfry chicken pieces in a small amount of hot oil—just enough to barely cover the bottom of the pan.

STIR-FRYING: Cut chicken into small even-size pieces, then cook quickly over high heat in a small amount of very hot oil, stirring constantly.

Lemon-Rosemary Roast Chicken

Prep: 10 minutes
Roast: About 1 hour

1 chicken (3½ pounds)
1 lemon, cut in half
1 bunch fresh rosemary
¾ teaspoon salt
½ teaspoon coarsely ground black pepper
¼ cup chicken broth

1. Preheat oven to 450°F. Remove giblets and neck from chicken; reserve for another use. Rinse chicken inside and out with cold running water; pat dry with paper towels.

2. Squeeze juice from lemon halves; set juice and lemon halves aside. Reserve 4 rosemary sprigs; chop enough remaining rosemary to equal 1 tablespoon. Place lemon halves and rosemary sprigs inside cavity of chicken. In cup, combine chopped rosemary, ¼ teaspoon salt, and ¼ teaspoon pepper. With fingertips, gently separate skin from meat on chicken breast and thighs. Rub rosemary mixture on meat under skin. Sprinkle remaining ½ teaspoon salt and remaining ¼ teaspoon pepper on chicken.

3. With breast side up, lift wings up toward neck, then fold wing tips under back of chicken so wings stay in place. With string, tie legs together. Place chicken, breast side up, on rack in medium roasting pan (14" by 10"). Pour lemon juice over chicken.

4. Roast chicken about 1 hour. Chicken is done when temperature on meat thermometer inserted in thickest part of thigh, next to body, reaches 175° to 180°F and juices run clear when thigh is pierced with tip of knife.

5. Transfer chicken to warm medium platter; let stand 10 minutes to set juices for easier carving.

6. Meanwhile, remove rack from roasting pan. Skim and discard fat from pan juices. Add broth to pan juices; heat to boiling over medium heat, stirring to loosen browned bits from bottom of pan. Carve chicken, arrange on platter, and serve with pan juices. Remove skin from chicken before eating, if you like. Makes 4 main-dish servings.

Each serving without skin: About 280 calories, 42 g protein, 1 g carbohydrate, 11 g total fat (3 g saturated), 129 mg cholesterol, 570 mg sodium.

Roast Chicken with 40 Cloves of Garlic

Prep: 15 minutes
Roast: About 1 hour

1 chicken (3½ pounds)
6 thyme sprigs
½ teaspoon salt
¼ teaspoon coarsely ground black pepper
40 garlic cloves (about 2 heads), unpeeled, with loose papery skin removed
1 cup chicken broth

1. Preheat oven to 450°F. Remove giblets and neck from chicken; reserve for another use. Rinse chicken inside and out with cold running water; pat dry with paper towels.

2. With fingertips, gently separate skin from meat on chicken breast. Place 4 thyme sprigs on meat under skin of chicken breast. Place remaining 2 thyme sprigs inside cavity of chicken. Sprinkle salt and pepper on chicken.

3. With breast side up, lift wings up toward neck, then fold wing tips under back of chicken so wings stay in place. With string, tie legs together. Place chicken, breast side up, on rack in medium roasting pan (14" by 10").

4. Roast chicken 30 minutes. Add garlic cloves to pan and roast about 30 minutes longer. Chicken is done when temperature on meat thermometer inserted in thickest part of thigh, next to body, reaches 175° to 180°F and juices run clear when thigh is pierced with tip of knife.

5. Transfer chicken to warm medium platter; let stand 10 minutes to set juices for easier carving.

6. Meanwhile, remove rack from roasting pan. With

slotted spoon, transfer garlic cloves to small bowl. Skim and discard fat from pan juices. Discard skin from 6 garlic cloves; add peeled garlic and broth to roasting pan. Heat broth mixture to boiling over medium heat, stirring to loosen browned bits from bottom of pan, and mashing garlic with spoon, until well blended.

7. Carve chicken, arrange on platter, and serve with pan juices, and remaining garlic cloves. Remove skin from chicken before eating, if you like. Makes 4 main-dish servings.

Each serving without skin: About 330 calories, 45 g protein, 10 g carbohydrate, 11 g total fat (3 g saturated), 129 mg cholesterol, 590 mg sodium.

Roast Chicken with
Creamy Mushroom Sauce

Prep: 15 minutes
Roast: About 1 hour

1 chicken (3½ pounds)
½ teaspoon salt
¼ teaspoon coarsely ground black pepper
1 package (8 ounces) white mushrooms, each trimmed and cut into quarters
1 package (3½ ounces) shiitake mushrooms, stems removed and each cap cut into quarters
1 tablespoon all-purpose flour
1¼ cups reduced-sodium chicken broth
2 tablespoons heavy or whipping cream
1 tablespoon chopped fresh parsley leaves

1. Preheat oven to 450°F. Remove giblets and neck from chicken; reserve for another use. Rinse chicken inside and out with cold running water; pat dry with paper towels. Sprinkle salt and pepper on chicken.

2. With breast side up, lift wings up toward neck, then fold wing tips under back of chicken so wings stay in place.

With string, tie legs together. Place chicken, breast side up, on rack in medium roasting pan (14" by 10").

3. Roast chicken 15 minutes; add mushrooms to roasting pan, stir to mix with pan juices, and roast about 45 minutes longer. Chicken is done when temperature on meat thermometer inserted in thickest part of thigh, next to body, reaches 175° to 180°F and juices run clear when thigh is pierced with tip of knife.

4. Transfer chicken to warm platter; let stand 10 minutes to allow juices to set for easier carving.

5. Meanwhile, remove rack from roasting pan. Skim and discard fat from pan juices. In small bowl, with wire whisk, mix flour and ¼ cup chicken broth until smooth; stir into mushroom mixture in roasting pan. Heat mushroom mixture over medium heat, stirring constantly, 1 minute. Slowly stir remaining 1 cup broth into roasting pan; cook, stirring constantly, until mixture boils and has thickened slightly, about 5 minutes.

6. Remove pan from heat; stir in cream and parsley. Carve chicken, arrange on platter, and serve with mushroom sauce. Remove skin from chicken before eating, if you like. Makes 4 main-dish servings.

Each serving without skin: About 330 calories, 45 g protein, 6 g carbohydrate, 14 g total fat (5 g saturated), 139 mg cholesterol, 570 mg sodium.

Mahogany Chicken

Prep: 10 minutes
Roast: 1 hour 15 minutes

1 chicken (3½ pounds)
¾ teaspoon salt
½ teaspoon coarsely ground black pepper
2 tablespoons balsamic vinegar
2 tablespoons dry vermouth
2 tablespoons dark brown sugar
¼ cup water

1. Preheat oven to 375°F. Remove giblets and neck from chicken; reserve for another use. Rinse chicken inside and out with cold running water and pat dry with paper towels.

2. With breast side up, lift wings up toward neck, then fold wing tips under back of chicken so wings stay in place. With string, tie legs together.

3. Place chicken, breast side up, on rack in medium roasting pan (14" by 10"); sprinkle salt and pepper on chicken. Roast chicken 45 minutes.

4. Meanwhile, prepare glaze: In small bowl, stir vinegar, vermouth, and brown sugar, until sugar has dissolved.

5. After chicken has roasted 45 minutes, brush with some glaze. Turn oven control to 400°F and roast chicken, brushing with glaze twice more during roasting, until chicken is a deep brown color, about 30 minutes longer. Chicken is done when temperature on meat thermometer inserted in thickest part of thigh, next to body, reaches 175° to 180°F and juices run clear when thigh is pierced with tip of knife. Transfer chicken to warm medium platter; let stand 10 minutes to set juices for easier carving.

6. Meanwhile, remove rack from roasting pan. Add water to pan juices; heat to boiling over medium heat, stirring to loosen browned bits from bottom of pan. Remove pan from heat; skim and discard fat from pan juices. Carve chicken, arrange on platter, and serve with pan juices. Makes 4 main-dish servings.

Each serving: About 405 calories, 43 g protein, 9 g carbohydrate, 21 g total fat (6 g saturated), 170 mg cholesterol, 530 mg sodium.

Roast Chicken with Herb Butter

Prep: 10 minutes
Roast: About 1 hour

1 chicken (3½ pounds)
3 tablespoons margarine or butter, softened
2 tablespoons chopped fresh chives
1 tablespoon chopped fresh parsley leaves
¼ teaspoon salt
¼ teaspoon coarsely ground black pepper

1. Preheat oven to 450°F. Remove giblets and neck from chicken; reserve for another use. Rinse chicken inside and out with cold running water; pat dry with paper towels.

2. In cup, stir margarine, chives, and parsley until blended. With fingertips, gently separate skin from meat on chicken breast and thighs. Rub herb mixture on meat under skin. Sprinkle salt and pepper on chicken.

3. With breast side up, lift wings up toward neck, then fold wing tips under back of chicken so wings stay in place. With string, tie legs together. Place chicken, breast side up, on rack in medium roasting pan (14" by 10").

4. Roast chicken about 1 hour. Chicken is done when temperature on meat thermometer inserted in thickest part of thigh, next to body, reaches 175° to 180°F and juices run clear when thigh is pierced with tip of knife.

5. Transfer chicken to warm medium platter; let stand 10 minutes to set juices for easier carving. To serve, carve chicken and arrange on platter. Remove skin from chicken before eating, if you like. Makes 4 main-dish servings.

Each serving without skin: About 350 calories, 42 g protein, 0 g carbohydrate, 19 g total fat (5 g saturated), 129 mg cholesterol, 370 mg sodium.

5 STEPS TO A PICTURE-PERFECT ROAST CHICKEN

1. Remove the giblets (usually packed in a paper bag) from cavity, then rinse the entire chicken inside and out under cold running water. Carefully pat dry inside and outside with paper towels.
2. Before roasting, use your fingers to remove the fatty flaps under the skin near the cavity (so there's less fat to trim later).
3. Lift wing tips up toward neck, then fold wing tips under back of chicken. This helps wings stay in place, prevents them from burning, and helps to steady the bird.
4. Bring the legs together and tie with kitchen string (or, in a pinch, heavy-duty thread) to secure. This helps the chicken brown evenly.
5. Using an instant-read thermometer, start testing the temperature of the chicken after 50 minutes of roasting, placing thermometer point in thickest part of thigh, next to the body. Chicken is done when thermometer reaches 175° to 180°F and the juices run clear when the thickest part of the thigh is pierced with the tip of a small, sharp knife. Because an instant-read thermometer isn't oven-safe, remove it if chicken needs to roast longer.

Plum-Glazed Chicken

Prep: 10 minutes
Roast: About 1 hour

1 chicken (3½ pounds)
¼ cup plum jam
½ teaspoon salt
¾ teaspoon Chinese five-spice powder
2 tablespoons margarine or butter, softened
¼ teaspoon coarsely ground black pepper

1. Preheat oven to 450°F. Remove giblets and neck from chicken; reserve for another use. Rinse chicken inside and out with cold running water; pat dry with paper towels.

2. In small bowl, stir plum jam, ¼ teaspoon salt, and ½ teaspoon five-spice powder. In another small bowl, stir margarine, pepper, remaining ¼ teaspoon salt, and remaining ¼ teaspoon five-spice powder until blended. With fingertips, gently separate skin from meat on chicken breast and thighs. Rub butter mixture on meat under skin.

3. With breast side up, lift wings up toward neck, then fold wing tips under back of chicken so wings stay in place. With string, tie legs together. Place chicken, breast side up, on rack in medium roasting pan (14" by 10").

4. Roast chicken about 1 hour, brushing occasionally with plum-jam mixture during last 10 minutes. Chicken is done when temperature on meat thermometer inserted in thickest part of thigh, next to body, reaches 175° to 180°F and juices run clear when thigh is pierced with tip of knife.

5. Place chicken on warm medium platter; let stand 10 minutes to set juices for easier carving. To serve, carve chicken and arrange on platter. Makes 4 main-dish servings.

Each serving: About 485 calories, 44 g protein, 14 g carbohydrate, 27 g total fat (7 g saturated), 174 mg cholesterol, 470 mg sodium.

Broiled Chicken Teriyaki

Prep: 10 minutes
Broil: 45 minutes

⅓ cup plus 1 tablespoon soy sauce
2 tablespoons vegetable oil
1 tablespoon dry sherry
1 large green onion, finely chopped
2 teaspoons freshly grated orange peel
1 small garlic clove, crushed with garlic press
¼ teaspoon ground ginger
¼ teaspoon crushed red pepper
1 chicken (3 pounds), cut in half
1 tablespoon brown sugar

1. Preheat broiler. Lightly oil rack in broiling pan. In small bowl, stir together ⅓ cup soy sauce, oil, sherry, green onion, orange peel, garlic, ginger, and crushed red pepper.

2. Place chicken halves, skin side down, in prepared broiling pan. Brush chicken halves with some soy-sauce mixture. Broil 7 to 9 inches from heat source until golden, about 25 minutes.

3. Turn chicken skin side up; broil about 20 minutes longer, brushing with soy-sauce mixture often during last 10 minutes of broiling time. Chicken is done when juices run clear when thickest part of chicken is pierced with tip of knife.

4. In cup, combine brown sugar and remaining 1 tablespoon soy sauce. Brush brown-sugar mixture on chicken halves; broil 30 seconds longer to glaze.

5. To serve, cut chicken into pieces with poultry shears and arrange on warm medium platter. Makes 4 main-dish servings.

Each serving: About 465 calories, 46 g protein, 6 g carbohydrate, 27 g total fat (7 g saturated), 178 mg cholesterol, 1,165 mg sodium.

Rosemary-Apricot Chicken

Prep: 20 minutes plus marinating
Bake: 45 minutes

4 garlic cloves, crushed with garlic press
2 teaspoons salt
½ teaspoon ground black pepper
1 teaspoon dried rosemary, crumbled
3 chickens (3 pounds each), each cut into quarters and skin removed
½ cup apricot jam
2 tablespoons fresh lemon juice
2 teaspoons Dijon mustard

1. In cup, combine garlic, salt, pepper, and rosemary; use to rub on chicken quarters. Place chicken in large bowl, cover and refrigerate about 2 hours to marinate.

2. Preheat oven to 350°F. Place chicken quarters,

skinned side up, in two large roasting pans (17" by 11½" each) or two jelly-roll pans (15½" by 10½" each). Bake chicken 25 minutes, rotating pans between upper and lower racks halfway through baking.

3. Meanwhile, in small bowl, stir apricot jam, lemon juice, and mustard until blended. Brush apricot mixture on chicken; bake 20 minutes longer, rotating pans between upper and lower racks halfway through baking. Chicken is done when juices run clear when thickest part of thigh is pierced with tip of knife. Arrange chicken on large platter and serve chicken hot, or cover and refrigerate to serve cold later. Makes 12 main-dish servings.

Each serving: About 275 calories, 36 g protein, 10 g carbohydrate, 9 g total fat (3 g saturated), 109 mg cholesterol, 485 mg sodium.

Zucchini-Stuffed Chicken Quarters

Prep: 20 minutes
Cook: 52 minutes

3 tablespoons margarine or butter
2 medium zucchini (about 8 ounces each), trimmed and shredded
3 slices white bread, torn into small pieces
1 large egg
2 ounces Swiss cheese, shredded (about ½ cup)
½ teaspoon salt
⅛ teaspoon ground black pepper
1 chicken (3 pounds), cut into quarters
2 tablespoons honey

1. In 2-quart saucepan, melt margarine over medium heat. Add zucchini and cook, stirring frequently, until tender, about 2 minutes. Remove from heat; stir in bread, egg, cheese, ½ teaspoon salt, and pepper.

2. Preheat oven to 400°F. With fingertips, gently separate skin from meat on chicken pieces to form a pocket; place some stuffing in each pocket. Place chicken, stuffing side up, in 13" by 9" baking pan. Sprinkle remaining ¼ teaspoon salt on chicken. Bake chicken until juices run clear when thickest part of chicken is pierced with tip of a knife, about 50 minutes. Brush chicken with honey, arrange on warm medium platter, and serve. Makes 4 main-dish servings.

Each serving: About 565 calories, 45 g protein, 22 g carbohydrate, 33 g total fat (10 g saturated), 212 mg cholesterol, 815 mg sodium.

Rosemary and Lemon-Broiled Chicken

Prep: 5 minutes
Broil: 45 minutes

¾ teaspoon salt
⅛ teaspoon coarsely ground black pepper
¾ teaspoon dried rosemary, crumbled
1 chicken (2½ pounds), cut into quarters
3 tablespoons margarine or butter, cut up
1 tablespoon fresh lemon juice

1. Preheat broiler. Sprinkle salt, pepper, and rosemary on chicken quarters. Place chicken, skin side down, in jelly-roll pan; dot with margarine. Pour lemon juice over chicken.

2. Broil 7 to 9 inches from heat source 5 minutes. Baste chicken with pan drippings and broil 20 minutes longer. Turn chicken and broil, basting occasionally with pan drippings, about 15 to 20 minutes longer. Chicken is done when juices run clear when thickest part of chicken is pierced with tip of knife.

3. To serve, arrange chicken quarters on warm medium platter; spoon pan juices over chicken. Makes 4 main-course servings.

Each serving: About 345 calories, 31 g protein, 1 g carbohydrate, 24 g total fat (6 g saturated), 121 mg cholesterol, 640 mg sodium.

Country Captain Casserole

Prep: 1 hour
Bake: 1 hour

2 tablespoons plus 1 teaspoon
vegetable oil
2 chickens (3½ pounds each),
each cut into 8 pieces and
skin removed
2 medium onions, chopped
1 large Granny Smith apple,
peeled, cored, and coarsely
chopped
1 large green pepper, chopped
3 large garlic cloves, finely
chopped

1 tablespoon grated, peeled
fresh ginger
3 tablespoons curry powder
½ teaspoon coarsely ground
black pepper
¼ teaspoon ground cumin
1 can (28 ounces) tomatoes in
puree
1 can (14½ ounces) chicken
broth
½ cup dark seedless raisins
1 teaspoon salt

1. In 8-quart Dutch oven, heat 2 tablespoons oil over medium-high heat until very hot. Add chicken, and cook, until chicken is browned, using tongs to transfer chicken to bowl as it is browned.

2. Preheat oven to 350°F. In same Dutch oven, heat remaining 1 teaspoon oil over medium-high heat. Add onions, apple, green pepper, garlic, and ginger and cook, stirring frequently, 2 minutes. Reduce heat to medium; cover and cook 5 minutes.

3. Stir in curry powder, pepper, and cumin; cook, stirring, 1 minute. Add tomatoes with their puree, broth, raisins, salt, and chicken pieces and any juices in bowl. Heat to boiling over high heat; boil 1 minute, breaking tomatoes up with side of spoon.

4. Cover, place in oven, and bake until chicken pieces lose their pink color throughout, about 1 hour. Makes 8 main-dish servings.

Each serving: About 325 calories, 39 g protein, 21 g carbohydrate, 10 g total fat (2 g saturated), 122 mg cholesterol, 710 mg sodium.

Chicken Curry with Papaya

Prep: 15 minutes
Cook: 1 hour

2 tablespoons all-purpose flour
1 chicken (3 pounds), cut into 8
    pieces
2 tablespoons vegetable oil
1 medium stalk celery, finely
    chopped
1 small onion, finely chopped
1 tablespoon curry powder
1 medium Granny Smith apple,
    peeled, cored, and coarsely
    chopped
1 cup water

¼ cup golden raisins
1 ½ teaspoons salt
¼ teaspoon coarsely ground
    black pepper
1 bay leaf
1 small garlic clove, crushed
    with garlic press
¼ cup heavy or whipping
    cream
1 papaya, peeled, seeded,
    and sliced
¼ cup salted peanuts

1. On waxed paper, place flour. Use to coat chicken, shaking off excess. In 12-inch skillet heat oil over medium-high heat until very hot. Add chicken in batches, and cook, until chicken is browned, using tongs to transfer pieces to plate as they are browned.

2. In drippings in same skillet, cook celery, onion, and curry powder over medium heat, until vegetables are tender-crisp, about 2 minutes. Stir in apple, water, raisins, salt, pepper, bay leaf, and garlic; add chicken and any juice on plate; heat to boiling. Reduce heat to low; cover and simmer, stirring occasionally, until chicken is fork-tender and loses its pink color throughout, about 45 minutes.

3. Discard bay leaf. Skim and discard fat from pan juices; stir in cream. Arrange papaya slices on chicken. Cover and simmer until papaya is heated through. Transfer to warmed serving dish, sprinkle with peanuts and serve. Makes 4 main-dish servings.

Each serving: About 630 calories, 45 g protein, 28 g carbohydrate, 38 g total fat (11 g saturated), 181 mg cholesterol, 1,040 mg sodium.

Baked "Fried" Chicken

Prep: 15 minutes
Bake: 35 minutes

Olive oil nonstick cooking spray
½ cup plain dried bread crumbs
¼ cup grated Parmesan cheese
2 tablespoons cornmeal
½ teaspoon ground red pepper (cayenne)
1 large egg white
½ teaspoon salt
1 chicken (3½ pounds), cut into 8 pieces and skin removed

1. Preheat oven to 425°F. Spray 15½" by 10½" jelly-roll pan with cooking spray.

2. On waxed paper, combine bread crumbs, Parmesan, cornmeal, and ground red pepper. In pie plate, beat egg white and salt.

3. Dip each piece of chicken in egg-white mixture letting excess drip off, then coat with crumb mixture, firmly pressing so mixture adheres. Arrange chicken in prepared pan; spray lightly with cooking spray.

4. Bake chicken until coating is crisp and juices run clear when thickest part of chicken is pierced with tip of knife, about 35 minutes. To serve, arrange on warm medium platter. Makes 4 main-dish servings.

Each serving: About 365 calories, 45 g protein, 14 g carbohydrate, 13 g total fat (4 g saturated), 126 mg cholesterol, 630 mg sodium.

Roasted Chicken and Vegetables

Prep: 20 minutes
Bake: 50 minutes

1 chicken (3 pounds), cut into 8 pieces and skin removed
1 pound all-purpose potatoes (3 medium), unpeeled and cut into
    2-inch chunks
1 medium fennel bulb (1½ pounds), trimmed and cut into
    8 wedges
1 large red onion, cut into 8 wedges
2 tablespoons olive oil
1 tablespoon chopped fresh thyme or 1 teaspoon dried thyme
1¼ teaspoons salt
½ teaspoon ground black pepper
⅓ cup water

1. Preheat oven to 450°F. In large roasting pan (17" by 11½"), place chicken pieces, potatoes, fennel, and red onion. Add oil, thyme, salt, and pepper, and toss to coat chicken and vegetables well.

2. Roast 20 minutes; baste chicken and vegetables with any pan juices. Roast 20 minutes longer, basting once, until juices run clear when thickest part of chicken breast is pierced with tip of knife. Transfer chicken breasts to warm large platter; cover and keep warm.

3. Continue roasting, until juices run clear when remaining chicken pieces are pierced with tip of knife, and vegetables are tender, about 10 minutes longer. Transfer chicken and vegetables to platter with breasts.

4. To pan juices, add water, stirring to loosen browned bits from bottom of pan. To serve, spoon pan juices over chicken and vegetables. Makes 4 main-dish servings.

Each serving: About 395 calories, 40 g protein, 33 g carbohydrate, 12 g total fat (2 g saturated), 114 mg cholesterol, 875 mg sodium.

Chicken in Wine

Prep: 25 minutes
Cook: 1 hour

4 ounces bacon, coarsely
  chopped
1 pound small white onions,
  trimmed and peeled
1 chicken, (2½ pounds), cut
  into 8 pieces
12 ounces mushrooms, each
  trimmed and cut in half
2 medium carrots, peeled and
  sliced

1 cup chicken broth
2 tablespoons dry sherry
½ teaspoon salt
½ teaspoon dried thyme
½ teaspoon sugar
1 tablespoon all-purpose flour
2 tablespoons water

1. In 5-quart Dutch oven, cook bacon over medium heat, until lightly browned and crisp, pressing it with back of spoon until all fat has been rendered. With slotted spoon, transfer bacon to paper towels to drain; reserve.

2. In drippings reserved in Dutch oven, cook onions until browned, stirring occasionally. With slotted spoon, transfer onions to bowl.

3. In drippings in Dutch oven, cook chicken, in small batches, over medium-high heat, until browned, using tongs to transfer pieces to bowl with onions as they are browned.

4. Return onions and chicken and any juice in bowl to Dutch oven; stir in mushrooms, carrots, broth, sherry, salt, thyme, and sugar. Heat to boiling over high heat, stirring to loosen browned bits from bottom of Dutch oven. Reduce heat to low; cover and simmer until chicken loses its pink color throughout and vegetables are tender, 30 to 35 minutes. Skim and discard fat from pan juices.

5. In cup, stir flour and water; stir into pan juices. Cook over medium heat, stirring, until pan juices boil and have thickened slightly. To serve, transfer stew to warmed serving dish; sprinkle bacon on top. Makes 4 main-dish servings.

Each serving: About 465 calories, 41 g protein, 19 g carbohydrate, 25 g total fat (8 g saturated), 142 mg cholesterol, 720 mg sodium.

Creole Chicken Stew

Prep: 17 minutes
Cook: 55 minutes

¼ cup olive oil
1 chicken (3 pounds), cut into 8 pieces
1 medium onion, chopped
1 medium green pepper, coarsely chopped
1 stalk celery, coarsely chopped
1 garlic clove, finely chopped
1 tablespoon all-purpose flour

1 can (28 ounces) tomatoes
1 package (10 ounces) frozen sliced okra
1 teaspoon salt
½ teaspoon hot pepper sauce
1 can (12 ounces) whole-kernel corn
1 cup regular long-grain rice

1. In 5-quart Dutch oven, heat oil over medium-high heat until very hot. Add chicken, in batches, and cook, until chicken is well browned, using tongs to transfer chicken to bowl as it is browned.

2. In drippings in Dutch oven, cook onion, green pepper, celery, and garlic, over medium heat, stirring occasionally, until lightly browned, about 15 minutes. With slotted spoon, transfer vegetables to bowl with chicken.

3. Into drippings in Dutch oven, stir flour; cook, stirring, 1 minute. Stir in tomatoes and their juice, breaking them up with side of spoon; stir in okra, salt, and hot pepper sauce. Return chicken, vegetables, and any juice in bowl to Dutch oven; heat to boiling. Reduce heat to low; cover and simmer, stirring occasionally, until chicken is fork-tender and loses its pink color throughout, about 30 minutes. Stir in corn and cook until heated through.

4. Meanwhile, prepare rice as label directs.

5. To serve, transfer stew to warmed dish and serve with rice. Makes 4 main-dish servings.

Each serving: About 825 calories, 45 g protein, 64 g carbohydrate, 44 g total fat (10 g saturated), 145 mg cholesterol, 1,125 mg sodium.

Beer-Batter Chicken

Prep: 7 minutes
Cook: 40 minutes

Vegetable oil for frying
⅔ cup all-purpose flour
1 teaspoon salt
½ teaspoon baking powder
⅓ cup beer
1 large egg
1 chicken (3 pounds), cut into 8 pieces

1. In heavy 12-inch skillet (at least 2 inches deep) heat ½ inch oil over medium heat, until temperature on deep-fat thermometer reaches 350°F.

2. Meanwhile, in medium bowl, stir together flour, salt, and baking powder. In another bowl, with fork, beat beer, egg, and 2 teaspoons oil; stir into flour mixture until blended.

3. Dip half of the chicken pieces into batter, turning to coat chicken completely. Carefully place chicken, skin side up, in hot oil. Cook until underside of chicken is golden, about 5 minutes; reduce heat to low, and cook 5 minutes longer. With slotted spatula, loosen chicken from pan bottom. Turn chicken skin side down. Increase heat to medium-high and cook until skin side of chicken is golden, about 5 minutes. Reduce heat to low; cook until juices run clear when thickest part of chicken is pierced with tip of knife, about 5 minutes longer. Drain chicken pieces, skin side up, on paper towels. Transfer to warm large platter and keep warm. Repeat with remaining batter and chicken. Serve chicken hot. Makes 4 main-dish servings.

Each serving: About 535 calories, 45 g protein, 17 g carbohydrate, 30 g total fat (7 g saturated), 218 mg cholesterol, 770 mg sodium.

Southern Fried Chicken

Prep: 10 minutes
Cook: 1 hour 15 minutes

Vegetable oil for frying
½ cup milk
2 cups all-purpose flour
1¼ teaspoons salt
½ teaspoon ground black pepper
2 chickens (3 pounds each), cut into 8 pieces
1½ cups chicken broth
1 cup half-and-half

1. In heavy 12-inch skillet (at least 2 inches deep) heat ½ cup oil, over medium heat, until temperature on a deep-fat thermometer reaches 350°F. Meanwile, pour milk into pie plate. On waxed paper, combine 1¾ cups flour, 1 teaspoon salt, and pepper. Dip chicken pieces in milk, then coat well with flour mixture, shaking off excess. Repeat, coating chicken pieces twice.

2. Carefully place one-third of chicken pieces, skin side up, in hot oil. Cook until underside of chicken is golden, about 5 minutes; reduce heat to low, and cook 5 minutes longer. With slotted spatula, loosen chicken from pan bottom. Turn chicken skin side down. Increase heat to medium-high and cook until skin side of chicken is golden, about 5 minutes. Reduce heat to low, and cook until juices run clear when thickest part of chicken is pierced with tip of knife, about 5 minutes longer. Drain chicken pieces, skin side up, on paper towels. Transfer to large platter and keep warm. Repeat twice more with remaining chicken.

3. When chicken is done, prepare gravy: In 2-quart saucepan, heat 3 tablespoons oil over medium heat. Stir in remaining ¼ cup flour until blended. Cook, stirring constantly, until flour is lightly browned. Gradually stir in broth, half-and-half, and remaining ¼ teaspoon salt; cook, stirring constantly, until gravy has thickened and boils. Boil

1 minute. Pour into a gravy boat. Serve chicken with gravy. Makes 8 main-dish servings.

Each serving: About 635 calories, 47 g protein, 26 g carbohydrate, 37 g total fat (9 g saturated), 178 mg cholesterol, 650 mg sodium.

Crispy Chicken with 3 Dipping Sauces

Prep: 30 minutes
Bake: 30 to 35 minutes

Olive-oil nonstick cooking spray
1¾ cups walnuts
1 cup plain dried bread crumbs
1½ teaspoons salt
¼ to ½ teaspoon ground red pepper (cayenne)
2 large eggs
8 medium bone-in chicken breast halves (3½ pounds), skin removed, each cut crosswise in half

8 medium chicken drumsticks (1¾ pounds), skin and fat removed
Blue-Cheese Sauce (see page 258)
Honey-Mustard Sauce (see page 258)
Apricot-Balsamic Sauce (see page 258)

1. Preheat oven to 450°F. Spray two 15½" by 10½" jelly-roll pans with olive-oil cooking spray.

2. In food processor with knife blade attached, process walnuts with ¼ cup bread crumbs until walnuts are finely ground. Place nut mixture, salt, ground red pepper, and remaining ¾ cup bread crumbs in medium bowl; stir well to combine.

3. In pie plate, with fork, beat eggs. One at a time, dip chicken-breast pieces and drumsticks in beaten egg letting excess drip off, then coat with crumb mixture, firmly pressing so mixture adheres. Arrange in prepared pans. Spray chicken pieces with olive-oil cooking spray.

4. Bake chicken, 30 to 35 minutes, rotating pans between upper and lower racks halfway through baking, until chicken is golden brown, and juices run clear when thickest part of chicken is pierced with tip of a knife.

5. While chicken is cooking, prepare sauces. Cover and refrigerate sauces if not serving right away.

6. Serve chicken hot with dipping sauces. Or, cool chicken slightly; cover and refrigerate to serve cold later with sauces. Makes 18 main-dish servings.

BLUE-CHEESE SAUCE: In medium bowl, stir together *4 ounces blue cheese,* crumbled (about 1 cup), *½ cup mayonnaise, ½ cup plain low-fat yogurt, ½ teaspoon hot pepper sauce,* and *¼ teaspoon coarsely ground black pepper.* Makes about 1½ cups.

HONEY-MUSTARD SAUCE: In medium bowl, stir together *⅔ cup Dijon mustard, ¼ cup sour cream, ¼ cup honey,* and *¾ teaspoon Worcestershire sauce.* Makes about 1¼ cups.

APRICOT-BALSAMIC SAUCE: In medium bowl, stir together *1 jar (12 ounces) apricot preserves* (1 cup), *2 tablespoons balsamic vinegar, 1 tablespoon soy sauce,* and *¼ teaspoon freshly grated orange peel.* Makes about 1¼ cups.

Each serving chicken without sauces: About 230 calories, 23 g protein, 7 g carbohydrate, 12 g total fat (2 g saturated), 84 mg cholesterol, 320 mg sodium.

Each tablespoon blue-cheese sauce: About 55 calories, 1 g protein, 0 g carbohydrate, 5 g total fat (2 g saturated), 6 mg cholesterol, 95 mg sodium.

Each tablespoon honey-mustard sauce: About 30 calories, 1 g protein, 4 g carbohydrate, 1 g total fat (0 g saturated), 1 mg cholesterol, 205 mg sodium.

Each tablespoon apricot-balsamic sauce: About 50 calories, 0 g protein, 12 g carbohydrate, 0 g total fat, 0 mg cholesterol, 55 mg sodium.

Chicken Bouillabaisse

Prep: 1 hour
Bake: 30 minutes

1 tablespoon olive oil
8 large bone-in chicken thighs
   (2½ pounds), skin and fat
   removed
2 large carrots, peeled and
   coarsely chopped
1 medium onion, chopped
1 medium fennel bulb (1¼
   pounds), trimmed and sliced
½ cup water
3 garlic cloves, finely chopped

1 can (14½ ounces) diced
   tomatoes
1 can (14½ ounces) chicken
   broth
½ cup dry white wine
2 tablespoons anise-flavored
   liqueur (optional)
½ teaspoon salt
⅛ teaspoon ground red pepper
   (cayenne)
¼ teaspoon dried thyme
1 bay leaf
Pinch saffron threads

1. In 5-quart Dutch oven, heat oil over medium-high heat until very hot. Add half of chicken thighs, and cook until browned, about 12 minutes, using tongs to transfer to bowl as it is browned. Repeat with remaining chicken.

2. In same Dutch oven cook carrots and onion over medium heat, until tender and golden, stirring occasionally, about 10 minutes; transfer to bowl with chicken.

3. Preheat oven to 350°F. Add fennel and water to Dutch oven, stirring to loosen browned bits from bottom of pan. Cook, stirring occasionally, until fennel is tender and browned, about 7 minutes; add garlic and cook, stirring frequently, 3 minutes longer.

4. Return chicken, carrot mixture, and any juice in bowl to Dutch oven; add tomatoes with their juice, broth, wine, anise liqueur, if using, salt, ground red pepper, thyme, bay leaf, and saffron. Heat to boiling over high heat. Cover, place in oven, and bake until chicken thighs lose their pink color throughout, about 30 minutes. Discard bay leaf. Serve chicken in shallow soup plates with vegetables and pan juices. Makes 4 main-dish servings.

Each serving: About 310 calories, 32 g protein, 24 g carbohydrate, 10 g total fat (2 g saturated), 119 mg cholesterol, 935 mg sodium.

Chicken Stew with Rosemary Dumplings

Prep: 20 minutes
Cook: 1 hour

2 teaspoons salt
6 medium bone-in chicken-breast halves (3¼ pounds), skin removed
2 tablespoons vegetable oil
4 large carrots, peeled and sliced 1 inch thick
2 large stalks celery, sliced ¼ inch thick
1 medium onion, chopped
1 cup plus 2 tablespoons all-purpose flour
2 teaspoons baking powder

1½ teaspoons chopped fresh rosemary or ½ teaspoon dried rosemary, crumbled
1½ cups milk
1 large egg
2 cups water
1 can (14½ ounces) chicken broth
¼ teaspoon ground black pepper
1 package (10 ounces) frozen peas

1. Sprinkle ½ teaspoon salt on chicken breasts. In 8-quart Dutch oven, heat 1 tablespoon oil over medium-high heat until very hot. Add 3 chicken-breast halves and cook until chicken is lightly browned, 8 to 10 minutes, using tongs to transfer chicken to bowl as it is browned. Repeat with remaining chicken breast halves.

2. Add remaining 1 tablespoon oil to Dutch oven. Stir in carrots, celery, and onion and cook, stirring frequently, until vegetables are browned and tender, about 10 minutes.

3. While vegetables are cooking, prepare dumplings: In

medium bowl, stir together 1 cup flour, baking powder, rosemary, and ½ teaspoon salt. In cup, with fork, mix ½ cup milk with egg. Stir milk mixture into flour mixture just until blended.

4. Return chicken and any juice in bowl to Dutch oven; add water, broth, pepper, and remaining 1 teaspoon salt; heat to boiling. Drop dumpling mixture by rounded tablespoons on top of chicken and vegetables to make 12 dumplings. Cover; reduce heat to low, and simmer 15 minutes.

5. With slotted spoon, carefully transfer dumplings, chicken, and vegetables to large bowl, reserving broth in Dutch oven.

6. In small bowl, stir remaining 2 tablespoons flour with remaining 1 cup milk until blended; stir into broth mixture. Heat to boiling over high heat, stirring constantly, until sauce has thickened slightly, 1 minute. Add peas and heat through. Return chicken, dumplings, and vegetables to Dutch oven; heat through and serve. Makes 6 main-dish servings.

Each serving: About 400 calories, 40 g protein, 37 g carbohydrate, 10 g total fat (3 g saturated), 124 mg cholesterol, 1230 mg sodium.

Tandoori-Style Chicken

Prep: 10 minutes plus marinating
Roast: 30 minutes

1 container (8 ounces) plain
    low-fat yogurt
2 tablespoons fresh lime juice
½ small onion, chopped
1 tablespoon minced, peeled
    fresh ginger
¾ teaspoon salt
¼ teaspoon ground red pepper
    (cayenne)

1 tablespoon paprika
1 teaspoon ground cumin
1 teaspoon ground coriander
Pinch ground cloves
6 medium bone-in chicken
    breast halves (3 pounds),
    skin removed
Lime wedges

1. In blender, process yogurt, lime juice, onion, ginger, salt, ground red pepper, paprika, cumin, coriander, and cloves until smooth. Place chicken in medium bowl or zip-tight plastic bag and pour in yogurt mixture. Turn to coat chicken with yogurt mixture. Cover chicken or close bag and refrigerate 30 minutes to marinate.

2. Preheat oven to 450°F. Place chicken on rack in medium roasting pan (14" by 10"). Spoon half of yogurt marinade over chicken; discard remainder. Roast chicken until juices run clear when thickest part of chicken breast is pierced with tip of knife, about 30 minutes. Arrange chicken on warm medium platter and serve with lime wedges to squeeze over each portion. Makes 6 main-dish servings.

Each serving: About 175 calories, 30 g protein, 4 g carbohydrate, 4 g total fat (1 g saturated), 79 mg cholesterol, 285 mg sodium.

Chicken with Asparagus and Mushrooms

Prep: 20 minutes
Cook: About 25 minutes

¾ teaspoon salt
¼ teaspoon coarsely ground black pepper
4 medium skinless, boneless chicken breast halves (about 1¼ pounds)
3 teaspoons olive oil
1 medium onion, chopped
4 ounces shiitake mushrooms, stems discarded and caps thinly sliced

4 ounces white mushrooms, trimmed and thinly sliced
1½ pounds asparagus, trimmed and cut into 2-inch pieces
¼ cup water
½ cup half-and-half or light cream

1. Sprinkle ¼ teaspoon salt and pepper on chicken.
2. In nonstick 12-inch skillet, heat 1 teaspoon oil over medium-high heat until very hot. Add chicken and cook 6

minutes. Reduce heat to medium; turn chicken and cook until chicken loses its pink color throughout, 6 to 8 minutes longer. Transfer chicken to warm medium platter; cover loosely with foil to keep warm.

3. In same skillet, heat remaining 2 teaspoons oil over medium heat. Add onion, shiitake and white mushrooms and cook, stirring often, until vegetables are tender and liquid has evaporated, about 5 minutes.

4. Add asparagus, water, and remaining ½ teaspoon salt to mushroom mixture; heat to boiling. Cook, stirring often, until asparagus is tender-crisp, about 5 minutes. Stir in half-and-half; heat through.

5. To serve, spoon asparagus mixture over chicken. Makes 4 main-dish servings.

Each serving: About 270 calories, 38 g protein, 11 g carbohydrate, 9 g total fat (3 g saturated), 92 mg cholesterol, 510 mg sodium.

Balsamic Chicken and Pears

Prep: 10 minutes
Cook: 20 minutes

2 teaspoons vegetable oil
4 small skinless, boneless chicken breast halves (1 pound)
2 Bosc pears, unpeeled, each cored and cut into 8 wedges
1 cup chicken broth
3 tablespoons balsamic vinegar
2 teaspoons cornstarch
1½ teaspoons sugar
½ teaspoon salt
¼ cup dried cherries or dark seedless raisins

1. In nonstick 12-inch skillet, heat 1 teaspoon oil over medium-high heat until very hot. Add chicken breasts and cook 4 to 5 minutes per side, until chicken just loses its pink color throughout. Transfer chicken to warm medium platter.

2. In same skillet, heat remaining 1 teaspoon oil. Add pear wedges and cook until lightly browned and tender.

3. In small bowl, stir together broth, vinegar, cornstarch, sugar and salt until blended. Add broth mixture and dried cherries to skillet with pears. Heat to boiling, stirring constantly; boil 1 minute. Return chicken to skillet; heat through. Serve chicken with pears and pan juices. Makes 4 main-dish servings.

Each serving: About 235 calories, 27 g protein, 22 g carbohydrate, 4 g total fat (1 g saturated), 69 mg cholesterol, 240 mg sodium.

Tarragon and Grape Chicken

Prep: 15 minutes
Cook: About 20 minutes

½ teaspoon salt
¼ teaspoon coarsely ground black pepper
4 medium skinless, boneless chicken breast halves (about 1¼ pounds)
1 teaspoon olive oil
2 teaspoons margarine or butter
3 medium shallots, finely chopped (about ⅓ cup)

¼ cup dry white wine
¼ cup chicken broth
¼ cup half-and-half or light cream
1 cup seedless red and/or green grapes, each cut in half
1 tablespoon chopped fresh tarragon

1. Sprinkle ¼ teaspoon salt and pepper on chicken.

2. In nonstick 12-inch skillet, heat oil over medium-high heat until very hot. Add chicken breasts and cook 6 minutes. Reduce heat to medium; turn chicken, and cook until chicken just loses its pink color throughout, 6 to 8 minutes. Transfer chicken to warm medium platter; cover loosely with foil to keep warm.

3. In same skillet, melt margarine over medium-low heat. Add shallots and remaining ¼ teaspoon salt and cook, stirring, until tender and golden, 3 to 5 minutes. Stir in wine; cook 30 seconds. Stir in chicken broth, half-and-half, grapes, and tarragon. Return chicken and any juice on platter to skillet; heat through. Serve chicken with grapes and pan juices. Makes 4 main-dish servings.

Each serving: About 255 calories, 34 g protein, 10 g carbohydrate, 8 g total fat (2 g saturated), 87 mg cholesterol, 455 mg sodium.

Chicken with Creamy Leek Sauce

Prep: 15 minutes
Cook: About 25 minutes

1 small bunch leeks (about 1 pound)
½ teaspoon salt
¼ teaspoon coarsely ground black pepper
4 medium skinless, boneless chicken breast halves
     (about 1¼ pounds)
1 teaspoon olive oil
1 tablespoon margarine or butter
½ cup chicken broth
¼ cup dry white wine
¼ cup heavy or whipping cream

1. Cut off roots and trim dark green tops from leeks; cut each leek lengthwise in half, then crosswise into ¼-inch-wide slices. Rinse leeks in large bowl of cold water, swishing to remove sand; transfer to colander to drain, leaving sand in bottom of bowl.

2. Sprinkle ¼ teaspoon salt and ⅛ teaspoon pepper on chicken.

3. In nonstick 12-inch skillet, heat oil over medium-high heat until very hot. Add chicken breasts and cook 6 minutes. Reduce heat to medium; turn chicken, and cook, until chicken just loses its pink color throughout, 6 to 8 minutes. Transfer chicken to warm medium platter; cover loosely with foil to keep warm.

4. In same skillet, melt margarine over medium-low heat. Add leeks and cook, stirring frequently, until tender and golden, 5 to 7 minutes. Add broth and wine; heat to boiling over medium-high heat. Boil until slightly reduced, about 1 minute. Add cream, remaining ¼ teaspoon salt, and remaining ⅛ teaspoon pepper; heat to boiling. Boil until sauce has thickened slightly, 1 to 2 minutes longer.

5. To serve, pour sauce over chicken. Makes 4 main-dish servings.

Each serving: About 285 calories, 35 g protein, 9 g carbohydrate, 12 g total fat (5 g saturated), 103 mg cholesterol, 510 mg sodium.

Chicken Breasts with Cumin, Coriander and Lime

Prep: 10 minutes
Cook: 10 to 12 minutes

3 tablespoons fresh lime juice (about 2 limes)
1 teaspoon salt
⅛ teaspoon ground red pepper (cayenne)
1 teaspoon ground cumin
1 teaspoon ground coriander
1 teaspoon sugar
4 small skinless, boneless chicken breast halves (1 pound)
Nonstick cooking spray
1 tablespoon chopped fresh cilantro leaves

1. In large bowl, combine lime juice, salt, ground red pepper, cumin, coriander, and sugar; add chicken, tossing to coat.

2. Spray grill pan or cast-iron skillet with nonstick cooking spray; heat over medium-high heat until very hot. Add chicken and cook 5 to 6 minutes per side, until chicken loses its pink color throughout, brushing with any remaining lime mixture halfway through cooking. Place chicken breast on platter; sprinkle with cilantro and serve. Makes 4 main-dish servings.

Each serving: About 150 calories, 27 g protein, 3 g carbohydrate, 3 g total fat (1 g saturated), 72 mg cholesterol, 600 mg sodium.

Skillet Lemon Chicken

Prep: 15 minutes
Cook: About 15 minutes

4 medium skinless, boneless
  chicken breast halves
  (1 ¼ pounds)
2 tablespoons plus 1 ½
  teaspoons all-purpose flour
½ teaspoon salt
1 large egg
2 teaspoons olive oil
2 tablespoons margarine or
  butter

3 garlic cloves, crushed with
  side of chef's knife
½ lemon, thinly sliced
½ cup chicken broth
¼ cup dry white wine
2 tablespoons fresh lemon juice
2 tablespoons capers, drained
1 tablespoon chopped fresh
  parsley leaves

1. With meat mallet, or between two sheets of plastic wrap or waxed paper, with rolling pin, pound chicken breasts to flatten slightly. On waxed paper, combine 2 tablespoons flour with salt. In pie plate, with fork, beat egg. Coat chicken with flour mixture, then dip in egg, turning to coat.

2. In nonstick 12-inch skillet, heat oil over medium-high heat. Add 1 tablespoon margarine and heat until melted. Add chicken; cook 5 minutes. Reduce heat to medium; turn chicken and cook until chicken loses its pink color throughout, about 8 to 10 minutes longer. Transfer chicken to warm medium platter; keep warm.

3. Add garlic and lemon slices to drippings in skillet; cook, turning often, until golden. In small bowl, stir broth, wine, lemon juice, and remaining 1 ½ teaspoons flour until smooth; stir into skillet. Heat sauce to boiling, stirring constantly; boil 1 minute. Stir in capers and remaining 1 tablespoon margarine until margarine has melted. Discard garlic. To serve, arrange browned lemon slices over and between chicken breasts. Pour sauce over chicken and sprinkle with parsley. Makes 4 main-dish servings.

Each serving: About 275 calories, 36 g protein, 5 g carbohydrate, 11 g total fat (2 g saturated), 136 mg cholesterol, 705 mg sodium.

New Chicken Cordon Bleu

Prep: 10 minutes
Cook: About 15 minutes

1 tablespoon margarine or butter
4 small skinless, boneless chicken breast halves (1 pound)
½ cup chicken broth
2 tablespoons balsamic vinegar
⅛ teaspoon coarsely ground black pepper
4 thin slices cooked ham (about 2 ounces)
4 thin slices part-skim mozzarella cheese (about 2 ounces)
1 bag (5 to 6 ounces) prewashed baby spinach

1. In nonstick 12-inch skillet, melt margarine over medium-high heat. Add chicken breasts and cook until golden brown, about 6 minutes. Turn chicken, cover, and reduce heat to medium. Cook chicken until chicken loses its pink color throughout, about 6 minutes longer.

2. Increase heat to medium-high. Stir in broth, vinegar, and pepper; cook 1 minute. Remove skillet from heat; top each chicken breast with a slice of ham, then a slice of cheese. Cover skillet until cheese melts, about 3 minutes.

3. To serve, place spinach on warm large platter; top with chicken breasts and drizzle with pan juices. Makes 4 main-dish servings.

Each serving: About 225 calories, 34 g protein, 5 g carbohydrate, 8 g total fat (3 g saturated), 82 mg cholesterol, 560 mg sodium.

Chicken Roulades

Prep: 30 minutes
Cook: 20 minutes

4 small skinless, boneless chicken breast halves (1 pound)
Half 7-ounce jar roasted red peppers, drained and sliced
2 ounces herb-and-garlic goat cheese, crumbled
½ cup loosely packed fresh basil leaves
¼ teaspoon salt
¼ teaspoon coarsely ground black pepper
1 tablespoon olive oil

1. Holding knife parallel to surface, and starting from a long side, cut each chicken breast lengthwise almost in half, being careful not to cut all the way through. Open up and spread flat like a book. With meat mallet, or between two sheets of plastic wrap or waxed paper with rolling pin, pound chicken to about ¼-inch thickness.

2. Place one-fourth of red-pepper slices, goat cheese, and basil leaves on each chicken breast half. Starting from a long side, roll each chicken breast jelly-roll fashion; secure with toothpicks.

3. Sprinkle salt and pepper on chicken roulades. In non-stick 12-inch skillet, heat olive oil over medium-high heat until very hot. Add chicken roulades and cook until chicken is browned on all sides. Reduce heat to medium; cover and cook until chicken loses its pink color throughout, 12 to 15 minutes longer. Transfer roulades to cutting board. Discard toothpicks. To serve, slice roulades crosswise into diagonal slices and arrange on warm large platter. Makes 4 main-dish servings.

Each serving: About 205 calories, 29 g protein, 1 g carbohydrate, 9 g total fat (3 g saturated), 85 mg cholesterol, 315 mg sodium.

Grilled Chicken Cutlets with Tomato-Olive Relish

Prep: 15 minutes
Grill: 10 to 12 minutes

2 medium tomatoes, coarsely chopped
¼ cup Kalamata olives, pitted and coarsely chopped
2 tablespoons minced red onion
2 tablespoons capers, drained
3 teaspoons olive oil
1 teaspoon red wine vinegar
4 small skinless, boneless chicken breast halves (1 pound)
¼ teaspoon salt
¼ teaspoon coarsely ground black pepper

1. Prepare grill. In small bowl, combine tomatoes, olives, red onion, capers, 1 teaspoon olive oil, and vinegar.

2. In medium bowl, toss chicken breasts with salt, pepper, and remaining 2 teaspoons olive oil until coated.

3. Place chicken on grill over medium heat and grill chicken 5 to 6 minutes per side or until chicken loses its pink color throughout. Serve chicken topped with relish. Makes 4 main-dish servings.

Each serving: About 205 calories, 27 g protein, 4 g carbohydrate, 9 g total fat (2 g saturated), 72 mg cholesterol, 490 mg sodium.

Chicken Breasts with Pecan Crust

Prep: 10 minutes
Cook: 17 minutes

2 tablespoons maple syrup or maple-flavored syrup
4 medium skinless, boneless chicken breast halves (1¼ pounds)
1 cup pecans, chopped
3 tablespoons all-purpose flour
1 teaspoon salt
2 tablespoons vegetable oil
2 tablespoons margarine or butter

1. Brush maple syrup on chicken breast halves. On waxed paper, combine pecans, flour, and salt. Coat chicken breasts with nut mixture, firmly pressing so mixture adheres.

2. In 12-inch skillet, heat oil and margarine over medium heat until butter melts. Add chicken breasts; cook 6 to 8 minutes per side until chicken is browned and has lost its pink color throughout. Serve hot. Makes 4 main-dish servings.

Each serving: About 470 calories, 38 g protein, 16 g carbohydrate, 27 g total fat (3 g saturated), 96 mg cholesterol, 705 mg sodium.

Hearty Chicken and Vegetable Stew

Prep: 45 minutes
Cook: 1 hour

2 medium leeks (about
　4 ounces each)
2 tablespoons olive oil
2 tablespoons margarine or
　butter
1 pound skinless, boneless
　chicken breast halves,
　trimmed and cut into
　1½-inch pieces
8 ounces mushrooms, trimmed
　and thickly sliced
1 small fennel bulb (1 pound),
　trimmed and cut lengthwise
　into thin wedges
3 medium carrots (about
　8 ounces), peeled and
　cut into 1-inch pieces

12 ounces red potatoes, not
　peeled, cut into 1-inch
　pieces
1 bay leaf
¼ teaspoon dried tarragon
½ cup dry white wine
1 can (14½ ounces) chicken
　broth
¼ cup water
3 tablespoons all-purpose flour
¾ cup half-and-half or light
　cream
1 cup frozen peas, thawed
¾ teaspoon salt

1. Cut off roots and trim dark green tops from leeks; cut each leek lengthwise in half, then crosswise into ¾-inch pieces. Rinse leeks in large bowl of cold water, swishing to remove sand; transfer to colander to drain, leaving sand in bottom of bowl.

2. In 5-quart Dutch oven, heat 1 tablespoon oil over medium-high heat until hot. Add 1 tablespoon margarine and melt. Add chicken and cook, tossing frequently, until chicken is golden and just loses its pink color throughout. With slotted spoon, transfer chicken to bowl.

3. To drippings in Dutch oven, add mushrooms and cook until golden (do not overbrown). With slotted spoon, transfer mushrooms to bowl with chicken.

4. To Dutch oven, add remaining 1 tablespoon oil; heat until hot. Add remaining 1 tablespoon margarine and melt. Add leeks, fennel, carrots, potatoes, bay leaf, and tarragon. Cook vegetables, stirring occasionally, until fennel is translucent and leeks are wilted, about 10 to 15 minutes.

5. Add wine; cook, stirring, 2 minutes. Add broth and water; heat to boiling over high heat. Reduce heat to low; cover and simmer until vegetables are tender, about 20 minutes.

6. In cup, stir flour and half-and-half until smooth. Stir half-and-half mixture into vegetable mixture; heat to boiling over high heat, stirring. Reduce heat to medium; cook until slightly thickened, about 1 minute. Stir in chicken, mushrooms, peas, and salt; heat through. Discard bay leaf. To serve, spoon into shallow soup plates. Makes 4 main-dish servings.

Each serving: About 530 calories, 37 g protein, 53 g carbohydrate, 20 g total fat (5 g saturated), 85 mg cholesterol, 985 mg sodium.

Jamaican Jerk Island Kabobs

Prep: 20 minutes plus marinating
Cook: 10 minutes

2 green onions, chopped
1 jalapeño chile, seeded and
  chopped*
1 tablespoon chopped, peeled
  fresh ginger
2 tablespoons white wine
  vinegar
2 tablespoons Worcestershire
  sauce
3 teaspoons vegetable oil

½ teaspoon plus ⅛ teaspoon
  salt
1 teaspoon ground allspice
1 teaspoon dried thyme
1 pound skinless, boneless
  chicken breast halves, cut
  into 12 pieces
2 medium red peppers, cut into
  1-inch pieces
4 metal skewers

1. In blender, process green onions, jalapeño, ginger, vinegar, Worcestershire, 2 teaspoons oil, ½ teaspoon salt, allspice, and thyme until well combined. Place chicken pieces in medium bowl or zip-tight plastic bag; add green-onion mixture and turn to coat. Cover chicken or close bag and refrigerate 30 minutes to marinate.

2. Meanwhile, in small bowl, toss pepper pieces with remaining 1 teaspoon vegetable oil and remaining ⅛ teaspoon salt; set aside.

3. Preheat broiler. Alternately thread chicken and pepper pieces on skewers.

4. Place kabobs on rack in broiling pan. Brush kabobs with any remaining marinade. Broil at closest position to heat source 5 minutes per side or until chicken loses its pink color throughout. To serve, slide kabobs off skewers onto plates. Makes 4 main-dish servings.

If you like spicy-hot food, leave some or all of the seeds in the jalapeño chile.

Each serving: About 195 calories, 27 g protein, 8 g carbohydrate, 6 g total fat (1 g saturated), 72 mg cholesterol, 385 mg sodium.

Stir-Fried Chicken and Vegetables

Prep: 30 minutes
Cook: 10 minutes

4 large skinless, boneless chicken breast halves (1½ pounds), cut crosswise into ⅛-inch-thick slices
¼ cup soy sauce
1 tablespoon dry sherry
2 teaspoons cornstarch
½ teaspoon sugar
Two 2-inch-long pieces fresh ginger, each about ¾ inch in diameter
¼ cup vegetable oil
8 ounces mushrooms, trimmed and sliced

2 medium carrots, peeled and thinly sliced
1 medium zucchini (about 8 ounces), trimmed and thinly sliced
4 green onions, cut into 2-inch pieces
¼ teaspoon salt
1 can (15½ ounces) whole baby corn, drained (optional)
½ cup water

1. In medium bowl, combine chicken, soy sauce, sherry, cornstarch, and sugar.

2. Peel ginger; cut lengthwise into very thin slices and cut slices into hair-thin strips. In 12-inch skillet heat oil over medium-high heat until very hot. Add ginger and cook, stirring, until lightly browned, 1 to 2 minutes. With slotted spoon, transfer ginger to paper towels to drain.

3. In oil in skillet, cook mushrooms, carrots, zucchini, green onions, and salt, stirring quickly and frequently, until vegetables are tender-crisp. With slotted spoon, transfer vegetables to another bowl.

4. In oil in skillet, stir-fry chicken mixture over high heat, until chicken loses its pink color throughout. Return vegetables to skillet, corn, if desired, and water; cook, stirring constantly, until juices are lightly thickened. Spoon chicken mixture into warm serving bowl, sprinkle with fried ginger and serve. Makes 4 main-dish servings.

Each serving: About 380 calories, 43 g protein, 15 g carbohydrate, 16 g total fat (2 g saturated), 99 mg cholesterol, 1,305 mg sodium.

Szechwan Chicken

Prep: 22 minutes
Cook: 8 minutes

4 small skinless, boneless
   chicken breast halves
   (1 ½ pounds), cut crosswise
   into ⅛-inch-thick slices
2 tablespoons soy sauce
2 tablespoons dry sherry
2 teaspoons cornstarch
¼ teaspoon sugar
¼ teaspoon ground ginger

¼ teaspoon crushed red
   pepper
4 tablespoons vegetable oil
6 green onions cut into 2-inch
   pieces
2 medium green peppers, cut
   into 1-inch pieces
⅓ cup dry-roasted peanuts

1. In medium bowl, toss together chicken, soy sauce, sherry, cornstarch, sugar, ginger, and crushed red pepper until chicken is well coated.

2. In 12-inch skillet, heat 2 tablespoons oil over medium-high heat until very hot. Add green onions and green peppers, and cook, stirring quickly and frequently, until vegetables are tender-crisp, about 2 minutes. With slotted spoon, transfer vegetables to bowl.

3. In same skillet, heat remaining 2 tablespoons oil over medium heat, until very hot. Add peanuts and cook, stirring frequently, until lightly browned. With slotted spoon, transfer peanuts to bowl with vegetables.

4. In oil remaining in skillet, stir-fry chicken mixture, over high heat, until chicken loses its pink color throughout, about 2 to 3 minutes. Return vegetables, peanuts, and any juices in bowl to skillet; heat through. Serve hot. Makes 4 main-dish servings.

Each serving: About 360 calories, 31 g protein, 12 g carbohydrate, 21 g total fat (3 g saturated), 66 mg cholesterol, 595 mg sodium.

Sweet-and-Sour Chicken

Prep: 10 minutes
Cook: 15 minutes

¼ cup cider vinegar
2 tablespoons soy sauce
2 tablespoons water
2 tablespoons brown sugar
1 tablespoon cornstarch
½ teaspoon salt
3 tablespoons vegetable oil
1 medium onion, sliced

4 large skinless, boneless chicken breast halves (1½ pounds), cut into 1½-inch pieces
1 can (20 ounces) pineapple chunks in juice
1 package (10 ounces) frozen peas

1. In small bowl, stir together vinegar, soy sauce, water, brown sugar, cornstarch, and salt until sugar has dissolved.

2. In 12-inch skillet heat oil over medium heat. Add onion and cook, stirring occasionally, until tender. Increase heat to medium-high; add chicken and cook, stirring, until chicken loses its pink color throughout, about 5 minutes.

3. Add pineapple chunks with their juice, peas, and cornstarch mixture; cook, stirring frequently, until juices boil and have thickened. Serve hot. Makes 4 main-dish servings.

Each serving: About 470 calories, 44 g protein, 45 g carbohydrate, 13 g total fat (2 g saturated), 99 mg cholesterol, 985 mg sodium.

Mock Buffalo Chicken Wings

Prep: 8 minutes
Cook: 10 minutes

Nonstick cooking spray
1 package (about 1 pound) chicken tenders
½ cup reduced-fat sour cream
1 ounce blue cheese, crumbled (about ¼ cup)
2 tablespoons light mayonnaise
2 tablespoons nonfat (skim) milk
½ teaspoon Worcestershire sauce
¼ teaspoon coarsely ground black pepper

¼ cup Louisiana-style cayenne pepper sauce*
1 tablespoon water
1 tablespoon light corn-oil spread (40% fat)
1 bag (12 ounces) precut carrot sticks
1 bag (12 ounces) precut celery sticks

1. Spray a 12-inch skillet with nonstick cooking spray. Heat skillet over medium-high heat until hot. Add chicken tenders, and cook, stirring occasionally, until chicken loses its pink color throughout, about 8 minutes.

2. Meanwhile, in small bowl, with fork, mix sour cream, blue cheese, mayonnaise, milk, Worcestershire, and black pepper until blended.

3. Transfer tenders to warm small platter. Add cayenne pepper sauce and water to skillet; heat to boiling. Remove skillet from heat; stir in margarine until blended. Pour sauce over chicken. Serve chicken tenders with carrot and celery sticks, and blue-cheese dip. Makes 4 main-dish servings.

Louisiana-style cayenne pepper sauce is a milder variety of hot pepper sauce that adds tang and flavor, not just heat.

Each serving: About 270 calories, 31 g protein, 17 g carbohydrate, 8 g total fat (2 g saturated), 81 mg cholesterol, 1,180 mg sodium.

Tortilla Chicken Tenders with Easy Southwest Salsa

Prep: 15 minutes
Bake: 10 minutes

2 ounces baked tortilla chips
2 teaspoons chili powder
¼ teaspoon salt
Olive oil nonstick cooking spray
1 pound chicken tenders
2 medium ears corn, husks and silk removed
1 jar (11 to 12 ounces) mild salsa
¼ cup loosely packed fresh cilantro leaves, chopped
Lime wedges

1. Place tortilla chips in zip-tight plastic bag. Crush tortilla chips with rolling pin to fine crumbs (about ½ cup crumbs). On waxed paper, combine tortilla-chip crumbs, chili powder, and salt.

2. Preheat oven to 450°F. Spray 15½" by 10½" jelly-roll pan with cooking spray. Place chicken tenders in medium bowl; spray with cooking spray, tossing to coat well. Coat chicken with crumb mixture; arrange in prepared pan, and spray again.

3. Bake chicken until chicken loses its pink color throughout, about 10 minutes.

4. Meanwhile, cut corn kernels from cobs; place in small bowl. Stir in salsa and cilantro until blended.

5. Serve chicken with salsa and lime wedges. Makes 4 main-dish servings.

Each serving: About 245 calories, 30 g protein, 24 g carbohydrate, 3 g total fat (0 g saturated), 66 mg cholesterol, 685 mg sodium.

Chicken Provençal

Prep: 30 minutes
Cook: 1 hour

2 pounds skinless, boneless
  chicken thighs, each
  trimmed and cut into
  quarters
¾ teaspoon salt
2 teaspoons olive oil
2 medium red peppers, cut into
  ¼-inch-thick slices
1 medium yellow pepper, cut
  into ¼-inch-thick slices
1 jumbo onion (1 pound), thinly
  sliced

3 garlic cloves, crushed with
  garlic press
1 can (28 ounces) Italian-style
  plum tomatoes
3 strips (3" by 1" each) orange
  peel
¼ teaspoon dried thyme leaves
¼ teaspoon fennel seeds,
  crushed
½ cup loosely packed fresh
  basil leaves, chopped

1. Sprinkle chicken thighs with ½ teaspoon salt. In non-stick 5-quart Dutch oven, heat 1 teaspoon oil over medium-high heat until very hot. Add half of chicken and cook until lightly browned, about 10 minutes, using slotted spoon to transfer chicken to bowl as it is browned. Repeat with remaining 1 teaspoon oil, and chicken.

2. In drippings in Dutch oven, place peppers, onion, and remaining ¼ teaspoon salt. Cook, stirring frequently, until tender and lightly browned, about 20 minutes. Add garlic; cook, stirring, 1 minute.

3. Return chicken and any juice in bowl to Dutch oven. Add tomatoes with their juice, orange peel, thyme, and fennel seeds, breaking up tomatoes with side of spoon; heat to boiling. Reduce heat to low; cover and simmer until chicken is tender and has lost its pink color throughout, about 15 minutes.

4. To serve, transfer to warm serving dish and sprinkle with basil. Makes 8 main-dish servings.

Each serving: About 200 calories, 25 g protein, 13 g carbohydrate, 6 g total fat (1 g saturated), 94 mg cholesterol, 460 mg sodium.

Sticky Drumsticks

Prep: 20 minutes
Bake: About 35 minutes

½ cup apricot preserves
¼ cup teriyaki sauce
1 tablespoon dark brown sugar
1 teaspoon cider vinegar
1 teaspoon cornstarch
¼ teaspoon salt
12 medium chicken drumsticks (3 pounds), skin removed

1. Preheat oven to 425°F. In large bowl, with wire whisk, mix apricot preserves, teriyaki sauce, brown sugar, vinegar, cornstarch, and salt until blended. Add chicken drumsticks, tossing to coat.

2. Transfer chicken and sauce to 15½" by 10½" jelly-roll pan. Bake 15 minutes. Brush chicken with sauce in pan. Bake chicken until it loses its pink color throughout 15 to 20 minutes longer, brushing with sauce every 5 minutes.

3. Remove chicken from oven; brush with sauce. Allow chicken to cool 10 minutes. To serve, place chicken on large platter, spoon sauce in jelly-roll pan over chicken. Makes 6 main-dish servings.

Each serving: About 120 calories, 13 g protein, 12 g carbohydrate, 2 g total fat (1 g saturated), 48 mg cholesterol, 330 mg sodium.

Buffalo-Style Chicken Wings

Prep: 20 minutes
Broil: 25 minutes

1 container (8 ounces) sour
   cream
4 ounces blue cheese,
   crumbled
¼ cup chopped fresh parsley
¼ cup mayonnaise
1 tablespoon milk
1 tablespoon fresh lemon juice
½ teaspoon salt

6 tablespoons margarine or
   butter
2 tablespoons hot pepper
   sauce
3 pounds chicken wings (about
   18), wing tips discarded if
   you like
1 medium bunch celery, cut into
   sticks

1. Preheat broiler. Meanwhile, in medium bowl, stir together sour cream, blue cheese, parsley, mayonnaise, milk, lemon juice, and ¼ teaspoon salt. Cover and refrigerate.

2. In small saucepan, heat margarine and hot pepper sauce over low heat, stirring occasionally, until butter melts.

3. In broiling pan, arrange chicken wings; sprinkle remaining ¼ teaspoon salt on wings. Brush with some margarine mixture. Broil 5 to 7 inches from heat source 10 minutes. Turn wings; brush with remaining margarine mixture. Broil, until wings are golden and tender and lose their pink color throughout, 10 to 15 minutes longer.

4. To serve, arrange chicken wings and celery sticks on large platter. Pass blue-cheese sauce as dip for wings and celery. Makes 6 main-dish servings.

Each serving: About 610 calories, 33 g protein, 5 g carbohydrate, 51 g total fat (16 g saturated), 120 mg cholesterol, 845 mg sodium.

Oven-Fried Chicken Wings

Prep: 15 minutes
Bake: 35 minutes

6 tablespoons margarine or butter
⅔ cup plain dried bread crumbs
⅔ cup whole-wheat or all-purpose flour
1½ teaspoons salt
¾ teaspoon dried rosemary, crumbled
⅛ teaspoon ground black pepper
½ cup buttermilk
2 pounds chicken wings (about 12), wing tips removed,
   if you like

1. Preheat oven to 425°F. In medium roasting pan (14"
by 10") place margarine; place pan in oven until margarine
has melted. Remove pan from oven.

2. On waxed paper, combine bread crumbs, flour, salt,
rosemary, and pepper. Pour buttermilk into small bowl. Dip
1 chicken wing at a time, into buttermilk, then coat with
crumb mixture, firmly pressing so mixture adheres.

3. Place chicken wings in melted margarine in roasting
pan, turning to coat evenly. Bake until chicken wings are
fork-tender and lose their pink color throughout, about 35
minutes. Makes 4 main-dish servings.

*Each serving: About 575 calories, 34 g protein, 29 g carbohy-
drate, 36 g total fat (9 g saturated), 87 mg cholesterol, 1,335 mg
sodium.*

Chicken Potpie with Corn-Bread Crust

Prep: 45 minutes
Bake: 35 minutes

Chicken Filling

1 tablespoon margarine or
    butter
2 medium carrots, peeled and
    cut into ½-inch pieces
1 medium onion, cut into
    ¼-inch pieces
1 can (14½ ounces) chicken
    broth
¾ teaspoon salt
¼ teaspoon coarsely ground
    black pepper

¼ teaspoon dried thyme
3 tablespoons cornstarch
1½ cups low-fat (1%) milk
3 cups shredded cooked
    chicken (12 ounces), without
    skin
1 package (10 ounces) frozen
    whole-kernel corn, thawed
1 package (10 ounces) frozen
    lima beans, thawed

Corn-Bread Crust

½ cup all-purpose flour
½ cup cornmeal
1 tablespoon sugar
1½ teaspoons baking powder
½ teaspoon salt
2 tablespoons cold margarine or butter
¾ cup low-fat (1%) milk

1. Preheat oven to 375°F. Prepare Chicken Filling: In 3-quart saucepan, melt margarine over medium-low heat. Add carrots and onion, and cook, stirring occasionally, 5 minutes. Add broth, salt, pepper, and thyme; heat to boiling over high heat. Reduce heat to low; cover and simmer until vegetables are tender, about 10 minutes.

2. Meanwhile, in small bowl, with wire whisk, mix cornstarch and ½ cup milk until blended. Stir cornstarch mixture and remaining 1 cup milk into saucepan with carrots; heat to boiling over high heat, stirring constantly. Boil, stirring, 1 minute. Stir in chicken, corn, and lima beans. Transfer mixture to shallow 2½-quart casserole.

3. Prepare Corn-Bread Crust: In medium bowl, stir flour, cornmeal, sugar, baking powder, and salt. With pastry blender or two knives used scissor-fashion, cut in margarine until mixture resembles coarse crumbs. Stir in milk until blended and mixture thickens slightly. Pour mixture over filling; spread to form an even layer. Bake casserole until filling is bubbling and top is golden, about 35 minutes. Let cool a few minutes before serving. Makes 6 main-dish servings.

Each serving: About 440 calories, 32 g protein, 51 g carbohydrate, 13 g total fat (3 g saturated), 67 mg cholesterol, 960 mg sodium.

Chicken Livers Marsala

Prep: 16 minutes
Cook: 15 minutes

2 tablespoons margarine or butter
1 medium onion, sliced
1 pound chicken livers, each cut in half and trimmed
8 ounces medium mushrooms, each trimmed and cut in half
¾ teaspoon salt
⅛ teaspoon ground black pepper
1 tablespoon all-purpose flour
½ cup water
2 tablespoons Marsala wine

1. In 12-inch skillet, melt margarine over medium heat. Add onion and cook, stirring occasionally, until tender, about 5 minutes. Add chicken livers, mushrooms, salt, and pepper. Cook, stirring often, until livers are tender and have just lost their pink color throughout, about 5 minutes.

2. In small bowl, stir together flour, water, and Marsala until blended; gradually stir into mixture in skillet. Cook, stirring constantly, until pan juices boil and have thickened slightly. Serve chicken livers hot. Makes 4 main-dish servings.

Each serving: About 140 calories, 10 g protein, 8 g carbohydrate, 8 g total fat (2 g saturated), 187 mg cholesterol, 550 mg sodium.

Capon

Herb-Roasted Capon

Prep: 20 minutes plus marinating
Roast: 2 hours 30 minutes

3 tablespoons salt
⅛ teaspoon cracked black pepper
1 teaspoon dried parsley flakes
¾ teaspoon dried thyme
½ teaspoon dried sage
1 fresh or frozen (thawed) capon or oven roaster (6 pounds),
    giblets and neck reserved for another use
3 tablespoons olive oil

1. Rinse capon inside and out with cold running water;
pat dry with paper towels. In small bowl, combine salt,
pepper, parsley, thyme, and sage. Use to rub on outside and
in body cavity of capon. Place capon in large bowl or pan;
cover and refrigerate capon at least 12 hours or overnight
to marinate.

2. Preheat oven to 325°F. Fold neck skin under capon
and fasten to back with skewers. With breast side up, lift
wings up toward neck, then fold wing tips under back of
capon so wings stay in place. Depending on brand of capon,
tie legs and tail together, push drumsticks under band of
skin, or use stuffing clamp.

3. Place capon, breast side up, on rack in large roasting
pan (17" by 11½"). Brush skin with oil. Roast capon about
2½ hours. Start checking for doneness during last 30
minutes of roasting.

4. When capon turns golden, cover loosely with a tent
of foil. Remove foil during last 20 minutes of roasting time,
and brush capon generously with pan drippings for an attractive sheen.

5. Capon is done when temperature on meat thermometer inserted in thickest part of thigh, next to body, reaches 175° to 180°F and juices run clear when thigh is pierced with tip of knife. Transfer to warm large platter; let stand 15 minutes to set juices for easier carving. To serve, carve capon and arrange on platter. Remove skin from capon before eating, if you like. Makes 8 main-dish servings.

Each serving: About 395 calories, 44 g protein, 0 g carbohydrate, 23 g total fat (6 g saturated), 132 mg cholesterol, 2,690 mg sodium.

∾Cornish Hens

Cornish Hens with Wild-Rice-and-Mushroom Stuffing

Prep: 25 minutes
Cook/Roast: 50 minutes

Wild-Rice-and-Mushroom Stuffing (below)
4 fresh or frozen (thawed) Cornish hens (1½ pounds each), giblets and neck reserved for another use
¼ cup honey
2 tablespoons fresh lemon juice
2 tablespoons dry vermouth
½ teaspoon salt
¼ teaspoon dried thyme

1. Prepare Wild-Rice-and-Mushroom Stuffing (page 287).

2. Preheat oven to 400°F. With kitchen shears, cut each hen in half, cutting along the backbone and breastbone.

3. With fingertips, gently separate skin from meat on hen halves to form a pocket; spoon some stuffing into each pocket. Place hen halves, cut side down, in two large roasting pans (each 17" x 11½").

4. In small bowl, stir honey, lemon juice, vermouth, salt, and thyme. Brush hen halves with some honey mixture. Bake hens about 50 minutes, basting occasionally with remaining honey mixture and drippings in pans, and rotating pans between upper and lower racks halfway through baking time so that hens are evenly browned. Hens are done when juices run clear when thickest part of thigh is pierced with tip of knife. Transfer hens to dinner plates and serve. Makes 8 main-dish servings.

Each serving: About 495 calories, 32 g protein, 33 g carbohydrate, 26 g total fat (7 g saturated), 149 mg cholesterol, 595 mg sodium.

WILD-RICE-AND-MUSHROOM STUFFING: In 3-quart saucepan melt 3 tablespoons margarine over medium heat; add 1 pound mushrooms, trimmed and chopped, and cook, stirring occasionally, until tender. In a sieve, rinse 1 box (8 ounces) wild rice (1½ cups); drain. To mushroom mixture in saucepan, add wild rice, 2 cups water, 1 cup chicken broth, and ¾ teaspoon salt; heat to boiling over high heat. Reduce heat to low; cover and simmer until rice is tender and liquid has been absorbed, 45 to 50 minutes.

Cornish Hens with Ginger-Plum Glaze

Prep: 25 minutes
Grill: About 30 minutes

⅔ cup plum jam or preserves
3 teaspoons grated, peeled fresh ginger
4 large plums, each cut in half and pitted
2 tablespoons soy sauce
2 small garlic cloves, crushed with garlic press
¾ teaspoon salt
¼ teaspoon coarsely ground black pepper
1 teaspoon Chinese five-spice powder
2 fresh or frozen (thawed) Cornish hens (1½ pounds each),
   giblets and neck reserved for another use

1. Prepare grill. In 1-quart saucepan, heat plum jam and 1 teaspoon ginger over low heat, stirring, until jam melts, 1 to 2 minutes. Spoon 2 tablespoons plum glaze into medium bowl; add fresh plums and toss to coat. Reserve glaze.

2. With kitchen shears, cut each hen in half, cutting along the backbone and breastbone. Pat hens dry.

3. In small bowl, stir remaining 2 teaspoons ginger with soy sauce, garlic, salt, pepper, and Chinese five-spice powder. Brush mixture on hen halves.

4. Place hen halves, skin side down, on grill over medium heat and grill 15 minutes, turning once. Brush skin side of hens with plum glaze from saucepan; turn hens, and grill 5 minutes. Brush hens with remaining glaze; turn, and grill until juices run clear when thickest part of thigh is pierced with tip of knife and hens are golden, about 10 minutes longer.

5. Just before hens are done, place plums on grill and grill about 3 minutes per side or until plums are hot and lightly browned. Serve hens with grilled plums. Makes 4 main-dish servings.

Each serving: About 435 calories, 29 g protein, 49 g carbohydrate, 15 g total fat (1 g saturated), 52 mg cholesterol, 985 mg sodium.

⌒Turkey

For general thawing and stuffing instructions, a roasting timetable, and how much turkey to buy, see pages 232–235.

Small turkeys, cut into serving-sized pieces, can be fried or oven-fried like chicken or cooked on a barbecue grill. Pieces from larger birds are better braised or stewed. Whole turkeys are usually roasted, but they can also be cooked on a rotisserie or in a covered barbecue grill, or they can be braised.

Turkey and turkey parts come fresh or frozen. There is no significant difference in quality between the two and your choice should be based on personal preference.

ROASTING TURKEY PIECES

Turkey breasts. Roast at 175° to 180°F on a meat thermometer (about 25 minutes per pound), to avoid drying out the meat.

Turkey halves and hindquarters roasts. Roast at 175° to 180°F on a meat thermometer (about 20 to 22 minutes per pound).

Turkey parts. Place the pieces in a single layer on a rack in a shallow roasting pan; cover loosely with foil. Roast at 175° to 180°F on a meat thermometer.

Roast Turkey with Pan Gravy

Prep: 45 minutes (not including time to prepare stuffing)
Roast: About 3 hours 45 minutes

Choice of stuffing (see pages 305–309)
1 fresh or frozen (thawed) turkey (14 pounds)
1½ teaspoons salt
½ teaspoon coarsely ground black pepper
Pan Gravy (see page 290)

1. Prepare any one of the recommended stuffings; set aside.

2. Preheat oven to 325°F. Remove giblets and neck from turkey; reserve for making Pan Gravy. Rinse turkey inside and out with cold running water; pat dry with paper towels.

3. Spoon some stuffing lightly into neck cavity (do not pack stuffing; it expands during cooking). Fold neck skin over stuffing; fasten neck skin to back with one or two skewers. With breast side up, fold wings under back of turkey so they stay in place.

4. Spoon some stuffing lightly into body cavity. (Bake any leftover stuffing in greased small covered casserole during last 45 minutes of roasting time.) Depending on brand of turkey, with string, tie legs and tail together, or push drumsticks under band of skin, or use stuffing clamp.

5. Place turkey, breast side up, on rack in large roasting pan (17" by 11½"). Sprinkle salt and pepper on turkey. Cover turkey with a loose tent of foil. Roast turkey about 3 hours 45 minutes; start checking for doneness during last hour of roasting.

6. While turkey is roasting, cook giblets and neck as directed below for Pan Gravy.

7. To brown turkey, remove foil during last 1 hour of roasting time and baste occasionally with pan drippings. Turkey is done when temperature on meat thermometer inserted in thickest part of thigh, next to body, reaches 175° to 180°F and juices run clear when thigh is pierced with tip of knife.

8. When turkey is done, transfer to warm large platter; cover loosely with foil to keep warm. Prepare Pan Gravy.

9. Carve turkey, arrange on platter and serve with gravy. Remove skin from turkey before eating, if you like. Makes 14 main-dish servings.

PAN GRAVY: In 3-quart saucepan, heat gizzard, heart, neck, and *enough water to cover* to boiling over high heat. Reduce heat to low; cover and simmer 45 minutes. Add liver and cook 15 minutes longer. Drain through sieve, reserving broth. Pull meat from neck; discard bones. Coarsely chop neck meat and giblets. Cover and refrigerate meat and broth separately.

To make gravy, remove rack from roasting pan. Pour pan

drippings through sieve into 4-cup measuring cup. Add 1 cup giblet broth to roasting pan and stir until browned bits are loosened from bottom of pan; add to drippings in measuring cup. Let stand a few seconds, until fat separates from pan juice. Skim off fat from pan juices; spoon about 2 tablespoons into 2-quart saucepan. Discard remainder, if any. Add remaining giblet broth and enough *water* to juice in cup to equal 3 cups.

Heat drippings in saucepan over medium heat; stir in 2 *tablespoons all-purpose flour* and *½ teaspoon salt* until blended. Cook, stirring, until flour turns golden brown. Gradually stir in juice mixture and cook, stirring, until gravy boils and has thickened slightly. Stir in reserved giblets and neck meat; heat through. Pour gravy into gravy boat.

Each serving of turkey without skin or gravy: About 330 calories, 57 g protein, 0 g carbohydrate, 10 g total fat (3 g saturated), 149 mg cholesterol, 250 mg sodium.

Each ¼ cup gravy: About 65 calories, 7 g protein, 2 g carbohydrate, 4 g total fat (1 g saturated), 63 mg cholesterol, 110 mg sodium.

Low-Stress Make-Ahead Gravy

Prep: 10 minutes
Cook: 1 hour 30 minutes

2 tablespoons vegetable oil
2 turkey wings (1½ pounds),
    separated at joints
1 large onion, cut into
    4 pieces
2 carrots, peeled and each cut
    into 4 pieces
2 stalks celery, each cut into 4
    pieces

½ cup dry white wine
2 cans (14½ ounces each)
    chicken broth
3 cups water
1 garlic clove, sliced
¼ teaspoon dried thyme
½ cup all-purpose flour

1. In 5-quart saucepot, heat oil over medium-high heat until very hot. Add turkey wings and cook, turning occasionally, until golden, about 10 minutes. Add onion, carrots, and celery and cook, stirring frequently, until vegetables and turkey wings are browned, 8 to 10 minutes. With slotted spoon, transfer turkey and vegetables to bowl.

2. Add wine to saucepot and stir until browned bits are loosened from bottom of pot; boil 1 minute. Return turkey and vegetables to saucepot; stir in broth, water, garlic, and thyme; heat to boiling over high heat. Reduce heat to low and simmer 45 minutes. Drain through sieve, reserving broth. Discard bones and vegetables.

3. Let broth stand a few seconds until fat separates from meat juice. Skim off fat from juices; spoon about ¼ cup fat into 2-quart saucepan. Discard remainder, if any.

4. Heat drippings in saucepan over medium heat. Stir in flour and cook, stirring, until flour turns golden brown. Gradually stir in reserved broth and cook, stirring, until gravy boils and has thickened slightly. Pour gravy into medium bowl; place plastic wrap directly on surface of gravy and refrigerate up to 3 days.

5. To serve, reheat on stove top or in microwave. If serving with a roast turkey or chicken, stir in some of the pan drippings. Makes about 6 cups without pan drippings.

Each ¼ cup: About 50 calories, 1 g protein, 2 g carbohydrate, 4 g total fat (1 g saturated), 3 mg cholesterol, 115 mg sodium.

Roast Turkey Breast with Caramelized Shallots

Prep: 40 minutes
Roast: 2 hours 30 minutes

1 tablespoon olive oil
8 ounces shallots or red onion, peeled and thinly sliced (2 cups)
4 garlic cloves, thinly sliced
1 tablespoon balsamic vinegar
2 tablespoons brown sugar
½ teaspoon salt

¼ teaspoon coarsely ground black pepper
1 bone-in turkey breast (6 to 7 pounds)
½ cup dry red wine
1 cup chicken broth
1 tablespoon cornstarch

1. In nonstick 10-inch skillet, heat oil over medium heat. Add shallots and cook, stirring occasionally, until tender and golden, 8 minutes. Add garlic and cook, stirring, 1 minute. Stir in vinegar, brown sugar, salt, pepper, and *1 tablespoon water;* cook 1 minute. Transfer to bowl and cool to room temperature.

2. Preheat oven to 325°F. With fingertips, gently separate skin from meat on turkey breast. Spread cooled shallot mixture on meat under skin.

3. Place turkey breast, skin side up, on rack in medium roasting pan (14" by 10"). Cover turkey breast with a loose tent of foil. Roast turkey 2 hours 30 minutes to 3 hours. Start checking for doneness during last 30 minutes of roasting.

4. To brown turkey breast, remove foil during last 1 hour of roasting and baste with pan drippings occasionally. Turkey breast is done when temperature on meat thermometer inserted in thickest part of breast registers 175° to 180°F and juices run clear when thickest part of breast is pierced with tip of knife. Transfer turkey to cutting board. Let stand 15 minutes to set juices for easier slicing.

5. Meanwhile, prepare sauce: Remove rack from roasting pan. Skim and discard fat from drippings in pan. In nonstick 2-quart saucepan, heat wine to boiling over high heat; boil 2 minutes. Stir in broth, *½ cup water,* and pan drippings; heat to boiling. In cup, dissolve cornstarch in *1 tablespoon water;* whisk into boiling sauce, and boil 1 minute. Pour sauce through sieve into gravy boat. Carve turkey breast, arrange on warm large platter, and serve with sauce. Makes 10 main-dish servings.

Each serving with sauce: About 445 calories, 60 g protein, 10 g carbohydrate, 17 g total fat (5 g saturated), 152 mg cholesterol, 320 mg sodium.

Rolled Turkey Breast with Basil Mayonnaise

Prep: 45 minutes
Roast: About 1 hour 15 minutes

Rolled Turkey Breast
1 whole turkey breast with bones (6 to 7 pounds)
2 teaspoons salt
1 teaspoon coarsely ground black pepper
1 jar (12 ounces) roasted red peppers, drained and sliced
1½ cups loosely packed fresh basil leaves
1 tablespoon olive oil

Basil Mayonnaise
2 cups loosely packed fresh basil leaves
1 cup light mayonnaise
1 cup reduced-fat sour cream
2 teaspoons fresh lemon juice
¼ teaspoon salt

1. Prepare Rolled Turkey Breast: Place turkey breast on cutting board, skin side up. With sharp knife, working with 1 side of breast, starting parallel and close to large end of rib bone, cut and scrape meat away from bone and rib cage, gently pulling back meat in one piece as you cut. Repeat with remaining side of breast; discard bones and skin.

2. To butterfly breast halves: Place 1 breast half, cut side up, on cutting board. Use sharp knife, starting at a long side, cut breast lengthwise almost in half, being careful not to cut all the way through, making sure that meat on other long side stays connected. Open and spread flat like a book. Place butterflied breast between 2 sheets of plastic wrap. With meat mallet or rolling pin, pound breast to about ¼-inch thickness. Repeat with second breast half.

3. Preheat oven to 350°F. Sprinkle ½ teaspoon salt and ¼ teaspoon pepper on each breast half. Arrange red-pepper slices evenly over breasts, leaving a 2-inch border all around edges of meat; top with basil leaves. Starting at a narrow end, roll each breast with filling, jelly-roll fashion. With string, tie each rolled turkey breast at 2-inch intervals. Brush rolls with oil and sprinkle with remaining 1 teaspoon salt and ½ teaspoon pepper.

4. Place rolls, seam sides down, on rack in large roasting pan (17" by 11½"). Roast turkey rolls about 1 hour and 15 minutes. Turkey is done when temperature on meat thermometer inserted in thickest part of breast reaches 175° to 180°F and turkey has lost its pink color throughout.

5. While turkey is roasting, prepare Basil Mayonnaise: In food processor with knife blade attached, or in blender, process basil, mayonnaise, sour cream, lemon juice, and salt until sauce is creamy. Cover and refrigerate sauce until ready to serve. Makes about 2 cups.

6. When turkey rolls are done, place on large platter. Let stand 10 minutes to set juices for easier carving if serving warm. If not serving right away, cool to room temperature, then wrap and refrigerate turkey rolls until ready to serve.

7. To serve, remove strings. Slice turkey rolls into ¼-inch-thick slices and serve with Basil Mayonnaise. Makes 12 main-dish servings.

Each serving of turkey: About 195 calories, 41 g protein, 2 g carbohydrate, 2 g total fat (1 g saturated), 112 mg cholesterol, 465 mg sodium.

Each tablespoon Basil Mayonnaise: About 55 calories, 1 g protein, 7 g carbohydrate, 3 g total fat (0 g saturated), 6 mg cholesterol, 245 mg sodium.

Sautéed Turkey Cutlets with Mushroom Sauce

Prep: About 15 minutes
Cook: About 15 minutes

¼ teaspoon salt
¼ teaspoon coarsely ground black pepper
1¼ pounds turkey cutlets
4 teaspoons olive oil
1 garlic clove, crushed with garlic press
1 pound mushrooms, trimmed and sliced
¼ teaspoon dried thyme
1 cup chicken broth
1 teaspoon cornstarch

1. Sprinkle salt and pepper on turkey cutlets. In nonstick 12-inch skillet, heat 2 teaspoons oil over medium-high heat until very hot. Add turkey cutlets and cook 1½ to 3 minutes per side, until lightly browned on the outside and cutlets have lost their pink color throughout. Transfer cutlets to warm medium platter; cover loosely with foil, and keep warm.
2. In same skillet, heat remaining 2 teaspoons olive oil over medium heat. Add garlic and cook, stirring, 10 seconds. Add mushrooms and thyme and cook, stirring occasionally, until mushrooms are golden and liquid has evaporated, about 10 minutes longer. In cup, stir broth and cornstarch until smooth. Add broth mixture to skillet and heat to boiling, stirring constantly. Cook 2 minutes. Spoon sauce over cutlets and serve. Makes 4 main-dish servings.

Each serving: About 245 calories, 37 g protein, 6 g carbohydrate, 8 g total fat (2 g saturated), 85 mg cholesterol, 420 mg sodium.

Turkey Cutlets à l'Orange

Prep: 10 minutes
Cook: About 6 minutes

½ teaspoon salt
¼ teaspoon coarsely ground black pepper
1 pound turkey cutlets
2 teaspoons olive oil
⅓ cup orange marmalade
2 tablespoons red wine vinegar
1 tablespoon grated, peeled fresh ginger
1 small navel orange, cut into wedges

1. Sprinkle salt and pepper on turkey cutlets. In nonstick 12-inch skillet, heat oil over medium-high heat until very hot. Add turkey cutlets and cook 2 minutes per side, until lightly browned on the outside and have lost their pink color throughout.

2. Meanwhile, in small bowl, combine marmalade, vinegar, and ginger.

3. Add marmalade mixture to turkey cutlets in skillet; heat to boiling. Transfer turkey to warm medium platter; spoon pan juices over turkey and serve with orange wedges. Makes 4 main-dish servings.

Each serving: About 220 calories, 27 g protein, 20 g carbohydrate, 4 g total fat (1 g saturated), 68 mg cholesterol, 340 mg sodium.

Spicy Turkey Chili

Prep: 5 minutes
Cook: 15 minutes

1 teaspoon olive oil
1 pound ground turkey breast
    meat
1 small onion, chopped
¼ teaspoon salt
1 teaspoon ground coriander
1 teaspoon ground cumin
2 cans (15 to 16 ounces each)
    no-salt-added navy or small
    white beans, rinsed and
    drained

1 can (14½ ounces) reduced-
    sodium chicken broth
1 package (10 ounces) frozen
    whole-kernel corn, thawed
1 can (4 to 4½ ounces)
    chopped mild green chiles,
    drained
2 tablespoons Louisiana-style
    cayenne pepper sauce*
1 cup chopped fresh cilantro
    leaves

1. In nonstick 12-inch skillet, heat oil over medium-high heat until very hot. Add ground turkey and onion; cook, breaking up meat with side of spoon, until meat loses its pink color throughout and the liquid has evaporated, about 10 minutes. Stir in salt, coriander, and cumin; cook, stirring, 1 minute.

2. Meanwhile, in small bowl, mash half of beans.

3. Add mashed and unmashed beans, broth, corn, and green chiles to turkey mixture. Heat to boiling over medium-high heat; stir in pepper sauce. Transfer chili to warm serving dish and sprinkle chili with cilantro. Makes about 6 cups or 6 main-dish servings.

Louisiana-style cayenne pepper sauce is a milder variety of hot pepper sauce that adds tang and flavor, not just heat.

Each serving: About 270 calories, 28 g protein, 33 g carbohydrate, 3 g total fat (1 g saturated), 45 mg cholesterol, 825 mg sodium.

Turkey Burgers

Prep: 10 minutes
Cook: 20 minutes

3 teaspoons olive oil
1 small onion, finely chopped
1 garlic clove, crushed with
    garlic press
1 pound ground turkey breast
    meat
1 large egg

2 tablespoons milk
1 slice firm white bread,
    crumbled
3 tablespoons mango chutney,
    chopped
½ teaspoon salt
¼ teaspoon dried sage

1. In nonstick 12-inch skillet, heat 1 teaspoon olive oil over medium heat. Add onion and garlic and cook, stirring often, until onion is tender, about 5 minutes. Transfer mixture to large bowl; set skillet aside.

2. Add ground turkey, egg, milk, bread, chutney, salt, and sage to onion mixture; combine just until well blended but not overmixed. With wet hands, shape mixture into four 1-inch-thick patties, handling meat as little as possible.

3. In same skillet, heat remaining 2 teaspoons oil over medium heat until very hot. Add patties and cook about 6 minutes per side, turning once, until browned and patties have lost their pink color throughout. Serve hot. Makes 4 main-dish servings.

Each serving: About 235 calories, 28 g protein, 13 g carbohydrate, 7 g total fat (2 g saturated), 113 mg cholesterol, 375 mg sodium.

Turkey-Meatball Pitas

Prep: 15 minutes
Bake: 12 to 15 minutes

Nonstick cooking spray
1 pound ground turkey meat
3 tablespoons water
1 large egg white
2 slices low-fat bread, chopped
2 tablespoons grated onion
1¼ teaspoons salt
1½ teaspoons ground cumin
5 (6 inch) whole-wheat pitas

1 container (8 ounces) nonfat
   plain yogurt
½ large cucumber, peeled and
   cut into ¾-inch pieces
2 tablespoons chopped fresh
   cilantro or 1 teaspoon dried
   mint leaves
4 cups thinly sliced romaine
   lettuce

1. Preheat oven to 425°F. Spray 15½" by 10½" jelly-roll pan with nonstick cooking spray.

2. In large bowl, with hands, mix ground turkey, water, egg white, bread, onion, ¾ teaspoon salt, and cumin until well blended but not overmixed.

3. With wet hands, shape turkey mixture into 25 meatballs. Place meatballs in prepared pan; bake until meatballs lose their pink color throughout, 12 to 15 minutes.

4. Meanwhile, cut about 1-inch from top of each pita; reserve cutoff pieces for another use. Wrap pitas in foil. After meatballs have baked 5 minutes, place pitas in oven to warm until meatballs are done.

5. In small bowl, stir together yogurt, cucumber, cilantro, and remaining ½ teaspoon salt.

6. To serve, fill pitas with lettuce and meatballs; top with cucumber sauce. Makes 5 main-dish servings.

Each serving: About 380 calories, 28 g protein, 44 g carbohydrate, 11 g total fat (3 g saturated), 46 mg cholesterol, 1,020 mg sodium.

Moo Shu Turkey

Prep: 20 minutes
Cook: About 15 minutes

8 (6 inch) low-fat flour tortillas
3 tablespoons hoisin sauce
2 tablespoons soy sauce
¾ teaspoon Asian sesame oil
1 bunch green onions
3 teaspoons olive oil
1 package (8 ounces) sliced
  mushrooms
1 package (16 ounces)
  shredded cabbage mix for
  coleslaw

½ medium red pepper, thinly
  sliced
1 garlic clove, crushed with
  garlic press
2 teaspoons grated, peeled
  fresh ginger
12 ounces cooked turkey meat,
  without skin, pulled into
  shreds (2 cups)

1. Warm tortillas as label directs.

2. Meanwhile, in small bowl, stir hoisin sauce, soy sauce, and sesame oil until smooth. Thinly slice 3 green onions; trim and reserve remaining green onions for garnish.

3. In nonstick 12-inch skillet, heat 1 teaspoon oil over medium-high heat. Add mushrooms and cook, stirring occasionally, until all liquid has evaporated and mushrooms are browned, about 8 minutes; transfer mushrooms to bowl.

4. In same skillet, heat remaining 2 teaspoons oil. Add cabbage mix, red pepper, and sliced green onions, and cook, stirring constantly, 3 minutes. Add garlic and ginger; cook, stirring constantly, 1 minute. Stir in shredded turkey, hoisin-sauce mixture, and mushrooms; heat through.

5. To serve, spoon turkey mixture onto warm tortillas and roll up. Garnish with reserved green onions. Makes 4 main-dish servings.

Each serving: About 405 calories, 35 g protein, 53 g carbohydrate, 7 g total fat (1 g saturated), 71 mg cholesterol, 1,140 mg sodium.

∾Duckling

Duckling à l'Orange

Prep: 20 minutes
Roast: 2 hours

2 fresh or frozen (thawed) ducklings (4½ pounds each), giblets and
    necks reserved for another use
2 teaspoons salt
1 jar (10 to 12 ounces) orange marmalade
2 tablespoons brandy
1 orange, sliced

1. Preheat oven to 350°F. Rinse ducklings inside and out
with cold running water; pat dry with paper towels. Cut
each duckling into quarters; trim excess skin and fat from
pieces.

2. Sprinkle 1½ teaspoons salt on duckling quarters;
place, skin side up, on rack in large roasting pan (17" by
11½"). Roast 2 hours. Ducklings are done when golden and
temperature on meat thermometer inserted in thickest part
of thigh, next to body, reaches 175° to 180°F and juices
run clear when thigh is pierced with tip of knife.

3. About 15 minutes before ducklings are done, prepare
sauce: In 1-quart saucepan, heat marmalade, brandy, and
remaining ½ teaspoon salt to boiling, over medium heat,
stirring frequently. Reduce heat to low; simmer 1 minute.
Remove saucepan from heat.

4. Brush some orange sauce on ducklings. Continue
roasting, brushing duckling pieces frequently with orange
sauce, (reserving about ¼ cup sauce) and turning them occasionally until well glazed.

5. To serve, arrange ducklings on warm large platter;
garnish with orange slices. Heat reserved orange sauce to
boiling. Makes 8 main-dish servings.

*Each serving: About 500 calories, 22 g protein, 30 g carbohy-
drate, 32 g total fat (11 g saturated), 95 mg cholesterol, 670 mg
sodium.*

Goose

Crispy Citrus Goose

Prep: 30 minutes
Roast: About 4 hours 30 minutes

1 fresh or frozen (thawed) goose (about 12 pounds), giblets and neck reserved for another use
1 bunch fresh thyme
4 bay leaves
5 medium oranges, each cut in half
1¼ teaspoons salt
½ teaspoon coarsely ground black pepper
½ teaspoon dried thyme
3 tablespoons orange-flavored liqueur
2 tablespoons cornstarch
½ cup orange marmalade
Orange wedges

1. Preheat oven to 400°F. Discard fat from body cavity and any excess skin. Rinse goose with cold running water and pat dry with paper towels.

2. With breast side up, fold wings under back of goose so they stay in place. Place thyme sprigs, bay leaves, and 6 orange halves in body cavity. With string, tie legs and tail together. Fold neck skin over back.

3. Place goose, breast side up, on rack in large roasting pan (17" by 11½"). With fork, prick skin all over. In cup, combine 1 teaspoon salt, pepper, and dried thyme; use to rub on goose.

4. Cover roasting pan with foil, and roast goose 1 hour 30 minutes. Turn oven control to 325°F and roast goose 2 hours longer.

5. Meanwhile, squeeze ¾ cup juice from remaining 4 orange halves. Stir 1 tablespoon orange liqueur, cornstarch, and remaining ¼ teaspoon salt into juice; set aside. In cup, mix orange marmalade with remaining 2 tablespoons orange liqueur.

6. Remove foil from goose and roast 45 minutes longer. Remove goose from oven and turn oven control to 450°F. Brush orange-marmalade mixture over goose. Roast goose until skin is golden and crisp, about 10 minutes longer. Goose is done when temperature on meat thermometer inserted in thickest part of thigh, next to body, reaches 175° to 180°F. and juices run clear when thigh is pierced with tip of knife.

7. Transfer goose to large platter; let stand 10 minutes to set juices for easier carving. Prepare sauce: Remove rack from roasting pan. Pour pan drippings through sieve into 8-cup glass measuring cup or large bowl. Let stand until fat separates from meat juice; pour off and discard fat. There should be about 5 cups fat and 1 cup meat juice; if necessary, add enough *water* to meat juice to equal 1 cup. Return meat juice to roasting pan and stir in reserved orange-juice mixture. Heat to boiling over medium heat, stirring constantly; boil 30 seconds. Pour sauce into gravy boat.

8. To serve, carve goose (see page 305) and arrange on platter with orange wedges; serve with orange sauce. Makes 10 main-dish servings.

Each serving of goose without skin: About 460 calories, 50 g protein, 12 g carbohydrate, 25 g total fat (8 g saturated), 170 mg cholesterol, 345 mg sodium.

Each tablespoon orange sauce: About 5 calories, 0 g protein, 1 g carbohydrate, 0 g total fat, 0 mg cholesterol, 20 mg sodium.

GOOSE-ROASTING TIPS

- Order goose from your butcher or supermarket meat manager at least 1 week ahead to get the proper-size bird.
- Most geese sold in the United States are frozen, so allow time for thawing. A 12-pound goose takes at least 2 days to thaw in the refrigerator. You can also thaw the goose in cold water in about 5 hours: Place the bird (in its original wrapping) in a sink with enough cold water to cover,

changing the water every half hour. When thawed, cook or refrigerate immediately.
• Before roasting, pierce the skin all over, with a fork. This will allow the fat to drain during roasting and help to crisp the skin. If necessary, spoon off fat from roasting pan occasionally during cooking to avoid splatters and spillovers.
• To carve the goose: Remove wings from the body. Cut through the leg joints to remove legs. Separate thighs from drumsticks. Cut down on one side of breastbone, continuing to cut along the bone toward the wing joint. Steady the breast meat and gradually cut the meat away from breastbone and rib cage. Repeat on the other side. Slice the breast meat on cutting board.

ᐧᐧ**Stuffings**

Northwest Fruit Stuffing

Prep: 40 minutes
Bake: 45 minutes

½ cup margarine or butter (1 stick)
1 large red onion, chopped
1 small fennel bulb (1¼ pounds), trimmed and coarsely chopped
2 large pears, peeled, cored, and coarsely chopped
1 large Granny Smith apple, peeled, cored, and coarsely chopped
1½ loaves (16 ounces each) sliced firm white bread, cut into ¾-inch cubes and lightly toasted

1 cup chicken broth
⅔ cup dried tart cherries
½ cup golden raisins
⅓ cup chopped fresh parsley
2 teaspoons chopped fresh thyme leaves
1 teaspoon chopped fresh sage leaves
1 teaspoon salt
½ teaspoon coarsely ground black pepper

1. In 12-inch skillet, melt margarine over medium-high heat. Add onion and fennel and cook, stirring occasionally, until golden, 10 to 12 minutes. Add pears and apple and cook 5 minutes longer.

2. In large bowl, combine onion mixture with toasted bread cubes, broth, cherries, raisins, parsley, thyme, sage, salt, and pepper; toss to mix well. Use to stuff 12- to 16-pound turkey. Or, spoon into 13" by 9" baking dish; cover with foil and bake in preheated 325°F oven until heated through, about 45 minutes. Makes about 12 cups.

Each ½ cup: About 155 calories, 3 g protein, 25 g carbohydrate, 5 g total fat (1 g saturated), 0 mg cholesterol, 330 mg sodium.

Country Sausage and Corn-Bread Stuffing

Prep: 45 minutes
Bake: 45 minutes

1 pound pork-sausage meat	¾ cup water
4 tablespoons margarine or butter	½ teaspoon coarsely ground black pepper
3 medium stalks celery, chopped	1 package (14 to 16 ounces) corn-bread stuffing mix
1 large onion, chopped	1 cup pecans, toasted and coarsely chopped
1 medium red pepper, coarsely chopped	¼ cup chopped fresh parsley
1 can (14½ ounces) chicken broth	

1. Heat 12-inch skillet over medium-high heat. Add sausage meat and cook, breaking sausage up with side of spoon, until browned, about 10 minutes. With slotted spoon, transfer sausage to large bowl.

2. Discard all but 2 tablespoons sausage drippings from skillet. Add margarine, celery, onion, and red pepper; cook, stirring occasionally, until vegetables are browned. Stir in broth, water, and black pepper; heat to boiling, stirring to loosen any browned bits from bottom of skillet.

3. Add vegetable mixture, corn-bread stuffing mix, pecans, and parsley to sausage; stir to mix well. Use to stuff 12- to 16-pound turkey. Or, spoon stuffing into 13" by 9" baking dish; cover with foil and bake in preheated 325°F oven until heated through, about 45 minutes. Makes 12 cups.

Each ½ cup: About 340 calories, 9 g protein, 33 g carbohydrate, 19 g total fat (4 g saturated), 18 mg cholesterol, 875 mg sodium.

Wild Rice Stuffing

Prep: 20 minutes
Cook: 1 hour

2 cans (14½ ounces each) chicken broth
1½ cups water
1 package (4 ounces) wild rice (⅔ cup)
1 teaspoon salt
½ teaspoon dried thyme or 2 teaspoons fresh thyme leaves
2 tablespoons vegetable oil

4 medium carrots, peeled and sliced
2 medium stalks celery, sliced
1 medium onion, chopped
1 package (10 ounces) medium mushrooms, trimmed and sliced
1½ cups regular long-grain rice
¼ cup chopped fresh parsley

1. In 4-quart saucepan, heat broth, water, wild rice, salt and thyme to boiling over high heat. Reduce heat to low; cover and simmer 35 minutes.

2. Meanwhile, in nonstick 10-inch skillet, heat 1 tablespoon oil over medium-high heat. Add carrots, celery, and onion and cook until tender-crisp, stirring occasionally. Transfer carrot mixture to bowl.

3. In same skillet, heat remaining 1 tablespoon oil over medium-high heat. Add mushrooms and cook, stirring occasionally, until golden brown and liquid has evaporated.

4. Stir long-grain rice, carrot mixture, and mushrooms into wild rice; heat to boiling over high heat. Reduce heat to low; cover and simmer until liquid has been absorbed and rice is tender, 20 minutes longer. Stir in chopped parsley. Use to stuff 12- to 16-pound turkey. Or, spoon into serving bowl; keep warm until ready to serve. Makes 8 cups.

Each ½ cup: About 125 calories, 4 g protein, 23 g carbohydrate, 2 g total fat (0 g saturated), 3 mg cholesterol, 290 mg sodium.

Chestnut and Apple Stuffing

Prep: 1 hour 30 minutes
Bake: 45 minutes

2 pounds chestnuts in the shell
12 cups day-old French bread, cut into ½-inch cubes (about one 16-ounce loaf)
6 tablespoons margarine or butter
2 large stalks celery, sliced
1 medium onion, chopped

3 large Rome Beauty or Crispin apples, peeled, cored, and coarsely chopped
2 teaspoons poultry seasoning
1 can (14½ ounces) chicken broth
1 cup water
1 teaspoon salt

1. In 3-quart saucepan place chestnuts and enough *water* to cover. Heat to boiling over high heat. Reduce heat to medium; cover and cook 10 minutes. Remove saucepan from heat. With slotted spoon, transfer 3 or 4 chestnuts at a time from water to cutting board. Cut each chestnut in half. With spoon or tip of small knife, scrape out chestnut meat from its shell (skin will stay in shell). Chop any large pieces of chestnut meat; place chestnuts in large bowl. Discard cooking water. Toss bread cubes with chestnuts.

2. In same saucepan, melt margarine over medium heat. Add celery and onion and cook, stirring occasionally, until vegetables are golden brown and tender, about 10 minutes. Add apples and poultry seasoning; cook, stirring occasionally, 2 minutes longer. Stir in broth, water and salt, and heat to boiling over high heat.

3. Pour apple mixture into chestnut mixture; toss to mix well. Use to stuff 12- to 16-pound turkey. Or, spoon stuffing into 13" by 9" baking dish; cover with foil and bake in preheated 325°F oven until heated through, about 45 minute. Makes 12 cups.

Each ½ cup: About 155 calories, 3 g protein, 27 g carbohydrate, 4 g total fat (1 g saturated), 1 mg cholesterol, 295 mg sodium.

Fish & Shellfish

~~~

Fish • Shellfish
Seafood Combinations

A rich source of protein, vitamins, and minerals, fish is also relatively low in fat and calories. Even fatty fish, such as tuna and salmon, contain only about 15 percent fat, far less than most meats, while white fish such as cod or flounder contain only 5 percent. Fish is highly perishable, so freshness (and a few simple guidelines for buying, storing, and handling) is key.

ᥟFish

HOW FISH IS SOLD

Cleaned and scaled: A whole fish that has been gutted and scaled but not boned.

Cleaned, scaled and head removed: Whole fish with scales, entrails, and perhaps fins removed; it is not boned. The head and tail may also be removed.

Fillet: A side of fish cut lengthwise away from the backbone so that it is boneless or contains only a few small bones. It may be skinned.

Steak: A crosscut section of a larger fish, usually cut at least ½ inch thick. If cut from very large fish, such as swordfish or tuna, the steaks are usually boneless and may be skinless as well.

HOW TO BUY FISH

Fresh fish (whole) should have bright, clear eyes, red gills, and bright, tight scales or shiny skin. The flesh should be firm and spring back when prodded, with a fresh, mild odor.

Fresh fillets or steaks should appear to be freshly cut, without a dried or brownish look, and have a firm texture and a fresh, mild odor.

Frozen fish should be tightly wrapped in moisture-proof material with little or no air space between the fish and its wrapping. The flesh should be solidly frozen, have a clear color, and be free of ice crystals, discoloration, or any brownish tinge. The odor, if any, should be mild. Breading on breaded fish should be crisp, not soggy.

HOW MUCH FISH TO BUY FOR EACH SERVING

Whole or drawn	1 pound
Dressed	8 to 12 ounces
Steaks	6 to 8 ounces
Fillets	6 to 8 ounces

HOW TO STORE FRESH FISH

Wrap fresh fish loosely and place in the coldest part of the refrigerator. Fresh fish is best used within 1 day. Always keep fish cold until you're ready to cook it—bacteria can multiply at room temperature. Don't leave it out while you're preparing the other ingredients. Do not store ungutted fish; bacteria in the guts will multiply and cause rapid spoilage.

If you must freeze fish, be sure it's impeccably fresh and of high quality. Rinse and dry, then carefully wrap it in moisture-proof and vapor-proof wrap, such as freezer paper, and freeze up to 3 months. Fish with skin left on, whether whole (gutted) or steak or fillets, freezes best, because the skin helps protect the flesh from the drying effects of the freezer.

HOW TO USE FROZEN FISH

Keep frozen fish for no more than 3 months. In many cases, frozen fish can be cooked while still frozen, but allow a few more minutes of cooking time.

Thaw frozen fish overnight in the refrigerator (on a plate to catch drips) in its original wrapping. Once thawed, drain well and pat dry with paper towels before cooking. (If you're short of time, hasten thawing by placing the wrapped fish under cold running water.) Never thaw frozen fish at room temperature, or you'll run the risk of bacterial contamination. For the same reason, never thaw fish under warm water.

HOW TO PREPARE FRESHLY CAUGHT FISH

To clean a whole fish start by removing the scales. With kitchen shears, cut off the fins. Place the fish on a board or in the sink, grip the fish firmly by the tail, and scrape the scales off with a fish scaler, a vegetable peeler, or the dull edge of a knife held almost at right angles to the body of the fish, working from the tail toward the head. Turn the fish over and scale the other side. Rinse the fish well with cold water after scaling.

Then, with a sharp knife, slit the belly of the fish open from the vent (anal opening) to the head. Remove the entrails and rinse the cavity clean. Thoroughly rinse the fish with running cold water and blot it dry with paper towels. It is now ready to cook (whole), pan-dress, or cut into fillets or steaks.

To fillet a fish it is not necessary to remove the head and tail; and if the fillets are to be skinned, the fish need not be scaled. With a sharp knife, cut through the fish along the backbone from just behind the head to tail, cutting right down to the bone, but not through the bone.

Holding the knife blade almost flat and parallel to the body of the fish, cut the flesh away from the backbone to the tail, as smoothly as possible, allowing the knife to run over the rib bones.

Lift the first fillet off in one piece. Turn the fish over and remove the other fillet in the same way.

To skin a fillet place it, skin side down, on a cutting board. With the tip of a knife, loosen enough skin at the tail end to give you a good grip. Holding down the loosened skin securely with one hand and with the knife held almost flat in the other hand, cut the flesh free from the skin.

HOW TO BREAD FISH

If the fish is frozen, thaw it before breading. Pat the fish dry with paper towels, then dip it in milk or egg beaten with a little milk; drain the fish slightly, and coat it with dried bread crumbs, cornflake crumbs, cornmeal, or flour, patting crumbs to cover. For a thicker coating, dust fish with flour before dipping in egg and coating with crumbs.

HOW TO COOK FISH

Fish should be cooked quickly, just long enough to co-agulate the protein and bring out the flavor. Overcooking makes it tough and tasteless. Fish is done as soon as the flesh just turns opaque throughout. With a whole fish or steak, check the flesh at the backbone; it should be just opaque throughout.

No matter which cooking method you choose, estimate the cooking time this easy way: Place the fish on the kitchen counter and measure it with a ruler at the thickest part, even if it is stuffed or rolled.

TIME THE COOKING AS FOLLOWS:

10 minutes per inch if fresh
15 minutes per inch if fresh and stuffed
20 minutes per inch if frozen

BROILING OR GRILLING: Use steaks, fillets, and pan-dressed whole fish. Place the fish on an oiled broiling-pan rack; brush it generously with a combination of lemon juice and melted butter, margarine, or olive oil, or with a sauce, before and during broiling. Broil the fish close to the heat source—2 to 4 inches; turn thicker pieces (steaks and pan-dressed fish) once halfway through broiling.

PANFRYING: Use fillets, thin steaks, and pan-dressed whole fish. Fish is usually breaded before frying (see How to Bread Fish, page 316). Fry over medium-high heat in a small amount of hot vegetable oil or butter; turn the fish once halfway through frying.

OVEN-FRYING: Preheat the oven to 450°F or as the recipe directs. Bread individual portions of fish and place them in a well-greased baking pan; drizzle them with some olive oil, melted margarine or butter, and bake the fish until just opaque throughout. No turning or basting the fish is necessary; the breading on fish prevents flavorful juices from escaping.

DEEP-FRYING: Heat 2 inches of vegetable oil or shortening in a deep, heavy saucepan or deep-fat fryer until temperature on a deep-fat thermometer reaches 350° to 370°F. Bread fillets or pan-dressed fish, or dip fish in batter. Gently lower the fish into the hot oil with a slotted spatula, or place it in a deep-frying basket in one layer and lower it into the hot oil. Fry fish until golden and just opaque throughout. Drain on paper towels.

BAKING: Preheat the oven to 450°F or as the recipe directs. To prevent fish from drying out during baking, brush a whole dressed fish, fillets, or steaks with melted margarine or butter, or olive oil, or cover with a sauce. Bake the fish, without turning it, until just opaque throughout.

POACHING: Cook fillets, steaks, and whole dressed fish in simmering, not boiling, liquid in a covered skillet or pan. Use lightly salted water, milk, a mixture of water and white wine, or a Court Bouillon (see Glossary, page 73), and start counting the cooking time when the liquid returns to a simmer after the fish has been added. After poaching fish, some of the liquid can be strained and used to make a sauce for the fish. Do not allow the poaching liquid to boil at any point as this will cause fish to toughen or even cause flesh to break up.

STEAMING: Use fillets, steaks, and pan-dressed fish, and a steamer or deep pan with a rack and a tight-fitting cover. Pour water into the pan to a level below the steamer liner or rack; heat the water to boiling. Place the fish in a greased, shallow baking dish and place it on the rack; cover the pan and simmer gently until the fish flakes easily when tested with a fork.

Broiled Cod Steaks Montauk

Prep: 7 minutes
Broil: 7 to 9 minutes

4 small cod steaks, each ½ inch thick
½ cup mayonnaise
½ teaspoon prepared mustard
¼ teaspoon salt
⅛ teaspoon ground black pepper
1 small lemon, sliced, slices cut crosswise in half

1. With tweezers, remove any small bones from cod steaks. Preheat broiler. In small bowl, stir mayonnaise, mustard, salt, and pepper.

2. Lightly oil rack in broiling pan. Place cod steaks on rack. Broil 2 to 4 inches from heat source until cod is just opaque throughout, 5 to 7 minutes. Remove broiling pan from broiler. Spread cod steaks with mayonnaise mixture; broil until mayonnaise mixture is lightly browned and bubbly, about 2 minutes longer.

3. Serve cod steaks with lemon slices. Makes 4 main-dish servings.

Each serving: About 335 calories, 29 g protein, 0 g carbohydrate, 25 g total fat (4 g saturated), 80 mg cholesterol, 380 mg sodium.

Swordfish Steaks Broiled with Herb Butter

Prep: 7 minutes
Broil: 17 minutes

2 swordfish or tuna steaks (12 ounces each), each 1 inch thick
4 tablespoons margarine or butter
2 tablespoons minced shallots or green onions
1 tablespoon fresh lemon juice
½ teaspoon salt
½ teaspoon dried tarragon
½ teaspoon dried basil

1. Preheat broiler.
2. Cut each swordfish steak crosswise in half. In 1-quart saucepan, melt butter over medium heat. Add shallots and cook, stirring, 1 minute. Remove saucepan from heat; stir in lemon juice, salt, tarragon, and basil.
3. Lightly oil rack in broiling pan. Place fish steaks on rack; brush fish on both sides with some margarine mixture. Broil 2 to 4 inches from heat source, basting occasionally with margarine mixture, until fish is just opaque throughout, about 8 to 10 minutes. To serve, transfer fish to plates and spoon pan juices over fish. Makes 4 main-dish servings.

Each serving: About 310 calories, 34 g protein, 1 g carbohydrate, 18 g total fat (4 g saturated), 66 mg cholesterol, 570 mg sodium.

California-Style Marinated Halibut

Prep: 5 minutes plus marinating
Broil: 10 minutes

4 small halibut steaks, each ¾ inch thick
¼ cup fresh lime juice
¼ cup olive oil
1 jalapeño chile, seeded and cut crosswise into thin strips
½ teaspoon salt
⅛ teaspoon crushed red pepper
½ teaspoon sugar
½ teaspoon dried oregano

1. With tweezers, remove any small bones from fish steaks. In large glass or stainless-steel bowl, stir lime juice, oil, jalapeño, salt, crushed red pepper, sugar, and oregano until well blended. Add halibut steaks and turn to coat. Cover and refrigerate halibut 2 hours to marinate, turning halibut steaks occasionally.

2. Lightly oil rack in broiling pan. Place steaks on rack, reserving marinade. Broil 2 to 4 inches from heat source, occasionally brushing some marinade on steaks, until halibut is just opaque throughout, about 8 to 10 minutes. Discard any remaining marinade. Transfer halibut steaks to plates to serve. Makes 4 main-dish servings.

Each serving: About 240 calories, 34 g protein, 1 g carbohydrate, 11 g total fat (1 g saturated), 53 mg cholesterol, 220 mg sodium.

Mustard-Dill Salmon with Herbed Potatoes

Prep: 20 minutes
Broil: 8 to 10 minutes

12 ounces small red potatoes, not peeled, cut into 1-inch chunks

12 ounces small white potatoes, not peeled, cut into 1-inch chunks

1½ teaspoons salt

3 tablespoons chopped fresh dill

½ teaspoon coarsely ground black pepper

4 pieces salmon fillet (6 ounces each), skin removed

2 tablespoons light mayonnaise

1 tablespoon white wine vinegar

2 teaspoons Dijon mustard

¾ teaspoon sugar

1. In 3-quart saucepan, place potatoes, 1 teaspoon salt, and enough *water to cover;* heat to boiling over high heat. Reduce heat to low; cover and simmer until potatoes are fork-tender, about 15 minutes. Drain potatoes; transfer to warm serving dish, and toss with 1 tablespoon dill, ¼ teaspoon salt, and ¼ teaspoon pepper. Keep potatoes warm.

2. Meanwhile, preheat broiler. Lightly oil rack in broiling pan. With tweezers, remove any small bones from salmon fillet. Sprinkle ⅛ teaspoon each salt and pepper on salmon. Place salmon on rack; Broil at closest position to heat source, just until fish is opaque throughout, 8 to 10 minutes.

3. While salmon is broiling, prepare sauce: In small bowl, stir together mayonnaise, vinegar, mustard, sugar, remaining 2 tablespoons dill, remaining ⅛ teaspoon salt, and remaining ⅛ teaspoon pepper.

4. Serve salmon with sauce and potatoes. Makes 4 main-dish servings.

Each serving: About 335 calories, 37 g protein, 31 g carbohydrate, 7 g total fat (1 g saturated), 86 mg cholesterol, 655 mg sodium.

Broiled Shad

Prep: 4 minutes
Broil: 7 to 10 minutes

4 shad fillets (about 1½ pounds)
4 tablespoons margarine or butter
2 tablespoons fresh lemon juice
1 teaspoon salt
1 tablespoon chopped fresh parsley
Lemon wedges

1. With tweezers, remove any small bones from shad fillet. Preheat broiler. Lightly oil rack in broiling pan. Place cut shad, skin side down, on rack.

2. In small saucepan, melt margarine over medium heat; stir in lemon juice and salt. Brush on shad. Broil 2 to 4 inches from heat source, until fish is just opaque throughout, about 7 to 10 minutes. Sprinkle parsley on shad and serve with lemon wedges. Makes 4 main-dish servings.

Each serving: About 440 calories, 31 g protein, 1 g carbohydrate, 34 g total fat (2 g saturated), 122 mg cholesterol, 610 mg sodium.

Jamaican Jerk Catfish with Grilled Pineapple

Prep: 15 minutes plus standing
Grill: 10 to 12 minutes

2 tablespoons white wine
  vinegar
2 tablespoons Worcestershire
  sauce
1 tablespoon vegetable oil
2 green onions, chopped
1 jalapeño chile, seeded and
  chopped
1 tablespoon minced, peeled
  fresh ginger
¼ teaspoon salt

1¼ teaspoons dried thyme
1 teaspoon ground allspice
4 catfish, sole or flounder fillets
  (5 ounces each)
1 small pineapple, not peeled,
  cored, and cut lengthwise
  into 4 wedges or crosswise
  into ½-inch-thick slices
2 tablespoons brown sugar

1. Prepare grill. In medium bowl, stir together vinegar, Worcestershire, oil, green onions, jalapeño chile, ginger, salt, thyme, and allspice until combined. Add catfish fillets to bowl, turning to coat; let stand 5 minutes.

2. Meanwhile, rub pineapple wedges or slices with brown sugar.

3. Place pineapple and catfish fillets on grill over medium-high heat. Spoon half of jerk mixture in bowl on catfish. Grill pineapple and catfish 5 minutes. Turn pineapple and catfish. Spoon remaining jerk mixture on fish and grill until fish is just opaque throughout and pineapple is golden brown, 5 to 7 minutes longer. Transfer fish and pineapple to warm large platter and serve. Makes 4 main-dish servings.

Each serving: About 300 calories, 22 g protein, 25 g carbohydrate, 13 g total fat (2 g saturated), 72 mg cholesterol, 305 mg sodium.

Tunisian Snapper

Prep: 5 minutes
Cook: 5 to 8 minutes

4 red snapper fillets (6 ounces each)
½ teaspoon salt
¼ teaspoon crushed red pepper
¼ teaspoon cumin seeds, crushed
¼ teaspoon coriander seeds, crushed
¼ teaspoon fennel seeds, crushed
2 teaspoons vegetable oil
Lime wedges

1. With tweezers, remove any small bones from snapper fillets.

2. On waxed paper, combine salt, crushed red pepper, cumin seeds, coriander seeds, and fennel seeds. Use to rub on flesh side of snapper fillets.

3. In nonstick 12-inch skillet, heat oil over medium-high heat until very hot. Add fillets and cook 2½ to 4 minutes per side, until fish is just opaque throughout. With narrow spatula, carefully transfer snapper fillets to plates and serve with lime wedges. Makes 4 main-dish servings.

Each serving: About 190 calories, 35 g protein, 0 g carbohydrate, 5 g total fat (1 g saturated), 62 mg cholesterol, 340 mg sodium.

Panfried Trout and Potatoes

Prep: 30 minutes
Cook: 1 hour

4 tablespoons olive oil
4 tablespoons margarine or butter
1 pound all-purpose potatoes (3 medium), peeled and cut into ¼-inch-thick slices
1 small onion, chopped
1 teaspoon salt
2 medium lemons
½ teaspoon ground black pepper

4 brook or rainbow trout (8 ounces each), cleaned and scaled, with tails left on
1 large egg
⅓ cup all-purpose flour
1 tablespoon chopped fresh parsley

1. In 10-inch skillet, heat 1 tablespoon oil and 1 tablespoon butter over medium heat until margarine melts. Add potatoes, onion, and ¼ teaspoon salt and cook until potato slices are golden on bottom. Reduce heat to low; cover and cook 5 minutes. With wide spatula, turn potato mixture; increase heat to medium, remove cover and cook until browned on other side. Reduce heat to low; cover and cook until potatoes are fork-tender, 5 to 10 minutes longer. Remove from heat and keep warm.

2. From 1 lemon, grate, peel, and squeeze 2 tablespoons juice; cut remaining lemon into wedges.

3. Sprinkle ¼ teaspoon each salt and pepper inside and outside trout. In pie plate, beat egg. On waxed paper, combine flour, lemon peel, remaining ½ teaspoon salt, and remaining ¼ teaspoon pepper. One at a time, dip trout in egg, letting excess drip off, then coat with flour mixture, patting to cover.

4. In 12-inch skillet, heat 2 tablespoons oil and 2 tablespoons butter over medium-high heat until butter has melted. Stir in 1 tablespoon lemon juice. Add 2 trout and cook 6 to 7 minutes per side, turning trout carefully with narrow spatula, until fish is just opaque throughout. With spatula, carefully transfer trout to warm large platter; keep warm. Repeat with remaining trout and remaining 1 tablespoon each oil, butter, and lemon juice.

5. Sprinkle trout with parsley and serve with lemon wedges. Makes 4 main-dish servings.

Each serving: About 535 calories, 42 g protein, 22 g carbohydrate, 30 g total fat (6 g saturated), 162 mg cholesterol, 780 mg sodium.

Fried Catfish

Prep: 25 minutes plus standing
Cook: 25 minutes

6 small catfish (10 ounces each), cleaned, with heads and tails left on
¾ cup cornmeal
2 tablespoons all-purpose flour
½ teaspoon salt
¼ teaspoon ground black pepper
¼ cup milk
Vegetable oil for frying
Lemon wedges

1. To skin catfish, using knife or scissors, cut off the sharp fins. Make a cut through the skin around the catfish's head. Peel skin away from flesh around head; using paper towel to grasp skin, pull skin firmly toward tail to remove it in one piece. Cut off head.

2. In plastic bag, combine cornmeal, flour, salt, and pepper. In pie plate, pour milk. One at a time, dip catfish in milk, moistening fish well. Add to cornmeal mixture and shake to evenly coat with cornmeal mixture. Place coated catfish on wire rack over waxed paper and let dry at room temperature 30 minutes. Repeat with remaining catfish.

3. In heavy 10-inch skillet (at least 2 inches deep), heat about ½ inch oil over medium heat until temperature reaches 370°F on deep-fat thermometer. Carefully place half of catfish in skillet and fry about 4 to 5 minutes per side until catfish are golden and just opaque throughout when knife is inserted at backbone. With slotted spoon, carefully transfer catfish to paper towels to drain. Repeat with remaining catfish.

4. Transfer catfish to large warm platter and serve with lemon wedges. Makes 6 main-dish servings.

Each serving: About 305 calories, 25 g protein, 16 g carbohydrate, 15 g total fat (3 g saturated), 80 mg cholesterol, 300 mg sodium.

Fried Smelts

Prep: 25 minutes
Cook: 15 minutes

2 pounds smelts, cleaned and heads removed
1½ cups plain dried bread crumbs
¾ teaspoon salt
½ teaspoon ground black pepper
4 large eggs
¼ cup water
½ cup vegetable oil
1 large lemon, cut into 6 wedges
Tartar Sauce (see page 769)

1. Rinse smelts and pat dry with paper towels. On waxed paper, combine bread crumbs, salt, and pepper. In pie plate, with fork beat eggs and water. One at a time, dip fish in egg, then coat with crumb mixture. Repeat, coating each fish twice, patting crumbs to cover. Place coated fish on another sheet of waxed paper.

2. In 12-inch skillet, heat oil over medium-high heat until very hot. Add fish, in small batches, and fry about 2 minutes per side, or until browned and just opaque throughout when knife is inserted at backbone. With slotted spoon, carefully transfer smelts to paper towels to drain. Repeat

with remaining smelts. Serve smelts with lemon wedges
and Tartar Sauce. Makes 6 main-dish servings.

*Each serving: About 285 calories, 24 g protein, 20 g carbohydrate,
12 g total fat (2 g saturated), 205 mg cholesterol, 620 mg sodium.*

Sautéed Shad Roe

Prep: 2 minutes
Cook: 8 minutes

4 tablespoons margarine or butter
2 shad roe (1 pound)
½ teaspoon salt
Lemon wedges

In 10-inch skillet melt margarine over medium heat. Add
shad roe, cover and cook (it splatters) 4 minutes per side,
until roe loses its pink color throughout and is tender when
tested with a fork. Sprinkle salt on roe and serve with lemon
wedges. Makes 4 main-dish servings.

*Each serving: About 260 calories, 25 g protein, 2 g carbohydrate,
19 g total fat (4 g saturated), 424 mg cholesterol, 545 mg sodium.*

Chili-Spiced Cod

Prep: 5 minutes
Cook: 10 minutes

1 tablespoon cornmeal
1 tablespoon all-purpose flour
1 teaspoon salt
1 tablespoon chili powder
4 pieces cod or scrod fillet (about 6 ounces each)
2 tablespoons margarine or butter

1. On waxed paper, combine cornmeal, flour, salt, and
chili powder; use to coat cod fillets, patting to cover.
2. Heat nonstick 12-inch skillet over medium-high heat

until hot. Add 1 tablespoon margarine and melt. Add cod fillets and cook 4 minutes. Reduce heat to medium; turn fillets. Add remaining 1 tablespoon margarine to skillet and cook cod until just opaque throughout, about 4 to 6 minutes longer. Transfer cod fillets to plates to serve. Makes 4 main-dish servings.

Each serving: About 210 calories, 31 g protein, 4 g carbohydrate, 7 g total fat (1 g saturated), 74 mg cholesterol, 720 mg sodium.

Lemon-Thyme Cod

Prep: 5 minutes
Cook: 10 minutes

2 large lemons
2 tablespoons all-purpose flour
2 teaspoons chopped fresh thyme leaves or ½ teaspoon dried thyme
½ teaspoon salt
¼ teaspoon coarsely ground black pepper
1 cod or scrod fillet (1¼ pounds), cut into 4 pieces
2 tablespoons margarine or butter

1. From 1 lemon, grate peel; cut remaining lemon into wedges.

2. On waxed paper, combine flour, thyme, grated lemon peel, salt, and pepper; use to coat cod fillets, patting to cover.

3. In nonstick 12-inch skillet, melt margarine over medium-high heat. Add cod fillets and cook 5 minutes per side or until just opaque throughout. Using narrow spatula, transfer cod fillets to plates. Serve cod with lemon wedges. Makes 4 main-dish servings.

Each serving: About 190 calories, 26 g protein, 6 g carbohydrate, 7 g total fat (1 g saturated), 61 mg cholesterol, 430 mg sodium.

Sole Amandine

Prep: 10 minutes
Cook: 12 minutes

4 sole or flounder fillets (6 ounces each)
½ cup plus 2 tablespoons sliced blanched almonds
1 large egg
1 tablespoon water
½ cup plain dried bread crumbs
1 tablespoon finely chopped fresh parsley
½ teaspoon salt
⅛ teaspoon ground black pepper
4 tablespoons margarine or butter

1. With tweezers, remove any small bones from flounder fillets. In food processor with knife blade attached, or in blender, process ½ cup almonds until finely ground. In 12-inch skillet cook remaining 2 tablespoons almonds, over medium heat, stirring frequently until golden and toasted. Transfer toasted almonds to small plate.

2. In pie plate, with fork, beat egg and water. On waxed paper, combine ground almonds, bread crumbs, parsley, salt, and pepper. Dip fillets in egg, letting excess drip off, then coat with almond mixture, patting crumbs to cover.

3. In same skillet, melt 2 tablespoons margarine over medium heat. Add half of fish fillets and cook about 2 minutes per side or until golden brown and fish is just opaque throughout. Use narrow spatula to transfer fish to warm dinner plates. Repeat with remaining fish and remaining 2 tablespoons margarine.

4. To serve, sprinkle sole fillets with toasted almonds. Makes 4 main-dish servings.

Each serving: About 455 calories, 40 g protein, 14 g carbohydrate, 26 g total fat (4 g saturated), 135 mg cholesterol, 715 mg sodium.

Five-Spice Salmon

Prep: 5 minutes
Cook: 10 minutes

4 pieces salmon fillet (4 ounces each), skin removed
1 teaspoon all-purpose flour
½ teaspoon salt
¼ teaspoon cracked black pepper
2 teaspoons Chinese five-spice powder
2 teaspoons olive oil

1. With tweezers, remove any small bones from salmon fillets. On waxed paper, combine flour, salt, pepper, and Chinese five-spice powder. Use to coat salmon fillets.

2. In nonstick 10-inch skillet, heat oil over medium heat. Add salmon; cook 4 to 5 minutes per side, until fish is just opaque throughout. Transfer salmon to plates with slotted spatula and serve. Makes 4 main-dish servings.

Each serving: About 175 calories, 22 g protein, 1 g carbohydrate, 8 g total fat (1 g saturated), 61 mg cholesterol, 330 mg sodium.

Teriyaki Salmon Burgers

Prep: 15 minutes
Cook: 10 minutes

5 sesame-seed hamburger buns
1 salmon fillet (1 pound), skin removed
2 tablespoons teriyaki sauce
2 medium green onions, chopped
1½ teaspoons grated, peeled fresh ginger

1. Coarsely grate 1 hamburger bun into bread crumbs. Measure ⅓ cup bread crumbs; set aside. Reserve remaining crumbs on waxed paper to coat patties.

2. With tweezers, remove any small bones from salmon fillet. Finely chop salmon and place in medium bowl. Add teriyaki sauce, green onions, ginger, and ⅓ cup bread crumbs.

3. On waxed paper, shape salmon mixture into four 3-inch round patties. Use reserved bread crumbs to coat patties, patting crumbs to cover.

4. In nonstick 10-inch skillet, cook patties over medium heat, 5 minutes per side, turning carefully with wide spatula, until patties are golden and just opaque throughout. Serve patties on hamburger buns. Makes 4 main-dish servings.

Each serving: About 340 calories, 28 g protein, 38 g carbohydrate, 12 g total fat (2 g saturated), 61 mg cholesterol, 695 mg sodium.

Salmon Cakes

Prep: 8 minutes
Cook: 10 minutes

1 can (14¾ ounces) red or pink salmon, drained and flaked
3 tablespoons bottled white horseradish
2 tablespoons plain dried bread crumbs
1 green onion, sliced
1 teaspoon soy sauce
¼ teaspoon coarsely ground black pepper
Nonstick cooking spray
4 sandwich buns, split
Lettuce leaves

1. In medium bowl, with fork, lightly mix salmon, horseradish, bread crumbs, green onion, soy sauce, and pepper until combined. Shape mixture into four 3-inch round patties. Spray both sides of patties with nonstick cooking spray.

2. Heat 10-inch nonstick skillet over medium heat until hot. Add salmon cakes, and cook about 5 minutes per side or until golden and heated through. Serve salmon cakes on buns with lettuce. Makes 4 main-dish servings.

Each serving: About 255 calories, 19 g protein, 26 g carbohydrate, 9 g total fat (2 g saturated), 50 mg cholesterol, 815 mg sodium.

Easy Fish and Chips with Special Slaw

Prep: 20 minutes
Cook: 12 minutes

½ cup mayonnaise
¼ cup milk
2 tablespoons cider vinegar
1 tablespoon Dijon mustard
½ teaspoon salt
¼ teaspoon coarsely ground
    black pepper
½ teaspoon sugar
1 medium head iceberg lettuce,
    finely sliced
    (8 cups)
1 medium cucumber, peeled
    and coarsely shredded

1 bag (6 ounces) radishes,
    trimmed and coarsely
    shredded
1 large egg
½ cup plain dried bread
    crumbs
4 flounder or haddock fillets
    (4 ounces each)
3 tablespoons vegetable oil
Potato chips

1. Prepare slaw: In medium bowl, stir together mayonnaise, milk, vinegar, mustard, salt, pepper, and sugar until blended and smooth. Add lettuce, cucumber, and radishes; with rubber spatula, toss to coat with dressing. Cover and refrigerate slaw while preparing fish.

2. In pie plate, with fork, beat egg. Place bread crumbs on waxed paper. Dip fish in egg, letting excess drip off, then coat with crumbs, patting crumbs to cover.

3. In 12-inch skillet heat oil over medium heat. Add half of fish and cook about 2½ minutes per side, until fish is browned and just opaque throughout. Use slotted spatula to transfer flounder to warm platter as it is cooked. Repeat with remaining fish.

4. Serve flounder with slaw and potato chips. Makes 4 main-dish servings.

Each serving: About 500 calories, 21 g protein, 19 g carbohydrate, 39 g total fat (6 g saturated), 109 mg cholesterol, 815 mg sodium.

Stir-Fried Swordfish with Broccoli and Mushrooms

Prep: 17 minutes
Cook: 8 minutes

1 swordfish steak (1 pound),
　　1 inch thick, cut into 1-inch
　　pieces
2 tablespoons dry sherry
1 tablespoon soy sauce
2 teaspoons cornstarch
½ teaspoon sugar
¼ teaspoon ground
　　ginger
⅛ teaspoon crushed red
　　pepper

4 tablespoons vegetable oil
½ small bunch broccoli,
　　flowerets cut into 2" by 1"
　　pieces, stems peeled and
　　cut into 2" by ½" match stick
　　strips
8 ounces mushrooms, trimmed
　　and sliced
4 green onions, cut into
　　3-inch pieces
½ teaspoon salt

1. In medium bowl, combine swordfish, sherry, soy sauce, cornstarch, sugar, ginger, and crushed red pepper.

2. In 5-quart Dutch oven, heat 2 tablespoons oil over medium-high heat until very hot. Add broccoli, mushrooms, green onions, and salt, and cook, stirring quickly and frequently, until vegetables are tender-crisp, about 5 minutes. With slotted spoon, transfer vegetables to bowl.

3. In same Dutch oven, heat remaining 2 tablespoons oil over medium-high heat until very hot. Add swordfish mixture and cook, stirring gently, until fish is just opaque throughout, about 2 minutes. Return vegetables and juices in bowl to Dutch oven; heat through. Serve hot. Makes 4 main-dish servings.

Each serving: About 305 calories, 25 g protein, 8 g carbohydrate, 19 g total fat (3 g saturated), 44 mg cholesterol, 665 mg sodium.

Red Snapper Veracruz

Prep: 25 minutes
Cook: 20 minutes

4 red snapper fillets (6 ounces each)
2 tablespoons olive oil
1 medium onion, chopped
1 garlic clove, finely chopped
1½ pounds ripe tomatoes (3 medium), coarsely chopped
¼ cup pitted small green olives, each cut crosswise in half
2 tablespoons capers, drained
1 large fresh or pickled jalapeño chile, finely chopped
½ teaspoon salt

1. With tweezers, remove any small bones from snapper fillets. In 12-inch skillet, heat oil over medium heat. Add onion and garlic, and cook, stirring occasionally, until lightly browned and tender. Stir in tomatoes, olives, capers, jalapeño, and salt; heat to boiling. Reduce heat to low; simmer, until flavors are blended, about 5 minutes.

2. Add red snapper fillets to tomato mixture; heat to boiling over high heat. Reduce heat to low; cover and simmer until snapper fillets are just opaque throughout, about 5 minutes. Serve snapper in shallow soup plates with sauce. Makes 4 main-dish servings.

Each serving: About 280 calories, 37 g protein, 8 g carbohydrate, 12 g total fat (2 g saturated), 63 mg cholesterol, 780 mg sodium.

Poached Trout

Prep: 10 minutes
Cook: 25 minutes

½ cup dry white wine
½ cup water
4 green onions, thinly sliced
1 small garlic clove, crushed with flat side of chef's knife
1 teaspoon salt
1 teaspoon Worcestershire sauce
4 brook or rainbow trout (8 ounces each), cleaned and scaled,
   with tails left on
1 large lemon, thinly sliced

1. In 12-inch skillet, combine wine, water, green onions, garlic, salt, and Worcestershire. Heat to boiling over high heat. Add 2 trout and heat to simmering. Reduce heat to low; cover and simmer until fish is just opaque throughout, 8 to 10 minutes.

2. With narrow spatula, carefully transfer trout to warm large platter; cover to keep warm. Repeat with remaining fish. Spoon pan juices on trout and serve with lemon slices. Makes 4 main-dish servings.

Each serving: About 255 calories, 37 g protein, 2 g carbohydrate, 10 g total fat (3 g saturated), 105 mg cholesterol, 660 mg sodium.

Chilled Salmon with Green Mayonnaise Dressing

Prep: 20 minutes plus chilling
Cook: 16 minutes

6 small salmon steaks, each ½
   inch thick
4 cups water
2 teaspoons salt
2 large cucumbers, thinly sliced
½ cup distilled white vinegar
2 tablespoons sugar
¼ teaspoon ground black
   pepper
1 small onion, sliced
Green-Mayonnaise Dressing
   (see page 336)
Romaine lettuce leaves

1. With tweezers, remove any small bones from salmon steaks. In 12-inch skillet, heat water and 1 teaspoon salt to boiling over high heat. Add half the salmon steaks; heat to simmering. Reduce heat to low; cover and simmer until fish is just opaque throughout, 5 to 8 minutes. With slotted spatula, carefully lift each salmon steak from water; drain salmon (still on spatula) on paper towels. Place on large platter. Repeat with remaining salmon steaks. Cover and refrigerate until salmon steaks are well chilled, about 1½ hours.

2. Meanwhile, prepare cucumbers: In medium bowl, with rubber spatula, combine cucumber slices with 1 teaspoon salt; let stand 30 minutes. Drain cucumbers in sieve; with spoon, press out extra liquid. Transfer cucumbers to bowl, add vinegar, sugar, pepper, and onion; gently toss to mix well. Cover and refrigerate.

3. Prepare Green-Mayonnaise Dressing; spoon into small bowl. Cover and refrigerate.

4. To serve, line large platter with lettuce leaves. Drain cucumbers. Arrange cucumbers and salmon steaks on lettuce leaves. Serve with Green-Mayonnaise Dressing. Makes 6 main-dish servings.

GREEN-MAYONNAISE DRESSING: In blender, process *2 cups mayonnaise, ½ teaspoon salt, ⅓ cup chopped fresh parsley, 2 green onions, cut up, and 4 teaspoons tarragon vinegar* until smooth, stopping blender occasionally and scraping down with rubber spatula. Makes about 2 cups.

Each serving salmon steak and cucumbers: 190 calories, 28 g protein, 6 g carbohydrate, 6 g total fat (2 g saturated), 74 mg cholesterol, 455 mg sodium.

Each two-teaspoon serving Green-Mayonnaise Dressing: 35 calories, 0 g protein, 0 g carbohydrate, 4 g total fat (1 g saturated), 3 mg cholesterol, 38 mg sodium.

Steamed Sea Bass with Ginger and Green Onions

Prep: 20 minutes plus marinating
Cook: 15 minutes

1 whole sea bass (2 pounds),
    cleaned and scaled, with
    head and tail left on
1 tablespoon dry sherry
½ teaspoon salt
¼ teaspoon ground black
    pepper
2 tablespoons soy sauce
1 tablespoon vegetable oil

1 teaspoon Asian sesame oil
1 teaspoon cornstarch
1 teaspoon sugar
3 green onions, cut into
    1-inch pieces
1 piece peeled fresh ginger,
    about 1 inch long and
    ½ inch in diameter, cut
    into slivers

1. Rinse sea bass inside and out with cold running water; pat dry with paper towels. With sharp knife, cut 3 or 4 crosswise slashes about ½ inch deep and ¾ inch apart on each side of fish to help fish to cook faster and more evenly.

2. Place fish in heat-safe deep oval platter or baking dish large enough to hold fish. Rub sherry, salt, and pepper over fish and inside cavity. Cover and refrigerate fish 1 hour to marinate.

3. In cup, stir soy sauce, vegetable oil, sesame oil, cornstarch, and sugar until smooth.

4. Place half the green onion pieces and half the ginger slivers in cavity of fish. Pour soy-sauce mixture over fish. Sprinkle top of fish with remaining green onions and remaining ginger slivers.

5. To steam: Pour *1 to 2 inches water* in large oval or rectangular roasting pan, wok, or steamer large enough to hold platter of fish. Place 3 custard cups, bottom sides up, in roasting pan; with wok or steamer, use a wire rack. Over high heat, heat water to boiling. Set platter with fish on custard cups or rack. Reduce heat to medium-high; cover and steam fish until just opaque throughout when knife is inserted in backbone, about 10 to 15 minutes. Serve portions of fish with accumulated juices in platter. Makes 4 main-dish servings.

Each serving: About 160 calories, 19 g protein, 4 g carbohydrate, 7 g total fat (1 g saturated), 41 mg cholesterol, 875 mg sodium.

Creamed Finnan Haddie

Prep: 5 minutes plus hard-cooking eggs
Cook: 20 minutes

1 pound finnan haddie or smoked cod fillets, cut into large pieces
2 tablespoons margarine or butter
2 teaspoons all-purpose flour
1 cup milk
½ cup heavy or whipping cream or half-and-half
2 hard-cooked eggs, shelled
Toast points

1. If using smoked cod, in large, shallow baking dish, place fillets and enough cold water to cover. Soak 1 hour, then drain.

2. In 12-inch skillet melt margarine over medium heat. Stir in flour until blended; cook, stirring, 1 minute. Gradually stir in milk and cream, and cook, stirring, until mixture has thickened slightly and boils; add fish. Cover; simmer, stirring occasionally, until fish flakes easily when tested with a fork, about 15 minutes.

3. Reserve 1 hard-cooked egg yolk. Chop whites and other egg yolk. Using a fork, coarsely flake fish; stir in chopped eggs, and pour into warm serving dish. Press reserved egg yolk through coarse sieve over top of dish. Serve warm with toast points. Makes 4 main-dish servings.

Each serving: About 365 calories, 35 g protein, 5 g carbohydrate, 23 g total fat (10 g saturated), 243 mg cholesterol, 1,015 mg sodium.

Tarragon Salmon with Caper Sauce

Prep: 20 minutes
Roast: About 40 minutes

Caper Sauce
¾ cup sour cream
½ cup mayonnaise
¼ cup milk
3 tablespoons capers, drained and chopped
2 tablespoons chopped fresh tarragon leaves
½ teaspoon freshly grated lemon peel
⅛ teaspoon coarsely ground black pepper

Salmon
2 large lemons, thinly sliced
1 whole salmon (5½ pounds), cleaned and scaled, with head and
    tail removed
2 tablespoons olive oil
½ teaspoon salt
½ teaspoon coarsely ground black pepper
1 large bunch fresh tarragon
1 small bunch fresh flat-leaf parsley
Lemon wedges

1. Prepare Caper Sauce: In medium bowl, stir together
sour cream, mayonnaise, milk, capers, tarragon, lemon peel,
and pepper until well blended. Cover and refrigerate up to
2 days or until ready to serve. Makes about 1⅓ cups.

2. Prepare Salmon: Preheat oven to 450°F. Line 15½"
by 10½" jelly-roll pan with foil.

3. Place one-third of lemon slices in a row down center
of pan. Rub outside of salmon with oil. Place salmon on
top of lemon slices. Sprinkle salt and pepper in cavity.
Place tarragon and parsley sprigs and half of remaining
lemon slices in cavity. Place remaining lemon slices on top
of fish.

4. Roast salmon until just opaque throughout when knife
is inserted at backbone, about 40 minutes. Remove and discard lemon slices and skin from top of salmon. Transfer

salmon to large platter. Serve with Caper Sauce and lemon wedges. Makes 10 main-dish servings.

Each serving of fish without sauce: About 180 calories, 25 g protein, 0 g carbohydrate, 8 g total fat (2 g saturated), 45 mg cholesterol, 160 mg sodium.

Each tablespoon of sauce: About 60 calories, 0 g protein, 1 g carbohydrate, 6 g total fat (2 g saturated), 6 mg cholesterol, 80 mg sodium.

Some helpful tips when roasting a whole salmon: To estimate cooking time for a whole fish, use the 10-minute rule. Allow 10 minutes per inch of thickness, measuring at the plumpest part—near the base of the head. To test for doneness, insert a small knife at the backbone to see if the flesh is just opaque throughout. For easier serving, peel off the top skin with a fork and knife. Slide a cake server under the front section of the top fillet on top of backbone and transfer to a platter. Slide the cake server under the backbone and lift it away from the bottom fillet. Slide the cake server between the bottom fillet and skin and transfer the bottom fillet to the platter.

Baked Whole Flounder with Savory Crumb Topping

Prep: 10 minutes
Bake: About 40 minutes

3 slices firm white bread, torn into fine crumbs
2 tablespoons chopped fresh parsley
½ cup dry white wine
1 whole flounder (2 pounds), cleaned and scaled, head and tail
    left on
¼ teaspoon salt
¼ cup mayonnaise

1. Preheat oven to 350°F. In small skillet, cook bread crumbs over medium heat, stirring frequently, until golden. Remove skillet from heat; stir in parsley.

2. Pour wine into 13" by 9" baking dish; place flounder in dish and turn to moisten each side with wine. Turn flounder so dark-skin side is up. Sprinkle salt on flounder and spread top with mayonnaise. Use crumb mixture to coat top of fish, patting crumbs to cover. Bake until crumbs are crisp and flounder is just opaque throughout when knife is inserted at backbone, 30 to 40 minutes. Serve hot. Makes 4 main-dish servings.

Each serving: About 245 calories, 17 g protein, 10 g carbohydrate, 15 g total fat (2 g saturated), 46 mg cholesterol, 510 mg sodium.

Asian-Style Flounder Packets

Prep: 10 minutes
Bake: 8 minutes

4 flounder fillets (6 ounces each)
2 large green onions
2 tablespoons soy sauce
2 tablespoons seasoned rice vinegar
2 teaspoons grated, peeled fresh ginger

1. With tweezers, remove any small bones from flounder fillets. Cut tops of green onions crosswise into 2-inch pieces, then cut each piece lengthwise into thin strips; reserve. Thinly slice white part of green onions.

2. In small bowl, stir soy sauce and rice vinegar.

3. Preheat oven to 425°F. From foil or parchment paper, cut four 15" by 12" sheets.

4. Arrange 1 flounder fillet on half of each piece of foil; sprinkle each with ½ teaspoon ginger. Spoon 1 tablespoon soy-sauce mixture over each flounder fillet; top with some sliced green onions. Fold other half of foil over fish. To seal packets, beginning at a corner where foil is folded, make small ½-inch-wide folds, with each new fold overlapping previous one, until packet is completely sealed. Packet will resemble a half circle. Repeat, making 4 packets. Place sealed packets in 15½" by 10½" jelly-roll pan. Bake packets 8 minutes.

5. To serve, with kitchen shears, cut an X in top of each packet to let steam escape before serving. (When packets are open, check that fish is opaque throughout.) Sprinkle fish with reserved green-onion strips. Makes 4 main-dish servings.

Each serving: About 175 calories, 33 g protein, 5 g carbohydrate, 2 g total fat (1 g saturated), 90 mg cholesterol, 855 mg sodium.

Baked Tilefish with Mushrooms

Prep: 15 minutes
Bake: 32 minutes

4 small tilefish or cod steaks, each 1 inch thick
¾ teaspoon salt
¼ teaspoon ground black pepper
6 tablespoons margarine or butter
1 pound medium mushrooms, trimmed and halved
2 tablespoons lemon juice
2 teaspoons Worcestershire sauce
½ teaspoon dry mustard
2 tablespoons chopped fresh chives

1. With tweezers, remove any small bones from tilefish steaks. Preheat oven to 350°F. Grease 13" by 9" baking dish; arrange tilefish steaks in prepared dish. Sprinkle ¼ teaspoon salt and pepper on tilefish; bake 10 minutes.

2. Meanwhile, in 10-inch skillet, melt margarine over medium-high heat. Add mushrooms, and cook, stirring frequently, until tender. Stir in lemon juice, Worcestershire, mustard, and remaining ½ teaspoon salt. Spoon mushroom mixture on fish steaks. Sprinkle chives on top.

3. Bake, basting steaks occasionally with pan juices, until fish is just opaque throughout, about 10 minutes longer. Serve tilefish with mushrooms and pan juices. Makes 4 main-dish servings.

Each serving: About 350 calories, 34 g protein, 5 g carbohydrate, 23 g total fat (4 g saturated), 85 mg cholesterol, 785 mg sodium.

Roasted Scrod with Tomato Relish

Prep: 10 minutes
Roast: 15 minutes

3 teaspoons vegetable oil
1 small onion, chopped
2 tablespoons water
1 can (28 ounces) plum tomatoes, drained, tomatoes cut into
    quarters
¼ cup red wine vinegar
2 tablespoons brown sugar
½ teaspoon salt
4 pieces scrod fillet (6 ounces each)
¼ teaspoon coarsely ground black pepper

1. Preheat oven to 450°F.

2. In 2-quart saucepan, heat 2 teaspoons oil over medium heat. Add onion and water and cook, stirring frequently, until tender and golden, about 10 minutes. Stir in tomatoes, vinegar, brown sugar, and ¼ teaspoon salt; heat to boiling over high heat. Cook, stirring frequently, until relish thickens, about 10 to 15 minutes.

3. Meanwhile, place scrod in 9" by 9" baking dish; drizzle remaining 1 teaspoon oil on scrod and sprinkle with pepper and remaining ¼ teaspoon salt. Roast until fish is just opaque throughout, 12 to 15 minutes. To serve, spoon tomato relish on scrod. Makes 4 main-dish servings.

Each serving: About 230 calories, 32 g protein, 15 g carbohydrate, 5 g total fat (1 g saturated), 73 mg cholesterol, 590 mg sodium.

Salmon Pie

Prep: 30 minutes
Bake: 55 minutes

4 tablespoons margarine or butter
1 pound all-purpose potatoes (3 medium), peeled and cut into ½-inch chunks
2 medium carrots, peeled and sliced
1 large onion, cut into 8 wedges
¼ cup all-purpose flour
½ teaspoon salt

¼ teaspoon ground black pepper
2 cups milk
1 can (15 ½ ounces) salmon, drained and separated into bite-size chunks
1 cup frozen peas
½ package (10 to 11 ounces) piecrust mix
1 large egg yolk
1 teaspoon water

1. In 3-quart saucepan, melt margarine over medium heat. Add potatoes, carrots, and onion and cook, stirring frequently, until nearly tender.

2. Stir in flour, salt, and pepper until blended; cook, stirring, 1 minute. Gradually stir in milk, and cook, stirring constantly, until mixture has thickened slightly and boils. Gently stir in salmon and peas. Spoon mixture into 2-quart round casserole.

3. Preheat oven to 375°F. Prepare piecrust mix for 1 crust pie as label directs.

4. On lightly floured surface, with floured rolling pin, roll pastry into a round about 1½ inches larger than top of casserole. Place pastry loosely over salmon mixture. With kitchen shears, trim pastry edge, leaving 1-inch overhang. Fold overhang under and press gently all around casserole rim to make a stand-up edge. Cut several 1-inch slits in pastry top to allow steam to escape during baking. In cup, with fork, beat egg yolk and water. Brush crust with egg-yolk mixture. If you like, reroll scraps and cut out designs to decorate top of pie; brush cutouts with yolk mixture. Place pie on foil-lined cookie sheet to catch any overflow. Bake pie until crust is golden and filling bubbles in center,

30 to 35 minutes. Transfer pie to wire rack and let stand a few minutes before serving. Makes 6 main-dish servings.

Each serving: About 435 calories, 21 g protein, 38 g carbohydrate, 22g total fat (6 g saturated), 70 mg cholesterol, 835 mg sodium.

ᴄᴏ Shellfish

CLAMS

Among the varieties of hard-shell clams are chowder clams (large), cherrystones (medium), and littlenecks (small) from Eastern waters; butter, razor, littleneck, and Pismo clams from the West Coast. Large clams are used in chowders and stews. Cherrystones and littlenecks are either eaten raw or used in cooked dishes. Soft-shell clams are also called steamers. They are usually steamed and served in their shells or used in cooked dishes.

Fresh clams are sold live in the shell, or shucked. The shells of live clams should be tightly closed; any partly opened shells should shut tightly if lightly tapped. Shucked clams should be plump, shiny, and fresh-smelling.

To open hard-shell clams

Clams need to be well scrubbed with a stiff brush and rinsed under cold running water to remove any sand. Discard any clams that remain open when tapped with fingers. Shuck as below.

Hold clam in one hand and, with the other hand, insert a clam-shucker or blunt knife between the two shell sections near hinge, and run it between the shells.

With twisting motions of the knife, pry the shells apart. Remove the top shell.

Run the knife under the clam muscle to loosen it from its shell; remove any bits of broken shell.

For soft-shell clams, pull the sections apart; slit the tough neck skin and pull it off.

Steamed Soft-Shell Clams

Prep: 25 minutes
Cook: 15 minutes

6 dozen steamer (soft-shell) clams
1 cup water
¾ cup (1½ sticks) margarine or butter, melted

1. With stiff brush, scrub clams with cold running water until free of sand. In steamer or saucepot, heat water or enough *water to cover bottom* of steamer or saucepot to boiling over high heat. On rack in steamer or in saucepot, place clams. Reduce heat to low, cover and *steam clams* 5 to 10 minutes until clams open, transferring clams to bowl as they open. Discard any clams that have not opened.

2. Place clams in 4 bowls. Let clam broth stand a few minutes until sand settles. Strain clam broth through sieve lined with paper towels. Pour margarine into 4 small dishes and clam broth into 4 mugs.

3. To eat, with fingers, pull clams from shells by neck; swish first in broth to remove any sand, then dip in butter. (All except the tough skin of the neck may be eaten.) When sand settles to bottom, the broth may be drunk, if desired. Makes 4 main-dish servings.

Each serving: About 450 calories, 26 g protein, 5 g carbohydrate, 36 g total fat (6 g saturated), 67 mg cholesterol, 565 mg sodium.

Chinese Steamed Clams

Prep: 15 minutes
Cook: 17 minutes

2 dozen cherrystone or littleneck clams
2 tablespoons vegetable oil
1 piece peeled fresh ginger, about ½ inch in diameter and
    1 inch long, cut into thin slices
¼ cup water
3 tablespoons dry sherry
2 tablespoons soy sauce
¾ cup regular long-grain rice, cooked as label directs but
    omit salt

1. With stiff brush, scrub clams under cold running water until free of sand.

2. In 8-quart Dutch oven, heat oil over high heat until very hot. Add ginger and cook, tossing, until browned. Add clams, water, sherry, and soy sauce; heat to boiling. Reduce heat to medium; cover and simmer about 5 minutes, stirring frequently, until clams open, transferring clams to bowl as they open. Discard any clams that have not opened. Serve clams and pan juices with rice. Makes 3 main-dish servings.

Each serving: About 335 calories, 16 g protein, 42 g carbohydrate, 10 g total fat (1 g saturated), 32 mg cholesterol, 740 mg sodium.

Clam Fritters

Prep: 20 minutes
Cook: 15 minutes

1 cup all-purpose flour
1½ teaspoons baking powder
¼ teaspoon salt
1 teaspoon sugar
2 dozen cherrystone clams, shucked, with their liquid (see page
    346)
2 large eggs
1 teaspoon grated onion
Vegetable oil for frying
Tartar Sauce (see page 769)

1. In medium bowl, stir together flour, baking powder, salt, and sugar. Drain clams in sieve, reserving ½ cup liquid; coarsely chop clams.

2. In another bowl, combine clams, eggs, onion, and reserved clam liquid; stir just until mixed. Stir clam mixture into flour mixture until just blended.

3. In 12-inch skillet heat 1 tablespoon oil over medium heat until very hot. In small batches, carefully place clam mixture, by tablespoons, into hot oil. Fry fritters, turning once with slotted spoon, until golden. Use slotted spoon to transfer fritters to paper towels to drain. Transfer to warm large platter and keep warm. Repeat with remaining clam mixture, adding additional oil to skillet as needed. Serve fritters hot with Tartar Sauce. Makes 4 main-dish servings or about 2 dozen fritters.

Each serving: About 300 calories, 16 g protein, 28 g carbohydrate, 14 g total fat (2 g saturated), 131 mg cholesterol, 365 mg sodium.

CRABS

Crabs are sold whole, cooked or live, and as fresh or frozen cooked legs, lumpmeat (whole pieces from the body), or flaked meat (light and dark meat from the body and claws.) When buying whole crabs, choose cooked ones with bright red shells or live crabs that are active. Cooked crabmeat should be white tinged with pink, and sweet-smelling; when preparing it, check for any small pieces of shell and cartilage. Frozen crabmeat is a convenient alternative to fresh.

Hard-shell varieties of crab should be cooked before you remove the meat. Soft-shell crabs, which are available fresh only from May through mid-September, are eaten shell and all, and must be cleaned before cooking.

To cook hard-shell crabs

Rinse the crabs with cold running water (if you like, wear rubber gloves). Plunge crabs into a large saucepot containing enough boiling water to cover them. When water boils again, reduce the heat to medium; cover and cook crabs for 5 to 10 minutes or until shells turn red.

To remove cooked crabmeat

1. Twist off claws and legs; then with a nut-cracker or hammer, crack claws all over. Pick out the meat and remove any cartilage from the meat.
2. Next, with fingers, pull off "apron" on the underside of the body and discard.
3. With the body in both hands, insert your thumb under the shell, by the apron hinge, and pull the top shell from the body.
4. Use a spoon to scrape the soft red roe or grayish green liver from the top shell into a small bowl, if you like. Discard the shell.
5. Spoon any roe or liver from body into same bowl. With fingers, remove and discard "dead-man's fingers" (spongy gills).
6. Now, break or cut the body in half down the center. With a lobster or nut pick, remove the meat between the shell sections. Use the meat, roe, and liver in recipes.

Panfried Soft-Shell Crabs

Prep: 20 minutes
Cook: 14 minutes

8 live soft-shell crabs
½ teaspoon salt
¼ teaspoon ground black pepper
4 tablespoons margarine or butter
1 tablespoon chopped fresh parsley
1 teaspoon fresh lemon juice
⅛ teaspoon Worcestershire sauce
Lemon wedges (optional)

1. Order crabs cleaned or, with kitchen shears, cut across crab ¼ inch behind eyes; discard. With fingers, remove the flat pointed appendage (apron) on the underside. Fold back but do not remove top shell from one of the points. Pull off spongy gills (dead-man's fingers) and discard. Fold top shell back. Repeat on other side of crab. Rinse crab with cold running water and pat dry with paper towels.

2. Sprinkle salt and pepper on crabs. In 12-inch skillet, melt butter over medium heat. Add half the crabs and cook about 3 minutes per side or until golden. With tongs, transfer crabs to warm large platter and keep warm. Repeat with remaining crabs.

3. Into margarine in skillet, stir parsley, lemon juice, and Worcestershire; pour mixture over crabs. If you like, serve crabs with lemon wedges. Entire crab, shell and all, is eaten. Makes 4 main-dish servings.

Each serving: About 210 calories, 23 g protein, 0 g carbohydrate, 13 g total fat (2 g saturated), 99 mg cholesterol, 820 mg sodium.

Little Crab Cakes with Guacamole

Prep: 45 minutes
Cook: 10 minutes per batch

Guacamole
3 ripe medium avocados
2 tablespoons fresh lime juice
2 green onions, thinly sliced
2 tablespoons chopped fresh cilantro leaves
½ teaspoon salt
¼ teaspoon green jalapeño sauce

Crab Cakes
1½ teaspoons fresh lemon juice
1 container (16 ounces) lump crabmeat, picked over
3 tablespoons olive oil
1 medium onion, finely chopped
⅛ teaspoon ground red pepper (cayenne)
3 large eggs
⅓ cup mayonnaise
1 tablespoon Dijon mustard with seeds
2 tablespoons chopped fresh parsley leaves
¾ teaspoon salt
¼ teaspoon dried thyme
4 cups cornflakes
Lemon or lime wedges

1. Prepare Guacamole: Cut each avocado lengthwise in half; remove pits and peel. Cut avocados into chunks.

2. In medium bowl, with fork, mash avocados with lime juice; stir in green onions, cilantro, salt, and jalapeño sauce. Cover surface of guacamole directly with plastic wrap to prevent discoloration. Refrigerate if not serving right away. (Makes about 1½ cups.)

3. Prepare Crab Cakes: Sprinkle lemon juice on crabmeat.

4. In nonstick 12-inch skillet, heat 1 tablespoon oil over medium heat. Add onion and ground red pepper, and cook, stirring frequently, until onion is tender, about 8 minutes. Remove skillet from heat.

5. In medium bowl, with wire whisk, blend 1 egg, mayonnaise, mustard, 1 tablespoon parsley, salt, and thyme.

Stir in crabmeat and onion mixture until well blended. With hands, shape crabmeat mixture into twenty-four 2-inch round cakes.

6. In food processor with knife blade attached, or in blender, pulse cornflakes to fine crumbs; transfer crumbs to large sheet of waxed paper and toss with remaining 1 tablespoon parsley.

7. In pic plate, with fork, beat remaining 2 eggs and *1 tablespoon water.* One at a time, dip each crab cake into beaten eggs, letting excess drip off, then coat with crumb mixture, patting crumbs to cover. (If not cooking right away, place crab cakes on large cookie sheet; cover with plastic wrap and refrigerate until ready to cook.)

8. In same skillet, heat 1 tablespoon oil over medium-high heat. Add 12 crab cakes and cook about 5 minutes, per side, until golden brown. Use narrow spatula to transfer crab cakes to warm large platter; cover loosely with foil to keep warm. Repeat with remaining 1 tablespoon oil and crab cakes. Serve crab cakes with guacamole and lemon or lime wedges. Makes 24 crab cakes, 8 main-dish servings.

Each crab cake without guacamole: About 85 calories, 5 g protein, 4 g carbohydrate, 5 g total fat (1 g saturated), 47 mg cholesterol, 205 mg sodium.

Each tablespoon guacamole: About 40 calories, 1 g protein, 2 g carbohydrate, 4 g total fat (1 g saturated), 0 mg cholesterol, 45 mg sodium.

CRAYFISH

The crayfish is a small freshwater shellfish that closely resembles the lobster in appearance and taste. Crayfish are sold live in their shells and the peeled cooked tailmeat is sold fresh and frozen. Only the meat from the tail and the small pocket of rich yellow or orange "fat" (roe) from the head are consumed.

Buy crayfish that are lively; and cook them the same day they are purchased. Five to 6 pounds of live crayfish equals 1 pound of peeled tail meat.

TO BOIL CRAYFISH: Place the crayfish in the sink and rinse them well with cold running water; discard any dead crayfish. In a large saucepot, heat enough water to boiling to cover the crayfish; plunge the crayfish into the boiling water and heat to boiling. Reduce the heat to medium, cover and cook for 5 minutes. Drain. Cool crayfish until easy to handle, then peel.

TO PEEL CRAYFISH: Separate the tail from the head by slightly twisting and firmly pulling them apart. Discard the head. Hold the tail between your forefinger and thumb and squeeze. You can usually hear the shell crack.

Grasp the first three segments of the tail shell from the side and loosen them by lifting up and pulling around the meat. These segments can easily be pulled off now and discarded. Firmly grasp the last tail segment and the tail fin between the thumb and forefinger of one hand, and the meat with the other hand, and gently pull them apart. The meat should slide out of the shell and the vein should pull free from the meat.

Crayfish Etouffée

Prep: 35 minutes
Cook: 35 minutes

3 pounds live crayfish	1 teaspoon salt
¼ cup olive oil	½ teaspoon ground red pepper
⅓ cup all-purpose flour	(cayenne)
¼ cup chopped onion	½ teaspoon dried basil
¼ cup chopped celery	½ teaspoon dried thyme
¼ cup chopped green pepper	1 cup regular long-grain rice, cooked as label directs

1. Rinse crayfish with cold running water; discard any crayfish that show no sign of life.

2. In 8-quart saucepot, heat *12 cups water* to boiling over high heat. Add crayfish; heat to boiling. Reduce heat to medium; cover and cook 5 minutes. Drain and cool crayfish until easy to handle. Peel and remove tail meat from crayfish (see page 354).

3. In 3-quart saucepan heat oil over medium-high heat until very hot. Stir in flour and cook, stirring frequently, until flour is dark brown, but not scorched, about 5 minutes. Reduce heat to medium; stir in onion, celery, green pepper, salt, ground red pepper, basil, and thyme; cook, stirring, 1 minute.

4. Gradually stir in ¾ *cup water;* cook, stirring constantly, until sauce has thickened slightly and boils. Reduce heat to low; cover and simmer, stirring occasionally, until vegetables are tender, about 5 minutes. Add crayfish meat; heat through, gently. Serve Etouffée with rice. Makes 4 main-dish servings.

Each serving: About 380 calories, 14 g protein, 47 g carbohydrate, 15 g total fat (2 g saturated), 68 mg cholesterol, 640 mg sodium.

SHRIMP ETOUFÉE: Prepare as above but use *1 pound medium shrimp,* shelled and deveined, (see page 366) instead of crayfish. In 2-quart saucepan, heat *1½ inches water* to boiling over high heat. Add shrimp; heat to boiling. Reduce heat to low; simmer, stirring frequently, 1 minute. Drain. Complete recipe as above following steps 3 through 5. Makes 3 main-dish servings.

Each serving: About 425 calories, 24 g protein, 47 g carbohydrate, 15 g total fat (2 g saturated), 180 mg cholesterol, 795 mg sodium.

LOBSTERS

The American lobster, most abundant in the waters of Maine, comes from the North Atlantic coast. It is usually sold live or cooked in the shell.

An uncooked lobster should be alive and lively, with the tail curling under, not hanging down, when the lobster is picked up. Cooked lobster should have a bright-red shell.

Buy a 1¼- to 1½-pound lobster per serving, which will yield about ¼ pound cooked meat.

Boiled Live Lobster

1. Allow one live *1¼- to 1½-pound lobster* per serving. In large saucepot, heat *3 inches water* to boiling over high heat. Plunge 2 or 3 lobsters at a time (depending on size of saucepot), headfirst into boiling water. Immediately cover with lid; cook until water boils again. Reduce heat to medium; cook 10 minutes, covered, frequently lifting lid to let steam escape and to prevent water from boiling over.

2. When lobster is done, with tongs, transfer to plate lined with paper towels to drain. Serve lobster hot with lobster cracker and fork. Accompany with small dishes of melted margarine or butter.

Broiled Live Lobster

1. Allow one live *1¼- to 1½-pound* lobster per serving. Order lobster split lengthwise and cleaned. Or split and clean as follows:

2. Place lobster on its back. Where tail and body meet, insert point of knife through to back shell (this immobilizes the lobster). With lobster cracker or heavy mallet, crack claws.

3. Then, split lobster from end of tail to head, cutting to, but not through, back shell. Spread lobster open. Remove dark vein in back of tail; leave in greenish-gray liver (tomalley) and roe (coral), if present. Roe turns red when cooked. Remove the sand sac from body of lobster.

4. Preheat broiler. Place lobster, cut side up, in broiling pan. Broil at closest position to heat source, brushing occasionally with melted margarine, until lobster meat is just opaque throughout, 8 to 15 minutes, depending on size of lobster. If broiling several lobsters, arrange them around sides of pan, with body sections in center. Serve with melted margarine or butter.

Each serving without additional margarine or butter for serving: About 275 calories.

To remove cooked lobster meat

Break off claws and legs. With lobster cracker, crack claws and remove meat.

Twist off head from tail and, using kitchen shears, cut away thin underside shell from tail and discard; gently pull meat from the shell.

Cut along the rounded backside of the tail meat, about ¼ inch deep, to expose the dark vein; remove the vein and discard. Reserve any dark roe (coral) or greenish-gray liver (tomalley).

Lift bony portion from the head shell. Discard the sac and spongy grayish gills from the top of the head. Break the bony portion into several pieces. Using a lobster pick, pick out the meat.

Lobster Newburg

Prep: 20 minutes
Cook: 25 minutes

3 tablespoons margarine or butter
1 package (10 ounces) medium mushrooms, each trimmed and cut into quarters
¼ teaspoon salt
2 tablespoons all-purpose flour
¼ teaspoon paprika
Pinch ground nutmeg
3 tablespoons dry sherry
1 cup chicken broth
1 cup heavy or whipping cream
12 ounces cooked lobster meat, cut into small pieces*
8 slices firm white bread, toasted and each cut diagonally in half
2 tablespoons fresh parsley leaves, chopped

1. In 12-inch skillet, melt 1 tablespoon margarine over medium-high heat. Add mushrooms and ⅛ teaspoon salt, and cook, stirring occasionally, until mushrooms are golden, about 10 minutes. With slotted spoon, transfer mushrooms to small bowl.

2. In same skillet, melt remaining 2 tablespoons margarine. Reduce heat to low; stir in flour, paprika, and nutmeg, and cook, stirring, 1 minute. Stir in sherry and cook 30 seconds. Increase heat to medium; gradually stir in broth and cream, and cook, stirring, until mixture boils and has thickened slightly. Stir in cooked lobster, mushrooms, and remaining ⅛ teaspoon salt, and heat through.

3. To serve, arrange toast on 4 large plates. Spoon lobster mixture on toast; sprinkle with parsley. Makes 4 main-dish servings.

We cooked 2½ pounds frozen lobster tails, which yielded ¾ pound of meat. Or, you can buy fresh or frozen cooked lobster meat from your fish store or supermarket.

Each serving: About 550 calories, 26 g protein, 35 g carbohydrate, 34 g total fat (16 g saturated), 144 mg cholesterol, 1,070 mg sodium.

Rock Lobster Tails

The tails are the commonly available portion of spiny lobsters. They usually come in the shell, uncooked and frozen. The cooked meat can be used in any recipe that calls for lobster meat.

Allow one 6- to 8-ounce tail or 2 or 3 smaller ones for each serving. One 8-ounce tail yields about 4 ounces cooked lobster meat.

TO COOK IN WATER FOR USE IN RECIPE: To cook, drop them, frozen or thawed, into boiling salted water in a saucepot and heat to boiling. Reduce heat to low and cook until shells turn bright red and the meat is tender.

TO REMOVE MEAT: With kitchen shears, cut away the thin underside shell. Grasp the meat and pull it away from shell.

TO BROIL: Thaw rock lobster tails, wrapped, in the refrigerator for several hours or overnight. Preheat the broiler. Lightly oil the rack in the broiling pan. With kitchen shears, cut away the thin underside shell of each lobster tail. Insert a skewer lengthwise through the meat so that the tail will lie flat and the meat won't curl while broiling. Place the tails, shell side up, on the rack. Broil the tails turning them once until the meat becomes opaque throughout. Serve the tails in their shells, meat side up, with melted margarine or butter.

MUSSELS

Mussels come to market live in their shells. Be sure to buy them from a reliable fish market or supermarket with a busy fish counter and a fast turnover. Like other shellfish, they are very perishable and should be used as soon after purchase as possible.

Buy mussels with unbroken, tightly closed shells, or shells that close when touched. Allow 18 to 24 mussels per serving if small, 12 per serving if large.

TO PREPARE: Rinse mussels well with cold running water to remove any sand; discard any that remain open. Under running water, scrub the shells clean with a stiff metal brush, scraping off any loose barnacles with a knife. Using rubber gloves, grasp the beard and pull hard to remove it or clip it off with kitchen scissors. This is "debearding" a mussel.

TO STEAM: Place mussels in a large pot with a small amount of boiling water, broth, or wine. Cover the pot tightly and simmer over medium heat for 5 to 10 minutes, stirring the mussels or shaking the pot occasionally, until the mussels open, transferring mussels to bowl as they open. Discard any mussels that do not open.

Mussels in Wine

Prep: 15 minutes
Cook: 17 minutes

3 tablespoons olive oil
1 small onion, chopped
1 garlic clove, finely chopped
1 can (14½ to 16 ounces) tomatoes
¾ cup dry white wine
¼ teaspoon dried basil
4 dozen large mussels, scrubbed and debearded
   (see page 359)
2 tablespoons chopped fresh parsley

In 5-quart Dutch oven, heat oil over medium heat. Add onion and garlic, and cook, stirring occasionally, until tender. Stir in tomatoes with their juice, wine, and basil; heat to boiling over high heat breaking tomatoes up with side of spoon. Add mussels; heat to boiling. Reduce heat to low; cover and simmer, 5 to 10 minutes, stirring occasionally, until mussels open, transferring mussels to bowl as they open. Discard any mussels that have not opened. Serve mussels in shallow soup plates with the pan juices. Sprinkle servings with parsley. Makes 4 main-dish servings.

Each serving: About 255 calories, 18 g protein, 13 g carbohydrate, 14 g total fat (2 g saturated), 40 mg cholesterol, 580 mg sodium.

Mussels in Saffron-Tomato Broth

Prep: 20 minutes
Cook: 30 minutes

3 tablespoons olive oil
2 garlic cloves, crushed with side of chef's knife
1 small bay leaf
½ teaspoon loosely packed saffron threads
⅛ to ¼ teaspoon crushed red pepper
1 can (14½ ounces) diced tomatoes
1 bottle (8 ounces) clam juice
½ cup dry white wine
5 dozen medium mussels, scrubbed and debearded .
   (see page 359)

1. In 8-quart saucepot, heat oil over medium heat. Add garlic and cook, stirring, until golden. Add bay leaf, saffron threads, and crushed red pepper; cook, stirring, 1 minute.

2. Add tomatoes with their juice, clam juice, and wine; heat to boiling over high heat. Reduce heat to low; cover and simmer 20 minutes.

3. Add mussels; heat to boiling over high heat. Reduce heat to medium; cover and simmer 5 minutes, stirring occasionally, until mussels open, transferring mussels to bowl as they open. Discard bay leaf and any mussels that do not open. Serve mussels in shallow soup plates with the pan juices. Makes 4 main-dish servings.

Each serving: About 220 calories, 15 g protein, 10 g carbohydrate, 13 g total fat (2 g saturated), 34 mg cholesterol, 795 mg sodium.

OYSTERS

Fresh oysters can be bought year-round but in most of the world are at their best during fall and winter.

Buy oysters with undamaged, tightly closed shells. Fresh shucked oysters are also available. They should be plump and uniform in size, smell fresh, and be packed in clear, not cloudy, liquid.

Cover live oysters with a damp kitchen towel and store flat, preferably on ice, in the refrigerator for up to 5 days. Refrigerate shucked oysters in a container with their liquor for up to 1 day. (The liquor should cover the oysters. If not, make your own to top it up by dissolving ½ teaspoon salt in 1 cup water.)

Clean oysters by scrubbing with a stiff brush under cold running water to remove any sand. Shuck oysters just before serving or cooking; discard open or damaged oysters. For serving raw on the half-shell, allow 6 oysters per diner.

To open oysters

Hold oyster in an oven mitt or kitchen towel, flat side up. Insert point of oyster knife between top and bottom shells next to the hinge. Push knife blade farther into the shell and then twist the knife to pry shells apart. Taking care not to spill any liquor, carefully loosen flesh from top shell. Discard top shell. Run knife blade under the oyster to loosen flesh from bottom shell. Remove any broken shell.

Panfried Oysters

Prep: 10 minutes
Cook: 10 minutes

1 pint shucked oysters
3 tablespoons vegetable oil
3 tablespoons margarine or butter
⅔ cup finely crushed saltine crackers
Lemon wedges

1. Drain oysters; pat dry with paper towels. In 10-inch skillet, heat oil and margarine over medium-high heat until margarine melts. On waxed paper, sprinkle half of crushed saltines. Place oysters on crumbs and sprinkle remaining saltines on top of oysters.

2. Lightly shaking off excess crumbs, add half of oysters to skillet and fry about 2 minutes per side or until oysters are golden brown and opaque throughout. With slotted spoon, gently remove oysters from skillet and (still on spoon) drain on paper towels. Transfer to warm platter; keep warm. Repeat with remaining oysters.

3. Serve oysters hot with lemon wedges. Makes 3 main-dish servings.

Each serving: About 425 calories, 11 g protein, 27 g carbohydrate, 31 g total fat (5 g saturated), 40 mg cholesterol, 770 mg sodium.

SCALLOPS

Bay scallops are small, about ½ inch in diameter, and they are more delicately flavored and tender than the larger sea scallops, which can be as big as 2 inches in diameter.

Buy scallops that are creamy-pink in color, moist, and shiny, with little or no liquid, and a slightly sweet odor.

Scallops with Saffron Cream

Prep: 4 minutes
Cook: 10 minutes

1 pound bay or sea scallops
3 tablespoons margarine or butter
1 tablespoon all-purpose flour
½ teaspoon salt
⅛ teaspoon ground white pepper
⅛ teaspoon crushed saffron threads
½ cup half-and-half
2 tablespoons dry vermouth or white wine

1. Pull tough crescent-shaped muscle from side of each scallop. Rinse with running cold water to remove sand from crevices. Pat scallops dry with paper towels. (If using sea scallops, cut each horizontally in half.)

2. In 10-inch skillet, melt margarine over medium-high heat. Add scallops and cook, stirring frequently, just until opaque throughout, about 5 minutes. With slotted spoon, transfer scallops to bowl.

3. Into margarine in same skillet, stir flour, salt, white pepper, and saffron, over medium heat, until blended; cook, stirring, 1 minute. Gradually stir in half-and-half and vermouth; cook, stirring constantly, until mixture has thickened slightly. Stir scallops and any juice in bowl into saffron cream; heat through. Serve scallops with saffron-cream sauce. Makes 4 main-dish servings.

Each serving: About 210 calories, 18 g protein, 5 g carbohydrate, 13 g total fat (4 g saturated), 44 mg cholesterol, 580 mg sodium.

Chili Scallops with Black-Bean Salsa

Prep: 15 minutes
Cook: 3 to 6 minutes

1 can (15 to 19 ounces) black beans, rinsed and drained
1 can (15¼ to 16 ounces) whole-kernel corn, drained
¼ cup finely chopped red onion
¼ cup loosely packed fresh cilantro leaves, chopped
2 tablespoons fresh lime juice
½ teaspoon salt
1 pound sea scallops, rinsed
1 tablespoon chili powder
1 teaspoon sugar
2 teaspoons vegetable oil
Lime wedges (optional)

1. In large bowl, stir together black beans, corn, red onion, cilantro, lime juice, and ¼ teaspoon salt. Set black-bean salsa aside.

2. Pull tough crescent-shaped muscle from side of each scallop. Rinse with cold running water to remove sand from crevices. Pat scallops dry with paper towels. In medium bowl, combine chili powder, sugar, and remaining ¼ teaspoon salt; add scallops, tossing to coat.

3. In nonstick 12-inch skillet, heat oil over medium-high heat until very hot. Add scallops and cook 1½ to 3 minutes per side or until scallops are lightly browned and just opaque throughout.

4. Arrange black-bean salsa and scallops on 4 dinner plates. Serve with lime wedges, if you like. Makes 4 main-dish servings.

Each serving: About 290 calories, 31 g protein, 40 g carbohydrate, 5 g total fat (1 g saturated), 38 mg cholesterol, 1,005 mg sodium.

Scallop and Asparagus Stir-Fry

Prep: 20 minutes
Cook: 15 minutes

1 pound sea scallops, rinsed
1 tablespoon minced, peeled fresh ginger
2 tablespoons reduced-sodium soy sauce
2 tablespoons vegetable oil
2 garlic cloves, sliced
1½ pounds asparagus, trimmed and cut into 2-inch pieces
¼ teaspoon crushed red pepper
½ cup packed fresh basil leaves, chopped

1. Pull tough crescent-shape muscle from side of each scallop. Rinse under cold running water to remove sand from crevices. Pat scallops dry with paper towels.

2. In large bowl, toss scallops with ginger and 1 table-spoon soy sauce.

3. In nonstick 12-inch skillet, heat 1 tablespoon oil over medium-high heat. Add garlic and cook, stirring often, until golden brown. With slotted spoon, transfer garlic to another bowl.

4. In same skillet, cook asparagus and crushed red pepper, stirring often, until asparagus is tender-crisp, about 7 minutes. With slotted spoon, transfer asparagus to bowl with garlic.

5. Add remaining 1 tablespoon oil to skillet; add scallop mixture and cook, stirring frequently, just until scallops are opaque throughout, 3 to 5 minutes.

6. Add asparagus, garlic, and remaining 1 tablespoon soy sauce to skillet; heat through. Toss with chopped basil.

Spoon mixture into warm dish and serve. Makes 4 main-dish servings.

Each serving: About 190 calories, 22 g protein, 6 g carbohydrate, 8 g total fat (1 g saturated), 38 mg cholesterol, 505 mg sodium.

SHRIMP

Shrimp vary in size and shell color. Depending on the variety, the shells can be light gray, brownish pink, or red. When cooked, shells become reddish and the meat turns pink and is just opaque throughout. Available all year, shrimp come fresh or frozen (or thawed, frozen) in the shell, or frozen, shelled, and deveined, either uncooked or cooked. Frozen shrimp are also sold breaded, either cooked or uncooked.

Buy shrimp that have a mild aroma and firm-textured meat. One pound unshelled shrimp yields 12 ounces cooked, shelled meat.

TO BOIL SHRIMP: Place unshelled or shelled raw shrimp in enough boiling water to cover. When the water returns to boiling, reduce heat to low and simmer, stirring frequently, for 1 to 3 minutes, depending on the size and amount, until the shrimp are reddish on the outside and just opaque throughout.

TO SHELL AND DEVEIN SHRIMP: Hold shrimp with curved side up and with tail away from you. Insert tip of sharp kitchen shears under shell and snip along back through to tail, cutting about ¼ inch deep to expose black or green vein.

Remove shrimp by peeling away sides of shell from the cut; gently pull shrimp free, keeping tail intact. Rinse shrimp with running cold water to remove vein.

Shrimp and Scallop Kabobs

Prep: 20 minutes
Grill: 6 to 8 minutes

12 ounces large sea scallops,
 rinsed
1 pound large shrimp, shelled
 and deveined, leaving tail
 part of shell on, if you like
 (see page 366)
3 tablespoons soy sauce
3 tablespoons seasoned rice
 vinegar
2 tablespoons grated, peeled
 fresh ginger

1 tablespoon brown sugar
1 tablespoon Asian sesame oil
2 garlic cloves, crushed with
 garlic press
1 bunch green onions, cut
 diagonally into 3-inch-long
 pieces
12 cherry tomatoes
6 (10-inch) metal skewers

1. Prepare grill. Pull tough crescent-shaped muscle from side of each scallop. Pat shrimp and scallops dry with paper towels.

2. In large bowl, stir together soy sauce, rice vinegar, ginger, brown sugar, sesame oil, and garlic; add shrimp and scallops, tossing to coat.

3. Alternately thread shrimp, scallops, green onions, and cherry tomatoes on skewers. Grill skewers over medium heat, turning skewers occasionally, spooning any remaining soy sauce mixture on shrimp and scallops halfway through grilling, just until shrimp and scallops are opaque throughout, 6 to 8 minutes. To serve, slide shrimp, scallops, and vegetables off skewers onto plates. Makes 6 main-dish servings.

Each serving: About 150 calories, 22 g protein, 10 g carbohydrate, 3 g total fat (0 g saturated), 119 mg cholesterol, 710 mg sodium.

Beer-Batter Fried Shrimp

Prep: 12 minutes
Cook: 1 minute per batch

½ cup all-purpose flour
½ cup beer
½ teaspoon salt
Vegetable oil for frying
1 ½ pounds large shrimp, shelled and deveined
    (see page 366)

1. In small bowl, with wire whisk, beat flour, beer, and salt until well blended.

2. In heavy 2-quart saucepan, heat 2 inches oil over medium heat until temperature on deep-fat thermometer reaches 375°F (or heat oil in deep-fat fryer set at 375°F).

3. One or two at a time, dip shrimp into batter, letting excess drip off, then carefully place in hot oil. Fry shrimp about 30 seconds per side, turning with slotted spoon, just until batter is golden and shrimp are opaque throughout. With slotted spoon, transfer shrimp to paper towels to drain. Transfer to large warm platter; keep warm. Repeat with remaining shrimp and batter. Makes 6 main-dish servings.

Each serving: About 220 calories, 20 g protein, 9 g carbohydrate, 11 g total fat (1 g saturated), 140 mg cholesterol, 330 mg sodium.

Cajun Shrimp

Prep: 10 minutes
Cook: 3 to 4 minutes

¼ teaspoon salt
¼ teaspoon ground red pepper (cayenne)
1 teaspoon paprika
½ teaspoon dried thyme
⅛ teaspoon ground nutmeg
2 teaspoons olive oil
1 garlic clove, crushed with side of chef's knife
12 extra large shrimp (about 8 ounces), shelled and deveined (see page 366)

1. In cup, combine salt, ground red pepper, paprika, thyme, and nutmeg.
2. In nonstick 10-inch skillet, heat oil over medium-high heat. Add garlic; cook, stirring, 1 minute. With slotted spoon, discard garlic. Add paprika mixture and cook, stirring constantly, 30 seconds. Add shrimp, stirring to coat evenly with spices, and cook, stirring frequently, until shrimp are just opaque throughout, 2 to 3 minutes. Transfer shrimp to dinner plates and serve. Makes 2 main-dish servings.

Each serving: About 145 calories, 19 g protein, 2 g carbohydrate, 6 g total fat (1 g saturated), 142 mg cholesterol, 405 mg sodium.

Shrimp with Two Sauces

Prep: 25 minutes
Cook: 20 minutes

Southwestern Dipping Sauce
1 cup seafood cocktail sauce
2 tablespoons minced fresh cilantro leaves
2 teaspoons fresh lime juice
1 jalapeño chile, seeded and minced

Dijon Dipping Sauce
1 cup reduced-fat sour cream
¼ cup Dijon mustard with seeds
3 tablespoons chopped fresh parsley leaves
¼ teaspoon grated fresh lemon peel
¼ teaspoon salt
⅛ teaspoon coarsely ground black pepper

Shrimp
1 lemon, thinly sliced
2 teaspoons salt
20 whole black peppercorns
10 whole allspice berries
4 bay leaves
48 large shrimp (about 2 pounds), shelled and deveined
   (see page 366)

1. Prepare Southwestern Dipping Sauce: In small bowl, stir cocktail sauce, cilantro, lime juice, and jalapeño until well blended. Cover and refrigerate up to 2 days. Makes about 1 cup.

2. Prepare Dijon Dipping Sauce: In small bowl, stir sour cream, mustard, parsley, lemon peel, salt, and pepper until well blended. Cover and refrigerate up to 2 days. Makes about 1 cup.

3. Prepare Shrimp: In 5- or 6-quart saucepot, stir *8 cups water*, sliced lemon, salt, peppercorns, allspice, and bay leaves to boiling over high heat. Cover and boil 15 minutes.

4. Add shrimp and cook, stirring frequently, just until

shrimp are opaque throughout, about 1 to 2 minutes. Drain shrimp in colander; rinse with cold running water to stop further cooking. Dry shrimp well on paper towels. Discard lemon slices, bay leaves, peppercorns, and allspice from shrimp.

5. Serve shrimp on platter with bowls of dipping sauces. Makes 8 main-dish servings.

Each serving of shrimp without sauces: About 45 calories, 9 g protein, 0 g carbohydrate, 1 g total fat (0 g saturated), 90 mg cholesterol, 105 mg sodium.

Each tablespoon Southwestern dipping sauce: About 15 calories, 0 g protein, 3 g carbohydrate, 0 g total fat, 0 mg cholesterol, 170 mg sodium.

Each tablespoon Dijon dipping sauce: About 20 calories, 1 g protein, 1 g carbohydrate, 1 g total fat (0 g saturated), 5 mg cholesterol, 140 mg sodium.

Thai Shrimp

Prep: 30 minutes
Cook: 15 minutes

2 medium limes
3 teaspoons vegetable oil
1 small onion, finely chopped
1 small red pepper, thinly sliced
2 teaspoons grated, peeled fresh ginger
⅛ to ¼ teaspoon ground red pepper (cayenne)
4 ounces medium mushrooms, trimmed, each cut into quarters

½ teaspoon salt
1 can (13¾ to 15 ounces) light coconut milk*
1 pound large shrimp, shelled and deveined (see page 366)
2 ounces snow peas, strings removed and cut into thin strips
⅓ cup loosely packed fresh cilantro leaves

1. From limes, with vegetable peeler, remove 6 strips (1" by ¾" each) peel and squeeze 2 tablespoons juice. In nonstick 12-inch skillet, heat 2 teaspoons oil over medium heat. Add onion and cook, stirring occasionally, until tender, 5 minutes; add sliced red pepper and cook 1 minute. Stir in ginger and ground red pepper; cook, stirring, 1 minute. Transfer onion mixture to bowl.

2. In same skillet, heat remaining 1 teaspoon oil over medium-high heat. Add mushrooms and salt and cook, stirring frequently, until tender and lightly browned, about 3 minutes. Stir in coconut milk, lime peel and juice, and onion mixture, and heat to boiling. Add shrimp and cook, stirring frequently, just until shrimp are opaque throughout. Stir in snow pea strips; heat through. Stir in cilantro. Spoon into warm dish and serve. Makes 4 main-dish servings.

Coconut milk is available regular or light (reduced-fat) in Asian or Hispanic grocery stores and some supermarkets. Don't confuse it with coconut cream that is sweetened and used for drinks such as piña coladas.

Each serving: About 425 calories, 25 g protein, 47 g carbohydrate, 14 g total fat (6 g saturated), 142 mg cholesterol, 420 mg sodium.

Shrimp Curry and Rice

Prep: 10 minutes
Cook: 20 minutes

2 teaspoons olive oil
1 medium onion, coarsely chopped
1 tablespoon curry powder
1 teaspoon mustard seeds
1 pound large shrimp, shelled and deveined, leaving tail part of shell on, if you like (see page 366)
½ cup light coconut milk (see above)

1 cup frozen whole baby carrots, thawed
¾ cup frozen peas, thawed
½ teaspoon salt
1 cup regular long-grain rice, cooked as label directs, omitting margarine or butter
Chopped fresh cilantro leaves (optional)

1. In nonstick 12-inch skillet, heat 1 teaspoon oil over medium-high heat. Reduce heat to medium; add onion and cook, stirring occasionally, until tender, about 8 minutes. Stir in curry powder and cook, stirring, 1 minute. Transfer onion mixture to bowl.

2. Increase heat to medium-high. In same skillet, heat remaining 1 teaspoon oil until very hot. Add mustard seeds; cook, shaking pan, 30 seconds. Add shrimp and cook, stirring frequently, just until opaque throughout, about 4 minutes.

3. Return onion mixture to skillet and stir in coconut milk, carrots, peas, and salt; heat through. Serve over rice. Sprinkle with cilantro, if you like. Makes 4 main-dish servings.

Each serving: About 390 calories, 30 g protein, 49 g carbohydrate, 8 g total fat (2 g saturated), 175 mg cholesterol, 490 mg sodium.

Shrimp Paella

Prep: 45 minutes
Bake: 30 minutes

1 tablespoon olive oil
1 medium onion, finely chopped
1 medium red pepper, finely chopped
2 garlic cloves, finely chopped
¼ teaspoon ground red pepper (cayenne)
1 can (14½ ounces) tomatoes in puree
½ cup dry white wine
2¼ cups water
2 bottles (8 ounces each) clam juice
2 cups medium-grain or regular long-grain rice

1 ounce fully cooked chorizo sausage or pepperoni, coarsely chopped (¼ cup)
1 teaspoon salt
⅛ teaspoon loosely packed saffron threads, crumbled
⅛ teaspoon dried thyme
1 bay leaf
1 package (10 ounces) frozen baby peas
1 pound large shrimp, shelled, deveined, and each cut lengthwise in half (see page 366)
¼ cup chopped fresh parsley leaves
Lemon wedges

1. Preheat oven to 350°F. In deep, oven-safe 12-inch skillet (if skillet is not oven-safe, wrap handle of skillet with double layer of foil), heat oil over medium heat. Add onion and red pepper, and cook, stirring occasionally, until vegetables are tender, about 10 minutes. Stir in garlic and ground red pepper, and cook, stirring, 30 seconds. Add tomatoes with their puree and wine; cook, stirring frequently, until mixture is very dry, breaking tomatoes up with side of spoon.

2. Stir water, clam juice, rice, chorizo, salt, saffron, thyme, and bay leaf, into tomato mixture; heat to boiling over high heat. Cover skillet, place in oven, and bake 15 minutes.

3. Stir in frozen peas. Tuck shrimp into rice mixture; cover and bake just until shrimp are opaque throughout, 10 to 15 minutes longer. Remove skillet from oven and let stand at room temperature 5 minutes. Discard bay leaf. Sprinkle paella with parsley and serve with lemon wedges. Makes 6 main-dish servings.

Each serving: About 400 calories, 22 g protein, 64 g carbohydrate, 5 g total fat (1 g saturated), 101 mg cholesterol, 975 mg sodium.

Shrimp Creole

Prep: 40 minutes
Bake: 30 minutes

1 tablespoon olive oil
1 large onion, coarsely chopped
1 medium red pepper, coarsely chopped
1 medium green pepper, coarsely chopped
8 ounces fully cooked chorizo sausage or pepperoni, cut into ¼-inch-thick slices
2 garlic cloves, finely chopped

1½ cups parboiled rice
1 can (14½ ounces) stewed tomatoes
1½ cups water
1 bottle (8 ounces) clam juice
1 pound medium-size shrimp, shelled and deveined (see page 366)
1 package (10 ounces) frozen whole okra, thawed

1. Preheat oven to 350°F. In 3- to 3½-quart Dutch oven, heat oil over medium heat. Add onion and green and red peppers and cook, stirring frequently, until tender and lightly browned, about 10 minutes. Add chorizo and garlic and cook, stirring frequently, until chorizo is lightly browned, 5 minutes longer.

2. Stir in rice, stewed tomatoes, water, and clam juice; heat to boiling over high heat. Cover; place in oven, and bake 20 minutes. Stir shrimp and okra into rice mixture; cover and bake until rice and shrimp are tender, 10 minutes longer. Makes 6 main-dish servings.

Each serving: About 445 calories, 27 g protein, 54 g carbohydrate, 15 g total fat (5 g saturated), 132 mg cholesterol, 1,020 mg sodium.

Greek Shrimp and Potatoes

Prep: 25 minutes
Cook: 40 minutes

2 teaspoons olive oil
1 large onion, chopped
1½ pounds all-purpose potatoes, peeled and cut into 1-inch pieces
1 large garlic clove, crushed with garlic press
⅛ teaspoon ground red pepper (cayenne)
1 cup water

½ teaspoon salt
1 can (14½ ounces) diced tomatoes
1 pound large shrimp, shelled and deveined (see page 366)
2 ounces crumbled feta cheese (about ½ cup)
2 tablespoons chopped fresh dill

1. In deep nonstick 12-inch skillet, heat oil over medium heat. Add onion and cook, stirring often, until tender, about 10 minutes.

2. Stir in potatoes, garlic, and ground red pepper, and cook, stirring, 30 seconds. Stir in water and salt; heat to boiling over high heat. Reduce heat to low; cover and simmer until potatoes are tender, 15 minutes.

3. Add tomatoes with their juice; heat to boiling over high heat. Reduce heat; cover and simmer 5 minutes. Remove cover; simmer 5 minutes longer.

4. Stir in shrimp; heat to boiling over high heat. Reduce heat to low; cover and simmer 3 to 5 minutes, just until shrimp are opaque throughout. Remove skillet from heat; stir in feta and dill. Spoon into bowls to serve. Makes 4 main-dish servings.

Each serving: About 310 calories, 25 g protein, 36 g carbohydrate, 7 g total fat (3 g saturated), 155 mg cholesterol, 740 mg sodium.

SQUID

Buy whole squid (calamari) that are small with bright white flesh, and a mild ocean smell. Fresh squid should be refrigerated in a tightly sealed container for no more than a day or two. Rinse thoroughly before and after cleaning. When estimating how much squid to buy, figure on about 1 pound cleaned meat from 1½ pounds whole squid. Allow ¼ pound meat per appetizer serving. Squid can also be purchased cleaned and ready to use at most fish markets. Rinse and pat dry before using.

TO CLEAN SQUID: Pull off tentacles from squid body. Cut off and discard portion of tentacles containing sac. Remove thin transparent cartilage and all loose pieces from inside body; with fingertips, gently pull off thin dark outer skin from squid. Rinse tentacles and body with cold running water.

Fried Calamari with Hot Sauce

Prep: 20 minutes
Cook: 20 minutes

Vegetable oil for frying
1 small onion, finely chopped
1 can (8 ounces) tomatoes, chopped
½ teaspoon crushed red pepper
¼ teaspoon sugar
1 pound cleaned squid (see page 376)
1 large egg
⅔ cup all-purpose flour
Salt

1. In 1-quart saucepan, heat 1 tablespoon oil over medium heat. Add onion and cook, stirring frequently, until tender. Add tomatoes, crushed red pepper, and sugar; heat to boiling. Reduce heat to low; cover and simmer 5 minutes. Remove from heat and keep warm.

2. Slice squid body crosswise into ¾-inch-thick rings. Cut tentacles into several pieces if they are large.

3. In large bowl, with fork, lightly beat egg. Add squid and stir to mix. On waxed paper, place flour.

4. In 10-inch skillet, heat ½ inch oil over medium heat until very hot. One piece at a time, remove squid from egg, letting excess drip off, then coat squid in flour, shaking off excess. In batches, carefully place squid in hot oil and fry, turning with slotted spoon, until golden and just opaque throughout. With slotted spoon, transfer squid to paper towels to drain; transfer to warm platter and sprinkle salt on squid to taste. Serve hot with sauce. Makes 3 main-dish servings.

Each serving: About 375 calories, 30 g protein, 32 g carbohydrate, 13 g total fat (2 g saturated), 424 mg cholesterol, 395 mg sodium.

∾Seafood Combinations

Mussels and Clams Fra Diavolo

Prep: 30 minutes
Cook: 25 minutes

3 dozen cherrystone or
　littleneck clams
3 dozen large mussels
1 cup water
1 tablespoon olive oil
3 tablespoons margarine or
　butter
1 small onion, finely chopped

1 garlic clove, finely chopped
½ teaspoon dried oregano
¼ teaspoon salt
¼ to ½ teaspoon crushed red
　pepper
¼ cup dry white wine
⅓ cup chopped fresh parsley

1. With stiff brush, scrub clams and mussels with cold running water until free of sand; scrape barnacles and remove beards from mussels (see page 359).

2. In 8-quart Dutch oven, heat water to boiling over high heat. Add clams and heat to boiling. Reduce heat to medium-low; cover and simmer, stirring occasionally, until clams open, using slotted spoon to transfer clams to large bowl as they open, about 6 to 8 minutes. To broth remaining in Dutch oven, add mussels; heat to boiling over high heat. Reduce heat to medium-low; cover and simmer, stirring occasionally, about 6 to 8 minutes, until mussels open, using slotted spoon to transfer mussels to bowl with clams as they open. Discard any mussels or clams that have not opened.

3. Meanwhile, in nonstick 2-quart saucepan, heat oil and margarine over medium heat until margarine melts. Stir in onion, garlic, oregano, salt, and crushed red pepper, and cook, stirring often, until onion is tender. Stir in wine and parsley; cook 2 minutes.

4. Discard top shell from each clam and mussel; rinse clams and mussels on half shell in cooking broth to remove any sand. Place clams and mussels on plate; cover with foil to keep warm. Let broth stand a few minutes until sand settles. Carefully strain clear broth through sieve lined with paper towels.

5. Rinse and dry Dutch oven. Pour clear shellfish broth into Dutch oven; add wine mixture in saucepan and reserved clams and mussels. Heat mixture through over medium-high heat. Spoon shellfish and broth into shallow soup plates and serve. Makes 4 main-dish servings.

Each serving: About 265 calories, 23 g protein, 9 g carbohydrate, 15 g total fat (3 g saturated), 56 mg cholesterol, 595 mg sodium.

Cioppino

Prep: 35 minutes
Cook: 35 minutes

1½ pounds striped bass fillets, skin removed and cut into 2-inch pieces
½ pound medium sea scallops, rinsed
1½ dozen cherrystone or littleneck clams
2 tablespoons olive oil
1 large onion, chopped
1 medium green pepper, chopped
1 garlic clove, finely chopped

1 can (28 ounces) tomatoes
½ cup dry white wine
¼ cup chopped fresh parsley
2 teaspoons salt
¼ teaspoon dried basil
1 pound large shrimp, shelled and deveined (see page 366)
1 package (12 ounces) frozen Alaska King crab split legs, thawed and cut into chunks

1. With tweezers, remove any small bones from fish fillets. Pull tough crescent-shaped muscle from side of each scallop. Cover and refrigerate until ready to use. With stiff brush, scrub clams with cold water running until free of sand. In 8-quart Dutch oven, heat *½ inch water* to boiling over high heat. Add clams; heat to boiling. Reduce heat to medium; cover and cook, about 5 minutes, just until clams open, transferring clams to bowl as they open. Discard any clams that have not opened.

2. Discard top shell from each clam; rinse clam on half shell in cooking broth to remove any sand and transfer to plate, cover and reserve. Let broth stand a few minutes until sand settles. Strain ¾ cup clear broth through sieve lined with paper towels. Discard remaining broth. Rinse and dry Dutch oven.

3. In same Dutch oven, heat oil over medium heat. Add onion, green pepper, and garlic and cook, stirring frequently, until tender. Stir in tomatoes with their juice, wine, parsley, salt, basil, and reserved clam broth; heat to boiling, breaking tomatoes up with side of spoon. Reduce heat to low; cover and simmer 15 minutes.

4. Increase heat to high; add shrimp, crab legs, striped bass and scallops. Heat to simmering. Cook, gently stirring, just until fish and seafood are opaque throughout, about 1 minute. Add reserved clams; heat through. Serve in deep bowls. Makes 8 main-dish servings.

Each serving: About 245 calories, 35 g protein, 9 g carbohydrate, 7 g total fat (1 g saturated), 156 mg cholesterol, 1,040 mg sodium.

Seafood Stew

Prep: 10 minutes
Cook: 20 minutes

12 ounces cod fillet
1¼ pounds all-purpose potatoes, peeled and cut into ½-inch
    pieces
1 can (14½ ounces) chunky tomatoes with olive oil, garlic, and
    spices
1 can (14½ ounces) chicken broth
⅓ cup dry white wine
16 large mussels, scrubbed and debearded (see page 359)
16 large shrimp, shelled and deveined, leaving tail part of shell
    on, if you like (see page 366)
1 tablespoon chopped fresh parsley leaves

1. With tweezers, remove any small bones from cod; cut cod into 2-inch pieces. In 2-quart saucepan, heat potatoes and enough *water to cover* to boiling over high heat. Reduce heat to low; cover and simmer until potatoes are tender, about 5 to 8 minutes. Drain.

2. Meanwhile, in 5-quart Dutch oven, heat tomatoes with their juice, broth, and wine to boiling over high heat. Add mussels; reduce heat to medium; cover and simmer 3 to 5 minutes, until mussels open, transferring mussels to bowl as they open. Discard any mussels that have not opened.

3. Add shrimp and cod to Dutch oven; simmer, gently stirring frequently, just until shrimp and cod are opaque throughout, 3 to 5 minutes longer. Add potatoes and mussels to Dutch oven; heat through. Sprinkle with parsley and serve in shallow soup plates. Makes 4 main-dish servings.

Each serving: About 305 calories, 35 g protein, 28 g carbohydrate, 5 g total fat (0 g saturated), 136 mg cholesterol, 965 mg sodium.

Peruvian Fisherman's Stew

Prep: 30 minutes
Cook: 25 minutes

1 tablespoon vegetable oil
1 medium onion, finely chopped
2 garlic cloves, finely chopped
2 serrano or jalapeño chiles, seeded and finely chopped
1 pound red potatoes, not peeled, cut into ¾-inch chunks
3 bottles (8 ounces each) clam juice

2 cups water
¾ teaspoon salt
⅛ teaspoon dried thyme
1 lime
1 pound monkfish, dark membrane removed, cut into 1-inch pieces
1 pound medium shrimp, shelled and deveined, leaving tail part of shell on, if you like (see page 366)
¼ cup chopped fresh cilantro leaves

1. In 4-quart saucepan, heat oil over medium heat. Add onion and cook, stirring often, until tender, 10 minutes. Stir in garlic and serrano chiles and cook, stirring, 30 seconds. Stir in potatoes, clam juice, water, salt, and thyme; heat to boiling over high heat. Reduce heat to medium; cook 10 minutes.

2. Cut lime in half; cut one half into wedges and set aside. Add other lime half and monkfish to pan; cover and cook 5 minutes. Stir in shrimp and cook, stirring frequently, just until shrimp are opaque throughout and monkfish is tender, 3 to 5 minutes longer.

3. Remove lime half, squeezing juice into pan. Sprinkle with cilantro; ladle into deep bowls and serve with lime wedges. Makes about 11 cups or 6 main-dish servings.

Each serving: About 215 calories, 26 g protein, 16 g carbohydrate, 5 g total fat (1 g saturated), 117 mg cholesterol, 640 mg sodium.

Party Paella

Prep: 45 minutes
Cook/Bake: 2 hours

2 dozen mussels, scrubbed and debearded (see page 359)

2 dozen littleneck clams, scrubbed

1 pound hot Italian-sausage links

1½ pounds large shrimp, shelled and deveined (see page 366)

1 chicken (2½ pounds), cut into 12 pieces

1 large garlic clove, finely chopped

¾ teaspoon salt

½ teaspoon dried thyme

2 tablespoons olive oil

1 large onion, chopped

1 large green pepper, cut into ½-inch strips

2¼ cups regular long-grain rice

1 can (14½ to 16 ounces) tomatoes

½ cup dry white wine

½ teaspoon crushed saffron threads

1 package (9 ounces) frozen whole or cut green beans, thawed

1. In 8-quart Dutch oven, heat *1 inch water* to boiling over high heat. Add mussels and clams; heat to boiling. Reduce heat to medium-low; cover and simmer, stirring occasionally, 5 to 10 minutes, until mussels and clams open, transferring shellfish to large bowl as they open. Discard any mussels and clams that have not opened.

2. Discard top shell from each mussel and clam; rinse mussels and clams on half shell in cooking broth to remove any sand. Place mussels and clams on plate; cover and refrigerate. Let broth stand a few minutes until sand settles. Strain 2 cups clear broth through sieve lined with paper towels. Rinse and dry Dutch oven.

3. In same Dutch oven, heat sausages and *¼ cup water* to boiling over medium heat. Reduce heat to low; cover and simmer 5 minutes. Remove cover; continue cooking, turning sausages frequently, until water has evaporated and sausages are well browned, about 20 minutes. Drain sausages on paper towels. Cut into 1-inch slices. Cover and reserve.

4. In drippings in Dutch oven, cook shrimp, over medium heat, stirring frequently, until pink and just opaque throughout, about 3 minutes. With slotted spoon, transfer shrimp to small bowl. Cover and refrigerate until ready to use.

5. In large bowl, toss chicken pieces with garlic, salt, and thyme. In same Dutch oven, heat oil over medium-high heat until very hot. Add chicken, in batches, and cook until browned, using slotted spoon to transfer chicken to bowl as it is browned.

6. In drippings in Dutch oven, cook onion and green pepper over medium heat, stirring frequently, until tender. Add rice, tomatoes with their juice, wine, saffron, chicken and any juice in bowl, and reserved broth; heat to boiling over high heat, breaking tomatoes up with side of spoon. Reduce heat to low; cover and simmer, stirring occasionally, until rice is tender and liquid has been absorbed, about 30 minutes.

7. Meanwhile, preheat oven to 350°F. Stir sausage, shrimp, and green beans into rice mixture. Tuck mussels and clams on half shell into rice. Cover and bake in oven until shellfish is heated through and the flavors have blended, about 10 minutes. Makes 12 main-dish servings.

Each serving: About 505 calories, 134 g protein, 35 g carbohydrate, 25 g total fat (7 g saturated), 154 mg cholesterol, 670 mg sodium.

Eggs & Cheese

~~~

Eggs • Cheese

❧Eggs

As a cooking ingredient, their uses are virtually endless—from thickening and enriching custards to aerating cakes and puffy soufflés. Nutritionally speaking, eggs are a good (and inexpensive) source of protein, iron, and vitamins. And, while the yolks are relatively high in fat and cholesterol, egg whites are completely fat- and cholesterol-free.

HOW TO CHOOSE EGGS

When buying eggs, pass on any that are dirty, cracked, or leaking. Move each egg in the carton to make sure it isn't stuck to the bottom. The "pack date" on the carton is the day the eggs were packed. It runs from 001 (for January) through 365 (for December 31). Eggs can be used up to 5 weeks beyond pack date. In some states and localities, the carton also indicates an expiration date after which the eggs should not be sold. Egg sizes—jumbo, extra large, large, medium, small—are based on minimum weight per dozen.

Shell color does not affect the quality of an egg; it depends simply on the breed of hen that laid the egg. Nor does the color of the yolk, which is determined by the diet of the hen, affect egg quality.

HOW TO STORE EGGS

IN THE REFRIGERATOR: Store whole eggs in their original carton, large end up (which helps keep yolks centered), and away from strong-smelling foods, such as onions or cheese, whose aromas might penetrate the porous egg shell.

Store leftover whites or broken yolks in small, tightly covered containers; use them within a week. To store unbroken yolks for a few days, cover them with cold water and refrigerate. Drain before using.

IN THE FREEZER: Pour enough egg whites for a favorite recipe into a freezer container and seal. Or freeze egg whites in plastic-wrap-lined 6-ounce custard cups, 1 white to a cup. After they are frozen, remove the whites from the cups and store them in a zip-tight plastic bag in the freezer. They will thaw quickly when needed.

Leftover egg yolks, and the yolks in whole eggs, thicken and gel if frozen alone. You can slow the thickening process this way: For every 1/4 cup yolks (4) or whole eggs (2), stir in 1/8 teaspoon salt if you plan to use them in savory dishes. Stir yolks or whole eggs with 1 1/2 teaspoons sugar or corn syrup if you expect to use them in baking and desserts. Be sure to label the container with the number of yolks or whole eggs and what and how much salt, sugar, or corn syrup has been added.

HOW TO TELL FRESH FROM STALE

To check the freshness of an egg, break it into a saucer and sniff it. If it is fresh, the egg will smell clean and faintly sweet, if there is any odor at all; if it has gone bad, the egg will have an unmistakable offensive odor. The white of a fresh egg should be translucent, thick, and firmly shaped; the yolk, smooth and well rounded. If the white runs thinly over the saucer and the yolk is flat, the egg is past its prime. Blood spots on the yolk, caused by the rupture of a blood vessel during formation of the egg, do not affect its quality or flavor and can be removed with the tip of a spoon before cooking, if you like. Stringy white fibers (chalazae), found in the whites of fresh eggs, are wholesome and normal; they anchor the yolk in the center of the egg, but usually disappear as the egg gets older.

HOW TO COOK EGGS

Always cook eggs at low to moderate temperatures, for the exact time called for in a recipe. Eggs cooked at too high a temperature or too long at a low temperature will be tough and rubbery.

COOKING IN THE SHELL: Place eggs in a saucepan wide enough to accommodate them without crowding and deep enough so that at least 1 inch of cold water covers the tops of the eggs. Heat the water just to a full boil over high heat. Immediately remove the saucepan from the heat and cover it tightly. (Never boil hard-cooked eggs; the yolks will become hard and turn greenish gray.) Let the eggs stand in the hot water, covered, for 15 minutes for hard-cooked eggs; 4 to 5 minutes, depending on the desired firmness, for soft-cooked eggs. For hard-cooked eggs pour off the hot water and run cold water over the eggs to cool them and make peeling easier.

To shell hard-cooked eggs, crack the entire surface of the shell by gently tapping the egg against a flat surface. Under cold running water, peel the egg, starting at the large end, where the air space makes starting to peel easier.

FRYING: Use a skillet large enough for the eggs to remain separate so that they can be turned easily; if the whites run together, the eggs will have to be cut apart. For tender fried eggs, use a moderate cooking temperature and as short a cooking time as possible to produce the desired firmness. Also use a minimum of fat; too much fat makes fried eggs greasy.

In a skillet (nonstick is a good choice) over medium heat, melt margarine or butter, or heat mild-flavored olive or vegetable oil (1 teaspoon for a small skillet, up to 1 tablespoon for a medium skillet). One at a time, break the eggs into a saucer, then slip them into the skillet. Reduce the heat to low. Cook the eggs slowly to the desired firmness, covering the skillet, if you like for sunny-side up eggs, or turning the eggs once to cook both sides ("over easy").

SCRAMBLING: Use a skillet, preferably nonstick, which is large enough so that the egg mixture is not more than ½ inch deep. For each serving, in a bowl with a wire whisk, beat 2 eggs slightly with 2 tablespoons water or milk; add salt and pepper to taste. In a medium skillet, heat 2 teaspoons margarine or butter, or mild-flavored olive oil or vegetable oil over medium heat. Pour in the egg mixture. As the mixture begins to set, with a spatula, stir the cooked portion slightly so that the uncooked part flows to the bottom. Avoid constant stirring. Cook until the eggs are thickened and set, about 3 to 5 minutes.

POACHING: In a wide, shallow saucepan or deep skillet over high heat, heat 1 to 1½ inches water to boiling. Reduce the heat to gentle simmer. Break cold eggs, 1 at a time, into a cup; holding cup close to water, slip in eggs. Cook 3 to 5 minutes, until whites are set and yolks begin to thicken. With a slotted spoon, lift out each egg; drain in spoon over paper towel.

BAKING: An attractive and easy way to prepare eggs with the yolks *soft* and the whites just set is baking.

Preheat the oven to 325°F. For each serving, generously butter an 8-ounce oven-safe baking dish or ramekin. Break 2 eggs into the dish; add 1 tablespoon of milk or cream, if desired; sprinkle with salt and pepper to taste. Bake the eggs until the desired firmness, about 15 to 20 minutes. Serve the eggs in the baking dish.

HOW TO SEPARATE EGGS

Many recipes call for separating eggs. Sharply tap the egg on the side of the bowl to crack the shell. With your thumbs, carefully pull open the shell along the crack, letting some of the white run into the bowl. Transfer the yolk carefully back and forth from one half-shell to the other until all the white has run into the bowl. When separating several eggs, transfer the whites to a different bowl as you go in case a yolk breaks.

HOW TO BEAT EGGS

Eggs are easiest to separate when they are cold, but whites beat to the fullest possible volume when they are at room temperature. Even a tiny bit of yolk in the whites will greatly reduce their foaming action. So carefully separate eggs directly from the refrigerator; let the whites stand at room temperature for about 45 minutes before beating them.

Egg whites increase in volume many times when beaten, so follow recipe directions for bowl size. Bowl and beaters must be perfectly clean, since even the slightest bit of fat prevents the whites from beating to their fullest volume.

If a recipe says to beat egg whites until "foamy" or "frothy," it means that you should beat until the whites are foamy but still unstable, reverting quickly back to liquid. For "soft peaks," beat until the whites form soft, rounded peaks when the beaters are lifted. For "stiff peaks," beat until the whites are snowy white and moist, forming stiff, straight peaks when the beaters are lifted; the peaks should be stable but not dry. Overbeaten whites are stiff and dry, and are likely to collapse when the mixture thcy are folded into is heated.

Cream of tartar is frequently added to unbeaten egg whites to make the foam more stable. When sugar is beaten in, it should be added a little at a time, as the whites are being beaten, so that it will not retard the foaming action.

French Omelet

Prep: 2 minutes
Cook: 3 minutes

4 large eggs
¼ cup water
½ teaspoon salt
⅛ teaspoon coarsely ground black pepper
4 teaspoons margarine or butter
choice of Omelet Fillings (below, optional)

1. In medium bowl, with wire whisk, beat eggs, water, salt, and pepper until well blended. In nonstick 10-inch skillet, melt margarine over medium-high heat, tilting skillet to grease sides. Pour egg mixture into skillet; cook until it begins to set around edge.

2. With heatproof rubber spatula, gently lift edge of egg as it sets, tilting skillet to allow uncooked eggs to run under omelet. Shake skillet occasionally to keep omelet moving freely in pan. When omelet is set but still moist on top, increase heat slightly to brown bottom of omelet.

3. If desired, add filling. Tilt skillet and, with spatula, fold omelet in half; slide onto warm platter. Makes 2 main-dish servings.

Each serving: About 215 calories, 13 g protein, 1 g carbohydrate, 18 g total fat (4 g saturated), 425 mg cholesterol, 520 mg sodium.

OMELET FILLINGS: Just before folding omelet and sliding it onto platter, spoon one of these fillings into omelet: *2 cups cooked cut-up asparagus; 2 ounces sharp Cheddar cheese,* shredded (about ½ cup); *3 slices bacon,* chopped and cooked crisp; *8 ounces mushrooms,* trimmed, sliced, and cooked in *1 tablespoon vegetable oil.*

Omelet Española

Prep: 45 minutes
Bake: 15 to 20 minutes

2 tablespoons olive oil
1 pound all-purpose potatoes (2 large), cut into ¼-inch pieces
1 medium onion, sliced
1 medium green pepper, coarsely chopped
¾ teaspoon salt

8 large eggs
½ cup water
¼ teaspoon coarsely ground black pepper
1 can (14½ ounces) diced tomatoes, drained
½ cup chopped pimiento-stuffed olives (salad olives)

1. In nonstick 10-inch oven-safe skillet (if skillet is not oven-safe, wrap handle of skillet with double layer of foil before placing in oven), heat oil over medium heat. Stir in potatoes, onion, green pepper, and ¼ teaspoon salt, and cook, stirring occasionally, until vegetables are tender, about 20 minutes.

2. Meanwhile, preheat oven to 400°F. In large bowl, with wire whisk, beat eggs, water, pepper, and remaining ½ teaspoon salt until well blended. Stir in tomatoes and olives. Stir egg mixture into potato mixture in skillet, cover and cook until egg mixture begins to set around edge, about 5 minutes. Remove cover and place skillet in oven; bake until omelet is set, about 15 to 20 minutes.

3. Carefully invert omelet onto large flat plate. Let cool before cutting into 4 wedges. Makes 4 main-course servings.

Each serving: About 340 calories, 16 g protein, 28 g carbohydrate, 19 g total fat (4 g saturated), 425 mg cholesterol, 1,115 mg sodium.

Herbed Vegetable Omelet

Prep: 15 minutes
Cook: 15 minutes

8 large eggs, separated (see page 390)
¼ cup water
1 teaspoon salt
2 tablespoons olive oil
1 medium zucchini (8 ounces), trimmed and cut into bite-size
    pieces
1 medium yellow straightneck squash (8 ounces), trimmed and cut
    into bite-size pieces
¼ teaspoon dried oregano
4 ounces Cheddar cheese, shredded (about 1 cup)

1. Preheat oven to 350°F. In large bowl with mixer at high speed, beat egg whites just until stiff peaks form when beaters are lifted. In small bowl, with same beaters, and with mixer at high speed, beat egg yolks, water, and ½ teaspoon salt until very thick and lemon-colored. With wire whisk or rubber spatula, gently fold egg yolk mixture into beaten egg whites.

2. In 12-inch nonstick oven-safe skillet (if skillet is not oven-safe, wrap handle of skillet with double layer of foil), heat 1 tablespoon oil over medium-low heat. Pour in egg mixture and cook until top is puffy and bottom is golden when gently lifted with a narrow spatula, about 3 minutes.

3. Place skillet in oven. Bake until omelet is golden and top springs back when lightly touched with finger, about 10 minutes.

4. Meanwhile, in 10-inch skillet, heat remaining 1 tablespoon oil over medium heat. Add zucchini, yellow squash, oregano, and remaining ½ teaspoon salt, and cook, stirring occasionally, until vegetables are tender. Remove skillet from heat; keep vegetables warm.

5. To serve, loosen side and bottom of omelet from skillet and spoon vegetable mixture over half of omelet. Sprinkle vegetables with cheese; fold omelet in half over filling.

Tilt skillet; with wide spatula, slide omelet onto warm platter. Makes 4 main-dish servings.

Each serving: About 345 calories, 21 g protein, 6 g carbohydrate, 26 g total fat (10 g saturated), 455 mg cholesterol, 885 mg sodium.

Classic Cheese Soufflé

Prep: 15 minutes
Bake: 1 hour

4 tablespoons margarine or butter
¼ cup all-purpose flour
½ teaspoon salt
⅛ teaspoon ground red pepper (cayenne)
1½ cups milk
8 ounces sharp Cheddar cheese, shredded (about 2 cups)
6 large eggs, separated (see page 390)

1. Prepare cheese sauce: In 2-quart saucepan, melt margarine over low heat. Stir in flour, salt, and ground red pepper until blended; cook, stirring constantly, 1 minute. With wire whisk, gradually mix in milk; cook, stirring constantly, until mixture has thickened slightly. Stir in cheese; cook, stirring, just until cheese has melted and sauce is smooth. Remove saucepan from heat.

2. In medium bowl, with wire whisk, beat egg yolks slightly; beat in small amount of hot cheese sauce. Gradually stir egg yolk mixture into cheese sauce in saucepan, stirring rapidly to prevent curdling. Cool slightly.

3. Preheat oven to 325°F. In large bowl with mixer at high speed, beat egg whites just until stiff peaks form when beaters are lifted. With rubber spatula, gently fold one-third of cheese mixture at a time into egg whites, folding just until blended.

4. Pour mixture into ungreased 2-quart soufflé dish. If desired, with back of spoon, make 1-inch-deep indentation in batter around inside of soufflé dish, about 1 inch from edge of dish (the center will rise higher than the edge, creating a top-hat effect when the soufflé is done). Bake until knife inserted under top hat or in center of soufflé comes out clean, about 55 to 60 minutes. Serve immediately. Makes 6 main-dish servings.

Each serving: About 375 calories, 20 g protein, 8 g carbohydrate, 29 g total fat (13 g saturated), 331 mg cholesterol, 645 mg sodium.

Tomato Soufflé

Prep: 50 minutes
Bake: 45 minutes

5 tablespoons margarine or butter
1 medium onion, chopped
2 pounds ripe tomatoes (6 medium), peeled and chopped
1¼ teaspoons salt
¼ teaspoon ground black pepper

½ teaspoon sugar
¼ cup all-purpose flour
1¼ cups milk
1 tablespoon plain dried bread crumbs
6 large eggs, separated (see page 390)
2 tablespoons freshly grated Parmesan cheese

1. In 12-inch skillet, melt 1 tablespoon margarine over medium heat. Add onion and cook, stirring frequently, until tender, about 10 minutes.

2. Add tomatoes with their juice, ½ teaspoon salt, pepper, and sugar. Increase heat to high and cook, stirring often, until tomato juices have evaporated, about 15 to 20 minutes.

3. Meanwhile, in 2-quart saucepan, melt remaining 4 tablespoons margarine over medium heat. Stir in flour and remaining ¾ teaspoon salt until blended; cook, stirring constantly, 1 minute. With wire whisk, gradually mix in milk and cook, stirring constantly, until mixture boils and has thickened. Remove saucepan from heat; stir in tomato mixture until blended.

4. Preheat oven to 325°F. Grease 2-quart soufflé dish; sprinkle inside of dish with bread crumbs. In large bowl, with wire whisk, beat egg yolks slightly; beat in a small amount of hot tomato mixture. Gradually stir yolk mixture into tomato mixture, stirring rapidly to prevent curdling. Pour mixture back into bowl.

5. In medium bowl, with mixer at high speed, beat egg whites to stiff peaks. With rubber spatula, gently fold beaten egg whites, one-third at a time, into tomato mixture just until blended; pour into soufflé dish. Sprinkle with Parmesan. Bake 45 minutes, or until puffy and golden. Serve immediately. Makes 8 accompaniment servings.

Each serving: About 200 calories, 8 g protein, 13 g carbohydrate, 13 g total fat (4 g saturated), 166 mg cholesterol, 540 mg sodium.

Quiche Lorraine

Prep: 20 minutes
Bake: 50 minutes

½ package (10 to 11 ounces) piecrust mix
1 tablespoon margarine or butter, softened
8 ounces sliced bacon, coarsely chopped
4 large eggs
2 cups heavy or whipping cream
¾ teaspoon salt
8 ounces Swiss cheese, shredded (about 1 cup)

1. Prepare piecrust mix as label directs for 1-crust pie; use dough to line 9-inch pie plate. Spread piecrust with margarine. Refrigerate while preparing filling.

2. Preheat oven to 425°F. In 3-quart saucepan, cook bacon over medium low heat, stirring frequently, until browned and crisp. With slotted spoon, transfer bacon to paper towels to drain.

3. In medium bowl, with wire whisk, mix eggs, cream, and salt until well blended; stir in cheese.

4. Sprinkle bacon in piecrust. Pour cream mixture over bacon. Place quiche on foil-lined cookie sheet to catch any overflow. Bake 15 minutes; turn oven control to 325°F, and bake quiche until knife inserted in center comes out clean, about 35 minutes longer. Transfer quiche to wire rack and let cool a few minutes before cutting and serving. Or serve quiche at room temperature. Makes 6 main-dish servings.

Each serving: About 665 calories, 21 g protein, 16 g carbohydrate, 58 g total fat (30 g saturated), 295 mg cholesterol, 830 mg sodium.

Spinach Strata

Prep: 15 minutes plus chilling
Bake: 1 hour

8 slices firm white bread
4 ounces mozzarella cheese, shredded (about 1 cup)
1 package (10 ounces) frozen chopped spinach, thawed and squeezed dry
1 tablespoon margarine or butter, softened
6 large eggs
2 cups milk
½ cup loosely packed fresh basil leaves, chopped
½ teaspoon salt
¼ teaspoon coarsely ground black pepper

1. Grease 8" by 8" baking dish. Place 4 slices bread in dish; top with ½ cup cheese, the spinach, then remaining ½ cup cheese. Spread margarine on each remaining 4 bread slices; place in dish, buttered side up.

2. In medium bowl, with wire whisk, beat eggs, milk, basil, salt, and pepper until blended. Slowly pour mixture over bread slices. Prick bread with fork and press slices down so that they absorb egg mixture.

3. Cover with plastic wrap and refrigerate at least 30 minutes or overnight.

4. To bake, preheat oven to 350°F. Uncover baking dish; bake strata until knife inserted in center comes out clean, about 1 hour. Transfer strata to wire rack and let cool 5 minutes before cutting and serving. Makes 6 main-dish servings.

Each serving: About 290 calories, 17 g protein, 22 g carbohydrate, 15 g total fat (6 g saturated), 240 mg cholesterol, 575 mg sodium.

Huevos Rancheros

Prep: 10 minutes
Cook: 20 minutes

1 tablespoon plus 2 teaspoons vegetable oil
1 medium onion, coarsely chopped
1 jalapeño chile, seeded and finely chopped
1 small garlic clove, finely chopped
1 can (14½ ounces) tomatoes
¼ teaspoon salt
8 large eggs
8 (6-inch) flour or corn tortillas, warmed as label directs
1 tablespoon chopped fresh cilantro leaves

1. In 2-quart saucepan, heat 1 tablespoon oil over medium-high heat. Add onion, jalapeño, and garlic, and cook, stirring occasionally, until onion is tender, about 8 minutes. Stir in tomatoes with their juice and salt; heat to boiling over high heat, breaking tomatoes up with side of spoon. Reduce heat to low; cover and simmer, stirring occasionally, 5 minutes. Remove from heat; cover and keep warm.

2. In nonstick 10-inch skillet, heat 1 teaspoon oil over medium heat. One at a time, break 4 eggs into a saucer, then slip into skillet. Reduce heat to low; cook eggs slowly, until whites are completely set and yolks begin to thicken but are not hard. Turn eggs, if you like. Transfer eggs to warm plate; keep warm. Repeat with remaining 1 teaspoon oil and remaining 4 eggs.

3. Arrange tortillas on 4 dinner plates. Place 1 fried egg on each tortilla. Spoon 2 tablespoons tomato sauce over each egg; sprinkle with cilantro. Serve with remaining tomato sauce. Makes 4 main-dish servings.

Each serving: About 395 calories, 18 g protein, 37 g carbohydrate, 20 g total fat (4 g saturated), 426 mg cholesterol, 665 mg sodium.

Crepes

Prep: 5 minutes plus chilling
Cook: 20 minutes

3 large eggs
1½ cups milk
⅔ cup all-purpose flour
½ teaspoon salt
4 tablespoons margarine or butter, melted
Suggested fillings: thinly sliced ham, smoked turkey, diced
  tomatoes, crumbled feta or goat cheese or sautéed vegetables

1. In blender at medium speed, mix eggs, milk, flour, salt, and 2 tablespoons melted margarine until completely smooth and free from lumps.

2. Transfer to bowl and refrigerate at least 1 hour, or overnight. Whisk batter thoroughly just before using.

3. Heat nonstick 10-inch skillet over medium-high heat; brush lightly with melted margarine. Pour scant ¼ cup batter into pan; tip pan to coat bottom. Cook crepe 1½ minutes, or until top is set and underside is lightly browned.

4. With plastic spatula, loosen crepe; turn and cook other side 30 seconds. Slip onto waxed paper. Repeat with remaining batter, brushing pan lightly with margarine before cooking each crepe; stack cooked crepes between layers of waxed paper. Makes 12 crepes.

Each crepe: About 95 calories, 3 g protein, 7 g carbohydrate, 6 g total fat (2 g saturated), 57 mg cholesterol, 180 mg sodium.

Scrambled Eggs Deluxe for a Crowd

Prep: 5 minutes not including toppings
Cook: 10 minutes

Caribbean Black-Bean Topping (see page 402)

French Pepper Topping (see page 403)

Scandinavian Smoked-Salmon Topping (see page 404)

18 large eggs
½ cup milk
½ teaspoon salt
2 tablespoons margarine or butter

1. Prepare toppings. Keep black-bean and pepper toppings warm if serving immediately or refrigerate to reheat later. (Salmon topping should be refrigerated.)
2. In large bowl, with wire whisk, beat eggs, milk, and salt until well blended.
3. In nonstick 12-inch skillet (at least 2 inches deep), melt margarine over medium-high heat. Add egg mixture to skillet. As egg mixture begins to set around edge, stir lightly with heat-safe rubber spatula or wooden spoon to allow uncooked egg mixture to flow toward side of pan. Continue cooking until eggs are set to desired doneness, about 5 to 7 minutes longer. Transfer eggs to warm serving bowl and serve with toppings. Makes 8 main-dish servings.

Each serving eggs without toppings: About 205 calories, 15 g protein, 2 g carbohydrate, 15 g total fat (4 g saturated), 480 mg cholesterol, 320 mg sodium.

Caribbean Black-Bean Topping

Prep: 15 minutes
Cook: 20 minutes

1 tablespoon olive oil
1 large onion, chopped
2 garlic cloves, crushed with
    garlic press
2 teaspoons chili powder
½ teaspoon ground cumin
½ cup chicken broth
3 cans (15 to 19 ounces each)
    black beans, rinsed and
    drained

1 can (4 to 4½ ounces)
    chopped mild green chiles
½ cup loosely packed fresh
    cilantro leaves, chopped
1 tablespoon fresh lime juice

1. In nonstick 12-inch skillet, heat oil over medium heat. Add onion and cook, stirring occasionally, until tender and golden, 10 minutes.

2. Stir in garlic, chili powder, and cumin, and cook, stirring, 2 minutes. Stir in broth, beans, and green chiles with their juice, and cook, stirring occasionally, 8 minutes longer. Remove from heat; keep warm until ready to serve, or refrigerate if not serving right away. Stir in cilantro and lime juice to serve. Makes about 6 cups.

Each ¼ cup: About 55 calories, 5 g protein, 11 g carbohydrate, 1 g total fat (0 g saturated), 4 g fiber, 0 mg cholesterol, 220 mg sodium.

French Pepper Topping

Prep: 20 minutes
Cook: 40 minutes

1 tablespoon olive oil
1 large onion, thinly sliced
1 large red pepper, thinly
   sliced
1 large yellow pepper, thinly
   sliced
2 garlic cloves, crushed with
   garlic press
¾ teaspoon salt
⅛ teaspoon ground red pepper
   (cayenne)

1 can (14½ to 16 ounces)
   diced tomatoes
½ cup water
1 medium zucchini (8 to 10
   ounces), trimmed and cut
   lengthwise in half, then
   crosswise into ¼-inch-thick
   slices
½ cup loosely packed fresh
   parsley leaves, chopped

1. In nonstick 12-inch skillet, heat oil over medium-high heat. Add onion and red and yellow peppers, and cook, stirring often, until vegetables are golden, about 20 minutes. Stir in garlic, salt, and ground red pepper, and cook, stirring, 1 minute longer.

2. Stir in tomatoes with their juice and water, and cook, stirring occasionally, 5 minutes. Add zucchini and cook, stirring gently, until tender, about 10 minutes longer. Remove from heat; keep warm until ready to serve or refrigerate if not serving right away. Serve at room temperature or reheat. Stir in parsley to serve. Makes about 4 cups.

Each ¼ cup: About 25 calories, 1 g protein, 4 g carbohydrate, 1 g total fat (0 g saturated), 0 mg cholesterol, 195 mg sodium.

Scandinavian Smoked-Salmon Topping

Prep: 10 minutes

4 ounces thinly sliced smoked salmon, chopped
¼ cup minced red onion
¼ cup loosely packed fresh dill sprigs, chopped
½ teaspoon freshly grated lemon peel
1 package (3 ounces) cream cheese, cut into small pieces

In small bowl, with fork, stir together smoked salmon, onion, dill, and lemon peel. Gently stir in cream cheese pieces just until combined. Cover and refrigerate until ready to serve. Makes about 1¼ cups.

Each tablespoon: About 25 calories, 1 g protein, 0 g carbohydrate, 2 g total fat (1 g saturated), 6 mg cholesterol, 60 mg sodium.

Capellini Frittata

Prep: 14 minutes
Bake: About 6 minutes

2 ounces capellini or angel hair pasta, broken into pieces (½ cup)
2 teaspoons olive oil
1 small onion, thinly sliced
1 small red pepper, chopped
6 large egg whites
2 large eggs
¼ cup fat-free (skim) milk
⅓ cup freshly grated Parmesan cheese
½ teaspoon salt
¼ teaspoon hot pepper sauce

1. In 2-quart saucepan, heat *3 cups water* to boiling over high heat. Add pasta and cook, stirring frequently, just until tender, about 2 minutes. Drain.

2. Meanwhile, preheat oven to 425°F. In nonstick 10-inch skillet with oven-safe handle (if skillet is not oven-safe, wrap handle of skillet with double layer of foil before placing in oven), heat oil over medium heat. Add onion

and red pepper, and cook, stirring frequently, until vegetables are tender, about 7 minutes.

3. In large bowl, with wire whisk, beat egg whites,
whole eggs, milk, Parmesan, salt, and hot pepper sauce; stir
in drained pasta. Pour egg mixture over onion mixture in
skillet; cover and cook until set around the edge, about 3
minutes. Uncover skillet and place skillet in oven. Bake
until frittata is set in center, about 6 minutes.

4. To serve, invert frittata onto cutting board and cut into
wedges. Makes 4 main-dish servings.

Each serving: About 190 calories, 15 g protein, 15 g carbohy-
drate, 8 g total fat (3 g saturated), 113 mg cholesterol, 545 mg
sodium.

～Cheese

The incredible range in the taste and texture of individual
cheeses is the result of the type of milk used, the manufac-
turing process, and the length of aging (in general, the
longer cheese has been aged, the stronger the flavor, the
harder the cheese, and the longer it will keep).

Cheese is also classified according to texture or consistency: hard-grating, such as Parmesan and Romano; hard
(or semi-firm), such as Cheddar and Swiss; semi soft, such
as Gouda and Monterey Jack; soft, such as Brie and Camembert; fresh, including such perishable mild-tasting
cheeses as ricotta, cottage cheese, mascarpone, and cream
cheese; goat and sheep milk cheeses, which may be fresh
and mild or aged and sharp; blue-veined cheeses, such as
Roquefort and Stilton; processed cheese, made by combin-
ing one or more cheeses with an emulsifier and pasteurizing
the mixture; and processed cheese spreads, which have ingredients added to make them soft, moist, and spreadable.

STORING CHEESE

The basic rule for storing cheese is to keep air out and
moisture in. Store all cheese in the refrigerator, tightly

wrapped to prevent drying. Leave it in its original wrapping, if possible; or rewrap it tightly in plastic wrap or foil. Cover cut surfaces tightly.

Hard cheeses keep longest. Unopened packages of hard cheese and wax-coated cheeses such as Cheddar, Edam, and Swiss will keep for 3 to 6 months; once opened, for 3 to 4 weeks, and 2 weeks if bought sliced. Semisoft cheeses such as Port du Salut will keep about 3 to 4 weeks in the refrigerator. Soft, ripened cheeses, such as Brie and Camembert, should be used as soon as possible.

If you are not sure how long a cheese will keep, buy only as much as you can use within 1 week. When buying packaged cheese, be sure to check the date on the package to see how long it can be stored.

Before serving hard and semisoft cheeses, remove them from the refrigerator and let them stand at room temperature for at least 30 minutes, preferably an hour, to develop their best flavor. Soft cheeses such as Brie and Camembert should be left out for an hour or two, until they are almost runny. Cottage and cream cheeses, however, should be refrigerator-cold when served.

If mold appears on the surface of hard cheese, cut off and discard the moldy part. The cheese will be fine to eat. However, soft cheeses with mold should be discarded, as the mold may have permeated the cheese.

FREEZING CHEESE

Freeze hard or semihard up to 3 months. Closely wrap cheese in foil or freezer-wrap, or seal in a zip-tight plastic freezer bag to prevent it from drying out. Hard cheese may become crumbly, but its flavor will not be affected; it's fine to use it in cooking.

COOKING WITH CHEESE

Cheese needs just enough heat to melt evenly and blend with other ingredients; high heat or long cooking makes cheese tough and leathery.

Grate, shred, or slice cheese for quick, even melting and for blending with other ingredients.

Stir cheese into sauces toward the end of the cooking time and cook over low heat or remove from the heat and stir just until the cheese has melted and the sauce is smooth. Broil cheese toppings several inches from the heat source, just until melted.

Add cheese toppings to skillet dishes at the end of the cooking time. Then turn off the heat and cover the skillet; the heat of the food will melt the cheese in just a few minutes. Add cheese toppings to baked dishes during the last few minutes of baking time and bake cheese dishes at low to moderate temperatures (325° to 350°F).

To blend cream cheese with other ingredients, let it stand, wrapped, at room temperature to soften.

CHEESE PRIMER

BLUE: A semisoft, ripened white cheese with blue-green veins and sometimes, a crumbly texture. The flavor is strong and piquant.

BOURSIN: A soft, white, triple-cream cheese, often flavored with garlic and herbs, or coated with pepper.

BRIE: A soft, ripened cheese with a creamy interior and chalky, edible crust. The flavor is mild to pungent. Brie is best when served at room temperature so the center is very soft, and almost (but not quite) runny. It comes in thin wheels or is sold in wedges.

CAMEMBERT: A soft, ripened cheese, with a creamy interior and a thin, chalky, edible crust; mild to pungent in flavor. Camembert is best served at room temperature. When ripe, it should feel tender and springy when pressed with a finger and, when cut, the soft center should bulge out from between the crusts.

CHEDDAR: A hard, ripened cheese, white to yellow orange; its nutty flavor ranges from mild to extrasharp, depending on the age of the cheese, and its texture varies from soft to firm and dry.

CHESHIRE: A hard, ripened cheese, orange, with a crumbly texture, mellow in flavor. Chesire is produced only in England.

COTTAGE CHEESE: Soft, unripened cheese made from skim milk, lumpy in appearance, mildly acidic in flavor. Curds can be large or small. Creamed cottage cheese has cream added; some has added flavoring such as pineapple or vegetables. It is available in low-fat and nonfat versions, as well. Uncreamed cottage cheese is also known as "pot cheese."

CREAM CHEESE: A soft, rich unripened cheese, white, with a smooth, buttery texture and mildly acidic flavor. Look for foil-wrapped bars or buy soft or whipped or low-fat cream cheese in tubs. Two of cream cheese's many uses are for cheesecakes and frostings.

DOUBLE GLOUCESTER: A type of Cheddar with a firm, dense texture; yellow, with a mellow or tangy flavor.

EMMENTALER (Swiss cheese): A firm, ripened, light-yellow cheese with large holes and a sweet, nutlike flavor.

EXPLORATEUR: A soft, triple-cream cheese with a delicate white rind and thick creamy-white interior; the flavor is rich and luxurious.

FARMER CHEESE: A fresh, soft, unripened cheese similar to cottage cheese but pressed to make a fine-grained, smooth, sliceable mass. The flavor is mild and slightly sour. Usually sold in plastic-wrapped packages.

FETA: A semisoft, ripened, flaky white cheese with a very salty, sharp flavor. Look for cheese packed in brine in containers or jars, or floating in brine at the cheese counter.

FONTINA: A semisoft to hard, ripened cheese, medium yellow with some small holes and a delicate, nutty flavor that may become slightly smoky when the cheese is aged.

GORGONZOLA: Italian semisoft, ripened cheese with a clay-colored outer crust, and marbled with blue-green veins in a creamy-white interior.

GOUDA: A hard, grainy, ripened cheese, with a yellow to yellow-orange interior; it has small holes and a mellow, nutlike flavor. Look for flattened balls with yellow or red wax coating.

GRUYÈRE: A hard, ripened cheese, with a hard, brownish rind; the interior is light yellow with tiny holes, or eyes. Its nutty flavor varies with age, becoming fuller and richer as it gets older.

JARLSBERG: A firm, ripened cheese with a light-yellow interior and large holes; its mild, nutlike flavor is similar to that of Emmentaler.

MASCARPONE: A soft, unripened, spreadable double-cream cheese, creamy in color, with a mild buttery flavor; packaged in containers. It is very perishable and should be used soon after purchase.

MONTEREY JACK: Cheddar-style semisoft, ripened cheese, off-white in color, with a smooth, open texture and mild flavor. It is sometimes flavored with jalapeño chiles and called Pepper Jack.

MONTRACHET (Chère du Montrachet): A soft, semi-fresh goat's milk cheese, white, with a moist texture similar to that of cottage cheese, and almost indiscernible rind. Look for logs, often ash-coated; may also be wrapped in grape or chestnut leaves in containers.

MOZZARELLA: A semisoft, unripened cheese, creamy white, with a smooth, rubbery texture, made from whole or part-skim milk. Look for small rounds or braided forms, slices; it is also packed shredded. Fresh mozzarella, with a rich creamy texture, is available either salted or unsalted in specialty stores and some supermarkets.

MUENSTER: A semisoft, ripened cheese, creamy white, with many small holes, and a yellow-tan surface. Flavor is mild to mellow.

NEUFCHÂTEL: A soft, unripened cheese, creamy white, resembling cream cheese in texture and flavor but often lower in fat. Look for foil-wrapped bars.

PARMESAN (Parmigiano): A very hard, ripened Italian cheese, creamy white or yellow, with a sharp to piquant flavor and a granular texture; the tough brownish or waxy black rind should be removed before using the cheese. Look for wedges, cut pieces, and packages or jars of grated cheese.

PECORINO ROMANO: A very hard, ripened Italian grating cheese, yellowish-white and granular, with a greenish-black surface and a sharp flavor.

PORT DU SALUT: A semisoft, ripened cheese, creamy yellow, smooth and buttery, with a thin orange rind. The flavor is mellow to robust.

PROVOLONE: A hard, ripened cheese, pale yellow to golden, compact and flaky, with a light-brown or golden surface. The flavor is mild to sharp, smoky, and salty. Look for pear, ball, or sausage shapes; it's also sold in wedges and slices.

RACLETTE: A semifirm, ripened cheese, with a pale-cream interior and thin brownish rind. When raclette is served cold, the flavor is mild and faintly salty; when melted and served hot, the cheese has a much stronger, unique flavor.

RICOTTA: A soft, unripened cheese, with very small white curds and a mild, sweetish flavor. Sold in containers like cottage cheese.

RICOTTA SALATA: A firm ricotta, slightly salty; good for grating.

ROQUEFORT: A French semisoft, ripened cheese, white, marbled with blue-green veins, and crumbly. The flavor is sharp and salty.

SAGA: A soft, ripened, double-cream cheese, creamy, with blue veins and light, downy surface mold. The flavor is mild and rich.

SAINT-ANDRÉ: A soft, ripened, triple-cream cheese, creamy white, with a light, downy surface mold. The flavor is rich and tangy.

SAMSOE: A firm, ripened cheese, yellow, with small holes, and a dry, yellow rind that is sometimes wax-coated. The flavor is mild, buttery, and nutlike.

SAPSAGO: A very hard, ripened cheese; powdered clover leaves give it a green color and the flavor is sharp, pungent, and cloverlike. Look for small foil-wrapped cones.

SCAMORZA: A semisoft, unripened cheese, pale yellow,

with a smooth, rubbery texture similar to mozzarella. The flavor is mild and nutty.

STILTON: A semisoft, ripened cheese, creamy white with blue-green veins, flaky and crumbly. Look for tall cylinders, wedges, or oblongs. The flavor is milder than Roquefort.

SWISS: See Emmentaler, page 408.

TILSIT: A medium-firm, ripened cheese, pale yellow, with many small holes; caraway seeds are sometimes added. Flavor is mild to very strong.

Classic Swiss Fondue

Prep: 15 minutes
Cook: 7 minutes

1 garlic clove, cut in half
1½ cups dry white wine
1 tablespoon kirsch, brandy, or lemon juice
1 pound Swiss cheese, shredded (about 4 cups)
3 tablespoons all-purpose flour
⅛ teaspoon ground black pepper
⅛ teaspoon ground nutmeg
1 loaf (16 ounces) crusty French bread, cut into 1-inch pieces

1. Rub inside of fondue pot or 2-quart nonstick saucepan with garlic; discard garlic. Pour wine into fondue pot; heat over low heat, until wine is hot but not boiling. Stir in kirsch. Meanwhile, in medium bowl, toss cheese with flour until blend.

2. Add cheese to wine by handfuls, stirring constantly, until cheese has melted and fondue is smooth. Stir in pepper and nutmeg. Remove from heat; keep warm.

3. Let each person spear pieces of French bread on long-handled fondue forks and dip in fondue. Makes 4 main-dish servings.

Each serving: About 780 calories, 43 g protein, 68 g carbohydrate, 34 g total fat (21 g saturated), 103 mg cholesterol, 990 mg sodium.

Spanakopita

Prep: 40 minutes
Bake: 35 to 40 minutes

6 tablespoons margarine or
   butter
1 jumbo onion (1 pound),
   chopped
4 packages (10 ounces each)
   frozen chopped spinach,
   thawed and squeezed dry
3 large eggs
1 package (8 ounces) feta
   cheese, well drained and
   crumbled

1 cup part-skim ricotta cheese
½ cup chopped fresh dill
¼ teaspoon salt
¼ teaspoon coarsely ground
   black pepper
10 sheets (about 16" by 12"
   each) fresh or frozen
   (thawed) phyllo

1. In 12-inch skillet, melt 2 tablespoons margarine over medium-high heat. Add onion and cook, stirring occasionally, until tender and lightly browned, about 15 minutes.

2. Transfer onion to large bowl. Stir in spinach, eggs, feta, ricotta, dill, salt, and pepper until well blended. (You can prepare the recipe a day in advance up to this point. If not using filling right away, cover and refrigerate.)

3. In small saucepan, melt remaining 4 tablespoons margarine over low heat. Preheat oven to 400°F. Remove phyllo from package; keep sheets covered with plastic wrap to prevent drying out. Lightly brush bottom and sides of 11" by 7" baking dish with some melted margarine. On waxed paper, lightly brush 1 phyllo sheet with some melted margarine. Place phyllo in baking dish, gently pressing phyllo against sides of dish and allowing edges to overhang sides. Lightly brush second sheet with some melted margarine; place over first sheet, pressing gently. Repeat layering with 3 more phyllo sheets.

4. Spread spinach filling evenly over phyllo in baking dish. Fold overhanging edges of phyllo over filling. Cut remaining 5 phyllo sheets crosswise in half. On waxed paper, lightly brush 1 half phyllo sheet with some melted margarine. Place on top of filling. Repeat with remaining cut phyllo sheets, brushing each sheet lightly with remaining margarine.

5. Bake Spanakopita until filling is hot in the center and top of phyllo is golden, about 35 to 40 minutes. Transfer to wire rack and let stand a few minutes before cutting and serving. Makes 8 main-dish servings.

Each serving: About 355 calories, 17 g protein, 28 g carbohydrate, 21 g total fat (8 g saturated), 114 mg cholesterol, 795 mg sodium.

Southwest Tortilla Casserole

Prep: 20 minutes
Bake: 37 minutes

1 can (15¼ to 16 ounces) whole-kernel corn, drained
1 can (14½ ounces) stewed tomatoes
1 can (4 to 4½ ounces) chopped mild green chiles
2 tablespoons vegetable oil
3 tablespoons all-purpose flour
2½ cups milk
12 ounces cooked chicken, cut into ½-inch cubes (2½ cups)

1 can (15 to 19 ounces) black beans, rinsed and drained
7 ounces Monterey Jack cheese with jalapeño chiles, shredded (about 1¾ cups)
¼ cup chopped fresh cilantro or parsley
8 (6-inch) corn tortillas, each cut in half

1. Preheat oven to 375°F. In medium bowl, combine corn, stewed tomatoes, and green chiles with their juice. Spoon half of corn mixture into bottom of 13" by 9" baking dish.

2. Prepare white sauce: In 2-quart saucepan, heat oil over medium heat. Stir in flour until blended; cook, stirring, 1 minute. With wire whisk, gradually mix in milk; cook, stirring constantly, until mixture boils and has thickened.

3. Into corn mixture remaining in bowl, stir chicken,

beans, 1 cup cheese, cilantro, and about half the white sauce.

4. Arrange half the tortillas over corn mixture in baking dish and spoon the chicken mixture on top. Arrange remaining tortillas over chicken mixture; top with remaining white sauce, then sprinkle remaining ¾ cup cheese on top.

5. Bake casserole until hot in the center and bubbling around the edges, 30 to 35 minutes. Transfer to wire rack and let stand at room temperature 15 minutes for easier serving. Makes 8 main-dish servings.

Each serving: About 430 calories, 30 g protein, 42 g carbohydrate, 19 g total fat (7 g saturated), 76 mg cholesterol, 865 mg sodium.

Cottage-Cheese Puff

Prep: 15 minutes
Bake: 45 minutes

6 slices bacon, chopped
3 tablespoons margarine or butter
3 tablespoons all-purpose flour
¼ teaspoon salt
¾ cup milk
4 large eggs, separated, at room temperature (see page 390)
1 container (8 ounces) creamed cottage cheese (1 cup)

1. In 10-inch skillet, cook bacon over medium heat, stirring frequently, until browned; with slotted spoon, transfer to paper towels to drain. Preheat oven to 325°F. Grease four 15-ounce (or one 2-quart) soufflé dishes.

2. In 2-quart saucepan, melt margarine over medium heat. Stir in flour and salt until blended; cook, stirring, 1 minute. With wire whisk, gradually mix in milk; cook, stirring constantly, until sauce has thickened and boils.

3. In medium bowl, with wire whisk, lightly beat egg yolks. Stir in small amount of hot white sauce until blended. Slowly pour yolk mixture into sauce, stirring rapidly to prevent curdling. Stir in cottage cheese.

4. In large bowl with mixer at high speed, beat egg whites until stiff peaks form when beaters are lifted. With rubber spatula, gently fold cheese sauce and bacon into egg whites; pour into prepared soufflé dishes. Bake small puffs 35 minutes, large puff 45 minutes or until golden. Serve immediately. Makes 4 main-dish servings.

Each serving: About 310 calories, 18 g protein, 9 g carbohydrate, 22 g total fat (7 g saturated), 235 mg cholesterol, 710 mg sodium.

Broiled Goat Cheese

Prep: 5 minutes
Broil: 2 to 3 minutes

½ teaspoon cracked black pepper
¼ teaspoon dried thyme
¼ teaspoon fennel seeds
¼ teaspoon paprika
⅛ teaspoon dried rosemary
⅛ teaspoon ground red pepper (cayenne), optional
¼ cup plain dried bread crumbs
2 tablespoons extravirgin olive oil
11 to 12 ounces plain goat cheese (chèvre), such as Montrachet

1. Prepare crumb topping: With mortar and pestle, crush black pepper, thyme, fennel seeds, paprika, rosemary, and ground red pepper. In small bowl, toss herb mixture, bread crumbs and oil; store in airtight container until ready to use.

2. Preheat broiler. Evenly crumble goat cheese into shallow 8-inch round gratin dish. Sprinkle crumb mixture over goat cheese.

3. Broil 5 to 7 inches from heat source until crumb topping is lightly browned, 2 to 3 minutes. Makes 12 appetizer servings.

Each serving: About 105 calories, 6 g protein, 2 g carbohydrate, 8 g total fat (5 g saturated), 13 mg cholesterol, 125 mg sodium.

Eggplant and Mozzarella

Prep: 20 minutes
Cook: 12 minutes

¼ cup olive oil
3 tablespoons balsamic or cider vinegar
1 teaspoon finely chopped fresh basil
1¼ teaspoons salt
1 teaspoon sugar
8 ounces ripe tomatoes, (2 small) sliced

3 tablespoons all-purpose flour
1 small eggplant (1 pound), trimmed and cut on the diagonal into four 1-inch-thick slices
1 package (8 ounces) mozzarella cheese, sliced
Basil leaves

1. In pie plate, stir together 1 tablespoon oil, vinegar, basil, ¼ teaspoon salt, and sugar until salt and sugar have dissolved. Add tomato slices, turning tomatoes to coat with dressing.

2. On waxed paper, combine flour and remaining 1 teaspoon salt. Coat eggplant slices with flour, shaking off excess.

3. In 12-inch skillet, heat remaining oil over medium heat. Add eggplant and cook until tender and browned on both sides. Transfer eggplant slices to paper towels to drain. Discard any remaining oil and wipe skillet clean with paper towels.

4. Return eggplant slices to skillet; top with tomato slices, then cheese slices. Cover and cook over medium heat until the cheese has melted. Arrange 1 or 2 basil leaves on each eggplant stack and serve. Makes 4 main-dish servings.

Each main-dish serving: About 360 calories, 13 g protein, 20 g carbohydrate, 26 g total fat (9 saturated), 44 mg cholesterol, 945 mg sodium.

Pasta

Pasta • Sauces

ᐱPasta

Most pasta falls into one of three basic types; spaghetti, a straight or twisted solid rod, available in different thicknesses; macaroni, usually tubular, available long or short, smooth or ridged; and noodles, flat and ribbonlike, sometimes curled on one or both edges, available in varying widths. All three types are made from essentially the same wheat flour-and-water dough; noodles contain eggs in addition. Vermicelli and fusilli are types of spaghetti; macaroni includes ziti and rotelle among others; fettuccine and lasagna fall into the noodle category.

However, there are also dozens of other shapes—rings, corkscrews, fans, shells, and many more—and varieties, such as ravioli and tortellini, filled with meat, cheese, and/or other ingredients. Some pasta is colored by the addition of special ingredients to the dough: for example, spinach for green pasta, tomato for red.

The term "enriched" on the label indicates that the pasta is rich in B vitamins and iron.

Asian-style noodles, such as cellophane and rice stick noodles, are usually made with ingredients other than wheat flour and they do not contain eggs. They cannot be substituted for regular noodles in pasta recipes.

DRIED VS. FRESH PASTA

Dried pasta is made with semolina, a flour milled from durum wheat, high in gluten, which gives it the strength to withstand the mechanical pasta-making process and hold its shape when cooked. Dried pasta has a slightly rough surface to which a sauce can cling. The long shapes, from fine angel hair to thick bucatini, are best with oil-based and tomato sauces that coat each strand. Short shapes are best served with chunky meat or vegetables sauces—their hollows and grooves hold the sauce well. Stored in a cool dry place, dried pasta will stay fresh for up to 2 years.

Fresh pasta, which you'll find in a refrigerated case at your market, is usually made with white flour and eggs. The term "fresh" doesn't imply superior quality; it simply means that the dough was made recently and must be kept refrigerated. The pasta has a soft, porous texture and is best paired with light sauces containing cream, butter, and cheese. Wrapped airtight, it will keep for a week refrigerated, or a month in the freezer.

Note: A pound of fresh pasta makes fewer servings than a pound of dried pasta because the fresh pasta absorbs less water during cooking. On package labels, a serving size for dried pasta is 2 ounces, while a serving size for fresh pasta is 3 ounces; both yield 1 cup cooked.

HOW MUCH PASTA TO USE

Noodles swell slightly when cooked; spaghetti and macaroni double in size. An 8-ounce package of elbow macaroni (2 cups) makes about 4½ cups when cooked; the same amount of spaghetti makes about 5 cups when cooked.

In recipes, you can interchange pastas of similar sizes and shapes; but measure by weight, not cup volume, because uncooked pastas differ in weight. Cooked pastas can be substituted cup for cup.

PASTA POINTERS

Everyone can cook pasta, right? But not everyone knows how to keep noodles from clumping or the secret to using the pasta cooking water in sauces. Follow our tips:

- **Make room.** Fill a large, 6- to 8-quart saucepot with cold water, at least 16 cups water per pound. This prevents the pasta from sticking and helps dilute the starch released during cooking so you don't end up with a gluey mess.
- **Put a lid on it.** When heating the water, cover the pot, and use high heat so water will reach the boiling point sooner (it still takes about 15 minutes).
- **Add salt.** When water begins to boil, add about 2 teaspoons salt. This only slightly affects the sodium content of the finished dish but noticeably boosts the flavor.
- **Go slow.** Add pasta gradually, stirring with a wooden spoon or fork to keep it from sticking together or to the bottom of the pot. If cooking long strands like spaghetti or linguine, use the spoon to bend them as they soften until completely submerged; stir well.
- **Boil again.** Partially cover the pot until water bubbles once more, then uncover and adjust the heat so water is boiling, but not so fast that will overflow.
- **Don't add oil.** Your mother may have told you it keeps noodles from sticking, but so does frequent stirring. Besides, an oily coating makes it harder for sauce to cling.
- **Test it.** Don't just go by the time on the package. Italians have been cooking their pasta al dente, literally, "to the tooth," for years, and with good reason: Pasta becomes gummy and absorbs too much sauce when overcooked. A noodle should offer some resistance—but never crunch—when you bite it. Package guidelines for pasta that are generally baked, like lasagna, manicotti, and jumbo shells, usually take into account the additional oven time and reduce boiling time accordingly. But if you're making a casserole with a pasta that isn't usually baked—such as Tuna-Melt Casserole, page 447, which calls for corkscrews—reduce stovetop cooking time by one-third to compensate for baking time.
- **Save the water.** It helps to reserve ½ to 1 cup of the pasta cooking water before draining in case you need more sauce for your finished dish (often the case with angel hair pasta, which seems to soak toppings right up). Gradually stir the water into tomato, vegetable, or cream sauce.

- **Serve pronto.** Drain pasta quickly and use it immediately. Rinsing in cold water is unnecessary unless noodles are to be served cold—the cool splash removes surface starch, which helps sauce hold on.

SHOULD YOU SALT THE WATER?

It's not only a matter of cooking technique, there's a health question as well: Are you turning virtuous dried pasta—which is sodium-free—into a salt-watcher's nightmare?

To get to the bottom of this kitchen debate, we cooked 3 separate pounds of dried penne, each in 16 cups of boiling water—the first potful had no salt; the second, 2 teaspoons; and the third, 2 tablespoons. When the pastas were al dente, we drained and tasted them. The consensus: The salt-free pasta was exceedingly bland; we longed to reach for the shaker and sprinkle away. The pasta that was cooked with 2 tablespoons salt—the amount packages recommended until recently—was a little too salty, especially since most pasta gets sauced or seasoned anyway. The penne cooked with 2 teaspoons salt—the amount we use in our test kitchens—was just right.

But we wanted to know how much sodium the pasta was actually absorbing (1 teaspoon of salt almost meets the 2,400 mg daily recommended limit for sodium). So we had the Chemistry Department do a sodium analysis of all three pastas. The results: Each main-dish serving (4 ounces, cooked) absorbed 92 mg sodium when boiled with 2 teaspoons salt, and 228 mg when boiled with 2 tablespoons salt.

The surprise: Only about 10 percent of the sodium added to the water was absorbed in both cases. So in the long run, you're probably better off lightly salting the water than compensating for dull pasta by oversalting at the table.

A PERFECT MATCH: PAIRING PASTAS AND SAUCES

Not every pasta works with every topping. Fragile angel hair can completely absorb a creamy sauce in the time it takes to turn around and get a serving spoon, and sturdy penne overpowers a delicate seafood sauce. Here's a general guide to using the most common shapes:

- **LONG** [spaghetti, vermicelli, linguine, spaghettini, capellini or angel hair]: Best with smooth tomato and oil-based sauces; these varieties don't carry a chunky topping well once you lift the fork. Save ultrathin capellini for light sauces, or use in broths.
- **LONG STRAWS** [perciatelli, bucatini]: Ideal for pesto, cheese, or cream sauces because the pasta gets coated inside and out.
- **SHORT** [farfalle (bow ties), fusilli (corkscrews), orecchiette (little ears), shells, gemelli, radiatore]: Serve with butter, cheese, tomato, meat, vegetable, and light oil-based sauces; they'll catch every drop.
- **SHORT TUBES** [penne, rigatoni, ziti]: Bite for bite, the most suitable partner for meat, vegetable, and chunky tomato sauces.
- **SMALL** [pastina, ditalini, orzo, stelline, tubettini, farfalline]: Use in broths or soups so you can spoon up every last morsel.
- **WIDE** [tagliatelle, fettuccine, pappardelle, lasagna, mafalda]: These noodles are substantial enough to support cream, cheese, and thick meat sauces.

MEAT PASTA

Rigatoni with "Sausage" Sauce

Prep: 5 minutes
Cook: 25 minutes

12 ounces rigatoni or ziti
12 ounces extralean ground beef
1 medium onion, chopped
¾ teaspoon salt
¼ teaspoon crushed red pepper
1 teaspoon fennel seeds, crushed
2 cans (14½ ounces each) Italian-style stewed tomatoes
Chopped fresh parsley for garnish

1. In large saucepot, cook rigatoni as label directs. Drain and keep warm.

2. Meanwhile, in nonstick 12-inch skillet, cook ground beef, onion, salt, crushed red pepper, and fennel seeds, over medium-high heat, stirring occasionally, and breaking up beef with side of spoon, until pan juices have evaporated and beef is well browned.

3. Stir in stewed tomatoes; heat to boiling over high heat. Reduce heat to low; cover and simmer, stirring occasionally, 10 minutes. In warm serving bowl, place rigatoni; add sauce and toss until well combined. Sprinkle with parsley. Makes 4 main-dish servings.

Each serving: About 585 calories, 29 g protein, 79 g carbohydrate, 16 g total fat (6 g saturated), 57 mg cholesterol, 1,120 mg sodium.

Corkscrew Pasta with Sausage and Butternut Squash

Prep: 15 minutes
Cook: 20 minutes

1 medium butternut squash (1¾ pounds)
12 ounces sweet Italian-sausage links, casings removed
1 package (16 ounces) corkscrew pasta
¼ teaspoon each salt and coarsely ground black pepper
⅓ cup packed fresh basil leaves
¼ cup freshly grated Parmesan cheese

1. Cut butternut squash lengthwise in half; discard seeds. Peel squash and cut into ½-inch pieces.

2. In nonstick 12-inch skillet, cook sausage over medium-high heat, breaking up sausage with side of spoon, until sausage is browned, about 7 minutes. With slotted spoon, transfer sausage to bowl; discard all but 2 table-spoons drippings from skillet.

3. Meanwhile, in large saucepot, cook pasta as label directs.

4. To drippings in skillet, stir in butternut squash, salt, and pepper. Reduce heat to medium; cover and cook until squash is tender, stirring occasionally, about 10 minutes.

5. Drain pasta, reserving ¾ cup pasta cooking water. Return pasta to saucepot; add sausage, butternut squash, basil, Parmesan, and reserved pasta water and toss to mix well. Transfer to warm large serving bowl. Makes 6 main-dish servings.

Each serving: About 505 calories, 20 g protein, 66 g carbohydrate, 17 g total fat (6 g saturated), 40 mg cholesterol, 645 mg sodium.

Ziti with Sausage and Zucchini

Prep: 10 minutes
Cook: 15 minutes

1 package (16 ounces) ziti rigate or wagon-wheel pasta
12 ounces sweet Italian-sausage links, casings removed
3 medium zucchini (8 ounces each), each cut lengthwise in half,
    then cut crosswise into ¼-inch-thick slices
¼ teaspoon each salt and coarsely ground black pepper
1 can (28 ounces) plum tomatoes
Freshly grated Parmesan cheese (optional)

1. In large saucepot, cook pasta as label directs. Drain.

2. Meanwhile, heat nonstick 12-inch skillet over medium-high heat. Add sausage and cook, breaking up sausage with side of spoon, until browned, about 5 minutes. With slotted spoon, transfer sausage to bowl.

3. Discard all but 1 tablespoon drippings from skillet. Add zucchini, salt, and pepper and cook, stirring occasionally, until zucchini is golden, about 5 minutes. Stir in tomatoes with their juice; heat to boiling, breaking tomatoes up with side of spoon. Return sausage to skillet. Reduce heat to low; cover and simmer, until flavors have blended, about 5 minutes.

4. In warm serving bowl, toss pasta with sausage mixture until well combined. Sprinkle with Parmesan, if you like. Makes 6 main-dish servings.

Each serving: About 475 calories, 21 g protein, 66 g carbohydrate, 15 g total fat (5 g saturated), 35 mg cholesterol, 785 mg sodium.

Mafalda with Veal and Rosemary

Prep: 15 minutes
Cook: 20 minutes

1 package (16 ounces)
 mafalda or spaghetti
1 tablespoon olive oil
1 medium onion, finely
 chopped
1 garlic clove, finely chopped
½ teaspoon dried rosemary,
 crumbled
1 pound ground veal
1 teaspoon salt

¼ teaspoon ground black
 pepper
½ cup dry white wine
1 can (14½ to 16 ounces)
 tomatoes
1 tablespoon margarine or
 butter
½ cup chopped fresh flat-leaf
 parsley

1. In large saucepot, cook pasta as label directs. Drain.

2. Meanwhile, in 12-inch skillet, heat oil over medium-high heat. Add onion and cook, stirring often, until almost tender, about 3 minutes. Stir in garlic and rosemary and cook, stirring, 30 seconds.

3. Increase heat to high. Add ground veal, salt, and pepper and cook, stirring often, and breaking up veal with side of spoon, until veal has browned, 5 to 7 minutes. Add wine and cook until almost evaporated, stirring to loosen browned bits from bottom of skillet. Stir in tomatoes with their juice; heat to boiling, breaking tomatoes up with side of spoon. Boil, stirring occasionally, 5 minutes. Remove skillet from heat; stir in margarine.

4. In warm serving bowl, toss pasta with veal sauce and parsley until well combined. Makes 6 main-dish servings.

Each serving: About 455 calories, 26 g protein, 62 g carbohydrate, 11 g total fat (3 g saturated), 62 mg cholesterol, 665 mg sodium.

Spaghetti with Bacon and Peas

Prep: 10 minutes
Cook: 10 minutes

1 pound thin spaghetti or vermicelli
4 slices bacon
1 medium onion, finely chopped
1 package (10 ounces) frozen peas
1 container (15 ounces) part-skim ricotta cheese
½ cup freshly grated Pecorino Romano or Parmesan cheese
½ teaspoon salt
¼ teaspoon coarsely ground black pepper

1. In large saucepot, cook pasta as label directs.

2. Meanwhile, in 12-inch skillet, cook bacon over medium heat until browned. Transfer to paper towels. Discard all but 1 tablespoon bacon fat from skillet. Add onion and cook, stirring frequently, until tender and golden, 8 to 10 minutes.

3. During last 2 minutes of pasta cooking time, add frozen peas and continue cooking until pasta and peas are done. Drain pasta and peas, reserving 1 cup pasta cooking water. Return pasta and peas to saucepot and toss with ricotta, Pecorino, salt, pepper, and reserved pasta cooking water until well blended. Crumble in bacon, toss again, and serve. Makes 4 main-dish servings.

Each serving: About 745 calories, 37 g protein, 103 g carbohydrate, 20 g total fat (10 g saturated), 54 mg cholesterol, 880 mg sodium.

Radiatore with Sweet and Spicy Picadillo Sauce

Prep: 10 minutes
Cook: 15 minutes

1 package (16 ounces)
   radiatore or corkscrew pasta
1 teaspoon olive oil
1 small onion, finely chopped
2 garlic cloves, crushed with
   garlic press
¼ teaspoon ground cinnamon
⅛ to ¼ teaspoon ground red
   pepper (cayenne)

12 ounces ground beef
   chuck
½ teaspoon salt
1 can (14½ ounces) tomatoes
   in puree
½ cup dark seedless raisins
¼ cup chopped pimiento-
   stuffed olives (salad olives)
Chopped fresh parsley leaves

1. In large saucepot, cook pasta as label directs. Drain, reserving 1 cup pasta cooking water.

2. Meanwhile, in nonstick 12-inch skillet, heat oil over medium heat. Add onion and cook, stirring frequently, until tender, 5 minutes. Stir in garlic, cinnamon, and ground red pepper; cook, stirring, 30 seconds. Increase heat to medium-high; add ground beef and salt, and cook, stirring frequently, and breaking up beef with side of spoon, until beef begins to brown, about 5 minutes. Spoon off fat, if necessary. Stir in tomatoes with their puree, raisins, and olives, breaking tomatoes up with side of spoon, and cook until sauce has thickened slightly, about 5 minutes longer.

3. In warm serving bowl, toss pasta with ground-beef sauce and reserved pasta cooking water until well combined. Sprinkle with chopped parsley to serve. Makes 6 main-dish servings.

Each serving: About 470 calories, 20 g protein, 71 g carbohydrate, 11 g total fat (4 g saturated), 35 mg cholesterol, 775 mg sodium.

Light Sesame Noodles

Prep: 10 minutes
Cook: 10 minutes

1 package (9 ounces)
   refrigerated angel hair pasta
2 cups packaged shredded
   carrots
2 teaspoons vegetable oil
12 ounces skinless, boneless
   chicken breasts halves or
   chicken breast tenders, cut
   into thin slices
2 garlic cloves, crushed with
   garlic press
1 medium orange
3 tablespoons seasoned rice
   vinegar

3 tablespoons soy sauce
2 teaspoons Asian sesame oil
1 teaspoon grated, peeled
   fresh ginger
1 teaspoon sugar
⅛ teaspoon ground red pepper
   (cayenne)
4 large radishes, each cut in
   half and thinly sliced
2 green onions, cut into thin
   diagonal slices
2 tablespoons sesame seeds,
   toasted (see page 29)

1. In large saucepot, cook pasta as label directs but do not add salt. Place shredded carrots in colander; drain pasta over carrots to soften them slightly. Transfer mixture to large serving bowl.

2. In nonstick 12-inch skillet, heat oil over medium-high heat until very hot. Add chicken and garlic; cook, stirring constantly, until chicken loses its pink color throughout, about 4 to 5 minutes. Transfer chicken to bowl with pasta.

3. Prepare vinaigrette: From orange, grate 1 teaspoon peel and squeeze ¼ cup juice. In small bowl, with wire whisk, mix orange peel and juice, vinegar, soy sauce, sesame oil, ginger, sugar, and ground red pepper until well blended.

4. Toss pasta mixture with vinaigrette, radish slices, and green onions; sprinkle with sesame seeds. Serve warm or refrigerate until ready to serve. Makes 4 main-dish servings.

Each serving: About 415 calories, 30 g protein, 51 g carbohydrate, 10 g total fat (2 g saturated), 121 mg cholesterol, 1,170 mg sodium.

SEAFOOD PASTA

Linguine with Asian-Style Clam Sauce

Prep: 30 minutes
Cook: 20 minutes

1 package (16 ounces) linguine
  or spaghetti
3 tablespoons olive oil
3 garlic cloves, crushed with
  side of chef's knife
1 tablespoon grated, peeled
  fresh ginger
¼ teaspoon crushed red
  pepper
3 dozen littleneck clams,
  scrubbed under cold running
  water until free of sand

1 bottle (8 ounces) clam juice
½ cup dry white wine
3 strips (3" by ¾" each) lemon
  peel, cut lengthwise into thin
  slivers
2 tablespoons butter or olive oil
¼ cup chopped fresh cilantro
  leaves

1. In large saucepot, cook linguine as label directs. Drain, reserving ¾ cup pasta cooking water. Return linguine to saucepot.

2. Meanwhile, in nonstick 12-inch skillet, heat 3 tablespoons oil over medium-high heat. Add garlic and cook, stirring, until golden. Add ginger and crushed red pepper; cook, stirring, 30 seconds. Stir in clams, clam juice, wine, and lemon peel strips; heat to boiling. Reduce heat to medium; cover and simmer 10 to 15 minutes, stirring occasionally, until clams open, transferring clams to bowl as they open. Discard any clams that have not opened. Stir 2 tablespoons butter or olive oil and reserved pasta cooking water into sauce in skillet.

3. Stir sauce and cilantro into saucepot of linguine; heat to boiling over high heat. Reduce heat to low; cook 1 minute. Add clams; cover and heat through. Ladle clams, pasta, and sauce into shallow soup plates and serve. Makes 4 main-dish servings.

Each serving: About 660 calories, 30 g protein, 90 g carbohydrate, 19 g total fat (5 g saturated), 55 mg cholesterol, 450 mg sodium.

Shells with Smoked Trout and Chives

Prep: 15 minutes
Cook: 15 minutes

1 package (16 ounces) medium pasta shells or linguine
12 ounces green beans, ends trimmed and cut crosswise in half
1 whole smoked trout (6 ounces)
½ cup half-and-half or light cream
½ teaspoon freshly grated lemon peel
¼ teaspoon each salt* and coarsely ground black pepper
5 tablespoons chopped fresh chives

1. In large saucepot, cook pasta as label directs. After pasta has cooked 5 minutes, add green beans to saucepot and continue cooking until pasta and beans are done. Drain pasta and beans, reserving ½ cup pasta cooking water. Return pasta and beans to saucepot; keep warm.
2. Meanwhile, remove and discard head, tail, skin, and bones from trout. Separate flesh into 1-inch pieces. In 2-quart saucepan, stir half-and-half, lemon peel, salt, pepper, and 1 tablespoon chives; to simmering over low heat. Remove saucepan from heat.
3. Add half-and-half mixture, trout, reserved pasta cooking water, and 3 tablespoons chives to pasta and beans; toss well. Sprinkle with remaining 1 tablespoon chives to serve. Makes 6 main-dish servings.

*Since the saltiness of the smoked fish can vary considerably, taste first before adding salt in step 2.

Each serving: About 350 calories, 15 g protein, 62 g carbohydrate, 5 g total fat (2 g saturated), 10 mg cholesterol, 360 mg sodium.

Linguine with Scallops and Saffron

Prep: 20 minutes
Cook: 15 minutes

1 package (16 ounces) linguine
  or spaghetti
1 pound leeks (3 medium)
1 pound sea scallops, rinsed
2 tablespoons margarine or
  butter
¾ teaspoon salt
¼ teaspoon coarsely ground
  black pepper
½ teaspoon freshly grated
  orange peel

Large pinch saffron threads,
  crumbled
¼ cup dry white wine
1 bottle (8 ounces) clam
  juice
¼ cup heavy or whipping
  cream
½ cup loosely packed fresh
  parsley leaves

1. In large saucepot, cook pasta as label directs. Drain.

2. Meanwhile, cut off roots and dark green tops from leeks; cut each leek lengthwise in half, then crosswise into ½-inch-thick slices. Rinse leeks in large bowl of cold water, to remove sand; transfer to colander to drain, leaving sand in bottom of bowl.

3. Pull tough crescent-shaped muscle from side of each scallop. Cut each scallop horizontally in half.

4. In 12-inch skillet, melt margarine over medium heat. Add leeks, salt, and pepper and cook, stirring frequently, until leeks are tender, about 8 minutes. Add orange peel and saffron and cook, stirring, 2 minutes. Add wine; cook 1 minute longer. Increase heat to medium-high; stir in clam juice and heat to boiling. Add scallops and cook, stirring often, until just opaque throughout, 3 to 4 minutes. Stir in cream and heat through.

5. In warm serving bowl, toss pasta with leek mixture. Sprinkle with parsley leaves to serve. Makes 6 main-dish servings.

Each serving: About 440 calories, 24 g protein, 66 g carbohydrate, 9 g total fat (3 g saturated), 40 mg cholesterol, 635 mg sodium.

Pad Thai

Prep: 25 minutes
Cook: 5 minutes

1 package (7 to 8 ounces) flat rice stick noodles,* broken in half, or 8 ounces angel hair pasta
8 ounces medium shrimp, shelled and deveined (see page 366)
¼ cup fresh lime juice
¼ cup Asian fish sauce†
2 tablespoons sugar
1 tablespoon vegetable oil
2 garlic cloves, crushed with garlic press
¼ teaspoon crushed red pepper
2 large eggs, lightly beaten
6 ounces fresh bean sprouts (2 cups), rinsed
2 tablespoons unsalted roasted peanuts, coarsely chopped
3 green onions, thinly sliced
½ cup loosely packed fresh cilantro leaves
Lime wedges

1. In large bowl, soak rice stick noodles in hot tap water to cover 20 minutes. (Or, break angel hair pasta in half; cook in large saucepot as label directs, drain, and rinse under cold running water. Drain again.)

2. Meanwhile, cut each shrimp horizontally in half. In small bowl, stir together lime juice, fish sauce, and sugar until sugar has dissolved. Assemble all remaining ingredients before beginning to cook.

3. Drain rice stick noodles. In nonstick wok or 12-inch skillet, heat oil over high heat until very hot. Add shrimp, garlic, and crushed red pepper, and cook, stirring, 1 minute. Add eggs and cook, stirring, until just set, about 20 seconds. Add noodles and cook, stirring, 2 minutes. Add lime-juice mixture, half of bean sprouts, half of peanuts, and half of green onions; cook, stirring, 1 minute.

4. Transfer Pad Thai to warm large platter; top with remaining bean sprouts, peanuts, and green onions. Sprinkle with cilantro leaves. Serve with lime wedges. Makes 4 main-dish servings.

*Rice stick noodles are available in Asian groceries.
†Asian fish sauce is available in the Asian sections of some supermarkets.

Each serving: About 395 calories, 19 g protein, 59 g carbohydrate, 9 g total fat (2 g saturated), 172 mg cholesterol, 1400 mg sodium.

Penne with Salmon and Asparagus

Prep: 15 minutes
Cook: About 15 minutes

1 package (16 ounces) penne rigate or bow-tie pasta	¼ teaspoon coarsely ground black pepper
1 piece salmon fillet (1 pound), skin removed	1 large shallot, finely chopped (about ¼ cup)
3 teaspoons olive oil	⅓ cup dry white wine
1 pound medium asparagus, trimmed and cut crosswise into 2-inch pieces	1 cup reduced-sodium chicken broth
½ teaspoon salt	1 tablespoon chopped fresh tarragon leaves

1. In large saucepot, cook pasta as label directs. Drain.
2. Meanwhile, with tweezers, remove any small bones from salmon. Cut salmon fillet crosswise into thirds, then cut each third lengthwise into ¼-inch-thick slices. In 12-inch skillet, heat 2 teaspoons oil over medium-high heat until very hot. Add asparagus, salt, and pepper, and cook until asparagus is almost tender-crisp, stirring frequently, about 5 minutes. Add shallot and remaining 1 teaspoon oil; cook, stirring constantly, 2 minutes longer. Add wine; heat to boiling over high heat. Stir in broth and heat to boiling. Place salmon slices in skillet; cover and cook, stirring gent-

ly, until salmon is just opaque throughout, 2 to 3 minutes. Remove skillet from heat; stir in tarragon.

3. In warm serving bowl, toss pasta with asparagus mixture until well combined. Makes 6 main-dish servings.

Each serving: About 460 calories, 27 g protein, 59 g carbohydrate, 12 g total fat (2 g saturated), 45 mg cholesterol, 420 mg sodium.

Shells with Tuna and Capers

Prep: 5 minutes
Cook: 15 minutes

1 package (16 ounces) medium pasta shells
1 medium lemon
2 tablespoons olive oil
2 garlic cloves, crushed with garlic press
¼ teaspoon crushed red pepper
2 cans (6 ounces each) tuna in water, drained and flaked
¼ cup capers, drained and chopped
¼ teaspoon salt
1 cup packed fresh flat-leaf parsley leaves, chopped

1. In large saucepot, cook pasta as label directs. Drain, reserving ½ cup pasta cooking water.

2. Meanwhile, from lemon, grate 1 teaspoon peel, and squeeze 2 tablespoons juice. In 10-inch skillet, heat oil over medium heat. Add garlic and crushed red pepper, and cook, stirring, 30 seconds. Add tuna, capers, salt, and lemon peel and juice, and cook, stirring gently, until heated through, about 2 minutes.

3. In warm serving bowl, toss pasta, parsley, tuna mixture, and reserved pasta cooking water until well combined. Makes 6 main-dish servings.

Each serving: About 395 calories, 26 g protein, 58 g carbohydrate, 6 g total fat (1 g saturated), 0 mg cholesterol, 590 mg sodium.

Vermicelli with Shrimp and Broccoli

Prep: 15 minutes
Cook: 15 minutes

1 package (16 ounces each)
  vermicelli or thin spaghetti
1 tablespoon vegetable oil
1 pound medium shrimp,
  shelled and deveined, with
  tail part of shell left on, if
  you like (see page 366)
1 tablespoon grated, peeled
  fresh ginger
2 garlic cloves, crushed with
  garlic press

¼ teaspoon crushed red
  pepper
2 packages (12 ounces each)
  broccoli flowerets
1 cup reduced-sodium chicken
  broth
2 tablespoons soy sauce
1 teaspoon Asian sesame oil

1. In large saucepot, cook pasta as label directs. Drain.
2. Meanwhile, in 10-inch skillet, heat oil over medium-high heat until very hot. Add shrimp, ginger, garlic, and crushed red pepper. Cook, stirring, until shrimp are just opaque throughout, about 2 minutes. With slotted spoon, transfer shrimp to bowl.
3. Add broccoli to skillet and cook, stirring, 1 minute. Stir in broth and heat to boiling over high heat. Cover and cook, stirring often, until broccoli is just tender, about 3 minutes. Stir in soy sauce, sesame oil, shrimp and any juice in bowl; heat through.
4. In warm serving bowl, toss pasta with shrimp mixture until well combined. Makes 6 main-dish servings.

Each serving: About 415 calories, 26 g protein, 65 g carbohydrate, 6 g total fat (1 g saturated), 95 mg cholesterol, 655 mg sodium.

Fusilli Puttanesca

Prep: 15 minutes
Cook: 15 minutes

1 package (16 ounces) fusilli or
    corkscrew pasta
3 tablespoons capers, drained
    and chopped
3 tablespoons finely chopped
    shallot
2 tablespoons red wine vinegar
1 tablespoon olive oil
½ teaspoon freshly grated
    lemon peel

½ teaspoon salt
¼ teaspoon coarsely ground
    black pepper
1 can (6 ounces) light tuna in
    olive oil
2 bunches watercress (4 ounces
    each); tough stems trimmed
½ cup loosely packed fresh
    basil leaves, chopped

1. In large saucepot, cook pasta as label directs. Drain, reserving ½ cup pasta cooking water. Return pasta to saucepot.

2. Meanwhile, in large bowl, stir capers, shallot, vinegar, oil, lemon peel, salt, and pepper until well mixed. Add undrained tuna and watercress; toss well to coat.

3. Add tuna mixture, reserved pasta cooking water, and basil to pasta in saucepot; toss well and serve. Makes 6 main-dish servings.

Each serving: About 375 calories, 17 g protein, 58 g carbohydrate, 8 g total fat (1 g saturated), 4 mg cholesterol, 540 mg sodium.

BAKED PASTA

Spaghetti Carbonara Pie

Prep: 15 minutes
Bake: 35 to 40 minutes

12 ounces spaghetti
4 ounces bacon (about 6
    slices), cut into ¼-inch
    pieces
2 cups milk
1 container (15 ounces) part-
    skim ricotta cheese
½ cup freshly grated Pecorino
    Romano cheese

2 large eggs
1 large egg yolk
½ teaspoon salt
½ teaspoon coarsely ground
    black pepper
Pinch ground nutmeg

1. Preheat oven to 375°F. In large saucepot, cook spaghetti as label directs. Drain and return to saucepot.
2. Meanwhile, in nonstick 10-inch skillet, cook bacon over medium heat, stirring frequently, until browned, about 10 minutes. With slotted spoon, transfer bacon to paper towels to drain.
3. In blender, blend ½ cup milk, ricotta, Pecorino, eggs, egg yolk, salt, pepper, and nutmeg until smooth.
4. Add ricotta mixture, bacon, and remaining 1½ cups milk to pasta in saucepot, stirring to combine.
5. Transfer pasta mixture to 2½-quart baking dish (about 2 inches deep). Bake until golden around the edges and almost set but still slightly liquid in center, 35 to 40 minutes. Transfer to wire rack and let pie stand 10 minutes before serving (liquid will be absorbed as it stands). Cut into wedges to serve. Makes 6 main-dish servings.

Each serving: About 470 calories, 25 g protein, 50 g carbohydrate, 18 g total fat (9 g saturated), 154 mg cholesterol, 595 mg sodium.

Baked Rigatoni and Peas for a Crowd

Prep: 45 minutes
Bake: 30 to 35 minutes

2 packages (16 ounces each) rigatoni or ziti
14 tablespoons margarine or butter (1¾ sticks)
½ cup all-purpose flour
7 cups milk
2 cups freshly grated Parmesan cheese
2 teaspoons salt
1 bag (20 ounces) frozen peas, thawed
2 cans (14½ ounces each) diced tomatoes
1 cup loosely packed fresh basil leaves, cut into strips
½ cup plain dried bread crumbs

1. In 12-quart saucepot, cook rigatoni as label directs. Drain and return to saucepot; cover to keep warm.

2. Meanwhile, prepare Parmesan sauce: In 3-quart saucepan, melt 10 tablespoons margarine over low heat. Stir in flour until blended; cook, stirring constantly, 3 minutes. With wire whisk, gradually mix in milk. Increase heat to medium; cook, stirring frequently, until sauce boils and has thickened slightly, about 20 minutes. Stir in 1½ cups Parmesan and salt. Remove from heat.

3. Preheat oven to 350°F. Pour Parmesan sauce into saucepot with rigatoni, stirring to combine. Stir in peas, tomatoes with their juice, and basil. Spoon rigatoni mixture into two shallow 3½- to 4-quart casseroles or two 13" by 9" baking dishes.

4. In small saucepan, melt remaining 4 tablespoons margarine over low heat; remove from heat and stir in bread crumbs and remaining ½ cup Parmesan. (Recipe can be prepared to this point up to 1 day ahead. Cover and refrigerate rigatoni and topping separately.) Sprinkle topping on rigatoni just before baking. Bake rigatoni until sauce is hot and bubbly and topping is golden, 30 to 35 minutes, if cooking right away, or about 1 hour if rigatoni was refrigerated. Transfer to wire rack and let rigatoni stand a few minutes before serving. Makes 20 main-dish servings.

Each serving: About 390 calories, 15 g protein, 49 g carbohydrate, 15 g total fat (5 g saturated), 20 mg cholesterol, 695 mg sodium.

Classic Lasagna with Meat Sauce

Prep: 1 hour
Bake: 30 minutes

Meat Sauce
8 ounces sweet Italian-sausage links, casings removed
8 ounces lean ground beef chuck
1 small onion, chopped
2 garlic cloves, finely chopped
1 can (28 ounces) tomatoes
1 can (14½ to 16 ounces) tomatoes
2 tablespoons tomato paste
½ teaspoon salt
2 tablespoons chopped fresh basil leaves

Cheese Filling
1 container (15 ounces) part-skim ricotta cheese
1 large egg
4 ounces part-skim mozzarella cheese, shredded (about 1 cup)
¾ cup freshly grated Parmesan cheese
¼ teaspoon ground black pepper

No-boil lasagna noodles (8 ounces)

1. Prepare Meat Sauce: Heat 4-quart saucepan over medium-high heat until hot. Add sausage and ground beef, and cook, stirring, 1 minute. Stir in onion and cook, stirring occasionally and breaking up sausage with side of spoon, until meat is browned and onion is tender, about 5 minutes. Pour off drippings from saucepan. Add garlic to saucepan and cook, stirring, 1 minute.
2. Stir in both cans of tomatoes with their juice, tomato paste, and salt, heat to boiling; breaking tomatoes up with

spoon. Reduce heat to medium and cook, stirring occasionally, 20 minutes. Stir in basil; remove saucepan from heat. Makes about 6 cups sauce.

3. Prepare Filling: In medium bowl, stir ricotta, egg, ½ cup mozzarella, ½ cup Parmesan, and pepper until blended.

4. Preheat oven to 350°F. In 13" by 9" baking dish, evenly spread 2 cups sauce. Arrange 3 lasagna noodles over sauce, making sure noodles do not touch sides of dish (they will expand during baking). Top with 1¼ cups ricotta mixture, 3 noodles, and 2 cups sauce. Arrange 3 noodles on top; spread with remaining ricotta mixture. Top with remaining noodles and remaining sauce. Sprinkle with remaining ½ cup mozzarella and remaining ¼ cup Parmesan. (If making a day ahead, cover and refrigerate.)

5. Cover lasagna with foil and bake until hot and bubbly, about 30 minutes (1 hour if lasagna was refrigerated). Transfer lasagna to wire rack and let stand stand 10 minutes for easier serving. Makes 10 main-dish servings.

Each serving: About 350 calories, 24 g protein, 27 g carbohydrate, 16 g total fat (8 g saturated), 78 mg cholesterol, 775 mg sodium.

Easy make-ahead tip: Complete lasagna and refrigerate overnight, then bake and serve the next day.

Butternut Squash Lasagna

Prep: 1 hour and 15 minutes
Bake: 40 minutes

12 lasagna noodles
1 large butternut squash (3 pounds), peeled, seeds removed, and
    cut into 1-inch pieces
2 tablespoons olive oil
¾ teaspoon salt
1 jumbo onion (1 pound), cut in half and thinly sliced
1 large bunch Swiss chard (1½ pounds), coarsely chopped, with
    tough stems trimmed, washed and dried very well

White Sauce
2 tablespoons margarine or butter
⅓ cup all-purpose flour
¼ teaspoon salt
¼ teaspoon coarsely ground black pepper
¼ teaspoon ground nutmeg
¼ teaspoon dried thyme
4 cups low-fat (1%) milk
¾ cup freshly grated Parmesan cheese

1. In large saucepot, cook lasagna noodles as label directs. Drain noodles and rinse with cold running water to stop cooking; drain again. Layer noodles between waxed paper.

2. Meanwhile, preheat oven to 450°F. In large bowl, toss butternut squash pieces with 1 tablespoon oil and ½ teaspoon salt. Spread squash in 15½" by 10½" jelly-roll pan or large cookie sheet. Roast squash until fork-tender, about 30 minutes, stirring halfway through cooking. Remove from oven, transfer to medium bowl, and, with potato masher, mash squash until almost smooth; cover and set aside. Turn oven control to 375°F.

3. Meanwhile, in 5-quart Dutch oven, heat remaining 1 tablespoon oil over medium heat. Add onion and ¼ teaspoon salt, and cook, stirring often, about 15 to 25 minutes, until golden. Add Swiss chard and cook, stirring often with two spoons, until wilted and liquid has evaporated, about 7 minutes. Remove Dutch oven from heat.

4. Prepare White Sauce: In 3-quart saucepan, melt margarine over medium heat. Stir in flour, salt, pepper, nutmeg, and thyme until blended, and cook, stirring constantly, 1 minute. With wire whisk, gradually mix in milk. Increase heat to medium-high; cook, stirring frequently, until sauce boils and has thickened slightly. Boil, stirring 1 minute. Whisk in all but 2 tablespoons Parmesan. Remove saucepan from heat.

5. In 13" by 9" baking dish, evenly spread about ½ cup white sauce until bottom of dish is covered. Arrange 4 lasagna noodles over sauce, overlapping to fit. Evenly spread Swiss chard mixture on noodles; top with about 1 cup white sauce. Arrange 4 lasagna noodles on top, then spoon 1 cup white sauce and the mashed butternut squash on noodles. Top with remaining noodles and remaining white sauce. Sprinkle with reserved 2 tablespoons Parmesan.

6. Cover lasagna with foil and bake 30 minutes; remove foil and bake until hot and bubbly, about 10 minutes longer. Transfer lasagna to wire rack and let stand 10 minutes for easier serving. Makes 10 main-dish servings.

Each serving: About 315 calories, 13 g protein, 47 g carbohydrate, 9 g total fat (3 g saturated), 10 mg cholesterol, 575 mg sodium.

Tuscan Lasagna Spirals

Prep: 1 hour
Bake: 55 minutes

12 lasagna noodles
1 tablespoon olive oil
1 jumbo onion (about 1
    pound), finely
    chopped
4 garlic cloves, crushed with
    garlic press
4 slices bacon, cut into ¼-inch
    pieces
1 pound white mushrooms,
    trimmed and finely chopped
1 pound portobello mushrooms,
    stems removed and caps
    finely chopped

1 package (10 ounces) frozen
    chopped spinach, thawed
    and squeezed dry
4 ounces Fontina cheese,
    shredded (about 1 cup)
½ cup freshly grated Parmesan
    cheese
½ teaspoon salt
¼ teaspoon coarsely ground
    black pepper
1 can (28 ounces) tomatoes in
    puree
1 can (14½ to 16 ounces)
    tomatoes in puree
⅓ cup water

1. In large saucepot, cook lasagna noodles as label directs. Drain noodles and rinse with cold running water to stop cooking; drain again. Layer noodles between waxed paper.

2. Meanwhile, preheat oven to 450°F. In nonstick 12-inch skillet, heat oil over medium heat. Add onion and cook, stirring frequently, until tender and golden, 12 to 15 minutes. Add garlic and cook, stirring frequently, 2 minutes. Reserve ⅓ cup onion mixture for sauce; transfer remainder to large bowl.

3. Add bacon to skillet and cook, stirring occasionally, until browned, about 7 to 8 minutes. With slotted spoon, transfer bacon to bowl with onion mixture.

4. Into each of two 15½" by 10½" jelly-roll pans, spoon 2 teaspoons bacon fat from skillet. Discard any remaining fat; but do not clean skillet. Place pans in oven to heat 3 minutes. Add white mushrooms to 1 hot pan and toss to coat. Add portobello mushrooms to other hot pan and toss to coat. Bake mushrooms 25 minutes, rotating pans between upper and lower racks halfway through baking or until mushrooms are slightly browned. Transfer white and portabello mushrooms to bowl with onion mixture; stir in spinach, Fontina, Parmesan, salt, and pepper until well blended. Turn oven control to 350°F.

5. Prepare sauce: In same skillet, heat both cans of tomatoes with their puree, water, and reserved ⅓ cup onion mixture to boiling over medium-high heat, stirring occasionally, and breaking tomatoes up with side of spoon. Reduce heat to low; cover and simmer 10 minutes. Stir ½ cup sauce into mushroom mixture in bowl. Spoon remaining sauce into 13" by 9" baking dish.

6. On surface, place 6 lasagna noodles. Spoon scant ½ cup mushroom filling down center of each noodle. Roll each noodle, from a long side, jelly-roll fashion. Place rolled noodles, seam-side down, in dish with sauce. Repeat with remaining 6 noodles and filling.

7. Cover lasagna with foil and bake until heated through, about 30 minutes. Transfer lasagna to wire rack and let cool a few minutes before serving. Makes 6 main-dish servings.

Each serving: About 500 calories, 24 g protein, 66 g carbohydrate, 18 g total fat (8 g saturated), 35 mg cholesterol, 1360 mg sodium.

Tuna-Melt Casserole

Prep: 40 minutes
Bake: 20 minutes

1 package (16 ounces)
   corkscrew or medium pasta
   shells
3 cups broccoli flowerets
2 tablespoons margarine or
   butter
2 tablespoons all-purpose flour
¾ teaspoon salt
¼ teaspoon ground black
   pepper

4 cups reduced-fat (2%) milk
4 ounces Swiss cheese,
   shredded (about 1 cup)
1 can (12 ounces) chunk light
   tuna in water, drained and
   flaked
1 pound ripe tomatoes
   (2 medium), cut into
   ¼-inch-thick slices

1. Preheat oven to 400°F. In large saucepot, cook pasta as label directs, but for 5 minutes; add broccoli to pasta and cook, stirring frequently, until broccoli is tender and pasta is al dente, about 5 minutes longer. Drain well and return to saucepot.

2. Meanwhile, prepare cheese sauce: In 3-quart saucepan, melt margarine over low heat. Stir in flour, salt, and pepper until blended and cook, stirring, 1 minute. With wire whisk, gradually mix in milk. Increase heat to medium-high and cook, stirring frequently, until mixture has thickened and boils. Boil, stirring frequently, 1 minute. Remove saucepan from heat and stir in ½ cup cheese until cheese has melted and sauce is smooth.

3. Add cheese sauce and tuna to pasta and broccoli in saucepot; toss until evenly mixed. Transfer mixture to shallow 3½-quart casserole or 13" by 9" baking dish. Arrange tomato slices on top, overlapping if necessary. Sprinkle with remaining ½ cup cheese.

4. Cover casserole with foil and bake until hot and bubbly, about 20 minutes. Transfer casserole to wire rack and let stand a few minutes before serving. Makes 6 main-dish servings.

Each serving: About 570 calories, 39 g protein, 71 g carbohydrate, 14 g total fat (6 g saturated), 29 mg cholesterol, 755 mg sodium.

Pasta e Fagioli Bake

Prep: 35 minutes
Bake: 15 minutes

8 ounces ditalini pasta (1¾ cups)
2 slices bacon, cut into ½-inch pieces
1 medium onion, coarsely chopped
2 teaspoons plus 1 tablespoon olive oil
3 garlic cloves, finely chopped
2 cans (15 to 19 ounces each) white kidney beans (cannellini), rinsed and drained

1 can (16 ounces) plum tomatoes
¾ cup chicken broth
¼ teaspoon coarsely ground black pepper
¼ cup plus 2 tablespoons freshly grated Pecorino Romano cheese
2 slices firm white bread, torn into ¼-inch pieces
1 tablespoon chopped fresh parsley leaves

1. Preheat oven to 400°F. In large saucepot, cook pasta as label directs. Drain, reserving ½ cup pasta cooking water. Return pasta to saucepot.

2. Meanwhile, in 4-quart saucepan, cook bacon over medium heat, stirring occasionally, until browned. With slotted spoon, transfer bacon to paper towels to drain.

3. Discard all but 1 teaspoon bacon fat from saucepan. Reduce heat to medium-low. Add onion and 2 teaspoons oil, and cook, stirring occasionally, until onion is tender, about 5 minutes. Stir in 1 teaspoon chopped garlic, and cook, stirring, 1 minute. Stir in beans, tomatoes with their juice, broth, pepper, and bacon; heat to boiling over high heat, breaking tomatoes up with side of spoon. Reduce heat to medium and simmer, uncovered, stirring occasionally, 5 minutes.

4. To pasta in saucepot, add bean mixture, ¼ cup Pecorino, and reserved pasta cooking water; toss until well combined. Transfer mixture to 3-quart casserole.

5. In small bowl, with fork, mix bread crumbs, parsley, remaining 1 tablespoon oil, remaining garlic, and remaining 2 tablespoons Pecorino until evenly combined. Sprinkle crumb mixture on top of casserole. Bake pasta until hot and bubbly and top is golden, about 15 minutes. Transfer casserole to wire rack and let stand a few minutes before serving. Makes 6 main-dish servings.

Each serving: About 405 calories, 19 g protein, 63 g carbohydrate, 9 g total fat (3 g saturated), 9 mg cholesterol, 815 mg sodium.

Seafood-Stuffed Shells

Prep: 1 hour and 15 minutes
Bake: 20 minutes

30 jumbo pasta shells
1 tablespoon olive oil
1 small onion, chopped
2 garlic cloves, finely chopped
1 bottle (8 ounces) clam juice
1 can (28 ounces) tomatoes in puree
2 tablespoons tomato paste
1 teaspoon sugar
¼ teaspoon crushed red pepper

⅓ cup heavy or whipping cream
1 pound medium shrimp, shelled, deveined, and coarsely chopped (see page 366)
1 pound scrod or cod fillet, coarsely chopped
1 package (10 ounces) frozen peas

Bread Crumb Topping
1 tablespoon olive oil
1 garlic clove, crushed with side of chef's knife
2 slices firm white bread, torn into ¼-inch pieces

1. In large saucepot, cook pasta shells as label directs. Drain shells and rinse with cold running water to stop cooking; drain again. Arrange shells in single layer on waxed paper.

2. Meanwhile, in 4-quart saucepan, heat oil over medium heat. Add onion and cook, stirring frequently, until tender, about 5 minutes. Add garlic and cook, stirring frequently, 1 minute. Increase heat to high, stir in clam juice and heat to boiling. Boil until reduced to ½ cup, about 7 minutes. Stir in tomatoes with their puree, breaking them up with side of spoon. Stir in tomato paste, sugar, and crushed red pepper; heat to boiling. Reduce heat to low; partially cover and simmer, stirring occasionally, about 20 minutes. Stir in cream and simmer 2 minutes longer; remove saucepan from heat.

3. Transfer 1 cup tomato sauce to 3-quart saucepan. Stir in shrimp and scrod, and cook over medium-high heat, gently stirring occasionally, until seafood is just opaque throughout, about 5 minutes. Remove saucepan from heat; stir 1 cup frozen peas into both saucepans.

4. Preheat oven to 400°F. Fill each pasta shell with 2 heaping tablespoons seafood mixture and arrange in 13" by 9" baking dish. Spoon tomato sauce over and around stuffed shells.

5. Prepare Bread Crumb Topping: In nonstick 10-inch skillet, heat oil and garlic over medium heat stirring, until garlic is fragrant. Add bread and cook, stirring often, until golden, about 5 minutes. Discard garlic.

6. Spoon crumb mixture over stuffed shells. Bake until filling is hot and sauce is bubbly, about 20 minutes. Transfer to wire rack and let stand a few minutes before serving. Makes 16 main-dish servings.

Each serving: About 325 calories, 23 g protein, 38 g carbohydrate, 9 g total fat (3 g saturated), 87 mg cholesterol, 450 mg sodium.

Family-Style Macaroni and Cheese

Prep: 20 minutes
Bake: 20 minutes

1 package (16 ounces) fusilli or rotini pasta
2 tablespoons margarine or butter
3 tablespoons all-purpose flour
½ teaspoon salt
¼ teaspoon coarsely ground black pepper
Pinch ground nutmeg
4 cups reduced-fat (2%) milk
1 package (8 ounces) pasteurized process-cheese spread, cut up
¼ cup freshly grated Parmesan cheese
6 ounces extrasharp Cheddar cheese, shredded (about 1½ cups)
1 package (10 ounces) frozen mixed vegetables

1. In large saucepot, cook pasta as label directs. Preheat oven to 400°F.

2. Meanwhile, in 3-quart saucepan, melt margarine over medium heat. Stir in flour, salt, pepper, and nutmeg until blended; cook, stirring, 1 minute. With wire whisk, gradually mix in milk. Increase heat to medium high and cook, stirring frequently, until sauce boils and has thickened slightly. Boil, stirring, 1 minute. Stir in cheese spread, Parmesan, and 1 cup Cheddar until cheeses have melted and sauce is smooth. Remove saucepan from heat.

3. Place frozen vegetables in colander; drain pasta over vegetables. Return pasta mixture to saucepot. Stir in cheese sauce until well blended. Transfer pasta mixture to 13" by 9" baking dish. Sprinkle with remaining ½ cup Cheddar. Bake until casserole is hot and bubbly and top is lightly browned, about 20 minutes. Transfer casserole to wire rack and let stand a few minutes before serving. Makes 8 main-dish servings.

Each serving: About 520 calories, 25 g protein, 58 g carbohydrate, 21 g total fat (12 g saturated), 52 mg cholesterol, 845 mg sodium.

Macaroni and Cheese Deluxe

Prep: 30 minutes
Bake: 25 minutes

1 package (16 ounces) penne
  pasta
3 tablespoons margarine or
  butter
1 medium onion, finely
  chopped
2 tablespoons all-purpose flour
¼ teaspoon salt
¼ teaspoon coarsely ground
  black pepper
¼ teaspoon ground red pepper
  (cayenne)

¼ teaspoon ground nutmeg
4 cups low-fat (1%) milk
½ cup freshly grated Parmesan
  cheese
1 cup frozen peas
4 ounces creamy blue cheese,
  such as Gorgonzola, cut up
  or crumbled into pieces
½ pint pear-shaped or round
  cherry tomatoes, each cut in
  half
½ cup walnuts, toasted

1. In large saucepot, cook pasta as label directs. Preheat oven to 400°F.

2. Meanwhile, in 3-quart saucepan, melt margarine over medium heat; add onion and cook, stirring occasionally, until tender, 8 to 10 minutes. Stir in flour, salt, black pepper, ground red pepper, and nutmeg, until blended and cook, stirring constantly, 1 minute. With wire whisk, gradaully mix in milk. Increase heat to medium-high and cook, stirring frequently, until sauce boils and has thickened slightly. Boil, stirring, 1 minute. Stir in ¼ cup Parmesan and remove saucepan from heat.

3. Place frozen peas in colander; drain pasta over peas. Return pasta mixture to saucepot. Stir in white sauce and blue cheese until well blended. Transfer pasta mixture to deep 3-quart casserole.

4. In small bowl, toss cherry tomato halves with remaining ¼ cup Parmesan. Sprinkle cherry tomato mixture on top of casserole. Bake until hot and bubbly and top is lightly browned, about 20 minutes. Transfer casserole to wire rack and let stand a few minutes. Sprinkle with walnuts, before serving. Makes 6 main-dish servings.

Each serving: About 610 calories, 26 g protein, 76 g carbohydrate, 23 g total fat (6 g saturated), 43 mg cholesterol, 965 mg sodium.

Bow Ties with Fennel and Leeks

Prep: 35 minutes
Bake: 20 minutes

4 medium leeks (1½ pounds)
2 tablespoons olive oil
2 small fennel bulbs (1 pound each), trimmed, and each cut lengthwise in half and crosswise into thin slices
2 garlic cloves, finely chopped
1 tablespoon sugar
1 package (16 ounces) bow-tie or gemelli pasta
1 cup chicken broth

¼ cup heavy or whipping cream
½ teaspoon salt
¼ teaspoon coarsely ground black pepper
½ cup freshly grated Parmesan cheese
1 medium ripe tomato (8 ounces), cut into ¼-inch pieces

1. Preheat oven to 400°F. Cut off roots and trim dark green tops from leeks; cut each leek lengthwise in half, then crosswise into ¼-inch-thick slices. Rinse leeks in large bowl of cold water, swishing to remove sand; transfer leeks to colander to drain, leaving sand in bottom of bowl.

2. In nonstick 12-inch skillet, heat 1 tablespoon oil over medium heat. Add leeks and cook, stirring frequently, until tender and golden, about 15 minutes.

3. Add fennel, garlic, sugar, and remaining 1 tablespoon oil to skillet, and cook, stirring frequently, until fennel is tender and light golden, about 20 minutes.

4. Meanwhile, in large saucepot. cook pasta as label directs. Drain.

5. When leeks are tender, stir in broth, cream, salt, pepper, and all but 2 tablespoons Parmesan. Heat to boiling; boil 1 minute.

6. Spoon pasta into deep 4-quart casserole. Add leek

mixture and toss well. Sprinkle tomato and remaining 2 tablespoons Parmesan on top of casserole. Cover and bake until hot and bubbly, about 20 minutes. Transfer casserole to wire rack and let stand a few minutes before serving. Makes 6 main-dish servings.

Each serving: About 460 calories, 15 g protein, 77 g carbohydrate, 11 g total fat (4 g saturated), 17 mg cholesterol, 560 mg sodium.

Cavatelli with Roasted Vegetables

Prep: 45 minutes
Bake: About 50 minutes

3 large red peppers, cut into 1-inch pieces
4 garlic cloves, peeled
2 tablespoons olive oil
½ teaspoon salt
1 large head cauliflower (2½ pounds), cut into 1-inch flowerets
12 ounces cavatelli or bow-tie pasta
1 tablespoon cornstarch
1 can (14½ ounces) chicken broth

⅓ cup loosely packed fresh parsley leaves, chopped
3 tablespoons freshly grated Parmesan cheese
¼ teaspoon ground red pepper (cayenne)
⅛ teaspoon dried thyme
4 ounces ricotta salata cheese, crumbled (about 1 cup)*

1. Preheat oven to 450°F. In 15½" by 10½" jelly-roll pan, toss red peppers, garlic, 1 tablespoon oil, and ¼ teaspoon salt until well coated. In another jelly-roll pan or large cookie sheet, toss cauliflower, remaining 1 tablespoon oil, and remaining ¼ teaspoon salt until well coated.

2. Roast vegetables 30 minutes, stirring vegetables and rotating pans between upper and lower racks halfway through roasting or until vegetables are browned. Turn oven control to 400°F.

3. Meanwhile, in large saucepot, cook pasta as label directs. Drain. Return pasta to saucepot.

4. In 2-quart saucepan, blend cornstarch, broth, and ½ *cup cold water* until smooth; heat to boiling over medium-high heat, stirring. Boil 1 minute.

5. Add roasted vegetables, broth mixture, parsley, Parmesan, ground red pepper, and thyme to pasta and toss to mix well. Transfer pasta mixture to deep 2½-quart baking dish or casserole.

6. Bake pasta 15 minutes. Sprinkle top with ricotta salata and bake until heated through, about 5 minutes longer. Transfer baking dish to wire rack and let cool a few minutes before serving cheese. Makes 4 main-dish servings.

*If you can't find ricotta salata, shredded Fontina or mozzarella would work well too.

Each serving: About 560 calories, 23 g protein, 81 g carbohydrate, 17 g total fat (7 g saturated), 29 mg cholesterol, 1120 mg sodium.

VEGETABLE PASTA

Bow Ties with Cannellini Beans and Spinach

Prep: 10 minutes
Cook: 15 minutes

12 ounces bow-tie pasta
1 tablespoon olive oil
1 jumbo onion (about 1 pound), thinly sliced
¾ cup chicken broth
1 teaspoon cornstarch
½ teaspoon salt
¼ teaspoon crushed red pepper

1 can (15 to 19 ounces) white kidney beans (cannellini), rinsed and drained
2 packages (10 ounces each) spinach, tough stems trimmed, washed
2 tablespoons freshly grated Pecorino Romano or Parmesan cheese

1. In large saucepot, cook pasta as label directs.

2. Meanwhile, in nonstick 12-inch skillet, heat oil over medium-high heat. Add onion and cook, stirring occasionally, until golden brown, about 10 to 12 minutes.

3. In 1-cup measuring cup, stir broth, cornstarch, salt, and crushed red pepper. Pour into skillet; add beans and cook, stirring constantly, until sauce boils and has thickened slightly, about 1 minute.

4. Just before draining pasta, stir in spinach just until wilted. Drain pasta and spinach; return to saucepot. Add sauce; toss to mix well. Sprinkle with Pecorino to serve. Makes 4 main-dish servings.

Each serving: About 545 calories, 24 g protein, 99 g carbohydrate, 7 g total fat (1 g saturated), 5 mg cholesterol, 925 mg sodium.

Cheese Tortellini with Pesto

Prep: 15 minutes
Cook: 10 minutes

2 packages (9 ounces each) refrigerated cheese tortellini
2 cups loosely packed fresh basil leaves
¼ cup pine nuts (pignoli), toasted
¼ cup freshly grated Parmesan cheese
1 tablespoon olive oil
1 small garlic clove, crushed with garlic press
¼ teaspoon salt
¼ teaspoon coarsely ground black pepper
½ pint cherry tomatoes, each cut in half or into quarters if large

1. In saucepot, cook tortellini as label directs. Drain, reserving ½ cup pasta cooking water. Return tortellini to saucepot; cover to keep warm.

2. In blender, combine basil, pine nuts, Parmesan, oil, garlic, salt, pepper, and reserved pasta cooking water and blend until mixture is smooth, stopping blender occasionally, and scraping down sides with rubber spatula.

3. Add basil mixture and tomatoes to tortellini; toss until evenly combined, and serve. Makes 6 main-dish servings.

Each serving: About 330 calories, 16 g protein, 42 g carbohydrate, 12 g total fat (4 g saturated), 43 mg cholesterol, 480 mg sodium.

Orecchiette with Tomato Cream

Prep: 15 minutes
Cook: 15 minutes

1 package (16 ounces) orecchiette or bow-tie pasta
1 can (14½ to 16 ounces) tomatoes, drained and chopped
½ cup heavy or whipping cream
½ cup milk
3 tablespoons vodka (optional)
4 teaspoons tomato paste
½ teaspoon salt
⅛ to ¼ teaspoon crushed red pepper
1 cup frozen peas, thawed
½ cup loosely packed fresh basil leaves, thinly sliced

1. In large saucepot, cook pasta as label directs.
2. Meanwhile, in 2-quart saucepan, stir together tomatoes, cream, milk, vodka, if you like, tomato paste, salt, and crushed red pepper. Heat just to simmering over medium-low heat. Stir in peas and heat through.
3. In warm serving bowl, toss pasta with tomato cream sauce until well combined. Sprinkle with basil to serve. Makes 4 main-dish or 8 accompaniment servings.

Each main-dish serving: About 590 calories, 19 g protein, 98 g carbohydrate, 15 g total fat (8 g saturated), 45 mg cholesterol, 635 mg sodium.

Quick Cincinnati Chili with Spaghetti

Prep: 15 minutes
Cook: 15 minutes

12 ounces spaghetti
2 teaspoons olive or vegetable
   oil
1 medium onion, chopped
3 tablespoons water
1 tablespoon chili powder
¼ teaspoon ground cinnamon
1 can (15 to 16 ounces) pink
   beans, rinsed and drained
1 can (14½ ounces) diced
   tomatoes

½ cup beef broth
1 tablespoon tomato paste
¼ teaspoon salt
½ teaspoon sugar
Toppings: 1 ounce reduced-fat
   Cheddar cheese, shredded
   (about ¼ cup),
   2 tablespoons nonfat sour
   cream, 3 green onions,
   chopped

1. In large saucepot, cook spaghetti as label directs. Drain, return to saucepot; cover and keep warm.

2. Meanwhile, in nonstick 10-inch skillet, heat oil over medium heat. Add onion and water; cook, stirring frequently, until onion is tender and golden, about 10 minutes. Stir in chili powder and cinnamon; cook, stirring, 1 minute.

3. Stir in beans, tomatoes with their juice, broth, tomato paste, salt, and sugar; heat to boiling over high heat. Reduce heat to low; simmer, 5 minutes.

4. To serve, divide spaghetti among 4 warm dinner plates. Spoon chili over spaghetti; serve with toppings. Makes 4 main-dish servings.

Each serving with toppings: About 490 calories, 21 g protein, 90 g carbohydrate, 6 g total fat (1 g saturated), 4 mg cholesterol, 885 mg sodium.

Gnocchi with Asparagus and Mushrooms

Prep: 15 minutes
Cook: 15 minutes

1 package (16 ounces) gnocchi or medium pasta shells
2 tablespoons margarine or butter
1 medium onion, chopped
4 ounces sliced smoked ham, cut into thin strips
1 package (8 ounces) sliced mushrooms

1 pound asparagus, trimmed and cut into 2-inch pieces
1 cup reduced-sodium chicken broth
½ cup heavy or whipping cream
⅛ teaspoon ground black pepper
Freshly grated Parmesan cheese (optional)

1. In large saucepot, cook pasta as label directs. Drain.
2. Meanwhile, in 10-inch skillet, melt margarine over medium-high heat. Add onion and ham and cook, stirring occasionally, until onion is tender, about 5 minutes.
3. Add mushrooms and cook, stirring frequently, until mushrooms are tender and liquid has evaporated, about 5 minutes. Stir in asparagus, broth, cream, and pepper; heat to boiling over high heat, stirring. Boil 3 to 5 minutes, until asparagus is tender.
4. In warm serving bowl, toss pasta with mushroom mixture until well combined. Serve with Parmesan, if you like. Makes 6 main-dish servings.

Each serving: About 435 calories, 17 g protein, 62 g carbohydrate, 13 g total fat (6 g saturated), 38 mg cholesterol, 455 mg sodium.

Wagon Wheels with Summer Squash and Mint

Prep: 15 minutes
Cook: 15 minutes

1 package (16 ounces) wagon-wheel or bow-tie pasta
1 tablespoon olive oil
1 tablespoon margarine or butter
3 medium yellow straightneck squash (8 ounces each), each cut lengthwise in half, then cut crosswise into ¼-inch-thick slices
3 medium zucchini (8 ounces each), each cut lengthwise in half, then cut crosswise into ¼-inch-thick slices

½ cup chopped fresh mint leaves
2 garlic cloves, crushed with garlic press
¾ teaspoon salt
¼ teaspoon coarsely ground black pepper
1 cup reduced-sodium chicken broth
¼ cup freshly grated Parmesan cheese, plus additional for serving

1. In large saucepot, cook pasta as label directs. Drain.

2. Meanwhile, in 12-inch skillet, heat oil and margarine over high heat until butter has melted. Add yellow squash, zucchini, ¼ cup chopped mint, garlic, salt, and pepper, and cook, stirring frequently, until vegetables are just tender, about 10 minutes.

3. Add broth and Parmesan to vegetables; stir well, and heat to boiling over high heat. Boil 1 minute.

4. In large warm serving bowl, toss pasta with vegetable mixture and remaining ¼ cup mint until well combined. Serve with additional Parmesan, if you like. Makes 4 main-dish or 8 accompaniment servings.

Each main-dish serving: About 565 calories, 22 g protein, 98 g carbohydrate, 11 g total fat (3 g saturated), 5 mg cholesterol, 845 mg sodium.

Penne with Caramelized Onions and Radicchio

Prep: 15 minutes
Cook: 20 minutes

1 package (16 ounces) penne or ziti pasta
2 teaspoons olive oil
1 jumbo onion (1 pound), thinly sliced
1 tablespoon balsamic vinegar
½ teaspoon salt
¼ teaspoon coarsely ground black pepper

1 large head radicchio (8 ounces), cut lengthwise in half, then crosswise into ½-inch slices
1 cup frozen peas, thawed
¼ cup crumbled ricotta salata or goat cheese

1. In large saucepot, cook pasta as label directs. Drain, reserving ¼ cup pasta cooking water. Return pasta to saucepot.

2. Meanwhile, in nonstick 12-inch skillet, heat oil over medium heat. Add onion and cook, stirring occasionally, until browned and tender, about 15 minutes. Stir in vinegar, salt, and pepper; cook 1 minute. Increase heat to medium-high; add radicchio and cook, stirring frequently, until wilted, about 2 to 3 minutes.

3. Add onion mixture, peas, and reserved pasta cooking water to pasta; toss to mix well. Sprinkle with cheese and serve. Makes 4 main-dish servings.

Each serving: About 550 calories, 20 g protein, 104 g carbohydrate, 6 g total fat (2 g saturated), 3 mg cholesterol, 510 mg sodium.

Vegetable Lo Mein

Prep: 20 minutes
Cook: 20 minutes

1 package (16 ounces) linguine
  or spaghetti
⅓ cup hoisin sauce
2 tablespoons reduced-sodium
  soy sauce
½ teaspoon cornstarch
3 teaspoons vegetable oil
1 package (10 ounces) sliced
  mushrooms
1 tablespoon grated, peeled
  fresh ginger
1 package (10 ounces)
  shredded carrots

3 small zucchini (6 ounces
  each), each cut lengthwise
  in half, then cut crosswise
  into ¼-inch-thick slices
3 green onions, cut into 1-inch
  pieces
1 cup reduced-sodium chicken
  broth
2 tablespoons seasoned rice
  vinegar

1. Prepare linguine as label directs but do not use salt. Drain.

2. Meanwhile, in cup, stir hoisin sauce, soy sauce, and cornstarch until smooth.

3. In nonstick 12-inch skillet, heat 2 teaspoons oil over medium-high heat. Add mushrooms and cook, stirring frequently, until mushrooms are golden and liquid has evaporated, about 5 minutes. Stir in ginger; cook, stirring, 30 seconds. Transfer mushroom mixture to bowl.

4. In same skillet, heat remaining 1 teaspoon oil, add carrots and cook, stirring frequently, 2 minutes. Stir in zucchini and green onions and cook, stirring frequently, until vegetables are tender-crisp, about 10 minutes. Stir cornstarch mixture; add to skillet. Stir in broth and mushroom mixture, and any juice in bowl. Heat to boiling, stirring, cook 1 minute.

5. In large serving bowl toss linguine with vegetable mixture and rice vinegar. Makes 4 main-dish servings.

Each serving: About 570 calories, 20 g protein, 111 g carbohydrate, 7 g total fat (1 g saturated), 0 mg cholesterol, 970 mg sodium.

Bow Ties with a Trio of Peas

Prep: 15 minutes
Cook: 15 minutes

1 package (16 ounces) bow-tie
  or corkscrew pasta
1 tablespoon olive oil
1 tablespoon margarine or
  butter
4 ounces snow peas, strings
  removed
4 ounces sugar snap peas,
  strings removed
1 garlic clove, crushed with
  garlic press
1 cup frozen baby peas
½ cup reduced-sodium chicken
  broth
¾ teaspoon salt
¼ teaspoon coarsely ground
  black pepper
½ teaspoon freshly grated
  lemon peel

1. In large saucepot, cook pasta as label directs. Drain.
2. Meanwhile, in 10-inch skillet, heat oil and margarine over medium-high heat until butter has melted. Add snow peas and sugar snap peas and cook, stirring, until tender-crisp, 1 to 2 minutes. Stir in garlic and cook, stirring, 30 seconds. Add baby peas, broth, salt, and pepper; heat to boiling. Stir in lemon peel.
3. In warm serving bowl, toss pasta with vegetable mixture until well combined. Makes 4 main-dish or 8 accompaniment servings.

Each main-dish serving: About 530 calories, 19 g protein, 95 g carbohydrate, 9 g total fat (1 g saturated), 0 mg cholesterol, 720 mg sodium.

Orecchini with Savoy Cabbage and Dill

Prep: 10 minutes
Cook: About 15 minutes

1 package (16 ounces)
orecchini or small pasta
shells
1 tablespoon margarine or
butter
1 medium onion, finely
chopped
½ medium head savoy
cabbage (1 pound), tough
outer leaves discarded,
cored, and very thinly sliced

¾ teaspoon salt
1 cup frozen baby peas
½ cup reduced-sodium chicken
broth
½ cup heavy or whipping
cream
¼ teaspoon coarsely ground
black pepper
¼ cup chopped fresh dill

1. In large saucepot, cook orecchini as label directs. Drain.

2. Meanwhile, in 12-inch skillet, melt margarine over medium-high heat. Add onion and cook, stirring often, or until tender, about 5 minutes.

3. Add cabbage and salt and cook, stirring often, until cabbage is tender-crisp, about 5 minutes. Stir in peas, broth, cream, and pepper; heat to boiling. Remove skillet from heat; stir in dill.

4. In warm serving bowl, toss pasta with cabbage mix ture. Makes 4 main-dish or 8 accompaniment servings.

Each main-dish serving: About 615 calories, 20 g protein, 100 g carbohydrate, 16 g total fat (8 g saturated), 41 mg cholesterol, 760 mg sodium.

Bow-Tie Pasta with
Baby Artichokes and Basil

Prep: 20 minutes
Cook: 25 minutes

12 baby artichokes (1½
   pounds)*
2 teaspoons olive oil
1 small onion, chopped
2 garlic cloves, finely chopped
1 can (14½ ounces) chicken
   broth
½ cup dry white wine
½ teaspoon salt

¼ teaspoon crushed red
   pepper
1 package (16 ounces) bow-tie
   or cavatelli pasta
½ teaspoon cornstarch
⅓ cup loosely packed fresh
   basil leaves, cut into thin
   strips

1. Trim baby artichokes: Bend back outer green leaves and snap them off at base until leaves are half green (at top) and half yellow (at bottom). Cut off stems. Cut across top of each artichoke at point where yellow meets green. Cut each artichoke lengthwise in half.

2. In nonstick 12-inch skillet, heat oil over medium heat. Add onion and cook, stirring frequently, 7 minutes; stir in garlic and cook, stirring frequently, 3 minutes longer.

3. Stir in 1½ cups broth, wine, salt, and crushed red pepper; heat to boiling over high heat. Add artichokes; heat to boiling. Reduce heat to medium-low; cover and simmer just until artichokes are tender and a knife inserted in bottom of artichoke goes through easily, about 15 minutes.

4. Meanwhile, in large saucepot, cook pasta as label directs. Drain.

5. In cup, stir cornstarch with remaining ¼ cup broth until smooth. Stir cornstarch mixture into artichoke mixture; heat to boiling over high heat, stirring. Boil 1 minute.

6. In large warm serving bowl, toss pasta with artichoke mixture and basil. Makes 4 main-dish or 8 accompaniment servings.

If baby artichokes are not available, use two regular artichokes and simply trim and remove chokes, cut each into eighths, and follow the recipe as written for baby artichokes.

Each main-dish serving: About 515 calories, 19 g protein, 99 g carbohydrate, 5 g total fat (1 g saturated), 5 mg cholesterol, 655 mg sodium.

Penne with Yellow Peppers and Sweet Onion

Prep: 15 minutes
Cook: 15 minutes

1 package (16 ounces) penne rigate or elbow twist pasta
2 tablespoons olive oil
2 medium yellow peppers, thinly sliced
1 jumbo sweet onion* (12 ounces) such as Walla Walla or Vidalia, thinly sliced
½ teaspoon salt
¼ teaspoon coarsely ground black pepper
1 tablespoon balsamic vinegar
½ cup chopped fresh basil leaves

1. In large saucepot, cook pasta as label directs. Drain, reserving ½ cup pasta cooking water.

2. Meanwhile, in 12-inch skillet, heat oil over medium heat. Add yellow peppers, onion, salt, and black pepper, and cook, stirring frequently, until vegetables are tender and golden, about 15 minutes. Remove skillet from heat; stir in vinegar and basil.

3. In serving bowl, toss pasta, yellow-pepper mixture, and reserved pasta cooking water until well combined. Makes 4 main-dish or 8 accompaniment servings.

Sweet onions are a thin-skinned onion with a high sugar and water content. They are mellower than storage onions, because they contain fewer of the sulfuric-acid compounds that give onions their characteristic bite. Varieties include Texas Spring Sweet, Sweet Imperial, Vidalia, Walla Walla, Maui, and OSO Sweet, and can be used interchangeably. Store them in a single layer in a well-ventilated area; they'll last 1 to 4 weeks. If you refrigerate them, individually wrap them in paper towels or newspaper.

Each main-dish serving: About 525 calories, 16 g protein, 95 g carbohydrate, 9 g total fat (1 g saturated), 0 mg cholesterol, 455 mg sodium.

Radiatore with Arugula, Tomatoes, and Pancetta

Prep: 15 minutes
Cook: About 15 minutes

1 package (16 ounces) radiatore or corkscrew pasta
4 ounces sliced pancetta or bacon, cut into ¼-inch pieces
1 garlic clove, crushed with garlic press
1 container (16 ounces) cherry tomatoes, each cut into quarters
½ teaspoon salt
¼ teaspoon coarsely ground black pepper
2 bunches arugula (4 ounces each), tough stems trimmed
¼ cup freshly grated Parmesan cheese
Freshly shredded Parmesan cheese

1. In large saucepot, cook pasta as label directs. Drain. Return pasta to saucepot.
2. Meanwhile, in 10-inch skillet, cook pancetta over medium heat, stirring occasionally, until lightly browned. (If using bacon, discard all but 1 tablespoon fat from skillet.) Add garlic; cook, stirring, 30 seconds. Add cherry tomatoes, salt, and pepper, and cook, gently stirring, 1 to 2 minutes. Remove skillet from heat.

3. Add pancetta mixture, arugula, and grated Parmesan to pasta and toss well. Serve with shredded Parmesan. Makes 4 main-dish or 8 accompaniment servings.

Each main-dish serving: About 560 calories, 22 g protein, 93 g carbohydrate, 12 g total fat (4 g saturated), 15 mg cholesterol, 680 mg sodium.

Bow Ties with Tomatoes, Herbs, and Lemon

Prep: 15 minutes
Cook: 15 minutes

2 pounds ripe tomatoes (6 medium), chopped
¼ cup loosely packed fresh mint leaves, chopped
¼ cup loosely packed fresh basil leaves, chopped
2 tablespoons olive oil
1 teaspoon freshly grated lemon peel
1 garlic clove, crushed with garlic press
1 teaspoon salt
¼ teaspoon coarsely ground black pepper
1 package (16 ounces) bow-tie or ziti pasta

1. In large serving bowl, stir tomatoes, mint, basil, oil, lemon peel, garlic, salt, and pepper. Set tomato mixture aside to allow flavors to develop.

2. Meanwhile, in large saucepot, cook pasta as label directs. Drain.

3. Add hot pasta to tomato mixture in bowl and toss until well combined. Serve. Makes about 11 cups or 4 main-dish servings.

Each serving: About 530 calories, 17 g protein, 96 g carbohydrate, 9 g total fat (1 g saturated), 0 mg cholesterol, 695 mg sodium.

Spaghetti with Cilantro Pesto

Prep: 15 minutes
Cook: 15 minutes

1 package (16 ounces) spaghetti or linguine
½ cup reduced-sodium chicken broth
2 tablespoons olive oil
1 tablespoon fresh lime juice
1 jalapeño chile, seeded and coarsely chopped
1 garlic clove, peeled
¼ cup pine nuts (pignoli), toasted
1 teaspoon salt
1½ cups packed fresh cilantro leaves with stems (about 2 bunches)
½ cup packed fresh parsley leaves

1. In large saucepot, cook pasta as label directs. Drain. Return pasta to saucepot.

2. Meanwhile, in food processor with knife blade attached, or in blender, place broth, oil, lime juice, jalapeño, garlic, 2 tablespoons pine nuts, and salt. Add cilantro and parsley and process until smooth.

3. Add cilantro mixture to pasta in saucepot and toss until well combined. Sprinkle with remaining 2 tablespoons pine nuts to serve. Makes 4 main-dish or 8 accompaniment servings.

Each main-dish serving: About 530 calories, 18 g protein, 87 g carbohydrate, 12 g total fat (2 g saturated), 0 mg cholesterol, 755 mg sodium.

Creste di Gallo with Sautéed Spring Onions

Prep: 15 minutes
Cook: 15 minutes

1 package (16 ounces) creste di gallo or orecchiette pasta
2 tablespoons margarine or butter
4 bunches green onions, chopped
½ teaspoon plus ⅛ teaspoon salt
¼ teaspoon coarsely ground black pepper
1 cup reduced-sodium chicken broth
1 container (8 ounces) plain low-fat yogurt
1 small garlic clove, crushed with garlic press

1. In large saucepot, cook pasta as label directs. Drain.
2. Meanwhile, in 12-inch skillet, melt margarine over high heat. Add green onions, ½ teaspoon salt, and pepper and cook, stirring often, 2 minutes. Reduce heat to medium-high and cook, stirring frequently, until green onions are tender, 4 to 5 minutes longer. Stir in broth; heat to boiling. Remove from heat; cover and keep warm.
3. In small bowl, stir yogurt, garlic, and ⅛ teaspoon salt until blended.
4. In serving bowl, toss pasta with green-onion mixture until well combined. Serve with yogurt mixture to spoon over each serving. Makes 4 main-dish or 8 accompaniment servings.

Each main-dish serving: About 540 calories, 20 g protein, 96 g carbohydrate, 9 g total fat (2 g saturated), 4 mg cholesterol, 735 mg sodium.

Buttered Noodles with Herbs

Prep: 10 minutes
Cook: 15 minutes

12 ounces wide egg noodles
2 tablespoons margarine or butter
¼ cup finely chopped fresh parsley
1 teaspoon finely chopped fresh rosemary leaves and/or other
    herb such as thyme, oregano, or sage
½ teaspoon salt
¼ teaspoon coarsely ground black pepper

1. In saucepot, cook egg noodles as label directs. Drain.
2. Add margarine, parsley, herbs, salt, and pepper to same saucepot, stirring until margarine melts. In warm serving bowl, toss noodles with herb mixture until well coated. Makes 6 accompaniment servings.

Each serving: About 250 calories, 8 g protein, 41 g carbohydrate, 6 g total fat (1 g saturated), 54 mg cholesterol, 240 mg sodium.

CHEESE PASTA

Gemelli with Feta, Mint and Olives

Prep: 15 minutes
Cook: 15 minutes

1 package (16 ounces) gemelli or penne pasta
4 ounces feta cheese, crumbled (about 1 cup)
¼ cup Kalamata olives, pitted and sliced*
¼ cup chopped fresh mint leaves
2 tablespoons extravirgin olive oil
1 tablespoon fresh lemon juice
⅛ teaspoon ground black pepper
1 bunch spinach (10 to 12 ounces), tough stems trimmed and
  leaves torn, washed and dried very well

1. In large saucepot, cook pasta as label directs. Drain, return to saucepot.

2. Meanwhile, in medium bowl, combine feta, olives, mint, oil, lemon juice, and pepper.

3. Add feta mixture and spinach to pasta in saucepot; toss well and serve. Makes 4 main-dish or 8 accompaniment servings.

Taste your olives before making this sauce—if they're very briny, you may want to omit the lemon juice.

Each main-dish serving: About 595 calories, 20 g protein, 90 g carbohydrate, 17 g total fat (6 g saturated), 25 mg cholesterol, 640 mg sodium.

Fettuccine Alfredo

Prep: 5 minutes
Cook: 12 minutes

12 ounces fettuccine noodles
1 cup heavy or whipping cream
⅓ cup freshly grated Parmesan cheese, plus additional for serving
4 tablespoons margarine or butter
¼ teaspoon salt
⅛ teaspoon coarsely ground black pepper

1. In large saucepot, cook fettuccine as label directs. Drain. Return fettuccine to saucepot.

2. Add cream, Parmesan, margarine, salt, and pepper to fettuccine. Heat over medium-low heat, tossing, until margarine has melted, pasta is coated, and sauce is warmed through. Serve with additional Parmesan, if you like. Makes 8 accompaniment servings.

Each serving: About 330 calories, 8 g protein, 33 g carbohydrate, 19 g total fat (9 g saturated), 44 mg cholesterol, 300 mg sodium.

Cavatelli with Ricotta and Fresh Tomato Sauce

Prep: 5 minutes
Cook: 25 minutes

1 bag (16 ounces) frozen cavatelli or frozen gnocchi
1 tablespoon olive oil
1 garlic clove, crushed with garlic press
1½ pounds ripe tomatoes (4 medium), coarsely chopped
½ teaspoon salt
¼ teaspoon coarsely ground black pepper
¾ cup part-skim ricotta cheese
¼ cup freshly grated Pecorino Romano or Parmesan cheese

1. In large saucepot, cook cavatelli as label directs. Drain.

2. Meanwhile, in nonstick 10-inch skillet, heat oil over medium heat. Add garlic and cook, stirring, 1 minute. Stir in tomatoes, salt, and pepper and cook, stirring occasionally, until tomatoes break up slightly, about 5 minutes.

3. In warm serving bowl, toss pasta with ricotta and Pecorino. Pour tomato mixture on top; toss before serving. Makes 4 main-dish servings.

Each serving: About 455 calories, 20 g protein, 71 g carbohydrate, 11 g total fat (5 g saturated), 40 mg cholesterol, 560 mg sodium.

Gemelli with Ricotta and Spinach

Prep: 10 minutes
Cook: 15 minutes

1 package (16 ounces) gemelli or corkscrew pasta	1 container (15 ounces) part-skim ricotta cheese
1 tablespoon olive oil	⅓ cup freshly grated Parmesan cheese
2 garlic cloves, crushed with side of chef's knife	½ teaspoon salt
2 packages (10 ounces each) prewashed spinach, tough stems trimmed	¼ teaspoon coarsely ground black pepper
	Shredded Parmesan cheese

1. In large saucepot, cook pasta as label directs. Drain, reserving 1 cup pasta cooking water. Return pasta to saucepot.

2. Meanwhile, in 12-inch skillet, heat oil over medium heat. Add garlic and cook, stirring, 1 minute. Gradually add spinach and *2 tablespoons water;* cook, tossing often with two spoons, just until spinach wilts. Remove skillet from heat.

3. Add ricotta, Parmesan, salt, pepper, spinach mixture, and reserved cooking water to pasta in saucepot. Heat over medium heat, tossing, until well combined. Sprinkle with shredded Parmesan cheese to serve. Makes 6 main-dish servings.

Each serving: About 445 calories, 23 g protein, 64 g carbohydrate, 11 g total fat (5 g saturated), 26 mg cholesterol, 565 mg sodium.

Farfalle with Gorgonzola and Walnuts

Prep: 5 minutes
Cook: 20 minutes

1 package (16 ounces) farfalle (bow tie) pasta
1 cup half-and-half or light cream
¾ cup chicken broth
4 ounces Gorgonzola or blue cheese, crumbled (about 1 cup)
¼ teaspoon coarsely ground black pepper
½ cup chopped walnuts, toasted

1. In large saucepot, cook pasta as label directs. Drain.
2. Meanwhile, in 2-quart saucepan, heat half-and-half and broth to boiling over medium-high heat. Reduce heat to medium; simmer 5 minutes. With wire whisk, mix Gorgonzola and pepper into saucepan, whisking constantly, until cheese has melted and sauce is smooth. Remove from heat.
3. In warm large serving bowl, toss pasta with sauce. Sprinkle with walnuts to serve. Makes 6 main-dish servings.

Each serving: About 460 calories, 17 g protein, 61 g carbohydrate, 17 g total fat (7 g saturated), 28 mg cholesterol, 455 mg sodium.

HOMEMADE PASTA

Spaetzle

Prep: 10 minutes
Cook: 3 minutes

2½ teaspoons salt
3 cups all-purpose flour
4 large eggs
Margarine or butter, melted (optional)

1. In 6-quart saucepot, heat *16 cups water* and 2 teaspoons salt to boiling over high heat. Meanwhile, in medium bowl, with spoon, beat flour, eggs, *¾ cup water,* and remaining ½ teaspoon salt until smooth.

2. Reduce heat to medium. With spaetzle maker, colander, or through the large holes of a flat grater, held over simmering water, press batter with rubber spatula through spaetzle maker into water. Stir gently so spaetzle pieces do not stick together. Cook, until tender but firm (al dente) 2 to 3 minutes; drain. If you like, toss with melted margarine or butter to serve. Makes 8 accompaniment servings.

Each serving: About 210 calories, 8 g protein, 36 g carbohydrate, 3 g total fat (1 g saturated), 106 mg cholesterol, 250 mg sodium.

Potato Gnocchi au Gratin

Prep: 20 minutes
Cook: 35 minutes

1½ pounds all-purpose
    potatoes (3 large), peeled
    and cut into 2-inch pieces
1 tablespoon margarine or
    butter
1 small onion, chopped
1 can (28 ounces) Italian plum
    tomatoes

1 teaspoon sugar
1 teaspoon dried basil
3½ teaspoons salt
1 container (8 ounces) part-skim
    ricotta cheese
1¼ cups all-purpose flour
2 ounces part-skim mozzarella
    cheese, thinly sliced

1. In 3-quart saucepan, heat potatoes and enough *water to cover* to boiling over high heat. Reduce heat to low; cover and simmer, until potatoes are fork-tender, 15 to 20 minutes; drain. Return potatoes to saucepan.

2. Meanwhile, in nonstick 12-inch skillet, melt margarine over medium heat. Add onion and *2 tablespoons water* and cook, stirring frequently, until liquid has evaporated and onion is tender and golden. Stir in tomatoes with their juice, sugar, basil, and ¼ teaspoon salt; heat to boiling over high heat, breaking tomatoes up with side of spoon. Reduce heat to low and simmer, 15 minutes. Keep sauce warm.

3. With potato masher, mash potatoes in saucepan until smooth. Add ricotta and 1¼ teaspoons salt; mash until smooth. With a spoon, stir in flour to make a soft dough.

4. Transfer dough to floured surface; divide dough in half. Shape each half into an 8" by 2" log. Cut each log into ½-inch-thick slices.

5. Preheat broiler. In 5-quart Dutch oven, heat *16 cups water* to boiling over high heat. Add remaining 2 teaspoons salt, gently drop gnocchi, 1 at a time, into boiling water. With slotted spoon, carefully remove gnocchi to jelly-roll pan as soon as they start to float.

6. Spoon all but 1 cup sauce into shallow 2½-quart broiler-safe baking or gratin dish. Arrange gnocchi, slightly overlapping, in sauce. Spoon remaining sauce randomly over gnocchi; top with mozzarella. Broil gnocchi at closest position to heat source, until cheese has melted and browned and sauce is bubbly. Serve hot. Makes 6 main-dish servings.

Each serving: About 315 calories, 13 g protein, 52 g carbohydrate, 7 g total fat (3 g saturated), 17 mg cholesterol, 880 mg sodium.

∾Sauces

TOMATO SAUCES

Marinara Sauce

Prep: 7 minutes
Cook: 25 minutes

2 tablespoons olive oil
1 small onion, chopped
1 garlic clove, finely chopped
1 can (28 to 35 ounces) tomatoes
1 can (6 ounces) tomato paste
½ teaspoon salt
2 tablespoons chopped fresh basil

1. In 2-quart saucepan, heat oil over medium-low heat. Add onion and garlic and cook, stirring occasionally, until tender.

2. Stir in tomatoes with their juice, tomato paste, salt, and basil. Heat to boiling, breaking tomatoes up with side of spoon. Reduce heat to low; cover and simmer, stirring occasionally until flavors have blended, about 20 minutes. Makes about 4 cups. Use sauce to coat 1 pound pasta for 4 accompaniment servings.

Each serving sauce without pasta: About 150 calories, 4 g protein, 21 g carbohydrate, 7 g total fat (1 g saturated), 0 mg cholesterol, 695 mg sodium.

Eggplant-and-Tomato Sauce

Prep: 7 minutes
Cook: 25 minutes

¼ cup olive oil
1 small eggplant (1 pound), cut into ¾-inch pieces
1 garlic clove, finely chopped
1 can (28 ounces) tomatoes
2 tablespoons chopped fresh basil
½ teaspoon salt
1 teaspoon sugar

1. In 3-quart saucepan, heat oil over medium heat. Add eggplant and cook, stirring often, until lightly browned. Add garlic, cook, stirring, 1 minute.

2. Stir in tomatoes with their juice, basil, salt, and sugar, breaking tomatoes up with spoon. Heat to boiling over high heat. Reduce heat to low; cover and simmer, stirring occasionally, until eggplant is very tender, about 20 minutes. Makes about 4½ cups. Use sauce to coat 8 ounces pasta for 6 accompaniment servings.

Each serving sauce without pasta: About 130 calories, 2 g protein, 1 g carbohydrate, 9 g total fat (1 g saturated), 0 mg cholesterol, 390 mg sodium.

Plum Tomato and Sage Sauce

Prep: 30 minutes
Cook: 1 hour 15 minutes

2 tablespoons olive oil
1 small onion, finely chopped
3 pounds ripe plum tomatoes (about 16 medium), peeled and
    chopped (see page 626)
½ cup chicken broth
⅓ cup dry white wine
2 tablespoons margarine (optional)
1 tablespoon chopped fresh sage leaves
1 teaspoon salt
Freshly shredded Parmesan cheese (optional)

1. In 10-inch skillet (about 2-inches deep), heat oil over medium-low heat. Add onion and cook, stirring frequently, until very tender and slightly golden, about 15 minutes.

2. To skillet, add tomatoes with their juice, broth, and wine; heat to boiling over high heat. Reduce heat to low; cover and simmer, stirring and pressing tomatoes with back of slotted spoon to crush them, about 30 minutes.

3. Remove cover and simmer, stirring occasionally, until sauce has reduced and thickened slightly, 25 to 30 minutes longer. Stir in margarine, if you like, sage, and salt. Serve with Parmesan if you like. Makes about 4 cups, enough to coat 1½ pounds pasta for 6 main-dish servings.

Each ½ cup sauce: About 75 calories, 2 g protein, 9 g carbohydrate, 4 g total fat (1 g saturated), 0 mg cholesterol, 330 mg sodium.

Roasted Tomato Sauce

Prep: 10 minutes plus cooling
Roast: 50 to 60 minutes

3 pounds ripe plum tomatoes (about 16 medium), each cut
    lengthwise in half
6 garlic cloves, unpeeled
2 tablespoons olive oil
¾ teaspoon salt
¼ teaspoon coarsely ground black pepper
Freshly grated Pecorino Romano cheese (optional)

1. Preheat oven to 450°F. In 15½" by 10½" jelly-roll pan, toss tomato halves and garlic cloves with 1 tablespoon olive oil. Arrange tomatoes, cut side down, in pan. Roast tomatoes and garlic, until tomatoes are well browned, and garlic is soft, about 50 to 60 minutes.

2. Let tomatoes and garlic cool in pan until easy to handle, about 20 minutes.

3. Over medium bowl, peel tomatoes. Place tomato pulp in bowl with any juice from pan. Squeeze garlic from skins into same bowl. With slotted spoon, crush tomatoes and garlic. Stir in salt, pepper, and remaining 1 tablespoon oil. Serve sauce at room temperature, or transfer to saucepan; heat over medium-low heat until hot. Serve with Pecorino, if you like. Makes about 3 cups sauce. Use sauce to coat 1 pound pasta for 4 main-dish servings.

Each ½ cup sauce: About 90 calories, 2 g protein, 12 g carbohydrate, 5 g total fat (1 g saturated), 0 mg cholesterol, 290 mg sodium.

Big-Batch Tomato Sauce

Prep: 30 minutes
Cook: About 1 hour

3 tablespoons olive oil
3 medium carrots, peeled and finely chopped
1 large onion, finely chopped
2 garlic cloves, finely chopped
3 cans (28 ounces each) Italian tomatoes in puree
¾ teaspoon salt
¼ teaspoon coarsely ground black pepper
1 bay leaf

1. In 5-quart Dutch oven, heat oil over medium heat. Add carrots and onion and cook, stirring occasionally, until vegetables are very tender and golden, about 20 minutes. Add garlic; cook, stirring, 2 minutes.

2. Meanwhile, place tomatoes with their puree in large bowl. With hands or slotted spoon, crush tomatoes well.

3. Add tomatoes with their puree, salt, pepper, and bay leaf to Dutch oven; heat to boiling over high heat. Reduce heat to low; cover and simmer 15 minutes. Remove cover and simmer sauce, stirring occasionally, 20 minutes longer. Discard bay leaf. Makes about 10 cups. Use 3 cups sauce to coat 1 pound pasta for 4 main-dish servings. Sauce may be frozen up to 6 months.

Each ½ cup sauce: About 25 calories, 1 g protein, 4 g carbo-hydrate, 1 g total fat (0 g saturated), 0 mg cholesterol, 240 mg sodium.

No-Cook Tomato Sauce

Prep: 15 minutes plus standing

2 pounds ripe tomatoes (6 medium), cut into ½-inch pieces
8 ounces fresh mozzarella cheese balls, cut into ½-inch pieces
1 cup packed fresh basil leaves, cut into strips
2 tablespoons olive oil
1 tablespoon red wine vinegar
1 teaspoon salt
¼ teaspoon coarsely ground black pepper

In medium bowl, combine tomatoes with their juice, mozzarella, basil, oil, vinegar, salt, and pepper, stirring gently to mix well. Let sauce stand at room temperature at least 15 minutes or up to 1 hour until flavors have developed. Makes about 7 cups. Use sauce to coat 1 pound pasta for 4 main-dish servings.

Each cup sauce: About 150 calories, 8 g protein, 8 g carbohydrate, 12 g total fat (4 g saturated), 26 mg cholesterol, 340 mg sodium.

Creamy Tomato Sauce

Prep: 10 minutes
Cook: 25 minutes

2 tablespoons olive oil
1 large red pepper, chopped
1 medium onion, chopped
1 garlic clove, finely chopped
1 tablespoon all-purpose flour
1 can (14½ to 16 ounces) tomatoes
1½ teaspoons salt
⅛ teaspoon crushed red pepper
1½ teaspoons sugar
¼ cup heavy or whipping cream

1. In 3-quart saucepan, heat oil over medium-low heat. Stir in red pepper, onion, and garlic and cook, stirring occasionally, until vegetables are tender.

2. Stir in flour until well blended; cook, stirring 1 minute. Add tomatoes with their juice, salt, crushed red pepper, and sugar. Heat to boiling over high heat, breaking tomatoes up with side of spoon. Reduce heat to low; cover and simmer until flavors have blended, about 15 minutes. Stir in cream; heat through but do not boil or sauce may curdle. Makes about 2½ cups. Use sauce to coat 8 ounces pasta for 6 accompaniment servings.

Each serving sauce without pasta: About 115 calories, 2 g protein, 9 g carbohydrate, 8 g total fat (3 g saturated), 11 mg cholesterol, 700 mg sodium.

Arrabbiata Sauce

Prep: 15 minutes
Cook: 1 hour

½ cup extravirgin olive oil
6 garlic cloves, crushed with side of chef's knife
4 cans (35 ounces each) Italian plum tomatoes
1 tablespoon salt
1 to 1½ teaspoons crushed red pepper

1. In 8-quart Dutch oven, heat oil over medium heat. Add garlic and cook, stirring, 2 minutes; do not brown. Stir in tomatoes with their juice, salt, and crushed red pepper; heat to boiling over high heat, breaking tomatoes up with side of spoon. Reduce heat to low; simmer, stirring occasionally, until sauce thickens slightly, about 50 minutes.

2. For smooth, traditional texture, press tomato sauce through food mill into large bowl. Or, leave sauce as is for a hearty, chunky texture. Cool sauce slightly. Spoon into jars. Makes about 14 cups. Use 2 cups sauce to coat 1 pound pasta for 4 main-dish servings. Store in refrigerator for up to 1 week. Or spoon into freezer-safe containers and freeze for up to 2 months.

Per ½ cup serving: About 70 calories, 1 g protein, 6 g carbohydrate, 4 g total fat (1 g saturated), 0 mg cholesterol, 550 mg sodium.

MEAT SAUCES

Hearty Meat Sauce

Prep: 10 minutes
Cook: 40 minutes

1 pound ground beef chuck
1 small onion, chopped
1 garlic clove, finely chopped
1 can (28 ounces) tomatoes
1 can (6 ounces) tomato paste
1 teaspoon sugar
1 teaspoon salt
½ teaspoon cracked black pepper
½ teaspoon dried oregano

1. In 4-quart saucepan or 12-inch skillet, cook ground beef, onion, and garlic, over high heat, stirring often, and breaking up beef with side of spoon until juices have evaporated and beef is browned, about 10 minutes.

2. Stir in tomatoes with their juice, tomato paste, sugar, salt, pepper, and oregano and heat to boiling, breaking tomatoes up with side of spoon. Reduce heat to low; cover and simmer 30 minutes. Makes about 4 cups. Use sauce to coat 1 pound of pasta for six main-dish servings.

Each serving sauce without pasta: About 290 calories, 15 g protein, 13 g carbohydrate, 20 g total fat (8 g saturated), 64 mg cholesterol, 660 mg sodium.

Sausage-Eggplant Sauce

Prep: 10 minutes
Cook: 35 minutes

1 pound hot or sweet Italian-sausage links, casings removed
1 small eggplant (1 pound), trimmed and cut into ¼-inch pieces
1½ cups water
1 can (28 ounces) tomatoes
2 tablespoons chopped fresh basil
½ teaspoon sugar
1 tablespoon chopped fresh parsley

1. In 12-inch skillet, cook sausage over medium-high heat, stirring frequently, and breaking up sausage with side of spoon, until sausage is browned and loses its pink color throughout. Drain sausage on paper towels. Discard all but 2 tablespoons drippings from skillet.

2. Add eggplant to skillet; stir to coat with drippings. Stir in water; heat to boiling over medium-high heat. Reduce heat to medium; cover and simmer until eggplant is very tender, about 15 to 20 minutes. Stir in sausage, tomatoes, basil, and sugar; cook, breaking tomatoes up with side of spoon, 10 minutes. Remove from heat and stir in parsley. Makes about 4½ cups. Use sauce to coat 1 pound pasta for 6 main dish servings.

Each serving sauce without pasta: About 255 calories, 13 g protein, 9 g carbohydrate, 19 g total fat (7 g saturated), 48 mg cholesterol, 630 mg sodium.

SEAFOOD SAUCE

White Clam Sauce

Prep: 8 minutes
Cook: 12 minutes

2 cans (10 ounces each) whole baby clams
¼ cup olive oil
4 tablespoons margarine or butter
2 garlic cloves, finely chopped
⅓ cup chopped fresh parsley
½ teaspoon salt
¼ teaspoon coarsely ground black pepper

1. Drain clams through sieve, reserving juice. In 2-quart saucepan, heat oil and margarine over low heat, until margarine has melted. Stir in garlic and cook, stirring, 1 minute.

2. Add clam juice and parsley to saucepan; heat to boiling. Reduce heat to low; cover and simmer 10 minutes to blend flavors. Stir in clams, salt, and pepper, and cook, stirring occasionally, until heated through. Makes about 3 cups. Use sauce to coat 1 pound pasta for 6 main-dish servings.

Each serving sauce without pasta: About 200 calories, 12 g protein, 0 g carbohydrate, 17 g total fat (3 g saturated), 32 mg cholesterol, 200 mg sodium.

VEGETABLE AND OTHER SAUCES

Sweet-Pepper Sauce

Prep: 15 minutes
Cook: 15 minutes

3 tablespoons olive oil
3 medium green peppers, cut into ¾-inch strips
3 medium red peppers, cut into ¾-inch strips
2 medium onions, sliced
1 can (14½ to 16 ounces) tomatoes
½ teaspoon salt
¼ teaspoon ground black pepper
½ teaspoon dried marjoram

1. In 4-quart saucepan, heat oil over medium-high heat. Add green and red peppers and onions and cook, stirring frequently, until tender.

2. Stir in tomatoes with their juice, salt, black pepper, and marjoram; heat to boiling over high heat, breaking tomatoes up with side of spoon. Reduce heat to medium; cook 5 minutes. Makes about 5 cups. Use sauce to coat 1 pound pasta for 6 accompaniment servings.

Each serving sauce without pasta: About 130 calories, 3 g protein, 16 g carbohydrate, 7 g total fat (1 g saturated), 0 mg cholesterol, 310 mg sodium.

Anchovy-and-Caper Sauce

Prep: 5 minutes
Cook: 4 minutes

⅓ cup olive oil
1 garlic clove, cut in half
1 can (2 ounces) anchovy fillets, drained and chopped
1 tablespoon capers, drained
1 teaspoon fresh lemon juice
2 tablespoons finely chopped fresh parsley

In small skillet, heat oil over medium heat. Add garlic and cook, stirring until golden. Remove skillet from heat; with slotted spoon, discard garlic. Into oil remaining in skillet, stir anchovies, capers, and lemon juice until blended; stir in parsley. Makes about ½ cup. Use to coat 8 ounces pasta for 6 accompaniment servings.

Each serving sauce without pasta: About 120 calories, 2 g protein, 0 g carbohydrate, 13 g total fat (2 g saturated), 6 mg cholesterol, 315 mg sodium.

Bacon, Egg, and Cheese Sauce

Prep: 7 minutes
Cook: 17 minutes

8 ounces sliced bacon, cut into ½-inch pieces
1 garlic clove, finely chopped
4 teaspoons all-purpose flour
1¼ cups milk
2 large eggs, slightly beaten
¾ cup freshly grated Parmesan cheese
¼ teaspoon cracked black pepper

1. In 2-quart saucepan, cook bacon over medium-low heat, stirring frequently, until bacon is browned, about 10 minutes. With slotted spoon, transfer bacon to paper towels to drain. Discard all but 3 tablespoons drippings from saucepan.

2. In drippings in saucepan, cook garlic over medium-low heat, stirring, 1 minute. Stir in flour; cook, stirring, 1 minute. With wire whisk, mix in milk, eggs, Parmesan, and pepper. Cook, whisking constantly, until sauce thickens, about 5 minutes, but do not boil or sauce may curdle. Remove from heat and stir in bacon. Makes about 2 cups. Use sauce to coat 8 ounces pasta for 6 accompaniment servings.

Each serving sauce without pasta: About 225 calories, 11 g protein, 5 g carbohydrate, 18 g total fat (8 g saturated), 101 mg cholesterol, 400 mg sodium.

Walnut Sauce

Prep: 10 minutes
Cook: 6 minutes

3 tablespoons margarine or butter
1 cup walnuts, coarsely chopped
½ cup milk
2 tablespoons finely chopped fresh parsley
½ teaspoon salt

1. In 2-quart saucepan, melt margarine over medium heat. Add walnuts, and cook, stirring frequently, until walnuts are lightly toasted, about 5 minutes.
2. Stir in milk, parsley, and salt; heat through. Makes about 1⅓ cups. Use sauce to coat 8 ounces pasta for 6 accompaniment servings.

Each serving sauce without pasta: About 190 calories, 4 g protein, 5 g carbohydrate, 19 g total fat (3 g saturated), 3 mg cholesterol, 285 mg sodium.

Pesto

Prep: 15 minutes

1 cup packed fresh basil leaves
⅓ cup olive oil
⅓ cup pine nuts (pignoli) or walnuts
⅓ cup freshly grated Parmesan cheese
1 garlic clove, peeled
¼ teaspoon salt

In blender, combine basil, oil, pine nuts, Parmesan, garlic, and salt and process until smooth. Makes about ¾ cup. Use pesto to coat 8 ounces pasta for 6 accompaniment servings.

Each serving sauce without pasta: About 175 calories, 4 g protein, 2 g carbohydrate, 17 g total fat (3 g saturated), 4 mg cholesterol, 200 mg sodium.

Beans, Rice &
Other Grains

❧

Beans • Rice • Wild Rice
Other Grains

∾Beans

Long a staple and source of protein in the cuisines of cultures around the globe, grains and beans have finally taken a prominent place on the American table—and it's easy to see why. Grains and beans are inexpensive, low in fat, rich in nutrients, and, if served together, form a complete protein. When it comes to meal planning, few foods are as versatile, creating satisfying side dishes and salads or hearty entrees in bold, robust flavors.

DRY BEANS

Many kinds of dry beans help add variety to meals. They are sold conveniently cooked and canned, as well as in their dry form.

BLACK BEANS: Also called turtle beans, these are a staple in Latin America and the Caribbean. With a slightly sweet taste, they partner well with rice.

BLACK-EYED PEAS: Also called cowpeas, they are oval, beige-colored beans with a black circular "eye"; they are mealy in texture with an earthy taste.

CRANBERRY BEANS: These plump beans are cream-colored with red streaks, but become uniform in color during cooking. Also called shell beans, they have a nutty flavor.

FAVA BEANS: Also called broad beans, these flat, light brown beans resemble lima beans. They have a tough skin that should be removed by blanching before cooking.

GARBANZO BEANS: Also called chickpeas, these creamy yellow, knobby beans remain fairly firm when cooked.

GREAT NORTHERN BEANS: These large white beans have a delicate flavor. They can be substituted for other white beans in most recipes.

LIMA BEANS: Also called butter beans, these large oval, cream-colored beans hold their shape well when cooked. They come both in baby limas and large limas.

NAVY BEANS: A small white bean, also called the pea or Yankee bean. These are the beans traditionally used for baked beans.

PINK BEANS: A smooth, reddish-brown dry bean, it can be used interchangeably with pinto beans.

PINTO BEANS: Named for the Spanish word for "speckled," these pale pink beans are splotched with reddish-brown streaks. They are interchangeable with pink beans.

RED KIDNEY: The choice for chili, this medium-size bean has firm, burgundy-colored skin, pale flesh, and a sweet meaty flavor.

SOYBEANS: These are small, round, tan-colored beans with a nutlike flavor. Even after lengthy cooking, they remain quite firm, almost crunchy.

SPLIT PEAS: Yellow or green in color, these dried peas have been peeled and split in half. They have a slightly sweet flavor that pairs well with ham. When cooked down they become thick with a pureed appearance.

WHITE KIDNEY: Also called cannellini beans, they have a creamy texture and milder taste than the red variety.

LENTILS

Lentils are protein-packed, cook up faster than most beans and require no pre-soaking.

BROWN LENTILS: The most common variety; they have a firm texture and mild nutty flavor.

GREEN LENTILS: Pale greenish-brown in color, these have a firm texture and nutty, earthy flavor.

RED LENTILS: A smaller, round variety, these lighten to yellow and become very soft when cooked.

SMALL GREEN FRENCH LENTILS (PUY): These tiny plump lentils are grown in central France. Considered to have the best flavor, they cook quickly, hold their shape, and have a nutty taste.

STORING BEANS

Dry beans, peas, and lentils should be stored in their original package in a cool, dry place. Once opened, they should be transferred to glass or plastic containers with tight-fitting covers.

If you use only part of a package, do not mix the remainder with the contents of other packages purchased at a different time, particularly if the packages have been bought several months apart. Mixing packages may result in uneven cooking, since older beans can take longer to cook.

DO DRY BEANS NEED TO BE SOAKED?

Soaking dry beans for hours before cooking shortens cooking time and improves texture, appearance, and even digestibility. But now some chefs are claiming soaking time can be reduced—even skipped. We tested the old-fashioned method against two shortcuts in the *Good Housekeeping* kitchens, using 3 batches of black beans and 3 of Great Northern beans, which were then cooked until tender. The results:

The winner is . . . overnight soaking. Grandma was right. For the best texture (not too hard or mushy) and appearance (beans held their shape, with practically no split skins), letting beans sit in a bowl of cool tap water overnight really works. Cooking time ranged from 1 hour and 10 minutes to 1 hour and 20 minutes for the soaked beans.

Second place: no soaking. This method yielded the second most tender and shapely beans, though it required the longest cooking time (1 hour and 35 minutes). But if beans pose digestive problems for you, it's probably better to soak them and discard the water, which helps remove the complex sugars that can cause bloating and gas.

Third place: quick soaking. Bringing the beans to a boil and boiling for 2 minutes, then allowing them to soak for an hour in the same water before cooking yielded the most broken beans but definitely the fastest cooking time, 1 hour. If you're preparing a bean soup or chili, where perfect-looking beans don't matter, this method is fine, but we don't recommend it for a bean salad.

Note: Whichever option you choose, remember that cooking time will vary depending on the age/dryness of the beans.

TRADITIONAL SOAKING: In a saucepan or Dutch oven large enough to allow the beans to expand 2½ times, place beans. Add enough cold tap water to cover the beans by 2 inches. Let stand at room temperature overnight; then drain the beans in a sieve and rinse. Add fresh cold water to cover beans by 2 inches and cook or add other ingredients, as the recipe directs.

QUICK-SOAKING: Place the beans and enough cold water to cover by 2 inches in a large saucepan. Heat to boiling over high heat; boil for 2 minutes. Remove the saucepan from the heat; cover and let the beans stand for 1 hour. Drain, rinse, and add fresh water, or other ingredients as the recipe suggests, and cook the beans.

COOKING TIPS: When cooking rinsed, drained, soaked beans, add fresh cold water to cover beans by 2 inches and cook following the timetable that follows. Actual cooking time will depend on age and dryness of the beans. Simmer the beans slowly; cooking them too fast can break their skins.

Dry Beans Cooking Times

1 cup dry beans, soaked	Simmering time
Black beans	1½-1¾ hours
Black-eyed peas	½-1 hour
Garbanzo beans (chickpeas)	1-2 hours
Great Northern beans	1¼-1¾ hours
Kidney beans	1-2 hours
Lentils	20-50 minutes
Lima beans, large or small	¾-1 hour
Navy (pea) beans	1½ hours
Whole peas	1 hour
Split peas	¾ hour
Pink beans	1-2 hours
Pinto beans	1-2 hours
Red beans	1-2 hours
Small white beans	1½ hours
Soybeans	1½ hours

RICE VARIETIES

A glossary of our favorites:

ARBORIO: The Italian-grown short-grain rice is a key ingredient in risotto. Its high starch content, which is released when the rice is heated, provides risotto with the requisite creamy texture. Another attribute that makes this an excellent choice for risotto: This rice absorbs up to 5 times its weight in liquid while other rices drink in only up to 3 times their weight. Please, don't rinse Arborio rice before cooking.

AROMATIC BROWN: These rices taste and smell like roasted nuts or popcorn (one variety is even called brown popcorn). Wild Pecan—which neither qualifies as a wild rice nor contains pecans—has a convincing toasted-nut flavor nonetheless, and a short, 20-minute cooking time. Wehani is a chewy, brownish-red rice that's great for stuffings, side dishes, and soups.

AROMATIC WHITE: This group includes imports from India and Pakistan, such as basmati, with its slender curved shape when cooked, and straighter-grained American-grown basmati. Thai and American jasmine both cook up moist, tender, and slightly sticky. These rices are delicately flavorful and don't need even a speck of butter on top. Serve them alongside chicken or fish, or with curries.

BLACK JAPONICA: This new variety is a cross between Japanese black short-grain rice and American brown medium-grain, with a musky, almost spicy aroma. It works well as an accompaniment or in chunky vegetable soups.

BROWN: The outer hull is removed from the rice kernel during processing, but the bran layers remain, giving this whole-grain rice its characteristic color, flavor, and chewiness. The bran acts as a barrier to heat and moisture, so this rice requires a longer cooking time. Try it in fried rice and stuffings.

LONG-GRAIN WHITE: The most popular rice in the United States, this has long, slender kernels that are ideal for pilafs and other dishes where you want to see distinct grains (unlike in pudding). Parboiled rice (also known as converted) is long-grain rice that has been soaked in water, steamed under pressure, and dried before milling. The grains are firmer and retain more nutrients than regular milled white rice but, as a result, take slightly longer to cook. Precooked (instant) rice is fully cooked and dried; the grains are porous, and boiling water quickly rehydrates them.

MEDIUM-GRAIN WHITE: Moister and more likely to hold together than long-grain rice, this is a good choice for creamy foods like puddings.

SHORT-GRAIN WHITE: These plump, almost round kernels cook up to a sticky consistency, just the thing you want for making sushi or stuffing.

STORING RICE

Rice should be stored at cool room temperature in a dry place. Once the package has been opened, transfer the rice to a glass or plastic container with a tight-fitting lid.

White rice keeps almost indefinitely. Because of the fat content of the bran, brown rice and aromatic brown rices should be refrigerated if they are to be stored for more than 6 months.

COOKING RICE

Rice is ready to cook right from the package and does not need rinsing. For maximum nutritional benefits, cook rice in just the amount of liquid that will be fully absorbed. Follow label directions exactly. For added flavor, chicken, vegetable, or beef broth can be substituted for some or all of the water when cooking.

Never rinse enriched rice or cook it in water that must be drained before serving. The rice is sprayed with a coating containing iron, B vitamins, and folic acid to replace nutrients lost during milling.

One cup of regular rice makes about 3 cups when cooked. One cup of parboiled, or converted rice yields 3 to 4 cups cooked; one cup of packaged precooked rice makes 1 to 2 cups cooked, depending upon the brand. One cup of brown rice yields 3 to 4 cups cooked.

STORING AND REHEATING LEFTOVER RICE

Cover leftover rice tightly so the grains will not dry out or absorb other food flavors, then refrigerate. Cooked rice will keep up to a week in the refrigerator. Reheat leftover rice, covered, with a little water or broth (about 2 table-spoons); cook it over low heat for a few minutes, until hot. Or reheat rice in a steamer or microwave oven.

OTHER POPULAR GRAINS AND GRAIN PRODUCTS

BARLEY is the most commonly available as "pearl barley," meaning, the husk has been removed and the grains polished. Barley is available in fine, medium, and coarse grains. Quick-cooking barley is pre-steamed and cooks in 10 minutes.

BUCKWHEAT GROATS are really a fruit related to sorrel and rhubarb, though they are used like a grain. Roasted groats may be labeled "kasha," sold as whole groats or in coarse, medium, and fine grinds. Kasha has a deep nutlike flavor and a crunchy texture.

BULGUR is a whole wheat kernel that has been parboiled and dried, with some of the bran removed. It is sold whole or cracked (crushed). It can be soaked in water and eaten without further cooking (see Basil Tabbouleh, page 549) or for pilafs or stuffings. Do not use cracked wheat in recipes which call for bulgur as it has not been precooked.

CORNMEAL is finely ground white or yellow dried corn kernels. Unless a recipe specifies a particular type, either kind may be used. In some areas, blue cornmeal, made from a blue strain of corn, may be found. When used instead of white or yellow cornmeal it gives foods a bluish color.

COUSCOUS (Moroccan pasta) takes its name from the North African dish in which it is traditionally used. It is a fine precooked semolina, made from durum wheat, that comes as small pale-yellow pellets.

FARINA (cream of wheat) is finely ground wheat from which the bran and germ have been removed. It is creamy in color and bland in flavor.

HOMINY is corn with the hull and germ removed; it comes cooked and canned as whole kernels, dried and ground (coarser than cornmeal) and sold as "hominy grits" or simply "grits."

OATS are hulled whole-oat grains. Rolled oats have been

partially cooked, then crushed into flakes by pressing between rollers. Quick-cooking oats are pressed into thinner flakes than the regular or "old-fashioned" oats and cut into smaller pieces. Instant oatmeal is cut into very small pieces and processed so that it needs no cooking at all, just the addition of boiling water. In recipes, use the type of oats called for.

QUINOA is a staple grain of the ancient Incas. It is rich in protein and vital nutrients. The tiny seeds cook quickly; they have a slightly earthy, green taste and springy texture.

WHEATBERRIES are unprocessed whole wheat kernels. They have a chewy texture; used for salads, pilafs, breakfast porridge, or baking.

WILD RICE is not a true rice; it is a cereal grain, but it is used like rice. The dark-brown grains have a crunchy, chewy texture and strong, distinctive, earthy flavor. Wild rice should be rinsed in several changes of cold water before cooking. It is very expensive as the grains are harvested by hand.

STORING GRAINS

Store stone- or water-ground cornmeal and whole-grain flakes in the refrigerator or freezer and try to use them within 6 months. Regular cornmeal and other grains and grain products should be stored like rice (see page 501).

COOKING GRAINS

Follow package or recipe directions for each variety. If you are cooking the grain in water, bring the water to a rapid boil; then, while stirring, sprinkle the grain slowly over the boiling water so that boiling does not stop and stir the grain as the mixture thickens so that it does not stick together. Reduce the heat, cover if directed, and continue cooking (or let the mixture stand) for the length of time given on the label.

If you use milk instead of water, use a little more than the amount of water called for (unless the label directs oth-

erwise), and heat the milk to just below the boiling point
before stirring in the grain.

Old-Fashioned Baked Beans

Prep: 15 minutes plus soaking beans
Bake: 2 hours 45 minutes

2 packages (16 ounces) dry navy (pea) beans, soaked and
    drained (see page 498)
7½ cups water
½ cup dark molasses
2 medium onions, chopped
4 slices bacon, cut into 1-inch pieces or 4 ounces salt pork,
    coarsely chopped
⅓ cup packed dark brown sugar
5 teaspoons salt
4 teaspoons dry mustard

1. Preheat oven to 350°F. In 8-quart Dutch oven, place
beans. Pour in water; heat to boiling over high heat. Cover,
place in oven, and bake 1 hour.

2. Into Dutch oven, stir molasses, onions, bacon, brown
sugar, salt, and mustard until well blended. Cover and bake,
stirring occasionally, 1 hour longer. Remove cover and
bake until beans are very tender and richly flavored, and
sauce has thickened, 15 to 30 minutes longer. Serve hot.
Makes 14 accompaniment servings.

*Each serving: About 335 calories, 16 g protein, 53 g carbohy-
drate, 8 g total fat (3 g saturated), 7 mg cholesterol, 930 mg
sodium.*

Fast Baked Beans

Prep: 10 minutes
Cook: 12 to 15 minutes

2 teaspoons olive oil
1 small onion, chopped
1 cup ketchup
½ cup water
3 tablespoons light (mild)
  molasses
1 tablespoon Dijon mustard
½ teaspoon Worcestershire
  sauce

¼ teaspoon salt
Pinch ground cloves
4 cans beans (15 to 19 ounces
  each), such as black,
  kidney, small white, pink,
  and/or pinto, rinsed and
  drained

1. In 4-quart saucepan, heat oil over medium-low heat. Add onion and cook, stirring occasionally, until tender and golden, 5 to 8 minutes.

2. Stir in ketchup, water, molasses, mustard, Worcestershire, salt, and cloves until blended. Increase heat to high; gently stir in beans and heat to boiling. Reduce heat to medium-low; cover and simmer 5 minutes. Serve hot. Makes about 6 cups or 8 accompaniment servings.

Each serving: About 320 calories, 19 g protein, 62 g carbohydrate, 2 g total fat (0 g saturated), 0 mg cholesterol, 1,085 mg sodium.

Southwestern Black-Bean Burgers

Prep: 10 minutes
Cook: About 6 minutes

1 can (15 to 19 ounces) black
  beans, rinsed and drained
2 tablespoons light mayonnaise
¼ cup packed fresh cilantro
  leaves, chopped
1 tablespoon plain dried bread
  crumbs
½ teaspoon hot pepper sauce

½ teaspoon ground cumin
Nonstick cooking spray
1 cup loosely packed sliced
  lettuce
4 (4-inch) mini whole-wheat
  pitas, warmed as label
  directs
½ cup mild salsa

1. In large bowl, with potato masher or fork, mash beans
and mayonnaise until almost smooth (some lumps should
remain). Stir in cilantro, bread crumbs, pepper sauce, and
cumin until blended. With lightly floured hands, shape bean
mixture into four 3-inch round patties. Spray both sides of
each patty lightly with nonstick cooking spray.

2. Heat 12-inch nonstick skillet over medium heat until
hot. Add patties and cook 3 minutes per side or until lightly
browned and heated through.

3. Arrange lettuce on pitas; top each with a burger and
some salsa. Makes 4 main-dish servings.

*Each serving: About 210 calories, 13 g protein, 42 g carbohy-
drate, 3 g total fat (0 g saturated), 0 mg cholesterol, 715 mg
sodium.*

Savory Black Beans

Prep: 15 minutes, plus soaking beans
Cook: 2 hours 10 minutes

8 ounces sliced bacon or salt pork, cut into ¼-inch pieces
1 medium onion, chopped
1 medium stalk celery, chopped
1 package (16 ounces) dry black beans, soaked and drained (see page 498)
5½ cups water
¼ teaspoon crushed red pepper
1½ teaspoons salt

1. In 5-quart Dutch oven, cook bacon over medium heat, stirring frequently, until lightly browned. Discard all but 2 tablespoons bacon fat. Add onion and celery, and cook, stirring occasionally, until vegetables are tender.

2. To Dutch oven, add beans, water, and crushed red pepper; heat to boiling over high heat. Reduce heat to low; cover and simmer, stirring occasionally, until beans are tender, about 1 hour 30 minutes to 2 hours. Stir in salt and serve. Makes 8 accompaniment servings.

Each serving: About 275 calories, 15 g protein, 37 g carbohydrate, 8 g total fat (3 g saturated), 10 mg cholesterol, 570 mg sodium.

Spinach and Garbanzo Bean Salad

Prep: 25 minutes

¼ cup fresh lemon juice (about 1 large lemon)
3 tablespoons olive oil
1 small garlic clove, crushed with garlic press
½ teaspoon salt
¼ teaspoon coarsely ground black pepper
½ teaspoon ground cumin
½ teaspoon sugar
1 large bunch (1 pound) spinach, tough stems trimmed, leaves torn into 2-inch pieces, washed and dried very well

1 can (15 to 19 ounces) garbanzo beans, rinsed and drained
3 medium nectarines, each pitted and cut into ¼-inch wedges
8 ounces sliced smoked turkey, cut into 2" by ½" matchstick strips

1. In large salad bowl, with fork or wire whisk, mix lemon juice, oil, garlic, salt, pepper, cumin, and sugar until well blended.

2. To dressing in bowl, add spinach, beans, nectarines, and turkey; toss to mix well and serve. Makes 4 main-dish servings.

Each serving: About 365 calories, 22 g protein, 42 g carbohydrate, 14 g total fat (2 g saturated), 23 mg cholesterol, 1,066 mg sodium.

Texas Caviar

Prep: 12 minutes plus soaking beans, hard cooking eggs, and chilling
Cook: 40 minutes

1 package (16 ounces) dry
    black-eyed peas soaked
    and drained (see page
    498)
½ cup cider vinegar
⅓ cup olive oil
1 small garlic clove, minced
2 teaspoons salt

¼ teaspoon ground red pepper
    (cayenne)
2 teaspoons sugar
½ cup chopped fresh parsley
2 celery stalks, thinly sliced
3 green onions, minced
1 hard-cooked egg, chopped

1. In 5-quart Dutch oven, place black-eyed peas. Add *6 cups water;* heat to boiling over high heat. Reduce heat to low; cover and simmer until beans are tender, about 30 minutes; drain.

2. In medium bowl, with wire whisk, beat vinegar, oil, garlic, salt, ground red pepper, and sugar, until well blended. Add black-eyed peas, parsley, celery, and green onions; toss gently to coat with dressing. Cover and refrigerate, until flavors have blended, stirring occasionally, at least 2 hours.

3. To serve, sprinkle Texas Caviar with chopped egg. Makes 10 accompaniment servings.

Each serving: About 230 calories, 12 g protein, 30 g carbohydrate, 8 g total fat (1 g saturated), 21 mg cholesterol, 490 mg sodium.

Hoppin' John

Prep: 15 minutes
Cook: 50 minutes

1 tablespoon vegetable oil
1 large onion, chopped
2 celery stalks, chopped
1 medium red pepper, chopped
2 garlic cloves, finely chopped
1 package (16 ounces) dry black-eyed peas
1 large smoked ham hock (12 ounces)

4 cups water
2 cans (14½ ounces each) chicken broth
2 teaspoons salt
¼ teaspoon crushed red pepper
1 bay leaf
2 cups regular long-grain rice
Chopped fresh parsley

1. In 4-quart saucepan, heat oil over medium-high heat. Add onion, celery, and red pepper; cook, until golden, 10 minutes. Stir in garlic; cook, stirring, 2 minutes.

2. Rinse peas with cold running water and discard any stones or shriveled peas. Stir peas, ham hock, water, broth, 1 teaspoon salt, crushed red pepper, and bay leaf, into celery mixture. Heat to boiling over high heat. Reduce heat to low; cover and simmer until peas are tender, about 40 minutes.

3. Meanwhile, prepare rice as label directs, using the remaining 1 teaspoon salt and omitting any butter.

4. In large bowl, gently stir together pea mixture and rice. Sprinkle with parsley, and serve hot.

Each serving: About 150 calories, 8 g protein, 26 g carbohydrate, 2 g total fat (0 g saturated), 9 mg cholesterol, 455 mg sodium.

Falafel Sandwiches

Prep: 10 minutes
Cook: 8 minutes per batch

4 green onions, cut into 1-inch pieces
½ cup packed fresh flat-leaf parsley leaves
2 garlic cloves, each cut in half
2 teaspoons dried mint
1 can (15 to 19 ounces) garbanzo beans, rinsed and drained
½ cup plain dried bread crumbs
1 teaspoon baking powder
½ teaspoon salt
¼ teaspoon ground red pepper (cayenne)
1 teaspoon ground coriander
1 teaspoon ground cumin
¼ teaspoon ground allspice
Olive oil nonstick cooking spray
4 (6- to 7-inch) pitas
Accompaniments: sliced romaine lettuce, sliced tomatoes, sliced cucumber, sliced red onion, plain low-fat yogurt

1. In food processor with knife blade attached, process green onions, parsley, garlic, and mint until finely chopped. Add beans, bread crumbs, baking powder, salt, ground red pepper, coriander, cumin, and allspice, and process to a coarse puree.

2. Shape bean mixture, by scant ½ cups, into eight 3-inch round patties; place on waxed paper. Spray both sides of patties with olive oil spray.

3. Heat nonstick 10-inch skillet over medium-high heat until hot. Add half of patties and cook 4 minutes per side or until dark golden brown. Transfer patties to plate; cover loosely with foil to keep warm. Repeat with remaining patties.

4. Cut off top third of each pita to form a pocket. Place 2 warm patties in each pita. Serve with choice of accompaniments. Makes 4 sandwiches.

Each sandwich without accompaniments: About 365 calories, 14 g protein, 68 g carbohydrate, 5 g total fat (1 g saturated), 0 mg cholesterol, 1,015 mg sodium.

Vegetarian Bean Burritos

Prep: 10 minutes
Cook: 7 to 8 minutes

2 teaspoon vegetable oil
4 small zucchini (5 ounces each), trimmed, each cut lengthwise in half, then thinly sliced crosswise
¼ teaspoon salt
¼ teaspoon ground cinnamon
1 can (15 to 19 ounces) black beans, rinsed and drained
1 can (15 ounces) Spanish-style red kidney beans, undrained

4 (10-inch) flour tortillas, warmed as label directs
4 ounces Monterey Jack cheese, shredded (about 1 cup)
½ cup loosely packed fresh cilantro leaves
1 jar (16 ounces) chunky-style salsa

1. In nonstick 12-inch skillet, heat oil over medium-high heat. Add zucchini, salt, and cinnamon and cook, stirring frequently, until zucchini is tender-crisp, about 5 minutes.

2. Meanwhile, in 2-quart saucepan, heat black beans and kidney beans with their sauce over medium heat just to simmering; remove from heat and keep warm.

3. To serve, allow each person to assemble a burrito as desired, using a warm flour tortilla, zucchini, bean mixture, cheese, and cilantro leaves. Pass salsa to serve with burritos. Makes 4 main-dish servings.

Each serving: About 550 calories, 29 g protein, 77 g carbohydrate, 17 g total fat (1 g saturated), 25 mg cholesterol, 1,943 mg sodium.

Lentil-Spinach Toss

Prep: 20 minutes plus chilling
Cook: 30 minutes

2 cups lentils
1 teaspoon salt
1 bay leaf
⅓ cup olive oil
3 tablespoons red wine vinegar
6 slices bacon
1 package (10 ounces) prewashed spinach, tough stems trimmed
    and leaves coarsely sliced

1. Rinse lentils with cold running water and discard any stones or shriveled lentils. In 3-quart saucepan, heat lentils, ½ teaspoon salt, and bay leaf, and *5 cups water* to boiling over high heat. Reduce heat to low; cover and simmer, stirring occasionally, until lentils are tender, 20 to 25 minutes. Drain lentils well. Discard bay leaf.

2. In large bowl, with wire whisk, beat oil, vinegar, and remaining ½ teaspoon salt. Add lentils; toss to combine. Cover and refrigerate until flavors have blended, about 2 hours.

3. Meanwhile, in 12-inch skillet, cook bacon over medium-low heat, until browned and crisp; transfer to paper towels to drain. Cool bacon slightly, then crumble into small pieces.

4. To serve, add spinach to lentil mixture; toss to combine well. Spoon onto salad plates and sprinkle each with crumbled bacon. Makes 8 accompaniment servings.

Each serving: About 270 calories, 16 g protein, 28 g carbohydrate, 12 g total fat (2 g saturated), 4 mg cholesterol, 335 mg sodium.

Two Bean and Tomato Salad

Prep: 25 minutes
Cook: 5 minutes

3 ounces thin French green beans (haricots verts) or green beans,
    trimmed
2 tablespoons extravirgin olive oil
2 tablespoons fresh lemon juice
1 medium shallot, finely chopped
½ teaspoon Dijon mustard
¼ teaspoon salt
¼ teaspoon coarsely ground black pepper
2 medium ripe tomatoes (about 12 ounces), each cut into 12
    wedges
1 can (15 to 19 ounces) Great Northern or cannellini (white
    kidney) beans, rinsed and drained

1. In 10-inch skillet, heat *¾ inch water* to boiling over
high heat. Add green beans; heat to boiling. Reduce heat
to medium; cook, stirring occasionally, until beans are
tender-crisp, 3 to 5 minutes. Drain beans and rinse with
cold running water; drain again.

2. In large salad bowl, with wire whisk, beat oil, lemon
juice, shallot, mustard, salt, and pepper until blended. Add
green beans, tomatoes, and white beans; with rubber spatula, gently toss to mix well and serve. Makes 8 accompaniment servings.

*Each serving: About 170 calories, 8 g protein, 27 g carbohydrate,
4 g total fat (1 g saturated), 0 mg cholesterol, 105 mg sodium.*

Caribbean Black Beans and Rice

Prep: 20 minutes
Cook: 40 minutes

1 tablespoon olive oil
3 medium carrots, peeled and
  cut into ¼-inch pieces
2 medium stalks celery, cut into
  ¼-inch pieces
1 large onion, chopped
3 garlic cloves, finely chopped
1 teaspoon salt
½ teaspoon ground allspice
¾ cup regular long-grain rice

1¼ cups water
¼ cup dry sherry
1 tablespoon Louisiana-style
  cayenne pepper sauce*
2 cans (15 to 19 ounces each)
  black beans, rinsed and
  drained
1 cup packed fresh cilantro
  leaves, chopped

1. In 5-quart Dutch oven, heat oil over medium heat. Add carrots, celery, and onion and cook, stirring often, until vegetables are tender, about 15 minutes. Add garlic, salt, and allspice; cook, stirring, 1 minute. Stir in rice, water, sherry, and cayenne pepper sauce; heat to boiling over medium-high heat. Reduce heat to low; cover and simmer until rice is tender and liquid has been absorbed, about 15 to 18 minutes.

2. Stir in black beans; cover and cook 5 minutes longer. Stir in cilantro just before serving. Serve with extra cayenne pepper sauce if you like. Makes about 7 cups or 4 main-dish servings.

*Louisiana-style cayenne pepper sauce is a milder variety of hot pepper sauce that adds tang and flavor, not just heat. It can be found in the condiment section of the supermarket, near the ketchup.

Each serving: About 400 calories, 23 g protein, 78 g carbohydrate, 5 g total fat (1 g saturated), 0 mg cholesterol, 1,360 mg sodium.

Red Beans and Rice

Prep: 15 minutes
Cook: 25 minutes

2 cups water
1 cup regular long-grain rice
½ teaspoon salt
2 slices bacon, coarsely
   chopped
2 medium celery stalks with
   leaves, thinly sliced
1 medium onion, coarsely
   chopped
¼ teaspoon dried thyme
2 garlic cloves, finely chopped

2 cans (15 to 19 ounces each)
   red kidney beans, rinsed
   and drained
1 cup chicken broth
1 teaspoon Worcestershire
   sauce
½ cup loosely packed fresh
   parsley leaves, chopped
1 teaspoon distilled white
   vinegar
¼ teaspoon hot pepper sauce

1. In 2-quart saucepan, heat water to boiling over high heat. Stir in rice and ¼ teaspoon salt; heat to boiling. Reduce heat to low; cover and simmer, without stirring or lifting lid, until rice is tender and liquid has been absorbed, 18 to 20 minutes. Remove from heat and let stand 5 minutes. Fluff rice with fork; keep warm.

2. Meanwhile, in 4-quart saucepan, cook bacon over medium heat, stirring occasionally, until browned, about 5 minutes.

3. To saucepan with bacon, add celery with leaves, onion, thyme, and remaining ¼ teaspoon salt and cook, stirring occasionally, until vegetables are tender, about 12 minutes. Add garlic and cook, stirring, 1 minute.

4. Increase heat to medium-high; stir in beans, broth, and Worcestershire sauce, and cook until heated through, about 5 minutes. Stir in parsley, vinegar, and hot pepper sauce. Serve bean mixture over rice. Makes 4 main-dish servings.

Each serving: About 465 calories, 20 g protein, 80 g carbohydrate, 8 g total fat (3 g saturated), 8 mg cholesterol, 1,105 mg sodium.

Dutch-Oven Beans for a Crowd

Prep: 40 minutes plus soaking beans
Cook: 1 hour 30 minutes

2 tablespoons vegetable oil
2 medium green peppers, cut
 into 1-inch-wide strips
2 medium onions, chopped
3 garlic cloves, finely chopped
1 package (16 ounces) dry
 navy (pea) beans, soaked
 and drained (see page
 498)
1 cup dry baby lima beans,
 soaked and drained (see
 page 498)
1 cup dry red kidney beans,
 soaked and drained (see
 page 498)

6 cups water
3 tablespoons brown sugar
4 teaspoons salt
½ teaspoon ground black
 pepper
¼ teaspoon ground cloves
1 can (28 ounces) tomatoes
1 can (12 ounces) tomato paste
1½ pounds kielbasa (smoked
 Polish sausage), cut into
 1½-inch pieces

1. In 8-quart Dutch oven, heat oil over medium-high heat. Stir in green peppers, onions, and garlic and cook, stirring occasionally, until tender. Add beans and water to Dutch oven; stir in brown sugar, salt, pepper, and cloves, heat to boiling over high heat. Reduce heat to low; cover and simmer, stirring occasionally, 1 hour.

2. Add tomatoes with their juice, tomato paste, and kielbasa, stirring to mix well, and breaking tomatoes up with side of spoon. Heat to boiling over medium-high heat. Reduce heat to low, cover and simmer until beans are tender, about 30 minutes longer. Skim and discard fat before serving. Makes 12 main-dish servings.

Each serving: About 510 calories, 26 g protein, 60 g carbohydrate, 20 g total fat (7 g saturated), 38 mg cholesterol, 1,450 mg sodium.

Meatless Chili

Prep: 30 minutes plus soaking beans
Bake: 1 hour 30 minutes

1½ pounds mixed dried beans, such as red kidney, white kidney (cannellini), and black beans (3 cups total), soaked and drained (see page 498)
1 tablespoon vegetable oil
3 medium carrots, peeled and cut into ¼-inch slices
2 medium onions, finely chopped
1 celery stalk, finely chopped
1 medium red pepper, finely chopped
3 garlic cloves, finely chopped
1 jalapeño chile, finely chopped, with seeds

2 teaspoons ground cumin
½ teaspoon ground coriander
1 can (28 ounces) tomatoes in puree
1 chipotle chile, canned in adobo sauce, finely chopped
2 teaspoons salt
¼ teaspoon dried oregano
1 package (10 ounces) frozen whole-kernel corn
1¼ cups loosely packed fresh cilantro leaves and stems, chopped

1. Preheat oven to 375°F. In 5-quart Dutch oven, place beans and *8 cups water;* heat to boiling over high heat. Cover, and place in oven, and bake, stirring occasionally, until beans are tender, about 1 hour. Drain beans and return to Dutch oven.

2. Meanwhile, in 10-inch skillet, heat oil over medium heat. Add carrots, onions, celery, and red pepper and cook, stirring frequently, until vegetables are tender, about 10 minutes. Stir in garlic, jalapeño, cumin, and coriander; cook, stirring, 30 seconds. Stir in tomatoes with their puree, chipotle chile, salt, and oregano, breaking tomatoes up with side of spoon; heat to boiling over high heat. Reduce heat to low; simmer, 10 minutes.

3. Stir tomato mixture, corn, and *2 cups water* into beans. Cover, place in oven, and bake 30 minutes longer.

Remove from oven. Stir in cilantro just before serving. Makes about 12½ cups or 6 main-dish servings.

Each serving: About 360 calories, 20 g protein, 66 g carbohydrate, 4 g total fat (0 g saturated), 0 mg cholesterol, 1195 mg sodium.

Stir-Fried Tofu with Vegetables

Prep: 10 minutes
Cook: 10 minutes

2 teaspoons vegetable oil
1 package (16 ounces) extrafirm tofu, patted dry and cut into 1" by ½" pieces
3 green onions
1 cup vegetable or chicken broth
1 tablespoon soy sauce
1 tablespoon dark brown sugar

2 teaspoons cornstarch
1 bag (10 ounces) shredded carrots
1 medium red pepper, thinly sliced
2 garlic cloves, crushed with garlic press
1 tablespoon grated, peeled fresh ginger
½ teaspoon salt

1. In nonstick 12-inch skillet, heat 1 teaspoon oil over medium-high heat until very hot. Add tofu and cook, gently tossing until heated through and lightly golden, about 4 minutes. Transfer tofu to plate.

2. Meanwhile, thinly slice green onions, separating white parts from green tops. In 2-cup measuring cup, stir broth, soy sauce, brown sugar, and cornstarch until smooth.

3. In same skillet, heat remaining 1 teaspoon oil. Add white parts of green onions, carrots, red pepper, garlic, ginger, and salt; cook, stirring frequently, 5 minutes.

4. Return tofu to skillet. Stir cornstarch mixture, and add to skillet; heat to boiling, stirring constantly. Boil, gently stirring, 30 seconds. Spoon into warm serving bowl and sprinkle with remaining green onions. Serve with rice, if you like. Makes 4 main-dish servings.

Each serving without rice: About 160 calories, 9 g protein, 20 g carbohydrate, 6 g total fat (1 g saturated), 0 mg cholesterol, 610 mg sodium.

∾Rice

Hot Fluffy Rice

Prep: 2 minutes
Cook: 20 minutes

2 cups water
1 cup regular long-grain rice
1 tablespoon margarine or butter (optional)
1 teaspoon salt

1. In 3-quart saucepan, heat water to boiling over high heat. Stir in rice, margarine, if you like, and salt; heat to boiling.
2. Reduce heat to low; cover pan and simmer, without stirring or lifting lid, until rice is tender and all liquid has been absorbed, 18 to 20 minutes. Remove from heat and let stand 5 minutes. Fluff rice with fork. Makes about 3 cups or 4 accompaniment servings.

Each serving: About 170 calories, 3 g protein, 37 g carbohydrate, 0 g total fat, 0 mg cholesterol, 585 mg sodium.

BROWN RICE: Prepare as above but use *2½ cups water, and 1 cup brown rice,* instead of white. Simmer rice about 45 minutes or as label directs. Makes about 4 cups or 5 to 6 accompaniment servings.

Each serving: About 140 calories, 3 g protein, 29 g carbohydrate, 1 g total fat (0 g saturated), 0 mg cholesterol, 470 mg sodium.

Rice with Mushrooms

Prep: 10 minutes
Cook: 30 minutes

2 tablespoons olive oil
1 medium onion, chopped
4 ounces mushrooms, trimmed and sliced
3 cups water
1½ cups regular long-grain rice
2 tablespoons soy sauce
⅛ teaspoon ground black pepper
½ cup frozen peas

1. In 3-quart saucepan, heat oil over medium heat. Add onion and mushrooms and cook, stirring occasionally, until tender.

2. Stir in water, rice, soy sauce, and pepper; heat to boiling over high heat. Reduce heat to low; cover and simmer, without stirring or lifting lid, until rice is tender and all liquid has been absorbed, about 20 minutes. Add frozen peas; heat through. Remove from heat and let stand 5 minutes. Fluff with fork before serving. Makes 8 accompaniment servings.

Each serving: About 175 calories, 4 g protein, 32 g carbohydrate, 4 g total fat (1 g saturated), 0 mg cholesterol, 270 mg sodium.

Green Rice

Prep: 7 minutes
Cook: 30 minutes

2 tablespoons margarine or butter
1 tablespoon finely chopped green onion
1 package (10 ounces) prewashed spinach, tough stems trimmed
    and leaves coarsely chopped
1½ cups chicken broth
¾ cup regular long-grain rice
Dash ground red pepper (cayenne)

1. In 3-quart saucepan, melt margarine over medium heat. Stir in green onion and cook, stirring, until tender. Stir in spinach; cook, tossing with two spoons, just until spinach wilts. Spoon spinach mixture into bowl; cover loosely.

2. In same saucepan, heat broth to boiling over high heat. Stir in rice and ground red pepper; heat to boiling. Reduce heat to low; cover and simmer until rice is tender and all liquid has been absorbed, about 20 minutes. Remove from heat and let rice stand 5 minutes. Fluff with a fork.

3. Stir spinach mixture into rice and heat through over low heat. Serve hot. Makes 4 accompaniment servings.

Each serving: About 200 calories, 6 g protein, 28 g carbohydrate, 7 g total fat (1 g saturated), 0 mg cholesterol, 440 mg sodium.

Chiles Rellenos Pie

Prep: 15 minutes
Cook: 70 minutes

2 cans (4 ounces each) whole mild green chiles, rinsed, drained, and patted dry with paper towels
⅔ cup bottled bean dip
4 large eggs
2 cups milk
½ teaspoon salt
½ cup regular long-grain rice, cooked as label directs but without salt
4 ounces Monterey Jack cheese, shredded (about 1 cup)

1. Preheat oven to 325°F. With knife, split each chile lengthwise in half, but not all the way through. Spoon 1 heaping tablespoon bean dip onto half of each chile; fold other half of chile over. In medium bowl, with wire whisk, mix eggs, milk, and salt until well blended.
2. Spoon rice into shallow 1½-quart casserole or 9½-inch deep-dish pie plate. Place stuffed chiles on top of rice. Pour egg mixture over chiles; sprinkle with cheese.
3. Bake pie until knife inserted in center comes out clean, about 50 minutes. Transfer casserole to wire rack and let stand a few minutes before serving. Makes 6 main-dish servings.

Each serving: About 255 calories, 14 g protein, 23 g carbohydrate, 12 g total fat (6 g saturated), 170 mg cholesterol, 795 mg sodium.

10 SPEEDY STIR-INS FOR RICE

To flavor rice without loading on the fat, to 3 to 4 cups freshly cooked rice, stir in:

- 3 chopped green onions, and ¼ cup chopped fresh basil, mint, or parsley

- 1 teaspoon curry powder and 1 coarsely chopped unpeeled Granny Smith apple
- 1 minced garlic clove, 3 tablespoons chopped fresh parsley, and 2 teaspoons freshly grated lemon peel
- 2 peeled, shredded carrots and 2 teaspoons chopped fresh thyme leaves
- 1 shredded zucchini and 1 teaspoon chopped fresh rosemary leaves
- ¼ cup freshly grated Parmesan cheese and 2 tablespoons chopped fresh basil leaves
- ⅓ cup dark seedless raisins, 1 teaspoon freshly grated orange peel, and ¼ cup chopped mango chutney
- 2 teaspoons soy sauce, 1 teaspoon grated, peeled fresh ginger, and ½ teaspoon Asian sesame oil
- 1 tablespoon chopped fresh mint leaves and ¼ cup crumbled feta cheese
- ⅓ cup bottled salsa and 2 tablespoons chopped fresh cilantro leaves

Curried Raisin-Nut Pilaf

Prep: 7 minutes
Cook: 25 minutes

3 tablespoons margarine or butter
1 small onion, coarsely chopped
2 teaspoons curry powder
2½ cups water
2 cups chicken broth
2 cups regular long-grain rice
½ cup dark seedless raisins
¾ teaspoon salt
⅔ cup sliced natural almonds

1. In 12-inch skillet, melt 2 tablespoons margarine over medium-high heat. Add onion and cook, stirring frequently, until tender. Add curry powder; cook, stirring, 1 minute. Stir in water, broth, rice, raisins, and salt; heat to boiling, stirring, over high heat. Reduce heat to low; cover and simmer, without stirring or lifting lid, until rice is tender and all liquid has been absorbed, about 20 minutes. Remove from heat and let stand 5 minutes. Fluff with a fork.

2. Meanwhile, in 10-inch skillet, melt remaining 1 tablespoon margarine over medium-low heat. Add almonds and cook, stirring often, until golden. Serve pilaf topped with toasted almonds. Makes 10 accompaniment servings.

Each serving: About 250 calories, 6 g protein, 38 g carbohydrate, 8 g total fat (1 g saturated), 0 mg cholesterol, 380 mg sodium.

Rice Pilaf with Vermicelli

Prep: 10 minutes
Cook: 1 hour 5 minutes

2 tablespoons margarine or butter
1½ ounces vermicelli or spaghettini, broken into 1-inch pieces (½ cup)
1 medium onion, finely chopped
1 cup long-grain brown rice
1 cup chicken broth
1 cup water
¼ teaspoon salt
Pine nuts (pignoli), toasted and chopped (optional)

1. In 3-quart saucepan, melt margarine over medium heat. Add vermicelli and cook, stirring occasionally, until lightly browned, 3 to 4 minutes. Reduce heat to medium-low; stir in onion and cook, stirring occasionally, until tender, about 10 minutes.

2. Stir brown rice, broth, water, and salt, into saucepan; heat to boiling over high heat. Reduce heat to low; cover and simmer, without stirring or lifting lid, until rice is tender and liquid has been absorbed, about 50 minutes. Remove from heat and let stand 5 minutes. Fluff rice with fork. If you like, sprinkle pilaf with pine nuts to serve. Makes about 4 cups or 4 accompaniment servings.

Each serving: About 280 calories, 7 g protein, 47 g carbohydrate, 8 g total fat (2 g saturated), 0 mg cholesterol, 410 mg sodium.

Weeknight Arroz Con Pollo

Prep: 15 minutes
Cook: About 45 minutes

1 tablespoon olive oil
1 medium onion, finely chopped
1 medium red pepper, cut into ½-inch pieces
1 cup regular long-grain white rice
1 garlic clove, finely chopped
⅛ teaspoon ground red pepper (cayenne)
1 can (14½ ounces) chicken broth

¼ cup dry sherry or water
1 strip lemon peel (3" by ½")
¼ teaspoon salt
1 pound chicken breast tenders, cut into 2-inch pieces
1 cup frozen peas
½ cup loosely packed fresh cilantro leaves or parsley leaves, chopped
¼ cup chopped pimiento-stuffed olives (salad olives)
Lemon wedges

1. In nonstick 12-inch skillet (about 2-inches deep), heat oil over medium heat. Add onion and red pepper and cook, stirring occasionally, until tender, about 12 minutes. Stir in rice, garlic, and ground red pepper; cook 2 minutes. Stir in broth, sherry, lemon peel, and salt; heat to boiling over medium-high heat. Reduce heat to low; cover and simmer 13 minutes.

2. Stir in chicken tenders; cover and simmer 13 minutes longer, stirring once halfway through cooking, until chicken has lost its pink color throughout, and rice is tender. Stir in frozen peas; cover and heat through. Remove skillet from heat; let stand 5 minutes.

3. To serve, sprinkle with cilantro and olives. Pass lemon wedges to squeeze over each serving. Makes about 7 cups or 4 main-dish servings.

Each serving: About 410 calories, 34 g protein, 49 g carbohydrate, 7 g total fat (2 g saturated), 66 mg cholesterol, 925 mg sodium.

Spring Risotto

Prep: 30 minutes
Cook: 55 minutes

1 can (14½ ounces) vegetable
   or chicken broth
3½ cups water
2 tablespoons olive oil
3 medium carrots, peeled and
   cut into ¼-inch pieces
12 ounces asparagus, trimmed
   and cut into 2-inch pieces
6 ounces sugar snap peas,
   strings removed and each
   cut in half

1 teaspoon salt
¼ teaspoon coarsely ground
   black pepper
1 small onion, chopped
2 cups Arborio rice (Italian short-
   grain rice) or medium-grain
   rice
½ cup dry white wine
½ cup freshly grated Parmesan
   cheese
¼ cup chopped fresh basil
   leaves or parsley

1. In 2-quart saucepan, heat broth and water to boiling over high heat. Reduce heat to low to maintain simmer; cover.

2. In 4-quart saucepan, heat 1 tablespoon oil over medium heat. Add carrots and cook 10 minutes. Stir in asparagus, sugar snap peas, ¼ teaspoon salt, and pepper; cover and cook, stirring frequently, until vegetables are tender-crisp, about 5 minutes. Transfer vegetables to bowl.

3. In same saucepan, heat remaining 1 tablespoon oil over medium heat. Add onion and cook, stirring frequently, until tender, about 7 minutes. Add rice and remaining ¾ teaspoon salt and cook, stirring frequently, until rice grains have become opaque. Add wine; cook, stirring, until wine has been absorbed. Add about ½ cup simmering broth to rice, and cook, stirring until liquid has been absorbed. Continue cooking, adding remaining broth, ½ cup at a time, and stirring after each addition, until all liquid has been absorbed and rice is tender but still firm, about 25 minutes (risotto should have a creamy consistency). Stir in vegeta-

bles, Parmesan, and basil and heat through. Serve hot.
Makes 4 main-dish servings.

Each serving: About 620 calories, 17 g protein, 106 g carbohydrate, 11 g total fat (3 g saturated), 10 mg cholesterol, 835 mg sodium.

Butternut-Squash Risotto with Sage

Prep: 20 minutes
Cook: 50 minutes

1 large butternut squash (2½
    pounds), peeled, cut into
    halves, and seeds removed
4 cups water
1 can (14½ ounces) chicken or
    vegetable broth
1 tablespoon margarine or
    butter
3 tablespoons chopped fresh
    sage leaves
1 teaspoon salt

¼ teaspoon coarsely ground
    black pepper
2 tablespoons olive oil
1 small onion, finely chopped
2 cups Arborio rice (Italian short-
    grain rice) or medium-grain
    rice
⅓ cup dry white wine
½ cup freshly grated Parmesan
    cheese

1. Cut enough squash into ½-inch pieces to equal 3 cups.
Coarsely shred enough remaining squash to equal 2 cups.
2. In 2-quart saucepan, heat water and broth to boiling
over high heat. Reduce heat to low to maintain simmer;
cover.
3. In 5-quart Dutch oven, melt margarine over medium
heat. Add butternut squash pieces, 2 tablespoons chopped
sage, ¼ teaspoon salt, and pepper. Cover and cook, stirring
occasionally, until squash is tender, about 10 minutes.
Transfer squash to bowl; cover loosely.
4. To Dutch oven, add oil, shredded squash, onion, and
remaining ¾ teaspoon salt and cook, stirring often, until
vegetables are tender. Add rice and cook, stirring frequently, 2 minutes. Add wine; cook, stirring, until wine has
been absorbed. Add about ½ cup simmering broth to rice,
and cook, stirring, until liquid has been absorbed.
5. Continue cooking, adding remaining broth, ½ cup at

a time, and stirring after each addition, until all liquid has been absorbed and rice is tender but still firm, about 25 minutes (risotto should have a creamy consistency). Stir in squash pieces, Parmesan, and remaining 1 tablespoon chopped sage and heat through. Serve hot. Makes 4 main-dish servings.

Each serving: About 700 calories, 17 g protein, 115 g carbohydrate, 14 g total fat (4 g saturated), 15 mg cholesterol, 1,105 mg sodium.

THE RIGHT WAY TO EAT RISOTTO

Italians serve this creamy rice in bowls to hold in the heat—and they eat around the perimeter (which cools off fastest) until they get to the middle. This way, every bits stays hot.

Green Risotto

Prep: 25 minutes
Cook: 50 minutes

1½ ounces pancetta, cut into ¼-inch pieces (⅓ cup) or 3 slices bacon, cut into ¼-inch pieces
1 can (14½ ounces) chicken broth
1 small onion, finely chopped
1 tablespoon olive oil
2 cups Arborio rice (Italian short-grain rice) or medium-grain rice
½ cup dry white wine

1 package (10 ounces) frozen chopped spinach, thawed and squeezed dry
½ cup packed fresh parsley leaves
½ cup packed fresh basil leaves
½ cup freshly grated Parmesan cheese
½ teaspoon salt
Shaved Parmesan cheese

1. Heat 12-inch skillet over medium heat. Add pancetta or bacon and cook, stirring occasionally, until browned, 5 minutes. With slotted spoon, transfer pancetta to paper towels to drain. Discard all but 1 teaspoon fat from pan.

2. Meanwhile, in 2-quart saucepan, heat broth and *3¼ cups water* to boiling over high heat. Reduce heat to low to maintain simmer; cover.

3. To same skillet, add onion and cook, stirring frequently, until tender, 5 minutes. Add oil and rice and cook, stirring often, until rice grains have become opaque, 2 to 3 minutes. Add wine; cook, stirring, until wine has been absorbed. Add about ½ cup simmering broth, stirring, until liquid has been absorbed.

4. Continue cooking, adding remaining broth, ½ cup at a time, and stirring after each addition, until all liquid has been absorbed and rice is tender but still firm, about 35 to 45 minutes (risotto should have a creamy consistency).

5. In blender, place spinach and *1½ cups water*. Blend until smooth, stopping blender occasionally, and scraping down sides as necessary. Add parsley and basil and blend until smooth.

6. Into rice in skillet, stir pureed greens, grated Parmesan, and salt; heat through. Sprinkle with pancetta or bacon and shaved Parmesan to serve. Makes about 6 cups or 4 main-dish servings.

Each serving: About 600 calories, 20 g protein, 98 g carbohydrate, 11 g total fat (4 g saturated), 15 mg cholesterol, 970 mg sodium.

Confetti Rice Pilaf

Prep: 10 minutes
Cook: 25 minutes

3 tablespoons margarine or butter
2 medium carrots, peeled and cut into ¼-inch pieces
2 cups regular long-grain rice
2 cups water
1 can (14½ ounces) chicken broth
½ teaspoon salt
¼ teaspoon coarsely ground black pepper
1 small bay leaf
1 package (10 ounces) frozen peas, thawed
2 medium green onions, sliced

1. In 3-quart saucepan, melt margarine over medium heat. Add carrots and cook, stirring occasionally, until slightly softened, 2 to 3 minutes. Add rice and cook, stirring, until grains are coated, about 1 minute. Stir in broth, salt, pepper, and bay leaf; heat to boiling over high heat. Reduce heat to low; cover and simmer, without stirring or lifting lid, until all liquid has been absorbed and rice is tender, 15 to 20 minutes.

2. Discard bay leaf; stir in peas and green onions.

3. Cook 2 minutes longer or until heated through. Makes about 8 cups or 12 accompaniment servings.

Each serving: About 165 calories, 4 g protein, 29 g carbohydrate, 3 g total fat (1 g saturated), 0 mg cholesterol, 260 mg sodium.

Chinese Fried Rice

Prep: 40 minutes
Cook: 20 minutes

3 teaspoons vegetable oil
2 large eggs, lightly beaten
8 ounces mushrooms, trimmed and thinly sliced
1 medium red pepper, finely chopped
1 tablespoon grated, peeled fresh ginger
2 garlic cloves, finely chopped
1½ cups medium-grain rice, cooked as label directs
1 cup frozen peas, thawed
4 ounces sliced cooked ham, cut into 1" by ¼" strips
½ cup chicken broth
2 green onions, thinly sliced
2 tablespoons soy sauce
1 teaspoon Asian sesame oil
½ cup loosely packed fresh cilantro leaves, chopped

1. In nonstick 12-inch skillet, heat 1 teaspoon vegetable oil over medium heat. Add eggs and cook, stirring with wooden spoon, until eggs are scrambled, about 2 minutes. Transfer eggs to plate; cover loosely.

2. In same skillet, heat remaining 2 teaspoons vegetable oil over medium-high heat. Add mushrooms and red pepper, and cook, stirring occasionally, until vegetables are tender and lightly golden, about 10 minutes. Add ginger and garlic, and cook, stirring, 1 minute.

3. Stir in rice, peas, ham, broth, green onions, soy sauce, sesame oil, and scrambled eggs, and cook, stirring and separating rice with spoon, until heated through, about 3 minutes. Toss with cilantro just before serving. Makes about 8 cups or 4 main-dish servings.

Each serving: About 470 calories, 18 g protein, 73 g carbohydrate, 11 g total fat (3 g saturated), 123 mg cholesterol, 1,055 mg sodium.

Polo

Prep: 5 minutes
Cook: 35 minutes

1 cup basmati or Texmati rice (see Aromatic White, page 500)
3 tablespoons margarine or butter
1 medium onion, finely chopped
½ teaspoon salt
Sliced green onions

1. In 3-quart saucepan, heat *6 cups water* to boiling over high heat. Add rice and cook, stirring occasionally, 10 minutes. Drain rice; rinse with cold water. Drain well.

2. Meanwhile, in nonstick 10-inch skillet, melt 1 tablespoon margarine over medium heat. Add onion and cook, stirring occasionally, until tender, about 10 minutes.

3. Add remaining 2 tablespoons margarine to skillet and melt. Add cooled rice, salt, and ¼ cup water and stir until rice is evenly coated. Spread mixture into even layer over bottom of skillet.

4. Cover skillet and cook until rice is tender and golden crust forms on the bottom, 15 to 20 minutes. With wide spatula, transfer rice to shallow serving bowl, crust side up.

Sprinkle sliced green onions on rice and serve. Makes 4 accompaniment servings.

Each serving: About 255 calories, 4 g protein, 40 g carbohydrate, 9 g total fat (2 g saturated), 0 mg cholesterol, 385 mg sodium.

Sushi

Prep: 1 hour 30 minutes plus chilling
Cook: 25 minutes

Fillings
4 ounces cooked, shelled and deveined shrimp, thinly sliced lengthwise
4 ounces imitation crab sticks (surimi), cut lengthwise into pencil-thin sticks
4 ounces thinly sliced smoked salmon
1 medium-ripe avocado, cut lengthwise in half, pitted and peeled, then thinly sliced lengthwise
1 medium carrot, peeled and cut crosswise in half, then lengthwise into pencil-thin sticks
1 small cucumber, cut lengthwise into pencil-thin sticks

Garnishes (optional)
Black sesame seeds
White sesame seeds, toasted
Minced chives

Accompaniments
Pickled sushi ginger
Soy sauce
Wasabi (Japanese horseradish)

Sushi Rice
2½ cups water
2 cups Japanese short-grain rice (see Short-grain White, page 501)
2 tablespoons sugar
1 teaspoon salt
½ cup seasoned rice vinegar

Sushi Nori (Seaweed Wrappers)

1 package (10 sheets) roasted seaweed for sushi (8" by 7" each)*

1. Assemble Fillings: Place each Filling in small bowl. Cover bowls with plastic wrap and place in jelly-roll pan for easy handling. Refrigerate Fillings until ready to use.

2. Assemble Garnishes and Accompaniments: Place each Garnish in small bowl. Place each Accompaniment in small serving dish. Cover and place in another jelly-roll pan, or a roasting pan for easy handling. If not serving right away, refrigerate pickled ginger and wasabi.

3. Prepare Sushi Rice: In 3-quart saucepan, heat water, rice, sugar, and salt to boiling over high heat. Reduce heat to low; cover and without stirring or lifting lid, cook until rice is tender and liquid has been absorbed, about 25 minutes (rice will be sticky). Remove saucepan from heat; stir in vinegar. Cover and keep warm.

4. Make sushi rolls: Place 12-inch-long piece plastic wrap on surface. Place small bowl of water within reach of work area; it is easiest to handle sticky sushi rice with damp hands.

5. Place 1 nori sheet, shiny (smooth) side down, on plastic wrap, with a short side facing you; top with generous ½ cup sushi rice. With small metal spatula and damp hands, gently spread and pat rice down to make an even layer over nori, leaving ¼-inch border all around sheet. (To make an inside-out roll, flip rice-covered nori sheet so that nori is on top.)

6. On top of rice (or nori), starting about 2 inches away from side facing you, arrange desired fillings crosswise in 1½-inch-wide strip.

7. Using end of plastic wrap closest to you, lift edge of sushi, then firmly roll sushi, jelly-roll fashion, away from you. Seal end of nori sheet with water-dampened finger. (If making inside-out roll, coat outside of roll in 1 of the Garnishes.) Place sushi roll on tray or platter.

8. Repeat steps 5 through 7 to make 10 sushi rolls in all, changing plastic wrap when necessary. Cover and refrigerate sushi rolls 30 minutes or up to 6 hours.

9. To serve, with serrated knife, slice off and discard ends from each sushi roll. Slice each roll crosswise into ½-inch-thick slices. Arrange sliced rolls on platter. Serve with accompaniments. Makes about 100 pieces, about 20 appetizer servings.

*Sushi ingredients are available in specialty food stores and the ethnic food section of some supermarkets.

Each piece: About 25 calories, 1 g protein, 4 g carbohydrate, 0 g total fat, 3 mg cholesterol, 70 mg sodium.

Asian Coconut Rice Salad

Prep: 15 minutes
Cook: 22 minutes

1 tablespoon vegetable oil
2 tablespoons matchstick strips
   (2" × ¼") peeled, fresh
   ginger
1½ cups regular long-grain rice
½ cup well-stirred canned
   unsweetened coconut milk
   (not cream of coconut)

2 cups water
½ teaspoon salt
¼ teaspoon hot pepper sauce
2 green onions, minced
3 tablespoons minced fresh
   cilantro leaves
2 tablespoons seasoned rice
   vinegar

1. In 2-quart saucepan, heat oil over medium-high heat until very hot. Add ginger and cook, stirring, 1 minute. Add rice and cook, stirring, 1 minute. Stir in coconut milk, water, salt, and hot pepper sauce; heat to boiling. Reduce heat to low; cover and simmer, without stirring or lifting lid, until rice is tender and liquid has been absorbed, 18 to 20 minutes. Remove from heat and let stand 5 minutes. Fluff with fork.
2. Transfer rice to serving bowl. Stir in green onions, cilantro, and vinegar. Cover and refrigerate if not serving

right away. Makes about 4 cups or 6 accompaniment servings.

Each serving: About 235 calories, 4 g protein, 41 g carbohydrate, 6 g total fat (3 g saturated), 0 mg cholesterol, 315 mg sodium.

∾Wild Rice

Boiled Wild Rice

Prep: 2 minutes
Cook: 50 minutes

2⅔ cups water
1⅓ cups wild rice, rinsed
1½ teaspoons salt
2 tablespoons margarine or butter (¼ stick)

1. In 2-quart saucepan, heat water to boiling over high heat. Stir in wild rice and salt; heat to boiling. Reduce heat to low.
2. Cover and simmer until grains are tender and all liquid has been absorbed, 45 to 50 minutes. With fork, lightly toss in margarine until it has melted. Serve hot. Makes 6 accompaniment servings.

Each serving: About 160 calories, 5 g protein, 27 g carbohydrate, 4 g total fat (1 g saturated), 0 mg cholesterol, 635 mg sodium.

Wild Rice with Mushrooms

Prep: 7 minutes
Cook: 50 minutes

2 tablespoons margarine or butter
8 ounces mushrooms, trimmed and sliced
1 cup wild rice, rinsed
2 cups chicken broth
¼ teaspoon salt

1. In 2-quart saucepan, melt margarine over medium-high heat. Add mushrooms and cook, stirring occasionally, 5 minutes.

2. Add wild rice, broth, and salt to mushrooms; heat to boiling over high heat. Reduce heat to low; cover and simmer until rice is tender and all liquid has been absorbed, 45 to 50 minutes. Serve hot. Makes 6 accompaniment servings.

Each serving: About 150 calories, 6 g protein, 22 g carbohydrate, 5 g total fat (1 g saturated), 0 mg cholesterol, 410 mg sodium.

Wild Rice and Orzo Pilaf

Prep: 25 minutes
Cook: 45 minutes

1¼ cups orzo pasta (8 ounces)
1 cup wild rice rinsed
3 tablespoons margarine or butter
1 small onion, chopped
1 medium celery stalk, chopped
1 pound medium mushrooms, trimmed and sliced
2 teaspoons chopped fresh thyme leaves
1 teaspoon salt
¼ teaspoon coarsely ground black pepper

1. Prepare orzo and wild rice, separately, as labels direct.
2. Meanwhile, in 12-inch skillet, melt margarine over me-

dium heat. Add onion and celery, and cook, stirring occasionally, until tender, about 10 minutes. Stir in mushrooms, thyme, salt, and pepper, and cook, stirring occasionally, until mushrooms are tender and liquid has evaporated, about 10 minutes longer.

3. Preheat oven to 350°F. In shallow 2½-quart baking dish, stir orzo, wild rice, and mushroom mixture until blended. Cover baking dish with foil.

4. Bake casserole until wild rice and orzo are heated through and flavors have blended, about 35 minutes. Serve hot. Makes about 9 cups or 12 accompaniment servings.

Each serving: About 155 calories, 5 g protein, 26 g carbohydrate, 3 g total fat (1 g saturated), 0 mg cholesterol, 220 mg sodium.

Breakfast Wild Rice

Prep: 2 minutes
Cook: 50 minutes

1 ⅓ cups water
⅔ cup wild rice, rinsed
½ teaspoon vanilla extract
½ teaspoon salt
Toppings: half-and-half, heavy or whipping cream, honey, maple syrup, coarsely chopped walnuts, dark seedless raisins, brown sugar, margarine or butter

1. In 2-quart saucepan heat water to boiling over high heat. Stir in wild rice, vanilla, and salt; heat to boiling. Reduce heat to low; cover and simmer until rice is tender and all liquid has been absorbed, about 45 to 50 minutes.

2. Serve wild rice warm for breakfast in individual bowls like oatmeal. Let each person choose one or more of the toppings to spoon onto wild rice. Makes 4 breakfast servings.

Each serving without topping: About 95 calories, 4 g protein, 20 g carbohydrate, 0 g total fat, 0 mg cholesterol, 295 mg sodium.

∿Other Grains

BARLEY

Baked Barley with Mushrooms

Prep: 15 minutes
Bake: 2 hours

2 cups chicken broth
2 cups water
¾ cup pearl barley
8 ounces mushrooms, trimmed and sliced
1 medium carrot, peeled and sliced
1 small onion, chopped
4 tablespoons margarine or butter, cut up
½ teaspoon salt

Preheat oven to 350°F. In 2-quart casserole, stir together broth, water, barley, mushrooms, carrot, onion, margarine, and salt until well blended. Cover casserole and bake, stirring often, until barley and vegetables are tender and the liquid has been absorbed, about 2 hours. Makes 8 accompaniment servings.

Each serving: About 140 calories, 4 g protein, 18 g carbohydrate, 6 g total fat (1 g saturated), 0 mg cholesterol, 420 mg sodium.

COUSCOUS

Couscous

Prep: 5 minutes plus standing
Cook: 5 minutes

1½ cups water
¼ cup dark seedless raisins or dried currants
1 tablespoon margarine or butter
¾ teaspoon salt
¼ teaspoon turmeric
1 cup couscous (Moroccan pasta)

In 3-quart saucepan, heat water, raisins, margarine, salt, and turmeric to boiling over high heat. Gradually stir couscous into boiling mixture until blended. Remove from heat; cover and let stand 5 minutes. Fluff with fork and serve. Makes 6 accompaniment servings.

Each serving: About 150 calories, 4 g protein, 29 g carbohydrate, 2 g total fat (0 g saturated), 0 mg cholesterol, 320 mg sodium.

Couscous Salad with Grapes and Thyme

Prep: 15 minutes
Cook: 5 minutes

1 package (10 ounces) couscous (Moroccan pasta)
1½ teaspoons fresh thyme leaves
¼ cup cider vinegar
2 tablespoons olive oil
1 teaspoon salt
1½ cups green and red seedless grapes (8 ounces), each cut into quarters
½ cup pine nuts (pignoli), toasted

1. Cook couscous as label directs, but do not add salt or butter. Stir thyme into couscous.

2. In large salad bowl, with wire whisk, beat vinegar, oil, and salt. Add grapes, pine nuts, and warm couscous; toss to coat well. Cover and refrigerate if not serving right away. Makes about 6 cups or 8 accompaniment servings.

Each serving: About 220 calories, 6 g protein, 34 g carbohydrate, 7 g total fat (1 g saturated), 0 mg cholesterol, 270 mg sodium.

HOMINY, GRITS, AND POLENTA

Polenta and Hominy Stew

Prep: 45 minutes
Bake: 1 hour 45 minutes

2 medium red peppers, roasted (see page 606)
3 pounds boneless pork shoulder, well trimmed and cut into 1½-inch pieces
1 cup water
1 jumbo onion (1 pound), chopped
1 cup loosely packed fresh cilantro leaves and stems, chopped
3 jalapeño chiles, seeded and finely chopped
4 garlic cloves, finely chopped
1½ teaspoons salt
¼ teaspoon ground red pepper (cayenne)
2 teaspoons ground cumin
½ teaspoon dried oregano
1 can (29 ounces) hominy, rinsed and drained
Chopped fresh cilantro leaves
Lime wedges

1. Preheat oven to 325°F. Cut peeled peppers into 1-inch pieces. In 5-quart Dutch oven, combine roasted peppers, pork, water, onion, cilantro, jalapeños, garlic, salt, ground red pepper, cumin, and oregano and stir until well combined. Heat to boiling over high heat. Cover, place in oven, and bake until pork is very tender.

2. Remove from oven; skim and discard fat from pan juices. Stir in hominy; cover and bake until heated through, about 15 minutes longer. Spoon stew into shallow soup plates, sprinkle with cilantro, and serve with lime wedges to squeeze over servings. Makes about 10 cups or 10 main-dish servings.

Each serving: About 300 calories, 38 g protein, 14 g carbohydrate, 9 g total fat (3 g saturated), 83 mg cholesterol, 565 mg sodium.

Puffy Cheddar Grits

Prep: 20 minutes
Bake: 45 minutes

3½ cups milk
2 cups water
2 tablespoons margarine or butter
1 teaspoon salt
1¼ cups quick-cooking grits
8 ounces shredded Cheddar cheese (about 2 cups)
5 large eggs
1 teaspoon hot pepper sauce
¼ teaspoon ground black pepper

1. In 3-quart saucepan, heat 1½ cups milk, water, margarine, and salt to boiling over medium-high heat. Gradually sprinkle in grits, beating constantly with wire whisk to prevent lumping. Reduce heat to low; cover and cook, stirring occasionally, 5 minutes. (Grits will be very stiff.) Remove saucepan from heat; blend in cheese.

2. In large bowl, with wire whisk, mix eggs, hot pepper sauce, black pepper, and remaining 2 cups milk until well blended. With whisk, gradually stir grits mixture into egg mixture.

3. Preheat oven to 325°F. Grease shallow 2½-quart casserole. Pour grits mixture into casserole. Bake uncovered, until knife inserted in center comes out clean, about 45 minutes. Transfer to wire rack and let cool a few minutes before serving. Makes 6 main-dish servings.

Each serving: About 230 calories, 12 g protein, 17 g carbohydrate, 13 g total fat (7 g saturated), 118 mg cholesterol, 385 mg sodium.

Polenta with Cheese

Prep: 5 minutes
Cook: 25 minutes

6½ cups water
1 teaspoon salt
1½ cups cornmeal
½ cup freshly grated Parmesan cheese
4 tablespoons margarine or butter

1. In 5-quart Dutch oven, heat water and salt to boiling over high heat. Reduce heat to medium; gradually sprinkle in cornmeal, beating constantly with wire whisk to prevent lumping. Reduce heat to low and cook, stirring frequently, until mixture is very thick, about 15 minutes.
2. Stir Parmesan and margarine into polenta until blended. Serve immediately. Makes 8 accompaniment servings.

Each serving: About 170 calories, 4 g protein, 20 g carbohydrate, 8 g total fat (2 g saturated), 4 mg cholesterol, 460 mg sodium.

Polenta Lasagna

Prep: 45 minutes
Bake: 30 minutes

1 tablespoon olive oil
1 small onion, finely chopped
1 garlic clove, finely chopped
1 can (28 ounces) tomatoes in juice
2 tablespoons tomato paste
2 tablespoons chopped fresh basil
1 teaspoon salt
1 package (10 ounces) frozen chopped spinach, thawed and squeezed dry
1 cup part-skim ricotta cheese
2 tablespoons freshly grated Parmesan cheese
¼ teaspoon coarsely ground black pepper
1 package (24 ounces) precooked polenta, cut into 16 slices
4 ounces part-skim mozzarella cheese, shredded (about 1 cup)

1. In 3-quart saucepan, heat oil over medium heat. Add onion and cook, stirring occasionally, until tender, about 8 minutes. Add garlic and cook, stirring, 30 seconds. Stir in tomatoes with their juice, tomato paste, basil, and ½ teaspoon salt; heat to boiling over high heat, breaking up tomatoes with side of spoon. Reduce heat to low and simmer, stirring occasionally, 20 minutes. Remove from heat.

2. Meanwhile, in medium bowl, stir together spinach, ricotta, Parmesan, pepper, and remaining ½ teaspoon salt until blended.

3. Preheat oven to 350°F. Grease 8" by 8" baking dish.

4. Arrange half of polenta slices, overlapping slightly, in prepared baking dish. Drop half of spinach mixture, by rounded tablespoons, on top of polenta (mixture will not completely cover slices). Pour half of sauce over spinach mixture; with narrow spatula, spread to form an even layer. Sprinkle with half of mozzarella. Repeat layering.

5. Bake casserole until hot and bubbling, about 30 minutes. Transfer to wire rack and let stand 10 minutes for easier serving. Makes 6 main-dish servings.

Each serving: About 270 calories, 16 g protein, 30 g carbohydrate, 10 g total fat (5 g saturated), 28 mg cholesterol, 1,210 mg sodium.

Creamy Polenta with Sausage
and Mushrooms

Prep: 25 minutes
Cook: 45 minutes

1 pound sweet Italian-sausage
links, casings removed
1 pound mushrooms, trimmed
and sliced
1 medium onion, chopped
2 garlic cloves, finely chopped
¼ teaspoon coarsely ground
black pepper
1 can (28 ounces) Italian plum
tomatoes in puree

2½ cups milk
2 cups cornmeal
2 cups water
1 can (14½ ounces) reduced-
sodium chicken broth
⅓ cup freshly grated Parmesan
cheese
2 tablespoons chopped fresh
parsley leaves

1. Heat 12-inch skillet over medium-high heat until hot. Add sausage and cook, breaking up sausage with side of spoon, until sausage is browned, about 10 minutes. With slotted spoon, transfer sausage to bowl.

2. Discard all but 1 tablespoon drippings from skillet. Add mushrooms, onion, garlic, and pepper; cook, stirring occasionally, until liquid has evaporated and vegetables are golden, about 10 minutes. Stir in tomatoes with their puree; heat to boiling over high heat, breaking tomatoes up with side of spoon. Return sausage to skillet. Reduce heat to low; cover and simmer 10 minutes. Remove from heat; cover to keep warm.

3. Meanwhile, prepare polenta: Into 3-quart saucepan, pour milk; with wire whisk, gradually beat in cornmeal until smooth. In 2-quart saucepan, heat water and broth to boiling over high heat. Whisk hot broth mixture into cornmeal mixture. Heat to boiling over medium-high heat, and cook polenta, stirring constantly until thick, about 5 minutes. Stir in Parmesan. Serve polenta topped with sausage mixture and sprinkle parsley on top. Makes 6 main-dish servings.

Each serving: About 520 calories, 24 g protein, 53 g carbohydrate, 22 g total fat (7 g saturated), 63 mg cholesterol, 1,270 mg sodium.

FARINA

Farina and Cheese Custard

Prep: 10 minutes
Bake: 25 minutes

2 cups milk
1 tablespoon margarine or butter
½ teaspoon salt
⅛ teaspoon ground black pepper
¼ teaspoon dry mustard
¼ cup quick-cooking farina
3 large eggs
4 ounces Monterey Jack cheese, shredded (about 1 cup)

1. Preheat oven to 350°F. Grease six 6-ounce custard cups.

2. In nonstick 2-quart saucepan, heat milk, margarine, salt, pepper, and dry mustard to boiling over medium-high heat. Gradually sprinkle in farina; heat to boiling, stirring constantly. Reduce heat to medium-low and cook, stirring constantly, until mixture thickens, about 2 to 3 minutes. Remove from heat.

3. In medium bowl, with wire whisk, beat eggs until blended. Beating eggs rapidly, gradually beat in hot farina mixture, then stir in cheese.

4. Pour farina mixture into prepared custard cups; place cups in 13" by 9" baking pan. Fill pan with *boiling water* to come halfway up side of cups. Bake custards until knife inserted in center comes out clean, about 25 minutes. Serve warm in custard cups. Makes 6 accompaniment servings.

Each serving: About 200 calories, 11 g protein, 10 g carbohydrate, 13 g total fat (6 g saturated), 134 mg cholesterol, 390 mg sodium.

KASHA

Kasha with Mushrooms

Prep: 20 minutes
Cook: 20 minutes

3 tablespoons margarine or butter
4 ounces mushrooms, trimmed and sliced
1 small red pepper, chopped
1 small onion, finely chopped
1 large egg
1 cup medium-grain kasha
2 cups chicken broth, boiling
¼ teaspoon salt

1. In 10-inch skillet, melt 2 tablespoons margarine over medium heat. Add mushrooms, red pepper, and onion and cook, stirring frequently, until tender, about 5 minutes. With slotted spoon, transfer vegetables to bowl.

2. Meanwhile, in small bowl, beat egg slightly. Add kasha and stir until grains are well coated.

3. In same skillet, melt remaining 1 tablespoon margarine. Add kasha mixture and cook, stirring constantly, until grains become separate and dry. Stir in vegetables and any juice in bowl, boiling broth, and salt; heat to boiling over high heat. Reduce heat to low; cover and simmer until kasha is tender, 10 to 12 minutes. Serve hot. Makes 8 accompaniment servings.

Each serving: About 140 calories, 5 g protein, 18 g carbohydrate, 6 g total fat (1 g saturated), 27 mg cholesterol, 335 mg sodium.

BULGUR

Bulgur Pilaf

Prep: 2 minutes
Cook: 10 to 15 minutes

1 can (14½ ounces) chicken broth
¼ cup water
¼ teaspoon dried thyme
Pinch ground nutmeg
1 cup bulgur

In 2-quart saucepan, heat broth, water, thyme, and nut-meg to boiling over high heat. Stir in bulgur; reduce heat to medium-low. Cover and simmer until liquid is absorbed, and bulgur is tender, 10 to 15 minutes. Serve hot. Makes 4 accompaniment servings.

Each serving: About 135 calories, 6 g protein, 27 g carbohydrate, 1 g total fat (0 g saturated), 0 mg cholesterol, 335 mg sodium.

Bulgur with Dried Cranberries

Prep: 5 minutes
Cook: 10 to 15 minutes

1 can (14½ ounces) reduced-sodium chicken broth
1 cup bulgur
⅓ cup dried cranberries
1 teaspoon freshly grated lemon peel
¼ teaspoon salt
⅛ teaspoon coarsely ground black pepper

In 2-quart saucepan, stir together broth, bulgur, cranberries, lemon peel, salt, and pepper; heat to boiling over high heat. Reduce heat to low; cover and simmer until liquid has been absorbed and bulgur is plump and tender, 10 to 15 minutes. Makes about 3 cups or 4 accompaniment servings.

Each serving: About 160 calories, 6 g protein, 35 g carbohydrate, 1 g total fat (0 g saturated), 0 mg cholesterol, 420 mg sodium.

Basil Tabbouleh

Prep: 45 minutes plus standing

¾ cup bulgur
¾ cup boiling water
¼ cup extravirgin olive oil
¼ cup fresh lemon juice
1 pound ripe tomatoes (2 medium), halved, seeds removed, and coarsely chopped
½ English (seedless) cucumber, unpeeled and coarsely chopped
1 medium red onion, minced

1 cup loosely packed fresh flat-leaf parsley leaves, chopped
1 cup loosely packed fresh mint leaves, chopped
¼ cup loosely packed fresh basil leaves, chopped
1 teaspoon salt
⅛ teaspoon ground red pepper (cayenne)
¼ teaspoon ground allspice

1. In large bowl, combine bulgur and water, stirring to mix. Let stand until water has been absorbed, about 30 minutes.

2. When bulgur is ready, stir in oil, lemon juice, tomatoes, cucumber, onion, parsley, mint, basil, salt, ground red pepper, and allspice. Cover and refrigerate if not serving right away. Makes about 5¼ cups or 6 accompaniment servings.

Each serving: About 170 calories, 3 g protein, 20 g carbohydrate, 10 g total fat (1 g saturated), 0 mg cholesterol, 370 mg sodium.

Vegetables

~~

Individual Vegetables
Vegetable Combinations

∿Vegetables

Vegetables are a good source of vitamins and minerals; many are high in fiber and most are low in calories. To preserve flavor and nutrients, cook vegetables as little as possible. For boiling, use the minimum amount of water, or steam or stir-fry them. Salad greens, sautéed just until wilted, can also be served as a vegetable.

∿Quick Guide to Steaming Vegetables

Steaming is an easy, low-calorie way to prepare many vegetables. Steamed vegetables retain their color and nutrients—and they taste fantastic. To begin, fill a steamer with ¾ to 1 inch of water. Insert the steamer basket or a trivet and add the vegetables. Over high heat, heat the water to boiling. Reduce the heat to medium-low; cover the steamer and cook for the time indicated below, or until tender. After cooking, season the vegetables as desired with lemon juice, margarine or butter, salt, and pepper.

Vegetable		Time
Artichokes	2 medium, whole	40
Aspargus	1 pound, whole	10
Beans (green and wax)	1 pound, whole	15
Beets	3 medium, sliced	20

Broccoli	1 bunch, spears	12
Brussels sprouts	1 container (10 ounces), whole	15
Cabbage	1 small head, cut in quarters	40
Carrots	1 pound, whole	15
	1 pound sliced	8
Cauliflower	1 medium head, separated into flowerets	15
Celery	1 small bunch, sliced	20
Corn on the cob	2 ears	5
Kohlrabi	2 medium, sliced	25
Onions (white)	½ pound, small	12
Peas (greens)	1 pound, shelled	10
Potatoes	4 small, whole and unpeeled	30
Rutabaga	1 medium, diced	40
Spinach	1 bag (10 ounces)	5
Squash (acorn, butternut, and spaghetti)	1 medium, cut in half and seeded	40
(zucchini and yellow straight-neck)	2 medium-sized, sliced	5
Turnips	2 medium, sliced	15

∾Individual Vegetables

ARTICHOKES

SEASON: All year. Supplies are best in March, April, and May.

LOOK FOR: Compact, plump artichokes that are heavy in relation to their size and have thick, tightly closed, blemish-free green leaves. Size is not an indication of quality. Avoid overmature artichokes with hard-tipped, spreading leaves.

TO STORE: Refrigerate artichokes; use within three days.

TO PREPARE: Rinse the artichokes. With a sharp knife, cut off the stems and about 1 inch straight across the top. With kitchen shears, trim the thorny tips of the leaves. Pull off any loose leaves from around the bottoms.

TO COOK: In a kettle, heat 1 inch of water to boiling over high heat. Place the artichokes on their stem ends; add a few lemon slices, if you like, and heat to boiling. Reduce heat to low; cover and simmer the artichokes until a leaf can be pulled off easily, about 30 minutes.

TO EAT: With your fingers, pluck off the leaves one by one, starting at the bottom. Dip the base of each leaf (the lighter-colored end) in melted butter or some other dip, then pull the leaf through your teeth, scraping off the pulp. Discard the leaves in a pile on your plate. Then cut out and discard the fuzzy center (the choke) of the artichoke; cut the solid heart into chunks and dip them in melted butter also.

SUGGESTED SAUCES: Basic Vinaigrette (see page 770).

Artichokes with Dill Sauce

Prep: 20 minutes
Cook: 45 minutes

4 medium artichokes
2 tablespoons olive oil
1 medium onion, finely chopped
½ cup fresh lemon juice (about 3 medium lemons)
¼ cup all-purpose flour
¼ cup chopped fresh dill
½ cup water
½ teaspoon salt

1. Remove tough outer leaves from artichokes. With serrated knife, cut about 1 inch across top of each artichoke; remove and discard stems. Trim thorny tops of leaves with kitchen shears. Cut each artichoke lengthwise in half; set artichokes aside.

2. In 8-quart Dutch oven or saucepot, heat oil over medium heat until hot. Add onion and cook until tender, about 5 minutes.

3. Meanwhile, in small bowl, stir lemon juice, flour, dill, and water until blended. When onion is tender, reduce heat to low and stir lemon-juice mixture into Dutch oven. Add artichokes and heat to boiling over high heat. Reduce heat to low; cover and simmer 20 minutes. Turn artichokes over. Cover and simmer until knife inserted in center of artichoke heart goes through easily, about 25 minutes longer.

4. To serve, transfer artichokes to deep platter. Stir salt into sauce and pour sauce over artichokes. Serve artichokes hot or cool slightly to serve warm. Makes 8 accompaniment servings.

Each serving: About 85 calories, 3 g protein, 12 g carbohydrate, 4 g total fat (1 g saturated), 0 mg cholesterol, 190 mg sodium.

ASPARAGUS

SEASON: Supplies are best from March through June.

LOOK FOR: Straight stalks with closed, compact tips and a bright green color along almost the entire length.

TO STORE: Trim ends and stand spears upright, loosely covered, in a tall glass with 1 inch of water in the bottom.

TO PREPARE: Hold the base of each asparagus stalk firmly and bend the stalk; the end will break off at the spot where the stalk becomes too tough to eat. Discard the tough ends; trim the scales if the stalks are gritty. Leave stalks whole, or cut into 1- to 2-inch-long pieces, or slice diagonally, if desired.

TO COOK: In a large skillet, heat ½ inch of water to boiling over high heat. Add asparagus; heat to boiling. Reduce heat to medium-low and cook the asparagus until tender-crisp, 3 to 5 minutes.

TO SERVE: Serve asparagus hot or cold, with or without a sauce. Or use asparagus in recipes for soup, main dishes, salads, and appetizers.

SUGGESTED SAUCE: Basic Vinaigrette (see page 770).

Stir-fried Asparagus

Prep: 10 minutes
Cook: 7 minutes

1 ½ pounds asparagus
2 tablespoons olive or vegetable oil
½ teaspoon salt

Prepare asparagus as directed in general information for asparagus. Cut asparagus diagonally into 3-inch-long pieces. In 3-quart saucepan or 12-inch skillet, heat oil over high heat until very hot. Add asparagus and cook, stirring frequently (stir-frying), until evenly coated with oil. Sprinkle with salt; continue stir-frying asparagus until tender-crisp, about 3 minutes longer. Makes 6 accompaniment servings.

Each serving: About 60 calories, 2 g protein, 2 g carbohydrate, 5 g total fat (1 g saturated), 0 mg cholesterol, 205 mg sodium.

Asparagus Gratin

Prep: 40 minutes
Broil: 3 to 5 minutes

1 large shallot, finely chopped
2 tablespoons plus 2 teaspoons olive oil
2 slices white bread
2 pounds asparagus, trimmed
¾ teaspoon salt
¼ cup freshly grated Parmesan cheese
1 tablespoon chopped fresh parsley
1 tablespoon fresh lemon juice
Lemon wedges (optional)

1. Preheat oven to 400°F. In 1-quart saucepan, cook shallot in 2 tablespoons oil over medium-low heat until golden, about 6 minutes. Remove saucepan from heat; cool slightly.

2. Tear bread into small crumbs. Spread crumbs on jelly-roll pan and bake until golden, 3 to 6 minutes.

3. In 12-inch skillet, heat *1 inch water* to boiling over high heat. Add asparagus and ½ teaspoon salt; heat to boiling. Reduce heat to medium-low and simmer, uncovered, until asparagus spears are tender, 5 to 10 minutes; drain. Place asparagus in shallow, broiler-safe dish; drizzle with remaining 2 teaspoons oil.

4. Preheat broiler if manufacturer suggests. In medium bowl, toss bread crumbs with Parmesan, parsley, lemon juice, shallot mixture, and remaining ¼ teaspoon salt. Sprinkle bread-crumb mixture over asparagus. Place dish in broiler 5 inches from heat source; broil until lightly browned, about 3 minutes. Transfer to platter and serve with lemon wedges, if you like. Makes 6 accompaniment servings.

Each serving: About 120 calories, 5 g protein, 8 g carbohydrate, 8 g total fat (2 g saturated), 4 mg cholesterol, 300 mg sodium.

AVOCADOS

ALSO CALLED: Alligator pears.

SEASON: All year.

LOOK FOR: Smooth green, or pebbly, purplish-black pear- or egg-shaped avocados, depending on variety. Firm avocados should ripen at room temperature in three to five days. They are ripe when they yield to gentle pressure on the skin. Avoid dark spots or broken skin. Irregular light brown skin markings do not affect quality.

TO STORE: Refrigerate avocados after they ripen and use them within three to five days.

TO PREPARE: Cut each avocado in half lengthwise to the seed and twist the halves apart. To remove the seed, strike it with a sharp knife so the blade lodges in the seed; twist gently to lift out the seed. Peel and slice or cut up, depending on use. To prevent browning if avocados are not to be eaten immediately, sprinkle them with lemon juice.

Corn and Avocado Salad

Prep: 10 minutes

1 package (10 ounces) frozen whole-kernel corn, thawed
1 medium ripe tomato, cut into ½-inch pieces
2 tablespoons chopped fresh cilantro
2 tablespoons fresh lime juice
1 tablespoon olive oil
¼ teaspoon salt
¼ teaspoon sugar
1 medium avocado
Lettuce leaves (optional)

In medium bowl, combine corn, tomato, cilantro, lime juice, oil, salt, and sugar. Just before serving, cut avocado in half lengthwise; remove seed and peel. Cut avocado into ½-inch pieces; stir into corn mixture. Serve on lettuce leaves, if you like. Makes 4 accompaniment servings.

Each serving: About 175 calories, 3 g protein, 20 g carbohydrate, 11 g total fat (2 g saturated), 0 mg cholesterol, 145 mg sodium.

GREEN AND WAX BEANS

SEASON: All year. The supply is best in June.

LOOK FOR: Crisp but tender beans without scars. Well-shaped pods with small seeds are the most desirable; the length is unimportant.

TO STORE: Refrigerate green and wax beans; use within two to five days.

TO PREPARE: Rinse beans with cold running water. Snap off end. Leave whole, or snap or cut into bite-size pieces; for French-style beans, pull them through a bean slicer.

TO COOK: In a saucepan, heat 1 inch of water to boiling over high heat. Add beans without crowding; heat to boiling. Reduce heat to low; cover and simmer whole or cut-up beans 5 to 10 minutes and French-style beans 5 minutes, or until tender-crisp.

Green Beans with Oregon Hazelnuts

Prep: 20 minutes
Cook: 10 minutes

⅔ cup hazelnuts (filberts)
1½ teaspoons salt
2 pounds green beans, trimmed
4 tablespoons margarine or butter
1 teaspoon grated lemon peel
1 teaspoon ground black pepper

1. Preheat oven to 375°F. Place hazelnuts in 9" by 9" metal baking pan. Bake until lightly toasted, 10 to 15 minutes. To remove skins, wrap hot hazelnuts in a clean, dry dishcloth and gently rub back and forth until skins come off. Discard skins; finely chop nuts.

2. Meanwhile, in 12-inch skillet, heat *1 inch water* and 1 teaspoon salt to boiling over high heat. Add green beans; heat to boiling. Reduce heat to low and simmer, uncovered, until beans are tender-crisp, 5 to 10 minutes; drain. Wipe skillet dry.

3. In same skillet, melt margarine over medium heat. Add hazelnuts and cook, stirring until butter just begins to brown, about 3 minutes. Add green beans, lemon peel, pepper, and remaining ½ teaspoon salt and cook, stirring often, until hot, about 5 minutes. Makes 8 accompaniment servings.

Each serving: About 150 calories, 3 g protein, 9 g carbohydrate, 13 g total fat (2 g saturated), 0 mg cholesterol, 250 mg sodium.

Roasted Green Beans in Dill Vinaigrette

Prep: 20 minutes
Roast: 20 to 30 minutes

2 pounds green beans or wax beans (or a combination), trimmed
3 tablespoons olive oil
¾ teaspoon salt
2 tablespoons white wine vinegar
2 tablespoons Dijon mustard
1 ½ teaspoons sugar
½ teaspoon coarsely ground black pepper
2 tablespoons chopped fresh dill

1. Preheat oven to 450°F. In large roasting pan (17" by 11½"), toss green beans with 1 tablespoon oil and ½ teaspoon salt. Roast beans, until tender and slightly browned, stirring twice, 20 to 30 minutes.

2. Meanwhile, prepare vinaigrette: In small bowl, with wire whisk, mix vinegar, mustard, sugar, pepper, and remaining ¼ teaspoon salt. While whisking, slowly add remaining 2 tablespoons oil; stir in dill.

3. When beans are done, in large bowl, toss beans with vinaigrette. Makes 8 accompaniment servings.

Each serving: About 80 calories, 2 g protein, 8 g carbohydrate, 5 g total fat (1 g saturated), 0 mg cholesterol, 230 mg sodium.

LIMA BEANS

SEASON: Supplies are best in August and September.

LOOK FOR: Well-filled, tender green pods; avoid dried, spotty, or yellowing ones. Shelled beans should be plump, with green to greenish-white skins.

TO STORE: Refrigerate lima beans; use within one or two days.

TO PREPARE: Snap off one end of each pod and open

the pod to remove the beans. Or, with a knife, cut off a thin strip from the inner edge of the pod and push the beans out.

TO COOK: In a saucepan, heat 1 inch of water to boiling over high heat. Add beans; heat to boiling. Reduce heat to low; cover and simmer the beans until they are tender, about 20 minutes.

Sautéed Lima Beans with Bacon

Prep: 30 minutes for fresh lima beans; 5 minutes for frozen
Cook: 25 minutes for fresh lima beans; 15 minutes for frozen

1½ pounds lima beans, shelled, or 1 package (10 ounces) frozen baby lima beans
4 slices bacon, diced
2 medium stalks celery, sliced
¼ teaspoon salt
⅛ teaspoon pepper
¾ cup water

1. If using fresh lima beans, prepare as directed in general information for lima beans.
2. In 10-inch skillet, cook bacon over medium-low heat until browned. With slotted spoon, transfer bacon to paper towels to drain. Discard all but 2 tablespoons bacon drippings from skillet.
3. To drippings remaining in skillet, add celery, fresh or frozen lima beans, salt, and pepper, separating frozen lima beans, if using, with fork; cook, over medium heat, stirring frequently, until vegetables are tender, about 10 minutes.
4. Add water; heat to boiling over high heat. Reduce heat to low; simmer 5 minutes. Spoon bean mixture into small warm bowl; sprinkle with diced bacon. Makes 4 accompaniment servings.

Each serving: About 190 calories, 8 g protein, 19 g carbohydrate, 10 g total fat (4 g saturated), 11 mg cholesterol, 300 mg sodium.

BEAN SPROUTS

SEASON: All year.
LOOK FOR: Fresh, long, crisp ivory-colored sprouts.
TO STORE: Place sprouts in a container with enough water to cover and refrigerate; change the water every day. Use within three days.
TO PREPARE: Rinse the sprouts with cold running water and discard loose hulls. If you like, remove the roots of bean sprouts.
TO SERVE: Use in tossed green salads or sandwiches. Sauté in oil to serve as a cooked vegetable.

BEETS

SEASON: All year. Supplies are best from March through August.
LOOK FOR: Smooth, rich red or golden beets of uniform size that have no ridges or blemishes; soft spots indicate decay. Green tops should be fresh.
TO STORE: Remove the tops; refrigerate tops and beets. Use the beets within a week, preferably less. Use the tops as soon as possible.
TO PREPARE: Cut off the tops; scrub under cold running water with a soft brush.
TO COOK: In a saucepan, heat beets and enough water to cover them to boiling over high heat. Reduce heat to low; cover and simmer whole beets until they are tender, 30 to 60 minutes (the cooking time depends on the maturity as well as the size of the beets). Drain beets and run cold water over them; when they are cool enough to handle, remove the skins. Or peel beets before cooking, and slice or dice them. Heat to boiling; cover and cook until tender, 15 to 20 minutes.

Orange-Glazed Beets

Prep: 20 minutes
Cook: 35 minutes

1½ pounds beets with tops
1 medium orange
½ cup orange marmalade
1½ teaspoons cornstarch
1½ teaspoons prepared mustard
⅛ teaspoon salt

1. Remove stems and leaves from beets. Wash beets and leaves well with cold running water; discard stems. If beets are large, cut into halves or quarters. Wrap leaves with plastic wrap and refrigerate for garnish.

2. In 3-quart saucepan, heat beets and *enough water to cover* to boiling over high heat. Reduce heat to low; cover and simmer until tender, about 30 minutes. Drain and peel.

3. Cut orange in half. From one half, grate 1½ teaspoons peel and squeeze ¼ cup juice. Slice remaining orange half.

4. In same saucepan, mix marmalade, cornstarch, mustard, salt, orange juice, and ½ teaspoon orange peel. Add beets and heat to boiling over medium heat; boil 1 minute, stirring.

5. Arrange orange slices and reserved leaves on platter. Spoon beets and sauce onto platter. Sprinkle with remaining teaspoon orange peel. Makes 6 accompaniment servings.

Each serving: About 105 calories, 1 g protein, 26 g carbohydrate, 0 g total fat, 0 mg cholesterol, 120 mg sodium.

Roasted Beets and Red Onions

Prep: 20 minutes
Roast: 1 hour 30 minutes

6 medium beets with tops
    (about 2 pounds, including
    tops)
3 small red onions (about
    1 pound)
2 tablespoons extravirgin olive
    oil
⅓ cup chicken broth

¼ cup balsamic vinegar
1 teaspoon dark brown sugar
1 teaspoon fresh thyme
¼ teaspoon salt
¼ teapoon coarsely ground
    black pepper
Minced fresh parsley

1. Trim tops from beets, leaving about 1 inch of stems attached. Scrub beets well with cold running water.
2. Preheat oven to 400°F. Place beets and unpeeled red onions in 10-inch skillet with oven-safe handle (if skillet is not oven-safe, wrap handle of skillet with double layer of foil) or in 13" by 9" metal baking pan; drizzle with oil. Roast vegetables, shaking skillet occasionally, until onions are soft to the touch and beets are fork-tender, at least 1 hour and 30 minutes, depending on size of vegetables. (Beets may take longer than onions to roast; remove onions as they are done and continue roasting beets.)
3. Transfer vegetables to plate; cool until easy to handle. Meanwhile, to same skillet, add broth, vinegar, brown sugar, and thyme; heat to boiling over high heat. Boil, stirring and scraping bottom of skillet, until liquid is dark brown and syrupy and reduced to about ¼ cup, 5 to 7 minutes; stir in salt and pepper. Remove skillet from heat
4. Peel beets and onions. Slice beets into julienne strips and onions into thin rings; place in bowl. Pour reduced liquid over vegetables. Serve at room temperature; garnish with parsley. Makes about 4 cups or 6 accompaniment servings.

Each serving: About 120 calories, 2 g protein, 18 g carbohydrate, 5 g total fat (1 g saturated), 0 mg cholesterol, 195 mg sodium.

Sautéed Beet Greens

Prep: 10 minutes
Cook: 4 minutes

6 cups packed, coarsely cut tender beet greens
2 tablespoons olive oil
½ teaspoon cider vinegar (optional)
Salt

1. Wash beet greens well with cold running water. Trim any tough stems.

2. In 4-quart saucepan, heat oil over high heat until hot. Add beet greens and cook, stirring frequently, until tender, about 3 minutes. Add vinegar; stir in salt to taste. Makes 2 accompaniment servings.

Each serving: About 140 calories, 2 g protein, 5 g carbohydrate, 14 g total fat (2 g saturated), 0 mg cholesterol, 375 mg sodium.

BROCCOLI

SEASON: All year. Supplies are lowest in August.

LOOK FOR: Tender, firm stalks and tightly closed dark green flowerets.

TO STORE: Refrigerate broccoli; use within two days.

TO PREPARE: Remove the large leaves and trim the end of the broccoli stalk if it is tough or woody. Because stalks cook more slowly than the buds, split them lengthwise two or three times. Rinse the broccoli well with cold running water.

TO COOK: In a skillet, heat 1 inch of water to boiling over high heat. Add broccoli; heat to boiling. Reduce heat to low; cover and simmer broccoli until tender-crisp, about 5 minutes.

Stir-Fried Broccoli

Prep: 10 minutes
Cook: 9 minutes

3 tablespoons olive oil
1 bunch broccoli, cut into 2" by ½" pieces
½ teaspoon salt
¼ teaspoon sugar
¼ cup water

1. In 5-quart Dutch oven, heat oil over high heat until very hot. Add broccoli and cook, stirring frequently (stir-frying), until evenly coated with oil.

2. Add salt, sugar, and water. Reduce heat to medium; cover and cook 2 minutes. Uncover and stir-fry until tender-crisp, about 5 minutes. Makes 6 accompaniment servings.

Each serving: About 75 calories, 2 g protein, 2 g carbohydrate, 7 g total fat (1 g saturated), 0 mg cholesterol, 210 mg sodium.

BROCCOLI RABE

SEASON: All year.

LOOK FOR: Leaves with thin green stalks, about 8 inches long, and small bud clusters. Avoid stalks with yellowish leaves.

TO STORE: Refrigerate broccoli rabe; use within two days.

TO PREPARE: Cut off the tough root ends; discard the tough outer leaves. Wash in several changes of cold water and drain.

TO COOK: In a large skillet, heat *1 inch water* to boiling over high heat. Add broccoli rabe; heat to boiling. Reduce heat to low; cook the broccoli rabe until tender-crisp, about 3 minutes. Drain.

TO SERVE: Serve hot with margarine or butter. Or, serve cold with Basic Vinaigrette (see page 770).

BRUSSELS SPROUTS

SEASON: Supplies are best from October to February.

LOOK FOR: Firm, fresh, bright green (not yellow) sprouts with tight-fitting outer leaves that are free from black spots. Puffy or soft sprouts are usually of poor quality.

TO STORE: Refrigerate Brussels sprouts; use within two days.

TO PREPARE: Trim off any yellow leaves and the stem; cut an "X" in the stem end to speed cooking. Rinse the Brussels sprouts with cold running water.

TO COOK: In a saucepan, heat 1 inch of water to boiling over high heat. Add Brussels sprouts; heat to boiling. Reduce heat to low; cover and simmer the Brussels sprouts until they are tender-crisp, about 10 minutes.

Brussels Sprouts with Bacon

Prep: 15 minutes
Cook: 15 minutes

3 containers (10 ounces each) Brussels sprouts, trimmed
6 slices bacon
1 tablespoon olive oil
2 garlic cloves, crushed with garlic press
½ teaspoon salt
¼ teaspoon coarsely ground black pepper
¼ cup pine nuts (pignoli), toasted

1. In 4-quart saucepan, heat 1 inch water to boiling over high heat. Add Brussels sprouts; heat to boiling. Reduce heat to low; cover and simmer until tender-crisp, about 5 minutes. Drain. (If you like, Brussels sprouts can be cooked a day ahead. After cooking, rinse with cold running water to stop the cooking, then cover and refrigerate until ready to stir-fry in step 3.)

2. In nonstick 12-inch skillet, cook bacon over medium-low heat until browned. With slotted spoon, transfer bacon to paper towels to drain; crumble. Discard all but 1 tablespoon bacon fat from skillet.

3. Heat bacon fat and oil over medium-high heat. Add Brussels sprouts, garlic, salt, and pepper; cook, stirring frequently, until Brussels sprouts are browned, about 5 minutes. Top with pine nuts and crumbled bacon. Makes 8 accompaniment servings.

Each serving: About 120 calories, 6 g protein, 10 g carbohydrate, 8 g total fat (2 g saturated), 6 mg cholesterol, 235 mg sodium.

CHINESE CABBAGE

ALSO CALLED: "Nappa" cabbage.
SEASON: All year.
LOOK FOR: Crisp, fresh-looking heads that are free from blemishes.
TO STORE: Refrigerate Chinese cabbage; use within three days.
TO PREPARE: Cut bottom from stalk. Separate into ribs; rinse and slice.

Stir-Fried Chinese Cabbage

Prep: 10 minutes
Cook: 10 minutes

1 medium head Chinese cabbage (2½ pounds)
3 tablespoons vegetable oil
1 teaspoon salt or 2 tablespoons soy sauce
½ teaspoon sugar

1. Trim both ends of cabbage. With sharp knife, cut cabbage crosswise into 1½-inch pieces; cut section with core lengthwise into thin wedges.

2. In 5-quart Dutch oven, heat oil over high heat until very hot. Add cabbage, and cook, stirring frequently (stir-frying), until evenly coated with oil. Sprinkle cabbage with salt and sugar. Reduce heat to medium; continue stir-frying until cabbage is tender-crisp, 5 to 8 minutes longer. Makes 4 accompaniment servings.

Each serving: About 120 calories, 3 g protein, 3 g carbohydrate, 11 g total fat (1 g saturated), 0 mg cholesterol, 610 mg sodium.

GREEN AND RED CABBAGE

SEASON: All year.

LOOK FOR: Firm heads with fresh, crisp-looking leaves. Green cabbage is often trimmed of its outer leaves and lacks bright green color, but it is satisfactory if not wilted or discolored. Savoy cabbage has finely crumpled green leaves and loosely formed heads; red varieties have a reddish-purple color.

TO STORE: Refrigerate cabbage; use within one week.

TO PREPARE: Discard any tough outer leaves; cut the head into wedges, then cut the core from each wedge, leaving just enough to retain the shape of the wedge. To slice (shred) cabbage, remove the core from the head and separate the leaves; cut out and discard the tough ribs Thinly slice the leaves.

TO COOK: For wedges, in a saucepot, heat 1 inch of water to boiling over high heat. Add cabbage; heat to boiling. Reduce heat to low; cover and simmer the wedges 10 to 15 minutes. For coarsely sliced cabbage, sauté the cabbage in a skillet, in a little margarine, butter, or vegetable oil, over medium heat until tender-crisp. Add salt to taste.

Southern-Style Cabbage

Prep: 25 minutes
Cook: 35 minutes

4 slices bacon, cut into 1-inch pieces
1 small head green cabbage (about 2 pounds), coarsely sliced
1 small onion, thinly sliced
½ teaspoon salt
½ cup water

In 5-quart Dutch oven or 12-inch skillet, cook bacon over medium heat, until browned. Add cabbage, onion, and salt; stir to coat cabbage evenly with bacon fat. Add water and reduce heat to medium-low; cover and cook, stirring occasionally, until cabbage is very tender and lightly browned, about 30 minutes. Makes 6 accompaniment servings.

Each serving: About 175 calories, 4 g protein, 8 g carbohydrate, 15 g total fat (5 g saturated), 17 mg cholesterol, 400 mg sodium.

∽∾

When cooking red cabbage in water, add a little vinegar or lemon juice to the water. The acid ingredient will help the cabbage retain its bright red color.

Sautéed Cabbage with Peas

Prep: 10 minutes
Cook: About 25 minutes

2 tablespoons margarine or butter
1 medium onion, thinly sliced
1 small head savoy cabbage (about 2 pounds), cored and cut into
    ½-inch-thick slices, with tough ribs discarded
¾ teaspoon salt
½ teaspoon sugar
¼ teaspoon coarsely ground black pepper
½ cup chicken broth
1 package (10 ounces) frozen baby peas
¼ cup chopped fresh dill

1. In 12-inch skillet, melt margarine over medium heat. Add onion and cook, stirring often, until tender and golden, about 8 minutes.

2. Add cabbage, salt, sugar, and pepper, and cook, stirring, until cabbage is tender-crisp, about 5 minutes. Stir in broth, and cook until cabbage is tender, about 10 minutes.

3. Add frozen peas and dill. Cook over medium heat, stirring frequently, until heated through, about 5 minutes. Makes about 6 cups or 8 accompaniment servings.

Each serving: About 90 calories, 4 g protein, 13 g carbohydrate, 3 g total fat (1 g saturated), 0 mg cholesterol, 345 mg sodium.

Sweet and Sour Cabbage

Prep: 20 minutes
Cook: 15 minutes

2 tablespoons margarine or butter
2 Granny Smith apples (about 8 ounces each), peeled, cored, and chopped
1 medium onion, finely chopped
1 medium head red cabbage (2 pounds), cut into quarters, cored, and coarsely chopped
3 tablespoons cider vinegar
1 teaspoon sugar
1 teaspoon salt
¼ teaspoon coarsely ground black pepper

1. In deep 12-inch skillet or 5-quart Dutch oven, melt margarine over medium heat. Add apples and onion, and cook, stirring occasionally, until soft, about 5 minutes.

2. Stir in cabbage, vinegar, sugar, salt, and pepper. Cook, stirring occasionally, until cabbage is tender but still slightly crunchy, about 12 minutes. Makes about 8 cups or 8 accompaniment servings.

Each serving: About 75 calories, 1 g protein, 12 g carbohydrate, 3 g total fat (1 g saturated), 0 mg cholesterol, 315 mg sodium.

CARDOON

ALSO CALLED: Cardoni.
SEASON: The fall and winter months.
LOOK FOR: Large, thick stalks with prickly leaves.
TO STORE: Refrigerate cardoon; use within five days
TO PREPARE: Separate the stalks and discard the stringy outer ones. Rinse the remaining stalks under cold running water; cut them in pieces.
TO COOK: In a medium saucepan, heat 1 inch of water to boiling over high heat. Add cardoon; heat to boiling. Reduce heat to low; cover and simmer cardoon until it is fork-tender, 20 minutes.

TO SERVE: Serve hot as a cooked vegetable, with margarine or butter. Or chill and serve with Basic Vinaigrette (see page 770).

Cardoon in Chive Sauce

Prep: 30 minutes
Cook: 30 minutes

1 bunch cardoon (about 3 pounds)
2 tablespoons margarine or butter
1 tablespoon all-purpose flour
¾ cup chicken broth
½ teaspoon salt
1 teaspoon chopped fresh chives
1 tablespoon chopped fresh parsley

1. Trim root and leaf ends of cardoon. Separate stalks and discard any tough outer stalks and all inner leafy stalks. With vegetable peeler, peel remaining stalks to remove strings. Rinse stalks with cold running water to remove all traces of sand. Cut each stalk crosswise into 1-inch pieces. Cut root-end pieces lengthwise in half if they are large.

2. In 4-quart saucepan, heat *1 inch water* to boiling. Add cardoon; heat to boiling. Reduce heat to low; cover and simmer until fork-tender, 20 minutes. Drain in colander.

3. In same saucepan, melt margarine over low heat. Add flour and stir until blended. Gradually stir in chicken broth and salt; cook, stirring constantly, until mixture thickens. Stir in cardoon, chives, and parsley. Heat through. Makes 8 accompaniment servings.

Each serving: About 50 calories, 1 g protein, 5 g carbohydrate, 3 g total fat (1 g saturated), 0 mg cholesterol, 255 mg sodium.

CARROTS

SEASON: All year.
LOOK FOR: Firm, well-formed, bright-colored carrots. Avoid flabby or shriveled carrots.

TO STORE: Remove and discard any tops. Refrigerate carrots; use within one to two weeks.

TO PREPARE: Scrub, using stiff vegetable brush, and rinse with cold running water, or scrape. Leave carrots whole; or dice, slice, or shred.

TO COOK: In a saucepan, heat 1 inch of water to boiling over high heat. Add carrots; heat to boiling. Reduce heat to low; cover and simmer whole carrots about 20 minutes, cut-up carrots 10 to 20 minutes, or until tender-crisp.

TO SERVE: Use uncooked in salads or for snacks; serve cooked with or without seasonings. Use in recipes for soups, stews, and casseroles.

Apricot-Ginger Carrots

Prep: 10 minutes
Cook: 20 minutes

2 bags (1 pound each) peeled baby carrots
2 tablespoons margarine or butter
2 green onions, minced
1 large garlic clove, minced
1 tablespoon minced, peeled fresh ginger
⅓ cup apricot jam
1 tablespoon balsamic vinegar
¼ teaspoon salt
Pinch ground red pepper (cayenne)

1. Place steamer basket in deep 12-inch skillet with *1 inch water*; heat to boiling over high heat. Add carrots and reduce heat to medium. Cover and cook just until carrots are tender, 10 to 12 minutes. Remove carrots and rinse with cold running water to stop cooking; drain well.

2. In 12-inch skillet, melt margarine over medium heat. Add green onions, garlic, and ginger, and cook, stirring often, until soft, about 3 minutes. Add apricot jam, vinegar, salt, and ground red pepper, and cook, stirring often, 3 to 4 minutes longer.

3. Add carrots to glaze in skillet, and cook over medium-high heat 5 minutes. Increase heat to high and cook, stirring occasionally, until carrots are well coated and heated through, 3 minutes. Makes about 6½ cups or 8 accompaniment servings.

Each serving: About 115 calories, 1 g protein, 22 g carbohydrate, 3 g total fat (1 g saturated), 0 mg cholesterol, 145 mg sodium.

CAULIFLOWER

SEASON: All year. Supplies are best from September through January.

LOOK FOR: Compact, creamy-white flowerets with a granular appearance. The leaves around the base should be fresh and green.

TO STORE: Refrigerate cauliflower; use within five days.

TO PREPARE: Remove the leaves and the core. Separate the head into flowerets or leave it whole. Rinse with cold running water.

TO COOK: In a saucepan, heat 1 inch of water to boiling over high heat. Add cauliflower; heat to boiling. Reduce heat to low; cover and simmer whole cauliflower 10 to 15 minutes, flowerets about 5 minutes, or until tender-crisp. Cauliflower can also be roasted; see Roasted Cauliflower with Onions and Rosemary (see page 578).

Cauliflower Polonaise

Prep: 22 minutes
Cook: 35 minutes

2 eggs
1 large head cauliflower (2½ pounds)
4 tablespoons margarine or butter
1 cup fresh bread crumbs (about 2 slices)
2 tablespoons chopped fresh parsley
2 tablespoons fresh lemon juice
½ teaspoon salt

1. Hard-cook eggs; drain, peel, and chop.

2. Meanwhile, remove leaves and core of cauliflower. In 5-quart saucepot, heat *1 inch water* to boiling over high heat. Add whole cauliflower; heat to boiling. Reduce heat to low; cover and simmer until tender, 10 to 15 minutes; drain. Place cauliflower on platter.

3. In small saucepan, melt margarine over medium heat. Add bread crumbs, and cook, stirring, until golden. Stir in chopped eggs, parsley, lemon juice, and salt.

4. To serve, sprinkle bread-crumb mixture over cauliflower. Makes 10 accompaniment servings.

Each serving: About 85 calories, 3 g protein, 6 g carbohydrate, 6 g total fat (1 g saturated), 42 mg cholesterol, 230 mg sodium.

Roasted Cauliflower with Onions and Rosemary

Prep: 20 minutes
Roast: 40 minutes

2 heads cauliflower (about 2 pounds each), separated into
    1-inch flowerets
2 medium red onions, peeled, each cut into 12 wedges
4 garlic cloves, crushed with side of chef's knife and peeled
2 tablespoons olive oil
1 tablespoon fresh rosemary, chopped
¾ teaspoon salt
¼ teaspoon coarsely ground black pepper
¼ cup fresh parsley leaves, chopped
Rosemary sprig

1. Preheat oven to 450°F. In large bowl, toss cauliflower,
red onions, garlic, olive oil, chopped rosemary, salt, and
pepper until evenly mixed. Divide mixture between two
15½" by 10½" jelly-roll pans. Roast vegetables on 2 oven
racks 40 minutes or until tender and browned, stirring occasionally and rotating pans between upper and lower racks
halfway through roasting time.

2. Transfer vegetables to platter. Sprinkle with parsley
to serve. Garnish with rosemary sprig. Makes about 8 cups
or 12 accompaniment servings.

*Each serving: About 55 calories, 2 g protein, 7 g carbohydrate,
3 g total fat (0 g saturated), 1 g fiber, 0 mg cholesterol, 160 mg
sodium.*

CELERIAC

ALSO CALLED: Celery root.
SEASON: October through April.
LOOK FOR: Firm, small celeriac (bulbs that are 4 inches
    or more in diameter are likely to be woody) without
    any sprouts on top of the bulb. Bulb roots should be
    clean.

TO STORE: Refrigerate celeriac; use within one week.

TO PREPARE: Scrub with a vegetable brush and rinse with cold running water. Cut off the roots; peel and slice the bulb.

TO COOK: In a medium saucepan, heat 1 inch of water to boiling over high heat. Add celeriac and a little lemon juice, and heat to boiling. Reduce the heat to low; cover and simmer the celeriac just until tender, 10 to 15 minutes. Drain.

TO SERVE: Serve raw in salads, cut into matchstick strips, or serve as a cooked vegetable.

Sautéed Celeriac with Green Pepper

Prep: 30 minutes
Cook: 15 minutes

3 medium celeriac (about 1¼ pounds)
1 small green pepper
2 tablespoons margarine or butter
¾ teaspoon salt

1. Peel celeriac; cut into matchstick strips. Cut green pepper into thin strips.

2. In 12-inch skillet, melt margarine over medium heat. Add celeriac, green pepper, and salt, and cook, stirring frequently, until celeriac is tender-crisp, 12 to 15 minutes. Makes 4 accompaniment servings.

Each serving: About 90 calories, 2 g protein, 9 g carbohydrate, 6 g total fat (1 g saturated), 0 mg cholesterol, 590 mg sodium.

CELERY

SEASON: All year.

LOOK FOR: Fresh, crisp, clean celery of medium length and size, pale green in color. Thin darker-green stalks may be stringy.

TO STORE: Refrigerate celery; use within one week.

TO PREPARE: Remove leaves (use in soups and stews); trim root end. Rinse with cold running water. Use outer stalks for cooking or cut up for salads; serve inner stalks raw.

TO COOK: In a saucepan, heat 1 inch water to boiling over high heat. Add cut up stalks; heat to boiling. Reduce heat to low; cover and simmer cut-up celery 3 to 4 minutes. Cook whole stalks in a skillet, until they are tender-crisp, 4 to 6 minutes.

TO SERVE: Serve uncooked celery for snacks or use in salads; use as a flavoring in casseroles and sauces. Serve celery as a cooked vegetable.

Braised Hearts of Celery

Prep: 20 minutes
Cook: 17 minutes

2 large bunches celery
1 medium onion, chopped
1½ cups chicken broth
3 tablespoons margarine or butter
¾ teaspoon dried oregano leaves
½ teaspoon salt
1 jar (2 ounces) diced pimientos, drained

1. Remove outer rows of celery stalks; trim root ends. Cut tops and leaves from celery 6 to 8 inches from root ends (save outer stalks, tops, and leaves to make soup another day). Cut each bunch of celery lengthwise into quarters.

2. In 12-inch skillet, heat celery, onion, and broth to boiling over high heat. Reduce heat to medium; cover and cook until celery is fork-tender, 15 minutes; drain. Stir in margarine, oregano, salt and pimientos. Makes 8 servings.

Each serving: About 70 calories, 2 g protein, 7 g carbohydrate, 5 g total fat (1 g saturated), 0 mg cholesterol, 360 mg sodium.

Crunchy Celery and Parsley Salad

Prep: 40 minutes

¼ cup olive oil
1 tablespoon white wine vinegar
1 teaspoon Dijon mustard
¼ teaspoon fennel seeds, crushed
¼ teaspoon salt
⅛ teaspoon coarsely ground black pepper
1 large shallot, minced (about ¼ cup)

1 garlic clove, minced
1 bunch fresh flat-leaf parsley leaves (about 3 cups loosely packed)
1 bunch fresh curly parsley leaves (about 3 cups loosely packed)
4 cups thinly sliced celery stalks with leaves
⅓ cup chopped fresh chives

1. In small bowl, with wire whisk, mix oil, vinegar, mustard, fennel seeds, salt, pepper, shallot, and garlic until blended.

2. In large salad bowl, toss parsley, celery, and chives with dressing. Makes 10 accompaniment servings.

Each serving: About 80 calories, 2 g protein, 6 g carbohydrate, 6 g total fat (1 g saturated), 0 mg cholesterol, 160 mg sodium.

CHAYOTE

ALSO CALLED: Mirliton, vegetable pear.

SEASON: All year.

LOOK FOR: A pear-shaped member of the squash family, with lengthwise furrows, about 3 to 6 inches long, with celery-green color. Choose firm ones.

TO STORE: Refrigerate chayote; use within one week.

TO PREPARE: Peel the skin, if you like. Cut the chayote in half and discard the seed. Use halves for baking or cut into smaller pieces for cooking in liquid.

TO COOK: In a saucepan, heat 1 inch of water to boiling over high heat. Add cut-up chayote; heat to boiling. Reduce heat to low; cover and simmer the chayote until tender, 20 to 30 minutes. Or bake chayote halves in a preheated 375°F. oven until fork-tender, 30 to 40 minutes.

Chayote and Peppers

Prep: 25 minutes
Cook: 40 minutes

2 tablespoons olive oil	½ cup chicken broth
1 small onion, minced	½ teaspoon dried basil
2 medium chayote (about 1½ pounds), peeled and cut into 1-inch chunks	½ teaspoon sugar
	½ teaspoon salt
1 medium green pepper, cut into 1-inch pieces	⅛ teaspoon pepper
	Minced fresh flat-leaf parsley
1 medium red pepper, cut into 1-inch pieces	

1. In 10-inch skillet, heat oil over medium heat until hot. Add onion, and cook, stirring occasionally, until tender.

2. Add chayote and green and red peppers; cook 5 minutes. Stir in broth, basil, sugar, salt, and pepper, and heat to boiling over high heat. Reduce heat to low; cover and simmer, stirring occasionally, until vegetables are tender, 30 minutes. Sprinkle mixture with minced parsley. Makes 6 accompaniment servings.

Each serving: About 90 calories, 2 g protein, 11 g carbohydrate, 5 g total fat (1 g saturated), 0 mg cholesterol, 265 mg sodium.

CORN

SEASON: Supplies are best from May through September.

LOOK FOR: Medium-size ears with bright, plump, milky kernels that are just firm enough to offer slight resistance to pressure. Tiny kernels indicate immaturity; very large, deep-yellow kernels may be overmature and tough.

TO STORE: Refrigerate corn; use as soon as possible.

TO PREPARE: Just before cooking, remove the husks and silk (a small vegetable brush helps) if not already removed at the market.

TO COOK: In a saucepot or kettle, heat 2 to 3 inches of

water to boiling. Add the corn; heat to boiling. Reduce
the heat to low; cover and simmer 5 minutes. Drain.

TO SERVE: Spread corn on the cob with margarine or
butter; sprinkle with salt or sugar.

Creamy Corn Pudding

Prep: 30 minutes
Bake: 1 hour 15 minutes

2 tablespoons margarine or butter	2 cups half-and-half or light cream
1 small onion, minced	1 cup milk
¼ cup all-purpose flour	1 package (10 ounces) frozen whole-kernel corn, thawed
1 teaspoon salt	4 large eggs
¼ teaspoon coarsely ground black pepper	Fresh thyme sprig (optional)

1. Preheat oven to 325°F. In 2-quart saucepan, melt margarine over medium heat. Add onion and cook until tender
and golden brown, about 10 minutes. Stir in flour, salt, and
pepper until blended. Gradually stir in half-and-half and milk,
and cook, stirring constantly, until mixture boils and thickens slightly. Remove saucepan from heat; stir in corn.

2. In 2-quart casserole, beat eggs slightly. Slowly add
corn mixture, beating constantly.

3. Set casserole in 13" by 9" baking pan; place pan on
oven rack. Pour enough *boiling water* into pan to come
halfway up side of casserole. Bake pudding until knife inserted in center comes out clean, about 1 hour and 15
minutes. Garnish with thyme sprig, if you like. Makes 12
accompaniment servings.

*Each serving: About 135 calories, 5 g protein, 11 g carbohydrate,
9 g total fat (4 g saturated), 86 mg cholesterol, 250 mg sodium.*

Corn Fritters

Prep: 7 minutes
Cook: 5 minutes per batch

Vegetable oil
1 can (16- to 17-ounces) whole-kernel corn, drained
1 cup all-purpose flour
¼ cup milk
1 teaspoon baking powder
½ teaspoon salt
2 large eggs
Confectioners' sugar or maple syrup

1. In heavy saucepan, heat ½ inch vegetable oil, over medium-high heat, to 400°F. on deep-fat thermometer (or heat oil in electric skillet set at 400°F.).
2. In medium bowl, stir 1 tablespoon vegetable oil, corn, flour, milk, baking powder, salt, and eggs just until blended. Drop batter by tablespoons into hot oil; fry, turning fritters once, until golden brown, 3 to 5 minutes. With slotted spoon, transfer fritters to paper towels to drain. Sprinkle with confectioners' sugar or serve with syrup. Makes 6 accompaniment servings.

Each serving: About 215 calories, 6 g protein, 27 g carbohydrate, 10 g total fat (2 g saturated), 72 mg cholesterol, 405 mg sodium.

Flavored Butters for Corn on the Cob

Chili Butter
In small bowl, with spoon, beat ½ cup margarine or butter (1 stick), softened, 1 teaspoon chili powder, and ¼ teaspoon pepper until well blended. Refrigerate until firm. Makes ½ cup.

Each tablespoon: About 100 calories, 0 g protein, 0 g carbohydrate, 11 g total fat (2 g saturated), 0 mg cholesterol, 155 mg sodium.

Chive Butter
Prepare as above, but substitute 2 teaspoons chopped fresh chives for chili powder. Makes ½ cup.

*Each tablespoon: About 100 calories, 0 g protein, 0 g carbohydrate,
11 g total fat (2 g saturated), 0 mg cholesterol, 150 mg sodium.*

CUCUMBERS

SEASON: All year.

LOOK FOR: Firm, well-shaped green cucumbers. Overmature cucumbers, generally seedy, are dull or yellow
and have an overgrown, puffy look. Smaller varieties,
such as Kirby, are preferred for pickling. Long, slender
seedless cucumbers, known as European cucumbers,
are preferred for salad.

TO STORE: Refrigerate cucumbers; use within one week.

TO PREPARE: Rinse with cold running water. Trim the
ends and cut the cucumber into any shape you like. If
the skin is tender, it is not necessary to peel cucumbers.
Slice, chop, or cut them into long wedges.

TO COOK: In a skillet, heat margarine or butter over medium heat. Add cucumbers, peeled, cut lengthwise into
halves, seeded and thickly sliced, and cook, stirring
occasionally, until tender-crisp, about 5 minutes.

Cucumbers with Yogurt and Dill

Prep: 10 minutes

1 container (8 ounces) plain yogurt
1 teaspoon fresh lemon juice
¼ teaspoon dried dill weed
¼ teaspoon salt
2 medium cucumbers, peeled and thinly sliced

In medium bowl, mix yogurt, lemon juice, dill weed, salt,
and sliced cucumbers; with rubber spatula, gently toss to
mix well. Makes 6 accompaniment servings.

*Each serving: About 35 calories, 3 g protein, 5 g carbohydrate,
1 g total fat (1 g saturated), 4 mg cholesterol, 130 mg sodium.*

Stir-Fried Cucumbers

Prep: 12 minutes
Cook: 6 minutes

3 medium cucumbers
3 tablespoons vegetable oil
¼ cup water
5 teaspoons soy sauce
¼ teaspoon sugar

1. Peel and cut each cucumber in half lengthwise; remove seeds. Then cut cucumber halves crosswise into 1-inch chunks.

2. In 4-quart saucepan heat oil over high heat until very hot. Add cucumbers and cook, stirring frequently, until evenly coated with oil. Add water, soy sauce, and sugar. Reduce heat to medium; cover and cook, stirring occasionally, until tender-crisp, about 5 minutes. Makes 4 accompaniment servings.

Each serving: About 120 calories, 2 g protein, 6 g carbohydrate, 11 g total fat (1 g saturated), 0 mg cholesterol, 435 mg sodium.

EGGPLANT

SEASON: All year.

LOOK FOR: Firm, heavy eggplant with a uniformly dark, rich purple color and a bright green cap that is free from scars or cuts.

TO STORE: Refrigerate; use within one week.

TO PREPARE: Rinse with cold running water. It is not necessary to peel an eggplant if it is fresh and tender. Also, do not soak eggplant in salt water (you'll lose nutrients). Slice or cut eggplant into any shape you like just before cooking (eggplant discolors quickly).

TO COOK: Sauté cut-up eggplant in hot vegetable oil just until tender, about 5 minutes.

Stuffed Eggplants

Prep: 30 minutes
Bake: 30 to 35 minutes

6 small or Italian eggplants
   (8 ounces each)
3 tablespoons olive oil
1 cup long-grain white rice
1¼ teaspoons salt
1 medium red onion, coarsely
   chopped
1 medium red pepper, finely
   chopped
1 garlic clove, minced

½ teaspoon dried mint
¼ teaspoon coarsely ground
   black pepper
1 tablespoon fresh lemon juice
2 ounces feta cheese, crumbled
   (½ cup)
6 large pitted green olives,
   coarsely chopped
Lemon wedges

1. Preheat oven to 450°F. Cut each eggplant lengthwise in half. Rub cut sides of eggplants with 2 tablespoons oil. Place eggplants, cut side down, in 15½" by 10½" jelly-roll pan and bake until tender, 20 to 25 minutes. Remove jelly-roll pan with eggplants from oven. Turn oven control to 400°F.

2. While eggplants are baking, in 2-quart saucepan, heat rice, ½ teaspoon salt, and *2 cups water* to boiling over high heat. Reduce heat to low; cover and simmer, until rice is tender and liquid is absorbed, 15 to 18 minutes.

3. With spoon, gently scoop out most of flesh from each eggplant half, leaving about ¼-inch-thick shell. Coarsely chop eggplant flesh and spoon into bowl. Sprinkle eggplant shells with ¼ teaspoon salt. Set eggplant flesh and shells aside.

4. In nonstick 12-inch skillet, heat remaining 1 tablespoon oil over medium heat until hot. Add onion and red pepper and cook, stirring frequently, until vegetables are tender, about 10 minutes. Add garlic, mint, black pepper, and remaining ½ teaspoon salt; cook 1 minute longer. Stir in eggplant flesh and cook, stirring often, 5 to 10 minutes. Stir in lemon juice.

5. Spoon cooked rice into eggplant shells; top with eggplant mixture. Return to same jelly-roll pan. Sprinkle feta cheese and chopped olives over filled eggplants. Bake until heated through, about 10 minutes. Serve with lemon wedges. Makes 6 main-dish servings.

Each serving: About 275 calories, 6 g protein, 42 g carbohydrate, 10 g total fat (3 g saturated), 1 g fiber, 8 mg cholesterol, 575 mg sodium.

Szechwan Eggplant

Prep: 17 minutes
Cook: 22 minutes

2 small eggplants (about 1 pound each)
Vegetable oil
1¾ cups chicken broth
1 tablespoon sugar
1 tablespoon cornstarch
2 tablespoons soy sauce
1 tablespoon minced, peeled gingerrooot or 1¼ teaspoons ground
    ginger
1 teaspoon hot-pepper sauce
1 green onion, finely chopped

1. Cut eggplants lengthwise into ½-inch-thick slices; cut each slice lengthwise in half.
2. In 12-inch skillet, heat ¼ cup vegetable oil over medium-high heat, until hot. Add eggplant, a few slices at a time, and cook until browned on both sides; transfer slices as they brown to paper towels to drain, adding more oil to skillet, if needed. Discard oil.
3. In same skillet, stir broth, sugar, cornstarch, soy sauce, gingerroot, hot-pepper sauce, and green onion. Cook over medium heat, stirring constantly, until mixture boils and thickens slightly. Return eggplant to skillet; heat through. Makes 8 accompaniment servings.

Each serving: About 100 calories, 3 g protein, 10 g carbohydrate, 6 g total fat (1 g saturated), 0 mg cholesterol, 435 mg sodium.

BELGIAN ENDIVE

ALSO CALLED: Witloof.
SEASON: September through May.
LOOK FOR: Small, compact heads of white leaves with pale green edges. Avoid wilted outer leaves.
TO STORE: Refrigerate Belgian endive; use within one week.
TO PREPARE: Rinse with cold running water. Trim any bruised leaves.

For chicory (curly endive), see *Greens* (page 590).

Butter-Braised Belgian Endive

Prep: 5 minutes
Cook: 20 minutes

6 large heads Belgian endive
6 tablespoons butter (no substitutions)
½ teaspoon sugar
¼ teaspoon salt

Cut each endive head lengthwise in half. In 12-inch skillet, melt butter, sugar, and salt over medium-low heat. Arrange endive in skillet in 1 layer. Cover and cook, turning endive occasionally, until tender and lightly browned, 15 to 20 minutes. Makes 6 accompaniment servings.

Each serving: About 120 calories, 1 g protein, 3 g carbohydrate, 12 g total fat (8 g saturated), 33 mg cholesterol, 220 mg sodium.

ESCAROLE

See *Greens* (page 590).

FENNEL

ALSO CALLED: Anise, finocchio.
SEASON: October through April.

LOOK FOR: Featherlike green leaves and pale green bulb.

TO STORE: Refrigerate fennel; use within one week.

TO PREPARE: Rinse with cold running water. Cut the root end and stalks from the bulb. Leave the bulb whole or slice it.

TO COOK: In a medium saucepan, heat *1 inch water* to boiling over high heat. Add fennel; heat to boiling. Reduce heat to low; cover and simmer cut-up fennel 5 to 10 minutes, whole fennel 15 to 20 minutes, or until tender.

TO SERVE: Separate the bulb into pieces. Serve uncooked fennel as a snack, or use in salads. Serve cooked pieces as a vegetable with melted margarine or butter and lemon juice.

GREENS

Varieties: Swiss chard, chicory, collards, escarole, kale, lettuce, mustard greens, turnip greens. See also Beets (page 563), Broccoli Rabe (page 567), Chinese Cabbage (page 569), Green and Red Cabbage (page 570), Belgian Endive (page 589), Spinach (page 618).

SEASON: All year.

LOOK FOR: Clean, crisp or tender leaves, free from decay or dirt. Injured, dried, or yellow leaves and coarse stems indicate poor quality.

TO STORE: Refrigerate greens in crisper or partially open plastic bag; use within two days.

TO PREPARE LETTUCE: See *Buying, Storing, and Preparing Salad Greens* (page 705).

TO PREPARE OTHER GREENS (Swiss chard, chicory, collards, escarole, kale, mustard and turnip greens): Wash in cold water; drain well. Trim tough stems or ribs.

TO COOK: In deep skillet or Dutch oven, heat ¼ inch of water to boiling over medium heat. Cook leafy salad greens, until wilted, stirring occasionally, 1 to 3 minutes; cook other greens until tender-crisp, 5 to 10 minutes.

Greens are also good stir-fried, or used in recipes for vegetable dishes, soups, and wilted salads.

For salad greens, see *Glossary of Salad Greens* (pages 703-705).

JICAMA

SEASON: Supplies are best in June and July.
LOOK FOR: Large (1 to 6 pounds) turnip-shaped jicama with thin brown skin and white flesh (if sold cut in pieces). Choose smaller ones to avoid woodiness. In taste and texture, jicama resembles the water chestnut.
TO STORE: Keep whole jicama in a cool, dry place; cover cut pieces with plastic wrap and refrigerate them. Use within one to two weeks.
TO PREPARE: Scrub under cold running water. Peel and slice thinly to substitute in salads or other recipes for water chestnuts; or cut into strips to serve as a raw-vegetable appetizer with a dip.

KALE

See Greens (above).

KOHLRABI

SEASON: May through November.
LOOK FOR: Small or medium, pale-green or purple kohlrabi, with a fresh top and tender skin.
TO STORE: Discard top. Refrigerate kohlrabi; use within one week.
TO PREPARE: Rinse with cold running water. Peel thinly and slice, sliver, or quarter.
TO COOK: In a saucepan, heat 1 inch of water to boiling over medium heat. Add kohlrabi; heat to boiling. Reduce the heat to low; cover and simmer kohlrabi until it is tender, 15 to 30 minutes.

Creamy Kohlrabi

Prep: 30 minutes

8 small kohlrabi with leaves (about 2 pounds)
1 medium lemon
1 medium carrot, peeled and grated
½ cup sour cream
½ cup mayonnaise
3 tablespoons milk

2 teaspoons minced fresh dill or ½ teaspoon dried dill weed
1 teaspoon salt
½ teaspoon sugar
¼ teaspoon ground black pepper
Fresh dill sprigs (optional)

1. Reserve kohlrabi leaves for lining serving bowl later. Peel and thinly slice kohlrabi. From lemon, grate 1 teaspoon peel and squeeze 2 teaspoons juice.

2. In medium bowl, combine sliced kohlrabi, lemon peel, lemon juice, grated carrot, sour cream, mayonnaise, milk, dill, salt, sugar, and pepper; with rubber spatula, gently toss to mix well. Cover bowl and refrigerate, stirring mixture occasionally, at least 1 hour to blend flavors.

3. To serve, line bowl with reserved kohlrabi leaves. Spoon kohlrabi mixture onto leaves. Garnish mixture with fresh dill sprigs, if desired. Makes 6 accompaniment servings.

Each serving: About 205 calories, 3 g protein, 9 g carbohydrate, 18 g total fat (4 g saturated), 19 mg cholesterol, 525 mg sodium.

LEEKS

SEASON: All year. Supplies are best from September through November.

LOOK FOR: A white bulb base with fresh green tops. (Leeks are larger and milder than green onions, and they impart a different flavor to cooked foods.)

TO STORE: Refrigerate leeks; use within three days.

TO PREPARE: Trim off the roots and the leaf end. With a knife, slash the bulb base lengthwise in half. Carefully wash with cold running water until all the sand is removed. Use leeks cut into halves or pieces.

TO COOK: In a saucepan heat 1 inch of water to boiling over medium heat. Add leeks; heat to boiling. Reduce the heat to low; cover and simmer the leeks until tender, 10 to 15 minutes.

Leeks Vinaigrette

Prep: 20 minutes
Cook: 10 minutes

16 slender leeks (4½ to 5 pounds)
2¼ teaspoons salt
2 tablespoons red wine vinegar
2 teaspoons Dijon mustard
¼ teaspoon coarsely ground black pepper
¼ cup olive oil
2 tablespoons chopped fresh parsley

1. In 8-quart Dutch oven, heat *5 quarts water* to boiling over high heat. Meanwhile, cut root ends from leeks. Trim leeks to 6 inches; discard tops (or save to make soup another day). Cut leeks lengthwise almost in half down to beginning of white part, keeping bottom 2 to 3 inches intact. Remove any bruised or tough dark green outer leaves. Rinse leeks thoroughly with cold running water to remove all sand, gently fanning cut part.

2. Add leeks and 2 teaspoons salt to Dutch oven; cook until tender when pierced with knife, about 10 minutes. With slotted spoon, transfer leeks to colander to drain; rinse with cold running water. Drain again and pat dry with paper towels.

3. Coarsely chop any loose pieces of leek and spread on platter; arrange leeks in a row, in a single layer, on top.

4. In small bowl, with wire whisk, mix vinegar, mustard, pepper, and remaining ¼ teaspoon salt. Gradually whisk in olive oil.

5. Spoon vinaigrette evenly over leeks; sprinkle with parsley. Makes 8 accompaniment servings.

Each serving: About 105 calories, 1 g protein, 11 g carbohydrate, 7 g total fat (1 g saturated), 0 mg cholesterol, 180 mg sodium.

LETTUCE

See *Greens* (page 590) and *Glossary of Salad Greens* (pages 703-705).

MUSHROOMS

SEASON: All year.

LOOK FOR: Firm, plump, cream-colored mushrooms with short stems and caps that are closed around the stem or slightly open and have pink or light-tan gills. Buy only cultivated mushrooms (varieties found growing wild may be poisonous). Look for other cultivated varieties such as shiitake, oyster, portobello.

TO STORE: Refrigerate mushrooms in their original fiberboard container, in a paper bag, or in a plastic bag in which holes have been punched. Mushrooms are best used within one or two days, but they will keep for one week.

TO PREPARE: Do not peel or soak mushrooms; rinse them with cold running water; drain well on paper towels. Cut a thin slice from the stem. Use mushrooms whole or slice them vertically; or prepare as recipe directs.

Creamed Jumbo Mushrooms

Prep: 15 minutes
Cook: 15 minutes

2½ pounds large mushrooms
2 medium green onions
6 tablespoons margarine or butter
¾ teaspoon salt
⅛ teaspoon ground black pepper
1 tablespoon all-purpose flour
2 tablespoons dry sherry
½ cup half-and-half

1. Trim ends from mushroom stems. Cut green onions into 1-inch pieces.

2. In 12-inch skillet, heat margarine over medium heat until hot. Add mushrooms, green onions, salt, and pepper, and cook, stirring frequently, until mushrooms are tender, about 10 minutes.

3. In cup, stir flour and sherry until blended. Gradually stir half-and-half and sherry mixture into mushroom mixture; cook, stirring often, until mixture boils and thickens slightly. Makes 10 accompaniment servings.

Each serving: About 110 calories, 3 g protein, 7 g carbohydrate, 9 g total fat (2 g saturated), 4 mg cholesterol, 275 mg sodium.

Sautéed Mixed Mushrooms

Prep: 15 minutes
Cook: 20 minutes

4 tablespoons margarine or
  butter
2 large shallots, minced (about
  ½ cup)
1 pound white mushrooms,
  each cut into quarters
8 ounces shiitake mushrooms,
  stems removed and caps cut
  into 1-inch wedges
8 ounces oyster mushrooms,
  each cut in half if large

¼ teaspoon dried thyme
¼ teaspoon salt
¼ teaspoon coarsely ground
  black pepper
1 garlic clove, crushed with
  garlic press
2 tablespoons chopped fresh
  parsley

1. In 12-inch skillet, melt 2 tablespoons margarine over medium-high heat. Add shallots and cook, stirring, 1 minute. Stir in white mushrooms, and cook, stirring often, until mushrooms are tender and liquid has evaporated, about 8 minutes. Transfer mushrooms to bowl. In same skillet, melt remaining 2 tablespoons margarine. Add shiitake and oyster mushrooms, and cook, stirring often, until mushrooms are tender and liquid has evaporated, about 6 minutes.

2. Return white mushrooms to pan; stir in ¼ *cup water*, and cook until liquid evaporates. Stir in thyme, salt, pepper, and garlic, and cook 1 minute longer.

3. Sprinkle with parsley to serve. Makes 8 accompaniment servings.

Each serving: About 95 calories, 3 g protein, 9 g carbohydrate, 6 g total fat (1 g saturated), 0 mg cholesterol, 150 mg sodium.

❦

Older mushrooms have the best flavor. Mushrooms lose moisture from the time they are picked, and this moisture loss is indicated by the darkening of the "veil," or underside, of the mushroom cap. As the veil darkens, the mushroom flavor becomes more concentrated and actually intensifies. Use older mushrooms in stews, soups, and cooked dishes for full flavor. Use firm, white mushrooms for eating raw in delicate salads.

To keep the creamy-white color of fresh mushrooms, add a little lemon juice to the margarine or butter in the skillet when you sauté them, either whole or cut.

OKRA

SEASON: Supplies are best from May through September.

LOOK FOR: Young, tender green pods that are less than 4½ inches long.

TO STORE: Refrigerate okra; use within two days.

TO PREPARE: Rinse okra with cold running water. Cut off stems, if any. Leave whole or slice.

TO COOK: In a saucepan heat 1 inch of water to boiling over high heat. Add okra; heat to boiling. Reduce the heat to low; cover and simmer whole okra 5 to 10 minutes, cut-up okra 3 to 5 minutes.

Marinated Okra

Prep: 10 minutes plus marinating
Cook: 5 minutes

¾ cup olive or vegetable oil
½ cup distilled white vinegar
¾ teaspoon dry mustard
¾ teaspoon dried thyme
½ teaspoon sugar
2 teaspoons salt
2½ pounds tender young okra

1. In large bowl, with wire whisk, mix oil, vinegar, dry mustard, thyme, sugar, and 1½ teaspoons salt; set marinade aside.

2. In 12-inch skillet, heat *½ inch water* to boiling over high heat. Add okra and remaining ½ teaspoon salt; over high heat, heat to boiling. Reduce heat to low; cover and simmer until tender-crisp, about 5 minutes. Drain.

3. Add okra to marinade. Cover bowl and refrigerate at least 4 hours or overnight, tossing occasionally. Drain before serving. Makes 8 accompaniment servings.

Each serving: About 100 calories, 3 g protein, 10 g carbohydrate, 7 g total fat (1 g saturated), 0 mg cholesterol, 185 mg sodium.

ONIONS

SEASON: All year.

LOOK FOR: Clean, firm onions with dry, brittle skin. Avoid onions with sprouts.

TO STORE: Store at a cool room temperature (60°F. or below) in a container that allows good circulation of air, or store in the refrigerator. Keep onions dry. They will last for several months.

TO PREPARE: Peel onion; slice under cold running water to prevent tears.

TO COOK: In a saucepan, heat 1 inch of water to boiling over medium heat. Add whole onions; heat to boiling.

Reduce heat to low; cover and simmer until tender, 10 minutes.

Pickled Onions

Prep: 45 minutes plus marinating
Cook: 15 minutes

3½ pounds small white onions
2 tablespoons mixed pickling spice
1 teaspoon crushed red pepper
4 cups cider vinegar
1 cup sugar
1 cup water
1 tablespoon salt

1. Peel onions, leaving a little of the root ends to help hold shape during cooking. Tie pickling spice and crushed red pepper in small square of cheesecloth.
2. In 4-quart nonaluminum saucepan, heat spice bag, vinegar, sugar, water, salt, and onions to boiling over high heat. Reduce heat to low; cover and simmer 10 minutes. Discard spice bag. Ladle onions and their liquid into bowl; cover and refrigerate at least 12 hours to blend flavors.
3. To serve, drain onions. If you like, cut each onion crosswise in half. Makes 16 accompaniment servings.

Each serving: About 40 calories, 1 g protein, 10 g carbohydrate, 0 g total fat, 0 mg cholesterol, 75 mg sodium.

Glazed Pearl Onions

Prep: 45 minutes
Cook: 20 minutes

2 pounds pearl onions
3 tablespoons margarine or butter
2 tablespoons currant jelly
2 teaspoons sugar
¼ teaspoon salt

1. In deep 12-inch skillet, heat *1 inch water* to boiling over high heat. Add onions; heat to boiling. Boil 1 minute; drain.

2. Peel onions, leaving a little of the root ends to help hold shape during cooking.

3. In same skillet, heat *1 inch water* to boiling over high heat. Add onions; heat to boiling. Reduce heat to low; cover and simmer until onions are tender, 5 to 10 minutes. Drain. Wipe skillet dry.

4. In same skillet, cook onions, margarine, currant jelly, sugar, and salt, over high heat stirring occasionally, until onions are browned and glazed, about 10 minutes. Makes 8 accompaniment servings.

Each serving: About 95 calories, 1 g protein, 13 g carbohydrate, 4 g total fat (1 g saturated), 0 mg cholesterol, 130 mg sodium.

French-fried Onion Rings

Prep: 12 minutes
Cook: 5 minutes per batch

3 large onions, peeled
Vegetable oil
1 cup milk
1 cup all-purpose flour
½ teaspoon salt

1. Slice onions ¼ inch thick. Separate onion slices into rings. In 3- to 4-quart saucepan, heat 2 inches vegetable oil over medium heat to 370°F. on deep-fat thermometer (or heat oil in deep-fat fryer set at 370°F.).

2. In small dish, place milk. In small bowl, mix flour and salt. Dip onion rings into milk, then into flour mixture. Repeat to coat twice.

3. Add onion rings in batches to hot oil and cook until golden brown. Drain thoroughly on paper towels. Serve immediately. Makes 6 accompaniment servings.

Each serving: About 180 calories, 4 g protein, 24 g carbohydrate, 8 g total fat (1 g saturated), 3 mg cholesterol, 205 mg sodium.

Creamed Onions

Prep: 30 minutes
Cook: 15 minutes

2 pounds small white onions
6 tablespoons margarine or butter
3 tablespoons all-purpose flour
1½ cups milk
¼ teaspoon salt
Paprika

1. Peel onions, leaving a little of the root ends to help hold shape during cooking.

2. In 3-quart saucepan, heat *1 inch water* to boiling over high heat. Add onions; heat to boiling. Reduce heat to low, cover and simmer until onions are tender, 10 to 15 minutes.

3. Meanwhile, in another saucepan melt margarine over medium heat. Stir in flour until smooth. Slowly stir in milk and salt, and cook, stirring constantly, until sauce thickens.

4. Drain onions and place in serving dish; pour on sauce and sprinkle with paprika, if you like. Makes 10 accompaniment servings.

Each serving: About 125 calories, 3 g protein, 11 g carbohydrate, 8 g total fat (2 g saturated), 5 mg cholesterol, 170 mg sodium.

GREEN ONIONS, SCALLIONS, AND SHALLOTS

GREEN ONIONS, shoots of any onion harvested before the bulb forms, are available all year. Eat fresh or use in recipes.

SCALLIONS, technically, are shoots of white onions only; in a few places in the United States, the word *scallion* is used to mean green onions.

SHALLOTS have distinctive bulbs made up of cloves like garlic. Green shallots are available in summer; dry bulbs are available year-round. Use in recipes as directed.

Sautéed Green Onions

Prep: 15 minutes
Cook: 10 minutes

1 tablespoon vegetable oil
5 bunches green onions, cut into 2-inch pieces
½ teaspoon freshly grated lemon peel
¼ teaspoon salt
¼ teaspoon coarsely ground black pepper
2 radishes, each cut in half and thinly sliced (optional)

In 12-inch skillet, heat oil over medium-high heat until hot. Add green onions, lemon peel, salt, and pepper, and cook, stirring frequently, 2 minutes. Add *½ cup water* and cook, stirring, until green onions are tender and lightly browned and liquid has evaporated, 5 to 7 minutes longer. Toss with radishes, if you like. Makes 4 accompaniment servings.

Each serving: About 60 calories, 2 g protein, 7 g carbohydrate, 4 g total fat (0 g saturated), 0 mg cholesterol, 140 mg sodium.

PARSNIPS

SEASON: All year.

LOOK FOR: Smooth, firm, well-shaped, medium-size parsnips. Avoid large, coarse roots or those with gray or soft spots.

TO STORE: Refrigerate parsnips; use within two weeks.

TO PREPARE: Scrub parsnips under cold running water. Trim the ends and peel them. Leave them whole; slice or cut them into halves or quarters.

TO COOK: In a saucepan, heat 1 inch of water to boiling over high heat. Add parsnips; heat to boiling. Reduce the heat to low; cover and simmer whole parsnips 20 to 30 minutes, cut-up parsnips 8 to 15 minutes. Serve parsnips as a cooked vegetable; use them in recipes for soups, stews, pot roasts; or mash and season them as you would potatoes.

PEAS

SEASON: All year. Supplies are best in spring and early summer.

LOOK FOR: Fresh, young pods that are light green, slightly velvety to the touch, and well-filled with well-developed peas. Pods with immature peas are usually flat, dark green, and wilted; overmature pods are swollen, light, and flecked with gray.

TO STORE: Refrigerate peas in pods; use within one or two days.

TO PREPARE: Shell peas by pressing the pods between your thumb and forefinger to open them.

TO COOK: In a saucepan, heat 1 inch of water to boiling over high heat. Add peas; heat to boiling. Reduce the heat to low; cover and simmer the peas until tender, 3 to 5 minutes.

Peas with Lettuce

Prep: 5 minutes
Cook: 10 minutes

2 tablespoons margarine or butter
½ medium head iceberg lettuce, thinly sliced
1 package (10 ounces) frozen peas
1 teaspoon sugar
½ teaspoon salt

In 4-quart saucepan, melt margarine over medium heat. Add lettuce and cook, stirring occasionally, until wilted, about 5 minutes. Add frozen peas, sugar, and salt; cook, stirring occasionally, until peas are tender, 5 minutes longer. Makes 4 accompaniment servings.

Each serving: About 120 calories, 4 g protein, 13 g carbohydrate, 6 g total fat (1 g saturated), 0 mg cholesterol, 435 mg sodium.

CHINESE PEA PODS

ALSO CALLED: Snow peas.
SEASON: May through September.
LOOK FOR: Fresh flat, green pea pods.
TO STORE: Refrigerate Chinese pea pods; use within two days.
TO PREPARE: Rinse with cold running water. Remove stem and strings along both edges of pod; do not shell.

Stir-Fried Chinese Pea Pods

Prep: 7 minutes
Cook: 4 minutes

1 pound Chinese pea pods
3 tablespoons vegetable oil
½ teaspoon salt

1. Remove stem and strings along both edges of each pea pod.

2. In 10-inch skillet or 3-quart saucepan, heat oil over high heat until very hot. Add Chinese pea pods, and cook, stirring frequently (stir-frying), until evenly coated with oil. Sprinkle with salt; continue stir-frying, until tender-crisp, 2 to 3 minutes longer. Makes 4 accompaniment servings.

Each serving: About 135 calories, 3 g protein, 8 g carbohydrate, 10 g total fat (1 g saturated), 0 mg cholesterol, 295 mg sodium.

Snap Peas are a variety of edible pea pods. They are shorter and rounder than Chinese pea pods, with fully formed peas and thick pods. The peas and pod are eaten together either raw, or quickly cooked, like Chinese pea pods.

SWEET PEPPERS

SEASON: All year.

LOOK FOR: Medium to dark green peppers that are firm, shiny, and thick-fleshed. Wilted or flabby peppers, with cuts or punctures, are of poor quality. Soft spots on the sides indicate decay. When mature, peppers turn red. Yellow and purple varieties are also available. The pimiento is a mild, sweet pepper.

TO STORE: Refrigerate sweet peppers; use within one week.

TO PREPARE: Rinse peppers with cold running water. Cut a slice from the stem end; remove the seeds and white membrane. Use green peppers whole or cut into halves to stuff; or cut them into strips or rings. They may also be diced or slivered.

TO COOK: Cook as recipe directs. When stuffing peppers, parboil them first: In a large saucepan, in enough boiling water to cover them, cook peppers over high heat 3 to 5 minutes, then drain.

TO ROAST: Preheat broiler. Line broiling pan (without rack) with foil. Cut each pepper lengthwise in half; discard stems and seeds. Arrange peppers, cut side down, in broiling pan. Place broiling pan in broiler 5 to 6 inches from heat source and broil peppers until charred and blistered, about 8 to 10 minutes. Wrap foil around peppers and allow to steam at room temperature until cool enough to handle; about 15 minutes. Peel off skin and discard.

Sautéed Peppers and Onions

Prep: 15 minutes
Cook: 20 minutes

¼ cup olive oil
4 large peppers (green and/or red), cut into ½-inch-wide strips
4 large onions (3 pounds), cut into ¼-inch-thick slices
½ teaspoon salt
½ teaspoon dried basil or thyme

In 12-inch skillet heat oil over medium heat until hot. Add peppers, onions, salt, and basil, and cook, stirring occasionally, until vegetables are tender, about 20 minutes. Serve hot, or cover and refrigerate to serve cold later. Makes 8 accompaniment servings.

Each serving: About 50 calories, 1 g protein, 6 g carbohydrate, 3 g total fat (0 g saturated), 0 mg cholesterol, 65 mg sodium.

Charred Peppers with Peaches

Prep: 30 minutes plus standing
Broil: 10 minutes

1 large yellow pepper, roasted (see page 606)
1 large red pepper, roasted (see page 606)
1 tablespoon olive oil
2 teaspoons fresh lemon juice
½ teaspoon ground cumin
¼ teaspoon salt
⅛ teaspoon ground red pepper (cayenne)
3 large ripe peaches

1. Cut peeled peppers lengthwise into ½-inch-wide strips. Pat dry with paper towels.

2. In bowl, stir peppers with oil, lemon juice, cumin, salt, and ground red pepper. Cover and refrigerate if not serving right away.

3. To serve, peel, pit, and slice peaches; stir into pepper mixture. Serve at room temperature. Makes about 3 cups or 4 first-course servings.

Each serving: About 100 calories, 2 g protein, 17 g carbohydrate, 4 g total fat (1 g saturated), 0 mg cholesterol, 135 mg sodium.

HOT PEPPERS

SEASON: All year.

LOOK FOR: Peppers that provide the right degree of "heat" for your recipe. Spiciness ranges from relatively mild to fiery hot, depending on the variety of pepper. Anaheim peppers—long, tapered, and usually green—are the mildest. Poblano peppers, resembling long, large, tapered green peppers, with shiny blackish-green skin, are also relatively mild. Jalapeño peppers, which are dark green and smooth skinned, are hot. Serrano peppers, which are small and tapered, with smooth, dark green skin, are hotter still. Scotch bonnet or habañero peppers, which are small and bumpy with a thin skin, are the hottest.

TO STORE: Refrigerate hot peppers; use within one week.

TO PREPARE: Hot peppers contain capsaicin, a colorless substance that can seriously irritate the skin and eyes. Wear rubber gloves when preparing hot peppers, and avoid touching your face or eyes; wash the gloves and your hands thoroughly afterward.

Remove the stems and seeds from peppers. Rinse peppers with cold running water. Roast and peel Anaheim and Poblano peppers before using them in recipes as directed.

POTATOES

SEASON: All year.

LOOK FOR: Smooth, well-shaped, firm potatoes that are free from blemishes or sprouts. Large cuts or bruises mean waste in peeling.

Potato varieties are classified by shape (long or round) and skin color, which can be white (ranging from white to buff), russet (with rough, scaly brownish skin), or red. Any potato can be used for a wide variety of dishes. However, russets, which are dry and mealy, are often used for baking; round reds, firmer and moister, are often used for boiling. Round or long whites are popular for baking or boiling. Use any type in recipes unless a particular type is specified.

New potatoes are not a variety, but simply potatoes sold right after harvest, without being placed in storage. They are usually smaller in size, with smooth thin skin.

TO STORE: Store potatoes in a dark, cool place (don't refrigerate). At 45° to 50°F. potatoes will keep for several weeks. At temperatures much over that, use within a week.

TO COOK: For boiled potatoes: In a saucepan, heat potatoes and enough water to cover them to boiling over high heat. Reduce the heat to low; cover and simmer small potatoes 15 to 20 minutes, medium potatoes 25 to 30 minutes, or until tender.

Baked Potatoes

Prep: 5 minutes
Bake: 45 minutes to 1 hour

6 medium baking potatoes, unpeeled
Shortening or vegetable oil (optional)
Toppings: sour cream, margarine or butter, shredded Cheddar
    cheese, chopped chives, crumbled cooked bacon

Preheat oven to 450°F. Wash and dry potatoes. If you
like, rub with shortening; for steamed texture, wrap potatoes in foil. Place in shallow pan. Bake until tender, about
45 minutes. If desired, slash top; serve with choice of toppings. Makes 6 accompaniment servings.

*Each serving: About 220 calories, 5 g protein, 51 g carbohydrate,
0 g total fat, 0 mg cholesterol, 15 mg sodium.*

Oven-Roasted Rosemary Potatoes

Prep: 20 minutes
Roast: 50 minutes

2 tablespoons margarine or butter
4 pounds small red potatoes (about 24), each cut into quarters
1 tablespoon olive oil
1 tablespoon chopped fresh rosemary or 1 teaspoon dried
    rosemary, crumbled
1½ teaspoons chopped fresh thyme or ½ teaspoon dried thyme
¾ teaspoon salt
¼ teaspoon coarsely ground black pepper
2 tablespoons chopped fresh parsley

1. Preheat oven to 450°F. Place margarine in large (17"
by 11½") roasting pan; place in oven until margarine melts.
Remove pan from oven. Add potatoes, oil, rosemary,
thyme, salt and pepper, and toss until evenly mixed.

2. Roast potatoes until tender and browned, stirring occasionally, about 50 minutes. Transfer potatoes to platter; sprinkle with parsley to serve. Makes 8 accompaniment servings.

Each serving: About 210 calories, 5 g protein, 38 g carbohydrate, 5 g total fat (1 g saturated), 4 g fiber, 0 mg cholesterol, 250 mg sodium.

Basic Mashed Potatoes

Prep: 30 minutes
Cook: 20 minutes

3 pounds all-purpose potatoes, peeled and cut into 1-inch chunks
4 tablespoons margarine or butter
1½ teaspoons salt
1 cup hot milk

1. In 3-quart saucepan, heat potatoes and *enough water to cover* to boiling over high heat. Reduce heat to low; cover and simmer until potatoes are fork-tender, about 15 minutes. Drain.

2. Return potatoes to pan. With potato masher, mash potatoes with margarine or butter and salt. Gradually add milk; mash until mixture is smooth and well blended. Keep warm. Makes 8 accompaniment servings.

Each serving: About 195 calories, 4 g protein, 30 g carbohydrate, 7 g total fat (2 g saturated), 4 mg cholesterol, 500 mg sodium.

Mashed Potatoes Plus

WITH GARLIC AND LEMON: Prepare Basic Mashed Potatoes as in Step 1. Meanwhile, with garlic press, press *2 cloves garlic* into 1-quart saucepan with the margarine or butter and salt called for in Step 2; heat over low heat until margarine melts, 2 to 3 minutes. Add garlic mixture to potatoes with the milk; mash. Stir in *2 tablespoons finely chopped fresh parsley* and *1 teaspoon freshly grated lemon peel.*

WITH HORSERADISH: Prepare Basic Mashed Potatoes, but add *2 tablespoons undrained prepared white horseradish* with the milk.

WITH PARSNIPS: Prepare Basic Mashed Potatoes, but substitute *1 pound parsnips,* peeled and cut into 1-inch pieces, for 1 pound potatoes, and use only ¾ cup milk.

Potato Pancakes

Prep: 20 minutes
Cook: 24 minutes (about 8 minutes per batch)

4 large potatoes (about 3 pounds)
1 small onion
2 large eggs
⅓ cup all-purpose flour
2 teaspoons salt
⅛ teaspoon ground black pepper
Vegetable oil

1. Rinse potatoes with cold running water; peel. Into large bowl half filled with cold *water,* coarsely shred potatoes and onion. In colander lined with clean towel or cheesecloth, drain potatoes and onion. Wrap potatoes and onion in towel; squeeze to remove as much water as possible.

2. In same large bowl, beat eggs; return potatoes and onion to bowl. Add flour, salt, and pepper; toss until well mixed.

3. In 12-inch skillet, heat ⅓ cup vegetable oil until hot. Drop potato mixture by scant ¼ cups into 4 mounds, 3 inches apart. With wide spatula, flatten each to make a 4-inch pancake. Cook pancakes until golden brown on 1 side, about 4 minutes; turn and brown other side. Transfer to paper-towel–lined cookie sheet to drain; keep warm in low oven. Repeat to make about 12 pancakes, stirring potato mixture occasionally and adding oil to skillet, if necessary. Makes about 16 pancakes or 8 accompaniment servings.

Each serving: About 195 calories, 5 g protein, 30 g carbohydrate, 7 g total fat (1 g saturated), 53 mg cholesterol, 605 mg sodium.

French-Fried Potatoes

Prep: 25 minutes
Cook: 20 minutes (about 5 minutes per batch)

8 medium potatoes (about 4 pounds)
Vegetable oil
Salt

1. In 3- to 4-quart saucepan, heat 2 inches vegetable oil over medium heat to 370°F. on deep-fat thermometer (or heat oil in deep-fat fryer set at 370°F.).

2. Meanwhile, peel potatoes; cut potatoes into ¼-inch-thick slices; cut slices into ¼-inch lengthwise strips (or use crinkle cutter to cut strips).

3. Fry potatoes in hot oil, about one-fourth at a time, until golden brown. With slotted spoon, transfer potatoes to paper towels to drain; keep warm. Repeat with remaining potatoes. Sprinkle lightly with salt to taste; serve immediately. Makes 8 accompaniment servings.

Each serving: About 210 calories, 4 g protein, 34 g carbohydrate, 7 g total fat (1 g saturated), 0 mg cholesterol, 155 mg sodium.

Home-Fried Potatoes

Prep: 10 minutes
Cook: 25 minutes

4 medium potatoes (about 2 pounds)
4 tablespoons margarine or butter
1 small onion, chopped
Salt

1. Leave potato skin on, if you like; cut potatoes into ¼-inch-thick slices.
2. In 12-inch skillet, melt margarine over medium heat. Add potato slices and sprinkle onion among slices; cook until potatoes are golden on bottom. Reduce heat to low; cover and cook 5 minutes. With pancake turner, turn potatoes; cook over medium heat until browned on other side. Reduce heat to low; cover and cook until potatoes are tender, 5 to 10 minutes longer. Sprinkle potatoes with salt to taste. Makes 4 accompaniment servings.

Each serving: About 275 calories, 5 g protein, 39 g carbohydrate, 12 g total fat (2 g saturated), 0 mg cholesterol, 315 mg sodium.

Hashed Brown Potatoes

Prep: 30 minutes
Cook: 25 minutes

½ cup (1 stick) margarine or butter
6 medium potatoes, peeled and diced or coarsely shredded (about 6 cups)
½ teaspoon paprika (optional)
¼ teaspoon ground black pepper
Salt

In 10-inch skillet heat margarine over medium heat until hot. Add potatoes and cook, covered, 10 minutes. Remove cover and sprinkle potatoes with paprika, pepper, and salt to taste. Continue cooking, uncovered, occasionally turning with a pancake turner, until potatoes are tender and brown, 15 minutes. Makes 6 accompaniment servings.

Each serving: About 225 calories, 3 g protein, 20 g carbohydrate, 15 g total fat (3 g saturated), 0 mg cholesterol, 305 mg sodium.

Scalloped Potatoes

Prep: 30 minutes
Bake: 1 hour

3 tablespoons margarine or butter
1 small onion, minced
3 tablespoons all-purpose flour
1 teaspoon salt
⅛ teaspoon ground black pepper
1½ cups milk
4 medium potatoes (about 2 pounds), peeled and thinly sliced
Paprika

1. Preheat oven to 375°F. In 2-quart saucepan, melt margarine over medium heat. Add onion and cook until tender, about 5 minutes. Stir in flour, salt, and pepper until blended. Gradually stir in milk, and cook, stirring constantly, until mixture thickens.

2. In 2-quart casserole, arrange half of the potatoes in 1 layer; pour half of the sauce on top; repeat. Sprinkle with paprika. Bake, covered, 45 minutes. Remove cover and bake until tender, about 15 minutes longer. Makes 6 accompaniment servings.

Each serving: About 205 calories, 5 g protein, 29 g carbohydrate, 8 g total fat (2 g saturated), 8 mg cholesterol, 500 mg sodium.

Oven Fries

Prep: 10 minutes
Bake: 20 minutes

Nonstick cooking spray
3 baking potatoes (about 1½ pounds)
½ teaspoon salt
¼ teaspoon coarsely ground black pepper

1. Preheat oven to 500°F. Spray two 15½" by 10½" jelly-roll pans or 2 large cookie sheets with nonstick cooking spray.

2. Scrub unpeeled potatoes well, but do not peel. Cut each potato lengthwise in half. With each potato half cut side down, cut lengthwise into ¼-inch-thick slices. Place potatoes in medium bowl and toss with salt and pepper.

3. Divide potato slices evenly between pans. Place pans on 2 oven racks and spray potatoes with nonstick cooking spray. Bake potatoes until tender and lightly browned, about 20 minutes. Makes 4 accompaniment servings.

Each serving: About 130 calories, 4 g protein, 28 g carbohydrate, 1 g total fat (0 g saturated), 0 mg cholesterol, 280 mg sodium.

PUMPKIN

SEASON: Supplies are best from September through December, with the peak in October.

LOOK FOR: Firm, bright-colored pumpkins that are free from blemishes.

TO STORE: Store pumpkins in a cool, dry place; use within one month.

TO PREPARE: Cut pumpkin into halves or quarters; remove the seeds and stringy portions. Cut into large portions, then peel.

TO COOK: In a saucepot, heat 1 inch of water to boiling, over high heat. Add cut up, peeled pumpkin; heat to boiling. Reduce the heat to low; cover and simmer the pumpkin until tender, 25 to 30 minutes.

TO SERVE: Mash; season with margarine or butter, brown sugar, and ground cinnamon to taste, if you like. Or use in recipes as directed.

RADISHES

VARIETIES: Red and white (Icicle).

SEASON: All year.

LOOK FOR: Firm, uniformly shaped radishes that are free of blemishes, firm and bright, deep red or white, depending on the variety.

TO STORE: Refrigerate radishes; use within one week.

TO PREPARE: Trim roots and tops. Remove the leaves or leave a few for decoration. Rinse with cold running water. If using radishes as a garnish or relish, cut as desired and chill them in ice water in the refrigerator.

Sautéed Radishes

Prep: 20 minutes
Cook: 10 minutes

3 bunches radishes with leaves
2 tablespoons margarine or butter
½ teaspoon salt

1. Cut off leaves from radishes, leaving 1-inch stems on each radish. Trim root ends; cut each radish into halves, or into quarters if very large.

2. In 3-quart saucepan, melt margarine over medium-high heat. Add radishes and salt, and cook until tender-crisp, about 10 minutes. Makes 6 accompaniment servings.

Each serving: About 40 calories, 0 g protein, 1 g carbohydrate, 4 g total fat (1 g saturated), 0 mg cholesterol, 250 mg sodium.

RUTABAGAS

ALSO CALLED: Yellow turnip, Swede.
SEASON: All year.
LOOK FOR: Rutabagas that have smooth skin, are heavy for their size, and are free of decay.
TO STORE: Store rutabagas at a cool room temperature and keep dry. Use within one month.
TO PREPARE: Cut rutabaga into quarters; peel and cut quarters into slices or cubes.
TO COOK: In a saucepan, heat 1 inch of water to boiling over high heat. Add cut-up rutabaga; heat to boiling. Reduce the heat to low; cover and simmer the rutabaga until it is fork-tender, 10 to 15 minutes.

Mashed Rutabagas with Brown Butter

Prep: 30 minutes
Cook: 17 minutes

2 rutabagas (about 1¼ pounds each)
¾ teaspoon salt
½ teaspoon sugar
4 tablespoons butter (no substitutions)
¼ cup hot milk

1. Cut each rutabaga into quarters; peel, then cut into ½-inch cubes. In 3-quart saucepan, heat *1 inch water* to boiling over high heat. Add rutabagas; heat to boiling. Reduce heat to low; cover and simmer until rutabagas are fork-tender, 10 to 15 minutes. Drain.

2. In large bowl, with mixer at low speed, beat rutabagas, salt, sugar, and 2 tablespoons butter until fluffy. Gradually add hot milk; beat until mixture is smooth.

3. In small saucepan, melt remaining 2 tablespoons butter over medium heat and cook, stirring (if butter gets too dark, it will be bitter), until butter turns golden brown.

4. To serve, spoon mashed rutabagas into warm bowl;

pour brown butter over mixture. Makes 6 accompaniment servings.

Each serving: About 135 calories, 2 g protein, 14 g carbohydrate, 8 g total fat (2 g saturated), 1 mg cholesterol, 425 mg sodium.

SALSIFY

ALSO CALLED: Oyster plant.
SEASON: October and November.
LOOK FOR: Firm, well-shaped, fresh-looking roots that are free from blemishes.
TO STORE: Refrigerate salsify; use within one week.
TO PREPARE: Scrub salsify with cold running water. Cut off tops; peel and slice. Drop slices into a pan of cold water with 1 or 2 teaspoons lemon juice added to prevent discoloration.
TO COOK: In a saucepan, heat 1 inch of water to boiling over high heat. Add sliced salsify; heat to boiling. Reduce the heat to low; cover and simmer until fork-tender, 10 to 15 minutes. Mash and serve salsify as you would potatoes.

SPINACH

SEASON: All year.
LOOK FOR: Fresh, tender, bright green leaves. Avoid spinach that is yellowish and wilted.
TO STORE: Refrigerate spinach; use within two days.
TO PREPARE: Cut off tough stems. Wash spinach well to remove any sand, and drain. To use spinach raw, dry it in a salad spinner or between paper towels.
TO COOK: In a saucepan, heat ¼ inch of water to boiling over high heat. Add spinach; heat to boiling. Reduce the heat to low; simmer the spinach, stirring occasionally, just until it wilts, 1 to 3 minutes. Or use in recipes as directed.

Spinach with Mushrooms

Prep: 15 minutes
Cook: 5 minutes

¼ cup olive oil
½ pound mushrooms, thinly sliced
1 pound spinach, tough stems trimmed and torn into bite-size
  pieces
1 tablespoon cider vinegar
1 tablespoon prepared mustard
1 teaspoon sugar
¾ teaspoon salt

In 4-quart saucepan, heat oil until hot. Add mushrooms
and cook, stirring often, until tender, about 5 minutes. Remove saucepan from heat. Add spinach, vinegar, mustard,
sugar, and salt; gently toss to coat well. Makes 6 accompaniment servings.

*Each serving: About 100 calories, 2 g protein, 3 g carbohydrate,
9 g total fat (1 g saturated), 0 mg cholesterol, 390 mg sodium.*

SUMMER SQUASH

ALSO CALLED: Soft-skinned squash.
VARIETIES: Zucchini, pattypan, yellow straightneck.
SEASON: All year.
LOOK FOR: Smooth-skinned young squash that are heavy
   for their size, with no soft spots or blemishes.
TO STORE: Refrigerate; use within a few days.
TO PREPARE: Scrub gently using a soft brush, with cold
   running water. Cut a slice from each end. Do not remove seeds or skin if tender and young. Cut into the
   shape desired.
TO COOK: In a saucepan, heat ½ inch of water to boiling
   over high heat. Add squash; heat to boiling. Reduce
   the heat to low; cover and simmer halved squash 5
   minutes, sliced squash 3 minutes.

Venetian-Style Zucchini

Prep: 20 minutes plus standing
Cook: 6 to 8 minutes per batch

3 tablespoons golden raisins	Vegetable oil for frying (at least 2 cups)
3 tablespoons balsamic vinegar	8 small zucchini (about 5 ounces each), cut crosswise into ¼-inch slices
1 tablespoon minced fresh mint	
1 teaspoon dark brown sugar	
½ teaspoon salt	
⅛ teaspoon ground black pepper	
1 garlic clove, peeled and cut in half	1 tablespoon pine nuts, toasted
	Mint sprigs (optional)

1. In large bowl, stir raisins, vinegar, mint, brown sugar, salt, pepper, and garlic; set aside.

2. In 10-inch skillet, heat ½ inch oil over medium-high heat until hot but not smoking. Add 2 cups zucchini; fry until golden, 6 to 8 minutes. With slotted spoon, transfer cooked zucchini to coarse sieve set over bowl to drain. While still hot, stir zucchini into vinegar mixture.

3. Repeat with remaining zucchini in batches of 2 cups each. Let stand at room temperature at least 1 hour. Or cover and refrigerate for up to 3 days.

4. Serve at room temperature, topped with pine nuts and garnished with mint, if you like. Makes about 3 cups or 6 accompaniment servings.

Each serving: About 140 calories, 3 g protein, 12 g carbohydrate, 10 g total fat (1 g saturated), 0 mg cholesterol, 185 mg sodium.

WINTER SQUASH

ALSO CALLED: Hard-skinned squash.

VARIETIES: Acorn, butternut, banana, Des Moines, Green and Golden Delicious, Green and Blue Hubbard, spaghetti.

SEASON: All year. Supplies are best in the fall.
LOOK FOR: Squash that is heavy for its size and has a hard skin; tender skin indicates immaturity and poor quality.
TO STORE: Refrigerate or store winter squash at room temperature; use within a few weeks.
TO PREPARE: Rinse with cold running water. Cut into halves or quarters; discard seeds.
TO COOK: For boiled squash, in a saucepan, heat 1 inch of water to boiling. Add squash; heat to boiling. Reduce the heat to low; cover and simmer squash halves 15 to 30 minutes. For baked squash, preheat oven to 350°F.; bake squash until tender, 45 to 90 minutes.

Baked Acorn Squash

Prep: 5 minutes
Bake: 45 minutes

1 medium acorn squash (about 2 pounds)
2 tablespoons margarine or butter
2 tablespoons brown sugar

1. Preheat oven to 350°F. Grease small baking pan.
2. Cut squash lengthwise in half; remove seeds. Place halves, cut side down, in baking pan; bake 30 minutes.
3. Turn squash cut side up. Place half of margarine and brown sugar in each cavity. Bake until squash is fork-tender and margarine and brown sugar have melted, about 15 minutes longer. Makes 2 accompaniment servings.

Each serving: About 280 calories, 3 g protein, 47 g carbohydrate, 12 g total fat (2 g saturated), 0 mg cholesterol, 165 mg sodium.

Maple Butternut Squash

Prep: 25 minutes
Cook: 20 minutes

2 medium butternut squash (about 1¾ pounds each)
½ cup maple or maple-flavored syrup
6 tablespoons margarine or butter

1. Cut each squash lengthwise in half; discard seeds. Then cut each squash half crosswise and peel. Cut into slices about 1 inch thick.

2. In 4- to 5-quart saucepot, heat *1 inch water* to boiling. Add squash; heat to boiling. Reduce heat to low; cover and simmer until squash is fork-tender, about 15 minutes. Drain.

3. In large bowl, with mixer at low speed, beat squash, maple syrup, and margarine until smooth. Spoon into warm bowl. Makes 10 accompaniment servings.

Each serving: About 155 calories, 1 g protein, 25 g carbohydrate, 7 g total fat (1 g saturated), 0 mg cholesterol, 100 mg sodium.

Home-Style Spaghetti Squash

Prep: 15 minutes
Cook: 30 minutes

1 medium spaghetti squash (about 2½ pounds)
6 tablespoons margarine or butter
¼ cup packed brown sugar
½ teaspoon salt

1. Cut spaghetti squash lengthwise in half; discard seeds. In 8-quart Dutch oven or saucepot, heat *1 inch water* to boiling. Place squash, cut side up, in pot; heat to boiling over high heat. Reduce heat to low; cover and simmer until squash is fork-tender, about 30 minutes.

2. When squash is done, remove from Dutch oven; drain

well. With 2 forks, lift up pulp of squash to form spaghetti-like strands; drain. Return squash pulp to Dutch oven; add margarine, brown sugar, and salt. With rubber spatula, gently toss until margarine and brown sugar have melted and are well mixed. Makes 6 accompaniment servings.

Each serving: About 165 calories, 1 g protein, 16 g carbohydrate, 12 g total fat (2 g saturated), 0 mg cholesterol, 370 mg sodium.

SUNROOTS

ALSO CALLED: Jerusalem artichokes, sunchokes.

SEASON: Supplies are best from October through March.

LOOK FOR: Firm, irregularly shaped sunroots that are free of mold.

TO STORE: Refrigerate sunroots; use within two weeks.

TO PREPARE: Scrub, using a vegetable brush, with cold running water. Peel and drop into a bowl of cold water to prevent discoloration.

TO COOK: In a medium saucepan, heat 1 inch of water to boiling over high heat. Add sunroots; heat to boiling. Reduce the heat to low; cover and simmer until they are fork-tender, about 20 minutes.

TO SERVE: Serve as a cooked vegetable in cream sauce or with melted margarine or butter. Or slice raw sunroots to use in a salad or to serve as a snack.

SWEET POTATOES

SEASON: All year. Supplies are best during the fall and winter months.

LOOK FOR: Firm, uniformly shaped sweet potatoes that are free of blemishes. Yams are not botanically related to sweet potatoes, but in the United States, canned sweet potatoes are often labeled yams; use in recipes as directed the same way you would sweet potatoes.

TO STORE: Do not refrigerate sweet potatoes. Store them in a cool, dry place; use within one week.

TO PREPARE: Scrub, using a soft brush with cold running water. When possible, do not peel before cooking (to save nutrients).

TO COOK: For boiled sweet potatoes, in a saucepan, heat sweet potatoes with enough water to cover them to boiling over high heat. Reduce the heat to low; cover and simmer the sweet potatoes until fork-tender, 30 to 40 minutes. For baked sweet potatoes, preheat the oven to 450°F. and bake the sweet potatoes until fork-tender, 45 minutes to 1 hour. If baking sweet potatoes with meat or other foods at a lower temperature, bake them longer.

Sweet-Potato Casserole

Prep: 20 minutes
Bake: 60 to 70 minutes

4 pounds sweet potatoes (5 large potatoes), peeled and cut
    crosswise into ¾-inch-thick slices
⅓ cup packed dark brown sugar
½ teaspoon salt
¼ teaspoon coarsely ground black pepper
4 tablespoons margarine or butter, cut into small pieces
½ cup coarsely chopped walnuts

1. Preheat oven to 400°F. Arrange half the potato slices in 13" by 9" ceramic or glass baking dish. Sprinkle with half the sugar, half the salt, and all the pepper. Dot with half the margarine. Arrange remaining potatoes in baking dish. Sprinkle with remaining sugar and salt, and dot with remaining margarine. Cover with foil and bake 30 minutes.
2. Remove foil; sprinkle with walnuts and bake, uncovered, 30 to 40 minutes longer, or until potatoes are tender, basting with syrup in baking dish 3 times during cooking. Makes 8 accompaniment servings.

Each serving: About 280 calories, 4 g protein, 45g carbohydrate, 10 g total fat (1 g saturated), 0 mg cholesterol, 225 mg sodium.

North Carolina Brown-Butter Sweet Potatoes

Prep: 15 minutes
Cook: 20 minutes

4 pounds sweet potatoes, peeled and cut into 2-inch chunks
6 tablespoons butter (do not use margarine)
¼ cup light molasses
½ teaspoon salt

1. In 5-quart saucepot, heat sweet potatoes and *enough water to cover* to boiling over high heat. Reduce heat to low; cover and simmer until sweet potatoes are fork-tender, about 20 minutes. Drain well and return sweet potatoes to saucepot.

2. Meanwhile, in 1-quart saucepan, cook butter over medium heat until brown but not burned, 5 to 7 minutes. (Butter should be the color of maple syrup.)

3. With potato masher, mash sweet potatoes, brown butter, molasses, and salt until smooth. Makes 12 accompaniment servings.

Each serving: About 180 calories, 2 g protein, 30 g carbohydrate, 6 g total fat (4 g saturated), 15 mg cholesterol, 160 mg sodium.

SWISS CHARD

See *Greens* (page 590).

TOMATOES

SEASON: All year.
LOOK FOR: Firm, plump, unblemished red or bright yellow tomatoes. Size does not indicate quality.
TO STORE: If tomatoes are not fully ripe, leave them at room temperature, stem end up, out of direct sunlight, until they ripen. Then for fullest flavor, do not refrig-

erate. Store at room temperature; they will keep several days. Green tomatoes can be used in recipes.

TO PREPARE: It is not necessary to peel tomatoes before using them. Rinse them with cold running water. If peeling is preferred, just dip tomatoes in boiling water for one minute, then cool them in cold water; the skin will peel off easily. Or, with a fork, hold the tomato over a direct flame, rotating it constantly until the skin pops, then peel the tomato. Juicy, ripe tomatoes stay firmer and lose less juice if you slice them from stem to blossom end rather than crosswise.

Broiled Tomato Halves

Prep: 16 minutes
Cook: 10 minutes

3 medium ripe tomatoes (about 1 ¼ pounds)
3 tablespoons margarine or butter
¾ cup fresh bread crumbs (about 1 ½ slices)
1 tablespoon minced fresh parsley
¼ teaspoon ground black pepper
¼ teaspoon salt

1. Preheat broiler. Cut out stem end of each tomato, then cut each tomato horizontally in half. Place tomato halves, cut side up, on broiler rack.

2. In small skillet, melt margarine over low heat. Brush each tomato half with a little of the melted margarine. Broil about 5 to 7 inches from heat source until tomatoes are heated through and soft on top, about 5 to 7 minutes. Remove from broiler.

3. Meanwhile, mix fresh bread crumbs, parsley, pepper, and salt into remaining margarine in skillet to make crumb topping.

4. Top each tomato half with about 1 tablespoon crumb topping; spread to cover each half evenly. Return tomato halves to broiler; continue broiling until tops are golden brown, about 3 to 5 minutes. Makes 6 accompaniment servings.

Each serving: About 75 calories, 1 g protein, 5 g carbohydrate, 6 g total fat (1 g saturated), 0 mg cholesterol, 200 mg sodium.

Skillet Cherry Tomatoes

Prep: 5 minutes
Cook: 5 minutes

3 tablespoons margarine or butter
1 pint cherry tomatoes, stems removed
¼ teaspoon sugar
⅛ teaspoon salt
Chopped fresh parsley for garnish

In large skillet, heat margarine over high heat until hot. Add tomatoes, sugar, and salt, and cook, stirring tomatoes and shaking skillet often, just until tomatoes are heated and skins start to wrinkle. Sprinkle with chopped parsley. Makes 4 accompaniment servings.

Each serving: About 95 calories, 1 g protein, 4 g carbohydrate, 9 g total fat (2 g saturated), 0 mg cholesterol, 195 mg sodium.

Fried Green Tomatoes

Prep: 10 minutes
Cook: 5 minutes per batch

¼ cup all-purpose flour or cornmeal
½ teaspoon salt
⅛ teaspoon ground black pepper
3 medium green tomatoes (about 1½ pounds), cut into ½-inch-thick slices
¼ cup vegetable oil

1. In pie plate, combine flour, salt, and pepper. Dip tomato slices in flour mixture to coat both sides thoroughly. Place floured slices on waxed paper.

2. In 10-inch skillet, heat oil over medium heat until hot. Add tomato slices, a few at a time, and cook until golden brown on both sides and heated through. Drain on paper towels. Makes 4 accompaniment servings.

Each serving: About 140 calories, 2 g protein, 11 g carbohydrate, 11 g total fat (1 g saturated), 0 mg cholesterol, 305 mg sodium.

TURNIPS

SEASON: All year.

LOOK FOR: Firm, unblemished turnips that are heavy for their size and have fresh tops.

TO STORE: Remove tops; refrigerate tops and turnips separately. Use turnips within one week; use tops as soon as possible.

TO PREPARE: Rinse turnips with cold running water. Peel turnips; leave them whole or cut them into slices or chunks, or dice them.

TO COOK: In a saucepan, heat 1 inch of water to boiling over high heat. Add turnips; heat to boiling. Reduce the heat to low; cover and simmer whole turnips 20 or 30 minutes, cut-up turnips 10 to 20 minutes.

Mashed Turnips

Prep: 10 minutes
Cook: 15 minutes

2½ pounds turnips, peeled and diced
4 tablespoons margarine or butter
2 teaspoons salt
1 teaspoon sugar
¼ teaspoon ground black pepper
Chopped fresh parsley for garnish

1. In 4-quart saucepan, heat *1 inch water* to boiling over high heat. Add turnips; heat to boiling. Reduce heat to low; cover and simmer, until tender, about 15 minutes. Drain.

2. Mash turnips. Add margarine, salt, sugar, and pepper; stir until well mixed. Garnish with chopped parsley. Makes 6 accompaniment servings.

Each serving: About 100 calories, 1 g protein, 8 g carbohydrate, 8 g total fat (1 g saturated), 0 mg cholesterol, 950 mg sodium.

᠔Vegetable Combinations

Potato and Artichoke Rösti

Prep: 15 minutes
Cook: 45 minutes

2½ pounds baking potatoes (about 4 large)
¾ teaspoon salt
¼ teaspoon coarsely ground black pepper
2 tablespoons olive oil
1 cup shredded Fontina or mozzarella cheese (4 ounces)
1 jar (8¼ ounces) marinated artichoke hearts, rinsed, well drained, and sliced

1. Preheat oven to 400°F. Peel and coarsely shred potatoes; pat dry with paper towels. In large bowl, toss potatoes with salt and pepper.

2. In nonstick 10-inch skillet with oven-safe handle (or wrap handle of skillet with a double thickness of foil), heat 1 tablespoon oil over medium heat. Working quickly, add half the potatoes, gently patting with rubber spatula to cover bottom of skillet. Leaving a ½-inch border, top potatoes with half the cheese, all the artichokes, then remaining cheese. Cover with remaining potatoes, gently patting to edge of skillet. Cook, gently shaking skillet from time to time to keep pancake from sticking, until browned, about 10 minutes.

3. Carefully invert potato pancake onto large, flat plate. Add remaining tablespoon of oil to skillet, then slide pancake back into skillet. Cook, gently shaking skillet from time to time, 10 minutes longer.

4. Place skillet, uncovered, in oven and bake until potatoes are tender throughout, 20 to 25 minutes. Makes 4 main-dish servings.

Each serving: About 410 calories, 14 g protein, 50 g carbohydrate, 18 g total fat (6 g saturated), 33 mg cholesterol, 760 mg sodium.

Harvest Casserole

Prep: 40 minutes
Bake: 1 hour

5 tablespoons margarine or butter
1 jumbo onion (about 1 pound), cut into ¼-inch-thick slices
2 garlic cloves, crushed with garlic press
1 small rutabaga (about 1 pound), peeled, quartered, and thinly sliced
6 medium carrots (about 1 pound), peeled and thinly sliced

6 medium parsnips (about 1 pound), peeled and thinly sliced
3 tablespoons all-purpose flour
1½ teaspoons salt
¼ teaspoon coarsely ground black pepper
¼ teaspoon ground nutmeg
2½ cups milk
¼ cup freshly grated Parmesan cheese

1. Preheat oven to 375°F. In nonstick 10-inch skillet, melt 3 tablespoons margarine over medium heat. Add onion and garlic, stirring occasionally, and cook, until onion is golden brown and tender, 15 to 20 minutes.

2. In shallow 2½-quart casserole, toss rutabaga, carrots, parsnips, and onion mixture. Cover and bake until vegetables are fork-tender, about 45 minutes.

3. After vegetables have baked 30 minutes, prepare sauce: In 2-quart saucepan, melt remaining 2 tablespoons margarine over medium heat; stir in flour, salt, pepper, and nutmeg until blended; cook 1 minute. Gradually stir in milk and cook, stirring constantly, until sauce boils and thickens.

4. Remove cover from baking dish. Stir sauce into vegetables; sprinkle with Parmesan. Bake, uncovered, until bubbly and golden, 15 minutes longer. Makes 8 accompaniment servings.

Each serving: About 250 calories, 7 g protein, 33 g carbohydrate, 11 g total fat (4 g saturated), 13 mg cholesterol, 630 mg sodium.

Curried Vegetable Stew

Prep: 10 minutes
Cook: 20 minutes

2 teaspoons olive oil
1 large sweet potato (about 12 ounces), peeled and cut into ½-inch chunks
1 medium onion, cut into ½-inch pieces
1 small zucchini (about 8 ounces), cut into 1-inch chunks
1 small green pepper, cut into ¾-inch pieces

1½ teaspoons curry powder
1 teaspoon ground cumin
1 can (15 to 19 ounces) garbanzo beans, rinsed and drained
1 can (14 ½ ounces) diced tomatoes
¾ cup vegetable broth
½ teaspoon salt

1. In nonstick 12-inch skillet, heat oil over medium-high heat. Add sweet potato, onion, zucchini, and green pepper; cook, stirring occasionally, until vegetables are golden, 8 to 10 minutes. Add curry and cumin; cook, stirring, 1 minute.

2. Add garbanzo beans, tomatoes with their juice, broth, and salt; heat to boiling over high heat. Reduce heat to medium-low; cover skillet and simmer until vegetables are fork-tender, about 10 minutes. Makes 4 main-dish servings.

Each serving: About 295 calories, 10 g protein, 55 g carbohydrate, 6 g total fat (1 g saturated), 0 mg cholesterol, 785 mg sodium.

Spinach and Potato Gratin

Prep: 40 minutes
Bake: 1 hour 30 minutes

1 tablespoon margarine or
   butter
3 large shallots, thinly sliced
2 packages (10 ounces each)
   frozen chopped spinach,
   thawed and squeezed dry
⅛ teaspoon ground nutmeg
1 teaspoon salt
½ teaspoon coarsely ground
   black pepper

3 pounds all-purpose potatoes
   (about 9 medium), peeled
   and cut into ¼-inch-thick
   slices
4 ounces Gruyère cheese,
   shredded (1 cup)
1½ cups milk
1 cup heavy or whipping
   cream
1 tablespoon cornstarch

1. Preheat oven to 350°F. Grease shallow 3-quart casserole.

2. In 10-inch skillet, melt margarine over medium heat. Add shallots and cook, stirring occasionally, until tender, 5 minutes. Remove skillet from heat; stir in spinach, nutmeg, ¼ teaspoon salt, and ¼ teaspoon pepper.

3. Arrange one-third of potato slices, overlapping, in casserole. Top with one-third of cheese and one-half of spinach mixture. Repeat layering with remaining ingredients, ending with cheese.

4. In large bowl, with wire whisk, mix milk, cream, cornstarch, remaining ¾ teaspoon salt, and ¼ teaspoon pepper until smooth. Pour milk mixture evenly over casserole.

5. Place sheet of foil underneath casserole; crimp foil edges to form a rim to catch any overflow during baking. Cover casserole and bake 30 minutes. Remove cover and bake until center is hot and bubbly, and top is golden, about 1 hour longer. Makes 12 accompaniment servings.

Each serving: About 230 calories, 8 g protein, 24 g carbohydrate, 13 g total fat (7 g saturated), 42 mg cholesterol, 315 mg sodium.

Sunday-Night Vegetable Hash

Prep: 15 minutes
Cook: 30 minutes

1½ pounds all-purpose potatoes (about 4 medium), peeled and cut into ½-inch cubes
6 slices bacon, cut into 1-inch pieces
1 large red pepper, cut into ½-inch pieces
Salt
1 can (10 to 15½ ounces) black beans, rinsed and drained
4 large eggs
Pepper (optional)

1. In 3-quart saucepan, heat potatoes and *enough water to cover* to boiling over high heat. Reduce heat to low; cover and simmer until potatoes are almost tender, about 4 minutes. Drain well.

2. In nonstick 12-inch skillet, cook bacon, red pepper, potatoes, and ¼ teaspoon salt over medium-high heat, stirring occasionally, until vegetables are tender and browned, about 15 minutes. Stir in black beans; heat through.

3. In nonstick 10-inch skillet, heat *1½ inches water* to boiling over high heat. Reduce heat to medium-low. One at a time, break eggs into a custard cup, then, holding cup close to water's surface, slip each egg into simmering water. Cook eggs until done as desired, 3 to 5 minutes. When done, carefully remove eggs from water with a slotted spoon. Drain each egg (still held in spoon) on paper towels.

Serve poached eggs on vegetable hash. Sprinkle eggs with salt and pepper, if desired. Makes 4 main-dish servings.

Each serving: About 480 calories, 22 g protein, 49 g carbohydrate, 26 g total fat (9 g saturated), 236 mg cholesterol, 750 mg sodium.

Green Beans and Mushrooms with Bacon

Prep: 25 minutes
Cook: 25 minutes

6 slices bacon
1 pound green beans, trimmed
1 pound medium mushrooms, each cut into quarters
1 large red onion (12 ounces), sliced
½ cup water
2 tablespoons cider vinegar
½ teaspoon salt
⅛ teaspoon crushed red pepper

1. In 12-inch skillet cook bacon over medium-low heat, until crisp. With slotted spoon, transfer to paper towels to drain.

2. To bacon drippings remaining in skillet, add whole green beans, mushrooms, onion, water, vinegar, salt, and crushed red pepper; cover skillet and cook over medium heat, stirring occasionally, until vegetables are tender, about 20 minutes.

3. To serve, spoon bean mixture into bowl. Crumble bacon and sprinkle over beans. Makes 6 accompaniment servings

Each serving: About 275 calories, 7 g protein, 14 g carbohydrate, 22 g total fat (8 g saturated), 25 mg cholesterol, 480 mg sodium.

Mashed Potatoes with Cabbage

Prep: 20 minutes
Cook: 35 minutes

6 medium potatoes (about 2 pounds)
1 medium head green cabbage (about 2 pounds)
5 tablespoons margarine or butter
1 small onion, diced
¾ cup milk
1 teaspoon salt
⅛ teaspoon ground black pepper

1. In 4-quart saucepan, heat potatoes and *enough water to cover* to boiling over high heat. Reduce heat to low; cover and simmer until potatoes are fork-tender, 25 to 30 minutes.

2. Meanwhile, discard tough outer leaves from cabbage; carefully remove 4 large leaves and reserve. Chop remaining cabbage. In 10-inch skillet, melt margarine over medium heat. Add chopped cabbage and onion, and cook, stirring occasionally, until very tender, about 25 minutes.

3. When potatoes are done, drain and peel. In large bowl, with mixer at low speed, beat potatoes, milk, salt, and pepper until light and fluffy. With rubber spatula, fold in cabbage mixture.

4. To serve, line platter or bowl with reserved cabbage leaves; spoon potato mixture onto cabbage leaves. Makes 10 accompaniment servings.

Each serving: About 155 calories, 3 g protein, 22 g carbohydrate, 7 g total fat (1 g saturated), 3 mg cholesterol, 335 mg sodium.

Succotash

Prep: 30 minutes
Cook: 35 minutes

4 slices bacon
6 medium potatoes (about 2 pounds), peeled and diced
1 medium green pepper, diced
1 small onion, minced
2 medium ripe tomatoes (¾ pound), chopped
1 package (10 ounces) frozen baby lima beans

1 package (10 ounces) frozen whole-kernel corn
¾ cup water
2 teaspoons salt
1½ teaspoons sugar
⅛ teaspoon ground black pepper

1. In 5-quart Dutch oven or saucepot, cook bacon until browned over medium-low heat. With slotted spoon, transfer to paper towels to drain. Crumble bacon; reserve.

2. In drippings remaining in Dutch oven, cook potatoes, green pepper, and onion over medium heat, stirring frequently, until pepper and onion are tender. Add tomatoes, lima beans, corn, water, salt, sugar, and pepper, and heat to boiling over high heat. Reduce heat to low; cover and simmer, stirring occasionally, until vegetables are tender and mixture thickens slightly, about 20 minutes.

3. To serve, spoon vegetable mixture into large bowl; sprinkle with reserved crumbled bacon. Makes 10 accompaniment servings.

Each serving: About 210 calories, 6 g protein, 28 g carbohydrate, 9 g total fat (3 g saturated), 10 mg cholesterol, 600 mg sodium.

Ratatouille

Prep: 35 minutes
Cook: 45 minutes

½ cup olive oil
1 large onion, diced
1 garlic clove, peeled and cut
  in half
1 medium eggplant (about 1½
  pounds), cut into 1-inch
  chunks
1 green or red pepper, cut into
  1-inch pieces

3 medium zucchini (about 10
  ounces each), cut into 1-inch-
  thick slices
½ cup water
2 teaspoons salt
2 teaspoons dried oregano
1 teaspoon sugar
2 large ripe tomatoes (1
  pound), cut into wedges

1. In 6-quart Dutch oven or saucepot, heat oil over medium heat. Add onion and garlic, and cook, stirring occasionally, until tender, about 10 minutes; discard garlic.

2. Add eggplant and green pepper; cook, stirring frequently, 5 minutes. Stir in zucchini, water, salt, oregano,
and sugar; heat to boiling. Reduce heat to medium-low;
cook, stirring occasionally, until vegetables are tender,
about 30 minutes. Stir in tomato wedges; heat through.
Serve hot, or cover mixture and refrigerate to serve chilled
later. Makes 8 accompaniment servings.

*Each serving: About 180 calories, 3 g protein, 14 g carbohydrate,
14 g total fat (2 g saturated), 0 mg cholesterol, 590 mg sodium.*

Vegetable Tempura

Prep: 25 minutes
Cook: 4 minutes plus 5 minutes per batch

1 pound green beans, trimmed
1 small head cauliflower, separated into flowerets
Vegetable oil
1 egg
1½ cups all-purpose flour
½ teaspoon salt
¼ teaspoon baking soda
1½ cups water
1 bunch fresh parsley
Sesame-Soy Sauce (recipe follows)

1. In 3-quart saucepan, heat *1 inch water* to boiling over high heat. Add green beans; heat to boiling. Reduce heat to low; cover and simmer, stirring occasionally, 4 minutes. Drain. Separate cauliflower into small flowerets; set aside.

2. In 4-quart saucepan, heat about 1 inch oil over medium heat to 375°F. on deep-fat thermometer (or heat oil in electric skillet set at 375°F.).

3. Meanwhile, prepare batter: In medium bowl, with wire whisk, mix egg, flour, salt, baking soda, and water until smooth (batter will be thin).

4. Reserve a few parsley sprigs for garnish, if you like. Dip remaining parsley, green beans, and cauliflower, a few pieces at a time, into batter and fry in hot oil until golden brown, about 3 to 5 minutes. Drain on paper towels. Arrange tempura on warm platter; garnish with reserved parsley sprigs. Serve with Sesame-Soy Sauce. Makes 8 accompaniment servings.

SESAME-SOY SAUCE: In small bowl, mix ¼ cup soy sauce, 1 tablespoon sugar, 1 tablespoon rice vinegar, 2 teaspoons sesame seeds, and 2 teaspoons sesame oil.

Each serving: About 195 calories, 6 g protein, 27 g carbohydrate, 8 g total fat (1 g saturated), 27 mg cholesterol, 725 mg sodium.

Moroccan Vegetable Stew

Prep: 15 minutes
Cook: 40 minutes

1 tablespoon olive oil
2 medium carrots, peeled and cut crosswise into ⅓-inch-thick slices
1 medium butternut squash (about 1¾ pounds), peeled and cut into 1-inch cubes
1 medium onion, chopped
1 can (15 to 19 ounces) garbanzo beans, rinsed and drained
1 can (14½ ounces) stewed tomatoes

½ cup pitted prunes, chopped
½ teaspoon ground cinnamon
½ teaspoon salt
⅛ to ¼ teaspoon crushed red pepper
1½ cups water
1 cup couscous (Moroccan pasta)
1 cup vegetable or chicken broth
2 tablespoons chopped fresh cilantro or parsley

1. In nonstick 12-inch skillet, heat oil over medium-high heat. Add carrots, squash, and onion, and cook until golden, about 10 minutes.

2. Stir in garbanzo beans, stewed tomatoes, prunes, cinnamon, salt, crushed red pepper, and water; heat to boiling. Reduce heat to low; cover and simmer until all vegetables are tender, about 30 minutes.

3. Meanwhile, prepare couscous as label directs, but use vegetable broth in place of the water called for on label.

4. Stir cilantro into stew. Spoon stew over couscous to serve. Makes 4 main-dish servings.

Each serving: About 485 calories, 16 g protein, 94 g carbohydrate, 7 g total fat (1 g saturated), 3 mg cholesterol, 1,030 mg sodium.

Fruits

~~~

Individual Fruits • Other Fruit Dishes

Many fruits are ripe and ready to eat when you buy them: apples, berries, cherries, citrus fruits, grapes, pineapples, pomegranates, and rhubarb. Other fruits, particularly those that are shipped long distances, usually need ripening at home. To ripen apricots, nectarines, peaches, pears, and plums, place them in a loosely closed paper bag or a covered fruit-ripening bowl and leave them at room temperature for a few days until ripe. Let bananas, kiwifruit, mangoes, melons, papayas, and Asian and American persimmons stand, uncovered, at room temperature away from direct sunlight until ripe. Refrigerate all ripe fruit.

Serve fruit instead of a vegetable with main dishes; tuck it into meat-, chicken-, or cheese-filled sandwiches; accompany it with cheese for dessert or snack. You'll find dozens of ways to use fruit to add flavor, color, texture contrast, and good nutrition to all types of foods.

The importing of fresh fruits from other growing areas around the world has, in many cases, vastly extended the time in which you can find them at your supermarket or specialty grocer. The "season" we give with each variety of fruit in this chapter is the one in which the fruit is most plentiful and at its best price.

DRIED FRUITS

Unopened packages of dried fruits can be stored at room temperature for up to six months. After opening, transfer to tightly closed containers. Eat out of hand or use in recipes for sauces, coffeecakes, breads, and desserts.

TO STEW DRIED FRUITS*

Fruit	Package size (in ounces)	Water (in cups)	Sugar (in cups)	Cooking time (in minutes)
Apples	8	3½ + ⅛ tsp. salt	¼	25
Apricots	8	2½	¼	15
	11 or 12	3	½	15
Figs	12	3 + 1 tbs lemon juice	0	35
Mixed Fruit	11 or 12	4	½	25
Peaches	11 or 12	4¼	½	25
Pears	11	3	¼	25
Prunes	16	4	0	20

Makes 4 to 6 servings.

ᔧ Individual Fruits

APPLES

SEASON: All year. Supplies are best from October through March.

LOOK FOR: Firm, crisp, well-shaped, and well-colored fruit, with color ranging from bright green to deep red, depending on the variety. Avoid apples that are shriveled, feel soft and mealy, or have brown, bruised spots.

TO STORE: Refrigerate apples; use them within two weeks.

TO PREPARE: Wash apples, then peel and core them, depending on use. To prevent browning, if apples are peeled or sliced and are to stand, sprinkle them with lemon juice.

Choosing the Best in the Bunch

The most perfect-looking apple is rarely the tastiest. Before you buy, consider this:

- Size doesn't always indicate flavor. Some people think that bigger is better; others, that smaller is sweeter. But neither is necessarily true; each apple variety has its own optimum size.
- Flawless lipstick-red skin isn't a guarantee. A Red Delicious, for one, can look gorgeous on the outside and be mealy and tasteless inside. Highly flavorful varieties come in a wide range of shades.
- Brown webbing on the skin isn't a bad sign. Called russeting, this discoloration on the skin of certain varieties is caused by preharvest conditions such as a cool and/or wet climate and doesn't affect taste.
- Freckles are fine. Apples breathe through small, pale vents on their skin called lenticels, which are sometimes visible to the naked eye as scattered brown dots. They have no effect on flavor.
- Shiny doesn't mean fresh. Apples straight from the tree have a natural dusty gray or white waxy "bloom," which seals in moisture. Apples destined for the supermarket are usually machine washed and brushed, which removes this protective coating and makes the apples shinier—not tastier. Apple packers often coat washed apples with an edible wax to make them more appealing and extend shelf life.

Homemade Applesauce

Prep: 10 minutes
Cook: 12 minutes

6 medium cooking apples (about 2 pounds)
½ cup water
⅓ cup sugar
1 teaspoon fresh lemon juice

1. Cut apples into quarters, but do not peel or remove core and seeds. In 3-quart saucepan, heat apples and water to boiling over high heat. Reduce heat to low; cover and simmer until apples are very tender, 10 to 12 minutes. Stir in sugar and lemon juice.

2. Into large bowl, press apple mixture through strainer or food mill to remove skin and seeds. Add more sugar if needed. (If red-skinned apples are used, applesauce will be pink.) Cover and refrigerate. Makes about 4 cups.

Each ½ cup: About 85 calories, 0 g protein, 22 g carbohydrate, 0 g total fat, 0 mg cholesterol, 0 mg sodium.

CHUNKY APPLESAUCE: About 2 hours before serving or early in day: Peel, core, and cut up *6 medium cooking apples.* In 3-quart saucepan, heat apples and *½ cup water* to boiling over high heat. Reduce heat to low; cover and simmer, stirring occasionally, until apples are tender, 8 to 10 minutes. Stir in *⅓ cup sugar, 1 teaspoon lemon juice,* and *dash ground cinnamon.* Cover and refrigerate. Makes about 3 cups.

Each ½ cup: About 115 calories, 0 g protein, 30 g carbohydrate, 0 g total fat, 0 mg cholesterol, 0 mg sodium.

Chunky Cranberry Applesauce

Prep: 10 minutes
Cook: 20 minutes

6 small McIntosh or Winesap apples (about 1½ pounds), peeled,
    cored, and cut into 1-inch chunks
½ cup apple juice
½ cup fresh or frozen cranberries
¼ cup sugar
¼ teaspoon ground cinnamon (optional)

About 30 minutes before serving or early in day: In 3-quart saucepan, heat apples, apple juice, cranberries, sugar, and cinnamon to boiling over high heat. Reduce heat to low; simmer, uncovered, stirring occasionally, until apples are very tender, 15 to 20 minutes. Serve warm or cover and refrigerate to serve chilled. Makes 3 cups or six ½-cup servings.

Each serving: About 100 calories, 0 g protein, 26 g carbohydrate, 0 g total fat (0 g saturated), 0 mg cholesterol, 1 mg sodium.

Fast Baked Apples with Oatmeal Streusel

Prep: 8 minutes
Microwave: 12 to 14 minutes

4 large Rome or Cortland apples (about 10 ounces each)
¼ cup packed brown sugar
¼ cup quick-cooking oats, uncooked
2 tablespoons chopped dates
½ teaspoon ground cinnamon
2 teaspoons margarine or butter

1. Core apples, cutting out a 1¼-inch-diameter cylinder from center of each, almost but not all the way through to bottom. Remove peel about one-third of the way down from top. Place apples in shallow, 1½-quart ceramic casserole or 8" by 8" glass baking dish.

2. In small bowl, combine brown sugar, oats, dates, and cinnamon. Fill each cored apple with equal amounts of oat mixture. (Mixture will spill over top of apples.) Place ½ teaspoon margarine on top of filling in each apple.

3. Microwave apples, covered, on Medium-High (70% power) until tender, 12 to 14 minutes, turning each apple halfway through cooking time. Spoon cooking liquid from baking dish over apples to serve. Makes 4 servings.

Each serving: About 240 calories, 2 g protein, 54 g carbohydrate, 3 g total fat (1 g saturated), 0 mg cholesterol, 30 mg sodium.

Outrageous Caramel Apples

Prep: 20 minutes plus chilling and softening
Cook: 5 minutes

5 (4-inch) ice-cream-bar sticks
5 medium McIntosh or Macoun apples (about 1¾ pounds)
¾ cup chopped peanuts (or miniature candy-coated chocolate
    pieces or semisweet-chocolate pieces, flaked coconut, colored
    sprinkles, toffee bits, or your favorite topping)
1 package (14 ounces) caramels
2 tablespoons water
3 squares (1 ounce each) semisweet or white chocolate, melted

1. Insert an ice-cream-bar stick in stem end of each apple. Place peanuts or other topping on sheet of waxed paper.

2. Line 15½" by 10½" jelly-roll pan with waxed paper; spray waxed paper with nonstick cooking spray.

3. In 2-quart saucepan, heat caramel candies and water over low heat, stirring constantly, until melted and smooth; remove saucepan from heat. Holding stick, dip 1 apple into caramel mixture, spooning mixture over apple to coat completely. (If caramel mixture in saucepan begins to harden, warm over low heat to soften.) Then, place caramel-coated apple on peanuts or other topping to coat bottom; place apple in jelly-roll pan. Repeat with remaining apples, caramel, and peanuts.

4. Spoon melted chocolate into heavy-weight plastic bag. With scissors, cut off corner of bag to make a small opening. Drizzle melted chocolate over apples. Refrigerate apples 15 minutes to allow chocolate to set. If not eating right away, refrigerate apples, loosely covered, up to 2 days. Let apples stand at room temperature 15 minutes to soften before eating. Makes 5 apples.

Each apple: About 610 calories, 9 g protein, 99 g carbohydrate, 23 g total fat (6 g saturated), 0 mg cholesterol, 400 mg sodium.

Gingered Apple Rings

Prep: 20 minutes
Cook: 12 minutes

1 large lemon
6 tablespoons margarine or butter
¼ cup packed brown sugar
2 tablespoons water
½ teaspoon ground ginger
4 medium Golden Delicious apples (1½ pounds), cored and cut into ½-inch rings

1. From lemon, grate 1 teaspoon peel and squeeze 2 tablespoons juice.

2. In 12-inch skillet, heat lemon peel, lemon juice, margarine, brown sugar, water, and ginger over medium heat until sugar dissolves. Add apples; cook until tender, turning apples occasionally, about 10 minutes. Makes 6 accompaniment servings.

Each serving: About 190 calories, 0 g protein, 24 g carbohydrate, 12 g total fat (2 g saturated), 0 mg cholesterol, 155 mg sodium.

Glazed Apple Wedges

Prep: 10 minutes
Cook: 10 minutes

3 large red cooking apples (1 ½ pounds)
4 tablespoons margarine or butter
3 tablespoons light brown sugar
2 teaspoons fresh lemon juice
¾ teaspoon ground cinnamon
¼ teaspoon salt
Heavy or whipping cream (optional)

1. Core apples; cut into ½-inch-thick wedges.

2. In 12-inch skillet, heat margarine over medium heat until hot. Add apples, brown sugar, lemon juice, cinnamon, and salt, and cook until apples are tender, 5 to 10 minutes.

3. Spoon apples and their syrup into 6 dessert bowls. If you like, serve with heavy cream. Makes 6 accompaniment servings.

Each serving, without cream: About 150 calories, 0 g protein, 21 g carbohydrate, 8 g total fat (1 g saturated), 0 mg cholesterol, 200 mg sodium.

Crunchy Apple Dessert

Prep: 20 minutes
Bake: 30 minutes

4 medium cooking apples (1 ½ pounds)
¼ cup dark seedless raisins
2 tablespoons fresh lemon juice
3 tablespoons margarine or butter
½ cup quick-cooking oats, uncooked
¼ cup packed brown sugar
3 tablespoons all-purpose flour
½ teaspoon ground cinnamon
⅛ teaspoon ground allspice
1 cup half-and-half (optional)

1. Preheat oven to 375°F. Grease 8" by 8" baking dish.

2. Peel apples and cut each in half; remove cores and slice. Combine apple slices, raisins, and lemon juice in baking dish.

3. In 1-quart saucepan, melt margarine over medium heat. Remove from heat; stir in oats, brown sugar, flour, cinnamon, and allspice until mixture forms large crumbs.

4. Spoon oat mixture on top of apple mixture. Bake until apples are tender and topping is crisp and lightly browned, about 30 minutes. Serve warm or chilled in dessert bowls. Pass half-and-half to pour over each serving, if you like. Makes 4 servings.

Each serving: About 330 calories, 5 g protein, 58 g carbohydrate, 10 g total fat (2 g saturated), 0 mg cholesterol, 120 mg sodium.

APRICOTS

SEASON: June and July.

LOOK FOR: Plump, juicy-looking orange-yellow fruit. Ripe apricots should yield to gentle pressure on the skin. Avoid dull-looking, shriveled, or soft fruit.

TO STORE: Refrigerate apricots; use within two to three days.

TO PREPARE: Wash apricots and cut in half to remove the pit; peel if desired. To prevent browning if apricots are not to be eaten immediately, sprinkle them with lemon juice.

Viennese Apricot Dumplings

Prep: 45 minutes plus chilling
Cook: 20 minutes

1 package (7½ ounces) farmer cheese
10 tablespoons margarine or butter (1¼ sticks)
¾ cup all-purpose flour
1 large egg
¼ teaspoon plus 1 tablespoon salt
1 cup packed brown sugar
1 teaspoon ground cinnamon
10 firm medium apricots
10 sugar tablets

1. With back of spoon, press farmer cheese through strainer into large bowl. In small saucepan, melt 2 tablespoons margarine over low heat. Add flour, egg, melted margarine, and ¼ teaspoon salt to bowl; mix with wooden spoon to form a soft dough. Wrap dough in plastic wrap and refrigerate until firm enough to handle, at least 3 hours or overnight.

2. About 1½ hours before serving, in small bowl, mix brown sugar and cinnamon; set aside. Cut short slit along seam of each apricot; open slightly to remove pit. Place 1 sugar tablet in cavity; reclose apricot.

3. Divide dough evenly into 10 pieces. With floured hands, on lightly floured surface, pat 1 piece of dough into a 5-inch round. Wrap dough around 1 apricot, pinching edges of dough to completely enclose apricot and seal edges. Set dumpling aside on floured surface; cover to prevent dough from drying out. Repeat to make 9 more dumplings, reserving remaining brown-sugar-and-cinnamon mixture for sprinkling over cooked dumplings later.

4. Fill 8-quart saucepot or Dutch oven three-fourths full with *water*. Add 1 tablespoon salt; heat to boiling over high heat. Carefully drop dumplings into boiling water. When dumplings rise to surface and float, cover saucepot and cook 10 minutes.

5. Meanwhile, in 1-quart saucepan, melt remaining ½

cup margarine (1 stick) over low heat. Remove saucepan from heat.

6. With slotted spoon, remove cooked dumplings from water and drain dumplings (still held in slotted spoon) on paper towels; place in warm deep platter. Pour melted margarine over dumplings. Sprinkle remaining brown-sugar mixture over dumplings. Serve warm. Makes 10 servings.

Each serving: About 330 calories, 7 g protein, 36 g carbohydrate, 18 g total fat (2 g saturated), 41 mg cholesterol, 390 mg sodium.

Honey-Cheese Apricots

Prep: 15 minutes

6 large apricots
2 tablespoons honey
2 packages (3 ounces each) cream cheese, softened
Ground cinnamon or minced preserved ginger

1. Cut apricots in half lengthwise; discard pits.
2. In small bowl, stir honey into softened cream cheese until smooth. Spoon dollop of cheese mixture into each apricot half; sprinkle with cinnamon. Makes 4 servings.

Each serving: About 215 calories, 4 g protein, 18 g carbohydrate, 15 g total fat (9 g saturated), 47 mg cholesterol, 125 mg sodium.

BANANAS

SEASON: All year.

LOOK FOR: Solid yellow bananas specked with some brown flecks if bananas are to be used immediately. Fruit with some green will ripen at home in a few days at room temperature. Brown skins usually indicate overripened fruit. Red bananas are a specialty in some areas.

TO STORE: Refrigerate bananas after ripening; use within two to three days. The skin will darken, but the fruit inside will be ripe and fresh. For longer storage, mash the fruit with a little lemon juice; pack it into freezer containers, leaving ½-inch head space, and freeze. To use, thaw the fruit in the refrigerator and use it in recipes for cakes, cookies, and breads.

TO PREPARE: Peel and slice or cut up bananas, depending on use. To prevent browning if peeled or sliced bananas are not to be eaten immediately, sprinkle them with a little lemon juice.

Broiled Brown-Sugar Bananas

Prep: 5 minutes
Broil: 5 minutes

4 ripe medium bananas (about 1½ pounds), unpeeled
2 tablespoons brown sugar
1 tablespoon margarine or butter
⅛ teaspoon ground cinnamon

1. Preheat broiler. Make a lengthwise slit in each unpeeled banana, being careful not to cut all the way through and leaving 1 inch uncut at banana ends.

2. In cup, with fork, blend brown sugar, margarine, and cinnamon. Place bananas, cut side up, on rack in broiling pan. Spoon brown-sugar mixture into split bananas.

3. Place pan in broiler at closest position to heat source; broil bananas until browned, about five minutes. Serve bananas in skins, and use spoons to scoop out fruit. Makes 4 servings.

Each serving: About 160 calories, 1 g protein, 34 g carbohydrate, 3 g total fat (1 g saturated), 0 mg cholesterol, 40 mg sodium.

BERRIES

A pretty presentation—whether you're scattering berries on cereal or making a shortcake—has a lot to do with how berries are selected and stored. Here are some tips:

PURCHASE POINTERS

- Choose plump, dry, firm berries that are uniformly colored. Check for withered, crushed, or moldy fruit (the mold can spread from berry to berry) and stained packages.
- Dewy, water-sprinkled berries may look picture-perfect, but they're not; moisture accelerates molding and decaying.

Blackberries

- Buy deeply colored berries. Choose from large maroon boysenberries with a rich, tart taste; deep-red loganberries, which are big, long, and tangy; medium to large dark-purple marionberries with small seeds and intense blackberry flavor; and large, glossy black olallieberries, ranging from sweet to tart.

Peak season: June through October
Cup for cup: ½ pint equals about 1 cup.

Blueberries

- Blueberries should be deep-blue; reddish ones are unripe and best saved for jams or pies. The silver-white bloom on the surface of the blueberries is a natural protective coating—not mold.
- Common blueberries are about ½ inch in diameter; wild berries (also called low-bush blueberries), are pea-size, much tarter, and hold their shape exceptionally well during baking.

Peak season: June through August (for wild blueberries, August and September)
Cup for cup: 1 pint equals about 2½ cups.

Boysenberries

- Large, dark, blackberrylike berries with a rich, tart, raspberry flavor. Available during the summer months.

Currants
- Small, round berries that are red, black, or white. Red currants are the most widely available; they are very tart but can be eaten fresh if sugared. Look for currants during the summer, mainly July and August.

Dewberries:
- Berries that resemble blackberries in appearance and flavor though they grow on trailing, ground-running vines. Look for them during the summer months.

Gooseberries
- Berries that resemble small, striped grapes and range in color from pale green to amber to brilliant red. They are tart and therefore are generally served cooked. Look for them in June and July.

Loganberries
- Large, long, reddish berries that taste like raspberries. They are available during the summer months.

Raspberries
- Select brightly colored berries without hulls. (When the color deepens to a dusky shade, the berries are past their prime.)
- Don't miss the sweeter, milder golden berries and moderately tart purple (black) varieties, which are becoming more widely available in farmers' markets and supermarkets.

Peak season: June, July, September, and October
Cup for cup: ½ pint equals about 1 cup.

Strawberries
- The sweetest berries are bright red with fresh green stems attached; pale, yellowish-white strawberries are unripe and sour.
- Leave caps on until after washing so berries don't get waterlogged. Use a huller, paring knife, or even your fingers to remove caps.

Peak season: April through June
Cup for cup: 1 pint equals about 3¼ cups whole, 2¼ cups sliced.

SMART STORAGE TIPS

- Because berries are more fragile and perishable than any other fruit, they can deteriorate within 24 hours of purchase. You can store them in their baskets for brief periods, but to keep for two to three days, place berries, unwashed, on a paper-towel–lined jelly-roll or baking pan, cover loosely with paper towels and plastic wrap, and refrigerate. (Blueberries are the exception: They last up to ten days in the fridge.) For fullest flavor, let berries come to room temperature before eating.
- To freeze berries, wash and drain, then spread in a single layer on a jelly-roll pan. Once they're frozen, transfer to a freezer-weight zip-tight plastic bag and freeze for up to one year. When using frozen berries for baking, there's no need to thaw, just extend cooking time for pies by 10 to 15 minutes; muffins and breads, 5 to 10 minutes. (Again, blues are the exception: They should be frozen unwashed, then quickly rinsed under cold water before using.)

Fresh Blueberry Fool

Prep: 10 minutes

1 pint fresh blueberries
⅓ cup confectioners' sugar
⅛ teaspoon ground cinnamon
½ cup heavy or whipping cream

1. Set aside about ¾ cup blueberries. In large bowl, with fork or potato masher, coarsely mash remaining blueberries. Stir in confectioners' sugar, cinnamon, and whole blueberries; set aside.
2. In small bowl, with mixer at medium speed, beat

cream until soft peaks form. Gently swirl blueberry mixture into whipped cream. Makes 4 servings.

Each serving: About 175 calories, 1 g protein, 19 g carbohydrate, 11 g total fat (7 g saturated), 42 mg cholesterol, 15 mg sodium.

Chocolate-Dipped Strawberries

4 pints large strawberries with stems
2 packages (8 ounces each) semisweet-chocolate squares

1. Rinse strawberries with cold running water but do not remove stems; pat completely dry with paper towels. Set aside. (For dipping, strawberries should be at room temperature.)

2. Into double-boiler top (not over water), grate semisweet-chocolate squares. Set candy thermometer in place; set aside. Heat *water* to boiling in double-boiler bottom; remove from heat. Place double-boiler top over hot water; melt chocolate, stirring chocolate constantly with rubber spatula, until smooth.

3. With fingers, hold 1 strawberry at a time and dip into chocolate, leaving part of strawberry uncovered. Shake off excess chocolate or gently scrape strawberry across rim of double boiler, being careful not to scrape too much chocolate from berry; place on waxed paper.

4. Let chocolate-covered strawberries stand until set, about 10 minutes; serve same day. Refrigerate if not serving right away. Makes about 5 dozen chocolate-covered strawberries.

Each chocolate-covered strawberry: About 40 calories, 0 g protein, 6 g carbohydrate, 2 g total fat (1 g saturated), 0 mg cholesterol, 1 mg sodium.

CACTUS PEARS

ALSO CALLED: Prickly pears.
SEASON: Supplies are best from September through November.

LOOK FOR: Thorny, tough-textured cactus pears that have had their sharp spines removed. (Handle carefully!) When cactus pears are ripe, their skin is red; the skin should yield to careful, gentle pressure. Avoid shriveled or dried fruit.

TO STORE: Keep cactus pears at room temperature; use within one to two days.

TO PREPARE: Peel the ripened cactus pears as you would an apple, being careful to avoid the thorns on the pear, and slice or cut them up for eating out of hand. Cactus pears can also be used in salads.

CHERIMOYAS

ALSO CALLED: Custard apples.

SEASON: November through May.

LOOK FOR: Uniformly green, large fruit, with rough, petallike indentations. Avoid fruit with cracks or dark brown skin.

TO STORE: If necessary, ripen cherimoyas at room temperature until they yield to gentle pressure. Refrigerate cherimoyas; use within one to two days.

TO PREPARE: Wash the fruit; cut it lengthwise into halves or quarters. Serve as you would melon wedges. Discard seeds when eating.

CHERRIES

SEASON: Supplies are best in June and July.

LOOK FOR: Plump, bright-looking cherries with color ranging from amber to red to purplish black, depending on the variety. Tart or sour cherries are best for cooking. Sweet cherries can be eaten fresh or used in cooking. Avoid fruit that is too soft or shriveled.

TO STORE: Refrigerate cherries; use within 1 week.

TO PREPARE: Wash and stem cherries; either leave them whole and unpitted, or cut each cherry in half to remove the pit (or use cherry pitter).

Cherries Jubilee

Prep: 10 minutes
Cook: 5 minutes

1½ pints vanilla ice cream
1 jar (10 ounces) red currant jelly
2 cans (17 ounces each) pitted dark sweet cherries, well drained
½ cup brandy

1. Scoop ice cream into 6 dessert bowls.
2. In medium skillet or chafing dish, heat currant jelly over medium heat, stirring gently, until melted and smooth. Add cherries; heat until simmering. Pour in brandy; heat, without stirring, 1 minute. At table, light brandy with match; spoon flaming cherries over ice cream. Makes 6 servings.

Each serving: About 415 calories, 3 g protein, 72 g carbohydrate, 12 g total fat (7 g saturated), 45 mg cholesterol, 60 mg sodium.

Cherry Cobbler

Prep: 25 minutes
Bake: 15 minutes

1 pound sweet cherries
1 cup water
2 tablespoons cornstarch
1 teaspoon freshly grated
    lemon peel
¼ teaspoon ground cinnamon
Sugar

¼ teaspoon salt
⅓ cup all-purpose flour
1 tablespoon vegetable oil
½ teaspoon baking powder
1 large egg
1 cup half-and-half

1. Reserve 6 cherries with stems for garnish. Stem and pit remaining cherries.
2. In 2-quart saucepan, blend water and cornstarch until smooth. Add pitted cherries, lemon peel, cinnamon, ¼ to ⅓ cup sugar (sweetness of cherries varies), and ⅛ teaspoon salt; cook, stirring, over medium heat, until mixture thick-

ens and boils, about 5 minutes. Spoon mixture into six 6-ounce custard cups.

3. Preheat oven to 375°F. In bowl, mix flour, oil, baking powder, egg, ¼ cup sugar, and remaining ⅛ teaspoon salt; spoon onto cherry mixture. Bake until golden, about 15 minutes. Garnish each cobbler with a reserved cherry. Pass half-and-half to serve over dessert. Makes 6 servings.

Each serving: About 230 calories, 4 g protein, 36 g carbohydrate, 8 g total fat (4 g saturated), 50 mg cholesterol, 155 mg sodium.

COCONUTS

SEASON: All year; supplies are best in November and December.

LOOK FOR: Coconuts that are heavy for their size; the liquid should slosh around inside when the coconut is shaken. Avoid fruit with moldy or wet "eyes."

TO STORE: Refrigerate coconuts; use them within one week. Shredded fresh coconut will keep in the refrigerator for one to two days.

TO PREPARE: Pierce the "eyes" (the three indentations at one end) with a clean screwdriver and hammer, and drain the liquid (reserve liquid if using it in a recipe). Bake coconut in a preheated 350°F. oven 30 minutes. With hammer, tap shell around middle to break it open. Pry the coconut meat in pieces from shell.

TO SHRED COCONUT MEAT: Peel the brown outer skin from the coconut meat. Shred the meat with a coarse grater or in a food processor. One 1½-pound coconut yields 4 to 5 cups of shredded coconut.

TO TOAST SHREDDED COCONUT MEAT: Prehe the oven to 350°F. Spread the shredded coconut in a shallow pan. Bake the coconut until it browned, 15 to 20 minutes, stirring toast it evenly.

CRANBERRIES

SEASON: Supplies are best ber.

LOOK FOR: Plump, firm, glossy, light to dark red berries. Avoid shriveled, discolored, or moist cranberries.

TO STORE: Refrigerate cranberries; use within one to two weeks. To freeze cranberries for longer storage, leave them in their original bag and place it in the freezer. Do not wash cranberries before freezing them.

TO PREPARE: Wash the cranberries and remove any stems; drain them well. Frozen cranberries do not need to thaw. When you wish to use them, just rinse with cold water and drain.

Buffet Cranberry Mold

Prep: 20 minutes plus chilling
Cook: 5 minutes

1 envelope unflavored gelatin
2 packages (6 ounces each) strawberry-flavored gelatin
3 medium oranges
1 package (12 ounces) fresh or frozen cranberries (3 cups)
1½ cups sugar

1. In 4-quart saucepan, evenly sprinkle unflavored gelatin over *2 cups water;* let stand 1 minute to soften slightly. Cook, stirring, over medium heat, until gelatin dissolves and mixture boils. Remove from heat; stir in strawberry gelatin until dissolved. Stir in *3 cups cold water.* Refrigerate until mixture mounds slightly when dropped from a spoon, about 1 hour.

2. Meanwhile, remove peel and white membrane from oranges; chop oranges and place in bowl. Chop cranberries; ˙dd cranberries and sugar to oranges. Stir mixture until ˙˙ar has dissolved.

˙˙˙old fruit mixture into thickened gelatin. Pour into ˙˙˙undt pan or mold. Cover and refrigerate until set, ˙˙˙˙˙s. To serve, unmold gelatin onto platter. Makes

˙˙75 calories, 3 g protein, 43 g carbohydrate, ˙˙˙terol, 55 mg sodium.

Cranberry Sauce with Port

Prep: 5 minutes plus chilling
Cook: 10 minutes

1 bag (12 ounces) cranberries (3 cups)
1 cup port wine
¾ cup sugar
½ teaspoon ground cinnamon
¼ teaspoon ground nutmeg
⅛ teaspoon ground cloves

In 2-quart saucepan, heat cranberries, port, sugar, cinnamon, nutmeg, and cloves to boiling over high heat, stirring occasionally. Reduce heat to medium and cook, uncovered, stirring occasionally, until most cranberries pop, about 5 to 8 minutes. (Mixture will thicken as it chills.) Spoon sauce into serving bowl; cover and refrigerate until well chilled, about 3 hours or up to 4 days. Makes about 2 cups.

Each ¼ cup: About 120 calories, 0 g protein, 28 g carbohydrate, 0 g total fat, 2 g fiber, 0 mg cholesterol, 2 mg sodium.

DATES

SEASON: All year.
LOOK FOR: Lustrous, plump, golden-brown fruit, lighter in color than dried dates. Both pitted and unpitted dates are sold prepackaged.
TO STORE: Keep dates tightly wrapped; when refrigerated, they will keep for several weeks.
TO PREPARE: Cut out the pits, if necessary.
TO SERVE: Eat dates out of hand; use them with fruit as a dessert; or use them in recipes cookies, and salads.

FIGS

SEASON: Summer and fall
LOOK FOR: Slightly firm

to gentle pressure on the skin. Varieties range in color from greenish yellow to purple to black. Avoid very soft fruit or fruit with a sour odor.

TO STORE: Refrigerate figs; use within one to two days.

TO PREPARE: Rinse gently; remove any stems.

TO SERVE: Eat figs out of hand; or serve them as a first course with prosciutto or as a dessert with cheese. Choose any of the following varieties:

Adriatic: Named for the Adriatic Sea, an arm of the Mediterranean, this fig has pale pink flesh and light green skin. Its high sugar content, retained as the fruit dries to a golden shade, makes this a blue-ribbon choice for fig bars and pastry fillings.

Black Mission (or **Mission**): Named for the Spanish missionaries who planted fig trees along the fertile California coast, this fruit has deep purple or black skin and tender, pink flesh. It's popular in recipes calling for dried or fresh figs, such as compotes or chutneys.

Calimyrna: The Smyrna fig comes from the ancient Turkish city that once went by that name, but the Calimyrna, its descendant, is grown in California. This large, greenish-yellow fig is known for its sweet crunch (thanks to many tiny edible seeds) and appealing nutlike flavor; it's the best-selling dried variety.

Kadota: A favorite for canning and preserving, this fig is the American version of the Italian Dattato. Its thick skin is a pretty amber when ripe; the flesh is purple and practically seedless.

Fresh Figs with Raspberry Cream

Prep: 15 minutes

6 medium figs, trimmed
½ cup heavy or whipping cream
⅛ teaspoon vanilla extract
2 tablespoons raspberry preserves

1. Cut deep "X" through top of each fig, being careful not to cut all the way through. Spread sections slightly apart; set aside.

2. In small bowl, with mixer at medium speed, beat cream and vanilla until stiff peaks form. Fold raspberry preserves into whipped cream.

3. Spoon whipped-cream mixture into large decorating bag with large rosette tip. Pipe whipped-cream mixture into center of each fig. Makes 6 servings.

Each serving: About 120 calories, 1 g protein, 15 g carbohydrate, 8 g total fat (5 g saturated), 27 mg cholesterol, 10 mg sodium.

Fig-Frangipane Tart

Prep: 30 minutes plus chilling
Bake: 45 to 50 minutes

Crust
¾ cup (1½ sticks) butter, softened (no substitutions)
⅓ cup sugar
2 large egg yolks
1 teaspoon vanilla extract
2 cups all-purpose flour

Frangipane Filling
1 tube or can (7 to 8 ounces) almond paste, broken into 1-inch
    pieces
4 tablespoons butter, softened (no substitutions)
2 large eggs
1 tablespoon all-purpose flour
2 pints small figs (about 1½ pounds), trimmed and each cut into
    quarters
1 tablespoon sugar

1. Prepare crust: In large bowl, with mixer at low speed, beat butter and sugar until blended. Increase speed to high; beat until creamy, about 2 minutes, constantly scraping bowl with rubber spatula. Beat in egg yolks, vanilla, and *1 tablespoon plus 1 teaspoon cold water*. At low speed, beat in flour until dough is just moist enough to hold together.

2. Shape dough into a disk; wrap and refrigerate until cold, about 30 minutes.

3. Preheat oven to 375°F. With floured hands, press dough into 11" by 8" by 1" rectangular or 11" by 1" round tart pan with removable bottom. Refrigerate while preparing filling.

4. Prepare frangipane filling: In medium bowl, with mixer at low speed, beat almond paste and butter until blended. Increase speed to high; beat until light and fluffy, about 2 minutes, constantly scraping bowl with rubber spatula. Reduce speed to medium; add eggs and beat until blended. (It's okay if there are tiny bits of almond paste in mixture.) With spoon, stir in flour. Spread filling over dough in pan. Arrange figs, cut side up, close together on filling; sprinkle with sugar.

5. Place sheet of foil under tart pan; crimp foil edges to form a rim to catch any overflow during baking. Bake tart until center is golden, 45 to 50 minutes. Cool tart in pan on wire rack. When cool, carefully remove side of pan. Makes 12 servings.

Each serving: About 390 calories, 6 g protein, 43 g carbohydrate, 23 g total fat (1 g saturated), 112 mg cholesterol, 170 mg sodium.

GRAPEFRUIT

SEASON: All year. Supplies are best from January through April.

LOOK FOR: Well-shaped fruit that is firm and heavy for its size. Brownish discolorations on the skin usually do not affect the eating quality. Varieties include seedless or with seeds, either pink-, red-, or white-fleshed. Avoid fruit that is soft or discolored at the stem end.

TO STORE: Refrigerate grapefruit; use within one to two weeks.

TO PREPARE: Cut the fruit in half parallel to the stem end. Then, cut the sections from the membranes, leaving them in place if you are serving the grapefruit in the shell. Remove any seeds.

Broiled Grapefruit

Prep: 5 minutes
Broil: 10 minutes

1 grapefruit, cut in half
1 teaspoon brown sugar
1 teaspoon margarine or butter, softened

Preheat broiler. Section grapefruit and remove seeds. Sprinkle each half with a little brown sugar; dot with softened margarine or butter. Broil until golden and heated through, about 10 minutes. Makes 2 servings.

Each serving: About 70 calories, 1 g protein, 14 g carbohydrate, 2 g total fat (0 g saturated), 0 mg cholesterol, 25 mg sodium.

BAKED GRAPEFRUIT: Prepare as above but bake in preheated 450°F. oven 20 minutes.

VARIATIONS: Instead of sugar, use *honey, maple* or *maple-flavored syrup,* or *dark corn syrup.*

GRAPES

SEASON: All year, depending on the variety.

LOOK FOR: Plump, fresh-looking fruit with individual grapes firmly attached to their stems. Avoid dry, brittle stems and shriveled grapes or ones leaking moisture. Varieties of table grapes—grapes eaten as is or in fruit cups, salads, and desserts—include:

ALMERIA: Large, firm, light green, oval grapes with a mild flavor; available from October through February.

BLACK BEAUTY: Medium to large grapes, similar in size to Thompson Seedless, known for juiciness. Earliest black seedless variety; available in May and June.

CALMERIA: Large, firm, light green, elongated grapes with a mild flavor; available from October through February.

CARDINAL: Very large, red, round grapes with a grayish bloom and a mild flavor; available May through August.

CONCORD: Large, purple, round, grapes with a distinctive aroma and flavor—a favorite choice for juice and jelly; available in September and October.

EMPEROR: Large, reddish grapes with a cherrylike flavor; available from September through March.

EXOTIC: Large, shiny-black, round grapes with a subtle mild flavor; available from June through August.

FLAME SEEDLESS: Medium to large, red, round, seedless grapes with a slightly tart flavor; available from mid-June through September.

ITALIA: Large, golden grapes with a whitish bloom and a distinctive full-bodied fruity flavor; available from August through October.

PERLETTE: Small, crisp, frosty-white, seedless grapes with a sweet, tangy flavor; available from mid-May through mid-July.

QUEEN: Large, uniformly red, slightly oval grapes, with a mild sweet flavor; available in August and September.

RIBIER: Very large, firm, jet-black, round grapes with a mild flavor; available from mid-July through mid-February.

RUBY SEEDLESS: Medium, brilliant red, round, seedless grapes with a very sweet flavor; available from mid-August through January.

THOMPSON SEEDLESS: Medium to large, light green to golden, oblong, seedless grapes with a light, sweet flavor; available from June through November.

TOKAY: Large, very firm, brilliant reddish orange grapes with a mild flavor; available from August through November.

TO STORE: Refrigerate grapes; use within one week.

TO PREPARE: Wash and pat dry with paper towels.

Green Grapes with Gingered Sour Cream

Prep: 10 minutes

1 pound seedless green grapes
Preserved ginger in syrup
1 container (8 ounces) sour cream

1. Cut each grape in half. Place grapes in 6 dessert bowls; set aside.

2. Mince enough preserved ginger to make 2 tablespoons. Reserve 1 teaspoon minced ginger for garnish. In small bowl, stir sour cream and remaining minced ginger.

Spoon a dollop of sour-cream mixture onto grapes in each bowl. Garnish with reserved minced ginger. Makes 6 servings.

Each serving: About 135 calories, 2 g protein, 16 g carbohydrate, 8 g total fat (5 g saturated), 17 mg cholesterol, 25 mg sodium.

GUAVAS

SEASON: September through November.

LOOK FOR: Fruit with green to yellowish red skin, depending on the variety. Ripe guavas should yield to gentle pressure on the skin. Avoid fruit with cracked skins.

TO STORE: Refrigerate guavas after ripening and use them within two to three days.

TO PREPARE: Wash the fruit; cut off the skin. Cut large guavas in pieces for eating out of hand.

KIWIFRUIT

ALSO CALLED: Chinese gooseberry.

SEASON: All year.

LOOK FOR: Slightly firm fruit with fuzzy skin. When fully ripe, kiwifruit should yield to gentle pressure on the skin.

TO STORE: Firm, unwashed kiwifruit may be stored by itself in a zip-tight plastic bag in the refrigerator for several months. Ripen kiwifruit at room temperature; refrigerate after ripening and use within one to two days.

TO PREPARE: With sharp knife, peel off skin; cut in wedges or slices. Or cut unpeeled fruit lengthwise in half to be eaten with a spoon.

KUMQUATS

SEASON: November through April with best supplies in early winter.

LOOK FOR: Firm, glossy, bright orange kumquats. Avoid blemished or shriveled fruit.

TO STORE: Refrigerate kumquats; use within one week.

TO PREPARE: Wash the fruit and remove the stems; cut in half to remove the seeds.

TO SERVE: Eat kumquats out of hand, peel and all; add cut-up kumquats to fruit salads; or leave them whole for a garnish.

LEMONS AND LIMES

SEASON: All year.

LOOK FOR: Firm, bright fruits that are heavy for their size. Pale or greenish yellow lemons usually indicate fruit of higher acidity. Limes should have glossy skin; irregular purplish brown marks on skins do not affect quality. Avoid soft, shriveled, or hard-skinned fruits.

TO STORE: Keep lemons and limes for a few days at room temperature, or refrigerate them and use them within two weeks.

TO PREPARE: Cut fruit in half, parallel to stem end, for squeezing; slice or cut into wedges for garnishes; remove seeds. When grating or shredding lemon or lime peel, be sure to grate only the zest, the thin, colored part of the peel, as the white pith underneath will add a bitter taste to food.

LOQUATS

SEASON: April and early May.

LOOK FOR: Deep-colored, orange-yellow fruit that yields to gentle pressure on the skin.

TO STORE: Refrigerate loquats; use within two to three days.

TO PREPARE: Pull off peel; remove seeds for eating out of hand; or use in salads.

LYCHEES

SEASON: Late May through July.

LOOK FOR: Firm, rough, reddish brown, rubbery-skinned fruit the size of a large strawberry, with no indication of decay at the stem end. Avoid blemished fruit.

TO STORE: Refrigerate lychees; use within one to two days.

TO PREPARE: Beginning at the stem, with your thumb, pull off the skin as you would an orange skin; remove the pit for eating lychees out of hand; or use fruit in salads or in Oriental stir-fry dishes.

MANGOES

SEASON: All year. Supplies are best from May through August.

LOOK FOR: Plump, yellowish or orange oval or round fruit, sometimes with speckled skin, and fresh aroma. Ripe mangoes should yield slightly to gentle pressure on the skin. (Unripe mangoes have very poor flavor.) Avoid soft or shriveled fruit and fruit with bruises or large black spots.

TO STORE: Let mangoes ripen at room temperature, then refrigerate and use them within two to three days.

TO PREPARE: With a sharp knife, cut a lengthwise slice from each side of the long flat seed as close to the seed as possible; set aside the section containing the seed. Peel the skin from the cut-off pieces and cut the mango crosswise into slices, or use a spoon to carefully scoop out the mango flesh in long, curved slices for salads, desserts or main-dish accompaniments. Cut the skin from the reserved mango section and carefully slice it from the seed into pieces.

MELONS

SEASON: April through December, depending on the variety.

LOOK FOR: Fully ripened melons that are heavy for their size for best sweetness and flavor. Avoid bruised or cracked fruit. Use these guidelines for selecting specific varieties:

Canary: Oval, with a bright yellow rind, this melon gives off a rich aroma when ripe. The sweet flesh tastes similar to honeydew. Look for canary melons from mid-June to mid-September.

Cantaloupe: Available June through September, this melon has a golden or greenish beige skin with thick, coarse netting. The scar at the stem end should be smooth, without any of the stem remaining. When ripe, cantaloupe has a pleasant aroma and salmon-colored flesh, and it feels tender but not mushy at the blossom end.

Casaba: Round, with a pointed end, the chartreuse-yellow casaba has lengthwise furrows, no netting, and cream colored flesh. When the fruit is ripe, the rind is a rich yellow and the blossom end yields to gentle pressure. Supplies are best in July through October.

Crenshaw: Globe-shaped and pointed at the stem end, with shallow furrows, the gold and green crenshaw melon has the rind that turns all gold when the melon is ripe and rich, aromatic pink flesh; blossom end yields to gentle pressure. Look for them July through October.

Honeydew, Honeyball: These melons are similar except that the honeyball is smaller. The rind is cream-colored with patches of netting. When the melon is ripe, the skin should feel velvety and the rind should give slightly. Look for honeyballs from July through November, honeydews all year.

Persian: Resembling the cantaloupe but larger and with finer netting, the Persian melon has a dark green background that turns lighter green when the fruit is ripe. The skin gives under slight pressure. The flesh is orange-pink, and the aroma is distinct. Persian melons are available from June through November.

Santa Claus: Available in December, this melon is a large, oblong fruit with yellow-green flesh and a green-gold, slightly netted rind that turns yellow when ripe. The blossom end will yield to gentle pressure.

See also *Watermelons* (page 690).

TO STORE: Let melons ripen at room temperature, then refrigerate them and use within two to three days. Keep them well wrapped after cutting.

Cantaloupe Boats

Prep: 10 minutes

¼ cup sliced almonds
¼ cup honey
1 ripe medium cantaloupe, cut into quarters, with seeds removed
1 pint vanilla frozen yogurt
½ pint raspberries

1. In small nonstick skillet, toast almonds over medium heat, stirring frequently, just until golden. Remove skillet from heat and stir in honey; set aside.

2. To serve, place cantaloupe quarters on 4 dessert plates. Top with frozen yogurt, raspberries, and warm almond mixture. Makes 4 servings.

Each serving: About 330 calories, 8 g protein, 64 g carbohydrate, 8 g total fat (3 g saturated), 2 mg cholesterol, 125 mg sodium.

Creamy Curried Melon

Prep: 15 minutes

½ medium cantaloupe
½ medium honeydew melon
2 tablespoons sugar
1 tablespoon fresh lemon juice
⅛ teaspoon salt
½ cup heavy or whipping cream
1 teaspoon curry powder

1. Cut cantaloupe and honeydew into bite-size chunks. In large bowl, toss melon chunks with sugar, lemon juice, and salt.

2. In small bowl, beat heavy or whipping cream and curry powder until soft peaks form.

3. Spoon whipped-cream mixture over fruit in bowl;

gently toss to mix well. Serve immediately, or dressing will
be watery. Makes 6 servings.

*Each serving: About 130 calories, 1 g protein, 17 g carbohydrate,
8 g total fat (5 g saturated), 27 mg cholesterol, 70 mg sodium.*

NECTARINES

SEASON: May through September. Best supplies are from
June through August.
LOOK FOR: Plump, richly colored, smooth-skinned fruit.
The color should be reddish to yellowish. Slightly firm
fruit should ripen well at room temperature. Avoid
hard, soft, or shriveled nectarines or those with a large
proportion of green skin.
TO STORE: Let nectarines ripen at room temperature;
then refrigerate them and use within three to five days.
TO PREPARE: Wash the fruit and cut it in half to remove
the pit. To prevent browning, if peeled or cut nectarines
are not to be eaten immediately, sprinkle them with
lemon juice.

Spiced Nectarine Slices

Prep: 10 minutes
Cook: 10 minutes

1½ cups water
¾ teaspoon whole cloves
¼ teaspoon ground cinnamon
¼ teaspoon ground ginger
4 large nectarines, peeled, pitted, and thinly sliced
½ cup sugar
3 tablespoons fresh lemon juice

1. In 10-inch skillet heat water, cloves, cinnamon, and
ginger to boiling; over medium heat; boil 2 minutes.
2. Add nectarine slices to spice mixture; cook, stirring
occasionally, until tender, about 7 minutes. Toward end of
cooking time, stir in sugar and lemon juice. Refrigerate.

Serve slices with roast meat. Makes 16 accompaniment servings.

Each serving: About 45 calories, 0 g protein, 11 g carbohydrate, 0 g total fat, 0 mg cholesterol, 0 mg sodium.

ORANGES

SEASON: All year. Best supplies in winter and early spring.

LOOK FOR: Firm oranges that are heavy for their size. Strict state regulations help assure tree-ripened fruit; a slight greenish color or russeting on the skin does not affect the quality. Navel and Temple oranges are easily peeled and sectioned; Valencias, Parson Browns, Pineapples, and Hamlins contain abundant juice.

TO STORE: Keep oranges at room temperature for a few days, or refrigerate them and use within two weeks.

TO PREPARE: Peel oranges and separate them into sections, slice them, or cut them up.

Caramel-Glazed Oranges

Prep: 30 minutes plus chilling
Cook: 10 minutes

6 large navel oranges
2 tablespoons brandy (optional)
1 cup sugar

1. From oranges, with vegetable peeler or small knife, remove six 3" by ¾" strips of peel. Cut strips lengthwise into very thin slivers.

2. Cut remaining peel and white pith from oranges. Slice oranges into ¼-inch-thick rounds and place in deep platter, overlapping slices. Sprinkle with brandy, if using, and orange peel.

3. In 10-inch skillet, cook sugar over medium heat, stirring to dissolve any lumps, until it melts and becomes deep amber in color. Drizzle caramelized sugar over oranges. Cover and refrigerate until caramel melts, about 2 hours. Makes 6 servings.

Each serving: About 210 calories, 2 g protein, 53 g total fat (0 g saturated), 0 mg cholesterol, 2 mg sodium.

PAPAYAS

SEASON: All year.

LOOK FOR: Greenish yellow to almost-yellow fruit that yields to gentle thumb pressure. Avoid shriveled or bruised fruit.

TO STORE: Refrigerate papayas; use within three to four days.

TO PREPARE: Cut papayas in half lengthwise and scoop out the seeds. Peel and slice or cut them up.

PASSION FRUIT

SEASON: February through July.

LOOK FOR: Fruit with leathery, mottled, purple skin and light orange flesh with numerous small, dark, edible seeds. The fruit is ripe and ready to eat when the skin becomes wrinkled; the flavor is somewhat like a sweet, delicately perfumed grapefruit.

TO STORE: Refrigerate passion fruit; use within three days.

TO PREPARE: Cut the fruit in half crosswise and spoon out the pulp and seeds.

PEACHES

SEASON: May through September.

LOOK FOR: Fairly firm to slightly soft fruit with a yellow or cream color and, depending on the variety, a red blush. Avoid green, shriveled, or bruised fruit. The pulp of freestone varieties is easily removed from the pit.

TO STORE: Refrigerate ripe peaches; use within three to five days.

TO PREPARE: Peel and cut the fruit in half to remove pit. To peel peaches, dip them in rapidly boiling water for about 15 seconds, then dip them immediately in a pan of cold water; pull off the skins. To prevent browning if peeled or cut peaches are not to be eaten immediately, sprinkle them with lemon juice.

Stewed Peaches

Prep: 5 minutes
Cook: 12 minutes

¾ cup water
¼ cup sugar
4 whole cloves
1½ pounds peaches

1. In medium saucepan, heat water, sugar, and cloves to boiling over medium heat.
2. Peel peaches; cut each in half, and remove pit. Add peach halves to syrup mixture; heat to boiling. Reduce heat to low; cover and simmer until peaches are tender, about 10 minutes. Serve warm. Or cover and refrigerate to serve later. Makes 6 servings.

Each serving: About 70 calories, 1 g protein, 18 g carbohydrate, 0 g total fat, 0 mg cholesterol, 0 mg sodium.

PEARS

SEASON: All year.
LOOK FOR: Well-shaped, fairly firm fruit; the color depends on the variety. Ripe pears yield readily to soft pressure in the palm of the hand. Avoid shriveled, discolored, cut, or bruised fruit. Select Bartlett, Anjou, and Bosc pears for eating fresh or cooking; Comice, Seckel, Nelis, and Kieffer for eating fresh.
TO STORE: Let firm pears ripen at room temperature for a few days, then refrigerate and use them within three to five days. To prevent browning if peeled or cut-up

pears are not to be eaten immediately, sprinkle them with lemon juice.

TO PREPARE: Peel pears if desired; cut the fruit lengthwise in half, and remove the seeds, core, and stem.

Roasted Vanilla Pears

Prep: 25 minutes plus cooling
Roast: 35 to 40 minutes

1 medium lemon
1 whole vanilla bean*
8 firm but ripe Bosc pears (about 3½ pounds), unpeeled
½ cup sugar
2 tablespoons butter, melted (no substitutions)
½ cup water

1. Preheat oven to 450°F. From lemon, with vegetable peeler or small knife, remove two 2" by 1" strips of peel. Squeeze 1 tablespoon juice from lemon. Cut vanilla bean crosswise in half, then cut each half lengthwise, without cutting all the way through to the other side. With knife, scrape out seeds. Reserve seeds and pod.

2. With melon baller or small knife, remove core and blossom end (bottom) of each pear, but do not remove stems. If necessary, cut thin slice from bottom of each pear so it will stand upright. Sprinkle ½ teaspoon sugar into cored area of each pear; swirl pears to coat insides with sugar. With pastry brush, brush pears with some melted butter; set aside.

3. In shallow 10-inch round ceramic or glass baking dish, mix lemon-peel strips, lemon juice, vanilla-bean pod, vanilla seeds, remaining sugar, any remaining melted butter, and water. Place pears, cored ends down, in baking dish.

4. Roast pears until fork-tender, 35 to 40 minutes. With meat baster or large spoon, baste pears several times during roasting with syrup in dish. Cool pears slightly to serve warm, or cover and refrigerate pears up to 1 day ahead. Reheat to serve warm. Makes 8 servings.

If not using vanilla bean, increase lemon peel to 3 strips and stir 2 teaspoons vanilla extract into syrup after pears have been roasted.

To remove the seeds from pears easily and without waste, use a melon baller to scoop them out. Then run the melon baller from the core to the stem and blossom ends of the pear to remove the stringy portion.

Each serving: About 160 calories, 1 g protein, 34 g carbohydrate, 3 g total fat (2 g saturated), 4 g fiber, 8 mg cholesterol, 30 mg sodium.

Napa Valley Poached Pears

Prep: 20 minutes plus chilling
Cook: 45 minutes

1 bottle (750 ml) red Zinfandel wine (about 3 cups)
2 cups cranberry-juice cocktail
1 ¼ cups sugar
1 cinnamon stick (3 inches)
2 whole cloves
½ teaspoon whole black peppercorns
8 medium Bosc pears with stems

1. In 5-quart Dutch oven, heat wine, cranberry juice, sugar, cinnamon stick, cloves, and peppercorns just to boiling over high heat, stirring to dissolve sugar.

2. Meanwhile, with apple corer, melon baller, or small knife, remove cores from blossom end (bottom) of pears. Peel pears but do not remove stems.

3. Place pears in wine mixture; heat to boiling. Reduce heat to low; cover and simmer until pears are tender but not soft, turning pears occasionally, 15 to 25 minutes.

4. Carefully transfer pears to platter. Strain wine mixture and return it to Dutch oven. Heat wine mixture to boiling over high heat. Cook, uncovered, until liquid is reduced to 1½ cups, 15 to 30 minutes.

5. Cover pears and syrup separately and refrigerate until well chilled, at least 6 hours. To serve, spoon syrup over pears. Makes 8 servings.

Each serving: About 235 calories, 1 g protein, 63 g carbohydrate, 0 g total fat, 0 mg cholesterol, 10 mg sodium.

PERSIMMONS

SEASON: October through December.

LOOK FOR: Slightly firm, plump fruit with smooth, unbroken skin and the stem cap attached. Avoid bruised or overly soft fruit. Asian varieties are most common; smaller, native persimmons are usually homegrown.

TO STORE: When ripe, refrigerate persimmons; use within one to two days.

TO PREPARE: Remove the caps. Press native persimmons through a food mill or strainer to remove the seeds and skin before using the fruit in recipes. For dessert or a snack, place an Asian persimmon, stem end down, on a plate; cut gashes through the top skin so that the pulp can be eaten with a spoon.

PINEAPPLES

SEASON: All year.

LOOK FOR: Firm fruit that is heavy for its size, with a distinct aroma and plump, glossy "eyes." The color will depend on the variety, but usually dark green indicates that fruit is not fully ripe (once picked, they will not ripen further). To tell if a pineapple is ripe and ready to eat; smell it. A pineapple with no aroma will have little flavor; one with a fresh, sweet odor should be juicy and ripe; one with fermented odor will be overripe.

TO STORE: If you like, refrigerate pineapples to chill them before serving.

TO PREPARE: For rings or chunks, cut off the crown and

stem ends; cut the fruit into ½- to 1-inch-thick cross-wise slices. Cut off the rind and remove the eyes. Core the pineapple with a biscuit cutter, knife, or pineapple corer; serve the fruit sliced into rings or cut up. For wedges, cut the fruit through the crown to the stem end into halves, then quarters. Cut off the core along the tops of the wedges; run a knife between the rind and the flesh close to the rind. Leaving the flesh in the shell, cut it into ¼- to ½-inch slices, or remove flesh and use the shell for serving salad.

Fresh Pineapple with Ginger-Maple Cream

Prep: 15 minutes

1 medium pineapple
1 container (8 ounces) sour cream (1 cup)
3 tablespoons maple or maple-flavored syrup
2 tablespoons minced crystallized ginger

1. Slice pineapple lengthwise, through crown to stem end, into 4 long wedges, leaving on leafy crown. Cut off tough core from top of each wedge, then loosen fruit by cutting close to rind. Leaving fruit in shell, cut flesh cross-wise into ½-inch slices.
2. In small bowl, stir sour cream, maple syrup, and ginger. Pass sour-cream mixture to spoon over pineapple wedges. Makes 4 servings.

Each serving: About 240 calories, 2 g protein, 32 g carbohydrate, 12 g total fat (7 g saturated), 25 mg cholesterol, 35 mg sodium.

Mint Julep Cups

Prep: 15 minutes plus chilling

¼ cup chopped fresh mint
¼ cup bourbon whiskey
2 tablespoons sugar
1 pint strawberries, hulled and thickly sliced
1 pineapple, pared, cut into 1-inch chunks

In medium bowl, stir mint, bourbon, and sugar until blended. Stir in strawberry slices and pineapple chunks. Refrigerate up to 2 hours to allow flavors to blend. Makes 6 servings.

Each serving: About 105 calories, 1 g protein, 21 g carbohydrate, 1 g total fat (0 g saturated), 0 mg cholesterol, 2 mg sodium.

PLANTAINS

ALSO CALLED: Cooking bananas.
SEASON: All year.
LOOK FOR: Large, firm, greenish yellow to dark brown fruit with some black spots. The skin of very ripe plantains is black, and the fruit yields to soft pressure.
TO STORE: Store at room temperature; plantain skin will blacken as it ripens.
TO PREPARE: Cut off the ends, then cut the skin lengthwise in strips. With your fingers, peel off the strips.
TO SERVE: Use cooked as a vegetable.

Fried Plantains

Prep: 5 minutes
Cook: 10 minutes per batch

4 very ripe plantains*
Margarine or butter
Salt
Sugar

1. Peel plantains. Cut plantains into ½-inch-thick diagonal slices.

2. In 12-inch skillet, heat 4 tablespoons margarine over medium-high heat until hot. Add about one-third of plantains, and cook until lightly browned on both sides, about 10 minutes. Transfer plantains to warm plate; sprinkle lightly with salt and sugar. Keep warm.

3. Repeat with remaining plantains, adding more butter as needed. Serve with roast ham, pork, lamb, or chicken. Makes 8 accompaniment servings.

If plantains are not available, very green, unripe bananas can be substituted; cooking time may be slightly shorter.

Each serving: About 210 calories, 1 g protein, 29 g carbohydrate, 12 g total fat (2 g saturated), 0 mg cholesterol, 0 mg sodium.

PLUMS

VARIETIES INCLUDE: Italian prune plums, greengage, Santa Rosa, President.

SEASON: June through September.

LOOK FOR: Plump fruit that yields to gentle pressure on the skin and is well colored. Color varies from bright yellow-green to reddish purple to purplish black, depending on the variety. Avoid hard, shriveled, or cracked fruit.

TO STORE: Refrigerate plums; use within five days.

TO PREPARE: Wash plums; cut into each center to remove the pit. Slice or cut up the fruit for serving, with or without skin. Varieties vary in tartness, and some need more sugar than others when cooked.

Plums in Port-Wine Sauce

Prep: 10 minutes
Cook: 5 minutes

2 pounds small plums, each halved and pitted
2 cups ruby port wine
6 whole cloves
1 cinnamon stick (3 inches)
1½ teaspoons freshly grated orange peel
1 cup sugar

1. In 4-quart saucepan, heat plums, port, cloves, cinnamon stick, and orange peel to boiling over high heat. Reduce heat to low; cover and simmer, until plums are tender, 3 to 5 minutes.
2. Gently stir in sugar until dissolved. Spoon plum mixture into bowl; cover and refrigerate until well chilled. Serve plums with syrup. Makes 6 servings.

Each serving: About 250 calories, 1 g protein, 57 g carbohydrate, 1 g total fat (0 g saturated), 0 mg cholesterol, 5 mg sodium.

Prune Plums in Syrup

Prep: 5 minutes
Cook: 10 minutes

12 medium Italian prune plums
1 cup water
⅓ cup sugar

1. With 4-tined fork, prick skin of each plum in several places.
2. In 2-quart saucepan, heat plums, water, and sugar to boiling over medium-high heat. Reduce heat to low; cover and simmer until tender, stirring occasionally, about 10 minutes. Cover and refrigerate until well chilled. Makes 4 servings.

Each serving: About 145 calories, 1 g protein, 35 g carbohydrate, 1 g total fat (0 g saturated), 0 mg cholesterol, 0 mg sodium.

POMEGRANATES

SEASON: September through December. Best supplies are in October.

LOOK FOR: Fresh-looking fruit that is heavy for its size. Avoid shriveled fruit or broken rinds.

TO STORE: Refrigerate pomegranates; use within one week.

TO PREPARE: With a sharp knife, make a shallow cut all around, 1 inch from and parallel to the blossom end. With your fingers, pull off the top. Score the fruit, through the peel only, into about six wedges. Break the wedges apart and gently remove the kernels (which are very juicy). To extract the juice, with a spoon, press the kernels through a strainer; discard the seeds.

TO SERVE: Use the juice in beverages. Eat the kernels out of hand, add them to fruit salad, or use them as a garnish.

QUINCES

SEASON: October and November.

LOOK FOR: Golden-yellow, round or pear-shaped fruit with rather fuzzy skin. Avoid small, knotty fruit and fruit with bruises.

TO STORE: Refrigerate quinces; use within two weeks.

TO PREPARE: Peel the fruit, cut it in half, and remove all the seeds and every bit of core. Slice the fruit. In a saucepan, heat 1 inch of water to boiling over medium heat. Add the slices, and return to a boil. Cover pan, reduce heat to low, and cook until tender. Add sugar to taste. The cooked fruit will remain firm though tender.

TO SERVE: Cooked fruit may be used as a sauce or a dessert as well as in puddings, pies, and tarts.

Baked Quinces with Brown-Sugar Butter

Prep: 10 minutes
Bake: 1 hour

4 medium quinces
½ teaspoon ground cinnamon
4 tablespoons margarine or butter, softened
¼ cup packed brown sugar
Heavy or whipping cream or milk (optional)

1. Preheat oven to 375°F. Do not peel quinces. Starting at stem end of each quince, remove core, being careful not to cut through blossom end. Place quince, cored end up, in 8" by 8" baking dish.

2. Bake quinces 45 minutes. Remove baking dish from oven. Sprinkle hollow center of each quince lightly with cinnamon. Place 1 tablespoon margarine and 1 tablespoon brown sugar in center of each quince, mounding any excess on top, if necessary.

3. Return baking dish to oven and continue baking until quinces are fork-tender, about 15 minutes longer, spooning any margarine mixture in baking dish over quinces occasionally.

4. To serve, place each quince in a dessert dish; spoon any margarine mixture in baking dish over quinces. Serve warm. If you like, pass heavy cream to pour over each serving. Makes 4 servings.

Each serving: About 205 calories, 1 g protein, 28 g carbohydrate, 11 g total fat (2 g saturated), 0 mg cholesterol, 160 mg sodium.

RHUBARB

SEASON: Supplies are best in April and May.
LOOK FOR: Firm, crisp, fairly thick stalks that are either red or pink, depending on the variety. Avoid flabby stalks.

TO STORE: Refrigerate rhubarb; use within three to five days.

TO PREPARE: Wash rhubarb and trim any discolored ends; cut off and discard any leaves (leaves should not be eaten).

Rhubarb-Strawberry Cobbler

Prep: 25 minutes plus cooling
Bake: 20 minutes

1¼ pounds rhubarb, cut into 1-inch chunks (4 cups)
¾ cup plus 1 teaspoon sugar*
¼ cup water
1 tablespoon cornstarch
1 pint strawberries, each cut into quarters
1½ cups all-purpose flour
1½ teaspoons baking powder
½ teaspoon baking soda
¼ teaspoon salt
¼ teaspoon ground cinnamon
⅛ teaspoon ground nutmeg
4 tablespoons margarine or butter
¾ cup plus 1 tablespoon heavy or whipping cream

1. Prepare filling: In 3-quart saucepan, heat rhubarb and ½ cup sugar to boiling over high heat, stirring constantly. Reduce heat to medium-low and continue cooking until rhubarb is tender, about 8 minutes.

2. In cup, blend water and cornstarch until smooth. Stir cornstarch mixture and strawberries into rhubarb mixture; continue cooking until mixture thickens slightly, about 2 minutes. Remove from heat.

3. Meanwhile, preheat oven to 400°F. Into medium bowl, measure flour, baking powder, baking soda, salt, cinnamon, nutmeg, and ¼ cup sugar; stir until combined. With pastry blender or 2 knives used scissor-fashion, cut in margarine until mixture resembles coarse crumbs. Add ¾ cup heavy cream; quickly stir just until mixture forms a soft dough that pulls away from side of bowl.

4. Turn dough onto lightly floured surface; knead 6 to 8 times to mix thoroughly. With floured rolling pin, roll out dough ½ inch thick. With floured 3-inch star-shaped cookie cutter, cut out as many biscuits as possible. Reroll trimmings and cut as above to make 8 biscuits in all.

5. Reheat rhubarb filling until hot; pour into shallow, 2-quart casserole or 11" by 7" glass baking dish. Place biscuits on top of rhubarb. Brush biscuits with remaining 1 tablespoon cream and sprinkle with remaining 1 teaspoon sugar. Place sheet of foil under baking dish; crimp edges to form rim to catch any overflow during baking. Bake until biscuits are golden brown and rhubarb filling is bubbly, about 20 minutes. Cool slightly on wire rack to serve warm, about 15 minutes. Makes 8 servings.

This makes a sweet-tart filling. For a sweeter filling, increase sugar in filling to ¾ cup.

Each serving: About 325 calories, 4 g protein, 45 g carbohydrate, 15 g total fat (7 g saturated), 33 mg cholesterol, 305 mg sodium.

Stewed Rhubarb

Prep: 7 minutes
Cook: 10 minutes

1 pound rhubarb, cut into 1-inch pieces (about 2½ cups), or 1
    package (16 ounces) frozen rhubarb
½ cup sugar
¼ cup strawberry jelly
¼ teaspoon ground cinnamon
⅛ teaspoon salt
½ cup heavy or whipping cream (optional)

1. In 2-quart saucepan, heat rhubarb, sugar, jelly, cinnamon, and salt to boiling over medium heat. Reduce heat to low; cover and simmer stirring often, until rhubarb is tender, about 10 minutes.

2. Spoon rhubarb mixture into 4 dessert dishes. Serve

warm or refrigerate to serve cold later. If you like, serve with cream. Makes 4 servings.

Each serving: About 160 calories, 1 g protein, 41 g carbohydrate, 0 g total fat, 0 mg cholesterol, 85 mg sodium.

TANGERINES AND TANGELOS

SEASON: Tangerines are in season from November through May, tangelos from December through April.

LOOK FOR: Tangerines that are deep yellow to deep orange and heavy for their size, often with loose skin that can be pulled away easily. Tangelos should be bright orange and firm and heavy for their size. They peel and section easily, have few seeds, and are juicy.

TO STORE: Keep at room temperature for a few days, or refrigerate and use within two weeks.

TO PREPARE: Starting from the stem end, with your fingers, pull off the skin. Break the fruit into its natural sections; if you like, cut the center of each section to remove the seeds.

UGLI FRUIT

SEASON: December through May.

LOOK FOR: Grapefruit-shaped citrus fruit that is yellow with greenish splotches and wrinkled, bumpy skin.

TO STORE: Refrigerate ugli fruit; use within one week.

TO PREPARE: Remove peel with your fingers as you would with tangerines, or cut the fruit in half and section it as you would grapefruit. Eat fruit out of hand or use it in salads.

WATERMELONS

SEASON: May through September.

LOOK FOR: Large (usually up to 20 pounds) or "icebox-size" (about 8 pounds) melons with red or yellow flesh; some are seedless. Melons should be firm, symmetrically shaped (round or oblong, depending on the variety). The side of the melon grown next to the ground will be yellowish or cream-colored, not pale green or white. The rind should have a velvety bloom, giving it a dull, not shiny, appearance.

To test a whole melon for ripeness, slap the side of the melon with the open palm of your hand; the sound should be deep and resonant. A dull thud indicates that the melon is underripe; a hollow sound indicates that it is overripe and mushy.

If you buy a cut piece of watermelon, the flesh should be firm and deep red with dark brown or black seeds. Avoid melons with a hard white streak running through the flesh.

TO STORE: Refrigerate watermelon; use within one week. After cutting, cover the cut surface with waxed paper or plastic wrap; use within one or two days.

TO SERVE: For wedges, cut whole melon from stem to blossom end in half; cut each half lengthwise in half, then cut each half crosswise into pieces of desired thickness. Or, cut melon into bite-size chunks; discard rind.

Watermelon Bowl

Prep: 30 minutes

1 long medium watermelon

1. With large, sharp knife, cut lengthwise slice about 2 inches from the top of watermelon; remove top section. With spoon, scoop out pulp from both sections of watermelon and cut into bite-size pieces, being careful to leave about ½ inch of pulp inside the rind to form a shell (or scoop pulp into balls). Reserve cut-up pieces; discard top section of rind.

2. With small, sharp knife, cut an even sawtooth pattern about 1 inch deep around top of watermelon shell. (If watermelon is not level, cut a thin slice of rind from the bottom.) Return watermelon pieces to shell. Cover with plastic wrap and refrigerate until serving time. Makes 16 servings.

Each serving: About 90 calories, 2 g protein, 20 g carbohydrate, 1 g total fat (0 g saturated), 0 mg cholesterol, 5 mg sodium.

↶Other Fruit Dishes

Fruit Salad with Vanilla-Bean Syrup

Prep: 30 minutes plus chilling
Cook: 10 minutes

1 large lemon
1 vanilla bean
¾ cup sugar
¾ cup water
3 ripe mangoes, peeled and cut into 1-inch chunks
2 pints strawberries, hulled and each cut in half or into quarters if
    large
1 medium honeydew melon (about 3½ pounds), cut into 1-inch
    chunks

1. From lemon, with vegetable peeler or small knife, re-move one 3" by 1" strip of peel; squeeze ¼ cup juice. Set aside. Cut vanilla bean lengthwise in half; spread pod open. Scrape seeds from inside of vanilla bean; reserve seeds and pod.

2. In 1-quart saucepan, heat lemon peel, vanilla-bean seeds, vanilla-bean pod, sugar, and water to boiling over high heat. Reduce heat to medium; cook, uncovered, until syrup is slightly thickened, about 5 minutes. Remove vanilla-bean pod and lemon. Pour syrup into small bowl; stir in lemon juice. Cover and refrigerate syrup until chilled, about 2 hours.

3. Place fruit in large bowl; toss with syrup. Makes 12 servings.

Each serving: About 120 calories, 1 g protein, 31 g carbohydrate, 0 g total fat, 0 mg cholesterol, 10 mg sodium.

Winter Fruit with Almond Cream

Prep: 25 minutes plus chilling
Cook: 20 minutes

3 cups heavy or whipping cream
6 egg yolks
⅓ cup sugar
¼ teaspoon almond extract
1 can (29 ounces) sliced cling peaches
6 large oranges
1 pint strawberries
4 medium bananas

1. Prepare almond cream: In 1-quart saucepan, heat heavy cream over medium heat until tiny bubbles form around edge of pan. In heavy 2-quart saucepan, with wire whisk, beat egg yolks and sugar until blended. Slowly stir in hot cream; cook, stirring constantly, over medium-low heat, until mixture coats the back of a spoon well, about 15 minutes. (Do not boil, or mixture will curdle.)

2. Stir almond extract into cream mixture; pour into medium bowl. Cover and refrigerate at least 6 hours or overnight to chill.

3. About 20 minutes before serving, prepare fruit: Drain peach slices; peel and section oranges; hull strawberries and cut each in half; peel bananas and cut into ¼-inch-thick slices. Arrange fruit in large bowl. Let each person help themselves to some fruit, then top with spoonful of almond cream. Makes 10 servings.

Each serving: About 455 calories, 5 g protein, 44 g carbohydrate, 30 g total fat (18 g saturated), 225 mg cholesterol, 35 mg sodium.

Summer Fruit Bowl

Prep: 45 minutes plus chilling
Cook: 15 minutes

2 cups water
1½ cups sugar
¼ cup fresh lime juice
¾ cup loosely packed mint leaves, minced
1 watermelon (20 pounds)
1 small cantaloupe
6 large plums
4 large nectarines
1 pound seedless green grapes

1. In 2-quart saucepan, cook water, sugar, and lime juice over medium heat, until mixture becomes a light syrup, about 15 minutes. Stir in mint leaves; cover and refrigerate until well chilled.

2. Cut watermelon into bite-size pieces; discard seeds. Cut cantaloupe into bite-size pieces; cut unpeeled plums and nectarines into wedges. Combine cut-up fruits with grapes and arrange in very large bowl. Pour chilled syrup through strainer over fruit; gently toss to mix well. Cover and refrigerate to blend flavors, stirring mixture occasionally. Makes 20 servings.

Each serving: About 180 calories, 2 g protein, 44 g carbohydrate, 2 g total fat (0 g saturated), 0 mg cholesterol, 5 mg sodium.

Summer Fruit Compote

Prep: 15 minutes

1 tablespoon sugar
1 tablespoon dark Jamaican rum
1 tablespoon fresh lime juice
2 large mangoes, peeled and cut into ¾-inch pieces
1 pint blueberries

In medium bowl, combine sugar, rum, and lime juice. Add mangoes and blueberries; toss to coat. Cover and refrigerate if not serving right away. Makes about 4 cups or 6 servings.

Each serving: About 85 calories, 1 g protein, 21 g carbohydrate, 0 g total fat, 0 mg cholesterol, 5 mg sodium.

Fruit Compote in Spiced Wine

Prep: 20 minutes plus chilling
Cook: 25 minutes

1 lemon
2 cups dry red wine
1¼ cups sugar
1 tablespoon whole black
   peppercorns
6 whole cloves
1 cinnamon stick (3 inches)
2 cups water
4 large Anjou or Bosc pears
   (about 2 pounds), peeled,
   cored, and each cut into
   12 wedges

4 large Granny Smith apples
   (about 2 pounds), peeled,
   cored, and each cut into
   16 wedges
2 cups cranberries

1. From lemon, with vegetable peeler or small knife, remove one 3" by 1" strip of peel.
2. In 4-quart saucepan, heat wine, sugar, peppercorns, cloves, cinnamon stick, lemon peel, and water to boiling

over high heat, stirring frequently, until sugar dissolves. Reduce heat to medium-low; cover and simmer, stirring occasionally, 10 minutes. Pour syrup through sieve set over bowl; discard peppercorns and cloves. Return syrup, lemon peel, and cinnamon to saucepan.

3. Add pears and apples to syrup, gently stirring to combine; heat to boiling over medium-high heat. Reduce heat to medium-low; cover and simmer until apples and pears are tender, about 5 minutes. Stir in cranberries and cook, covered, 5 minutes longer.

4. Pour fruit mixture into heat-safe bowl and refrigerate at least 4 hours to blend flavors, or up to 4 days. Makes 12 cups or 16 servings.

Each serving: About 125 calories, 0 g protein, 30 g carbohydrate, 0 g total fat (0 g saturated), 2 g fiber, 0 mg cholesterol, 5 mg sodium.

Dried Apricot, Prune, and Cherry Compote

Prep: 10 minutes plus cooling
Cook: 8 minutes

4 cups apple cider or apple juice
1 cup dried apricots (6 ounces), each cut into 3 strips
¼ cup packed light brown sugar
3 strips (3" by 1" each) lemon peel
1 cinnamon stick (3 inches)
1 cup pitted prunes (8 ounces), each cut in half
½ cup dried tart cherries
½ teaspoon vanilla extract

1. In 3-quart saucepan, heat apple cider, apricots, brown sugar, lemon peel, and cinnamon stick to boiling over high heat. Reduce heat to low; simmer, uncovered, 5 minutes.

2. Spoon mixture into large bowl; stir in prunes, dried cherries, and vanilla. Serve at room temperature or cover and refrigerate. Store in refrigerator up to 1 week. Makes 10 servings.

Each serving: About 175 calories, 2 g protein, 46 g carbohydrate, 1 g total fat (0 g saturated), 0 mg cholesterol, 7 mg sodium.

Fall Fruit Compote

Prep: 10 minutes
Cook: 20 minutes

⅔ cup sugar
1 tablespoon anise seeds
4 cups water
4 firm but ripe Bartlett or Anjou pears (about 1¾ pounds), peeled, cored, and cut into ¼-inch-thick wedges
⅔ cup dried apricot halves (about 3 ounces)
½ cup dried tart cherries
½ cup golden raisins
2 tablespoons fresh lemon juice

1. In 3-quart saucepan, heat sugar, anise seeds, and water over high heat, stirring frequently, until syrup boils and sugar dissolves. Reduce heat to medium and cook, stirring occasionally, 10 minutes. Pour syrup through sieve into bowl; discard seeds and return syrup to saucepan.

2. Add pears to syrup; heat to boiling over medium-high heat. Reduce heat to medium-low; cover and simmer until pears are tender, about 5 minutes. Stir in apricots, cherries, and raisins, and cook, covered, 1 minute longer. Remove saucepan from heat; stir in lemon juice. Serve compote warm, or cover and refrigerate to serve cold later. Makes about 6½ cups or 6 servings.

Each serving: About 260 calories, 2 g protein, 67 g carbohydrate, 1 g total fat (0 g saturated), 3 g fiber, 0 mg cholesterol, 4 mg sodium.

Chocolate-Fruit Fondue

Prep: 20 minutes
Cook: 5 minutes

1 package (6 ounces) semisweet-chocolate pieces (1 cup)
¼ cup half-and-half
½ teaspoon vanilla extract
4 small bananas, peeled
2 to 3 small pears
1 pint strawberries
½ cup finely chopped almonds

1. In heavy 1-quart saucepan, heat chocolate pieces and half-and-half over low heat, stirring frequently, until chocolate is melted and mixture is smooth. Stir in vanilla; keep sauce warm.

2. To serve, arrange bananas, pears, and strawberries on large dessert platter. Spoon sauce into a small bowl; place nuts in another small bowl. Let each person cut fruit and dip into chocolate sauce with fork or toothpick, then into nuts. Makes 6 servings.

Each serving: About 320 calories, 4 g protein, 48 g carbohydrate, 14 g total fat (7 g saturated), 4 mg cholesterol, 35 mg sodium.

Sacramento Fruit Bowl

Prep: 40 minutes plus chilling
Cook: 15 minutes

2 cups water
1½ cups sugar
2 tablespoons anise seeds
3 tablespoons fresh lemon juice
¼ teaspoon salt
1 small pineapple
1 small honeydew melon

1 small cantaloupe
2 oranges
2 large nectarines
2 large purple plums
½ pound green grapes
2 kiwifruit

1. In 2-quart saucepan, cook water, sugar, anise seeds, lemon juice, and salt over medium heat until mixture becomes a light syrup, about 15 minutes. Refrigerate until syrup is cool.

2. Meanwhile, remove peel from pineapple, honeydew melon, and cantaloupe. Cut pulp from pineapple and melons into bite-size chunks. Peel and section oranges. Slice unpeeled nectarines and plums into wedges. Cut grapes in half; remove seeds, if any.

3. In large bowl, combine cut-up fruit. Pour cooled syrup through strainer over fruit. Cover and refrigerate, stirring occasionally, until well chilled.

4. To serve, peel and slice kiwifruit. Gently stir kiwifruit slices into fruit mixture. Makes 12 servings.

Each serving: About 185 calories, 1 g protein, 47 g carbohydrate, 1 g total fat (0 g saturated), 0 mg cholesterol, 55 mg sodium.

Salads & Salad Dressings

~◦~

Accompaniment Salads
Main-Dish Salads • Salad Dressings

Choose from the many different kinds of greens described below to make salads delightfully varied and tasty. To mix greens, combine mild greens with tangy ones, tender with crisp, light-colored with dark for tempting contrasts in flavor, texture, and color.

ᴄ᷃Glossary of Salad Greens

Arugula (rocket): Sprigs of rich green, intensely flavored, somewhat spicy leaves. Combine with milder-flavored greens or use alone with oil-and-vinegar dressing.

Belgian endive (French endive, witloof): Small, smooth, compact heads of tapered white leaves, with a slight greenish tinge. Crisp, with a delicately bitter flavor. One of the most expensive greens, but it goes a long way because there is no waste. Use the leaves whole or cut into bite-size pieces or julienne strips, alone or with other greens. Endive is so compact it takes very little cleaning, just a quick rinse with cold running water.

Bibb lettuce (limestone lettuce): Small heads of cup-shaped, tender-crisp, buttery-feeling green leaves that are white near the core. Delicate, sweet flavor. Bibb lettuce is usually quite sandy and should be rinsed carefully with cold running water to wash away every trace of grit. Use alone or with other greens, with a light dressing.

Boston lettuce (butterhead lettuce): Soft, tender, buttery-feeling leaves, pale green, in a loose head, with a sweet, delicate flavor.

Chicory (curly endive): Lacy, fringed leaves with a somewhat bitter taste. The outer leaves are darker and stronger in flavor than the bleached inner leaves. Attractive as a garnish, or mix chicory with other greens.

Chinese cabbage (Nappa or Napa): Tightly closed head of wide-ribbed, tapered stalks with crinkly edged, celery-colored, white-ribbed leaves. Serve alone with vinaigrette dressing or mix with other greens.

Dandelion greens: Early spring favorite from wild or cultivated plants. Leaves are sharply indented, tender, slightly bitter. Choose the youngest, freshest leaves; wash thoroughly.

Escarole: Wide, flat leaves that are slightly curled at the edges: Outer leaves are green; inner ones, yellow or cream-colored. They should be crisp and snap easily. Slightly bitter; combine with other greens.

Fennel: Feathery leaves on stalks of fennel bulb, with anise flavor. Snip; add sparingly to mixed greens. Thinly slice bulb for salad too.

Fiddleheads: An edible fern that grows along stream banks. Available in some areas in early spring when very young and tender. The flavor is a cross between asparagus and mushrooms.

Iceberg lettuce (crisphead lettuce): Large heads of crisp, broad, green leaves outside, pale green leaves near core. Heads should be medium-heavy for their size and give a little to pressure. Mild flavor. Serve alone or mix with other greens.

Leaf lettuce: Varieties may be curly or green- or red-tipped. Broad, tender, loose leaves that grow from a short central stem. Delicate flavor.

Mâche (lamb's lettuce, corn salad): A wild or cultivated spring and summer salad green. Spoon-shaped leaves are tangy; good with other greens.

Nasturtium leaves: Pungent, peppery leaves from the familiar garden plant. Use the stems also. The flower is also edible.

Radicchio (pronounced ra-DEE-kee-o): Small, firm-textured heads of ruby-red leaves. Slightly bitter flavor. Use for flavor and color with other greens. Very expensive. A little goes a long way.

Radish sprouts: Cloverlike, tiny, dark green leaves with a peppery, radishlike flavor. Discard the roots; use only the leaves and stems to add crunch and flavor to salads and sandwiches.

Romaine (cos): Long, loose heads of firm, crisp, dark green leaves. Nutty flavor. Sauté in a little hot salad oil to serve as a wilted salad.

Sorrel (dock, sour grass): Long, arrow-shaped green leaves with sour, pungent flavor. Choose young, crisp, bright green leaves. Combine sparingly with milder greens.

Spinach: Dark green, flat or crinkled crisp leaves. Wash to remove all sand. Trim off any tough stems or ribs.

Watercress: Sold in bunches. Crisp sprigs of small, deep green leaves with refreshing, peppery flavor. Use alone or combine with other greens.

∾Buying, Storing, and Preparing Salad Greens

Buy greens that are fresh and crisp-looking, without bruised, yellowish, or brown-tipped leaves. Iceberg lettuce should feel firm but springy; cabbage should be firm and heavy.

Store lettuce and other greens in plastic bags in the crisper drawer of the refrigerator. Make sure to leave plastic bags slightly open; too much moisture promotes spoilage. Use iceberg lettuce and hardy greens within three to five days; use loose, leafier greens within one to two days. Rinse greens just before using.

To clean greens, remove any bruised or wilted outer

leaves but trim sparingly; dark green outer leaves are the most nutritious. Use a sharp knife to cut out, in cone shape, the core of firm heads of iceberg lettuce and cabbage. Or core iceberg lettuce this way: Place the head, core up, on the counter, and whack it firmly with the heel of your hand to loosen the core; or hold the head, core down, and whack it on the counter. Twist out the core with your fingers. Hold head, cored side up, under cold running water to clean and help separate the leaves.

Swish the leaves of lettuce, spinach, chicory, watercress, and similar greens through cold water. Drain them thoroughly and pat dry or use a salad spinner, then cut out any tough ribs or stems. To make bite-size pieces, it is okay to cut greens with a knife if you are planning to serve them right away. Torn lettuce edges will not darken as quickly as cut edges, so tear lettuce when preparing salad in advance.

ᑌᐧAccompaniment Salads

Salinas Mixed Greens with Tarragon-Vinegar Dressing

Prep: 25 minutes

¼ cup olive oil
2 tablespoons tarragon vinegar
½ teaspoon Dijon mustard
¼ teaspoon salt
¼ teaspoon coarsely ground black pepper
3 green onions, thinly sliced

1 head romaine lettuce, torn into bite-size pieces
1 head Boston lettuce, torn into bite-size pieces
1 bunch watercress, tough stems trimmed
⅓ cup chopped fresh parsley

1. In small bowl, with wire whisk or fork, mix oil, vinegar, mustard, salt, and pepper; mix well.

2. To serve, in large salad bowl, toss green onions, romaine, Boston lettuce, watercress, and parsley with dressing until well coated. Makes 8 accompaniment servings.

Each serving: About 75 calories, 1 g protein, 2 g carbohydrate, 7 g total fat (1 g saturated), 0 mg cholesterol, 80 mg sodium.

Spinach Salad with Hot Mushroom Dressing

Prep: 10 minutes
Cook: 5 minutes

1 bag (10 ounces) spinach, tough stems removed
¼ cup olive oil
½ pound mushrooms, sliced
1 tablespoon cider vinegar
1 tablespoon prepared mustard
1 teaspoon sugar
¾ teaspoon salt

1. Into bowl, tear spinach into pieces.
2. In 2-quart saucepan, heat oil over medium-high heat until hot. Add mushrooms, and cook, stirring often, until tender, about 5 minutes.
3. Stir in vinegar, mustard, sugar, and salt. Pour mixture over spinach; toss to coat well. Makes 6 accompaniment servings.

Each serving: About 100 calories, 2 g protein, 3 g carbohydrate, 9 g total fat (1 g saturated), 0 mg cholesterol, 370 mg sodium.

Fennel, Pear, and Endive Salad

Prep: 45 minutes

¼ cup extravirgin olive oil
¼ cup tarragon vinegar
1 tablespoon Dijon mustard
¾ teaspoon salt
¼ teaspoon coarsely ground black pepper
5 medium Bartlett pears (about 2 pounds)
2 fennel bulbs (about 1 pound each)
4 medium heads Belgian endive (2 red, if available)
¾ cup walnuts, toasted and coarsely chopped

1. In small bowl, prepare dressing: With wire whisk or fork, mix oil, vinegar, mustard, salt, and pepper; set aside. (If you like, combine dressing ingredients in jar with tight-fitting lid; refrigerate overnight.)

2. Remove core and slice each pear into 12 wedges, leaving skin on. Place pear wedges in large bowl.

3. Trim top and bottom from each fennel bulb. Slice each bulb lengthwise in half; remove core. Slice halves crosswise into paper-thin slices; place in bowl with pear wedges.

4. Cut 1 yellow and 1 red endive crosswise into ⅛-inch-thick slices; toss with fennel mixture. Separate leaves from remaining heads of endive.

5. Toss dressing with fennel mixture. Arrange endive leaves around edge of large shallow bowl or platter; top with fennel salad. Sprinkle with toasted walnuts. Makes 8 accompaniment servings.

Each serving: About 235 calories, 4 g protein, 27 g carbohydrate, 15 g total fat (2 g saturated), 0 mg cholesterol, 310 mg sodium.

Citrus Salad with Sherry Dressing

Prep: 30 minutes

2 tablespoons dry sherry
1 tablespoon red wine vinegar
1 teaspoon Dijon mustard
¼ teaspoon salt
⅛ teaspoon coarsely ground
   black pepper
2 tablespoons olive oil

1 large Granny Smith apple,
   cored and cut into paper-
   thin slices
2 large navel oranges
1 large pink grapefruit
1 bunch watercress, tough
   stems trimmed

1. In large bowl, with wire whisk or fork, beat sherry, vinegar, mustard, salt, and pepper until blended. Gradually whisk in olive oil.

2. Add apple slices to dressing in bowl and toss to coat.

3. Remove peel and white pith from oranges and grapefruit. Holding oranges and grapefruit over medium bowl to catch juice, cut sections from between membranes. (If you like, squeeze juice from membranes for use another day.) Add orange and grapefruit sections to dressing; toss to coat.

4. Spread watercress on platter. Spoon fruit mixture and dressing over watercress; toss before serving. Makes 6 accompaniment or first-course servings.

Each serving: About 100 calories, 1 g protein, 14 g carbohydrate, 5 g total fat (1 g saturated), 0 mg cholesterol, 115 mg sodium.

Mrs. Mary's Marinated Mushrooms

Prep: 20 minutes plus chilling
Cook: 5 minutes

3 cups distilled white vinegar
3 cups water
2 pounds medium mushrooms
1 tablespoon extravirgin olive oil
¼ teaspoon dried oregano
¼ teaspoon salt
¼ teaspoon coarsely ground black pepper

1. In 4-quart saucepan, heat vinegar and water to boiling over high heat. Add mushrooms and cook, stirring constantly to help keep mushrooms submerged in liquid, 3 minutes.

2. Drain mushrooms, reserving *1 cup cooking liquid*. Place drained mushrooms and reserved cooking liquid in large bowl. Stir in oil, oregano, salt, and pepper. Cool slightly; cover and refrigerate 2 hours or overnight. Makes about 5 cups or 10 first-course servings.

Each serving: About 25 calories, 2 g protein, 5 g carbohydrate, 1 g total fat (0 g saturated), 0 mg cholesterol, 55 mg sodium.

Spinach and Tangerine Salad

Prep: 30 minutes

4 medium tangerines or small oranges
1 large bunch spinach (about 1 pound), tough stems trimmed
2 small heads Bibb lettuce (about 8 ounces)
3 tablespoons extravirgin olive oil
3 tablespoons cider vinegar
1 teaspoon sugar
1 teaspoon Dijon mustard
⅛ teaspoon salt
⅛ teaspoon coarsely ground black pepper

1. Grate peel from 1 tangerine. Remove remaining peel and pith from all tangerines; discard. Cut each tangerine in half, then cut each half crosswise into ¼-inch-thick slices. Tear spinach and Bibb lettuce into bite-size pieces.

2. In large bowl, with wire whisk or fork, mix oil, vinegar, sugar, mustard, salt, pepper, and tangerine peel. Add spinach, lettuce, and tangerine slices; toss well. Makes 8 first-course servings.

Each serving: About 80 calories, 2 g protein, 8 g carbohydrate, 5 g total fat (1 g saturated), 0 mg cholesterol, 95 mg sodium.

Kirby Cucumber Salad

Prep: 30 minutes plus standing and chilling

4 pounds kirby cucumbers (about 16), unpeeled and thinly sliced
1 tablespoon salt
¾ cup distilled white vinegar
2 tablespoons sugar
2 tablespoons chopped fresh dill
Dill sprigs

1. In large colander set over large bowl, sprinkle cucumbers with salt; toss to mix. Let stand 30 minutes at room temperature. Discard liquid in bowl. Pat cucumbers dry with paper towels.

2. In same bowl, with fork, mix vinegar, sugar, and chopped dill. Add cucumbers and stir to coat. Cover and refrigerate, stirring occasionally, at least 2 hours. Garnish with dill. Makes 12 accompaniment servings.

Each serving: About 30 calories, 1 g protein, 7 g carbohydrate, 0 g total fat, 0 mg cholesterol, 270 mg sodium.

Creamy Cucumber and Dill Salad

Prep: 15 minutes plus standing and chilling

2 English (seedless), cucumbers, unpeeled and thinly sliced
2 teaspoons salt
½ cup sour cream
2 tablespoons minced fresh dill
2 teaspoons minced fresh mint
1 teaspoon distilled white vinegar
⅛ teaspoon ground black pepper

1. In large colander set over large bowl, toss cucumber slices with salt. Let stand 30 minutes at room temperature, stirring occasionally. Discard liquid in bowl. Pat cucumbers dry with paper towels.

2. In same bowl, with fork, mix sour cream, dill, mint, vinegar, and pepper. Stir in cucumbers. Cover and refrigerate at least 1 hour. Makes about 4 cups or 6 accompaniment servings.

Each serving: About 60 calories, 2 g protein, 5 g carbohydrate, 4 g total fat (3 g saturated), 9 mg cholesterol, 455 mg sodium.

Summer Greens with Beets and Mustard Vinaigrette

Prep: 25 minutes
Cook: 45 to 60 minutes

12 medium golden or red beets with tops (about 4 pounds, including tops)
3 tablespoons red wine vinegar
1 tablespoon Dijon mustard
1 small shallot, minced (1 tablespoon)
½ teaspoon salt
¼ teaspoon coarsely ground black pepper
⅓ cup extravirgin olive oil
12 cups loosely packed mixed salad greens

1. Trim tops from beets, leaving about 1 inch of stems attached. (Reserve tops for use another time, if you like.) Scrub beets well with cold running water.

2. In 8-quart Dutch oven or saucepot, place whole beets and *enough cold water to cover*; heat to boiling over high heat. Reduce heat to medium-low; cover and simmer, until beets are fork-tender (time depends on age as well as size of beets), 30 to 45 minutes.

3. Meanwhile, in small bowl, with wire whisk, mix vinegar, mustard, shallot, salt, and pepper. Gradually whisk in oil until vinaigrette is blended.

4. Drain beets in colander; rinse with cold water until easy to handle. Remove beet skins under cold running water. Slice beets; place in medium bowl. Cover and refrigerate beets if not using right away.

5. Just before serving, toss beet slices with half of vinaigrette. In large salad bowl, toss mixed salad greens with remaining vinaigrette; top with beet slices. Makes 12 accompaniment servings.

Each serving: About 90 calories, 2 g protein, 8 g carbohydrate, 6 g total fat (1 g saturated), 0 mg cholesterol, 170 mg sodium.

Carrot Salad

Prep: 30 minutes plus chilling

1 bag (16 ounces) carrots, peeled and coarsely grated
1 cup freshly squeezed orange juice (about 2 large oranges)
¼ cup golden raisins
1 tablespoon minced, peeled fresh ginger
1 teaspoon salt
¼ teaspoon crushed red pepper
2 medium avocados

1. In large bowl, combine carrots, orange juice, raisins, ginger, salt, and crushed red pepper; toss to mix. Cover and refrigerate at least 1 hour or up to 8 hours.

2. To serve, remove pit and peel from avocados. Cut avocados into very thin slices. Place some carrot salad and avocado slices on each plate. Makes about 2 cups or 8 accompaniment servings.

Each serving: About 140 calories, 2 g protein, 20 g carbohydrate, 7 g total fat (1 g saturated), 0 mg cholesterol, 290 mg sodium.

Moroccan Carrot Salad

Prep: 20 minutes

1 pound (about 2 bunches) carrots, peeled and coarsely shredded
2 tablespoons extravirgin olive oil
2 teaspoons fresh lemon juice
¼ teaspoon ground coriander
¼ teaspoon ground cumin
¼ teaspoon salt
⅛ teaspoon ground black pepper
2 tablespoons chopped fresh cilantro

1. In medium bowl, combine carrots, oil, lemon juice, coriander, cumin, salt, and pepper; toss to mix. Cover and refrigerate if not serving right away.

2. To serve, stir in cilantro. Makes about 2½ cups or 4 accompaniment servings.

Each serving: About 110 calories, 1 g protein, 11 g carbohydrate, 7 g total fat (1 g saturated), 0 mg cholesterol, 170 mg sodium.

Three-Pepper Salad

Prep: 20 minutes
Cook: 10 minutes

1 large mild sweet onion (about
   1 pound)
2 medium red peppers
2 medium green peppers
2 medium yellow peppers
2 tablespoons olive oil
2 tablespoons balsamic vinegar

1 teaspoon sugar
¾ teaspoon salt
½ teaspoon fennel seeds,
   crushed
¼ cup Kalamata olives, pitted
   and halved
4 ounces feta cheese, crumbled
   (about 1 cup)

1. Peel onion; cut onion from top to bottom into 8 wedges; separate each wedge to loosen onion layers. Cut red, green, and yellow peppers into ½-inch-wide strips.

2. In 12-inch skillet, heat oil over medium heat until hot. Add onion and cook 5 minutes. Add peppers; cook, stirring occasionally, until tender. Remove from heat.

3. In large bowl, combine vinegar, sugar, salt, and fennel seeds. Add vegetable mixture, olives, and cheese; toss gently to mix well. Serve salad warm. Or cover and refrigerate to serve chilled later. Makes 6 accompaniment servings.

Each serving: About 175 calories, 5 g protein, 20 g carbohydrate, 10 g total fat (4 g saturated), 17 mg cholesterol, 550 mg sodium.

Tomato and Mint Tabbouleh

Prep: 35 minutes plus chilling

1½ cups bulgur (cracked
    wheat)
¼ cup fresh lemon juice
3 medium ripe tomatoes (about
    1 pound)
1 medium cucumber (about 8
    ounces)
3 green onions

¾ cup loosely packed fresh
    parsley leaves, chopped
½ cup loosely packed fresh
    mint leaves, chopped
1 tablespoon olive oil
¾ teaspoon salt
¼ teaspoon coarsely ground
    black pepper

1. In medium bowl, combine bulgur, lemon juice, and
1½ cups boiling water; stir to mix. Let stand until liquid
is absorbed, about 30 minutes.

2. Meanwhile, cut tomatoes into ½-inch pieces. Peel and
cut cucumber into ½-inch pieces. Chop green onions.

3. When bulgur mixture is ready, stir in tomatoes, cucumber, onion, parsley, mint, oil, salt, and pepper. Cover
and refrigerate at least 1 hour or up to 24 hours to blend
flavors. Makes 12 accompaniment servings.

*Each serving: About 85 calories, 3 g protein, 16 g carbohydrate,
2 g total fat (0 g saturated), 0 mg cholesterol, 145 mg sodium.*

Marinated-Tomato and Arugula Salad

Prep: 10 minutes plus chilling

⅔ cup olive oil
¼ cup cider vinegar
1 tablespoon sugar
½ teaspoon salt
2 pounds ripe tomatoes (4 large), cut into wedges
2 large bunches arugula, trimmed
2 teaspoons sesame seeds, toasted

1. In medium bowl, with wire whisk or fork, mix oil,
vinegar, sugar, and salt. Add tomato wedges; toss to coat

with dressing. Cover and refrigerate at least 1 hour.

2. To serve, arrange arugula on large platter; top with tomatoes with their dressing. Sprinkle with sesame seeds. Makes 8 accompaniment servings.

Each serving: About 195 calories, 1 g protein, 8 g carbohydrate, 19 g total fat (3 g saturated), 0 mg cholesterol, 160 mg sodium.

Greek-Style Tomato Salad

Prep: 20 minutes plus chilling

2½ pounds ripe tomatoes (6 medium), sliced
4 ounces feta cheese, crumbled (about 1 cup)
1 small red onion, thinly sliced
⅓ cup Kalamata olives, pitted

⅓ cup olive oil
¼ cup red wine vinegar
2 tablespoons minced fresh mint
2 teaspoons sugar
¼ teaspoon salt
Lettuce leaves

1. Place tomato slices in 13" by 9" baking dish; top with cheese, onion slices, and olives.

2. In small bowl, with wire whisk or fork, mix oil, vinegar, mint, sugar, and salt; pour over tomato mixture. Gently lift tomato slices to coat with dressing. Cover baking dish and refrigerate at least 2 hours to blend flavors.

3. To serve, line chilled large platter with lettuce leaves. Arrange tomato mixture on lettuce. Makes 8 accompaniment servings.

Each serving: About 160 calories, 3 g protein, 10 g carbohydrate, 13 g total fat (3 g saturated), 13 mg cholesterol, 285 mg sodium.

Coleslaw Vinaigrette

Prep: 15 minutes plus chilling

1 medium head green cabbage (2½ pounds)
1 large red pepper
⅓ cup olive oil
¼ cup red wine vinegar
1 tablespoon sugar
1 teaspoon salt
½ teaspoon caraway seeds, crushed

1. Separate leaves from cabbage. Cut out and discard tough ribs from cabbage leaves. Thinly slice cabbage to make about 6 cups, packed. Cut red pepper into very thin strips.
2. Prepare dressing: In large bowl, with wire whisk or fork, mix oil, vinegar, sugar, salt, and caraway seeds. Add cabbage and red pepper; toss to coat well with dressing. Cover and refrigerate at least 1 hour. Makes 6 accompaniment servings.

Each serving: About 160 calories, 3 g protein, 13 g carbohydrate, 12 g total fat (2 g saturated), 0 mg cholesterol, 415 mg sodium.

Asian Coleslaw

Prep: 30 minutes

⅓ cup seasoned rice vinegar
2 tablespoons vegetable oil
2 teaspoons Oriental sesame oil
¾ teaspoon salt
1 head savoy cabbage (about 2½ pounds), tough ribs discarded
    and thinly sliced
1 bag (16 ounces) carrots, peeled and shredded
4 green onions, thinly sliced
½ cup chopped fresh cilantro

1. In large bowl, with wire whisk or fork, mix rice vinegar, vegetable oil, sesame oil, and salt.

2. Add cabbage, carrots, green onions, and cilantro; toss well. If not serving right away, cover and refrigerate. Makes 16 accompaniment servings.

Each serving: About 55 calories, 2 g protein, 9 g carbohydrate, 2 g total fat (0 g saturated), 0 mg cholesterol, 260 mg sodium.

Lemon-Chive Potato Salad

Prep: 25 minutes plus cooling
Cook: 15 minutes

5 pounds medium red potatoes, cut into 1½-inch chunks
4 teaspoon salt
2 medium lemons
3 tablespoons olive oil
1 teaspoon sugar
¾ cup light mayonnaise
½ cup milk
⅓ cup sour cream
5 large stalks celery, thinly sliced
½ cup chopped fresh chives or green-onion tops
Chopped fresh chives

1. In 8-quart saucepot, heat potatoes, 2 teaspoons salt, and enough *water* to cover to boiling. Reduce heat to low; cover and simmer until potatoes are fork-tender, 10 to 12 minutes.

2. Meanwhile, from lemons, grate 1½ teaspoons peel and squeeze ¼ cup juice. In large bowl, with wire whisk, mix lemon peel, lemon juice, oil, sugar, and 1½ teaspoons salt.

3. Drain potatoes. Add hot potatoes to lemon dressing. With rubber spatula, stir gently to coat. Let potatoes cool at room temperature, stirring occasionally, 30 minutes.

4. In small bowl, stir mayonnaise, milk, sour cream, and remaining ½ teaspoon salt until smooth. Add mayonnaise mixture, celery, and chopped chives to potatoes; stir gently to coat well. If not serving right away, cover and refrigerate. Garnish with chopped chives. Makes 16 accompaniment servings.

Each serving: About 165 calories, 4 g protein, 28 g carbohydrate, 5 g total fat (1 g saturated), 3 mg cholesterol, 435 mg sodium.

Red Potato Salad

Prep: 20 minutes plus cooling
Cook: 15 minutes

4 pounds small red potatoes, each cut into quarters (or eighths, if large)	⅓ cup cider vinegar
	¼ cup olive oil
	2 teaspoons sugar
1 tablespoon plus 1½ teaspoons salt	2 teaspoons Dijon mustard
4 slices bacon	¼ teaspoon coarsely ground black pepper
3 large shallots, chopped	2 green onions, chopped

1. In 5-quart saucepot, heat potatoes, 1 tablespoon salt, and enough *water* to cover to boiling over high heat. Reduce heat to low; cover and simmer, until potatoes are fork-tender, 10 to 12 minutes.

2. Meanwhile, in 10-inch skillet, cook bacon over medium-low heat until browned. With slotted spoon, transfer bacon to paper towels to drain. Discard all but 1 teaspoon bacon fat from skillet. Reduce heat to low. Add shallots and cook, stirring, until shallots are soft, about 5 minutes.

3. In large bowl, with wire whisk, mix shallots, vinegar, oil, sugar, mustard, pepper, and remaining 1½ teaspoons salt.

4. Drain potatoes. Add hot potatoes to shallot dressing. With rubber spatula, stir gently to coat. Let potatoes cool at room temperature, stirring occasionally, 30 minutes.

5. Stir in green onions. Serve salad at room temperature or cover and refrigerate until ready to serve. Sprinkle with crumbled bacon. Makes 12 accompaniment servings.

Each serving: About 170 calories, 4 g protein, 21 g carbohydrate, 6 g total fat (1 g saturated), 2 mg cholesterol, 375 mg sodium.

Warm Caesar Potato Salad

Prep: 5 minutes
Cook: 15 minutes

1¼ pounds red potatoes, cut into ¾-inch chunks
2 tablespoons light mayonnaise
1 tablespoon freshly grated Parmesan cheese
2 teaspoons cider vinegar
1 teaspoon Dijon mustard
½ teaspoon salt
½ teaspoon coarsely ground black pepper
⅛ teaspoon anchovy paste
1 green onion, sliced

1. In 3-quart saucepan, place potatoes and *enough water to cover*; heat to boiling over high heat. Cover, and reduce heat to low; simmer 15 minutes or until potatoes are fork-tender.

2. Meanwhile, in medium bowl, mix mayonnaise, Parmesan, vinegar, mustard, salt, pepper, anchovy paste, and green onion.

3. Drain potatoes; gently toss with dressing in bowl. Makes 4 accompaniment servings.

Each serving: About 165 calories, 4 g protein, 31 g carbohydrate, 3 g total fat (1 g saturated), 4 mg cholesterol, 380 mg sodium.

German Hot-Potato Salad

Prep: 25 minutes
Cook: 35 minutes

6 medium potatoes (about 2 pounds)
6 slices bacon, cut into ½-inch pieces
½ cup chopped onion
2 teaspoons sugar
1½ teaspoons salt
1 teaspoon all-purpose flour
⅛ teaspoon ground black pepper
3 tablespoons red wine vinegar
Minced fresh parsley

1. In 4-quart saucepan, heat unpeeled potatoes and enough *water* to cover to boiling over high heat. Reduce heat to low; cover and simmer until potatoes are fork-tender, 25 to 30 minutes. Drain; cool potatoes slightly. Peel and dice potatoes.

2. Meanwhile, in nonstick 10-inch skillet, cook bacon until brown over medium-low heat. With slotted spoon, transfer bacon to paper towels to drain.

3. Prepare dressing: Discard all but 2 tablespoons bacon fat from skillet; add onion and cook over medium heat until tender. Stir in sugar, salt, flour, and pepper; cook 1 minute. Gradually stir in vinegar and *½ cup water*; cook, stirring constantly, until mixture thickens slightly and boils.

4. Gently stir in potatoes and bacon until well coated with dressing; heat through. Garnish with minced parsley. Serve warm. Makes 6 accompaniment servings.

Each serving: About 205 calories, 5 g protein, 31 g carbohydrate, 8 g total fat (3 g saturated), 9 mg cholesterol, 690 mg sodium.

Summer Corn Salad

Prep: 30 minutes
Cook: 10 minutes

12 ears corn, husks and silk removed
¾ pound green beans, trimmed and cut into ¼-inch pieces
½ cup cider vinegar
¼ cup olive oil
¼ cup chopped fresh parsley
1 teaspoon salt
½ teaspoon coarsely ground black pepper
1 medium red pepper, diced
1 small sweet onion (about 4 ounces), finely chopped

1. In 8-quart saucepot, in *2 inches boiling water*, heat corn to boiling over high heat. Reduce heat to low; cover and simmer 5 minutes. Drain corn; set aside to cool. When cool enough to handle, cut off kernels.

2. Meanwhile, cook green beans: In 2-quart saucepan, in *1 inch boiling water*, heat green beans to boiling over high heat. Reduce heat to low; simmer, uncovered, until beans are tender-crisp, about 5 minutes. Drain.

3. In large salad bowl, with wire whisk or fork, mix vinegar, oil, parsley, salt, and pepper until blended.

4. To dressing in bowl, add corn kernels, green beans, red pepper, and onion; toss well. If not serving right away, cover and refrigerate. Makes 12 accompaniment servings.

Each serving: About 135 calories, 3 g protein, 23 g carbohydrate, 6 g total fat (1 g saturated), 0 mg cholesterol, 195 mg sodium.

Celery and Olive Salad

Prep: 15 minutes

1 cup drained giardiniera (Italian pickled mixed vegetables),
   coarsely chopped
6 large stalks celery with leaves, coarsely chopped (about 3 cups)
¼ cup pitted green olives, chopped
2 tablespoons olive oil
2 tablespoons fresh chopped flat-leaf parsley leaves
1 garlic clove, minced
¼ teaspoon coarsely ground black pepper
Celery leaves

In large bowl, combine giardiniera, chopped celery, olives, oil, parsley, garlic, and pepper; toss well. Cover and refrigerate if not serving right away. Garnish with celery leaves to serve. Makes about 4 cups or 6 accompaniment servings.

Each serving: About 70 calories, 1 g protein, 5 g carbohydrate, 5 g total fat (1 g saturated), 0 mg cholesterol, 565 mg sodium.

Orzo with Sun-Dried Tomatoes

Prep: 10 minutes plus cooling
Cook: 15 minutes

1 package (16 ounces) orzo (rice-shaped pasta)
2 green onions, chopped
½ cup drained oil-packed sun-dried tomatoes with herbs, coarsely
    chopped, with 1 tablespoon oil from tomatoes reserved
2 tablespoons red wine vinegar
2 teaspoons Dijon mustard
½ teaspoon salt
¼ teaspoon coarsely ground black pepper
½ cup loosely packed fresh basil leaves, cut into thin strips

1. Prepare orzo in *boiling salted water* as label directs.
2. Meanwhile, in large bowl, combine green onions, tomatoes, reserved oil from tomatoes, vinegar, mustard, salt, and pepper.
3. Drain orzo. Add warm orzo to green-onion mixture in bowl; stir to coat evenly. Let orzo mixture cool slightly, then stir in basil. Cover and refrigerate if not serving right away. Makes about 7 cups or 8 accompaniment servings.

Each serving: About 240 calories, 8 g protein, 44 g carbohydrate, 4 g total fat (0 g saturated), 0 mg cholesterol, 220 mg sodium.

Tubetti Macaroni Salad

Prep: 15 minutes
Cook: 15 minutes

1 package (16 ounces) tubetti or ditalini pasta
4 medium carrots, peeled and cut into 2" by ¼" sticks
1 lemon
⅔ cup light mayonnaise
⅓ cup milk
¾ teaspoon salt
2 medium stalks celery, cut into 2" by ¼" sticks
2 green onions, thinly sliced

1. Prepare pasta as label directs in *boiling salted water.* After pasta has cooked 10 minutes, add carrot sticks to pasta cooking water and cook until carrots are just tender-crisp and pasta is done, 1 to 2 minutes longer.

2. Meanwhile, from lemon, grate 1 teaspoon peel and squeeze 3 tablespoons juice. In large bowl, with wire whisk, mix lemon peel, lemon juice, mayonnaise, milk, and salt.

3. Drain pasta and carrots well. Add to mayonnaise mixture with celery and green onions; toss well. Serve at room temperature or cover and refrigerate until ready to serve. Makes 12 accompaniment servings.

Each serving: About 180 calories, 5 g protein, 35 g carbohydrate, 2 g total fat (0 g saturated), 1 mg cholesterol, 320 mg sodium.

Rice Salad with Black Beans

Prep: 10 minutes
Cook: 20 minutes

¾ cup regular long-grain rice
2 large limes
2 cans (15 to 19 ounces each)
    black beans, rinsed and
    drained
1 bunch watercress, tough
    stems trimmed
½ cup bottled salsa
1 cup fresh corn kernels (about
    2 medium ears corn)

¼ cup packed fresh cilantro
    leaves, chopped
1 tablespoon olive oil
½ teaspoon salt
¼ teaspoon coarsely ground
    black pepper

1. Prepare rice as label directs. Meanwhile, from limes, grate ½ teaspoon peel and squeeze 3 tablespoons juice.

2. In large bowl, combine black beans, cooked rice, watercress, salsa, corn, cilantro, oil, lime peel and juice, salt, and pepper; toss well. Cover and refrigerate if not serving right away. Makes about 7 cups or 4 main-dish servings.

Each serving: About 405 calories, 24 g protein, 81 g carbohydrate, 6 g total fat (1 g saturated), 0 mg cholesterol, 1,125 mg sodium.

Two-Bean Salad

Prep: 15 minutes plus cooling
Cook: 10 minutes

1 ¼ teaspoons salt
½ pound wax beans, trimmed
½ pound green beans, trimmed
1 medium lemon
1 tablespoon olive oil
⅛ teaspoon ground black pepper
⅛ teaspoon ground coriander
3 tablespoons minced fresh mint

1. In 12-inch skillet, heat *1 inch water* and 1 teaspoon salt to boiling over high heat. Add beans and cook until tender-crisp, 8 to 10 minutes.

2. Meanwhile, from lemon, grate ½ teaspoon peel and squeeze 2 teaspoons juice.

3. Drain beans; transfer to bowl. Stir in olive oil, pepper, coriander, and ¼ teaspoon salt. Cool slightly.

4. Just before serving, stir in mint, lemon peel, and lemon juice. Makes about 4 cups or 6 accompaniment servings.

Each serving: About 40 calories, 1 g protein, 5 g carbohydrate, 2 g total fat (0 g saturated), 0 mg cholesterol, 140 mg sodium.

Couscous Salad with Grapes and Thyme

Prep: 15 minutes
Cook: 5 minutes

1 package (10 ounces) couscous (Moroccan pasta)
1 ½ teaspoons chopped fresh thyme
¼ cup cider vinegar
2 tablespoons olive oil
1 teaspoon salt
1 ½ cups green and red seedless grapes (about ½ pound), each
    cut into quarters
½ cup pine nuts (pignoli), toasted
Thyme sprigs

1. Prepare couscous as label directs, but do not add salt or butter. Stir in chopped thyme with couscous.

2. In large bowl, with wire whisk or fork, mix vinegar, oil, and salt. Add grapes, pine nuts, and warm couscous; toss well to coat. Cover and refrigerate if not serving right away. Garnish with thyme sprigs to serve. Makes about 6 cups or 8 accompaniment servings.

Each serving: About 220 calories, 6 g protein, 34 g carbohydrate, 7 g total fat (1 g saturated), 0 mg cholesterol, 270 mg sodium.

Fruit and Barley Salad

Prep: 30 minutes
Cook: 35 to 45 minutes

1 package (16 ounces) pearl
   barley
2¾ teaspoons salt
4 medium limes
⅓ cup olive oil
1 tablespoon sugar
¾ teaspoon coarsely ground
   black pepper

1½ pounds nectarines (about 4
   medium), pitted and cut into
   ½-inch pieces
1 pound ripe tomatoes (about 2
   large), seeded and cut into
   ½-inch pieces
4 green onions, thinly sliced
½ cup chopped fresh mint

1. In 4-quart saucepan, heat *6 cups water* to boiling over high heat. Add barley and 1½ teaspoons salt; heat to boiling. Reduce heat to low; cover and simmer until barley is tender and liquid is absorbed, 35 to 45 minutes (barley will have a creamy consistency).

2. Meanwhile, from limes, grate 1 tablespoon peel and squeeze ½ cup juice. In large bowl, with wire whisk or fork, mix lime peel, lime juice, oil, sugar, pepper, and remaining 1¼ teaspoons salt.

3. Rinse barley with cold running water; drain well. Add barley, nectarines, tomatoes, green onions, and chopped mint to lime dressing; with rubber spatula, stir gently to coat. If not serving right away, cover and refrigerate. Makes 16 accompaniment servings.

Each serving: About 170 calories, 4 g protein, 28 g carbohydrate, 5 g total fat (1 g saturated), 0 mg cholesterol, 375 mg sodium.

Black-Eyed Pea Salad

Prep: 15 minutes
Cook: 30 minutes

1 package (16 ounces) dry black-eyed peas
⅓ cup cider vinegar
2 tablespoons olive oil
1 tablespoon cayenne pepper sauce*
2 teaspoons sugar
1½ teaspoons salt
2 medium stalks celery, diced
1 medium red onion, diced
1 package (10 ounces) frozen peas, thawed

1. Rinse black-eyed peas with cold running water and discard any stones or shriveled peas. In 8-quart Dutch oven, heat black-eyed peas and *12 cups water* to boiling over high heat. Reduce heat to low; cover and simmer until peas are just tender, 25 to 30 minutes.

2. Meanwhile, prepare dressing: In large bowl, with wire whisk or fork, mix vinegar, oil, pepper sauce, sugar, and salt until blended.

3. Drain black-eyed peas. Gently toss warm black-eyed peas with dressing in bowl. Add celery, onion, and thawed peas; toss. Serve salad at room temperature or cover and refrigerate until ready to serve. Makes 12 accompaniment servings.

Cayenne pepper sauce is a milder variety of hot pepper sauce that adds tang and flavor, not just heat. It can be found in the condiment section of the supermarket.

Each serving: About 135 calories, 8 g protein, 21 g carbohydrate, 3 g total fat (1 g saturated), 0 mg cholesterol, 360 mg sodium.

Grape Salad Mold

Prep: 30 minutes plus chilling

3 packages (3 ounces each) lemon-flavored gelatin
½ pound seedless red grapes
½ pound seedless green grapes
1 container (16 ounces) cottage cheese (2 cups)

1. In medium bowl, stir 2 packages of gelatin with 2½ *cups boiling water* until gelatin has dissolved completely. Refrigerate until mixture mounds slightly when dropped from a spoon, about 1 hour. Meanwhile, cut each red and green grape in half.

2. Fold grapes into thickened gelatin mixture; pour into 6-cup ring mold. Cover and refrigerate until almost set, about 30 minutes.

3. In small bowl, stir remaining package of gelatin with ½ *cup boiling water* until gelatin has dissolved completely. In blender at high speed, blend gelatin mixture and cottage cheese until smooth. Pour cottage-cheese mixture over gelatin layer in mold. Cover and refrigerate until set, at least 3 hours.

4. To serve, carefully unmold gelatin onto chilled platter. Makes 12 accompaniment servings.

Each serving: About 140 calories, 7 g protein, 27 g carbohydrate, 1 g total fat (1 g saturated), 3 mg cholesterol, 205 mg sodium.

ᘯUnmolding Gelatin Salads

1. Fill the sink or a large bowl with warm, not hot, water. Carefully loosen edges of the gelatin from mold with a metal spatula or knife.
2. Dip the mold into the warm water just to the rim for about 10 seconds. Be careful not to melt the gelatin.
3. Lift the mold out of the water and shake it gently to loosen the gelatin.
4. Invert the serving platter on top of the mold, then

quickly invert the mold and platter and gently lift off the mold.

Cranberry-Orange Mold

Prep: 30 minutes plus chilling

1 envelope (1 ounce) unflavored gelatin
2 packages (6 ounces each) strawberry-flavored gelatin
3 medium-sized oranges
1 package (12 ounces) fresh or frozen cranberries (3 cups)
1¼ cups sugar
Lettuce leaves

1. In 4-quart saucepan, evenly sprinkle unflavored gelatin over *2 cups water*; let stand 1 minute to soften gelatin slightly. Cook over medium heat, stirring frequently, until gelatin has dissolved completely. Remove saucepan from heat; add strawberry-flavored gelatin, stirring until it has dissolved completely. Stir in *3 cups cold water*. Refrigerate until mixture mounds slightly when dropped from a spoon, about 1 hour.
2. Meanwhile, prepare orange rose for garnish: With vegetable peeler or sharp knife, peel continuous 1-inch-wide strip of peel from each orange; reserve oranges. Roll peels tightly, skin side out, to resemble a large rose; hold end in place with toothpick. Wrap and refrigerate.
3. With sharp knife, remove white membrane from oranges; chop oranges and place in medium bowl. Chop cranberries; add cranberries and sugar to oranges; stir until sugar has dissolved completely. Fold fruit mixture into thickened gelatin. Pour into 10-inch Bundt pan or 12-cup mold. Cover and refrigerate until set, at least 3 hours.
4. To serve, unmold gelatin onto platter; garnish with orange roses and lettuce leaves. Makes 16 accompaniment servings.

Each serving: About 165 calories, 3 g protein, 40 g carbohydrate, 0 g total fat, 0 mg cholesterol, 55 mg sodium.

∾Main-Dish Salads

Thai Beef

Prep: 45 minutes
Cook: 10 minutes

2 large bunches cilantro
2 large bunches mint
1 head Boston lettuce
¼ cup seasoned rice vinegar
3 tablespoons vegetable oil
4 teaspoons Asian fish sauce*
4 teaspoons grated, peeled
  fresh ginger
1 jalapeño chile, seeded and
  minced
⅛ teaspoon plus ¼ teaspoon
  salt

1 large carrot, peeled and cut
  into 2-inch-long matchstick
  strips
1 medium red pepper, cut into
  2-inch-long matchstick strips
2 large green onions, cut into
  2-inch-long matchstick strips
1 pound ground beef chuck
1 garlic clove, crushed with
  garlic press

1. From cilantro, remove enough leaves to equal ½ cup loosely packed; chop enough remaining leaves to equal ¼ cup. Repeat with mint to get ½ cup loosely packed mint leaves and ¼ cup chopped mint. Separate Boston lettuce into leaves. Tear very large leaves into bite-size pieces.

2. In medium bowl, with wire whisk, combine chopped cilantro, chopped mint, vinegar, oil, fish sauce, ginger, jalapeño, and ⅛ teaspoon salt. Spoon half of dressing into large bowl; set aside. To dressing remaining in medium bowl, add carrot, red pepper, and green onions.

3. In nonstick 10-inch skillet, cook ground beef over medium-high heat, stirring to break up beef into nickel-size pieces, until browned. Spoon off fat from beef; add garlic and remaining ¼ teaspoon salt and cook, stirring, 1 minute. Toss hot beef mixture with carrot mixture.

4. To large bowl with dressing, add Boston lettuce, cilantro leaves, and mint leaves; toss well. Spoon lettuce mixture onto 4 dinner plates; top with beef mixture. Makes 4 main-dish servings.

Asian fish sauce (nuoc nam) *is a thin, translucent, salty brown liquid extracted from salted, fermented fish. This condiment is used predominantly in Thai and Vietnamese cooking. It can be purchased in the Oriental section of some grocery stores.*

Each serving: About 425 calories, 25 g protein, 15 g carbohydrate, 29 g total fat (8 g saturated), 72 mg cholesterol, 1105 mg sodium.

Chicken Caesar Salad

Prep: 20 minutes
Broil: 2 minutes

2 small garlic cloves
1 tablespoon fresh lemon juice
1 teaspoon Worcestershire
   sauce
1 teaspoon Dijon mustard
½ teaspoon anchovy paste
½ teaspoon salt
¼ teaspoon coarsely ground
   black pepper
3 tablespoons olive oil

½ loaf French bread
   (4 ounces)
12 ounces skinless, boneless
   rotisserie chicken, cut into
   thin strips
12 cups loosely packed bite-
   size pieces romaine lettuce
   or other favorite lettuce
   (about 1 pound)
¼ cup freshly grated Parmesan
   cheese

1. Into large salad bowl, crush 1 garlic clove with garlic press. With wire whisk, mix crushed garlic, lemon juice, Worcestershire, mustard, anchovy paste, salt, and pepper until blended. Slowly whisk in 2 tablespoons oil until dressing thickens slightly; set aside.

2. Preheat broiler. Cut bread horizontally in half. Brush cut surface with remaining 1 tablespoon oil. Place bread, cut side up, on rack in broiling pan. Place pan in broiler 5 to 7 inches from heat source and broil bread, until lightly toasted, 2 to 3 minutes.

3. Cut remaining garlic clove lengthwise in half. Rub cut sides of toasted bread lightly with garlic-clove halves; discard garlic. Cut bread into 1-inch cubes for croutons; set aside.

4. To serve, add chicken to dressing; toss to coat. Add lettuce, garlic croutons, and Parmesan; toss again. Makes 4 main-dish servings.

Each serving: About 390 calories, 33 g protein, 20 g carbohydrate, 20 g total fat (5 g saturated), 82 mg cholesterol, 720 mg sodium.

Shrimp and Watercress Salad

Prep: 45 minutes
Cook: 1 to 2 minutes

1 pound large shrimp
1½ teaspoon salt
2 medium oranges
1 medium jicama (about 1¼ pounds), peeled and cut into 1½" by ¼" sticks
2 bunches watercress (each about 4 ounces), tough stems trimmed

1 large lime
1 cup loosely packed fresh cilantro leaves
¼ cup mayonnaise
1 teaspoon sugar
¼ teaspoon ground red pepper (cayenne)
½ cup plain low-fat yogurt

1. Shell and devein shrimp, leaving on tail part of shell, if you like. Cut each shrimp horizontally in half; rinse with cold running water. In 3-quart saucepan, heat *3 inches water* to boiling over high heat. Add shrimp and 1 teaspoon salt; heat to boiling. Cook until shrimp turn opaque throughout, about 1 minute. Drain shrimp; rinse with cold running water to cool slightly, and drain well. Refrigerate until ready to use.

2. Remove peel and white pith from oranges. Holding oranges over medium bowl to catch juice, cut sections from between membranes. In large salad bowl, combine orange sections (without juice), jicama, and watercress; set aside.

3. From lime, grate 1 teaspoon peel and squeeze 2 tablespoons juice. In food processor with knife blade attached or in blender at medium speed, process lime peel, lime juice, cilantro leaves, mayonnaise, sugar, ground red pepper, and remaining ½ teaspoon salt until blended, about 30 seconds. Add yogurt; pulse just until blended.

4. Add shrimp to bowl with jicama mixture; toss with yogurt dressing. Makes 4 main-dish servings.

Each serving: About 325 calories, 24 g protein, 28 g carbohydrate, 13 g total fat (2 g saturated), 152 mg cholesterol, 660 mg sodium.

Couscous and Smoked-Turkey Salad

Prep: 10 minutes
Cook: 5 minutes

1 teaspoon ground cumin
1 package (10 ounces)
    couscous (Moroccan pasta)
⅓ cup dried tart cherries
3 tablespoons fresh lemon juice
2 tablespoons olive oil
1 tablespoon Dijon mustard

¾ teaspoon salt
¼ teaspoon coarsely ground
    black pepper
3 ripe medium nectarines
    (about 1 pound), diced
4 ounces smoked turkey breast
    (in 1 piece), cut into ¼-inch
    pieces
Boston lettuce leaves

1. In 3-quart saucepan, heat cumin over medium-high heat until fragrant, 1 to 3 minutes. In saucepan with cumin, prepare couscous as label directs, adding cherries but no salt or butter.

2. In large bowl, with wire whisk or fork, mix lemon juice, oil, mustard, salt, and pepper until dressing is blended.

3. Toss warm couscous mixture, diced nectarines, and turkey with dressing.

4. Spoon couscous onto large platter lined with Boston lettuce leaves. Makes about 7½ cups or 6 main-dish servings.

Each serving: About 300 calories, 11 g protein, 51 g carbohydrate, 6 g total fat (1 g saturated), 3 mg cholesterol, 470 mg sodium.

Panzanella Salad

Prep: 30 minutes
Cook: 15 minutes

¼ pound pancetta or bacon, cut into ¼-inch pieces
1 tablespoon olive oil
6 ounces sourdough bread, cut into ½-inch cubes
2 tablespoons freshly grated Parmesan cheese
¼ teaspoon ground black pepper
Tomato Vinaigrette (recipe follows)
4 bunches arugula (about 1 pound), trimmed
1½ pints red and/or yellow cherry tomatoes, each cut in half

1. In nonstick 12-inch skillet, cook pancetta or bacon over medium heat until lightly browned. With slotted spoon, transfer pancetta to large salad bowl.

2. To drippings in skillet, add olive oil and bread cubes and cook until bread is lightly browned, about 10 minutes. Toss toasted bread cubes, Parmesan, and pepper with pancetta; set aside.

3. Prepare Tomato Vinaigrette.

4. Add arugula and cherry tomatoes to bread cubes in bowl; toss with Tomato Vinaigrette. Makes 6 main-dish servings.

TOMATO VINAIGRETTE: Coarsely cut up *1 small ripe tomato,* peeled, and *1 small shallot.* In blender at medium speed, blend tomato, shallot, *2 tablespoons olive oil, 1 tablespoon red-wine vinegar, 1 tablespoon balsamic vinegar, 1 teaspoon sugar, 1 teaspoon chopped fresh oregano, 2 teaspoons Dijon mustard with seeds, ¼ teaspoon salt,* and *¼ teaspoon ground black pepper* just until smooth. Makes about 1 cup. Store in refrigerator for up to 2 days.

Each serving with dressing: About 300 calories, 8 g protein, 25 g carbohydrate, 20 g total fat (6 g saturated), 14 mg cholesterol, 500 mg sodium.

Tomato and Shrimp Salad

Prep: 45 minutes
Cook: About 7 minutes

1 pound large shrimp
4¾ teaspoons salt
¾ pound green beans, trimmed
    and each cut crosswise in
    half
1 pound ripe tomatoes (about
    4 small), each cut into
    8 wedges
1 pound Kirby cucumbers
    (about 4), peeled and each
    cut lengthwise into quarters,
    then cut crosswise into
    1-inch pieces

1 large lemon
2 tablespoons olive oil
1 tablespoon finely chopped
    shallot
1 tablespoon finely chopped
    fresh oregano
1 teaspoon Dijon mustard
½ teaspoon sugar
½ teaspoon coarsely ground
    black pepper
4 ounces feta cheese, crumbled
    (about 1 cup)

1. Shell and devein shrimp, leaving tails on, if you like. Rinse with cold running water. In 4-quart saucepan, heat *2 inches water* to boiling over high heat. Add shrimp and 2 teaspoons salt; cook until shrimp turn opaque throughout, or 1 minute. Drain shrimp; rinse with cold running water to cool and drain again. Place shrimp in large serving bowl.

2. In 10-inch skillet, heat *¼ inch water* to boiling over high heat. Add beans and 2 teaspoons salt; heat to boiling. Reduce heat to medium; cook, uncovered, until beans are tender-crisp, about 5 minutes. Drain beans; rinse under cold running water to cool and drain again. Place beans, tomatoes, and cucumbers in bowl with shrimp.

3. Prepare dressing: From lemon, grate ½ teaspoon peel and squeeze 3 tablespoons juice. In small bowl, with wire whisk or fork, mix lemon peel, lemon juice, oil, shallot, oregano, mustard, sugar, pepper, and remaining ¾ teaspoon salt. Toss dressing with shrimp and vegetables in bowl. Sprinkle with feta cheese. Makes 4 main-dish servings.

Each serving: About 300 calories, 27 g protein, 18 g carbohydrate, 14 g total fat (5 g saturated), 205 mg cholesterol, 1,105 mg sodium.

Salmon and Asparagus Salad

Prep: 20 minutes
Cook: 40 minutes

2 large lemons
2 tablespoons capers, drained and chopped
2 tablespoons Dijon mustard with seeds
2 tablespoons chopped fresh dill
1 teaspoon sugar
½ teaspoon salt
¼ teaspoon coarsely ground black pepper
⅓ cup olive oil

1 salmon fillet (1 pound)
1 teaspoon whole black peppercorns
1 pound small red potatoes
1 pound asparagus, trimmed and cut into 2-inch pieces
1 medium head green-leaf lettuce, torn into bite-size pieces
2 large hard-cooked eggs, shelled and each cut into quarters

1. Prepare dressing: From lemons, grate 1 teaspoon peel and squeeze ⅓ cup juice. In small bowl, combine lemon juice and lemon peel, capers, mustard, dill, sugar, salt, and ground pepper. With wire whisk, slowly beat in olive oil until mixture thickens slightly. Set dressing aside.

2. Remove any small bones and skin from salmon fillet. In 10-inch skillet, heat *1 inch water* to boiling over high heat. Add salmon fillet and peppercorns; heat to boiling. Reduce heat to low; cover and simmer until fish turns opaque throughout, 8 to 10 minutes. Drain fish; refrigerate until ready to assemble salad.

3. Meanwhile, in 3-quart saucepan, heat unpeeled potatoes and enough *water* to cover to boiling over high heat. Reduce heat to low; cover and simmer until potatoes are fork-tender, 15 to 20 minutes. Drain; cut each potato into quarters. While potatoes are still warm, toss with ¼ cup dressing.

4. In 2-quart saucepan, heat asparagus and *1 inch water* to boiling. Reduce heat to low; simmer, uncovered, until tender-crisp, about 5 minutes. Drain; refrigerate until ready to assemble salad.

5. To serve, into medium bowl, pour ¼ cup dressing. Add potatoes and asparagus; toss to coat. Divide lettuce among 4 dinner plates; top with potato mixture, egg quarters, and chunks of salmon. Drizzle remaining dressing over salads. Makes 4 main-dish servings.

Each serving: About 480 calories, 33 g protein, 29 g carbohydrate, 27 g total fat (5 g saturated), 169 mg cholesterol, 730 mg sodium.

Nordic Herring Salad

Prep: 30 minutes plus chilling
Cook: 30 minutes

2 medium potatoes (about ¾ pound)
1 jar (16 ounces) herring bits and pieces in wine sauce
1 medium Granny Smith apple
1 medium dill pickle
¼ cup olive oil
2 tablespoons white wine vinegar
2 tablespoons heavy or whipping cream
1 tablespoon prepared mustard
½ teaspoon salt
¼ cup chopped dill
3 large hard-cooked eggs
1 can (8 ounces) diced beets

1. In 3-quart saucepan, heat unpeeled potatoes and enough *water* to cover to boiling over high heat. Reduce heat to low; cover and simmer until potatoes are fork-tender, 25 to 30 minutes. Drain. Cool potatoes until easy to handle. Peel; cut potatoes into ½-inch chunks.

2. Meanwhile, drain herring. Cut apple into ½-inch chunks; dice pickle.

3. Prepare dressing: In large bowl, with wire whisk or fork, mix oil, vinegar, heavy cream, mustard, and salt. Add potatoes, herring, apples, pickle, and dill to dressing; gently toss to mix well. Cover and refrigerate salad at least 1 hour to blend flavors.

4. To serve, peel eggs. Separate egg yolks from whites. Chop whites. Drain beets; add beets with egg whites to herring salad. With back of spoon, press egg yolks through fine sieve over salad. Makes 4 main-dish servings.

Each serving: About 485 calories, 20 g protein, 39 g carbohydrate, 28 g total fat (7 g saturated), 214 mg cholesterol, 1,395 mg sodium.

Tuscan Tuna Salad

Prep: 25 minutes
Cook: 10 minutes

2 tablespoons plus ¼ cup olive oil
½ long loaf Italian bread (4 ounces), cut into 1-inch cubes
2 large garlic cloves, crushed with side of chef's knife
½ pound green beans, trimmed
¼ cup red wine vinegar
2 tablespoons capers, drained and chopped
1 teaspoon sugar
1 teaspoon Dijon mustard
½ teaspoon salt
¼ teaspoon coarsely ground black pepper

1 can (12 ounces) solid white tuna in water, drained and broken into large pieces
1 can (16 to 19 ounces) white kidney beans (cannellini), rinsed and drained
2 ripe tomatoes (1 pound), each cut into 8 wedges
1 head green-leaf lettuce, torn into 2-inch pieces
½ small head chicory, torn into 2-inch pieces
1 small red onion (4 ounces), cut in half and thinly sliced

1. In nonstick 12-inch skillet, heat 2 tablespoons oil over medium heat. Add bread cubes and garlic and cook, stirring occasionally, until bread is lightly browned. Remove skillet from heat; discard garlic.

2. In 2-quart saucepan, in *1 inch boiling water,* heat green beans to boiling over high heat. Reduce heat to low; simmer until beans are tender-crisp, 5 to 10 minutes. Drain and rinse beans under cold running water to cool slightly.

3. In large salad bowl, with fork or wire whisk, mix vinegar, capers, sugar, mustard, salt, pepper, and ¼ cup oil until blended.

4. To dressing in bowl, add tuna, kidney beans, tomatoes, lettuce, chicory, red onion, green beans, and croutons; toss to serve. Makes 4 main-dish servings.

Each serving: About 520 calories, 31 g protein, 48 g carbohydrate, 24 g total fat (4 g saturated), 29 mg cholesterol, 1,195 mg sodium.

Salade Niçoise

Prep: 25 minutes
Cook: 25 minutes

1 pound small red potatoes	2 heads Boston lettuce
1 package (9 ounces) frozen French-style green beans	1 can (12 ounces) tuna, drained
4 large hard-cooked eggs	½ cup Kalamata olives, pitted
½ cup olive oil	2 medium ripe tomatoes
⅓ cup red wine vinegar	(1 pound), cut into wedges
2 tablespoons Dijon mustard	1 can (2 ounces) anchovy
1 teaspoon salt	fillets, drained
½ teaspoon dried basil	1 tablespoon capers, drained

1. In 3-quart saucepan, heat unpeeled potatoes and enough *water* to cover to boiling over high heat. Reduce heat to low; cover and simmer until potatoes are fork-tender, about 15 minutes. Drain. Cut potatoes into bite-size pieces (do not peel).

2. Meanwhile, cook frozen green beans as label directs; drain.

3. Peel hard-cooked eggs. Separate yolks from whites; coarsely chop whites; set aside.

4. Prepare dressing: In small bowl, mash hard-cooked egg yolks; stir in oil, vinegar, mustard, salt, and basil.

5. To serve, arrange lettuce leaves on large platter. On lettuce leaves, arrange in separate piles potatoes, green beans, tuna, olives, tomato wedges, and anchovy fillets; garnish with capers and chopped egg whites. Let each person help himself to some salad and spoon on some dressing. Makes 8 main-dish servings.

Each serving: About 300 calories, 17 g protein, 17 g carbohydrate, 19 g total fat (3 g saturated), 122 mg cholesterol, 845 mg sodium.

Rice Pilaf Salad

Prep: 20 minutes
Cook: 50 minutes

½ cup wild rice
4 tablespoons olive oil
4 green onions, sliced
½ pound mushrooms, sliced
1 ¼ teaspoons salt
½ cup regular long-grain rice
½ pound oven-roasted boneless turkey breast
½ pound cooked ham
½ pound seedless green grapes
¼ cup red wine vinegar
1 ¼ teaspoons sugar
2 teaspoons Dijon mustard
½ teaspoon dried thyme
¼ teaspoon coarsely ground black pepper
½ cup slivered blanched almonds, toasted
2 medium avocados

1. Rinse wild rice well; drain. In 2-quart saucepan, heat *1 cup water* to boiling over high heat; stir in wild rice. Reduce heat to low; cover and simmer until rice is tender and all liquid is absorbed, about 45 minutes. Remove saucepan from heat.

2. Meanwhile, in 4-quart saucepan, heat 2 tablespoons oil over medium-high heat. Add green onions, mushrooms, and ¼ teaspoon salt, and cook, stirring frequently, until mushrooms are tender and lightly browned. Add long-grain rice and *1 cup water*; heat to boiling over high heat. Reduce heat to low; cover and simmer until rice is tender and all liquid is absorbed, about 20 minutes. Remove saucepan from heat.

3. Cut turkey and ham into long, thin strips. Cut each grape in half.

4. Prepare dressing: In large bowl, with fork, mix vinegar, sugar, mustard, thyme, pepper, 2 tablespoons oil, and remaining 1 teaspoon salt. Add turkey, ham, grapes, toasted nuts, and wild and white rice to dressing in bowl; toss to coat well. Serve salad at room temperature, or cover and refrigerate to serve chilled later.

5. To serve, peel, pit, and cut avocados into wedges. Arrange salad and avocado wedges on platter. Makes 8 main-dish servings.

Each serving: About 390 calories, 21 g protein, 29 g carbohydrate, 22 g total fat (3 g saturated), 36 mg cholesterol, 830 mg sodium.

Portobello and Prosciutto

Prep: 30 minutes
Broil: 8 to 10 minutes

1 small wedge Parmesan cheese	¼ teaspoon salt
2 bunches arugula, trimmed	¼ teaspoon coarsely ground black pepper
2 tablespoons balsamic vinegar	4 portobello mushrooms (about 1½ pounds), stems removed
2 tablespoons olive oil	8 ounces thinly sliced prosciutto
2 tablespoons minced shallots	
2 tablespoons chopped fresh parsley	

1. Preheat broiler.

2. With vegetable peeler, shave enough curls from Parmesan wedge to equal ½ cup (about 1 ounce). Reserve remaining Parmesan for use another day. Arrange arugula on platter.

3. In small bowl, with wire whisk or fork, mix vinegar, oil, shallots, parsley, salt, and pepper until blended.

4. Place mushrooms, top side up, on rack in broiling pan. Brush mushroom tops with 1 tablespoon dressing.

Place pan in broiler at closest position to heat source; broil mushrooms 4 minutes. Turn mushrooms over; brush with 2 more tablespoons dressing and broil until tender, about 5 minutes longer.

5. Thickly slice mushrooms and arrange on arugula. Spoon remaining dressing over salad. Arrange prosciutto on platter with salad. Top with Parmesan curls. Makes 4 main-dish servings.

TO GRILL: Prepare outdoor grill for barbecuing. Follow recipe steps 2 and 3. Place mushrooms, top side up, on grill over medium heat. Brush mushroom tops with 1 tablespoon dressing. Grill 4 minutes. Turn mushrooms and brush with 2 tablespoons dressing. Grill until tender, about 5 minutes longer. Complete recipe step 5.

Each serving: About 200 calories, 18 g protein, 11 g carbohydrate, 11 g total fat (3 g saturated), 38 mg cholesterol, 885 mg sodium.

∾Salad Dressings

Classic French Dressing

Prep: 3 minutes

¾ cup olive oil
¼ cup wine vinegar or cider vinegar
¾ teaspoon salt
Coarsely ground black pepper

Into small bowl or jar, measure oil, vinegar, salt, and pepper; mix with wire whisk or fork (or cover jar and shake) until well blended. Cover and refrigerate. Stir or shake before using. Serve on lettuce, mixed greens, or chilled, cooked vegetables. Makes 1 cup.

Each tablespoon: About 90 calories, 0 g protein, 0 g carbohydrate, 10 g total fat (1 g saturated), 0 mg cholesterol, 110 mg sodium.

ROQUEFORT OR BLUE-CHEESE DRESSING: Prepare as above but add *½ cup crumbled Roquefort or blue cheese.* Serve as above. Makes about 1⅓ cups.

Each tablespoon: About 80 calories, 1 g protein, 0 g carbohydrate, 9 g total fat (2 g saturated), 2 mg cholesterol, 130 mg sodium.

MIXED-HERB DRESSING: Prepare as above but add *2 teaspoons chopped parsley* and *½ teaspoon dried tarragon or basil.* Serve as above. Makes 1 cup.

Each tablespoon: About 90 calories, 0 g protein, 0 g carbohydrate, 10 g total fat (1 g saturated), 0 mg cholesterol, 110 mg sodium.

Mustard-Shallot Vinaigrette

Prep: 5 minutes

¾ cup olive oil
⅔ cup red wine vinegar
3 tablespoons Dijon mustard
1 large shallot, minced
1 teaspoon salt
1 teaspoon coarsely ground black pepper
1 teaspoon sugar

In large jar (about 2 cups) with tight-fitting lid, combine oil, vinegar, mustard, shallot, salt, pepper, and sugar; shake well. Refrigerate if not serving right away. Bring to room

temperature and shake well before using. Serve dressing
with greens. Refrigerate any remaining dressing to use up
within 3 days. Makes about 1⅔ cups.

Each tablespoon: About 55 calories, 0 g protein, 1 g carbohydrate, 6 g total fat (1 g saturated), 0 mg cholesterol, 120 mg sodium.

Russian Dressing

Prep: 5 minutes

1 cup mayonnaise
¼ cup ketchup
1 tablespoon minced fresh parsley
1 tablespoon milk
1 tablespoon grated onion (optional)
¼ teaspoon dry mustard
¼ teaspoon Worcestershire sauce
3 drops hot-pepper sauce

In small bowl, with fork, stir mayonnaise, ketchup, parsley, milk, onion, if using, dry mustard, Worcestershire, and hot-pepper sauce until well mixed. Cover and refrigerate. Serve on lettuce wedges, hard-cooked eggs, cold poultry, chilled, cooked vegetables, corned beef, and in sandwiches. Makes about 1¼ cups.

Each tablespoon: About 85 calories, 0 g protein, 1 g carbohydrate, 9 g total fat (1 g saturated), 7 mg cholesterol, 100 mg sodium.

Creamy Blue-Cheese Dressing

Prep: 5 minutes

4 ounces blue cheese, crumbled (1 cup)
3 tablespoons half-and-half
½ cup mayonnaise
⅓ cup olive oil
¼ cup white wine vinegar
1 teaspoon prepared mustard
⅛ teaspoon salt
⅛ teaspoon ground black pepper

In small bowl, with fork, mash cheese and half-and-half until creamy. Add mayonnaise, oil, vinegar, mustard, salt, and pepper; with wire whisk, beat until well mixed. Cover and refrigerate. Serve on mixed greens, lettuce wedges, chilled, cooked vegetables, tomato wedges, cold roast-beef slices, and hard-cooked eggs. Makes about 1 cup.

Each tablespoon: About 120 calories, 2 g protein, 1 g carbohydrate, 12 g total fat (3 g saturated), 10 mg cholesterol, 160 mg sodium.

Thousand Island Dressing

Prep: 5 minutes
Cook: 10 minutes

1 hard-cooked egg
1 cup mayonnaise
3 tablespoons chili sauce
2 tablespoons sweet-pickle relish
2 tablespoons milk
1 tablespoon minced fresh parsley
½ teaspoon paprika

1. Peel and chop egg.

2. In small bowl, stir chopped egg, mayonnaise, chili sauce, relish, milk, parsley, and paprika until well mixed. Cover and refrigerate. Serve on lettuce wedges, mixed greens, chilled, cooked vegetables, and in sandwiches. Makes about 1½ cups.

Each tablespoon: About 75 calories, 1 g protein, 1 g carbohydrate, 8 g total fat (1 g saturated), 14 mg cholesterol, 90 mg sodium.

Green Goddess Dressing

Prep: 7 minutes

¾ cup mayonnaise
2 anchovy fillets, minced
1 tablespoon chopped fresh parsley
1 tablespoon chopped fresh chives
1 tablespoon chopped green onion
1 tablespoon tarragon vinegar
¾ teaspoon dried tarragon

In small bowl, stir mayonnaise, anchovies, parsley, chives, green onion, vinegar, and tarragon until well mixed. Cover and refrigerate. Serve on mixed greens, chilled, cooked vegetables, cold seafood, or poultry. Makes about 1 cup.

Each tablespoon: About 75 calories, 0 g protein, 0 g carbohydrate, 8 g total fat (1 g saturated), 7 mg cholesterol, 75 mg sodium.

Honey-Caraway Dressing

Prep: 5 minutes

¾ cup mayonnaise
2 tablespoons honey
1 tablespoon fresh lemon juice
1 tablespoon caraway seeds

In small bowl, stir mayonnaise, honey, lemon juice, and caraway seeds until blended; cover and refrigerate. Stir before using. Serve on fruit salad, melon or papaya wedges. Makes about 1 cup.

Each tablespoon: About 85 calories, 0 g protein, 3 g carbohydrate, 8 g total fat (1 g saturated), 6 mg cholesterol, 60 mg sodium.

Mint-Lime Dressing

Prep: 7 minutes

1 cup loosely packed fresh mint leaves
¼ cup fresh lime juice
2 packages (3 ounces each) cream cheese, softened
⅓ cup sugar

In blender at medium speed, blend mint and lime juice until mint is finely chopped. Add cream cheese and sugar; blend at medium speed just until smooth. (Do not overblend, or dressing will be thin.) Serve on fruit salad or berries. Makes about 1⅓ cups.

Each tablespoon: About 40 calories, 1 g protein, 4 g carbohydrate, 3 g total fat (2 g saturated), 9 mg cholesterol, 25 mg sodium.

Poppy-Seed Dressing

Prep: 5 minutes

1 cup vegetable oil
½ cup sugar
⅓ cup cider vinegar
1 tablespoon poppy seeds
1 tablespoon grated onion
1 teaspoon salt
1 teaspoon dry mustard

In blender at medium speed, blend oil, sugar, vinegar, poppy seeds, onion, salt, and dry mustard until thoroughly mixed. Dressing will be thick. Store in tightly covered jar in refrigerator. Stir well before using. Serve dressing on tossed greens or fruit salad. Makes about 1½ cups.

Each tablespoon: About 90 calories, 0 g protein, 2 g carbohydrate, 9 g total fat (1 g saturated), 0 mg cholesterol, 95 mg sodium.

SIX SKINNY SALAD DRESSINGS

Buttermilk-Chive Dressing

Prep: 5 minutes

½ cup reduced-fat buttermilk
2 tablespoons distilled white vinegar
2 tablespoons chopped fresh chives
1 tablespoon low-fat mayonnaise dressing
¼ teaspoon salt
¼ teaspoon coarsely ground black pepper

In small bowl, with wire whisk or fork, mix buttermilk, vinegar, chives, mayonnaise dressing, salt, and pepper until blended. Makes about ¾ cup.

Each tablespoon: About 6 calories, 0 g protein, 1 g carbohydrate, 0 g total fat, 0 mg cholesterol, 65 mg sodium.

Tomato-Orange Vinaigrette

Prep: 5 minutes

½ cup tomato juice
1 tablespoon balsamic vinegar
¼ teaspoon freshly grated orange peel
¼ teaspoon sugar
⅛ teaspoon coarsely ground black pepper

In small bowl, with wire whisk or fork, mix tomato juice, vinegar, orange peel, sugar, and pepper until blended. Makes about ½ cup.

Each tablespoon: About 5 calories, 0 g protein, 1 g carbohydrate, 0 g total fat, 0 mg cholesterol, 55 mg sodium.

Honey-Lime Vinaigrette

Prep: 5 minutes

⅓ cup fresh lime juice
4 teaspoons honey
1 tablespoon rice vinegar
⅛ teaspoon salt

In small bowl, with wire whisk or fork, mix lime juice, honey, rice vinegar, and salt until blended. Makes about ½ cup.

Each tablespoon: About 15 calories, 0 g protein, 4 g carbohydrate, 0 g total fat, 0 mg cholesterol, 35 mg sodium.

Spicy Tomato Dressing

Prep: 5 minutes

1 can (5 ounces) spicy-hot vegetable juice
3 tablespoons red wine vinegar
1 tablespoon olive oil
1 garlic clove, crushed with garlic press
½ teaspoon sugar
½ teaspoon dry mustard

Into small bowl or jar, measure vegetable juice, vinegar, oil, garlic, sugar, and mustard; mix with wire whisk or fork (or cover jar and shake) until blended. Cover and refrigerate. Stir or shake before using. Makes about 1 cup.

Each tablespoon: About 15 calories, 0 g protein, 1 g carbohydrate, 1 g total fat (0 g saturated), 0 mg cholesterol, 35 mg sodium.

Creamy Ranch Dressing

Prep: 5 minutes

¾ cup plain nonfat yogurt
¼ cup low-fat mayonnaise
1 tablespoon cider vinegar
2 teaspoons Dijon mustard
¼ teaspoon coarsely ground black pepper
¼ teaspoon dried thyme
1 green onion, minced

Into small bowl, measure yogurt, mayonnaise, vinegar, mustard, pepper, thyme, and green onion; mix with wire whisk or fork until blended. Cover and refrigerate. Stir before using. Makes about 1 cup.

Each tablespoon: About 15 calories, 1 g protein, 2 g carbohydrate, 0 g total fat, 0 mg cholesterol, 60 mg sodium.

Orange-Ginger Dressing

Prep: 5 minutes

½ cup seasoned rice vinegar
½ cup fresh orange juice
½ teaspoon grated, peeled fresh ginger
½ teaspoon soy sauce
⅛ teaspoon Asian sesame oil

Into small bowl or jar, measure vinegar, orange juice, ginger, soy sauce, and sesame oil; mix with wire whisk or fork (or cover jar and shake) until blended. Cover and refrigerate. Stir or shake before using. Makes about 1 cup.

Each tablespoon: About 10 calories, 0 g protein, 3 g carbohydrate, 0 g total fat, 0 mg cholesterol, 110 mg sodium.

Sauces, Condiments & Garnishes

~∽∾~

Savory Sauces
Dessert Sauces • Condiments

In this chapter, you will find the finishing touches that enhance the good taste and good looks of your main dishes, vegetables, salads, desserts, and beverages. Use them to supply the contrasts in flavor, color, and texture that make foods more enjoyable.

ᏑSavory Sauces

White Sauce (Béchamel Sauce)

Prep: 2 minutes
Cook: 7 minutes

2 tablespoons margarine or butter
2 tablespoons all-purpose flour
½ teaspoon salt
Dash paprika
1 cup milk or half-and-half

1. In 1-quart nonstick saucepan, melt margarine over low heat; stir in flour, salt, and paprika until blended; cook 1 minute.

2. Gradually stir in milk; cook, stirring constantly, until mixture thickens and is smooth. Serve over hot, cooked vegetables, shrimp, cut-up hard-cooked eggs. Makes about 1 cup.

Each ¼ cup with milk: About 100 calories, 3 g protein, 6 g carbohydrate, 8 g total fat (2 g saturated), 8 mg cholesterol, 395 mg sodium.

THIN WHITE SAUCE: Prepare White Sauce as above but use only *1 tablespoon margarine or butter* and *1 tablespoon all-purpose flour*. Makes 1 cup.

Each ¼ cup with milk: About 70 calories, 2 g protein, 4 g carbohydrate, 5 g total fat (2 g saturated), 8 mg cholesterol, 360 mg sodium.

THICK WHITE SAUCE: Prepare White Sauce as above but use *4 tablespoons margarine or butter* and *¼ cup all-purpose flour*. Makes scant cup.

Each ¼ cup with milk: About 165 calories, 3 g protein, 9 g carbohydrate, 14 g total fat (3 g saturated), 8 mg cholesterol, 475 mg sodium.

VELOUTÉ: Prepare White Sauce as above but substitute *1 cup chicken broth* for the milk. Makes 1 cup.

Each ¼ cup: About 75 calories, 2 g protein, 3 g carbohydrate, 6 g total fat (1 g saturated), 0 mg cholesterol, 560 mg sodium.

CHEESE SAUCE: Prepare White Sauce as above. Into hot sauce, stir *¼ pound American or Cheddar cheese*, shredded (1 cup), and *¼ teaspoon dry mustard*. Cook over very low heat, stirring, just until cheese melts. Serve over hot, cooked vegetables, poached eggs, and baked potatoes. Makes 1¼ cup.

Each ¼ cup with milk: About 170 calories, 7 g protein, 5 g carbohydrate, 13 g total fat (6 g saturated), 28 mg cholesterol, 640 mg sodium.

CURRY SAUCE: Prepare White Sauce as above but cook *¼ cup minced onion, 2 teaspoons curry powder, ¾ teaspoon sugar,* and *⅛ teaspoon ground ginger* in the melted margarine until onion is tender, then proceed as directed. Serve over hot, cooked vegetables, cooked shrimp, or poached fish or eggs. Makes 1 cup.

Each ¼ cup with milk: About 110 calories, 3 g protein, 8 g carbohydrate, 8 g total fat (2 g saturated), 8 mg cholesterol, 400 mg sodium.

Polonaise Sauce

Prep: 7 minutes
Cook: 4 minutes

2 tablespoons margarine or butter
½ cup fresh white bread crumbs (1 slice)
1 hard-cooked egg, chopped
1 tablespoon fresh lemon juice
1 tablespoon chopped fresh parsley
¼ teaspoon salt

In small saucepan or skillet, melt margarine over medium heat. Add bread crumbs and cook, tossing lightly, until golden. Stir in chopped egg, lemon juice, parsley, and salt. Serve sauce over hot cooked vegetables. Makes about ¾ cup.

Each ¼ cup: About 110 calories, 3 g protein, 4 g carbohydrate, 10 g total fat (2 g saturated), 71 mg cholesterol, 350 mg sodium.

Beurre Blanc with Herbs

Prep: 5 minutes
Cook: 10 minutes

½ cup dry white wine
2 teaspoons white wine vinegar
1 teaspoon minced fresh tarragon or ¼ teaspoon dried tarragon
2 shallots, peeled and sliced
½ cup (1 stick) butter (no substitutions)
2 tablespoons heavy or whipping cream

1. In 1-quart nonstick saucepan, heat white wine, vinegar, tarragon, and shallots to boiling over medium-high heat; boil until liquid is reduced to about 2 tablespoons, about 5 minutes. Push through a sieve; discard shallots.

2. Reduce heat to medium; add butter, 1 tablespoon at a time (do not use margarine; sauce will not thicken), beating constantly with wire whisk until butter melts and mixture thickens slightly. Remove saucepan from heat; stir in heavy or whipping cream. Serve over broiled or grilled fish steaks, lobster, shrimp, poached fish fillets, or hot cooked vegetables. Makes about ¾ cup.

Each tablespoon: About 85 calories, 0 g protein, 0 g carbohydrate, 9 g total fat (6 g saturated), 25 mg cholesterol, 85 mg sodium.

Cumberland Sauce

Prep: 10 minutes
Cook: 6 minutes

1 medium orange	1 tablespoon orange
1 small lemon	marmalade
½ cup red-currant jelly	⅛ teaspoon ground ginger
¼ cup port wine	⅛ teaspoon dry mustard
1 tablespoon cornstarch	⅛ teaspoon salt
2 tablespoons red wine	⅛ teaspoon ground black
vinegar	pepper

1. Squeeze orange to make about ½ cup juice. From lemon, grate ¼ teaspoon peel and squeeze 1 tablespoon juice.

2. In 1-quart saucepan, mix orange and lemon juice, lemon peel, red currant jelly, wine, cornstarch, vinegar, marmalade, ginger, dry mustard, salt, and pepper. Cook over medium heat, stirring, until mixture boils and thickens slightly; boil 1 minute. Serve with baked ham, corned beef, roast venison, or tongue. Makes about 1½ cups.

Each ¼ cup: About 100 calories, 0 g protein, 25 g carbohydrate, 0 g total fat, 0 mg cholesterol, 60 mg sodium.

Creamy Mushroom Sauce

Prep: 8 minutes
Cook: 12 minutes

2 tablespoons margarine or butter
½ pound mushrooms, thinly sliced
1 tablespoon all-purpose flour
½ teaspoon salt
⅛ teaspoon ground black pepper
1¼ cups half-and-half or milk
1 tablespoon dry sherry
2 tablespoons sour cream

1. In 10-inch nonstick skillet, melt margarine over medium-high heat. Add mushrooms and cook, stirring occasionally, until tender. Stir in flour, salt, and pepper; cook 1 minute.

2. Gradually stir in half-and-half and sherry. Cook, stirring constantly, until sauce thickens slightly. Remove skillet from heat; stir in sour cream. Serve with roast beef, broiled pork chops, hamburgers, hot, cooked broccoli, Brussels sprouts, or asparagus. Makes about 1½ cups.

Each ¼ cup: About 125 calories, 3 g protein, 5 g carbohydrate, 11 g total fat (5 g saturated), 20 mg cholesterol, 270 mg sodium.

Chunky BBQ Sauce

Prep: 20 minutes
Cook: 20 minutes

1 tablespoon vegetable oil
1 large onion, diced
3 garlic cloves, minced
2 tablespoons minced, peeled
  fresh ginger
1 teaspoon ground cumin
1 can (14½ ounces) whole
  tomatoes in puree, chopped,
  with puree reserved

1 bottle (12 ounces) chili sauce
⅓ cup cider vinegar
2 tablespoons brown sugar
2 tablespoons light molasses
2 teaspoons dry mustard
1 tablespoon cornstarch

1. In 12-inch skillet, heat oil over medium heat until hot. Add diced onion and cook, stirring occasionally, until tender, about 10 minutes. Add garlic and ginger and cook 1 minute, stirring. Stir in cumin and cook 1 minute longer.

2. Stir in chopped tomatoes, reserved tomato puree, chili sauce, vinegar, brown sugar, molasses, and dry mustard; heat to boiling over high heat. Reduce heat to medium-high and cook, uncovered, 5 minutes, stirring occasionally.

3. In cup, with fork, mix cornstarch and *2 tablespoons water* until blended. After sauce has cooked 5 minutes, stir in cornstarch mixture and cook until sauce boils and thickens, 1 to 2 minutes longer. Cover and refrigerate if not using right away. Makes about 4 cups.

Each cup: About 240 calories, 5 g protein, 48 g carbohydrate, 5 g total fat (0 g saturated), 0 mg cholesterol, 1,500 mg sodium.

Secret-Recipe BBQ Sauce

Prep: 25 minutes
Cook: 40 minutes

1 tablespoon olive oil	1 can (28 ounces) crushed
1 jumbo onion (12 ounces),	tomatoes in puree
chopped	⅓ cup ketchup
2 tablespoons chopped, peeled	¼ cup cider vinegar
fresh ginger	3 tablespoons dark brown
3 tablespoons chili powder	sugar
3 garlic cloves, crushed with	3 tablespoons mild molasses
garlic press	2 teaspoons dry mustard
1 can (8 ounces) crushed	1 teaspoon salt
pineapple in juice	

1. In 5- to 6-quart saucepot, heat oil over medium heat until hot. (Do not use a smaller pan; sauce bubbles up and splatters during cooking—the deeper the pan, the better.) Add onion and ginger, and cook until onion is tender and golden, about 10 minutes. Add chili powder and cook, stirring, 1 minute. Add garlic and crushed pineapple with its juice, and cook 1 minute longer.

2. Remove saucepot from heat. Stir in tomatoes with their puree, ketchup, vinegar, dark brown sugar, molasses, mustard, and salt. Spoon one-fourth of sauce into blender. At low speed, blend sauce until smooth. Pour sauce into bowl; repeat with remaining sauce.

3. Return sauce to saucepot; heat to boiling over high heat. Reduce heat to medium-low and cook, partially covered, until reduced to about 4¾ cups, 25 minutes, stirring occasionally.

4. Cover and refrigerate if not using right away. Sauce will keep up to 1 week in refrigerator or up to 2 months in freezer. Makes about 4¾ cups.

Each ¼ cup: About 60 calories, 1 g protein, 12 g carbohydrate, 1 g total fat (0 g saturated), 0 mg cholesterol, 310 mg sodium.

Chinese Sparerib Sauce

Prep: 5 minutes
Cook: 8 minutes

2 tablespoons vegetable oil
2 green onions, sliced
⅔ cup packed light brown sugar
½ cup soy sauce
¼ cup dry sherry
1 tablespoon cornstarch
1 teaspoon ground ginger

1. In 1-quart saucepan, heat oil over medium heat until hot. Add green onions and cook until tender and lightly browned, about 5 minutes.

2. Stir in brown sugar, soy sauce, sherry, cornstarch, and ginger. Cook over medium-high heat until mixture boils and thickens slightly; cook, stirring constantly, 1 minute.

3. Cover and refrigerate sauce if not using right away. Use sauce to brush on pork spareribs, pork chops, or chicken or turkey parts during cooking. Makes about 1¼ cups.

Each ¼ cup: About 190 calories, 2 g protein, 34 g carbohydrate, 6 g total fat (1 g saturated), 0 mg cholesterol, 1,660 mg sodium.

Lemon Butter

Prep: 5 minutes
Cook: 3 minutes

4 tablespoons margarine or butter
1 tablespoon fresh lemon juice
1 tablespoon chopped fresh parsley
½ teaspoon salt
Dash ground red pepper (cayenne)

In small saucepan, melt margarine over medium heat.
Stir in lemon juice, parsley, salt, and ground red pepper.
Serve over hot, cooked vegetables or broiled, fried, or
poached fish or shellfish. Makes about ⅓ cup.

*Each tablespoon: About 80 calories, 0 g protein, 0 g carbohydrate,
9 g total fat (2 g saturated), 0 mg cholesterol, 355 mg sodium.*

Orange-Chive Butter

Prep: 15 minutes plus chilling or freezing

½ cup (1 stick) butter, softened
2 tablespoons minced fresh chives
1 teaspoon freshly grated orange peel

In bowl, with spoon, mix butter with chives and orange
peel until blended. Spoon mixture into a 6-inch-long strip
across the width of sheet of plastic wrap or waxed paper.
Freeze until slightly firm, about 20 minutes. Roll mixture,
covered with plastic wrap or waxed paper, back and forth,
to make a 6-inch-long log. Wrap well and refrigerate up to
2 days, or freeze up to 2 months. Serve a slice over cooked
vegetables, poultry, meat, or fish. Makes 8 accompaniment
servings.

*Each serving: About 100 calories, 0 g protein, 0 g carbohydrate,
12 g total fat (2 g saturated), 0 mg cholesterol, 135 mg sodium.*

Tarragon Butter

Prep: 15 minutes plus chilling or freezing

½ cup (1 stick) butter, softened
2 tablespoons finely chopped fresh tarragon
¼ teaspoon freshly grated lemon peel
⅛ teaspoon coarsely ground black pepper

In bowl, with spoon, mix butter with tarragon, lemon peel, and pepper until blended. Spoon mixture into a 6-inch-long strip across the width of sheet of plastic wrap or waxed paper. Freeze until slightly firm, about 20 minutes. Roll mixture, covered with plastic wrap or waxed paper, back and forth, to make a 6-inch-long log. Wrap well and refrigerate up to 2 days, or freeze up to 2 months. Serve a slice over cooked vegetables, poultry, or fish. Makes 8 accompaniment servings.

Each serving: About 100 calories, 0 g protein, 0 g carbohydrate, 12 g total fat (2 g saturated), 0 mg cholesterol, 135 mg sodium.

Honey-Pecan Butter

Prep: 15 minutes plus chilling or freezing
Bake: 10 minutes

½ cup pecans
½ cup (1 stick) butter, softened
2 tablespoons honey
½ teaspoon coarsely ground black pepper

1. Preheat oven to 375°F. Place nuts in 8" by 8" metal baking pan. Bake pecans until lightly toasted, 8 to 10 minutes. Cool completely. In food processor, with knife blade attached, process pecans until finely ground.

2. In bowl, with spoon, mix butter with honey, pepper, and ground pecans until blended. Spoon mixture into a 6-inch-long strip across the width of sheet of plastic wrap or waxed paper. Freeze until slightly firm, about 20 minutes. Roll mixture, covered with plastic wrap or waxed paper, back and forth, to make a 6-inch-long log. Wrap well and refrigerate up to 2 days, or freeze up to 2 months. Serve a slice over hot, cooked vegetables. Makes 8 accompaniment servings.

Each serving: About 165 calories, 0 g protein, 6 g carbohydrate, 16 g total fat (3 g saturated), 0 mg cholesterol, 135 mg sodium.

Hazelnut Butter

Prep: 20 minutes plus chilling or freezing
Bake: 15 minutes

½ cup hazelnuts (filberts)
½ cup (1 stick) butter, softened
2 teaspoons freshly grated lemon peel
¼ teaspoon ground black pepper

1. Preheat oven to 375°F. Place hazelnuts in 8" by 8" metal baking pan. Bake until lightly toasted, 10 to 15 minutes. To remove skins, wrap hot hazelnuts in clean cloth towel. With hands, roll hazelnuts back and forth until most of skins come off. Discard skins; let nuts cool. In food processor with knife blade attached, finely grind nuts.

2. In bowl, with spoon, mix butter with ground nuts, lemon peel, and pepper until blended. Spoon mixture into a 6-inch-long strip across the width of sheet of plastic wrap or waxed paper. Freeze until slightly firm, about 20 minutes. Roll mixture, covered with plastic wrap or waxed paper, back and forth, to make a 6-inch-long log. Wrap well and refrigerate up to 2 days, or freeze up to 2 months. Serve a slice over hot, cooked vegetables. Makes 8 accompaniment servings.

Each serving: About 145 calories, 1 g protein, 1 g carbohydrate, 16 g total fat (3 g saturated), 0 mg cholesterol, 135 mg sodium.

Sauce Rémoulade

Prep: 12 minutes

½ cup mayonnaise
3 tablespoons minced dill pickle
2 tablespoons sour cream
1 tablespoon minced fresh parsley
1 teaspoon Dijon mustard
1 teaspoon chopped capers
¾ teaspoon minced fresh tarragon or ¼ teaspoon dried tarragon
½ teaspoon chopped fresh chives
1 anchovy fillet, minced

In small bowl, stir mayonnaise, pickle, sour cream, parsley, mustard, capers, tarragon, chives, and anchovy until blended. Serve with hot or cold roast beef, broiled seafood, cold chicken, or cold, cooked vegetables. Makes about ¾ cup.

Each tablespoon: About 70 calories, 0 g protein, 1 g carbohydrate, 8 g total fat (1 g saturated), 7 mg cholesterol, 125 mg sodium.

Tartar Sauce

Prep: 10 minutes

½ cup mayonnaise
3 tablespoons minced dill pickle
1 tablespoon minced fresh parsley
2 teaspoons milk
1 teaspoon minced onion
½ teaspoon Dijon mustard

In small bowl, stir mayonnaise, pickle, parsley, milk, onion, and mustard until blended. Serve with fried shrimp or with poached, baked, broiled, or fried fish. Makes about ¾ cup.

Each tablespoon: About 70 calories, 0 g protein, 1 g carbohydrate, 7 g total fat (1 g saturated), 6 mg cholesterol, 100 mg sodium.

Basic Vinaigrette

Prep: 5 minutes

¾ cup olive oil
⅓ cup red wine, balsamic, or cider vinegar
2 tablespoons chopped fresh parsley
½ teaspoon salt

In blender, at low speed, blend oil, vinegar, parsley, and salt 1 minute. (Or in medium bowl, combine vinegar with parsley and salt; slowly pour in oil, beating with wire whisk or fork until well mixed.) Serve over chilled or hot, cooked vegetables, or salad. Makes about 1¼ cups.

Each tablespoon: About 70 calories, 0 g protein, 0 g carbohydrate, 8 g total fat (1 g saturated), 0 mg cholesterol, 60 mg sodium.

Tomato Salsa

Prep: 20 minutes plus chilling

1 large lime
1½ pounds ripe tomatoes (about 4 large), diced
½ small red onion, diced
1 small jalapeño chile, seeded and finely chopped
2 tablespoons chopped fresh cilantro
¾ teaspoon salt
¼ teaspoon coarsely ground black pepper

From lime, grate ½ teaspoon peel and squeeze 2 tablespoons juice. In medium bowl, combine lime peel and juice, tomatoes, onion, chile, cilantro, salt, and pepper; stir gently. Cover and refrigerate at least 1 hour to blend flavors. May be refrigerated up to 2 days. Makes about 3 cups.

Each ¼ cup: About 15 calories, 1 g protein, 3 g carbohydrate, 0 g total fat, 0 mg cholesterol, 140 mg sodium.

Olive and Lemon Salsa

Prep: 10 minutes

2 lemons
2 small navel oranges
¼ cup coarsely chopped pimiento-stuffed olives
2 tablespoons chopped shallot
2 tablespoons chopped fresh parsley
½ teaspoon sugar
¼ teaspoon coarsely ground black pepper

1. Remove peel and white pith from lemons and oranges. Cut fruit into ¼-inch slices, discarding seeds. Cut slices into ½-inch pieces.
2. In small bowl, combine lemon and orange pieces, olives, shallot, parsley, sugar, and pepper; stir gently. Cover and refrigerate if not serving right away. Makes about 2 cups.

Each ¼ cup: About 130 calories, 3 g protein, 28 g carbohydrate, 3 g total fat (1 g saturated), 0 mg cholesterol, 705 mg sodium.

Fresh Cherry Salsa

Prep: 30 minutes plus chilling

1 pound cherries, pitted and chopped
⅓ cup diced yellow pepper
1 green onion, chopped
2 tablespoons seasoned rice vinegar
1 teaspoon grated, peeled fresh ginger
⅛ teaspoon salt

In medium bowl, combine cherries, yellow pepper, green onion, vinegar, ginger, and salt; stir gently. Cover and refrigerate at least 1 hour to blend flavors. May be refrigerated up to 2 days. Makes about 3 cups.

Each ¼ cup serving: About 25 calories, 1 g protein, 6 g carbohydrate, 0 g total fat, 0 mg cholesterol, 20 mg sodium.

Peach Salsa

Prep: 30 minutes plus chilling

1¾ pounds ripe peaches (about 6 medium), peeled, pitted, and
  coarsely chopped
2 tablespoons finely chopped red onion
1 tablespoon chopped fresh mint
1 tablespoon fresh lime juice
1 teaspoon seeded, finely chopped jalapeño chile
⅛ teaspoon salt

In medium bowl, combine peaches, red onion, mint, lime juice, chile, and salt; stir gently. Cover and refrigerate at least 1 hour to blend flavors. May be refrigerated up to 2 days. Makes about 3 cups.

Each ¼ cup serving: About 25 calories, 0 g protein, 6 g carbohydrate, 0 g total fat, 0 mg cholesterol, 20 mg sodium.

Watermelon Salsa

Prep: 30 minutes plus chilling

1 piece watermelon (about 2½ pounds), seeds and rind removed
  and flesh coarsely chopped
1 tablespoon finely chopped red onion
1 tablespoon chopped fresh cilantro
2 tablespoons fresh lime juice
2 teaspoons seeded, finely chopped jalapeño chile
⅛ teaspoon salt

In medium bowl, combine watermelon, red onion, cilantro, lime juice, jalapeño, and salt; stir gently. Cover and refrigerate at least 1 hour to blend flavors. May be refrigerated up to 2 days. Makes about 3 cups.

Each ¼ cup serving: About 15 calories, 0 g protein, 3 g carbohydrate, 0 g total fat, 0 mg cholesterol, 25 mg sodium.

Plum Salsa

Prep: 30 minutes plus chilling

1 ½ pounds ripe plums (6 to 8 medium), pitted and coarsely
    chopped
1 green onion, chopped
1 tablespoon coarsely chopped fresh basil
2 tablespoons balsamic vinegar
⅛ teaspoon salt

In medium bowl, combine plums, green onion, basil, vinegar, and salt; stir gently. Cover and refrigerate at least 1 hour to blend flavors. May be refrigerated up to 2 days. Makes about 3 cups.

Each ¼ cup serving: About 30 calories, 0 g protein, 8 g carbohydrate, 0 g total fat, 0 mg cholesterol, 25 mg sodium.

Salsa Verde

Prep: 15 minutes

1 garlic clove, peeled and cut in half
¼ teaspoon salt
2 cups packed fresh Italian parsley leaves (about 3 bunches)
⅓ cup olive oil
3 tablespoons capers, drained
3 tablespoons fresh lemon juice
1 teaspoon Dijon mustard
⅛ teaspoon coarsely ground black pepper

In food processor with knife blade attached, or in blender, combine garlic, salt, parsley, oil, capers, lemon juice, mustard, and pepper, and process until finely chopped. If not using sauce right away, cover and refrigerate up to 3 days. Makes about ¾ cup.

Each tablespoon: About 60 calories, 0 g protein, 1 g carbohydrate, 6 g total fat (1 g saturated), 0 mg cholesterol, 140 mg sodium.

Chimichurri Sauce

Prep: 20 minutes

1 large garlic clove, minced
½ teaspoon salt
1½ cups loosely packed fresh Italian parsley leaves, minced
1 cup loosely packed fresh cilantro leaves, minced
¾ cup olive oil
2 tablespoons red wine vinegar
½ teaspoon crushed red pepper

1. On cutting board, with side of chef's knife, mash garlic with salt into a smooth paste.
2. In small bowl, stir garlic mixture, parsley, cilantro,

oil, vinegar, and red pepper until well blended. Makes about 1 cup.

Each tablespoon: About 90 calories, 0 g protein, 1 g carbohydrate, 10 g total fat (1 g saturated), 0 mg cholesterol, 70 mg sodium.

Cocktail Sauce

Prep: 5 minutes

1 cup bottled chili sauce
1 tablespoon prepared horseradish
¼ teaspoon Worcestershire sauce
Hot-pepper sauce to taste

In small bowl, stir chili sauce, horseradish, Worcestershire, and hot-pepper sauce until blended. Serve with cold, cooked shrimp, lobster meat, crabmeat, or with oysters or clams on the half shell. Makes about 1 cup.

Each tablespoon: About 25 calories, 1 g protein, 6 g carbohydrate, 0 g total fat, 0 mg cholesterol, 325 mg sodium.

Horseradish Cream

Prep: 5 minutes

1 cup mayonnaise
⅓ cup prepared mustard
1 bottle (4 ounces) prepared white horseradish
½ cup heavy or whipping cream, whipped

In small bowl, with wire whisk, mix mayonnaise, mustard, and horseradish. Fold in whipped cream. Serve with roast turkey, baked ham, or roast beef. Makes about 2⅔ cups.

Each tablespoon: About 50 calories, 0 g protein, 1g carbohydrate, 5 g total fat (1 g saturated), 7 mg cholesterol, 55 mg sodium.

⌒Dessert Sauces

Butterscotch Sauce

Prep: 5 minutes
Cook: 10 minutes

4 cups packed light brown sugar
2 cups heavy or whipping cream
1⅓ cups light corn syrup
½ cup (1 stick) margarine or butter
4 teaspoons distilled white vinegar
½ teaspoon salt
4 teaspoons vanilla extract

In 5-quart nonstick Dutch oven (do not use smaller pan because mixture bubbles up during cooking), heat brown sugar, heavy cream, corn syrup, margarine, vinegar, and salt to boiling over high heat, stirring occasionally. Reduce heat to low; simmer, uncovered, 5 minutes, stirring frequently. Remove pan from heat; stir in vanilla. Sauce will have thin consistency when hot but will thicken when chilled. Cool completely. Store in refrigerator for up to 2 weeks. Reheat to serve warm over ice cream. Makes about 6 cups.

Each tablespoon: About 75 calories, 0 g protein, 13 g carbohydrate, 3 g total fat (1 g saturated), 7 mg cholesterol, 35 mg sodium.

Our Sublime Hot Fudge Sauce

Prep: 5 minutes
Cook: 10 minutes

1 cup heavy or whipping cream
¾ cup sugar
4 squares (4 ounces) unsweetened chocolate, chopped
2 tablespoons light corn syrup
2 tablespoons margarine or butter
2 teaspoons vanilla extract

1. In heavy 2-quart saucepan, heat heavy cream, sugar, chocolate, and corn syrup over medium heat, stirring occasionally, until mixture comes to a boil. Cook, stirring constantly, until sauce thickens slightly (mixture should be gently boiling), 4 to 5 minutes longer.

2. Remove saucepan from heat; stir in margarine and vanilla until smooth and glossy. Serve immediately, or let cool completely, cover, and refrigerate. (Do not cover sauce until it is cold, or the water from condensation will make it grainy.) Makes about 1¾ cups.

Each tablespoon: About 85 calories, 1 g protein, 8 g carbohydrate, 6 g total fat (3 g saturated), 12 mg cholesterol, 15 mg sodium.

Bittersweet Chocolate Sauce

Prep: 2 minutes
Cook: 10 minutes

⅓ cup sugar
⅓ cup water
2 squares (2 ounces) unsweetened chocolate
2 squares (2 ounces) semisweet chocolate
2 tablespoons margarine or butter
¾ teaspoon vanilla extract

In heavy 1-quart saucepan, heat sugar, water, unsweetened and semisweet chocolates, and margarine to boiling over medium heat, stirring frequently. Reduce heat to medium-low; simmer, uncovered, stirring, until mixture thickens and is smooth, about 3 minutes. Remove from heat; stir in vanilla. Serve warm over ice cream, pound cake, poached pears, or sautéed bananas. Makes about 1 cup.

Each tablespoon: About 60 calories, 1 g protein, 7 g carbohydrate, 4 g total fat (2 g saturated), 0 mg cholesterol, 20 mg sodium.

Praline Sauce

Prep: 5 minutes
Cook: 7 minutes

½ cup (1 stick) margarine or butter
1 cup pecans, finely chopped
½ cup packed dark brown sugar
¾ cup water
2 teaspoons cornstarch

1. In 2-quart saucepan, melt margarine over medium-low heat. Add pecans and cook until brown. Stir in brown sugar.
2. In cup, stir water and cornstarch until smooth. Stir into pecan mixture; cook, stirring, over medium-high heat until mixture thickens slightly and boils. Serve warm over French toast, pancakes, waffles, ice cream, sliced banana, or rice or vanilla pudding. Makes about 2 cups.

Each tablespoon: About 60 calories, 0 g protein, 4 g carbohydrate, 5 g total fat (1 g saturated), 0 mg cholesterol, 40 mg sodium.

No-Cook Berry Sauce

Prep: 20 minutes

3 cups raspberries, blackberries, strawberries, or blueberries
½ to ⅔ cup confectioners' sugar, depending on sweetness of
   berries
1 to 2 teaspoons fresh lemon or lime juice, or to taste

1. In food processor with knife blade attached, process berries until pureed. Sift ½ cup confectioners' sugar over berries; pulse until smooth. Press berry mixture through medium-mesh sieve to remove seeds; discard seeds.

2. Stir in 1 teaspoon lemon or lime juice. Taste and adjust sugar and citrus juice. Cover and refrigerate if not serving immediately. Sauce will thicken upon standing; whisk just before serving, if necessary. Keep sauce refrigerated and use within 3 days. Makes about 1½ cups.

Each tablespoon: About 15 calories, 0 g protein, 4 g carbohydrate, 0 g total fat, 0 mg cholesterol, 0 mg sodium.

Custard Sauce

Prep: 5 minutes
Cook: 20 minutes

4 egg yolks
⅓ cup sugar
⅛ teaspoon salt
2 cups milk
1 teaspoon vanilla extract

In heavy, nonstick 2-quart saucepan over low heat, or in double boiler over hot, not boiling, water, with wire whisk, beat egg yolks, sugar, and salt. Gradually stir in milk and cook, stirring constantly, until mixture thickens and coats the back of a spoon, about 20 minutes. Stir in vanilla extract. Serve warm or cold over apple pie, fruitcake, cut-up fruit, or ice cream. Makes about 2¼ cups.

Each ¼ cup: About 90 calories, 3 g protein, 10 g carbohydrate, 4 g total fat (2 g saturated), 102 mg cholesterol, 60 mg sodium.

Hard Sauce

Prep: 5 minutes

1 cup confectioners' sugar
⅓ cup margarine or butter, softened
½ teaspoon vanilla extract

In small bowl, with mixer at medium speed, beat sugar and margarine until creamy; beat in vanilla. Spoon into small bowl; refrigerate if not serving right away. Serve on steamed pudding or warm fruit pie. Makes about ⅔ cup.

Each tablespoon: About 85 calories, 0 g protein, 9 g carbohydrate, 6 g total fat (1 g saturated), 0 mg cholesterol, 75 mg sodium.

DELUXE HARD SAUCE: Prepare as above but fold in ¼ cup *heavy or whipping cream,* whipped. Makes about 1 cup.

Each tablespoon: About 70 calories, 0 g protein, 6 g carbohydrate, 5 g total fat (2 g saturated), 5 mg cholesterol, 50 mg sodium.

BRANDIED HARD SAUCE: Prepare as above but use *½ cup (1 stick) margarine or butter, 1½ cups confectioners' sugar, 2 tablespoons brandy,* and *½ teaspoon vanilla extract.* Makes about 1 cup.

Each tablespoon: About 90 calories, 0 g protein, 9 g carbohydrate, 6 g total fat (1 g saturated), 0 mg cholesterol, 75 mg sodium.

Peanut-Butter Sundae Sauce

Prep: 4 minutes
Cook: 7 minutes

⅔ cup packed light brown sugar
½ cup half-and-half
1 tablespoon honey
¾ cup chunky or creamy peanut butter

1. In heavy 1-quart saucepan, heat brown sugar, half-and-half, and honey to boiling over medium heat, stirring occasionally.

2. Remove saucepan from heat. Stir in peanut butter until blended and smooth. Serve warm over ice cream, pancakes, or waffles, or refrigerate sauce. Reheat in heavy 1-quart saucepan over low heat, stirring constantly. Makes about 1½ cups.

Each tablespoon: About 80 calories, 2 g protein, 9 g carbohydrate, 5 g total fat (1 g saturated), 2 mg cholesterol, 45 mg sodium.

Melba Sauce

Prep: 7 minutes
Cook: 7 minutes

1 package (10 ounces) frozen raspberries in syrup
¼ cup red-currant jelly
4 teaspoons cornstarch
1 tablespoon water

1. In 2-quart saucepan, heat frozen raspberries and their syrup and currant jelly over low heat until berries thaw and mixture is hot.

2. In cup, stir cornstarch and water until smooth; stir into berries. Cook over medium heat, stirring constantly, until mixture boils and thickens slightly; boil 1 minute. If you like, press mixture through fine sieve to remove seeds.

Serve warm over ice cream or poached peaches or pears. Makes about 1 cup.

Each tablespoon: About 35 calories, 0 g protein, 9 g carbohydrate, 0 g total fat, 0 mg cholesterol, 2 mg sodium.

Sweetened Whipped Cream

Prep: 5 minutes

1 cup heavy or whipping cream, well chilled
1 to 2 tablespoons confectioners' sugar
½ teaspoon vanilla extract

In bowl, with hand beater or with mixer at medium speed, beat cream, sugar, and vanilla until soft peaks form (overbeating causes cream to curdle and turn to butter). On hot days, chill bowl and beaters. Serve on fruit or nut pies, cobblers, puddings, or ice-cream sundaes. Makes about 2 cups.

Each tablespoon: About 30 calories, 0 g protein, 1 g carbohydrate, 3 g total fat (2 g saturated), 10 mg cholesterol, 3 mg sodium.

CHOCOLATE WHIPPED CREAM: In small bowl, combine *2 tablespoons confectioners' sugar* and *2 tablespoons cocoa*; stir until blended. Gradually add *1 cup heavy or whipping cream.* Beat as above. Makes about 2 cups.

Each tablespoon: About 30 calories, 0 g protein, 1 g carbohydrate, 3 g total fat (2 g saturated), 10 mg cholesterol, 3 mg sodium.

COFFEE WHIPPED CREAM: In small bowl, combine *2 teaspoons instant-coffee powder* and *2 tablespoons confectioners' sugar*; stir until blended. Add *1 cup heavy or whipping cream.* Beat as above. Makes about 2 cups.

Each tablespoon: About 30 calories, 0 g protein, 1 g carbohydrate, 3 g total fat (2 g saturated), 10 mg cholesterol, 3 mg sodium.

Three-Berry Skillet Jam

Prep: 5 minutes plus chilling
Cook: 10 minutes

1 cup blackberries, crushed
1 cup raspberries, crushed
1 cup sliced strawberries, crushed
1 tablespoon plus 1 teaspoon powdered fruit pectin
½ teaspoon margarine or butter
1 cup sugar

1. Into bowl, press half of crushed blackberries and crushed raspberries through medium-mesh sieve to remove seeds; discard seeds.

2. In 12-inch skillet, stir strawberries, sieved berry mixture, remaining crushed blackberries and raspberries, pectin, and margarine. Heat over medium-high heat, stirring constantly, until mixture boils. Stir in sugar; heat to boiling. Boil 1 minute; remove skillet from heat.

3. Pour jam into two ½-pint jars with tight-fitting lids. Cover and refrigerate until jam is set, about 6 hours. Keep jam refrigerated and use within 3 weeks. Makes about 2 cups.

Each tablespoon: About 30 calories, 0 g protein, 10 g carbohydrate, 0 g total fat, 0 mg cholesterol, 2 mg sodium.

Blackberry-Blueberry Skillet Jam

Prep: 5 minutes plus chilling
Cook: 10 minutes

2 cups blackberries, crushed
2 cups blueberries, crushed
2 tablespoons powdered fruit pectin
½ teaspoon margarine or butter
¾ cup sugar

1. Into bowl, press half of crushed blackberries through medium-mesh sieve to remove seeds; discard seeds.

2. In 12-inch skillet, stir blueberries, sieved blackberries, remaining crushed blackberries, pectin, and margarine. Heat over medium-high heat, stirring constantly, until mixture boils. Stir in sugar; heat to boiling. Boil 1 minute; remove skillet from heat.

3. Pour jam into two ½-pint jars with tight-fitting lids. Cover and refrigerate until jam is set, about 6 hours. Keep jam refrigerated and use within 3 weeks. Makes about 2 cups.

Each tablespoon: About 25 calories, 0 g protein, 6 g carbohydrate, 0 g total fat, 0 mg cholesterol, 2 mg sodium.

∽Condiments

Sweet Corn Relish

Prep: 20 minutes plus chilling
Cook: 30 seconds

8 ears corn, husks and silk removed, or 4 cups frozen whole-kernel
   corn (one 20-ounce package), thawed
3 tablespoons fresh lime juice
2 tablespoons olive oil
¾ teaspoon ground cumin
¾ teaspoon ground coriander
¾ teaspoon salt
½ teaspoon chili powder
1 large red pepper, diced

1. If using fresh corn, with sharp knife, cut kernels from cobs (you should have about 4 cups). Fill large saucepot with water and heat to boiling over high heat. Add fresh corn; heat to boiling. Boil 30 seconds. Drain corn; rinse with cold running water and drain again.

2. In medium bowl, with wire whisk or fork, mix lime juice, oil, cumin, coriander, salt, and chili powder. Add corn and red pepper; toss well. Cover and refrigerate until chilled, about 2 hours. Makes about 5 cups.

Each ¼ cup: About 50 calories, 1 g protein, 8 g carbohydrate, 2 g total fat (0 g saturated), 0 mg cholesterol, 85 mg sodium.

Watermelon Pickles

Prep: 1 hour plus standing and chilling
Cook: About 25 minutes

12 pounds watermelon (about ½ large watermelon)
¾ cup salt
5 cups sugar
2½ cups distilled white vinegar
6 whole cloves
6 whole allspice
4 cinnamon sticks (3 inches)
1 teaspoon cracked black pepper

1. Cut watermelon into large chunks. With sharp knife, trim dark green outer skin from watermelon rind and discard. Cut off most of red flesh, leaving about 1/8-inch-thick layer. Reserve watermelon flesh for fruit salad another day. Cut watermelon rind into 1-inch cubes (you should have 12 cups).

2. In large bowl, dissolve salt in *8 cups water.* Add rind and let stand 4 to 5 hours at room temperature.

3. Drain rind; rinse with cold running water and drain again. In nonstick 5-quart Dutch oven or heavy saucepot, heat rind with *water* to cover to boiling over high heat. Reduce heat to medium and cook, uncovered, until rind is tender-crisp, about 10 minutes. Drain.

4. In same Dutch oven, combine sugar, vinegar, cloves, allspice, cinnamon sticks, pepper, and *2½ cups water.* Heat to boiling over high heat; boil 3 minutes. Add rind and cook, skimming any foam, until tender, about 10 minutes. Remove Dutch oven from heat and cool pickles to room temperature. Cover and refrigerate up to 2 weeks. Drain before serving. Makes about 5 cups, drained.

Each ¼ cup: About 45 calories, 0 g protein, 11 g carbohydrate, 0 g total fat, 0 mg cholesterol, 220 mg sodium.

Blushing Apple Butter

Prep: 30 minutes
Cook: About 1 hour 10 minutes

1 lemon
3¾ pounds Granny Smith apples (about 8 large), peeled, cored,
  and thinly sliced
1½ cups apple cider or apple juice
1 cup cranberries
1½ cups sugar

1. From lemon, with vegetable peeler or small knife, remove three 3" by 1" strips of peel and squeeze 3 tablespoons juice.

2. In 5-quart Dutch oven, heat apples, cider, cranberries, lemon peel, and lemon juice to boiling over high heat. Reduce heat to low; simmer, uncovered, until apples are very soft, 10 minutes, stirring occasionally.

3. Stir in sugar; heat to boiling over high heat. Reduce heat to medium; cook, partially covered, until apple butter is very thick, about 1 hour, stirring occasionally (mixture may sputter and splash, so be careful when stirring).

4. Spoon apple butter into blender in small batches and blend (with center part of blender cover removed to allow steam to escape) until smooth.

5. Spoon apple butter into jars or crocks for gift giving. Store tightly covered in refrigerator for up to 3 weeks. Makes about 4½ cups.

Each tablespoon: About 30 calories, 0 g protein, 8 g carbohydrate, 0 g total fat, 0 mg cholesterol, 0 mg sodium.

Green-Tomato and Pepper Relish

Prep: 40 minutes plus chilling
Cook: 2 hours 10 minutes

⅓ cup vegetable oil
3 large onions, diced
1 garlic clove, minced
8 large green tomatoes (about 4 pounds), cut into bite-size chunks
4 medium green peppers, cut into ¼-inch-wide strips

4 medium red peppers, cut into ¼-inch-wide strips
3 cups cider vinegar
1½ cups packed light brown sugar
1 tablespoon salt
1 teaspoon ground cinnamon
1 teaspoon ground ginger

1. In 8-quart Dutch oven or heavy saucepot, heat oil over medium heat until hot. Add onions and garlic, and cook, stirring occasionally, until tender. Add green tomatoes, green and red peppers, vinegar, brown sugar, salt, cinnamon, and ginger; heat to boiling over high heat. Reduce heat to medium-low; cook, uncovered, stirring occasionally, until mixture thickens, about 2 hours.

2. Spoon relish into large bowl; cover and refrigerate. Serve relish with barbecued or roasted poultry, meat, or fish. Makes about 8 cups.

Each ¼ cup: About 90 calories, 1 g protein, 18 g carbohydrate, 3 g total fat (0 g saturated), 0 mg cholesterol, 230 mg sodium.

Onion Relish

Prep: 15 minutes plus chilling
Cook: 25 minutes

6 medium onions (about 2 pounds), diced
1 medium red pepper, diced
½ cup packed light brown sugar
½ cup apple juice
⅓ cup white-wine vinegar
1 tablespoon salt
1 tablespoon prepared white horseradish
1 tablespoon vegetable oil
2½ teaspoons prepared mustard

1. In 3-quart nonstick saucepan, heat onions, red pepper, brown sugar, apple juice, vinegar, salt, horseradish, oil, and mustard to boiling over medium-high heat. Reduce heat to low; simmer, uncovered, stirring occasionally, 20 minutes.
2. Spoon relish into bowl; cover and refrigerate. Serve relish with hamburgers, frankfurters, or broiled steak or chicken. Makes about 3 cups.

Each ¼ cup: About 85 calories, 1 g protein, 18 g carbohydrate, 1 g total fat (0 g saturated), 0 mg cholesterol, 600 mg sodium.

No-Cook Cranberry-Orange Relish

Prep: 15 minutes plus chilling

1 bag (12 ounces) cranberries (3 cups)
1 medium-size orange, cut up
½ cup dark seedless raisins
½ cup sugar

In food processor with knife blade attached, combine cranberries, orange, raisins, and sugar and pulse until mixture is coarsely chopped. Cover and refrigerate relish until well chilled, about 2 hours. If you like, transfer relish to an airtight container and refrigerate up to 2 days. Makes about 3 cups.

Each ¼ cup: About 70 calories, 1 g protein, 18 g carbohydrate, 0 g total fat, 0 mg cholesterol, 1 mg sodium.

Cranberry-Pear Relish

Prep: 5 minutes plus chilling
Cook: 10 minutes

1 bag (12 ounces) cranberries (3 cups)
1¼ cups packed light brown sugar
¼ cup balsamic vinegar
½ cup water
1 medium pear, peeled, cored, and diced

In 3-quart nonstick saucepan, heat cranberries, sugar, vinegar, and water to boiling over high heat, stirring occasionally. Reduce heat to low; simmer, uncovered, until most of cranberries pop, about 8 minutes. Add diced pear, cover and cook 2 to 3 minutes longer. Cover and refrigerate relish until well chilled, about 4 hours. If you like, transfer relish to an airtight container and refrigerate up to 2 days. Makes about 3 cups.

Each ¼ cup: About 115 calories, 0 g protein, 29 g carbohydrate, 0 g total fat, 0 mg cholesterol, 10 mg sodium.

Cape Cod Cranberry Sauce

Prep: 5 minutes plus chilling
Cook: 10 minutes

1 bag (12 ounces) cranberries (3 cups)
1 cup packed brown sugar
½ cup golden raisins
2 tablespoons cider vinegar
1 cinnamon stick (3 inches long)
Pinch ground cloves
Pinch salt
1 large Rome Beauty apple, peeled, cored, and diced

In 3-quart nonstick saucepan, heat cranberries, brown sugar, raisins, vinegar, cinnamon stick, cloves, salt, and *¾ cup water* to boiling over high heat. Reduce heat to medium-low and cook, uncovered, stirring occasionally, 6 minutes. Add diced apple and cook until most of cranberries pop and mixture thickens slightly, about 4 minutes longer. Discard cinnamon stick. Spoon into serving bowl; cover and refrigerate until well chilled, about 3 hours. Makes about 4 cups.

Each ¼ cup: About 85 calories, 0 g protein, 22 g carbohydrate, 0 g total fat, 0 mg cholesterol, 15 mg sodium.

Red-Pepper Chutney

Prep: 25 minutes plus chilling
Cook: 40 minutes

1½ cups cider vinegar
1 cup sugar
6 large red peppers, diced
3 firm, medium pears, peeled and cut into ½-inch pieces
1 small red onion, diced
⅓ cup dark seedless raisins
1½ teaspoons mustard seeds
1 teaspoon salt
⅛ teaspoon ground allspice

In 5-quart nonstick Dutch oven, heat vinegar and sugar to boiling over high heat; boil 10 minutes. Add peppers, pears, onion, raisins, mustard seeds, salt, and allspice; heat to boiling. Reduce heat to medium-high and cook, uncovered, stirring occasionally, until syrupy, about 30 minutes. Cover and refrigerate until chilled, about 4 hours. Makes about 6 cups.

Each ¼ cup: About 65 calories, 1 g protein, 17 g carbohydrate, 0 g total fat, 0 mg cholesterol, 90 mg sodium.

Heirloom Chutney

Prep: 30 minutes
Cook: 1 hour

2 large cooking apples, diced
2 medium onions, diced
1 medium green or red pepper, cut into ½-inch pieces
1 garlic clove, crushed
¾ cup sugar
¾ cup distilled white vinegar
½ cup water
1 package (12 ounces) pitted prunes, each cut in half
1 tablespoon grated peeled fresh ginger
2 teaspoons mustard seeds
½ teaspoon salt
½ teaspoon crushed red pepper

1. In 3-quart nonstick saucepan over medium-high heat, heat apples, onions, green pepper, garlic, sugar, vinegar, and water to boiling. Reduce heat to low; simmer, uncovered, stirring occasionally, until vegetables are tender, about 15 minutes.

2. Add prunes, ginger, mustard seeds, salt, and crushed red pepper to mixture; cook until mixture thickens slightly and becomes syrupy, about 35 minutes. Spoon chutney into bowl; cover and refrigerate until well chilled. Serve with roast meats or poultry. Makes about 4 cups.

Each tablespoon: About 30 calories, 0 g protein, 8 g carbohydrate, 0 g total fat, 0 mg cholesterol, 20 mg sodium.

Tomato Chutney

Prep: 25 minutes
Cook: 45 to 50 minutes

3 pounds ripe tomatoes (about 9 medium), peeled and cut into ½-inch pieces
2 garlic cloves, minced
1 medium Granny Smith apple, peeled and grated
1 small onion, chopped
½ cup cider vinegar
⅓ cup packed light brown sugar
⅓ cup golden raisins
2 tablespoons minced, peeled fresh ginger
½ teaspoon salt
¼ teaspoon coarsely ground black pepper

In 12-inch nonstick skillet, heat tomatoes, garlic, apple, onion, vinegar, brown sugar, raisins, ginger, salt, and pepper to boiling over high heat. Reduce heat to medium; cook, uncovered, stirring occasionally, until mixture thickens, 45 to 50 minutes. Spoon chutney into bowl; cover and refrigerate until well chilled. Use within 2 weeks. Makes about 3½ cups.

Each ¼ cup: About 60 calories, 1 g protein, 15 g carbohydrate, 0 g total fat, 0 mg cholesterol, 90 mg sodium.

Quick Breads

~~~

Biscuits & Scones • Muffins
Corn Breads • Popovers
Tea Breads & Coffee Cakes
Pancakes & Waffles
Special Quick Breads

"Quick breads" means exactly that. Quick-acting leavening agents such as baking powder, baking soda, and eggs—plus the steam created by heat—permit these breads to be baked or cooked as soon as they are mixed. Even the mixing should be quick; overmixing results in coarse-textured or tough bread that won't rise to full volume and will have unattractive tunnels.

Most quick breads are at their best fresh from the oven. Remove loaves and muffins from their baking pan or cups as soon as they are baked or they will steam and become soggy. The exceptions are fruit and nut loaves. These are hard to slice when they are right out of the oven. Allow them to cool slightly before slicing. Or cool, then wrap loaves and leave them overnight: They will develop a mellower flavor and won't crumble when sliced.

∾Success Tips

Biscuits: Biscuit dough doubles in height when baked, so roll it half as thick as you want the finished biscuits to be. Dough rolled ½ inch thick produces inch-high, fluffy biscuits; rolled ¼ inch thick, it makes thin, crusty ones. To avoid making lopsided biscuits, cut the dough by pressing a floured cutter straight down without twisting it, or, using a floured knife, cut the dough with firm downward strokes. Cut the biscuits close together to keep rerolling to a minimum, then press (don't knead) the trimmings together, reroll them, and cut more biscuits. Use a wide spatula to transfer the cut-out biscuits to a cookie sheet. Place the biscuits 1 inch apart on the cookie sheet for crusty sides, close together in a shallow baking pan for tender sides.

Muffins: First, mix the dry ingredients together, then add liquid ingredients all at once and stir just a few strokes to moisten the flour. The batter will be lumpy, but the lumps will disappear during baking. Spoon the batter into muffin-pan cups and half-fill any empties with water. After baking, remove the muffins from the cups at once so they don't steam and soften.

Tea Breads and Coffee Cakes: Test tea breads for doneness by inserting a toothpick into the center of the loaf at the end of the minimum baking time. If the recipe states that the toothpick should come out clean, there should be no crumbs sticking to it; if it should come out "almost clean," the bread is done when only a few crumbs cling to the toothpick.

Don't worry if loaf is cracked on top; a deep crack down the center of quick-bread loaves is typical.

There is no single way to test coffee cakes for doneness; follow the individual recipe.

Pancakes and Waffles: Mix as you would muffins. Use an electric pancake griddle or a waffle baker as the manufacturer directs. Test the temperature of a nonelectric griddle or waffle baker by sprinkling it with a few drops of water; the drops should sizzle. After pouring the batter for pancakes, cook them until the bubbles that appear begin to burst and the edges look dry, then turn them and brown the undersides. For a waffle, pour the batter into the center of the grid, then close the lid and don't open it again until the waffle stops steaming or the light on the waffle baker goes out. As pancake or waffle batter stands, it may thicken; thin it to proper pouring consistency with a little more of the liquid used in the recipe. Leftover batter can be refrigerated, covered, and used the next day; stir the batter well before using it.

Doughnuts: For tender doughnuts, the dough should be soft, not stiff. Cut doughnuts as close together as possible to minimize rerolling; press the trimmings together, reroll them, and cut more doughnuts. Lift the doughnuts with a wide spatula and place them in deep hot fat; turn them as soon as they rise to the surface, using tongs or a slotted spoon. (Don't use a fork; if a doughnut is pricked, it will absorb fat.) Then fry the doughnuts, turning them occasionally, until both sides are golden; transfer them to paper towels to drain.

ᑌ Storing Quick Breads

Biscuits, Muffins, and Doughnuts: These taste best if they're served the day they're made. Wrap any leftovers tightly with plastic wrap or foil, and store at room temperature. Reheat and use leftovers within a day or two.

Fruit and Nut Loaves: These are best if they're made the day before they're served. Cool the loaves completely, wrap them tightly, and store them at room temperature.

ᑌ Reheating Quick Breads

Biscuits, Scones, Muffins, and Coffee Cake: Preheat the oven to 400°F. Wrap leftover or baked-ahead biscuits, etc., in a single layer in foil and heat until hot: 10 to 15 minutes for biscuits, scones, and muffins; about 20 to 30 minutes for coffee cake.

Biscuits, Scones, Muffins, or Corn Bread: Split and spread them with margarine or butter, and toast them in the broiler until they're hot and golden. If desired, spread them before toasting with shredded cheese cheese spread, or jelly.

Boston Brown Bread: Homemade or removed from the can if store-bought, Boston brown bread can be reheated in a covered double boiler or in a colander set over a pan of simmering water. Slices can be buttered and toasted in the broiler.

ᓚ Freezing Quick Breads

Biscuits: Up to one month ahead, prepare the biscuits but do not bake them. Place the biscuits on cookie sheets; cover and freeze them. Place the frozen biscuits in plastic bags and keep them frozen. About 30 minutes before serving, remove as many biscuits as needed and bake the frozen biscuits on a cookie sheet in a preheated oven as the recipe directs, but increase the baking time by 5 minutes, or until the biscuits are golden.

Muffins: Up to one month ahead, bake and cool muffins completely. Wrap them in a single layer tightly with foil and freeze. To serve the muffins, preheat the oven to 350°F. and heat the foil-wrapped frozen muffins for about 20 minutes.

Scones: Up to one month ahead, bake and cool scones completely. Wrap the scones tightly in a single layer with foil and freeze. To serve the scones, preheat the oven to 350°F. and heat the foil-wrapped frozen muffins for about 20 minutes.

Fruit and Nut Loaves: Up to three months ahead, bake loaves and cool them completely; pack in zip-tight bags, label, date and freeze them. To thaw, let the loaves stand, unwrapped, at room temperature for about 1½ hours.

Waffles: Up to two months ahead, bake waffles only until lightly browned. Cool them on wire racks or freeze them on cookie sheets, then seal them in zip-tight bags and freeze. To serve, toast the frozen waffles until golden brown in the toaster.

✑Biscuits & Scones

Baking-Powder Biscuits

Prep: 20 minutes
Bake: 12-15 minutes

2 cups all-purpose flour
1 tablespoon baking powder
1 teaspoon salt
¼ cup shortening
¾ cup milk

1. Preheat oven to 450°F. Into large bowl, stir flour, baking powder, and salt; stir until combined. With pastry blender or 2 knives used scissor-fashion, cut in shortening until mixture resembles coarse crumbs. Stir in milk; quickly mix just until mixture forms soft dough that leaves side of bowl.
2. Turn dough onto lightly floured surface; knead 6 to 8 strokes to mix thoroughly. With floured rolling pin, roll out dough ½ inch thick for high, fluffy biscuits, or ¼ inch thick for thin, crusty ones.
3. With floured 2-inch biscuit cutter, cut out biscuits. With wide spatula, place biscuits on ungreased cookie sheet 1 inch apart for crusty biscuits, nearly touching for soft-sided ones.
4. Press trimmings together; roll and cut as above. Bake until golden, 12 to 15 minutes. Makes about 1½ dozen biscuits.

Each biscuit: About 85 calories, 2 g protein, 11 g carbohydrate, 3 g total fat (1 g saturated), 1 mg cholesterol, 200 mg sodium.

DROP BISCUITS: Prepare Baking-Powder Biscuits as above, but use *1 cup milk*. Stir dough just until ingredients are blended. Onto ungreased cookie sheet, drop heaping tablespoons of mixture 1 inch apart. Bake as for Baking-Powder Biscuits. Makes about 20 biscuits.

Each biscuit: About 75 calories, 2 g protein, 10 g carbohydrate, 3 g total fat (1 g saturated), 2 mg cholesterol, 180 mg sodium.

BISCUITS PLUS: Prepare Baking-Powder Biscuits as on page 801, but add one of the following ingredients to flour mixture before adding liquid: *½ cup crumbled cooked bacon*; *¼ to ½ cup shredded sharp Cheddar cheese*; *2 tablespoons chopped chives*; *1 teaspoon curry powder*; *⅔ cup chopped cooked smoked ham*. Makes about 20 biscuits.

Cheddar-Jalapeño Biscuits

Prep: 15 minutes
Bake: About 15 minutes

2 cups all-purpose flour
1 tablespoon baking powder
½ teaspoon salt
½ teaspoon paprika
3 tablespoons cold margarine or butter, cut into pieces
2 tablespoons shortening
4 ounces shredded sharp or extrasharp Cheddar cheese (about 1 cup)
3 tablespoons drained and chopped picked jalapeño chiles
¾ cup milk

1. Preheat oven to 450°F. In large bowl, combine flour, baking powder, salt, and paprika. With pastry blender or 2 knives used scissor-fashion, cut in margarine and shortening until mixture resembles coarse crumbs. Stir cheese, chiles, and milk into flour mixture just until ingredients are blended and mixture forms a soft dough that leaves side of bowl.

2. Turn dough onto lightly floured surface. With lightly floured hands, pat dough into a 10" by 4" rectangle. With floured knife, cut rectangle lengthwise in half, then cut each half crosswise into five 2-inch squares. Cut each square diagonally in half to make 20 triangles in all. Place biscuits on ungreased large cookie sheet.

3. Bake biscuits, until golden, 13 to 15 minutes. Serve warm, or transfer to wire rack to cool completely. Makes 20 biscuits.

Each biscuit: About 100 calories, 3 g protein, 10 g carbohydrate, 5 g total fat (2 g saturated), 7 mg cholesterol, 200 mg sodium.

Southern-Style Biscuits

Prep: 10 minutes
Bake: About 15 minutes

3 cups self-rising cake flour (unsifted)*
⅓ cup shortening
1 cup milk

1. Preheat oven to 450°F. In large bowl, measure flour. With pastry blender or 2 knives used scissor-fashion, cut in shortening until mixture resembles coarse crumbs.

2. Stir milk into flour mixture just until ingredients are blended.

3. Scoop dough by scant ¼ cup onto ungreased large cookie sheet. If you like, with floured hands, lightly pat scoops of dough to smooth slightly.

4. Bake biscuits, until lightly browned, about 15 minutes. Serve warm, or, cool on wire rack to serve later. Reheat before serving, if desired. Makes 12 biscuits.

*If not using self-rising cake flour in Step 1, substitute 1½ cups all-purpose flour, 1½ cups cake flour (not self-rising), 1 tablespoon baking powder, and 1 teaspoon salt; place in large bowl, then cut in shortening. Continue as in Steps 2 through 4.

Each biscuit: About 175 calories, 4 g protein, 24 g carbohydrate, 7 g total fat (2 g saturated), 3 mg cholesterol, 405 mg sodium.

Whole-Wheat Sesame Biscuits

Prep: 15 minutes
Bake: 12 to 15 minutes

2 tablespoons sesame seeds
1 cup whole-wheat flour
1 cup all-purpose flour
1 tablespoon baking powder
¾ teaspoon salt
4 tablespoons margarine or butter, cut into pieces
¾ cup plus 3 tablespoons milk

1. In small skillet, toast sesame seeds over medium heat, stirring occasionally, until lightly browned, about 5 minutes.

2. Preheat oven to 425°F. Lightly grease large cookie sheet. Into large bowl, combine whole-wheat and all-purpose flours, baking powder, salt, and 5 teaspoons toasted sesame seeds; stir until combined. With pastry blender or 2 knives used scissor-fashion, cut in margarine or butter until mixture resembles coarse crumbs. Stir in ¾ cup plus 2 tablespoons milk, stirring just until mixture forms soft dough that leaves side of bowl.

3. Turn dough onto lightly floured surface; knead 8 to 10 strokes to mix thoroughly. With floured rolling pin, roll out dough ½ inch thick.

4. With floured 2½-inch round biscuit cutter, cut out biscuits. Place biscuits, about 2 inches apart, on cookie sheet.

5. Press trimmings together; roll and cut as above. Brush tops of biscuits with remaining 1 tablespoon milk; sprinkle with remaining 1 teaspoon sesame seeds. Bake until golden, 12 to 15 minutes. Makes 12 biscuits.

Each biscuit: About 125 calories, 3 g protein, 17 g carbohydrate, 6 g total fat (1 g saturated), 3 mg cholesterol, 285 mg sodium.

Featherlight Buttermilk Biscuits

Prep: 10 minutes
Bake: 12 to 15 minutes

3 cups cake flour (not self-rising)
2¼ teaspoons baking powder
¾ teaspoon baking soda
¾ teaspoon salt
6 tablespoons vegetable shortening
1 cup buttermilk

1. Preheat oven to 450°F. In large bowl, combine cake flour, baking powder, baking soda, and salt. With pastry blender or 2 knives used scissor-fashion, cut in shortening until evenly combined.

2. Add buttermilk to flour mixture; mix together with hand just until dough forms. (Do not overmix; biscuits will be tough.)

3. On lightly floured surface, pat dough into 7-inch square. Cut dough into 4 strips, then cut each strip cross-wise into 4 pieces to make 16 biscuits.

4. Place biscuits on ungreased large cookie sheet. Bake biscuits until lightly golden, 12 to 15 minutes. Serve warm, or cool on wire rack to serve later. Reheat before serving, if desired. Makes 16 biscuits.

Each biscuit: About 125 calories, 2 g protein, 17 g carbohydrate, 5 g total fat (2 g saturated), 1 mg cholesterol, 225 mg sodium.

Scones

Prep: 15 minutes
Bake: 10 to 15 minutes

3½ cups all-purpose flour
5 teaspoons baking powder
1 teaspoon salt
2 tablespoons sugar plus ¼ cup
¾ cup (1½ sticks) margarine or butter, cut into pieces
4 large eggs
½ cup milk

1. Preheat oven to 425°F. Grease 2 large cookie sheets.

2. In large bowl, combine flour, baking powder, salt, and 2 tablespoons sugar. With pastry blender or 2 knives used scissor-fashion, cut in margarine until mixture resembles coarse crumbs.

3. In small bowl, beat eggs. Reserve 2 tablespoons beaten egg for brushing on scones later. Stir milk into remaining beaten eggs. Stir egg mixture into flour mixture just until ingredients are blended.

4. Turn dough onto lightly floured surface; with floured rolling pin, lightly roll dough into 12" by 8" rectangle. Cut dough into 4-inch squares; cut each square into 2 triangles. With wide spatula, place triangles 2 inches apart on prepared cookie sheets. Brush tops with reserved beaten egg and sprinkle evenly with ¼ cup sugar.

5. Bake scones until golden, 10 to 15 minutes. Serve warm, or cool them on wire rack; wrap in single layer of foil. Reheat before serving, if desired. Makes 1 dozen scones.

Each scone: About 290 calories, 6 g protein, 35 g carbohydrate, 14 g total fat (3 g saturated), 72 mg cholesterol, 535 mg sodium.

Blueberry Hill Scones

Prep: 15 minutes
Bake: 22 to 25 minutes

2 cups all-purpose flour
¼ cup packed brown sugar
1 tablespoon baking powder
¼ teaspoon salt
4 tablespoons cold margarine or butter, cut into pieces
1 cup blueberries
⅔ cup heavy or whipping cream
1 large egg
½ teaspoon finely grated lemon peel

1. Preheat oven to 375°F. Into large bowl, combine flour, brown sugar, baking powder, and salt; stir until combined. With pastry blender or 2 knives used scissor-fashion, cut in margarine until mixture resembles coarse crumbs. Add blueberries and toss to mix.

2. In small bowl, with fork, mix cream, egg, and lemon peel until blended. Slowly pour cream mixture into dry ingredients and stir with rubber spatula just until a soft dough forms.

3. With lightly floured hand, knead dough in bowl just until it comes together, about 3 to 4 times; do not overmix. Divide dough in half. On lightly floured surface, shape each half into a 6-inch round. With floured knife, cut each round into 6 wedges. Transfer wedges to ungreased large cookie sheet.

4. Bake scones, until golden brown, 22 to 25 minutes. Serve warm, or cool on wire rack to serve later. Reheat before serving, if desired. Makes 12 scones.

Each scone: About 185 calories, 3 g protein, 23 g carbohydrate, 9 g total fat (4 g saturated), 36 mg cholesterol, 200 mg sodium.

Williamsburg Peppered Cornmeal Scones

Prep: 20 minutes
Bake: 15 minutes

2¼ cups all-purpose flour
½ cup yellow cornmeal
1 tablespoon sugar
2 teaspoons baking powder
1¼ teaspoons coarsely ground
    black pepper

1 teaspoon salt
½ teaspoon baking soda
6 tablespoons cold margarine
    or butter, cut into pieces
¾ cup milk
1 large egg

1. Preheat oven to 425°F. In large bowl, combine flour, cornmeal, sugar, baking powder, black pepper, salt, and baking soda. With pastry blender or 2 knives used scissor-fashion, cut in margarine until mixture resembles coarse crumbs.

2. In cup, with fork mix milk and egg; stir egg mixture into flour mixture just until ingredients are blended.

3. Turn dough onto lightly floured surface. Divide dough in half. With floured hands, pat each half into a 5½-inch round. Cut each round into 6 wedges. With wide spatula, transfer wedges to ungreased large cookie sheet.

4. Bake scones until lightly browned, 15 minutes. Serve warm, or cool on wire rack to serve later. Reheat before serving, if desired. Makes 12 scones.

Each scone: About 175 calories, 4 g protein, 25 g carbohydrate, 7 g total fat (2 g saturated), 20 mg cholesterol, 380 mg sodium.

∽**Muffins**

Old-Fashioned Muffins

Prep: 15 minutes
Bake: 20 minutes

2 cups all-purpose flour
2 tablespoons sugar
1 tablespoon baking powder
½ teaspoon salt
1 large egg
1 cup milk
¼ cup vegetable oil

1. Preheat oven to 400°F. Grease twelve 2½" by 1¼" muffin-pan cups.

2. In large bowl, combine flour, sugar, baking powder, and salt. In small bowl, beat egg, milk, and vegetable oil until blended; stir into flour mixture just until moistened (batter will be lumpy).

3. Spoon batter into muffin-pan cups. Bake until golden and toothpick inserted in center comes out clean, about 20 minutes. Immediately remove muffins from pan. Serve warm, or cool on wire rack to serve later. Reheat before serving, if desired. Makes 12 muffins.

Each muffin: About 145 calories, 3 g protein, 19 g carbohydrate, 6 g total fat (1 g saturated), 21 mg cholesterol, 210 mg sodium.

CHEDDAR-CHEESE MUFFINS: Prepare and bake as above, but add *6 ounces Cheddar cheese,* shredded (about 1½ cups) to flour. Makes 12 muffins.

Each muffin: About 200 calories, 7 g protein, 19 g carbohydrate, 11 g total fat (4 g saturated), 35 mg cholesterol, 300 mg sodium.

JAM-FILLED MUFFINS: Prepare and bake as above, but fill muffin-pan cups one-third full of batter. Drop *1 rounded* *teaspoon strawberry preserves* in center of each; top with remaining batter. Makes 12 muffins.

Each muffin: About 165 calories, 3 g protein, 25 g carbohydrate, 6 g total fat (1 g saturated), 21 mg cholesterol, 215 mg sodium.

WHOLE-WHEAT MUFFINS: Prepare and bake as above, but use only *¾ cup all-purpose flour;* add *1 cup whole-wheat flour.* Use *¼ cup sugar* and *4 teaspoons baking powder.* Makes 12 muffins.

Each muffin: About 140 calories, 3 g protein, 19 g carbohydrate, 6 g total fat (1 g saturated), 21 mg cholesterol, 245 mg sodium.

Bran Muffins

Prep: 20 minutes
Bake: 15 minutes

3 cups bran flakes
1¼ cups all-purpose flour
½ cup sugar
1¼ teaspoons baking soda
¼ teaspoon salt
1 large egg
1 cup buttermilk
¼ cup vegetable oil

1. Preheat oven to 400°F. Grease sixteen 2½" by 1¼" muffin-pan cups.
2. In large bowl, combine bran flakes, flour, sugar, soda, and salt. In small bowl, beat egg, buttermilk, and vegetable oil until blended. Stir egg mixture into flour mixture just until moistened (batter will be lumpy).
3. Spoon batter into muffin-pan cups. Bake until browned and toothpick inserted in center comes out clean, about 15 minutes. Immediately remove muffins from pan.

Serve warm, or cool on wire rack to serve later. Reheat before serving, if desired. Makes 16 muffins.

Each muffin: About 125 calories, 3 g protein, 20 g carbohydrate, 4 g total fat (1 g saturated), 14 mg cholesterol, 210 mg sodium.

Kansas Pecan-Topped Pumpkin Muffins

Prep: 10 minutes
Bake: 25 to 30 minutes

2¼ cups all-purpose flour
2½ teaspoons baking powder
2 teaspoons pumpkin-pie spice
¾ teaspoon salt
1 cup milk
¾ cup solid-pack pumpkin (not pumpkin-pie mix)
½ cup packed dark brown sugar
4 tablespoons margarine or butter, melted
2 teaspoons vanilla extract
2 large eggs
½ cup pecans, toasted and chopped

1. Preheat oven to 400°F. Grease twelve 2½" by 1¼" muffin-pan cups.

2. In large bowl, combine flour, baking powder, pumpkin-pie spice, and salt. In medium bowl, with wire whisk, mix milk, pumpkin, brown sugar, melted margarine, vanilla, and eggs until blended; stir into flour mixture until just moistened.

3. Spoon batter into muffin-pan cups. Sprinkle tops with chopped pecans. Bake until toothpick inserted in center of muffin comes out clean, 25 to 30 minutes. Immediately remove from pan. Serve warm, or cool completely on wire rack to serve later. Reheat before serving, if desired. Makes 12 muffins.

Each muffin: About 220 calories, 5 g protein, 31 g carbohydrate, 9 g total fat (2 g saturated), 38 mg cholesterol, 285 mg sodium.

Banana-Nut Muffins

Prep: 25 minutes
Bake: 20 minutes

2½ cups all-purpose flour
¾ cup sugar
1 tablespoon baking powder
¾ teaspoon salt
6 tablespoons margarine or
   butter, cut into pieces
walnuts (1 4-ounce cup),
   chopped

3 ripe small bananas, cut into
   pieces
2 large eggs
⅓ cup milk
½ teaspoon vanilla extract

1. Preheat oven to 400°F. Grease twelve 2½" by 1¼" muffin-pan cups.

2. In large bowl, combine flour, sugar, baking powder, and salt. With pastry blender or 2 knives used scissor-fashion, cut in margarine until mixture resembles coarse crumbs; stir in walnuts; set aside.

3. In blender at high speed or in food processor with knife blade attached, blend bananas, eggs, milk, and vanilla, until bananas are chopped, only a few seconds. Stir banana mixture into flour mixture just until flour is moistened (batter will be lumpy).

4. Spoon batter into muffin-pan cups (batter will fill cups completely). Bake until golden and toothpick inserted in center comes out clean (muffins will rise very high), 15 to 20 minutes. Immediately remove muffins from pan. Serve warm, or cool on wire rack to serve later. Reheat before serving, if desired. Makes 12 muffins.

Each muffin: About 295 calories, 6 g protein, 40 g carbohydrate, 13 g total fat (2 g saturated), 36 mg cholesterol, 335 mg sodium.

Blueberry Muffins

Prep: 20 minutes
Bake: 20 minutes

1¾ cups all-purpose flour
⅔ cup sugar
1 tablespoon baking powder
¾ teaspoon salt
6 tablespoons margarine or
   butter, cut into pieces
1 large egg

½ cup milk
1 teaspoon grated lemon peel
½ teaspoon vanilla extract
1 cup fresh or frozen
   blueberries*

1. Preheat oven to 400°F. Grease twelve 2½" by 1¼" muffin-pan cups.

2. Into large bowl, combine flour, sugar, baking powder, and salt. With pastry blender or 2 knives used scissor-fashion, cut in margarine until mixture resembles fine crumbs. In small bowl, beat egg, milk, lemon peel, and vanilla until blended. Stir egg mixture into flour mixture just until flour is moistened (batter will be lumpy). Fold blueberries into batter.

3. Spoon batter into muffin-pan cups. Bake until golden and toothpick inserted in center comes out clean, about 20 minutes. Immediately remove muffins from pan. Serve warm, or cool on wire rack to serve later. Reheat before serving, if desired. Makes 12 muffins.

If frozen blueberries are used, do not thaw before adding them to batter.

Each muffin: About 180 calories, 3 g protein, 27 g carbohydrate, 7 g total fat (1 g saturated), 19 mg cholesterol, 330 mg sodium.

Apple-Buttermilk Muffins

Prep: 15 minutes
Bake: 25 minutes

2 cups all-purpose flour
½ cup packed light brown
  sugar
2 teaspoons baking powder
1 teaspoon baking soda
½ teaspoon salt
1 cup buttermilk
¼ cup vegetable oil
2 teaspoons vanilla extract

1 large egg
2 medium Golden Delicious or
  Winesap apples, peeled,
  cored, and diced (about 2
  cups)
½ cup walnuts, chopped
  (optional)
1 teaspoon ground cinnamon
1 tablespoon sugar

1. Preheat oven to 400°F. Grease twelve 2½" by 1¼" muffin-pan cups.

2. Into large bowl, combine flour, brown sugar, baking powder, baking soda, and salt. In small bowl, with wire whisk or fork, beat buttermilk, oil, vanilla extract, and egg until blended; stir into flour mixture just until flour is moistened (batter will be lumpy). Fold in apples and walnuts, if using.

3. In cup, mix cinnamon and sugar. Spoon batter into muffin cups; sprinkle with cinnamon-sugar. Bake muffins until toothpick inserted in center comes out clean, about 25 minutes. Immediately remove from pan. Serve warm, or cool on wire rack to serve later. Reheat before serving, if desired. Makes 12 muffins.

Each muffin: About 185 calories, 3 g protein, 31 g carbohydrate, 5 g total fat (1 g saturated), 18 mg cholesterol, 300 mg sodium.

Raspberry Corn Muffins

Prep: 15 minutes
Bake: 20 to 25 minutes

1 cup all-purpose flour
1 cup yellow cornmeal
½ cup sugar
2 teaspoons baking powder
1 teaspoon baking soda
½ teaspoon salt

1 cup buttermilk
¼ cup vegetable oil
2 teaspoons vanilla extract
1 large egg
1¼ cups raspberries or 1½
  cups blueberries

1. Preheat oven to 400°F. Grease twelve 2½" by 1¼" muffin-pan cups.

2. In large bowl, combine flour, cornmeal, sugar, baking powder, baking soda, and salt. In small bowl, with wire whisk or fork, beat buttermilk, oil, vanilla, and egg until blended; stir into flour mixture just until flour is moistened (batter will be lumpy). Fold in berries.

3. Spoon batter into muffin cups. Bake muffins until toothpick inserted in center of muffin comes out clean, 20 to 25 minutes. Immediately remove muffins from pans. Serve warm, or cool on wire rack to serve later. Makes 12 muffins.

Each muffin: About 180 calories, 3 g protein, 29 g carbohydrate, 6 g total fat (1 g saturated), 19 mg cholesterol, 285 mg sodium.

Cranberry-Almond Muffins

Prep: 25 minutes
Bake: 20 minutes

3 cups all-purpose flour
½ cup sugar
2 teaspoons baking powder
1 teaspoon baking soda
¼ teaspoon salt
1 container (16 ounces) sour cream
⅓ cup milk

¼ cup vegetable oil
¼ teaspoon almond extract
2 large eggs
1½ cups fresh or frozen cranberries, coarsely chopped
2 tablespoons sliced blanched almonds

1. Preheat oven to 400°F. Grease and flour twenty-four 2½" by 1¼" muffin-pan cups.

2. In large bowl, combine flour, sugar, baking powder, baking soda, and salt. In medium bowl, beat sour cream, milk, oil, almond extract, and eggs until blended. Stir sour-cream mixture into flour mixture just until flour is moistened (batter will be lumpy). With rubber spatula, gently fold in cranberries.

3. Spoon batter into muffin-pan cups; sprinkle with sliced almonds. Bake 20 minutes or until golden and toothpick inserted in center comes out clean, Immediately remove muffins from pans. Serve warm, or cool on wire rack to serve later. Reheat before serving, if desired. Makes 24 muffins.

Each muffin: About 150 calories, 3 g protein, 18 g carbohydrate, 7 g total fat (3 g saturated), 27 mg cholesterol, 125 mg sodium.

ᗧᕦCorn Breads

Golden Corn Bread

Prep: 10 minutes
Bake: 25 minutes

1 cup all-purpose flour
¾ cup cornmeal
3 tablespoons sugar
1 tablespoon baking powder
1 teaspoon salt
1 large egg
⅔ cup milk
6 tablespoons margarine or butter, melted, or 6 tablespoons
   vegetable oil

1. Preheat oven to 425°F. Grease 8" by 8" baking pan.
2. In medium bowl, combine flour, cornmeal, sugar, baking powder, and salt. In small bowl, beat egg, milk, and margarine until blended. Stir egg mixture into flour mixture just until flour is moistened (batter will be lumpy).
3. Spread batter evenly in pan. Bake until golden and toothpick inserted in center comes out clean, about 25 minutes. Cut into 9 squares. Serve warm, or cool in pan on wire rack to serve later. Reheat before serving, if desired. Makes 9 servings.

Each serving: About 195 calories, 4 g protein, 25 g carbohydrate, 9 g total fat (2 g saturated), 26 mg cholesterol, 510 mg sodium.

CORN MUFFINS: Grease twelve 2½" by 1¼" muffin-pan cups. Prepare as above; spoon into cups, filling each two-thirds full. Bake until golden and toothpick inserted in center of muffin comes out clean, about 20 minutes. Immediately remove muffins from pans. Serve warm. Makes 1 dozen muffins.

Each muffin: About 150 calories, 3 g protein, 19 g carbohydrate, 7 g total fat (1 g saturated), 20 mg cholesterol, 380 mg sodium.

Corn Bread with Chives

Prep: 10 minutes
Bake: 20 minutes

2¼ cups buttermilk
½ cup (1 stick), margarine or
    butter, melted and cooled
3 large eggs
2 cups yellow cornmeal
1 cup all-purpose flour

2 tablespoons sugar
2½ teaspoons baking powder
¾ teaspoon salt
½ teaspoon baking soda
⅓ cup snipped fresh chives

1. Preheat oven to 400°F. Grease 13" by 9" metal baking pan.

2. In medium bowl, with fork, combine buttermilk, melted margarine, and eggs until blended. In large bowl, combine cornmeal, flour, sugar, baking powder, salt, and baking soda.

3. With fork, stir buttermilk mixture and chives into cornmeal mixture just until blended. Spoon batter into baking pan; spread evenly. Bake corn bread until toothpick inserted in center comes out clean, about 20 minutes. Cool in pan on wire rack 10 minutes to serve warm, or cool completely in pan to serve later. Reheat before serving, if desired. Makes 20 servings.

Each serving: About 140 calories, 4 g protein, 18 g carbohydrate, 6 g total fat (1 g saturated), 33 mg cholesterol, 255 mg sodium.

Spoon Bread

Prep: 20 minutes
Bake: 45 minutes

1½ cups milk
1 cup cornmeal
1 teaspoon salt
1½ cups water
4 tablespoons margarine, butter, or butter-flavored shortening
4 large eggs, separated, at room temperature

1. In 2-cup measuring cup or small bowl, stir milk, corn-meal, and salt until well mixed. In 2-quart saucepan, heat water to boiling over high heat. Reduce heat to low; with wire whisk or rubber spatula, stir in cornmeal mixture, and cook, stirring constantly, until very thick and bubbly. Remove saucepan from heat; stir in margarine until mixed.

2. In small bowl, with fork or wire whisk, beat egg yolks; beat in a small amount of hot cornmeal mixture until blended. Gradually pour egg-yolk mixture back into cornmeal mixture in saucepan, stirring rapidly to prevent lumping. Over low heat, cook, stirring constantly, until mixture thickens and bubbles just form. Remove saucepan from heat; cool cornmeal mixture slightly.

3. Preheat oven to 350°F. Grease 1½-quart casserole. In large bowl, with mixer at high speed, beat egg whites until stiff peaks form. With rubber spatula, gently fold cornmeal mixture into beaten egg whites just until blended.

4. Pour mixture into casserole. Bake until golden brown and knife inserted in center comes out clean, 40 to 45 minutes. Serve immediately. Makes 8 servings.

Each serving: About 180 calories, 6 g protein, 16 g carbohydrate, 10 g total fat (3 g saturated), 113 mg cholesterol, 420 mg sodium.

❧Popovers

Giant Popovers

Prep: 7 minutes
Bake: 1 hour 10 minutes

6 tablespoons margarine or butter
6 large eggs
2 cups milk
2 cups all-purpose flour
1 teaspoon salt

1. Preheat oven to 375°F. In small saucepan, melt margarine. Grease well 8 deep 7-ounce ceramic custard cups. Set custard cups in jelly-roll pan for easier handling.

2. In large bowl, with mixer at low speed, beat eggs until frothy; beat in milk and margarine until blended. Beat in flour and salt until batter is smooth.

3. Fill each custard cup three-fourths full with batter. Bake 1 hour, then quickly make small slit in top of each popover to let out steam. Bake 10 minutes longer. Immediately remove popovers from cups. Serve piping hot. Makes 8 popovers.

Each popover: About 285 calories, 10 g protein, 27 g carbohydrate, 15 g total fat (4 g saturated), 168 mg cholesterol, 485 mg sodium.

REGULAR POPOVERS: About 1 hour and 15 minutes before serving, grease twelve 2½-inch muffin-pan cups. Prepare as above but cut amounts of ingredients in half. Bake 50 minutes before cutting slit in top. Makes 1 dozen popovers.

ᑐTea Breads & Coffee Cakes

Michigan Orange-Cranberry Bread

Prep: 20 minutes plus cooling
Bake: 55 to 60 minutes

1 large orange
2½ cups all-purpose flour
1 cup sugar
2 teaspoons baking powder
½ teaspoon baking soda
½ teaspoon salt
2 large eggs

4 tablespoons margarine or
   butter, melted
2 cups cranberries, coarsely
   chopped
¾ cup walnuts, chopped
   (optional)

1. Preheat oven to 375°F. Grease 9" by 5" metal loaf pan. Grate peel from orange and squeeze ½ cup juice.

2. In large bowl, combine flour, sugar, baking powder, baking soda, and salt. In small bowl, with wire whisk or fork, beat eggs, margarine, orange peel, and juice. With spoon, stir egg mixture into flour mixture until batter is just blended (batter will be stiff). Fold in cranberries, and walnuts, if using.

3. Spoon batter into loaf pan. Bake until toothpick inserted in center of bread comes out clean, 55 to 60 minutes.

4. Cool bread in pan on wire rack 10 minutes; remove from pan and cool completely on wire rack. Makes 1 loaf, 12 slices.

Each slice without walnuts: About 220 calories, 4 g protein, 41 g carbohydrate, 5 g total fat (1 g saturated), 36 mg cholesterol, 265 mg sodium.

Lemon Loaf

Prep: 25 minutes
Bake: 1 hour 15 minutes

1 large lemon
2¼ cups all-purpose flour
1½ teaspoons baking powder
¾ teaspoon salt
1½ cups plus 2 tablespoons sugar
¾ cup (1½ sticks) margarine or butter, cut into pieces
3 large eggs
¾ cup milk

1. Preheat oven to 350°F. Grease 9" by 5" loaf pan. From lemon, grate 1 tablespoon peel and squeeze 4½ teaspoons juice.

2. In large bowl, combine flour, baking powder, salt, and 1½ cups sugar. With pastry blender or 2 knives used scissor-fashion, cut in margarine until mixture resembles coarse crumbs. Stir in lemon peel.

3. In small bowl, beat eggs slightly; stir in milk. Stir egg mixture into flour mixture just until flour is moistened.

4. Spoon batter evenly into pan. Bake until toothpick inserted in center comes out clean, about 1 hour and 15 minutes. Cool in pan on rack 10 minutes; remove from pan.

5. In 1-quart saucepan, heat lemon juice and remaining 2 tablespoons sugar to boiling over medium-high heat. Cook, stirring frequently, until mixture thickens slightly, about 5 minutes. With pastry brush, brush sugar mixture evenly over top of bread. Finish cooling bread on wire rack. Makes 1 loaf, 12 slices.

Each slice: About 315 calories, 5 g protein, 45 g carbohydrate, 13 g total fat (3 g saturated), 55 mg cholesterol, 370 mg sodium.

Banana-Pecan Bread

Prep: 25 minutes
Bake: 55 minutes

1¾ cups all-purpose flour
⅔ cup sugar
1 teaspoon baking powder
½ teaspoon salt
¼ teaspoon baking soda
½ cup (1 stick) margarine or
   butter, softened
1 cup mashed bananas (about
   2 ripe large bananas)

½ cup pecans, coarsely
   chopped
1 teaspoon freshly grated
   lemon peel
2 large eggs, slightly beaten

1. Preheat oven to 350°F. Grease 9" by 5" loaf pan.

2. In large bowl, combine flour, sugar, baking powder, salt, and baking soda. With pastry blender or 2 knifes used scissor-fashion, cut in margarine until mixture resembles coarse crumbs. Stir in bananas, pecans, lemon peel, and eggs just until flour is moistened.

3. Spoon batter evenly into loaf pan. Bake until toothpick inserted into center of bread comes out clean, about 55 minutes. Cool bread in pan on wire rack 10 minutes; remove from pan and finish cooling on wire rack. Makes 1 loaf, 12 slices.

Each slice: About 240 calories, 4 g protein, 31 g carbohydrate, 12 g total fat (2 g saturated), 35 mg cholesterol, 270 mg sodium.

Zucchini Bread

Prep: 25 minutes
Bake: 1 hour

3 cups all-purpose flour
1½ cups sugar
4½ teaspoons baking powder
1 teaspoon salt
4 ounces walnuts (1 cup), chopped
4 large eggs
⅔ cup vegetable oil
2 cups shredded zucchini
2 teaspoons freshly grated lemon peel

1. Preheat oven to 350°F. Grease two 8½" by 4½" loaf pans.

2. In large bowl, combine flour, sugar, baking powder, salt, and chopped walnuts. In medium bowl, beat eggs slightly; stir in oil, shredded zucchini, and grated lemon peel. Stir into flour mixture just until flour is moistened.

3. Spoon batter evenly into pans. Bake until toothpick inserted in center comes out clean, about 1 hour. Cool bread in pans on wire racks 10 minutes; remove from pans and finish cooling on wire racks. Makes 2 loaves, 24 slices.

Each slice: About 205 calories, 4 g protein, 26 g carbohydrate, 10 g total fat (1 g saturated), 35 mg cholesterol, 185 mg sodium.

Zucchini and Cheese Bread

Prep: 25 minutes
Bake: 50 to 55 minutes

4 ounces sharp Cheddar
   cheese, shredded (about 1
   cup)
½ cup freshly grated Parmesan
   cheese
2½ cups all-purpose flour
4 teaspoons baking powder
1 tablespoon sugar
1½ teaspoons salt
½ teaspoon coarsely ground
   black pepper

1 small zucchini (about 5
   ounces), coarsely shredded
   (1 cup)
1 medium red pepper, finely
   chopped (½ cup)
3 small green onions, finely
   chopped
2 large eggs
½ cup milk
3 tablespoons olive oil

1. Preheat oven to 350°F. Grease 9" by 9" metal baking
pan.

2. In small bowl, combine ¼ cup Cheddar and 2 tablespoons Parmesan; set aside.

3. In large bowl, combine flour, baking powder, sugar,
salt, and black pepper. Stir zucchini, red pepper, green onions, and remaining cheeses into flour mixture.

4. In medium bowl, with wire whisk, beat eggs, milk,
and oil until blended; add to flour mixture and stir just until
evenly moistened.

5. Spoon batter into pan and spread evenly. Sprinkle top
with reserved cheese mixture. Bake until toothpick inserted
in center comes out clean, 50 to 55 minutes. Cool bread in
pan on wire rack 5 minutes. With small metal spatula,
loosen bread from side of pan. Invert bread onto large plate
and remove pan. Immediately invert bread onto wire rack
to cool completely. Makes 1 loaf, 16 slices.

*Each slice: About 155 calories, 7 g protein, 17 g carbohydrate,
7 g total fat (3 g saturated), 38 mg cholesterol, 405 mg sodium.*

Blueberry-Lemon Tea Bread

Prep: 20 minutes plus cooling
Bake: 1 hour 5 minutes

½ cup (1 stick) margarine or butter, softened
1⅓ cups sugar
2 cups all-purpose flour
2 teaspoons baking powder
½ teaspoon salt
2 large eggs
½ cup milk
1½ cups blueberries
¼ cup fresh lemon juice

1. Preheat oven to 350°F. Grease and flour 9" by 5" loaf pan.

2. In large bowl, with mixer at low speed, beat margarine and 1 cup sugar just until blended. Increase speed to medium; beat until light and fluffy, about 5 minutes.

3. Meanwhile, in medium bowl, combine flour, baking powder, and salt.

4. Reduce speed to low; add eggs, 1 at a time, beating after each addition until well blended, occasionally scraping bowl with rubber spatula. Alternately add flour mixture and milk, mixing just until blended. Gently stir in blueberries.

5. Spoon batter into loaf pan. Bake until toothpick inserted in center comes out clean, about 1 hour and 5 minutes. Cool loaf in pan on wire rack 10 minutes; remove from pan.

6. With skewer, prick top and sides of warm cake in many places. In small bowl, mix lemon juice and remaining ⅓ cup sugar. With pastry brush, brush top and sides of warm cake with lemon glaze. Cool cake on wire rack. Makes 1 loaf, 16 slices.

Each slice: About 195 calories, 3 g protein, 31 g carbohydrate, 7 g total fat (1 g saturated), 28 mg cholesterol, 200 mg sodium.

Pumpkin-Spice Bread

Prep: 15 minutes
Bake: 1 hour 15 minutes

3 cups all-purpose flour
2 teaspoons baking powder
1¼ teaspoons salt
1 teaspoon baking soda
1 teaspoon ground cinnamon
¼ teaspoon ground allspice
2 large eggs
1 can (16 ounces)
　solid-pack pumpkin
　(not pumpkin-pie mix)

1 cup packed brown sugar
½ cup maple or maple-flavored
　syrup
¼ cup vegetable oil
½ cup dark seedless or golden
　raisins
½ cup chopped pecans

1. Preheat oven to 350°F. Grease 9" by 5" loaf pan.

2. In large bowl, combine flour, baking powder, salt, baking soda, cinnamon, and allspice. In medium bowl, beat eggs, pumpkin, brown sugar, maple syrup, and oil. Stir pumpkin mixture into flour mixture just until flour is moistened. Gently stir in raisins and pecans.

3. Spoon batter evenly into loaf pan. Bake until toothpick inserted in center comes out clean, about 1 hour and 15 minutes. Cool bread in pan on wire rack 10 minutes; remove from pan and finish cooling on wire rack. Makes 1 loaf, 16 slices.

Each slice: About 250 calories, 4 g protein, 45 g carbohydrate, 7 g total fat (1 g saturated), 27 mg cholesterol, 325 mg sodium.

Irish Soda Bread

Prep: 20 minutes
Bake: 1 hour 20 minutes

4 cups all-purpose flour
3 tablespoons sugar
1 tablespoon baking powder
1 teaspoon salt
1 teaspoon baking soda
6 tablespoons margarine or butter, cut into pieces
1½ cups golden raisins
2 large eggs
1½ cups buttermilk

1. Preheat oven to 350°F. Grease 2-quart round casserole.

2. In large bowl, combine flour, sugar, baking powder, salt, and baking soda; stir until combined. With pastry blender or 2 knives used scissor-fashion, cut in margarine until mixture resembles coarse crumbs; stir in raisins.

3. In cup, beat eggs slightly; remove 1 tablespoon beaten egg and reserve. Stir buttermilk and remaining beaten eggs into flour mixture just until flour is moistened (dough will be sticky).

4. Turn dough onto well-floured surface; with floured hands, knead 8 to 10 strokes to mix thoroughly. Shape dough into ball; place in casserole. In center of ball, cut a 4-inch cross about ¼ inch deep. Brush dough with reserved egg.

5. Bake until toothpick inserted in center of loaf comes out clean, about 1 hour and 20 minutes. Cool in casserole on wire rack 10 minutes; remove from casserole and finish cooling on wire rack. Makes 1 loaf, 12 slices.

Each slice: About 305 calories, 7 g protein, 52 g carbohydrate, 7 g total fat (2 g saturated), 37 mg cholesterol, 520 mg sodium.

New England Brown Bread

Prep: 15 minutes
Bake: 55 to 60 minutes

1 cup all-purpose flour
1 cup whole-wheat flour
¾ cup dark seedless raisins
¼ cup sugar
1¼ teaspoons baking soda
½ teaspoon salt
1¼ cups buttermilk or plain low-fat yogurt
¾ cup light molasses
1 large egg

1. Preheat oven to 350°F. Grease 9" by 5" metal loaf pan.

2. In large bowl, combine all-purpose and whole-wheat flours, raisins, sugar, baking soda, and salt. Stir in buttermilk, molasses, and egg until batter is just mixed (batter will be very wet).

3. Pour batter into loaf pan. Bake until toothpick inserted in center comes out clean, 55 to 60 minutes.

4. With spatula, loosen bread from sides of pan. Remove bread from pan. Cool slightly on wire rack to serve warm, or, cool completely to serve later. Makes 1 loaf, 12 slices.

Each slice: About 180 calories, 4 g protein, 41 g carbohydrate, 1 g total fat (0 g saturated), 19 mg cholesterol, 255 mg sodium.

Golden Raisin and Dried Cranberry Soda Bread

Prep: 15 minutes
Bake: 50 to 55 minutes

2½ cups all-purpose flour
½ cup whole-wheat flour
2 teaspoons baking soda
¼ teaspoon salt
½ cup plus 2 teaspoons sugar
4 tablespoons cold margarine or butter, cut into pieces
½ cup golden raisins
½ cup dried cranberries
1½ cups buttermilk

1. Preheat oven to 350°F. Grease 9" by 5" metal loaf pan.

2. In large bowl, combine all-purpose and whole-wheat flours, baking soda, salt, and ½ cup sugar. With pastry blender or 2 knives used scissor-fashion, cut in margarine until mixture resembles fine crumbs. With spoon, stir in raisins and cranberries, then buttermilk just until batter is combined.

3. Spoon batter into loaf pan. Sprinkle top with remaining 2 teaspoons sugar. Bake until toothpick inserted in center comes out clean, 50 to 55 minutes. Cool loaf in pan on wire rack 10 minutes; remove from pan and finish cooling on wire rack. Makes 1 loaf, 12 slices.

Each slice: About 230 calories, 5 g protein, 44 g carbohydrate, 5 g total fat (1 g saturated), 1 mg cholesterol, 340 mg sodium.

Sour Cream–Pear Coffee Cake

Prep: 25 minutes plus cooling
Bake: 40 to 45 minutes

Streusel
⅔ cup packed light brown sugar
½ cup all-purpose flour
1 teaspoon ground cinnamon
4 tablespoons margarine or butter, softened
⅔ cup walnuts, toasted and chopped

Cake
2½ cups all-purpose flour
1½ teaspoons baking powder
½ teaspoon baking soda
½ teaspoon salt
1¼ cups sugar
6 tablespoons margarine or butter, softened

2 large eggs
1½ teaspoons vanilla extract
1⅓ cups sour cream
3 firm but ripe Bosc pears (about 1¼ pounds), peeled, cored, and cut into 1-inch pieces

1. Preheat oven to 350°F. Grease 13" by 9" metal baking pan; dust with flour.
2. Prepare streusel: In medium bowl, with fork, mix brown sugar, flour, and cinnamon until well blended. With fingertips, work in margarine until evenly distributed. Add walnuts and toss to mix; set aside.
3. Prepare cake: Into another medium bowl, measure flour, baking powder, baking soda, and salt; stir until combined. Set aside.
4. In large bowl, with mixer at low speed, beat sugar and margarine until blended, scraping bowl often with rubber spatula. Increase speed to high; beat until creamy, about 2 minutes, occasionally scraping bowl. Reduce speed to low; add eggs, 1 at a time, beating well after each addition. Beat in vanilla.
5. With mixer at low speed, alternately add flour mixture and sour cream, beginning and ending with flour mixture,

occasionally scraping bowl, until batter is smooth. With rubber spatula, fold in pears.

6. Spoon batter into pan; spread evenly. Sprinkle top with streusel mixture. Bake until toothpick inserted in center comes out clean, 40 to 45 minutes. Cool cake in pan on wire rack 1 hour to serve warm, or cool completely in pan to serve later. Makes 16 servings.

Each serving: About 345 calories, 5 g protein, 49 g carbohydrate, 15 g total fat (4 g saturated), 35 mg cholesterol, 260 mg sodium.

Classic Crumb Cake

Prep: 40 minutes plus cooling
Bake: 40 to 45 minutes

Crumb Topping
2 cups all-purpose flour
½ cup granulated sugar
½ cup packed light brown sugar
1½ teaspoons ground cinnamon
1 cup (2 sticks) margarine or butter, softened

Cake
2¼ cups all-purpose flour
2¼ teaspoons baking powder
½ teaspoon salt
1¼ cups granulated sugar
½ cup margarine or butter (1 stick), softened
3 large eggs
¾ cup milk
2 teaspoons vanilla extract

1. Preheat oven to 350°F. Grease two 9-inch round cake pans; dust with flour.

2. Prepare topping: In medium bowl, combine flour, granulated sugar, brown sugar, and cinnamon. With fingertips, work in margarine until evenly distributed; set aside.

3. Prepare cake: Into another medium bowl, measure

flour, baking powder, and salt; stir until combined. Set aside.

4. In large bowl, with mixer at low speed, beat sugar and margarine, scraping bowl often with rubber spatula, until blended. Increase speed to medium; beat until well mixed, about 2 minutes, occasionally scraping bowl. Reduce speed to low; add eggs, 1 at a time, beating well after each addition.

5. In small bowl, combine milk and vanilla. With mixer at low speed, alternately add flour mixture and milk mixture, beginning and ending with flour mixture, and beat until batter is smooth, occasionally scraping bowl.

6. Pour batter into pans. Press topping into large chunks; evenly sprinkle over batter. Bake until toothpick inserted in centers comes out clean, 40 to 45 minutes. Cool cakes in pans on wire racks 15 minutes. With small metal spatula, loosen cakes from sides of pans. Invert onto plates, then immediately invert crumb side up onto wire racks to cool completely. Makes 2 coffee cakes, 10 slices per cake.

Each slice: About 325 calories, 4 g protein, 44 g carbohydrate, 15 g total fat (3 g saturated), 33 mg cholesterol, 295 mg sodium.

Simple Stollen

Prep: 25 minutes plus cooling
Bake: 1 hour

2¼ cups all-purpose flour
½ cup sugar
1½ teaspoons baking powder
¼ teaspoon salt
6 tablespoons cold margarine
  or butter
1 cup ricotta cheese
1 large egg
1 large egg yolk

½ cup diced candied lemon
  peel
½ cup dark seedless raisins
⅓ cup slivered blanched
  almonds, toasted
1 teaspoon vanilla extract
½ teaspoon freshly grated
  lemon peel
2 cups confectioners' sugar

1. Preheat oven to 325°F. Grease large cookie sheet.

2. In large bowl, combine flour, sugar, baking powder, and salt. With pastry blender or 2 knives used scissor-fashion, cut in margarine until mixture resembles fine crumbs.

3. In small bowl, with spoon, mix ricotta, egg, and egg yolk. Stir ricotta mixture into flour mixture until moistened. Stir in candied lemon peel, raisins, almonds, vanilla, and grated lemon peel until well mixed.

4. On lightly floured surface, gently knead dough 2 or 3 times to thoroughly blend ingredients. With floured rolling pin, roll dough into 10" by 8" oval. Fold lengthwise almost in half, letting bottom half extend about 1 inch beyond edge of top half.

5. Place stollen on cookie sheet. Bake until toothpick inserted in center comes out clean, about 1 hour. Transfer stollen from cookie sheet to wire rack. Cool completely.

6. In medium bowl, with wire whisk, mix confectioners' sugar and *3 tablespoons plus 1½ teaspoons water* until blended. Place waxed paper under wire rack to catch any drips. Pour glaze over stollen. Allow glaze to set about 20 minutes. Makes 12 servings. To make ahead, prepare through Step 5 and freeze for up to 2 months. After thawing, prepare glaze as in Step 6.

Each serving: About 370 calories, 7 g protein, 60 g carbohydrate, 12 g total fat (3 g saturated), 46 mg cholesterol, 205 mg sodium.

Pear and Ginger Coffee Cake

Prep: 25 minutes plus cooling
Bake: 55 to 60 minutes

2½ cups cake flour (not self-
    rising)
2 teaspoons baking powder
¼ teaspoon salt
1½ cups sugar
¾ cup (1½ sticks) margarine or
    butter, softened
3 large eggs
1 cup milk

1 teaspoon vanilla extract
½ cup crystallized ginger
    (about 3 ounces), finely
    chopped*
3 medium Anjou pears, peeled,
    cored, and thinly sliced
2 tablespoons brown sugar

1. Preheat oven to 350°F. Grease 13" by 9" metal baking
pan; dust with flour. In medium bowl, combine flour, baking powder, and salt. Set aside.

2. In large bowl, with mixer at low speed, beat sugar
and margarine until blended, scraping bowl often with
rubber spatula. Increase speed to high; beat until creamy,
about 2 minutes, occasionally scraping bowl. Reduce speed
to low; add eggs, 1 at a time, beating well after each addition.

3. In small bowl, stir milk and vanilla. With mixer at
low speed, alternately add flour mixture and milk mixture
until batter is smooth, occasionally scraping bowl. With
spoon, stir in chopped ginger.

4. Spread batter evenly in pan. Arrange pear slices, overlapping slightly, on top. Sprinkle brown sugar over batter
and pears.

5. Bake until toothpick inserted in center comes out
clean, 55 to 60 minutes. Cool cake in pan on wire rack 30
minutes to serve warm, or cool completely in pan to serve
later. Makes 15 servings.

*Candied ginger can be found in the spice section of your super-
market.*

*Each serving: About 300 calories, 3 g protein, 48 g carbohydrate,
11 g total fat (2 g saturated), 45 mg cholesterol, 230 mg sodium.*

ᐰPancakes & Waffles

Pancakes

Prep: 15 minutes
Cook: 12 minutes

1¼ cups all-purpose flour
2 tablespoons sugar
2 teaspoons baking powder
¾ teaspoon salt
1⅓ cups milk
1 large egg, slightly beaten
3 tablespoons margarine or butter, melted
Margarine or butter for topping
Maple or maple-flavored syrup

1. In large bowl, combine flour, sugar, baking powder, and salt. Add milk, egg, and 3 tablespoons melted margarine, and stir just until flour is moistened. (For thicker pancakes, use only 1 cup milk.)

2. Heat griddle or skillet over medium heat until drop of water sizzles (or use electric griddle or skillet); brush lightly with vegetable oil. Pour batter by scant ¼-cupfuls onto hot griddle, making a few pancakes at a time; cook until tops are bubbly and bubbles burst (edges will look dry). With wide spatula, turn and cook until undersides are golden. Place on warm platter; keep warm.

3. Repeat until all batter is used, brushing griddle with more vegetable oil, if necessary. Serve pancakes with margarine or butter and syrup or other topping, as desired. Makes about twelve 4-inch pancakes or 4 servings.

Each serving: About 325 calories, 8 g protein, 40 g carbohydrate, 14 g total fat (4 g saturated), 64 mg cholesterol, 805 mg sodium.

BLUEBERRY PANCAKES: Prepare thicker pancakes as above but add ½ *cup blueberries* to batter. Makes about 12 pancakes.

Each serving: About 320 calories, 8 g protein, 42 g carbohydrate, 13 g total fat (3 g saturated), 61 mg cholesterol, 795 mg sodium.

BUCKWHEAT PANCAKES: Prepare as at left but substitute ½ cup buckwheat flour for ½ cup all-purpose flour. Makes about 12 pancakes.

Each serving: About 315 calories, 9 g protein, 39 g carbohydrate, 14 g total fat (4 g saturated), 64 mg cholesterol, 805 mg sodium.

DOLLAR PANCAKES: Prepare as above but pour batter by tablespoons onto hot griddle. Makes about twenty-four 2-inch pancakes.

Puffy Apple Pancake

Prep: 25 minutes
Bake: 15 minutes

2 tablespoons margarine or butter
½ cup plus 2 tablespoons sugar
¼ cup water
6 medium Granny Smith or Newtown Pippin apples (about 2
   pounds), peeled, cored, and each cut into 8 wedges
3 large eggs
¾ cup milk
¾ cup all-purpose flour
¼ teaspoon salt

1. Preheat oven to 425°F. In 12-inch oven-safe skillet (if skillet is not oven-safe, wrap handle of skillet with double layer of foil), heat margarine, ½ cup sugar, and water to boiling over medium-high heat. Add apple wedges; cook, stirring occasionally, until apples are golden and sugar mixture begins to caramelize, about 15 minutes.

2. Meanwhile, in blender at medium speed or in food processor with knife blade attached, blend eggs, milk, flour, salt, and remaining 2 tablespoons sugar until batter is smooth.

3. When apple mixture in skillet is golden and lightly caramelized, pour batter over apples. Place skillet in oven;

bake pancake until puffed and golden, about 15 minutes. Serve immediately. Makes 10 servings.

Each serving: About 180 calories, 4 g protein, 32 g carbohydrate, 5 g total fat (1 g saturated), 66 mg cholesterol, 110 mg sodium.

Buttermilk Waffles

Prep: 10 minutes
Cook: 20 minutes

1¾ cups all-purpose flour
1 teaspoon baking powder
1 teaspoon baking soda
½ teaspoon salt
2 cups buttermilk
⅓ cup margarine or butter, melted
2 large eggs
Margarine or butter
Maple or maple-flavored syrup

1. Preheat waffle baker as manufacturer directs. In large bowl, combine flour, baking powder, baking soda, and salt. Add buttermilk, margarine, and eggs; beat until smooth.

2. When waffle baker is ready, pour batter into center of lower half until it spreads to 1 inch from edges. Cover and bake as manufacturer directs; do not lift cover during baking.

3. When waffle is done, lift cover; loosen waffle with fork. Serve at once with margarine or butter and syrup. Reheat baker before pouring in next waffle. If batter becomes too thick while standing, thin with a little more buttermilk. Makes about 5 waffles.

Each waffle: About 355 calories, 10 g protein, 39 g carbohydrate, 15 g total fat (3 g saturated), 88 mg cholesterol, 855 mg sodium.

SWEET-MILK WAFFLES: Prepare as above but use *2 teaspoons baking powder, omit soda;* use *milk* for buttermilk.

Each waffle: About 360 calories, 10 g protein, 39 g carbohydrate, 18 g total fat (4 g saturated), 98 mg cholesterol, 705 mg sodium.

∽Special Quick Breads

Dumplings for Stew

Prep: 5 minutes
Cook: 20 minutes

1 ⅓ cups all-purpose flour
2 teaspoons baking powder
½ teaspoon salt
⅔ cup milk
2 tablespoons vegetable oil

1. In large bowl, combine flour, baking powder, and salt. In cup, stir milk and oil; slowly stir into flour mixture just until mixture forms soft dough (stir as little as possible).

2. Drop dough by heaping tablespoons onto chicken, meat, or vegetables (so they don't sink) in simmering stew in Dutch oven or kettle.

3. Cook dumplings 10 minutes, uncovered; then cover and cook 10 minutes longer. With slotted spoon, remove dumplings from stew. Spoon stew into serving dish; top with dumplings. Makes about 6 dumplings.

Each dumpling: About 160 calories, 4 g protein, 23 g carbohydrate, 6 g total fat (1 g saturated), 4 mg cholesterol, 340 mg sodium.

HERBED DUMPLINGS: Prepare as above but add *¼ cup chopped fresh parsley* or *1 to 2 tablespoons chopped fresh chives* to flour mixture.

Each dumpling: About 160 calories, 4 g protein, 23 g carbohydrate, 6 g total fat (1 g saturated), 4 mg cholesterol, 340 mg sodium.

Lemon-Pepper Crisps

Prep: 50 minutes plus cooling
Bake: 15 to 18 minutes per batch

2¼ cups all-purpose flour
1 cup packed fresh parsley leaves, finely chopped
1 tablespoon freshly grated lemon peel
1½ teaspoons baking powder
¼ teaspoon coarsely ground black pepper
2½ teaspoons kosher salt
¾ cup water
2 tablespoons olive oil

1. In medium bowl, stir flour, parsley, lemon peel, baking powder, pepper, and 2 teaspoons salt. Add water; stir until dough comes together in a ball. With hand, knead dough in bowl until smooth, about 2 minutes. Divide dough in half; cover each half and let rest 10 minutes.

2. Preheat oven to 350°F. On floured surface, with floured rolling pin, roll half of dough into paper-thin rectangle, about 18" by 12" (don't worry if edges are irregular). With pizza wheel or sharp knife, cut dough lengthwise in half to form two 18" by 6" rectangles. Cut rectangles crosswise into 2-inch-wide strips.

3. Transfer strips to 2 ungreased large cookie sheets (it's all right if dough stretches a little); let rest 10 minutes. With pastry brush, brush strips lightly with 1 tablespoon olive oil; sprinkle with ¼ teaspoon salt.

4. Place cookie sheets on 2 oven racks. Bake strips until lightly browned, 15 to 18 minutes, rotating cookie sheets between upper and lower racks halfway through baking time. Immediately transfer crisps to wire racks to cool.

5. Repeat with remaining dough, oil, and salt. Store crisps in tightly covered container to use within 2 weeks. Makes 3 dozen crisps.

Each crisp: About 35 calories, 1 g protein, 6 g carbohydrate, 1 g total fat (0 g saturated), 0 mg cholesterol, 90 mg sodium.

Old-Fashioned Doughnuts

Prep: 20 minutes plus chilling
Cook: 4 to 6 minutes per batch

3 cups all-purpose flour
2 large eggs
1 cup sugar
¾ cup buttermilk
2 tablespoons shortening
2 teaspoons baking powder

1 teaspoon baking soda
1 teaspoon salt
½ teaspoon ground nutmeg
Vegetable oil
Confectioners' sugar

1. In large bowl, combine 1½ cups flour, eggs, sugar, buttermilk, shortening, baking powder, baking soda, salt, and nutmeg. With mixer at low speed, beat just until blended, constantly scraping bowl. Increase speed to medium; beat 1 minute. Stir in remaining 1½ cups flour. Refrigerate dough at least 1 hour to make it easier to handle.

2. On well-floured surface, with floured rolling pin, roll out dough ½ inch thick. With floured 3½-inch doughnut cutter, cut dough into rings. Press centers (''holes'') and other trimmings together; roll and cut until all dough is used.

3. Meanwhile, in 3-quart saucepan, heat 3 inches vegetable oil over medium heat to 370°F. on deep-fat thermometer (or heat oil in deep-fat fryer set at 370°F.). Fry doughnuts, a few at a time, in hot oil, turning with slotted spoon as soon as they rise to surface and turning often until golden, 4 to 6 minutes. Drain on paper towels. Sprinkle with confectioners' sugar. Makes about 2 dozen doughnuts.

Each doughnut: About 130 calories, 2 g protein, 21 g carbohydrate, 4 g total fat (1 g saturated), 18 mg cholesterol, 195 mg sodium.

Beignets

Prep: 20 minutes
Cook: 3 to 5 minutes per batch

1 cup water
½ cup (1 stick) margarine or butter
1 teaspoon sugar
¼ teaspoon salt
1 cup all-purpose flour
4 large eggs
1 teaspoon vanilla extract
Vegetable oil
Confectioners' sugar
Maple or maple-flavored syrup

1. In 2-quart saucepan, heat water, margarine, sugar, and salt over medium heat until margarine melts and mixture boils. Remove pan from heat. Add flour all at once; vigorously stir until mixture forms a ball.

2. Add eggs, 1 at a time, beating well with wooden spoon after each addition until mixture is smooth and glossy. Beat in vanilla.

3. Meanwhile, in another 2-quart saucepan, heat about 1½ inches vegetable oil over medium heat to 375°F. on deep-fat thermometer (or heat oil in deep-fat fryer set at 375°F.). Drop dough by heaping teaspoons into oil, a few at a time; fry until golden. Drain on paper towels.

4. To serve, sprinkle warm beignets with confectioners' sugar. Serve with syrup. Makes about 3 dozen beignets.

Each beignet: About 55 calories, 1 g protein, 3 g carbohydrate, 4 g total fat (1 g saturated), 24 mg cholesterol, 55 mg sodium.

Yeast Breads

~~~

Breads & Rolls
Sweet Breads & Rolls
Special Yeast Breads

Making breads with yeast is easy. The measuring, mixing, kneading, and shaping of dough usually can be done in less than half an hour; and while the bread rises and bakes, filling the house with its delicious aroma, you can be doing other things.

⌒Ingredients

Yeast: A living plant that feeds on the sugar in dough and produces a gas that makes the dough rise. Active dry yeast is available in granular form in individual packages and in 4-ounce jars. Compressed yeast comes in .6- and 2-ounce cakes. One package of active dry yeast equals 2½ teaspoons or the equivalent of one .6-ounce cake or one-third of a 2-ounce cake. One 4-ounce jar of active dry yeast contains the equivalent of 16 packages.

Flour: Wheat flour is best for making yeast breads; it contains gluten, which stretches when beaten and kneaded, and traps the gas formed by the yeast, producing a light, airy result. All-purpose flour is wheat flour. Whole-wheat flour, which contains less gluten, and other special flours such as rye make small, heavy, compact loaves when used alone; usually they are mixed with all-purpose flour for larger, lighter loaves.

Liquid: Milk—whole, skimmed, evaporated, or reconstituted nonfat dry—and water, or a combination of the two, are generally used for yeast breads. Milk gives bread a creamy white crumb and a soft crust; water makes bread crusty. The liquid must be at the temperature specified in the recipe if the yeast is to dissolve properly.

Sugar: When used in small quantities, sugar helps yeast grow and leaven the dough; it also adds flavor and makes the crust brown. Too much sugar slows down the action of the yeast; as a result, sweet doughs usually need longer rising times than plain doughs. White sugar is used most often, but brown sugar, molasses, and honey give good results when called for.

Fat: Butter, margarine, shortening, vegetable oil, and lard improve flavor and make dough stretch more easily; they also make bread tender and help it stay soft longer.

Eggs: A dough including eggs has added flavor, color, and nutrients. Eggs soften the crust and produce a fine crumb.

Salt: A small amount of salt adds and enhances flavor. It also controls the growth of the yeast, making the dough or batter rise more slowly. It is important not to add too much salt.

Other Ingredients: Herbs, seeds, fruits, and nuts add flavor and texture, and increase the food value; however, they may also increase the rising time needed.

ᛆSuccess Tips

Adding Flour: Many yeast-bread recipes do not give the exact amount of flour needed. Add flour as directed; more will be worked in during kneading. On very humid days the dough may need more flour than the recipe calls for.

Kneading: Knead the dough this way: Shape it into a ball and, on a lightly floured surface, fold it over toward you. With heels of your hands, push the dough away with a rolling motion and give it a quarter turn. Continue kneading 8 to 10 minutes, flouring the board and your hands as needed. When kneading is completed, the dough should be smooth and elastic, with little blisters under the surface; it shouldn't stick to the surface or to your hands.

Letting Dough Rise: Let the kneaded dough rest on the work surface while you wash, dry, and lightly grease the mixing bowl. Place dough in the mixing bowl, smooth side (top) down, to lightly grease the top so that it doesn't dry out, then turn the dough top side up. Cover the bowl with a towel and put it in a cozy, warm place away from drafts; the temperature should be 80° to 85°F. If your kitchen is cool, place the bowl in an unheated oven with a large pan of hot water on the shelf below, replenishing the water as it cools; or you can place the bowl on a wire rack set over a large roasting pan filled two-thirds full with hot tap water. For batter breads, leave the batter in the mixing bowl; cover it and let it rise in a warm place.

Testing for Doubling: When the dough looks almost doubled, quickly and lightly press two fingertips into it to a depth of ½ inch. If dents remain, the dough has doubled. If they fill in quickly, let the dough rise longer; test again in 15 minutes. Mixtures for batter breads look bubbly and moist, with an uneven, slightly rounded, soft top when doubled.

Punching or Stirring Down: When the dough has doubled, punch it down by pushing your fist deep into the center, then pull the edges to the center and turn the dough over in the bowl. Mixtures for batter breads should be "stirred down" with a wooden spoon until they are nearly their original size.

Letting the Dough "Rest": After it has been punched down, resting relaxes dough, making it easier to shape into loaves or braids.

Choosing Baking Pans: For a brown bottom crust, use pans made of dull metal or anodized aluminum. Or use glass baking pans and reduce the temperature called for by 25°F. For well-shaped loaves, be sure to use pans of the size called for.

Shaping Loaves: Rolling method: With a floured rolling pin on a lightly floured surface, roll the dough into a 12" by 8" rectangle. Starting at a narrow end, roll the dough up tightly to press out any air and pinch the seam to seal it. Press the ends with the sides of your hands to seal them and fold them under. Place the roll, seam side down, in a 9" by 5" loaf pan.

Stretching method: When the dough is ready, place it on a lightly floured surface. With floured hands, pat the dough into an oval about 5 inches wide. Pick up both ends of the dough and, gently shaking, stretch it into a 15-inch strip. Fold the ends over so that they overlap a little in the center; pinch the ends lightly together. Then, starting with a long side, roll up the dough, jelly-roll fashion, completely pressing out air as you roll to prevent large holes from forming in the loaf as it bakes. Pinch the seams to seal them. Place the roll seam side down in a loaf pan.

For a round loaf, hold the ball of dough and pull the sides under until the ball is evenly rounded and smooth on top; place it on a cookie sheet and flatten it slightly.

Testing Shaped Dough for Doubling: Press a finger lightly against the dough; the dent should remain.

Glazing Bread: With a pastry brush, brush glaze on the dough lightly so that the bread does not fall.

Baking: Place loaves on the middle shelf of a preheated oven 2 inches apart so that the heat can circulate. If baking on 2 shelves, stagger the pans. If the top crust browns too quickly, cover it loosely with foil. Test the bread after the minimum time given in the recipe has elapsed; if the bread is not done, bake it a few minutes longer and test again.

Testing for Doneness: Tap the top of the loaf or roll lightly. If it sounds hollow and is well browned, it is done.

Cooling Bread: Remove the bread or rolls from the pan or cookie sheet so that the bottom doesn't get soggy; cool on a wire rack.

Storing Bread: Wrap cooled bread or rolls in foil or plastic wrap, or seal in a plastic bag. Leave bread at room temperature (if it is stored in the refrigerator, bread goes stale quickly). Or you can freezer-wrap and freeze the bread to be used within three months.

Reheating Bread: Wrap bread or rolls in foil and reheat in a preheated 375°F. oven about 20 minutes. Or for soft rolls, pour ¼ cup of water into a skillet; place a rack in the skillet and put rolls on the rack. Cover the skillet and heat over low heat 8 to 10 minutes.

Thawing Frozen Bread: Frozen bread slices can be toasted without thawing. Unwrap a loaf and let it stand at room temperature 2 to 3 hours. Or wrap the loaf in foil and thaw it in a preheated 375°F. oven 20 minutes. For a crisp crust, unwrap the loaf for the last 5 minutes of heating time.

❧Breads & Rolls

White Bread

Prep: 30 minutes plus rising and cooling
Bake: 35 minutes

2 packages active dry yeast
¼ cup sugar
2¼ cups milk
6 tablespoons margarine or butter
about 8½ cups all-purpose flour
1 tablespoon salt

1. In small bowl, combine yeast, 1 tablespoon sugar, and *½ cup warm water* (105° to 115°F.). Let stand about 5 minutes, or until foamy.

2. Meanwhile, in 2-quart saucepan, heat milk, 4 tablespoons margarine and 3 tablespoons sugar over low heat until very warm (120° to 130°F.). Margarine does not need to melt completely.

3. In large bowl, with mixer at low speed, beat 3 cups flour and salt until blended. Gradually beat in liquid mixture and yeast mixture. Increase speed to medium; beat 2 minutes. Beat in 1¼ cups flour to make a thick batter; continue beating 2 minutes, scraping bowl often. With wooden spoon, stir in 4 cups flour.

4. Turn dough onto lightly floured surface and knead until smooth and elastic, about 10 minutes, working in more flour (about ¼ cup) while kneading. Shape dough into ball; place in greased large bowl, turning dough to grease top. Cover and let rise in warm place (80° to 85°F.) until doubled, about 1 hour.

5. Punch down dough. Turn dough onto lightly floured surface and cut in half; cover and let rest 15 minutes. Grease two 9" by 5" loaf pans.

6. Shape each half of dough into loaf; place, seam side down, in loaf pan. Cover and let rise in warm place until doubled, about 1 hour.

7. Preheat oven to 400°F. Brush loaves with remaining 2 tablespoons melted margarine. Bake until golden and loaves test done, 30 to 35 minutes. Remove loaves from pans; cool on wire racks. Makes 2 loaves, 16 slices per loaf.

Each slice: About 155 calories, 4 g protein, 28 g carbohydrate, 3 g total fat (1 g saturated), 2 mg cholesterol, 255 mg sodium.

Crusty Farmhouse Bread

Prep: 1 hour 30 minutes plus rising and cooling
Bake: About 25 minutes

Sponge Starter
3 cups all-purpose flour
½ teaspoon active dry yeast

Dough

¾ teaspoon active dry yeast
¼ teaspoon sugar
1 tablespoon plus 1 teaspoon salt
3⅓ cups all-purpose flour

1. Prepare sponge starter: Into large bowl, measure flour, yeast, and *1⅓ cups warm water* (105° to 115°F.). With mixer at low speed, beat until batter is smooth and elastic, about 3 minutes. Scrape starter into large bowl; cover with plastic wrap and refrigerate 15 to 24 hours. (Starter is ready to use when it has thinned out slightly, the volume has tripled, and small bubbles appear on the surface.)

2. When starter is ready, let stand, covered, 30 minutes at room temperature before using. Meanwhile, prepare dough: Into very large bowl, measure *1 cup warm water* (105° to 115°F.); stir in yeast and sugar until dissolved. Let stand about 10 minutes, or until foamy.

3. Add starter to yeast mixture in bowl, breaking up starter with hand (mixture will not be completely blended). Stir in salt and 3 cups flour. With floured hands, knead to combine in bowl.

4. Turn dough onto lightly floured surface and knead until smooth and elastic, 10 to 12 minutes, working in more flour (about ⅓ cup) while kneading, if necessary. Shape dough into ball and place in greased large bowl, turning dough over to grease top. Cover and let rise in warm place (80° to 85°F.) until doubled, about 1 hour.

5. Punch down dough. In same bowl, shape dough into a ball. Cover and let rise again until doubled, about 1 hour.

6. Turn dough onto floured surface; cut in half. Cover and let rest 15 minutes for easier shaping. Sprinkle large cookie sheet with flour.

7. Shape each half of dough into 7-inch round loaf. Place loaves, about 3 inches apart, in opposite corners on cookie sheet. Cover and let rise in refrigerator at least 3 hours, or up to 15 hours.

8. Preheat oven to 500°F. Remove loaves from refrigerator. Sprinkle loaves with flour. With serrated knife or single-edge razor, cut 2 parallel lines, 1½ inches apart, on top of each loaf, then cut 2 more lines, perpendicular to first lines (pattern should resemble a tic-tac-toe board). Place 12 ice cubes in 13" by 9" metal baking pan. Place pan in bottom of oven. Bake loaves on middle rack 10 minutes. Turn oven control to 400°F. Bake until loaves are golden brown, about 15 minutes longer. Cool loaves on wire rack. Makes 2 loaves, 12 slices per loaf.

Each slice: About 120 calories, 4 g protein, 25 g carbohydrate, 0 g total fat, 0 mg cholesterol, 355 mg sodium.

Whole-Wheat Bread

Prep: 25 minutes plus rising and cooling
Bake: 35 minutes

2 packages active dry yeast
3 tablespoons sugar
1¾ cups milk
6 tablespoons margarine or butter
⅓ cup light molasses
4 cups whole-wheat flour
3½ cups all-purpose flour
4 teaspoons salt

1. In small bowl, combine yeast, 1 tablespoon sugar, and *½ cup warm water* (105° to 115°F.). Let stand 5 minutes, or until foamy.

2. Meanwhile, in 2-quart saucepan, heat milk, margarine, light molasses, and 2 tablespoons sugar over low heat until mixture is very warm (120° to 130°F.). Margarine does not need to melt completely.

3. In large bowl, with mixer at low speed, beat 2 cups whole-wheat flour, 1 cup all-purpose flour, and salt until blended. Gradually beat in liquid mixture and yeast mixture. Increase speed to medium; beat 2 minutes, occasionally scraping bowl with rubber spatula. Continue beating 2 minutes, scraping bowl often. With wooden spoon, stir in 2 cups whole-wheat and 2 cups all-purpose flour to make a soft dough.

4. Turn dough onto lightly floured surface and knead until smooth and elastic, about 10 minutes, working in a little more all-purpose flour (about ½ cup) while kneading. Shape dough into ball; place in greased large bowl, turning to grease top. Cover and let rise in warm place (80° to 85°F.) until doubled, about 1 hour.

5. Punch down dough. Turn dough onto lightly floured surface; cut in half. Cover and let rest 15 minutes. Grease two 9" by 5" loaf pans.

6. Shape each half of dough into loaf; place, seam side down, in loaf pan. Cover and let rise in warm place until doubled, about 1 hour.

7. Preheat oven to 400°F. Bake until golden and loaves test done, 30 to 35 minutes. Remove from pans; cool on wire racks. Makes 2 loaves, 16 slices per loaf.

Each slice: About 140 calories, 4 g protein, 26 g carbohydrate, 3 g total fat (1 g saturated), 2 mg cholesterol, 330 mg sodium.

Walnut and Raisin Whole-Wheat Bread

Prep: 30 minutes plus rising and cooling
Bake: 20 to 25 minutes

1 package active dry yeast
1 teaspoon plus 3 tablespoons honey
2 teaspoons salt
3½ cups whole-wheat flour
3 tablespoons vegetable oil
¾ cup dark seedless raisins
¾ cup walnuts, chopped

1. In cup, combine yeast, 1 teaspoon honey and ½ *cup warm water* (105° to 115°F.); stir to dissolve. Let stand 5 minutes or until foamy.

2. In large bowl, combine salt and 3 cups whole-wheat flour. With spoon, beat in yeast mixture, oil, remaining 3 tablespoons honey, and *¾ cup warm tap water.*

3. On floured surface, knead dough until smooth and elastic, about 10 minutes, working in raisins, walnuts, and more flour (about ½ cup). Shape dough into ball; place in greased bowl, turning to grease top. Cover and let rise in warm place (80° to 85°F.) until doubled, about 1 hour.

4. Punch down dough. Turn dough onto lightly floured surface; cut in half. Cover and let rest 15 minutes. Grease large cookie sheet.

5. Shape each half of dough into a 5-inch round loaf. Place loaves on opposite corners of cookie sheet, about 2 inches from sides. Cover; let rise in warm place until doubled, about 1 hour.

6. Preheat oven to 400°F. Bake until golden, 20 to 25 minutes. Transfer to wire rack to cool. Makes 2 loaves, 8 slices per loaf.

Each slice: About 185 calories, 5 g protein, 29 g carbohydrate, 7 g total fat (1 g saturated), 0 mg cholesterol, 270 mg sodium.

Round Rye Bread

Prep: 30 minutes plus rising and cooling
Bake: 35 minutes

2 packages active dry yeast
1 teaspoon sugar
2 cups buttermilk
⅓ cup plus 2 tablespoons margarine or butter
⅓ cup light molasses
4 cups all-purpose flour
2 cups rye flour
2 tablespoons caraway seeds
1½ teaspoons salt

1. In small bowl, combine yeast, sugar, and *½ cup warm water* (105° to 115°F.). Let stand 5 minutes, or until foamy.

2. Meanwhile, in 2-quart saucepan, over low heat, heat buttermilk, ⅓ cup margarine, and light molasses until mixture is very warm (120° to 130°F.). Margarine does not need to melt completely, and mixture will appear curdled.

3. In large bowl, with mixer at low speed, beat 1 cup all-purpose flour, 1 cup rye flour, caraway seeds, and salt until blended. Gradually beat in liquid mixture and yeast mixture. Increase speed to medium; beat 2 minutes, occasionally scraping bowl with rubber spatula. Continue beating 2 minutes, scraping bowl often. With wooden spoon, stir in 2½ cups all-purpose flour and 1 cup rye flour to make a soft dough.

4. Turn dough onto well-floured surface and knead until smooth and elastic, about 10 minutes, working in a little more all-purpose flour (about ½ cup) while kneading. Shape dough into ball; place in greased large bowl, turning to grease top. Cover and let rise in warm place (80° to 85°F.) until doubled, about 1 hour.

5. Punch down dough. Turn dough onto lightly floured surface; cut in half. Cover and let rest 15 minutes. Grease large cookie sheet.

6. Shape each half of dough into a ball; place balls on

cookie sheet and flatten slightly. Cover and let rise in warm place until doubled, about 1 hour.

7. Preheat oven to 350°F. Melt remaining 2 tablespoons margarine. Brush loaves with melted margarine. Bake until loaves test done, about 35 minutes. Remove loaves from cookie sheet; cool on wire racks. Makes 2 round loaves, 16 slices per loaf.

Each slice: About 120 calories, 3 g protein, 20 g carbohydrate, 3 g total fat (1 g saturated), 1 mg cholesterol, 160 mg sodium.

Portuguese Peasant Bread

Prep 20 minutes plus rising and cooling
Bake: 35 minutes

2 packages active dry yeast
2 tablespoons sugar
1 package (8 ounces) barley cereal (about 4½ cups),*
   uncooked
2½ cups stone-ground cornmeal, preferably white
4 teaspoons salt
4¾ cups all-purpose flour

1. In small bowl, combine yeast, sugar, and *½ cup warm water* (105° to 115°F.). Let stand 5 minutes, or until foamy.

2. In large bowl, combine barley cereal, cornmeal, salt, and 4 cups flour. With wooden spoon, stir in yeast mixture and *2½ cups warm water* (105° to 115°F.) until combined. With floured hands, shape dough into a ball in bowl. Cover and let rise in warm place (80° to 85°F.) until doubled, about 1 hour.

3. Punch down dough. Turn onto well-floured surface and knead until smooth, about 5 minutes, working in more flour (about ¾ cup) as necessary while kneading.

4. Grease large cookie sheet. Cut dough in half and shape each half into a 6-inch round. Coat each round with flour; place on cookie sheet. Cover and let rise in warm place until doubled, about 1 hour.

5. Preheat oven to 400°F. Bake until golden brown,

about 35 minutes, using spray bottle to spritz loaves with water after first 5 minutes of baking, and again 10 minutes later. Cool on wire racks. Makes 2 loaves, 12 slices per loaf.

Barley cereal can be found in the baby-food section of supermarkets.

Each slice: About 170 calories, 5 g protein, 36 g carbohydrate, 1 g total fat (0 g saturated), 0 mg cholesterol, 360 mg sodium.

Colonial Oatmeal Bread

Prep: 30 minutes plus rising and cooling
Bake: 40 minutes

2 packages active dry yeast
1 teaspoon sugar
½ cup honey
4 tablespoons margarine or butter
4 cups whole-wheat flour
2¾ cups all-purpose flour
1 tablespoon salt
1 large egg
1 cup quick-cooking oats, uncooked

1. In small bowl, combine yeast, sugar, and *½ cup warm water* (105° to 115°F.). Let stand 5 minutes, or until foamy.

2. Meanwhile, in 2-quart saucepan, heat *1¾ cups water,* honey, and margarine, over low heat until mixture is very warm (120° to 130°F.). Margarine does not need to melt completely.

3. In large bowl, with mixer at low speed, beat 2 cups whole-wheat flour, 1 cup all-purpose flour, and salt until blended. Gradually beat in liquid mixture, yeast mixture, egg, and 1 cup whole-wheat flour. Increase speed to medium; beat 2 minutes, occasionally scraping bowl with rubber spatula. Continue beating 2 minutes, scraping bowl often. With wooden spoon, stir in oats, 1 cup whole-wheat flour, and 1 cup all-purpose flour to make a soft dough.

4. Turn dough onto lightly floured surface and knead until smooth and elastic, about 10 minutes, working in more all-purpose flour (about ¾ cup) while kneading the dough. Shape dough into ball; place in greased large bowl, turning to grease top. Cover and let rise in warm place (80° to 85°F.) until doubled, about 1 hour.

5. Punch down dough. Turn dough onto lightly floured surface and cut in half; cover and let rest 15 minutes. Grease large cookie sheet.

6. Shape each half of dough into 7" by 4" oval, tapering ends slightly; place on cookie sheet. Cover and let rise in warm place until doubled, about 1 hour.

7. Preheat oven to 350°F. With serrated knife or a single-edge razor, cut 3 to 5 crisscross slashes across top of each loaf; lightly dust tops of loaves with some all-purpose flour. Bake until loaves test done, 35 to 40 minutes. Remove loaves from cookie sheet; cool on wire racks. Makes 2 loaves, 16 slices per loaf.

Each slice: About 140 calories, 4 g protein, 27 g carbohydrate, 3 g total fat (0 g saturated), 7 mg cholesterol, 240 mg sodium.

Quick-and-Easy Anadama Bread

Prep: 25 minutes plus rising and cooling
Bake: 35 minutes

1 package active dry yeast
½ teaspoon sugar
¼ cup light molasses
3 tablespoons margarine or butter
3 cups all-purpose flour
⅓ cup cornmeal
1 teaspoon salt
1 large egg

1. In small bowl, combine yeast, sugar, and ¼ *cup warm water* (105° to 115° F.). Let stand 5 minutes, or until foamy.

2. In 1-quart saucepan, heat ¾ *cup water,* molasses, and margarine over low heat until mixture is very warm (120°

to 130°F.). Margarine does not need to melt completely. Meanwhile, grease 2-quart soufflé dish or casserole.

3. In large bowl, with mixer at low speed, beat 2 cups flour, cornmeal, and salt until blended. Beat in liquid mixture, yeast mixture, and egg. Increase speed to medium; beat 2 minutes, occasionally scraping bowl with rubber spatula. Continue beating 2 minutes, scraping bowl often. With wooden spoon, stir in remaining 1 cup flour to make a soft dough. Shape dough into ball and place in soufflé dish, turning to grease top. Cover, and let rise in warm place (80° to 85°F.) until doubled, about 1 hour.

4. Preheat oven to 375°F. Bake until browned and loaf tests done, 30 to 35 minutes. Remove loaf from soufflé dish; cool on wire rack. Makes 1 loaf, about 10 slices.

Each slice: About 215 calories, 5 g protein, 38 g carbohydrate, 4 g total fat (1 g saturated), 21 mg cholesterol, 290 mg sodium.

Whole-Grain Bread

Prep: 40 minutes plus rising and cooling
Bake: 50 to 60 minutes

2 cups rye flour	¾ cup milk
1 cup unprocessed bran	½ cup (1 stick) margarine or
½ cup wheat germ	butter
4¼ cups whole-wheat flour	⅓ cup dark molasses
4 teaspoons salt	2 eggs
3 tablespoons sugar	2 tablespoons yellow cornmeal
2 packages active dry yeast	1 teaspoon caraway seeds

1. In large bowl, combine rye flour, unprocessed bran, wheat germ, 3 cups whole-wheat flour, and salt. In another large bowl, combine sugar, yeast, and 3 cups flour mixture.

2. In 2-quart saucepan over low heat, heat milk, margarine, molasses, and *1 cup water* until very warm (120° to 130°F.). Margarine does not need to melt.

3. With mixer at low speed, gradually beat liquid into yeast mixture just until blended. Increase speed to medium;

beat 2 minutes, occasionally scraping bowl with rubber spatula. Reserve 1 egg white; beat in remaining egg and egg yolk and 2 cups rye flour mixture; continue beating 2 minutes, scraping bowl often. With spoon, stir in remaining flour mixture and ¾ cup whole-wheat flour to make a soft dough.

4. Lightly sprinkle work surface with whole-wheat flour; turn dough onto surface and knead until smooth and elastic, about 10 minutes, working in more whole-wheat flour (about ½ cup) while kneading. Shape dough into ball; place in greased large bowl, turning to grease top. Cover and let rise in warm place (80° to 85°F.) until doubled, about 1 hour.

5. Punch down dough. Turn onto surface lightly floured with whole-wheat flour; cover and let rest 15 minutes. Sprinkle cookie sheet with cornmeal.

6. Shape dough into oval loaf, tapering ends; place on cookie sheet. Cover and let rise in warm place until doubled, about 1 hour.

7. Preheat oven to 350°F. With serrated knife or single-edge razor, cut 3 diagonal slashes on top of loaf. In cup, mix reserved egg white with *1 tablespoon water*; brush over loaf. Sprinkle loaf with caraway seeds. Bake until loaf tests done, 50 to 60 minutes. Remove loaf from cookie sheet; cool on wire rack. Makes 1 oval loaf, about 16 servings.

Each serving: About 280 calories, 9 g protein, 47 g carbohydrate, 8 g total fat (2 g saturated), 28 mg cholesterol, 675 mg sodium.

Olive-Rosemary Bread

Prep: 30 minutes plus rising and cooling
Bake: 30 minutes

2 packages active dry yeast
1 tablespoon sugar
4 tablespoons extravirgin olive oil
1 cup Kalamata or green olives, pitted and chopped
2 tablespoons finely chopped fresh rosemary
2 teaspoons salt
5 cups bread flour

1. In small bowl, combine yeast, sugar, 3 tablespoons olive oil, and *½ cup warm water* (105° to 115°F.). Let stand 5 minutes, or until foamy.

2. Meanwhile, in large bowl, with wooden spoon, mix olives, rosemary, salt, and 4 cups flour. Add yeast mixture and *1 cup warm water* (105° to 115°F.); stir until combined.

3. Turn dough onto lightly floured surface and knead until smooth and elastic, about 8 minutes, working in more flour (½ to 1 cup) while kneading. Shape dough into ball; place in greased large bowl, turning to grease top. Cover and let rise in warm place (80° to 85°F.), until doubled, about 1 hour.

4. Punch down dough. Turn dough onto lightly floured surface and cut in half; cover and let rest 15 minutes for easier shaping. Grease large cookie sheet.

5. Shape each half of dough into a 7½" by 4" oval and place on cookie sheet, about 3 inches apart. Cover and let rise in warm place until doubled, about 1 hour.

6. Preheat oven to 400°F. Brush tops of loaves with remaining 1 tablespoon oil. With serrated knife or single-edge razor, cut 3 diagonal slashes across top of each loaf. Bake until golden, about 30 minutes. Remove loaves from pan. Cool on wire rack. Makes 2 loaves, 12 slices per loaf.

Each slice: About 140 calories, 4 g protein, 22 g carbohydrate, 4 g total fat (1 g saturated), 0 mg cholesterol, 265 mg sodium.

Ciabatta

Prep: 30 minutes plus rising and cooling
Bake: 25 to 30 minutes

1 package active dry yeast
1 teaspoon sugar
5 cups all-purpose flour
1 tablespoon salt
2 tablespoons milk
2 tablespoons extravirgin olive oil

1. In cup, combine yeast, sugar, and *¼ cup warm water* (105° to 115°F.). Let stand 5 minutes, or until foamy.

2. Into bowl of heavy-duty mixer, measure flour and salt. With wooden spoon, stir in milk, olive oil, yeast mixture, and *2 cups warm water* (105° to 115°F.) until blended. With dough hook, mix on medium speed until dough becomes elastic, about 15 minutes. (Or, if you prefer to mix by hand, in very large bowl, combine ingredients as above and stir with wooden spoon until dough becomes elastic, about 15 minutes.) This is a very sticky and moist dough; resist the urge to add more flour, and do not knead or stir for less than the suggested time.

3. Scrape dough into greased large bowl; with greased hand, pat top of dough to coat. Cover and let rise in warm place (80° to 85°F.) until doubled, 1 to 1½ hours.

4. Flour large cookie sheet. With floured hands punch down dough and divide it in half. Turn pieces of dough onto cookie sheet, about 3 inches apart; cover and let rest 15 minutes for easier shaping.

5. With hands, pull 1 piece of dough into 14" by 4" oval. Repeat with remaining piece of dough, still keeping loaves 3 inches apart. With floured fingers, make deep indentations all over each loaf, making sure to press all the way down to cookie sheet. Sprinkle loaves lightly with flour. Cover and let rise in warm place until doubled, about 30 minutes.

6. Preheat oven to 425°F. Place 12 ice cubes in 13" by 9" metal baking pan; place pan in bottom of oven. Bake loaves on middle rack 25 to 30 minutes until golden, using spray bottle to spritz loaves with water 3 times during first 10 minutes of baking. Remove loaves from cookie sheet. Cool on wire rack. Makes 2 loaves, 12 slices per loaf.

Each slice: About 105 calories, 3 g protein, 20 g carbohydrate, 1 g total fat (0 g saturated), 0 mg cholesterol, 270 mg sodium.

Tomato Focaccia

Prep: 20 minutes plus rising
Bake: 35 to 40 minutes

1 package quick-rise yeast
4 cups all-purpose flour
2 teaspoons salt
6 tablespoons olive oil
1 tablespoon cornmeal
1 pound ripe plum tomatoes (about 5 medium), sliced ¼ inch thick
1 tablespoon chopped fresh rosemary or 1 teaspoon dried
    rosemary leaves, crumbled
½ teaspoon coarsely ground black pepper

1. In large bowl, combine yeast, 1½ cups flour, and 1½ teaspoons salt.

2. In 1-quart saucepan, heat 4 tablespoons oil and *1⅓ cups water* over medium heat until very warm (120° to 130°F.).

3. With mixer at low speed, beat liquid into dry ingredients just until blended. Increase speed to medium; beat 2 minutes, scraping bowl often with rubber spatula. Add ½ cup flour; beat 2 minutes. With spoon, stir in 1½ cups flour to make a soft dough.

4. Turn dough onto lightly floured surface, and, with floured hands, knead until smooth and elastic, about 8 minutes, working in more flour (about ½ cup) while kneading. Cover and let rest in a warm place (80° to 85°F.) 15 minutes.

5. Grease 15½" by 10½" jelly-roll pan; sprinkle with cornmeal. Press dough evenly into pan; cover and let rise in warm place until doubled, about 30 minutes.

6. Preheat oven to 400°F. Press fingers into dough almost to bottom of pan, making indentations 1 inch apart. Drizzle with 1 tablespoon olive oil. Arrange sliced tomatoes over top; sprinkle with chopped rosemary, pepper, and remaining ½ teaspoon salt. Bake focaccia in top third of oven until top is lightly browned, about 35 to 40 minutes. Remove foccaccia from jelly-roll pan and place on wire rack; drizzle with remaining 1 tablespoon olive oil. Cool slightly to serve warm. Makes 1 loaf, 12 slices.

Each slice: About 225 calories, 5 g protein, 35 g carbohydrate, 7 g total fat (1 g saturated), 0 mg cholesterol, 300 mg sodium.

Semolina Focaccia

Prep: 20 minutes plus rising and cooling
Bake: About 20 minutes

1 package active dry yeast
6 tablespoons olive oil
1 teaspoon plus 2 tablespoons sugar
2 teaspoons salt
1½ cups plus 2 tablespoons patent durum or finely ground semolina flour*
1½ cups plus 3 tablespoons all-purpose flour
¾ cup golden raisins
1 tablespoon fennel seeds, crushed

1. In cup, combine yeast, 3 tablespoons oil, 1 teaspoon sugar, and *l cup warm water* (105° to 115°F.). Let stand 5 minutes, or until foamy.

2. Meanwhile, in large bowl, combine remaining 2 tablespoons sugar, salt, 1½ cups patent durum or semolina flour, and 1½ cups all-purpose flour; stir to blend. With wooden spoon, stir in yeast mixture. With floured hands, knead to combine.

3. Turn dough onto lightly floured surface and knead until smooth and elastic, about 8 minutes, working in more all-purpose flour (about 3 tablespoons) while kneading, if necessary. Knead in raisins and fennel seeds. Shape dough into ball; place in greased large bowl, turning to grease top. Cover and let rise in warm place (80° to 85°F.) until doubled, about 40 minutes.

4. Grease 15½" by 10½" jelly-roll pan; sprinkle with remaining 2 tablespoons patent durum or semolina flour. With floured rolling pin, roll dough evenly in jelly-roll pan; press dough into corners with fingers. Cover and let rise in warm place until doubled, about 30 minutes.

5. Preheat oven to 425°F. With fingers, make deep indentations, about 1 inch apart, over surface of dough. Drizzle focaccia with remaining 3 tablespoons oil. Bake focaccia until golden, about 20 minutes. Remove focaccia from jelly-roll pan and cool on wire rack. Makes 1 loaf, 12 slices.

Patent durum or semolina flour is a high-protein, high-gluten flour milled from durum wheat. It is available in Italian grocery stores.

Each slice: About 240 calories, 5 g protein, 40 g carbohydrate, 7 g total fat (1 g saturated), 0 mg cholesterol, 360 mg sodium.

Oatmeal Batter Bread

Prep: 25 minutes plus rising and cooling
Bake: 40 minutes

2 packages active dry yeast
1 teaspoon sugar
1 cup quick-cooking oats, uncooked
½ cup light molasses
1 tablespoon margarine or butter
5 cups all-purpose flour
2 teaspoons salt

1. In small bowl, combine yeast, sugar, and ½ *cup warm water* (105° to 115° F.). Let stand 5 minutes, or until foamy.

2. In 2-quart saucepan, heat *1¾ cups water*, oats, molasses, and margarine over low heat until mixture is very warm (120° to 130°F.). Margarine does not need to melt completely.

3. In large bowl, with mixer at slow speed, beat 2 cups flour and salt until blended. Beat in liquid mixture and yeast mixture. Increase speed to medium; beat 2 minutes. Beat in ½ cup flour to make a thick batter; continue beating, scraping bowl often, 2 minutes. With spoon, stir in about 2½ cups flour to make a stiff dough that leaves side of bowl. Cover and let rise in warm place (80° to 85°F.) until doubled, about 1 hour. Grease two 2-quart round, shallow casseroles.

4. Stir down dough; divide in half and turn into casseroles. With greased fingers, turn each dough half over to grease top; shape into ball. Cover and let rise in warm place until doubled, about 45 minutes.

5. Preheat oven to 350°F. Bake until loaves test done, about 40 minutes. Remove loaves from casseroles; cool on wire racks. Makes 2 loaves, about 12 slices.

Each slice: About 130 calories, 3 g protein, 27 g carbohydrate, 1 g total fat (0 g saturated), 0 mg cholesterol, 205 mg sodium.

Country-Style Pizzas

Prep: 45 minutes plus rising
Bake: 25 to 30 minutes

2 cups all-purpose flour
¾ teaspoon salt
1 package quick-rise yeast
Cornmeal
1 small eggplant (¾ pound)
1 jar (6 ounces) marinated artichoke hearts
3 small ripe tomatoes or 1 medium tomato, cut into thin wedges

¼ cup loosely packed basil leaves, sliced
6 ounces goat cheese, such as Montrachet, broken into large chunks, or mozzarella cheese, sliced
¼ teaspoon cracked black pepper

1. In large bowl, combine flour, salt, and yeast. Stir in
¾ *cup very warm water* (120° to 130°F.) until blended and
dough comes away from side of bowl. On lightly floured
surface, knead dough 5 minutes until smooth and elastic.

2. Sprinkle large cookie sheet with cornmeal. Shape
dough into 2 balls; place in diagonally opposite corners of
cookie sheet, each about 3 inches from edges of sheet.
Cover and let rest in warm place (80° to 85°F.) 15 minutes.

3. Preheat broiler. Cut eggplant lengthwise in half. Cut
each half crosswise into ¼-inch-thick slices. Drain artichokes, reserving marinade. Cut each artichoke in half, if
large.

4. In 15½" by 10½" jelly-roll pan, toss eggplant slices
with 2 tablespoons artichoke marinade. Arrange eggplant
in single layer. With jelly-roll pan 5 to 7 inches from heat
source, broil eggplant, turning slices once, until tender and
brown, 7 to 10 minutes. Remove from broiler. Turn oven
control to 425°F.

5. In large bowl, toss eggplant, artichokes, tomatoes,
and half of basil with remaining marinade.

6. Pat and stretch 1 ball of dough into a 10-inch round.
Arrange half of eggplant mixture and half of cheese on
crust, leaving 1-inch border. Bring edge of dough up; pinch
to make a rim. Repeat to make second pizza. Cover and let
rise in a warm place 15 minutes.

7. Bake on bottom rack in oven, until topping is hot and
crust is browned and crisp, 25 to 30 minutes. Sprinkle with
cracked pepper and remaining basil. Makes 4 main-dish
servings.

*Each serving. About 380 calories, 16 g protein, 62 g carbohy-
drate, 8 g total fat (3 g saturated), 8 mg cholesterol, 785 mg
sodium.*

Bistro Pizza

Prep: 1 hour
Bake: 25 to 30 minutes

2 cups all-purpose flour
1 package quick-rise yeast
1 teaspoon salt
2½ teaspoons olive oil
Cornmeal
½ pound thin asparagus, trimmed*
6 ounces smoked mozzarella cheese, shredded (about 1½ cups)
2 medium red peppers, roasted (see page 606) and cut into thin strips
½ teaspoon coarsely ground black pepper

1. In large bowl, combine flour, yeast, and ¾ teaspoon salt. Stir in *¾ cup very warm water* (120° to 130°F.) and 2 teaspoons oil until blended and dough comes away from side of bowl. On lightly floured surface, knead dough 5 minutes until smooth and elastic.

2. Sprinkle large cookie sheet with cornmeal. Shape dough into 2 balls; place in diagonally opposite corners of cookie sheet, each 3 inches from edges of sheet. Cover and let rest 15 minutes.

3. Cut each asparagus stalk into 2-inch pieces. In small bowl, toss asparagus with ½ teaspoon oil and remaining ¼ teaspoon salt.

4. Preheat oven to 425°F. With dough on cookie sheet, pat and stretch 1 ball into a 10-inch round. Bring edge of dough up, folding to make 1-inch rim. Arrange half of cheese, half of red-pepper strips, and half of uncooked asparagus on crust. Repeat to make second pizza. Cover and let rest 15 minutes.

5. Bake on bottom rack in oven until topping is hot and crust is browned and crisp, 25 to 30 minutes. Sprinkle pizzas with black pepper. Makes 4 main-dish servings.

If thin asparagus is unavailable, use medium asparagus, cutting each stalk lengthwise in half before proceeding with Step 4.

Each serving: About 395 calories, 17 g protein, 52 g carbohydrate, 13 g total fat (6 g saturated), 33 mg cholesterol, 730 mg sodium.

Refrigerator Potato Rolls

Prep: 1 hour 30 minutes plus rising and chilling
Bake: 25 minutes

3 medium all-purpose potatoes (about 1 pound), peeled and cut
   into 1-inch chunks
2 tablespoons sugar
1 tablespoon salt
2 packages quick-rise yeast
9¾ cups all-purpose flour
4 tablespoons margarine or butter
2 large eggs

1. In 2-quart saucepan, heat potatoes and *4 cups water* to boiling over high heat. Reduce heat to low; cover and simmer until potatoes are fork-tender, about 15 minutes. Drain potatoes, reserving 1 cup potato cooking water. Return potatoes to saucepan. With potato masher, mash potatoes until smooth.

2. In large bowl, combine sugar, salt, yeast, and 3 cups flour. In 1-quart saucepan, heat margarine, *1 cup water*, and reserved potato water over low heat until very warm (120° to 130°F.). Margarine does not need to melt completely.

3. With mixer at low speed, gradually beat liquid into dry ingredients just until blended. Increase speed to medium; beat 2 minutes, occasionally scraping bowl with rubber spatula. Gradually beat in 1 egg, 1 egg yolk, and 1 cup flour to make a thick batter; continue beating, scraping bowl often, 2 minutes. Refrigerate egg white to brush on rolls later. With wooden spoon, stir in mashed potatoes then 5 cups flour, 1 cup at a time, to make a soft dough. (You may want to transfer mixture to a larger bowl for easier mixing.)

4. Turn dough onto well-floured surface and knead until smooth and elastic, about 10 minutes, working in more flour (about ¾ cup) while kneading. Cut dough into 24 equal pieces; cover and let rest 15 minutes for easier shaping. Grease 17" by 11½" roasting pan.

5. Shape dough into balls and place in roasting pan. Cover and refrigerate overnight. When ready to bake, remove wrap; cover with towel and let rise in warm place (80° to 85°F.) until doubled, about 30 minutes. (If you like, you can bake rolls the same day. After shaping into balls, cover and let rise in warm place until doubled, about 40 minutes, then bake as directed in Step 6.)

6. Preheat oven to 400°F. With fork, beat reserved egg white. Brush rolls with egg white. Bake until golden and rolls sound hollow when lightly tapped, 25 to 30 minutes. Cool slightly to serve warm, or remove rolls from pan and cool on wire rack to serve later. Reheat before serving, if desired. Pull rolls apart to serve. Makes 2 dozen rolls.

Each roll: About 225 calories, 6 g protein, 43 g carbohydrate, 3 g total fat (1 g saturated), 18 mg cholesterol, 300 mg sodium.

Dinner Rolls

Prep: 50 minutes plus rising and cooling
Bake: 15 minutes

2 packages active dry yeast
⅓ cup sugar
1 cup milk
4 tablespoons margarine or butter
5 cups all-purpose flour
1½ teaspoons salt
2 large eggs
Egg Glaze (see page 871)

1. In small bowl, combine yeast, 1 teaspoon sugar from the ⅓ cup, and *½ cup warm water* (105° to 115° F.). Let stand 5 minutes, or until foamy.

2. In 1-quart saucepan, heat 1 cup milk and margarine over low heat until mixture is very warm (120° to 130°F.). Margarine does not need to melt completely.

3. In large bowl, with mixer at slow speed, beat 1½ cups flour, salt, and remaining 5 tablespoons sugar until blended. Beat in liquid mixture and yeast mixture. Increase speed to medium; beat 2 minutes, occasionally scraping bowl with rubber spatula. Beat in eggs and ½ cup flour to make a thick batter; continue beating 2 minutes, scraping bowl often. With wooden spoon, stir in 2¼ cups flour to make a soft dough.

4. Turn dough onto lightly floured surface and knead until smooth and elastic, about 10 minutes, working in more flour (about ¾ cup) while kneading. Shape dough into ball; place in greased large bowl, turning to grease top. Cover and let rise in warm place (80° to 85°F.) until doubled, about 1 hour.

5. Punch down dough. Turn dough onto lightly floured surface; cover and let rest 15 minutes.

6. Grease large cookie sheets or muffin-pan cups, depending on type of rolls desired. Shape dough into rolls as directed below. Cover and let rise in warm place until doubled, about 30 minutes. Brush with Egg Glaze or melted margarine or butter as directed below.

7. Preheat oven to 400°F. Bake until golden and rolls test done, 10 to 15 minutes. Remove from cookie sheets or pans. Serve rolls warm or cool on wire racks to serve later. Makes 2 dozen rolls.

Each roll: About 140 calories, 4 g protein, 23 g carbohydrate, 3 g total fat (1 g saturated), 28 mg cholesterol, 185 mg sodium.

EGG GLAZE: In small bowl, beat *1 egg* and *1 tablespoon milk* until blended.

DINNER BUNS: Grease cookie sheets. Cut dough into 24 pieces. Shape each piece into 2-inch ball; with floured hands, roll each ball 4 inches long, tapering ends slightly. Place rolls, 2 inches apart, on cookie sheets; with serrated knife or single-edge razor, make a slash lengthwise through center of each roll. Let rise; brush with Egg Glaze. Makes 2 dozen rolls.

Each roll: About 140 calories.

VIENNA ROLLS: Prepare as for Dinner Buns. Let rise; brush with Egg Glaze; sprinkle with *caraway seeds*. Makes 2 dozen rolls.

Each roll: About 140 calories.

CRESCENT ROLLS: Roll half of dough into 9-inch circle. With sharp knife, cut circle into 12 wedges; brush wedges with melted margarine or butter. Starting at side opposite point, roll up wedge toward each point. Place rolls on cookie sheet; curve ends toward each other. Repeat. Let rise; brush with Egg Glaze. Makes 2 dozen rolls.

Each roll: About 140 calories.

CLOVERLEAFS: Grease twenty-four 2½- or 3-inch muffin-pan cups. Cut half of dough into 36 equal pieces; shape each piece into ball. Place 3 balls in each muffin-pan cup. Repeat. Let rise; brush with Egg Glaze or melted margarine or butter. Makes 2 dozen rolls.

Each roll: About 150 calories, 4 g protein, 23 g carbohydrate, 4 g total fat (1 g saturated), 28 mg cholesterol, 195 mg sodium.

Whole-Wheat Pitas

Prep: 1 hour 45 minutes plus chilling, rising, and cooling
Bake: 5 minutes per batch

1 large baking potato (about 10 ounces), peeled and cut into
    1-inch chunks
1 tablespoon honey
1 package active dry yeast
1 container (8 ounces) plain low-fat yogurt
1¼ teaspoons salt
¾ cup whole-wheat flour
3¼ cups all-purpose flour

1. In 2-quart saucepan, place potato chunks and *enough water to cover;* heat to boiling over high heat. Reduce heat to low; cover and simmer until potato chunks are fork-tender, about 15 minutes. Drain potatoes. Return to saucepan; heat over medium heat, shaking pan constantly, until excess liquid evaporates, about 30 seconds. With potato masher, mash potatoes until smooth. Set aside until cool, about 20 minutes.

2. In small bowl, combine honey, yeast and ¼ *cup warm water* (105° to 115°F.). Let stand 5 minutes, or until foamy.

3. In large bowl, with wooden spoon, stir cooled mashed potatoes, yeast mixture, yogurt, and salt until combined. Stir in whole-wheat flour and about 2¼ cups all-purpose flour or enough to make a soft dough. With floured hands, mix dough in bowl and shape into a ball. Cover and refrigerate overnight.

4. When ready to bake, turn dough onto well-floured surface and knead until smooth and elastic, about 10 minutes, working in more all-purpose flour (about 1 cup) while kneading (dough will be sticky). Cut dough into 16 equal pieces; with floured hands, shape each into a ball and place in 15½" by 10½" jelly-roll pan. Cover and let rise in warm place (80° to 85°F.) until doubled, about 40 minutes.

5. Preheat oven to 450°F. Place oven rack in center of oven. On floured surface, with floured rolling pin, roll 1 piece of dough into a 6-inch round, being careful to keep thickness of dough even. (If dough is too thick or too thin, pitas will not rise uniformly when baked.) Repeat with 3 more pieces of dough. With pastry brush, remove excess flour from pitas.

6. Heat large cookie sheet in oven 5 to 7 minutes. Place 4 pita rounds on preheated cookie sheet; bake until golden and puffed (some pitas will puff more than others), about 5 minutes. Cool on wire rack. Repeat with remaining dough. Makes 16 pitas.

Each pita: About 130 calories, 4 g protein, 27 g carbohydrate, 1 g total fat (0 g saturated), 1 mg cholesterol, 145 mg sodium.

Great Plains Oatmeal-Molasses Rolls

Prep: 1 hour plus rising
Bake: 40 to 45 minutes

1 cup plus 2 tablespoons old-fashioned oats, uncooked
1 package active dry yeast
1 teaspoon sugar
5 tablespoons margarine or butter, slightly softened
⅓ cup plus 2 teaspoons light molasses
1½ teaspoons salt
4¼ cups all-purpose flour

1. In medium bowl, pour *1 cup boiling water* over 1 cup oats, stir to combine. Let stand until oats absorb water, about 10 minutes.

2. Meanwhile, in small bowl, combine yeast, sugar, and *¾ cup warm water* (105° to 115°F.). Let stand 5 minutes, or until foamy.

3. In large bowl, with mixer at low speed, beat 4 tablespoons margarine until smooth; add ⅓ cup molasses, beating until combined. Beat in oat mixture, yeast mixture, and salt just until blended. Gradually beat in 2 cups flour, 1 cup at a time, just until blended. With wooden spoon, stir in 2 more cups flour.

4. Turn dough onto lightly floured surface and knead until smooth and elastic, about 5 minutes, working in more flour (about ¼ cup) while kneading. Place in greased bowl, turning to grease top. Cover and let rise in warm place (80° to 85°F.) until doubled, about 1 hour.

5. Punch down dough. On lightly floured surface, divide dough into 18 equal pieces. Shape each piece into a ball and place in greased 13" by 9" metal baking pan in 3 rows of 6 balls each. Cover and let rise in warm place until doubled, about 1 hour.

6. Preheat oven to 350°F. Bake rolls until very lightly browned, about 30 minutes.

7. Meanwhile, melt remaining 1 tablespoon margarine; stir in remaining 2 teaspoons molasses.

8. After rolls have baked 30 minutes, remove from oven and brush with molasses mixture; sprinkle with remaining 2 tablespoons oats. Bake until golden, about 15 minutes longer. Remove rolls from pan to wire rack. Cool slightly to serve warm, or cool completely to serve later. Reheat before serving, if desired. Makes 18 rolls.

Each roll: About 195 calories, 5 g protein, 35 g carbohydrate, 4 g total fat (1 g saturated), 0 mg cholesterol, 220 mg sodium.

Rosemary-Fennel Breadsticks

Prep: 40 minutes
Bake: 20 minutes per batch

2 packages quick-rise yeast
2½ teaspoons salt
2 teaspoons fennel seeds, crushed
1 teaspoon dried rosemary, crumbled
½ teaspoon coarsely ground black pepper
4¾ cups all-purpose flour
½ cup olive oil

1. In large bowl, combine yeast, salt, fennel seeds, rosemary, pepper, and 2 cups flour. With spoon, stir in *1⅓ cups* *very warm water* (120° to 130°F.); beat vigorously with spoon 1 minute. Stir in olive oil. Gradually stir in 2¼ cups flour.

2. Turn dough onto floured surface and knead until smooth and elastic, about 8 minutes, working in more flour (about ½ cup) while kneading. Cover loosely and let rest 10 minutes.

3. Preheat oven to 375°F. Grease 2 large cookie sheets. Divide dough in half. Keeping remaining dough covered, cut dough half into 32 pieces. Shape each piece into 12-inch-long rope. Place ropes on cookie sheets, about 1 inch apart.

4. Place cookie sheets on 2 oven racks and bake breadsticks 20 minutes, or until golden and crisp throughout, rotating cookie sheets between upper and lower racks halfway through baking time. Remove breadsticks from sheets; cool on wire racks. Repeat with remaining dough. Makes 64 breadsticks.

Each breadstick: About 50 calories, 1 g protein, 7 g carbohydrate, 2 g total fat (0 g saturated), 0 mg cholesterol, 85 mg sodium.

❧Sweet Breads & Rolls

Cinnamon Bubble Ring

Prep: 45 minutes plus rising and cooling
Bake: 35 minutes

2 packages active dry yeast
1 teaspoon plus 1 cup sugar
1 cup milk
6 tablespoons margarine or butter
6 cups all-purpose flour
1 teaspoon salt
2 large eggs
1 teaspoon ground cinnamon

1. In small bowl, combine yeast, 1 teaspoon of the sugar, and ½ *cup warm water* (105° to 115° F.). Let stand 5 minutes, or until foamy.

2. In 1-quart saucepan, heat milk and 4 tablespoons margarine over low heat until mixture is very warm (120° to 130°F.). Margarine does not need to melt completely.

3. In large bowl, with mixer at low speed, beat 2 cups flour, salt, and ½ cup sugar until blended. Beat in liquid mixture and yeast mixture. Increase speed to medium, beat 2 minutes. Beat in eggs and 1 cup flour; beat 2 minutes, scraping bowl often. Stir in 2½ cups flour.

4. Turn dough onto floured surface and knead until smooth and elastic, about 10 minutes, working in more flour (½ cup). Shape into ball; place in greased large bowl, turning to grease top. Cover and let rise in warm place (80° to 85°F.) until doubled, about 1 hour.

5. Punch down dough. Turn onto lightly floured surface; cut in half and cut each half into 16 pieces. Cover and let rest 15 minutes.

6. Meanwhile, in small bowl, combine cinnamon and remaining ½ cup sugar. In small saucepan over low heat, melt 2 tablespoons margarine; set aside. Grease 10-inch tube pan.

7. Shape each piece of dough into a ball. Place half of balls in tube pan. Brush with half of melted margarine; sprinkle with half of sugar mixture. Repeat. Cover and let rise in warm place until doubled, about 45 minutes.

8. Preheat oven to 350°F. Bake until browned and loaf tests done, 30 to 35 minutes. If top browns too quickly, cover with foil during last 10 minutes of baking time. Cool loaf in pan on wire rack 5 minutes; remove from pan. Serve warm, or cool loaf on wire rack to serve later. Reheat before serving, if desired. Serve as coffee cake. Makes 1 coffee cake, 16 slices.

Each slice: About 280 calories, 7 g protein, 49 g carbohydrate, 6 g total fat (1 g saturated), 29 mg cholesterol, 220 mg sodium.

Chocolate-Cherry Bread

Prep: 20 minutes plus rising and cooling
Bake: About 20 minutes

1 package active dry yeast
3 teaspoons granulated sugar
⅓ cup unsweetened Dutch-process cocoa
⅓ cup packed dark brown sugar
1¾ teaspoons salt
3½ cups all-purpose flour
1 cup warm brewed coffee (105° to 115°F.)

4 tablespoons margarine or butter, softened
1 large egg, separated
¾ cup dried tart cherries
3 ounces bittersweet chocolate, coarsely chopped

1. In cup, combine yeast, 1 teaspoon granulated sugar, and ¼ *cup warm water* (105° to 115°F.). Let stand 5 minutes, or until foamy.

2. Meanwhile, in large bowl, combine cocoa, brown sugar, salt, and 3 cups flour; stir to blend.

3. With wooden spoon, stir warm coffee, margarine, egg yolk (cover and refrigerate egg white to use later), and yeast mixture into flour mixture. With floured hands, knead to combine.

4. Turn dough onto lightly floured surface and knead until smooth and elastic, about 10 minutes, working in more flour (about ½ cup) while kneading if necessary. Knead in cherries and chocolate. Shape into ball. Place in greased bowl, turning dough to grease top. Cover and let rise in warm place (80° to 85°F.) until doubled, about 1½ hours.

5. Punch down dough. Turn dough onto lightly floured surface and cut in half; cover and let rest 15 minutes for easier shaping.

6. Shape each half of dough into a 5-inch round loaf. Place loaves, about 3 inches apart, in opposite corners on ungreased large cookie sheet. Cover and let rise in warm place until doubled, about 1 hour.

7. Preheat oven to 400°F. In cup, beat egg white with *1 teaspoon water;* brush mixture on tops of loaves. Sprinkle loaves with remaining 2 teaspoons granulated sugar. With serrated knife or single-edge razor, cut shallow X on top of each loaf. Bake until crusty, about 20 minutes. Remove from pan, cool on wire rack. Makes 2 loaves, 12 slices per loaf.

Each slice: About 135 calories, 3 g protein, 23 g carbohydrate, 4 g total fat (1 g saturated), 9 mg cholesterol, 30 mg sodium.

Overnight Sticky Buns

Prep: 1 hour plus rising and cooling
Bake: About 30 minutes

Dough
1 package active dry yeast
1 teaspoon plus ¼ cup granulated sugar
1 cup cake flour (not self-rising)
¾ cup milk
4 tablespoons margarine or butter, softened
1 teaspoon salt
3 large egg yolks
3 cups all-purpose flour

Filling
½ cup packed dark brown sugar
¼ cup dried currants
1 tablespoon ground cinnamon
4 tablespoons margarine or butter, melted

Topping
⅔ cup packed dark brown sugar
3 tablespoons margarine or butter
2 tablespoons light corn syrup
2 tablespoons honey
1¼ cups pecans, coarsely chopped

1. Prepare dough: In cup, combine yeast, 1 teaspoon sugar, and *¼ cup warm water* (105° to 115°F.). Let stand 5 minutes, or until foamy.

2. In large bowl, with mixer at low speed, beat yeast mixture with cake flour, milk, margarine, salt, egg yolks, 2 cups all-purpose flour, and remaining ¼ cup sugar until blended. With wooden spoon, stir in ¾ cup all-purpose flour.

3. Turn dough onto lightly floured surface and knead until smooth and elastic, about 5 minutes, working in more flour if necessary (about ¼ cup) while kneading. Shape dough into ball; place in greased large bowl, turning to grease top. Cover and let rise in warm place (80° to 85°F.) until doubled, about 1 hour.

4. Meanwhile, prepare filling: In small bowl, combine brown sugar, currants, and cinnamon. Reserve melted margarine or butter.

5. Prepare topping: In 1-quart saucepan, heat brown sugar, margarine, corn syrup, and honey over low heat, stirring occasionally, until melted. Grease 13" by 9" metal baking pan; pour melted brown-sugar mixture into pan and sprinkle evenly with pecans; set aside.

6. Punch down dough. Turn dough onto lightly floured surface; cover and let rest 15 minutes. Roll dough into an 18" by 12" rectangle. Brush dough with reserved melted margarine or butter and sprinkle with filling. Starting at one long side, roll dough jelly-roll fashion; place seam side down. Cut dough crosswise into 20 slices.

7. Place slices, cut sides down, in baking pan with topping, in 4 rows of 5 slices each. Cover and refrigerate at least 12 hours or up to 15 hours.

8. Preheat oven to 375°F. Remove cover from pan. Bake buns until golden, about 30 minutes. Remove pan from oven. Immediately place serving tray or jelly-roll pan over top of baking pan and invert; remove pan. Let buns cool slightly to serve warm, or cool completely to serve later. Makes 20 buns.

Each bun: About 280 calories, 4 g protein, 40 g carbohydrate, 12 g total fat (2 g saturated), 33 mg cholesterol, 205 mg sodium.

Scandinavian Tea Ring

Prep: 50 minutes plus rising and cooling
Bake: 25 minutes

1 package active dry yeast
½ cup granulated sugar
¾ cup milk
10 tablespoons (1¼ sticks)
  margarine or butter
4½ cups all-purpose flour
¾ teaspoon ground cardamom
½ teaspoon salt

2 large eggs
½ cup packed brown sugar
½ cup blanched almonds,
  toasted, and chopped
½ teaspoon ground cinnamon
Confectioners' Glaze (see page
  883)

1. In small bowl, combine yeast, 1 teaspoon of the sugar, and *¼ cup warm water* (105° to 115° F.). Let stand 5 minutes, or until foamy.

2. In 1-quart saucepan, heat milk and 8 tablespoons margarine (1 stick) over low heat until mixture is very warm (120° to 130°F.). Margarine does not need to melt completely.

3. In large bowl, with mixer at low speed, beat 1 cup flour, cardamom, salt, and remaining sugar until blended. Beat in liquid mixture and yeast mixture. Increase speed to medium, beat 2 minutes, occasionally scraping bowl with rubber spatula. Beat in eggs and 1½ cups flour to make a thick batter; continue beating 2 minutes, occasionally scraping bowl. With wooden spoon, stir in 1½ cups flour to make a soft dough.

4. Turn dough onto lightly floured surface and knead until smooth and elastic, about 10 minutes, working in more flour (about ½ cup) while kneading. Shape dough into ball; place in greased large bowl, turning to grease top. Cover and let rise in warm place (80° to 85°F.) until doubled, about 1 hour.

5. Punch down dough. Turn dough onto lightly floured surface; cover and let dough rest 15 minutes. Grease large cookie sheet. In 1-quart saucepan over medium heat, melt remaining 2 tablespoons margarine.

6. On lightly floured surface with floured rolling pin, roll dough into an 18-inch square. With pastry brush, brush dough with melted margarine or butter; sprinkle with brown sugar, almonds, and cinnamon. Roll dough up jelly-roll fashion; place on cookie sheet. Shape roll into ring; press ends together to seal and tuck them under. With kitchen shears, cut ring up to but not through inside edge at 1-inch intervals. Starting at top of ring and moving cookie sheet clockwise, gently pull and twist each cut piece, arranging in slightly overlapping pattern. Cover and let rise in warm place until doubled, about 45 minutes.

7. Preheat oven to 375°F. Bake ring until golden and bread tests done, about 25 minutes. Remove ring from cookie sheet; cool on wire rack. Frost with Confectioners' Glaze. Makes 1 tea ring, 12 slices.

Each serving: About 450 calories, 8 g protein, 67 g carbohydrate, 17 g total fat (3 g saturated), 38 mg cholesterol, 275 mg sodium.

CONFECTIONERS' GLAZE: In small saucepan, melt *2 tablespoons margarine or butter;* stir in *1½ cups confectioners' sugar, 3 tablespoons milk,* and *¼ teaspoon vanilla extract* until blended and smooth.

Apple-Filled Coffee Braid

Prep: 50 minutes plus rising and cooling
Bake: 30 minutes

5 tablespoons margarine or butter
2 medium Rome Beauty or Crispin apples (about 1¼ pounds), peeled, cored, and diced
¼ cup dark seedless raisins
¼ teaspoon ground cinnamon
½ cup sugar
¼ teaspoon salt
1 package quick-rise yeast
2¾ cups all-purpose flour
⅓ cup plus 4 teaspoons milk
1 large egg
¾ cup confectioners' sugar

1. In 10-inch skillet, heat 2 tablespoons margarine over medium-high heat until hot. Add apples, raisins, cinnamon, and ¼ cup sugar, and cook until apples are tender, about 10 minutes. Remove skillet from heat.

2. Meanwhile, into large bowl, measure salt, yeast, ½ cup flour, and remaining ¼ cup sugar; stir until combined. In 1-quart saucepan over low heat, heat ⅓ cup milk, remaining 3 tablespoons margarine, and *2 tablespoons water* until very warm (120° to 130°F.). Margarine does not need to melt completely.

3. With mixer at low speed, beat liquid into dry ingredients just until blended. Increase speed to medium; beat 2 minutes. Beat in egg and ½ cup flour to make a thick batter; beat 2 minutes, scraping bowl often. With spoon, stir in 1½ cups flour to make a soft dough.

4. Turn dough onto floured surface. With floured hands, knead dough until smooth and elastic, about 15 minutes, working in more flour (about ¼ cup) while kneading. Shape dough into ball; cover and let rest 10 minutes.

5. On large cookie sheet (17" by 14"), with floured rolling pin, roll dough into a 14" by 10" rectangle (placing a damp towel under cookie sheet will help prevent cookie sheet from moving when rolling out dough). Spread apple filling in 3-inch-wide strip lengthwise down center of dough rectangle. With sharp knife, cut dough on both sides of filling crosswise into 1-inch-wide strips just to filling.

6. Place strips at an angle across filling, alternating sides for braided effect and making sure that end of each strip is covered by the next strip so strips stay in place as dough rises. Pinch last strip to bottom of braid to seal.

7. Cover braid loosely with towel; let rise in warm place (80° to 85°F.) away from draft, until doubled, about 40 minutes.

8. Preheat oven to 350°F. Bake braid until golden, about 30 minutes. Carefully remove braid from cookie sheet; cool completely on wire rack.

9. When braid is cool, prepare icing: In cup, mix remaining 4 teaspoons milk with confectioners' sugar. Spoon icing over cooled braid. Makes 1 braid, about 12 slices.

Each slice: About 240 calories, 4 g protein, 44 g carbohydrate, 6 g total fat (1 g saturated), 19 mg cholesterol, 120 mg sodium.

∾Special Yeast Breads

Challah (Sabbath Braided Loaf)

Prep: 45 minutes plus rising and cooling
Bake: 35 minutes

1 package active dry yeast
1 tablespoon sugar
3½ cups all-purpose flour
¾ teaspoon salt
3 tablespoons vegetable oil
3 large eggs

1. In small bowl, combine yeast, sugar, and *¼ cup warm water* (105° to 115° F.). Let stand 5 minutes, or until foamy.

2. In large bowl, with mixer at low speed, beat 1 cup flour and salt, until blended. Beat in vegetable oil, *½ cup warm water* (105° to 115°F.), and yeast mixture. Increase speed to medium; beat 2 minutes, occasionally scraping bowl with rubber spatula. Reserve 1 egg yolk for brushing top of loaf; add remaining egg white and eggs, and 1 cup flour to make a thick batter; continue beating 2 minutes, scraping bowl often. With wooden spoon, stir in 1¼ cups flour to make a soft dough.

3. Turn dough onto lightly floured surface and knead until smooth and elastic, about 10 minutes, working in more flour (about ¼ cup) while kneading. Shape dough into ball; place in greased large bowl, turning to grease top. Cover and let rise in warm place (80° to 85°F.) until doubled, about 1 hour.

4. Punch down dough. Turn dough onto lightly floured surface; cover and let rest 15 minutes for easier shaping. Meanwhile, grease large cookie sheet.

5. For bottom part of loaf, cut two-thirds of dough into 3 pieces; with hands, roll each piece into a 13-inch-long rope. Place ropes side by side on cookie sheet (so loaf won't have to be moved once ropes are braided). Start braiding from the middle of the ropes. When you reach one end, turn the braid and finish braiding from the middle. Pinch ends to seal.

6. For top part of loaf, cut remaining piece of dough into 3 equal pieces. With hands, roll each piece into a 14-inch-long rope. Place ropes side by side and braid as above. Carefully place braid down center top of large braid on cookie sheet; tuck ends of top braid under bottom braid, stretching top braid if necessary, and pinch to seal well. Cover and let rise in warm place until doubled, about 45 minutes.

7. Preheat oven to 375°F. In cup, beat reserved egg yolk; use to brush top and sides of loaf. Bake loaf until golden and loaf sounds hollow when lightly tapped, about 35 minutes. Remove from cookie sheet; cool completely on wire rack. Makes 1 braided loaf, about 16 slices.

Each slice: About 140 calories, 4 g protein, 22 g carbohydrate, 4 g total fat (1 g saturated), 40 mg cholesterol, 120 mg sodium.

Stollen

Prep: 45 minutes plus rising and cooling
Bake: 25 to 30 minutes per batch

2 packages active dry yeast
1 teaspoon sugar
¾ cup milk
¾ cup (1½ sticks) margarine or butter
6 cups all-purpose flour
1½ teaspoons salt

3 large eggs
1 cup toasted slivered almonds
1 cup cut-up candied cherries
½ cup cut-up candied citron
⅓ cup golden raisins
Confectioners' sugar

1. In small bowl, combine yeast, 1 teaspoon sugar, and *½ cup warm water* (105° to 115° F.). Let stand 5 minutes, or until foamy.

2. In 1-quart saucepan, heat milk and margarine until very warm (120° to 130°F.) over low heat. Margarine does not need to melt completely.

3. In large bowl, with mixer at low speed, beat 2 cups flour and salt until blended. Beat in liquid mixture and yeast mixture. Increase speed to medium; beat 2 minutes, occasionally scraping bowl with rubber spatula. Beat in eggs and ½ cup flour to make a thick batter; continue beating 2 minutes, scraping bowl often. With wooden spoon, stir in 2¾ cups flour to make a soft dough.

4. Turn dough onto lightly floured surface and knead until smooth and elastic, about 10 minutes, working in more flour (about ¾ cup) while kneading. Shape dough into ball; place in greased large bowl, turning to grease top. Cover and let rise in warm place (80° to 85°F.) until doubled, about 1 hour. In small bowl, mix almonds, cherries, citron, and raisins.

5. Punch down dough. Turn dough onto lightly floured surface; knead nut mixture into dough. Cut dough into 3 pieces. Cover 1 piece and refrigerate.

6. With floured rolling pin, roll 1 piece of dough into 12" by 7" oval. Fold in half lengthwise; place on large cookie sheet. Repeat with second piece of dough, placing it on same cookie sheet about 3 inches from first. Cover and let rise in warm place until doubled, about 1 hour. After 30 minutes of rising time, repeat with third piece of dough using another cookie sheet.

7. Preheat oven to 350°F. Bake first 2 stollen until they test done, 25 to 30 minutes. Remove from cookie sheet; cool on wire racks. Bake third stollen; cool on wire rack. Sprinkle stollen with confectioners' sugar. Makes 3 stollen, 8 slices per loaf.

Each slice: About 250 calories, 6 g protein, 37 g carbohydrate, 9 g total fat (2 g saturated), 28 mg cholesterol, 240 mg sodium.

Festive Christmas Tree Rolls

Prep: 45 minutes plus rising and cooling
Bake: 20 to 25 minutes

2 packages active dry yeast
½ cup sugar
1½ teaspoons ground
  cardamom
4¾ cups all-purpose flour
1½ teaspoons salt
½ cup (1 stick) margarine or
  butter

2 large eggs
½ cup golden raisins
½ cup diced mixed candied
  fruit
¾ cup confectioners' sugar

1. In large bowl, combine yeast, sugar, cardamom, 1½ cups flour, and 1½ teaspoons salt. In 1-quart saucepan, heat margarine and *1 cup water* until very warm (120° to 130°F.) over low heat. Margarine does not need to melt completely.

2. With mixer at low speed, gradually beat liquid into dry ingredients just until blended. Increase speed to medium; beat 2 minutes, occasionally scraping bowl with rubber spatula. Beat in 1 egg, 1 egg yolk, and ½ cup flour to make a thick batter; continue beating 2 minutes, scraping bowl often. Refrigerate remaining egg white to brush on rolls later. With wooden spoon, stir in 2½ cups flour to make a soft dough.

3. Turn dough onto lightly floured surface and knead until smooth and elastic, about 10 minutes, working in more flour (about ¼ cup) if needed to keep dough from sticking to surface. Shape dough into ball; place in greased large bowl, turning to grease top. Cover and let rise in warm place (80° to 85°F.) until doubled, about 1 hour.

4. Punch down dough. Knead in raisins and candied fruit. Cut dough into 25 equal pieces; let rest 15 minutes for easier shaping. Shape into balls.

5. To make Christmas tree: Place 1 dough ball at top of lightly greased large cookie sheet. Make a second row by centering 2 dough balls directly under first ball and placing balls about ¼ inch apart to allow space for rising. Continue making rows by increasing each row by 1 ball and centering balls directly under previous row, until there are 6 rows in all. Leave space to allow for rising. Use last 4 balls to make trunk of tree. Cover and let rise until doubled, about 40 minutes.

6. Preheat oven to 375°F. In cup, with fork, beat reserved egg white. Brush rolls with egg white. Bake until golden and rolls sound hollow when lightly tapped, 20 to 25 minutes. Remove rolls from cookie sheet. Cool on wire rack, about 1 hour.

7. When cool, prepare glaze: In bowl, mix confectioners' sugar and *1 tablespoon water*. With spoon, drizzle glaze in zigzag pattern over tree. Makes 25 rolls.

Each roll: About 180 calories, 3 g protein, 32 g carbohydrate, 4 g total fat (1 g saturated), 17 mg cholesterol, 195 mg sodium.

Hot Cross Buns

Prep: 25 minutes plus rising and cooling
Bake: 25 minutes

2 packages active dry yeast
1 teaspoon sugar
1 cup milk
½ cup (1 stick) margarine or butter
5½ cups all-purpose flour
1 teaspoon salt
2 large eggs
1 cup dark seedless raisins
Confectioners'-Sugar Icing (see page 890)

1. In small bowl, combine yeast, 1 teaspoon sugar, and *½ cup warm water* (105° to 115° F.). Let stand 5 minutes, or until foamy.

2. In 1-quart saucepan, heat milk and margarine until very warm (120° to 130°F.) over low heat. Margarine does not need to melt completely.

3. In large bowl, with mixer at low speed, beat 1½ cups flour and salt until blended. Beat in liquid mixture and yeast mixture. Increase speed to medium; beat 2 minutes, occasionally scraping bowl with rubber spatula. Beat in 1 egg and 1 cup flour to make a thick batter; continue beating 2 minutes, scraping bowl often. With wooden spoon, stir in raisins and 2½ cups flour.

4. Turn dough onto lightly floured surface and knead until smooth and elastic, about 10 minutes, working in more flour (about ½ cup) while kneading. Shape dough into ball; place in greased large bowl, turning to grease top. Cover and let rise in warm place (80° to 85°F.) until doubled, about 1 hour.

5. Punch down dough. Turn dough onto lightly floured surface; cut into 15 equal pieces; cover and let rest 15 minutes. Grease 13" by 9" baking pan.

6. Shape dough into balls; place in baking pan in 3 rows of 5 balls. Cover and let rise in warm place until doubled, about 1 hour.

7. Preheat oven to 350°F. In small bowl, beat remaining egg. With serrated knife or single-edge razor cut a cross in each bun; brush with egg. Bake until golden, about 25 minutes.

8. Remove pan from oven to wire rack; cool buns 15 minutes. Prepare Confectioners'-Sugar Icing; spoon into decorating bag with medium writing tip. Fill cross in each bun with icing. Makes 15 buns.

Each bun: About 325 calories, 7 g protein, 58 g carbohydrate, 8 g total fat (2 g saturated), 31 mg cholesterol, 255 mg sodium.

CONFECTIONERS'-SUGAR ICING: In bowl, stir ¾ cup confectioners' sugar and 1 tablespoon milk until blended and smooth.

Herbed Toast

Prep: 15 minutes
Bake: 15 minutes

16 thin slices white bread
½ cup (1 stick) margarine or butter
½ teaspoon dried savory
½ teaspoon fennel seeds, crushed

1. Cut crusts from bread slices (reserve crusts for making bread crumbs another day). Arrange bread slices on cookie sheets.

2. Preheat oven to 400°F. In small saucepan, heat margarine, savory, and fennel seeds over medium heat until margarine melts. Brush both sides of bread slices with margarine mixture; bake 15 minutes, or until golden on both sides, turning bread slices once. Makes 8 servings.

Each serving: About 195 calories, 39 g protein, 17 g carbohydrate, 13 g total fat (2 g saturated), 0 mg cholesterol, 335 mg sodium.

Caraway-Salt Sticks

Prep: 40 minutes plus rising
Bake: 10 to 15 minutes

1 package (16 ounces) hot-roll mix
1 large egg, beaten
1 tablespoon caraway seeds
1 tablespoon coarse or kosher salt

1. Prepare hot-roll mix as label directs through kneading step. Let dough rest 15 minutes for easier handling. Meanwhile, grease 2 large cookie sheets.

2. Divide dough into 24 pieces. On lightly floured surface, with floured hands, roll each piece of dough into an 8-inch-long stick and place on cookie sheets. Cover and let rise in warm place (80° to 85°F.) until doubled, about 30 minutes.

3. Preheat oven as label directs. Brush sticks with beaten egg; sprinkle with caraway seeds and salt. Bake 2 inches apart until golden, 10 to 15 minutes. Remove sticks to wire racks. Serve sticks warm, or cool and reheat to serve warm later. Makes 24 sticks.

Each stick: About 80 calories, 2 g protein, 14 g carbohydrate, 1 g total fat (0 g saturated), 10 mg cholesterol, 345 mg sodium.

Desserts

~~~

Cheesecakes • Soufflés
Meringue Desserts
Trifles & Cream Desserts
Steamed, Bread, Rice & Other
Puddings • Other Desserts • Candies

There are many kinds of dessert. This chapter includes mousses, cheesecakes, soufflés, meringues, and many kinds of puddings. Sometimes just a piece of homemade candy is all that's needed to finish off a satisfying meal, and so you will find a selection of candy recipes at the end of this chapter. Cakes and Frostings have a chapter all to themselves (page 961), as do Pies (page 1025), Cookies (page 1099), and Frozen Desserts (page 1151).

Keep the rest of the meal in mind when you plan dessert, choosing a substantial sweet for lighter meals, a light dessert for hearty ones. You can also use dessert to help keep the meal's nutritional balance—to supply fruit, milk, or grain products, for example, when these are missing from other dishes. Remember, desserts do not just taste good—they can be good for you, too.

∾Success tips

Puddings with Milk: To keep a skin from forming as a pudding cools, press waxed paper or plastic wrap right down onto the surface of the hot pudding, then cool the pudding; when the pudding is cold, remove the paper. For an extralight, fluffy texture, beat the pudding with a hand beater or wire whisk just before serving.

Gelatin Desserts: It is important to dissolve the gelatin completely if the dessert is to set properly. Undissolved gelatin can be seen as little granules in the hot liquid.

Stir gelatin gently, not vigorously, while it dissolves. Gelatin that splashes on the side of the bowl or pan is difficult to dissolve, and vigorous stirring can produce bubbles of air in the mixture, in which case the gelatin will not be crystal clear when set.

While the mixture chills, stir it occasionally so that it cools and thickens evenly. If it thickens too much before other ingredients are added or before it is poured into a mold, melt the mixture over low heat and chill it again.

When the recipe calls for refrigerating the mixture until it mounds, test it this way: Drop some from a spoon back into the mixture. If it forms a small mound that does not quickly blend back into the mixture, it is the right consistency.

For faster setting, place the bowl containing the mixture in a larger bowl of ice water. Stir the mixture often until it reaches the desired consistency, or put the bowl in the freezer and stir occasionally until the mixture is of the desired consistency. Do not leave it in the freezer until it sets; ice crystals may form and make the gelatin watery.

Do not use fresh kiwifruit, papaya, or pineapple in gelatin mixtures. Each of these contains an enzyme that prevents setting. Canned or cooked pineapple can be used, however.

Meringues: Have the egg whites at room temperature so that they can be beaten to their fullest volume. The egg-white-and-sugar mixture should be beaten until it forms stiff, glossy peaks when the beaters are lifted; the sugar should be completely dissolved. Make sure to beat the sugar into the egg whites gradually, about 2 tablespoons at a time, beating after each addition for about 2 minutes, or until the sugar dissolves. To test, rub a bit of the mixture between your thumb and forefinger. If it feels grainy, continue beating. Follow the recipe for the correct proportion of sugar to egg whites. For our meringue recipes that call for ¾ cup sugar to 3 egg whites, it may take about 15 minutes to beat in all the sugar.

Folding Beaten Egg Whites: Folding ingredients into beaten egg whites is easy if you use a rubber spatula or a wire whisk. To fold, cut down through the center of the egg whites, across the bottom, and up the side of the bowl; then give the bowl a quarter turn and repeat just until the mixture is uniformly blended. Fold ingredients gently so that the mixture remains light and fluffy.

Melting Chocolate: Use a heavy saucepan over low heat, and stir the chocolate frequently with a rubber spatula. In a lightweight saucepan, chocolate heats too quickly and can scorch, become bitter, and develop a stiff, grainy texture. You can also melt chocolate in the top of a double boiler over hot, not boiling, water; do not let the simmering water touch the bottom of the double-boiler top.

Chocolate Substitutions: If you do not have unsweetened chocolate on hand, you can substitute cocoa. For each square (1 ounce) of unsweetened chocolate, substitute 3 tablespoons of unsweetened cocoa plus 1 tablespoon of shortening, vegetable oil, butter, or margarine.

⌒Cheesecakes

Deluxe Cheesecake

Prep: 25 minutes plus standing and chilling
Bake: 55 minutes

¾ cup (1½ sticks) margarine or butter, softened
1¼ cups plus 3 tablespoons all-purpose flour
2 cups sugar
3 egg yolks
Grated peel of 2 small lemons
5 packages (8 ounces each) cream cheese, softened
5 large eggs
¼ cup milk
Cheesecake topping (optional): sour cream, canned cherry pie
    filling, or fresh berries brushed with melted jelly

1. In small bowl, with mixer at low speed, beat margarine, 1¼ cups flour, ¼ cup sugar, 1 egg yolk, and one-half of grated lemon peel until well mixed. Shape dough into ball; flatten into disk. Wrap and refrigerate 1 hour.

2. Preheat oven to 400°F. Press one-third of dough onto bottom of 10" by 2½" springform pan. Bake 8 minutes; cool on wire rack.

3. Turn oven control to 475°F. In large bowl, with mixer at medium speed, beat cream cheese just until smooth; slowly beat in remaining 1¾ cups sugar. Reduce speed to low; beat in eggs, milk, 3 tablespoons flour, remaining 2 egg yolks, and remaining lemon peel. Increase speed to medium; beat 5 minutes.

4. Press remaining two-thirds of dough around side of pan to within 1 inch of top; do not bake. Pour cream-cheese mixture into pan; bake 12 minutes. Turn oven control to 300°F.; bake 35 minutes longer. Turn off oven; let cheesecake remain in oven 30 minutes. Remove; cool in pan on wire rack. Refrigerate cheesecake until well chilled at least 4 hours.

5. To serve, carefully remove cake from pan; top with one of the cheesecake toppings, if you like. Makes 20 servings.

Each serving: About 395 calories, 7 g protein, 28 g carbohydrate, 29 g total fat (14 g saturated), 148 mg cholesterol, 280 mg sodium.

Espresso Cheesecake

Prep: 25 minutes plus chilling
Bake: 45 minutes

1 ½ cups crushed amaretti cookies (about 40 cookies)
6 tablespoons margarine or butter, softened
1 package (8 ounces) semisweet-chocolate squares
4 packages (8 ounces each) cream cheese, softened
3 large eggs
⅔ cup sugar
½ cup milk
2 teaspoons instant espresso-coffee powder

1. In 9" by 3" springform pan, with hand, mix amaretti cookies and margarine; press onto bottom and around side of pan to within 1 inch of top and set aside.
2. Preheat oven to 350°F. In heavy small saucepan, melt 6 squares semisweet chocolate, stirring frequently, over low heat. Cool at room temperature. In large bowl, with mixer at low speed, beat cream cheese just until smooth. Add melted chocolate, eggs, sugar, milk, and coffee powder; beat until blended. Increase speed to medium; beat 3 minutes, occasionally scraping bowl with rubber spatula.
3. Pour cream-cheese mixture into crust in pan. Bake 45 minutes; cool in pan on wire rack. Cover and refrigerate cheesecake until well chilled, at least 4 hours.
4. To serve, carefully remove cheesecake from pan. Coarsely grate remaining 2 squares semisweet chocolate. Garnish top of cake with grated chocolate. Makes 20 servings.

Each serving: About 310 calories, 6 g protein, 22 g carbohydrate, 24 g total fat (13 g saturated), 83 mg cholesterol, 195 mg sodium.

Pumpkin Cheesecake

Prep: 30 minutes plus chilling
Bake: About 1 hour 25 minutes

Crumb Crust
1 cup graham-cracker crumbs
3 tablespoons margarine or butter, melted
2 tablespoons sugar

Pumpkin Filling
2 packages (8 ounces each) cream cheese, softened
1 ¼ cups sugar
1 can (16 ounces) solid-pack pumpkin (not pumpkin pie mix)
¾ cup sour cream
2 tablespoons bourbon or 2 teaspoons vanilla extract
1 teaspoon ground cinnamon
½ teaspoon ground allspice
¼ teaspoon salt
4 large eggs

Sour-Cream Topping
1 cup sour cream
3 tablespoons sugar
1 teaspoon vanilla extract
Crystallized ginger strips

1. Prepare Crumb Crust: Preheat oven to 350°F. In 9" by 3" springform pan, with fork, stir graham-cracker crumbs, melted margarine, and sugar until moistened. With hand, press mixture onto bottom of pan. Tightly wrap outside of pan with heavy-duty foil to prevent leakage when baking in water bath later. Bake crust 10 minutes. Cool completely in pan on wire rack.

2. Prepare Pumpkin Filling: In large bowl, with mixer at medium speed, beat cream cheese until smooth; slowly beat in sugar until blended, about 1 minute, scraping bowl often with rubber spatula. Reduce speed to low; beat in pumpkin, sour cream, bourbon or vanilla, cinnamon, allspice, and salt. Add eggs, 1 at a time, beating just until blended after each addition.

3. Pour pumpkin mixture into crust and place in large roasting pan. Place pan on oven rack. Carefully pour enough boiling water into pan to come 1 inch up side of springform pan. Bake until center barely jiggles, about 1 hour 10 minutes.

4. Meanwhile, prepare Sour-Cream Topping: In small bowl, with wire whisk, beat sour cream, sugar, and vanilla until blended. Remove cheesecake from water bath, leaving water bath in oven, and spread sour-cream mixture evenly over top. Return cake to water bath and bake 5 minutes longer.

5. Remove cheesecake from water bath and transfer to wire rack; discard foil. With small knife, loosen cheesecake from side of pan to help prevent cracking during cooling. Cool cheesecake completely. Cover and refrigerate cheesecake at least 6 hours or overnight, until well chilled.

6. To serve, remove side of pan. Garnish with crystallized ginger. Makes 16 servings.

Each serving: About 310 calories, 5 g protein, 30 g carbohydrate, 20 g total fat (10 g saturated), 95 mg cholesterol, 225 mg sodium.

Creamy Lemon-Ricotta Cheesecake

Prep: 20 minutes plus cooling and chilling
Bake: 1 hour 25 minutes

30 vanilla wafers
2 lemons
4 tablespoons margarine or
 butter
1¼ cups sugar
¼ cup cornstarch
2 packages (8 ounces each)
 cream cheese, softened
1 container (15 ounces) ricotta
 cheese
4 large eggs
2 cups half-and-half or light
 cream
2 teaspoons vanilla extract
Lemon-peel strips and mint
 sprigs

1. Preheat oven to 375°F. In food processor with knife blade attached or in blender at medium speed, blend vanilla wafers until fine crumbs form. (You should have about 1 cup crumbs.)

2. From lemons, grate 4 teaspoons peel and squeeze ⅓ cup juice.

3. In small saucepan, melt margarine over low heat; stir in 1 teaspoon lemon peel. In 9" by 3" springform pan, with fork, stir wafer crumbs and melted margarine mixture until moistened. With hand, press mixture firmly onto bottom of pan. Bake crust 10 minutes. Cool completely in pan on wire rack, about 30 minutes. Wrap outside of pan with foil.

4. Turn oven control to 325°F. In small bowl, stir sugar and cornstarch until blended. In large bowl, with mixer at medium speed, beat cream cheese and ricotta cheese until smooth, about 5 minutes; slowly beat in sugar mixture. Reduce speed to low, beat in eggs, half-and-half, lemon juice, vanilla, and remaining 3 teaspoons lemon peel just until blended, scraping bowl often with rubber spatula.

5. Pour cream-cheese mixture onto crust. Bake 1 hour and 15 minutes. Turn off oven; let cheesecake remain in oven 1 hour longer. Remove cheesecake from oven. Cool completely in pan on wire rack. Cover and refrigerate cheesecake at least 6 hours or overnight until well chilled.

6. To serve, remove side of pan. Garnish with lemon peel and mint sprigs. Makes 16 servings.

Each serving: About 315 calories, 8 g protein, 27 g carbohydrate, 22 g total fat (11 g saturated), 112 mg cholesterol, 200 mg sodium.

Ricotta Pie

Prep: 50 minutes plus chilling
Bake: 35 to 40 minutes

Crust
¾ cup (1½ sticks) margarine or butter, softened
⅓ cup sugar
1 large egg
2 teaspoons vanilla extract
2 cups all-purpose flour
¼ teaspoon salt

Ricotta Filling
1 package (8 ounces) cream cheese, softened
¾ cup sugar
¼ teaspoon ground cinnamon
1 container (32 ounces) ricotta cheese
5 large egg whites, lightly beaten

1. Prepare crust: In large bowl, with mixer at low speed, beat margarine with sugar until blended. Increase speed to high; beat until light and creamy, occasionally scraping bowl with rubber spatula. Reduce speed to medium; beat in egg until blended. Beat in vanilla. With wooden spoon, stir in flour and salt until dough begins to form. With hands, press dough together. Shape dough into disk; wrap and refrigerate until dough is firm enough to handle, about 30 minutes.

2. Meanwhile, prepare filling: In large bowl, with mixer at low speed, beat cream cheese, sugar, and cinnamon until blended. Increase speed to high; beat until light and creamy. Reduce speed to medium; add ricotta cheese and all but 1 tablespoon egg whites, and beat just until blended. Set filling aside.

3. Preheat oven to 400°F. Lightly grease 13" by 9" glass baking dish.

4. With floured hands, press dough onto bottom and up sides of baking dish. Brush reserved egg white over dough.

5. Pour in ricotta mixture; spread evenly. With fingers, gently push edge of dough into scalloped design around top of filling. Bake 25 minutes; reduce heat to 350°F. and bake until center barely jiggles, 10 to 15 minutes longer. Cool completely in pan on wire rack. Cover and refrigerate until well chilled, 6 hours or overnight. Makes 20 servings.

Each serving: About 275 calories, 8 g protein, 22 g carbohydrate, 17 g total fat (8 g saturated), 46 mg cholesterol, 210 mg sodium.

∾Soufflés

Fresh Apple Soufflé

Prep: 15 minutes plus chilling
Bake: 15 minutes

3 medium cooking apples (about 1 pound), peeled, cored, and cut
    into bite-size chunks
¼ cup water
3 tablespoons granulated sugar
¼ teaspoon almond extract
5 egg whites, at room temperature
Confectioners' sugar

1. In 2-quart saucepan, heat apples and water to boiling over high heat. Reduce heat to low; cover and simmer, stirring occasionally, until apples are tender, 8 to 10 minutes. Stir in granulated sugar and almond extract. Remove saucepan from heat; cool apple mixture in saucepan in refrigerator 10 minutes.

2. Meanwhile, preheat oven to 450°F. In large bowl, with mixer at high speed, beat egg whites until stiff peaks form when beaters are lifted. With rubber spatula, gently fold cooled apple mixture into beaten egg whites. Spoon mixture into 1½-quart soufflé dish. Bake until soufflé puffs and begins to brown, about 15 minutes.

3. Lightly sprinkle soufflé with confectioners' sugar and serve immediately. Makes 4 servings.

Each serving: About 125 calories, 5 g protein, 27 g carbohydrate, 0 g total fat, 0 mg cholesterol, 70 mg sodium.

Chocolate Soufflé

Prep: 25 minutes
Bake: 40 minutes

½ cup all-purpose flour
½ cup plus 2 tablespoons
  granulated sugar
1½ cups milk
3 squares (3 ounces)
  unsweetened chocolate,
  coarsely chopped or
  grated

6 large eggs, separated, at
  room temperature
Margarine or butter
¼ teaspoon salt
2 teaspoons vanilla extract
1 cup heavy or whipping
  cream (optional)
Confectioners' sugar

1. Into 2-quart saucepan, measure flour and ¼ cup granulated sugar; slowly stir in milk until smooth. Cook over medium heat, stirring constantly, until mixture thickens and boils; continue to cook, stirring, 1 minute. Remove saucepan from heat.

2. Stir chocolate into mixture until melted. Rapidly beat in egg yolks all at once until well mixed; refrigerate to cool to lukewarm, stirring occasionally.

3. Preheat oven to 375°F. Grease 2½-quart soufflé dish with margarine, sprinkle with 2 tablespoons granulated sugar.

4. In large bowl, with mixer at high speed, beat egg whites and salt until soft peaks form when beaters are lifted; gradually sprinkle in ¼ cup granulated sugar, beating until sugar has completely dissolved and whites stand in stiff peaks. With rubber spatula, gently fold chocolate mixture, one-third at a time, and vanilla into egg whites until blended.

5. Pour mixture into soufflé dish. With back of spoon, about 1 inch from edge of dish, make 1-inch-deep indentations all around in soufflé mixture (the center will rise higher than the edge, making a top-hat effect when the soufflé is done). Bake until knife inserted under top hat comes out clean, 35 to 40 minutes.

6. Meanwhile, if using heavy cream, beat until soft peaks form; cover and refrigerate.

7. When soufflé is done, lightly sprinkle with confectioners' sugar and serve immediately, with whipped cream, if you like. Makes 8 servings.

Each serving: About 245 calories, 8 g protein, 28 g carbohydrate, 12 g total fat (6 g saturated), 166 mg cholesterol, 155 mg sodium.

Orange-Liqueur Soufflé

Prep: 25 minutes
Bake: 35 minutes

4 tablespoons (½ stick) margarine or butter
⅓ cup all-purpose flour
⅛ teaspoon salt
1½ cups milk
5 tablespoons sugar
4 egg yolks
⅓ cup orange-flavored liqueur

1 tablespoon freshly grated or finely shredded orange peel
6 egg whites, at room temperature
1 cup heavy or whipping cream (optional)

1. In 2-quart saucepan, melt margarine over low heat. Stir in flour and salt until blended; gradually stir in milk. Cook, stirring constantly, until mixture thickens and boils; continue to cook 1 minute. Remove saucepan from heat.

2. With wire whisk, beat 3 tablespoons sugar into milk mixture. Rapidly beat in egg yolks all at once until well mixed. Refrigerate egg-yolk mixture to cool to lukewarm, stirring mixture occasionally. Stir in orange liqueur and grated orange peel.

3. Preheat oven to 375°F. Grease 2-quart soufflé dish with margarine; sprinkle with 2 tablespoons sugar.

4. In large bowl, with mixer at high speed, beat egg whites until stiff peaks form when beaters are lifted. With rubber spatula or wire whisk, gently fold egg-yolk mixture, one-third at a time, into beaten egg whites.

5. Pour mixture into soufflé dish. With back of spoon, about 1 inch from edge of dish, make 1 inch-deep indentations all around in soufflé mixture (the center will rise higher than the edge, making a top-hat effect when the soufflé is done). Bake until knife inserted under top hat comes out clean, 30 to 35 minutes.

6. Meanwhile, if using cream, beat until soft peaks form; cover and refrigerate.

7. When soufflé is done, serve immediately. Pass whipped cream in bowl to spoon onto each serving, if you like. Makes 8 servings.

Each serving: About 185 calories, 6 g protein, 15 g carbohydrate, 11 g total fat (3 g saturated), 113 mg cholesterol, 190 mg sodium.

Individual Ginger-Pear Soufflés

Prep: 45 to 50 minutes
Bake: 12 to 15 minutes

4 cups peeled, cored, and coarsely chopped fully ripe pears (5 to 6 pears)
1 tablespoon fresh lemon juice
2 teaspoons minced, peeled fresh ginger
1 tablespoon margarine or butter, melted
2 tablespoons plus ¼ cup sugar
6 large egg whites
½ teaspoon cream of tartar
1 teaspoon vanilla extract

1. In 2-quart saucepan, toss chopped pears with lemon juice and ginger. Cook over medium-high heat, covered, until pears are very tender, about 15 minutes. Remove cover and cook, stirring occasionally, until mixture is almost dry and reduced to about 1 cup, 10 to 15 minutes longer. Transfer to blender or food processor with knife blade attached and blend until pureed. Place puree in large bowl; let cool to room temperature.

2. Meanwhile, preheat oven to 425°F. Brush six 6-ounce ramekins or custard cups with melted margarine; sprinkle with 2 tablespoons sugar.

3. In large bowl, with mixer at high speed, beat egg whites and cream of tartar until soft peaks form. Beat in vanilla. Gradually sprinkle in remaining ¼ cup sugar and beat until sugar has dissolved and whites stand in stiff peaks when beaters are lifted.

4. With rubber spatula, fold one-third of whites into pear mixture. Fold in remaining whites. Spoon mixture into ramekins. Place ramekins in jelly-roll pan for easier handling. Bake 12 to 15 minutes, until soufflés puff and begin to brown. Serve immediately. Makes 6 servings.

Each serving: About 180 calories, 4 g protein, 38 g carbohydrate, 3 g total fat (0 g saturated), 0 mg cholesterol, 80 mg sodium.

BANANA SOUFFLÉS: Prepare soufflés as above, but instead of pear mixture, make banana puree: In food processor with knife blade attached, blend *3 large, very ripe bananas, 1 tablespoon fresh lemon juice,* and *¼ teaspoon ground cinnamon* until smooth (about 1 cup). Fold beaten egg whites into banana puree; spoon into ramekins and bake as above. Makes 6 servings.

Each serving: About 150 calories, 4 g protein, 30 g carbohydrate, 2 g total fat (1 g saturated), 0 mg cholesterol, 80 mg sodium.

PEACH OR APRICOT SOUFFLÉS: Prepare soufflés as above, but instead of pear mixture, make peach or apricot puree: Drain *1 can (1 pound, 13 ounces) peaches in heavy syrup* or *2 cans (16 ounces each) apricots in heavy syrup.* In blender or food processor with knife blade attached, blend peaches or apricots until smooth. Transfer to 4-quart saucepan and heat to boiling over medium-high heat. Reduce heat to medium-low and cook, stirring occasionally, until puree is reduced to 1 cup, 15 to 20 minutes. Transfer fruit puree to large bowl to cool. Stir in *1 tablespoon fresh lemon juice* and *⅛ teaspoon almond extract.* Fold beaten egg whites into fruit puree; spoon into ramekins and bake as above. Makes 6 servings.

Each serving: About 155 calories, 4 g protein, 32 g carbohydrate, 2 g total fat (0 g saturated), 0 mg cholesterol, 85 mg sodium.

∾Meringue Desserts

Meringue Shells

Prep: 20 minutes
Bake: About 3 hours 30 minutes

3 egg whites, at room temperature
⅛ teaspoon cream of tartar
¾ cup sugar
½ teaspoon vanilla extract

1. In small bowl, with mixer at high speed, beat egg whites and cream of tartar until soft peaks form when beaters are lifted; gradually sprinkle in sugar, 2 tablespoons at a time, beating well after each addition until sugar dissolves and whites stand in stiff, glossy peaks. Beat in vanilla extract.

2. Preheat oven to 200°F. Line large cookie sheet with foil. Onto cookie sheet, spoon meringue to make 6 mounds. Spread each mound into a 4-inch round. With tablespoon, shape each meringue round to form a nest.

3. Bake until meringues are crisp but not brown, about 3 hours and 30 minutes. Cool completely on cookie sheet on wire rack. Carefully remove foil and discard. If not using right away, store shells in tightly covered container. Makes 6 shells.

Each shell: About 105 calories, 2 g protein, 24 g carbohydrate, 0 g total fat, 0 mg cholesterol, 30 mg sodium.

MINIATURE MERINGUE SHELLS: Prepare meringue as above in Step 1. Spoon meringue into decorating bag with medium writing tip. Pipe meringue into 1½-inch rounds, about 1 inch apart, on foil-lined cookie sheet. With teaspoon, shape each meringue round to form a nest. Bake until meringues are crisp but not brown, about 1 hour. Cool and store as above. Makes 30 miniature shells.

Each shell: About 20 calories, 0 g protein, 5 g carbohydrate, 0 g total fat, 0 mg cholesterol, 5 mg sodium.

Strawberry-Filled Miniature Meringues

Prep: 30 minutes
Bake: About 1 hour

Miniature Meringue Shells (above)
30 large strawberries
¾ cup heavy or whipping cream
2 teaspoons sugar
2 tablespoons orange-flavored liqueur

1. Prepare Miniature Meringue Shells.
2. Wash and hull strawberries.
3. In small bowl, with mixer at medium speed, beat heavy cream and sugar until soft peaks form when beaters are lifted; stir in orange-flavored liqueur. Spoon some whipped-cream mixture into center of each meringue; arrange a whole strawberry, stem end down, in cream. Makes 15 servings.

Each serving: About 100 calories, 1 g protein, 13 g carbohydrate, 5 g total fat (3 g saturated), 17 mg cholesterol, 15 mg sodium.

Strawberry Dacquoise

Prep: 1 hour plus chilling
Bake: 1 hour plus 1 hour 15 minutes
standing to dry in oven

1 cup pecans, toasted
2 tablespoons cornstarch
1½ cups plus 3 tablespoons
　confectioners' sugar
6 large egg whites
½ teaspoon cream of tartar
1 package (10 ounces) frozen
　quick-thaw strawberries in
　light syrup, thawed

1 envelope unflavored gelatin
2 cups heavy or whipping
　cream
1 pint strawberries

1. In food processor with knife blade attached, or in blender at medium speed, blend pecans, cornstarch, and ¾ cup confectioners' sugar until pecans are finely ground.

2. Line large cookie sheet with foil. With toothpick, outline three 13" by 4" rectangles on foil. Spray lightly with nonstick cooking spray.

3. Preheat oven to 275°F. In large bowl, with mixer at high speed, beat egg whites and cream of tartar until soft peaks form when beaters are lifted. Sprinkle in ¾ cup confectioners' sugar, 2 tablespoons at a time, beating well after each addition, until sugar completely dissolves and whites stand in stiff glossy peaks.

4. With rubber spatula, carefully fold ground pecan mixture into egg-white mixture. With metal spatula, spread one-third of meringue inside each rectangle on cookie sheet. Bake meringues 1 hour. Turn oven off; leave meringues in oven 1 hour and 15 minutes to dry.

5. Cool meringues on cookie sheet on wire rack 10 minutes. Carefully remove foil and discard. Cool completely. Store in airtight container at room temperature (to prevent sogginess) until ready to assemble.

6. In 2-quart saucepan, with potato masher or fork, mash quick-thaw strawberries with their syrup. Sprinkle gelatin evenly over crushed strawberries; let stand 5 minutes to soften gelatin. Place saucepan over medium heat and cook strawberry mixture until gelatin dissolves completely, stirring constantly, 2 to 3 minutes. Pour mixture into small bowl; chill over bowl of ice, stirring occasionally, until mixture thickens slightly to the consistency of egg whites, about 15 minutes.

7. In small bowl, with mixer at medium speed, beat heavy cream and remaining 3 tablespoons confectioners' sugar until stiff peaks form when beaters are lifted. Gently fold in thickened strawberry mixture.

8. On serving plate, place 1 meringue layer; spread with one-third of strawberry-cream filling. Repeat with remaining meringue layers and strawberry filling, ending with strawberry filling. Refrigerate dacquoise 4 hours to soften meringue layers for easier cutting.

9. To serve, wash and hull strawberries. Cut one-third of strawberries in half; slice remaining berries. Arrange halved and sliced berries on top of dacquoise. Dust with confectioners' sugar, if you like. Makes 12 servings.

Each serving: About 305 calories, 4 g protein, 28 g carbohydrate, 21 g total fat (10 g saturated), 54 mg cholesterol, 45 mg sodium.

Ice-Cream Meringues

Prep: 35 minutes
Bake: 3 hours 30 minutes

Meringue Shells (see page 909)
1 ½ pints ice cream
¼ cup shelled pistachios or pecans, chopped

1. Prepare Meringue Shells.

2. Using ice-cream scoop or large spoon, scoop ice cream into 6 balls onto cookie sheet; freeze.

3. To serve, top each Meringue Shell with an ice-cream ball and sprinkle with chopped nuts. Makes 6 servings.

Each serving: About 310 calories, 6 g protein, 42 g carbohydrate, 15 g total fat (8 g saturated), 45 mg cholesterol, 70 mg sodium.

∾Trifles & Cream Desserts

Raspberry-Pear Trifle

Prep: 1 hour
Chill: At least 5 hours

2¼ cups milk
¾ cup plus 3 tablespoons
    sugar
¼ cup cornstarch
⅛ teaspoon salt
6 large egg yolks
¼ cup almond-flavored liqueur
    (amaretto)
3 cans (16 ounces each) pear
    halves in extralight syrup
1 package (10 ounces) frozen
    raspberries in light syrup,
    thawed

1 cup heavy or whipping
    cream
8 pairs amaretti cookies,
    coarsely crushed (about 1¼
    cups)
1 frozen ready-to-serve pound
    cake (10.75 to 12 ounces),
    thawed and cut into 1-inch
    cubes
1 cup fresh raspberries

1. Prepare custard: In 3-quart saucepan, heat 1¾ cups milk and ¾ cup sugar just to boiling over medium heat. Remove saucepan from heat.

2. Meanwhile, in medium bowl, with wire whisk, mix remaining ½ cup milk, cornstarch, and salt until smooth; beat in egg yolks until blended.

3. Into yolk mixture, stir small amount of hot milk mixture; gradually stir yolk mixture back into milk mixture in saucepan. Cook over medium heat, stirring constantly, until mixture thickens and boils. Stir in liqueur. Pour custard into clean bowl. Cover surface directly with plastic wrap to prevent skin from forming. Refrigerate until cold, at least 3 hours.

4. Drain pear halves, reserving ⅓ cup syrup (discard remaining pear syrup). In blender at low speed, blend frozen raspberries with their syrup and reserved syrup from pears.

5. In small bowl, with mixer at medium speed, beat heavy cream, gradually adding remaining 3 tablespoons sugar, until stiff peaks form when beaters are lifted. Reserve 1 rounded cup whipped cream for garnish. Gently fold remaining whipped cream into chilled custard.

6. Reserve ¼ cup amaretti cookie crumbs for garnish. In 4-quart glass trifle or serving bowl, place half of pound cake cubes; spoon half of raspberry mixture over pound cake. Arrange half of pear halves over raspberry mixture; sprinkle with half the remaining cookie crumbs. Spread half the custard over crumb layer. Repeat layering.

7. Spoon reserved whipped cream onto trifle; sprinkle with fresh raspberries and reserved cookie crumbs. Cover and refrigerate at least 2 hours or up to 24 hours for flavors to blend. Makes 16 servings.

Each serving: About 305 calories, 4 g protein, 42 g carbohydrate, 13 g total fat (6 g saturated), 105 mg cholesterol, 110 mg sodium.

Mocha-Banana Trifle

Prep: 1 hour plus chilling
Cook: 10 minutes

Custards
1 tablespoon instant espresso-coffee powder
1 tablespoon hot tap water
6 large eggs
¾ cup sugar
⅓ cup cornstarch
4 cups milk
4 tablespoons margarine or butter
2 tablespoons vanilla extract

Fudge Sauce
⅔ cup sugar
½ cup heavy or whipping cream
⅓ cup unsweetened cocoa
3 tablespoons margarine or butter

1 package (12 ounces) vanilla-wafer cookies (about 90 cookies)
6 small ripe bananas (1¾ pounds), sliced
1 cup heavy or whipping cream

1. Prepare custards: In cup, blend espresso powder and water until smooth. In large bowl, with wire whisk, beat eggs.

2. In 3-quart saucepan, stir sugar and cornstarch until blended. With wire whisk, beat in milk until blended. Heat mixture to simmering over medium-high heat. While constantly beating with whisk, gradually pour about half of simmering milk mixture into eggs. Return egg mixture to saucepan and cook over low heat, whisking constantly, until mixture thickens and begins to bubble around edge of pan (mixture will not appear to boil vigorously); simmer 1 minute. Remove saucepan from heat; stir in margarine and vanilla.

3. Pour half of custard into medium bowl; cover surface directly with plastic wrap to prevent skin from forming. Pour remaining custard into another medium bowl; stir in espresso mixture until blended; cover surface with plastic wrap. Do not refrigerate.

4. Prepare sauce: In 1-quart saucepan, cook sugar, heavy cream, cocoa, and margarine over medium heat until mixture is smooth and boils; set aside.

5. To layer trifle: In 4-quart glass trifle or deep serving bowl, place 1 layer of vanilla-wafer cookies (about 30 cookies). Spoon warm espresso custard on top of cookies; top with half of sliced bananas and half of warm fudge. Place another layer of cookies (about 30) on top of fudge; top with warm vanilla custard. Top with remaining bananas, fudge, and cookies.

6. In small bowl, with mixer at medium speed, beat heavy cream until stiff peaks form when beaters are lifted;

spoon over top layer of cookies. Cover trifle loosely and refrigerate 6 hours or overnight. Makes 24 servings.

Each serving: About 270 calories, 4 g protein, 33 g carbohydrate, 14 g total fat (6 g saturated), 88 mg cholesterol, 125 mg sodium.

Crème Caramel

Prep: 15 minutes plus chilling
Bake: 55 minutes

½ cup sugar
4 large eggs
2 cups milk
1 teaspoon vanilla extract
¼ teaspoon salt

1. Preheat oven to 325°F. Grease six 6-ounce custard cups. In small saucepan heat ¼ cup sugar over medium heat, stirring constantly, until melted and a light caramel color. Immediately pour into prepared custard cups; swirl to coat bottoms.

2. In large bowl, with wire whisk or fork, beat eggs and remaining ¼ cup sugar until well blended. Beat in milk, vanilla, and salt until well mixed; pour mixture into custard cups.

3. Place custard cups in 13" by 9" baking pan; fill pan with enough *boiling water* to come halfway up sides of custard cups. Bake until knife inserted in center of each custard comes out clean, 50 to 55 minutes. Remove cups from water in baking pan; cover and refrigerate until chilled, about 2 hours.

4. To serve, with small spatula, carefully loosen custard from cups and invert each custard onto a chilled dessert plate, allowing caramel syrup to drip from cup onto custard. Makes 6 servings.

Each serving: About 165 calories, 7 g protein, 20 g carbohydrate, 6 g total fat (3 g saturated), 153 mg cholesterol, 180 mg sodium.

Pumpkin Crème Caramel

Prep: 30 minutes plus chilling
Bake: 55 minutes

6 strips (about 3" by 1" each)
   orange peel
1¼ cups sugar
¼ cup water
1 can (12 ounces) evaporated
   milk
1 cup heavy or whipping
   cream

1 cup solid-pack pumpkin (not
   pumpkin pie mix)
6 large eggs
¼ cup orange-flavored liqueur
1 teaspoon vanilla extract
1 teaspoon ground cinnamon
Pinch nutmeg
Pinch salt

1. In 1-quart saucepan, heat orange peel, ¾ cup sugar, and water to boiling over high heat; cover and cook 10 minutes. With fork, remove orange-peel strips and discard. Continue cooking sugar mixture, uncovered, until it has turned amber in color, about 3 minutes longer. Pour caramel into 9" by 5" loaf pan, swirling to coat bottom. (Hold pan with pot holders to protect hands from heat of caramel.) Set aside.

2. In heavy 2-quart saucepan, heat evaporated milk, heavy cream, and remaining ½ cup sugar just to boiling over medium-high heat.

3. Meanwhile, preheat oven to 350°F. In large bowl, with wire whisk, mix pumpkin, eggs, orange liqueur, vanilla, cinnamon, nutmeg, and salt until blended.

4. Gradually whisk hot milk mixture into pumpkin mixture until blended. Pour pumpkin mixture through strainer into medium bowl with pouring spout, then into caramel-coated loaf pan. Place loaf pan in roasting pan; place on oven rack. Pour enough *boiling water* into roasting pan to come three-fourths of the way up side of loaf pan. Bake until knife comes out clean when inserted 1 inch from edge of custard (center will jiggle slightly), about 55 minutes.

5. Carefully remove loaf pan from water. Cool 1 hour in pan on wire rack. Refrigerate crème caramel overnight. To unmold, run small spatula around sides of loaf pan; invert crème caramel onto serving plate, allowing caramel syrup to drip down from pan (some caramel may remain in pan). Makes 12 servings.

Each serving: About 180 calories, 4 g protein, 21 g carbohydrate, 9 g total fat (5 g saturated), 106 mg cholesterol, 61 mg sodium.

Crème Brûlée

Prep: 10 minutes plus chilling
Cook: 18 minutes

3 cups heavy or whipping cream
6 egg yolks
⅓ cup sugar
1 teaspoon vanilla extract
¼ cup packed brown sugar

1. In 1-quart saucepan, heat heavy cream over medium heat until tiny bubbles form around edge of pan.

2. Meanwhile, in 2-quart saucepan, with wire whisk or spoon, beat yolks with sugar until blended. Slowly stir in warm cream. Cook over medium-low heat, stirring constantly, until mixture coats back of spoon, about 15 minutes (do not boil or mixture will curdle). Stir in vanilla. Pour into 1½-quart broiler-safe casserole; refrigerate until well chilled, about 6 hours.

3. About 1 to 2 hours before serving, preheat broiler. Sift brown sugar over top of chilled cream mixture; broil, until sugar melts, making shiny crust, 3 to 4 minutes. Chill.

4. To serve, with spoon, tap to break brown-sugar crust. Makes 10 servings.

Each serving: About 330 calories, 3 g protein, 14 g carbohydrate, 30 g total fat (18 g saturated), 226 mg cholesterol, 35 mg sodium.

Panna Cotta with Raspberry Sauce

Prep: 20 minutes plus chilling
Cook: 10 minutes

1 envelope unflavored gelatin
1 cup milk
½ vanilla bean or 1½
  teaspoons vanilla extract
1¾ cups heavy or whipping
  cream
¼ cup sugar

1 strip (3" by 1") lemon peel
1 cinnamon stick (3 inches)
1 package (10 ounces) frozen
  raspberries in syrup
2 tablespoons red currant jelly
2 teaspoons cornstarch
Fresh raspberries

1. In 2-cup measuring cup, sprinkle gelatin over milk; set aside to allow gelatin to soften. Scrape inside of vanilla bean and reserve seeds.

2. In 1-quart saucepan, heat cream, sugar, lemon peel, cinnamon stick, vanilla-bean seeds, and vanilla-bean pod to boiling over high heat, stirring occasionally. (If using vanilla extract, stir in after removing lemon peel.) Reduce heat to low; simmer, stirring occasionally, 5 minutes. Stir in milk mixture; heat until gelatin dissolves, 2 to 3 minutes.

3. Remove lemon peel, cinnamon stick, and vanilla-bean pod from cream mixture. Pour mixture into medium bowl set in large bowl of ice water. Stir mixture until it just begins to set, about 10 to 12 minutes.

4. Pour cream mixture into eight 4-ounce ramekins or custard cups. Place ramekins on jelly-roll pan for easier handling. Refrigerate until well chilled, at least 4 hours or overnight.

5. Meanwhile, prepare the raspberry sauce: Into 2-quart saucepan, press frozen raspberries and their syrup through coarse sieve to remove seeds. Discard seeds. Stir in currant jelly and cornstarch. Cook over medium heat, stirring, until mixture boils and thickens; boil 1 minute. Pour sauce into bowl; cover and refrigerate.

6. Invert each ramekin onto a dessert plate. Spoon some raspberry sauce around each panna cotta. Garnish with raspberries. Makes 8 servings.

Each serving: About 270 calories, 3 g protein, 19 g carbohydrate, 20 g total fat (13 g saturated), 75 mg cholesterol, 35 mg sodium.

Cappuccino Cream with Warm Chocolate Sauce

Prep: 20 minutes plus chilling
Cook: 5 minutes

Cappuccino Cream
1 envelope unflavored gelatin
¼ cup milk
¾ cup finely ground espresso-coffee beans (about ¾ cup whole coffee beans)
1 cinnamon stick (3 inches)
1¼ cups water
½ cup sugar
1¾ cups heavy or whipping cream

Chocolate Sauce
2 squares (2 ounces) semisweet chocolate
¼ cup heavy or whipping cream

1. Prepare Cappuccino Cream: In 1-cup measuring cup, sprinkle gelatin over milk; set aside to allow gelatin to soften.

2. In 1-quart saucepan, heat ground coffee, cinnamon stick, and water, over high heat, stirring often, just until mixture begins to boil. Remove saucepan from heat; cover and let steep 10 minutes.

3. Line sieve with coffee filter or paper towel and place over 2-cup measuring cup. Pour coffee mixture into sieve to drain; discard cinnamon stick.

4. Return liquid coffee to same saucepan. Add gelatin mixture and sugar, and heat over medium-low heat, stirring frequently, until gelatin and sugar have completely dissolved, about 1 minute.

5. Pour coffee mixture and cream into medium bowl set in large bowl of ice water. Stir mixture until it just begins to set, about 20 minutes.

6. Immediately pour cream mixture into eight 4-ounce ramekins or custard cups. Place ramekins on jelly-roll pan for easier handling. Cover and refrigerate until well chilled, at least 4 hours or overnight.

7. Meanwhile, prepare Chocolate Sauce: In 1-quart saucepan, heat chocolate and cream over low heat, stirring constantly, until chocolate melts. Remove saucepan from heat; cool 5 minutes. (If making ahead, cover and reheat before using.)

8. To unmold each Cappuccino Cream, warm small knife under hot water; run along inside edge of ramekin. Then, firmly tap side of ramekin against palm of hand to break seal completely. Invert each ramekin onto a dessert plate. Spoon warm Chocolate Sauce over each dessert to serve. Makes 8 servings.

Each serving: About 295 calories, 3 g protein, 20 g carbohydrate, 24 g total fat (14 g saturated), 83 mg cholesterol, 30 mg sodium.

ᥫ᭡Steamed, Bread, Rice & Other Puddings

Christmas Pudding with Hard Sauce

Prep: 1 hour
Cook: About 2 hours

Plum Pudding

2¼ cups all-purpose flour
1 cup fresh bread crumbs
1 teaspoon baking powder
1 teaspoon ground cinnamon
½ teaspoon salt
¼ teaspoon ground nutmeg
¼ teaspoon ground cloves
1 cup pitted prunes, chopped
1 cup pitted dates, chopped
¾ cup dark seedless raisins
½ cup walnuts, toasted and chopped
1 medium Granny Smith apple, peeled, cored, and coarsely shredded

1 teaspoon freshly grated lemon peel
1 cup (2 sticks) margarine or butter, softened
1 cup packed light brown sugar
2 large eggs
⅔ cup buttermilk
½ cup dark molasses
⅓ cup dark rum or brandy

Hard Sauce

1 cup (2 sticks) butter, softened (do not use margarine)
2 cups confectioners' sugar
¼ cup dark rum or brandy
1 teaspoon vanilla extract

1. Heavily grease two 1-quart heat-safe bowls. Cut 2 pieces of foil, one to cover top of each bowl, allowing 1-inch overhang. Grease one side of each piece of foil; set aside.

2. Prepare Plum Pudding: In large bowl, combine flour, bread crumbs, baking powder, cinnamon, salt, nutmeg, and cloves; stir until combined. Add prunes, dates, raisins, walnuts, apple, and lemon peel to flour mixture. With hands, thoroughly toss mixture until fruits are well coated and separate. Set aside.

3. In another bowl, with mixer at low speed, beat margarine and brown sugar. Increase speed to high; beat until creamy, about 1 minute. Reduce speed to medium; add eggs, 1 at a time, beating well after each addition. Beat in buttermilk, molasses, and rum (mixture will look curdled). With spoon, stir margarine mixture into flour mixture until blended.

4. Spoon batter into prepared bowls; cover with foil, greased side down. Tie foil tightly in place with string around outside of bowls so pudding surface does not get wet from steam.

5. Place a metal cookie cutter in each of two 5- or 6-quart saucepots. (The cookie cutters keep bowls elevated during steaming.) Pour in *enough water to measure 1½ inches*. Set bowls on top of cookie cutters. Cover saucepots and heat water to boiling over high heat. Reduce heat to low; simmer puddings until toothpick inserted through foil into center comes out clean, about 2 hours.

6. Meanwhile, prepare Hard Sauce: In small bowl, with mixer at medium speed, beat butter until smooth. Reduce speed to low; gradually beat in confectioners' sugar until creamy. Beat in rum or brandy and vanilla. Spoon into 1 or 2 decorative crocks or bowls. Cover and chill until serving time. Makes about 2 cups.

7. When puddings are done, cool in bowls on wire racks 5 minutes. Remove foil; loosen puddings with small spatula or sharp knife and invert onto serving dishes. Serve hot with Hard Sauce. Makes 2 puddings, 8 servings each.

Each serving of pudding without Hard Sauce: About 365 calories, 4 g protein, 56 g carbohydrate, 15 g total fat (3 g saturated), 27 mg cholesterol, 290 mg sodium.

Each tablespoon Hard Sauce: About 85 calories, 0 g protein, 8 g carbohydrate, 6 g total fat (4 g saturated), 15 mg cholesterol, 60 mg sodium.

Bread Pudding with Warm Banana-Maple Sauce

Prep: 20 minutes, plus chilling
Bake: About 45 minutes

1 loaf (about 1 pound) unsliced rich egg bread, such as challah, cut into 1-inch-thick slices
3 cups milk
½ teaspoon salt
10 large eggs
¼ cup plus 1 tablespoon sugar

1 teaspoon ground cinnamon
4 tablespoons margarine or butter
6 medium firm bananas, peeled and sliced into ¼-inch-thick slices
1 cup (8 ounces) maple syrup

1. Grease shallow 3½- to 4-quart ceramic casserole or 13" by 9" glass baking dish. Arrange bread slices, overlapping slightly, in dish.

2. In medium bowl, with wire whisk or fork, beat milk, salt, eggs, and ¼ cup sugar until well mixed. Slowly pour egg mixture over bread slices; prick bread slices with fork and press slices down to absorb egg mixture. Spoon any egg mixture that bread has not absorbed back over bread slices.

3. In cup, with fork, mix cinnamon and remaining 1 tablespoon sugar; sprinkle over top of bread pudding and dot with 2 tablespoons margarine. Cover and refrigerate overnight.

4. Preheat oven to 325°F. Remove cover and bake pudding until knife inserted in center comes out clean, about 45 minutes.

5. Meanwhile, prepare sauce: In nonstick 12-inch skillet melt remaining 2 tablespoons margarine over medium-high heat. Add banana slices and cook until lightly browned, about 3 minutes. Pour maple syrup over bananas; heat to boiling. Boil until mixture thickens slightly, 2 to 3 minutes. Serve warm sauce in bowl with bread pudding. Makes 12 servings.

Each serving: About 365 calories, 11 g protein, 52 g carbohydrate, 13 g total fat (4 g saturated), 205 mg cholesterol, 410 mg sodium.

Black and White Bread Pudding

Prep: 40 minutes plus standing
Bake: 1 hour 20 minutes

1 loaf (16 ounces) sliced firm white bread
4 cups milk
½ cup sugar
1 tablespoon vanilla extract
½ teaspoon salt
9 large eggs
3 squares (3 ounces) white chocolate, grated
3 squares (3 ounces) bittersweet chocolate, grated
White-Chocolate Custard Sauce (below)

1. Preheat oven to 325°F. Grease 13" by 9" glass or ceramic baking dish; set aside. Place bread slices on large cookie sheet; lightly toast in oven, turning once, 20 to 30 minutes. Place bread slices in baking dish, overlapping slightly.

2. Meanwhile, in very large bowl, with wire whisk or fork, beat milk, sugar, vanilla, salt, and eggs until blended. Stir in grated white and bittersweet chocolates. Pour milk mixture evenly over bread; let stand 30 minutes for bread to absorb most of the milk mixture, occasionally spooning mixture over bread.

3. Cover baking dish with foil; bake 1 hour. Remove cover and bake until top is golden, 15 to 20 minutes longer.

4. While pudding is baking, prepare White-Chocolate Custard Sauce. Serve bread pudding warm, or refrigerate to serve cold later. Makes 16 servings.

WHITE-CHOCOLATE CUSTARD SAUCE: Finely chop *3 squares (3 ounces) white chocolate*; place in large bowl. In small bowl, with wire whisk, beat *4 large egg yolks*. Gradually whisk in *¼ cup sugar* until combined; set aside. In heavy 2-quart saucepan, heat *1 cup milk* and *¾ cup heavy or whipping cream*, over medium heat until small bubbles form around edge of pan. Into egg mixture, beat small amount of hot milk mixture. Slowly pour egg mixture back into milk mixture, stirring rapidly to prevent lumping. Reduce heat to low; cook, stirring constantly, until mixture thickens slightly and coats back of a spoon, about 5 minutes. (Mixture should be about 160°F., but do not boil or it will curdle.) Pour mixture over white chocolate, stirring to combine. Serve custard sauce warm or refrigerate to serve cold. Makes about 2½ cups.

Each serving of bread pudding without sauce: About 240 calories, 9 g protein, 28 g carbohydrate, 11 g total fat (5 g saturated), 129 mg cholesterol, 285 mg sodium.

Each tablespoon White-Chocolate Custard Sauce: About 40 calories, 1 g protein, 3 g carbohydrate, 3 g total fat (2 g saturated), 29 mg cholesterol, 5 mg sodium.

Baked Lemon-Cake Pudding

Prep: 15 minutes
Bake: About 1 hour 5 minutes

2 lemons
2 large eggs, separated, at room temperature
¼ teaspoon salt
¾ cup sugar
1 cup milk
3 tablespoons all-purpose flour
2 tablespoons margarine or butter, melted
Whipped cream (optional)

1. Preheat oven to 350°F. Grease 1-quart casserole. From lemons, grate 1 tablespoon peel and squeeze ⅓ cup juice; set aside.

2. In small bowl, with mixer at high speed, beat egg whites with salt until soft peaks form when beaters are lifted. Gradually sprinkle in ½ cup sugar, 2 tablespoons at a time, beating after each addition, until sugar has completely dissolved and whites stand in stiff peaks.

3. In another small bowl, with same beaters and with mixer at medium speed, beat egg yolks and remaining ¼ cup sugar; add milk, lemon peel and juice, flour and margarine, and beat until well mixed. With rubber spatula or wire whisk, gently fold egg-yolk mixture into egg whites just until mixed. Pour batter into casserole.

4. Set casserole in 13" by 9" baking pan; place on oven rack. Fill baking pan halfway up with *boiling water*. Bake until top is golden and firm, 55 to 65 minutes. (Pudding separates into cake layer on top, sauce layer underneath.) Cool casserole on wire rack. Serve as is or topped with whipped cream, if you like. Makes 6 servings.

Each serving without cream: About 195 calories, 4 g protein, 30 g carbohydrate, 7 g total fat (2 g saturated), 76 mg cholesterol, 190 mg sodium.

INDIVIDUAL LEMON-CAKE PUDDINGS: Grease six 6-ounce custard cups. Prepare as above; pour into custard cups. Bake puddings as above, 40 to 45 minutes.

Brownie Pudding

Prep: 20 minutes
Bake: 30 minutes

2 teaspoons instant-coffee granules or powder
2 tablespoons hot tap water
1 cup all-purpose flour
½ cup sugar
2 teaspoons baking powder
¼ teaspoon salt
¾ cup unsweetened cocoa

½ cup milk
4 tablespoons margarine or butter, melted
1 teaspoon vanilla extract
½ cup packed light brown sugar
1¾ cups boiling water
Vanilla ice cream (optional)

1. Preheat oven to 350°F. In cup, blend instant coffee and hot tap water until smooth; set aside.

2. In medium bowl, combine flour, sugar, baking powder, salt, and ½ cup cocoa. In 2-cup measuring cup, with fork, mix milk, melted margarine, vanilla, and dissolved instant coffee. With spoon, stir liquid mixture into dry mixture just until blended. Pour batter into ungreased 8" by 8" glass baking dish.

3. In small bowl, with spoon, combine brown sugar and remaining ¼ cup cocoa; sprinkle over batter. Carefully pour water over brownie mixture in baking dish; do not stir.

4. Bake 30 minutes (dessert will separate into cake and pudding layers). Cool in pan on wire rack 10 minutes, then serve right away. Top with ice cream, if you like. Makes 8 servings.

Each serving without ice cream: About 235 calories, 4 g protein, 44 g carbohydrate, 7 g total fat (2 g saturated), 2 mg cholesterol, 250 mg sodium.

Chocolate Pudding

Prep: 5 minutes
Cook: 6 minutes

⅓ cup sugar
¼ cup cornstarch
3 tablespoons unsweetened cocoa
Pinch salt
2 cups milk
1 square (1 ounce) semisweet chocolate, finely chopped
1 teaspoon vanilla extract

1. In 2-quart saucepan, combine sugar, cornstarch, cocoa, and salt. Whisk in milk until blended. Heat mixture to boiling over medium heat, stirring constantly. Add chocolate and cook, stirring, until chocolate melts and pudding thickens slightly, about 1 minute.

2. Remove saucepan from heat; stir in vanilla. Spoon pudding into custard cups. Serve warm, or cover surface of pudding directly with plastic wrap and refrigerate to serve later. Makes 4 servings.

Each serving: About 215 calories, 5 g protein, 35 g carbohydrate, 6 g total fat (4 g saturated), 17 mg cholesterol, 100 mg sodium.

Cool Berry Pudding

Prep: 20 minutes plus cooling and overnight to chill
Cook: 8 to 10 minutes

12 slices firm white bread, crusts removed
2 cups blueberries, washed and picked over
⅔ cup sugar
2 cups sliced strawberries
2 cups raspberries
1 cup blackberries
Whipped cream (optional)
Berries

1. Arrange bread slices on wire rack to dry out while preparing filling.

2. Meanwhile, in 3-quart saucepan, heat blueberries and sugar to boiling over medium heat, stirring often; boil 1 minute. Stir in strawberries, raspberries, and blackberries, and cook, stirring, 1 minute longer. Remove saucepan from heat; cool berry filling to room temperature.

3. Line deep 1½-quart bowl with plastic wrap, allowing ends of plastic wrap to hang over side of bowl. Line bowl with some bread slices, trimming to fit and using scraps to fill in spaces. Spoon 2 cups berry filling into bowl. Cover with a layer of bread, trimming to fit. Spoon remaining filling into bowl and top with remaining bread.

4. Cover bowl loosely with plastic wrap. Place a saucer small enough to fit just inside rim of bowl on plastic wrap. Place several heavy cans on top of saucer to weight down pudding. Place bowl on plate to catch any overflow; refrigerate until pudding is firm and bread is saturated with berry juices, about 24 hours.

5. Remove cans, saucer, and top layer of plastic wrap. Invert pudding onto serving plate; remove and discard plastic wrap. Spoon juices over pudding. Serve with whipped cream, if you like. Garnish with berries. Makes 8 servings.

Each serving without whipped cream: About 195 calories, 3 g protein, 44 g carbohydrate, 2 g total fat (0 g saturated), 0 mg cholesterol, 150 mg sodium.

Rich Rice Pudding

Prep: 5 minutes plus chilling
Cook: 1 hour 5 minutes

7 cups milk
1 cup regular long-grain rice
½ cup sugar
½ teaspoon salt
1 cup heavy or whipping cream
1 teaspoon vanilla extract

In 4-quart saucepan, heat milk, rice, sugar, and salt to boiling over medium heat. Reduce heat to low; cover and simmer, stirring occasionally, until rice is very tender, about 1 hour. Pour rice mixture into medium bowl; stir in cream and vanilla. Refrigerate until well chilled. Makes 8 servings.

Each serving: About 365 calories, 9 g protein, 41 g carbohydrate, 18 g total fat (11 g saturated), 70 mg cholesterol, 265 mg sodium.

Coconut Rice Pudding

Prep: 10 minutes plus chilling
Cook: 25 minutes

1 cup Japanese or other short grain rice
½ cup sugar
½ teaspoon salt
3 cups water
1 can (14 to 15 ounces) unsweetened light coconut milk (not
    cream of coconut)
1 large mango, peeled and sliced
½ cup shaved, peeled fresh coconut, toasted, or ¼ cup
    sweetened flaked coconut, toasted

1. In 3-quart saucepan, heat rice, sugar, salt, and water
to boiling over high heat. Reduce heat to low; cover and
simmer 15 minutes.

2. Increase heat to medium; stir in coconut milk and
cook, uncovered, stirring occasionally, until rice is tender,
about 10 minutes.

3. Transfer rice pudding to serving bowl; cover and refrigerate at least 3 hours or overnight to serve cold. Top
with mango slices and toasted coconut before serving.
Makes about 5 cups or 8 servings.

*Each serving: About 225 calories, 2 g protein, 40 g carbohydrate,
6 g total fat (3 g saturated), 0 mg cholesterol, 145 mg sodium.*

Cherries and Cream Rice Pudding

Prep: 15 minutes plus chilling
Cook: About 1 hour 15 minutes

½ vanilla bean or 1 tablespoon vanilla extract
6 cups milk
¾ cup sugar
¾ cup Arborio rice (Italian short-grain rice) or regular long-grain rice
½ cup dried cherries or raisins
2 tablespoons dark rum (optional)
¼ teaspoon salt
½ cup heavy or whipping cream

1. With knife, cut vanilla bean lengthwise in half. Scrape out and reserve seeds from inside both halves.

2. In 4-quart saucepan, heat milk, sugar, vanilla-bean seeds, and vanilla-bean halves to boiling over medium-high heat, stirring occasionally. (If using vanilla extract, add in Step 3 with rum.) Stir in rice; heat to boiling. Reduce heat to low; cover and simmer, stirring occasionally, until mixture is very creamy and slightly thickened (pudding will firm up upon chilling), about 1 hour and 15 minutes. Remove and discard vanilla-bean halves.

3. Spoon rice pudding into large bowl; stir in dried cherries, rum if using, and salt. Cool slightly, then cover and refrigerate until well chilled, at least 6 hours.

4. Up to 2 hours before serving, whip cream until stiff peaks form when beaters are lifted. Fold whipped cream, half at a time, into rice pudding. Makes 12 servings.

Each serving with rum: About 230 calories, 5 g protein, 34 g carbohydrate, 8 g total fat (5 g saturated), 30 mg cholesterol, 110 mg sodium.

Nantucket Indian Pudding

Prep: 30 minutes plus cooling
Bake: About 2 hours

⅔ cup yellow cornmeal
4 cups milk
½ cup light molasses
4 tablespoons margarine or
    butter, cut up
¼ cup sugar

1 teaspoon ground ginger
1 teaspoon ground cinnamon
½ teaspoon salt
¼ teaspoon ground nutmeg
Whipped cream or vanilla ice
    cream (optional)

1. Preheat oven to 350°F. Grease shallow 1½-quart glass or ceramic baking dish.

2. In small bowl, stir cornmeal and 1 cup milk until combined. In 4-quart saucepan, heat remaining 3 cups milk to boiling over high heat. Stir in cornmeal mixture; heat to boiling. Reduce heat to low and cook, stirring often to avoid lumps, 20 minutes. (Mixture will be very thick.) Remove saucepan from heat; stir in molasses, margarine, sugar, ginger, cinnamon, salt, and nutmeg until blended.

3. Pour batter evenly into baking dish. Place baking dish in roasting pan; place on oven rack. Carefully pour *enough boiling water* into roasting pan to come halfway up side of baking dish. Cover with foil and bake pudding 1 hour. Remove foil and bake until lightly browned and just set, about 1 hour longer.

4. Carefully remove baking dish from water. Cool pudding in pan on wire rack for 30 minutes. Serve pudding warm with whipped cream or vanilla ice cream if you like. Makes 8 servings.

Each serving without whipped or ice cream: About 245 calories, 5 g protein, 34 g carbohydrate, 10 g total fat (4 g saturated), 17 mg cholesterol, 275 mg sodium.

∽Other Desserts

Strawberry Shortcake

Prep: 30 minutes
Bake: 15 minutes

2 cups all-purpose flour
2 teaspoons baking powder
½ teaspoon salt
2 tablespoons plus ½ cup sugar
⅓ cup shortening
⅔ cup milk
2 pints strawberries
3 tablespoons margarine or butter, softened
1 cup heavy or whipping cream

1. Preheat oven to 425°F. Grease 8-inch round cake pan.

2. In medium bowl, combine flour, baking powder, salt, and 2 tablespoons sugar. With pastry blender or 2 knives used scissor-fashion, cut in shortening until mixture resembles coarse crumbs. Add milk; quickly stir just until mixture forms soft dough and leaves side of bowl.

3. On lightly floured surface, knead dough 10 times. Pat dough evenly into cake pan. Bake until golden, about 15 minutes.

4. Wash strawberries. Reserve 4 whole strawberries for garnish; hull and halve or quarter remaining strawberries. In medium bowl, mix cut-up strawberries and remaining ½ cup sugar until sugar has dissolved (do not let strawberries stand too long or they will become very liquid).

5. Invert shortcake on work surface. With long, serrated knife, carefully split hot shortcake horizontally. Spread both cut surfaces of shortcake with margarine. Cool to room temperature.

6. In small bowl, with mixer at medium speed, beat heavy cream until soft peaks form when beaters are lifted.

7. Place bottom half of shortcake, cut side up, on dessert platter; top with half of strawberry mixture. Arrange top cake half, cut side down, on strawberry mixture. Spoon remaining strawberry mixture over top of cake, then pile whipped cream on top of strawberries. Garnish cream with reserved whole strawberries. Makes 10 servings.

Each serving: About 340 calories, 4 g protein, 37 g carbohydrate, 20 g total fat (8 g saturated), 35 mg cholesterol, 260 mg sodium.

Brown Sugar–Pear Shortcakes

Prep: 45 minutes
Bake: 12 to 15 minutes

1 cup all-purpose flour
¾ cup cake flour (not self-rising)
3 tablespoons sugar
2½ teaspoons baking powder
½ teaspoon salt
9 tablespoons cold margarine or butter
⅔ cup milk
2½ pounds ripe Bosc pears (about 6 medium), peeled, cored, and cut lengthwise into ¾-inch wedges
¼ cup packed light brown sugar
¼ teaspoon ground cinnamon
2 strips (2½" by ½" each) lemon peel
¼ cup water
1 cup heavy or whipping cream, whipped

1. Preheat oven to 425°F. Prepare biscuits:

2. In large bowl, combine all-purpose flour, cake flour, sugar, baking powder, and salt. With pastry blender or 2 knives used scissor-fashion, cut in 5 tablespoons cold margarine, until mixture resembles coarse crumbs. Add milk; quickly stir just until mixture forms a soft dough that comes together (dough will be sticky).

3. Turn dough onto floured surface; knead gently 6 to 8 times to mix thoroughly. With floured hands, pat dough 1 inch thick.

4. With floured 2½-inch round biscuit cutter, cut out as many biscuits as possible. With wide spatula, place biscuits, 1 inch apart, on ungreased cookie sheet. Press trimmings together; cut as above to make 6 biscuits in all. Bake until golden, 12 to 15 minutes.

5. Meanwhile, prepare pears: In nonstick 12-inch skillet, melt remaining 4 tablespoons margarine over medium-high heat. Add pears and cook, stirring carefully with rubber spatula, 10 to 15 minutes, until pears are brown and tender. Stir in brown sugar, cinnamon, lemon-peel strips, and water; cook 1 minute. Discard lemon peel.

6. To serve, with fork, split each warm biscuit horizontally in half. Spoon pear mixture onto bottom halves of biscuits; top with whipped cream, then biscuit tops. Makes 6 servings.

Each serving: About 580 calories, 6 g protein, 67 g carbohydrate, 34 g total fat (13 g saturated), 58 mg cholesterol, 590 mg sodium.

Country Apple Crisp

Prep: 15 minutes
Bake: 35 minutes

1 large orange
7 medium Golden Delicious or Cortland apples (about 2½ pounds), peeled, cored, and cut into 1-inch-thick slices
½ cup dried cherries or raisins
1 teaspoon ground cinnamon
½ teaspoon salt

¼ teaspoon ground nutmeg
⅓ cup plus ¼ cup packed light brown sugar
2 tablespoons plus ⅓ cup all-purpose flour
½ cup quick-cooking or old-fashioned oats, uncooked
3 tablespoons margarine or butter

1. Preheat oven to 425°F. From orange, grate ½ teaspoon peel; squeeze ⅓ cup juice.

2. In 2-quart glass or ceramic baking dish, toss orange peel, orange juice, apple slices, cherries, cinnamon, salt, nutmeg, ⅓ cup brown sugar, and 2 tablespoons flour.

3. In small bowl, mix oats, remaining ⅓ cup flour, and remaining ¼ cup brown sugar. With pastry blender or 2 knives used scissor-fashion, cut in margarine until mixture resembles coarse crumbs. Sprinkle over apple mixture.

4. Bake apple crisp, covering with foil if necessary to prevent overbrowning, until apples are tender and topping is lightly browned, 30 to 35 minutes. Cool crisp slightly on wire rack to serve warm, or, cool crisp completely on rack to serve later. Reheat before serving, if desired. Makes 8 servings.

Each serving: About 260 calories, 3 g protein, 52 g carbohydrate, 6 g total fat (1 g saturated), 0 mg cholesterol, 195 mg sodium.

Apple Brown Betty

Prep: 35 minutes plus standing
Bake: About 50 minutes

8 slices firm white bread, torn into ½-inch pieces
½ cup (1 stick) margarine or butter, melted
1 teaspoon ground cinnamon
2½ pounds Granny Smith apples (about 6 medium), peeled, cored, and thinly sliced
⅔ cup packed light brown sugar
2 tablespoons fresh lemon juice
1 teaspoon vanilla extract
¼ teaspoon ground nutmeg

1. Preheat oven to 400°F.

2. Grease shallow 2-quart ceramic or glass baking dish. In 15½" by 10½" jelly-roll pan, bake bread pieces, stirring occasionally, until very lightly toasted, 12 to 15 minutes.

3. In medium bowl, stir melted margarine and ½ teaspoon ground cinnamon until blended. Add toasted bread; toss gently until evenly moistened.

4. In large bowl, toss sliced apples, brown sugar, lemon

juice, vanilla, ground nutmeg, and remaining ½ teaspoon
ground cinnamon.

5. Place ½ cup bread pieces in baking dish. Top with
half the apple mixture, then 1 cup bread pieces. Place remaining apple mixture on top; sprinkle with remaining
bread pieces, leaving a 1-inch border all around edge.

6. Cover dish with foil and bake 40 minutes. Remove
foil and bake until apples are tender and crumbs on top are
brown, about 10 minutes longer. Let stand 10 minutes before serving. Serve warm. Makes 8 servings.

*Each serving: About 305 calories, 2 g protein, 48 g carbohydrate,
13 g total fat (2 g saturated), 0 mg cholesterol, 275 mg sodium.*

Country Plum Cobbler

Prep: 20 minutes plus cooling
Bake: 50 to 60 minutes

2½ pounds ripe red or purple plums (about 10 medium), each
    pitted and cut into quarters
½ cup sugar
2 tablespoons all-purpose flour
1¾ cups reduced-fat all-purpose baking mix
¼ cup yellow cornmeal
¾ cup water

1. Preheat oven to 400°F. In large bowl, toss plums with
sugar and flour. Spoon plum mixture into shallow 2-quart
ceramic or glass baking dish. Cover loosely with foil. Bake
until plums are very tender, 30 to 35 minutes.

2. Remove baking dish from oven. In medium bowl, stir
baking mix, cornmeal, and water just until combined. Drop
10 heaping spoonfuls of batter randomly on top of plum
mixture.

3. Bake cobbler, uncovered, until biscuits are browned
and plum mixture is bubbly, 20 to 25 minutes longer. Cool
slightly to serve warm, or cool completely to serve later.
Reheat before serving, if desired. Makes 10 servings.

Each serving: About 190 calories, 3 g protein, 41 g carbohydrate, 2 g total fat (0 g saturated), 0 mg cholesterol, 230 mg sodium.

Puffy Apple Pancake

Prep: 20 minutes
Bake: 15 minutes

2 tablespoons margarine or butter
½ cup plus 2 tablespoons sugar
¼ cup water
6 medium Granny Smith or Newtown Pippin apples (about 2
    pounds), peeled, cored, and each cut into 8 wedges
3 large eggs
¾ cup milk
¾ cup all-purpose flour
¼ teaspoon salt

1. Preheat oven to 425°F. In 12-inch oven-safe skillet (if skillet is not oven-safe, wrap handle of skillet with double layer of foil), heat margarine, ½ cup sugar, and water to boiling over medium-high heat. Add apple wedges; cook, stirring occasionally, until apples are golden and sugar mixture begins to caramelize, about 15 minutes.
2. Meanwhile, in blender at medium speed or in food processor with knife blade attached, blend eggs, milk, flour, salt, and remaining 2 tablespoons sugar until batter is smooth.
3. When apple mixture in skillet is golden and lightly caramelized, pour batter over apples. Place skillet in oven; bake until puffed and golden, about 15 minutes. Serve immediately. Makes 10 servings.

Each serving: About 180 calories, 4 g protein, 32 g carbohydrate, 5 g total fat (1 g saturated), 66 mg cholesterol, 110 mg sodium.

Skillet Blueberry Crisps

Prep: 10 minutes
Cook: 5 minutes

1 medium lemon
2 tablespoons brown sugar
2 teaspoons cornstarch
2 teaspoons almond-flavored liqueur
½ cup cold water
1 tablespoon margarine or butter, softened
1 pint (about 2½ cups) blueberries, picked over and rinsed
10 amaretti cookies, coarsely crushed
Confectioners' sugar

1. From lemon, grate ¼ teaspoon peel and squeeze 1 teaspoon juice.

2. In 2-quart saucepan, with spoon, stir lemon peel, lemon juice, brown sugar, cornstarch, almond liqueur, and water. Add margarine and half of blueberries; lightly crush blueberries with potato masher or side of spoon. Cook blueberry mixture over medium heat, stirring constantly, until mixture boils. Stir in remaining blueberries and boil, stirring, 2 minutes longer.

3. Spoon hot blueberry mixture into 4 dessert or custard cups; top with amaretti-cookie crumbs and sprinkle with confectioners' sugar. Serve warm. Makes 4 servings.

Each serving: About 160 calories, 1 g protein, 30 g carbohydrate, 4 g total fat (1 g saturated), 0 mg cholesterol, 50 mg sodium.

Rhubarb-Apple Crumble

Prep: 20 minutes
Bake: About 45 minutes

⅓ cup granulated sugar
1 tablespoon cornstarch
1¼ pounds rhubarb, cut into
   ½-inch pieces (about 4
   cups)
3 medium Golden Delicious
   apples (about 1¼ pounds),
   peeled, cored, and cut into
   1-inch pieces

½ cup packed brown sugar
2 tablespoons margarine or
   butter, softened
¼ teaspoon ground cinnamon
⅓ cup old-fashioned or quick-
   cooking oats, uncooked
¼ cup all-purpose flour

1. Preheat oven to 375°F. In large bowl, stir granulated
sugar and cornstarch until blended. Add rhubarb and apples; toss to coat. Spoon fruit mixture into 11" by 7" glass
baking dish or shallow 2-quart casserole.

2. In medium bowl, with fingers, mix brown sugar, margarine, and cinnamon until blended. Stir in oats and flour
until evenly combined.

3. Sprinkle oat topping evenly over fruit in baking dish.
Bake crumble until filling is hot and bubbly and topping is
browned, about 45 minutes. Serve warm. Makes 6 servings.

*Each serving: About 255 calories, 3 g protein, 53 g carbohydrate,
5 g total fat (1 g saturated), 0 mg cholesterol, 60 mg sodium.*

Summer Peach Cobbler

Prep: 45 minutes
Bake: About 45 minutes

Peach Filling
16 to 18 ripe medium peaches (about 6 pounds), peeled, pitted,
    and sliced (about 13 cups)
⅔ cup granulated sugar
½ cup packed dark brown sugar
¼ cup cornstarch
¼ cup fresh lemon juice

Lemon Biscuits
2 cups all-purpose flour
2½ teaspoons baking powder
1 teaspoon grated lemon peel
¼ teaspoon salt
½ cup plus 1 teaspoon granulated sugar
4 tablespoons cold margarine or butter, cut into pieces
⅔ cup plus 1 tablespoon half-and-half or light cream

1. Preheat oven to 425°F. Prepare Peach Filling: In 8-quart Dutch oven, combine peaches, granulated sugar, brown sugar, cornstarch, and lemon juice. Heat to boiling over medium heat, stirring occasionally; boil 1 minute. Spoon hot peach mixture into 13" by 9" glass baking dish. Place sheet of foil under baking dish and crimp edges to catch any overflow during baking. Bake 10 minutes.

2. Meanwhile, prepare Lemon Biscuits: In medium bowl, combine flour, baking powder, lemon peel, salt, and ½ cup granulated sugar. With pastry blender or 2 knives used scissor-fashion, cut in margarine until mixture resembles coarse crumbs. Stir ⅔ cup half-and-half into flour mixture just until ingredients are blended and mixture forms soft dough that leaves side of bowl.

3. Turn dough onto lightly floured surface. With lightly floured hands, pat dough into a 10" by 6" rectangle. With floured knife, cut rectangle lengthwise in half, then cut each half crosswise into 6 pieces.

4. Remove baking dish from oven. Place biscuits on top of hot fruit filling. Brush biscuits with remaining 1 tablespoon half-and-half and sprinkle with remaining 1 teaspoon granulated sugar. Return cobbler to oven and bake until filling is hot and bubbly and biscuits are golden brown, about 35 minutes longer. Cool cobbler on wire rack about 1 hour to serve warm, or cool completely to serve cold later. Reheat before serving, if desired. Makes 12 servings.

Each serving: About 330 calories, 4 g protein, 69 g carbohydrate, 6 g total fat (2 g saturated), 5 mg cholesterol, 180 mg sodium.

∾What's In a Name?

Old-fashioned cobblers, crisps, pandowdies, and other fruit desserts are popping up on menus everywhere. To brush up on your after-dinner vocabulary:

- *Brown Betty:* a layered mixture of buttered bread crumbs, fruit, and spices that is covered and baked until tender.
- *Buckle:* a coffee cake with berries in the batter and crumbly topping. (Sometimes, the batter is poured over the fruit and baked.)
- *Cobbler:* a deep-dish fruit dessert (in a casserole) that is topped with a thick layer of biscuit dough or with individual pieces ("cobbles") of dough; it can also have a bottom crust.
- *Crisp:* fruit that is covered with a rich crumb topping (a homemade mixture or bread, cookie, or cracker crumbs blended with butter, sugar, and sometimes nuts) and baked until the topping is browned and the fruit is bubbly.
- *Crumble:* British cousin to the crisp, but with oats and brown sugar added to the topping.
- *Grunt (or slump):* similar to the cobbler, except the fruit is usually simmered on the stove in a saucepan, not baked. The dough is dropped on top, where it steams to a dumpling consistency. (The word *grunt* comes from the sound the fruit makes as it bubbles and stews.)

- *Pandowdy:* a deep dish of sliced fruit that is covered with tender pastry. Before the crust is baked completely, it's cut into pieces and pressed back into the fruit to absorb the juices. The name is sometimes traced to the dessert's plain ("dowdy") appearance.
- *Shortcake:* "short" (rich) biscuit sliced in half and filled with sweetened fruit and whipped cream. Strawberries are the traditional filling, but other fruits work beautifully.

Apple Strudel

Prep: 50 minutes plus cooling
Bake: 40 minutes

3 large green cooking apples (1¼ pounds)	¼ teaspoon salt
½ cup sugar	¾ cup dried bread crumbs
½ cup dark seedless raisins	½ package (16 ounces) fresh or frozen (thawed) phyllo
½ cup walnuts, chopped	½ cup (1 stick) margarine or butter, melted
½ teaspoon ground cinnamon	Confectioners' sugar
¼ teaspoon ground nutmeg	

1. Grease large cookie sheet. Peel, core, and thinly slice apples. In large bowl, toss apples, sugar, raisins, walnuts, cinnamon, nutmeg, salt, and ¼ cup bread crumbs.

2. Cut two 24-inch lengths of waxed paper; overlap 2 long sides about 2 inches; fasten with cellophane tape.

3. On waxed paper, arrange 1 sheet (about 18" by 12") of phyllo; brush with some melted margarine; sprinkle with scant tablespoon bread crumbs. Continue layering phyllo, brushing each sheet with melted margarine and sprinkling every other sheet with crumbs.

4. Preheat oven to 375°F. Starting along 1 long side of phyllo, spoon apple mixture to within about ½ inch from edges to cover about half of phyllo rectangle. From apple-mixture side, roll phyllo, jelly-roll fashion.

5. Place roll, seam side down, on cookie sheet. Brush

with remaining melted margarine. Bake until golden, about 40 minutes. Cool on cookie sheet 30 minutes.

6. To serve, sprinkle strudel lightly with confectioners' sugar; cut into slices. Serve warm or at room temperature. Makes 16 servings.

Each serving: About 195 calories, 2 g protein, 27 g carbohydrate, 9 g total fat (2 g saturated), 0 mg cholesterol, 225 mg sodium.

Galatoboureko (Greek Custard Pastry)

Prep: 35 minutes plus cooling
Bake: About 1 hour

4 cups milk
2 cups heavy or whipping cream
½ cup plus 1 tablespoon quick enriched farina
½ cup sugar
6 egg yolks
1 tablespoon vanilla extract
½ package (16 ounces) fresh or frozen (thawed) phyllo
¾ cup (1½ sticks) margarine or butter, melted
Lemon Syrup (see page 946)

1. Preheat oven to 375°F. Grease 13" by 9" baking pan.

2. In 3-quart saucepan, heat milk and heavy cream to boiling over medium-high heat. In bowl, stir farina and sugar until blended; gradually sprinkle into milk mixture, stirring with spoon. Heat to boiling over medium-high heat. Reduce heat to medium-low; cook, stirring, until mixture thickens slightly, 5 to 10 minutes. Remove saucepan from heat.

3. In large bowl, with mixer at high speed, beat egg yolks and vanilla well. Reduce speed to medium and gradually beat in farina mixture.

4. In baking pan, place 1 sheet of phyllo, allowing it to extend up side of pan; brush with melted margarine. Repeat to make about 5 more layers. Pour farina mixture into phyllo-lined pan.

5. Cut remaining phyllo into approximately 13" by 9"

rectangles. Place 1 sheet of phyllo on farina; brush with margarine. Repeat with remaining phyllo and margarine, overlapping small strips of phyllo to make rectangles, if necessary. Cut top phyllo layers lengthwise into 4 strips; cut each strip into 6 pieces. Bake until top is golden brown and puffy, about 35 minutes.

6. Meanwhile, prepare Lemon Syrup. Pour hot syrup over baked dessert. Cool on wire rack at least 1 hour before serving.

7. To serve, finish cutting through layers. Serve warm or refrigerate to serve cold. Makes 24 servings.

Each serving: About 245 calories, 4 g protein, 21 g carbohydrate, 16 g total fat (7 g saturated), 86 mg cholesterol, 150 mg sodium.

LEMON SYRUP: In 1-quart saucepan, heat *¾ cup sugar* and *⅓ cup water* to boiling over medium heat, stirring occasionally. Reduce heat to low; simmer until syrup thickens slightly, 8 minutes. Stir in *1 tablespoon lemon juice*.

Baklava

Prep: 25 minutes
Bake: 1 hour 25 minutes

16 ounces walnuts (4 cups), finely chopped
½ cup sugar
1 teaspoon ground cinnamon
1 package (16 ounces) fresh or frozen (thawed) phyllo
1 cup (2 sticks) margarine or butter, melted
1 jar (12 ounces) honey

1. Preheat oven to 300°F. Grease 13" by 9" baking dish. In large bowl, mix walnuts, sugar, and cinnamon.

2. Cut phyllo into 13" by 9" rectangles. In baking dish, place 1 sheet of phyllo; brush with some margarine. Repeat to make 5 more layers of phyllo; sprinkle with 1 cup walnut mixture.

3. Place 1 sheet of phyllo in baking dish over walnut mixture; brush with melted margarine. Repeat to make at least 6 layers, overlapping any small strips of phyllo to make rectangles, if necessary. Sprinkle 1 cup walnut mixture over phyllo. Repeat layering 2 times, ending with walnut mixture.

4. Place remaining phyllo on top of last walnut layer; brush with margarine. With sharp knife, cut just halfway through layers in triangle pattern to make 24 servings: Cut lengthwise into 3 strips; cut each strip crosswise into 4 rectangles, then cut each rectangle diagonally into 2 triangles. Bake until top is golden brown, about 1 hour and 25 minutes.

5. In small saucepan, heat honey over medium-low heat until hot but not boiling. Spoon hot honey evenly over hot baklava. Cool Baklava in pan on wire rack at least 1 hour, then cover with foil and let stand at room temperature until serving.

6. To serve, with sharp knife, finish cutting through layers. Makes 24 servings.

Each serving: About 310 calories, 4 g protein, 29 g carbohydrate, 21 g total fat (3 g saturated), 0 mg cholesterol, 195 mg sodium.

Mini Éclairs

Prep: 1 hour plus chilling
Bake: 35 minutes

Pastry Cream
3 large egg yolks
⅓ cup sugar
3 tablespoons cornstarch
1½ cups milk
1 tablespoon margarine or butter
2 teaspoons vanilla extract

Cream-Puff Dough
6 tablespoons margarine or butter
1 cup water
1 cup all-purpose flour
1 tablespoon sugar
¼ teaspoon salt
4 large eggs

Chocolate Glaze
4 squares (4 ounces) semisweet chocolate
1 tablespoon margarine or butter
1 tablespoon milk
1 tablespoon light corn syrup

1. Prepare Pastry Cream: In medium bowl, with wire whisk, beat egg yolks, sugar, and cornstarch; set aside. In 2-quart saucepan, heat milk just to boiling. While constantly beating with whisk, gradually pour about half of hot milk into yolk mixture. Pour yolk mixture back into milk in saucepan and cook over medium-low heat, whisking constantly, until mixture thickens and begins to bubble around edge of pan (mixture will not boil vigorously). Simmer pastry cream, whisking constantly, 1 minute; it must reach at least 160°F. Remove saucepan from heat; stir in margarine and vanilla. Transfer mixture to bowl; cover surface directly with plastic wrap to prevent skin from forming and refrigerate until cold, at least 2 hours.

2. Meanwhile, prepare Cream-Puff Dough: Preheat oven to 400°F. Grease and flour large cookie sheet (17" by 14"). In 2-quart saucepan, heat margarine and water over high heat until mixture boils. Reduce heat to low; add flour, sugar, and salt all at once, and stir vigorously with wooden spoon until mixture forms a ball and leaves side of saucepan. Remove saucepan from heat. Add eggs, 1 at a time, beating well with wooden spoon after each addition, until mixture is smooth and shiny.

3. Spoon dough into decorating bag with large round tip (about ½ inch in diameter). Pipe dough in five 12-inch-long strips (about 1 inch wide) lengthwise down cookie sheet, leaving 1½ inches between strips. Bake until golden, about 30 minutes. Remove cookie sheet from oven; poke strips in several places with fork to let out steam. Bake 5 minutes longer.

4. Remove strips from cookie sheet. While strips are warm, with serrated knife slice each strip horizontally in half to make top and bottom halves. Cool completely on wire rack. When cool, with fingertips, remove some of soft centers from top and bottom halves.

5. While strips are cooling, prepare Chocolate Glaze: In heavy small saucepan, melt semisweet chocolate, margarine, milk, and corn syrup over low heat, stirring frequently. Spoon warm glaze into sturdy zip-tight bag. Cut tip of bag to make small hole; use to drizzle glaze in crosshatch pattern over éclair-strip tops.

6. With clean decorating bag and tip, fill cooled éclair-strip bottoms with Pastry Cream. (Do not overfill—you may have a small amount of cream left over.) Top with glazed tops and refrigerate until ready to serve, up to 1 hour.

7. To serve, cut strips crosswise with serrated knife into 2-inch-long pieces. Makes 30 éclairs.

Each éclair: About 100 calories, 2 g protein, 11 g carbohydrate, 6 g total fat (1 g saturated), 51 mg cholesterol, 15 mg sodium.

Easy Napoleons

Prep: 45 minutes
Bake: 10 minutes

1 large egg white	⅓ cup plus 1 tablespoon sugar
Pinch salt	½ cup sliced natural almonds
1 teaspoon water	1 pint strawberries
4 sheets (about 16" by 12" each) fresh or frozen (thawed) phyllo	¾ cup heavy or whipping cream
2 tablespoons margarine or butter, melted	½ teaspoon vanilla extract

1. Preheat oven to 375°F. In small bowl, lightly beat egg white, salt, and water; set aside.

2. Place 1 phyllo sheet on work surface; brush with melted margarine and sprinkle with 1 rounded tablespoon sugar. Top with a second phyllo sheet; brush with melted margarine and sprinkle with 1 rounded tablespoon sugar. Repeat layering with phyllo, melted margarine, and sugar 1 more time. Top with remaining phyllo and brush with egg-white mixture.

3. Cut phyllo stack lengthwise into 3 strips, then cut each strip crosswise into 4 squares. Cut each square diagonally in half to make 24 triangles in all. Place triangles on ungreased large cookie sheet; sprinkle with sliced almonds and 1 rounded tablespoon sugar. Bake phyllo triangles until golden, 10 minutes; transfer to wire racks to cool.

4. Just before serving, wash, hull, and thinly slice strawberries. In small bowl, with mixer at medium speed, beat cream, vanilla, and remaining 1 tablespoon sugar until stiff peaks form.

5. To assemble, place 1 phyllo triangle in center of each of 8 dessert plates. Top each with about 1 tablespoon whipped cream and about 1 rounded tablespoon sliced strawberries. Place a second phyllo triangle on top of each, rotating it so that points of second triangle are angled slightly away from points of first triangle. Repeat with remaining cream and strawberries; top with a third triangle. Serve immediately. Makes 8 servings.

*Each serving: About 220 calories, 4 g protein, 19 g carbohydrate,
15 g total fat (6 g saturated), 31 mg cholesterol, 115 mg sodium.*

Blueberry-Lemon Tiramisu

Prep: 50 minutes plus chilling
Cook: 15 minutes

Lemon Curd
2 large lemons
3 large egg yolks
2 large eggs
⅓ cup granulated sugar
6 tablespoons margarine or butter

Blueberry Sauce
6 cups blueberries, washed and picked over
1 to 1½ cups confectioners' sugar, depending on sweetness of
   berries
6 tablespoons water
2 to 4 teaspoons fresh lemon or lime juice, or to taste

Syrup
1 large lemon
¼ cup granulated sugar
¼ cup water

1 package (7 ounces) Italian-style ladyfingers (savoiardi)
8 ounces mascarpone cheese
½ cup heavy or whipping cream

1. Prepare Lemon Curd: From 2 lemons, finely grate 1
tablespoon peel and squeeze ⅓ cup juice. In heavy 2-quart
saucepan, with wire whisk, beat peel, juice, yolks, eggs,
and granulated sugar just until mixed. Add margarine and
cook over low heat, stirring constantly, until mixture coats
the back of a spoon. (Do not boil or mixture will curdle.)
Pour Lemon Curd through sieve into bowl; cover surface

directly with plastic wrap and refrigerate until cool, about 45 minutes.

2. Meanwhile, make Blueberry Sauce: In 2-quart saucepan, cook blueberries, 1 cup confectioners' sugar, and water over medium heat, stirring occasionally, until sauce has thickened slightly, 5 to 8 minutes. Remove saucepan from heat; stir in 2 teaspoons lemon juice. Taste and adjust sugar and juice; cool to room temperature.

3. Make Syrup: With vegetable peeler, remove 3 strips peel (about 3" by ¾" each) from lemon. In small saucepan, heat lemon-peel strips, granulated sugar, and water over medium heat, stirring occasionally, until mixture boils and sugar has dissolved. Pour sugar syrup into small bowl; cool to room temperature.

4. Line bottom of 13" by 9" glass baking dish with ladyfingers. Discard peel from syrup. Brush ladyfingers with syrup. Spread sauce over ladyfingers.

5. In large bowl, with wire whisk, mix Lemon Curd, mascarpone, and cream until smooth; spoon evenly over sauce and spread to cover top. Cover and refrigerate at least 6 hours or overnight. Makes 12 servings.

Each serving: About 380 calories, 5 g protein, 49 g carbohydrate, 21 g total fat (9 g saturated), 133 mg cholesterol, 130 mg sodium.

Strawberry-Waffle Chantilly

Prep: 15 minutes plus thawing

1 package (10 ounces) frozen strawberries in quick-thaw pouch
½ cup heavy or whipping cream
¼ teaspoon vanilla or almond extract
4 frozen waffles, toasted

1. Thaw frozen strawberries as label directs. Drain, reserving 2 tablespoons liquid.

2. Meanwhile, in small bowl, with mixer at medium speed, beat heavy cream and vanilla extract until stiff peaks form when beaters are lifted.

3. Reserve 4 strawberries for garnish. With rubber spatula or wire whisk, gently fold remaining strawberries and reserved liquid into whipped cream just until blended.

4. To serve, place each waffle on an individual dessert plate. Spoon some strawberry mixture on top of each waffle. Garnish with reserved strawberries. Makes 4 servings.

Each serving: About 245 calories, 39 g protein, 28 g carbohydrate, 14 g total fat (7 g saturated), 50 mg cholesterol, 295 mg sodium.

Almond-Cordial Parfaits

Prep: 15 minutes plus softening

1 pint coffee ice cream
¼ cup almond-flavored liqueur
¼ cup crushed amaretti cookies (about 6 cookies)
½ cup heavy or whipping cream, whipped

1. Let ice cream stand at room temperature until softened, about 15 minutes.

2. Into four 6-ounce freezer-safe parfait glasses, spoon one-third of ice cream; top with one-half of almond-flavored liqueur, then another one-third of ice cream. Sprinkle with one-half of cookies; top with remaining ice cream and almond-flavored liqueur. Spoon all of the whipped cream on top; sprinkle with remaining cookies. Serve immediately or place in freezer to serve later. Makes 4 servings.

Each serving: About 450 calories, 6 g protein, 33 g carbohydrate, 30 g total fat (18 g saturated), 161 mg cholesterol, 100 mg sodium.

∽Candies

Dark Chocolate–Rum Truffles

Prep: 25 minutes plus chilling

8 squares (8 ounces) bittersweet chocolate*
½ cup heavy or whipping cream
3 tablespoons unsalted butter, softened and cut into pieces
    (no substitutions)
2 tablespoons dark Jamaican rum (optional)
⅓ cup hazelnuts (filberts), toasted, with skins removed and finely
    chopped
3 tablespoons unsweetened cocoa

1. In food processor with knife blade attached, process chocolate until finely ground.

2. In 1-quart saucepan, heat heavy cream to boiling over medium-high heat. With food processor running, add hot cream, butter, and rum, if using, to chocolate and process until blended and smooth.

3. Grease 9" by 5" metal loaf pan; line with plastic wrap. Pour chocolate mixture into pan; spread evenly. Refrigerate until cool and firm enough to cut, about 3 hours, or freeze 1 hour.

4. Remove chocolate mixture from pan by lifting edges of plastic wrap and inverting chocolate block onto cutting board; discard plastic wrap. Cut chocolate into thirty-two pieces. (To cut chocolate mixture easily, dip knife in hot water and wipe dry.)

5. Place chopped hazelnuts in small bowl; place cocoa in another small bowl. One at a time, dip 16 chocolate pieces in hazelnuts to coat. Dip remaining chocolate pieces in cocoa. Store in tightly covered container, with waxed paper between layers, in refrigerator. Makes 32 truffles. Truffles may be made ahead and stored in refrigerator for up to 2 weeks, or frozen for up to 1 month. Remove from freezer 10 minutes before serving.

Each truffle: About 70 calories, 1 g protein, 5 g carbohydrate, 6 g total fat (3 g saturated), 8 mg cholesterol, 2 mg sodium.

*Or, in place of bittersweet chocolate, use 7 ounces semisweet and 1 ounce unsweetened chocolate.

Chocolate-Nut Fudge

Prep: 15 minutes plus cooling
Cook: 15 minutes

3 cups sugar
1 cup half-and-half
¾ cup unsweetened cocoa
3 tablespoons light corn syrup
¼ teaspoon salt
4 tablespoons margarine or butter
1 teaspoon vanilla extract
4 ounces walnuts (1 cup), coarsely chopped

1. In heavy 3-quart saucepan, heat sugar, half-and-half, cocoa, corn syrup, and salt to boiling over medium-high heat, stirring frequently, until sugar has completely dissolved. Set candy thermometer in place; reduce heat to low and continue cooking, without stirring, until temperature reaches 238°F., or soft-ball stage (when small amount of mixture dropped into very cold water forms soft ball that flattens on removal from water).

2. Remove saucepan from heat; add margarine and vanilla but do not stir. Cool mixture to 110°F. or until outside of saucepan feels lukewarm. Lightly butter 8" by 8" baking pan.

3. When chocolate mixture is lukewarm, with wooden spoon, beat until fudge becomes thick and begins to lose its gloss. Quickly stir in nuts; pour fudge into prepared pan. (Don't scrape saucepan; mixture on side may be grainy.)

4. Cool fudge in pan on wire rack. When cold, cut fudge into 6 strips, then cut each strip crosswise into 6 pieces.

Store in tightly covered container. Makes 3 dozen squares or about 2 pounds.

Each square: About 115 calories, 1 g protein, 19 g carbohydrate, 4 g total fat (1 g saturated), 3 mg cholesterol, 40 mg sodium.

Pecan Penuche

Prep: 15 minutes plus cooling
Cook: 15 minutes

2 cups packed light-brown sugar
2 cups granulated sugar
1 cup milk
3 tablespoons margarine or butter
1½ teaspoons vanilla extract
3 ounces pecans (1 cup), chopped

1. In heavy 3-quart saucepan, heat brown and granulated sugars and milk to boiling over medium heat, stirring constantly, until sugars have completely dissolved. Set candy thermometer in place and continue cooking, without stirring, until temperature reaches 238°F., or soft-ball stage (when small amount of mixture dropped into very cold water forms soft ball that flattens on removal from water).

2. Remove saucepan from heat; add margarine and vanilla but do not stir. Cool mixture to 110°F. or until outside of saucepan feels lukewarm. Meanwhile, lightly butter 8" by 8" baking pan.

3. When mixture is lukewarm, with wooden spoon, beat until it becomes thick and begins to lose its gloss. Quickly stir in pecans; pour into pan. (Don't scrap saucepan; mixture on side may be grainy.)

4. Cool candy in pan on wire rack. When cold, cut into 6 strips, then cut each strip crosswise into 6 pieces. Store tightly covered. Makes 3 dozen squares or about 2 pounds.

Each square: About 120 calories, 1 g protein, 23 g carbohydrate, 3 g total fat (1g saturated), 1 mg cholesterol, 20 mg sodium.

Peanut Brittle

Prep: 15 minutes plus cooling
Cook: 20 minutes

1 cup sugar
½ cup light corn syrup
¼ cup water
¼ teaspoon salt
1 cup shelled raw peanuts
2 tablespoons margarine or butter
1 teaspoon baking soda

1. In heavy 2-quart saucepan, heat sugar, corn syrup, water, and salt to boiling over medium heat, stirring constantly until sugar has completely dissolved. Stir in peanuts. Set candy thermometer in place and continue cooking, stirring frequently, until temperature reaches 300°F., or hard-crack stage (when small amount of mixture dropped into very cold water separates into hard and brittle threads), about 20 minutes.

2. Meanwhile, lightly butter large cookie sheet.

3. Remove saucepan from heat; stir in margarine and baking soda; immediately pour onto cookie sheet. With 2 forks, quickly lift and stretch peanut mixture into rectangle about 14" by 12".

4. Cool brittle completely on cookie sheet on wire rack. With hands, break brittle into small pieces. Store in tightly covered container. Makes about 1 pound brittle.

Each 1-ounce serving: About 140 calories, 2 g protein, 21 g carbohydrate, 6 g total fat (1 g saturated), 0 mg cholesterol, 150 mg sodium.

Toffee Crunch

Prep: 1 hour plus cooling
Cook: 30 minutes

1¾ cups sugar
⅓ cup light corn syrup
¼ cup water
1 cup (2 sticks) margarine or butter
8 ounces slivered blanched almonds (2 cups), lightly toasted and finely chopped
2 squares (2 ounces) unsweetened chocolate, coarsely chopped
2 squares (2 ounces) semisweet chocolate, coarsely chopped
1 teaspoon shortening

1. In heavy 2-quart saucepan, heat sugar, corn syrup, and water to boiling over medium heat, stirring occasionally. Stir in margarine. Set candy thermometer in place and continue cooking, stirring frequently, until temperature reaches 300°F. or hard-crack stage (when small amount of mixture dropped into very cold water separates into hard and brittle threads), about 20 minutes.

2. Meanwhile, lightly grease 15 ½" by 10 ½" jelly-roll pan.

3. Remove saucepan from heat. Reserve ⅓ cup chopped almonds. Stir remaining almonds into hot syrup. Immediately pour mixture into jelly-roll pan; spread evenly. Cool in pan on rack.

4. Prepare chocolate glaze: In heavy small saucepan over low heat, heat unsweetened and semisweet chocolates and shortening, stirring occasionally, until melted. Remove saucepan from heat; cool slightly.

5. Remove candy in one piece from pan to cutting board. Spread chocolate over candy; sprinkle with reserved almonds, pressing them gently into chocolate. Set candy aside to allow glaze to set, about 1 hour. Break candy into pieces. Store in layers, separated by waxed paper, in tightly covered container to use up within 2 weeks. Makes about 1¾ pounds candy.

Each 1-ounce serving: About 180 calories, 2 g protein, 19 g carbohydrate, 12 g total fat (2 g saturated), 0 mg cholesterol, 90 mg sodium.

Bourbon Balls

Prep: 15 minutes

Confectioners' sugar
2½ cups finely crushed vanilla wafers (about 60 wafers)
4 ounces walnuts (1 cup), finely chopped
¼ cup bourbon
3 tablespoons corn syrup
2 tablespoons unsweetened cocoa

1. In large bowl, stir 1 cup confectioners' sugar, vanilla wafers, walnuts, bourbon, corn syrup and cocoa until combined.

2. Sprinkle some confectioners' sugar onto waxed paper. With hands, shape mixture into 1-inch balls. Roll each ball in confectioners' sugar. Wrap each ball in plastic wrap. Store in tightly covered container. Makes about 3½ dozen.

Each piece: About 65 calories, 1 g protein, 8 g carbohydrate, 3 g total fat (1 g saturated), 0 mg cholesterol, 25 mg sodium.

Cakes & Frostings

❧❦

Layers, Loaves, & Special Cakes
Chiffon, Angel-food, & Sponge Cakes
Dried & Fresh Fruitcakes
Frostings & Fillings

Nothing shows off your baking skills as well as a beautiful cake. Recipes for cakes are carefully balanced, so be sure to follow them exactly for successful results.

ᴄ∾Tips for Perfect Cakes

Ingredients: In our recipes we use large eggs and measure the flour—without sifting—right from the sack or canister.

Pans: Make sure pans are the size called for in the recipe, and prepare them before you start mixing the batter. If the pans are greased and floured, grease them with shortening, and use crumpled waxed paper or paper towels to grease them evenly. Then sprinkle them generously with flour or, for dark-colored batter, with cocoa so the cake doesn't have a white coating. Invert pan and tap lightly to remove any excess flour or cocoa. Do not grease pans for angel-food, chiffon, and sponge cakes; in an ungreased pan, the batter will cling to the sides and rise to its full height. For fruitcakes, grease pans generously and line with foil; smooth out the foil as much as possible so the cake does not have wrinkles on its sides and bottom, then grease the foil also.

Oven Space: For cakes baked in tube pans which are deep, set the oven rack lower so that the cake is in the middle of the oven. For loaves and layers that fit on one rack, set the rack so that the center of the loaf or layers is close to the center of the oven. For three or four cake layers, two oven racks are needed; place them so they divide the oven into thirds, and stagger the pans so that one is not directly underneath another. Place pans so they don't touch the sides of the oven or each other.

Preheat the oven so that it is at the temperature called for in the recipe when the cake is put into it.

Cakes Made With Butter, Margarine, or Shortening: When mixing the batter, be sure to beat at the recommended mixer speed for the specified length of time. Scrape the bowl often with a rubber spatula so that all ingredients are mixed thoroughly. If you use a wooden spoon instead of a mixer, you will need to give ingredients 150 vigorous strokes for every minute of beating time to blend the ingredients.

Pour the batter into the prepared pan(s) and cut through it several times with a rubber spatula or knife to break any large air bubbles that might be present.

Once a cake is in the oven, do not open the oven door until the minimum baking time has passed, then test for doneness by inserting a cake tester or toothpick into the center of the cake. If it comes out clean, the cake is done and should be removed at once to cool. Otherwise, bake the cake 5 to 10 minutes longer and test it again.

Most cakes should be cooled in the pan for 10 minutes on a wire rack before removing them from the pan (a hot cake might be too tender and might break when the pan is removed). Then loosen the edges from the pan sides and invert a second wire rack over the top of the pan. Now invert the pan and both racks; the cake should drop from the pan. Remove the upper rack and the pan, then place the inverted wire rack over the cake bottom and again invert the cake and both racks. Remove the upper rack, leaving the cake top side up. This way there will not be any marks from the wire rack on the top of the cake. Let the cake cool completely on the rack before frosting or storing it.

Follow recipe directions for cooling fruitcakes.

Chiffon, Angel-Food, and Sponge Cakes: The bowl and beaters for egg whites must be absolutely free from grease or any specks of egg yolk, which contains fat, or the egg whites cannot be beaten stiff.

Fold ingredients into beaten egg whites with a rubber spatula or wire whisk by cutting down through the center of the egg whites, across the bottom, and up the side of the bowl. Give the bowl a quarter turn; repeat until the mixture is uniformly blended.

When the batter is mixed, push it into the cake pan with a rubber spatula, smooth and level it very lightly, then cut through it to break any large air bubbles.

When the minimum baking time is up, check the cake for doneness. It is done if the top springs back when very lightly pressed with a finger and the cracks in the top (typical of these cakes) look dry, not moist. If the cake is not done, bake it a few minutes longer and check again.

To cool the cake, invert the pan on a bottle neck or funnel so that its top does not touch the counter; air can then circulate underneath as well as over and around it and it will cool evenly. Also, this helps the cake to hold its shape while cooling; if cooled top side up, it will fall. Let the cake cool completely in the pan, then remove it by cutting around the side and tube of the pan with a metal spatula, using an up-and-down motion and pressing the spatula firmly against the pan. Invert the pan and gently shake the cake out onto a plate.

FROSTING CAKES

Brush off any crumbs and trim any crisp edges from the cooled cake. To keep the cake plate clean, arrange strips of waxed paper to form a square covering the plate edges; center the cake on the strips and frost it, then gently pull out the strips. Turning a cake as you work makes frosting it easier; place the cake on a turntable, lazy Susan, or bowl.

Layer Cake: Place the first layer, top side down, on a cake plate; spread the layer with filling or frosting almost to the edge. Place the second layer, top side up, on the frosted layer so that the flat bottoms of the two layers face each other. Thinly frost the cake side to set the crumbs so that they will not show in the finished frosting, then frost the sides again, generously, bringing the frosting up to make a ½-inch ridge at the cake top. Now frost the cake top, and decorate it if you wish.

To split layers before frosting, use a ruler and toothpicks to mark the midpoint all around; cut the layer horizontally in two with a long, sharp, serrated knife and remove the toothpicks.

Tube Cake: Place the cake, top side down, on waxed paper strips on a cake plate. Brush off any crumbs and thinly frost the side as above, then spread the side and top generously with frosting. Also frost the inside center of the cake. A tube cake can be split into layers as above.

To glaze a cake, brush the crumbs from the top only. Drizzle glaze over the top of the cake from a spoon, letting it drip down the sides.

Bundt and Ring Cakes: Place the cake, top side down, on waxed paper strips on a cake plate. Glaze as you would a tube cake (above).

Cupcakes: Dip the top of each cupcake in frosting, turning the cake slightly to coat it. If the cupcakes have been baked in paper or foil liners, leave the liners on.

STORING CAKES

Layer and tube cakes frosted with fudge or butter cream–type frostings or a confectioners' sugar glaze should be kept in a cake keeper or under an inverted large bowl or pan.

Cakes made with fluffy frosting should be served the same day they are made, since the frosting gradually disintegrates during storage. Store leftovers in a cake keeper or under an inverted bowl, but insert a spoon or knife handle under the top so that air can circulate and help to keep the frosting fluffy.

Cakes made with whipped-cream or cream-cheese frosting or cream fillings should be kept refrigerated.

Wrap fruitcakes tightly in plastic wrap or foil and keep them in a cool place. If desired brush them first with wine or brandy, or wrap them in a wine- or brandy-dampened cloth, then overwrap them with foil. Redampen the cloth weekly. Glaze or decorate a fruitcake just before serving.

FREEZING CAKES

Don't freeze cake batter, cakes with fillings made with cornstarch or flour, or fruit fillings; they may be soggy when thawed.

Unfrosted cakes should be tightly wrapped with freezer wrap, plastic wrap, or foil, and sealed with tape. Frozen, they will keep four to six months; fruitcakes will keep up to twelve months in the freezer.

Cakes frosted with butter-cream, fudge, or whipped-cream frostings should be placed on foil-wrapped cardboard and frozen unwrapped until the frosting is hard, then wrapped, sealed, and stored in the freezer for two to three months.

THAWING CAKES

Unwrap cakes with whipped-cream frostings or fillings, and thaw them in the refrigerator for 3 to 4 hours. Unwrap cakes with other types of frosting, and thaw them at room temperature. Thaw cakes without frosting, still wrapped, at room temperature. Unfrosted layers thaw in 1 hour, frosted tube and layer cakes in 2 to 3 hours, cupcakes in 30 minutes.

～Layers, Loaves, & Special Cakes

Yellow Cake

Prep: 25 minutes plus cooling
Bake: 23 to 25 minutes

2¼ cups cake flour (not self-rising)
2½ teaspoons baking powder
¼ teaspoon salt
¾ cup milk
1½ teaspoons vanilla extract
1½ cups sugar
¾ cup (1½ sticks) margarine or butter, softened
3 large eggs

1. Preheat oven to 350°F. Grease two 9-inch round cake pans. Line bottoms of pans with waxed paper; grease paper. Dust pans with flour.

2. In medium bowl, combine flour, baking powder, and salt; set aside. In measuring cup, with fork, mix milk and vanilla.

3. In large bowl, with mixer at low speed, beat sugar and margarine until blended. Increase speed to high; beat until creamy, 2 minutes. Reduce speed to medium-low; add eggs, 1 at a time, beating well after each addition. Alternately add flour mixture and milk mixture, beginning and ending with flour mixture; beat until batter is smooth, occasionally scraping bowl with rubber spatula.

4. Divide batter evenly among pans. Bake until toothpick inserted in center of layer comes out almost clean with a few moist crumbs attached, 23 to 25 minutes. Cool in pans on wire racks 10 minutes. With small knife, loosen layers from sides of pans; invert onto racks. Remove and discard waxed paper. Cool completely. Makes 12 servings.

Each Serving: About 300 calories, 4 g protein, 41 g carbohydrate, 13 g total fat (3 g saturated), 55 mg cholesterol, 305 mg sodium.

*Fill and frost cake with: Any Buttercream Frosting (page 1014),
or fill with Creamy-Custard Filling (page 1022) or Lemon-Curd
Filling (page 1024) and frost with Seven-Minute Frosting (page
1017).*

YELLOW CUPCAKES: Preheat oven to 375°F. Place paper
liners in 2 dozen 3-inch muffin-pan cups or grease and flour
cups. Prepare Yellow Cake batter as above but pour it into
cups, filling each half full. Bake until toothpick inserted in
center comes out clean, 15 minutes. Cool in pans on wire
racks 10 minutes. Remove from pans; cool completely.
Frost as for cake.

Silver-White Cake

Prep: 25 minutes plus cooling
Bake: 25 to 28 minutes

2¼ cups cake flour (not self-rising)
1 tablespoon baking powder
¼ teaspoon salt
1 cup milk
1 teaspoon vanilla extract
4 large egg whites, at room temperature
1½ cups sugar
½ cup (1 stick) margarine or butter, softened

1. Preheat oven to 350°F. Grease two 8-inch round cake
pans. Line bottoms of pans with waxed paper; grease paper.
Dust pans with flour.

2. In medium bowl, combine flour, baking powder, and
salt; set aside. In measuring cup, with fork, mix milk and
vanilla.

3. In large bowl, with mixer at high speed, beat egg
whites until soft peaks form. Beating at high speed, sprinkle
in ½ cup sugar, 2 tablespoons at a time, beating until sugar
has dissolved and whites stand in stiff peaks when beaters
are lifted. Set aside.

4. In large bowl, with mixer at low speed, beat remaining 1 cup sugar and margarine until blended. Increase speed to high; beat until creamy, 2 minutes. Alternately add flour mixture and milk mixture, beginning and ending with flour mixture; beat until batter is smooth, occasionally scraping bowl with rubber spatula. With a rubber spatula, gently fold egg white mixture into batter.

5. Divide batter evenly among pans. Bake until toothpick inserted in center of each layer comes out almost clean with a few moist crumbs attached, 25 to 28 minutes. Cool in pans on wire racks 10 minutes. With small knife, loosen layers from sides of pans; invert onto racks. Remove and discard waxed paper. Cool completely. Makes 12 servings.

Each serving: About 255 calories, 4 g protein, 41 g carbohydrate, 8 g total fat (2 g saturated), 3 mg cholesterol, 280 mg sodium.

Fill and frost cake with: Any Buttercream Frosting (page 1014), or fill with Creamy-Custard Filling (page 1022) or Fresh-Orange Filling (page 1023) and frost with Seven-Minute Frosting (page 1017).

Old-Fashioned Cocoa Cake

Prep: 30 minutes plus cooling
Bake: 35 to 40 minutes

2½ cups all-purpose flour	¾ cup mayonnaise
1½ cups sugar	1 tablespoon vanilla extract
¾ cup unsweetened cocoa	2 large eggs
1½ teaspoons baking soda	Rich Chocolate Frosting
¾ teaspoon salt	(see page 971)
1½ cups buttermilk	

1. Preheat oven to 350°F. Grease 13" by 9" metal baking pan.

2. In large bowl, combine flour, sugar, cocoa, baking soda, and salt.

3. In medium bowl, with wire whisk, mix buttermilk, mayonnaise, vanilla, and eggs until almost smooth.

4. With spoon, stir buttermilk mixture into flour mixture until batter is smooth. Spoon batter into baking pan. Bake until toothpick inserted in center of cake comes out clean, 35 to 40 minutes. Cool cake in pan on wire rack.

5. Prepare Rich Chocolate Frosting. When cake is cool, spread with frosting. Makes 18 servings.

RICH CHOCOLATE FROSTING: In heavy small saucepan, melt *4 squares (4 ounces) semisweet chocolate* and *2 squares (2 ounces) unsweetened chocolate* over low heat. Remove saucepan from heat; cool chocolate to room temperature. In large bowl, with mixer at low speed, beat *2 cups confectioners' sugar, 3/4 cup (1 1/2 sticks) margarine or butter,* softened, and *1 teaspoon vanilla extract* until almost combined. Add melted, cooled chocolate. Increase speed to high and beat until light and fluffy, about 1 minute.

Each serving: About 385 calories, 5 g protein, 52 g carbohydrate, 20 g total fat (4 g saturated), 28 mg cholesterol, 380 mg sodium.

Devil's Food Cake

Prep: 25 minutes plus cooling
Bake: 25 to 30 minutes

2 cups cake flour (not self-rising)	1 1/2 cups sugar
1 1/2 teaspoons baking soda	1/2 cup (1 stick) margarine or butter, softened
1/2 teaspoon baking powder	
1/4 teaspoon salt	3 large eggs
1 1/4 cups buttermilk	3 squares (3 ounces) unsweetened chocolate, melted and cooled
1 teaspoon vanilla extract	

1. Preheat oven to 350°F. Grease two 9-inch round cake pans. Line bottoms of pans with waxed paper; grease paper. Dust pans with flour.

2. In medium bowl, combine flour, baking soda, baking powder, and salt; set aside. In measuring cup, with fork, mix buttermilk and vanilla.

3. In large bowl, with mixer at low speed, beat sugar and margarine until blended. Increase speed to high; beat, until creamy, 2 minutes. Reduce speed to medium-low; add eggs, 1 at a time, beating well after each addition. Beat in chocolate. Alternately add flour mixture and buttermilk mixture, beginning and ending with flour mixture; beat until batter is smooth, occasionally scraping bowl with rubber spatula.

4. Divide batter evenly among pans. Bake until toothpick inserted in center of each layer comes out almost clean with a few moist crumbs attached, 25 to 30 minutes. Cool in pans on wire racks 10 minutes. With small knife, loosen layers from sides of pans; invert onto racks. Remove and discard waxed paper. Cool completely. Makes 12 servings.

Fill and frost cake with: Any Buttercream Frosting (page 1014).

Each serving: About 295 calories, 5 g protein, 42 g carbohydrate, 13 g total fat (4 g saturated), 54 mg cholesterol, 370 mg sodium.

Triple Chocolate-Cherry Cake

Prep: 40 minutes plus cooling
Bake: About 1 hour 10 minutes

1¾ cups all-purpose flour
¾ cup unsweetened cocoa
1½ teaspoons baking soda
½ teaspoon salt
1 cup dried tart cherries
1 tablespoon instant espresso-coffee powder
1 tablespoon very hot water
1½ cups buttermilk
2 teaspoons vanilla extract
1¾ cups sugar

1 cup (2 sticks) butter, softened (no substitutions)
3 large eggs
2 squares (2 ounces) unsweetened chocolate, melted
1 package (6 ounces) semisweet-chocolate chips (1 cup)
Confectioners' sugar
Whipped cream (optional)

1. Preheat oven to 325°F. Grease and flour 10-inch Bundt pan.

2. In medium bowl, combine flour, cocoa, baking soda, and salt; set aside.

3. In small bowl, place cherries with enough *very hot water* just to cover; let stand at least 5 minutes to soften cherries. In 2-cup measuring cup, blend espresso powder and water until smooth; stir in buttermilk and vanilla. Set aside.

4. In large bowl, with mixer at low speed, beat sugar and butter until blended, scraping bowl often with rubber spatula. Increase speed to medium; beat 2 minutes, occasionally scraping bowl. Reduce speed to low; add eggs, 1 at a time, beating well after each addition. At low speed, alternately add flour mixture and buttermilk mixture, beginning and ending with flour mixture; beat until smooth, occasionally scraping bowl.

5. Drain cherries and pat with paper towels to remove excess water. With rubber spatula, fold melted chocolate into batter. Then fold in chocolate chips and drained cherries.

6. Pour batter into pan. Bake until toothpick inserted in center of cake comes out clean, 1 hour to 1 hour 10 minutes. Cool cake in pan on wire rack 10 minutes. With small knife, loosen cake from side of pan; invert onto rack. Cool completely. Turn cake top side up.

7. To serve, sift confectioners' sugar over cake. Pass whipped cream to spoon over each serving, if you like. Makes 16 servings.

Each serving without whipped cream: About 365 calories, 5 g protein, 52 g carbohydrate, 17 g total fat (8 g saturated), 72 mg cholesterol, 345 mg sodium.

Spice Cake with Brown-Butter Frosting

Prep: 1 hour plus cooling
Bake: 25 to 30 minutes

Cake

2⅔ cups all-purpose flour
2½ teaspoons baking powder
2 teaspoons ground cinnamon
1 teaspoon ground ginger
½ teaspoon ground nutmeg
½ teaspoon salt

¼ teaspoon ground cloves
1 cup packed dark brown sugar
1 cup granulated sugar
1 cup (2 sticks) margarine or butter, softened
5 large eggs
1 cup milk

Brown-Butter Frosting

½ cup (1 stick) butter, (no substitutions)
1 box (16 ounces) confectioners' sugar
¼ cup milk
1½ teaspoons vanilla extract

1 cup walnuts, toasted and finely chopped

1. Preheat oven to 350°F. Grease three 8-inch round cake pans. Line bottoms with waxed paper; grease paper. Dust pans with flour.

2. In medium bowl, combine flour, baking powder, cinnamon, ginger, nutmeg, salt, and cloves.

3. In large bowl, combine brown and granulated sugars, breaking up any lumps of brown sugar. Add margarine and, with mixer at low speed, beat until blended, scraping bowl often with rubber spatula. Increase speed to medium; beat 4 minutes, or until light and creamy, occasionally scraping bowl. Add eggs, 1 at a time, beating well after each addition. At low speed, alternately add flour mixture and milk, beginning and ending with flour mixture; beat until blended.

4. Pour batter into pans and spread evenly. Stagger pans on 2 oven racks, placing 2 on upper rack and 1 on lower rack, so that layers are not directly above each other. Bake until toothpick inserted in center of each layer comes out clean, 25 to 30 minutes. Cool layers in pans on wire racks 10 minutes. With small knife or metal spatula loosen layers from sides of pans; invert onto racks. Remove and discard waxed paper. Cool completely.

5. Prepare Brown-Butter Frosting: In small skillet, melt butter over medium-low heat and cook, stirring occasionally, until butter is golden-brown, about 10 minutes. Pour butter into large bowl; cool to room temperature, about 30 minutes.

6. To cooled butter, add confectioners' sugar, milk, and vanilla; with mixer at medium speed, beat ingredients until smooth. With mixer at high speed, beat frosting until light and fluffy, about 1 minute. Makes about 2⅓ cups.

7. Place 1 cake layer, rounded side down, on cake plate; spread with scant ½ cup frosting. Top with second cake layer; spread with another scant ½ cup frosting, then top with remaining cake layer. Frost top and side of cakes with remaining frosting. With hand, press walnuts around side of cake. Refrigerate if not serving right away. Makes 16 servings.

Each serving: About 525 calories, 6 g protein, 73 g carbohydrate, 24 g total fat (7 g saturated), 85 mg cholesterol, 370 mg sodium.

Chocolate Truffle Cake

Prep: 1 hour plus overnight to chill
Bake: 35 minutes

1 cup (2 sticks) butter (no substitutions)
14 squares (14 ounces) semisweet chocolate
2 squares (2 ounces) unsweetened chocolate
9 large eggs, separated
½ cup sugar
¼ teaspoon cream of tartar
Confectioners' sugar

1. Preheat oven to 300°F. Remove bottom from 9" by 3" springform pan and cover with foil, wrapping foil around to the underside (this will make it easier to remove cake from pan). Replace bottom. Grease and flour foil bottom and side of pan.

2. In large glass bowl, combine butter and semisweet and unsweetened chocolates. In microwave oven, cook, uncovered, on Medium (50%), 2½ minutes; stir. Return chocolate mixture to microwave oven; cook 2 to 2½ minutes longer, until almost melted. Stir until smooth. (Or, in heavy 2-quart saucepan, heat butter and both kinds of chocolate over low heat until melted, stirring frequently. Pour chocolate mixture into large bowl.)

3. In small bowl, with mixer at high speed, beat egg yolks and sugar until very thick and lemon-colored, about 5 minutes. Add egg-yolk mixture to chocolate mixture, stirring with rubber spatula until blended.

4. In another large bowl, with clean beaters, and with mixer at high speed, beat egg whites and cream of tartar until soft peaks form when beaters are lifted. With rubber spatula or wire whisk, gently fold beaten egg whites into chocolate mixture, one-third at a time.

5. Pour batter into pan, spreading evenly. Bake 35 minutes. (Do not overbake. The cake will firm upon standing and chilling.) Cool cake completely in pan on wire rack; then cover and refrigerate overnight in pan.

6. To remove cake from pan, with a hot knife, loosen cake from side of pan, then lift off side. Invert cake onto cake plate; unwrap foil from bottom and lift off bottom of pan. Carefully remove foil and discard.

7. Let cake stand 1 hour at room temperature before serving. Just before serving, decorate cake: Sprinkle confectioners' sugar through fine sieve over star stencil,* or dust top of cake with confectioners' sugar. Makes 24 servings.

*A store-bought doily makes an easy stencil, or you can create your own design on lightweight cardboard or a manila file folder. Cut cardboard at least 1 inch larger all around than the cake's surface. Cut out stars of different sizes or your own design using *a mat knife. Place stencil over cake and sprinkle with confectioners' sugar, as we did, or try cocoa, ground nuts, or grated chocolate. Carefully remove stencil to avoid marring the design.*

Each serving without confectioners' sugar: About 200 calories, 4 g protein, 17 g carbohydrate, 14 g total fat (6 g saturated), 100 mg cholesterol, 110 mg sodium.

Chocolate Layer Cake with White Chocolate Frosting

Prep: 40 minutes plus cooling
Bake: 20 to 25 minutes

1¾ cups sugar
¾ cup (1½ sticks) margarine or butter, softened
3 large eggs
1½ teaspoons vanilla extract
2¾ cups cake flour (not self-rising)

1½ cups milk
¾ cup unsweetened cocoa
1½ teaspoons baking soda
½ teaspoon salt
White-Chocolate Buttercream Frosting (see page 978)

1. Preheat oven to 350°F. Grease three 9-inch round cake pans. Line bottom of cake pans with waxed paper; grease and flour paper.

2. In large bowl, with mixer at medium speed, beat sugar and margarine until light and fluffy, about 5 minutes. Beat in eggs and vanilla until smooth, about 2 minutes. Reduce speed to low. Add cake flour, milk, cocoa, baking soda, and salt; beat until combined. Increase speed to medium; beat 1 minute, occasionally scraping bowl.

3. Pour batter into pans. Stagger cake pans on 2 oven racks, placing 2 on upper rack and 1 on lower rack, so that layers are not directly over one another. Bake until toothpick inserted in center of each layer comes out clean, 20 to 25 minutes. Cool layers in pans on wire racks 10 minutes. With small knife, loosen layers from sides of pans; invert onto racks. Remove and discard waxed paper. Cool completely.

4. Prepare White-Chocolate Buttercream Frosting.

5. Place 1 cake layer on cake plate; spread with ¾ cup buttercream. Repeat layering, ending with a cake layer. Frost side and top of cake with remaining butter cream. Refrigerate cake if not serving right away. Makes 16 servings.

WHITE-CHOCOLATE BUTTERCREAM FROSTING: In large bowl, with mixer at high speed, beat *1 cup (2 sticks) butter*, slightly softened, *2½ cups confectioners' sugar*, *6 ounces white chocolate*, melted but still slightly warm, *¼ cup milk*, and *1½ teaspoons vanilla extract* just until mixed. Increase speed to high; beat until light and fluffy, 2 minutes.

Each serving: About 500 calories, 5 g protein, 65 g carbohydrate, 26 g total fat (12 g saturated), 76 mg cholesterol, 455 mg sodium.

Country Spice Cake

Prep: 30 minutes plus cooling
Bake: 20 to 25 minutes

1½ cups sugar	2 teaspoons ground ginger
¾ cup shortening	2 teaspoons ground cinnamon
3 large eggs	1 teaspoon salt
1 tablespoon vanilla extract	½ teaspoon ground cloves
2½ cups cake flour (not self-rising)	Molasses Buttercream (see page 979)
1¼ cups milk	
2½ teaspoons baking powder	

1. Preheat oven to 350°F. Grease and flour three 8-inch round cake pans.

2. In large bowl, with mixer at high speed, beat sugar and shortening, constantly scraping bowl with rubber spatula, until mixture has a sandy appearance, about 2 minutes. Beat in eggs and vanilla extract until smooth, about 2 minutes. Reduce speed to low. Add cake flour, milk, baking powder, ginger, cinnamon, salt, and cloves; beat until just combined. Increase speed to medium; beat 1 minute, occasionally scraping bowl.

3. Pour batter into pans. Stagger cake pans on 2 oven racks, placing 2 on upper rack and 1 on lower rack, so that layers are not directly over one another. Bake until toothpick inserted in center of each layer comes out clean, 20 to 25 minutes. Cool layers in pans on wire racks 10 minutes. With small knife, loosen layers from sides of pans; invert onto racks. Cool completely on racks.

4. Prepare Molasses Buttercream.

5. Place 1 cake layer on cake plate; spread with scant 1 cup buttercream. Repeat layering, ending with a cake layer. Frost side and top of cake with remaining buttercream. Refrigerate cake if not serving right away. Makes 16 servings.

MOLASSES BUTTERCREAM: In large bowl, with mixer at high speed, beat *1 cup (2 sticks) butter*, slightly softened, and *1 package (8 ounces) light cream cheese* (Neufchatel), slightly softened, until smooth. With mixer at low speed, beat in *1 package (16 ounces) confectioners' sugar* and *¼ cup light molasses* until mixture begins to come together. Increase speed to medium-high; beat until smooth with an easy spreading consistency.

Each serving: About 510 calories, 5 g protein, 66 g carbohydrate, 26 g total fat (13 g saturated), 84 mg cholesterol, 385 mg sodium.

Checkerboard Cake

Prep: 40 minutes plus cooling
Bake: 25 to 30 minutes

1 cup (2 sticks) margarine or
    butter, softened
2 cups sugar
3½ cups cake flour (not self-
    rising)
1¼ cups milk
1 tablespoon baking powder
1 tablespoon vanilla extract
½ teaspoon salt
8 large egg whites
1 package (8 ounces)
    semisweet-chocolate
    squares, melted and cooled
Chocolate Buttercream Frosting
    (see page 981)

1. Preheat oven to 350°F. Grease three 8-inch round cake pans. Line bottoms of cake pans with waxed paper. Grease waxed paper; dust with flour.

2. In large bowl, with mixer at low speed, beat margarine and 1½ cups sugar until blended. Increase speed to high; beat until light and fluffy, about 5 minutes. Reduce speed to low. Add flour, milk, baking powder, vanilla, and salt; beat until just combined. Increase speed to medium; beat 2 minutes, occasionally scraping bowl.

3. In another large bowl, with mixer at high speed, beat egg whites and remaining ½ cup sugar until stiff peaks form when beaters are lifted. Gently fold beaten egg whites into flour mixture until blended. Spoon half of batter into medium bowl. Into batter remaining in large bowl, fold melted chocolate until blended.

4. Spoon vanilla batter into 1 large decorating bag with ½-inch opening (or use a heavy-duty plastic bag with corner cut to make ½-inch opening). Repeat with chocolate batter and a second large decorating bag with ½-inch opening. Pipe one ½-inch-wide band of chocolate batter around inside edge of 2 cake pans. Then, pipe one ½-inch-wide band of vanilla batter next to each chocolate band. Pipe enough chocolate batter to fill in the center. In third cake pan, repeat piping, alternating rings of batter, but starting with vanilla around edge of pan.

5. Stagger cake pans on 2 oven racks, placing 2 on upper rack and 1 on lower rack, so that layers are not directly over one another. Bake until toothpick inserted in center of each cake layer comes out clean, 25 to 30 minutes. Cool layers in pans on wire racks 10 minutes. With small knife, loosen layers from sides of pans; invert onto racks. Remove and discard waxed paper. Cool completely on racks.

6. Meanwhile, prepare Chocolate Buttercream Frosting.

7. Place one of the two identical cake layers on cake plate; spread with ½ cup buttercream. Top with the reverse-design cake layer. Spread with another ½ cup buttercream. Top with remaining cake layer; frost side and top of cake with remaining buttercream. Makes 16 servings.

CHOCOLATE BUTTERCREAM FROSTING: Melt, then cool *6 squares (6 ounces) semisweet chocolate.* In large bowl, with mixer at low speed, beat *2 cups confectioners' sugar, 1 cup (2 sticks) margarine or butter,* softened, *3 tablespoons milk, 1 teaspoon vanilla extract,* and cooled chocolate just until mixed. Increase speed to high; beat 2 minutes, or until light and fluffy, scraping bowl often with rubber spatula.

Each serving: About 585 calories, 6 g protein, 78 g carbohydrate, 29 g total fat (5 g saturated), 3 mg cholesterol, 495 mg sodium.

Black Forest Cake

Prep: 1 hour plus chilling
Bake: About 25 minutes

Chocolate Cake
2 cups all-purpose flour
1 cup unsweetened cocoa
2 teaspoons baking powder
1 teaspoon baking soda
½ teaspoon salt
2 cups sugar
1 cup (2 sticks) margarine or butter, softened
4 large eggs
1⅓ cups milk
2 teaspoons vanilla extract

Cherry Filling
2 cans (16½ ounces each) pitted dark sweet cherries (Bing) in heavy syrup
⅓ cup kirsch (cherry brandy)

Cream Filling
1½ cups heavy or whipping cream
½ cup confectioners' sugar
2 tablespoons kirsch (cherry brandy)
1 teaspoon vanilla extract

1. Position 2 oven racks in center of oven. Preheat oven to 350°F. Grease three 9-inch round cake pans. Line bottoms with waxed paper; grease paper. Dust pans with flour.

2. Prepare Chocolate Cake: In medium bowl, combine flour, cocoa, baking powder, baking soda, and salt; set aside.

3. In large bowl, with mixer at low speed, beat sugar and margarine until blended. Increase speed to high; beat until creamy, about 2 minutes. Reduce speed to medium-low; add eggs, 1 at a time, beating well after each addition.

4. In 2-cup measuring cup, with fork, mix milk and vanilla. Reduce speed to low; alternately add flour mixture and milk mixture to margarine mixture, beginning and ending with flour mixture, and beat until batter is smooth, occasionally scraping bowl with rubber spatula.

5. Divide batter among cake pans; spread evenly. Stagger cake pans on 2 oven racks, placing 2 on upper rack and 1 on lower rack, so that layers are not directly over one another. Bake until toothpick inserted in center of each layer comes out almost clean, about 25 minutes. Cool in pans on wire racks 10 minutes. With small knife or metal spatula, loosen cake from sides of pans; invert onto racks. Remove and discard waxed paper. Cool layers completely.

6. Meanwhile, prepare Cherry Filling: Drain cherries well in sieve set over bowl to catch syrup. Reserve ½ cup syrup; stir in kirsch. Set syrup mixture aside.

7. Prepare Cream Filling: In small bowl, with mixer at medium speed, beat cream, confectioners' sugar, kirsch, and vanilla until stiff peaks form when beaters are lifted.

8. Assemble cake: Place 1 cake layer on cake stand or serving plate; brush with one-third syrup mixture. Spread with one-third whipped-cream mixture, then top with half of cherries.

9. Place second cake layer on top of cherries. Brush with half of remaining syrup mixture, half of remaining cream mixture, and all of remaining cherries. Top with third cake layer; brush with remaining syrup mixture. Spoon remaining cream mixture onto center of top layer, leaving a border of cake around edge.

10. For best flavor cover and refrigerate cake overnight. Makes 16 servings.

Each serving: About 450 calories, 6 g protein, 58 g carbohydrate, 22 g total fat (8 g saturated), 87 mg cholesterol, 380 mg sodium.

German Gold Pound Cake

Prep: 20 minutes plus cooling
Bake: About 1 hour

3½ cups cake flour (not self-rising)
1½ teaspoons baking powder
¼ teaspoon salt
1¼ cups milk
2 teaspoons vanilla extract
2 cups sugar
1 cup (2 sticks) margarine or butter, softened
6 large egg yolks

1. Preheat oven to 350°F. Grease and flour 10-inch Bundt pan.

2. In medium bowl, combine flour, baking powder, and salt. In 2-cup measuring cup, with fork, mix milk and vanilla.

3. In large bowl, with mixer at medium speed, beat sugar and margarine until blended. Beat until light and creamy, 5 minutes longer. Add egg yolks, 1 at a time, beating well after each addition. Reduce speed to low; alternately add flour mixture and milk mixture, beginning and ending with flour mixture. Beat until batter is smooth, occasionally scraping bowl with rubber spatula.

4. Spoon batter into pan. Bake until toothpick inserted in center of cake comes out clean, about 1 hour. Cool cake in pan on wire rack 10 minutes. With small knife, loosen cake from sides of pan; invert onto rack. Cool completely on rack. Makes 16 servings.

Each serving: About 315 calories, 4 g protein, 44 g carbohydrate, 14 g total fat (3 g saturated), 82 mg cholesterol, 240 mg sodium.

Kentucky Bourbon Brown-Sugar Pound Cake

Prep: 30 minutes plus cooling
Bake: 1 hour 20 minutes

3 cups all-purpose flour
¾ teaspoon salt
½ teaspoon baking powder
½ teaspoon baking soda
¾ cup milk
2 teaspoons vanilla extract
6 tablespoons bourbon whisky

1½ cups packed dark brown sugar
½ cup plus ⅓ cup granulated sugar
1 cup (2 sticks) margarine or butter, softened
5 large eggs
2 tablespoons orange juice

1. Preheat oven to 325°F. Grease and flour 12-cup fluted tube pan.

2. In medium bowl, combine flour, salt, baking powder, and baking soda. In 1-cup measuring cup, with fork, mix milk, vanilla, and 4 tablespoons bourbon.

3. In large bowl, with mixer at medium speed, beat brown sugar and ½ cup granulated sugar until free of lumps. Increase speed to high; add margarine and beat until light and creamy, about 5 minutes. Add eggs, 1 at a time, beating well after each addition. Reduce speed to low; alternately add flour mixture and milk mixture, beginning and ending with flour mixture, and beat until batter is smooth, occasionally scraping bowl.

4. Pour batter into pan. Bake until cake springs back when lightly touched with finger and toothpick inserted in center comes out clean, about 1 hour and 20 minutes. Cool cake in pan on wire rack 10 minutes. With small knife, loosen cake from side of pan; invert onto rack.

5. In small bowl, combine orange juice, remaining ⅓ cup granulated sugar, and remaining 2 tablespoon bourbon; brush mixture over warm cake. Cool cake completely. Makes 24 servings.

Each serving: About 230 calories, 3 g protein, 33 g carbohydrate, 9 g total fat (5 g saturated), 66 mg cholesterol, 200 mg sodium.

Almond Pound Cake

Prep: 20 minutes plus cooling
Bake: 60 to 65 minutes

3 cups cake flour (not self-rising)
1 tablespoon baking powder
½ teaspoon salt
1 cup milk
2 teaspoons vanilla extract
1 tube or can (7 to 8 ounces)
    almond paste, crumbled

1¾ cups sugar
¾ cup (1½ sticks) margarine or
    butter, softened
4 large eggs
⅓ cup sliced natural almonds

1. Preheat oven to 350°F. Grease and flour 10-inch tube pan.

2. On waxed paper, combine flour, baking powder, and salt. In 1-cup measuring cup, with fork, mix milk and vanilla.

3. In large bowl, with heavy-duty mixer at low speed, beat almond paste and sugar until they have a sandy consistency. (If heavy-duty mixer is unavailable, place almond paste and sugar in food processor with knife blade attached and pulse until fine crumbs form. Transfer almond-paste mixture to large bowl and proceed as directed in recipe.) Beat in margarine. Increase speed to high; beat until well blended, about 5 minutes, scraping bowl often with rubber spatula. Reduce speed to low; add eggs, 1 at a time, beating well after each addition.

4. With mixer at low speed, alternately add flour mixture and milk mixture, beginning and ending with flour mixture; beat until batter is smooth, occasionally scraping bowl.

5. Pour batter into pan. Sprinkle almonds evenly on top. Bake until toothpick inserted in center of cake comes out clean, 60 to 65 minutes. Cool cake in pan on wire rack 10 minutes. With small knife, loosen cake from side of pan; invert onto rack. Cool completely on wire rack. Makes 16 servings.

Each serving: About 340 calories, 6 g protein, 46 g carbohydrate, 15 g total fat (3 g saturated), 55 mg cholesterol, 275 mg sodium.

Marble Loaf Cake with Espresso Glaze

Prep: 20 minutes plus cooling and standing
Bake: About 1 hour

1 ½ cups all-purpose flour
½ teaspoon baking powder
¼ teaspoon baking soda
¼ teaspoon salt
1 ¼ cups sugar
¾ cup (1 ½ sticks) margarine or
   butter, softened

2 large eggs
1 teaspoon vanilla extract
½ cup sour cream
¼ cup unsweetened cocoa
Espresso Glaze (below)

1. Preheat oven to 350°F. Grease 9" by 5" metal loaf pan.

2. In medium bowl, combine flour, baking powder, baking soda, and salt.

3. In large bowl, with mixer at low speed, beat sugar and margarine until blended. Increase speed to high; beat until creamy, 2 minutes. Reduce speed to medium-low; add eggs, 1 at a time, beating well after each addition. Beat in vanilla. Alternately add flour mixture and sour cream, beginning and ending with flour mixture; beat until batter is smooth, occasionally scraping bowl with rubber spatula.

4. Remove half of batter to medium bowl. Beat cocoa into batter remaining in large bowl until blended.

5. Alternately spoon vanilla and chocolate batters into pan. With knife, cut and twist through batters to obtain marbled effect. Bake until toothpick inserted in center of cake comes out clean, about 1 hour. Cool cake in pan on wire rack 10 minutes. With small knife, loosen cake from side of pan; invert onto rack. Cool completely on rack.

6. When cake is cool, prepare Espresso Glaze. With spoon, drizzle glaze over top of cake in crisscross pattern. Let cake stand until glaze is set. Makes 12 servings.

ESPRESSO GLAZE: In small saucepan over low heat, heat *1 tablespoon margarine or butter, 1 tablespoon water,* and *2 teaspoons instant espresso-coffee powder* until butter melts and coffee dissolves; remove saucepan from heat. Stir in *⅓ cup confectioners' sugar* until smooth; add more water if necessary to make glaze of drizzle consistency.

Each serving: About 290 calories, 4 g protein, 36 g carbohydrate, 15 g total fat (4 g saturated), 39 mg cholesterol, 270 mg sodium.

Lemon-Poppyseed Pound Cake

Prep: 25 minutes plus cooling
Bake: About 1 hour 20 minutes

2 cups all-purpose flour	¾ cup (1½ sticks) margarine or
2 tablespoons poppyseeds	butter, softened
½ teaspoon baking powder	1½ cups plus ⅓ cup sugar
¼ teaspoon baking soda	4 large eggs
¼ teaspoon salt	1 teaspoon vanilla extract
2 large lemons	½ cup sour cream

1. Preheat oven to 325°F. Grease and flour 9" by 5" metal loaf pan.

2. In medium bowl, combine flour, poppyseeds, baking powder, baking soda, and salt. From lemons, grate 1 tablespoon peel and squeeze 3 tablespoons juice.

3. In large bowl, with mixer at low speed, beat margarine and 1½ cups sugar until blended. At high speed, beat until light, about 5 minutes. Add eggs, 1 at a time, beating well after each addition. Beat in lemon peel and vanilla. Reduce speed to low; alternately add flour mixture and sour cream, beginning and ending with flour mixture, and beat until batter is smooth.

4. Spoon batter into pan. Bake until toothpick inserted in center of cake comes out clean, about 1 hour 20 minutes.

5. Cool cake in pan on wire rack 10 minutes. With small knife, loosen cake from sides of pan; invert onto rack. Mix lemon juice and remaining ⅓ cup sugar; brush over top and sides of warm cake. Cool completely. Makes 16 servings.

Each serving: About 265 calories, 4 g protein, 36 g carbohydrate, 12 g total fat (3 g saturated), 56 mg cholesterol, 200 mg sodium.

Colonial Gingerbread

Prep: 15 minutes
Bake: About 55 minutes

½ cup sugar
½ cup (1 stick) margarine or butter, softened
2 cups all-purpose flour
1 cup light or dark molasses
2 teaspoons ground ginger

1 teaspoon ground cinnamon
1 teaspoon baking soda
½ teaspoon salt
1 large egg
¾ cup buttermilk

1. Preheat oven to 325°F. Grease 9" by 9" metal baking pan. Line bottom of pan with waxed paper; grease paper. Dust pan with flour.

2. In large bowl, with mixer at low speed, beat sugar and margarine until blended. Increase speed to high; beat until creamy, 1 minute. Reduce speed to low; beat in flour, molasses, ginger, cinnamon, baking soda, salt, egg, and buttermilk until blended. Increase speed to high; beat 1 minute, occasionally scraping bowl with rubber spatula.

3. Pour batter into pan. Bake until toothpick inserted in center of gingerbread comes out clean, about 55 minutes. Cool in pan on wire rack 10 minutes. With small knife, loosen cake from sides of pan; invert onto rack. Remove and discard waxed paper. Serve warm, or cool completely to serve later. Makes 12 servings.

Each serving: About 260 calories, 3 g protein, 43 g carbohydrate, 8 g total fat (2 g saturated), 18 mg cholesterol, 335 mg sodium.

Apple-Walnut Bundt Cake

Prep: 20 minutes plus cooling
Bake: 1 hour 15 minutes

3 cups all-purpose flour
1¾ cups granulated sugar
1 teaspoon baking soda
1 teaspoon ground cinnamon
¾ teaspoon salt
¼ teaspoon ground nutmeg
1 cup vegetable oil
½ cup apple juice
2 teaspoons vanilla extract
3 large eggs

3 medium Golden Delicious or
    Granny Smith apples (about
    1 pound), peeled, cored,
    and coarsely chopped
1 cup walnuts, coarsely
    chopped
1 cup golden raisins
Confectioners' sugar

1. Preheat oven to 350°F. Grease and flour 10-inch Bundt pan.

2. In large bowl, combine flour, granulated sugar, baking soda, cinnamon, salt, nutmeg, oil, apple juice, vanilla extract, and eggs. With mixer at low speed, beat until well mixed, constantly scraping bowl with rubber spatula. Increase speed to medium; beat 2 minutes, occasionally scraping bowl. Stir in apples, walnuts, and raisins.

3. Spoon batter into pan, spreading evenly. Bake until cake pulls away from side of pan and toothpick inserted in center of cake comes out clean, about 1 hour 15 minutes. Cool cake in pan on wire rack 10 minutes. With small knife, loosen cake from side of pan; invert onto rack. Cool completely. If you like, wrap cake well and freeze up to 1 month. Sprinkle with confectioners' sugar to serve. Makes 16 servings.

Each serving: About 400 calories, 5 g protein, 55 g carbohydrate, 19 g total fat (2 g saturated), 40 mg cholesterol, 195 mg sodium.

New England Maple-Walnut Cake

Prep: 50 minutes plus cooling
Bake: 25 to 30 minutes

⅔ cup walnuts
1 cup sugar
2¼ cups cake flour (not self-rising)
2 teaspoons baking powder
½ teaspoon salt
¼ teaspoon baking soda
¾ cup pure maple syrup or maple-flavored syrup

½ cup milk
½ teaspoon imitation maple flavor
¾ cup (1½ sticks) margarine or butter, softened
3 large eggs
Maple Buttercream (see page 992)
Walnut halves (optional)

1. Preheat oven to 350°F. Grease three 8-inch round cake pans. Line bottoms with waxed paper; grease paper. Dust pans with flour.

2. In food processor with knife blade attached, or in blender at medium speed, blend walnuts and 2 tablespoons sugar until walnuts are finely ground.

3. In medium bowl, combine flour, baking powder, salt, and baking soda. In 2-cup measuring cup, with fork, mix maple syrup, milk, and maple flavor until blended.

4. In large bowl, with mixer at low speed, beat margarine and remaining sugar until blended. Increase speed to high; beat until mixture has a sandy appearance, about 2 minutes, occasionally scraping bowl with rubber spatula. At medium-low speed, add eggs, 1 at a time, beating well after each addition.

5. Alternately add flour mixture and maple-syrup mixture, beginning and ending with flour mixture, until batter is smooth, occasionally scraping bowl with rubber spatula. Fold in ground-walnut mixture.

6. Pour batter into pans. Stagger cake pans on 2 oven racks, placing 2 on upper rack and 1 on lower rack, so that layers are not directly over one another. Bake until toothpick inserted in center of each layer comes out clean, 25 to 30 minutes. Cool layers in pans on wire racks 10 minutes.

With small knife, loosen layers from sides of pans; invert onto racks. Cool completely on wire racks.

7. Meanwhile, prepare Maple Buttercream.

8. Place 1 cake layer on cake plate; spread with ⅔ cup buttercream. Repeat layering, ending with a cake layer. Frost side and top of cake with remaining buttercream. Garnish with walnut halves if you like. Refrigerate cake if not serving right away. Makes 16 servings.

MAPLE BUTTERCREAM: In 2-quart saucepan, with wire whisk, mix *½ cup all-purpose flour* and *⅓ cup sugar* until blended. Gradually whisk in *1 cup milk* and *⅔ cup pure maple syrup* or maple-flavored syrup until smooth. Cook over medium-high heat, stirring often, until mixture thickens and boils. Reduce heat to low and cook stirring constantly, 2 minutes. Cool completely. In large bowl, with mixer at medium speed, beat *1 cup (2 sticks) margarine or butter*, softened, until creamy. Gradually beat in cooled milk mixture. Beat in *¼ teaspoon imitation maple flavor*. Increase speed to medium-high; beat until smooth with an easy spreading consistency.

Each serving: About 440 calories, 4 g protein, 52 g carbohydrate, 25 g total fat (5 g saturated), 43 mg cholesterol, 425 mg sodium.

Peanut-Butter Cupcakes

Prep: 15 minutes plus cooling
Bake: 18 to 20 minutes

1¾ cups all-purpose flour
1 tablespoon baking powder
½ teaspoon salt
1 cup milk
¾ teaspoon vanilla extract
¾ cup sugar
½ cup chunky or creamy peanut butter
¼ cup margarine or butter, softened
2 large eggs

1. Preheat oven to 350°F. Grease twenty-four 2½-inch muffin-pan cups.

2. In medium bowl, combine flour, baking powder, and salt. In 1-cup measuring cup, with fork, mix milk and vanilla.

3. In large bowl, with mixer at low speed, beat sugar, peanut butter, and margarine until blended. Increase speed to high; beat until creamy, 2 minutes. Reduce speed to medium-low; add eggs, 1 at a time, beating well after each addition. Add flour mixture, alternating with milk mixture; beat until batter is smooth, occasionally scraping bowl with rubber spatula.

4. Spoon batter into cups. Bake until toothpick inserted in center of 1 cupcake comes out clean, 18 to 20 minutes. Cool in pans on racks 10 minutes. With small knife, loosen cupcake from side of cups; invert onto racks. Cool completely on racks. Makes 24 cupcakes.

Each serving: About 120 calories, 3 g protein, 15 g carbohydrate, 5 g total fat (1 g saturated), 19 mg cholesterol, 160 mg sodium.

Ambrosia Layer Cake

Prep: 1 hour 30 minutes plus cooling
Bake: 35 to 40 minutes

Orange Filling (see page 995)
2½ cups cake flour (not self-
    rising)
1½ teaspoons baking powder
1 teaspoon baking soda
¼ teaspoon salt
1½ cups sugar

¾ cup (1½ sticks) margarine or
    butter, softened
2 teaspoons vanilla extract
3 large eggs
1 cup buttermilk*
Fluffy White Frosting
    (see page 995)
1 cup flaked coconut

1. Prepare Orange Filling. Refrigerate until cold, about 2 hours.

2. Meanwhile, preheat oven to 350°F. Grease and flour 13" by 9" metal baking pan.

3. In medium bowl, combine flour, baking powder, baking soda, and salt.

4. In large bowl, with mixer at low speed, beat sugar and margarine just until blended. Increase speed to high; beat 5 minutes until light and fluffy, scraping bowl often with rubber spatula. Reduce speed to low; add vanilla extract and eggs, 1 at a time, and beat until blended. Alternately add flour mixture and buttermilk, beginning and ending with flour, and beat until batter is well mixed, occasionally scraping bowl.

5. Spread batter in pan. Bake until toothpick inserted in center of cake comes out clean, 35 to 40 minutes. Cool in pan on wire rack 10 minutes. With small knife, loosen cake from sides of pan; invert onto wire rack. Cool completely on rack.

6. Prepare Fluffy White Frosting.

7. To assemble cake, use a serrated knife to cut cake horizontally in half. To remove top cake layer, carefully place cookie sheet in between cut layers and lift off top layer. With metal spatula, spread cooled Orange Filling on bottom layer. Carefully transfer top layer of cake onto bottom layer by gently sliding cake onto filling. Frost top and sides of cake with Fluffy White Frosting. Sprinkle with coconut. Makes 20 servings.

ORANGE FILLING: From *4 large oranges,* grate 1 tablespoon peel and squeeze 1⅓ cups juice. From *1 lemon,* squeeze 1 tablespoon juice. In heavy 3-quart saucepan, mix orange peel, orange juice, lemon juice, *1 cup sugar,* and *3 tablespoons cornstarch* until blended. Add *½ cup (1 stick) margarine or butter* and cook over medium heat until mixture boils; boil 1 minute. In small bowl, beat *6 large egg yolks* slightly. Into yolks, beat a small amount of orange mixture; pour egg mixture back into orange mixture in saucepan. Reduce heat to low; cook, stirring constantly, until mixture is very thick, about 3 minutes. Pour filling into medium bowl; cover surface directly with plastic wrap to prevent skin from forming. Refrigerate until well chilled.

FLUFFY WHITE FROSTING: In top of double boiler, over simmering water, with handheld mixer at high speed, beat *2 large egg whites, 1 cup sugar, ¼ cup water, 2 teaspoons lemon juice, 1 teaspoon light corn syrup,* and *¼ teaspoon cream of tartar* until soft peaks form, 7 to 10 minutes. Remove double-boiler top from double-boiler bottom; continue beating at high speed until stiff peaks form, 7 to 10 minutes.

*Buttermilk Substitute: If you don't have a cup of buttermilk on hand, in 1-cup glass measuring cup, place 1 tablespoon lemon juice, then add enough milk to equal 1 cup. Let mixture stand until thickened, about 5 minutes.

Each serving: About 355 calories, 4 g protein, 52 g carbohydrate, 15 g total fat (4 g saturated), 96 mg cholesterol, 300 mg sodium.

Carrot Cake

Prep: 20 minutes plus cooling
Bake: 50 to 55 minutes

2 cups all-purpose flour
2 teaspoons baking soda
2 teaspoons ground cinnamon
1 teaspoon salt
4 large eggs
1½ cups sugar
¾ cup vegetable oil

2 teaspoons vanilla extract
2 cups shredded carrots
1 cup pecans (about 4 ounces),
    chopped
½ cup chopped dates
1 small red cooking apple,
    coarsely shredded
Cream-Cheese Frosting
    (see page 1018)

1. Preheat oven to 350°F. Grease and flour 10-inch Bundt pan.

2. In medium bowl, combine flour, baking soda, cinnamon, and salt.

3. In large bowl, with mixer at medium-high speed, beat eggs until blended. Gradually add sugar; beat 2 minutes, frequently scraping bowl with rubber spatula. Beat in oil and vanilla. Reduce speed to low; add flour mixture and beat about 1 minute, until smooth, frequently scraping bowl. Fold in carrots, pecans, dates, and apple.

4. Pour batter into pan. Bake until toothpick inserted in center of cake comes out clean, with a few moist crumbs attached, 50 to 55 minutes. Cool cake in pan on wire rack 10 minutes. With small knife, loosen cake from side of pan; invert onto rack. Cool completely on rack.

5. Prepare Cream-Cheese Frosting. Transfer cake to large platter. Spread frosting over sides and top of cake. Makes 16 servings.

Each serving: About 455 calories, 5 g protein, 56 g carbohydrate, 24 g total fat (5 g saturated), 65 mg cholesterol, 415 mg sodium.

Gingerbread Bûche de Noël with Orange Buttercream Frosting

Prep: 1 hour 30 minutes plus cooling and chilling
Bake: 15 to 17 minutes

Gingerbread Cake

½ cup all-purpose flour
2 teaspoons ground ginger
1 teaspoon baking powder
½ teaspoon baking soda
½ teaspoon ground
  cinnamon

¼ teaspoon ground nutmeg
4 large eggs, separated
¼ teaspoon salt
½ cup granulated sugar
¼ cup light molasses
Confectioners' sugar

Orange Buttercream Frosting

¾ cup granulated sugar
6 tablespoons all-purpose flour
¾ cup milk
¾ cup (1½ sticks) margarine or butter, softened
2 tablespoons orange-flavored liqueur
1½ teaspoons vanilla extract
½ teaspoon freshly grated orange peel

1. Prepare Gingerbread Cake: Preheat oven to 375°F. Grease 15½" by 10½" jelly-roll pan; line bottom only with waxed paper. Grease paper and dust pan with flour.

2. On waxed paper, combine flour, ginger, baking powder, baking soda, cinnamon, and nutmeg.

3. In small bowl, with mixer at high speed, beat egg whites and salt until soft peaks form when beaters are lifted. Beating at high speed, gradually sprinkle in ¼ cup granulated sugar, beating until sugar has dissolved and whites stand in stiff peaks.

4. In large bowl, using same beaters and with mixer at high speed, beat egg yolks and remaining ¼ cup granulated sugar until very thick and lemon-colored, and ribbons form when beaters are lifted, about 8 to 10 minutes. Beat in molasses until blended.

5. With rubber spatula, gently fold beaten egg whites

into beaten egg-yolk mixture, one-third at a time. Then fold flour mixture into egg mixture, one-third at a time.

6. Spread batter evenly in pan. Bake until top of cake springs back when lightly touched with finger, 15 to 17 minutes.

7. Sprinkle clean cloth towel with confectioners' sugar. When cake is done, with small metal spatula, loosen cake from sides of pan; immediately invert hot cake onto towel. Gently remove waxed paper and discard. Starting from a long side, roll cake with towel jelly-roll fashion. Place cake roll, seam side down, on wire rack; cool completely, about 45 minutes.

8. Meanwhile, prepare Orange Buttercream Frosting: In 2-quart saucepan, combine sugar and flour; whisk in milk until smooth. Cook over medium-high heat, stirring often, until mixture thickens and boils. Reduce heat to low and cook, stirring constantly, 2 minutes. Transfer mixture to pie plate; cover surface directly with plastic wrap and refrigerate until cool, about 1 hour.

9. In large bowl, with mixer at medium speed, beat margarine until creamy. Gradually beat in cooled milk mixture. When mixture is smooth, beat in liqueur, vanilla, and orange peel until blended. Makes about 2 cups.

10. Assemble cake: Gently unroll cooled cake. With metal spatula, spread 1 cup frosting almost to edges. Starting from same long side, roll cake without towel. With sharp knife, cut 1-inch-thick diagonal slice off each end of roll; set aside. Place rolled cake, seam side down, on long platter. Using about 1⅔ cups orange frosting, spread thin layer of frosting over roll, leaving cut sides unfrosted. Place 1 end piece on side of roll to resemble a cut branch. Place remaining end piece on top of roll to resemble another cut branch. Spread remaining ⅓ cup frosting over roll and branches, leaving cut side of branches unfrosted. With metal spatula or tines of fork, mark frosting to resemble bark of tree. Refrigerate until ready to serve. If dessert is very cold, let stand at room temperature 20 minutes to allow frosting to soften slightly. To make ahead, frost cake and refrigerate up to a day in advance. Before covering with plastic wrap, stick toothpicks or wooden skewers into top to prevent plastic wrap from touching frosting. Makes 14 servings.

Each serving: About 240 calories, 3 g protein, 30 g carbohydrate, 12 g total fat (3 g saturated), 63 mg cholesterol, 270 mg sodium.

Chocolate-Hazelnut Cake

Prep: 1 hour plus cooling
Bake: 25 to 28 minutes

6 squares (6 ounces) semisweet chocolate
1 square (1 ounce) unsweetened chocolate
⅔ cup hazelnuts (filberts), toasted and skinned (see page 19)
4 tablespoons plus ⅓ cup sugar
½ cup cake flour (not self-rising)
½ cup (1 stick) margarine or butter, slightly softened
3 large eggs, separated
1 teaspoon vanilla extract
¼ teaspoon cream of tartar
⅓ cup heavy or whipping cream
1 teaspoon light corn syrup

1. Preheat oven to 375°F. Grease and flour 8-inch round cake pan.

2. In small saucepan over low heat, heat 3 squares semisweet chocolate and unsweetened chocolate, stirring frequently, until melted and smooth. Remove saucepan from heat. Set aside to cool.

3. In food processor with knife blade attached, or in blender at medium speed, blend ½ cup toasted hazelnuts and 2 tablespoons sugar until hazelnuts are very finely ground (reserve remaining hazelnuts for garnish). Blend in cake flour.

4. In large bowl, with mixer at low speed, beat margarine and ⅓ cup sugar just until blended. Increase speed to high; beat until light and fluffy, about 1 minute. Reduce speed to low; beat in egg yolks, vanilla extract, and melted chocolate mixture until blended, about 1 minute, scraping bowl often with rubber spatula.

5. In small bowl, with clean beaters and mixer at high speed, beat egg whites and cream of tartar until soft peaks form when beaters are lifted. Sprinkle in remaining 2 tablespoons sugar, beating until whites stand in stiff, glossy peaks.

6. With rubber spatula, fold hazelnut mixture into yolk mixture just until blended. Gently fold beaten egg whites into yolk mixture, one-third at a time.

7. Spread batter in pan. Bake until toothpick inserted in cake, about 2 inches from edge, comes out clean, 25 to 28 minutes. (The center of cake will still be slightly soft.) Cool cake in pan on wire rack 15 minutes. With small knife, loosen cake from side of pan; invert onto wire rack. Cool completely. (The recipe can be prepared up to this point 2 days in advance. If not using cake right away, wrap well and refrigerate.)

8. Coarsely chop remaining 3 squares semisweet chocolate; place in small bowl. In small saucepan over low heat, heat heavy cream just to boiling. Pour cream over chopped chocolate; let stand 1 minute. Gently stir until chocolate melts; stir in corn syrup. Let stand at room temperature until glaze begins to thicken, about 5 minutes. Meanwhile, coarsely chop reserved hazelnuts.

9. Place cake on cake plate. Tuck strips of waxed paper under edge of cake to keep plate clean when glazing cake. Pour chocolate glaze over cake. With metal spatula, spread glaze to completely cover top and side of cake. Sprinkle chopped hazelnuts around top edge of cake. Chill cake 20 minutes to set glaze. Remove and discard waxed-paper strips. Refrigerate cake if not serving right away. Makes 10 servings.

Each serving: About 330 calories, 4 g protein, 30 g carbohydrate, 22 g total fat (5 g saturated), 74 mg cholesterol, 155 mg sodium.

∿Chiffon, Angel-Food, & Sponge Cakes

Tangerine Chiffon Cake

Prep: 30 minutes plus cooling and standing
Bake: About 1 hour 15 minutes

5 tangerines or 3 large oranges
2 ¼ cups cake flour (not self-
   rising)
1 tablespoon baking powder
1 teaspoon salt

1 ½ cups sugar
½ cup vegetable oil
5 large egg yolks
7 large egg whites
½ teaspoon cream of tartar
Tangerine Glaze
   (see page 1002)

1. Preheat oven to 325°F. Grate 4 teaspoons peel and squeeze ¾ cup juice from tangerines.

2. In large bowl, combine flour, baking powder, salt, and 1 cup sugar; whisk in oil, egg yolks, peel, and juice until smooth.

3. In another large bowl, with mixer at high speed, beat egg whites and cream of tartar until soft peaks form when beaters are lifted. With mixer at high speed, gradually sprinkle in remaining ½ cup sugar until whites hold stiff peaks. Fold one-third of whites into yolk mixture; fold in remaining whites.

4. Pour batter into ungreased 10-inch tube pan. Bake until top springs back when touched, about 1 hour and 15 minutes. Invert cake in pan on funnel or bottle; cool completely in pan. With small knife, loosen cake from side of pan; invert onto rack.

5. Place cake on cake plate. Tuck strips of waxed paper under edge of cake to keep plate clean while glazing. Prepare Tangerine Glaze; spread over top of cake. Let stand 1 hour or until set. Makes 16 servings.

TANGERINE GLAZE: With spoon, mix *1 cup confectioners' sugar*, and *1 teaspoon grated tangerine or orange peel*. Stir in *5 to 6 teaspoons tangerine or orange juice* until glaze is spreadable.

Each serving: About 250 calories, 4 g protein, 40 g carbohydrate, 9 g total fat (1 g saturated), 67 mg cholesterol, 230 mg sodium.

Angel-Food Cake

Prep: 10 minutes plus cooling
Bake: 30 to 35 minutes

1¼ cups confectioners' sugar
1 cup cake flour (not self-rising)
1⅔ cups egg whites (12 to 14 egg whites), at room temperature
1½ teaspoons cream of tartar
½ teaspoon salt
2 teaspoons vanilla extract
½ teaspoon almond extract
1¼ cups granulated sugar

1. Preheat oven to 375°F. In small bowl, stir confectioners' sugar and cake flour; set aside.

2. In large bowl, with mixer at high speed, beat egg whites, cream of tartar, and salt until soft peaks form when beaters are lifted; beat in extracts. With mixer at high speed, sprinkle in granulated sugar, 2 tablespoons at a time, beating until sugar has completely dissolved and whites stand in stiff peaks. Sift flour mixture over egg whites, one-third at a time, folding in with rubber spatula after each addition, just until flour disappears.

3. Pour batter into ungreased 10-inch tube pan. Bake until cake springs back when lightly touched, 30 to 35 minutes. Invert cake in pan on funnel or bottle; cool completely in pan. With small knife, carefully loosen cake from side of pan; invert onto cake plate. Makes 16 servings.

Each serving: About 130 calories, 4 g protein, 28 g carbohydrate, 0 g total fat, 0 mg cholesterol, 120 mg sodium.

Seattle Cappuccino Angel-Food Cake

Prep: 10 minutes plus cooling
Bake: 35 to 40 minutes

1 cup cake flour (not self-rising)
½ cup plus 1 tablespoon confectioners' sugar
1⅔ cups egg whites (about 12 large), at room temperature
4 teaspoons instant espresso-coffee powder
1½ teaspoons cream of tartar
½ teaspoon salt
½ plus ⅛ teaspoon ground cinnamon
1½ teaspoons vanilla extract
1¼ cups granulated sugar

1. Preheat oven to 375°F. On waxed paper, mix flour and ½ cup confectioners' sugar; set aside.

2. In large bowl, with mixer at high speed, beat egg whites, instant espresso-coffee powder, cream of tartar, salt, and ½ teaspoon cinnamon until soft peaks form when beaters are lifted; beat in vanilla. With mixer at high speed, sprinkle in granulated sugar, 2 tablespoons at a time, beating until sugar has completely dissolved and egg whites stand in stiff, glossy peaks. Sift flour mixture over egg whites, one-third at a time, folding in with rubber spatula after each addition, just until flour disappears.

3. Spoon batter into ungreased 10-inch tube pan. Bake cake until top springs back when lightly touched with finger, 35 to 40 minutes. Invert cake in pan on funnel or bottle; cool completely in pan.

4. With small knife, carefully loosen cake from side of pan; invert onto cake plate. In cup, mix remaining 1 tablespoon confectioners' sugar and remaining ⅛ teaspoon cinnamon; sprinkle over cake. Makes 16 servings.

Each serving: About 120 calories, 3 g protein, 26 g carbohydrate, 0 g total fat, 0 mg cholesterol, 110 mg sodium.

Walnut Torte

Prep: 45 minutes plus cooling
Bake: 25 to 30 minutes

3¼ cups walnuts
1 cup plus 2 tablespoons sugar
3 tablespoons all-purpose flour
1 teaspoon baking powder
¼ teaspoon salt
6 large eggs, separated
½ teaspoon almond extract
1 cup heavy or whipping cream

1. Preheat oven to 350°F. Grease two 8-inch round cake pans. Line bottoms of pans with waxed paper; grease paper. Dust with flour.

2. Remove ¼ cup walnuts; coarsely chop. In food processor with knife blade attached, or in blender in batches, grind remaining 3 cups walnuts and ¼ cup sugar. (Nuts should be finely ground but not pastelike.) Transfer nut mixture to medium bowl; stir in flour, baking powder, and salt.

3. In large bowl, with mixer at high speed, beat egg whites until soft peaks form when beaters are lifted. Sprinkle in ¾ cup sugar, 2 tablespoons at a time, until whites stand in stiff peaks.

4. In small bowl, with mixer at medium speed, beat yolks and almond extract 3 minutes, frequently scraping bowl. Fold nut mixture and yolk mixture into egg whites, just until blended.

5. Divide batter evenly among pans. Bake until toothpick inserted in center of each layer comes out clean, 25 to 30 minutes. Cool in pans on wire racks 10 minutes. With small knife, loosen layers from sides of pans; invert onto racks. Remove and discard waxed paper. Cool completely.

6. In small bowl, with mixer at medium speed, beat cream and remaining 2 tablespoons sugar until stiff peaks form when beaters are lifted. Place 1 cake layer on cake plate; spread with about half of whipped cream. Top with second cake layer. Spread top of cake with remaining whipped cream; sprinkle with chopped walnuts. Refrigerate until ready to serve. Makes 12 servings.

Each serving: About 395 calories, 8 g protein, 2 g carbohydrate, 30 g total fat (7 g saturated), 134 mg cholesterol, 125 mg sodium.

Jelly Roll

Prep: 25 minutes plus cooling
Bake: About 15 minutes

¾ cup cake flour (not self-rising)
1 teaspoon baking powder
¼ teaspoon salt
4 large eggs, separated
¾ cup granulated sugar
¾ teaspoon vanilla extract
Confectioners' sugar
1 jar (10 to 12 ounces) jelly or jam

1. Preheat oven to 350°F. Grease 15½" by 10½" jelly-roll pan. Line pan with waxed paper; grease paper.

2. In small bowl, combine flour, baking powder, and salt; set aside. In large bowl, with mixer at high speed, beat egg whites until soft peaks form when beaters are lifted. Beating at high speed, gradually sprinkle in ¼ cup granulated sugar, beating until sugar has completely dissolved and whites stand in stiff peaks.

3. In large bowl, with mixer at high speed, beat egg yolks, remaining ½ cup granulated sugar, and vanilla until very thick and lemon-colored. Reduce speed to low; beat in flour mixture just until combined. With rubber spatula, fold yolk mixture into beaten whites.

4. Spread batter evenly in pan; bake until cake is golden and top springs back when lightly touched, about 15 minutes.

5. Meanwhile, sprinkle large clean cloth towel with confectioners' sugar. When cake is done, immediately invert cake onto towel. Carefully remove waxed paper and discard. If you like, cut off crisp edges. Starting at a narrow end, roll cake with towel, jelly-roll fashion. Cool cake roll, seam side down, on wire rack, until completely cool, about 30 minutes.

6. To serve, unroll cooled cake. Spread cake evenly with jelly. Starting from same narrow end, roll cake without towel. Sprinkle roll with confectioners' sugar; place, seam side down, on platter. Makes 16 servings.

Each serving: About 135 calories, 2 g protein, 29 g carbohydrate, 1 g total fat (0 g saturated), 53 mg cholesterol, 85 mg sodium.

LEMON ROLL: About 4 hours before serving or early in day, prepare *Lemon-Curd Filling* (see page 1024). Prepare Jelly Roll through Step 5. When ready to fill cake, unroll and spread evenly with Lemon-Curd Filling almost to edges. Roll cake and sprinkle with confectioners' sugar as above. Refrigerate until serving time.

Each serving: About 215 calories, 3 g protein, 27 g carbohydrate, 11 g total fat (2 g saturated), 93 mg cholesterol, 205 mg sodium.

Cannoli Cake Roll

Prep: 1 hour 30 minutes plus cooling and chilling
Bake: About 10 minutes

Cake
5 large eggs, separated
1 teaspoon vanilla extract
½ cup plus 1 tablespoon granulated sugar
¼ teaspoon cream of tartar
¼ teaspoon salt
¾ cup cake flour (not self-rising)
2 tablespoons orange-flavored liqueur
1 tablespoon water
Confectioners' sugar

Ricotta Filling
1¼ cups ricotta cheese
4 ounces reduced-fat cream cheese (Neufchatel)
½ cup confectioners' sugar
½ teaspoon vanilla extract
¼ teaspoon ground cinnamon
¼ cup semisweet-chocolate mini pieces

Frosting
¾ cup heavy or whipping cream
3 tablespoons confectioners' sugar
2 tablespoons orange-flavored liqueur
½ teaspoon vanilla extract
¼ cup pistachio nuts, chopped
1 tablespoon semisweet-chocolate mini pieces

1. Prepare Cake: Preheat oven to 375°F. Grease 15½" by 10½" jelly-roll pan. Line pan with waxed paper; grease paper and dust with flour.

2. In small bowl, with mixer at high speed, beat egg yolks, vanilla, and ¼ cup granulated sugar until very thick and lemon-colored, about 5 minutes. Transfer beaten yolk mixture to a large bowl and set aside.

3. In another large bowl, with clean beaters and with

mixer at high speed, beat egg whites, cream of tartar, and salt until soft peaks form when beaters are lifted. Beating at high speed, gradually sprinkle in ¼ cup granulated sugar until sugar has dissolved and whites stand in stiff peaks.

4. With rubber spatula or wire whisk, gently fold beaten egg whites into beaten egg yolks, one-third at a time. Sift and fold flour, one-third at a time, into egg mixture.

5. With metal spatula, spread batter evenly in pan. Bake until top of cake springs back when lightly touched with finger, about 10 minutes.

6. Meanwhile, in cup, with fork, mix orange liqueur, water, and remaining 1 tablespoon granulated sugar until sugar has dissolved.

7. Sprinkle clean cloth towel with confectioners' sugar. When cake is done, immediately invert hot cake onto towel. Carefully remove waxed paper and discard. Brush cake with orange-liqueur mixture. Starting from a long side, roll cake with towel jelly-roll fashion. Cool cake roll, seam side down, on wire rack until completely cool, about 1 hour.

8. Meanwhile, prepare Ricotta Filling: In food processor with knife blade attached, process ricotta, cream cheese, confectioners' sugar, vanilla extract, and cinnamon, until smooth. Transfer filling to bowl; stir in chocolate pieces. Cover and refrigerate filling while cake cools.

9. Assemble cake: Gently unroll cooled cake. With metal spatula, spread filling over cake almost to edges. Starting from same long side, roll cake without towel. Place rolled cake, seam side down, on platter.

10. Prepare Frosting: In small bowl, with mixer at medium speed, beat heavy cream and confectioners' sugar until soft peaks form when beaters are lifted. With rubber spatula, fold in orange liqueur and vanilla. Spread whipped-cream frosting over cake. Refrigerate cake at least 2 hours before serving. Sprinkle top of cake with pistachios and chocolate pieces just before serving. Makes 14 servings.

Each serving: About 255 calories, 7 g protein, 26 g carbohydrate, 13 g total fat (7 g saturated), 111 mg cholesterol, 120 mg sodium.

◦∿Dried & Fresh Fruitcakes

Cranberry-Raisin Fruitcake

Prep: 20 minutes plus cooling
Bake: About 1 hour 15 minutes

2⅔ cups walnuts, toasted	5 large eggs
1½ cups golden raisins	½ cup brandy
1 cup dried cranberries	1 tablespoon vanilla extract
1 tablespoon plus 2 cups all-purpose flour	2 teaspoons baking powder
1¼ cups sugar	1 teaspoon salt
1 cup (2 sticks) margarine or butter, softened	⅓ cup apple jelly

1. Preheat oven to 325°F. Grease 9-inch tube pan with removable bottom.

2. Set aside ⅔ cup walnut halves or large pieces to decorate top of cake; coarsely chop remaining walnuts. In medium bowl, toss chopped walnuts, raisins, dried cranberries, and 1 tablespoon flour; set aside.

3. In large bowl, with mixer at low speed, beat sugar and margarine until blended. Increase speed to high; beat until creamy, about 2 minutes, constantly scraping bowl with rubber spatula. Reduce speed to low; add eggs, brandy, vanilla, baking powder, salt, and remaining 2 cups flour; beat until well blended. With spoon, stir in raisin mixture (batter may look curdled).

4. Spoon batter into pan. Scatter reserved walnuts on top of batter. Bake cake until wooden skewer or toothpick inserted in center comes out clean, about 1 hour and 15 minutes. Cool cake in pan on wire rack 10 minutes. With small metal spatula, loosen cake from side of pan. Invert cake onto plate and remove side of pan. Loosen bottom of pan from cake and remove. Immediately invert cake onto wire rack. Cool completely.

5. When fruitcake is cold, melt apple jelly in small

saucepan over low heat. Brush cake with melted apple jelly. Or, wrap and refrigerate cake up to 1 month, then brush with jelly before serving. Makes 24 servings.

Each serving: About 315 calories, 5 g protein, 37 g carbohydrate, 17 g total fat (3 g saturated), 44 mg cholesterol, 240 mg sodium.

Golden Fruitcake

Prep: 1 hour plus cooling
Bake: About 3 hours

2 cups golden raisins
1 package (12 ounces) dried figs (1½ cups), chopped
1 cup diced candied citron (8 ounces)
1 cup diced candied lemon peel (8 ounces)
1 cup diced candied orange peel (8 ounces)
1 package (10 ounces) pitted dates, chopped (2 cups)
1 cup slivered blanched almonds (4 ounces)
½ cup candied pineapple, diced (4 ounces)
½ cup candied cherries, each cut in half (4 ounces)
3¾ cups all-purpose flour
2 teaspoons baking powder
½ teaspoon salt
2 cups sugar
1 cup (2 sticks) margarine or butter, softened
6 large eggs
1 cup sherry or orange juice
1 teaspoon lemon or orange extract

1. Preheat oven to 300°F. Line 10-inch tube pan with foil.

2. In large bowl, stir together raisins, figs, citron, lemon peel, orange peel, dates, almonds, pineapple, cherries, and ¾ cup of flour. Toss until evenly coated.

3. In medium bowl, combine remaining 3 cups flour, baking powder, and salt. In another large bowl, with mixer at low speed, beat sugar and margarine until blended. Increase speed to high; beat until light and fluffy. Add eggs, 1 at a time, beating well after each addition. Beat in sherry and lemon extract. Beat in flour mixture. Stir batter into fruit mixture.

4. Pour batter into pan. Bake until toothpick inserted in center of cake comes out clean, about 3 hours. Cool cake completely in pan on wire rack. Invert onto rack and carefully remove foil. Wrap fruitcake tightly; refrigerate overnight so cake will be firm and easy to slice. Makes one 7-pound fruitcake, or 56 servings.

Each serving: About 205 calories, 3 g protein, 38 g carbohydrate, 5 g total fat (1 g saturated), 23 mg cholesterol, 95 mg sodium.

Apricot-Pecan Fruitcake

Prep: 20 minutes plus cooling
Bake: About 1 hour 15 minutes

2½ packages (6 ounces each) dried apricot halves (2½ cups), cut into ½-inch pieces
2 cups coarsely chopped pecans plus ⅔ cup pecan halves
1 tablespoon plus 2 cups all-purpose flour
1¼ cups sugar

1 cup (2 sticks) margarine or butter, softened
5 large eggs
½ cup brandy
1 tablespoon vanilla extract
2 teaspoons baking powder
1 teaspoon salt
⅓ cup apricot preserves, melted and strained

1. Preheat oven to 325°F. Grease 9-inch tube pan.
2. In medium bowl, toss apricots, 2 cups coarsely chopped pecans, and 1 tablespoon flour; set aside.
3. In large bowl, with mixer at low speed, beat sugar and margarine until blended. Increase speed to high; beat until light and fluffy, about 2 minutes, constantly scraping bowl with rubber spatula. Reduce speed to low; add eggs, brandy, vanilla, baking powder, salt, and remaining 2 cups flour; beat until well blended. Stir in dried apricot mixture.
4. Spoon batter into pan. Arrange the pecan halves on top of batter in 2 concentric circles. Bake cake until wooden skewer or toothpick inserted in center comes out clean,

1 hour and 10 minutes to 1 hour and 20 minutes. Cool cake in pan on wire rack 10 minutes. With small knife, loosen cake from side of pan; invert onto rack. Cool completely on rack.

5. When cold, brush cake with melted apricot preserves, or wrap and refrigerate it for up to 1 week, then brush with preserves before serving. Makes 24 servings.

Each serving: About 295 calories, 4 g protein, 33 g carbohydrate, 17 g total fat (2 g saturated), 44 mg cholesterol, 235 mg sodium.

Caramelized Plum Cake

Prep: 1 hour plus cooling
Bake: 55 to 60 minutes

Fruit Topping
5 medium plums or 2 large Granny Smith apples (about 1 pound)
2 tablespoons margarine or butter
⅔ cup packed dark brown sugar

Cake
1½ cups cake flour (not self-rising)
1½ teaspoons baking powder
¼ teaspoon salt
6 tablespoons margarine or butter, softened
¾ cup granulated sugar
4 ounces almond paste (about half 7- to 8-ounce can or tube)
2 large eggs
1½ teaspoons vanilla extract
½ cup milk

1. Preheat oven to 350°F. Wrap outside of 10" by 3" springform pan with foil to prevent batter from leaking. Grease side of pan.

2. Prepare topping: Cut each unpeeled plum into thin wedges (or peel, core, and thinly slice each apple). Place margarine in springform pan and heat in oven until melted, about 4 minutes; remove from oven. In small bowl, with fork, stir brown sugar and melted margarine until blended, spreading mixture to coat bottom of pan. Arrange fruit on top of brown-sugar mixture, overlapping pieces slightly; set aside.

3. Prepare cake: In medium bowl, combine cake flour, baking powder, and salt; set aside.

4. In large bowl, with mixer at low speed, beat margarine, granulated sugar, and almond paste until blended, about 2 to 3 minutes, scraping bowl often with rubber spatula. Increase speed to medium; beat until well mixed, occasionally scraping bowl. Gradually beat in eggs and vanilla, just until blended.

5. With mixer at low speed, alternately add flour mixture and milk to almond-paste mixture, starting and ending with flour mixture; beat until just mixed.

6. Pour batter over fruit in pan. Bake until toothpick inserted in center of cake comes out clean, 55 to 60 minutes. Cool cake in pan on wire rack 10 minutes. With small knife, loosen cake from side of pan. Invert cake onto large plate; remove side and bottom of pan. Let cake cool at least 1 hour before serving. Makes 12 servings.

Each serving: About 295 calories, 4 g protein, 45 g carbohydrate, 12 g total fat (2 g saturated), 37 mg cholesterol, 215 mg sodium.

Skillet Pear Upside-Down Cake

Prep: 40 minutes plus cooling
Bake: 40 to 45 minutes

⅓ cup packed dark brown
    sugar
8 tablespoons (1 stick)
    margarine or butter, softened
5 firm but ripe Bartlett or Bosc
    pears (about 2 pounds),
    peeled, cored, and each cut
    into 8 wedges

1 cup cake flour (not self-rising)
1 teaspoon baking powder
¼ teaspoon salt
⅔ cup granulated sugar
1 large egg
1 teaspoon vanilla extract
⅓ cup milk

1. Preheat oven to 325°F. In nonstick 10-inch skillet with oven-safe handle (if skillet is not oven-safe, wrap handle of skillet with double layers of foil), heat brown sugar and 2 tablespoons margarine over medium-high heat until melted, stirring occasionally. Add pear wedges and cook, stirring occasionally, until pears are golden and tender, and sugar mixture has thickened slightly, about 10 minutes. Remove skillet from heat. With tongs, gently arrange pear wedges in concentric circles in skillet.

2. On sheet of waxed paper, combine flour, baking powder, and salt. In large bowl, with mixer at high speed, beat granulated sugar and remaining 6 tablespoons margarine until smooth, scraping bowl often with rubber spatula. Reduce mixer speed to low; beat in egg and vanilla. Alternately beat in flour mixture and milk, beginning and ending with flour mixture.

3. Pour batter over pears. Bake 40 to 45 minutes, until toothpick inserted in center of cake comes out clean. Cool cake in pan on wire rack, 5 minutes. Invert cake onto large plate. With a small metal spatula loosen sides of cake and underside of fruit to release. Carefully lift skillet. Serve warm or at room temperature. Makes 8 servings.

Each serving: About 325 calories, 3 g protein, 52 g carbohydrate, 13 g total fat (2 g saturated), 28 mg cholesterol, 290 mg sodium.

∿Frostings & Fillings

Buttercream Frosting

Prep: 7 minutes

1 package (16 ounces) confectioners' sugar
6 tablespoons margarine or butter, softened
3 tablespoons milk or half-and-half
1½ teaspoons vanilla extract

In large bowl, with mixer at medium speed (or with spoon), beat sugar, margarine, milk, and vanilla extract, adding more milk if necessary, until frosting is smooth and has an easy spreading consistency. Makes enough to fill and frost 2-layer cake or frost tube cake, 13" by 9" cake, or 2 dozen cupcakes.

Each serving: About 200 calories, 0 g protein, 38 g carbohydrate, 6 g total fat (1 g saturated), 1 mg cholesterol, 80 mg sodium.

LEMON BUTTERCREAM FROSTING: Prepare as above but use *3 tablespoons lemon juice* instead of milk and omit vanilla.

Each serving: About 200 calories, 0 g protein, 38 g carbohydrate, 6 g total fat (1 g saturated), 1 mg cholesterol, 80 mg sodium.

MOCHA BUTTERCREAM FROSTING: Prepare as above but add *½ cup unsweetened cocoa.* Substitute *⅓ cup hot coffee* for milk and reduce vanilla to ½ teaspoon.

Each serving: About 210 calories, 1 g protein, 39 g carbohydrate, 6 g total fat (1 g saturated), 0 mg cholesterol, 80 mg sodium.

BURNT BUTTERCREAM FROSTING: In small skillet over medium heat, cook margarine until lightly browned; cool. Prepare as above.

Each serving: About 200 calories, 0 g protein, 38 g carbohydrate, 6 g total fat (1 g saturated), 1 mg cholesterol, 80 mg sodium.

Decorating Buttercream

Prep: 10 minutes

1 cup (2 sticks) margarine or butter, softened
1½ packages (16 ounces each) confectioners' sugar (6 cups)
½ cup half-and-half or light cream
1 tablespoon vanilla extract

In large bowl, with mixer at low speed, beat margarine, confectioners' sugar, half-and-half, and vanilla extract just until blended. Increase speed to medium and beat until frosting is smooth and fluffy, about 1 minute, constantly scraping bowl with rubber spatula. Makes about 3¾ cups.

Each tablespoon: About 60 calories, 0 g protein, 9 g carbohydrate, 3 g total fat (1 g saturated), 1 mg cholesterol, 35 mg sodium.

Whipped-Cream Frosting

Prep: 5 minutes

2 cups heavy or whipping cream
¼ cup confectioners' sugar
Dash salt
1 teaspoon vanilla extract

In small bowl, with mixer at medium speed, beat heavy cream, sugar, and salt until stiff peaks form when beaters are lifted; fold in vanilla extract. Makes enough to fill and frost 2-layer cake or frost tube cake, 13" by 9" cake, or 2 dozen cupcakes.

Each serving: About 145 calories, 1 g protein, 3 g carbohydrate, 14 g total fat (9 g saturated), 55 mg cholesterol, 25 mg sodium.

CHOCOLATE WHIPPED-CREAM FROSTING: Prepare as above but fold in *1 package (6 ounces) semisweet-chocolate pieces* (1 cup), melted and cooled.

Each serving: About 205 calories, 2 g protein, 12 g carbohydrate, 18 g total fat (11 g saturated), 55 mg cholesterol, 25 mg sodium.

COFFEE WHIPPED-CREAM FROSTING: Prepare as above but add *1 teaspoon instant-coffee granules or powder* with sugar.

Each serving: About 145 calories, 1 g protein, 3 g carbohydrate, 14 g total fat (9 g saturated), 55 mg cholesterol, 25 mg sodium.

ORANGE WHIPPED-CREAM FROSTING: Prepare as above but add *1 teaspoon shredded orange peel* and *⅛ teaspoon orange extract* with vanilla extract.

Each serving: About 145 calories, 1 g protein, 3 g carbohydrate, 14 g total fat (9 g saturated), 55 mg cholesterol, 25 mg sodium.

Seven-Minute Frosting

Prep: 5 minutes
Cook: 7 minutes

1½ cups sugar
½ cup water*
1 tablespoon light corn syrup
1 teaspoon vanilla extract
½ teaspoon salt
2 egg whites, at room temperature

1. In top of double boiler, with mixer at high speed, beat sugar, water, corn syrup, vanilla, salt, and egg whites until blended, about 1 minute. Place top over rapidly boiling water; beat at high speed until soft peaks form when beaters are lifted (this may take more than 7 minutes).
2. Pour mixture into large bowl; beat at high speed until thick enough to spread. Makes enough to fill and frost 2-layer cake or frost tube cake, 13" by 9" cake, or 2 dozen cupcakes.

*For crusty surface, use only ⅓ cup water.

Each serving: About 100 calories, 1 g protein, 25 g carbohydrate, 0 g total fat, 0 mg cholesterol, 110 mg sodium.

CHOCOLATE SEVEN-MINUTE FROSTING: Melt *2 squares (2 ounces) unsweetened chocolate*; cool. Prepare as above; fold in (do not beat) melted chocolate.

Each serving: About 125 calories, 1 g protein, 27 g carbohydrate, 3 g total fat (2 g saturated), 0 mg cholesterol, 110 mg sodium.

HARVEST-MOON SEVEN-MINUTE FROSTING: Prepare as above but use *1½ cups packed brown sugar* instead of granulated sugar.

Each serving: About 110 calories, 1 g protein, 28 g carbohydrate, 0 g total fat, 0 mg cholesterol, 120 mg sodium.

Cream-Cheese Frosting

Prep: 10 minutes

3 cups confectioners' sugar
2 packages (3 ounces each) cream cheese, slightly softened
6 tablespoons (¾ stick) margarine or butter, softened
1½ teaspoons vanilla extract

In large bowl, with mixer at low speed, beat confectioners' sugar, cream cheese, margarine, and vanilla just until blended. Increase speed to medium and beat until frosting is smooth and fluffy, about 1 minute, constantly scraping bowl with rubber spatula. Makes about 2½ cups frosting.

Each tablespoon: About 65 calories, 0 g protein, 9 g carbohydrate, 3 g total fat (1 g saturated), 5 mg cholesterol, 35 mg sodium.

Ornamental Frosting

1 package (16 ounces) confectioners' sugar
3 tablespoons meringue powder*
⅓ cup warm water
Assorted food-color pastes (optional)*

1. In bowl, with mixer at medium speed, beat confectioners' sugar, meringue powder, and warm water until blended and mixture is so stiff that knife drawn through it leaves a clean-cut path, about 5 minutes.

2. If you like, tint frosting with food colorings; keep covered with plastic wrap to prevent drying out. With small metal spatula, artist's paintbrush, or decorating bag with small writing tip, decorate cookies with frosting. (You may need to thin frosting with a little *warm water* to obtain the right consistency.)

*Meringue powder and food-color pastes are available in specialty stores wherever cake-decorating equipment is sold.

Each cookie: About 40 calories, 0 g protein, 10 g carbohydrate, 0 g total fat, 0 mg cholesterol, 3 mg sodium.

Semisweet-Chocolate Icing

Prep: 3 minutes
Cook: 5 minutes

1 package (6 ounces) semisweet-chocolate pieces (1 cup)
2 tablespoons shortening
2 tablespoons light corn syrup
3 tablespoons milk

1. In heavy 2-quart saucepan over low heat, or in double boiler over hot, not boiling, water, heat semisweet-chocolate pieces and shortening until melted and smooth. Remove pan from heat.
2. With wire whisk or fork, beat in corn syrup and milk until mixture is smooth. Spread while still warm. Makes enough to ice top and sides of 2-layer cake or ice a rolled cake.

Each serving: About 90 calories, 1 g protein, 12 g carbohydrate, 6 g total fat (3 g saturated), 1 mg cholesterol, 5 mg sodium.

Chocolate Glaze

Prep: 5 minutes
Cook: 5 minutes

2 squares (2 ounces) semisweet chocolate
1 tablespoon margarine or butter
½ cup confectioners' sugar
2 to 3 tablespoons milk

1. In heavy 1-quart saucepan, heat semisweet chocolate and margarine over low heat until melted and smooth. Remove saucepan from heat.

2. With wire whisk or fork, beat in confectioners' sugar and milk until glaze is smooth and has an easy spreading consistency.

Each serving: About 45 calories, 1 g protein, 7 g carbohydrate, 2 g total fat (1 g saturated), 1 mg cholesterol, 15 mg sodium.

Broiled Praline Topping

Prep: 5 minutes
Broil: 2 minutes

½ cup (1 stick) margarine or butter
1⅓ cups (3½ ounces) flaked coconut, chopped
¾ cup chopped nuts
¾ cup packed brown sugar
¾ teaspoon vanilla extract

1. About 10 minutes before 13" by 9" cake has finished baking, in 2-quart saucepan, heat margarine over low heat, until melted. Stir in coconut, chopped nuts, brown sugar, and vanilla extract until mixed. Remove saucepan from heat.

2. When cake is done, turn oven control to broil. Spread coconut mixture over hot cake. Broil cake until golden, about 2 minutes. Makes enough to spread on top of 13" by 9" cake.

Each serving: About 205 calories, 2 g protein, 18 g carbohydrate, 15 g total fat (4 g saturated), 0 mg cholesterol, 110 mg sodium.

FOR ONE 8- OR 9-INCH CAKE LAYER: Prepare topping as above, but use *⅓ cup margarine, butter, or shortening, 1 cup chopped coconut, ½ cup chopped nuts, ½ cup packed brown sugar,* and *½ teaspoon vanilla extract.*

Each serving: About 280 calories, 3 g protein, 25 g carbohydrate, 20 g total fat (6 g saturated), 0 mg cholesterol, 145 mg sodium.

Easy Cream Filling

Prep: 5 minutes
Cook: 10 minutes

1 package (3 to 3¼ ounces) regular vanilla-flavored pudding and
    pie filling
1½ cups milk
½ cup heavy or whipping cream
Vanilla or almond extract

1. Prepare pudding mix as label directs but use only 1½
cups milk. Cover surface directly with plastic wrap and
refrigerate until chilled.
2. When pudding is cold, beat heavy or whipping cream
until stiff peaks form when beaters are lifted. Fold whipped
cream and a few drops of extract into pudding until
blended. Makes enough to fill and spread on top of 3-layer
cake or fill 4-layer cake.

*Each serving: About 60 calories, 1 g protein, 6 g carbohydrate,
4 g total fat (2 g saturated), 13 mg cholesterol, 50 mg sodium.*

EASY ORANGE-CREAM FILLING: Prepare as above but use
1½ cups orange juice instead of milk. Fold in *1 tablespoon
grated orange peel* with whipped cream

*Each serving: About 55 calories, 0 g protein, 8 g carbohydrate,
3 g total fat (2 g saturated), 10 mg cholesterol, 35 mg sodium..*

EASY CHOCOLATE-CREAM FILLING: Prepare as above but
substitute *1 package (3½ to 3⅝ ounces) regular chocolate-
flavored pudding and pie filling* for vanilla pudding; use
only *1½ cups milk.* Into hot pudding, stir *2 tablespoons
brown sugar.* Omit cream if you prefer a less rich filling.

*Each serving: About 70 calories, 1 g protein, 9 g carbohydrate,
4 g total fat (2 g saturated), 14 mg cholesterol, 35 mg sodium.*

Mocha-Cream Filling

Prep: 5 minutes

1½ cups heavy or whipping cream
½ cup unsweetened cocoa
¼ cup confectioners' sugar
2 tablespoons coffee-flavored liqueur

In large bowl, with mixer at medium speed, beat heavy cream, cocoa, confectioners' sugar, and liqueur until stiff peaks form when beaters are lifted. Makes enough to fill and spread on top of 2-layer cake or fill a rolled cake.

Each serving: About 135 calories, 1 g protein, 5 g carbohydrate, 11 g total fat (7 g saturated), 41 mg cholesterol, 15 mg sodium

Creamy Custard Filling

Prep: 5 minutes
Cook: 15 minutes

¼ cup sugar
2 tablespoons cornstarch
Dash salt
1 cup milk
2 large eggs
1 teaspoon vanilla extract

1. In 2-quart saucepan, combine sugar, cornstarch, and salt; stir in milk until smooth. Over medium heat, cook, stirring constantly, until mixture thickens and boils; boil 1 minute.

2. In small bowl, beat eggs slightly. Into eggs, beat small amount of hot milk mixture. Reduce heat to low; slowly pour egg mixture back into milk mixture, stirring rapidly to prevent lumping. Cook, stirring constantly, until custard thickens and coats the back of a spoon well (do not boil or mixture will curdle).

3. Remove saucepan from heat; stir in vanilla extract. Pour custard into a bowl; cover surface directly with plastic wrap and refrigerate until well chilled. Makes enough to fill 2-layer cake.

Each serving: About 45 calories, 2 g protein, 6 g carbohydrate, 2 g total fat (1 g saturated), 38 mg cholesterol, 30 mg sodium.

Fresh-Orange Filling

Prep: 10 minutes
Cook: 5 minutes

1 medium orange
½ cup water
¼ cup sugar
4 teaspoons cornstarch
½ teaspoon fresh lemon juice
¼ teaspoon salt
1 tablespoon margarine or butter

1. From orange, grate 1 tablespoon peel and squeeze ¼ cup juice.

2. In 1-quart saucepan, stir orange peel, orange juice, water, sugar, cornstarch, lemon juice, and salt until blended. Cook over medium heat, stirring constantly, until mixture thickens and boils; boil 1 minute.

3. Remove saucepan from heat; stir in margarine. Cool filling at room temperature. (If filling becomes too thick upon standing to spread easily, stir until it reaches spreading consistency.) Makes enough to fill 2-layer cake.

Each serving: About 30 calories, 0 g protein, 6 g carbohydrate, 1 g total fat (0 g saturated), 0 mg cholesterol, 60 mg sodium.

Lemon-Curd Filling

Prep: 10 minutes
Cook: 20 minutes

1 large lemon
¾ cup (1½ sticks) margarine or butter
1 cup sugar
3 large eggs

1. From lemon, grate 1 tablespoon peel and squeeze 3 tablespoons juice.

2. In double boiler over hot, not boiling, water, or in heavy 2-quart saucepan over low heat, stir lemon juice, lemon peel, margarine, and sugar until margarine melts.

3. In small bowl, beat eggs slightly. Add eggs to margarine mixture and cook, stirring constantly, until mixture is very thick and coats the back of a spoon well, about 15 minutes (do not boil or mixture will curdle).

4. Pour filling into a bowl; cover surface directly with plastic wrap and refrigerate until filling is well chilled, about 3 hours. Makes enough to fill rolled cake or 4-layer cake.

Each tablespoon: About 135 calories, 1 g protein, 13 g carbohydrate, 9 g total fat (2 g saturated), 40 mg cholesterol, 125 mg sodium.

Pies

~~~

Pastry & Piecrusts • Fruit Pies
Nut Pies • Cheese Pies
Custard Pies • Cream Pies
Mousse Pies

Crunchy crumb and nut crusts, flaky pastry, fruit, cream—there are pies of all types here, and you do not have to be a professional pastry chef to make them.

∾Tips for Baking Success

- Use nonshiny metal or glass pie plates for nicely browned bottom crusts. Shiny metal pans reflect the heat and keep crusts from browning properly.
- If you find that a recipe makes too much filling for your pie plate, bake the extra in a custard cup along with the pie. Cover the cup with foil if the pie has a top crust.
- If the top crust or edges seem to be browning too quickly, cover the pie loosely with foil and continue baking for the amount of time directed in the recipe.
- Before baking a 2-crust or deep-dish pie or cobbler, brush the top lightly with milk, half-and-half, or undiluted evaporated milk to enrich the browning. For a shiny top, brush the dough with slightly beaten egg white; for a golden-brown glazed top, brush with beaten whole egg or, for an even richer color, with beaten egg yolk. To add a bit of sparkle to a pie, sprinkle it lightly with granulated sugar.
- To keep a pie shell, baked without filling, from puffing and shrinking during baking, first prick dough in pie plate all over with a fork. Then, weight down pie shell with pie weights, dry beans or uncooked rice spread evenly

over foil-lined dough. Remove beans and foil several minutes before baking time is over to complete browning.

❧Keeping Pies Fresh

- Most fruit pies can be kept at room temperature overnight, even in warm weather, covered with foil or plastic wrap. For longer storage, refrigerate them, then freshen by warming them in the oven.
- Meringue-topped pies should be served the day they are made.
- To avoid spoilage, refrigerate pies with cream or custard fillings as soon as they have cooled, especially in warm weather. After serving, refrigerate any leftovers immediately.

❧Freezing Pastry

Pastry: Roll dough into rounds about 2 inches larger than the pie plate you will use, stack them with two sheets of waxed paper between each, freezer-wrap, and freeze. To use, remove dough rounds as needed, place them on pie plates, and allow them to thaw (10 to 15 minutes) before shaping. Use frozen dough within 2 months.

Pie Shells: If making several shells at one time, use reusable foil pie plates. Freeze unbaked or baked pie shells in their pie plates; wrap them, then stack them with crumpled waxed paper between each. Store unbaked pie shells in the freezer for two to three months. To use a shell, do not thaw; prick it many times with a fork, then bake it for 15 to 20 minutes in a preheated 425°F. oven, or fill it, then bake it as directed in the recipe.

∾Making Perfect Piecrust

1. Combine flour and salt. Cut in shortening with a pastry blender or with 2 knives used scissor-fashion until mixture forms coarse crumbs, making sure shortening is distributed evenly (this is what produces a flaky crust). Do not overhandle dough or shortening may become too soft and blend with the flour, making a sticky dough that will bake into a hard, tough crust.

2. Use very cold or ice water to help keep shortening cold; sprinkle over the crumb mixture 1 tablespoon at a time, tossing quickly with a fork. Too much water will make the dough sticky; too little water will make the dough crack at the edges as you roll it. When mixture is still crumbly but moist enough to hold together with slight pressure, stop tossing (too much handling will produce a tough crust with a pale, smooth surface). Flatten dough into a disk and chill before rolling.

3. To prevent sticking, place dough on a lightly floured surface (or on a pastry cloth sprinkled with flour). Flatten dough; roll it out with a rolling pin from the center to the edge, in all directions, for a round piecrust. Use light, even strokes, lifting pin up as it comes to the edge to keep edge from becoming too thin. Occasionally loosen dough with a metal spatula and sprinkle flour underneath. If bits of dough gather on the rolling pin, remove them immediately so that they will not tear holes in dough when rolling it.

4. To transfer the rolled pastry dough to a pie plate: Wrap the dough loosely around the rolling pin, then unroll it onto the plate. Or carefully fold it in half and lift it into the pie plate, placing the fold in the center of the plate. Unfold the dough and fit it loosely.

5. Ease the dough onto the bottom and side of the pie plate. The dough will shrink as it bakes, so be sure not to stretch or pull it. Pat the dough gently over the entire surface with your fingers to ease out any air pockets underneath.

6. With kitchen shears, trim the dough even with the pie-

plate rim or leave the overhang as the recipe directs. To repair tears, moisten the edges with a little water and press them firmly together.

7. If you have left the dough overhanging the rim of the pie plate, fold it under inside the pan rim, and pinch the fold firmly to seal it. Then turn the folded edge up to make a high stand-up edge. If the pie has a top crust, fold the top-crust dough under the overhang on the bottom crust before pinching and turning the fold-up.

ᔈFood-Processor Pie Crust the Right Way

• Be sure shortening, margarine or butter, and water are well-chilled; the motor will heat them up.
• Pulse dry ingredients (flour, sugar, and salt).
• Add fat, then pulse only until mixture resembles very coarse crumbs.
• With machine running, add water gradually, stopping just before the dough forms a ball. Beware: The food processor works so quickly that it's easy to add too little liquid; be sure to use what the recipe calls for, so the dough is moist enough to roll and transfer to a dish.

∾Pastry & Piecrusts

Crust for 8- or 9-inch Pie

For 1-Crust Pie or Baked Pie Shell
1 cup all-purpose flour
½ teaspoon salt
¼ cup plus 2 tablespoons shortening
2 to 3 tablespoons cold water

Each serving: About 1,135 calories, 13 g protein, 95 g carbohydrate, 78 g total fat (19 g saturated), 0 mg cholesterol, 1,165 mg sodium.

For 2-Crust Pie
2 cups all-purpose flour
1 teaspoon salt
¾ cup shortening
5 to 6 tablespoons cold water

1. In medium bowl, combine flour and salt. With pastry blender or 2 knives used scissor-fashion, cut in shortening until mixture resembles coarse crumbs.

2. Sprinkle cold water, 1 tablespoon at a time, into mixture, mixing lightly with a fork after each addition until pastry is just moist enough to hold together. Shape pastry into ball; flatten into disk. Wrap and refrigerate 30 minutes, or overnight (if chilled overight let stand at room temperature 30 minutes before rolling). Proceed as directed below for 1-crust pie, baked pie shell, no-roll piecrust, or 2-crust pie.

1-CRUST PIE: After preparing dough (above), on lightly floured surface, with floured rolling pin, roll dough into round about 2 inches larger than pie plate. Transfer round to pie plate and ease into plate. Trim edge, leaving 1-inch overhang. Fold overhang under, then bring up over pie-plate rim; pinch to form high edge, then make decorative edge (see page 1034). Fill and bake pie as recipe directs.

BAKED PIE SHELL: Preheat oven to 425°F. Prepare dough and line pie plate as for 1-crust pie (see page 1031); with fork, prick bottom and side of pastry all over to prevent puffing and shrinking during baking. Line with foil and pie weights. Bake shell until golden, about 15 minutes. Remove foil and weights; bake 2 to 3 minutes longer until browned. Cool before adding filling.

NO-ROLL PIECRUST: Prepare dough as for 1-crust pie (above). Do not roll out but press dough onto bottom and up side of pie plate.

2-CRUST PIE: After preparing dough (see page 1031), divide dough into 2 pieces, 1 slightly larger. Shape each into ball; flatten into disk, wrap and refrigerate 30 minutes. To line pie plate, roll larger disk into round 2 inches larger than pie plate. Transfer round to pie plate and ease into plate. Fill pie as recipe directs. For top crust, roll smaller disk as for bottom crust but cut a few short slashes or a design in center of round, then center over filling in bottom crust. Trim edge of dough, leaving 1-inch overhang. Fold overhang under, then bring up over pie-plate rim; pinch to form high edge, then make decorative edge (see page 1034).

Oil Crust for 8- or 9-inch Pie

Prep: 30 minutes plus chilling
Bake: 15 minutes

For 1-crust Pie or Baked Pie Shell
1 ⅓ cups all-purpose flour
½ teaspoon salt
⅓ cup vegetable oil
2 tablespoons cold water

Each serving: About 1,240 calories, 17 g protein, 127 g carbohydrate, 73 g total fat (7 g saturated), 0 mg cholesterol, 1,165 mg sodium.

For 2-Crust Pie
2⅓ cups all-purpose flour
1 teaspoon salt
½ cup plus 1 tablespoon vegetable oil
3 to 4 tablespoons cold water

Each serving: About 2,140 calories, 30 g protein, 222 g carbohydrate, 125 g total fat (12 g saturated), 0 mg cholesterol, 2,330 mg sodium.

1. In medium bowl, combine flour and salt. Stir in oil until mixture resembles coarse crumbs.

2. Sprinkle cold water, 1 tablespoon at a time, into mixture, mixing lightly with fork after each addition until dough is moist and cleans side of bowl. Shape dough into ball; flatten into disk. Proceed as directed below for 1-crust pie, baked pie shell, or 2-crust pie.

1-CRUST PIE: After preparing dough (above), dampen countertop slightly; place 12-inch square of waxed paper on dampened surface. Center disk on waxed paper; cover with second waxed-paper square. With rolling pin, roll dough into round about 2 inches larger than pie plate. If top waxed-paper sheet wrinkles, lift it off carefully, smooth it out, and replace on dough; continue rolling.

Gently remove top sheet of paper. Lift up dough on bottom sheet and place in pie plate, dough side down; remove paper and ease dough onto bottom and up side of plate. Trim edge of dough, leaving 1-inch overhang. Fold overhang under; pinch to form high edge, then make decorative edge (see page 1034). Fill and bake pie as recipe directs.

BAKED PIE SHELL: Preheat oven to 425°F. Prepare dough and line pie plate as for 1-crust pie; with fork, prick dough all over to prevent puffing and shrinking during baking. Bake shell until golden, 15 minutes. Line with foil and pie weights. Remove foil and weights; bake 2 to 3 minutes longer until browned. Cool before filling.

2-CRUST PIE: After preparing dough (above), divide dough into 2 pieces, one slightly larger. Shape each into ball; flatten into disk. To line pie plate, roll larger disk between 2 sheets of waxed paper and transfer to pie plate as above; ease into pie plate. Fill pie as recipe directs.

For top crust, roll smaller disk in same manner; remove top sheet of waxed paper and cut a few short slashes or a design in center of dough. Center round, dough side down, over filling in bottom crust; remove waxed paper. Trim edges of dough, leaving 1-inch overhang. Fold overhang under, then bring up over pie-plate rim; pinch to form high edge, then make decorative edge (see page 1034).

PIE TOPS

Cobbler or Deep-Dish: Prepare dough for 1-crust pie (see page 1033). Roll 2 inches larger than 9½" by 1½" deep pie plate; place over filling. Trim edge, leaving 1-inch overhang; pinch to form high edge and make decorative edge. Cut 4-inch "X" in center of crust; fold back points to make square opening.

Lattice: Prepare dough for 2-crust pie (see page 1033). Prepare bottom crust; fill. Trim dough, leaving 1-inch overhang. Roll top crust into 12-inch circle; cut into ½-inch strips. Moisten edge of bottom crust with water. Place dough strips about ¾ inch apart across pie; press each at both ends to seal. Repeat with an equal number of strips placed at right angles to first ones to make lattice design. Turn overhang up over ends of strips; pinch to seal. Make high stand-up edge that will hold juices in; flute.

DECORATIVE EDGES

Old-Fashioned Forked: Trim dough even with rim of pie plate. With back of floured 4-tined fork, press dough to plate rim all around edge.

Fluted: Trim dough, leaving 1-inch overhang; fold overhang under to make stand-up edge. Firmly place left index finger on inside edge of dough; with right thumb and index finger, pinch dough at that point. Repeat every ¾ inch around edge. Leave flutes rounded or pinch again to sharpen. (This makes a high edge, especially suitable for pumpkin, custard, and fruit pies that are very juicy.)

Rope: Trim dough, leaving 1-inch overhang; fold overhang under to make stand-up edge. Press right thumb into dough at angle, then pinch dough between the thumb and knuckle of index finger. Place thumb in groove left by index finger and repeat all around edge.

Scalloped: Trim dough, leaving 1-inch overhang; fold overhang under to make stand-up edge. Position left thumb and index finger about 1¼ inches apart on edge. Using floured round-bowl measuring tablespoon, gently push dough between fingers outward to form scallop. Gently press dough against spoon to round evenly. Repeat around edge. Pinch points between scallops to sharpen.

No-Roll Nut Crust

Prep: 15 minutes
Bake: 12 minutes

For 8- or 9-Inch Pie Shell
1 cup all-purpose flour
½ cup (1 stick) margarine or butter, softened
¼ cup confectioners' sugar
¼ cup walnuts, finely chopped

1. Preheat oven to 400°F. In pie plate, with fork, mix all ingredients until soft and pliable. Press mixture evenly onto bottom and up side of pie plate. With fork, prick bottom of crust all over to prevent puffing during baking.

2. Bake shell until golden, about 12 minutes. Cool on wire rack. Fill as recipe directs or with chilled pie filling.

Each serving: About 1,550 calories, 18 g protein, 125 g carbohydrate, 110 g total fat (18 g saturated), 0 mg cholesterol, 1,225 mg sodium.

Tart Shell

Prep: 20 minutes plus chilling
Bake: 25 minutes

For 9- or 10-Inch Tart Shell
1¼ cups all-purpose flour
¼ cup shortening
4 tablespoons cold margarine or butter
1 tablespoon sugar
¼ teaspoon salt
3 to 4 tablespoons cold water

1. In medium bowl, combine flour, shortening, margarine, sugar, and salt. With fingertips, blend mixture until it resembles coarse crumbs. Sprinkle cold water, 1 tablespoon at a time, mixing with fork after each addition until just moist enough to hold together. Shape dough into ball; flatten into disk. Wrap and refrigerate until well chilled, 1 hour.

2. Preheat oven to 425°F. On floured surface, with floured rolling pin, roll dough into round about 1 inch larger than tart pan with removable bottom. Line pan with dough, pressing dough onto bottom and up side of pan; trim edge. With fork, prick dough all over to prevent puffing during baking. Line dough with foil and weight it with pie weights, dry beans, or uncooked rice to prevent puffing or slipping during baking.

3. Bake shell 10 minutes. Remove foil; again prick shell. Bake until golden, 15 minutes. (If shell puffs up during baking, gently press to pan with back of spoon.) Cool tart shell in pan on wire rack. Fill as recipe directs.

Each serving: About 1,470 calories, 17 g protein, 132 g carbohydrate, 98 g total fat (21 g saturated), 0 mg cholesterol, 1,195 mg sodium.

Baked Graham-Cracker Crumb Crust

Prep: 10 minutes
Bake: 8 minutes

For 8-inch Pie Shell
1 ¼ cups graham-cracker crumbs
4 tablespoons margarine or butter, melted
3 tablespoons sugar

Each serving: About 1,075 calories, 14 g protein, 123 g carbohydrate, 59 g total fat (11 g saturated), 0 mg cholesterol, 1,610 mg sodium.

For 9-inch Pie Shell
1 ½ cups graham-cracker crumbs
6 tablespoons margarine or butter, melted
¼ cup sugar

1. Preheat oven to 375°F. If you would like to make your own graham-cracker crumbs, pulverize crackers in blender or in food processor with knife blade attached as manufacturer directs; or place them in sturdy plastic bag and roll into fine crumbs with rolling pin.

2. In pie plate or bowl, with fork, mix crumbs, margarine, and sugar. If you like, set aside 3 tablespoons mixture for topping. With hand, press mixture onto bottom and up side of pie plate.

3. Bake crust 8 minutes; cool on wire rack. Fill as recipe directs or with chilled pie filling; top with reserved crumb mixture or garnish as recipe directs.

VANILLA- OR CHOCOLATE-WAFER CRUMB CRUST: For 8-inch pie, use *1 ¼ cups vanilla- or chocolate-wafer crumbs* and *4 tablespoons margarine or butter*, melted. For 9-inch pie, use *1 ½ cups vanilla- or chocolate-wafer crumbs* and *6 tablespoons margarine or butter*, melted.

GINGERSNAP CRUMB CRUST: Use *gingersnap crumbs* instead of graham-cracker crumbs for Baked Graham-Cracker Crumb Crust.

NUT-CRUMB CRUST: Use *½ cup finely chopped nuts* (such as walnuts, almonds, pecans, and filberts) instead of ½ cup crumbs in any of above recipes.

Baked Coconut Crust

For 8- or 9-Inch Pie Shell
2 tablespoons margarine or butter, softened
1⅓ cups (3½ ounces) shredded coconut

1. Preheat oven to 300°F. Onto bottom and side of pie plate, evenly spread margarine. Pat coconut into margarine.
2. Bake shell until golden, 15 minutes. Cool on wire rack. Fill as recipe directs or with chilled pie filling.

Each serving: About 835 calories, 4 g protein, 65 g carbohydrate, 66 g total fat (34 g saturated), 0 mg cholesterol, 475 mg sodium.

UNBAKED COCONUT CRUST: In pie plate or medium bowl, combine coconut, *¼ cup confectioners' sugar*, and *3 tablespoons margarine or butter*. Press mixture onto bottom and up side of pie plate, making a small rim. Refrigerate until firm, 1 hour. Fill as recipe directs or with chilled pie filling.

Each serving: About 640 calories, 4 g protein, 41 g carbohydrate, 54 g total fat (32 g saturated), 0 mg cholesterol, 325 mg sodium.

Baked Nut Crust

For 8-inch Pie Shell
1 cup blanched almonds, Brazil nuts, peanuts, pecans, or walnuts, finely ground
2 tablespoons sugar
1½ tablespoons margarine or butter, softened

Each serving: About 1,215 calories, 34 g protein, 53 g carbohydrate, 97 g total fat (10 g saturated), 0 mg cholesterol, 240 mg sodium.

For 9-inch Pie Shell
1½ cups blanched almonds, Brazil nuts, peanuts, pecans, or
    walnuts, finely ground
3 tablespoons sugar
2 tablespoons margarine or butter, softened

1. Preheat oven to 400°F. In pie plate or small bowl, stir ground nuts, sugar, and margarine until blended. With hand, press mixture onto bottom and up side of pie plate.

2. Bake shell just until golden, about 8 minutes. Cool on rack. Fill as recipe directs or with chilled pie filling.

∾Fruit Pies

Fruit Pie

Prep: 45 minutes
Bake: 40 to 50 minutes

Pastry for 9-inch 2-crust pie (page 1031) or 1 package (10 to 11
    ounces) piecrust mix
1 fruit filling (see pages 1039–1041)
1 tablespoon margarine or butter, cut into pieces

1. Prepare dough and line 9-inch pie plate as directed for 2-crust pie. Preheat oven to 425°F.

2. Spoon filling into piecrust; dot filling with margarine.

3. Place top crust on filling; make a decorative edge (see page 1034).

4. Bake pie until golden, 40 to 50 minutes. Cool slightly on wire rack to serve warm, or cool pie completely to serve later.

APPLE PIE FILLING: Peel, core, and thinly slice *6 medium cooking apples* (about 2 pounds) to make 6 to 7 cups slices. In large bowl, toss apple slices, *⅔ cup sugar* (half brown sugar, if you like), *2 tablespoons all-purpose flour, 1 to 2 teaspoons lemon juice, ½ teaspoon ground cinnamon, ½ teaspoon freshly grated lemon peel*, and *¼ teaspoon ground nutmeg* until well mixed.

Each serving: About 335 calories, 3 g protein, 45 g carbohydrate, 17 g total fat (4 g saturated), 0 mg cholesterol, 250 mg sodium.

BLUEBERRY PIE FILLING: In large bowl, with rubber spatula, toss *2 pints blueberries* (about 5 cups), washed and picked over, *¾ cup sugar, ⅓ cup all-purpose flour, ½ teaspoon ground cinnamon, ½ teaspoon freshly grated lemon peel*, and *⅛ teaspoon salt*.

Each serving: About 220 calories, 7 g protein, 35 g carbohydrate, 7 g total fat (2 g saturated), 30 mg cholesterol, 170 mg sodium.

CHERRY-PIE FILLING: Remove pits from *2 pounds fresh tart cherries*. In large bowl, toss cherries, *1 cup sugar, ¼ cup cornstarch*, and *½ teaspoon salt* until well mixed.

Each serving: About 365 calories, 3 g protein, 51 g carbohydrate, 17 g total fat (4 g saturated), 0 mg cholesterol, 370 mg sodium.

CANNED CHERRY PIE FILLING: Drain *2 cans (16 ounces each) pitted tart cherries*, reserving *½ cup juice*. In medium bowl, stir *1 cup sugar, 3 tablespoons quick-cooking tapioca, ¼ teaspoon salt*, and *¼ teaspoon ground cinnamon*; stir in reserved cherry juice, cherries, and *½ teaspoon vanilla extract*. Let mixture stand 15 minutes to soften tapioca.

Each serving: About 375 calories, 3 g protein, 54 g carbohydrate, 17 g total fat (4 g saturated), 0 mg cholesterol, 310 mg sodium.

PEACH PIE FILLING: Peel, pit, and slice *8 medium peaches* (about 2 pounds) to make 6 cups slices. In large bowl, toss peach slices, *¾ cup sugar, ⅓ cup all-purpose flour, 1 tablespoon fresh lemon juice, ½ teaspoon ground cinnamon*, and *½ teaspoon freshly grated lemon peel* until well mixed.

Each serving: About 395 calories, 5 g protein, 60 g carbohydrate, 17 g total fat (4 g saturated), 0 mg cholesterol, 250 mg sodium.

PEAR PIE FILLING: Prepare as for Apple Pie Filling (see pages 1039–1040), but substitute *6 pears (about 2 pounds)*, peeled, cored, and thinly sliced, instead of apples.

Each serving: About 350 calories, 3 g protein, 48 g carbohydrate, 17 g total fat (4 g saturated), 0 mg cholesterol, 250 mg sodium.

RHUBARB PIE FILLING: Prepare filling before making pastry: In large bowl, stir *1½ cups sugar, ¼ to ⅓ cup all-purpose flour, 1 tablespoon fresh orange peel* (optional), and *¼ teaspoon salt*. Add *1 pound rhubarb* (without tops), cut into 1-inch pieces (about 4 cups); toss lightly to mix well.

Each serving: About 375 calories, 4 g protein, 53 g carbohydrate, 17 g total fat (4 g saturated), 0 mg cholesterol, 310 mg sodium.

Deep-Dish Apple Pie

Prep: 40 minutes plus cooling
Bake: 1 hour 15 minutes

Apple Filling
6 pounds Granny Smith apples (about 12 large apples), peeled, cored, and each cut into 16 wedges
¾ cup sugar
⅓ cup all-purpose flour
2 tablespoons fresh lemon juice
½ teaspoon ground cinnamon

Pie Crust
2 cups all-purpose flour
2 teaspoons baking powder
½ teaspoon salt
¼ cup plus 1 tablespoon sugar
4 tablespoons margarine or butter
1 large egg, beaten
⅔ cup plus 2 tablespoons heavy or whipping cream

1. Prepare filling: In large bowl, combine apples, sugar, flour, lemon juice, and cinnamon; toss to coat well. Spoon apple mixture into 13" by 9" glass baking dish; set aside.

2. Preheat oven to 400°F. Prepare pie crust: In medium bowl, combine flour, baking powder, salt, and ¼ cup sugar. With pastry blender or 2 knives used scissor-fashion, cut in margarine until mixture resembles coarse crumbs. Stir in egg and ⅔ cup cream until blended.

3. With floured hands, shape dough into ball. Divide dough into 6 pieces; flatten each to about ½-inch thickness and arrange on top of apple mixture. (It is not necessary to completely cover top; as dough bakes, it will spread.) Brush dough with remaining 2 tablespoons cream, and sprinkle with 1 tablespoon sugar.

4. Place sheet of foil underneath baking dish; crimp foil edges to form a rim to catch any overflow during baking. Bake pie until apples are tender when pierced with knife, filling is bubbly, and crust is golden, about 1 hour 15 minutes. Cover pie loosely with foil to prevent over-browning if necessary halfway through baking time. Cool pie on wire rack 1 hour to serve warm, or cool completely to serve later. Makes 12 servings.

Each serving: About 355 calories, 4 g protein, 64 g carbohydrate, 11 g total fat (5 g saturated), 39 mg cholesterol, 210 mg sodium.

Apple Crumb Pie

Prep: 40 minutes
Bake: About 1 hour 45 minutes

1½ cups all-purpose flour
½ teaspoon salt
4 tablespoons margarine or butter
¼ cup shortening
4 tablespoons cold water
3 pounds Granny Smith apples (about 7 large)
⅔ cup sugar

⅓ cup dark seedless raisins
3 tablespoons cornstarch
½ teaspoon ground cinnamon
Crumb Topping (see page 1043)
1 container (8 ounces) sour cream
1 teaspoon vanilla extract

1. In medium bowl, combine flour and salt. With pastry blender or 2 knives used scissor-fashion, cut in margarine and shortening until mixture resembles coarse crumbs. Sprinkle cold water, 1 tablespoon at a time, into flour mixture, mixing lightly with fork after each addition until dough is just moist enough to hold together. Shape dough into ball; flatten into disk. Wrap and refrigerate until firm enough to roll, about 30 minutes.

2. Meanwhile, peel, core, and cut apples into ¾-inch chunks. In large bowl, toss apples, sugar, raisins, cornstarch, and cinnamon until well combined. Set aside.

3. Preheat oven to 400°F. On lightly floured surface, with floured rolling pin, roll dough into a round 2 inches larger in diameter than inverted 9½-inch deep-dish pie plate. Ease dough into pie plate; trim edge, leaving 1-inch overhang. Fold overhang under; pinch to form decorative edge. Cover and refrigerate.

4. While crust is chilling, prepare Crumb Topping.

5. Add sour cream and vanilla to apple mixture and toss well to coat evenly. Spoon apple mixture into chilled pie crust. Sprinkle top of apples evenly with Crumb Topping.

6. Place sheet of foil underneath pie plate; crimp foil edges to form a rim to catch any overflow during baking. Bake pie 1 hour. Turn oven control to 350°F. and bake until filling is bubbly and top is golden, 35 to 45 minutes longer. Cover pie loosely with foil to prevent overbrowning if necessary during last 20 minutes of baking. Remove from oven and cool slightly on wire rack to serve warm, or cool completely to serve at room temperature later. Makes 10 servings.

CRUMB TOPPING: In medium bowl, combine *⅔ cup all-purpose flour, ⅓ cup packed brown sugar,* and *¼ teaspoon ground cinnamon.* With pastry blender or 2 knives used scissor-fashion, cut in *3 tablespoons cold margarine* until mixture resembles coarse crumbs.

Each serving: About 410 calories, 4 g protein, 65 g carbohydrate, 16 g total fat (5 g saturated), 10 mg cholesterol, 175 mg sodium.

Cheddar-Crust Vermont Apple Pie

Prep: 1 hour plus cooling
Bake: About 1 hour 15 minutes

2½ cups all-purpose flour
3 ounces shredded extrasharp
    Cheddar cheese (¾ cup)
½ teaspoon salt
3 tablespoons shortening
10 tablespoons (1¼ sticks)
    margarine or butter
4 to 6 tablespoons cold water

6 large Cortland apples (about
    3¼ pounds)
1 tablespoon fresh lemon juice
⅔ cup sugar
¼ teaspoon ground cinnamon

1. In medium bowl, combine 2¼ cups flour, Cheddar cheese, and salt. With pastry blender or 2 knives used scissor-fashion, cut in shortening and 8 tablespoons margarine until mixture resembles coarse crumbs. Sprinkle cold water, 1 tablespoon at a time, into flour mixture, mixing lightly with a fork after each addition until dough is just moist enough to hold together. Shape dough into 2 balls, 1 slightly larger than the other; flatten into disks. Wrap and refrigerate smaller disk until ready to use.

2. On lightly floured surface, with floured rolling pin, roll larger disk of dough into a round 2 inches larger all around than inverted 9½-inch deep-dish pie plate. Gently ease dough into pie plate; trim edge leaving 1-inch overhang. Cover and refrigerate at least 30 minutes.

3. Meanwhile, peel, core, and cut apples into ⅜-inch-thick slices. Place apple slices in large bowl; toss with lemon juice. In small bowl, mix sugar and cinnamon with remaining ¼ cup flour. Add sugar mixture to apple slices; toss well to coat. Spoon apple mixture into chilled piecrust; dot with remaining 2 tablespoons margarine.

4. Preheat oven to 425°F. Roll remaining dough for top crust into 11-inch round. Center round over filling in bottom crust. Trim edge, leaving 1-inch overhang. Fold overhang under; bring up over pie-plate rim and pinch to form high decorative edge. Cut short slashes in top crust to allow steam to escape during baking.

5. Place sheet of foil underneath pie plate; crimp foil edges to form a rim to catch any overflow during baking. Bake pie until apples are tender when pierced with a knife and pie is bubbly, about 1 hour and 15 minutes. Cover pie loosely with foil to prevent overbrowning if necessary during last 10 minutes of baking. Cool pie on wire rack 1 hour; serve warm, or cool completely to serve later. Makes 10 servings.

Each serving: About 405 calories, 6 g protein, 56 g carbohydrate, 19 g total fat (5 g saturated), 9 mg cholesterol, 315 mg sodium.

French Apple Tart

Prep: 35 minutes
Bake: 25 minutes

1 package (10 ounces) frozen ready-to-bake puff-pastry shells
10 medium Golden Delicious apples (about 3½ pounds)
1 cup sugar
½ cup (1 stick) butter (no substitutions)
¼ teaspoon almond extract
Heavy or whipping cream (optional)

1. Let frozen puff-pastry shells stand at room temperature to thaw slightly.

2. Meanwhile, peel and core apples (Golden Delicious apples with greener skin retain shape best; do not use other apples); cut each apple lengthwise in half. In heavy 10-inch skillet with heat-safe handle (or with handle covered with heavy-duty foil), heat sugar, butter, and almond extract over medium heat, stirring occasionally, until butter melts (Do not use margarine because it separates from sugar during cooking.) Sugar will not completely dissolve.

3. Remove skillet from heat. Arrange apple halves on their sides around side and in center of skillet, fitting apples very tightly together. Heat apple mixture to boiling over medium heat; boil until sugar mixture becomes caramel-colored, 20 to 40 minutes, depending on juiciness of apples. Remove from heat.

4. Preheat oven to 450°F. On floured surface, stack puff-pastry shells, one on top of the other, pressing firmly together. With floured rolling pin, roll pastry into 12-inch round. Arrange pastry round on apples; with fork, press pastry to edge of skillet. Cut slits in pastry. Bake until pastry is golden, 20 to 25 minutes.

5. Remove skillet from oven; let cool on wire rack 10 minutes. Place a dessert platter upside down over skillet and, grasping them firmly together, carefully invert tart onto dessert platter (do this over sink since tart may be extremely juicy). If you like, serve with heavy cream. Makes 12 servings.

Each serving without cream: About 325 calories, 2 g protein, 43 g carbohydrate, 17 g total fat (7 g saturated), 22 mg cholesterol, 140 mg sodium.

Raspberry-Peach Pie

Prep: 30 minutes plus cooling
Bake: 1 hour 15 minutes

1¼ cups all-purpose flour
½ plus ⅛ teaspoon salt
2 tablespoons shortening
6 tablespoons cold margarine
   or butter
4 tablespoons cold water
1¼ cups sugar

⅓ cup cornstarch
9 ripe medium peaches (about
   3 pounds)
2½ cups raspberries
1 tablespoon fresh lemon juice

1. In medium bowl, combine flour and ½ teaspoon salt. With pastry blender or 2 knives used scissor-fashion, cut in shortening and 4 tablespoons margarine until mixture resembles coarse crumbs. Sprinkle cold water, 1 tablespoon at a time, into flour mixture, mixing lightly with a fork after each addition until dough is just moist enough to hold together. Shape dough into balls; flatten into disk and refrigerate until ready to use.

2. Preheat oven to 425°F. In large bowl, combine sugar, cornstarch, and remaining ⅛ teaspoon salt. Peel, pit, and slice peaches; add peaches to sugar mixture and toss to coat evenly. With rubber spatula, gently stir in raspberries and lemon juice. Spoon peach mixture into 6-cup baking dish or 9½-inch deep-dish pie plate; dot with remaining 2 tablespoons margarine.

3. On lightly floured surface, with floured rolling pin, roll dough 1½ inches larger all around than top of baking dish. Center dough over filling. Trim edge of dough, leaving 1-inch overhang. Fold overhang under; pinch dough onto rim of baking dish to seal. With tip of knife, cut slits in piecrust to allow steam to escape during baking.

4. Place sheet of foil underneath baking dish; crimp foil edges to form a rim to catch any overflow during baking. Bake pie until filling begins to bubble and crust is golden, 1 hour and 15 minutes. Cover pie loosely with foil to prevent overbrowning if necessary during last 15 minutes of baking. Cool pie on wire rack 1 hour to serve warm. Or cool completely to serve later. Makes 10 servings.

Each serving: About 315 calories, 3 g protein, 56 g carbohydrate, 10 g total fat (2 g saturated), 0 mg cholesterol, 225 mg sodium.

Deep-Dish Peach Pie

Prep: 40 minutes
Bake: About 50 minutes

8 large peaches (about 3½ pounds)
1 cup sugar
⅓ cup all-purpose flour
¼ teaspoon ground cinnamon
Pastry for 9-inch 2-crust Pie (see page 1031) or 1 package (10 to 11 ounces) piecrust mix
1 tablespoon margarine or butter, cut into pieces
1 tablespoon milk

1. Peel, pit, and thinly slice peaches. In large bowl, toss peaches with sugar, flour, and cinnamon.

2. Prepare dough for 2-crust pie. On lightly floured surface with floured rolling pin, roll two-thirds of dough into round about 2½ inches larger than 9½" by 1½" deep pie plate. Line pie plate with dough; trim edge of dough, leaving 1-inch overhang. Spoon peach mixture into piecrust; dot with margarine.

3. Preheat oven to 425°F. Roll remaining dough into 12-inch round. With floured pastry wheel or knife, cut dough round into ½-inch-wide strips; then prepare top crust as for Lattice Pie Top (see page 1034). Brush lattice (not edge) with milk.

4. Bake pie until peach mixture begins to bubble and crust is golden, about 50 minutes. Cool pie on wire rack 1 hour to serve warm, or cool completely to serve later. Makes 10 servings.

Each serving: About 380 calories, 4 g protein, 55 g carbohydrate, 17 g total fat (4 g saturated), 0 mg cholesterol, 250 mg sodium.

Pear Tarte Tatin

Prep: 1 hour plus cooling
Bake: 25 minutes

1½ cups all-purpose flour
½ teaspoon salt
2 tablespoons plus ¾ cup sugar
¼ cup shortening
10 tablespoons (1¼ sticks) margarine or butter
4 tablespoons cold water
1 tablespoon fresh lemon juice
7 firm, slightly ripe Bosc pears (about 3½ pounds), peeled, cored, and each cut lengthwise in half

1. In medium bowl, combine flour, salt, and 2 tablespoons sugar. With pastry blender or 2 knives used scissor-fashion, cut in shortening and 4 tablespoons margarine until mixture resembles coarse crumbs. Sprinkle cold water, 1 tablespoon at a time, into flour mixture, mixing lightly with fork after each addition until dough is just moist enough to hold together. Shape dough into ball; flatten into disk. Wrap and refrigerate until firm enough to roll, about 30 minutes.

2. Meanwhile, in heavy 12-inch oven-safe skillet (preferably cast iron; if skillet is not oven-safe, wrap handle of skillet with double layer of foil), heat lemon juice, ¾ cup sugar, and remaining 6 tablespoons margarine over medium-high heat until mixture boils. Place pears in skillet, cut side down; cook 12 minutes. Carefully turn pears over; cook until syrup is caramelized and thickened, 10 minutes longer.

3. Preheat oven to 425°F. Just before pears are done, on lightly floured surface, with floured rolling pin, roll dough into a 14-inch round. Place dough on top of pears in skillet; fold edge of dough under to form a rim around pears. With knife, cut six ¼-inch slits in dough to allow steam to escape during baking. Bake tart until crust is golden, 25 minutes.

4. When tart is done, place large platter over top of tart. Quickly turn skillet upside down to invert tart onto platter. Cool tart about 1 hour to serve warm, or cool completely to serve later. Makes 12 servings. If you like, you may substitute 11 firm, slightly ripe medium peaches (about 3¾ pounds), peeled, pitted, and halved for the pears.

Each serving: About 295 calories, 2 g protein, 42 g carbohydrate, 14 g total fat (3 g saturated), 0 mg cholesterol, 215 mg sodium.

Streusel-Topped Pear Pie

Prep: 40 minutes plus chilling
Bake: 1 hour

2¼ cups all-purpose flour
1¼ teaspoons salt
1 cup (2 sticks) margarine or butter
2½ to 3 tablespoons cold water
5 medium pears (about 1½ pounds)
½ cup granulated sugar

2 tablespoons fresh lemon juice
½ cup packed light brown sugar
1 teaspoon ground cinnamon
¼ teaspoon ground nutmeg
¼ teaspoon ground cloves
2 ounces Cheddar cheese, shredded (½ cup)

1. Prepare piecrust: In medium bowl, combine 2 cups flour and 1 teaspoon salt. With pastry blender or 2 knives used scissor-fashion, cut in ¾ cup margarine until mixture resembles coarse crumbs. Measure 1 cup mixture into another medium bowl; set aside.

2. Sprinkle cold water, 1 tablespoon at a time, into remaining flour mixture, mixing lightly with fork after each addition until dough is moist enough to hold together. Shape dough into ball; flatten into disk. Chill 30 minutes.

3. On lightly floured surface, with floured rolling pin, roll dough into round about 2 inches larger than 9-inch pie plate; use to line pie plate. Trim edges, leaving 1-inch overhang. Fold overhang under, then bring up over pie-plate rim; pinch to form a high fluted edge.

4. Peel, core, and cut pears into thick slices to make about 4½ cups. In large bowl, toss pears, granulated sugar, lemon juice, remaining ¼ cup flour, and ¼ teaspoon salt; spoon mixture into piecrust.

5. Preheat oven to 425°F. In medium bowl, combine reserved flour mixture, brown sugar, cinnamon, nutmeg, and cloves. With pastry blender or 2 knives used scissor-fashion, cut in cheese and remaining 4 tablespoons margarine until mixture resembles coarse crumbs and ingredients are well blended. Sprinkle over pears.

6. Bake pie 40 minutes. Cover pie loosely with foil to prevent overbrowning if necessary; bake 20 minutes longer. Cool on wire rack 1 hour to serve warm, or cool completely to serve later. Makes 10 servings.

Each serving: About 415 calories, 5 g protein, 55 g carbohydrate, 21 g total fat (5 g saturated), 6 mg cholesterol, 575 mg sodium.

Double Blueberry Pie

Prep: 30 minutes plus chilling
Bake: 8 minutes

30 gingersnaps
2 tablespoons plus ½ cup sugar
5 tablespoons margarine or butter, melted
2 tablespoons cornstarch
2 teaspoons cold water
3 pints blueberries, washed and picked over
whipped cream (optional)

1. In food processor with knife blade attached or in blender at high speed, blend gingersnaps and 2 tablespoons sugar until fine crumbs form.

2. Preheat oven to 375°F. In 9-inch pie plate, with fork, stir crumbs and melted margarine until moistened. With hand, press mixture onto bottom and up side of pie plate, making a small rim. Bake crust 8 minutes. Cool on wire rack.

3. Meanwhile, in 2-quart saucepan, blend cornstarch and cold water until smooth. Add half the blueberries and remaining ½ cup sugar to cornstarch mixture; heat to boiling over medium-high heat, pressing blueberries against side of saucepan with back of spoon. Boil 1 minute, stirring constantly. Remove saucepan from heat; stir in remaining blueberries.

4. Pour blueberry mixture into crust. Cover and refrigerate until well chilled, about 5 hours. Serve with whipped cream, if you like. Makes 10 servings.

Each serving without whipped cream: About 240 calories, 2 g protein, 42 g carbohydrate, 8 g total fat (2 g saturated), 0 mg cholesterol, 220 mg sodium.

Buttery Plum Tart

Prep: 30 minutes
Bake: 45 minutes

½ cup (1 stick) margarine or butter, softened
1½ cups plus 2 tablespoons all-purpose flour
⅓ cup plus ½ cup sugar
¾ teaspoon ground cinnamon
1½ pounds purple plums, pitted and sliced
¼ teaspoon almond extract
¼ cup slivered almonds
½ cup heavy or whipping cream (optional)

1. Prepare tart shell: In medium bowl, combine margarine, 1½ cups flour, ⅓ cup sugar, and ¼ teaspoon cinnamon. With hand, knead mixture until blended. Press dough onto bottom and up side of 9-inch tart pan with removable bottom or onto bottom and 1 inch up side of 9-inch springform pan.
2. Preheat oven to 375°F. In bowl, toss plums, almond extract, ½ cup sugar, remaining 2 tablespoons flour, and remaining ½ teaspoon cinnamon. Arrange plum slices, closely overlapping, to form concentric circles in pan. Sprinkle with almonds.
3. Bake tart until shell is golden and plums are tender, 45 minutes. Cool tart in pan on wire rack.
4. To serve, carefully remove side of pan. Cut tart into wedges. If you like, pass heavy cream to pour over servings. Makes 10 servings.

Each serving: About 270 calories, 3 g protein, 40 g carbohydrate, 11 g total fat (2 g saturated), 0 mg cholesterol, 125 mg sodium.

Lattice-Top Pineapple Tart

Prep: 45 minutes plus chilling and cooling
Bake: 35 to 40 minutes

Cookie Crust
¾ cup (1 ½ sticks) butter, softened (no substitutions)
⅓ cup plus 1 teaspoon granulated sugar
1 large egg, beaten
2 teaspoons vanilla extract
2 cups all-purpose flour
¼ teaspoon salt
1 teaspoon water

Pineapple Filling
1 can (20 ounces) crushed pineapple in unsweetened pineapple juice
⅓ cup packed light brown sugar
2 tablespoons fresh lemon juice
1 tablespoon butter, softened (no substitutions)

1. Prepare Cookie Crust: In large bowl, with mixer at low speed, beat butter and ⅓ cup granulated sugar until blended. Increase speed to high; beat until light and creamy, occasionally scraping bowl with rubber spatula. Reduce speed to medium; beat in all but 1 tablespoon egg (cover and refrigerate remaining egg). Beat in vanilla. With wooden spoon, stir in flour and salt until dough begins to form. With hands, press dough together. Divide dough into 2 pieces, 1 slightly larger than the other. Shape each piece into ball; flatten into disk. Wrap and refrigerate until dough is firm enough to roll, about 30 minutes.
2. While dough is chilling, prepare Pineapple Filling: In 10-inch skillet, heat pineapple with its juice, brown sugar, and lemon juice to boiling over medium-high heat. Cook, stirring often, until liquid evaporates, about 15 minutes. Stir in butter. Spoon pineapple mixture into medium bowl; cover and refrigerate until cooled.
3. Preheat oven to 375°F. Remove both pieces of dough from refrigerator. With floured hands, press larger disk into

9-inch round tart pan with removable bottom. Cover and refrigerate 15 minutes.

4. Meanwhile, on lightly floured waxed paper, roll remaining disk into 10-inch round. With pastry wheel or knife, cut dough into ten ¾-inch-wide strips. Refrigerate strips until easy to handle, about 15 minutes.

5. Spread pineapple mixture over dough in tart pan to ½ inch from edge. Prepare remaining dough as in Lattice Pie Top (see page 1034). With hands, roll dough trimmings into ¼-inch-thick ropes. Press ropes around edge of tart to create a finished edge. (If ropes break, just press pieces together.)

6. In cup, beat water and reserved egg. Brush egg mixture over lattice and edge of tart; sprinkle lattice and edge with remaining 1 teaspoon granulated sugar.

7. Bake tart until crust is golden, 35 to 40 minutes. Cool tart in pan on wire rack. Makes 10 servings.

Each serving: About 320 calories, 4 g protein, 43 g carbohydrate, 16 g total fat (9 g saturated), 61 mg cholesterol, 215 mg sodium.

Rustic Apricot Crostata

Prep: 45 minutes plus chilling and cooling
Bake: 40 to 45 minutes

½ cup blanched almonds, toasted
3 tablespoons cornstarch
2½ cups all-purpose flour
¼ teaspoon salt
1 cup (2 sticks) butter, softened (no substitutions)
½ cup plus 2 teaspoons sugar
1 large egg
1 large egg yolk
2 teaspoons vanilla extract
1 jar (12 ounces) apricot preserves (about 1 cup)
1 tablespoon water

1. In food processor with knife blade attached, or in blender at high speed, blend toasted almonds and cornstarch until finely ground. In medium bowl, combine nut mixture, flour, and salt.

2. In large bowl, with mixer at high speed, beat butter and ½ cup sugar until creamy. Add whole egg and vanilla; beat until almost combined (mixture will look curdled). With spoon, stir in flour mixture until dough begins to form. With hands, press dough together. Divide dough into 2 pieces, 1 slightly larger than the other. Shape each piece into ball; flatten into disk. Wrap and refrigerate until dough is firm enough to roll, 1½ to 2 hours.

3. Preheat oven to 375°F. Remove both pieces of dough from refrigerator. On lightly floured surface, roll larger disk into an 11-inch round. Press dough into 11-inch tart pan with removable bottom.

4. On lightly floured waxed paper, roll remaining disk into 12-inch round. With pastry wheel or knife, cut dough into twelve 1-inch-wide strips. Refrigerate 15 minutes.

5. Spread apricot preserves over dough in tart pan to ½ inch from edge. Prepare remaining dough as in Lattice Pie Top (see page 1034). Press ends to seal. With hands, roll dough trimmings and remaining strips of dough into about ¼-inch-thick ropes. Press ropes around edge of tart to create a finished edge. (If ropes break, just press pieces together.)

6. In cup, beat egg yolk and water. Brush egg-yolk mixture over lattice and edge of tart; sprinkle lattice and edge with remaining 2 teaspoons sugar.

7. Bake tart until deep golden, 40 to 45 minutes. If crust puffs up during baking (check occasionally during first 30 minutes of baking), press it to pan with back of spoon. Transfer tart to wire rack to cool completely. Makes 12 servings.

Each serving: About 395 calories, 5 g protein, 52 g carbohydrate, 19 g total fat (10 g saturated), 76 mg cholesterol, 210 mg sodium.

Old-Fashioned Strawberry-Rhubarb Pie

Prep: 45 minutes plus standing and cooling
Bake: 50 minutes

2 pints strawberries, hulled and
  halved
1 pound rhubarb (without tops),
  cut into ½-inch pieces, or 1
  package (16 ounces) frozen
  rhubarb
1 ¼ cups sugar
⅓ cup all-purpose flour
2 tablespoons quick-cooking
  tapioca

½ teaspoon vanilla extract
¼ teaspoon salt
Pastry for 9-inch 2-crust pie (see
  page 1031) or 1 package
  (10 to 11 ounces) piecrust
  mix
1 tablespoon margarine or
  butter, cut into pieces
1 tablespoon milk or half-and-
  half

1. In large bowl, with rubber spatula, gently toss strawberries, rhubarb, sugar, flour, tapioca, vanilla, and salt until well mixed. Let mixture stand 30 minutes to soften tapioca, stirring occasionally so tapioca will be evenly moistened.

2. Prepare piecrust for 2-crust pie. On lightly floured surface, with floured rolling pin, roll two-thirds of pastry into round about 2½ inches larger than 9½" by 1½" deep pie plate. Line pie plate with pastry; trim edge of pastry, leaving 1-inch overhang. Spoon fruit mixture into piecrust; dot fruit with margarine or butter.

3. Preheat oven to 425°F. Prepare remaining dough as in Lattice Pie Top (see page 1034). Brush lattice (not edge) with milk or half-and-half.

4. Bake pie until fruit mixture begins to bubble and crust is golden, 50 minutes. Cool pie on wire rack 1 hour to serve warm, or cool completely to serve later. Makes 10 servings.

Each serving: About 375 calories, 4 g protein, 53 g carbohydrate, 17 g total fat (4 g saturated), 0 mg cholesterol, 310 mg sodium.

Farm-Stand Cherry Pie

Prep: 45 minutes plus chilling and cooling
Bake: 45 to 50 minutes

1 ½ cups all-purpose flour
⅓ cup plus 1 tablespoon cornmeal
⅔ cup plus 1 teaspoon sugar
½ teaspoon plus ⅛ teaspoon salt
½ cup (1 stick) cold margarine or butter
4 to 5 tablespoons cold water
2 tablespoons plus 1 teaspoon cornstarch
1 ½ pounds dark sweet cherries, pitted
1 large egg white

1. In medium bowl, combine flour, ⅓ cup cornmeal, ⅓ cup sugar, and ½ teaspoon salt. With pastry blender or 2 knives used scissor-fashion, cut in margarine until mixture resembles coarse crumbs. Sprinkle cold water, 1 tablespoon at a time, into flour mixture, mixing with hands until dough comes together (it will feel dry at first). Shape into ball; flatten into disk.

2. Sprinkle large cookie sheet with remaining 1 tablespoon cornmeal. Place dampened towel under cookie sheet to prevent it from slipping. With floured rolling pin, roll dough, on cookie sheet, into a 13-inch round. With long metal spatula, gently loosen round from cookie sheet.

3. In large bowl, combine ⅓ cup sugar and cornstarch. Sprinkle half of sugar mixture over center of dough round, leaving a 2½-inch border all around. Add cherries and any cherry juice to sugar mixture remaining in bowl; toss well. With slotted spoon, spoon cherry mixture over sugared area on dough round (reserve any cherry-juice mixture in bowl). Fold dough up around cherries, leaving a 4-inch opening in center. Pinch dough to seal any cracks.

4. In cup, beat egg white and remaining ⅛ teaspoon salt. Brush egg-white mixture over dough; sprinkle with remaining 1 teaspoon sugar. Pour cherry-juice mixture through opening in top of pie. Refrigerate until well chilled, about 30 minutes. Meanwhile, preheat oven to 425°F.

5. Bake pie until crust is golden brown and cherry mixture is gently bubbling, 45 to 50 minutes. Cover pie loosely with foil to prevent overbrowning if necessary during last 10 minutes of baking.

6. As soon as pie is done, use long metal spatula to loosen it from cookie sheet to prevent sticking. Cool pie on cookie sheet 15 minutes, then slide onto wire rack to cool completely. Makes 6 servings.

Each serving: About 460 calories, 6 g protein, 74 g carbohydrate, 17 g total fat (3 g saturated), 0 mg cholesterol, 435 mg sodium.

Mince Pie

Prep: 30 minutes
Bake: 30 to 40 minutes

1 jar (28 ounces) ready-to-use mincemeat
1 large cooking apple, cored and diced
4 ounces walnuts (1 cup), coarsely broken
½ cup packed brown sugar
¼ cup brandy or rum (optional)
1 tablespoon fresh lemon juice
Pastry for 9-inch 2-crust Pie (see page 1031) or 1 package (10 to 11 ounces) piecrust mix
Hard Sauce (see page 922) or sliced sharp Cheddar cheese

1. In medium bowl, stir mincemeat, apple, walnuts, brown sugar, brandy, and lemon juice until well mixed.

2. Prepare piecrust and line 9-inch pie plate as directed for 2-crust pie.

3. Preheat oven to 425°F. Spoon undrained mincemeat mixture into piecrust. Prepare top crust.

4. Bake pie until golden, 30 to 40 minutes. Cool pie on wire rack 1 hour. Serve warm, topped with Hard Sauce, or cool completely to serve later. Makes 10 servings.

Each serving: About 500 calories, 5 g protein, 71 g carbohydrate, 25 g total fat (6 g saturated), 0 mg cholesterol, 415 mg sodium.

∾**Nut Pies**

Double Peanut Pie

Prep: 25 minutes plus cooling
Bake: 55 to 60 minutes

Pastry for 9-inch 1-crust pie (see page 1031) or ½ package (10 to
    11 ounces) piecrust mix
3 large eggs
1 cup dark corn syrup
½ cup sugar
½ cup creamy peanut butter
½ teaspoon vanilla extract
1 cup salted peanuts
Whipped cream

1. Prepare piecrust for 1-crust pie; use to line 9-inch pie
plate. Make decorative edge (see page 1034).
2. Preheat oven to 350°F. In large bowl, with mixer at
medium speed, beat eggs, corn syrup, sugar, peanut butter,
and vanilla until smooth; stir in peanuts. Place pie plate on
oven rack; pour peanut mixture into piecrust.
3. Bake pie until knife inserted 1 inch from edge of pie
comes out clean, 55 to 60 minutes. Cool on rack. Garnish
with whipped cream. Makes 12 servings.

*Each serving: About 355 calories, 9 g protein, 41 g carbohydrate,
19 g total fat (4 g saturated), 53 mg cholesterol, 245 mg sodium.*

Maple-Walnut Pie

Prep: 30 minutes plus cooling
Bake: 1 hour

Pastry for 9-inch 1-crust pie (see page 1031) or ½ package (10 to 11 ounces) piecrust mix
4 tablespoons margarine or butter
½ cup maple or maple-flavored syrup
½ cup dark corn syrup
3 tablespoons sugar
¼ teaspoon salt
3 large eggs
2 cups walnuts (8 ounces)

1. Prepare piecrust for 1-crust pie; use to line 9-inch pie plate. Make high stand-up edge.

2. Preheat oven to 350°F. In 2-quart saucepan, melt margarine over low heat; remove saucepan from heat. With wire whisk, beat in maple syrup, corn syrup, sugar, salt, and eggs.

3. Arrange walnuts on bottom of piecrust; carefully pour egg mixture over walnuts. Bake pie until knife inserted 1 inch from edge comes out clean, 1 hour. Cool pie on wire rack. Makes 10 servings.

Each serving: About 430 calories, 7 g protein, 41 g carbohydrate, 29 g total fat (5 g saturated), 64 mg cholesterol, 280 mg sodium.

Chocolate-Brownie Pie

Prep: 30 minutes plus cooling
Bake: 30 minutes

Pastry for 9-inch 1-crust pie (see page 1031) or ½ package (10 to 11 ounces) piecrust mix
4 tablespoons margarine or butter
2 squares unsweetened chocolate
½ cup sugar
½ cup milk
¼ cup all-purpose flour
2 tablespoons light corn syrup
1 teaspoon vanilla extract
½ teaspoon salt
3 large eggs
1 cup (4 ounces) walnuts, chopped
1 pint vanilla ice cream (optional)

1. Prepare piecrust for 1-crust pie; use to line 9-inch pie plate. Make high stand-up edge.

2. Preheat oven to 350°F. In heavy 2-quart saucepan, melt margarine and chocolate over low heat, stirring occasionally. Remove saucepan from heat. With wire whisk, beat in sugar, milk, flour, corn syrup, vanilla, salt, and eggs until blended. Stir in walnuts.

3. Pour chocolate mixture into piecrust. Bake pie until filling is set and puffed, 30 minutes. Cool pie slightly on wire rack to serve warm, or cool completely to serve later. If you like, serve pie with ice cream. Makes 10 servings.

Each serving without ice cream: About 350 calories, 6 g protein, 29 g carbohydrate, 25 g total fat (6 g saturated), 65 mg cholesterol, 325 mg sodium.

Warm Banana-Pecan Tart

Prep: 45 minutes plus chilling
Bake: 30 minutes

1 ½ cups all-purpose flour
½ teaspoon salt
½ cup plus 3 tablespoons
    sugar
¼ cup shortening
6 tablespoons margarine or
    butter
4 tablespoons cold water
½ cup pecans, toasted

3 large egg yolks
1 tablespoon cornstarch
¾ cup half-and-half or light
    cream
1 teaspoon vanilla extract
5 ripe medium bananas (about
    2 pounds), thinly sliced on
    diagonal

1. In medium bowl, combine flour, salt, and 2 table-spoons sugar. With pastry blender or 2 knives used scissor-fashion, cut in shortening and 4 tablespoons margarine until mixture resembles coarse crumbs. Sprinkle cold water, 1 tablespoon at a time, into flour mixture, mixing lightly with fork after each addition until dough is just moist enough to hold together. Shape dough into ball; flatten into disk. Wrap and refrigerate until firm enough to roll, about 30 minutes.

2. Meanwhile, prepare toasted pecan cream: In food processor with knife blade attached or in blender at medium speed, blend pecans with ¼ cup sugar until very finely ground. In small bowl, with wire whisk, mix egg yolks, cornstarch, and ¼ cup sugar until blended. In 2-quart saucepan, heat half-and-half to simmering over medium heat. While constantly beating with wire whisk, gradually pour about half of simmering cream into bowl with yolk mixture. Reduce heat to low. Return yolk mixture to sauce-pan and cook, whisking constantly, until thickened, 4 to 5 minutes. Stir in toasted pecan mixture, vanilla, and remaining 2 tablespoons margarine. Transfer toasted pecan cream to medium bowl; cover surface directly with plastic wrap to prevent skin from forming and refrigerate at least 30 minutes.

3. While cream is chilling, preheat oven to 425°F. On lightly floured surface, with floured rolling pin, roll dough into a 14-inch round. Press dough onto bottom and up side of 11" by 1" round tart pan with removable bottom. Fold overhang in and press against side of tart pan to form a rim ⅛ inch above edge of pan. With fork, prick dough all over to prevent puffing and shrinking during baking.

4. Line tart shell with foil and fill with pie weights, dry beans, or uncooked rice. Bake tart shell 20 minutes; remove foil with weights and bake until golden, about 10 minutes longer. (If crust puffs up during baking, gently press it to pan with back of spoon.) Turn oven control to broil.

5. Arrange banana slices, overlapping slightly, in tart shell. Spoon toasted pecan cream evenly on top of bananas and sprinkle with remaining 1 tablespoon sugar. Cover edge of crust loosely with foil to prevent overbrowning. Place tart on oven rack at closest position to source of heat and broil until top is lightly caramelized, 1 to 2 minutes. Serve tart warm. Makes 12 servings.

Each serving: About 295 calories, 4 g protein, 36 g carbohydrate, 16 g total fat (4 g saturated), 58 mg cholesterol, 175 mg sodium.

Southern Pecan Pie

Prep: 30 minutes plus cooling
Bake: 1 hour

Pastry for 9-inch 1-crust pie (see page 1031) or ½ package (10 to 11 ounces) piecrust mix
4 tablespoons margarine or butter
1 cup dark corn syrup
¼ cup sugar
1 teaspoon vanilla extract
3 large eggs
1 cup pecan halves (4 ounces)
Whipped cream

1. Prepare piecrust for 1-crust pie; use to line 9-inch pie plate. Make high stand-up edge.

2. Preheat oven to 350°F. In 2-quart saucepan, melt margarine over low heat; remove saucepan from heat. With wire whisk, beat in corn syrup, sugar, vanilla, and eggs until blended.

3. Arrange pecans on bottom of piecrust; carefully pour egg mixture over pecans. Bake pie until knife inserted 1 inch from edge comes out clean, 1 hour. Cool pie on wire rack. Garnish with whipped cream. Makes 10 servings.

Each serving: About 360 calories, 4 g protein, 41 g carbohydrate, 21 g total fat (4 g saturated), 64 mg cholesterol, 235 mg sodium.

Georgia Chocolate-Pecan Pie

Prep: 45 minutes plus cooling
Bake: 1 hour 10 minutes

1¼ cups all-purpose flour
½ teaspoon salt
2 tablespoons shortening
8 tablespoons (1 stick)
   margarine or butter
3 to 4 tablespoons cold water
2 squares (2 ounces)
   unsweetened chocolate

1¾ cups pecan halves
¾ cup packed dark brown
   sugar
¾ cup dark corn syrup
1 teaspoon vanilla extract
3 large eggs

1. In medium bowl, combine flour and salt. With pastry blender or 2 knives used scissor-fashion, cut in shortening and 4 tablespoons margarine until mixture resembles coarse crumbs. Sprinkle cold water, 1 tablespoon at a time, into flour mixture, mixing lightly with fork after each addition until dough is just moist enough to hold together. Shape dough into ball; flatten into disk. Wrap and refrigerate 30 minutes or overnight. If chilled overnight bring to room temperature 30 minutes before rolling.

2. On lightly floured surface, with floured rolling pin, roll dough into a round 1½ inches larger all around than inverted 9-inch pie plate. Gently ease dough into pie plate; trim edge, leaving 1-inch overhang. Fold overhang under; pinch to form decorative edge (see page 1034). With fork, prick bottom and side of piecrust all over to prevent puffing during baking. Wrap and refrigerate piecrust at least 30 minutes.

3. Meanwhile, preheat oven to 425°F. In heavy 1-quart saucepan, melt unsweetened chocolate and remaining 4 tablespoons margarine over low heat, stirring frequently. Set aside to cool slightly.

4. Line pie shell with foil and fill with pie weights, dry beans, or uncooked rice. Bake 10 minutes; remove foil with weights and bake until lightly browned, about 10 minutes longer. If shell puffs up during baking, gently press it to pie plate with back of spoon. Cool piecrust on wire rack at least 10 minutes. Turn oven control to 350°F.

5. Coarsely chop 1 cup pecans; reserve remaining pecan halves.

6. In large bowl, with wire whisk, mix cooled chocolate mixture, brown sugar, corn syrup, vanilla, and eggs until blended. Stir in chopped pecans and pecan halves.

7. Pour pecan mixture into cooled crust. Bake pie until edges of filling are set (center will jiggle slightly), 45 to 50 minutes. Cool pie on wire rack. Makes 12 servings.

Each serving: About 395 calories, 5 g protein, 43 g carbohydrate, 24 g total fat (4 g saturated), 53 mg cholesterol, 225 mg sodium.

Cranberry-Almond Tart

Prep: 40 minutes plus cooling
Bake: 50 minutes

¼ teaspoon salt
1 cup plus 3 tablespoons all-purpose flour
4 tablespoons cold margarine or butter plus 4 tablespoons softened
2 to 3 tablespoons plus ⅓ cup cold water

½ cup almond paste (about 5 ounces)
1¼ cups sugar
2 large eggs
½ teaspoon grated orange peel
1 bag (12 ounces) cranberries (3 cups)

1. In medium bowl, combine salt and 1 cup flour. With pastry blender or 2 knives used scissor-fashion, cut in 4 tablespoons cold margarine until mixture resembles coarse crumbs. Add 2 to 3 tablespoons cold water, 1 tablespoon at a time, mixing lightly with fork after each addition until dough is just moist enough to hold together. Shape dough into ball; flatten into disk. Wrap and freeze until firm enough to roll, about 15 minutes.

2. Meanwhile, in food processor with knife blade attached, blend almond paste, ½ cup sugar, and remaining 4 tablespoons softened margarine until smooth. Add eggs and remaining 3 tablespoons flour; blend until mixed.

3. Preheat oven to 425°F. On lightly floured surface, with floured rolling pin, roll dough into a 12-inch round. Press dough onto bottom and up side of 10" by 1" round tart pan with removable bottom. Fold overhang in and press against side of tart pan to form a thicker edge. With fork, prick dough all over to prevent puffing and shrinking during baking. Freeze until dough is firm, 10 minutes.

4. Line tart shell with foil and fill with pie weights, dry beans, or uncooked rice. Bake tart shell 15 minutes; remove foil with weights and bake until golden, about 10 minutes longer. (If shell puffs up during baking, gently press it to pan with back of spoon.) Turn oven control to 350°F.

5. Fill hot tart shell with almond filling. Bake until almond filling is slightly puffed and golden, 20 to 25 minutes longer. Cool in pan on wire rack.

6. While tart shell is baking, in 2-quart saucepan over high heat, heat orange peel, 1 cup cranberries, remaining ¾ cup sugar, and remaining ⅓ cup water to boiling. Reduce heat to medium-low; simmer until mixture thickens slightly and cranberries pop, about 5 minutes. Stir in remaining 2 cups cranberries. Set aside until cool.

7. Remove almond-filled tart shell from pan; place on cake plate. Spoon cranberry topping over almond filling. Makes 10 servings.

Each serving: About 340 calories, 5 g protein, 48 g carbohydrate, 15 g total fat (2 g saturated), 43 mg cholesterol, 190 mg sodium.

Holiday Nut Tart

Prep: 20 minutes plus cooling
Bake: 55 minutes

1½ cups all-purpose flour	3 tablespoons margarine or
2 tablespoons sugar	butter, melted
¼ teaspoon salt	2 teaspoons vanilla extract
½ cup shortening	2 large eggs
3 to 4 tablespoons cold water	1 can (10 to 11 ounces) salted
½ cup packed light brown	deluxe mixed nuts (about 2
sugar	cups)
½ cup light corn syrup	Whipped cream (optional)

1. Preheat oven to 375°F. In medium bowl, combine flour, sugar, and salt. With pastry blender or 2 knives used scissor-fashion, cut in shortening until mixture resembles coarse crumbs. Add cold water, 1 tablespoon at a time, mixing lightly with fork after each addition, until dough is just moist enough to hold together. Shape dough into ball; flatten into disk.

2. On lightly floured surface, with floured rolling pin, roll dough into a 14-inch round. Press dough onto bottom and up side of 11" by 1" round tart pan with removable bottom. Fold overhang in and press against side of tart pan to form a rim ⅛ inch above edge of pan.

3. Line tart shell with foil and fill with pie weights, dry beans, or uncooked rice. Bake tart shell 15 minutes; remove foil with weights and bake until golden, 8 to 10 minutes longer. (If crust puffs up during baking, gently press it to pan with back of spoon.) Cool on wire rack.

4. Meanwhile, in medium bowl, with wire whisk, mix brown sugar, corn syrup, margarine, vanilla, and eggs until smooth. Stir in nuts.

5. Pour mixture into tart shell. Bake until set and tart is a deep golden brown, 25 to 30 minutes. Cool tart in pan on wire rack. When cool, carefully remove side from pan. Serve with whipped cream, if you like. Makes 16 servings.

Each serving without whipped cream: About 310 calories, 5 g protein, 29 g carbohydrate, 20 g total fat (4 g saturated), 27 mg cholesterol, 215 mg sodium.

Plum Frangipane Tart

Prep: 20 minutes plus cooling
Bake: 1 hour 35 minutes

1¾ cups all-purpose flour
3 tablespoons plus ½ cup sugar
¾ teaspoon salt
½ cup shortening
3 to 4 tablespoons cold water
1 tube or can (7 to 8 ounces) almond paste, broken into 1-inch pieces

4 tablespoons butter, softened (no substitutions)
2 large eggs
2 teaspoons vanilla extract
1¼ pounds ripe plums (about 5 medium), each pitted and cut into 6 wedges

1. Preheat oven to 375°F. In medium bowl, combine 1½ cups flour, 3 tablespoons sugar, and ½ teaspoon salt. With pastry blender or 2 knives used scissor-fashion, cut shortening into flour mixture until mixture resembles coarse crumbs. Add cold water, 1 tablespoon at a time, mixing lightly with fork after each addition, until dough is just moist enough to hold together. Shape dough into ball; flatten into disk.

2. On lightly floured surface, with floured rolling pin, roll dough into a 14-inch round. Ease dough round into 11" by 1" round tart pan with removable bottom. Fold overhang in and press against side of tart pan to form a rim ⅛ inch above edge of pan.

3. Line tart shell with foil and fill with pie weights, dry beans, or uncooked rice. Bake tart shell 20 minutes; remove foil with weights and bake until golden, 10 to 15 minutes longer. (If shell puffs up during baking, gently press it to pan with back of spoon.)

4. Meanwhile, prepare filling: In large bowl, with mixer at low speed, beat almond paste, butter, remaining ½ cup sugar, and remaining ¼ teaspoon salt until crumbly. Increase speed to medium-high and beat until blended, constantly scraping bowl with rubber spatula, about 3 minutes. (It's okay if there are tiny lumps.) Add eggs and vanilla;

beat until smooth. With spoon, stir in remaining ¼ cup flour.

5. Pour filling into warm tart shell. Arrange plums in concentric circles over filling. Bake tart, until golden, 50 to 60 minutes. Cool tart in pan on wire rack. When cool, carefully remove side from pan. Makes 12 servings.

Each serving: About 340 calories, 5 g protein, 38 g carbohydrate, 19 g total fat (4 g saturated), 36 mg cholesterol, 195 mg sodium.

Pine Nut Tart

Prep: 30 minutes plus chilling and cooling
Bake: 50 minutes

1½ cups all-purpose flour	¾ cup slivered blanched
2 tablespoons plus ⅔ cup sugar	almonds
	¼ cup cornstarch
¾ teaspoon salt	½ teaspoon baking powder
¼ cup shortening	3 large eggs
4 tablespoons cold margarine or butter plus 6 tablespoons softened	2 teaspoons vanilla extract
	¼ teaspoon almond extract
	1 cup pine nuts (pignoli),
4 tablespoons cold water	toasted

1. In medium bowl, combine flour, 2 tablespoons sugar, and ½ teaspoon salt. With pastry blender or 2 knives used scissor-fashion, cut in shortening and 4 tablespoons cold margarine until mixture resembles coarse crumbs. Sprinkle cold water, 1 tablespoon at a time, into flour mixture, mixing lightly with fork after each addition until dough is just moist enough to hold together. Shape dough into ball; flatten into disk. Wrap and refrigerate until firm enough to roll, about 30 minutes.

2. Preheat oven to 425°F. On lightly floured surface, with floured rolling pin, roll dough into 14-inch round. Press dough onto bottom and up side of 11" by 1" round tart pan with removable bottom. Fold overhang in and press against side of tart pan to form a rim ⅛ inch above edge of pan. With fork, prick dough in many places to prevent puffing and shrinking during baking.

3. Line tart shell with foil and fill with pie weights, dry beans, or uncooked rice. Bake tart shell 20 minutes; remove foil with weights and bake until golden, about 10 minutes longer. (If shell puffs up during baking, press it to pan with back of spoon.) Turn oven control to 375°F.

4. In food processor with knife blade attached, pulse almonds, cornstarch, baking powder, and remaining ¼ teaspoon salt until almonds are very finely ground.

5. In large bowl, with mixer at low speed, beat almond mixture, remaining ⅔ cup sugar, and remaining 6 tablespoons softened margarine until crumbly. Increase speed to medium-high and beat until well combined, about 3 minutes, constantly scraping bowl with rubber spatula. Add eggs, 1 at a time, vanilla, and almond extract; beat until smooth.

6. Pour filling into warm tart shell. Arrange pine nuts evenly over filling. Bake tart until golden and filling is firm, about 20 minutes. Cool tart in pan on wire rack. When cool, carefully remove side from pan. Makes 12 servings.

Each serving: About 360 calories, 8 g protein, 32 g carbohydrate, 24 g total fat (5 g saturated), 53 mg cholesterol, 290 mg sodium.

∾**Cheese Pies**

Deluxe Cheese Pie

Prep: 20 minutes plus chilling
Bake: 35 minutes

Baked Graham-Cracker Crumb Crust for 8-inch pie shell
   (see page 1037)
1½ packages (8 ounces each) cream cheese, softened
2 large eggs
½ cup sugar
½ teaspoon vanilla extract
1 container (8 ounces) sour cream

1. Preheat oven to 350°F. Grease 9-inch pie plate. Prepare graham-cracker crumb crust as recipe directs; but do not bake. Press onto bottom and up side of pie plate.

2. In small bowl, with mixer at low speed, beat cream cheese, eggs, sugar, and vanilla just until mixed. Beat at high speed until cream-cheese mixture is smooth; pour into crumb crust.

3. Bake pie until set, 35 minutes. Spread sour cream over top of hot pie. Cool pie on wire rack. Refrigerate. Makes 10 servings.

Each serving: About 320 calories, 6 g protein, 24 g carbohydrate, 23 g total fat (11 g saturated), 88 mg cholesterol, 285 mg sodium.

CHERRY-CHEESE PIE: Prepare pie as above but omit sour cream; cool pie. Meanwhile, prepare cherry glaze: Drain *1 can (16 ounces) pitted tart cherries,* reserving 1 cup cherries and ½ cup liquid (save rest of cherries and liquid for use another day). In small saucepan, stir *2 tablespoons sugar* and *1 tablespoon cornstarch*; slowly stir in reserved cherry liquid. Cook over medium heat, stirring, until mixture thickens and boils; boil 1 minute. Stir in reserved cherries, *1 teaspoon fresh lemon juice,* and *¼ teaspoon almond extract;* cool. Spread over top of cooled pie.

Each serving: About 325 calories, 6 g protein, 35 g carbohydrate, 19 g total fat (9 g saturated), 80 mg cholesterol, 275 mg sodium.

STRAWBERRY-CHEESE PIE: Prepare Deluxe Cheese Pie (see page 1071) but omit sour cream; cool pie. Arrange *1 pint strawberries,* hulled and sliced, on top of pie. In small saucepan, melt *½ cup red-currant jelly* over low heat; brush over strawberries.

Each serving: About 330 calories, 5 g protein, 36 g carbohydrate, 19 g total fat (9 g saturated), 80 mg cholesterol, 280 mg sodium.

∿Custard Pies

Cherry-Custard Tart

Prep: 35 minutes
Bake: About 50 minutes

Pastry for 9-inch 1-crust pie (see page 1031) or ½ package (10 to 11 ounces) piecrust mix
3 large eggs
¾ cup heavy or whipping cream
⅓ cup sugar
2 tablespoons almond-flavored liqueur
1½ teaspoons freshly grated lemon peel
¼ teaspoon salt
1 pound dark sweet cherries, pitted

1. Prepare piecrust for 1-crust pie. On lightly floured surface with floured rolling pin, roll dough into round 1 inch larger than 10-inch tart pan with removable bottom. Line tart pan with dough; trim edge of dough even with top of pan.

2. Preheat oven to 425°F. Line tart shell with foil and fill with pie weights, dry beans, or uncooked rice. Bake tart shell until edges are lightly browned, about 20 minutes. Remove foil with weights; set tart shell in pan on wire rack. Turn oven control to 350°F.

3. In large bowl, with wire whisk or fork, beat eggs, heavy cream, sugar, liqueur, lemon peel, and salt until blended. Place cherries in tart shell. Place tart shell on oven rack; pour egg mixture over cherries. Bake tart until knife inserted 1 inch from edge comes out clean, 30 minutes.

4. Cool tart slightly in pan on wire rack. Remove side of pan. Serve warm, or refrigerate. Makes 10 servings.

Each serving: About 255 calories, 4 g protein, 23 g carbohydrate, 16 g total fat (7 g saturated), 88 mg cholesterol, 200 mg sodium.

Italian Triple-Berry Tart

Prep: 40 minutes plus chilling and cooling
Bake: About 30 minutes

Tart Shell
1 ½ cups all-purpose flour
2 tablespoons sugar
½ teaspoon salt
¼ cup shortening
4 tablespoons (½ stick) cold margarine or butter
4 tablespoons cold water

Pastry Cream
3 large egg yolks
⅓ cup sugar
2 tablespoons cornstarch
1 cup milk
2 tablespoons margarine or butter
1 teaspoon vanilla extract
½ cup heavy or whipping cream

2 cups blueberries
2 cups raspberries
2 cups blackberries
Confectioners' sugar

1. Prepare Tart Shell: In medium bowl, combine flour, sugar, and salt. With pastry blender or 2 knives used scissor-fashion, cut in shortening and margarine until mixture resembles coarse crumbs. Sprinkle cold water, 1 tablespoon at a time, into flour mixture, mixing lightly with a fork after each addition until dough is just moist enough to hold together. Shape dough into ball; flatten into disk; Wrap and refrigerate until firm enough to roll, about 30 minutes.

2. Meanwhile, prepare Pastry Cream: In small bowl, with wire whisk, mix egg yolks, sugar, and cornstarch until blended. In 2-quart saucepan, heat milk to simmering over medium heat. While constantly beating with wire whisk, gradually pour about half of simmering milk into yolk mixture. Reduce heat to low. Return yolk mixture to saucepan and cook, whisking constantly, until pastry cream thickens and boils; boil 1 minute. Remove saucepan from heat; stir in margarine and vanilla. Transfer pastry cream to medium bowl; cover surface directly with plastic wrap to prevent skin from forming, and refrigerate until cold, at least 2 hours.

3. Preheat oven to 425°F. On lightly floured surface, with floured rolling pin, roll dough into a 14-inch round. Press dough onto bottom and up side of 11" by 1" tart pan with removable bottom. Fold overhang in and press against side of tart pan to form a rim ⅛ inch above edge of pan. With fork, prick dough in many places to prevent puffing and shrinking during baking.

4. Line tart shell with foil and fill with pie weights, dry beans, or uncooked rice. Bake tart shell 20 minutes; remove foil with weights and bake until golden, 10 minutes longer. (If shell puffs up during baking, press it to pan with back of spoon.) Cool completely on wire rack.

5. Up to 2 hours before serving, in small bowl, with mixer at medium speed, beat cream just until stiff peaks form. Whisk pastry cream until smooth; fold in whipped cream. Fill tart shell with pastry-cream mixture; top with berries and sprinkle with confectioners' sugar. Makes 12 servings.

Each serving: About 285 calories, 4 g protein, 32 g carbohydrate, 16 g total fat (6 g saturated), 70 mg cholesterol, 180 mg sodium.

Cherry-Almond Clafouti

Prep: 20 minutes
Cook: 40 to 45 minutes

1 pound dark sweet cherries, pitted
⅔ cup all-purpose flour
⅓ cup sugar
2 tablespoons almond-flavored liqueur
4 large eggs
2 cups half-and-half or light cream
Confectioners' sugar

1. Preheat oven to 350°F. Grease 10" by 1½" round ceramic baking dish.

2. Place pitted cherries in baking dish. In blender at low speed, blend flour, sugar, amaretto, eggs, and 1 cup half-and-half 30 seconds. With motor running, gradually add remaining 1 cup half-and-half; blend 30 seconds longer.

3. Pour egg mixture over cherries in baking dish. Bake until custard is set and knife inserted 1 inch from edge comes out clean (center will still jiggle), 40 to 45 minutes. Serve hot, sprinkled with confectioners' sugar. Makes 12 servings.

Each serving: About 150 calories, 4 g protein, 19 g carbohydrate, 6 g total fat (3 g saturated), 84 mg cholesterol, 40 mg sodium.

Custard Pie

Prep: 30 minutes plus cooling
Bake: 20 to 25 minutes

Pastry for 9-inch 1-crust Pie (see page 1031) or ½ package (10 to 11 ounces) piecrust mix
1 tablespoon margarine or butter, softened
2½ cups milk
½ cup sugar
3 large eggs
1 teaspoon vanilla extract
½ teaspoon salt
¼ teaspoon ground nutmeg
Whipped cream, toasted coconut, or chopped nuts

1. Prepare piecrust for 1-crust pie; use to line 9-inch pie plate. With fingertips gently rub margarine evenly over piecrust; refrigerate.

2. Preheat oven to 425°F. In medium bowl, with wire whisk or fork, beat milk, sugar, eggs, vanilla, salt, and nutmeg until blended. Place pie plate on oven rack; pour milk mixture into piecrust.

3. Bake pie until knife inserted 1 inch from edge comes out clean, 20 to 25 minutes. Cool pie on wire rack; refrigerate.

4. To serve, top with whipped cream, toasted coconut, or chopped nuts. Makes 10 servings.

Each serving without garnish: About 225 calories, 5 g protein, 22 g carbohydrate, 13 g total fat (4 g saturated), 72 mg cholesterol, 295 mg sodium.

Pear Custard Tart

Prep: 1 hour plus cooling
Bake: About 1 hour 30 minutes

Sweet Pastry
1½ cups all-purpose flour
2 tablespoons sugar
½ teaspoon salt
4 tablespoons vegetable shortening
4 tablespoons cold margarine or butter
4 tablespoons cold water

Custard Filling
2 large eggs
8 ounces sour cream or crème fraîche
½ cup sugar
½ cup heavy or whipping cream
¼ teaspoon almond extract

Pears and Glaze
3 firm but ripe Bosc pears (about 1¼ pounds), unpeeled
⅓ cup apricot preserves

1. Preheat oven to 425°F. Prepare Sweet Pastry: In medium bowl, combine flour, sugar, and salt. With pastry blender or 2 knives used scissor-fashion, cut in shortening and margarine until mixture resembles coarse crumbs. Sprinkle cold water, 1 tablespoon at a time, into flour mixture, mixing lightly with fork after each each addition until dough is just moist enough to hold together. Shape dough into ball; flatten into disk. Wrap and refrigerate until firm enough to roll.

2. Meanwhile, prepare Custard Filling: In large bowl, with wire whisk, beat eggs. Remove 2 tablespoons beaten eggs to cup; reserve and refrigerate to brush over crust later. Add sour cream, sugar, heavy cream, and almond extract to eggs in bowl; beat until well mixed. Cover and refrigerate.

3. On lightly floured surface, with floured rolling pin, roll dough into 13-inch round. Press dough onto bottom and up side of 11" by 1" round tart pan with removable bottom. Fold overhang in and press against side of tart pan to form a rim ⅛ inch above edge of pan. With fork, prick dough all over to prevent puffing and shrinking during baking.

4. Line tart shell with foil; fill with pie weights, dry beans, or uncooked rice. Bake tart shell 15 minutes; remove foil with weights and bake 10 minutes longer. (If shell puffs up during baking, press it to pan with back of spoon.) Remove tart shell from oven; brush with reserved beaten egg. Bake 5 minutes longer. Cool on wire rack while preparing pears. Turn oven control to 375°F.

5. To prepare Pears: Cut each pear lengthwise in half and remove cores. Then, cut each half lengthwise into 10 slices. Arrange pear slices in concentric circle in tart shell, with narrow tops toward center of tart, reserving a few slices to cut to fit center of tart.

6. Slowly pour custard over pears. Bake tart until custard is set and top is puffy and lightly browned around edge, 55 to 60 minutes.

7. With back of spoon, press preserves through small strainer set over small bowl. With pastry brush, brush strained preserves over hot tart. Let tart cool at least 1 hour to serve warm, or refrigerate to serve later. Makes 12 servings.

Each serving: About 305 calories, 4 g protein, 36 g carbohydrate, 17 g total fat (7 g saturated), 58 mg cholesterol, 165 mg sodium.

Pilgrim Pumpkin Pie

Prep: 35 minutes plus chilling
Bake: About 40 minutes

Pastry for 9-inch 1-crust Pie (see
   page 1031) or ½ package
   (10 to 11 ounces) piecrust
   mix
1 can (16 ounces) solid-pack
   pumpkin (not pumpkin pie
   mix) or 2 cups mashed
   cooked pumpkin
1 can (12 ounces) evaporated
   milk
2 large eggs

¾ cup packed brown sugar
1½ teaspoons ground
   cinnamon*
½ teaspoon ground ginger*
½ teaspoon ground nutmeg*
½ teaspoon salt
¼ cup heavy or whipping
   cream (optional)

1. Prepare piecrust for 1-crust pie; use to line 9-inch pie plate. Make high stand-up edge. Set aside.

2. Preheat oven to 400°F. In large bowl, with mixer at medium speed, beat pumpkin, evaporated milk, eggs, brown sugar, cinnamon, ginger, nutmeg, and salt.

3. Place pie plate with pie shell on oven rack; pour in pumpkin mixture. Bake pie until knife inserted 1 inch from edge comes out clean, about 40 minutes. Cool pie on wire rack about 1½ hours.

4. To serve, in small bowl, with mixer at medium speed, beat heavy cream until stiff peaks form; use to garnish pie, if desired. Makes 10 servings.

*Or instead of cinnamon, ginger, and nutmeg, use 2 teaspoons pumpkin-pie spice.

Each serving without cream: About 255 calories, 5 g protein, 33 g carbohydrate, 12 g total fat (4 g saturated), 53 mg cholesterol, 290 mg sodium.

Pumpkin Pie with Pecan-Caramel Topping

Prep: 1 hour plus cooling
Bake: About 1 hour 30 minutes

Crust
½ cup pecans, toasted
2 tablespoons sugar
1¼ cups all-purpose flour
¼ teaspoon salt
4 tablespoons cold margarine or butter
2 tablespoons vegetable shortening
3 tablespoons ice water

Pumpkin Filling
1 can (16 ounces) solid-pack pumpkin (not pumpkin pie mix)
¾ cup heavy or whipping cream
½ cup milk
½ cup packed light brown sugar
1½ teaspoons ground cinnamon
½ teaspoon salt
¼ teaspoon ground nutmeg
¼ teaspoon ground ginger
¼ teaspoon ground cloves
3 large eggs

Pecan-Caramel Topping
1 cup packed light brown sugar
¼ cup heavy or whipping cream
2 tablespoons light corn syrup
2 tablespoons margarine or butter
1 teaspoon distilled white vinegar
1 cup pecans, toasted and broken
1 teaspoon vanilla extract

1. Prepare piecrust: In food processor with knife blade attached, blend toasted pecans and sugar until finely ground. Add flour and salt to nut mixture and pulse to blend. Add margarine and shortening, and pulse just until mixture resembles very coarse crumbs. With processor running, add ice water, stopping just before dough forms a ball. Shape dough into ball; flatten into disk.

2. Preheat oven to 400°F. Between lightly floured sheets of waxed paper, with rolling pin, roll dough into a round 1½ inches larger in diameter than inverted 9-inch pie plate. Dough will be very tender; refrigerate if too soft to roll. Gently ease dough into pie plate; trim edge, leaving 1-inch overhang. Fold overhang under; bring up over pie-plate rim and pinch to form high decorative edge (see page 1034). With fork, prick bottom and side of pie shell all over to prevent puffing and shrinking during baking. Refrigerate pie shell about 30 minutes.

3. Line pie shell with foil and fill with pie weights, dry beans, or uncooked rice. Bake pie shell 20 minutes; remove foil with weights and bake until lightly browned, about 10 minutes longer. (If shell puffs up during baking, press it to pan with back of spoon.) Cool on wire rack at least 15 minutes. Turn oven control to 350°F.

4. Prepare Pumpkin Filling: In large bowl, with wire whisk, beat pumpkin, heavy cream, milk, brown sugar, cinnamon, salt, nutmeg, ginger, cloves, and eggs.

5. Pour filling into cooled pie shell. Bake pie until knife inserted 1 inch from edge of pie comes out clean, 50 to 60 minutes. Transfer pie to wire rack until it cools and becomes slightly firm, about 1 hour.

6. Prepare Pecan-Caramel Topping: In 2-quart saucepan, heat brown sugar, cream, corn syrup, margarine, and vinegar to boiling over high heat, stirring occasionally. (Do not use smaller pan; mixture bubbles up during cooking.) Reduce heat to low; simmer, uncovered, stirring frequently, 5 minutes. Remove saucepan from heat; stir in pecans and vanilla. (Topping will be very thin when hot but will thicken as it cools.) Pour hot topping over cooled pie. Refrigerate pie at least 4 hours or overnight. Makes 12 servings.

Each serving: About 435 calories, 5 g protein, 49 g carbohydrate, 25 g total fat (7 g saturated), 80 mg cholesterol, 254 mg sodium.

Butternut Squash Pie

Prep: 30 minutes plus cooling
Bake: 40 to 45 minutes

Piecrust
1½ cups all-purpose flour
2 tablespoons sugar
½ teaspoon salt
4 tablespoons cold margarine or butter
¼ cup shortening
4 tablespoons cold water

Squash Filling
1½ cups cooked, mashed butternut squash (from about a 1½-pound squash)*
1 cup milk
⅔ cup packed brown sugar
½ cup heavy or whipping cream
2 tablespoons granulated sugar
1 tablespoon margarine or butter, melted
1¼ teaspoons ground cinnamon
½ teaspoon ground ginger
½ teaspoon ground nutmeg
¼ teaspoon ground cloves
⅛ teaspoon salt
2 large eggs

1. Prepare Piecrust: In medium bowl, combine flour, sugar, and salt. With pastry blender or 2 knives scissor-fashion, cut in margarine and shortening until mixture resembles coarse crumbs. Sprinkle cold water, 1 tablespoon at a time, into flour mixture, mixing lightly with fork after each addition until dough is just moist enough to hold together. Shape dough into ball; flatten into disk.

2. On lightly floured surface, with floured rolling pin, roll dough into a round 2 inches larger in diameter than inverted 9-inch pie plate. Ease dough into pie plate; trim edge, leaving 1-inch overhang. Fold overhang under; pinch to form decorative edge (see page 1034). Wrap and refrigerate pie shell.

3. Meanwhile, preheat oven to 425°F. Make a foil shield

for edge of crust: Cut 12-inch square piece of foil; fold into quarters. Cut out center and round off edges, leaving a 2½-inch-wide ring. Unfold ring; set aside.

4. Prepare Squash Filling: In large bowl, with wire whisk, beat squash, milk, brown sugar, cream, granulated sugar, melted margarine, cinnamon, ginger, nutmeg, cloves, salt, and eggs until blended.

5. Pour squash mixture into chilled pie shell. Place foil shield over edge of crust to prevent overbrowning. Bake pie until knife inserted 1 inch from edge comes out clean, 40 to 45 minutes. Cool pie on wire rack. Makes 10 servings.

*To cook squash in microwave oven: Cut squash lengthwise in half; remove seeds. In shallow, microwave-safe baking dish, place squash cut side down in ½ inch water. Cook on High about 6 minutes; turn squash over and cook until fork-tender, about 6 minutes longer. Or, to cook in conventional oven, place squash halves in shallow pan, add ⅓ cup water, and bake at 400°F. until tender, 35 to 45 minutes.

Each serving: About 325 calories, 5 g protein, 39 g carbohydrate, 17 g total fat (6 g saturated), 62 mg cholesterol, 245 mg sodium

Alabama Sweet-Potato Meringue Pie

Prep: 1 hour plus cooling
Bake: 1 hour 30 minutes

1¼ cups all-purpose flour
1 teaspoon salt
4 tablespoons margarine or butter
2 tablespoons shortening
3 to 4 tablespoons cold water
1½ pounds sweet potatoes (about 3 large), peeled and cut into 1-inch chunks
3 large eggs, separated

¾ cup packed light brown sugar
1½ cups half-and-half or light cream
2 tablespoons light molasses
1¼ teaspoons ground cinnamon
¼ teaspoon ground nutmeg
¼ teaspoon cream of tartar
⅓ cup granulated sugar

1. In medium bowl, combine flour and ½ teaspoon salt. With pastry blender or 2 knives used scissor-fashion, cut in margarine and shortening until mixture resembles coarse crumbs. Sprinkle cold water, 1 tablespoon at a time, into flour mixture, mixing lightly with a fork after each addition until dough is just moist enough to hold together. Shape dough into ball; flatten into disk.

2. On lightly floured surface, with floured rolling pin, roll dough into a round 2 inches larger all around than inverted 9½-inch deep-dish pie plate. Gently ease dough into pie plate; trim edge, leaving 1-inch overhang. Fold overhang under; pinch to form decorative edge. With fork, prick bottom and side of piecrust all over to prevent puffing and shrinking during baking. Cover and refrigerate at least 30 minutes.

3. Meanwhile, preheat oven to 425°F. In 2-quart saucepan, heat sweet potatoes and enough water to cover to boiling over high heat. Reduce heat to low; cover and simmer until sweet potatoes are fork-tender, about 10 minutes. Drain and mash sweet potatoes; you will have about 2 cups.

4. Line pie shell with foil; fill with pie weights, dry beans, or uncooked rice. Bake 10 minutes; remove foil with weights and bake 10 minutes longer or until lightly browned. (If pastry puffs up during baking, gently press it to pan with back of spoon.) Cool pie shell on wire rack at least 10 minutes. Turn oven control to 375°F.

5. In large bowl, with wire whisk, beat mashed sweet potatoes, egg yolks, brown sugar, half-and-half, molasses, cinnamon, nutmeg, and remaining ½ teaspoon salt until blended. Cover and refrigerate egg whites until ready to use.

6. Pour sweet-potato mixture into cooled crust. Bake pie until knife inserted 1 inch from edge of pie comes out clean, 55 to 60 minutes. Transfer pie to wire rack while preparing meringue. Turn oven control to 400°F.

7. In small bowl, with mixer at high speed, beat egg whites and cream of tartar until soft peaks form when beaters are lifted. Gradually sprinkle in granulated sugar, 2 tablespoons at a time, beating until whites stand in stiff peaks.

8. Spread meringue over hot filling to edge of crust;

swirl meringue with back of spoon to make attractive top. Bake until meringue is golden, about 10 minutes. Cool pie on wire rack. Makes 10 servings.

Each serving: About 355 calories, 6 g protein, 55 g carbohydrate, 13 g total fat (4 g saturated), 75 mg cholesterol, 325 mg sodium.

Chess Pie

Prep: 25 minutes plus cooling
Bake: About 1 hour

Pastry for 8-inch 1-crust pie (see page 1031) or ½ package (10 to 11 ounces) piecrust mix
5 tablespoons margarine or butter
3 large eggs
1¼ cups sugar
½ cup milk
2 tablespoons all-purpose flour
2 tablespoons cornmeal
1 teaspoon vanilla extract
¼ teaspoon salt
Ground nutmeg

1. Prepare piecrust for 1-crust pie; use to line 8-inch pie plate and make high stand-up edge. Set aside.

2. Preheat oven to 300°F. In 2-quart saucepan, melt margarine over low heat. With wire whisk or fork, beat in eggs, sugar, milk, flour, cornmeal, vanilla, salt, and ⅛ teaspoon ground nutmeg until blended. Pour egg mixture into piecrust; sprinkle with nutmeg.

3. Bake pie until knife inserted 1 inch from edge comes out clean, about 1 hour. Cool pie on wire rack. Refrigerate. Makes 10 servings.

Each serving: About 300 calories, 4 g protein, 37 g carbohydrate, 15 g total fat (4 g saturated), 65 mg cholesterol, 275 mg sodium.

∾Cream Pies

Coconut Cream Pie

Prep: 35 minutes plus chilling
Bake: 20 minutes

Piecrust
1 cup all-purpose flour
½ cup sweetened shredded coconut, toasted
6 tablespoons cold margarine or butter, cut into small pieces
2 tablespoons sugar
1 tablespoon cold water
Nonstick cooking spray

Filling
2 cups milk
1 can (8½ ounces) cream of coconut* (not coconut milk)
⅓ cup cornstarch
¼ teaspoon salt
4 large egg yolks
2 tablespoons margarine or butter
1 teaspoon vanilla extract

Topping
1 cup heavy or whipping cream
2 tablespoons sugar
½ teaspoon vanilla extract
2 tablespoons sweetened shredded coconut, toasted

1. Prepare piecrust: Preheat oven to 375°F. Combine flour, coconut, margarine, sugar, and cold water into food processor with knife blade attached. Blend ingredients, pulsing processor on and off, until dough just comes together.

2. Spray 9-inch pie plate with nonstick cooking spray. Press dough evenly onto bottom and up side of pie plate, making a small rim. Bake pie shell 20 minutes, or until golden, covering edge loosely with foil if necessary during last 10 minutes to prevent overbrowning. Cool on wire rack.

3. While pie shell is cooling, prepare filling: In 3-quart saucepan, with wire whisk, mix milk, cream of coconut, cornstarch, and salt until blended. Cook over medium heat, stirring constantly, until mixture thickens and begins to bubble around side of pan, about 7 minutes; boil 1 minute.

4. In small bowl, with wire whisk or fork, beat egg yolks slightly. Into yolks, beat small amount of hot milk mixture. Slowly pour yolk mixture back into milk mixture, stirring rapidly to prevent lumping. Cook over low heat, about 2 minutes, stirring constantly, until very thick (mixture should be about 160°F.).

5. Remove saucepan from heat; stir in margarine and vanilla. Spoon hot filling into pie shell. Place plastic wrap directly on surface of filling and refrigerate pie until filling is cold and set, about 4 hours.

6. To serve, prepare topping: In bowl, with mixer at medium speed, beat cream and sugar until stiff peaks form when beaters are lifted. Beat in vanilla. Spread whipped cream over filling. Sprinkle with coconut. Makes 10 servings.

*Coconut cream, available in Asian and Hispanic specialty stores, is pressed and rehydrated coconut meat. It resembles vegetable shortening, and is used in some Asian and Caribbean cooking for deep-frying. Cream of coconut, a sweeter, thicker version of coconut milk, contains added sugar and stabilizers. It's used in piña coladas (and similar drinks) and in our Coconut Cream Pie (above); you'll find it where cocktail mixers are sold.

Each serving: About 425 calories, 5 g protein, 40 g carbohydrate, 28 g total fat (14 g saturated), 124 mg cholesterol, 235 mg sodium.

Banana Cream Pie

Prep: 35 minutes plus chilling
Bake: About 25 minutes

1 ¼ cups all-purpose flour
1 tablespoon plus ¾ cup sugar
¾ teaspoon salt
¼ cup butter-flavored shortening
6 tablespoons margarine or butter
3 to 4 tablespoons cold water

⅓ cup cornstarch
3¾ cups milk
5 large egg yolks
1¾ teaspoons vanilla extract
3 medium, ripe bananas
¾ cup heavy or whipping cream

1. In medium bowl, combine flour, 1 tablespoon sugar, and ½ teaspoon salt. With pastry blender or 2 knives used scissor-fashion, cut in shortening and 4 tablespoons margarine until mixture resembles coarse crumbs. Sprinkle cold water, 1 tablespoon at a time, into flour mixture, mixing lightly with a fork after each addition until dough is just moist enough to hold together. Shape dough into ball; flatten into disk.

2. Preheat oven to 425°F. On floured surface, with floured rolling pin, roll dough into a round 1½ inches larger all around than inverted 9-inch pie plate. Ease dough into pie plate; trim edge, leaving 1-inch overhang. Fold overhang under; pinch to form high fluted edge (see page 1034). With fork, prick bottom and side of piecrust all over to prevent puffing during baking. Line pie shell with foil and fill with pie weights, dry beans, or uncooked rice. Bake pie shell 10 minutes; remove foil with weights and bake until golden, 10 to 15 minutes longer. If shell puffs up during baking, gently press it to pie plate with back of spoon. Cool on wire rack.

3. In 3-quart saucepan, mix cornstarch, remaining ¾ cup sugar, and ¼ teaspoon salt; stir in milk until smooth. Cook over medium heat, stirring constantly, until mixture boils and thickens; boil 1 minute.

4. In small bowl, beat egg yolks slightly. Into yolks, beat small amount of hot milk mixture. Slowly pour yolk mixture back into milk mixture, stirring rapidly to prevent lumping. Over low heat, cook mixture stirring constantly, until mixture is very thick, about 2 minutes.

5. Remove saucepan from heat; stir in remaining 2 tablespoons margarine and 1½ teaspoons vanilla. Slice 2 bananas. Pour half the filling into cooled pie shell. Arrange sliced bananas over custard; spoon remaining filling over banana layer. Place plastic wrap directly on surface of filling and refrigerate pie until filling is cold and set, about 4 hours.

6. To serve, in small bowl, with mixer at medium speed, beat heavy cream and remaining ¼ teaspoon vanilla until stiff peaks form when beaters are lifted. Spread whipped cream over filling. Slice remaining banana and arrange around edge of pie. Makes 10 servings.

Each serving: About 425 calories, 7 g protein, 45 g carbohydrate, 25 g total fat (10 g saturated), 143 mg cholesterol, 310 mg sodium.

Chocolate Truffle Tart

Prep: 20 minutes plus cooling
Bake: 45 to 50 minutes

1 cup all-purpose flour	¼ cup sugar
½ teaspoon salt	1 teaspoon vanilla extract
3 tablespoons shortening	½ cup heavy or whipping
3 tablespoons plus ½ cup (1 stick) margarine or butter	cream
	3 large eggs
3 tablespoons cold water	White-Chocolate Hearts (see
6 squares (6 ounces) semisweet chocolate	page 1090)

1. Preheat oven to 400°F. In medium bowl, combine flour and salt. With pastry blender or 2 knives used scissor-fashion, cut in shortening and 3 tablespoons margarine until mixture resembles coarse crumbs. Add cold water, 1 tablespoon at a time, tossing with fork just until mixture is moist enough to hold together. Shape into ball; flatten into disk.

2. On floured surface, with floured rolling pin, roll

dough into an 11-inch round. Press dough onto bottom and up side of 9-inch tart pan with removable bottom. Trim edge even with rim of pan. With fork, prick dough all over to prevent puffing and shrinking during baking.

3. Line tart shell with foil and fill with pie weights, dry beans or uncooked rice. Bake tart shell 15 minutes; remove foil with weights and bake until golden, 10 to 15 minutes longer. Cool in pan on wire rack 15 minutes. Turn oven control to 350°F.

4. While tart shell is cooling, prepare filling: In 1-quart measuring cup, combine semisweet chocolate and remaining ½ cup margarine; cover with waxed paper. In microwave oven, cook on High until almost melted, 1½ to 2½ minutes; stir until smooth. Stir in sugar and vanilla. In small bowl, with fork or wire whisk, lightly beat heavy or whipping cream and eggs. Blend some warm chocolate mixture into egg mixture; stir egg mixture back into chocolate mixture until blended.

5. Pour warm chocolate mixture into cooled tart shell. Bake until custard is just set (center will appear jiggly), about 20 minutes.

6. While tart is baking, prepare White-Chocolate Hearts.

7. Cool tart on wire rack. Cover and refrigerate to serve cold. Garnish with White-Chocolate Hearts. Makes 12 servings.

WHITE-CHOCOLATE HEARTS: With pencil, draw outline of 12 hearts, each about 1½ inches all around, on piece of waxed paper. Place waxed paper, pencil-side down, on cookie sheet; tape to cookie sheet. In heavy small saucepan, melt *1½ ounces white chocolate,* * coarsely chopped, over low heat. Spoon warm white chocolate into small decorating bag with small writing tip; use to pipe heart-shaped outlines on waxed paper. Set aside to dry.

*Or, use ½ Swiss confectionery bar (3 ounces) or ¼ package (6 ounces) white baking bar.

Each serving without chocolate hearts: About 315 calories, 4 g protein, 25 g carbohydrate, 23 g total fat (6 g saturated), 68 mg cholesterol, 260 mg sodium.

Blueberry-Cassis Tart

Prep: 40 minutes plus chilling
Bake: 27 minutes

Tart Shell (see page 1036)
2 tablespoons cornstarch
2 tablespoons water
¼ teaspoon salt
⅓ cup plus 2 teaspoons sugar
2 pints blueberries, washed and picked over
3 tablespoons plus 2 teaspoons crème de cassis or black raspberry-
    flavored liqueur
½ cup heavy or whipping cream

1. Prepare and bake 10-inch Tart Shell as directed; cool.
2. While tart shell is baking, prepare filling: In 3-quart
saucepan, stir cornstarch, water, salt, and ⅓ cup sugar until
blended. Stir in 4½ cups blueberries; reserve remaining
blueberries for garnish. Cook over medium heat, stirring
constantly, until mixture thickens and boils; boil 1 minute.
3. Remove saucepan from heat; stir in 3 tablespoons
crème de cassis; cool mixture slightly. Spoon blueberry
mixture into cooled tart shell. Refrigerate tart until chilled,
about 3 hours.
4. To serve, in small bowl, with mixer at medium speed,
beat heavy cream, remaining 2 teaspoons sugar, and remaining 2 teaspoons crème de cassis until soft peaks form
when beaters are lifted. Top tart with whipped cream and
remaining blueberries. Makes 10 servings.

*Each serving: About 275 calories, 2 g protein, 33 g carbohydrate,
15 g total fat (5 g saturated), 17 mg cholesterol, 185 mg sodium.*

Chocolate Angel Pie

Prep: 20 minutes plus cooling
Bake: 1 hour

3 large egg whites
¼ teaspoon salt
¼ teaspoon cream of tartar
2½ teaspoons vanilla extract
2¼ cups confectioners' sugar
½ cup unsweetened cocoa
1 teaspoon instant espresso-coffee powder
1 teaspoon hot tap water
2 cups heavy or whipping cream
2 tablespoons milk

1. Preheat oven to 300°F. Grease and flour 9-inch metal pie pan.

2. In small bowl, with mixer at high speed, beat egg whites, salt, and cream of tartar until soft peaks form when beater are lifted. Beating at high speed, add 1 teaspoon vanilla and sprinkle in 1 cup confectioners' sugar, 2 tablespoons at a time, beating well after each addition until sugar has dissolved and whites stand in stiff, glossy peaks.

3. With metal spatula, evenly spread meringue over bottom and up side of pie pan, making an edge above pie pan rim. Bake meringue 1 hour. Turn off oven and let meringue remain in oven 1 hour to dry out. Cool meringue shell in pie pan on wire rack.

4. Meanwhile, prepare filling: Sift cocoa with remaining 1¼ cups confectioners' sugar. In cup, stir espresso powder and hot tap water until blended. In large bowl, with mixer at medium speed, beat heavy or whipping cream, dissolved espresso, and remaining 1½ teaspoons vanilla just until soft peaks form when beaters are lifted. Reduce speed to low; gradually beat in cocoa mixture until thoroughly blended and stiff peaks form (do not overbeat). Beat in milk.

5. With rubber spatula, spread chocolate cream into cooled meringue shell. If not serving pie right away, cover and refrigerate until ready to serve. Makes 10 servings.

Each serving: About 290 calories, 3 g protein, 31 g carbohydrate, 18 g total fat (11 g saturated), 66 mg cholesterol, 95 mg sodium.

Lemon Meringue Pie

Prep: 40 minutes plus chilling
Bake: 25 minutes

Pastry for 9-inch baked pie shell (see page 1031) or ½ package
   (10 to 11 ounces) piecrust mix
2 or 3 medium lemons
⅓ cup cornstarch
⅛ teaspoon salt
1¼ cups sugar
1½ cups water
4 large eggs, separated, at room temperature
1 tablespoon margarine or butter
¼ teaspoon cream of tartar

1. Prepare baked pie shell as directed; cool.

2. Meanwhile, prepare filling: Grate 1 tablespoon peel and squeeze ½ cup juice from lemons. Set peel and juice aside. In 2-quart saucepan, combine cornstarch, salt, and ¾ cup sugar. Stir in water; cook over medium heat, stirring constantly, until mixture thickens and boils; boil 1 minute. Remove saucepan from heat.

3. In small bowl, beat egg yolks; stir in small amount of hot cornstarch mixture until blended. Slowly pour yolk mixture back into hot cornstarch mixture in saucepan, stirring rapidly to prevent lumping. Return saucepan to heat; cook, stirring constantly, until filling is very thick, about 5 minutes. Remove from heat; stir in margarine, then gradually stir in lemon juice and peel. Pour into cooled pie shell.

4. Preheat oven to 400°F. Prepare meringue: In small bowl, with mixer at high speed, beat egg whites and cream of tartar until soft peaks form when beaters are lifted. Gradually sprinkle in remaining ½ cup sugar, 2 tablespoons at a time, beating until sugar has completely dissolved and whites stand in stiff peaks.

5. Spread meringue over filling to edge of crust; swirl meringue with back of spoon to make attractive top. Bake until meringue is golden, about 10 minutes. Cool pie on wire rack away from draft. Makes 10 servings.

Each serving: About 265 calories, 4 g protein, 39 g carbohydrate, 11 g total fat (3 g saturated), 85 mg cholesterol, 185 mg sodium.

Chocolate-Cream Pie

Prep: 40 minutes plus chilling
Bake: 15 minutes

Pastry for 9-inch baked pie shell (see page 1031) or ½ package (10 to 11 ounces) piecrust mix
3 tablespoons cornstarch
¼ teaspoon salt
½ cup plus 1 teaspoon sugar
2 cups milk
3 squares (3 ounces) unsweetened chocolate, coarsely chopped

2 egg yolks
2 tablespoons margarine or butter
1 teaspoon vanilla extract
½ cup heavy or whipping cream
¼ cup walnuts, toasted and chopped

1. Prepare baked pie shell as directed; cool.

2. Meanwhile, prepare filling: In heavy 3-quart saucepan, combine cornstarch, salt, and ½ cup sugar. Stir in milk and chopped chocolate. Cook over medium heat until chocolate melts and mixture thickens and boils; boil 1 minute, stirring constantly. Remove saucepan from heat.

3. In cup, beat egg yolks; stir in small amount of hot chocolate mixture. Slowly pour yolk mixture back into chocolate mixture, stirring rapidly to prevent lumping. Return saucepan to heat; cook over low heat, stirring constantly, until mixture is very thick, about 2 minutes. Stir in margarine and vanilla until blended. Pour chocolate filling into cooled pie shell. Place plastic wrap directly on surface of filling. Refrigerate pie at least 3 hours or until well chilled.

4. To serve, in small bowl, with mixer at medium speed, beat heavy cream with 1 teaspoon sugar until soft peaks form, when beaters are lifted. Spoon whipped cream onto filling and swirl to make an attractive design. Sprinkle whipped-cream top with toasted walnuts. Makes 10 servings.

Each serving: About 330 calories, 5 g protein, 27 g carbohydrate, 24 g total fat (9 g saturated), 66 mg cholesterol, 235 mg sodium.

⌒Mousse Pies

Strawberry-Rhubarb Mousse Pie

Prep: 20 minutes plus chilling
Bake: 15 minutes

1 pound rhubarb, cut into
    1-inch chunks (3½ cups)
1 cup sugar
¾ cup cold water
2 envelopes unflavored gelatin
1 pint strawberries, hulled
1 tablespoon fresh lemon juice

2 cups shortbread cookie
    crumbs (about thirty-six
    1½-inch-square cookies)
6 tablespoons margarine or
    butter, melted
½ pint heavy or whipping
    cream
Whole strawberries with leaves

1. In 2-quart saucepan, heat rhubarb, sugar, and ¼ cup water to boiling over high heat, stirring constantly. Reduce heat to medium-low and continue cooking until rhubarb is very tender, about 10 minutes. In food processor, with knife blade attached, blend rhubarb until smooth; return rhubarb to saucepan.

2. Sprinkle gelatin over remaining ½ cup cold water; let stand 2 minutes to soften.

3. In bowl, with potato masher or fork, mash strawberries. Stir softened gelatin, mashed strawberries, and lemon juice into rhubarb; simmer 3 minutes until gelatin has dissolved.

4. Pour rhubarb mixture into bowl and refrigerate, stirring occasionally, until mixture mounds slightly when dropped from a spoon, about 2½ hours. (Or, for quicker setting, place bowl with rhubarb mixture in a larger bowl of ice water and stir every 10 minutes until mixture mounds, about 1 hour.)

5. Meanwhile, preheat oven to 350°F. In deep-dish 9-inch pie plate, with hand, mix cookie crumbs and margarine. Press mixture onto bottom and up side of pie plate. Bake until golden, about 15 minutes. Cool on wire rack.

6. When rhubarb mixture is ready, beat cream until stiff peaks form when beaters are lifted. With spatula, fold whipped cream into rhubarb mixture until blended. Spoon mixture into pie shell. Refrigerate until pie is well chilled and set, 3 hours or overnight. Garnish with whole strawberries to serve. Makes 10 servings.

Each serving: About 370 calories, 4 g protein, 42 g carbohydrate, 22 g total fat (8 g saturated), 39 mg cholesterol, 215 mg sodium.

Three-Berry Tart

Prep: 45 minutes plus chilling
Bake: 27 minutes

Tart Shell (see page 1036)
1½ pints strawberries, hulled
½ cup water
¼ cup sugar
1 envelope unflavored gelatin
½ cup heavy or whipping cream

1 pint blueberries or blackberries
1 pint raspberries
¼ cup red-currant jelly
1 teaspoon fresh lemon juice

1. Prepare and bake 10-inch Tart Shell as directed; cool.

2. In blender at medium speed or in food processor with knife blade attached, blend 1 pint strawberries until smooth (about 1½ cups puree).

3. In 2-quart saucepan, stir water and sugar. Sprinkle gelatin evenly over mixture; let stand 1 minute to soften gelatin slightly. Cook over medium-low heat, stirring occasionally, until sugar and gelatin have completely dissolved. Remove saucepan from heat; stir in strawberry puree. Refrigerate, stirring occasionally, until mixture mounds slightly when dropped from a spoon, 20 to 25 minutes.

4. In small bowl, with mixer at medium speed, beat heavy cream until soft peaks form when beaters are lifted. With rubber spatula or wire whisk, fold strawberry mixture into whipped cream. Evenly spread mixture in cooled tart shell. Refrigerate until mixture is set, about 1 hour.

5. Slice remaining ½ pint strawberries. Arrange blueberries, raspberries, and sliced strawberries on strawberry filling.

6. Prepare glaze: In small saucepan, heat currant jelly and lemon juice over low heat until jelly melts. Brush fruit with jelly mixture; refrigerate tart about 15 minutes longer to set glaze (if glaze is placed on dessert too early, glaze will become watery). Carefully remove side from pan and place tart on serving plate. Makes 10 servings.

Each serving: About 270 calories, 3 g protein, 24 g carbohydrate, 15 g total fat (5 g saturated), 17 mg cholesterol, 130 mg sodium.

Cookies

～⌘～

Bar Cookies • Drop Cookies
Molded Cookies
Refrigerator Cookies
Rolled Cookies
Pressed Cookies

Cookies fall into six basic categories, depending on the consistency of the dough and method of shaping.

Bar Cookies are the easiest. Soft dough is spread in a shallow pan, baked, cooled slightly, then cut into bars, squares, or diamonds.

Drop Cookies are shaped by dropping soft dough from a spoon onto a cookie sheet.

Molded Cookies are made from stiff dough that is shaped by hand into balls, logs, pretzels, and similar shapes before baking, or they are baked in small molds.

Refrigerator Cookies are made from stiff, rich dough that is shaped, chilled, then sliced and baked. The dough keeps for several days in the refrigerator or six months in the freezer, ready to be sliced and baked on short notice.

Rolled Cookies are made from stiff dough that has been rolled out, then cut into fancy shapes with floured cookie cutters, a knife, or a pastry wheel.

Pressed Cookies are formed by forcing moderately stiff dough through a cookie press or decorating bag to make designs.

ᴖSuccess Tips

• Chill the dough if the recipe so directs. Chilling makes dough easier to handle and helps cookies hold their shape while they bake.

- Use shiny, clean aluminum cookie sheets that are at least 2 inches smaller all around than your oven, so that heat can circulate and the cookies can bake evenly.
- Grease cookie sheets only if the recipe calls for it; otherwise, cookies will spread too much.
- Always place dough on a cool cookie sheet; it spreads on a hot one. If you need extra cookie sheets, use inverted baking pans; or, while a sheet of cookies is baking, place the next batch on heavy-duty foil cut to fit the cookie sheet. As soon as baked cookies have been removed from the cookie sheet, place the foil with dough on it on the cookie sheet and bake immediately.
- When dough must be chilled before using, remove only the amount needed for one batch and keep the rest refrigerated until needed.
- Spoonfuls of dough for drop cookies should be placed 2 inches apart unless the recipe directs otherwise.
- Save trimmings from rolled cookie dough and reroll all at once, to keep cookies from becoming tough.
- If you bake one sheet of cookies at a time, place the oven rack in the center of the oven; if two sheets, place racks so they divide the oven into thirds, and switch the cookie sheets once during baking so that cookies brown evenly.
- As soon as the minimum baking time is up, test cookies for doneness.
- Unless the recipe directs otherwise, remove cookies from cookie sheets as soon as they come from the oven. Don't overlap cookies on wire racks, but cool them in a single layer. When they are cold, decorate them if you wish and store them. Cool bar cookies in the pan.

ᴄᴡHow to Store Cookies

Store soft and crisp cookies in separate containers with tight-fitting lids. Crisp cookies that soften can be recrisped in a 300°F. oven for 3 to 5 minutes. Soft cookies can be kept soft by adding a piece of apple or bread to the container, and changing it every other day or so. Store bar cookies, if you like, in the pan they bake in, tightly covered with foil or plastic wrap.

How to Freeze Cookies

Baked Cookies should be thoroughly cooled, then packed in sturdy containers, with a cushion of crumpled waxed paper, if necessary. If cookies have been decorated, freeze them until hard in a single layer on a cookie sheet, then pack them for storage. To thaw, unwrap cookies and let them stand for about 10 minutes at room temperature.

Unbaked Cookie Dough can be packed in containers or, for refrigerator cookies, shaped into rolls and wrapped tightly in foil or plastic wrap, then frozen. To use frozen dough, thaw it until soft enough to handle, then shape the cookies and bake them. Leave frozen refrigerator-cookie dough in the refrigerator until it softens just enough to be sliced.

Bar Exam: 12 Tips for Never-Fail Results

DO:

1. Let margarine or butter stand at room temperature if it must be softened. Leave stick(s) wrapped on counter or unwrapped in mixing bowl, cut into small pieces, to speed up the process. Softening can take up to an hour. (Popping cold butter into the microwave is tempting, but our food editors caution that zapping can soften it unevenly, creating hot spots, or melt the butter in a blink. And if butter is melted or nearly melted it will be too soft to cream properly and will affect a cookie's texture.)

2. Prepare the pan before you start mixing the batter. Some rising occurs as soon as ingredients are moistened. If you line and grease the pan after making the

batter, the mixture might start to swell and be harder to spread evenly.

3. Dip knife or scissors in flour often when chopping sticky foods like figs or dates.

4. Allow bars to cool completely before cutting with a chef's knife, to avoid jagged edges and broken pieces. Use a gentle sawing motion to avoid squashing squares.

5. For fudgy, cheesecakelike, or topped bars, dip knife blade in hot water; quickly dry blade with a paper towel and redip between cuts.

6. Keep soft bar cookies from getting stale by storing them in a cookie tin or jar with a slice of plain bread (replace the bread every other day). The bars should keep for up to 3 days. Or wrap and freeze the treats individually for up to 1 month to pop into a lunch box or briefcase.

DON'T:

7. Substitute light margarines, vegetable-oil spreads, or whipped butters for regular stick margarine or butter; they contain more water (or air) than standard sticks and are likely to throw off the recipe.

8. Measure ingredients over the bowl. If you slip while measuring and add too much, you may have to start all over again.

9. Use liquid measures for dry ingredients, or vice versa. Cup for cup, liquid measures have more volume.

10. Choose a different pan size than the recipe calls for; the timing (and test to see if cookies are done) is based on specific bakeware dimensions.

11. Open the oven door to check on bar cookies while they bake. The temperature can drop, and the cookies may not rise properly. Wait until the minimum baking time is up before taking a peek.

12. Wrap warm cookies or place them in any closed container. The heat will cause condensation and make the tops wet, so the bars stick together. Always let them cool completely first.

∿Bar Cookies

Fudgy *GH* Brownies

Prep: 10 minutes plus cooling
Bake: 30 minutes

¾ cup (1 ½ sticks) margarine or butter
4 squares (4 ounces) unsweetened chocolate
4 squares (4 ounces) semisweet chocolate
2 cups sugar
1 tablespoon vanilla extract
5 large eggs, beaten
1 ¼ cups all-purpose flour
½ teaspoon salt

1. Preheat oven to 350°F. Grease 13" by 9" metal baking pan. Line pan with foil; grease foil.

2. In heavy 3-quart saucepan, melt margarine and unsweetened and semisweet chocolates over low heat, stirring frequently. Remove saucepan from heat. With wooden spoon, stir in sugar and vanilla, then stir in eggs until well blended.

3. In small bowl, combine flour and salt; stir into chocolate mixture just until blended.

4. Spread batter evenly in pan. Bake 30 minutes (toothpick inserted in center will not come out clean). Cool completely in pan on wire rack.

5. When cool, transfer with foil to cutting board. Cut lengthwise into 4 strips, then cut each strip crosswise into 6 pieces. Makes 2 dozen bars.

Each bar About 200 calories, 3 g protein, 27 g carbohydrate, 10 g total fat (2 g saturated), 44 mg cholesterol, 135 mg sodium.

Blondies

Prep: 10 minutes plus cooling
Bake: 30 minutes

6 tablespoons margarine or butter
1¾ cups packed light brown sugar
2 teaspoons vanilla extract
2 large eggs
1 cup all-purpose flour
2 teaspoons baking powder
1 teaspoon salt
1½ cups pecans, coarsely chopped

1. Preheat oven to 350°F. Grease 13" by 9" metal baking pan. Line pan with foil; grease foil.

2. In heavy 3-quart saucepan, melt margarine over low heat. Remove saucepan from heat. With wooden spoon, stir in brown sugar and vanilla, then stir in eggs until well blended.

3. In small bowl, combine flour, baking powder, and salt; stir into sugar mixture just until blended. Stir in chopped pecans.

4. Spread batter evenly in pan. Bake until toothpick inserted 2 inches from edge of pan comes out clean, 30 minutes. Do not overbake; blondies will become firm as they cool. Cool completely in pan on wire rack.

5. When cool, transfer with foil to cutting board. Cut lengthwise into 4 strips, then cut each strip crosswise into 6 pieces. Makes 2 dozen bars.

Each bar: About 155 calories, 2 g protein, 21 g carbohydrate, 8 g total fat (1 g saturated), 18 mg cholesterol, 170 mg sodium.

Peanut-Butter Rocky-Road Bars

Prep: 15 minutes plus cooling
Bake: About 25 minutes

¾ cup packed light brown
   sugar
⅔ cup creamy peanut butter
½ cup granulated sugar
4 tablespoons margarine or
   butter, softened
1¼ cups all-purpose flour
1 teaspoon baking powder

1 teaspoon vanilla extract
2 large eggs
1 cup miniature marshmallows
½ cup salted cocktail peanuts,
   chopped
½ cup semisweet-chocolate
   pieces

1. Preheat oven to 350°F. Grease 13" by 9" metal baking pan. Line pan with foil; grease foil.

2. In large bowl, with mixer at low speed, beat brown sugar, peanut butter, granulated sugar, and margarine until blended. Increase speed to high; beat until creamy. Reduce speed to low, beat in flour, baking powder, vanilla, and eggs until well blended, constantly scraping bowl with rubber spatula.

3. With hand, press dough onto bottom of pan. Bake 20 minutes. Sprinkle marshmallows, peanuts, and chocolate pieces over top; bake until golden, 5 minutes longer. Cool completely in pan on wire rack.

4. When cool, transfer with foil to cutting board. Cut lengthwise into 4 strips, then cut each strip crosswise into 6 pieces. Makes 2 dozen bars.

Each bar: About 175 calories, 4 g protein, 22 g carbohydrate, 8 g total fat (1 g saturated), 18 mg cholesterol, 100 mg sodium.

Turtle Bars

Prep: 35 minutes plus cooling
Bake: 15 to 20 minutes

Pastry Crust
1 cup all-purpose flour
¼ cup granulated sugar
⅛ teaspoon salt
6 tablespoons cold butter (no substitutions)
3 tablespoons cold water

Caramel
1⅓ cups packed light brown sugar
½ cup heavy or whipping cream
⅓ cup light corn syrup
3 tablespoons butter (no substitutions)
1 teaspoon distilled white vinegar
⅛ teaspoon salt
1 teaspoon vanilla extract
¾ cup pecans, toasted and chopped

Topping
3 ounces semisweet chocolate

1. Preheat oven to 425°F. Grease 9" by 9" metal baking pan. Line pan with foil; grease foil.

2. Prepare Pastry Crust: In medium bowl, combine flour, sugar, and salt. With pastry blender or 2 knives used scissor-fashion, cut in butter until mixture resembles coarse crumbs. Sprinkle cold water, 1 tablespoon at a time, into flour mixture, mixing lightly with fork after each addition until dough is just moist enough to hold together.

3. With lightly floured hands, press dough evenly onto bottom of pan. With fork, prick dough all over to prevent puffing and shrinking during baking. Bake crust until golden (crust may crack slightly during baking), 15 to 20 minutes. Cool completely in pan on wire rack.

4. When crust is cool, prepare Caramel: In 2-quart saucepan, heat brown sugar, cream, corn syrup, butter, vinegar, and salt to boiling over high heat, stirring occasionally. Reduce heat to medium-low and cook, uncovered, 5 minutes, stirring frequently. Remove saucepan from heat; stir in vanilla until blended and bubbling subsides, about 20 seconds.

5. Pour hot caramel evenly over cooled crust; sprinkle with pecans. Set aside to allow caramel to cool, about 1 hour.

6. To prepare Topping, place chocolate in 2-cup measuring cup or medium glass bowl. In microwave oven, cook, covered with waxed paper, on High, until almost melted, 1 to 2 minutes; stir until smooth. (Or, in heavy 1-quart saucepan, heat chocolate over low heat, stirring frequently, until melted and smooth.) Cool chocolate 5 minutes; drizzle over pecans. Place pan in refrigerator until chocolate is set, about 30 minutes.

7. When set, transfer with foil to cutting board. Cut into 6 strips, then cut each strip crosswise into 6 pieces. Store bars in refrigerator. Makes 3 dozen bars.

Each bar: About 120 calories, 1 g protein, 16 g carbohydrate, 6 g total fat (3 g saturated), 12 mg cholesterol, 50 mg sodium.

Scottish Shortbread

Prep: 20 minutes
Bake: About 40 minutes

3 cups cake flour (not self-rising)
¾ cup confectioners' sugar
¼ teaspoon salt
1½ cups (3 sticks) margarine or butter, softened, cut into small
    pieces

1. Preheat oven to 325°F. In large bowl, combine flour, confectioners' sugar, and salt. With hand, knead margarine into flour mixture until well blended and mixture holds together.

2. Pat dough evenly into two 8-inch round cake pans.

With fork, prick dough to make an attractive pattern. Bake shortbread until golden, about 40 minutes. Remove shortbread from oven; immediately cut each round in pan into 16 wedges. Cool shortbread in pans on wire racks.

3. When cold, carefully remove cookies from pans. Store in tightly covered container in refrigerator. Makes 32 cookies.

Each cookie: About 120 calories, 1 g protein, 10 g carbohydrate, 9 g total fat (2 g saturated), 0 mg cholesterol, 130 mg sodium.

Fresh Lemon Bars

Prep: 15 minutes plus cooling
Bake: 30 to 32 minutes

1½ cups plus 3 tablespoons all-purpose flour
½ cup plus 1 tablespoon confectioners' sugar
¾ cup (1½ sticks) margarine or butter, cut into small pieces
2 large lemons
3 large eggs
1 cup granulated sugar
½ teaspoon baking powder
½ teaspoon salt

1. Preheat oven to 350°F. Line 13" by 9" metal baking pan with foil; lightly grease foil.

2. In medium bowl, combine 1½ cups flour and ½ cup confectioners' sugar. With pastry blender or 2 knives used scissor-fashion, cut in margarine until mixture resembles coarse crumbs.

3. Sprinkle crumb mixture evenly in pan. With floured hands, firmly pat crumbs onto bottom of pan to form a crust. Bake crust until lightly browned, 15 to 17 minutes.

4. Meanwhile, from lemons, grate 1 teaspoon peel and squeeze ⅓ cup juice. In large bowl, with mixer at high speed, beat eggs until thick and lemon-colored, about 3 minutes. Reduce speed to low; add lemon juice, lemon peel, granulated sugar, baking powder, salt, and remaining 3 tablespoons flour, and beat until blended, occasionally scraping bowl.

5. Pour lemon filling over warm crust. Bake until filling is just set and golden around edges, about 15 minutes. Transfer pan to wire rack. Place remaining 1 tablespoon confectioners' sugar in sieve and sprinkle over warm filling. Cool completely in pan on wire rack.

6. When cool, cut lengthwise into 3 strips, then cut each strip crosswise into 12 pieces. To store, cover pan and refrigerate. Makes 36 bars.

Each bar: About 90 calories, 1 g protein, 12 g carbohydrate, 4 g total fat (1 g saturated), 18 mg cholesterol, 90 mg sodium.

Apricot Squares

Prep: 25 minutes
Bake: 50 minutes

⅔ cup dried apricots
½ cup (1 stick) margarine or butter, softened
¼ cup granulated sugar
1⅓ cups all-purpose flour
1 cup packed light brown sugar
2 large eggs
½ cup walnuts, chopped
½ teaspoon baking powder
½ teaspoon vanilla extract
¼ teaspoon salt
Confectioners' sugar

1. In 1-quart saucepan, heat apricots and enough *water to cover* to boiling over high heat. Reduce heat to low; cover and cook apricots 15 minutes; drain. Finely chop apricots; set aside.

2. Preheat oven to 350°F. Grease 8" by 8" baking pan.

3. In large bowl, combine margarine, granulated sugar, and 1 cup flour. With mixer at medium speed, beat until well mixed (mixture will be crumbly). Pat dough evenly into pan. Bake until golden, about 25 minutes.

4. Meanwhile, in same bowl, combine apricots, brown sugar, eggs, walnuts, baking powder, vanilla, salt, and remaining ⅓ cup flour. With mixer at medium speed, beat until mixed, scraping bowl often.

5. Remove baking pan from oven; pour apricot mixture over baked layer and return to oven. Bake until golden, about 25 minutes. Cool completely in pan on wire rack.

6. When cold, cut lengthwise into 4 strips, then cut each strip crosswise into 4 pieces. Sprinkle with confectioners' sugar. Store in tightly covered container. Makes 16 squares.

Each square: About 200 calories, 3 g protein, 29 g carbohydrate, 9 g total fat (1 g saturated), 27 mg cholesterol, 140 mg sodium.

Granola Breakfast Bars

Prep: 15 minutes plus cooling
Bake: 30 to 35 minutes

2 cups old-fashioned oats, uncooked	¾ teaspoon salt
1 cup all-purpose flour	¾ teaspoon ground cinnamon
¾ cup packed light brown sugar	½ cup vegetable oil
¾ cup dark seedless raisins	½ cup honey
½ cup toasted wheat germ	2 teaspoons vanilla extract
	1 large egg

1. Preheat oven to 350°F. Grease 13" by 9" metal baking pan. Line pan with foil; grease foil.

2. In large bowl, combine oats, flour, brown sugar, raisins, wheat germ, salt, and cinnamon. Stir in vegetable oil, honey, vanilla, and egg until blended.

3. With wet hand, pat oat mixture into pan. Bake until pale golden around edges, 30 to 35 minutes. Cool completely in pan on wire rack.

4. When cool, transfer with foil to cutting board. Cut lengthwise into 4 strips, then cut each strip crosswise into 6 pieces. Makes 2 dozen bars.

Each bar: About 185 calories, 4 g protein, 30 g carbohydrate, 6 g total fat (1 g saturated), 9 mg cholesterol, 75 mg sodium.

Hermit Bars

Prep: 10 minutes plus cooling
Bake: 18 to 22 minutes

2 cups all-purpose flour
⅔ cup packed dark brown
   sugar
2 teaspoons ground cinnamon
1½ teaspoons ground ginger
½ teaspoon baking soda

½ teaspoon salt
⅔ cup light molasses
6 tablespoons margarine or
   butter, melted
2 teaspoons vanilla extract
2 large eggs, lightly beaten
¾ cup dark seedless raisins

1. Preheat oven to 375°F. Grease 13" by 9" metal baking pan. Line pan with foil; grease foil.

2. In large bowl, combine flour, brown sugar, cinnamon, ginger, baking soda, and salt. Stir in molasses, melted margarine, vanilla, and eggs just until blended. Stir in raisins.

3. Spread mixture evenly in pan. Bake until golden around edges, 18 to 22 minutes. Cool completely in pan on wire rack.

4. When cool, transfer with foil to cutting board. Cut lengthwise into 6 strips, then cut each strip crosswise into 4 pieces. Makes 2 dozen bars.

Each bar: About 130 calories, 2 g protein, 24 g carbohydrate, 3 g total fat (1 g saturated), 18 mg cholesterol, 120 mg sodium.

〜Drop Cookies

Double-Chocolate Chunk Cookies

Prep: 40 minutes plus cooling
Bake: 25 to 30 minutes per batch

1 package (12 ounces)
   semisweet-chocolate chunks
   (2 cups)
1 cup (2 sticks) margarine or
   butter, softened
⅔ cup packed light brown
   sugar
⅓ cup granulated sugar

1 teaspoon baking soda
2 teaspoons vanilla extract
½ teaspoon salt
1 large egg
2 cups all-purpose flour
2 cups walnuts, coarsely
   chopped

1. In heavy small saucepan, heat 1 cup chocolate chunks over low heat, stirring frequently, until melted and smooth. Remove saucepan from heat; cool to room temperature.

2. In large bowl, with mixer at low speed, beat margarine, brown sugar, granulated sugar, baking soda, vanilla, and salt until crumbly. Add melted chocolate and egg; beat until well blended, occasionally scraping bowl with rubber spatula. With spoon, stir in flour, walnuts, and remaining 1 cup chocolate chunks.

3. Preheat oven to 350°F. Drop dough by level ¼ cups, about 3 inches apart, onto 2 ungreased large cookie sheets. Place cookie sheets on 2 oven racks. Bake 25 to 30 minutes, rotating cookie sheets between upper and lower racks halfway through baking time, or until edges of cookies are set but centers are still soft. With wide spatula, transfer cookies to wire racks to cool completely. Store cookies in tightly covered container. Makes about 1½ dozen cookies.

Each cookie: About 365 calories, 5 g protein, 38 g carbohydrate, 23 g total fat (3 g saturated), 12 mg cholesterol, 285 mg sodium.

Fruitcake Drops

Prep: 30 minutes plus cooling
Bake: 10 to 12 minutes per batch

1¾ cups all-purpose flour
½ teaspoon baking soda
¼ teaspoon salt
1 cup packed light brown
   sugar
6 tablespoons margarine or
   butter, softened
2 tablespoons shortening
1 large egg
1 cup pitted prunes, coarsely
   chopped

1 cup golden raisins
½ cup red candied cherries,
   coarsely chopped
½ cup sweetened shredded
   coconut
3 ounces white chocolate,
   Swiss confectionery bar, or
   white baking bar

1. Preheat oven to 375°F. Grease large cookie sheet.

2. In large bowl, combine flour, baking soda, and salt; set aside.

3. In another large bowl, with mixer at low speed, beat brown sugar, margarine, and shortening until blended, occasionally scraping bowl with rubber spatula. Increase speed to high; beat until creamy, about 2 minutes. Reduce speed to low; beat in egg until blended. Add flour mixture, prunes, raisins, cherries, and coconut, and beat just until blended.

4. Drop dough by rounded tablespoons, about 2 inches apart, onto cookie sheet. Bake until golden around edges (cookies will be soft), 10 to 12 minutes. Transfer cookies to wire rack to cool. Repeat with remaining dough.

5. In heavy small saucepan, melt white chocolate over very low heat, stirring frequently, until smooth. On sheet of waxed paper, arrange cookies in 1 layer. Using spoon, drizzle white chocolate over cookies. Allow white chocolate to set, refrigerating if necessary. Store cookies in tightly covered container with waxed paper between layers. Makes about 3 dozen cookies.

Each cookie: About 130 calories, 1 g protein, 22 g carbohydrate, 4 g total fat (2 g saturated), 6 mg cholesterol, 70 mg sodium.

Darlene's Oatmeal Cookies

Prep: 20 minutes plus cooling
Bake: 12 to 15 minutes per batch

2 cups old-fashioned oats, uncooked	1 cup (2 sticks) margarine or butter, softened
1 cup dark seedless or golden raisins	1 cup granulated sugar
2 cups all-purpose flour	1 cup packed light brown sugar
1 teaspoon baking soda	2 large eggs
½ teaspoon salt	2 teaspoons vanilla extract

1. Preheat oven to 350°F. In food processor with knife blade attached, pulse oats and raisins until ground. Transfer oat mixture to medium bowl; stir in flour, baking soda, and salt.

2. In large bowl, with mixer at low speed, beat margarine and granulated and brown sugars until blended. Increase speed to high; beat until light and creamy. Reduce speed to low; beat in eggs and vanilla, then beat in oat mixture.

3. Drop dough by rounded tablespoons, about 2 inches apart, onto ungreased large cookie sheet. Bake until cookies are browned, 12 to 15 minutes. Cool on wire rack. Repeat with remaining dough. Makes about 3 dozen cookies.

Each cookie: About 165 calories, 3 g protein, 26 g carbohydrate, 6 g total fat (1 g saturated), 12 mg cholesterol, 140 mg sodium.

Chocolate-Hazelnut Macaroons

Prep: 30 minutes plus cooling
Bake: 10 to 12 minutes per batch

1 cup hazelnuts (filberts), toasted
1 cup sugar
¼ cup unsweetened cocoa
1 square (1 ounce) unsweetened chocolate, chopped
⅛ teaspoon salt
2 large egg whites
1 teaspoon vanilla extract

1. Preheat oven to 350°F. Line large cookie sheet with kitchen parchment or foil

2. In food processor with knife blade attached, pulse toasted hazelnuts, sugar, cocoa, chocolate, and salt until finely ground. Add egg whites and vanilla, and process until blended.

3. Drop dough by rounded teaspoons, 2 inches apart, onto cookie sheet. If necessary, with moistened fingertip, push dough from teaspoon. Bake cookies until tops feel firm when lightly pressed, 10 minutes. Cool cookies completely on cookie sheet on wire rack. If you want to reuse cookie sheet right away, let cookies cool slightly, about 5 minutes, then slide parchment or foil, with cookies attached, onto wire rack and let cookies cool completely.

4. When cool, carefully peel cookies off parchment or foil. Store cookies in tightly covered container up to 2 weeks. Makes about 3 dozen cookies.

Each cookie: About 50 calories, 1 g protein, 7 g carbohydrate, 3 g total fat (1 g saturated), 0 mg cholesterol, 10 mg sodium.

Moravian Spice Crisps

Prep: 30 minutes plus cooling
Bake: 8 to 10 minutes per batch

¾ cup all-purpose flour
½ teaspoon baking powder
½ teaspoon ground cinnamon
½ teaspoon ground ginger
½ teaspoon ground white pepper
¼ teaspoon ground cloves
¼ teaspoon baking soda
¼ teaspoon salt
⅓ cup packed light brown sugar
3 tablespoons margarine or butter, softened
¼ cup light molasses

1. Preheat oven to 350°F. Grease large cookie sheet.
2. In large bowl, combine flour, baking powder, cinnamon, ginger, white pepper, cloves, baking soda, and salt; set aside.
3. In another large bowl, with mixer at low speed, beat brown sugar and margarine until blended. Increase speed to high; beat until creamy, about 2 minutes. Reduce speed to medium; beat in molasses until blended. Stir in flour mixture until blended.
4. Drop dough by rounded teaspoons, about 4 inches apart, onto cookie sheet. With finger, press each into a 2-inch round. Bake until cookies spread and darken, 8 to 10 minutes. Let cookies remain on cookie sheet on wire rack 3 minutes to cool slightly. Transfer cookies to wire rack to cool completely. Repeat with remaining dough. Store cookies in tightly covered container. Makes about 3 dozen cookies.

Each cookie: About 30 calories, 0 g protein, 6 g carbohydrate, 1 g total fat (0 g saturated), 0 mg cholesterol, 45 mg sodium.

Wooden Spoon Cookies

Prep: 25 minutes plus cooling
Bake: 5 to 7 minutes per batch

¾ cup blanched almonds, ground
½ cup (1 stick) margarine or butter, softened
½ cup sugar
1 tablespoon all-purpose flour
1 tablespoon heavy or whipping cream

1. Preheat oven to 350°F. Grease and flour 2 large cookie sheets.
2. In 2-quart saucepan, combine ground almonds, margarine, sugar, flour, and cream. Heat over low heat, stirring occasionally, until margarine melts. Keep mixture warm over very low heat.
3. Working with one cookie sheet at a time, drop batter by rounded teaspoons, about 3 inches apart, onto cookie sheet. (Do not place more than 6 on cookie sheet because, after baking, cookies must be shaped quickly before hardening.) Bake cookies, one sheet at a time, until edges are lightly browned and centers are just golden, 5 to 7 minutes. Let cookies remain on cookie sheet 30 to 60 seconds, until edges are just set.
4. With long, flexible metal spatula, flip cookies over quickly so lacy texture will be on outside after rolling. Working as quickly as possible, roll each cookie into a cylinder around handle of wooden spoon; transfer to wire rack. If cookies become too hard to roll, return to oven briefly to soften. As each cookie is shaped, transfer from spoon handle; cool on wire rack. Repeat until all batter is used. Makes about 3 dozen cookies.

Each cookie About 50 calories, 1 g protein, 3 g carbohydrate, 4 g total fat (1 g saturated), 1 mg cholesterol, 35 mg sodium.

Chocolate-Chip Cookies

Prep: 25 minutes
Bake: 12 to 15 minutes per batch

1¼ cups all-purpose flour
½ cup packed light brown
  sugar
½ cup (1 stick) margarine or
  butter, softened
¼ cup granulated sugar
1 tablespoon water
1 teaspoon vanilla extract

½ teaspoon baking soda
½ teaspoon salt
1 large egg
1 package (6 ounces)
  semisweet-chocolate pieces
½ cup walnuts, chopped

1. Preheat oven to 375°F. In large bowl, combine flour, brown sugar, margarine, granulated sugar, water, vanilla, baking soda, salt, and egg. With mixer at low speed, beat ingredients until mixed. Stir in chocolate and nuts.

2. Drop mixture by rounded tablespoons, 2 inches apart, onto ungreased cookie sheet. Bake until lightly browned, 12 to 15 minutes. With wide spatula, transfer cookies to wire racks to cool. Repeat with remaining dough. Store cookies in tightly covered container. Makes about 2 dozen cookies.

Each cookie: About 130 calories, 2 g protein, 17 g carbohydrate, 7 g total fat (2 g saturated), 9 mg cholesterol, 130 mg sodium.

Florentines

Prep: 45 minutes plus cooling
Bake: 10 minutes per batch

1 cup slivered almonds
1 container (3½ ounces) candied orange peel (about ½ cup)
6 tablespoons butter (no substitutions)
½ cup sugar
¼ cup heavy or whipping cream
2 tablespoons all-purpose flour
1 tablespoon light corn syrup
8 squares (8 ounces) semisweet chocolate, melted and cooled

1. Preheat oven to 350°F. Line large cookie sheet with kitchen parchment. In food processor with knife blade attached, pulse almonds and orange peel until finely chopped.

2. In 1-quart saucepan, combine butter, sugar, cream, flour, and corn syrup; heat to boiling over medium heat, stirring frequently. Remove saucepan from heat; stir in almond mixture.

3. Drop batter by rounded teaspoons about 3 inches apart, onto cookie sheet. (Do not place more than 6 on cookie sheet because, after baking, cookies must be removed quickly before hardening.) Bake cookies until lacy and lightly browned, about 10 minutes. Remove cookie sheet from oven. Let cookies remain on cookie sheet on wire rack about 2 minutes to set slightly.

4. With wide metal spatula, transfer cookies to wire rack to cool completely. (If cookies become too hard to remove, reheat on cookie sheet in oven 1 minute to soften.) Repeat with remaining batter.

5. With small metal spatula, gently spread flat side of each cookie with chocolate. Return cookies to wire rack, chocolate side up, and let stand at room temperature until chocolate has set, about 30 minutes. Store cookies, with waxed paper between layers, in tightly covered container up to 1 week. Makes about 4 dozen cookies.

Each cookie: About 70 calories, 1 g protein, 8 g carbohydrate, 4 g total fat (1 g saturated), 6 mg cholesterol, 20 mg sodium.

∽Molded Cookies

Mexican Wedding Cakes

Prep: 30 minutes plus chilling
Bake: 10 to 12 minutes

2¼ cups all-purpose flour
1 cup (2 sticks) margarine or butter, softened
1 teaspoon vanilla extract
⅛ teaspoon salt
1 cup confectioners' sugar
¾ cup walnuts, finely chopped

1. In medium bowl, combine flour, margarine, vanilla, salt, and ½ cup confectioners' sugar; knead until blended. Stir in chopped walnuts. Shape dough into ball; wrap and refrigerate until firm enough to handle, about 1 hour.

2. Preheat oven to 400°F. Shape dough into 1-inch balls. Place balls, about 1 inch apart, on ungreased cookie sheet. Bake cookies until set but not brown, 10 to 12 minutes. With spatula, transfer cookies to wire racks to cool. Repeat with remaining dough.

3. Place remaining ½ cup confectioners' sugar on sheet of waxed paper. When cookies are cold, roll them in confectioners' sugar to coat completely. Store cookies in tightly covered container. Makes about 4 dozen cookies.

Each cookie: About 75 calories, 1 g protein, 7 g carbohydrate, 5 g total fat (1 g saturated), 0 mg cholesterol, 55 mg sodium.

Walnut Crescents

Prep: 45 minutes plus chilling and cooling
Bake: 20 minutes per batch

1 cup walnuts
½ cup granulated sugar
1 cup (2 sticks) butter, softened (no substitutions)
2 cups all-purpose flour
½ cup sour cream
2 teaspoons vanilla extract
¼ teaspoon salt
½ cup confectioners' sugar

1. In 10-inch skillet, lightly toast walnuts over medium heat, shaking skillet frequently. Set skillet aside until walnuts are cool.

2. In food processor with knife blade attached, pulse walnuts and ¼ cup granulated sugar until walnuts are very finely chopped.

3. In large bowl, with mixer at low speed, beat butter and remaining ¼ cup granulated sugar until blended, occasionally scraping bowl with rubber spatula. Increase speed to high; beat until light and fluffy, about 5 minutes. Reduce speed to low; gradually beat in flour, sour cream, vanilla, salt, and walnut mixture until blended.

4. Divide dough in half; wrap each half and refrigerate until dough is firm enough to handle, about 1 hour. (Or, place dough in freezer 30 minutes.)

5. Preheat oven to 325°F. Working with half of dough at a time, with lightly floured hands, shape dough by rounded teaspoons into 1" by ½" crescents. Place crescents, about 1½ inches apart, on 2 ungreased large cookie sheets. Place cookie sheets on 2 oven racks. Bake cookies 20 minutes, rotating cookie sheets between upper and lower racks halfway through baking time or until lightly browned around the edges. Cool cookies on cookie sheets on wire racks 2 minutes.

6. Place confectioners' sugar in small bowl. While still warm, gently roll cookies in sugar, 1 at a time, to coat. Place cookies on wire racks to cool completely. Repeat with remaining dough. Store cookies in tightly covered containers. Makes about 6 dozen cookies.

Each cookie: About 60 calories, 1 g protein, 5 g carbohydrate, 4 g total fat (2 g saturated), 8 mg cholesterol, 35 mg sodium.

Molasses Cookies

Prep: 40 minutes plus chilling
Bake: 10 to 12 minutes per batch

¾ cup (1½ sticks) margarine or butter
¼ cup light (mild) molasses
1¼ cups sugar
1 large egg
2 cups all-purpose flour

2 teaspoons baking soda
1 teaspoon ground cinnamon
½ teaspoon ground ginger
½ teaspoon salt
¼ teaspoon ground cloves

1. Preheat oven to 375°F. In 3-quart saucepan, melt margarine over low heat. Remove saucepan from heat. With wire whisk, beat in molasses and 1 cup sugar until blended; whisk in egg. With spoon, stir in flour, baking soda, cinnamon, ginger, salt, and cloves until blended. Transfer dough to medium bowl and freeze until firm enough to handle, about 15 minutes.

2. Spread remaining ¼ cup sugar on waxed paper. Roll dough into 1-inch balls; roll balls in sugar to coat. Place balls, 2½ inches apart, on ungreased large cookie sheet. Bake until cookies spread and darken, 10 to 12 minutes. Let cookies remain on cookie sheet on wire rack 1 minute to cool slightly. Transfer cookies to wire rack to cool completely. Repeat with remaining dough. Store cookies in tightly covered container up to 2 weeks. Makes about 6 dozen cookies.

Each cookie: About 45 calories, 1 g protein, 7 g carbohydrate, 2 g total fat (0 g saturated), 3 mg cholesterol, 75 mg sodium.

Raspberry Linzer Thumbprint Cookies

Prep: 45 minutes plus cooling
Bake: 20 minutes per batch

1 cup hazelnuts (filberts), toasted (see page 19), plus ⅓ cup not
    toasted
½ cup sugar
¾ cup (1½ sticks) margarine or butter, cut into pieces
1 teaspoon vanilla extract
¼ teaspoon salt
1¾ cups all-purpose flour
¼ cup seedless red raspberry jam

1. Preheat oven to 350°F. In food processor with knife
blade attached, pulse toasted hazelnuts and sugar until hazelnuts are finely ground. Add margarine, vanilla, and salt,
and process until blended. Add flour and process until
evenly mixed. Remove knife blade, and press dough together with hand.

2. Finely chop remaining ⅓ cup hazelnuts; spread on
sheet of waxed paper. Roll dough into 1-inch balls (dough
may be slightly crumbly), using about 2 teaspoons dough
for each ball. Roll balls in nuts, gently pressing nuts into
dough.

3. Place balls, about 1½ inches apart, on ungreased large
cookie sheet. With thumb, make small indentation in center
of each ball. Fill each indentation with ¼ teaspoon jam.
Bake cookies until lightly golden around edges, 20 minutes.
Transfer cookies to wire rack to cool. Repeat with remaining balls and jam. Store cookies in tightly covered container. Makes about 4 dozen cookies.

*Each cookie: About 75 calories, 1 g protein, 7 g carbohydrate, 5
g total fat (1 g saturated), 0 mg cholesterol, 50 mg sodium.*

Chocolate Sambuca Cookies

Prep: 30 minutes plus chilling and cooling
Bake: 10 to 12 minutes per batch

12 squares (12 ounces) semisweet chocolate
4 tablespoons margarine or butter
3 large eggs
⅓ cup sambuca (anise-flavored liqueur)
1 cup granulated sugar
1 cup blanched almonds, finely ground
⅔ cup all-purpose flour
¾ teaspoon baking soda
⅓ cup confectioners' sugar

1. In 2-quart saucepan, melt chocolate and margarine over low heat, stirring frequently. Remove saucepan from heat; cool chocolate mixture slightly.

2. In medium bowl, with wire whisk, mix eggs, sambuca, and ½ cup granulated sugar; stir in chocolate mixture until blended. With spoon, stir ground almonds, flour, and baking soda into chocolate mixture until combined (dough will be very soft). Cover bowl and refrigerate at least 4 hours or overnight.

3. Preheat oven to 350°F. In small bowl, combine confectioners' sugar and remaining ½ cup granulated sugar. With lightly floured hands, roll dough by rounded tablespoons into balls. Roll balls in sugar mixture to coat.

4. Place balls, about 2 inches apart, on ungreased large cookie sheet. Bake until cookies are just set and look puffed and cracked, 10 to 12 minutes. Let cookies remain on cookie sheet 1 minute to cool slightly. With spatula, transfer cookies to wire rack to cool completely. Repeat with remaining dough and sugar mixture. Makes about 4 dozen cookies.

Each cookie: About 85 calories, 2 g protein, 12 g carbohydrate, 4 g total fat (0 g saturated), 13 mg cholesterol, 20 mg sodium.

Peanut-Butter Cookies

Prep: 25 minutes
Bake: 15 minutes

1 jar (12 ounces) creamy peanut butter (about 1¼ cups)
2¼ cups all-purpose flour
1 cup (2 sticks) margarine or butter, softened
¾ cup granulated sugar
¾ cup packed light brown sugar
1 teaspoon baking powder
1 teaspoon baking soda
½ teaspoon vanilla extract
2 large eggs

1. In large bowl, combine peanut butter, flour, margarine, granulated and brown sugars, baking powder, baking soda, vanilla, and eggs. With mixer at low speed, beat ingredients just until blended. Increase speed to medium; beat until well mixed, occasionally scraping bowl with rubber spatula.

2. Preheat oven to 375°F. With hands, shape dough into 1½-inch balls. Place balls, 2 inches apart, on ungreased large cookie sheet; flatten each ball slightly with fingers.

3. Dip a 4-tined fork into flour and press across top of each cookie; repeat at right angles to flatten cookie to 2 inches in diameter. Bake cookies just until lightly browned, about 15 minutes. Cool cookies slightly on cookie sheet on wire rack. With spatula, transfer cookies to wire racks to cool completely. Repeat with remaining dough. Store in tightly covered container. Makes about 4½ dozen cookies.

Each cookie: About 110 calories, 2 g protein, 11 g carbohydrate, 7 g total fat (1 g saturated), 8 mg cholesterol, 110 mg sodium.

Cream Cheese-Walnut Cookies

Prep: 30 minutes
Bake: 14 to 18 minutes per batch

1 cup sugar
½ cup (1 stick) margarine or butter, softened
1 package (3 ounces) cream cheese
1 teaspoon vanilla extract
1 cup all-purpose flour
½ cup walnuts, finely chopped

1. Preheat oven to 350°F. In large bowl, with mixer at low speed, beat sugar, margarine, and cream cheese until blended. Increase speed to high; beat until creamy, about 2 minutes, occasionally scraping bowl with rubber spatula. Beat in vanilla. With spoon, stir in flour and walnuts just until blended.

2. With lightly floured hands, roll dough into 1-inch balls. Place balls, 2 inches apart, on ungreased large cookie sheet. With floured fingertips, flatten balls into 1¼-inch rounds. Bake cookies until golden, 14 to 18 minutes. Let cookies remain on cookie sheet on wire rack 2 minutes to cool slightly. Transfer cookies to wire rack to cool completely. Repeat with remaining dough. Store cookies in tightly covered container up to 2 weeks. Makes about 5 dozen cookies.

Each cookie: About 45 calories, 1 g protein, 5 g carbohydrate, 3 g total fat (1 g saturated), 2 mg cholesterol, 25 mg sodium.

Lemon Madeleines

Prep: 20 minutes plus cooling
Bake: 10 to 15 minutes per batch

½ cup (1 stick) margarine or
   butter
2 large eggs
¾ cup sugar
¼ cup plain low-fat yogurt
1 teaspoon lemon extract

½ teaspoon vanilla extract
1 cup all-purpose flour
1 teaspoon freshly grated
   lemon peel
¼ teaspoon salt
Confectioners' sugar

1. In small saucepan, melt margarine over low heat; set aside to cool.

2. Preheat oven to 400°F. Grease 1 madeleine pan (twelve 3⅜" by 2" shells).

3. In large bowl, with mixer at low speed, beat eggs, sugar, yogurt, and lemon and vanilla extracts until blended, occasionally scraping bowl with rubber spatula. Increase speed to high; beat until very light and lemon-colored, about 5 minutes, occasionally scraping bowl. Reduce speed to low; beat in flour, lemon peel, salt, and melted margarine until blended.

4. Spoon 1 tablespoon batter into each madeleine shell. Bake until madeleines are golden brown, 10 to 15 minutes. Immediately remove madeleines from shells to wire racks to cool. Repeat until all batter is used, greasing madeleine pan each time.

5. Sprinkle madeleines lightly with confectioners' sugar. Store madeleines in tightly covered container if not serving right away to prevent them from becoming soggy. Makes about 2 dozen madeleines.

Each madeleine: About 85 calories, 1 g protein, 11 g carbohydrate, 4 g total fat (1 g saturated), 18 mg cholesterol, 80 mg sodium.

Greek Cinnamon Paximadia

Prep: 1 hour plus cooling
Bake: 50 minutes

½ cup (1 stick) margarine or butter, softened
½ cup shortening
1 ½ cups sugar
3 large eggs
1 teaspoon vanilla extract
2 teaspoons baking powder
½ teaspoon baking soda
4 cups all-purpose flour
1 ½ teaspoons ground cinnamon

1. In large bowl, with mixer at low speed, beat margarine, shortening, and 1 cup sugar until blended. Increase speed to high; beat until light and fluffy, about 5 minutes. Reduce speed to low; add eggs, 1 at a time, and vanilla, and beat until well mixed. Gradually add baking powder, baking soda, and 3 cups flour, and beat until well blended. With wooden spoon, stir in remaining 1 cup flour until soft dough forms. If necessary, add additional flour (up to ½ cup) until dough is easy to handle.

2. Preheat oven to 350°F. Divide dough into 4 equal pieces. On lightly floured surface, shape each piece of dough into an 8-inch-long log. Place 2 logs, about 4 inches apart, on each of 2 ungreased large cookie sheets. Flatten each log to 2½ inches wide. Place cookie sheets on 2 oven racks. Bake cookies 20 minutes, rotating cookie sheets between racks halfway through baking, or until lightly browned and toothpick inserted in center comes out clean.

3. Meanwhile, in pie plate, mix cinnamon and remaining ½ cup sugar; set aside.

4. Remove cookie sheets from oven. Transfer hot loaves (during baking, logs will spread and become loaves) to cutting board; with serrated knife, cut diagonally into ½-inch-thick slices. Coat slices with cinnamon sugar.

5. Return slices, cut side down, to same cookie sheets. Bake 15 minutes. Turn slices over and return to oven, ro-

tating cookie sheets between upper and lower racks, and
bake until golden, about 15 minutes longer. Transfer cookies to wire racks to cool. Makes about 4 dozen cookies.

*Each cookie: About 105 calories, 1 g protein, 14 g carbohydrate,
5 g total fat (1 g saturated), 13 mg cholesterol, 60 mg sodium.*

Chocolate-Cherry Biscotti

Prep: 30 minutes plus cooling
Bake: 50 minutes

2½ cups all-purpose flour
¾ cup unsweetened cocoa
1 tablespoon baking powder
½ teaspoon salt
1⅓ cups sugar
½ cup (1 stick) margarine or
    butter, softened
3 large eggs

2 squares (2 ounces) semisweet
    chocolate, melted
1 teaspoon instant espresso-
    coffee powder
1 teaspoon hot water
¾ cup dried tart cherries,
    coarsely chopped

1. Preheat oven to 350°F. Grease and flour large cookie
sheet. In large bowl, combine flour, cocoa, baking powder,
and salt.

2. In another large bowl, with mixer at medium speed,
beat sugar and margarine until creamy. Reduce speed to
low; add eggs, 1 at a time, then chocolate, and beat until
blended.

3. In small cup, blend espresso-coffee powder and hot
water until dissolved; beat into chocolate mixture. Add
flour mixture and beat just until blended. With hands, knead
in cherries until combined.

4. On floured surface, with floured hands, divide dough
in half. Shape each half into a 12" by 3" log. With pastry
brush, brush off excess flour. Place logs, about 3 inches
apart, on cookie sheet. Bake logs 30 minutes. Cool logs on
cookie sheet on wire rack until easy to handle, about 10
minutes.

5. Place 1 log on cutting board. With serrated knife, cut log crosswise on diagonal into ¾-inch-thick slices. Repeat with remaining log. Place slices, cut side down, on same cookie sheet. Bake 20 to 25 minutes to allow biscotti to dry out. Transfer biscotti to wire racks to cool completely. (Biscotti will harden as they cool.) Store biscotti in tightly covered container. Makes about 3 dozen biscotti.

Each biscotti: About 110 calories, 2 g protein 18 g carbohydrate, 4 g total fat (1 g saturated), 18 mg cholesterol, 100 mg sodium.

∾Refrigerator Cookies

Peanut Circles

Prep: 25 minutes plus chilling
Bake: 8 to 10 minutes per batch

1 cup unsalted peanuts
2 cups all-purpose flour
1 cup (2 sticks) margarine or butter, softened
¾ cup packed light brown sugar
½ teaspoon vanilla extract
¼ teaspoon salt
¼ teaspoon baking soda
1 large egg

1. In blender at medium speed or in food processor with knife blade attached, grind ¾ cup peanuts, a few portions at a time. Reserve remaining peanuts.

2. Into large bowl, combine flour, margarine, brown sugar, vanilla, salt, baking soda, and egg. With mixer at low speed, beat ingredients until well blended, occasionally scraping bowl with rubber spatula. Stir in ground peanuts until well mixed.

3. With hands, roll dough into three 5-inch-long logs. Wrap each log and refrigerate until dough is firm enough to slice, about 2 hours. (Dough can be refrigerated up to 1 week before baking.)

4. Preheat oven to 350°F. Grease large cookie sheets. Slice 1 log crosswise into ¼-inch-thick slices. Place slices, ½ inch apart, on cookie sheets; press a reserved peanut into top of each cookie. Bake cookies until lightly browned, 8 to 10 minutes, rotating cookie sheets between upper and lower racks. With spatula, transfer cookies to wire racks to cool. Repeat with remaining logs and peanuts. Store cookies in tightly covered container. Makes about 5 dozen cookies.

Each cookie: About 70 calories, 1 g protein, 6 g carbohydrate, 4 g total fat (1 g saturated), 4 mg cholesterol, 60 mg sodium.

Coconut Buttons

Prep: 45 minutes plus chilling and cooling
Bake: 20 to 25 minutes per batch

1 cup (2 sticks) butter, softened (no substitutions)
½ cup sugar
2 tablespoons milk
1 teaspoon coconut extract
¾ teaspoon baking powder
½ teaspoon salt

2⅔ cups all-purpose flour
1½ cups flaked coconut, chopped
1 squares (1 ounces) semisweet chocolate
1 tablespoon shortening

1. In large bowl, with mixer at medium-high speed, beat butter, sugar, milk, coconut extract, baking powder, and salt until light and fluffy. With wooden spoon, stir in flour and chopped coconut (dough will be a bit crumbly).

2. With hands, squeeze dough together. Divide dough into 4 equal pieces. Shape each piece into a 10" by 1" log. Wrap each log and slide onto small cookie sheet for easier handling. Refrigerate dough until firm, at least 1 hour.

3. Preheat oven to 325°F. Cut each log crosswise into ½-inch-thick slices. Place slices, 1 inch apart, on 2 ungreased large cookie sheets. With toothpick, make 4 holes in each cookie to resemble a button. Place cookie sheets on 2 oven racks. Bake cookies 20 to 25 minutes, rotating cookie sheets between upper and lower racks halfway through baking time until lightly golden. Transfer cookies to wire racks to cool.

4. When cookies are cool, melt chocolate and shortening. Dip bottom of each cookie into melted chocolate so that the chocolate comes slightly up side of the cookie. With small metal spatula, scrape excess chocolate from bottom of cookie, leaving a thin layer. Place cookies, chocolate side up, on waxed paper. Set cookies aside 30 minutes to allow chocolate to set. Store cookies in tightly covered container. Makes about 6½ dozen cookies.

Each cookie: About 55 calories, 1 g protein 6 g carbohydrate, 3 g total fat (2 g saturated), 6 mg cholesterol, 45 mg sodium.

NOTE: You can make the cookie dough and keep it wrapped in the refrigerator for up to 2 weeks before slicing and baking. Or, you can freeze the dough for up to 2 months.

Sally Ann Cookies

Prep: 1 hour plus freezing and cooling
Bake: 15 to 20 minutes per batch

1½ cups sugar
1 cup (2 sticks) margarine or butter
5½ cups all-purpose flour
1 cup light molasses
½ cup cold strong coffee
2 teaspoons baking soda
2 teaspoons ground ginger
½ teaspoon ground nutmeg
½ teaspoon salt
¼ teaspoon ground cloves
Sally Ann Frosting (see page 1135)
Holiday décors (optional)

1. In large bowl, with mixer at low speed, beat sugar and margarine until blended. Increase speed to high; beat until creamy. Reduce speed to low; beat in flour, molasses, coffee, baking soda, ginger, nutmeg, salt, and cloves until well blended. Cover bowl and freeze until firm enough to handle, about 1 hour.

2. Divide dough into thirds. On lightly floured surface, shape each third into a 12-inch-long log. Wrap each log and freeze until firm enough to slice, at least 4 hours or overnight. (Or freeze up to 2 months.)

3. Preheat oven to 350°F. Grease large cookie sheet. Slice 1 log crosswise into ¼-inch-thick slices. Place slices, 1½ inches apart, on cookie sheet. Bake until set and lightly browned around edges, 15 to 20 minutes. Cool on cookie sheet 1 minute. With spatula, transfer to wire rack to cool completely. Repeat with remaining dough.

4. When cookies are cool, prepare Sally Ann Frosting. With small metal spatula or knife, spread frosting on cookies. If you like, sprinkle cookies with décors. Set cookies aside to allow frosting to dry completely, about 1 hour. Makes about 12 dozen cookies.

SALLY ANN FROSTING: In 2-quart saucepan, stir *1 cup sugar* and *1 envelope unflavored gelatin* until well mixed. Stir in *1 cup cold water;* heat to boiling over high heat. Reduce heat to low; simmer, uncovered, 10 minutes. Into small bowl, measure *2 cups confectioners' sugar.* With mixer at low speed, gradually add gelatin mixture to confectioners' sugar, beating until blended. Increase speed to high; beat until frosting is smooth and fluffy, and has an easy spreading consistency, about 10 minutes. Beat in *¼ teaspoon vanilla extract.* Keep bowl covered with plastic wrap to prevent frosting from drying out.

Each cookie without décors: About 55 calories, 0 g protein, 10 g carbohydrate, 1 g total fat (0 g saturated), 0 mg cholesterol, 40 mg sodium.

Gwen's Almond Slices

Prep: 25 minutes plus chilling
Bake: 10 minutes per batch

1¾ cups sugar
1 cup (2 sticks) margarine or
   butter, softened
¼ cup light molasses
1 tablespoon ground ginger
1 tablespoon vanilla extract

1 teaspoon baking soda
1 teaspoon salt
2 large eggs
4 cups all-purpose flour
2 cups sliced almonds

1. In large bowl, with mixer at medium speed, beat sugar, margarine, molasses, ginger, vanilla, baking soda, salt, eggs, and 2 cups flour until blended. With wooden spoon, stir in almonds and remaining 2 cups flour (if necessary use hands to mix thoroughly, as dough will be very stiff.)

2. Divide dough in half. Shape each half into 10" by 3" by 1" brick; wrap each brick and refrigerate until firm enough to slice, about 4 hours. (Or freeze up to 2 months.)

3. Preheat oven to 400°F. Grease large cookie sheet. With serrated knife, cut 1 brick into scant ¼-inch-thick slices. Place slices, 1 inch apart, on cookie sheet. Bake until golden, about 10 minutes. Transfer cookies to wire rack to cool. Repeat with remaining brick. Store cookies in tightly covered container up to 2 weeks. Makes about 7 dozen cookies.

Each cookie: About 75 calories, 1 g protein, 10 g carbohydrate, 3 g total fat (1 g saturated), 5 mg cholesterol, 70 mg sodium.

⌒◦Rolled Cookies

Anna's Spice Thins

Prep: 45 minutes plus chilling and cooling
Bake: 10 to 12 minutes per batch

1 cup (2 sticks) butter, softened
  (no substitutions)
1 cup sugar
½ cup dark corn syrup
½ cup heavy or whipping
  cream
2½ teaspoons baking soda

2 teaspoons ground cinnamon
2 teaspoons ground cloves
2 teaspoons ground ginger
4 cups all-purpose flour
Ornamental Frosting (see page
  1018), optional

1. In large bowl, with mixer at low speed, beat butter and sugar until blended. Increase speed to high; beat until light and creamy, occasionally scraping bowl with rubber spatula. Reduce speed to low; beat in corn syrup, cream, baking soda, cinnamon, cloves, and ginger until blended. Gradually beat in flour until well mixed.

2. Divide dough into 8 pieces; wrap each piece and refrigerate overnight.

3. Preheat oven to 350°F. On lightly floured surface, with floured rolling pin, roll 1 piece of dough at a time to ⅛-inch thickness. With floured 3-inch round fluted cookie cutter, cut dough into as many cookies as possible. Reserve trimmings.

4. Place cookies, 1 inch apart, on ungreased large cookie sheet. Bake cookies until lightly browned, 10 to 12 minutes. Transfer cookies to wire rack to cool. Repeat with remaining dough and reserved trimmings to make more cookies.

5. If you like, prepare Ornamental Frosting and use to pipe border around cookies. Allow frosting to dry completely, about 1 hour. Store cookies in tightly covered container up to 2 weeks. Makes about 7½ dozen cookies.

Each cookie without frosting: About 55 calories, 1 g protein, 8 g carbohydrate, 3 g total fat (2 g saturated), 7 mg cholesterol, 60 mg sodium.

Christmas Butter Cookies

Prep: 45 minutes plus chilling, cooling, and decorating
Bake: 10 to 12 minutes per batch

1 cup (2 sticks) butter, softened (no substitutions)
½ cup sugar
1 large egg
1 tablespoon vanilla extract
3 cups all-purpose flour
½ teaspoon baking powder
Assorted colored granulated sugar for decorating
Ornamental Frosting (see page 1018), optional

1. Preheat oven to 350°F. In large bowl, with mixer at low speed, beat butter and sugar until blended. Increase speed to high; beat until light and creamy. Reduce speed to low; beat in egg and vanilla. Beat in flour and baking powder just until blended.

2. Divide dough into 4 equal pieces. Wrap each piece and refrigerate until firm enough to roll, about 1 hour.

3. On lightly floured surface, with floured rolling pin, roll 1 piece of dough to ⅛-inch thickness. With floured 2- to 3-inch assorted cookie cutters, cut dough into as many cookies as possible; wrap and refrigerate trimmings.

4. Place cookies, 1 inch apart, on large ungreased cookie sheet; sprinkle cookies with colored sugar now if you like, or frost with Ornamental Frosting after baking. Bake cookies until lightly browned, 10 to 12 minutes. Transfer cookies to wire rack to cool. If you like, brush colored sugar remaining on cookie sheets onto piece of waxed paper to use again. Repeat with remaining dough and reserved trimmings.

5. When cookies are cool, prepare Ornamental Frosting, if you like; use to decorate cookies as desired. Sprinkle colored sugars as desired on frosting before it dries. Allow frosting to dry completely, about 1 hour. Store cookies in tightly covered container up to 2 weeks. Makes about 8 dozen cookies.

Each cookie without colored sugar or frosting: About 40 calories, 1 g protein, 5 g carbohydrate, 2 g total fat (1 g saturated), 7 mg cholesterol, 20 mg sodium.

Gingerbread Cutouts

Prep: 55 minutes plus cooling and decorating
Bake: About 12 minutes per batch

½ cup sugar
½ cup light molasses
2 teaspoons ground ginger
1½ teaspoons ground
  cinnamon
½ teaspoon ground cloves
½ teaspoon ground nutmeg
¼ teaspoon ground black
  pepper

2 teaspoons baking soda
½ cup (1 stick) margarine or
  butter, cut into pieces
1 large egg, beaten
3½ cups all-purpose flour
Ornamental Frosting
  (see page 1018)

1. In 3-quart saucepan, heat sugar, molasses, ginger, cinnamon, cloves, nutmeg, and pepper to boiling over medium heat, stirring occasionally. Remove saucepan from heat; stir in baking soda (mixture will foam up in the pan). Stir in margarine until melted. With fork, stir in egg, then flour.

2. On lightly floured surface, knead dough until thoroughly mixed. Divide dough in half; wrap half of dough and set aside.

3. Preheat oven to 325°F. With floured rolling pin, roll half of dough slightly thinner than ¼ inch. With floured 3- to 4-inch assorted cookie cutters, cut dough into as many cookies as possible; reserve trimmings.

4. Place cookies, ½ inch apart, on ungreased large cookie sheet. Bake cookies until edges begin to brown, about 12 minutes. Transfer cookies to wire racks to cool. Repeat with remaining dough and reserved trimmings.

5. When cookies are cool, prepare Ornamental Frosting; use to decorate cookies as desired. Allow frosting to dry completely, about 1 hour. Store in tightly covered container up to 2 weeks. Makes about 3 dozen cookies.

Each cookie without frosting: About 90 calories, 1 g protein, 15 g carbohydrate, 3 g total fat (1 g saturated), 6 mg cholesterol, 105 mg sodium.

Holiday Sugar Cookies

Prep: 1 hour plus cooling and decorating
Bake: 10 to 12 minutes per batch

3 cups all-purpose flour
1 teaspoon baking powder
¼ teaspoon salt
1 cup sugar
½ cup (1 stick) margarine or butter, softened
½ cup shortening
2 large eggs
2 teaspoons vanilla extract
Ornamental Frosting (see page 1018)

1. In large bowl, combine flour, baking powder, and salt. In another large bowl, with mixer at medium speed, beat sugar, margarine, and shortening until creamy. Reduce speed to low; add eggs, 1 at a time, and vanilla; beat until blended. Beat in flour mixture just until blended.

2. Divide dough into 4 equal pieces. Wrap each piece and refrigerate 30 minutes (dough will be soft).

3. Preheat oven to 350°F. On well-floured surface, with

floured rolling pin, roll 1 piece of dough to ⅛-inch thickness. With floured 3- to 4-inch assorted cookie cutters, cut dough into as many cookies as possible; reserve trimmings.

4. With spatula, place cookies, about 1 inch apart, on large ungreased cookie sheet. Bake cookies until lightly browned, 10 to 12 minutes. Transfer cookies to wire rack to cool. Repeat with remaining dough and trimmings.

5. When cookies are cool, prepare Ornamental Frosting; use to decorate cookies as desired. Set cookies aside to allow frosting to dry completely, about 1 hour. Store cookies in tightly covered container. Makes about 5 dozen cookies.

Each cookie without frosting: About 65 calories, 1 g protein, 8 g carbohydrate, 4 g total fat (1 g saturated), 7 mg cholesterol, 40 mg sodium.

Great-Granny's Old-Time Spice Cookies

Prep: 1 hour 10 minutes plus chilling, cooling, and decorating
Bake: 8 to 10 minutes per batch

5½ cups all-purpose flour
1 teaspoon ground cinnamon
1 teaspoon ground allspice
½ teaspoon ground nutmeg
½ teaspoon baking soda
½ teaspoon salt
1 cup (2 sticks) margarine or butter, softened

1¼ cups packed light brown sugar
1 jar (12 ounces) dark molasses
Ornamental Frosting (see page 1018), optional

1. In large bowl, combine flour, cinnamon, allspice, nutmeg, baking soda, and salt. In another large bowl, with mixer at low speed, beat margarine and brown sugar until blended. Increase speed to high; beat until light and creamy. Reduce speed to low; beat in molasses until blended, then beat in 3 cups flour mixture. With spoon, stir in remaining flour mixture.

2. Divide dough into 4 equal pieces. Wrap each piece and freeze at least 1 hour or refrigerate overnight, until dough is firm enough to roll.

3. Preheat oven to 350°F. On well-floured surface, with floured rolling pin, roll 1 piece of dough to ⅛-inch thickness, keeping remaining dough refrigerated (dough will be soft). With floured 3- to 4-inch assorted cookie cutters, cut dough into as many cookies as possible; reserve trimmings.

4. Place cookies, about 1 inch apart, on ungreased large cookie sheet. Bake cookies until just browned, 8 to 10 minutes. Cool cookies on cookie sheet 5 minutes. With spatula, transfer cookies to wire rack to cool completely. Repeat with remaining dough and reserved trimmings.

5. When cookies are cool, if you like, prepare Ornamental Frosting. Use to decorate cookies as desired. Set cookies aside to allow frosting to dry completely, about 1 hour. Makes about 4 dozen cookies.

Each cookie without frosting: About 120 calories, 2 g protein, 21 g carbohydrate, 4 g total fat (1 g saturated), 0 mg cholesterol, 95 mg sodium.

Jelly Centers

Prep: 45 minutes plus chilling and cooling
Bake: 10 to 12 minutes per batch

1 cup (2 sticks) margarine or butter, softened
1¼ cups sugar
2 large eggs, separated
2 teaspoons vanilla extract
3 cups all-purpose flour
⅛ teaspoon baking powder
⅛ teaspoon salt
1 cup raspberry preserves

1. In large bowl, with mixer at low speed, beat margarine and 1 cup sugar until blended, occasionally scraping bowl with rubber spatula. Increase speed to high; beat until light and fluffy, about 3 minutes. Reduce speed to low; beat in egg yolks and vanilla until blended. Gradually beat in flour, baking powder, and salt.

2. Shape dough into 2 balls; flatten each slightly. Wrap each ball and refrigerate until firm enough to roll, 1 hour.

3. Preheat oven to 350°F. Between 2 sheets of floured waxed paper, roll half of dough to ⅛-inch thickness, keeping remaining dough refrigerated. With floured 2-inch cookie cutter (we like rounds or stars) cut out as many cookies as possible; reserve trimmings.

4. Place cookies, about ½ inch apart, on ungreased large cookie sheet. With ½-inch round or star-shaped cookie cutter, cut out centers from half of cookies. Remove centers; add to trimmings.

5. In cup, with fork, beat egg whites slightly. With pastry brush, brush cookies with cutout centers with some egg white, then sprinkle with some of remaining ¼ cup sugar. Bake all cookies until lightly browned, 10 to 12 minutes. With spatula, transfer cookies to wire rack to cool. Repeat with remaining dough and reserved trimmings.

6. When cookies are cool, spread center of each cookie without cutout center with ¼ to ½ teaspoon preserves; top each with a cookie with a cutout center, gently pressing cookies together to form a sandwich. Makes about 4½ dozen sandwich cookies.

Each sandwich cookie: About 95 calories, 1 g protein, 14 g carbohydrate, 4 g total fat (1 g saturated), 8 mg cholesterol, 55 mg sodium.

Sand Tarts

Prep: 1 hour 30 minutes plus chilling, cooling, and decorating
Bake: 12 to 15 minutes per batch

1 cup (2 sticks) butter, softened (no substitutions)
1½ cups sugar
2 large eggs
1 teaspoon vanilla extract
3 cups all-purpose flour
½ teaspoon baking powder
½ teaspoon salt
Ornamental Frosting (see page 1018), optional

1. In large bowl, with mixer at low speed, beat butter and sugar until blended. Increase speed to high; beat until light and creamy. Reduce speed to low; beat in eggs and vanilla until mixed, then beat in flour, baking powder, and salt until blended, occasionally scraping bowl with rubber spatula.

2. Shape dough into 4 balls; flatten each slightly. Wrap each and freeze at least 1 hour or refrigerate overnight until dough is firm enough to roll.

3. Preheat oven to 350°F. On lightly floured surface, with floured rolling pin, roll 1 piece of dough slightly thinner than ¼ inch, keeping remaining dough refrigerated. With floured 3- to 4-inch assorted cookie cutters, cut dough into as many cookies as possible; reserve trimmings.

4. Place cookies, about 1 inch apart, on ungreased large cookie sheet. Bake cookies until golden around edges, 12 to 15 minutes. With spatula, transfer cookies to rack to cool. Repeat with remaining dough and trimmings.

5. When cookies are cool, if you like, prepare Ornamental Frosting; use to decorate cookies as desired. Set cookies aside to allow frosting to dry completely, about 1 hour. Makes about 6 dozen cookies.

Each cookie without frosting: About 60 calories, 1 g protein, 8 g carbohydrate, 3 g total fat (2 g saturated), 13 mg cholesterol, 45 mg sodium.

⌒Pressed Cookies

Peppermint Meringues

Prep: 15 minutes plus drying
Bake: 2 hours

4 large egg whites
¼ teaspoon cream of tartar
1 cup confectioners' sugar
¼ teaspoon peppermint extract*
Red and green food coloring

1. Preheat oven to 225°F. Line 2 large cookie sheets with foil.

2. In small bowl, with mixer at high speed, beat egg whites and cream of tartar until soft peaks form when beaters are lifted; gradually sprinkle in sugar, beating until whites stand in stiff, glossy peaks. Beat in peppermint extract.

3. Transfer half of meringue mixture to another bowl. Add enough red food coloring to meringue in 1 bowl to tint it a pale red. Add enough green food coloring to remaining meringue to tint it a pale green. Spoon red meringue into large zip-tight plastic bag; cut ¼-inch opening at corner. Repeat with green meringue in separate bag.

4. Fit large decorating bag (we used a 14-inch bag) with basketweave or large round tip (½- or ¾-inch-diameter opening). Place decorating bag in 2-cup measuring cup to stabilize bag; fold top third of bag over top of cup to keep top of bag clean. Simultaneously, squeeze meringues from both plastic bags into decorating bag, filling decorating bag no more than two-thirds full.

5. Pipe meringue onto cookie sheets, leaving 1 inch between each meringue. If using basketweave tip, pipe meringue into 3- to 4-inch long pleated ribbons; if using round tip, pipe meringue into 2-inch rounds. Bake meringues 2 hours. Turn oven off. Leave meringues in oven at least 30 minutes or overnight to dry.

6. Let meringues cool completely before removing from foil with wide metal spatula. Store meringues in tightly covered containers up to 3 weeks. Makes about 4½ dozen meringues.

*Do not use peppermint extract containing peppermint oil; the meringue mixture will quickly deflate. We had good results using imitation peppermint extract.

Each meringue: About 10 calories, 0 g protein, 2 g carbohydrate, 0 g total fat, 0 mg cholesterol, 5 mg sodium.

Vanilla Spritz Cookies

Prep: 15 minutes plus cooling
Bake: 12 to 14 minutes per batch

1 cup (2 sticks) margarine or butter, softened
¾ cup sugar
1 large egg yolk
1 teaspoon vanilla extract
2 cups all-purpose flour
Red candied cherries, each cut in half (optional)

1. Preheat oven to 375°F. In large bowl, with mixer at medium speed, beat margarine and sugar until creamy. Beat in egg yolk and vanilla until blended. Reduce speed to low; beat in flour just until blended, occasionally scraping bowl with rubber spatula.

2. Spoon half of dough into large decorating bag with large star tip (¾-inch-diameter opening). Pipe dough into rosettes (about 1½ inches in diameter), about 1 inch apart, onto ungreased large cookie sheet. If you like, place a cherry half in center of some or all of the cookies before baking.

3. Bake cookies until lightly browned around the edges,

12 to 14 minutes. Let cookies remain on cookie sheet on wire rack 3 minutes to cool slightly, then transfer cookies to wire rack to cool completely. Repeat with remaining dough. Store cookies in tightly covered container. Makes about 4½ dozen cookies.

Each cookie without candied cherry: About 60 calories, 1 g protein, 6 g carbohydrate, 4 g total fat (1 g saturated), 4 mg cholesterol, 45 mg sodium.

Chocolate-Raspberry Almond Spritz

Prep: 1 hour 15 minutes plus cooling
Bake: 12 to 14 minutes per batch

½ cup blanched whole almonds
¾ cup sugar
2¼ cups all-purpose flour
1 cup (2 sticks) butter, softened (no substitutions)
1½ teaspoons almond extract
¼ teaspoon salt
1 large egg
Chocolate-Raspberry Filling (see page 1148)

1. In food processor with knife blade attached, pulse almonds and sugar until almonds are finely ground. (Or, in blender, grind almonds and sugar in batches.)

2. Preheat oven to 350°F. In large bowl, with mixer at low speed, beat almond mixture, flour, butter, almond extract, salt, and egg just until blended, scraping bowl occasionally with rubber spatula.

3. Spoon dough into large decorating bag with large star tube (about ¾-inch-diameter opening). Pipe dough into teardrop shapes (about 2" by 1½"), 1 inch apart, onto 2 ungreased large cookie sheets.

4. Place cookie sheets on 2 oven racks. Bake cookies 12 to 14 minutes, rotating cookie sheets between upper and lower racks halfway through baking time, or until lightly browned around edges. Allow cookies to cool slightly on cookie sheets. With spatula, transfer cookies to wire racks to cool completely. Repeat with remaining dough.

5. When cookies are cool, prepare Chocolate-Raspberry Filling. With small spatula, spread about 1 rounded teaspoon filling onto flat side of half of cookies. Top with remaining cookies, flat side down, to make filled cookies. Makes about 2½ dozen filled cookies.

CHOCOLATE-RASPBERRY FILLING: In 1-quart saucepan, heat *¼ cup plus 2 tablespoons heavy or whipping cream* over low heat, to boiling. Meanwhile, finely chop *6 squares (6 ounces) semisweet chocolate* and place in small bowl with *3 tablespoons seedless raspberry jam*. Pour hot cream over chocolate mixture; let stand 1 minute. Stir chocolate mixture until smooth. Cover and refrigerate until chocolate mixture is firm enough to spread, about 15 to 18 minutes. If mixture becomes too firm, let stand at room temperature until slightly softened.

Each filled cookie: About 165 calories, 2 g protein, 18 g carbohydrate, 10 g total fat (5 g saturated), 28 mg cholesterol, 85 mg sodium.

Pignoli Cookies

Prep: 45 minutes
Bake: 10 to 12 minutes per batch

1 tube or can (7 to 8 ounces) almond paste, crumbled into large
    pieces
¾ cup confectioners' sugar
1 large egg white
1 tablespoon plus 1 teaspoon honey
⅓ cup pine nuts (pignoli)

1. Preheat oven to 350°F. In food processor with knife blade attached, process crumbled almond paste and confectioners' sugar until mixture resembles fine crumbs.

2. In large bowl, with mixer at low speed, beat almond-paste mixture, egg white, and honey until blended. Increase speed to high; beat 5 minutes or until very smooth, occasionally scraping bowl with rubber spatula (mixture will be thick).

3. Line large cookie sheet with kitchen parchment or greased foil. Spoon almond mixture into large decorating bag with large round tip (½-inch-diameter opening). Pipe mixture into 1¼-inch rounds, 2 inches apart, onto lined cookie sheet. With moistened fingertip, gently smooth surface of cookie. Sprinkle with pine nuts; lightly press to cover tops of cookies.

4. Bake cookies until golden brown, 10 to 12 minutes. Cool cookies completely on cookie sheet on wire rack. If you want to reuse cookie sheet right away, slide parchment or foil, with cookies attached, onto wire rack, and let cookies cool completely on parchment or foil. Repeat with remaining almond mixture.

5. When cool, carefully peel cookies off parchment or foil. Store cookies in tightly covered container up to 2 weeks. Makes about 2 dozen cookies.

Each cookie: About 70 calories, 2 g protein, 9 g carbohydrate, 3 g total fat (0 g saturated), 0 mg cholesterol, 5 mg sodium.

Frozen Desserts

～⌘～

Ice Creams & Ice Milks
Sherbet & Ices
Ice-Cream Bombes, Cakes & Pies
Other Frozen Desserts

Ice cream, sherbet, bombes, sorbets, mousses, and ice-cream pies and cakes are all easily made in your freezer and stored there for use at a moment's notice.

∾How to Keep Ice Cream at Its Best

- Ice cream, whether store-bought or homemade, keeps best in the freezer at 0°F. or lower. It will keep about one month in the freezer compartment of your refrigerator, and up to two months in a home freezer.
- To store open containers of ice cream, press some plastic wrap over the exposed surface to protect the ice cream from refrigerator odors and prevent the development of a "skin" (caused by evaporation) or ice crystals (caused by condensation in the container).
- Do not refreeze partially melted ice cream, or a coarse, icy texture will result.
- Ice-cream desserts are more sensitive to temperature than ice cream because of the presence of other ingredients (fruit, cake, whipped cream, etc.). Wrap these desserts well and keep them as cold as your freezer allows.

∿Ice Creams & Ice Milks

Vanilla Ice Cream

Prep: 10 minutes plus chilling and freezing
Cook: 15 minutes

2 cups sugar
⅓ cup all-purpose flour
1½ teaspoons salt
6 cups milk
6 large eggs
3 cups heavy or whipping cream
2 tablespoons vanilla extract

1. In heavy 4-quart saucepan, combine sugar, flour, and salt; stir in milk. Cook over medium heat, stirring frequently, until mixture thickens slightly and boils.

2. In medium bowl, beat eggs slightly; stir in small amount of hot mixture. Slowly pour egg mixture back into hot mixture, stirring rapidly to prevent lumping. Cook over low heat, stirring constantly, until mixture thickens, about 5 minutes (do not boil or mixture will curdle). Remove saucepan from heat. Stir in heavy cream and vanilla. Cover and refrigerate, stirring occasionally, until well chilled, about 2 hours.

3. Pour chilled mixture into ice-cream can or freezer chamber of ice-cream maker. Freeze as manufacturer directs. Serve immediately or freeze to harden. Use within 2 weeks. Makes about 3½ quarts ice cream or 28 servings.

Each serving: About 200 calories, 4 g protein, 18 g carbohydrate, 12 g total fat (7 g saturated), 88 mg cholesterol, 175 mg sodium.

CHOCOLATE ICE CREAM: Prepare egg mixture as in Steps 1 and 2 for Vanilla Ice Cream, except add *1 package (8 ounces) semisweet-chocolate squares,* chopped, with milk

in Step 1. Follow Step 3. Makes about 3¾ quarts ice cream
or 30 servings.

*Each serving: About 215 calories, 4 g protein, 22 g carbohydrate,
13 g total fat (8 g saturated), 82 mg cholesterol, 160 mg sodium.*

CHOCOLATE-FUDGE-SWIRL ICE CREAM: Prepare Chocolate Ice Cream as above. While ice cream is freezing, prepare fudge sauce: In 2-quart saucepan heat *1 cup sugar, 1
cup heavy or whipping cream, 2 tablespoons margarine or
butter (¼ stick), 1 tablespoon light corn syrup,* and *4
squares (4 ounces) unsweetened chocolate,* chopped, to
boiling, over medium-high heat, stirring constantly. Reduce
heat to medium; cook 5 minutes, stirring occasionally. Remove saucepan from heat; stir in *1 teaspoon vanilla extract.*
Let sauce stand at room temperature to cool slightly, stirring occasionally. After freezing, spoon ice cream into
15½" by 10½" roasting pan or 6-quart bowl. With spoon,
quickly swirl fudge sauce into ice cream to create marbled
effect. Cover surface of ice cream with plastic wrap, then
cover pan with foil. Place pan in freezer for 2 to 3 hours
to harden. Makes about 4 quarts ice cream or 32 servings.

*Each serving: About 280 calories, 4 g protein, 28 g carbohydrate,
18 g total fat (10 g saturated), 87 mg cholesterol, 165 mg sodium.*

PEACH ICE CREAM: Prepare egg mixture as in Steps 1 and
2 for Vanilla Ice Cream. While egg mixture is chilling, in
blender at medium speed or in food processor with knife
blade attached, blend *10 to 12 medium ripe peaches,*
peeled, pitted and cut up, and *½ cup sugar* until smooth to
make 3 cups puree. Follow Step 3 but add peach puree,
vanilla, and *¼ teaspoon almond extract.* Makes about 4
quarts ice cream or 32 servings.

*Each serving: About 200 calories, 4 g protein, 23 g carbohydrate,
11 g total fat (6 g saturated), 77 mg cholesterol, 150 mg sodium.*

Old-Fashioned Raspberry Ice Cream

Prep: 10 minutes plus chilling and freezing

4 cups raspberries
⅜ cup sugar
⅛ teaspoon salt
1 cup heavy or whipping cream
1 cup milk

1. In food processor with knife blade attached, process raspberries until pureed (about 1½ cups puree). With spoon, press raspberries through medium-mesh sieve into large bowl; discard seeds.

2. With wire whisk, beat sugar and salt into raspberry puree until sugar has dissolved. Add cream and milk and whisk until blended. Cover and refrigerate until well chilled, about 1 hour.

3. Pour chilled mixture into ice-cream can or freezer chamber of ice-cream maker. Freeze as manufacturer directs. Serve immediately or freeze to harden. Use within 2 weeks. Makes about 1 quart or 8 servings.

Each serving: About 225 calories, 2 g protein, 28 g carbohydrate, 12 g total fat (8 g saturated), 45 mg cholesterol, 60 mg sodium.

GH's Best Strawberry Ice Cream

Prep: 15 minutes plus freezing

2 cups milk
1 cup sugar
¼ teaspoon salt
2 cups heavy cream
1½ teaspoons vanilla extract
1 pint strawberries

1. In saucepan, heat milk over medium heat until bubbles form around edge. Remove from heat; stir in sugar and salt until completely dissolved. Stir in cream and vanilla. Transfer to large bowl; cover and refrigerate for at least 30 minutes.

2. In blender at medium speed, blend strawberries until smooth.

3. Pour chilled mixture and strawberry puree into ice-cream can or freezer chamber of ice-cream maker. Freeze as manufacturer directs. Serve immediately or freeze to harden. Makes 2 quarts or 16 servings.

Each ½ cup serving: About 175 calories, 2 g protein, 15 g carbohydrate, 12 g total fat (7 g saturated), 45 mg cholesterol, 60 mg sodium.

Peach Ice Milk

Prep: 10 minutes plus freezing and softening
Cook: 3 minutes

1 envelope unflavored gelatin
1 cup half-and-half
3 cups milk
¾ cup sugar
¼ teaspoon almond extract
⅛ teaspoon salt
6 to 8 medium ripe peaches, peeled, pitted, and diced (4 cups)
¼ cup fresh lemon juice

1. In 3-quart saucepan, sprinkle gelatin evenly over half-and-half; let stand 1 minute to soften gelatin slightly. Cook over medium-low heat, stirring, until gelatin dissolves. Remove from heat; stir in milk, sugar, almond extract, and salt.

2. In blender at medium speed, or in food processor with knife blade attached, blend peaches and lemon juice until smooth. Stir into milk mixture (mixture may look curdled).

3. Pour peach mixture into 13" by 9" baking pan. Cover and freeze, stirring occasionally, until partially frozen, about 3 hours.

4. Spoon peach mixture into chilled large bowl; with mixer at medium speed, beat until smooth but still frozen. Return mixture to pan; cover and freeze until firm, about 3 hours.

5. To serve, let ice milk stand at room temperature 15 minutes to soften slightly. Makes about 2 quarts ice milk or 16 servings.

Each serving: About 120 calories, 3 g protein, 22 g carbohydrate, 3 g total fat (2 g saturated), 12 mg cholesterol, 50 mg sodium.

STRAWBERRY ICE MILK: Prepare milk mixture as above in Step 1, but use *2 teaspoons vanilla extract* instead of almond extract. In Step 2 in place of peaches, stir *1 pint strawberries*, hulled and pureed, into milk mixture, and omit lemon juice. Complete recipe as above in Steps 3 and 4. Makes about 1½ quarts ice milk or 12 servings.

Each serving: About 120 calories, 3 g protein, 22 g carbohydrate, 3 g total fat (2 g saturated), 12 mg cholesterol, 50 mg sodium.

∾Sherbet & Ices

5-Minute Peach Sherbet

Prep: 5 minutes

1 package (20 ounces) frozen sliced peaches
1 container (8 ounces) plain low-fat yogurt
1 cup confectioners' sugar
1 tablespoon fresh lemon juice
⅛ teaspoon almond extract

1. In food processor with knife blade attached, process frozen peaches until fruit resembles finely shaved ice, stopping processor occasionally to scrape down side of bowl.

If fruit is not finely shaved, dessert will not be smooth.

2. With processor running, add yogurt, confectioners' sugar, lemon juice, and almond extract, and process until mixture is smooth and creamy. Stop processor and scrape down side occasionally.

3. Serve the sherbet immediately or freeze to serve later. If refrozen, let stand at room temperature for about 30 minutes before scooping. Makes about 4 cups or 6 servings.

Each serving: About 190 calories, 3 g protein, 45 g carbohydrate, 1 g total fat (0 g saturated), 2 mg cholesterol, 35 mg sodium.

Orange Sherbet

Prep: 12 minutes plus freezing and softening
Cook: 3 minutes

3 large oranges
1 envelope unflavored gelatin
5 cups milk
1½ cups sugar
¼ cup fresh lemon juice
⅛ teaspoon salt

1. From oranges, grate ¼ cup peel and squeeze 1 cup juice; set aside.

2. In 3-quart saucepan, sprinkle gelatin evenly over 1 cup milk; let stand 1 minute to soften gelatin slightly. Cook over medium-low heat, stirring, until gelatin has completely dissolved. Remove from heat; stir in sugar, orange peel and juice, lemon juice, salt, and remaining milk until sugar has dissolved (mixture may look curdled).

3. Pour mixture into 13" by 9" baking pan. Cover and freeze, stirring occasionally, until partially frozen, about 3 hours.

4. Spoon orange mixture into chilled large bowl; with mixer at medium speed, beat until smooth but still frozen. Return mixture to pan. Cover and freeze until firm, about 3 hours.

5. To serve, let sherbet stand at room temperature 15 minutes to soften slightly. Makes about 2 quarts sherbet or 16 servings.

Each serving: About 130 calories, 3 g protein, 24 g carbohydrate, 3 g total fat (2 g saturated), 10 mg cholesterol, 55 mg sodium.

Strawberry-Orange Ice

Prep: 10 minutes plus freezing and softening

3 pints strawberries, hulled
1¾ cups fresh orange juice
1¾ cups sugar
½ cup fresh lemon juice
⅛ teaspoon salt

1. In blender at high speed or in food processor with knife blade attached, blend one-third of all ingredients at a time until smooth. Pour strawberry mixture into 13" by 9" baking pan (or, if you like, press strawberries through food mill into large bowl; stir in remaining ingredients).
2. Cover pan with foil or plastic wrap and freeze, stirring occasionally, until partially frozen, about 4 hours.
3. Spoon strawberry mixture into chilled large bowl; with mixer at medium speed, beat until smooth but still frozen. Return mixture to pan; cover and freeze until firm, about 3 hours.
4. To serve, let strawberry ice stand at room temperature 15 minutes to soften slightly. Makes about 10 cups ice or 20 servings.

Each serving: About 90 calories, 0 g protein, 23 g carbohydrate, 0 g total fat, 0 mg cholesterol, 15 mg sodium.

Peach Granita

Prep: 20 minutes plus freezing

1 cup sugar
1 ¼ cups water
5 medium peaches or nectarines (about 1 ¾ pounds), unpeeled,
   pitted and cut into wedges
2 tablespoons fresh lemon juice

1. In 1-quart saucepan, heat sugar and water to boiling over high heat, stirring occasionally. Reduce heat to medium; cook mixture until sugar has dissolved completely, about 1 minute. Transfer syrup to small bowl to cool.

2. In blender at medium speed, blend peach wedges until smooth. Pour fruit puree into medium-mesh sieve set over medium bowl. With spoon, press peach puree against sieve to push through pulp and juice; discard skin. You should have 3 cups puree. Stir lemon juice and sugar syrup into puree.

3. Pour peach mixture into 9" by 9" metal baking pan. (Mixture will freeze faster in shallow pans than in deep ones.) Cover with foil or plastic wrap. Freeze until partially frozen, about 2 hours (It should be frozen to 1 inch from the edge; the center, however, will still be mushy and soft.) Stir with fork; freeze until completely frozen, at least 3 hours longer or overnight.

4. To serve, let granita stand at room temperature 15 minutes to soften slightly. Then, with spoon or fork, scrape across surface of granita to create pebbly texture. Makes about 8 cups or 16 servings.

Each serving: About 65 calories, 0 g protein, 17 g carbohydrate, 0 g total fat, 0 mg cholesterol, 0 mg sodium.

BLUEBERRY GRANITA: Prepare and serve as above but substitute *3 pints blueberries*, washed and picked over, for peaches. Makes about 8 cups or 16 servings.

Each serving: About 80 calories, 0 g protein, 20 g carbohydrate, 0 g total fat, 0 mg cholesterol, 5 mg sodium.

WATERMELON GRANITA: Prepare and serve as on page 1161 but substitute *5½ pounds watermelon,* seeded and cut into chunks (about 9 cups), and *2 tablespoons fresh lime juice* for peaches and lemon juice. When making the sugar syrup, use only *¾ cup water* instead of 1¼ cups. Makes about 9 cups or 18 servings.

Each serving: About 70 calories, 1 g protein, 17 g carbohydrate, 0 g total fat, 0 mg cholesterol, 2 mg sodium.

Lemon Granita

Prep: 10 minutes plus freezing and softening
Cook: 7 minutes

2 cups water
1 cup sugar
4 large lemons

1. In 2-quart saucepan, heat water and sugar to boiling over high heat. Reduce heat to medium; cook 5 minutes.

2. Meanwhile, from lemons, grate 2 teaspoons peel and squeeze ¾ cup juice. Stir lemon peel and juice into sugar syrup.

3. Pour mixture into 8" by 8" baking pan. Cover with foil or plastic wrap; freeze, stirring occasionally, until firm, about 5 hours.

4. To serve, let granita stand at room temperature 15 minutes to soften slightly. Then, with spoon or ice cream scoop, scrape across surface of granita to create pebbly texture; spoon into bowls. Makes about 3 cups or 6 servings.

Each serving: About 130 calories, 0 g protein, 35 g carbohydrate, 0 g total fat, 0 mg cholesterol, 0 mg sodium.

ORANGE GRANITA: Prepare sugar syrup as above in Step 1. Meanwhile, from *3 large oranges,* grate 2 teaspoons peel and squeeze 1 cup juice. Stir orange peel, juice, and *2 tablespoons fresh lemon juice* into sugar syrup. Freeze and serve as above. Makes about 3¼ cups or 6 servings.

Each serving: About 145 calories, 0 g protein, 37 g carbohydrate, 0 g total fat, 0 mg cholesterol, 1 mg sodium.

STRAWBERRY GRANITA: Prepare sugar syrup as above in Step 1, but use only *1 cup water* and *½ cup sugar*. Stir *2 pints strawberries*, hulled and pureed, and *1 tablespoon fresh lemon juice* into sugar syrup. Freeze and serve as above. Makes about 6 cups or 12 servings.

Each serving: About 45 calories, 0 g protein, 12 g carbohydrate, 0 g total fat, 0 mg cholesterol, 1 mg sodium.

COFFEE GRANITA: Prepare sugar syrup as above in Step 1 but use *3 cups water, ⅓ cup sugar,* and *¼ cup instant espresso-coffee powder.* Freeze and serve as above. Makes about 3 cups or 6 servings.

Each serving: About 50 calories, 0 g protein, 12 g carbohydrate, 0 g total fat, 0 mg cholesterol, 1 mg sodium.

Cassis Sorbet

Prep: 10 minutes plus chilling, freezing, and softening
Cook: 7 minutes

2¼ cups water
½ cup sugar
1 package (10 ounces) frozen raspberries in quick-thaw pouch, thawed
⅓ cup cassis (black currant–flavored liqueur)
3 tablespoons fresh lemon juice
⅛ teaspoon salt

1. In 2-quart saucepan, heat water and sugar to boiling over medium heat; boil 5 minutes, stirring occasionally. Refrigerate sugar syrup until chilled, about 2 hours.
2. In blender at medium speed, blend raspberries, liqueur, lemon juice, and salt until smooth. With spoon, press

raspberry mixture through medium-mesh sieve into medium bowl; discard seeds. Stir purée into cooled syrup.

3. Pour mixture into 8" by 8" baking pan. Cover pan and freeze, stirring occasionally, until firm, about 3½ hours.

4. To serve, let sorbet stand at room temperature 15 minutes to soften slightly. Makes about 3½ cups or 7 servings.

Each serving: About 135 calories, 0 g protein, 30 g carbohydrate, 0 g total fat, 0 mg cholesterol, 45 mg sodium.

Pink Grapefruit Sorbet

Prep: 20 minutes plus freezing
Cook: 5 minutes

3 large pink or red grapefruit
1 cup sugar
¼ cup light corn syrup
4 cups water

1. With vegetable peeler, remove 4 strips peel (4" by ¾" wide each) from grapefruit, then squeeze 2 cups juice. In 2-quart saucepan, heat sugar, corn syrup, peel, and water until sugar has dissolved and syrup boils. Pour sugar syrup and grapefruit juice through strainer into large bowl. Discard peel and pulp.

2. Pour juice mixture into 9" by 9" metal baking pan; cover with foil. Freeze until partially frozen, about 4 hours, stirring occasionally.

3. In food processor with knife blade attached, process sorbet until smooth but still frozen. Return to pan; cover and freeze until almost firm, at least 3 hours.

4. Just before serving, return mixture to food processor and process until smooth. Makes about 5 cups or 10 servings.

Each serving: About 120 calories, 0 g protein, 31 g carbohydrate, 0 g total fat, 0 mg cholesterol, 5 mg sodium.

∾**Ice-Cream Bombes, Cakes & Pies**

Vanilla-Pecan Ice-Cream Torte

Prep: 25 minutes plus cooling, freezing and softening
Bake: 8 minutes

1 cup pecan halves, toasted and cooled
20 gingersnap cookies
2 tablespoons sugar
3 tablespoons margarine or butter, melted
3 pints vanilla ice cream
2 tablespoons plus 1 teaspoon pumpkin-pie spice

1. Preheat oven to 375°F. Reserve 16 pecan halves for garnish. In food processor with knife blade attached, process remaining pecan halves with gingersnaps and sugar until mixture is finely ground.

2. In 9-inch springform pan, with fork, stir cookie mixture and melted margarine until moistened. With hand, press mixture onto bottom of pan. Bake crust 8 minutes. Cool completely on wire rack.

3. Let ice cream soften on counter 20 minutes. In large bowl, mix softened ice cream and pumpkin-pie spice until blended; spread over crust. Place pecan halves around top edge of torte. Cover torte and freeze at least overnight or up to 1 week.

4. To serve, let frozen torte stand at room temperature about 15 minutes for easier slicing. Remove side of springform pan. Makes 16 servings.

Each serving: About 240 calories, 3 g protein, 22 g carbohydrate, 17 g total fat (7 g saturated), 34 mg cholesterol, 115 mg sodium.

Banana-Split Cake

Prep: 25 minutes plus softening and freezing
Cook: 5 minutes

1 pint vanilla ice cream
¾ cup walnuts
½ cup graham-cracker crumbs
7 tablespoons margarine or
  butter
2 tablespoons plus ¾ cup
  sugar

½ cup unsweetened cocoa
1 cup heavy or whipping
  cream
1 teaspoon vanilla extract
4 medium bananas
1 pint chocolate ice cream
1 pint strawberry ice cream
6 Maraschino cherries

1. Place vanilla ice cream in refrigerator until slightly softened, about 40 minutes. Meanwhile, finely chop ½ cup walnuts (reserve remaining ¼ cup walnuts for garnish).

2. In 9" by 3" springform pan, mix chopped walnuts, graham-cracker crumbs, 3 tablespoons margarine, and 2 tablespoons sugar. With fingers, press mixture onto bottom of pan. Evenly spread vanilla ice cream on top of crust; cover pan and freeze until firm, about 45 minutes.

3. While waiting for vanilla ice cream to harden, prepare fudge sauce: In 2-quart saucepan, cook cocoa, remaining ¾ cup sugar, ½ cup heavy cream, and 4 tablespoons margarine, over medium heat, stirring constantly, until mixture is smooth and boils. Remove saucepan from heat; stir in vanilla. Cool fudge sauce to room temperature.

4. Split 3 bananas lengthwise in half. Remove pan from freezer. Pour fudge sauce over vanilla ice cream; top with split bananas. Return cake to freezer; freeze until fudge sauce is firm, about 1 hour. Place chocolate ice cream in refrigerator until slightly softened.

5. Spread chocolate ice cream over fudge and bananas. Return cake to freezer; freeze about 20 minutes to harden slightly.

6. Place strawberry ice cream in medium bowl; let stand at room temperature, stirring occasionally, until smooth enough to spread but not melted. Spread strawberry ice cream over chocolate ice cream. Cover cake and return to freezer; freeze until firm, about 3 hours.

7. To serve, break reserved ¼ cup walnuts into small pieces. Whip remaining ½ cup heavy cream until soft peaks form when beaters are lifted. Cut remaining banana diagonally into slices. Run knife or metal spatula, dipped in hot water, around edge of pan to loosen ice cream. Remove side of pan. Spread top of cake with whipped cream. Arrange banana slices, cherries, and broken walnuts on whipped cream. Makes 16 servings.

Each serving: About 340 calories, 4 g protein, 37 g carbohydrate, 21 g total fat (9 g saturated), 42 mg cholesterol, 130 mg sodium.

Jiffy Peanut Ice-Cream Bombe

Prep: 15 minutes
Cook: 5 minutes

1 cup finely chopped salted peanuts
1 quart vanilla ice cream
4 tablespoons margarine or butter
2 squares (2 ounces) semisweet chocolate
½ teaspoon vanilla extract

1. Spread chopped peanuts on waxed paper. With spatula, gently remove ice cream from container in 1 piece. With knife, slice ice cream crosswise into 3 slices. Working quickly, coat ice-cream slices with peanuts. Reassemble ice-cream slices; place large end down on plate. Cover and freeze until ready to serve.

2. Meanwhile, in 1-quart saucepan, melt margarine and chocolate over medium-low heat. Remove from heat; stir in vanilla.

3. To serve, spoon chocolate sauce over ice-cream bombe. Cut bombe into wedges. Makes 8 servings.

Each serving: About 390 calories, 9 g protein, 25 g carbohydrate, 31 g total fat (11 g saturated), 45 mg cholesterol, 215 mg sodium.

Sorbet and Cream Cake

Prep: 1 hour plus freezing
Bake: 10 minutes

30 vanilla wafers
4 tablespoons margarine or butter, melted
½ teaspoon freshly grated lime peel
2 pints vanilla ice cream
1 pint strawberry sorbet
1 pint mango sorbet
1 pint lemon sorbet
1 ripe mango, peeled and sliced
Fresh raspberries

1. In food processor with knife blade attached or in blender at medium speed, blend vanilla wafers until fine crumbs form. (about 1 cup crumbs).

2. Preheat oven to 375°F. In small saucepan, melt margarine over low heat; stir in lime peel.

3. In 9" by 3" springform pan, with fork, stir wafer crumbs and melted margarine mixture until moistened. With hand, press mixture firmly onto bottom of pan. Bake crust 10 minutes. Cool completely in pan on wire rack, about 30 minutes.

4. When crust comes out of oven, place 1 pint vanilla ice cream and all sorbets in refrigerator until slightly softened, about 30 minutes.

5. Spoon alternating scoops of vanilla ice cream and sorbets into springform pan in 2 layers; press mixture down to eliminate air pockets. Cover pan and place in freezer to harden mixture slightly, about 30 minutes.

6. Meanwhile, place remaining vanilla ice cream in refrigerator to soften slightly.

7. With metal spatula, evenly spread softened vanilla ice cream over frozen layers. Cover and freeze until firm, at least 4 hours.

8. To serve, place warm dampened towels around side of pan for about 20 seconds to slightly soften ice cream. Remove side of pan and place cake on platter. (If you like, remove pan bottom also.) Cover and keep cake frozen if not serving right away, or let stand at room temperature about 10 minutes for easier slicing. Before serving, garnish top of cake with slices of mango and fresh berries. Makes 20 servings.

Each serving: About 175 calories, 1 g protein, 26 g carbohydrate, 6 g total fat (2 g saturated), 15 mg cholesterol, 65 mg sodium.

Holiday Baked Alaska with Red-Raspberry Sauce

Prep: 1 hour 30 minutes plus freezing
Bake: 2 to 3 minutes

Ice-Cream Cake
2 pints vanilla ice cream
3 packages (3 to 4½ ounces each) sponge-type ladyfingers
2 pints raspberry sorbet

Red-Raspberry Sauce
1 package (10 ounces) frozen raspberries in quick-thaw pouch, thawed
2 tablespoons seedless raspberry jam
1 tablespoon orange-flavored liqueur

Meringue
4 large egg whites
¾ cup sugar
¼ teaspoon salt
¼ teaspoon cream of tartar
4 teaspoons water

1. Prepare Ice-Cream Cake: Place vanilla ice cream in large bowl; let stand at room temperature to soften slightly, stirring occasionally, until spreadable.

2. Meanwhile, split each ladyfinger in half lengthwise. Line bottom and side of 10" by 1½" scalloped round baking dish, shallow 1 ½-quart round casserole, or 9½-inch deep-dish pie plate with about two-thirds of ladyfingers, placing ladyfingers with rounded side out around side and allowing ladyfingers to extend above rim of baking dish.

3. Spoon vanilla ice cream into lined dish; smooth with small metal spatula. Place in freezer until ice cream is firm, about 30 minutes.

4. Place raspberry sorbet in large bowl; let stand at room temperature to soften slightly, stirring occasionally, until spreadable. Spoon raspberry sorbet on top of ice cream, smoothing with spatula. Top sorbet with remaining ladyfingers. Cover cake with waxed paper and foil; freeze until firm, at least 6 hours. Cake may be made ahead up to this point and frozen up to 2 weeks.

5. Prepare Red-Raspberry Sauce: In food processor, process raspberries, jam, and orange-flavored liqueur until blended and smooth. Pour sauce into small pitcher to serve. Refrigerate until ready to use. Makes about 1⅓ cups sauce.

6. About 30 minutes before serving, prepare Meringue: Preheat oven to 500°F. In large bowl set over simmering water or in top of double boiler, with handheld mixer at medium speed, beat egg whites, sugar, salt, cream of tartar, and water, until soft peaks form when beaters are lifted and temperature on thermometer reaches 160°F, 12 to 14 minutes. Transfer bowl with meringue to work surface. Beat meringue until stiff peaks form, 8 to 10 minutes longer.

7. Remove cake from freezer. Spoon meringue over top of cake, swirling with spoon to make attractive top. Bake until meringue top is lightly browned, 2 to 3 minutes. Place cake on heat-safe platter. Serve immediately with Red-Raspberry Sauce on side. Makes 16 servings.

Each serving About 250 calories, 4 g protein, 40 g carbohydrate, 5 g total fat (3 g saturated), 73 mg cholesterol, 95 mg sodium.

Frozen Strawberry Margarita Pie

Prep: 25 minutes plus freezing
Bake: 10 minutes

Crumb Crust
1½ cups vanilla wafer crumbs
5 tablespoons margarine or butter, melted
½ teaspoon freshly grated lime peel

Strawberry Filling
1 pint strawberries
2 limes
1 can (14 ounces) sweetened condensed milk
2 tablespoons orange-flavored liqueur
1 cup heavy or whipping cream

1. Prepare Crumb Crust: Preheat oven to 375°F. In 9-inch pie plate, with fork, stir wafer crumbs, melted margarine, and lime peel until crumbs are moistened. Press mixture onto bottom and up side of pie plate, making a slight rim. Bake crust 10 minutes. Cool crust in pie plate on wire rack.

2. Prepare Strawberry Filling: Hull 2 cups strawberries; reserve remaining berries for garnish. From limes, grate 1 teaspoon peel and squeeze ¼ cup juice. In food processor with knife blade attached, pulse hulled berries with lime peel and juice, undiluted sweetened condensed milk, and liqueur until almost smooth. Transfer mixture to large bowl.

3. In small bowl, with mixer at medium speed, beat ⅔ cup cream until stiff peaks form when beaters are lifted; reserve remaining unwhipped cream for garnish. Gently fold whipped cream into strawberry mixture, one-third at a time.

4. Pour filling into cooled crust. Freeze until almost firm, at least 4 hours. (If not serving pie on the same day, wrap frozen pie in foil or plastic wrap and freeze up to 1 week.)

5. If pie freezes completely, let it stand at room temperature 10 minutes before serving for easier slicing. Meanwhile, cut each reserved strawberry in half. In small bowl, with mixer at medium speed, beat remaining ⅓ cup cream just until stiff peaks form when beaters are lifted. Mound whipped cream in center of pie and top with strawberry halves. Makes 10 servings.

Each serving: About 360 calories, 5 g protein, 39 g carbohydrate, 21 g total fat (9 g saturated), 57 mg cholesterol, 180 mg sodium

Fudge-Sundae Pie

Prep: 20 minutes
Bake: 10 minutes

2 cups walnuts, finely chopped
2 tablespoons brown sugar
7 tablespoons margarine or butter
1 pint vanilla ice cream
½ cup unsweetened cocoa
½ cup heavy or whipping cream
1 ¼ cups granulated sugar
1 teaspoon vanilla extract
1 pint chocolate or coffee ice cream
4 large egg whites, at room temperature
¼ teaspoon salt
⅛ teaspoon cream of tartar

1. Preheat oven to 400°F. In 9-inch pie plate, with hand, mix walnuts, brown sugar, and 3 tablespoons margarine. Press mixture onto bottom and up side of pie plate. Bake 8 minutes. Cool crust completely on wire rack. Meanwhile, place vanilla ice cream in refrigerator to soften slightly.

2. Evenly spread softened vanilla ice cream on crust; cover and freeze until firm, about 1½ hours.

3. In 2-quart saucepan, cook cocoa, heavy cream, ¾ cup granulated sugar, and remaining 4 tablespoons margarine over medium heat, stirring constantly, until mixture is smooth and boils. Remove saucepan from heat; stir in vanilla. Cool fudge sauce to room temperature.

4. Pour fudge sauce over ice-cream layer. Return pie to freezer; freeze until fudge sauce hardens, about 30 minutes.

5. Transfer chocolate ice cream from container to medium bowl; let stand at room temperature, stirring occasionally, until smooth enough to spread but not melted. Spread chocolate ice cream over fudge. Cover and freeze until firm, at least 3 hours.

6. About 20 minutes before serving, preheat oven to 500°F. Prepare meringue: In small bowl, with mixer at high speed, beat egg whites, salt, and cream of tartar until soft peaks form when beaters are lifted; beat in ½ cup granulated sugar, 2 tablespoons at a time, beating until sugar has completely dissolved and whites stand in stiff, glossy peaks. With spoon, quickly spread meringue over top of pie, sealing to edge and swirling meringue with back of spoon to make attractive top. Bake until meringue is lightly browned, 2 to 3 minutes. Serve pie immediately. Makes 12 servings.

Each serving: About 435 calories, 7 g protein, 40 g carbohydrate, 29 g total fat (9 g saturated), 36 mg cholesterol, 195 mg sodium.

Sugar-and-Spice Ice-Cream Sandwiches

Prep: 10 minutes plus chilling and freezing
Bake: 10 to 12 minutes per batch

1½ cups all-purpose flour	1 cup packed dark brown
½ cup unsweetened cocoa	sugar
2 teaspoons ground ginger	½ cup (1 stick) margarine or
1 teaspoon ground cinnamon	butter, softened
1 teaspoon baking powder	1 large egg
½ teaspoon baking soda	1 teaspoon vanilla extract
½ teaspoon finely ground black	1 pint strawberry ice cream,
pepper	softened
½ teaspoon salt	

1. In medium bowl, combine flour, cocoa, ginger, cinnamon, baking powder, baking soda, pepper, and salt.

2. In large bowl, with mixer at medium speed, beat brown sugar and margarine until creamy. Reduce speed to low; beat in egg and vanilla until well blended. Add flour mixture, beating just until blended.

3. Divide dough into 4 equal pieces. Shape each piece of dough into 3" by 2" rectangular block 1½" inches high.

Wrap each block and freeze until very firm, at least 1 hour or overnight.

4. Preheat oven to 350°F. Slice 1 cookie-dough block lengthwise into 8 equal slices. Place slices, about 1 inch apart, on large ungreased cookie sheet. Repeat with another block of dough. (Work quickly with dough to prevent cookies from becoming misshapen as the dough softens.) Bake cookies 10 to 12 minutes. Cool completely on cookie sheet. Transfer cookies to plate. Repeat with remaining dough.

5. To make sandwiches, place 16 cookies on 15½" by 10½" jelly-roll pan. Place about 1 heaping tablespoon softened ice cream on top of each cookie. With small metal spatula, spread ice cream on each cookie, almost to edges. Top with remaining cookies to make 16 sandwiches in all. Wrap individually in foil and freeze at least 1 hour or up to 1 week. Makes 16 sandwiches.

Each sandwich: About 200 calories, 3 g protein, 30 g carbohydrate, 9 g total fat (3 g saturated), 29 mg cholesterol, 240 mg sodium.

ᴄ∾Other Frozen Desserts

Dacquoise Glacée

Prep: 1 hour plus softening and chilling
Bake: 1 hour 30 minutes

5 large egg whites, at room
   temperature
¼ teaspoon cream of tartar
⅛ teaspoon salt
1 cup granulated sugar
1 teaspoon vanilla extract
3 tablespoons unsweetened
   cocoa
1 tablespoon cornstarch

½ cup sliced blanched
   almonds
2 pints coffee ice cream
2 cups heavy or whipping
   cream
¼ cup confectioners' sugar
2 tablespoons coffee-flavored
   liqueur

1. Line 1 large and 1 small cookie sheet with foil. Using 8-inch round plate as guide, with toothpick, outline 2 circles on large cookie sheet and 1 circle on small cookie sheet.

2. In large bowl, with mixer at high speed, beat egg whites, cream of tartar, and salt until soft peaks form when beaters are lifted. Add granulated sugar, 2 tablespoons at a time, beating until sugar has completely dissolved. Add vanilla and continue beating until meringue stands in stiff, glossy peaks. In cup, combine cocoa and cornstarch. With rubber spatula or wire whisk, fold cocoa mixture into meringue until blended.

3. Preheat oven to 275°F. Spoon one-third of meringue inside each circle on cookie sheets; with metal spatula, evenly spread meringue to cover whole circle. Bake until meringues are crisp, about 1¼ hours. Cool meringues on cookie sheets on wire racks 10 minutes. Carefully loosen and remove meringues from foil; transfer to wire racks to cool completely.

4. Meanwhile, spread almonds in 13" by 9" baking pan. Bake almonds until browned, stirring occasionally, about 15 minutes. Cool; set aside.

5. To assemble dessert: Chill meringue layers in freezer about 30 minutes for easier handling. Place 1 pint coffee ice cream in refrigerator until slightly softened, about 30 minutes.

6. Place 1 meringue layer on freezer-safe cake plate; quickly spread with softened ice cream. Place meringue with ice cream in freezer until firm, about 30 minutes. Meanwhile, place a second pint of coffee ice cream in refrigerator to soften.

7. Remove meringue with ice cream from freezer; top with second meringue layer; spread with second pint of ice cream; top with remaining meringue layer. Freeze dessert until completely frozen, at least 4 hours.

8. In small bowl, with mixer at medium speed, beat cream, confectioners' sugar, and liqueur until stiff peaks form when beaters are lifted. Frost side and top of dessert with whipped cream; sprinkle almonds on top. Return to freezer but do not cover until whipped cream has hardened, then cover; return to freezer until ready to serve. To serve, let cake stand at room temperature 15 minutes to soften slightly. Makes 16 servings.

Each serving: About 265 calories, 4 g protein, 25 g carbohydrate, 17 g total fat (10 g saturated), 54 mg cholesterol, 65 mg sodium.

Rocky-Road Freeze

Prep: 10 minutes plus freezing and softening

1 can (14 ounces) sweetened condensed milk
½ cup chocolate-flavored syrup
2 cups heavy or whipping cream
1 cup miniature marshmallows
½ package (6 ounces) semisweet-chocolate pieces (½ cup), chopped
½ cup salted peanuts, chopped

1. In small bowl, stir condensed milk and chocolate syrup until blended; set aside.

2. In large bowl, with mixer at medium speed, beat heavy cream until stiff peaks form when beaters are lifted. With rubber spatula, fold chocolate mixture, marshmallows, chocolate pieces, and chopped peanuts into whipped cream until blended. Cover bowl with plastic wrap; freeze until firm, about 5 hours.

3. To serve, let mixture stand at room temperature 15 minutes for easier scooping. Makes 12 servings.

Each serving: About 350 calories, 6 g protein, 36 g carbohydrate, 23 g total fat (13 g saturated), 66 mg cholesterol, 95 mg sodium.

Individual Baked Alaskas

Prep: 10 minutes
Bake: About 3 minutes

2 pints vanilla or other ice cream
4 large egg whites, at room temperature
⅛ teaspoon cream of tartar
½ cup sugar
6 baker's or packaged dessert shells

1. Preheat oven to 500°F. Place ice cream in refrigerator to soften slightly. Meanwhile, in small bowl, with mixer at high speed, beat egg whites and cream of tartar until soft peaks form when beaters are lifted. Add sugar, 2 tablespoons at a time, beating until sugar has completely dissolved and whites stand in stiff, glossy peaks.

2. Place dessert shells on chilled cookie sheet. Scoop a ball of ice cream on top of each shell. Quickly spread each with meringue to completely cover right down to cookie sheet. Bake until meringue is lightly browned, about 3 minutes. Transfer dessert to chilled plates. Serve immediately. Makes 6 servings.

Each serving: About 380 calories, 8 g protein, 52 g carbohydrate, 17 g total fat (10 g saturated), 100 mg cholesterol, 145 mg sodium.

Banana-Praline Sundaes

Prep: 10 minutes
Cook: 10 minutes

1 pint vanilla ice cream
⅓ cup packed dark-brown sugar
3 tablespoons margarine or butter
¼ cup golden raisins
2 medium-sized bananas, sliced
⅓ cup pecans, chopped

1. Let ice cream stand at room temperature to soften slightly.

2. Meanwhile, in 10-inch skillet over low heat, heat brown sugar and margarine until mixture melts, stirring frequently. Add raisins and bananas; cook 5 minutes, gently turning fruit, until fruit is heated through.

3. To serve, spoon ice cream into 4 dessert bowls; top with banana mixture, then nuts. Makes 4 servings.

Each serving. About 470 calories, 4 g protein, 58 g carbohydrate, 27 g total fat (10 g saturated), 45 mg cholesterol, 165 mg sodium.

Ice-Cream Bonbons

Prep: 20 minutes plus chilling
Cook: 5 minutes

1 pint vanilla or other ice cream
1½ cups walnuts, finely chopped
1 package (6 ounces) semisweet-chocolate pieces (1 cup)
3 tablespoons margarine or butter
1 tablespoon light corn syrup
¼ cup confectioners' sugar
1 teaspoon water

1. Place ice cream in refrigerator until slightly softened, about 30 minutes. Chill small cookie sheet in freezer. Place walnuts on sheet of waxed paper.

2. Line chilled cookie sheet with waxed paper. Working quickly, with medium ice-cream scoop, scoop a ball of ice cream; roll in walnuts; place on waxed-paper-lined cookie sheet. Repeat with remaining ice cream and walnuts to make 8 ice-cream balls. Freeze until firm, about 1½ hours.

3. In double boiler over hot, not boiling, water, heat chocolate pieces, margarine, and corn syrup, stirring occasionally, until chocolate melts and mixture is smooth. Turn off heat, but leave top of double boiler over hot water in bottom of double boiler to keep chocolate warm for easier coating.

4. With 2 forks, quickly dip each ice-cream ball into chocolate mixture to coat completely; place on same cookie sheet. Return to freezer; freeze until chocolate is firm, about 1 hour.

5. In small bowl, mix confectioners' sugar and water until smooth and spreadable. With spoon, drizzle sugar mixture over bonbons to make an attractive design. Return bonbons to freezer. If not serving on same day, when sugar glaze has hardened, wrap bonbons with foil or plastic wrap and return to freezer.

6. To serve, let bonbons stand at room temperature 10 minutes to soften slightly. Makes 8 bonbons.

Each bonbon: About 390 calories, 5 g protein, 30 g carbohydrate, 30 g total fat (9 g saturated), 23 mg cholesterol, 85 mg sodium.

Tartufo

Prep: 35 minutes plus softening and chilling
Cook: 5 minutes

2 pints vanilla ice cream
2 tablespoons almond-flavored liqueur
6 amaretti cookies
1 package (6 ounces) semisweet-chocolate pieces (1 cup)
3 tablespoons margarine or butter
1 tablespoon light corn syrup
¾ cup whole almonds, toasted and finely chopped

1. Place ice cream in refrigerator until slightly softened, about 30 minutes. Chill small cookie sheet in freezer.

2. Meanwhile, on plate, pour almond-flavored liqueur over amaretti cookies; let stand until liqueur is absorbed, turning cookies occasionally.

3. Line chilled cookie sheet with waxed paper. Working quickly, with large ice-cream scoop, scoop a ball of ice cream. Gently press a cookie into center of ball; reshape ball around cookie; place on waxed-paper-lined cookie sheet. Repeat to make 6 balls. Freeze until firm, at least 1½ hours.

4. In double boiler over hot, not boiling, water, heat chocolate pieces, margarine, and corn syrup, stirring occasionally, until chocolate melts and mixture is smooth. Turn off heat, but leave top of double boiler over hot water in bottom of double boiler to keep chocolate warm for easier coating.

5. Remove 1 ice-cream ball from freezer; place on a chilled plate. Using pastry brush, quickly coat ice-cream ball with chocolate. Firmly pat some almonds onto chocolate-coated ice-cream ball; return to freezer. Repeat with remaining ice-cream balls, chocolate, and nuts. Freeze until chocolate is firm, about 1 hour. If not serving on same day, when chocolate is firm, wrap ice-cream balls with foil or plastic wrap and return to freezer.

6. To serve, let ice-cream balls stand at room temperature 10 minutes to soften slightly. Makes 6 ice-cream balls.

Each ball: About 565 calories, 9 g protein, 51 g carbohydrate, 39 g total fat (16 g saturated), 60 mg cholesterol, 140 mg sodium.

Beverages

~⚬~

Coffee & Tea
Chocolate Drinks
Smoothies & Shakes
Fruit Drinks
Party Punches & Eggnogs

What you serve beverages in can make them seem special. Hot drinks will stay hot and look inviting in mugs, steins, brulot cups, or demitasse cups. For cold drinks, try pilsners, water goblets, brandy snifters, or champagne or wine glasses. Ladle punches and party beverages from glass or silver punch bowls, glass salad bowls, or pour them from attractive pitchers.

～Coffee

- Buy enough beans only for the immediate future. Unless they are vacuum-packed, whole beans are at their peak for only 3 weeks, ground beans for only about 1 week. Vacuum-packed beans will keep a year.
- Despite what you've heard, don't store coffee in the fridge or freezer. The beans absorb the condensation that forms when they're exposed to temperature changes from cold to warm. Best bet: Keep coffee in an opaque, airtight container in a cool, dry place.
- Follow the manufacturer's directions for brewing in your coffeemaker. Generally, 1 to 2 tablespoons ground coffee per ¾ cup cold water is sufficient for a good cup.
- Don't leave brewed coffee on the burner for longer than 20 minutes. The heat causes the coffee to deteriorate, leaving a bitter taste. Instead, pour it into an insulated pitcher.

∽Tea

BUYING TEA

The thousands of varieties of tea offer flavors ranging from strong and smoky to delicate and flowery. Teas fall into three basic types, depending on how the leaves are processed: black tea, oolong tea, and green tea.

Black tea is the favorite type consumed in this country. It is made by fermenting (oxidizing) the leaves so that they turn black and make a hearty, flavorful amber brew. Well-known blends include Assam, which is full-bodied and robust; Ceylon, delicate and fragrant; Darjeeling, the finest black tea from India, flavorful and aromatic; Earl Grey, from India and Sri Lanka, aromatic and hearty; English Breakfast, a mellow, fragrant blend; Keemun, a fine Chinese tea, mild but robust; Lapsang Souchong, from Formosa, pungent and strong, with a smoky flavor.

Oolong tea is only partially fermented; the leaves are partly green, partly brown, and make a light-colored brew. Varieties include Formosa Oolong, subtle and slightly winelike in flavor, and Jasmine tea, delicate and scented with white jasmine blossoms.

Green tea consists of leaves that are not fermented and thus retain their green color; they make a greenish-yellow brew. Common varieties include Basket Fired tea from Japan, which has a light flavor; Gunpowder tea, so called because the leaves are rolled into small pellets, makes a delicate, pale green brew.

The terms *pekoe* and *orange pekoe* on tea labels refer to the size of the tea leaves, not to the variety of tea, and indicate that these are the choice leaves.

STORING TEA

Loose tea and tea bags should be stored at room temperature. After opening the tea, transfer it to an airtight container and use it within 6 months. Store jars of instant tea at room temperature; close tightly after each use.

HERBAL TEA

Herbal teas are blends of herbs, spices, aromatic ingredients such as citrus peels, and flower buds and petals. They are caffeine free (this is usually stated on the label) unless blended with black tea and/or maté (a South American holly whose leaves are brewed as a beverage).

If the name of the blend does not suggest the basic flavor (orange or mint, for example), check the list of ingredients on the label. The herbs most frequently used in blends supply these flavors and/or colors and fragrances: hibiscus flowers—citruslike flavor and rosy color; chamomile flowers—flowery taste, applelike fragrance, and golden color; lemongrass and verbena—lemony taste and fragrance; strawberry leaves—soft, fruity strawberry flavor; carob—chocolatelike taste; fenugreek—maple flavor.

Follow package directions for brewing herbal teas, hot or iced. Let the mixture brew at least 3 minutes to develop its full flavor.

∾Coffee & Tea

THE ULTIMATE AT-HOME COFFEE BAR

Nothing goes better with bacon and eggs—or, for that matter, dessert—than steaming hot coffee. So arrange your cups and saucers (or mugs) and spoons, and set up a mini bar your friends will love. You'll need:

Beverages: Regular and decaf coffees, including a fragrant flavored one such as hazelnut or French vanilla if you like, a selection of teas, and a carafe of freshly boiled water. (Java flavor drops within 20 minutes of brewing, so have coffee machines ready to go before guests arrive, then brew just prior to serving. Or, transfer coffee to thermal carafes to keep it piping hot.)

Sweeteners: Granulated sugar, turbinado or Demerara sugar (tan and unrefined), artificial sweetener, honey, rock-sugar stirring sticks (sold in candy or fancy-food stores), and candy canes. Snow-white vanilla sugar is a tempting addition too. You can buy it or make your own: Place half of a split vanilla bean in a jar of granulated sugar; store, covered, for a few days. The longer the flavor steeps, the better. Remove vanilla bean before serving.

Pour-ins: Choices from skinny to rich: nonfat milk, whole milk, and half-and-half. If it's a late brunch, pamper guests with liqueurs like amaretto, Grand Marnier, sambuca, or crème de menthe to stir into coffee for a wonderful depth of flavor.

Add-ons: Shakers of cocoa powder or sweetened hot cocoa mix, nutmeg (ground or a whole nut to grate individually), shaved semisweet chocolate, ground cinnamon, cinnamon sticks, chocolate stirrers, and for the premium indulgence, a bowl of fluffy whipped cream.

Café au Lait: Prepare Hot Coffee. To serve this breakfast drink in the French manner, hold the pot of coffee in one hand, a pot of hot milk in the other; pour both at the same time to fill large cups. Serve sugar separately.

SECRETS FOR THE BEST ICED COFFEE

To Make Iced Coffee: Brew regular or decaf coffee, cool slightly, and refrigerate. Stir in milk and sugar as desired and serve over ice. Shortcut: Double the amount of grounds, then add ice to the hot coffee. If you're a die-hard caffeine fan and don't want to water down your drink with ice, make coffee cubes: Pour the cooled brew into ice-cube trays and freeze.

For Spiced Iced Coffee: Put a cinnamon stick or some cardamom pods in with the ground beans before brewing.

Frosty Cappuccino

Prep: 5 minutes

1 cup low-fat (1%) milk
1 tablespoon chocolate-flavored syrup
1 teaspoon instant espresso-coffee powder
2 ice cubes
Sugar (optional)
⅛ teaspoon ground cinnamon

In blender at high speed, blend milk, syrup, espresso-coffee powder, and ice cubes. Pour into 2 chilled glasses. If you like, add sugar to taste. Sprinkle with cinnamon for garnish. Makes 2 servings.

Each serving: About 75 calories, 4 g protein, 12 g carbohydrate, 1 g total fat (1 g saturated), 5 mg cholesterol, 65 mg sodium.

Hot Tea

Prep: 5 minutes
Cook: 5 minutes

1. Preheat a teapot by rinsing it out with boiling water. Use ¾ cup boiling water and 1 teaspoon loose tea or 1 tea bag for each 6-ounce cup. Measure loose tea into hot teapot (or into tea ball before putting into teapot); pour boiling water over tea. Cover teapot and brew 3 to 5 minutes. Do not judge strength of tea by its color; some fully brewed teas are light, some dark.

2. After brewing, stir tea to make sure flavor is uniform. Pour tea through small strainer into teacup (or remove tea ball or tea bag before pouring).

Spiced Hot Tea

Prep: 5 minutes
Cook: 5 minutes

4 cups cold water
¼ teaspoon whole cloves
¼ teaspoon whole allspice
1 cinnamon stick (3 inches)
5 teaspoons loose Earl Grey or Darjeeling tea or 5 tea bags
Honey
Lemon or orange wedges (optional)

1. In 2-quart saucepan, heat water, cloves, allspice, and cinnamon stick to boiling over high heat. Remove saucepan from heat.

2. Add tea to hot spice mixture in saucepan; cover and brew 3 to 5 minutes.

3. To serve, pour spiced tea through strainer into 4 mugs. Into each mug, stir about 1½ teaspoons honey or to taste. Serve with lemon or orange wedges, if you like. Makes 4 cups or four 1-cup servings.

Each serving: About 35 calories, 0 g protein, 10 g carbohydrate, 0 g total fat, 0 mg cholesterol, 10 mg sodium.

Classic Iced Tea

Prep: 5 minutes
Brew: 5 minutes

8 cups cold water
8 tea bags, tags removed
Ice cubes
Granulated or superfine sugar (optional)
Thin lemon slices (optional)

1. In 3-quart saucepan, heat 4 cups cold water to boiling over high heat. Remove saucepan from heat and stir in tea bags. Cover and brew 5 minutes.

2. Stir tea. Remove tea bags and pour tea into 2½-quart pitcher with remaining 4 cups cold water. Cover and let stand until ready to serve. (Do not refrigerate or tea will become cloudy. If this happens, add boiling water, gradually, until tea clears.)

3. To serve, pour tea over ice cubes in tall glasses. Serve with sugar and lemon slices, if you like. Makes about 8 cups or 8 servings.

Each serving classic iced tea: About 2 calories, 0 g protein, 1 g carbohydrate, 0 g total fat, 0 mg cholesterol, 5 mg sodium.

FRUIT TEA: Prepare Classic Iced Tea as above, except in Step 2, after pouring tea into pitcher, stir in *4 cups cold fruit juice* (such as peach, cranberry, raspberry, or white grape) instead of water. Garnish with fresh fruit. Makes about 8 cups or 8 servings.

Each serving fruit tea: About 65 calories, 0 g protein, 16 g carbohydrate, 0 g total fat, 0 mg cholesterol, 15 mg sodium.

∾**Chocolate Drinks**

Hearty Hot Cocoa

Prep: 5 minutes
Cook: 10 minutes

¾ cup water
⅔ cup unsweetened cocoa
½ cup sugar
5¼ cups milk
½ teaspoon vanilla extract
6 regular-sized marshmallows or whipped cream

1. In 3-quart saucepan, stir water, cocoa, and sugar until smooth; heat mixture to boiling over medium heat. Stir in milk; heat until tiny bubbles form around edge (do not boil). Remove saucepan from heat; add vanilla.

2. Pour into mugs or cups. Top each serving with marshmallow or whipped cream. Makes about 6 cups or six 1-cup servings.

Each serving: About 250 calories, 9 g protein, 36 g carbohydrate, 8 g total fat (5 g saturated), 29 mg cholesterol, 115 mg sodium.

French Hot Chocolate

Prep: 10 minutes plus cooling
Cook: 10 minutes

4 squares (4 ounces) semisweet chocolate, coarsely chopped
¼ cup light corn syrup
½ teaspoon vanilla extract
4 cups milk
1 cup heavy or whipping cream

1. In heavy 1-quart saucepan, heat chocolate and corn syrup over low heat, stirring until mixture is smooth. Cover and refrigerate until cool, about 30 minutes. Stir in vanilla.

2. In 2-quart saucepan, heat milk over medium-low heat until it is very hot and small bubbles form around edge (do not boil). Meanwhile, in small bowl, with mixer at medium-low speed, beat heavy cream and cooled chocolate mixture until soft peaks form when beaters are lifted.

3. To serve, spoon whipped-cream mixture into 8 cups; fill cups with hot milk. Makes about 6 cups or eight ¾-cup servings.

Each serving: About 365 calories, 7 g protein, 31 g carbohydrate, 26 g total fat (16 g saturated), 77 mg cholesterol, 115 mg sodium.

∾Smoothies & Shakes

Peach Smoothie

Prep: 5 minutes

1 cup peeled, pitted, and sliced peaches (about 2 medium)
1 cup peach juice or nectar
½ cup vanilla low-fat yogurt
3 ice cubes

In blender, combine peaches, juice, yogurt, and ice cubes and blend until mixture is smooth and frothy. Pour into 2 tall glasses. Makes about 2¾ cups or 2 servings.

Each serving: About 160 calories, 3 g protein, 36 g carbohydrate, 1 g total fat (1 g saturated), 3 mg cholesterol, 45 mg sodium.

Mango-Strawberry Smoothie

Prep: 5 minutes

1 medium ripe mango, peeled and cut into chunks
1 cup hulled, cut-up strawberries
½ cup vanilla low-fat yogurt
6 ice cubes

In blender, combine mango, strawberries, yogurt, and ice cubes, and blend until mixture is smooth and frothy. Pour into 2 tall glasses. Makes about 2½ cups or 2 servings.

Each serving: About 145 calories, 4 g protein, 32 g carbohydrate, 2 g total fat (1 g saturated), 3 mg cholesterol, 40 mg sodium.

Chocolate-Banana Cooler

Prep: 5 minutes

2 cups milk
1 large banana, sliced
¼ cup chocolate-flavored syrup
½ teaspoon vanilla extract
Grated chocolate (optional)

In blender at low speed, blend milk, banana, chocolate syrup, and vanilla until smooth. Pour into three 10-ounce glasses; sprinkle with grated chocolate, if you like. Makes about 3 cups or three 1-cup servings.

Each serving: About 200 calories, 6 g protein, 34 g carbohydrate, 6 g total fat (4 g saturated), 22 mg cholesterol, 105 mg sodium.

Chocolate-Banana Cooler Deluxe: Prepare as above but use only *1 cup milk* and add *1 cup vanilla or chocolate ice cream* with ingredients when blending. Makes about 3 cups or three 1-cup servings.

Each serving: About 270 calories, 5 g protein, 41 g carbohydrate, 11 g total fat (7 g saturated), 41 mg cholesterol, 90 mg sodium.

Vanilla Milk Shake

Prep: 5 minutes

1 pint vanilla ice cream
½ cup milk
½ teaspoon vanilla extract

1. In blender at medium speed, blend ice cream, milk, and vanilla until mixture is smooth and frothy.

2. Pour milk shakes into 2 tall 10-ounce glasses. Serve with straws, if you like. Makes 2 servings.

Each serving: About 300 calories, 7 g protein, 36 g carbohydrate, 26 g total fat (16 g saturated), 99 mg cholesterol, 115 mg sodium.

❧Fruit Drinks

Lemonade

Prep: 10 minutes plus chilling
Cook: 5 minutes

2 cups sugar
2 cups cold water
2 cups fresh lemon juice (from about 10 medium lemons)
Ice cubes

1. Prepare sugar syrup: In 2-quart saucepan, heat sugar and cold water to boiling over high heat, stirring occasionally. Cover saucepan and boil 3 minutes. Remove saucepan from heat.

2. Stir lemon juice into sugar syrup. Pour mixture into pitcher or measuring cup; cover and refrigerate until cold, about 3 hours.

3. Serve over ice, stirring in *additional water*, if you like. Makes about 5 cups or 10 servings.

FRESH MINT LEMONADE: Prepare sugar syrup for Lemonade as in Step 1. After removing saucepan from heat, stir in 1 cup loosely packed fresh mint leaves and let stand, covered, 10 minutes. Strain mixture and discard mint leaves. Complete recipe as in Steps 2 and 3. Garnish with mint sprigs.

Each serving: About 170 calories, 0 g protein, 44 g carbohydrate, 0 g total fat, 0 mg cholesterol, 1 mg sodium.

Limeade

Prep: 10 minutes plus chilling
Cook: 5 minutes

2 cups sugar
3½ cups cold water
1¼ cups fresh lime juice (from about 10 medium limes)
Ice cubes
Lime slices (optional)

1. Prepare sugar syrup: In 2-quart saucepan, heat sugar and cold water to boiling over high heat, stirring occasionally. Cover saucepan and boil 3 minutes. Remove saucepan from heat.

2. Stir lime juice into sugar syrup. Pour mixture into pitcher or measuring cup; cover and refrigerate until cold, about 3 hours.

3. Serve over ice, with lime slices, stirring in *additional water*, if you like. Makes about 6 cups or 12 servings.

GINGER LIMEADE: Prepare sugar syrup for Limeade as in Step 1, adding *6 slices* (each ⅛ inch thick) *peeled, fresh ginger* to sugar-and-water mixture. Cover and boil 5 minutes instead of 3. Remove saucepan from heat and let stand, covered, 5 minutes. Strain mixture and discard ginger. Complete recipe as in Steps 2 and 3.

Each serving: About 125 calories, 0 g protein, 33 g carbohydrate, 0 g total fat, 0 mg cholesterol, 1 mg sodium.

Warm Spiced Cider

Prep: 10 minutes
Cook: 15 minutes

1 large orange
12 whole cloves
1 medium lemon
1 gallon apple cider
6 cinnamon sticks (3 inches each)

1. Cut two ½-inch-thick slices from center of orange. Stick cloves into skin around each orange slice. Cut remaining orange into thin slices for garnish. Remove a 1-inch-wide continuous strip of peel from lemon (reserve peeled lemon for another use).

2. In 5-quart saucepot over high heat, heat orange slices with cloves, lemon peel, apple cider, and cinnamon sticks to boiling. Reduce heat to low; cover and simmer 15 minutes.

3. Pour hot cider into large heat-safe punch bowl (about 5 quarts). Place remaining orange slices in cider for garnish. Makes about 16 cups or 20 servings.

Each serving: About 105 calories, 0 g protein, 28 g carbohydrate, 0 g total fat, 0 mg cholesterol, 5 mg sodium.

∾Party Punches & Eggnog

Orange-Cranberry Fizz

Prep: 10 minutes

1 quart cranberry-raspberry juice blend, chilled
2 cups cranberry- or plain ginger ale, chilled
2 cups fresh orange juice
2 cups lemon-lime seltzer, chilled
Orange and lime slices, and whole cranberries (optional)

1. In large pitcher (about 3 quarts), mix cranberry-raspberry juice, ginger ale, and orange juice. Refrigerate until ready to serve.
2. Just before serving, stir in seltzer. If you like, garnish with orange and lime slices, and cranberries. Makes about 10 cups or 10 servings.

Each serving: About 95 calories, 0 g protein, 24 g carbohydrate, 0 g total fat, 0 mg cholesterol, 20 mg sodium.

Italian Lemon Cordial

Prep: 10 minutes plus steeping
Cook: About 5 minutes

6 lemons
1 bottle (750 ml) 100-proof vodka (3¼ cups)
1¾ cups sugar
3¼ cups water

1. With vegetable peeler, remove peel from lemons (reserve peeled lemons for another use). Pour vodka into 8-cup measuring cup or large glass bowl and add lemon peels. Cover with plastic wrap and let stand at room temperature 1 week.

2. After 1 week, line sieve with paper towels and place over a large bowl. Pour vodka mixture through sieve; discard lemon peels.

3. In 2-quart saucepan, stir sugar and water; heat to boiling over high heat, stirring. Boil 2 minutes. Cool completely. Add cool syrup to vodka mixture.

4. Pour cordial into small decorative bottles with tight-fitting stoppers or lids. Although it is not necessary to refrigerate cordial, we recommend storing it in the freezer where it can keep indefinitely. Makes about 6½ cups or 34 servings.

Each serving: About 100 calories, 0 g protein, 10 g carbohydrate, 0 g total fat, 0 mg cholesterol, 0 mg sodium.

Sangria

Prep: 10 minutes

2 oranges
2 lemons
1 bottle (750 ml) dry red wine (about 3¼ cups)
⅓ cup sugar
¼ cup brandy
¼ cup orange-flavored liqueur
1 bottle (1 liter) plain seltzer
Ice cubes (optional)

1. With vegetable peeler, remove peel in 1-inch-wide strips from 1 orange and 2 lemons. Squeeze juice from both oranges.

2. In 2½-quart pitcher, stir wine, sugar, brandy, liqueur, and orange juice until sugar has dissolved. Stir in orange and lemon peels. If not serving right away, cover and refrigerate.

3. Just before serving, stir in seltzer. Serve over ice if you like. Makes about 7 cups or 14 servings.

Each serving: About 85 calories, 0 g protein, 9 g carbohydrate, 0 g total fat, 0 mg cholesterol, 50 mg sodium.

WHITE SANGRIA: Prepare Sangria as on page 1197, but use *white wine* instead of red and add *3 peaches*, peeled, pitted and cut into thin wedges, and *1 orange*, thinly sliced. Makes about 7 cups or 14 servings.

Each serving: About 90 calories, 0 g protein, 9 g carbohydrate, 0 g total fat, 0 mg cholesterol, 20 mg sodium.

Mock Sangria

Prep: 15 minutes

2 bottles (24 ounces each) purple, red, or white grape juice, chilled
1 liter club soda, chilled
½ small pineapple, cut into bite-size chunks
1 large orange, sliced
1 tray ice cubes

In 4-quart pitcher, combine grape juice and club soda. Add fruit and ice cubes. Makes about 12 cups or twenty-four ½-cup servings.

Each serving: About 25 calories, 0 g protein, 7 g carbohydrate, 0 g total fat, 0 mg cholesterol, 10 mg sodium.

Sparkling Strawberry Punch

Prep: 10 minutes

2 packages (10 ounces) frozen strawberries in quick-thaw pouch,
    thawed
1 can (6 ounces) frozen lemonade concentrate, slightly thawed
1 bottle (750 ml) rosé wine (about 3¼ cups), chilled
2 liters ginger ale, chilled
1 liter club soda, chilled
2 trays ice cubes
¼ cup sugar
Orange slices

1. In blender at high speed, blend strawberries and undiluted lemonade concentrate until strawberries are pureed.

2. Pour strawberry mixture into a chilled 6-quart punch
bowl. Add wine, ginger ale, club soda, ice cubes, and sugar;
stir punch until sugar is completely dissolved. Garnish
punch with orange slices. Makes about 18 cups or thirty-
six ½-cup servings.

*Each serving: About 65 calories, 0 g protein, 13 g carbohydrate,
0 g total fat, 0 mg cholesterol, 10 mg sodium.*

Cranberry-Zinfandel Punch

Prep: 5 minutes

1 bottle (64 ounces) cranberry-juice cocktail, chilled
1 bottle (750 milliliter) red Zinfandel wine, chilled
⅓ cup bottled sweetened lime juice
1 liter seltzer, chilled
Lime slices

1. In large pitcher or punch bowl (about 5 quarts), combine cranberry-juice cocktail, Zinfandel, and lime juice. Refrigerate until ready to serve.

2. Just before serving, stir in seltzer. Garnish with lime slices. Makes about 16 cups or 20 servings.

Each serving: About 90 calories, 0 g protein, 16 g carbohydrate, 0 g total fat, 0 mg cholesterol, 30 mg sodium.

Sparkling Orange Sunrises

Prep: 5 minutes plus chilling

1 quart orange juice
2 cups seltzer or club soda, chilled
2 tablespoons orange-flavored liqueur
2 tablespoons pomegranate syrup or grenadine syrup
Ice cubes

In 2-quart pitcher, combine orange juice, seltzer, liqueur, and syrup. Refrigerate until ready to serve, up to 30 minutes. Add ice cubes just before serving. Makes 6 cups or 8 servings. If you like, combine orange juice, orange-flavored liqueur, and pomegranate syrup several hours ahead and chill. Add cold seltzer and ice at serving time.

Each serving: About 70 calories, 1 g protein, 16 g carbohydrate, 0 g total fat, 0 mg cholesterol, 15 mg sodium.

Hot Mulled Wine

Prep: 10 minutes
Cook: 20 minutes

4 cups sugar
2 cups water
1 tablespoon ground cinnamon or 6 cinnamon sticks (3 inches each)
1 teaspoon ground cloves or whole cloves
3 medium oranges, thinly sliced
1 medium lemon, thinly sliced
1 bottle (4 liters) dry red wine (about 17 cups)

In 8-quart saucepot heat sugar, water, cinnamon, cloves, oranges, and lemon to boiling over high heat; boil 5 minutes, stirring occasionally. Reduce heat to medium; pour in wine and heat, stirring occasionally, until hot but not boiling. Serve hot. Makes about 22 cups or forty four ½-cup servings.

Each serving: About 140 calories, 0 g protein, 21 g carbohydrate, 0 g total fat, 0 mg cholesterol, 5 mg sodium.

Wassail Bowl

Prep: 10 minutes
Cook: 25 minutes

2 quarts apple cider or apple juice
3 cinnamon sticks (3 inches each)
2 teaspoons whole allspice
2 teaspoons whole cloves
1 small orange, sliced
1 small lemon, sliced
1 can (6 ounces) frozen orange-juice concentrate
1 can (6 ounces) frozen lemonade concentrate
1 bottle (750 ml) dry white wine (about 3¼ cups)
4 cups water
¾ cup packed brown sugar

1. In 5-quart saucepot, heat apple cider, cinnamon sticks, allspice, and cloves to boiling over high heat. Reduce heat to low; cover and simmer 15 minutes.

2. Meanwhile, place orange and lemon slices in heat-safe 5-quart punch bowl; set aside.

3. To cider mixture, add orange-juice concentrate, lemonade concentrate, white wine, water, and brown sugar; heat to boiling over high heat. Pour hot mixture over fruit in bowl. Makes about 16 cups or thirty-two ½-cup servings.

Each serving: About 90 calories, 0 g protein, 19 g carbohydrate, 0 g total fat, 0 mg cholesterol, 5 mg sodium.

Holiday Eggnog

Prep: 10 minutes plus chilling
Cook: 25 minutes

12 large eggs
1¼ cups sugar
½ teaspoon salt
2 quarts milk
1 cup dark rum (optional)
2 tablespoons vanilla extract
1 teaspoon ground nutmeg plus extra for sprinkling
1 cup heavy or whipping cream

1. In heavy 4-quart saucepan, with wire whisk, beat eggs, sugar, and salt until blended. Gradually stir in 1 quart milk and cook over low heat, stirring constantly, until custard thickens and coats the back of a spoon well, about 25 minutes (mixture should be about 160°F.). Do not boil, or custard will curdle.

2. Pour custard into large bowl; stir in rum, if using, vanilla, 1 teaspoon ground nutmeg, and remaining 1 quart milk. Cover and refrigerate until well chilled, at least 3 hours.

3. To serve, in small bowl, with mixer at medium speed, beat heavy or whipping cream until soft peaks form when beaters are lifted. With wire whisk, gently fold whipped cream into custard mixture.

4. Pour eggnog into chilled 5-quart punch bowl; sprinkle with nutmeg for garnish. Makes about 16 cups or 32 servings.

Each serving: About 125 calories, 5 g protein, 11 g carbohydrate, 7 g total fat (4 g saturated), 98 mg cholesterol, 90 mg sodium.

Menus

HOLIDAY DINNERS

∿St. Patrick's Day

Mustard-Glazed Corned Beef with Cabbage
    (page 136)
Mashed Potatoes Plus (page 610)
Irish Soda Bread (page 828)
Country Spice Cake (page 978)

∿Easter

Leg of Lamb with Pistachio Topping (page 210)
Asparagus Gratin (page 557)
Mrs. Mary's Marinated Mushrooms (page 710)
Oven Roasted Rosemary Potatoes (page 609)
Salinas Mixed Greens with Tarragon-Vinegar Dressing
    (page 706)

∿Mother's Day Brunch

Capellini Frittata (page 404)
Spinach and Tangerine Salad (page 710)
Rosemary-Fennel Breadsticks (page 875)

❧Father's Day Dinner

❧July 4th Picnic/BBQ

❧Thanksgiving

Apple Crumb Pie (page 1042)
Kentucky Bourbon Brown-Sugar Pound Cake
  (page 985)

∾Hanukkah

Salmon Pâté (page 47)
Potato Pancakes (page 611)
Chunky Applesauce (page 646)
Sour Cream
Moroccan Carrot Salad (page 714)
Two-Bean Salad (page 728)
Old-Fashioned Doughnuts (page 841)

∾Christmas

Shrimp Cocktail with Tangy Dip (page 64)
Crispy Citrus Goose (page 303)
North Carolina Brown-Butter Sweet Potatoes
  (page 625)
Creamed Onions (page 601)
Peas with Lettuce (page 604)
Chestnut and Apple Stuffing (page 308)
Holiday Baked Alaska with Red-Raspberry Sauce
  (page 1169)
Gingerbread Bûche de Noël with Orange
  Buttercream Frosting (page 997)

∾New Year's Eve Buffet

Roasted Red Pepper and Walnut Dip (page 44)
GH Guacamole (page 43)
Tortilla Chips
Parmesan Toasts (page 51)

Sesame Pita Toasts (page 52)
Mushroom Turnovers (page 58)
Salmon Pâté (page 47)
Tortilla Spirals (page 46)
Chicken Liver Pâté (page 67)
Spiced Nut and Pretzel Mix (page 55)
Mini Eclairs (page 948)

New Year's Eve Dinner

Champagne
Alaskan Salmon Spread (page 68)
Pepper-Crusted Beef Tenderloin with Red Wine Gravy
   (page 112)
Green Beans with Oregon Hazelnuts (page 560)
Apricot-Ginger Carrots (page 575)
Sautéed Mixed Mushrooms (page 596)
Dinner Rolls (page 870)
Roasted Vanilla Pears (page 679)
Strawberry Granita (page 1163)
Chocolate-Cherry Biscotti (page 1131)
Italian Lemon Cordial (page 1196)

Pizza and Salad Party

Country-Style Pizzas (page 866)
Bistro Pizza (page 868)
Tuscan Tuna Salad (page 742)
Marinated Tomato-and-Arugula Salad (page 716)
Three-Pepper Salad (page 715)
Lemon Granita (page 1162)
Chocolate Sambuca Cookies (page 1126)

∾Kid's Birthday Party

Sticky Drumsticks (page 280)
Banana-Split Cake (page 1160)
Sugar-and-Spice Ice-Cream Sandwiches (page 1173)
Lemonade (page 1193)
Mock Sangria (page 1198)

∾Ice Cream and Cake Party

GH's Best Strawberry Ice Cream (page 1156)
Old-Fashioned Raspberry Ice Cream (page 1156)
Vanilla Ice Cream (page 1154)
Almond Pound Cake (page 986)
Old-Fashioned Cocoa Cake (page 970)
Yellow Cake (page 968)
The Ultimate At-Home Coffee Bar (page 1185)

∾Brunch

Omelet Española (page 393)
Spinach Strata (page 398)
Oven-Roasted Rosemary Potatoes (page 609)
Overnight Sticky Buns (page 880)
Classic Crumb Cake (page 832)
Café au Lait (page 1186)
Spiced Hot Tea (page 1188)

∾Any Occasion Soup and Bread

Shrimp and Sausage Gumbo (page 89)
Hearty Mushroom-Barley Soup (page 94)
Curried Lentil Soup (page 96)
Crusty Farmhouse Bread (page 850)
Round Rye Bread (page 855)
Colonial Oatmeal Bread (page 857)

ᦞQuick Week-Night Dinners

Penne with Salmon & Asparagus (page 435)
Citrus Salad with Sherry Dressing (page 709)
Fast Baked Apples with Oatmeal Streusel (page 647)

Quickie Vegetable Cream Soup (page 81)
Couscous and Smoked Turkey Salad (page 737)
Spiced Nectarine Slices (page 675)

Steak Pizzaiolo (page 120)
Stir-Fried Broccoli (page 567)
Dinner Rolls (page 870)
Chunky Applesauce (page 646)

Tortilla Chicken Tenders with Easy Southwest Salsa
    (page 278)
Hot Fluffy Rice (page 520)
Jiffy Peanut Ice-Cream Bombe (page 1167)

Stir-Fried Chicken and Vegetables (page 274)
Hot Fluffy Rice (page 520)
Broiled Brown-Sugar Bananas (page 654)

Weeknight Arroz con Pollo (page 526)
Skillet Cherry Tomatoes (page 627)
Fruit Salad with Vanilla-Bean Syrup (page 692)

ᦞVegetarian Dinners

Meatless Chili (page 518)
Corn and Avocado Salad (page 559)
Brown Rice (page 500)
Country Apple Crisp (page 936)

Vegetarian Bean Burritos (page 512)
Sauteed Mixed Mushrooms (page 596)
Brown Rice (page 500)
Caramel-Glazed Oranges (page 676)

Stir-Fried Tofu with Vegetables (page 519)
Mixed Green Salad (pages 703–706)
Hot Fluffy Rice (page 520)
Napa Valley Poached Pears (page 680)

Sunday Night Vegetable Hash (page 633)
Zucchini and Cheese Bread (page 825)
Brownie Pudding (page 927)

Moroccan Vegetable Stew (page 639)
Hot Fluffy Rice (page 520)
Semolina Foccacia (page 864)
Ricotta Pie (page 903)

Classic Cheese Soufflé (page 395)
Marinated Tomato and Arugula Salad (page 716)
Herbed Toast (page 891)
Prune Plums in Syrup (page 685)

~Family Suppers

Chicken Potpie in Corn Bread Crust (page 283)
Mixed Green Salad (pages 703–706)
Rocky-Road Freeze (page 1176)

Family Mac (page 451)
Roasted Green Beans in Dill Vinaigrette (page 561)
Apple Brown Betty (page 937)

Spaghetti Carbonara Pie (page 439)
Skillet Cherry Tomatoes (page 627)
Cantaloupe Boats (page 674)

Home-Style Meat Loaf (page 145)
Mashed Potatoes Plus (page 610)
Sautéed Peppers and Onions (page 606)
Cherry Cobbler (page 660)

Index

⁓⚬⁓